6 -

American State Government

AMERICAN STATE GOVERNMENT

By

W. BROOKE GRAVES

CHIEF OF THE STATE LAW SECTION
LEGISLATIVE REFERENCE SERVICE
LIBRARY OF CONGRESS

THIRD EDITION

D. C. HEATH AND COMPANY : Boston

Offices:	Boston	New York	Chicago
Atlanta	Dallas	San Francisco	London

Preface to the Third Edition

THE cordial reception which the two earlier editions of this book received has encouraged the author and the publishers to offer this Third Edition in which full recognition has been given to changes in state government brought about by the war and the problems of the postwar period. Some changes have been made in the arrangement of material, and two entirely new chapters have been added, while others have been very largely rewritten.

Somewhat greater emphasis has been placed on the administrative aspects of the subject than in the earlier editions, and one of the new chapters attempts to give a bird's-eye view of the administrative services rendered by the state governments. The changes which have occurred in the financial field are so great that the two chapters on this subject have been very extensively revised.

The concluding chapter on the future of the states appearing in earlier editions has been broadened to include not only Federal-state relations, but other phases of federalism in the United States today. A new concluding chapter on the states in the war and the postwar attempts for the first time to bring together in compact form an account of the contribution which the states made to the war effort and, in turn, to discuss the effect of the war upon the states. Their postwar plans for social and economic reconstruction, their plans for highway and building construction and other public works, as well as their programs for the assistance of returning veterans, are also included.

The extensive reference lists previously included seem to have met with widespread approval. They have accordingly been retained, after thorough revision. New publications have been inserted in the book lists at appropriate places, and some of the older titles have been dropped. The lists of articles in professional and legal journals have been restricted, with very rare exceptions, to items appearing in 1940 or later. It is believed that students wishing to consult earlier articles will usually have access to previous editions of the book.

As always, I am deeply grateful to a host of public officials, research bureaus, and members of university faculties who have so generously answered my questions and supplied reports, reprints of articles, and other information. I am especially indebted to Professor Harold M. Dorr of the University of Michigan for his continued interest and helpfulness, and to Professor Frank Paddock, my colleague for many years at Temple University, for numerous constructive suggestions, the adoption of which has contributed to the improvement of the book.

Most of all, I am indebted to my wife, Hazel W. Graves, whose alertness in detecting faults in style and choice of words has contributed greatly to the improvement of the text, and whose unfailing loyalty has enabled her to survive once more the ordeal of preparing a manuscript for publication.

W. Brooke Graves

Bryn Mawr College,
October 1, 1945.

Contents

PART THREE
The Process of Lawmaking

PART FOUR
Executive and Administrative Problems

PART FIVE
Financial Problems

PART SIX
Judicial and Legal Problems

PART SEVEN
Intergovernmental Relations

Part One

CONSTITUTIONAL BASES OF STATE GOVERNMENT

INTRODUCTION

The Importance of State Government

IT would be difficult to overemphasize the importance of state government from the points of view of its relations to the individual citizen, its fundamental position in the American system of federal government, and the contributions of the states as laboratories for political experimentation and the training of Federal officials and officeholders. There has been, in fact, for many years a tendency to underestimate its importance. Prior to 1900 little attention was given to either the organization or the functioning of state government. While there had been some increase in the scope of activity of the states before this date, the increases in activity subsequent to it were much greater, both in number and in extent. The rather dramatic development of the reorganization plan in Illinois in 1917 served to focus attention upon the problems of the states. Since that date there has been evidence of a steadily increasing interest in problems of both state government and state administration.

EXPANDING SERVICES AND INCREASED EXPENDITURES

We have long permitted ourselves to regard the states simply as local units, and thus to minimize the importance both of the states and of the truly local units. In the present century great advances have been made in preventive medicine and in the treatment of disease, in agriculture and forestry, in new techniques and skills in industry, in new developments in transportation and communications, and in new concepts of social welfare. As these were all reflected in expanded public services, the costs of government increased by leaps and bounds.

The figures in the accompanying table, furnished by the Governments Division of the United States Bureau of the Census, show these increased costs from 1902 through 1942, the first full year of war. In year after year the states and the local units spent more than 50 per cent of the total expended for governmental purposes. While it is true that the states are more local in character than the Federal government, the real units of local government are the counties, cities and boroughs, towns and townships. If anyone doubts this let him observe the reactions of the ordinary citizen to the steady transfer of functions from local communities to agencies at the state capitol.

GOVERNMENTAL EXPENDITURE: SELECTED YEARS 1902 TO 1942
(In millions)

Year	Total Expenditure [1]			Fiscal Aid Paid		Net Expenditure [2]	
	Federal, State, and Local	State	Local	By Federal to State Governments	By State to Local Governments	Federal, State, and Local	State
1902	$ 1,771	$ 183	$ 971 [3]	$ 6	$ 52	$ 1,710	$ 131
1913	2,635	379	1,569 [3]	10	87	2,538	292
1922	. . . . [4]	1,278	. . . . [4]	94	133 [5]	. . . . [4]	1,145
1932	13,984	2,606	6,842	249	841	12,260	2,246
1938	20,427	4,936	7,865	627 [6]	1,543	18,059	3,393
1942	47,328	5,844	7,164	837 [6]	1,789	44,681	4,740

Note: Figures for provision for debt retirement are unavailable for 1902, 1913, and 1922, but are included for 1932, 1938, and 1942 for state and local governments. Federal debt retirements for the last cited years were refundings, and hence are excluded from expenditures.

[1] Includes aid paid to other governments. [2] Excludes aid paid; includes payments from aid received. [3] Excludes incorporated places with populations under 2,500. [4] No data available. [5] School and highway aid for 1923. [6] Includes a small amount of local aid to states.

Sources: Bureau of the Census for all years except 1938; Treasury Department estimates for 1938.

Much has been said and written about the tremendous increases that have taken place in recent years, both in the expenditures for government and in the scope of services performed by government. Many whose tendency is to cling to old traditions and established ways have protested at what they regard as government extravagance and the development of a policy of paternalism. While it is desirable to preserve long-established traditions when they are sound and to follow familiar ways when these ways are suitable, those who express this view usually fail to consider that we are living in a world quite different from that of our fathers — or even from that with which as children we became familiar. This new world created by science and the useful arts has, as everyone knows, brought fundamental changes in our daily lives and in the organization and functioning of our social institutions. These people are in reality urging that in this changing world government should remain static.

Of course this cannot happen. Government cannot — and it should not if it could — remain changeless, uninfluenced by a society that is in a continual state of flux. It cannot do this because government itself is both a phase of life and a social institution. As such, it cannot be separated from life, nor from the influences that are everywhere else bringing change in established modes of thought and ways of doing things. If it did so it would fail to perform one of the chief functions for which it was established.

From the point of view of the individual and of society as a whole, these increased expenditures and expanding services can be justified. Socially, they are justifiable because they make possible the accomplishment of purposes designed to promote the public welfare, in the broadest sense in which that term is used, including education, health, welfare, protection of labor, et cetera. From the point of view of the individual, they represent, in the first place, a more efficient and economical use of one's financial resources. In one necessary activity of life after another we have discovered that we could get more and better service per dollar expended by spending through the agency of government than by spending the money ourselves as individuals. It is impossible for every family to hire tutors to educate its children; for every property owner to build the street which passes by his property; for every person to check and test the accuracy of weights and measures used in the vending of the commodities he buys; for every householder to control individually anything like all the factors affecting his own health and that of the members of his family. This list might be extended indefinitely. As science develops and society grows more complex, the number of things which the welfare of the people requires should be done and which the people as individuals cannot do for themselves increases. If they are not undertaken by the government the chances are that they will not be done at all. To perform these services costs money, and the greater the number of services, the larger the expenditures will be.

Government expenditures represent not merely a more efficient use of the individual's financial resources but also a more efficient use of his time. If the citizen were to undertake to render for himself the services which government now provides for him, he would have little time left for the business or profession by which he now makes his livelihood. If government did not provide for the collection of ashes and garbage, the citizen would either have to perform this service for himself or hire it done at a much greater cost than he now pays in the form of taxes. If the city did not shovel the walks in winter and keep the streets paved and clean, the citizen would have to do these things also. If he desired to take out an insurance policy he would not only have to ascertain whether the company was registered and licensed to do business within the state in which he lived, but also to make or have made a thorough investigation of its affairs and financial standing. If he required drugs he would have to employ a chemist to analyze them and determine whether or not they were pure and fit for use. In similar manner, he would be obliged to test, or have tested, the water and milk which were brought into his home. As standards of living are raised, as the development of both natural and social science brings about more requirements designed to protect the health and well-being of the people, the services rendered by the state governments and by their local subdivisions increase in both number and importance.[1]

Reference has already been made to the scope of these governmental services. There is no doubt that governments now do many more things than they formerly did, nor that many of these things are of a nature heretofore undreamed of. It has often been said that the aim and purpose of government should be to bring about the greatest good to the greatest number of people. Those who criticize the expanding scope of governmental activity, who talk about paternalism, bureaucracy, the invasion of the rights of the individual, and the danger to " the American way of life," fail to realize that it is frequently possible to further the welfare of the group or to retain rights for the individual only through the exercise of methods of social control. They fail to realize that the right of the rank and file to a reasonable measure of security is paramount over the rights of any small coterie to amass great wealth at the expense of their employees or of the general public. They mistakenly assume that these concepts are something new in the development of society. It is true that their development has of late progressed more rapidly, but it is also true

[1] Theodore Roosevelt well described this transformation when he wrote: " The government has been forced to take the place of the individual in a hundred ways; in, for instance, such matters as the prevention of fires, the construction of drainage systems, the supply of water, light, and transportation. In a primitive community every man or family looks after his or its interests in all these matters. In a city it would be an absurdity to expect every man to continue to do this, or to say that he had lost the power of individual initiative because he relegated any or all of these matters to the province of public officers." Quoted by Beard, Charles A., *American Government and Politics*, Sixth Edition, p. 3 (Macmillan, New York, 1931).

that throughout the ages this development has been a part of the story of the progress of the human race.

CLOSE RELATION OF THE STATES TO THE CITIZEN

The importance of the problems of state government will become more and more evident as our discussion proceeds. It has been said that these questions are uninteresting — perhaps upon the basis of an assertion by a distinguished American publicist that the interests of the people are not always the things that interest the people most. While in general this statement is true — while it may be true that many citizens are apparently uninterested in the problems of their state governments — it is doubtful whether these problems are themselves uninteresting. It is true that the Federal government is larger, that its operations are on a more extensive scale, that they often relate to more spectacular subjects, and that consequently the citizen may believe that he is more interested in them. This belief is fostered periodically by the ballyhoo which accompanies a Presidential election. There is no intention here of minimizing the importance of the Federal government, nor of belittling the honest and efficient administration of its services, but until the last few years, the average individual rarely came in contact with them at frequent intervals, except perhaps in the case of the Post Office Department and the Collector of Internal Revenue.

In the decade of the thirties this situation was somewhat changed by the entry of the Federal government into a large number of new fields. Not only did the Department of Agriculture continue to supply information to the farmer and his wife on all kinds of subjects relating to the farm and the farm home, but it undertook to give him parity payments and other forms of financial assistance. Under the credit agencies, farm owners, farm operators, and home owners were assisted in the solution of their problems. The development of the social security program resulted in each wage earner in industry being given a social security number and brought into close and vital contact with the Federal government. The operation of the Civilian Conservation Corps and the public works program brought thousands more into contact with the central government, not to mention other thousands who have been the recipients of direct relief, supported in part by Federal funds.

During the war every individual had his ration book from the Office of Price Administration, and his gasoline coupons if he owned a car. He could not secure employment or change jobs without the approval of the War Manpower Commission, nor obtain a raise in pay except with the approval of the National War Labor Board. The War Production Board established priorities under which it was determined how much material and what kind of materials he could obtain for the operation of his business. The Office of Defense Transportation, in the effort to conserve cars, tires, and gasoline, imposed restrictions upon the delivery service he might provide. In brief, the citizen could not eat, drink, smoke, work or play, or travel, without confronting some regulation imposed by the emergency war agencies.

In spite of these changes of the last few years, the relation of the citizen to the functions and services of his state government is still very close, as Charles A. Beard has vividly pointed out.[2] It is impossible for a business or professional man to go from the building in which his office is located without coming directly in contact with evidences of the authority of his state government. The traffic sign at the corner or the traffic officer on duty is an evidence of this authority. When he stops in a restaurant for his noonday lunch, he would find upon inquiry that the establishment was inspected by state or local officers or both, and that it was subject to the provisions of the law governing public eating places. If his residence is at some distance from his office or place of business, he will be subject to the law governing the operation of motor vehicles if he drives back and forth; or if he travels by street car, bus, or train, the conveyances upon which he rides will be owned and operated by companies subject to the provisions of the public service company law. The electric current which furnishes the light by which he works will be supplied either by a municipally owned and operated plant or by a private company whose rates and service are subject to the regulatory power of the state. All through the day and night, the properties in which he works and lives, as well as his personal safety, will be in charge of local police officers.

It is indeed impossible for an individual to escape from the authority of the state government. The application of this authority is sometimes direct, and sometimes so indirect that the individual is unaware of it. Sometimes it is exercised by the state itself or its

[2] Beard, Charles A., *American Government and Politics*, Fifth Edition, p. 5 (Macmillan, New York, 1928). See also Brown, Vernon J., " The Growth of State Government," *State Government*, February, 1944, pp. 276–277, 283, a comment on fifteen years of personal experience and observation of the evolution of state government services in Michigan.

officers, and sometimes by the local units of government which have been created by and which are, to some extent at least, responsible to the state authority. This is true from the moment the individual is born until the moment that he is laid in his final resting place. The infant at birth is attended by a physician examined and licensed by the state for the practice of his profession. In all probability the physician is assisted by one or more trained nurses, whose registry with a state board authorizes them to practice their profession. In other cases the birth may be attended by a midwife, but midwives are subject to licensure and their work is carefully inspected and supervised by visiting nurses. As soon as the infant is born, a solution of nitrate of silver is placed in his eyes, in accordance with the provisions of state law, to prevent blindness. The fact of his birth must, in accordance with state law, be registered with the state bureau of vital statistics or with a local bureau. From this time until his death the individual citizen is in constant contact either directly or indirectly with an officer of the state or with someone authorized by it to engage in the practice of a trade or profession.

As the child grows older he comes in contact with dentists and other professional persons examined and licensed for the practice of their respective callings and professions. Some states require a vaccination certificate before the child is permitted to enroll in either private or public schools. The food which the child eats and the clothing which he wears are subject to a wide variety of laws covering adulteration, misbranding, unfair competitive practices, sanitary conditions in shops, hours of labor, and many other points. The child attends either a public school supported by tax moneys or a private school. In either case the subjects studied and other matters affecting standards of instruction and the physical equipment of the school plant are subject to state authority. Upon the completion of the work in secondary school, many students continue with college or university work. In a large number of states this work is taken in a state university supported chiefly by state funds and requiring very small payments by way of tuition and fees. The university course may be followed by postgraduate training for professional life, at the conclusion of which the applicant will submit himself to the state examining and licensing board for authorization to practice. At this time he becomes eligible to vote; he registers, subject to the provisions of the law of the state in which he lives, and in due time participates in Federal, state, and local elections — all held in accordance with rules laid down by the state legislature.

Having come of age and desiring to establish a home of his own, he applies to a local officer who, under the provisions of the state marriage law, is authorized to issue a marriage license under certain conditions. If the venture proves to be an unhappy one, the individual may apply, under the provisions of the divorce law of the state, to the proper state judicial authority to have the marriage ties dissolved. So it continues until the date of his death, when the law prescribes the treatment of his body and declares that the embalming fluid can be injected into his circulatory system only by the undertaker who has attained the age of twenty-one years, has a grammar school education, and has been examined and licensed under the authority of state law. Finally, he will be buried by a minister, priest, or rabbi whose right to officiate is recognized by the state.

This is, as President Cleveland observed in quite a different connection, a condition and not a theory that confronts us. To many of us it seems a natural, more or less inevitable, and not particularly alarming aspect of modern life. In the minds of others it raises serious questions as to the right of the state to interfere with the rights of individuals. They recognize the right of society to impose regulations which it is thought will be generally beneficial; yet they believe that there can be no real progress for the community as a whole unless, in some way, we manage to preserve and protect the rights and liberties of the individual. This point of view was well stated some years ago in an address by Samuel Seabury:

We should guard against the illusion that human ills can be cured by panaceas, or that the increase of the power of the State is the efficient remedy for all existing evils. Real improvement comes not from the growth of State power but from the growth of education and the development of individual character among the people. These qualities give better assurances of relief than that which comes from augmenting State power.

This State power may become so great that it will be repressive of the personalities within it and aggressive and threatening toward neighboring States. The present proportions which it has assumed and the rate at which it is growing is one of the most amazing facts in the history of civilization, as it is one of the most alarming incidents of our times, and carries with it a threat to the prosperity, happiness and peace of mankind.[3]

FUNDAMENTAL POSITION OF THE STATES IN THE FEDERAL SYSTEM

The importance of state government is not to be measured, however, solely in terms of its cost, the extent of its services, or its con-

[3] At the 1934 Annual Dinner of the National Institute of Social Services; reported in *New York Times*, May 13, 1934.

stant relationship to the everyday life of the individual. From the point of view of our governmental structure as a whole, the states are perhaps the most important units. It should not be forgotten that the Federal government was established by, and is still maintained through the cooperation of the states; that in many particulars the Constitution of the United States was based on the original state constitutions; nor that the Federal Constitution limits the powers of the Federal government to those subjects upon which the states thought it necessary or desirable that the Federal government should be authorized to act. In the course of the years, particularly in the older sections of the country, it is to the states that the people have developed, to a high degree, a kind of sentimental attachment. Many individuals and families pride themselves upon being natives of some particular state and upon the part which that state has played in the history of the nation. From a more practical point of view, the states have in our own time come to be important as administrative areas for many of the undertakings of the Federal government. In many instances the states have cooperated with Federal agencies, sometimes upon their own initiative and sometimes upon that of the Federal agencies concerned.

On the other hand, it is equally important to remember that the local units have been created by the action of the states, and that the nature and extent of their powers are defined by enactments of the state legislature, at whose will the powers and duties of these units may be changed or the units themselves modified or abolished (subject to certain constitutional restrictions). Thus the legislatures of the several states have provided for the organization of cities, counties, towns, townships, villages, boroughs, and administrative districts for schools, health, highways, and many other purposes. In more recent times constitutions have imposed restrictions upon the freedom of the legislatures to change the boundary lines of some of these units, particularly the counties, but they were none the less originally created by this power. Likewise, in every state, laws or codes of laws have been enacted for the government of these several types of local unit, specifying what officers shall be chosen, what their duties shall be, by what method and how much they shall be paid, et cetera. In the more progressive states nearly all the services rendered by these units are subject to state supervision and control. While this aspect of state government is discussed at length in a later chapter, what has been said here is sufficient to emphasize the point that the powers of local government rest in the states, and that the powers exercised by the local units are powers that the states have delegated to them or permitted or required them to exercise.

In still another way the states render to the Federal government a service of inestimable value. Aside from those persons who at an early age enter the Federal civil service, practically all the leaders in national affairs and nearly all the major officeholders acquire some considerable portion of their political experience in state or local offices or in both. Many serve first in local offices, and then move on to the state legislature or to some position in the administrative end of the state government, later being elected to Congress or transferring into the Federal service. Two thirds of our Presidents have served in the legislatures of their respective states. Of the five Presidents elected since the beginning of the World War in 1914, Wilson, Coolidge, and Roosevelt had previously served as governors of their states, and Harding had once made an unsuccessful race for the governorship of Ohio. Of the defeated candidates in the same period, Hughes, Cox, Smith, Landon, and Dewey had served, or were serving, as governors. Many who have been schooled in state government and politics find their way into the Senate, the Cabinet, the Foreign Service, the higher Federal courts, and the departments and administrative boards and commissions of the Federal government.

Truly it may be said that the states are a training school out of which come the leaders of the nation.[4] Woodrow Wilson wrote in his *Constitutional Government* many years ago: " The governorship of a state is very like a smaller Presidency; or, rather, the Presidency is

[4] John Brown Mason has made a number of interesting studies in this field; see especially his " State Legislatures: The Proving-Grounds of American Statesmanship," in *State Government*, December, 1938, pp. 230–231, 239; and " The State Legislature as Training for Further Public Service," in *Annals* of the American Academy of Political and Social Science (cited hereafter as *Annals*), January, 1938, pp. 172–186. In 1933 it was reported that there were 195 former state legislators in the preceding Congress; see *State Government*, January, 1933, pp. 23–24. The following year Professor Mason showed (in " 184 of Us in Congress," *State Government*, June, 1934, pp. 126–128) " that 34% of the nation's present Senators, 36% of its Representatives, have learned the ropes ' back home.' " The 184 (35% of all the members) include 35 Senators and 149 Representatives who can " recall the eras when they shouted ' Here ' in the humbler halls in St. Paul, Frankfort, Nashville, Oklahoma City, Columbus, Trenton, Little Rock, Salem, and the rest. The average length of time which they served in state legislatures was: Senators, 3.2 years, Representatives, 5.6 years." The average length of service in the home capitol was 4.4 years — surely a sufficient period of time to give a member some preparation for his new duties in Washington. In August, 1937, the number of Congressmen with state legislative experience was somewhat reduced, the number of Senators being 37, Representatives 34. But there were 16 Senators and 4 Representatives who had been governors of their respective states. Similar data might be presented to show that many members of Congress have served as prosecuting attorneys, as judges in the state courts, and in various administrative positions.

very like a big governorship. Training in the duties of one fits for the duties of the other." Clearly the states are the key units in the system of government under which we live in the United States. Both the Federal government on the one hand and the local units of government on the other owe their origins, powers, and continued existence largely to the governments of the states. More than that, the states and the local units combined serve as a training school for the development of Federal officeholders and the leaders in national affairs. No study of American government which omits the states can possibly be either complete or adequate.

THE STATES AS LABORATORIES

One of the most interesting, and surely not one of the least important, aspects of state government is to be found in the function of these units as laboratories for the trial of new political policies and the development of new administrative methods and techniques. This phase of state government has rarely been adequately emphasized. In 1910 Justice Holmes referred to " the insulated laboratories of the states " in the course of his opinion in the case of Noble State Bank v. Haskell,[5] in which the Court upheld the validity of an Oklahoma statute creating a state banking board and directing it to levy upon every bank existing under the laws of the state an assessment of 1 per cent of the bank's average daily deposits, with certain deductions, for the purpose of creating a depositors' guarantee fund.

The history of American government is replete with illustrations of problems with which the states have experimented for a time, following which the Federal government has been able to enact legislation representing a relatively permanent policy. This has been particularly true in recent years. Mention has just been made of bank deposit guarantee laws; eleven states adopted legislation of this character, but none of the laws were regarded by students as notably successful. They were, in fact, so unsatisfactory in operation that, one by one, they were repealed. Yet in 1933 Congress was able to frame and adopt the Federal Deposit Guarantee Act. This measure, originally temporary in character, now operates on a permanent basis. In the summer of 1934, when the report of the first six months of the operation of the act was made public, it was shown that there had been only one failure among the approximately 14,000 banks insured, and that the cost had been only about six cents per $1,000

[5] 219 U. S. 104, 1910.

of deposits.[6] The report of the F.D.I.C. covering the first five years of its operation, from 1934 to 1938 inclusive, showed that the total number of suspensions, receiverships, and mergers of insured banks for this period was 178, an average of about thirty-five a year. Probably the success of this act was due in part to the experience of the states with legislation of this character, and in part to a more rigid supervision of insured banks than had been practiced in some states.[7]

Again, in the field of legislation, the adoption of the Federal Budget and Accounting Act of 1921 provides another illustration. For years students of government had been urging the adoption of budgetary legislation. Such systems had long been in use in the more important European countries, and in this country there had been one commission and investigating committee after another through the forty years preceding the passage of the act, all recommending such legislation. Notable among these was the report, in 1913, of President Taft's Commission on Economy and Efficiency, headed by Frederick A. Cleveland. During the administration of President Wilson a budget act was passed, but for technical reasons he felt obliged to veto it. The Republicans made budget legislation a campaign issue in 1920, and the present act was adopted early in the Harding administration. Meanwhile, however, the states had been experimenting with every conceivable type of budgetary procedure, and the executive budget had come to be recognized as the most desirable.

Similar experiences occurred with regard to the development of radio and aviation law. In the former case the stations were at first purely local in character. As their number and power increased and conflicts developed in air channels, it became apparent that some kind of central control would be required. An effort was made to exercise this control through the United States Department of Commerce; in 1927 the Federal Radio Commission was created, to be replaced in 1934 by the Federal Communications Commission. In the early stages of this development the Federal government was able to profit by the attempts of the states to regulate and control radio. Likewise the states made the exploratory first attempts to control aviation. When it became apparent that aviation itself was growing out of the experimental stage and that it was destined to be a new and important means of transportation on an interstate basis, a large part of the control gradually shifted from the states to the Federal

---

[6] *Philadelphia Record,* Financial Section, August 9, 1934.
[7] The provisions of the Federal act are outlined and appraised in Smith, Arthur Alvin, " The Guaranty of Bank Deposits," *Social Science,* Summer Number, 1934, pp. 279–293.

government, but not until the Federal government had had an opportunity to select from the state laws those elements of sound policy upon which its own efforts at regulation were to be based.

This question was well stated by President Hoover before a joint session of the Illinois General Assembly, at Springfield, June 17, 1931:

> . . . Our state legislatures occupy a position of dominant importance to the Nation as a whole . . . for the legislatures are the laboratories in which new ideas are developed and in which they are tried out.
>
> A study of national legislation and national action will show that an overwhelming proportion of the ideas which have been developed nationally have first been born in the state legislatures, as the result of problems which have developed within the states. . . . It is true that not all of the ideas come through this successfully, but even the negative values of the trial . . . are of themselves of inestimable value to the Nation, and the ideas which develop with success become of vital importance to our people at large.

Justice Brandeis's View. It is scarcely necessary to present further concrete instances of the manner in which the states serve as laboratories in which the Federal agencies are able to observe the operation of various types of legislative and administrative policies. Let us turn now to a consideration of the philosophy which underlies this interesting aspect of American governmental procedure. Nowhere has this philosophy been better stated than in the dissenting opinion of Mr. Justice Brandeis in the case of the New State Ice Company v. Liebmann,[8] in which a majority of the Court held invalid, as an unreasonable interference with private business, an Oklahoma statute forbidding the State Corporation Commission to license persons or corporations for the manufacture, sale, or distribution of ice, except on proof of necessity, and authorizing the denial of license where existing facilities were sufficient.

The attorneys for the defendant, and the majority opinion of the Court, argued that the manufacturing of ice for sale and distribution is a common calling, and that the right to engage in a common calling is one of the fundamental liberties guaranteed by the due process clause in Amendment XIV. To this Mr. Brandeis replies: " To think of the ice-manufacturing business as a common calling is difficult; so recent is it in origin and so peculiar in character. Moreover, the Constitution does not require that every calling which has been common shall ever remain so. The liberty to engage in a common calling, like other liberties, may be limited in the exercise of the police power." And elsewhere: " The business of supplying to others, for

[8] 285 U. S. 262, 1932.

compensation, any article or service whatsoever may become a matter of public concern. Whether it is, or is not, depends upon the conditions existing in the community affected." And in this connection he quotes with approval: " Plainly circumstances may so change in time or so differ in space as to clothe with such an [public] interest what at other times or in other places would be a matter of purely private concern." [9]

This brilliant dissenting opinion discusses at length the local situation which prompted the enactment of this Oklahoma statute, and traces the history of previous efforts at control by the State Corporation Commission in the seventeen years prior to its enactment. It traces the gradual and comparatively recent extension of the practice, among the states, of requiring the issuance of certificates of public convenience and necessity in an increasing number and for a variety of types of business. It points out that, under the due process clause, the Court has by unanimous decisions ruled that a state or a city may engage " in the business of supplying its inhabitants with articles in general use, when it is believed that they cannot be secured at reasonable prices from the private dealers," and it continues:

. . . As states may engage in a business, because it is a public purpose to assure to their inhabitants an adequate supply of necessary articles, may they not achieve this public purpose, as Oklahoma has done, by exercising the lesser power of preventing single individuals from wantonly engaging in the business and thereby making impossible a dependable private source of supply? As a state so entering upon a business may exert the taxing power, all individual dealers may be driven from the calling by the unequal competition. If states are denied the power to prevent the harmful entry of a few individuals into a business, they may thus, in effect, close it altogether to private enterprise.

While these excerpts are from a minority opinion, they are presented deliberately, since repeatedly in the nation's history, noteworthy minority opinions have been transformed into majority opinions.

The significance of the opinion can best be shown by a further quotation from its concluding paragraphs. Mr. Brandeis reviews the seriousness of the then existing economic emergency, noting how unusual situations give rise to the warranted exercise of unusual governmental powers. He reviews the suggestions for economic planning, citing an extensive bibliography, and the various proposals for economic control, and then raises the fundamental question whether the act before the Court may not be a step in this direction. His conclu-

[9] Block v. Hirsh, 256 U. S. 135, 155, 1920.

sions to the planning program in general, and to its relations to the states, are significant:

Whether that view [concerning economic planning] is sound nobody knows. The objections to the proposal are obvious and grave. The remedy might bring evils worse than the present disease. The obstacles to success seem insuperable. The economic and social sciences are largely uncharted seas. We have been none too successful in the modest essays in economic control already entered upon. The new proposal involves a vast extension of the area of control. Merely to acquire the knowledge essential as a basis for the exercise of this multitude of judgments would be a formidable task; and each of the thousands of these judgments would call for some measure of prophecy. Even more serious are the obstacles to success inherent in the demands which execution of the project would make upon human intelligence and upon the character of men. Man is weak and his judgment is at best fallible.

Yet the advances in the exact sciences and the achievements in invention remind us that the seemingly impossible sometimes happens. There are many men now living who were in the habit of using the age-old expression: " It is as impossible as flying." The discoveries in physical science, the triumphs in invention, attest the value of the process of trial and error. In large measure, these advances have been due to experimentation. In those fields experimentation has, for two centuries, been not only free but encouraged. Some people assert that our present plight is due in part, to the limitations set by courts upon experimentation in the fields of social and economic science; and to the discouragement to which proposals for betterment there have been subjected otherwise. There must be power in the states and the nation to remould, through experimentation, our economic practices and institutions to meet changing social and economic needs. I cannot believe that the framers of the Fourteenth Amendment, or the states which ratified it, intended to deprive us of the power to correct the evils of technological unemployment and excess productive capacity which have attended progress in the useful arts.

To stay experimentation in things social and economic is a grave responsibility. Denial of the right to experiment may be fraught with serious consequences to the nation. It is one of the happy incidents of the federal system that a single courageous state may, if its citizens choose, serve as a laboratory; and try novel social and economic experiments without risk to the rest of the country. This Court has the power to prevent an experiment. We may strike down the statute which embodies it on the ground that, in our opinion, the measure is arbitrary, capricious, or unreasonable. We have power to do this, because the due process clause has been held by the Court applicable to matters of substantive law as well as to matters of procedure. But, in the exercise of this high power, we must ever be on our guard, lest we erect our prejudices into legal principles. If we would guide by the light of reason, we must let our minds be bold.

CHAPTER I

The States in the Federal Union

THE NATURE OF THE FEDERAL SYSTEM

BEFORE considering certain characteristics of the American federal system, it seems desirable to note briefly the meaning of certain terms used in describing different types of governmental organization. First among these is the concept of a federal system. Professor Ogg has defined a federal government as one in which " the political sovereign has made a distribution of the powers of government among certain agencies, central and divisional, and has done so through the medium of constitutional provisions which neither the central nor the divisional government has made, and which are beyond the power of either to alter or rescind." [1] If one restates this in the terms of American conditions, it is evident that " We, the people " have, in our Federal Constitution, made a division of the powers of government between the Federal government in Washington and the governments of the several states. The division of powers so prescribed was not devised by either the previously existing central government or the states acting alone, nor can it be amended or abrogated by the action of either type of governmental agency acting alone.

In this connection, it should be noted that our use of the term " state " is somewhat confusing, at least to beginners in the study of government. A state is technically regarded as a governmental unit possessing full powers of sovereignty and recognized as a regular member of the family of nations. This concept of the state is obviously inapplicable to the forty-eight subdivisions of the American Union. The confusion in terminology might have been avoided had the majority of the states chosen to follow the example of Kentucky,

[1] Ogg, Frederic A., *Governments of Europe,* p. 53 (Macmillan, New York, 1924).

Massachusetts, Pennsylvania, and Virginia, all of which are officially known as Commonwealths. The term " commonwealth " is more accurately descriptive of the kind of governmental unit which the so-called states represent. It implies a separate political entity, but does not necessarily indicate the existence of a complete sovereignty. While at this late date it is impossible to consider seriously the changing of a national practice supported by a century and a half of usage, it is essential that one understand the manner in which the everyday use of the term " state " differs from what might be called a scientific connotation.

The Tenth Amendment. In the American federal system, the sum total of all the powers of government are divided between the Federal government and the states by application of the principle set forth in Amendment X to the Federal Constitution. This amendment provides that " the powers not delegated to the United States by the Constitution, nor prohibited by it to the States, are reserved to the States respectively, or to the people." By the terms of this amendment, it is apparent that those powers of government not conferred upon the Federal government in Article I, Section 8, in Article IV, and elsewhere, nor denied by it to the states in Article I, Section 10, belong to the states or to the people. Thus the Federal government is commonly described as one of delegated or enumerated powers — a government, in other words, that may do those things and only those things which are expressly authorized by the Constitution or which, under the doctrine of implied powers set forth by Chief Justice Marshall in the case of McCulloch v. Maryland,[2] may be reasonably implied from the powers definitely granted. By the same token, the states are described as governments of residuary powers. They may, in other words, exercise all the powers of government except those definitely eliminated by the provisions of Amendment X. Under these conditions, the powers of our state governments may be determined by a process of elimination.

If it be found that any given power has been neither conferred upon the Federal government nor prohibited to the states, it may properly be assumed that this subject is one falling within the scope of state power. Take, for instance, the power over education. Search of those sections of the Constitution which confer powers upon the Federal government does not reveal that the control over this important activity has been vested in the central government. Search of the provisions of Article I, Section 10, does not reveal that this

[2] 4 Wheaton 316, 1819.

power has been denied to the states. Therefore we may assume that this power, like that over health, welfare, highways, and many other activities, has been left to the states. These powers are all examples of residuary or inherent powers.

This suggests at least one fundamental distinction between the unitary and federal types of government. Under a plan such as ours, the administrative areas (states) possess powers which cannot be alienated from them except by Constitutional amendment. Even here, unless there is specific provision for such change, the Court assumes, as in the famous Slaughter House Cases [3] involving the interpretation of Amendment XIV, that it was not the intention of the Congress which proposed the amendment nor of the states which ratified it to disturb in any fundamental way the existing governmental structure by a general redistribution of the powers of government. Similarly, in interpreting the sweeping phrase of Amendment XVI, " from whatever source derived," the Court long refused to sanction the taxation of Federal judges' salaries, on the ground that to do so would result in a diminution of their salaries, contrary to the Constitutional guarantee as then understood.[4]

It should be remembered too that the Constitution contemplated an " indestructible union of indestructible states " — to use the famous phrase from Chief Justice Chase.[5] It may be that a terrible civil war was necessary to secure a full realization of this intention, but the reality of such a union can scarcely now be questioned. Looking toward the permanency of the Federal government, on the one hand, we find established, as a result of the supreme law clause (Article VI, Section 2), the principle of a Constitutional review of state laws, and the imposing of definite duties upon the states as members of the Federal Union. Looking toward the permanency of the states, on the other, we find the whole doctrine of delegated powers for the Federal government and of residuary powers for the states. Not only has the system enjoyed an uninterrupted existence since the date of its establishment, but during this time it has been subjected to few drastic changes in form. There have been some amendments, and of course changes have been made in practice through the operation of the system of grants-in-aid and through other extensions of Federal

[3] 16 Wallace 36, 1873.
[4] In O'Malley v. Woodrough, 307 U. S. 277, 1939, the Court overruled Miles v. Graham, 268 U. S. 501, 1925, and virtually overruled the parent case, Evans v. Gore, 253 U. S. 245, 1920.
[5] Texas v. White, 7 Wallace 700, 1868. For contemporary statements of the arguments on the secession question, see Perkins, Howard C., *Northern Editorials on Secession,* 2 vols., and Dumond, Dwight L., *Southern Editorials on Secession* (both, Appleton-Century, New York, 1942) .

power. Reference has already been made to the refusal of the Court in the Slaughter House Cases to sanction an interpretation of Amendment XIV that would have caused a significant change in the balance of power as between the Federal government and the states.

Advantages and Disadvantages of the Federal System. It may be well to list briefly the arguments for and against such a form of federalism as exists in the United States, as contrasted with a unitary system. These arguments have been well stated by Professor Benson in a recent article.[6] The federal plan insures " (1) the prevention, by division of the agencies possessing political power, of the acquisition by any one agency of power sufficient to overthrow democratic, constitutional government; (2) opportunity for experimentation in governmental matters [discussed in the previous chapter]; (3) an opportunity to adapt governmental programs to needs of different localities; (4) an opportunity to train our citizenry in state institutions before selecting them for national responsibilities; (5) the administrative advantages attendant upon a forced administrative decentralization."

Professor Benson goes on to say that " recognition of the desirability of these goals does not, however, deny the validity of certain basic criticisms of a federal form of government. The most obvious disadvantages are: (1) The tendency of freedom of commerce — almost universal within federal systems — to place economic handicaps on progressive social legislation by members of the system. These handicaps frequently operate to prevent the establishment of even minimum nationwide standards. (2) The great variations in financially feasible governmental programs of member states which result from the unequal economic resources of different members of federal systems. These variations adversely affect establishment of nationwide minimum levels of government personnel. (3) The central government almost inevitably possesses a predominance in financial resources over most of the member units, simply because most taxes can be collected more effectively over an entire economic area than over portions of such an area. (4) A problem, if not a disadvantage, arises from the fact that the financial strength of the federal government often exceeds its responsibilities. Federal financial supremacy often results in higher-salaried personnel and hence better administrative standards."

Federalism in Other Lands. The student of American government

6 Benson, George C. S., " Federal-State Personnel Relations," *Annals,* January, 1940, pp. 38-43.

should be aware of the fact that this is only one of the plans in accordance with which a federal government may be constructed. The American federal system is much older than any of the others; other peoples have, therefore, been able to profit to some extent by our experience. The British North America Act, which serves as a constitution for the Dominion of Canada, was drafted in 1867. Its framers had before them the then very recent and very distressing spectacle of the American Civil War. It is only natural that they should have sought to prevent the occurrence in Canada of an experience similar to our own. In their effort to do this they completely reversed the provisions contained in Amendment X. In their fundamental law they provided that the powers not delegated to the provinces should be reserved to the government of the Dominion. In this way they sought to avoid many of the difficulties which we have experienced in the effort to distinguish, in commerce and in other fields, between interstate and intrastate matters. In addition to those of the United States and Canada, the best known federal systems are found in Australia and Switzerland; others exist in Brazil, Russia, and South Africa. Germany, under the Weimer Constitution, had a federal system.[7]

RELATION OF THE STATES TO THE FEDERAL GOVERNMENT

There are three or four different phases which must be considered in discussing the states in relation to other units of government. There are the relations of the states to the Federal government, the relations of the states with each other, and the relations of the states to the local subdivisions within their own borders. In addition, there may occasionally develop questions concerning the relation of the states to the governments of foreign nations. The first and last of these problems will be discussed in the present chapter, while questions of interstate relations and of relations to local units will be reserved for later consideration.

The position of the states in our federal system involves several reciprocal relationships. While the states have certain definite duties and responsibilities by virtue of their membership in the Federal Union, they receive from the Federal government guarantees of as-

[7] *State Government* published in 1945 a series of articles on federalism abroad; Hazard, John N., " Federalism in the U. S. S. R.," June, pp. 92–94; Hodgetts, John E., " Problems of Canadian Federalism," *ibid.*, pp. 95–99; May, Henry J., " The Union of South Africa: The Provinces and the Central Government," July, pp. 115–119; Walker, Harvey, " Federalism in Brazil," March, pp. 43–44, 52.

sistance and protection with regard to several vital matters. Among the duties of the states should be noted the requirement that they participate in the election of representatives to both houses of Congress and of Presidential electors; that they maintain the public peace within their borders; and that they maintain a republican form of government.

Duties and Responsibilities of the States. It is definitely to the advantage of the states to discharge promptly their duty of participation in the choice of Presidential electors and of members of Congress. While it is of course true that the Federal government could not continue to function for any considerable length of time if any large number of states refrained from the discharge of this responsibility, it is also true that the states would by such failure be denying themselves their proper influence in the conduct of the affairs of the Federal government. This is especially true in the case of the selection of Senators, where a failure to choose one Senator deprives a state of 50 per cent of its voting strength in the upper chamber. This fact is so well recognized throughout the country that Senatorial vacancies are rarely permitted to exist for any considerable time. Exceptions may occur in a contested election, such as the William S. Vare case in Pennsylvania in 1926. Occasional vacancies create no serious problem, but if any considerable number were permitted to continue indefinitely, the Federal government would find itself unable to function as the government of a united people.

Among the responsibilities attaching to the status of membership in the Federal Union, the maintenance of the public peace was listed. The states are definitely responsible for the maintenance of peace and order within their borders, for the protection of the lives and property of persons (not merely citizens) within their jurisdictions. The principle has, however, been established that in instances where an individual state may be unable to discharge this responsibility, the Federal government may, either with or without the consent of the state, send in Federal troops. The Constitution, in Article IV, Section 4, authorizes the President to dispatch troops for the purpose of quieting domestic violence, at the request of the legislature or the governor of the state concerned. An illustration of the use of this power occurred in West Virginia when Governor John J. Cornwall requested assistance from President Harding in 1921 for the quieting of disturbance in the coal fields. Such a request from the governor of a state makes for harmonious relations between the states and the Federal government. It is, however, well established that in case of necessity Federal troops may be sent into a state to preserve order, not only without the request of the governor, but in spite of his protest and opposition. The most famous illustration of this is found in the decision of President Cleveland to send Federal troops into Illinois at the time of the Pullman strike, against the vigorous protest of Governor John P. Altgeld. The power of the President in this case was upheld by the Supreme Court in its opinion in *In re Debs*,[8] on the ground that the interference of the strikers with the free flow of interstate commerce and with transportation of the mail justified this exercise of Federal power.

It is the duty of the states to maintain a republican form of government. No particular government is designated as republican, nor is the exact form to be guaranteed in any manner described; the question as to what constitutes such government is in most cases a political one, coming within the authority of Congress, or perhaps of the President, rather than a judicial one coming within the power of the courts. In repeated instances where the question has been under consideration in Congress, it has been decided that the guarantee of a republican form of government contained in the Constitution in Article IV, Section 4, is in effect a guarantee of a representative form of government. In the Pacific States Telephone and Telegraph Company v. Oregon,[9] a public service corporation succeeded in getting this question before the Supreme Court. The voters of Oregon enacted by use of the initiative a tax law affecting this corporation. The company paid the tax under protest, filing suit to recover the tax money on the ground that the law under which the tax was paid was unconstitutional, being a violation of the clause guaranteeing a republican form of government. The opinion of the Court took the position that the Constitutional guarantee was being fulfilled as long as the state maintained its representative institutions. If, in any state, the citizens should decide that they wished to supplement the work of these representative institutions by resort to methods of direct legislation, the Court said that they would be entirely within the

    8 158 U. S. 564, 1894.
    9 223 U. S. 118, 1912; see also Ohio v. Hildebrant, 241 U. S. 565, 1916. "All of the States had governments when the Constitution was adopted. In all, the people participated to some extent, through their representatives elected in the manner specially provided. These governments the Constitution did not change. They were accepted precisely as they were, and it is therefore to be presumed that they were such as it is the duty of the States to provide. Thus we have unmistakable evidence of what was republican in form, within the meaning of that term as employed in the Constitution." From *Constitution of the United States of America*, revised and annotated, pp. 533–534 (Government Printing Office, 1924) — hereafter referred to as *Constitution*.

limits of their authority. The Oregon decision seems reasonable, but it was no less expedient politically than it was wise. At the time, the processes of direct legislation were held in high regard in many of the states. If the Court had undertaken to uproot these methods of popular lawmaking by declaring that they were unconstitutional, it is difficult to visualize the probable consequences of their decision.

The States and Amendment of the Constitution. Finally, the states must on occasion participate in the procedure of amending the Federal Constitution. The two methods by which Constitutional amendments may be proposed, and the two methods either of which may be designated by Congress for their ratification, are set forth in Article V.[10]. These provisions may be presented in outline form as follows:

Proposal	*Ratification*
1. By two-thirds vote of both houses of Congress.	1. By affirmative action of the legislatures of three fourths of the states.
2. By a convention called by Congress at request of the legislatures of two thirds of the states.	2. By affirmative action of conventions called in at least three fourths of the states for the purpose of considering the proposed amendment.

A study of this outline in connection with the history of the use made of these provisions indicates that while our Constitution was framed by the second method of proposal and put in effect by the second method of ratification, all the amendments thus far have been proposed by the first method, and all except Amendment XXI have been ratified by the first method. In the case of Amendment XXI, Congress specified the second method, ratification by convention, in order to avoid the recurrence of the charges so frequently made concerning Amendment XVII — that it had been " put over " by a powerful and aggressive minority, and that it did not represent the will of a majority of the people at any given time.[11]

[10] " The Congress, whenever two-thirds of both Houses shall deem it necessary, shall propose Amendments to this Constitution, or, on the Application of the Legislatures of the two-thirds of the several States, shall call a Convention for proposing Amendments, which, in either Case, shall be valid to all Intents and Purposes, as Part of this Constitution, when ratified by the Legislatures of three-fourths of the several States, or by Conventions in three-fourths thereof, as the one or the other Mode of Ratification may be proposed by the Congress; Provided that no Amendment which may be made prior to the Year One thousand eight hundred and eight shall in any Manner affect the first and fourth Clauses in the Ninth Section of the first Article; and that no State, without its Consent, shall be deprived of its equal Suffrage in the Senate." *Constitution*, p. 539.

[11] See Brown, Everett S., *Ratification of the Twenty-first Amendment to the*

The extent to which the amendment procedure has been used to date is indicated in the following table:

Period	Amendment Number	Subject Matter
1791–1804	I–X	Bill of Rights
	XI	Limiting Power of Federal Courts
	XII	Election of the President
1865–1870	XIII–XV	War Amendments
1913–1933	XVI	Income Tax
	XVII	Direct Election of Senators
	XVIII, XXI	Liquor Control
	XIX	Woman Suffrage
	XX	Lame Duck Amendment

It thus appears that for long periods of time no amendments have been added to the Constitution. After some necessary changes immediately following the establishment of the government under it, none were made for a period of sixty-one years, from 1804 to 1865. Again, after the changes incorporated in the Constitution by the War Amendments, no changes were made during a period of forty-three years, from 1870 to 1913. Since the latter date, we have apparently been able to use the amending process with greater facility — a condition which it is hoped may continue, unless a general revision of the Constitution is undertaken.

In the course of the years the courts have been called upon to answer many questions involving the interpretation of the provisions of Article V. As early as 1797 the question was raised whether or not the approval of the President was necessary when a Constitutional amendment was being submitted to the states for adoption; the Court held in Hollingsworth v. Virginia that since the Constitution did not require such approval, it was not necessary.[12] More recently the Court was asked to decide the meaning of the requirement of a two-thirds vote, necessary for the passage of resolutions proposing amendments. In Missouri Pacific Railway Company v. Kansas, and later in the National Prohibition Cases,[13] the Court took the position that two thirds meant two thirds of the members present (if the number present constituted a quorum), rather than two thirds

Constitution of the United States (University of Michigan Press, 1938). In United States v. Chambers, et al., 291 U. S. 217, 1934, the Court dealt with the interpretation of Article V, in connection with the effect of Amendment XXI on Amendment XVIII.

[12] 3 Dallas 378, 1798.

[13] 248 U. S. 276, 1919; 253 U. S. 350, 1920.

of the members elected. In support of this view they cited the fact
that the first ten amendments had been proposed by two thirds of
those present. Many of the members of the First Congress had served
in the Constitutional Convention, and might therefore be presumed
to know the intent of that body. Furthermore, a motion had been
made in the Convention to require a two-thirds vote of all the Senators elected in order to ratify a treaty, but the motion had failed of
adoption. It was pointed out also that in 1861 the Senate had, by a
vote of thirty-three to one, determined that two thirds meant two
thirds of a quorum — not two thirds of the members elected. Finally,
this interpretation was in harmony with that commonly followed in
the several states, where a similar clause in the state constitutions had
been interpreted by the courts.

In Dillon v. Gloss [14] the question was raised as to the exact time
at which an amendment should take effect. Does an amendment become effective at the moment when the last one of the required number of states has approved it, or not until it has been proclaimed by
the Secretary of State? The Court accepted the first of these alternatives. It is significant, however, that when Amendment XXI was
adopted, the Secretary of State issued his proclamation immediately
upon receipt of official information regarding the action of the thirty-
sixth state — Utah. In this same case the question arose as to the
constitutionality of a clause in the proposing resolution for Amendment XVIII, limiting the time during which the amendment might
be ratified by the states to a period of seven years. The Court upheld this provision, noting that a time limit was not prohibited by
Article V, and that as a matter of fact such a limitation would seem
to be in accord with the spirit of the Constitution. The Court accepted the view that such a clause would operate to prevent the
adoption of an amendment by a series of minority groups over a
long period of time. The intention of the Fathers that amendments,
when adopted, would represent the will of the majority at the time
of their adoption was aided rather than hindered by the inclusion
of a time limit in the proposing resolution.

In 1939 this question was presented to the Supreme Court in a
new and different form in Coleman v. Miller. The Court ruled that
the proposed child labor amendment to the Federal Constitution
was still subject to ratification by the states, despite the lapse of time
since it was proposed by Congress in 1924.[15] In Kansas and Kentucky
the validity of ratification was challenged and diametrically opposite

[14] 256 U. S. 368, 1921.   [15] 307 U. S. 433, 1939.

opinions were handed down by the two state courts. The main points involved in the cases were, first, whether a state can ratify a proposed amendment after prior rejection, and second, whether the proposed amendment has lost its potency because of the lapse of time since it was submitted by Congress to the states. In 1937 the Kansas Supreme Court upheld the validity of ratification, while less than a month later the Kentucky Court of Appeals ruled ratification " void and ineffective." Both cases were appealed; the Supreme Court rejected the contention that more than " a reasonable length of time " had elapsed; that one action by a state on a given proposal exhausts its power; and that since more than one fourth of the states had definitely rejected the proposed child labor amendment, it was no longer subject to ratification. This decision is significant from the point of view of the time that had already elapsed since the child labor amendment was proposed — approximately 180 months at the time the decision was handed down. The shortest period required for ratification in the past has been approximately eight months, in the case of Amendment XII; the longest forty-two months, in the case of Amendment XVI. At that time the child labor proposal had already been before the states four and one half times as long as had been taken to ratify the amendment that had required the longest period of time previously. In 1939, after 150 years, the legislature of Massachusetts ratified the first amendment to the Constitution.

The question of the limits of the amending power has been presented to the Court a number of times. In the National Prohibition Cases the Court dealt with the question whether or not there are limits to the nature of the contents of proposed amendments. The Court held that, with the exception of that clause in Article V which provides that no state shall be deprived of its equal suffrage in the Senate without its own consent, there were no such limits. It therefore seems clear that any proposal for amendment regularly made and regularly ratified in accordance with the provision of Article V may become a part of the fundamental law. This decision represents not only good law but good sense, for it is to be remembered that there is no necessary correlation between the wisdom and desirability of a policy on the one hand, and its constitutionality on the other. Several years later, in United States v. Sprague,[16] the Court was asked to decide whether an amendment properly proposed and properly ratified could itself be unconstitutional. This question was answered in the negative; it would obviously create a ridiculous situation if such

[16] 282 U. S. 716, 1931.

a provision could be thrown out on grounds of constitutionality. Again, such a provision might be different in character from those previously adopted, it might be unwise or be judged by many to represent an unsound public policy, and still if regularly proposed and ratified be a valid part of the fundamental law.[17] It was also argued that this amendment involving a major change in the Constitution was invalid because it was ratified by state legislatures rather than by state ratifying conventions; this contention the Court also rejected.

In Hawke v. Smith [18] the Court was obliged to pass upon the constitutionality of an Ohio law requiring a popular referendum on proposals for amending the Federal Constitution. In this case the referendum was held subsequent to legislative action approving the amendment; when the popular vote indicated a public opinion contrary to the action taken by the legislature, the Secretary of State of Ohio sought to withdraw the previously indicated approval of Amendment XVIII. The Supreme Court noted that nowhere does Article V mention the referendum as part of the established amending procedure. The conclusion may therefore be drawn that a state may, if it chooses, use the referendum *prior to* the action of its legislature as a guide to that body, but that so far as the provisions of the Federal Constitution are concerned, the results of such a referendum are entirely extra-constitutional and of no legal effect.

A Maryland case, Leser v. Garnett,[19] raised the question of the right of a state to refuse observance of an amendment which it had failed to approve. This question presents a strong reminder of the debates in the middle of the last century over nullification and states' rights. The Court gave the only answer which it reasonably could give; namely, that all states were bound by the provisions of amendments duly and regularly ratified. An Oklahoma case, Guinn and Beal v. United States,[20] raised the interesting question whether a

[17] See Orfield, Lester B., " The Scope of the Federal Amending Power," *Michigan Law Review*, March, 1930, pp. 550–585, for a summary of the arguments in favor of unlimited scope rather than of implied limitations. In Fairchild v. Hughes, 258 U. S. 126, 1921, the Court upheld the validity of Amendment XIX.

[18] 253 U. S. 231, 1921. The Supreme Court of Alabama held that a statute requiring delegates to a convention to ratify Amendment XXI, to abide by the results of a statewide referendum, was not violative of Article V, basing their opinion on Hawke v. Smith (*In re* Opinion of the Justices, on Mullins Convention Act, 226 Ala. 565, 148 So. 107, 1933) .

[19] 258 U. S. 130, 1922; it also reaffirmed the doctrine of the National Prohibition Cases in upholding the validity of the amendment, noting that Amendment XV, of comparable effect in enlarging the electorate, had been recognized as valid fifty years before.

[20] 238 U. S. 347, 1915.

state may actually, although not specifically, violate an amendment to the Federal Constitution. The case grew out of grandfather clause provisions incorporated in the Constitution of Oklahoma, under which the plaintiffs in this appeal had, as election inspectors, excluded Negro citizens in their district from registering and voting. The Court ruled that while the provisions of Amendment XV were not specifically violated, the reference to the year 1866 in the Oklahoma Constitution made it obvious to any reasonable person that it was the deliberate intent of the framers of this provision to evade Amendment XV to the Federal Constitution. This the Court was quite rightly unwilling to permit.

Guarantees of Assistance and Protection to the States. Thus is concluded a discussion of the duties of the states as members of the Federal Union. As already noted, the states receive certain compensations for the discharge of their duties. If they cannot or do not maintain a republican form of government, there is assurance that the Federal government will intervene to see that such a government is established. If they are unable to maintain domestic peace, or to protect themselves against invasion, there is the guarantee of assistance from the Federal government. After providing that Congress shall have the power to admit new states into the Union, the Constitution says in Article IV, Section 3, that " no new State shall be formed or erected within the jurisdiction of any other States; nor shall any State be formed by the junction of two or more States, or parts of States, without the consent of the legislatures of the States concerned as well as of the Congress." Thus the states have a guarantee of territorial integrity. Again, there is the assurance of equal representation in the Senate, based upon the guarantee in Article V. Certain other clauses attempt to insure an equality of the states in the possession of the same kinds and degrees of political power — an attempt which the Supreme Court has in every way tried to sustain. Finally, the adoption in 1798 of Amendment XI brought to the states the promise of immunity from suits in the Federal courts, at least without their own consent.[21]

EXPANSION OF FEDERAL POWER

Due largely to the changing character of modern civilization, the power of the Federal government has in recent years been very

[21] Orth, Samuel P., and Cushman, Robert E., *American National Government,* pp. 709–712 (Crofts, New York, 1931).

greatly increased — often at the expense of the states.[22] There are a number of ways in which this has happened. In the first place, each of the major branches of the Federal government has contrived over a period of years to bring about this result. In the second place, the balance of power between the Federal government and the states may be changed by the process of amendment. Occasionally the treaty-making power may be so exercised as to bring about the same result. Under the strain of the depression certain emergency agencies of the Federal government undertook to influence the action of the state legislatures. Each of these influences will be discussed in turn.

Through Legislative Influence. The expansion of Federal power through Congressional influence has developed most notably out of legislation based upon the grant-in-aid or subsidy principle. Under this principle the states which accept the offer of Federal funds are required to match the Federal grant dollar for dollar, or in some other proportion specified in the act. In addition the states are required to expend the whole sum so provided for the exact purposes specified in the act, and in accordance with the conditions therein prescribed. The net result of this procedure has been gently to coerce the states into the making of expenditures which they might not have made otherwise, or into increasing the amount of their expenditures for the purposes specified in the act. In spite of vigorous criticism of this policy in some quarters and a certain amount of resentment on the part of some of the states, it has none the less been steadily extended since 1862, and particularly since 1912, with regard to both the amount of the expenditures involved and the number of purposes to which it has been applied. These include agricultural extension work, highways, forest fire prevention, vocational education and rehabilitation, public employment offices, infant and maternity hygiene, et cetera.

During the depression years enormous expenditures of money for purposes of unemployment relief, public works construction, and other purposes were handled in this way. The total amounts expended increased from $6,000,000 in 1912 to $215,000,000 a year at the close of the Hoover administration. In the last decades they have increased rapidly because of Federal programs for public works, relief, social security, et cetera; but they still constitute less than 10 per cent of the national budget. The amount expended in 1930 was

22 See Wooddy, Carroll H., *The Growth of the Federal Government, 1915–1932* (McGraw-Hill, New York, 1934) ; also Thompson, Walter, *Federal Centralization* (Harcourt, Brace, New York, 1923) .

$134,802,944; in 1935, $342,030,546; while in 1940, $582,519,319 was expended for twenty-one different purposes, of which highways, national guard, agricultural extension, and social security received the largest allocations. These grants were continued during World War II, and were not greatly affected by it. The result of this policy has been in practically every case to diminish the power of the states and to extend the policy-determining power of the Federal government to a large number of subjects formerly thought to be exclusively within the power and control of the state governments.[23]

Many of the so-called emergency activities undertaken during the depression later assumed a settled and more or less permanent character. Whereas the administrative set-up of Federal-aid activities prior to 1933 appeared to have achieved a rather stable and permanent form, new techniques were necessary when the providing of jobs became a primary consideration. Thus the method of extending Federal financial assistance to state and local units depends to a large extent on the purposes for which allotments are made. The Federal Emergency Relief Administration, several times reorganized and finally discontinued, was for a time the most important dispenser of Federal funds. When all Federal relief activities were put on a works basis, its place was taken by the Public Works Administration and the Works Progress Administration, both of which likewise dispensed huge sums. Legislation authorizing the various Federal agencies interested in housing had the threefold purpose of providing better housing, stimulating the construction industries, and providing employment. The establishment of the Civilian Conservation Corps provided funds for needed work in forests and on public lands. The social security program likewise made funds available, but as in the other cases mentioned, participation by the states was possible only after legislation on lines clearly indicated and prescribed had been adopted by the legislature of each cooperating state. The objectives of these programs have all been highly commendable, but they have made great inroads upon what have previously been regarded as the powers of the state governments.

[23] See Macdonald, Austin F., " Federal Aid to the States: 1940 Model," *American Political Science Review*, June, 1940, pp. 489–499, and *Federal Aid* (Crowell, New York, 1928) ; Williams, J. Kerwin and Edward A., " New Techniques in Federal Aid," *American Political Science Review*, October, 1940, pp. 947–954. For other excellent discussions, see Harris, Joseph P., " The Future of Federal Grants-in-Aid," *Annals*, January, 1940, pp. 14–26; also Bitterman, Henry J., *State and Federal Grants-in-Aid* (Mentzer, Bush, Chicago, 1938) ; Key, V. O., Jr., *The Administration of Federal Grants to States* (Public Administration Service, Chicago, 1937) . On its constitutionality, see Massachusetts v. Mellon, and Frothingham v. Mellon, 262 U. S. 447, 1923.

Through Executive Influence. In the executive departments the prestige if not the power of the Federal government has been enhanced at the expense of the states through the leadership and initiative of its administrative agencies. This has happened in one field after another; sometimes the Federal agencies have had their hand strengthened by subsidy legislation, and sometimes not. In the collection of crop estimates and market statistics, the United States Department of Agriculture took the lead in inducing the state departments to render a more efficient service and to secure reports that are uniform in character. The Office of Agricultural Experiment Stations in similar manner cooperates with the experiment stations in the several states. The Bureau of Public Roads supervises the layout of roads under subsidy appropriations, and has cooperated with the National Highway Users Conference and the American Association of State Highway Officials for the purpose of securing a uniform traffic code, uniform numbering of important highways, and uniform highway markings. Similarly, the Food and Drug Administration has taken the initiative in the calling of sectional and regional conferences of food and drug administrators, as well as national and state conferences for the purpose of securing cooperation and, where possible, a uniform handling of common administrative problems.

Illustrations of this type might be continued almost indefinitely. The United States Public Health Service assumed the initiative in organizing the Conference of State and Territorial Health Officers, and it has largely, through the Surgeon General of the United States, retained the leadership and control of this organization. The Census Bureau has worked for the development of the Federal Registration Service, through cooperation with the states, until we have now a uniform system for the reporting of vital statistics that is practically nationwide. The United States Department of Labor has been a powerful stimulating factor in the organization and development of what is now the Association of Government Officials in Industry. It has cooperated with the state officials for the improvement of labor legislation, and with the aid of the subsidy it has worked with them for the improvement of the system of public employment offices. The extension of Federal control in the administration of relief and in the control of crimes such as kidnapping and racketeering has been based in part on legislation and in part on a liberal interpretation of the powers of Federal officers.

Cooperative and concerted action between the Interstate Commerce Commission and the state railroad commissions in the regulation of railroads and other public utilities has been advocated at every convention of the National Association of Railroad and Utility Commissioners since that Association was organized in 1889. Judge Thomas M. Cooley, first chairman of the Interstate Commerce Commission and first president of the Association, at the initial meeting urged that " it is of the highest importance that there should be harmony in the legislation of control, so that the system . . . as nearly as local conditions " will permit, may operate harmoniously as a unit.[24] These comments with regard to utility control are true in large measure of each of the other important administrative fields in which both the Federal government and the states are active. Just as six presidents of this Association in eight years pointed out the desirability of cooperation, so similar statements might be found in the records of other associations of state administrative officials.

It is clear that of late a large number of Federal departments have been attempting to exert a more positive influence on the course of legislation in the states; an investigator, however, is confronted by a curious situation. With rare exceptions Federal agencies will vigorously deny any attempt to influence state legislation. A few agencies, however, frankly point out that the very nature of the subsidy system has made it necessary for them from time to time to call the attention of state authorities to conditions in the Federal law. For instance, the Chief of the Bureau of Public Roads explained:

In several instances it has been necessary to direct the attention of State legislatures to provisions of the Federal act requiring the enactment of concurrent or complying State legislation. One example is the provision of the Federal Highway Act requiring: " That before any project shall be approved by the Secretary of Agriculture for any State such State shall make provisions for State funds required each year of such States by this act for construction and maintenance of Federal-aid highways within the State, which funds shall be under the direct control of the State Highway Department."

It was necessary to draw attention to this provision in several States in which under existing laws the funds provided for construction and maintenance of Federal-aid highways were obtained from county and other local sources and were not " under the direct control of the State Highway Department." [25]

[24] McChord, C. C., *Twentieth Report,* National Association of Railroad and Utility Commissioners, p. 10.
[25] Letter from the Chief of the Bureau of Public Roads, August 10, 1934. See also Fesler, James W., *The Independence of State Regulatory Agencies* (Public Administration Service, Chicago, 1942).

In cases of this sort the procedure seems to be quite simple. The Federal agency sees something which needs to be done and which only a few states are doing well. The appeal is made to Congress for aid through a subsidy. Having secured the law and being anxious to get the work done, the agency then faces the task of getting the states to qualify under the terms of the act. No one will deny that the objectives of these Federal agencies have been laudable and that, in the main, they have worked for the enactment of laws of a desirable type. Even so, some questions important to the student of government arise.[26]

Through Judicial Influence. The influence of the Federal courts in the gradual expansion of Federal power has long been recognized, and much has been written about it. In an excellent article on this subject Professor Oliver P. Field makes the following observations:

The Supreme Court of the United States has been as impartial an umpire in national-state disputes as one of the members of two contending teams could be expected to be. This is not to impugn the wisdom or the fairness of the Supreme Court, but it is to say that the Supreme Court has been partial to the national government during the past one hundred and forty-four years of our experience with a federal system in the United States. The states, as members of the federal system, have had to play against the umpire as well as against the national government itself. The combination has long been too much for them.[27]

After pointing out the fact that the distribution of powers between the Federal government and the states has in fact been greatly modified, compared with the original provisions of the Constitution and the intentions of the Fathers, he continues:

This increase in Federal power, and this place of dominance of the national government in the Federal system, has been aided by the Supreme Court. For the time being, such changes do not necessarily mean that the states lose power, although they have already lost position, so far as the Federal system is concerned.

Somewhat facetiously, perhaps, he suggests that we might restate the rule on express, implied, and delegated powers in some such form as the following: "The national government has all those powers of

---

[26] For a fuller discussion of these questions, see Graves, W. Brooke, "Stroke Oar," *State Government*, December, 1934, pp. 259–262; "Federal Leadership in State Legislation," *Temple Law Quarterly*, July, 1936, pp. 385–405; and "Influence of Congressional Legislation on Legislation in the States," *Iowa Law Review*, May, 1938, pp. 519–538; also Key, V. O., Jr., "State Legislation Facilitative of Federal Action," *Annals*, January, 1940, pp. 7–13.

[27] Field, Oliver P., "States versus Nation, and the Supreme Court," *American Political Science Review*, April, 1934, pp. 233–245.

government not specifically denied it. In case of doubt, the national government shall be deemed to have the power. In case of conflict between national and state power, the national government shall be deemed superior. In case of war or emergency, these rules apply particularly, but in case of doubt a state of emergency shall be deemed to exist."

This attitude on the part of the Court toward the states has been illustrated in numerous ways and with regard to numerous subjects. In Texas v. White [28] the Court accepted the results of the Civil War, taking the constitutionally logical position that the Southern states had never been out of the Union, and that, in future, states once in could not leave the Union unless by a general dissolution. The Federal government may bring actions against the states in the Supreme Court, but the states may not sue the Federal government without its consent. This distinction appears to rest " upon the assumption that the national government is sovereign and therefore not subject to suit, while the states are assumed not to be sovereign, and therefore are subject to the indignity of being made parties defendant in the Supreme Court." Again, the states as such may not challenge the actions of the Federal government, having to rely rather upon suits instituted by individual citizens whose interests are injured by such actions. This attitude has been further illustrated by the manner in which the Court has handled various questions in the fields of taxation, control over commerce, questions involving the health, safety, and welfare of citizens, et cetera. It is significant also that this attitude is not new — it was expressed first by the Court as early as 1793 in Chisholm v. Georgia,[29] in which it was held that suit might be brought against the states in the Federal courts. The fact that the effect of this decision was overcome by the provisions of Amendment XI does not in any way diminish the importance of the case as an indicator of the attitude of the Court toward the states. An examination of the cases in the intervening years indicates clearly that the general attitude of the Court has not greatly changed.

Through Constitutional Amendment. Another influence toward the expansion of Federal power is the transfer of power from the states to the Federal government by the amendment of the Federal Constitution. Amendments XV and XIX imposed certain limitations upon the powers of the states with respect to the suffrage. The income tax amendment gave the Federal government a new source of revenue; it was supposed at the time that the states gave up their

[28] 7 Wallace 700, 1868.   [29] 2 Dallas 419, 1793.

claim to this type of tax, but later developments indicate that they have not done so. Amendment XVIII, while it was in effect, greatly extended the powers of the Federal government with regard to control over the manufacture and sale of intoxicating liquors — a subject always supposed to fall within the police powers of the states. The amendment to prohibit child labor, if it had been ratified, would have represented a similar invasion of the rights of the states as previously interpreted. Most important of all, the powers of the states have been definitely limited, and those of the Federal government frequently indirectly enlarged, through the interpretation which has been given to the due process and equal protection clauses of Amendment XIV. These are discussed at some length in a later chapter.

Through Exercise of the Treaty Power. The treaty power of the United States " extends to all proper subjects of negotiation between this Government and those of other nations, and to protecting the ownership, transfer, and inheritance of property which citizens of one country may have in another. It is unlimited under the Constitution, except as to restraints found in that instrument, and except those which arise from the nature of the Government itself and as to those of the states." [30] It occasionally happens, however, that the Federal government negotiates and ratifies treaties with regard to subjects that are proper in themselves but which, under our system of allocation of powers, are commonly regarded as state powers. An illustration is that of the Migratory Bird Treaty between the United States and Great Britain, certain questions with regard to which were considered by the Supreme Court in Missouri v. Holland.[31] Under the terms of this treaty Congress passed the Act of July 3, 1918, which prohibited the destruction of migratory birds passing between the United States and Canada. The act authorized the Secretary of Agriculture to execute the law and to make the necessary regulations. The Missouri authorities objected to the activities of one Holland, United States Game Warden, who was proceeding under the terms of the treaty, the act of Congress, and the regulations of the Secretary of Agriculture. The state contended that the Federal act was unconstitutional, since the control of wild game was a subject reserved to the states or to the people under the terms of Amendment X. Mr. Justice Holmes, at the conclusion of an opinion upholding the act and emphasizing the fact that the Federal power to make treaties was broader and covered a wider range of subjects than the lawmaking power, used the following significant language:

[30] *Constitution,* p. 391.   [31] 252 U. S. 416, 1920.

Here a national interest of very nearly the first magnitude is involved. It can be protected only by national action in concert with that of another power. The subject-matter is only transitory within the State and has no permanent habitat therein. But for the treaty and the statute there soon might be no birds for any powers to deal with. We see nothing in the Constitution that compels the Government to sit by while a food supply is cut off and the protectors of our forests and our crops are destroyed. It is not sufficient to rely upon the States. The reliance is vain, and were it otherwise, the question is whether the United States is forbidden to act. We are of opinion that the treaty and statute must be upheld.

In recent years a number of proposals have been made for the application of this power to other subjects; in 1938, for instance, a plan was worked out for a treaty with Canada regarding uniform commercial fishing regulations on the Great Lakes.[32]

CONSTITUTIONAL LIMITATIONS UPON STATE POWER

The Federal Constitution in various ways imposes restrictions and limitations upon the powers of the states. As has been shown in the discussion of the nature of the Federal system, the powers of the states are diminished to the extent that powers are granted to the Federal government. These powers include the various types listed in Article I, Section 8, as well as certain others noted in other parts of the Constitution. The states may not make treaties or alliances with foreign nations, nor even formal agreements in the form of compacts among themselves, unless sanctioned by Congress. They may not keep troops or ships of war in time of peace, nor unless they are faced by such imminent danger as will not admit of delay. The Federal government is given power to collect taxes, duties, imposts, and excises, and by judicial interpretation the states were for more than 100 years prohibited from taxing the officers, agencies, or instrumentalities of the Federal government. Recent decisions have modified this rule. They may regulate and control intrastate commerce, but when such control in any way interferes with the control of Congress over interstate commerce, they are likely to find that they have exceeded the bounds of their authority. So one might continue through all the clauses of the Constitution conferring power upon the Federal government, showing in turn how each indirectly imposes limitations upon the powers of the states; in some cases specific prohibitions are included in the Constitution.

Further limitations upon the powers of the states are to be found

[32] See " Going Places," *State Government,* March, 1938, p. 58.

in the list of prohibitions in Article I, Section 10. No state, for instance, may make or enforce any law impairing the obligation of contract. If the states had not found ways of evading the declared intentions of the Court as expressed in Dartmouth College v. Woodward,[33] they would have been unable to control the corporate bodies which they had created. By constitutional provisions prohibiting the granting of unconditional charters and in other ways the states have succeeded in protecting themselves in spite of the decision. Other limitations forbid the states to issue letters of marque and reprisal (also prohibited to the Federal government); to coin money and emit bills of credit (which the states succeeded in evading through the operations of state banks, prior to the decision in Veazie Bank v. Fenno); [34] to make anything but gold or silver coin a legal tender in the payment of debts; and to pass any bill of attainder or ex post facto law, or confer any title of nobility. These latter prohibitions are also applied to the Federal government.[35]

Other restrictions prohibit the states from levying any imposts, or duties upon imports and exports, except such as may be necessary for the execution of their inspection laws, without the consent of Congress. At the time the Constitution was adopted this provision was urgently required in order to prevent the recurrence of the trade barriers which had so hampered the commercial and economic development of the colonies. New Jersey and North Carolina had no ports of their own, and were obliged to buy their imported goods, from New York and Pennsylvania in the one case and from Virginia and South Carolina in the other. With high duties imposed, these two states were entirely at the mercy of their neighbors; the situation became so serious that contemporaries likened one of the states to a cask tapped at both ends, and the other to a man bleeding at both arms. It was also provided that no state should, without the consent of Congress, lay any duty on tonnage.

[33] 4 Wheaton 518, 1819.
[34] 8 Wallace 533, 1869.
[35] Letters of marque and reprisal and bills of attainder are no longer important. The first was an authorization to private parties to conduct private warfare against a public enemy; the second was a legislative act declaring an individual to be guilty of a crime and prescribing his punishment, all in the same act and without opportunity on his part to be heard or to offer testimony in his own defense. An ex post facto law may still be a matter of practical and vital importance; such an act is one which, in the field of the criminal law, applies retroactively, with the effect of making criminal an act which was innocent at the time it was committed, which increases the penalty imposed, which removes defenses permissible at the time the act was committed, or which in some other way operates to the disadvantage of the accused, as compared with his position at the time the act was committed.

In still another field the powers of the states are restricted by grants of power to the central government. In Article I, Section 8, Clause 17, and in Article IV, Section 3, Paragraph 2, Congress is given broad powers over " the territories and other property belonging to the United States." As a result of these provisions, no one of the forty-eight states has jurisdiction over all of•the territory within its borders. Each has surrendered to the Federal government some territory over which it once exercised its general governmental power. There are, in fact, a few states which never possessed this power over all the territory within their borders. " In each of the states are enclaves, some small, some very large, over which the Federal government has a power fully as broad as that of the state, and to the exclusion of the latter." [36]

All the limitations thus far mentioned are based upon grants of power to the Federal government, and thereby denied to the states, or are express limitations in the Constitution itself. Still others are, in various ways, either implied or inferred. When, for instance, the Constitution guarantees to each state a republican form of government, " it necessarily follows that every other form of government is prohibited." Although it is not expressly prohibited by the Constitution, the Supreme Court long held that for the states to impose taxes upon the officers, agencies, or instrumentalities of the Federal government was inherently opposed to the nature of the Federal system. After the Civil War the Supreme Court in the case of Texas v. White, already cited, gave its approval to the doctrine of the constitutional impossibility of secession from the Union. Recent authors have classified all these restrictions as designed to prevent state encroachment on Federal authority, while certain others, presently to be discussed, are intended to restrict the states for the purpose of protecting the civil liberties of the individual.[37]

To the original meager list of restrictions upon the states for the purpose of protecting these civil rights — the passage of bills of attainder, ex post facto laws, and laws impairing the obligations of contract — the War Amendments made important additions; these are discussed at some length in later chapters, but the general nature of their contents may be noted here. The prohibition of slavery and involuntary servitude, contained in Amendment XIII, applies to the states as well as the Federal government and individuals. Amend-

[36] Chute, Charlton F., " Areas Lying within the States and over Which the Federal Government Has Exclusive Jurisdiction," ms. of an unpublished article, prepared in 1941.
[37] Orth and Cushman, *op. cit.*, pp. 704–709.

ment XIV attempts to guarantee the privileges and immunities of citizens as well as their right to due process of law and the equal protection of the laws. A second section of this amendment, which has never been enforced, attempted to guarantee to the newly created group of Negro citizens the right to vote. This effort to prevent discrimination, so far as race, color, and previous conditions of servitude were concerned, was continued in Amendment XV; so far as sex was concerned, it was continued much later in Amendment XIX.

Confusion sometimes arises when the states attempt to exercise power over matters granted to the Federal government, but concerning which the Federal government has not acted. In general, it is assumed that the states may act in a given area unless or until the Federal government acts. Thus while the power to regulate interstate and foreign commerce is unquestionably a Federal power, the Court held, before Congress assumed control of the matter, that the states and even cities might impose reasonable regulations designed to promote the public safety.[38] In many cases the states may act after the Federal government has acted, provided that the action taken by them is supplementary to or at least not in conflict with that taken by the Federal government. The regulation of the sale of food and drugs represents such an area. In this field of Federal regulation, the states and municipalities can and do render valuable assistance toward the accomplishment of the national purpose represented by the Pure Food and Drug Act of June 30, 1906, as amended.

Occasionally, however, it is assumed that when no action is taken by the Congress under a particular grant of power, the very failure to take action is to be construed as indicating a desire on the part of the Congress that no action be taken. The same decision has been made when Congress has acted and when the administrative department has refrained from taking the action contemplated by Congress.[39] By following such a policy, it is possible to create governmental voids — areas in which the Federal government does not act, and in which it will not permit the states to act, even though it would appear that somebody ought to do something.

[38] Cooley v. Port Wardens of Philadelphia, 12 Howard 299, 1824.
[39] Such a situation was presented in Oregon-Washington Railroad and Navigation Company v. State of Washington, 270 U. S. 87, 1926. The Congress had directed the Secretary of Agriculture to take certain action. He did not act, so the state did. The Court held that the state had no right to act, although the action taken was proper and was urgently needed under the existing conditions.

ADMISSION OF NEW STATES

While at the present time it seems unlikely that any important additions will be made to the territory of the United States proper by the admission of new states, for many years the question was one of the utmost importance, since nearly three fourths of the states came into the Union by this process. It has commonly been assumed that Congress has the power to deny statehood to any territory seeking admission to the Union; and apparently it may compel a territory to become a state, even though the people thereof prefer to retain the territorial status. The original thirteen states were the charter members of the Federal Union; the other thirty-five have come into the Union since the date of its establishment, through a process now to be described. Many years ago Mr. Justice Lamar said that while the states were in 1789 in a very real sense the creators of the Federal government, by 1861 or later the Federal government had created most of the states.

There has been little uniformity through the years regarding the requirements as to size or population essential to a territory in order to qualify for admission as a state. The process of admission has begun in a formally organized territory when its inhabitants have become impatient at a further continuance of their territorial status. Under such circumstances, the territorial legislature has addressed a petition to Congress, requesting authority to hold an election of delegates to a constitutional convention and to submit the work of such convention to the citizens of the territory. In the instances in which Congress has considered such petitions favorably, the result has been the passage of an enabling act authorizing the voters to call a convention and to apply for admission. These enabling acts have sometimes specified that certain things should be included in the constitution; in Utah, for instance, it was required that polygamy should forever be prohibited.[40]

Thus authorized by Congress, the residents of the territory may proceed, upon proper notice, to elect the delegates to the convention. This body meets in due time and drafts a constitution which includes any conditions that may have been prescribed by Congress. If the constitution so framed is satisfactory to the electorate of the territory, it is then submitted to Congress with the plea that it be accepted and that the state be formally admitted as a member of the Union.

---

[40] This irrevocable ordinance is found in Article III; compare the compacts with the United States in the constitutions of New Mexico (Article XXI) and North Dakota (Article XVI).

This Congress does by the passage of a resolution. A number of questions regarding the power of Congress to impose conditions upon a state have arisen and have been decided by the courts. Some of the more interesting cases will be discussed briefly at this point.

When Oklahoma was admitted to the Union in 1907, Congress specified that the state capital should not be removed from Guthrie before 1913. The purpose of this provision was to prevent the recurrence in Oklahoma of a practice common in a number of the western states — namely, the moving of the capital as an aid to land speculation. In 1910 the capital was removed from Guthrie to Oklahoma City. This change was tested in the case of Coyle v. Smith,[41] in which the Court ruled that the condition imposed by Congress could not be enforced, since the matter which Congress sought to regulate was one of internal and domestic concern. Arizona and New Mexico were admitted in 1912; in the constitution of the former as drafted and submitted to Congress were provisions for the initiative, referendum, and recall. Congress passed a resolution admitting these states, but this was vetoed by President Taft in a vigorous message presenting in classic form the arguments against the recall as applied to the judiciary. The objectionable clauses were removed by the Territory, only to be reinstated after the condition of statehood had been achieved. On the basis of the doctrine in the Oklahoma case, it would have been useless to contest the state's right to make such reinstatement.

If this rule had not been adopted, it would have been possible for Congress to expand its power tremendously, in a manner and to an extent never intended by the Constitutional Fathers. The adoption of any other policy would, in addition, have resulted in the creation of different classes of states, or at least of states having different degrees of control over their own problems. It is obvious that this would have resulted in a lack of uniformity with regard to the powers of the states, as well as in the creation of other undesirable conditions. As one writer has observed,[42] this decision does not mean " that the states are free to do whatever they wish, once inside the Union, but holds that one state may do whatever the other states may do, politically, despite bargains to the contrary with Congress in connection with admission. This still leaves the states subject to all of the restrictions which rested upon the original thirteen which formed the Union, in addition to such other restrictions as have been imposed on them since." In the later case of United States v. Sandoval [43]

[41] 221 U. S. 559, 1911.   [42] Field, *op. cit.*, p. 235.   [43] 231 U. S. 28, 1913.

the Court was obliged to deal again with the same fundamental problem. In this decision it was held that Congressional regulation in an enabling act which a state is required to accept as a condition of admission into the Union remains in force after such admission if, and only if, the subject is one within the regulatory power of Congress. It thus seems clear that the obligation imposed on the newly created state is an ethical or moral one, not enforceable at law after the territory has achieved the coveted position of statehood. The state ought to recognize the obligation and respect it, but if it ignores it there is not much that can be done about it.

Another phase of the question of the extent of the power which Congress may exercise over members of the Federal Union is illustrated by Ervien v. United States [44] — a case which might be considered with equal propriety under the heading of the subsidy system. While this is not a problem growing out of conditions of admission, it does involve matters of internal policy. New Mexico had been given a liberal grant of land by Congress, the proceeds from it to be used only for schools, highways, and other definitely specified purposes. The state accepted the grant and then proceeded to use 3 per cent of the annual income from this land for the purpose of advertising and publicizing the state, with the idea of attracting new settlers. The Court held that a property fund granted by Congress under a condition or with reservations was to be distinguished from the police power which a state possesses over its own affairs. The legal doctrine here is in harmony with a well-established principle of law; namely, that gifts, grants, and bequests may ordinarily be accepted and used only in accordance with the conditions accompanying them.

Similar judgments have been rendered in cases involving matters of a commercial character or a promise concerning tax exemptions.[45] Under the Homestead Act of 1863, Minnesota Territory sold tax-exempt homestead land for ten years. Then Minnesota was admitted into the Union as a state. Did she have the right to tax the land? In passing upon this question, the Supreme Court invoked the long-standing principle of international law that, when a government enters into agreement with private parties, the succeeding government is bound thereby. This same principle had been relied upon in the Dartmouth College Case. The point is that the equality of the states — important as that is — is not the only consideration involved in the determination of some of these cases.

44 251 U. S. 41, 1919.   45 Stearns v. Minnesota, 179 Minn. 223, 1900.

Interesting constitutional questions with regard to the admission of new states developed in connection with the partition of Virginia and the admission of West Virginia in 1863. Aside from the somewhat irregular procedure by which this separation was affected during the troublous days of the Civil War, these questions were not peculiar to the Virginia-West Virginia situation; they had occurred in earlier instances and might easily occur again — if, for instance, Texas were to exercise the option contained in the resolution of Congress for its annexation, that four more states might eventually be formed from it. Most important of these questions, perhaps, was the apportionment of the debt. For more than fifty years West Virginia failed to assume its equitable portion, quite in contrast to the arrangements with regard to this matter when Maine was separated from Massachusetts and admitted into the Union in 1820. Virginia was in fact forced " to resort to a long and painful litigation before the United States Supreme Court in order to overcome an obstructive attitude on the part of the younger commonwealth which at times verged upon defiance." Again, there was the question of the boundary. Since Virginia was not consulted on the terms of the separation, since the provisions of the Constitution on this point in Article IV, Section 3, were not complied with (although they are quite definite), the final arrangement was in some respects unfair to the older state. This also was quite in contrast to the Massachusetts-Maine separation. Questions of this character provide an interesting field for study in those states whose history provides incidents of somewhat parallel character.[46]

RELATIONS OF THE STATES TO FOREIGN GOVERNMENTS

Mention has been made of the relations of the states to the governments of foreign nations. The states have little or no occasion to conduct relations with such nations, and are prohibited by a clause in Article I, Section 10, of the Federal Constitution from entering into treaty arrangements. Nevertheless the states can, and sometimes do, seriously imperil the peaceful relations of the Federal government with foreign nations. Instances in point include the Italian Mafia incident in 1891, the California school case in 1906, and the numerous controversies with foreign governments over repudiated state debts.

[46] These questions are discussed in Randall, James G., *Constitutional Problems under Lincoln*, Chapter 18 (Appleton, New York, 1926).

The latter controversies are the oldest. They grew out of extensive loans negotiated abroad for internal improvements in the period following the War of 1812, and out of loans made in the reconstruction period following the Civil War. As a result of these loans, there were numerous state defaults in the forties and in the seventies and eighties; for almost a century those in the first group have been the subject of international controversy. They raise in pointed fashion the question of the international responsibility of states (in the technical sense) for the acts of their political subdivisions — a basic question of international law which the United States was long able to evade. The question was squarely presented to the Supreme Court in 1934, when the Principality of Monaco brought suit against Mississippi on bonds issued by that state. The motion was denied by the Court in an opinion written by Chief Justice Hughes, holding that Article III, Section 2, Clause 1, of the Constitution gives the Supreme Court jurisdiction of such suits only in the event of the state's consent to be sued. Thus a state of the Union is immune from suits which are brought against it by a foreign state without its consent.[47]

The Italian Mafia incident grew out of the murder of the Chief of Police of New Orleans, John C. Hennessey. Investigation revealed the fact that certain Italian residents of the city, members of the Black Hand or Mafia Society, were guilty of the crime. These persons were arrested and confined in the parish jail. One morning prior to the date of their trial, one of the local papers announced that there would be a meeting of citizens on the plaza in front of the jail at four o'clock that afternoon. The crowd assembled, and after a series of harangues descended upon the jail, battered down the gates, went inside and seized five of the accused persons, carried them off and lynched them. Since some of these persons were citizens of Italy, the Italian government protested. While the identity of the leaders of the mob was known, both the governor and the local authorities were in sympathy with the lynchers, and refused to take any effective action looking toward their arrest and conviction. Secretary of State Blaine was placed in the painful and embarrassing position of having to explain to the Italian government that, reprehensible as the crime

[47] Monaco v. Mississippi, 292 U. S. 313, 1934. See McGrane, Reginald C., *Foreign Bondholders and American State Debts* (Macmillan, New York, 1935), and " Some Aspects of American State Debts in the Forties," *American Historical Review*, July, 1933, pp. 673–686; also Ratchford, B. U., " An International Debt Settlement: the North Carolina Debt to France," *American Historical Review*, October, 1934, pp. 63–69, and *American States Debts* (Duke University Press, 1941) .

was and much as the Federal authorities regretted its occurrence, there was nothing they could do about it, since under our Federal system it was a matter falling entirely within the authority of the state government. Even though the Secretary of State literally begged the state authorities to take action for the purpose of avoiding complications between the United States and Italy, they obdurately refused. Italy severed diplomatic relations and recalled its ambassador. For some time there was serious danger of war between the United States and Italy.[48]

In the California school case a controversy between the United States and Japan developed through the refusal of California to comply with certain treaty arrangements existing between Japan and the United States. In these treaties the United States had agreed to accord to Japanese citizens equality of treatment. The San Francisco Board of Education passed, and attempted to enforce, a race segregation ordinance in its public schools. In this case also the Secretary of State, Elihu Root, was obliged to plead with the California officials for such a modification of the resolution as would enable the United States to live up to its treaty obligations, and as would avoid a possible conflict with Japan.[49]

In the summer of 1934 citizens of the Salt River Valley in Arizona became exercised over the fact that Hindus and Japanese were moving up from the Imperial Valley. In spite of Arizona land laws which forbid aliens ineligible for United States citizenship from owning, leasing, or farming land except as laborers, yellow men and brown were already farming 8,000 acres. When the Aryans served notice upon them that they would have to leave or be run out, the Japanese vice consul and half a dozen Japanese businessmen from Los Angeles, as well as the British consul, arrived on the scene. " Protests flashed East and West and overseas." The governor and the state's attorney general went into action to enforce the law, prevent violence, and avoid international complications.[50]

Even more embarrassing to the government of the United States was an incident which occurred in New York City in the summer and

[48] This account is based upon a study of the State Papers made by the author some years ago; a fuller printed summary appears in Curtis, William E., *The United States and Foreign Powers*, Chapter 16 (Scribner's, New York, 1900).

[49] See Root, Elihu, " The Real Question under the Japanese Treaty and the San Francisco School Board Resolution," *American Journal of International Law*, April, 1907, pp. 274–283. For a valuable discussion of the background and the constitutional aspects of the race problem in California, see Swisher, Carl Brent, *Motivation and Political Technique in the California Constitutional Convention, 1878–1879*, Chapter 6 (Pomona College, Claremont, California, 1930).

[50] *Time*, September 3, 1934, p. 15.

fall of 1935. The German liner *Bremen* arrived in New York harbor
on July 26, flying the new flag of the Nazi government. A riot occurred, in the course of which the flag was hauled down and treated
with disrespect. The German government filed a vigorous formal
protest with the Department of State, and relations between the two
governments became somewhat strained. In due course six prisoners
charged with participation in the riot were brought for a hearing
before Magistrate Louis B. Brodsky. Five of them he discharged,
commenting, as he did so, upon the Nazi regime in language " offensive to another government with which we have official relations " —
as Secretary of State Hull was to say shortly after in an official apology
to the German government, whose protest at the words of the magistrate was even more vigorous than before. Three paragraphs from the
statement of Secretary Hull to the Counselor of the German Embassy
are worthy of quotation:

The complaint of the German Government is specifically directed at the
statements made by the magistrate in rendering his decision which that
Government interprets as an unwarranted reflection upon it.

The Department is constrained to feel that the magistrate, in restating
contentions of the defendants in the case and in commenting upon the
incident, unfortunately so worded his opinion as to give the reasonable and
definite impression that he was going out of his way adversely to criticize
the government, which criticism was not a relevant or legitimate part of his
judicial decision.

I may explain that State and municipal officials are not instrumentalities
of the Federal Government. Although in this country the right of freedom
of speech is well recognized by our fundamental law, it is to be regretted
that an official having no responsibility for maintaining relations between
the United States and other countries should, regardless of what he may
personally think of the laws and policies of other governments, thus indulge
in expressions offensive to another government with which we have official
relations.[51]

It is a serious weakness of our federal system that it should be
possible for a state so to conduct its affairs as to involve the Federal
government in diplomatic difficulties with other nations. The question has often been discussed but no remedial measures have ever been
adopted. Perhaps the most promising solution is one proposed by
Attorney General Daugherty in 1922; his suggestion was that Congress should by law provide that all cases involving questions arising
under the treaty obligations of the United States, regardless of the
subject with which they dealt, should be taken immediately and automatically into the Federal courts for adjudication. This proposal

[51] *New York Times,* September 15, 1935.

has the merit of being simple, effective, and of not requiring any modification of the Constitution; it should be adopted.

SELECTED REFERENCES

Ames, Herman V., *State Documents on Federal Relations* (University of Pennsylvania, 1911).

Beman, Lamar T., *Selected Articles on State Rights* (Wilson, New York, 1926).

Benson, George C. S., *The New Centralization* (Farrar and Rinehart, New York, 1941).

Bitterman, Henry J., *State and Federal Grants-in-Aid* (Mentzer, Bush and Company, Chicago, 1938).

Brown, Everett S., *Ratification of the Twenty-first Amendment to the Constitution of the United States* (University of Michigan Press, 1938).

Burdick, Charles K., *The Law of the American Constitution* (Putnam, New York, 1922).

Burger, Alvin A., *Should the Federal Government Subsidize Education?* (New Jersey State Chamber of Commerce, Newark, 1945).

Clark, Jane Perry, *The Rise of a New Federalism* (Columbia University Press, 1938).

Council of State Governments, *Grants-in-Aids and Other Federal Expenditures within the States* (Chicago, 1945).

Dunning, William A., "Are the States Equal under the Constitution?" *Essays on the Civil War and Reconstruction*, pp. 304–352 (Macmillan, New York, 1898).

Editorial Research Reports, *Revision of the Constitution* (Washington, 1937).

Graves, W. Brooke, *Uniform State Action* (University of North Carolina Press, 1934).

—— Ed., "Intergovernmental Relations in the United States," *Annals,* January, 1940. (See extensive bibliography, pp. 210–218.)

—— Ed., *Centralization in the United States, 1933–1939,* being the proceedings of a round table, 1939 Annual Meeting, American Political Science Association (Philadelphia, 1940).

Greenough, Katherine C., *The Amending Process: The Orderly Method of Change* (National League of Women Voters, Washington, 1938).

Hehmeyer, Alexander, *Time for Change: A Proposal for a Second Constitutional Convention* (Farrar and Rinehart, New York, 1943).

Heinberg, John G., *Manual on Federal-State Relations* (Missouri Constitutional Convention of 1943, Columbia, 1943).

Howard, George E., *Preliminaries of the Revolution, 1763–1775* (Harper, New York, 1905).

Howell, Roger, *The Privileges and Immunities of State Citizenship* (Johns Hopkins University Studies, Series XXXVI, No. 3, 1918).

Kenyon, Dorothy, *Changing the Constitution: A Study of the Amending Process* (National League of Women Voters, Washington, 1926).

Key, V. O., Jr., *The Administration of Federal Grants to States* (Public Administration Service, Chicago, 1937).

Leigh, Robert D., *Federal Health Administration in the United States* (Harper, New York, 1927).

Macdonald, Austin F., *Federal Aid* (Crowell, New York, 1928).

McLaughlin, Andrew C., *Confederation and Constitution* (Harper, New York, 1905).

Merriam, Charles E., *History of American Political Theories* (Macmillan, New York, 1903).

Mitchell, Nicholas P., *State Interests in American Treaties* (Garrett and Massie, Richmond, 1936).

Nevins, Allan, *The American States During and After the Revolution* (Macmillan, New York, 1924).

Patterson, Ernest M., Ed., " Federal versus State Jurisdiction in American Life," *Annals,* January, 1927.

Quattlebaum, Charles A., *Federal Aid to the States for Education* (Library of Congress, Legislative Reference Series, 1944).

Stephens, Harry R., *The Government of the Indians in South Dakota* (University of South Dakota, Governmental Research Bureau, 1942).

Summers, Harrison B. and Robert E., *Increasing Federal Power* (Wilson, New York, 1940).

Swisher, Carl B., *American Constitutional Development* (Houghton Mifflin, Boston, 1943).

Thompson, Walter, *Federal Centralization* (Harcourt, Brace, New York, 1923).

United States Senate, Committee on Commerce, *Federal Aid for Public Airports,* Hearings on S 2 and S 34 (Washington, 1945).

Willoughby, W. W., *Constitutional Law of the United States,* Second Edition, 3 vols. (Baker, Voorhis, New York, 1929).

Wooddy, Carroll H., *The Growth of the Federal Government, 1915–1932* (McGraw-Hill, New York, 1934).

Benson, George C. S., " Federal-State Personnel Relations," *Annals,* January, 1940, pp. 38–43.

Harris, Joseph P., " The Future of Federal Grants-in-Aid," *Annals,* January, 1940, pp. 14–26.

Hazard, John N., " Federalism in the U.S.S.R.," *State Government,* June, 1945, pp. 92–94.

Hodgetts, John E., " Problems of Canadian Federalism," *State Government,* June, 1945, pp. 95–99.

Key, V. O., Jr., " State Legislation Facilitative of Federal Action," *Annals,* January, 1940, pp. 7–13.

Macdonald, Austin F., " Federal Aid to the States: 1940 Model," *American Political Science Review,* June, 1940, pp. 489–499.

May, Henry J., " The Union of South Africa: The Provinces and the Central Government," *State Government,* July, 1945, pp. 115–119.

Walker, Harvey, " Federalism in Brazil," *State Government,* March, 1945, pp. 43–44, 52.

Williams, J. Kerwin and Edward A., " New Techniques of Federal Aid," *American Political Science Review,* October, 1940, pp. 947–954.

CHAPTER II

State Constitutions

HISTORY AND CHARACTERISTICS

THE supreme law clause in Article VI of the Federal Constitution provides that this Constitution shall be " the supreme law of the land." While the states, therefore, are bound by the provisions of this document, each of them has an instrument of government of its own. These state constitutions serve as the fundamental law of the states in somewhat the same manner in which the Federal Constitution serves as the fundamental law of the Federal government, or the municipal charter as the fundamental law of a municipality. It is important, therefore, that one be familiar with the characteristics of the original state constitutions, with their development, with the essential elements of the present state constitutions, and with recent tendencies in constitution making.

The Original Constitutions and Their Background. A study of the origins of the American state constitutions carries one back into the history of the Middle Ages; these constitutions are in reality the oldest instruments of government on this continent. The trading companies of the Middle Ages were obliged eventually to establish trading posts, for they discovered that it was too difficult for the operators of their vessels to sell the cargoes which they brought with them and buy up a new cargo of goods to take back to their native land. In the effort to expedite the trading process, outposts were established at which the cargo was sold and a new cargo of native products collected. As these posts increased in size, questions arose as to the exercise of governmental authority. The companies exercised such authority as seemed necessary without much supervision. As the significance of the problem was recognized, the charters of trading companies were amended to include provisions regarding the government of such outposts as the company might establish.

In accordance with these practices, developed over a period of many years, trading companies exercised governmental authority over colonies and trading posts established in America. Many of these charters continued in use with slight modification during the entire colonial period; their life approximately equaled the life of our existing governmental machinery. When it became apparent that the struggle for independence would be a long one, the colonies realized that they must have a better organization. Before the Declaration of Independence had actually been adopted, seven of the states had independent governments; four of them were contemplating changes. Massachusetts retained its provisional government until 1780, at which date it adopted a constitution which remained in effect — with many amendments — for more than 140 years. Upon the recommendation of Congress, all the colonies applied themselves to the task of establishing state governments. New Hampshire and South Carolina adopted such plans on January 5 and March 26, 1776, respectively; they proved defective and were soon replaced.

When the states acquired a status of independence as a result of the Declaration of Independence and of the successful prosecution of the Revolutionary War, several of them continued to use their previously existing charters as instruments of government under the new regime. This was true of Connecticut and Rhode Island; a few changes were made with reference to the King and short bills of rights were added, but Connecticut did not adopt a new constitution until 1819, nor Rhode Island until 1842. The student of American constitutional development must be impressed by two significant facts in this general situation. In the first place, there was no sharp break in the development of our institutions before and after the achievement of independence. The original constitutions were, like most things governmental, a result of generations — and in some cases centuries — of human experience. They were, in fact, little more than the previously existing constitutions adapted to changed conditions. In the second place, it is significant that the state constitutions antedated the Constitution of the Federal government. Accustomed to acknowledging the debt of the states to the Federal government, one may forget that originally the situation was reversed — that the provisions of the Federal Constitution were based upon the experience of the states and the provisions of their constitutions in effect when the Federal Convention met.

The ideas of government in the original state constitutions were very similar. Eight of them contained a bill of rights, and all provided for three branches of government and severe restrictions on the exercise of the suffrage. Provision for amendment was made in eight constitutions but was omitted in five. An authority in the history of this period describes the original constitutions in the following terms:

. . . In all there were the three departments, — the Executive, Legislative, and Judicial; and these were rendered independent of one another. In most of the States the executive was hampered by a council. In Pennsylvania and Georgia the legislature consisted of one branch; in the others of two branches, according to the custom of the colonial period. In four States the Governor was to be chosen by the people; in the others, by the legislature.

These constitutions were said to be " ordained, declared, established," and were not to be altered except in the manner pointed out. Thus they assume to be modes of action different from ordinary acts of legislation. They were universally recognized and held to be such. They were really decrees of the people as constituting the sovereignty. They prescribed the degrees and spheres of power by which their agents or " trustees " periodically chosen to make or administer the laws were to be governed in their various departments. Their sphere is internal government. Their provisions give validity and continuity to the body of local law. In no instance is there power conferred on these local agents to deal with foreign nations. This function had been vested by the same sovereignty in a congress; and the constitutions contain provisions for the appointment of members to compose it.

These governments went immediately into operation. Well-known characters were selected to fill the high offices. . . . These names gave *éclat* to the new governments. This field of labor and honor proved more attractive than the national council; and the work of enfranchising the local law from features derived from European traditions — the abolition of entails, primogeniture, and an established church — worthily employed the time and thought of the most able statesmen. The spectacle of republican order was a novelty in the political world.[1]

Their Characteristics. Although the original constitutions were alike in their recognition of three distinct branches of government, the principle of the separation of powers was not always fully observed in practice. Pennsylvania and Georgia approached more nearly the democratic ideal. Members were elected annually, except in South Carolina, where the term was two years. In one state members of the upper house were chosen by the members in office at the time of the election. The term in the upper house was usually three or five years. Property qualifications for members of the upper house

[1] Frothingham, Richard, *The Rise of the Republic of the United States,* pp. 567–568 (Little, Brown, Boston, 1899) .

were high, and religious qualifications for governor and for members of the legislature were prescribed. In four states the governor had to be a Protestant, in two a Christian; in Delaware it was necessary that he believe in the Trinity. Property qualifications for officeholding in this state were established on a sliding scale arrangement, the amount of the requirement depending upon the importance of the office. The names given the legislative bodies reflected the earlier history of the colonies, as in North Carolina, where the name " House of Commons " was used, and in New Jersey, which had a " Legislative Council." The executive was called the Governor in all but two states — Pennsylvania and New Hampshire; but Massachusetts was the only state to give him a limited veto power. The judiciary was not, as a rule, fully provided for, the completion of the plan being left to the legislatures. Georgia was the only state to elect its judges by popular vote. The term of judges was usually good behavior. Their salary was fixed by the legislature, a provision which, under conditions then existing, made the judiciary lacking in independence and security. Rhode Island failed to re-elect judges who refused to sanction a law making paper money legal tender. One has only to read over these descriptive features of the early constitutions to realize how far we have changed our concepts of desirable public policy.

The framers of these constitutions, in addition to providing for the three major departments of government in separate and watertight compartments, believed that the check and balance system would prevent the concentration of power in the hands of any one officer or department of government. They were greatly worried lest such a concentration of power should lead to the establishment of a dictatorship or an oligarchy. Consequently, while only one state gave the governor the veto power, all of them conferred extensive powers upon the legislative branch, including the power to pass upon appointments recommended by the governor. The courts were to serve as a check upon both the governor and the legislature. It is conceivable that this system of checks and balances, if used extensively enough, might undermine the separation of powers. This, however, the framers of these early constitutions avoided, resorting to the check and balance system only to such an extent as would in practice strengthen and protect the separation of powers. Both of these principles are still in evidence in the present-day constitutions, although many governmental practices have developed which make them much less effective than they were originally intended to be, and although the confidence of students in their soundness has greatly diminished.

Comparison with Present-day Constitutions. The characteristics of the original state constitutions and of the more recent ones can best be presented by a series of comparisons and contrasts, covering such points as length, content, relations of executive and legislative branches, et cetera. The basic principles remain much the same. The original constitutions were brief and concise; the modern ones are lengthy and verbose, being padded with great quantities of legislative material. The original constitutions were confined to the statement of fundamental principles, whereas present-day constitutions include great numbers of detailed provisions on an ever increasing number of subjects. Many of them have been expanded until they would fill a moderate-sized volume if the same size type and format were used as in trade publications. The Constitution of California, for instance, contains approximately 70,000 words, that of Oklahoma 50,000 words, while that of Louisiana takes 130 printed pages. This excessive length can be traced directly to the steadily diminishing confidence with which, over a period of many years, the people regarded their legislative bodies and to the increasing number and complexity of governmental functions. These innumerable restrictions and limitations are an interesting development of our democracy. They limit the subject matter with which the legislature may deal, the number of its sessions, and the number of days the sessions may last. They impose restrictions upon corporations, and limitations upon the financial powers of both states and cities with regard to methods of raising money, tax limits, debt limits, et cetera.

There were certain basic principles of government which were generally accepted by those who framed the original state constitutions; many of these have remained a part of the American political tradition. Among them were the bill of rights, the principle of the separation of powers, the check and balance system, the concept of the relation of the executive and legislative branches of the government, and the general distrust of popular control. Many of those who participated in the framing of the Federal Constitution had previously given similar service in their respective states; their adherence to the principle of the separation of powers, under the influence of the writing of the French political philosopher Montesquieu, was in evidence in the state conventions as well as in the Federal Convention. Their respect for and knowledge of English institutions prompted them to adopt what they believed to be an

essential element in the success of the English system. Professor
Becker writes of the attitude of the colonists in general toward the
mother country:

> It is this aspect of the Revolution that gives it its chief significance for
> modern democracy. The privileged classes in the Colonies, generally speak-
> ing, never really desired separation from Great Britain. They took old
> England as their ideal. Outside of New England most educated men were
> educated in England, and wished for nothing better than to fashion their
> clothes, their houses, their minds, and their manners on the best English
> models. They opposed parliamentary taxation because they wanted to
> manage their own affairs in miniature parliaments, where they could carry
> on miniature contests with the governors for control of the purse, after
> the manner of the English Parliament in the seventeenth century. In no
> sense were they democrats; and they were as much afraid of radical move-
> ments in the Colonies as they were of British oppression. They wanted
> to preserve their *liberties* against parliament, without sharing their *privi-
> leges* with the people in the Colonies. They wanted home rule, but they
> wanted to rule at home. Left to themselves, the governing classes in America
> would never have carried the contest to the point of rebellion, would never
> have created an independent state.[2]

It is in the relations of the executive and legislative branches of the
government that the greatest contrasts are to be found between the
original and present-day constitutions. The framers of the early
constitutions had a deep and profound distrust of the executive authority. When one recalls their experience during the years preceding the Revolution, this is not difficult to explain. The Royal Governors were the agents of the King and of Parliament in America.
In their efforts to enforce the orders of the Crown and the acts of
Parliament in America, these governors came to be a veritable per-
sonification of the idea of oppression. Whether the acts to which the
colonists objected were in fact oppressive or whether the colonists
merely believed that they were makes no difference — the psychological effect is the same in either case. In view of this experience it
is not strange that the framers of these early constitutions sought by
every means at their command to limit and restrict the powers of
their governors. They were determined that these officials should no
longer have the power to do wrong; the fact that the withholding of
such power inevitably withheld from them the power to do things
necessary and proper for the effective functioning of their government had not yet impressed itself upon them.

At the same time that the inhabitants of these newly established

[2] Becker, Carl, *The United States, An Experiment in Democracy*, pp. 45–46
(Harper, New York, 1920).

states were seeking to curb the exercise of executive power, they were conferring almost unlimited powers upon their legislative bodies. The historical background of this fact is likewise easy to discover.[3] Time and time again throughout the period preceding the Revolution, it had been the representative assemblies that had offered protest against the oppressive acts of the Crown, the Parliament, and the Royal Governors. On one occasion after another these bodies had drafted and adopted resolutions of protest, had organized committees of correspondence, and finally had organized and contributed to the financing of the troops in the Revolutionary War. It was therefore quite natural that the framers of the early constitutions should confer broad powers upon their legislative bodies. In doing so they did no differently from what we would have done had we lived in their day and been subjected to their experience.

In the course of the last century and a half, significant changes have occurred in the relative positions of the executive and legislative branches of the government. While the prestige of the executive has steadily increased, that of the legislature has constantly declined. This change has been due largely to the failure of the legislatures to respond to the trust imposed in them; their personnel included too many persons lacking either the intellectual and educational requirements or the integrity essential to the operation of government on an honest and effective basis. They failed so often to deal adequately with pressing problems that they gradually lost the confidence of the public. Instances of fraud and dishonesty were not rare. As the prestige of the legislatures declined, the people were more and more disposed to regard the executive as their champion. This tendency has been accentuated since the inauguration of the movement for administrative reorganization — a movement which has made governors of states, in fact as well as in name, the responsible heads of their respective state governments.

The early constitutions differ from modern ones also in their attitude toward popular participation in government. The Founding Fathers were exceedingly cautious in this respect. Their conception of democracy bore a striking resemblance to what might now be

---

[3] Senator George Woodward has a very simple explanation: " We all know that it was Thomas Jefferson or someone of the Fathers who could read French who read M. Montesquieu's essay on three compartments in government. The Father thought it over in English and put it in all our constitutions. It is therefore customary for the legislative, executive and judicial compartments to abstain from one another's society and to try to misunderstand one another as far as possible. This promotes business in the art of government and adds zest to elections." *The Pennsylvania Legislator*, May, 1935.

called "mobocracy." They did not believe in "government of the people, by the people, and for the people," preferring rather a government of the people by the best people. They took extreme care in their effort to protect the people from what they feared might be the results of their own folly. The election of many officials was placed on an indirect basis. In New Jersey, which may be taken as a typical example, nearly all the state officials were chosen by the Council and Assembly in joint meeting; they were commissioned by the governor after such election. A very small number of minor officials were elected by the direct vote of the people.[4]

In most states the suffrage was restricted to men who were members in good standing, contributing to the support of the predominant religious sect of the state in which they lived, and to those who owned property. Even the majority of white persons could not vote. South Carolina limited the suffrage to those who believed in God and a future state of rewards and punishments. Property qualifications were higher to vote for senator than to vote for a member of the lower house. Although religious freedom was granted, there was everywhere a close connection between Church and State, and in Massachusetts the Congregational Church was practically the established one until the middle of the nineteenth century. The modern constitutions differ greatly with respect to the suffrage, for by long and laborious effort, not merely a universal manhood suffrage, but universal suffrage has been established. Important steps toward this goal were Amendment XV, which has been partially successful in extending the suffrage to the Negro; Amendment XIX, which made woman suffrage nationwide; and the general removal of religious and property qualifications for voting.

ESSENTIAL ELEMENTS OF A STATE CONSTITUTION

A constitution is a body of *fundamental law*. It is established for the purpose of providing a set of governmental machinery, on the one hand, and of protecting citizens from an unfair or improper use of governmental authority, on the other. There are in all constitutions — old and new alike — certain essential features which must be included if the constitution is to meet in a satisfactory manner the needs which led to its adoption. These fundamentals may be grouped

---

[4] The list of the New Jersey officers indirectly chosen, together with their terms of office, follows: Judges and Clerks of the Supreme Court and of the Inferior Court of Common Pleas, and Justices of the Peace — all seven years; Attorney General and Provincial Secretary, both five years; Provincial Treasurer, one year; and field and general officers of the State Militia.

for purposes of discussion under four headings: the bill of rights, the framework of government, its powers, and provision for piece-meal amendment.

Bill of Rights. In the United States we have become definitely attached to the idea of a written bill of rights incorporated in the body of a constitution. The idea of the bill of rights owes its origin to a period of political philosophy during which great stress was laid upon the doctrine of natural rights. Its purpose was then, and is now, to guarantee to the individual the enjoyment of certain rights and privileges against possible infringement by governmental authority. Eight of the Revolutionary constitutions had bills of rights, either as a preamble or as a postscript. The first bill of rights in America was drafted by George Mason, who presented it to the Virginia Constitutional Convention of 1776, by which it was adopted and from which the idea spread rapidly to the other states. The Declaration of the Rights of Man was copied from these bills of rights, which, in turn, went back to the English Bill of Rights.[5]

In general, it may be said that provisions of the bills of rights in the state constitutions run parallel to the provisions of the Bill of Rights of the Federal Constitution. They serve the purpose of protecting the individual from infringement by the state governments of substantially the same rights against whose infringement by the Federal government he is guaranteed by the first ten amendments of the Federal Constitution. While these rights are everywhere regarded as fundamental, they are subject to some modification with the passage of time. Rights which are vital to the people of one age may become either unimportant or so widely recognized that they are rarely if ever questioned in another. Similarly, new conditions give rise to the demand for the protection of new rights. Present-day Americans are little concerned with some of the older rights, but they are vitally interested in the protection of certain social and economic rights which the development of an industrial civilization has made vital. Among these are old age pensions, unemployment insurance, public assistance, and social security legislation generally. They are concerned with the elimination of child labor, with maximum hours, minimum wages and conditions of labor, with housing conditions, and with programs of social and economic planning. Such questions have assumed an importance quite as great as that of ancient rights won in the long struggle for human liberty.

The bill of rights protects both personal and property rights.

5 See Hill, Helen, *George Mason, Constitutionalist* (Harvard University Press, 1938).

With regard to personal rights, its provisions are of two types: those relating to the protection of individuals in the normal course of life, and those relating to the protection of persons accused of crime. Among the former are the ordinary personal and civil rights such as religious freedom,[6] freedom of speech, freedom of assemblage, freedom of the press, and other rights once much more important than they are now: freedom from the quartering of troops in times of peace, freedom from unreasonable searches and seizures, the right to bear arms, et cetera. Most of the rights accorded to persons accused of crime fall under the heading of due process of law — the right to indictment by grand jury, to trial where the offense was committed, to trial by jury, to a speedy and public trial; freedom from the necessity for self-incrimination and from double jeopardy, from excessive bails and fines, and from cruel and unusual punishments. In addition to all these, there are miscellaneous safeguards of accused persons, which vary according to the jurisdiction in which the offense is being tried.[7]

In connection with the protection of property, the clauses with regard to due process and eminent domain are most important. Although the due process clause in Amendment XIV applies only to the states, the majority of the state constitutions contain a provision of similar purpose and intent — often in the identical words: " No person shall be deprived of life, liberty, or property without due process of law." There is also the provision that private property shall not be taken for public use without just compensation. These guarantees are so essential to the well-being of the individual that their occasional repetition does no harm.

Framework of the Government. The second essential of a state constitution includes the provisions outlining the framework of government. These must provide for the establishment of the three branches of government, and should provide for necessary extensions of government service by legislative act, and the means by which incumbents of higher offices should be selected. The most frequent difficulty has been that the framers of constitutions have attempted to establish specific offices — a practice which has made it difficult to adapt the machinery of government to changed conditions and

[6] The epitaph inscribed on the monument at the tomb of Thomas Jefferson at Monticello was written by himself; in it he mentions his authorship of this provision but not the fact that he was twice President.

[7] Excellent analyses of the bills of rights have been made in connection with recent constitutional conventions in Georgia, Missouri, and New York. See also, National Lawyers Guild, New York City Chapter, *Report* of the Special Committee . . . Concerning the Bill of Rights Article (New York, 1938) .

changing needs. Essential services should be provided for in such general terms that the legislature will be free to provide such organization and personnel as it may deem necessary. The progress of the reorganization movement has been hampered in many states by constitutional officers, provisions as to salaries, and other matters.

The framers of the state constitutions might well take a leaf from the experience of the nation under the Federal Constitution. The office of the President is created, and its powers outlined. There is no mention of a cabinet — only the statement that the President may require reports in writing of the heads of his departments. The provision is also made that his salary shall be neither increased nor diminished during his term of office. The legislative power is vested in Congress, the scope of that power being limited to the subjects entrusted to the control of the Federal government. Similarly, the judicial power is vested by the Constitution in a Supreme Court and such inferior courts as Congress may from time to time ordain and establish, with a clause on salaries similar to that applying to the President. The makers of state constitutions should deal with these essential subjects with the same brevity and clarity.

Powers of the Government. The third essential relates to the powers which shall be exercised by the machinery so established. Either the constitution should enumerate the several types of power to be entrusted to the government agencies, or it should state definitely and clearly some principle by means of which these powers may be determined. In some cases a combination of these two methods might be used. The result should be that the state is free to exercise all the powers belonging to it under our federal system, minus only such powers as the convention sees fit to deny to the state government altogether. Such an ideal solution of this problem has rarely, if ever, been achieved. Many of the constitutions now in effect were framed in the latter half of the last century. The movement to increase the power and responsibility of the governor had not yet begun. For reasons to be discussed more fully later, the legislatures were at a low ebb in public esteem, and every effort was made, not to give them power to perform their task well, but to limit their powers in such a way that they might be able to do a minimum amount of harm. During this period the judicial branch suffered less than either of the other two.

This question has much more than a mere theoretical significance. The constitutions have, in fact, gone into such greater detail in the enumeration of the powers which the government might exercise and of those which were prohibited that it has been found repeatedly that this practice, coupled with prevailing doctrines of judicial interpretation, has prevented the enactment of desirable social and economic legislation. Illustrations were numerous during the depression in states whose constitutions were more than a quarter of a century old.

Provisions for Amendment. The fourth essential of a state constitution is a workable method of piecemeal amendment. This item is, in fact, so important that a separate section of this chapter is devoted to its consideration. The amending processes of many state constitutions furnish striking and indisputable evidence of the fact that unworkable amending provisions constitute a barrier to the progress of the state. Government is a changing, growing, developing, dynamic institution, in need of continuous adaptation to changed social and economic conditions. A constitution whose amending provisions make it impossible to make necessary modifications in governmental institutions comes to be a sort of constitutional straitjacket. We cannot prevent governmental changes by failing to make adequate constitutional provision for them. The alternative method is likely to be a revolutionary upheaval caused by the accumulation of grievances and social and economic maladjustments. This alternative is not pleasing to a society whose governmental tradition is based upon the orderly processes characteristic of Anglo-Saxon institutions.

Analysis of the Contents of Existing Constitutions. With a view to getting a picture of the scope of the constitutions now in force, an effort was made to classify the headings of the various articles of these constitutions. The results are indicated in the following table:

1. Agriculture and Public Lands — 16 articles in 12 states.
2. Amending the Constitution — 48 articles in 44 states.
3. Banks and Banking; Insurance — 6 articles in 5 states.
4. Corporations Other than Municipal — 39 articles in 37 states.
5. Counties (see Local Government) — 21 articles in 19 states.
6. Declaration of Rights — 49 articles in 48 states.
7. Education (School Taxes, Funds, and Lands) — 44 articles in 42 states.
8. Executive Department — 51 articles in 48 states.
9. Federal-State Relations—6 articles in 6 states.
10. Health — 12 articles in 11 states.
11. Homesteads and Exemptions — 15 articles in 12 states.
12. Impeachment (see Removal from Office) — 21 articles in 21 states.
13. Institutions and Public Buildings — 22 articles in 22 states.
14. Intoxicating Liquors — 6 articles in 5 states.
15. Judiciary — 50 articles in 48 states.
16. Labor — 6 articles in 6 states.

17. Legislative Department — 52 articles in 48 states.
18. Local Government — 13 articles in 12 states.
19. Militia — 39 articles in 37 states.
20. Mines and Mining — 6 articles in 5 states.
21. Miscellaneous Provisions — 57 articles in 41 states.
22. Municipal Corporations — 27 articles in 24 states.
23. Oath of Office — 8 articles in 8 states.
24. Officers of Government — 27 articles in 20 states.
25. Powers of Government, Distribution of — 34 articles in 33 states.
26. Public Debt (State) — 18 articles in 18 states.
27. Public Salaries — 6 articles in 5 states.
28. Public Works — 5 articles in 5 states.
29. Railroads, Canals, and Turnpikes — 5 articles in 5 states.
30. Removal from Office (including Impeachment) — 11 articles in 11 states.
31. Representation, Apportionment of; Census — 15 articles in 14 states.
32. Road Bond Issues and Taxes — 8 articles in 6 states.
33. School Taxes, Funds, and Lands — 11 articles in 10 states.
34. State and County Boundaries, State Capital — 28 articles in 24 states.
35. Suffrage and Elections — 52 articles in 46 states.
36. Taxation and Revenue, Finance — 41 articles in 37 states.
37. Water Rights, Harbors, etc. — 11 articles in 8 states.

In the framing of a modern constitution an effort at brevity should be made. This in turn will mean less legislative matter in the constitution and greater discretion for the legislature. There should be an easier and more workable amending process, although it is also likely that, if other provisions are properly framed, there will be less need for using it. The aim should be, in the words of Mr. Justice Cardozo, to "state principles of government for an expanding future."

PROVISIONS FOR AMENDMENT

The emergency of the depression repeatedly illustrated the dangers that arise in the absence of workable provisions for piecemeal amendment. In many states needed funds for relief were held up and desirable social legislation delayed because of the difficulty or the impossibility of getting necessary constitutional changes with any reasonable speed. The more detailed matter the constitution contains, the more urgent is the need for an easy amending process; this is clearly evident even in so-called normal times. A few years ago the Holland Tunnel between New York and New Jersey and the Delaware River Bridge between Camden and Philadelphia were under construction at the same time. The cost of the two projects was about the same. New Jersey promptly provided its part of the money for both of them, but the construction of the bridge was repeatedly delayed because Pennsylvania could not provide the necessary funds out of current revenues, and could not operate an antiquated amending procedure with sufficient speed. In this state, loans for more than $1,000,000 may not be made except by amending the constitution; amendments require the action of two successive legislatures and, for a period of sixteen years, could not be submitted oftener than once in five years. This was frequently referred to as the time-lock provision. Illustrations of the ill effects of a slow and cumbersome amending process can be readily found in many states.

Proposal of Amendments by Conventions. In 1919, when Walter F. Dodd prepared his analysis of the amending provisions of state constitutions for the Illinois Convention, he listed six different types of amending procedure in existence among the several states at that time.[8] Changes may have since occurred in individual states but the types of methods used have not been substantially changed. The first method is used in New Hampshire, where amendment of the constitution is possible by constitutional convention only. Against this method must be noted its extreme costliness and its time-consuming and cumbersome nature. What happens in practice is that individual changes are not made when needed, but are permitted to accumulate, since it is impractical to place upon the state the financial burden of a convention for relatively minor changes. Nevertheless, conventions have been held at frequent intervals — in 1930, 1938, and 1941, respectively.

While in New Hampshire all amendments to the constitution emanate from conventions, some amendments may come before the people from this source in other states. It is assumed that the work of constitutional convention will ordinarily result in a proposed new instrument of government, but this does not necessarily follow. Very often a convention will propose the retention of the existing constitution, and will propose a series of amendments thereto. Even when the number of amendments is so extensive as to result in a thorough revision of the constitution, it may still be held by the courts that the original constitution, as amended, is in effect. Thus the New York Constitution of 1938 is still referred to as the Constitution of 1894.

[8] Illinois Constitutional Convention, *Bulletin* No. 3, " The Amending Article of the Constitution " (Springfield, 1919) ; Rohlfing, Charles C., " Amendment and Revision of State Constitutions," *Annals*, September, 1935, pp. 180–187. In the *Book of the States*, beginning 1941–1942, there has been a biennial report on current developments in state constitutions and constitutional conventions, by W. Brooke Graves and Irving J. Zipin, giving full information on amending procedures.

Methods of Legislative Proposal. Under Dodd's classification there are four different methods of legislative proposal of amendments. The first of these is used in Delaware, which permits amendment by two successive legislatures without a direct popular vote. This method, like amendment by special convention, preserves the valuable distinction between constitutional provisions and ordinary statutory law; its chief defect lies in the fact that it violates an almost universal practice of the American states; namely, the submission of constitutional provisions to a popular referendum for their approval or rejection.

The second method of legislative proposal involves technicalities which have fortunately appeared in only two states. In South Carolina, amendments may be proposed by the legislature, with a popular vote upon the proposal but with the ultimate approval or rejection of the proposal left to the legislature. A similar provision exists in Mississippi. The objection to this procedure is obvious. There would seem to be little justification for the expenditures incident to the conduct of a referendum if, after the people have rendered their decision, the legislature is at liberty to disregard it.

The third method, with certain modifications to be noted below, is used in more than half the states. Under this plan, amendments are proposed by the legislature subject to popular approval, but with the amending process subject to such restrictions as to make amendment of the constitution difficult. These restrictions are of three types, the first of which requires the action of two successive legislatures for the proposal of amendments, upon the theory that such proposals will be of sufficient importance to influence the selection of legislative personnel. The second imposes limitations upon the number, frequency, and character of proposals. Thus it may happen, as was the case in Pennsylvania for many years, that amendments may not be voted upon oftener than once in five years; that, as in Indiana, only one proposal may be voted on at a time; or, as in Illinois, that the legislature may not propose amendments to more than one article of the constitution; or that the same proposal may not be resubmitted within a specified period of time. In some cases any other proposal to amend the same article is prohibited within a specified period of time. One serious disadvantage of permitting amendments only at periodic intervals is the fact that often ten, twelve, or more amendments appear on a ballot to be voted upon at a single election.

The third type of restriction requires a popular vote greater than that of a majority of all the persons voting on the amendment. In other words, instead of permitting the ratification of an amendment by a majority of the persons voting thereon, this provision requires the affirmative vote of a majority of those participating in the election. It is a matter of common knowledge that not many more than half the people who participated in an election of public officials vote on referendum proposals submitted at the same time. When, in addition to this, one recalls the general tendency of voters to vote " No " on propositions submitted in this way, it is possible to get some idea of the handicaps that such a system imposes upon the use of the amending process. It is also significant that some states have all three of these restrictive measures in force in their constitutions, thereby making any piecemeal amendment exceedingly difficult, if not practically impossible.

The fourth method of amendment permits unrestricted proposals by one legislative action only, and adoption by the majority of the persons voting thereon. If constitutions must be weighed down by great masses of detail, this is, of all the possible methods of constitutional amendment, the most satisfactory. If state constitutions were better framed, the question of the nature of the amending provisions would not be so important. This method has the merit of preserving the worthwhile distinction between constitutional and statutory law, without at the same time erecting impossible barriers to the use of the amending procedure.

Of the forty-seven states providing for the proposal of amendments by the legislature, all but eight authorize introduction in either house.[9] In five states — Arkansas, Florida, Kentucky, New Mexico, and Texas — proposals for amendment may be introduced only at regular sessions of the legislature. Louisiana prescribes that no proposal may be considered unless introduced within the first thirty days of the session, whether regular or special. Provision is regularly made with regard to the size of the vote necessary to approve proposals for amendment. A two-thirds vote of each house is necessary in nineteen states. In eighteen states the requirement is a majority of those elected. Six states require a three-fifths majority. Nebraska requires a favorable vote of three fifths of those elected to its single-chambered legislative body.[10]

[9] Connecticut permits introduction in the lower house only; Vermont in the upper house only. Minnesota, Mississippi, Missouri, North Carolina, Rhode Island, and Texas are silent on this subject.

[10] *Two-thirds vote:* California, Colorado, Connecticut, Delaware, Georgia, Idaho, Illinois, Kansas, Louisiana, Maine, Michigan, Montana, South Carolina, Tennessee, Texas, Utah, Washington, West Virginia, and Wyoming. *Majority of those elected:* Arizona, Arkansas, Indiana, Iowa, Missouri, Nevada, New Jersey,

The Constitutional Initiative. The final method of amendment exists in thirteen states, which, in addition to the legislative power of proposal, permit the popular initiation of constitutional amendments. One's judgment concerning the desirability of this supplementary amending procedure will depend largely upon his attitude toward direct legislation in general. If he regards the initiative, referendum, and recall as devices vital to effective popular control of government, he will doubtless approve their application to the problem of constitutional amendment. If, on the other hand, he has serious objections to the use of these methods in other fields, he is not likely to approve their application to the problem of constitutional modification. Further doubts may be raised by the oppressive labor measures and the " ham and eggs " proposals that were brought before the voters of the Pacific Coast states in 1938 and other recent years.

Under the initiative plan, any individual or group of individuals may draft a proposed amendment and, by securing the signatures of a certain number of qualified voters to a petition, bring about its submission to a popular vote. This method originated in Oregon in 1902 and has now spread to thirteen states. The percentage of signatures that must be secured varies from eight to fifteen, and other limitations have been imposed upon the operation of this method. These involve such matters as the geographical distribution of the signatures to the petition (Missouri) , scrutiny of the proposal by the legislature (Massachusetts) , and requirements as to the size of the popular vote necessary for approval. Except in California and Oregon, no very extensive use has been made of this device, as is shown in the table on page 68.[11]

There appears to be a general tendency for voters to be more wary of amendments submitted by petition than of amendments submitted by the legislature. This is true for California (29 per cent as against 57 per cent since 1911) and, according to Professor Gosnell, for the country as a whole (27 per cent as against 64 per cent) .

New Mexico, New York, North Dakota, Oklahoma, Oregon, Pennsylvania, Rhode Island, South Dakota, Vermont, Virginia, and Wisconsin. *Three-fifths vote:* Alabama, Florida, Kentucky, Maryland, North Carolina, and Ohio. See Steinbicker, Paul G., and Faust, Martin L., *Manual on the Amending Procedure and the Initiative and Referendum* (Missouri Constitutional Convention of 1943, Columbia, 1943) .

[11] See New York State Constitutional Convention Committee, *Problems Relating to Legislative Organization and Powers,* Chapter 9 (Albany, 1938) , on the constitutional initiative; also Crouch, Winston W., " The Constitutional Initiative in Operation," *American Political Science Review,* August, 1939, pp. 634–645, and Hallett, George H., Jr., " The Constitutional Initiative Starts a New Advance," *National Municipal Review,* May, 1935, pp. 254–257.

Use Made of the Constitutional Initiative

State	Date of Adoption	Amendments Submitted to 1939	Amendments Adopted to 1939
Arizona	1911	15	8
Arkansas	1910	24	7
California	1911	56	15
Colorado	1910	36	10
Massachusetts	1918	1	0
Michigan	1913	25	3
Missouri	1908	27	8
Nebraska	1912	6	3
Nevada	1904	0	0
North Dakota	1914	18	8
Ohio	1912	24	7
Oklahoma	1907	25	5
Oregon	1902	70	25

Other Classifications of Amending Procedures. It is possible to classify differently the methods of amending state constitutions. In fact, Professor Dodd himself, in his *State Government,* presents a different classification, noting three methods of change which have developed in this country, as follows: (1) the constitutional convention; (2) legislative proposal of specific amendments; and (3) proposal of such amendments by initiative petition.[12] To this list, in the opinion of the author, should be added revision by commission, and a definite distinction should be noted between piecemeal amendment on the one hand, and general revision on the other. This distinction will be discussed in the concluding section of the chapter. It should be noted also that the methods of constitutional change by convention and by commission are best suited to general revision, while the methods of legislative proposal and of proposal by initiative petition are best suited to occasional or piecemeal amendment. Of the methods listed above, the first — the constitutional convention — is discussed in the following chapter. The legislative proposal of specific amendments includes the first four methods in the classification by Professor Dodd which begins on page 65, while his sixth method is the constitutional initiative, discussed on the preceding page.

Popular Referenda on Proposed Changes. From the beginning of the period of statehood, it has been customary to submit the work of

[12] Dodd, Walter F., *State Government,* Second Edition, p. 93 (Century, New York, 1928) ; the same classification is used by Ogg, Frederic A., and Ray, P. Orman, *Introduction to American Government,* Eighth Edition, p. 722 ff. (Appleton-Century, New York, 1945) .

constitutional conventions and proposals for constitutional amendment, no matter how initiated, to a popular referendum. Some of the limitations imposed on such referenda have already been referred to. It is often required that such proposals must be advertised; thus the Pennsylvania Constitution of 1873 provides (Article XVIII) : ". . . and the Secretary of the Commonwealth shall cause the same to be published three months before the next general election, in at least two newspapers in every county in which such newspapers shall be published." [13] Submission must usually take place at a general election, although a few states permit submission at special elections. In some states a simple majority of those present and voting thereon is sufficient to ratify; others specify a majority of those voting in the election, while Rhode Island requires three fifths and New Hampshire two thirds of those present and voting in the election. Such provisions make the use of the amending process too difficult.

Tests of a Desirable Plan. The two practical methods which are available for piecemeal amendment have now been considered — proposal by legislative act and by initiative petition. Some method of legislative proposal is provided in all states except New Hampshire, while in about one fourth of them initiative proposal is also permitted. There are important questions to be considered by the people of a state when they are called upon to select the amending procedure under which they are to live. Will the plan or combination of plans work? Can practical use be made of it, so that actual changes in the fundamental law may be secured? If not, the plan is defective. In Tennessee, for instance, the Constitution of 1870, although containing provisions for amendment (Article XI, Section 3) , has not been changed during the first seventy-five years of its existence. Between 1870 and 1935 ten amendments were proposed, but only the first of these received an affirmative vote more than one fourth of that cast for governor. With the exception of Tennessee, however, there is not a state whose organic law has not been amended since 1912 — although many are in serious need of revision.[14]

In the second place, does the plan recognize and tend to maintain the distinction between ordinary statutory law on the one hand, and the fundamental law of the constitution on the other? If not, again

[13] In a recent case the Secretary of the Commonwealth had distributed the text of the proposed amendments, but a few papers had not printed them although the material was distributed in sufficient time. The State Supreme Court held in *Tausig v. Lawrence*, 197 Pa. 235, 1938, that this was all that was necessary.

[14] See Combs, William H., " An Unamended State Constitution: The Tennessee Constitution of 1870," *American Political Science Review*, June, 1938, pp. 514–524.

the plan is defective. Finally, is the plan of such a nature as to be reasonably responsive to the popular will? This does not necessarily mean that the initiative method of proposal must be included in the plan, for there are methods of legislative proposal in connection with which effective popular control is possible. But it does mean that a plan under which popular control is impossible or ineffective is a poor plan for the American states.

For purposes of discussion it may be well to include at this point a brief summary of the recommendations with regard to the amending procedure contained in the Model State Constitution, which would, in the first place, permit proposal of amendments either by use of the initiative or by the legislature (Article XII). In the latter case a simple majority vote in either a regular or a special session is sufficient, while the proposal from either source may be ratified by a majority of the voters voting thereon if 20 per cent of those participating in the election vote in the affirmative. The question of a constitutional convention may emanate either from the legislature or from the people by initiative petitions, which must be signed by 5 per cent of the total number voting in the last election, the signers to reside in not less than half the counties of the state.

Use Made of the Amending Procedure. Most of the changes made by individual amendments grow out of problems and situations arising in the states and their local units, but pressure groups also contribute to the grist of constitutional amendments, as they do to the volume of legislation. The National Highway Users Conference, for instance, reported in January, 1945, the text of amendments adopted in sixteen states, from 1920 on (most of them since 1938), dedicating special motor vehicle taxes to highway purposes. While the number of proposals voted on in many states is small, there are exceptions; the totals for all of the states run, in even-numbered years (following legislative sessions in most states in the odd-numbered years), into sizeable figures.

The United States Bureau of the Census reported that in the calendar year 1938, 154 proposals of constitutional amendment were submitted to the voters of thirty-six states; in 1939, fifty measures were submitted in twelve states, but of these, thirty-three were submitted in Georgia and many were of local application only. In both years the average number per state was four. In the former year ninety-seven proposals were approved and fifty-seven rejected; in the latter, forty-three were approved and seven rejected. Thirty states voted on 113 proposals in 1942, while seventy-seven were on the ballots in 1943. Thirty-eight of these were constitutional amendments, thirty-five of which were approved.

In 1944 voters were asked to pass upon more than 100 proposals, in approximately thirty states. Rejection of the " $60 at 60 " old-age assistance plans by Arizona, California, Oregon, and Washington, and approval of anti-closed shop amendments in Arkansas and Florida, were conspicuous in the results of the voting in November of that year. The anti-closed shop proposal was defeated in California. Other proposals had to do with airports and airways development, poll taxes and voting, taxation, prohibition, municipal retirement plans, horse and dog racing, postwar planning, veterans' preference, and bank operations.

Thus it is that practically all of the usual types of subject matter are represented each year, by one or more proposals.[15] The number of proposals in some states is confusing to the voters and, if the proposals are approved, may have a serious effect upon the constitutions involved. In 1938 the voters of Georgia had to pass upon thirty-three proposals. In 1939 the voters of Louisiana had to pass upon twenty-eight, those of California on twenty-five, those of Georgia on twenty-three. While these may be extreme cases, they indicate a serious problem that has developed in a few states — a problem which was well stated by the California Constitutional Committee reporting in 1930 to Governor C. C. Young:

> When it comes to the form of the Constitution, we find that its constant amendment has produced an instrument bad in form, inconsistent in particulars, loaded with unnecessary detail, encumbered with provisions of no permanent value and replete with matter which might more properly be contained in the law of the state. . . .

The condition which this committee found existing in California likewise exists in many other states. It was largely responsible for the constitutional revision in Georgia in 1944 and 1945. It suggests again the importance of care in the framing of a constitution, the importance of moderation in the use of the amending procedure, and the need for periodic revision.

Public Interest in the Amending Process. Most of the amendments to state constitutions that are adopted receive the approval of only a minority of the population — often even a minority of the voting population — and that approval is given in a perfunctory and

[15] For current information on these matters, see the annual issue of *State Proposals Voted upon in the 19— General Elections.* For results of balloting on constitutional amendments, referenda, and initiated measures in 1944, see " Legislation in the 1944 Elections," *State Government,* January, 1945, pp. 13–14.

halfhearted manner by voters who know little or nothing about the nature of the proposals upon which they are voting. One has no cause for wonder at this when he examines a typical list of the propositions submitted. A list submitted in New York in 1927 is used here for reasons that will presently be explained,[16] while the table below for Illinois shows the results of the voting on amendments in that state during the life of the present constitution.

STATE OF ILLINOIS

VOTE ON AMENDMENTS AND ON CALLING OF A CONSTITUTIONAL CONVENTION 1870–1941 [17]

Year	Issue	Result	Election Percentages		
			For	Against	Not Voting
Period of the party ballot (1870–1890)					
1878	Drainage and ditching (Art. IV, Sec. 31)	Carried	65.9	14.4	20.7
1880	County officers (Art. X, Sec. 8)	Carried	51.7	16.7	31.6
1884	Veto of appropriation items (Art. V, Sec. 16)	Carried	63.6	8.9	27.5
1886	Anti-contract convict labor (Separate article following Art. XIV)	Carried	53.4	29.5	17.1
1890	World's Fair bonds (Art. IX, Sec. 13)	Carried	73.8	8.1	18.1
Amendments printed at bottom of ballot (1891–1898)					
1892	Gateway amendment	Failed	9.7	10.7	79.6
1894	Labor legislation	Failed	17.8	6.8	75.4
1896	Gateway amendment	Failed	14.9	6.1	79.0
Amendments printed on separate ballot (1899–1928)					
1904	Chicago charter	Carried	62.3	8.2	29.5
1908	Deep waterway bonds	Carried	59.2	17.7	24.1
1916	Revenue amendment	Failed	48.9	22.0	29.1
1918	Constitutional convention	Carried	57.6	16.6	25.8
1924	Gateway amendment	Failed	27.3	15.4	57.3
1926	Revenue amendment	Failed	34.1	24.9	41.0
Amendments printed at upper left corner of ballot (since 1929)					
1930	Revenue amendment	Failed	15.9	22.0	62.1
1932	Gateway amendment	Failed	31.2	7.9	60.9
1934	Constitutional convention	Failed	23.5	20.0	56.5
1938	Banking amendment	Failed	28.2	10.8	61.0

[16] For a comment on the campaign for these amendments, see Godshall, W. Leon, " Amendment of State Constitutions in 1927," *American Political Science Review,* February, 1929, pp. 102–106.

[17] From Illinois Legislative Council, Research Department, *Problems of Constitutional Revision in Illinois,* p. 13 (Springfield, November, 1941).

STATE OF NEW YORK —
CONSTITUTIONAL AMENDMENTS SUBMITTED, 1927

No. *Subject of Proposal*

1. Establishing a state executive budget system.
2. Authorizing New York City to borrow $300,000,000 outside its existing debt limit for rapid transit construction and equipment purposes; also expanding the debt-incurring power of certain other cities.
3. Making counties, instead of towns and villages, the local units in the apportionment of costs in grade crossing eliminations.
4. Fixing the salary of the governor at $25,000, that of the lieutenant governor at $10,000, and that of the members of the legislature at $2,500.
5. Designating the governor as the head of the executive department of the state.
6. Providing four-year terms for elective state officers and state senators and two-year terms for assemblymen, the first election thereunder to be held in 1928.
7. Authorizing the construction of a state highway in Essex County, from Wilmington to the top of Whiteface Mountain.
8. Authorizing the legislature to confer upon counties powers of excess condemnation in connection with public improvements.
9. Providing that no territory shall be annexed to a city without the consent of a majority in the territory obtained by a referendum vote.

These were the amendments which Governor Alfred E. Smith advocated during his last term to make possible effective reorganization of the state government. In this list Proposals No. 1, 4, 5, and 6 related definitely to the reorganization plan; they involved important structural changes in the government and are proper subjects for referendum. There is serious question as to the wisdom of constitutional salaries (see Proposal No. 4) , but in this case an amendment was necessary to change similar provisions already in the constitution. Proposals No. 3, 7, and 9 involve matters of general interest but less fundamental than the structure and powers of the government, and might well have been left to the legislature by the framers of the constitution. With regard to Proposal No. 2, which relates chiefly to the debt limits of the City of New York, one wonders why the people in the up-state counties should be consulted, for it is a question which concerns them remotely if at all.

The fault, of course, was not with the framers of the amendments, but with the constitution itself, which, by dealing with these subjects in detail, made amendment necessary if the provisions were to be changed. Proposal No. 8 deals with excess condemnation, a highly technical and difficult subject concerning which the ordinary voter could scarcely be expected to have any real comprehension. Under ordinary circumstances these proposals would have aroused little popular interest, but in this case the interest was tremendous in New York City and throughout the state. It was estimated that there were between 40,000 and 50,000 people in Times Square on election night watching the returns on these various proposals as they were flashed on the screen. This interest was due almost solely to the genius which Mr. Smith showed as governor in presenting in an interesting manner, abstract principles and problems of government. In other elections and in other states, where such leadership has been lacking, the author has been unable to find the final returns on amendments in the daily press, and has had to write to the Secretary of the Commonwealth for such information. Leadership is important, but the uninteresting, detailed, and sometimes relatively unimportant subject matter of constitutional proposals has often been such as would defy even the talents of a great popular leader.

RECENT QUESTIONS IN CONSTITUTIONAL REVISION

Piecemeal Amendment v. General Revision. There are a number of important problems of constitutional modification concerning which some comment should be made. The first is the question of the relative merits of constitutional change through piecemeal amendment and widespread changes made through a general constitutional revision. If one's judgment on this subject were governed wholly by regard for a logical and methodical program of revision, he would undoubtedly choose the second method. When, however, one faces the practical situation involved in securing the adoption of a new constitution where a thoroughgoing revision has been made, he is apt to prefer the energetic and continuous use of the provisions for piecemeal amendment, provided these are workable. The experience of New York in 1915, of Illinois in 1919, and of other states shows conclusively the difficulty of securing popular approval for a new constitution, no matter how well drafted or how modern the ideas upon which it is based. General revisions widely recognized as good may be defeated at the polls through the cumulative effect of various disgruntled elements objecting to individual provisions. No one of these groups alone would be powerful enough to defeat the proposed constitution; all of them together, though they may have little or nothing in common, can defeat it by their united opposition.

Piecemeal amendment would therefore seem to be more practical for those who wish to get things done — unless, of course, the pro-

posals are split up as was done in New York in 1938. The procedure
followed in Massachusetts is interesting; the Constitution of 1780
remained in force without general revision until 1919, when a rearrangement of the document was effected in which obsolete provisions
were struck out and the remaining portions still in effect were arranged in accordance with a logical and coherent plan. This revision
was approved by the voters of the Commonwealth, with the assurance that the substance of the constitution had not been modified.
The Supreme Court held that this rearrangement was for convenience only, and that in case of conflict the wording of the original
constitution should control.

Revision by Convention v. Revision by Commission. A state undertaking a general revision of its constitution must consider seriously the relative merits of revision by convention and by constitutional commission. While revision by commission is a newer method,
it has been tried in a number of states with notable success. Governor Harry F. Byrd of Virginia was instrumental in securing a revision
of the constitution of that state by this method in 1929. The advantages which he claimed for it in Virginia at that time are equally
applicable in other jurisdictions. A commission, being a far smaller
body — the Virginia Commission had seven members — can command the services of the ablest men available. Because of this fact the
deliberations of a commission are likely to result in a much more
thorough piece of work and to give much more satisfactory results
than are procurable from a large and unwieldy convention. Equally
important is the financial saving which may be made by the use of
the commission method. The total cost of a convention amounts usually to several hundred thousand dollars; a commission requires only
a few thousand dollars for the payment of actual expenses. In Virginia this meant a saving of approximately $475,000 — the difference
between the $500,000 which might have been spent for a convention
and the $25,000 actually expended for the commission. In Virginia
the commission plan had the additional advantage of evading the
possibility of a promulgated constitution, such as the one of 1911.[18]

The relative advantages and disadvantages of the convention and
commission forms for constitutional revision are summarized in the
following table:

[18] See discussion in Walker, Harvey, *Law Making in the United States*, pp. 76–
78 (Ronald Press, New York, 1934) ; also " Renovating Used Constitutions," *State
Government*, March, 1931, pp. 8–9, in which the work of the California and West
Virginia commissions is compared. Charles Aikin describes the method of operation of the former in " The Movement for Revision of the California Constitu-
ton," *American Political Science Review*, May, 1931, pp. 337–342.

CONSTITUTIONAL CONVENTION	CONSTITUTIONAL COMMISSION
Advantages	*Advantages*

CONSTITUTIONAL CONVENTION

Advantages

1. Adheres to democratic tradition.
2. Conforms to previous practice in most states.

Disadvantages

1. Large in size.
2. Unwieldy.
3. Expensive.
4. Inferior personnel.
5. Time-consuming.
6. Makes for log-rolling and compromise.
7. More susceptible to influence of pressure groups.
8. Unnecessary unless for sweeping revision.

CONSTITUTIONAL COMMISSION

Advantages

1. Small, compact body.
2. High-caliber personnel.
3. Inexpensive.
4. Superior type of work produced.
5. Supported by recent successful use in several states.
6. Can work more expeditiously.
7. Not so susceptible to log-rolling.
8. More independent, and less susceptible to influence of pressure groups.
9. Can study more effectively the experiences of other states.

Disadvantages

1. Undemocratic according to generally accepted standards.
2. Commissions in Pennsylvania and other states not successful.

The Legislature in the Role of a Convention. The role of the legislature in the business of constitution making is always an important one. It must ordinarily put in motion the machinery of a referendum on the question of revision. It must make legislative provision for the convention or commission, and must appropriate the funds necessary for the payment of expenses. It must approve the draft of the revised constitution to be submitted to the electorate. The attempt to revise the Constitution of New Jersey, concluded unsuccessfully in 1944, brings the legislature to light in a new role — that of a legislature itself serving in the role of a constitutional convention.

In November, 1941, the legislature created a seven-man Commission on Revision of the New Jersey Constitution. After a winter of hard work, the Commission reported in May, 1942, a sample draft of a thoroughly revised constitution. No hearings were held, but the Commission invited and received suggestions from citizens and civic associations, and availed itself of the technical assistance of the Princeton Government Surveys. In its report the Commission suggested " that the people be asked at a referendum whether or not they wished to direct the legislature, acting as a constitutional convention, to submit a revised constitution for adoption or rejection at the following general election." Such a vote was held in November, 1943, the result being overwhelmingly in favor of revision. The legislature proceeded to appoint a joint committee to hold public hearings and to prepare a draft of a constitution. The constitution was endorsed by the legislature in January, 1944.

Here was a revision commission doing preliminary work, not for a convention as had been attempted in Pennsylvania in 1919–1920, but for the legislature, and here was the legislature of a state acting in the role of a constitutional convention. The experiment worked out successfully — that is to say, the legislature did an adequate job, presenting an instrument vastly superior to the century-old existing constitution. The defeat of the proposed constitution at the polls in November, 1944, was in no wise attributable to the fact that the legislature had assumed a new and unusual role in the revision procedure.[19]

Current Needs for Constitutional Revision. The problem of constitutional revision became acute in many states during the depression. More than one third of the constitutions now in effect were framed during the period of reconstruction following the Civil War; they are weighed down by provisions that are useless and obsolete on the one hand, and they lack provisions essential for the proper handling of present-day questions on the other. The Constitution of Pennsylvania, for instance, framed in 1873, guarantees that soldiers shall not be quartered in the homes of citizens in time of peace, that canals shall ever be held open as public highways, that citizens shall not be denied the right to bear arms; but it has no word to say on the vital issues of our time. Again and again, as the people of this state have tried to cope with these issues, they have found themselves prevented from taking effective action by the dead hand of the past — by the constitutional convention of a generation which in its own time exercised the power to make a fundamental law, but which, by the adoption of a rigid and inelastic constitution, sought to withhold from future generations powers which it itself had enjoyed.[20] Other states find themselves in a similar situation. In a new

---

19 See Bebout, John E., " New Task for a Legislature," in *National Muncipal Review*, January, 1944, pp. 17–21.

20 William A. Schnader, an able former Attorney General of the Commonwealth, said in 1935: " I consider we have a dangerous Constitution at the present moment as it is hamstringing the legislature from making immediate and important changes demanded by the electorate." See Sears, Kenneth C., " Voting on Constitutional Conventions and Amendments," *University of Chicago Law Review*, June, 1935, pp. 612–618, who rightly points out that it may not be fair to accuse the framers of these constitutions of a desire to make them practically incapable of amendment. " In 1870, the mechanics of voting were very different from those of today. . . . In 1870, there was no official ballot in this state (Illinois) . Ballots were printed by the parties and handed to the voters by party workers at the polls. Consequently, if a party organization printing ballots was favorable to a proposed

era it is essential that the provisions of the fundamental law in the several states should be so revised as to make it possible for the people to deal effectively with the problems which confront them.

Numerous illustrations may be gathered from the recent history of many states; the following have occurred recently in Pennsylvania. The State Supreme Court has specifically ruled that graded income and inheritance taxes are unconstitutional. It was impossible to provide pensions for the blind without amending the constitution. When the momentous banking crisis developed in March, 1933, requiring immediate action, there was no constitutional way of softening the required legislative procedure. It was necessary for the legislature, by joint resolution, to instruct the Secretary of Banking to violate the existing law, and at the same time promise him immunity for so doing. The state has been faced in recent years with an unprecedented crime wave, but it has been necessary to proceed precariously before magistrates whose offices are created by the constitution, and to await the slow and uncertain outcome of grand jury consideration of such cases. The list might be extended almost indefinitely.

The need, as has been said, is for the framing of constitutions which state principles of government for an expanding future. In doing so, we must not abandon that which time has proved to be suited to our needs, but we must not hesitate to break new trails in order to make suitable provision for the handling of the newer social and economic problems of our time, and to modernize our governmental machinery in keeping with the needs of an industrial civilization. In 1932 a writer who had our existing Federal Constitution particularly in mind, made some observations which are equally applicable to the constitutions of the states. He recommends that a new constitution should contain five things: provision for economic liberty, social security, more efficient government, personal liberty and the protection of property, and a planned economy.[21] It will take years to work out and secure the adoption of provisions of this character in the constitutions, but the need for the effort is very plain.

Elsewhere it has been observed that constitutional revision is urgently needed, not in one state but in many, and that the time to

amendment a statement to this effect was printed on that party's ballot. The person who expressed himself by using that ballot voted in favor of the amendment unless he used some diligence to ' scratch ' that statement from the ballot. True, another party could take the contrary action or, do what was the same in effect, omit any statement of the proposal from its ballot."

[21] Wallace, William Kay, *Our Obsolete Constitution* (John Day, New York, 1932).

act is now, in preparation for the new era, the coming of which we confidently await. In the second World War our men fought in distant parts of the world to preserve the democratic way of life. We do not want to save democracy in far away lands, only to discover that we have failed to preserve it at home. We shall not strengthen the democratic tradition by declaring a moratorium on progress in state and local affairs.

Thomas Jefferson wrote many years ago:

Some men look at constitutions with sanctimonious reverence, and deem them like the ark of the covenant — too sacred to be touched. They ascribe to the men of the preceding age a wisdom more than human, and suppose what they did to be beyond amendment. I knew that age well; I belonged to it and labored with it. It deserved well of its country. It was very like the present but without the experience of the present. . . . I am certainly not an advocate of frequent and untried changes in laws and constitutions. . . . But I know also that laws and institutions must go hand in hand with the progress of the human mind.[22]

The task of constitutional revision requires courage and initiative as well as competent leadership. The obstacles to be overcome are tremendous — an undue reverence for the past, fear of the loss of existing privileges, fear of " radical " ideas, et cetera. To some, the time for revision is never ripe. If existing conditions are favorable, they see no need of " rocking the boat "; if existing conditions are bad, they feel that the serious task of revision should not be undertaken when men's minds are unsettled and disturbed. If one were to be guided by these prophets of disaster, a long period of constitutional stagnation would certainly result. Dr. George Woodward, veteran of many an attempt to modify the Constitution of Pennsylvania, must have felt this strongly when, in whimsical mood, he wrote:

There is a well known hymn with the title, " Abide with Me." It is a great favorite for funerals. One line says, " change and decay in all around I see. O Thou who changest not, abide with me." I always hum this hymn whenever I try to amend the Pennsylvania Constitution. We may be filled with a noble discontent. We may be burning with a crusader zeal to put a patch on the covenant of the Commonwealth but believe me, our Constitution seems to be immutable, immobile, and immortal.[23]

Model State Constitution. The text of the Model Constitution, as revised in 1941, appears as an Appendix to this volume. The use

[22] Quoted in *Journal* of the American Judicature Society, August, 1934, p. 62.
[23] Woodward, George, " Pay as You Come," *The Pennsylvania Legislator,* May, 1941.

of the word "model" is unfortunate, but there seems to be no alternative. The instrument itself is by no means perfect, and it has sometimes been severely criticized,[24] but it represents the judgment of some of the ablest students of state government. Frequent reference to it in connection with the various topics to be considered will be helpful. That it has had a great influence on the development of state institutions in the last twenty-five years there can be no doubt. While no state has adopted, and probably no state will try to adopt, its provisions in their entirety, various recommendations contained in the Model Constitution have gained wide acceptance. Specific mention might be made of the proposals for legislative councils and judicial councils, as well as of the establishment of the unicameral legislature in Nebraska.

SELECTED REFERENCES

American Year Book, annually, 1924 to date (Macmillan, New York).

Brennan, Ellen E., *Plural Office-Holding in Massachusetts, 1760–1780; A Study in the Separation of Powers* (University of North Carolina Press, 1944).

Callender, Clarence N., Carter, Edward W., and Rohlfing, Charles C., Eds., "The State Constitution of the Future," *Annals,* September, 1935.

Cloud, Archibald J., and Meany, Edmond S., *Our Constitutions, National and State* (Scott, Foresman, Chicago, 1926).

Combs, William H., and Cole, William E., *Tennessee, A Political Study,* Chapters 1 and 2 (University of Tennessee Press, 1940).

Dealey, James Q., *Growth of American State Constitutions* (Ginn, Boston, 1915).

Dodd, Walter F., *Revision and Amendment of State Constitutions* (Johns Hopkins Press, 1910).

——, "The Amending Article of the Constitution," *Bulletin* No. 3, Illinois Constitutional Convention (Springfield, 1919).

Erdman, Charles R., Jr., *The New Jersey Constitution — A Barrier to Governmental Efficiency and Economy* (Princeton University Press, 1934).

Fiske, John, *The Critical Period* (Houghton Mifflin, Boston, 1888).

Frothingham, Richard, *The Rise of the Republic of the United States* (Little, Brown, Boston, 1899).

Green, Fletcher M., *Constitutional Development in the South Atlantic States, 1776–1860* (University of North Carolina Press, 1930).

Hicks, John D., *The Constitutions of the Northwest States* (Univeristy of Nebraska Studies, Vol. XXIII, 1925).

Hill, Helen, *George Mason; Constitutionalist* (Harvard University Press, 1938).

Kettleborough, Charles, *The State Constitutions* (Bobbs-Merrill, Indianapolis, 1918).

[24] See, for instance, the letter of Senator George W. Norris, *National Municipal Review,* September, 1927, pp. 553–554.

Kies, Harry B., and McCandless, Carl A., *Manual on the Bill of Rights and Suffrage and Elections* (Missouri Constitutional Convention of 1943, Columbia, 1943).

McCarthy, Sister M. Barbara, *The Widening Scope of American Constitutions* (Catholic University of America, Washington, 1928).

McLaughlin, Andrew C., *A Constitutional History of the United States* (Appleton-Century, New York, 1935).

Mussey, Henry R., Ed., "Revision of the State Constitution," Parts I and II, *Proceedings, Academy of Political Science, Vol. V* (1914–1915), pp. 1–215.

Nevins, Allan, *The American States During and After the Revolution* (Macmillan, New York, 1924).

New York State Constitutional Convention Committee, *Report,* 12 vols. (Albany, 1938).

Osgood, Herbert L., *The American Colonies in the Eighteenth Century,* 4 vols. (Columbia University Press, 1924).

Poore, Ben Perley, *The Federal and State Constitutions,* 2 vols. (Government Printing Office, Washington, 1877).

Selsam, J. Paul, *The Pennsylvania Constitution of 1776, A Study in Revolutionary Democracy* (University of Pennsylvania Press, 1936).

Steinbicker, Paul G., and Faust, Martin L., *Manual on the Amending Procedure and the Initiative and Referendum* (Missouri Constitutional Convention of 1943, Columbia, 1943).

Thorpe, Francis N., *The Federal and State Constitutions,* 7 vols. (Government Printing Office, Washington, 1909).

Walker, Harvey, *Law Making in the United States* (Ronald Press, New York, 1934).

———————

Bebout, John E., "New Task for a Legislature," *National Municipal Review,* January, 1944, pp. 17–21.

Council of State Governments, "Legislation in the 1944 Elections," *State Government,* January, 1945, pp. 13–14.

DeLancy, Frances P., "West Virginia Explores Judicial and Administrative Reforms," *State Government,* May, 1940, pp. 87–88, 96–97.

Gallagher, Hubert R., "State Constitutional Development in 1938–1939," *American Political Science Review,* June, 1940, pp. 506–512.

Graves, W. Brooke, and Zipin, Irving J., "State Constitutions and Constitutional Conventions," *Book of the States,* 1945–1946, pp. 69–80.

Spencer, Richard C., "Proposals Voted on in 1944," *Elections: 1944* (United States Bureau of the Census, Washington, April, 1945).

CHAPTER III

State Constitutional Conventions

STATE constitutions, generally speaking, have been much longer-lived than is commonly supposed. They remain in force for an average of more than sixty years. The table which appears on the following page shows that five of the present constitutions were drafted prior to 1850, that thirty-one were drafted in the last half of the nineteenth century, while only twelve have been drawn up in the twentieth century. Thus roughly one eighth of the states fall in the first age group, five eights in the second, and two eights, or one fourth, in the third. This does not mean, of course, that these constitutions have not been amended many times — most of them have — or that various unsuccessful attempts may not have been made to revise them.

The states have, on the whole, been extremely conservative in the matter of constitutional revision. Approximately one third of them have never had but one constitution; this group is made up chiefly of states most recently admitted, although three New England states are included. One fourth have had only two constitutions. Seven states have had three constitutions, six states have had four, Alabama and New York have had five each, South Carolina has had seven, and Louisiana nine. Of the ten states that have had four or more, all but New York and Pennsylvania have some claim to being classified as southern; the changes in constitutions in these states are accounted for by the disturbances of the Civil War period. In some cases constitutions bearing a relatively recent date are not really new. The Massachusetts Constitution of 1919, for instance, was merely a rearrangement of the Constitution of 1780; the Supreme Court held that the rearrangement was for convenience only and that, in any case of conflict, the wording of the original constitution should control. Similarly, Maine's Constitution of 1876 is merely a rearrangement of the Constitution of 1820.

Dates of Adoption of Existing State Constitutions [1]

I. *Prior to 1850 — five states.*
    Prior to 1800 — one state.
        New Hampshire (1784).
    1800–1840 — one state.
        Connecticut (1818).
    1840–1849 — three states.
        Rhode Island (1843); New Jersey (1844); Wisconsin (1848).

II. *1850–1899 — thirty-one states.*
    1850–1859 — five states.
        Indiana and Ohio (1851); Iowa and Minnesota (1857); Oregon (1859).
    1860–1869 — three states.
        Kansas (1861); Nevada (1864); Maryland (1867).
    1870–1879 — eleven states.
        Illinois and Tennessee (1870); West Virginia (1872); Arkansas and Pennsylvania (1874); Nebraska (1875); Colorado, Maine,[2] North Carolina, and Texas (1876); California (1879).
    1880–1889 — six states.
        Florida (1887); Montana, North Dakota, South Dakota, Washington, and Wyoming (1889).
    1890–1899 — six states.
        Idaho and Mississippi (1890); Kentucky (1891); South Carolina and Utah (1895); Delaware (1897).

III. *1900 to date — twelve states.*
    1900–1909 — three states.
        Alabama (1901); Oklahoma (1907); Michigan (1909).
    1910–1919 — four states.
        Arizona and New Mexico (1912); Vermont [2] (1913); Massachusetts[2] (1919).
    1920–1929 — two states.
        Louisiana (1921); Virginia [2] (1929).
    1930–1939 — one state.
        New York [2] (1938).
    1940 to date — two states.
        Missouri (1944); Georgia (1945).

[1] Follows, to 1938, Mott, Rodney L., Ed., *Constitutions of the States and United States* (New York State Constitutional Convention Committee, Albany, 1938).

[2] The Maine Constitution of 1876 is still regarded as the Constitution of 1820, the Massachusetts Constitution of 1919 as the Constitution of 1780, the New York Constitution of 1938 as the Constitution of 1894, the Vermont Constitution of 1913 as the Constitution of 1793, and the Virginia Constitution of 1929 as the Constitution of 1902. The Maine and Vermont rearrangements were made by the Supreme Court of the states concerned, those in Massachusetts and New York by conventions, and that in Virginia by a commission.

THE CALLING AND COMPOSITION OF CONVENTIONS

Exactly one fourth of the states fail to make provision for the calling of constitutional conventions, and in these there is often a question as to whether the legislature alone can call a convention.[3] In two of the remaining thirty-six, Georgia and Maine, conventions may be called by the legislature alone, although in every other case a vote of the people is required. In nine states a majority vote of the legislature and the referendum are sufficient, but Nebraska requires a three-fifths vote and the referendum. Seventeen states require a vote of two thirds and the referendum,[4] but New Mexico requires a three-fourths vote plus the referendum. A majority vote of two successive legislatures plus a referendum is necessary in Kentucky, and a convention may be brought about by initiative petition in Oregon. Eight constitutions contain provisions in accordance with which the voters may, at periodic intervals, indicate whether or not they consider revision necessary.[5]

Just as there is no uniformity in the practice of the several states with regard to the calling of conventions, so likewise one finds none within particular states. Pennsylvania is one of those states which has had four constitutions. The first of these, that of 1776, was framed by what was essentially a revolutionary body chosen at the call of an informal committee of gentlemen who had no legal mandate to speak for the people. The convention which drafted the Constitution of 1790 was called into being by the legislature of the state. First the legislature passed a resolution expressing the opinion that the constitution was in need of amendment and declaring that, if the people concurred in this opinion, it would call a convention. About six months later, without actually submitting the question to a popular vote, the legislature concluded that the people favored a convention and provided for the election of convention delegates. The conventions of 1837–1838 and 1872–1873 were called by the legislature after it had submitted to the people the question whether

[3] See Shenton, Clarence G., " Can the Legislature Alone Call a Constitutional Convention? " *Temple Law Quarterly*, November, 1935, pp. 25–40. These states are: Arkansas, Connecticut, Indiana, Louisiana, Massachusetts, Mississippi, New Jersey, North Dakota, Pennsylvania, Rhode Island, Texas, and Vermont.

[4] *Majority vote:* Alabama, Arizona, New York, Oklahoma, Oregon, Tennessee, Virginia, West Virginia, and Wisconsin. *Two-thirds vote:* California, Colorado, Delaware, Florida, Idaho, Illinois, Kansas, Minnesota, Montana, Nevada, North Carolina, Ohio, South Carolina, South Dakota, Utah, Washington, and Wyoming.

[5] The submission of the question of calling a convention is mandatory every seven years in New Hampshire, every ten years in Iowa, every sixteen years in Michigan, and every twenty years in Maryland, Missouri, New York, Ohio, and Oklahoma.

there should be a convention and the people had voted affirmatively thereon.[6]

In any case, the decision to revise the constitution by means of a convention having been made, it is necessary for the legislature to provide for the holding of the convention.[7] The provisions of these acts depend in part on the nature of the constitutional provisions regarding conventions. Twenty-six constitutions require that the legislature provide for the convention, and twenty-one specify that this must be done at the next session after the popular referendum at which the proposition for holding the convention was approved. Fourteen constitutions specify the time at which the convention shall assemble; if the constitution does not do so, the legislative act must. The place at which the convention will meet is specified as the state capitol in Delaware, Kentucky, Michigan, and New York; elsewhere this question is determined by legislative act, the usual provision being that the convention will assemble in the hall of the House. The legislative act must make provision for the nomination and election of delegates, the manner of filling vacancies, the compensation of delegates to the convention (unless, as in seven states, this point is covered in the constitution), the necessary expenses of the convention,[8] and its temporary organization.

Conventions vary greatly in size; most of them are larger than they would be if the size of the membership were restricted to the limits of an effective working group. How should the delegates be chosen? The usual practice is to select one or more members from each senatorial district; in the larger states, from each Congressional district or from each county. The practice may not be uniform, however, even within a single state. To refer again to the experience of Pennsylvania, eight of the delegates to the Convention of 1776 were from the city of Philadelphia, while eight more were elected from each county by the then qualified voters. Those who framed the Constitution of 1790 were the same in number, and were elected and

[6] Philadelphia Bureau of Municipal Research, *Citizens' Business*, November 6; 1934.

[7] The Massachusetts Convention Act of 1916 is reprinted in Ewing, Cortez A. M., and Dangerfield, Royden J., Eds., *Source Book in Government and Politics*, pp. 608–610 (Heath, Boston, 1931). The Illinois Act of 1919 appears in Mathews, John M., and Berdahl, Clarence A., *Documents and Readings in American Government*, pp. 569–573 (Macmillan, New York, 1928). On this whole question of proposals for calling conventions, and the convention act, see Walker, Harvey, *Law Making in the United States*, pp. 66–73 (Ronald Press, New York, 1934).

[8] Conventions cost money; the New York legislature in 1938 appropriated $1,300,000 on the basis of the estimate of a session of 150 days. Governor Harry F. Byrd of Virginia estimated in 1929 that a convention would have cost that state half a million dollars.

apportioned in the same manner as the members of the General Assembly, which at that time consisted of only one chamber. The delegates to the Convention of 1837–1838 were also the same in number, and were elected and apportioned in the same manner as the members of the legislature; but the legislature was then, as it is now, a two-chambered body. The Convention of 1872–1873 was composed of 133 delegates, 28 elected at large, 6 from Philadelphia at large, and 99 from senatorial districts. Representation of minority parties was made possible by limiting the number of candidates a voter could vote for to less than the total number of delegates to be elected.[9]

The caliber of the personnel of conventions is usually higher than that of the legislature for the reason that the work of framing a constitution is regarded as being highly important. Since it does not have to be done often, and since the duration of the convention is not great, it is possible to enlist the services of outstanding business and professional men who often would not be willing to serve as members of the legislature.

PREPARATION FOR THE CONVENTION

Before taking up the powers and duties of the convention, it is desirable to consider the preparation which is necessary before the delegates assemble. In a day when American life was relatively simple and when the tasks imposed upon government were correspondingly fewer in number and less technical in nature, the work of framing a constitution was not nearly so difficult as it is under modern conditions. Under these conditions it would be impossible for any group of men possessing anything less than omniscient wisdom to deal intelligently and wisely with the multitude of problems confronting them, on the basis of their own information. Consequently it is necessary to prepare, in advance of the meeting of the convention, information and working materials for the members. Until recently such preparation consisted largely in making collections of state constitutions, from which members of the convention might determine how the questions facing them had been handled by the constitution makers of other states. Of late a more thorough and detailed preparation has been necessary.

Thus in Illinois in 1919 an extensive series of bulletins was prepared by the Legislative Reference Bureau for the use of the consti-

[9] *Citizens' Business,* loc. cit.

tutional convention in that state. These bulletins dealt with such subjects as the procedure and problems of the constitutional convention; the amending article of the constitution; the executive, legislative, and judicial branches of the government; problems of finance, local government, et cetera. The complete list appears in the table on page 88.[10] Each of them analyzed provisions of the then existing constitution on the subject with which it dealt, pointing out their merits and defects; each called attention to significant practices in other states, and made clear the different methods by which these various problems of constitution making might be handled. It would seem to be a necessary prerequisite to a high grade of work by a constitutional convention that information of this character should be carefully collected and made available in convenient form for the use of the delegates.

When there seemed to be a possibility of holding a constitutional convention in Pennsylvania in 1935, a citizens' committee under the leadership of Dr. William Draper Lewis worked out a plan embodying three major proposals. In preparation for the New York Convention of 1915, an *Index Digest of State Constitutions* had been prepared. Although there had been few new constitutions adopted since that date, numerous amendments had rendered the volume out of date and it had long since been out of print. The first proposal was, therefore, to revise this volume and bring it up to date. The second proposal was to have prepared by leading political scientists of the state a series of pamphlets generally similar to those prepared in Illinois in 1919, referred to above. Finally, the State Constitutional Revision Commission of 1919–1920 had prepared a proposed draft of a revised constitution which had been printed in the report of the Commission in a column parallel with the text of the existing constitution. It was proposed to reprint this material, including in a third column all of the suggestions of proposed changes in the existing constitution that could be gathered from responsible citizens or organizations throughout the state. The plan was presented to the Governor and the Attorney General, but no action was taken.

Quite in contrast to this Pennsylvania situation was the action of Governor Herbert H. Lehman of New York in 1937. Not long after the voters of the state had decided that a convention should be held,

[10] The first four of these bulletins were distributed to delegates before the convention assembled, and complete sets, together with a consolidated index, were distributed immediately upon the assembling of the convention. The bulletins were later issued in a single bound volume, a copy of which was sent to each delegate. Delegates were also furnished with an interleaved text of the Constitution of 1870. (Illinois Constitutional Convention, *Delegates' Manual,* 1920, p. 78.)

Preparation for a Constitutional Convention

Illinois — 1919
Fifteen Pamphlets

1. *The Procedure and Problems of the Constitutional Convention*
2. *The Initiative, Referendum, and Recall*
3. *The Amending Article of the Constitution*
4. *State and Local Finance*
5. *The Short Ballot*
6. *Municipal Home Rule*
7. *Eminent Domain and Excess Condemnation*
8. *The Legislative Department*
9. *The Executive Department*
10. *The Judicial Department, Jury, Grand Jury, and Claims against the State*
11. *Local Government in Chicago and Cook County*
12. *County and Local Government in Illinois*
13. *Farm Tenancy and Rural Credits*
14. *Social and Economic Problems*
15. *Bill of Rights, Education, Militia, Suffrage and Elections, Preamble, Boundary, Distribution of Powers, Schedule*

New York — *1938*
Twelve Bound Volumes

Vol. I   *The New York State Constitution Annotated*
Vol. II   *Amendments Proposed to New York Constitution, 1895–1937*
Vol. III   *Constitutions of the States and United States*
Vol. IV   *State and Local Government in New York*
Vol. V   *New York City Government — Functions and Problems*
Vol. VI   *Problems Relating to Bill of Rights and General Welfare*
Vol. VII   *Problems Relating to Legislative Organization and Powers*
Vol. VIII   *Problems Relating to Executive Administration and Powers*
Vol. IX   *Problems Relating to Judicial Administration and Organization*
Vol. X   *Problems Relating to Taxation and Finance*
Vol. XI   *Problems Relating to Home Rule and Local Government*
Vol. XII   *General Index*

Missouri — *1943*
Eight Pamphlet Manuals

1. *Organization Manual*
2. *County Government Manual*
3. *Manual on Federal-State Relations*
4. *Manual on the Executive Article*
5. *Manual on Education*
6. *Manual on the Legislative Article*
7. *Manual on the Bill of Rights, and Suffrage and Elections*
8. *Manual on the Amending Procedure, and the Initiative and Referendum*

he appointed the New York State Constitutional Convention Committee, composed of forty-two members distinguished for their public service. This Committee, organized in August, 1937, created six smaller working subcommittees, each of which, with a research staff, made a study of one or two specific subjects likely to be considered at the convention. Upon each of these subjects a volume of the resultant research was published. In addition, the chairman was authorized to initiate five general reference volumes. In all, a set of twelve volumes was published, the titles of which appear in the table on page 88, to provide the factual basis for discussion by the delegates.[11] The Committee had less than a year in which to complete its work, which followed in general the pattern established by the New York Convention of 1915, and of other states in recent years.

Similar procedures have been followed in the Missouri Convention in 1943 and the Georgia Commission of 1944. The University of Missouri assumed responsibility for the preparation of a series of manuals for the information of the delegates; the titles of these appear in the table on page 88. In Georgia the Constitutional Revision Commission of twenty-five members was broken up into a series of seven subcommittees, each of which made a report with recommendations. The subcommittees were assigned to bill of rights and judiciary, suffrage and elections, taxation and finance, the executive, the legislature, education, and county and local government.[12] Compilations such as these are not only a necessary prerequisite to a high grade of work by the bodies for which they are prepared; they are valuable for years to come as reference works for citizens and public officials of the state and for students and research workers in state government in other states throughout the country.

POWERS OF THE CONVENTION

Questions as to the scope of the powers of a constitutional convention and as to the relations of the convention to the legislature may

---

[11] The first five volumes were for general reference; the last six (exclusive of the general index) contained the studies and reports of the six subcommittees. Three thousand copies were prepared for distribution; sets are available in most good libraries. For a description of the procedure followed, see Poletti, Charles, " First Steps in Streamlining a Constitution," *State Government*, August, 1938, pp. 148–149, 157.

[12] Reports of each of these subcommittees were published. See also Arnall, Governor Ellis, " Twenty-five Study Georgia Basic Law," *National Municipal Review*, January, 1944, pp. 11–13, and " A New Constitution for Georgia," *State Government*, July, 1945, pp. 109–110; also Saye, Albert B., " Georgia's Proposed New Constitution," *American Political Science Review*, June, 1945, pp. 459–463.

arise in any state when a constitutional convention meets. These are troublesome questions. In powers, as well as in form, constitutional conventions differ from state legislatures. As Professor Walker observes:

The convention is universally unicameral, the legislature is almost universally bicameral. Otherwise the two bodies are similar. Each chooses its own officers and prescribes its rules of procedure. The powers of the convention relate to a single object, the framing and submission to the people of a new constitution or a series of amendments. The legislature's powers relate to general purposes of government. The convention in no way supersedes or suspends the operation of any of the regular organs of government. These continue to function as before. The convention may propose that these be changed, but such changes go into effect only when approved by the people. Constitutional conventions do not meet, as do legislatures, at stated times; nor do they serve for a fixed term, as two or four years. They convene for a special task. When this is accomplished they adjourn *sine die.* Even if a new constitution were deemed necessary soon after, the old convention would not serve. The whole process of calling the convention would begin anew.[13]

As a practical matter, a convention once seated is hard to control. Its delegates are likely to feel that they have a direct and unlimited mandate from the sovereign people. The law may be against them on this, but the law and the practice may be very different things, because a convention has ways of doing things that are not always approved by the books. For instance, it is said that some of the delegates to the Pennsylvania Convention of 1873, annoyed by Supreme Court interference, wanted to submit to the people a constitution that would curb the powers of the Court. If the convention had done this, the people could have voted down the proposed constitution, but that would not have given them the new constitution they wanted. The point is that a convention can submit its proposals in such form that if the people want the good they must take the bad along with it. Moreover, the proposals of conventions often become effective without being submitted to the people.[14]

Relation of a Convention to the Legislature. J. F. Jameson, in his work on constitutional conventions, asserts that such a body is absolutely bound by any restrictions which may appear in the legislative act by which it is called, but even he admits that these limitations " must be in harmony with the principles of the convention system, or, rather, not inconsistent with the exercise by the conven-

[13] Walker, Harvey, *op. cit.,* p. 66.
[14] On these points, see Philadelphia Bureau of Municipal Research, *Citizens' Business,* February 19, 1935.

tion, to some extent, of its essential and characteristic function." [15]
An important decision with regard to this question was handed
down by the Supreme Court of Pennsylvania many years ago in the
case of Wood's Appeal, which revolved around certain acts of the
convention which framed the Pennsylvania Constitution of 1873.[16]
An act of the General Assembly of Pennsylvania, passed in 1871, submitted to the people the question of constitutional revision. The
popular vote being in the affirmative, an act passed the following
year provided for the election of delegates and authorized the convention to propose " a new constitution or amendments to the present one, or specific amendments to be voted for separately." The act
also required that the election for passing upon the work of the convention should be held according to the general election law of the
Commonwealth. The convention chose to prepare a new constitution, and passed an ordinance providing for the submission of this
document to the voters according to the general election law (except
in Philadelphia, where different provisions were made) . The plaintiffs sought an injunction in the Allegheny County Court of Common Pleas to prevent various state officers from holding the election
under the convention ordinance, alleging that the ordinance was
illegal. The Court was faced with the question of the extent to which
the legislature could impose restrictions upon a constituent assembly. In its opinion it distinguished clearly between the constitution-
making power of a convention on the one hand, and the statute-
making power of a legislative body on the other. Each is supreme
within its own field, when acting within the limits of its powers. If
the convention felt, as it did, that there was adequate reason for prescribing a special election in all or part of the state for the purpose
of passing upon the proposals which it wished to submit, the convention was — in so far as this court was concerned — acting entirely
within its rights, and attempts at the restriction of such action on
the part of the legislature were without effect.

THE WORK OF THE CONVENTION

When the convention assembles, its first problem is that of organization. It has the same power as a legislature to determine its rules,

[15] Jameson, J. F., *The Constitutional Convention*, Section 338, p. 310 (Scribner's, New York, 1867) . Cited by Walker, *op. cit.*, p. 72.
[16] 75 Pa. 59, 1874. Conveniently accessible in Hall, James Parker, *Cases on Constitutional Law* (West Publishing Company, St. Paul, 1926) — the first case in
the book.

choose its officers and employees, and provide for its printing; it is, however, dependent upon the legislature for its funds, since it has no appropriating or taxing power. On the organization and work of the convention, Professor Walker says:

When the convention meets, it usually organizes in much the same manner as the lower house of a state legislature. Officers are elected, rules adopted, and committees appointed. There is usually a committee for each article of the existing constitution, with others to consider special questions. There were thirty-one committees in the New York convention in 1894; sixteen in that of Virginia in 1901–1902; twenty-nine in Michigan in 1907–1908; twenty-five in Ohio in 1912; and thirty-nine in Illinois in 1869–1870.[17] The same reasons for few committees of small size apply in a constitutional convention as in a state legislature. Parts of the existing constitution are referred to the committees as are also proposals from the floor for new sections or for the amendment of old ones.

When the committees are ready to report, they present their recommendations to the convention, where they are usually debated in committee of the whole. Then, after amendment, they are usually referred to a special committee on arrangement and phraseology, which is responsible for presenting the final draft of the constitutional document to the convention for its approval.

The vote necessary for the submission of amendments by a convention is specified only in the constitutions of Michigan and New York, where the assent of a majority of the delegates is required. This matter would ordinarily in other states be left to the decision of the convention. No doubt a mere majority of a quorum could be established as the requisite vote. Upon conclusion of the business of the convention, it is required to adjourn in Kentucky, Michigan, and New York. Such action would presumably be taken in any state and the convention itself would be the sole judge of whether or not its business had been completed.[18]

Usually the first committee to report is the committee on rules; these are commonly based upon those of the lower house of the legislature, but may be modified in such manner as to provide more ample opportunity for discussion and deliberation. Party groups may set up unofficial steering committees to aid in determining their stand on proposals. The regular procedure for proposals adopted by the Michigan Convention of 1907 was as follows:

1. Introduction, first reading, and reference to a committee.
2. Report of committee and placing in the general order.
3. Consideration in committee of the whole in order of reference.

17 Dodd, Walter F., " Revision of the State Constitution," *Proceedings,* Academy of Political Science, Vol. V (1914–1915) pp. 54–72.

18 Walker, *op. cit.,* pp. 73–74; see also Illinois Constitutional Convention, *Bulletin* No. 1, " The Procedure and Problems of the Constitutional Convention," pp. 23–30 (Springfield, 1919) .

4. Report by committee of the whole, and reference to the committee on arrangement and phraseology.
5. Report of committee on arrangement and phraseology.
6. Second reading, vote on passage by roll call.
7. Reference to committee on arrangement and phraseology.
8. Report of the complete revision by the committee on arrangement and phraseology.
9. Consideration of the complete revision in committee of the whole, by sections.
10. Report of the committee of the whole.
11. Third reading and passage (on roll call) by articles and as a whole.[19]

Problems of Draftsmanship. Many state constitutions show slight evidence of care in arrangement of material or in draftsmanship. The Federal Constitution has continued to be reasonably satisfactory during a century and a half, due in no small measure to the fine work of the Committee on Style and Arrangement. The failure of state conventions to exert similar care in the drafting of most of the state constitutions, through the use of like committees, has been productive of much uncertainty and of much expense and annoyance due to resultant litigation. Many questions present themselves: Should the convention rewrite or merely amend? How much detail should be included? Should changes be made solely for the purpose of achieving more effective expression?

As a general principle it may be urged that changes in the existing constitution should not be made unless it is desired to change the meaning. Most of the provisions of the old constitution have been interpreted and clarified by the courts; to the extent, therefore, that these provisions, as interpreted, are satisfactory, they should be permitted to remain unchanged. To rewrite them for any reason, however worthy, is likely to result only in substituting the unknown and the uncertain for what is known and relatively certain. The old wording may sometimes seem quaint and antiquated as compared with modern usage. Many of these phrases, however, have come down through generations and centuries; to change them will necessitate new litigation to interpret them, while the time-honored phrases have already been interpreted.

Just as old phrases are to be preferred where applicable and satisfactory, so should the draftsmen of a new constitution strive for brevity. This objective is more difficult to achieve as the functions of the states increase in number and complexity. But unnecessary de-

[19] Fairlie, John A., "The Michigan Constitutional Convention," *Michigan Law Review,* May, 1908, pp. 533–551.

tails not only expand the length of the document; they are likely to cause a lack of flexibility, to encourage a rigidity which may become a distinct handicap to the effective functioning of the government. They will likewise assure the need for numerous amendments in the future, and increase the probability of an extensive amount of litigation. The more details the constitution includes, the more opportunities there are for doubt, change, modification, and interpretation.

Extreme care must be exercised in the effort to have the text say what the framers wanted to have said — nothing more and nothing less. Where, in two or more different places in the constitution, it is intended to convey the same idea, the same phraseology should be used; for the courts are likely to assume that where the wording is different, a different meaning was intended. Some language permits or leads to technical constructions; some may grant more or less power than was intended. A bulletin prepared for the Illinois Convention of 1919 aptly illustrates these points.[20] In the Illinois Constitution of 1870 frequent reference is made to the requirement of a two-thirds vote on certain types of legislative measures. In some cases the wording indicated that the usual interpretation of the two-thirds rule was intended — namely, two thirds of the members present, providing that the number present constituted a quorum. In another case the wording was not clear, although it did not seem that any difference in meaning had been intended.

In the same constitution, boards of county commissioners of three members each were provided for each of the counties of the state except Cook County, in which Chicago is located. The powers and duties of these boards were definitely described. The convention evidently believed that Cook County should be treated differently and provided in this case for a board of county commissioners consisting of fifteen members. They failed, however, to specify that the powers and duties of the Cook County Board should be the same as the powers and duties of the smaller boards created for the other counties of the state. In both of these cases litigation resulted to determine the meaning of these carelessly drawn constitutional provisions — litigation which would never have occurred had the convention exerted sufficient care in draftsmanship. It is essential that, where the same meaning is intended, the same language shall be consistently used, and that every effort shall be made to state in clear, accurate, and concise form the purpose and intent of the convention. It is perhaps needless to observe that these illustrations cited from

[20] See Illinois Constitutional Convention, *Bulletin* No. 1, pp. 15–22.

an Illinois constitution could be easily duplicated in the constitutions of many of the other states.

The same constitution contains a number of provisions — no less than eight — with respect to popular votes. " In some of these provisions differences in language were clearly intended to adopt different rules, but this was not true in all cases." The Illinois pamphlet continues:

For example, Article X, Section 5, provides for the adoption of the township system " by a majority of the legal voters of such county, voting at any general election," and for the abolition of the township system if at a general election " a majority of all the votes cast upon that question shall be against township organization." It seems pretty clear that no difference in meaning was intended here, and that the purpose of the Constitutional Convention of 1870 was that merely of adding a provision for the abolition of the township system by the same vote as that required to establish the system. . . .

Similarly, there are six different provisions with respect to private legislation. " To find what is prohibited as special legislation therefore requires a search of the whole text of the Constitution." In some cases judicial construction of these clauses has restricted their application, in others it has made them mean much more than the language seems to mean.

Spotlighting Major Issues. Whether or not a state gets a new constitution as a result of a convention, the convention itself may be worth while if it serves to spotlight major issues and focus public attention upon them. Before the New York Convention met in 1938, the *National Municipal Review* said editorially that the constitution of that state was " in fair shape, far ahead of the constitutions of most of the forty-eight states." [21] The *Review* went on to say that major issues of our time should have a thorough airing, with able advocates on both sides. What are these major issues — the issues with which a state convention should now concern itself? While such a list may vary in different states and sections of the country, and with time and circumstance, the following is suggested:

1. Reorganization of the state administrative departments, and a review of the merits of proposals for new departments, such as justice, commerce, public assistance, et cetera.
2. Improvement of the functioning of the legislature, which is at the very core of the democratic process. Should there be one house or two? How can this body be made more responsive to the wishes of the people? How can its organization be improved to make it function more effectively?

21 October, 1937, p. 465.

3. **Reorganization** of the judicial system, in order to provide more efficient machinery for the administration of justice.

4. **City-county relations** and the reorganization of the system of local government, including consolidation, reallocation of functions, long-range planning, proper land utilization, et cetera.

5. **Popular control** of government, including the short ballot principle and proportional representation.

6. **Budgetary methods and procedure**, including the possibility of provision for a capital outlay budget, a reserve fund, annual v. biennial budgeting, and other problems.

7. **State aid.** The question of the extent, method, and purposes of state aid to political subdivisions warrants careful and discriminating study, as well as the relation of this whole question to the burden of taxation on real estate.

8. **Taxation.** Taxation is always a vitally important issue; with an increasing burden of Federal taxes and overlapping of state levies with both Federal and local levies this question deserves careful study indeed.

9. **Labor relations.** In view of extended Federal activity in this field, what should be the function of the states? Should unions be incorporated? Should " a bill of rights for labor " be written into the constitution?

10. **Social welfare.** Recent and possible future extensions of governmental activity in this field may well receive consideration. Should housing be dealt with in the constitution, and if so, in what manner?

If the convention finally accomplishes nothing more than to arouse public interest and discussion of these and other issues, it will have served a useful purpose. If the proposed new constitution should be defeated, there is still the possibility of securing the desired changes by individual amendments.

In its treatment of the major issues a convention naturally reflects the temper of the time. This is particularly noticeable in states that have had a number of constitutions, where the movement from liberalism to conservatism and back again operates with an almost pendulumlike regularity. The Pennsylvania Constitution of 1776 was a liberal, almost a revolutionary, document. That of 1790 was conservative. A liberal constitution of 1838 was followed by the conservative one of 1873, which is still in force. The experience of New York has been similar. Its Constitution of 1777 was conservative; the conventions of 1821 and 1846 were devoted largely to undoing the work of the first convention. The reform of the judiciary was the chief work of the Convention of 1867. The Convention of 1894 showed a more conservative tone, while the conventions held in 1915 and 1938 were generally liberal in their point of view.[22]

22 There is no point in arguing here the meaning of " liberal " and " conservative "; an examination of the constitutions mentioned will show differences which justify the use of these or similar terms.

MOTIVATION AND CONTROL OF CONSTITUTIONAL CONVENTIONS

During recent years much has been written on the influence of pressure groups and propagandist methods in their relations to legislative bodies, but almost nothing has been done on the subject of the influence of these groups and methods upon the deliberations of constituent assemblies. It appears, in fact, to have been assumed that the members of conventions are in some way drawn from a different species than that from which the members of other law-making bodies are selected, and that they function in another sphere, quite remote from the mundane influence of political parties, lobbies, and pressure groups. Such clearly is not the case.

Under these circumstances, students of state government as well as those of propaganda and pressure groups are much indebted to Professor Swisher for his excellent study of these influences in the California Convention of 1878,[23] in the introduction to which Professor Russell M. Story points out that " the ability of man to identify the public welfare with his own desire and to rationalize the latter in terms of the former is almost unlimited." This work is intended to " provide the reader with perspective and generate insight into the life process by which constitutions come into being."

It is interesting to compare Mr. Swisher's findings with those of Charles A. Beard in his analysis of the Federal Convention of 1787. In California also there was the conflict between the established propertied classes and the representatives of the " plain people "; the legal profession was likewise heavily represented. The convention met in a period of rapid corporate development, and the representatives of the property-owning group had the moral and ethical standards that characterized the railroad and other corporate organizations throughout the country at that time. The state was greatly disturbed by the recent organization of a so-called Workingmen's Party, led by the irresponsible agitator, Dennis Kearney.[24]

These two groups clashed in the choice of delegates, and again when the convention met and attempted to organize and select its officers. There was a bitter struggle on the effort to regulate corporations, particularly the railroads. In this the small business interests

[23] Swisher, Carl B., *Motivation and Political Technique in the California Constitutional Convention, 1878–1879* (Pomona College, Claremont, California, 1930) .

[24] Bryce, James, in his *American Commonwealth,* First Edition, Vol. III, Chapter 90 (Macmillan, New York, 1888) , has a very interesting discussion of " Kearneyism in California."

sided with the popular party. There were others, not extensive
property owners, who supported the conservative group because they
felt the railroads had been largely responsible for the rapid development of the state, and that, therefore, they ought to be allowed a
good deal of freedom. There was much dissatisfaction with the existing system of taxation, for the economic depression in the decade of
the seventies had thrown added weight upon those who bore the
burden of the taxes levied in the state. The taxation of mortgagers
had been unfair, and a large part of the mortgager group was made
up of farmers. Then there was the clash of interests over the taxation
of the mining industry, which may have been inspired in part by
the hostility of the farmers toward the mines, due to their pollution
of streams. There were also questions of race relations, involving
land ownership and the competition of Asiatic with white labor in
agriculture and elsewhere. This situation was made more difficult
by the agitation of Kearney and his supporters. In addition, there
were numerous lesser problems. The purpose of this comment is
simply to call attention to the fact that in every convention there
is a conflict of economic interests, and that these interests resort to
the same use of the press and of other types of pressure group influence that is characteristic of their dealings with other governmental agencies.

The New York Convention of 1938. That pressure groups as well
as citizen organizations can take an active and helpful interest in the
work of a constitutional convention is well illustrated by the recent
experience in New York. One state association after another established a constitutional convention committee. This was due largely
to the leadership of the New York State Committee of the National
Municipal League. Much of the work of these committees was done
before the convention met, simultaneously with that of the official
New York State Constitutional Convention Committee appointed
by the Governor. The League's Committee performed a twofold
function — first, in promoting organization throughout the state for
the study of the problems of the convention, and second, in the
development of certain recommendations of its own. This Committee included the presidents of all the universities and colleges of
the state. In each institution a speaker's committee was set up to
send interested faculty members and specially trained students to
discuss and debate constitutional questions before ready-made audiences in churches, schools, and lodges and before farm organizations,
chambers of commerce, and other similar groups. This work was

tremendously valuable in stimulating interest among both the speakers and the audiences, and in informing citizens of the nature and importance of the work of the convention.

Not only the League's Committee, but numerous other civic organizations like the Citizens Union, formulated recommendations for the consideration of the convention. The League's Committee sponsored regional conferences of leaders interested in constitutional revision and mimeographed numerous papers and addresses for general circulation.[25] Members of university faculties prepared several special studies dealing with constitutional questions.[26] The *New York Times* issued a *Constitutional Convention Almanac* containing much useful information. The New York League of Women Voters put out a pamphlet on convention issues and carried constant reference to these problems in its monthly bulletin.[27] The Women's City Club and the State Federation of Business and Professional Women's Clubs organized committees and conducted forums. The City Club of New York published an impressive series of bulletins dealing with important topics.[28]

The work of preparation for the convention and the interest of citizens were not by any means confined to civic organizations. Businessmen were interested; chambers of commerce and the Merchants' Association of New York undertook studies of many questions which were not closely connected with their obvious interests, as, for example, *A Unicameral Legislature Elected by Proportional Representation*, and *Recommendations Concerning Housing and Slum Clearance*, which favored the recognition of housing as a public purpose.[29] The New York State Automobile Association made an extensive study of the diversion of highway funds and published

[25] Examples: Crawford, Finla G., *Problems and Possibilities of the New York Constitutional Convention*, October 20, 1937; Evans, S. Howard, *The New York Constitutional Convention: An Opportunity for Citizen Participation in Government*, October 25, 1937; Graves, W. Brooke, *What Should a Constitution Contain?* December 20, 1937.

[26] Example: Hurd, T. N., *Some Facts Concerning the Constitution of the State of New York* (New York State College of Agriculture, Ithaca, February, 1938).

[27] Winternitz, Sibyl, *"We the People" Resolve* — (New York League of Women Voters, New York, February, 1938); also *Monthly News*, of the same organization.

[28] Examples: *Home Rule; Property Assessment Review; Solving the Mortgage Moratorium Problem; Apportionment; City Residence and the Right to Vote;* and *The Next Step in Community Planning* (New York, at intervals during early months of 1938).

[29] Other titles were *Recommendations Concerning the State Judicial System; Recommendations Concerning State and Local Finances;* and *Further Recommendations Concerning State Finances* (New York, at intervals during early months of 1938).

its results.[30] While this organization may not have been wholly disinterested, it rendered a public service in accordance with the ideal of democracy which accords to every man and group the right to present his case. Other groups, like the State Charities Aid Association, compiled pertinent data on subjects within their range of interest.[31] Further illustrations are unnecessary, although many might be offered; it is evident that there was widespread interest in the convention and its problems, and that a tremendous amount of valuable work was done by citizen groups to insure its success.

RATIFICATION OF THE CONSTITUTION

When all other problems of constitution making have been disposed of, there still remains the question of ratification. In every state but Delaware proposals for amending the constitution must be submitted to a popular vote, although in Virginia and a few other states new constitutions have been promulgated. The time of the election or the method of fixing it may be set forth in the constitution or determined by the legislature or the convention. Since a convention has no taxing power and the holding of an election involves expense, it is better for the legislature to assume the responsibility. The size of the vote necessary to insure adoption varies considerably from state to state; unless otherwise provided, such changes take effect immediately upon canvass of the vote, if they have been adopted by the required majority. In some cases where the extent of revision made by the convention has been extensive, there arises a question whether the changes should be submitted as a whole or whether they should be voted upon separately. Professor Walker suggests that it is sometimes possible to adopt a combination of these two methods, as when Illinois in 1870 submitted eight proposals separately, besides the question of the approval of the constitution as a whole.[32]

While it is almost the universal practice to ask the voters of a state whether they want a constitutional convention, it is not nearly so universal a practice, however, for conventions to submit their

[30] Gottlieb, William J., *Basic Facts with Relation to the Need for a Constitutional Amendment Dedicating All Motor Vehicle Revenues to Highway Purposes* (New York, 1938) .

[31] State Charities Aid Association, *Existing Constitutional Provisions Affecting Public Welfare, Public Health, and Mental Hygiene, and Some Questions Relating Thereto* (New York, 1937) .

[32] For a discussion of all these questions with illustrations, see Walker, *op. cit.,* pp. 74–76.

proposals to the people. Thus of thirteen new constitutions adopted from 1890 to 1912, only seven were submitted to the people — Utah, 1895; New York, 1894; Alabama, 1901; Oklahoma, 1907; Michigan, 1908; Arizona, and New Mexico, 1912. In four of these states — Utah, Oklahoma, Arizona, and New Mexico — submission was required by Congressional acts granting statehood. In five states there was no submission — Mississippi, 1890; South Carolina, 1895; Delaware, 1897; Louisiana, 1898; and Virginia, 1902. In Kentucky in 1902 the convention met and altered the constitution after the people had approved it. Promulgation of the Virginia Constitution of 1902 without submission to the voters occurred notwithstanding the fact that the legislation calling the convention directed such submission.[33]

Ratification of Pennsylvania Constitutions. Reference has been made twice to the Pennsylvania experience. Just as the practice differs in different states, so it differs from one generation to another in the same state. The Pennsylvania constitutions of 1776 and 1790 were never submitted to the people for approval — a practice more common in the early days than it is today. In its resolution calling the Convention of 1789–1790, the legislature suggested that the convention publish its draft and then adjourn for at least four months before confirming it, so that the people might have an opportunity to examine the draft. The convention accordingly adjourned on February 26, 1790, and reconvened on August 9 of the same year. On the following September 2 it formally proclaimed the new constitution. The constitutions of 1838 and 1873 were submitted to a vote of the people and did not therefore become effective until after their approval.[34] The trend in this state, as in others, has been toward a greater direct participation by the people in the constitution-making process. Whereas, in creating the first two constitutions the people voted only in the election of convention delegates, in making the last two they voted also to call the conventions and approve their work.

Experience in New York in 1938. The experience of New York in 1915 and 1938 provides a striking illustration of the wisdom of using the plan followed by Illinois in 1870. New York in 1915 and Illinois in 1919 had conventions that did a splendid job of constitution drafting, but both of them made the mistake of submitting their

---

[33] See Philadelphia Bureau of Municipal Research, *Citizens' Business,* April 23, 1935.
[34] *Citizens' Business, loc. cit.,* and November 6, 1934. See Sears, Kenneth C., " Voting on Constitutional Conventions and Amendments," *University of Chicago Law Review,* June, 1935, pp. 612–618.

work to the electorate in its entirety. In both cases it was rejected, not because it was not good, not because it was not generally recognized to be good, but because pressure groups and vested interests such as those which were active in California in 1878 were able to unite in their opposition to particular features. Thus the work as a whole was rejected, and both states were denied the benefits of needed constitutional revision.

Profiting by the 1915 experience, the New York Convention of 1938 submitted to the voters one omnibus proposal containing forty-nine miscellaneous changes proposed in the existing constitution and eight specific proposals. The omnibus proposals were, on the whole, noncontroversial, and were generally admitted by representatives of all parties and groups to be desirable. At least there were not enough important groups actively opposed to any particular items to bring about the defeat of the whole. All of the eight specific proposals were highly controversial. These dealt, respectively, with legislative reapportionment, grade crossing elimination, low-rent housing and slum clearance, the creation of a new judicial district, the rights of labor, proportional representation, social security, and the debt limit of the City of New York. Three of these were generally regarded as objectionable by impartial and informed persons, and these three — but only these three — proposals were rejected by the electorate. The proposed legislative reapportionment was of a clearly partisan character; the additional judicial district was not needed; and the proposal to outlaw proportional representation, which had already been approved by the voters of the City of New York and incorporated in their new municipal charter, was uncalled for. The result of the election bore testimony to the wisdom of the convention in choosing this method of submitting its proposals, to the discrimination of the voters in being able to approve the desirable proposals and reject the undesirable, and to the effectiveness of intelligent citizen organization in bringing about this result.

This constructive type of civic influence during the campaign for ratification is illustrated by the work of the New York State Committee of the National Municipal League. As soon as the convention adjourned, the Committee prepared a pamphlet containing a summary of the amendments to be voted on. This summary was prepared by a technical committee, whose statement of the arguments for and against each of the proposals was submitted to interested persons and groups, to insure fairness and accuracy of statement. Ultimately, about 25,000 copies of this pamphlet were distributed to key people, leaders of opinion in their respective groups and communities throughout the state. Included were teachers, ministers, editors, political leaders, and others whose position was influential and imposed upon them a responsibility for having accurate information. Considering the millions of voters in the state, the number of pamphlets distributed was not large, but the results of the referendum indicated that they had gone to the right people. The work of this Committee was one of the most constructive and effective pieces of civic leadership on record. The Citizens Union included recommendations on the amendments in its annual *Voters' Directory*, while the Merchants Association of New York and many other groups as well as the press were active in the campaign.[35]

Missouri and New Jersey Campaigns of 1944. Campaigns for the adoption of new constitutions were carried on in Missouri and New Jersey in 1944. The first campaign, in the Middle West, was successful; the second, in the East, failed. Both were well organized and well conducted. In Missouri the Statewide Committee for the Revision of the Missouri Constitution, with the full cooperation of press, radio, and civic associations, did splendid work both before the referendum on the holding of a convention and after the convention had completed its work. A statewide Constitution Day was marked by a radio program broadcast over a state network from the capitol, and leading newspapers issued special editions devoting much space to the discussion of constitutional questions.[36]

In New Jersey, the revision of the state's century-old constitution was begun with a State Commission on Revision of the New Jersey

[35] National Municipal League, *What's in the Proposed Constitution?* (New York, 1938) ; and Citizens Union, *Voters' Directory* (New York, October, 1938). See O'Rourke, Vernon A., and Campbell, D. W., *Constitution Making in a Democracy* (Johns Hopkins Press, 1943) , and McKinney, Madge M., " Constitutional Amendment in New York State," *Public Opinion Quarterly*, October, 1939, pp. 635–645, for discussions of the public opinion aspects of the New York referendum.

[36] For a step by step account of what happened in connection with the Missouri Constitutional revision, see the following articles: " Missouri Campaigns for a New Constitution," *National Municipal Review*, July, 1942, pp. 403–405; Morgenthau, Hans J., Ed., *University of Kansas City Law Review*, December, 1942, entire issue; Morton, Stratford L., " Missouri Picks Delegates to Revise Constitution," *National Municipal Review*, May, 1943, pp. 263–265; " Missouri Constitutional Convention Gets under Way," *ibid.*, November, 1943, p. 549, describing set-up of twenty-six committees; Loeb, Tess, " Constitution by Convention," *ibid.*, January, 1944, pp. 14–16, 26; Bradshaw, William L., " Missouri's Proposed New Constitution," *American Political Science Review*, February, 1945, pp. 61–65; Sparlin, Estal E., " Missouri Adopts a New Constitution," *Bulletin* of the National Tax Association, March, 1945, pp. 185–188; Loeb, Tess, " New Constitution for Missouri," *National Municipal Review*, April, 1945, pp. 164–167, 178; Chute, Charlton F., " The New Constitution of Missouri," *State Government*, July, 1945, pp. 111–112, 119.

Constitution, which reported to the legislature in 1943. The Joint Legislative Committee to Formulate a Draft of a Proposed Revised Constitution for the State of New Jersey completed its draft in January, 1944, and this was approved by the legislature for submission to the electorate in November. Reference is made later to the volume of educational work done in behalf of the new constitution, which had the support of the retiring Democratic governor, Charles Edison, and the incoming Republican governor, Walter E. Edge. It was defeated largely through the chicanery of Boss Hague of Jersey City.

Leadership in the campaign was assumed by the Constitution Foundation, which had the assistance and support of practically all responsible organizations — the State Bar Association, the State League of Women Voters, and many others. Democratic Discussions, a public forum program operated as a phase of the work of the New Jersey Education Association, put out discussion outlines and held scores of local meetings on the topics, " Should We Revise Our State Constitution? " and " Our State Constitution: How Shall We Vote in November? " The speeches of Governor Edison in favor of revision were published in pamphlet form and widely distributed, while many other radio speeches were mimeographed for further distribution. The Foundation put out a six-page *Summary of Major Changes Embodied in the Proposed Revised Constitution,* and the full text of the proposed constitution was widely distributed. Neither work nor expense was spared in promoting the new constitution. Defeat came chiefly because the unfounded charges of Boss Hague raised doubts in the minds of many citizens at so late a date that the supporters of the new constitution lacked time sufficiently to publicize the answers to his charges.[37]

Pressure Group Influences. If and when the convention does decide to submit its proposals to the people, the same economic groups whose representatives have been trying to arrive at some kind of agreement in the convention are active in the campaign for and against ratification of the new constitution. According to the nature

[37] A blow by blow account of the four-year effort to revise the New Jersey constitution will be found in the notes in the monthly issues of the *National Municipal Review*. Hon. Robert C. Hendrickson, chairman of the Commission on Revision, reviewed the report of the Commission in " New Jersey Considers a New Constitution," *State Government,* December, 1942, pp. 231–232, 249–251. John E. Bebout, leader in the campaign, wrote extensively on the problems involved: " How Can New Jersey Get a New Constitution? " *University of Newark Law Review,* March, 1941, pp. 1–69; " New Jersey Commission on Constitutional Revision Reports," *National Municipal Review,* July, 1942, pp. 243–245; and *The Making of the New Jersey Constitution* (MacCrellish and Quigley Company, Trenton, 1945).

of the provisions of the proposed instrument, one can list those groups which are in favor and those which are opposed. The California Convention, previously discussed, turned out what was for the time a fairly liberal constitution; therefore it was possible for a San Francisco newspaper to classify as follows the sources of the opposition:

1. Corporations, railroads, et cetera.
2. Banks, which had been virtually exempt from taxation.
3. Dealers in mining stocks now to be taxed.
4. Land monopolies.
5. Pro-Chinese aristocrats.
6. Newspapers who sell out to the above classes.
7. Preachers who serve the above.[38]

The making of constitutions is a very human thing, as is shown in any state by a study of the attitudes of important social and economic groups toward constitutional revision.

The antidotes for these pressure group influences are more and more and more public information and more and more and more public discussion. That such objectives are being realized, even in cases where the result of the voting on the new constitution is unfavorable, is evidenced by comparison of past practice with that of the present day. Highway Commissioner Spencer Miller, Jr., President of the New Jersey Constitution Foundation, revealed some interesting facts on this subject in a radio address closing the campaign in New Jersey. He made the statement that, " in the last four years, there has been more public discussion of the principles of constitutional government and the structure and substance of a new constitution for New Jersey than ever before in our entire history." In support of this claim, he continues:

Recently I made some researches into the amount of public discussion which took place in 1844, when a new constitution was adopted by a vote of 20,276 to 3,526. In those days, there was a population of approximately 400,000 people in New Jersey. There was no radio, no motion pictures, and no widely circulated newspapers. The facilities for widespread public discussion were limited. The two leading newspapers at that time were the *Newark Daily Advertiser* and the *State Gazette* of Trenton. Their total circulation was little more than 15,000. The Constitution of 1844, which was drafted by a Constitutional Convention in thirty-seven days, was well reported in the *Newark Daily Advertiser* and the *State Gazette*. It was presented to the people for their adoption at a special election, however, just six weeks after it had been drafted. In these six weeks, for example, there

[38] Swisher, *op. cit.*, p. 102. See also Seabury, Samuel, " Property Representation and the Constitutional Convention," *National Municipal Review*, December, 1937, pp. 567–571.

were just 136½ inches of space devoted to the discussion of the new constitution in the *Daily Advertiser.* The constitution itself was printed in full fourteen times.

In contrast, the *Newark Evening News* for today (November 6, 1944) contains no less than 213½ inches of space devoted to the discussion of constitutional revision in news articles, in editorials, in advertising space. This means that in a single day in one issue of one newspaper with a circulation of 215,000, there was nearly twice as much space devoted to the discussion of constitutional revisions as in the whole six-weeks campaign of 1844. During the six weeks prior to the Special Election in 1844, there were but two public meetings reported in the *Newark Daily Advertiser.*

In contrast, there have been thousands of town meetings in this State during the past four years in every county and before every kind of group. The New Jersey Constitution Foundation alone has supplied speakers for hundreds of meetings since the 1944 revision was completed by the legislature. There have been innumerable radio broadcasts; the printed word has been widely circulated; copies of the new constitution have been printed in over 400 newspapers of the State. The State itself has published and distributed 1,100,000 copies of the proposed constitution and 600,000 summaries. The Constitution Foundation and other organizations have distributed hundreds of thousands of summaries and explanations of the new constitution.[39]

Selected References

Ambler, Charles H., and others, Eds., *Debates and Proceedings of the First Constitutional Convention of West Virginia, 1861–1864,* 3 vols. (Gentry Brothers, Huntington, 1943).

Anderson, William, and Lobb, A. J., *History of the Constitution of Minnesota* (University of Minnesota Press, 1921).

Bebout, John E., *The Making of the New Jersey Constitution* (MacCrellish and Quigley Company, Trenton, 1945).

Bridgman, R. L., *The Massachusetts Constitutional Convention of 1917* . . . (Houghton Mifflin, Boston, 1923).

Bryce, James, *The American Commonwealth,* First Edition, Vol. III, Chapter 90, " Kearneyism in California " (Macmillan, New York, 1888).

Callendar, Carence N., Carter, Edward W., and Rohlfing, Charles C., Eds., " The State Constitution of the Future," *Annals,* September, 1935.

Carey, Charles H., Ed., *The Oregon Constitution and Proceedings and Debates of the Constitutional Convention of 1857* (State Printing Department, Salem, 1926).

Chafee, Zechariah, Jr., *The Constitutional Convention That Never Met,* First Part, 1935; Second Part, 1936 (Booke Shop, Providence, 1938, 1939).

Choate, Joseph H., *Arguments and Addresses* (Hicks, Frederick L., Ed.), pp. 675–699, Presidential addresses before New York Convention of 1894 (West, St. Paul, 1926).

Dealey, James Q., *Growth of American State Constitutions* (Ginn, Boston, 1915).

Dodd, Walter F., *Revision and Amendment of State Constitutions* (Johns Hopkins Press, 1922).

[39] Note in Bebout, *The Making of the New Jersey Constitution,* p. A.

Dorr, Harold M., Ed., *The Michigan Constitutional Convention of 1835–1836* (University of Michigan Press, 1940).

Erdman, Charles R., Jr., *The New Jersey Constitution of 1776* (Princeton University Press, 1929).

Faust, Martin L., *Organization Manual* (Missouri Constitutional Convention of 1943, Columbia, 1943).

Frothingham, Louis A., *A Brief History of the Constitution and Government of Massachusetts* (Houghton Mifflin, Boston, 1925).

Green, F. M., *Constitutional Development in the South Atlantic States, 1778–1860* (University of North Carolina Press, 1930).

Hapgood, Norman, and Moskowitz, Henry, *Up From the City Streets: Alfred E. Smith,* Chapter 4 (Harcourt, Brace, New York, 1927).

Hart, Albert B., Ed., *Commonwealth of Massachusetts,* Vol. V (The States History Company, New York, 1927–1930).

Hoar, Roger S., *Constitutional Conventions: Their Nature, Powers and Limitations* (Little, Brown, Boston, 1917).

Illinois Legislative Council, Research Department, *Problems of Constitutional Revision in Illinois* (Springfield, 1941).

Jameson, J. F., *The Constitutional Convention* (Scribner's, New York, 1867).

Jameson, John A., *A Treatise on Constitutional Conventions; Their History, Powers, and Modes of Proceeding,* Fourth Edition (Callaghan, Chicago, 1887).

Jessup, Philip C., *Elihu Root* (Dodd, Mead, New York, 1938).

Kettleborough, Charles, *Constitution-making in Indiana: A Source Book of Constitutional Documents,* 3 vols. (Indiana Historical Commission, Indianapolis, 1916–1930).

——, Ed., *The State Constitutions* (Bobbs-Merrill, Indianapolis, 1918).

Kuhlman, A. F., Comp., *Official Publications Relating to American State Constitutional Conventions* (Wilson, New York, 1935).

Lewis, William D., Secretary, Commission on Constitutional Amendment and Revision, *Report,* 4 vols. (Harrisburg, 1920).

Loeb, Isador, and Shoemaker, Floyd C., Eds., *Debates of the Missouri Constitutional Convention of 1875* (State Historical Society, Columbia, 1930).

McDaniel, R. M., *Virginia Constitutional Convention, 1901–1902* (Johns Hopkins University Press, 1928).

McKay, Seth S., *Making the Texas Constitution of 1876* (University of Pennsylvania, 1924).

——, Ed., *Debates in the Texas Constitutional Convention of 1875* (University of Texas Press, 1930).

McLaughlin, Andrew C., *A Constitutional History of the United States* Appleton-Century, New York, 1935).

National Municipal League, *What's in the Proposed Constitution?* (New York, 1938).

New York State Constitutional Convention, *Record of the Constitutional Convention of 1915,* 4 vols. (Albany, 1915).

New York State Constitutional Convention Commission, *Index Digest of State Constitutions* (Albany, 1915).

New York State Constitutional Convention Committee, *Report,* 12 vols. (Albany, 1938).

Perlman, Philip B., Comp., *Debates of the Maryland Constitutional Convention of 1867* (Hepron, Baltimore, 1923).

O'Rourke, Vernon A., and Campbell, D. W., *Constitution Making in a Democracy* (Johns Hopkins Press, 1943).

Selsam, J. Paul, *The Pennsylvania Constitution of 1776* (University of Pennsylvania Press, 1936).

Shambaugh, Benjamin F., Ed., *The Constitution of Iowa* (Iowa State Historical Society, Iowa City, 1935).

Swisher, Carl B., *Motivation and Political Technique in the California Constitutional Convention, 1878–1879* (Pomona College, Claremont, California, 1930).

Walker, Harvey, *Law Making in the United States* (Ronald Press, New York, 1934).

Wallace, D. D., *The South Carolina Constitution of 1895* (University of South Carolina Press, 1927).

———

Arnall, Ellis, "Twenty-five Study Georgia Basic Law," *National Municipal Review*, January, 1944, pp. 11–13.

———, "A New Constitution for Georgia," *State Government*, July, 1945, pp. 109–110.

Bebout, John E., "New Jersey Commission on Constitutional Revision Reports," *National Municipal Review*, July, 1942, pp. 243–245.

———, and Kass, Julius, "How Can New Jersey Get a New Constitution?" *University of Newark Law Review*, March, 1941, pp. 1–69.

Bradshaw, William L., "Missouri's Proposed Constitution," *American Political Science Review*, February, 1945, pp. 61–65.

Chute, Charlton F., "The New Constitution for Missouri," *State Government*, July, 1945, pp. 111–112, 119.

Council of State Governments, "New Jersey Considers a New Constitution," *State Government*, December, 1942, pp. 231–232, 249–251.

Gooch, R. K., "The Recent Limited Constitutional Convention in Virginia," *Virginia Law Review*, June, 1945, pp. 708–726.

Loeb, Tess, "Constitution by Convention," *National Municipal Review*, January, 1944, pp. 14–16, 26.

———, "New Constitution for Missouri," *National Municipal Review*, April, 1945, pp. 164–167, 178.

Morganthau, Hans J., Ed., "Constitutional Reform in Missouri," *University of Kansas City Law Review*, December, 1942, entire issue.

Morton, Stratford L., "Missouri Picks Delegates to Revise Constitution," *National Municipal Review*, May, 1943, pp. 263–265.

———, "Missouri Wins Constitutional Revision," *National Municipal Review*, December, 1943, pp. 591–594.

Peterson, Henry J., "The Constitutional Convention of Wyoming," *University of Wyoming Publications*, Vol. III, May, 1940, pp. 101–131.

Saye, Albert B., "Georgia's Proposed New Constitution," *American Political Science Review*, June, 1945, pp. 459–463.

Sparlin, Estal E., "Missouri Adopts a New Constitution," *Bulletin* of the National Tax Association, March, 1945, pp. 185–188.

Part Two

POLITICAL PARTIES AND POPULAR CONTROL

CHAPTER IV

Parties and Elections

WHILE, in a volume devoted to the organization and functioning of state government, extensive discussion of the party system is impossible, some attention must be given to it. Brief consideration will therefore be given to the scheme of organization used by political parties in the states, the relation of this machinery to that in the national and local fields, and finally, the methods and techniques by which political parties manage to maintain control over the people. It will be necessary also to examine the general qualifications for the suffrage, and such special problems as Negro suffrage and woman suffrage as well as the subject of registration, of nominating systems, and of the conduct of elections, including campaign methods, ballot forms and voting machines, election officers, election frauds, the cost of elections, et cetera.

THE AMERICAN PARTY SYSTEM

The organization of political parties runs parallel with the structure of the several levels of government. Just as the Federal government is established in Washington with the President, the Cabinet, and the Congress, so in the field of party organization one finds the national chairman, the national committee, and the national convention. Just as the governor, the cabinet, and the legislature function in the state governments, so in the state party organization there is the state chairman, the state committee, and the state convention. In the cities the organization is elaborate, but constructed along similar lines. Just as the city committee is composed of representatives from the various wards of the city, so the ward committee is composed of representatives from the various election districts or voting precincts, each of which has its own committeemen. Thus there develops a hierarchy of party leaders, beginning with the smallest local districts and extending to the national organization. The state party organizations become cogs in the great national political party machinery. In addition, the party may organize itself in special districts, as in Congressional or state senatorial districts, for the purpose of conducting more effectively the party campaigns for legislative officers. Most significant of all is the fact that the party organization in the upper units is unable to function effectively without a strong foundation in the districts where the voters live. It is because of the lack of such organization that reform movements, as Amos Pinchot once said, like a queen bee, sting once and die. Many of them do not even sting once. It is impossible to build a party from the top down, for the strength of the party depends upon its strength at the grassroots, in the local communities where the people live.

A strong local organization with a large controlled vote can be used by the party on many occasions. While the connection between national issues and those of the state and local units is relatively slight, local organizations function with equal effectiveness in behalf of the party candidates in all three fields. The techniques and methods by which the organization maintains control over the voters are interesting and important. These controls are exercised more effectively, on the whole, in urban than in rural districts, and decrease in effectiveness in urban districts as the economic and educational status of the people advances. Party ties seem to be taken more seriously in the older states along the Atlantic seaboard; their strength is greatly diminished in the Middle West, and is apparently nonexistent in the Pacific coast states. The farther west one travels, the less he finds of this effective party organization with its relentless discipline and almost complete domination. Here, indeed, is a striking political phenomenon.

Methods of Control. In the large eastern cities, the control of the party organization rests very largely upon two things. In the first place, the division committeeman knows intimately and personally all the people in his district. He calls them by their first names, and they greet him in the same familiar fashion. He knows whether or not a man is married, and if so, how many children he has, and what their ages are. He knows whether there are any in-laws residing with the family, or any roomers or boarders. He knows where the man works, what he does, how much he earns, and all the personal and more or less intimate details of the family's affairs. If anyone is ill, the committeeman is solicitous in inquiring for his welfare. If there is a birth, christening, marriage, or death, the committeeman is on hand with congratulations or condolences. No detail in the life of his people is too insignificant to demand his attention. He is interested, too, in the group life of the neighborhood. If there is a street carnival, a dance, a baseball game, or a strawberry festival at the church, he always buys a ticket, and if at all possible he attends.

A large number of the party workers are on the public payroll, holding either city or county jobs as a rule, although some of them are able to secure state and Federal positions.[1] Those who are not on the public payroll usually maintain some kind of small business or professional practice. This may be a tap room, a real estate office, an insurance office, a lawyer's office, or an undertaking establishment. The leader may not sell much insurance or much real estate, or practice much law, but he must have some kind of business, for appearance's sake; and more important, he must have some convenient and accessible place in the neighborhood where his constituents may be sure of finding him. A tap room serves this purpose well, since it will enable him to see fairly frequently a considerable portion of his constituents. An undertaking establishment gives him an opportunity to render service to his people at a time when, perhaps, they appreciate it most, while, on the other hand, the fact that he is in politics assists him in the development of his business. One leader in a Philadelphia division runs a small local movie house; in the evening he stands outside to greet and talk with his patrons.

It has long been customary to refer to such political leaders as bosses, the term having acquired in the minds of many people an unpleasant connotation. Students of government and politics have come to realize that these men are not wholly vicious, and that their activities are not without some social justification. Take, for instance, the following comment by Professor William Bennett Munro:

For it is the boss who serves, almost single-handed, as the mediator between poverty and power, between the people of the tenements and those who try to be their oppressors. He is the protector of the people against profiteering landlords, avaricious employers, crooked policemen, iron-fisted magistrates, shyster lawyers, and other predatory folks. He is the real friend

[1] For an able and thorough study of this problem in the Philadelphia Republican organization, see Kurtzman, David H., *Methods of Controlling Votes in Philadelphia* (University of Pennsylvania, 1935).

of the forgotten man. It is to him that the unprivileged go when they are in any kind of trouble. And rarely do they come away empty-handed. To see that they are helped, one and all of them, is what the boss is there for.[2]

This brings us to the second method of control. The leader not only knows his people intimately and personally and identifies himself with the problems of their everyday lives, but he endeavors by every means at his disposal to place them under obligation — financially, if possible — to him. The nature of this obligation depends very largely upon the general social and economic status of his constituents, but whatever their status, there is an economic appeal which may be effectively used. In the lower strata of society, this may consist in normal times in getting a man a job or getting a clerical position for his son or his daughter, of sending in a ton of coal, a basket of food, or some clothing, or of paying a month's rent. In the upper strata of society, this appeal may be used through influencing the awarding of contracts for supplies and equipment or for public works, by failure to enforce uniformly and fairly the inspection laws, by reducing the assessment on property, by conferring some special privilege not ordinarily enjoyed, or by any one of a hundred other methods. In the former case, a family may be counted on for an average of five votes, while in the latter the persons benefited may be influential in the community and therefore able to sway a considerable number of voters at election time.

The party worker is at the disposal of his people practically twenty-four hours a day. In addition to the rendering of service which places the voter under financial obligation to him, the leader performs other favors of every conceivable sort. If one of his constituents is arrested, he goes to the station house to secure his release on a copy of the charge. If a constituent in a foreign district needs a vendor's license from City Hall, he takes care of it. If the street needs repair, if the citizen wants an additional street light installed or a traffic light at a dangerous intersection, he goes to the party worker in his district. If a young man desires to be admitted to law school, he gets in touch with his committeeman, who takes up the case with someone more influential than himself; if he desires a Senatorial scholarship, he

[2] Munro, William Bennett, *Personality in Politics,* pp. 76–77 (Macmillan, New York, 1934). See also Graves, W. Brooke, *Readings in Public Opinion,* Chapter 25 (Appleton, New York, 1928). Significant researches into the organization and methods of municipal machines have been conducted in Chicago under the supervision of Professors Charles E. Merriam and Harold F. Gosnell; in New York by Professor Roy V. Peel; in Philadelphia by Professor John T. Salter and Dr. David H. Kurtzman; and in Jersey City by Professor Dayton D. McKean. See Selected References for titles.

begins his negotiations (in states where the competitive examination system is not in use) with the local party worker.

Although people who are not especially familiar with the system may not realize it, the bases or sources of the bosses' power are not necessarily corrupt. Their power rests upon — in addition to financial and personal obligations — personal friendship, sometimes on fear, and very often on the fact that their followers get out to vote in primary and general elections, while the " good " citizens stay at home and moan that " politics are so dirty." Their power rests upon their interest in people and their aptitude for doing the job. It is well to remember that a ward leader is not a good politician because he is a ward leader, but rather that he is ward leader because he is able to carry his ward.

It is by such methods as these that the party workers are able to produce results which have given rise to the phrase, the " zero wards." In the Pennsylvania Senatorial primary of May, 1934, one ward leader in Philadelphia suddenly swung his support from one candidate to the other; when the returns came in, the candidate whom he had originally supported had eighteen votes, while the one to whom he turned had over 13,000. In one division after another, not a single vote was recorded for the candidate he opposed. The late Governor Alfred E. Smith had a good story on zero wards. After one of his campaigns he was going over the returns in New York City with some of the ward leaders. In one ward there were thousands of votes for him, and one against. The ward leader was very indignant at this blot upon his record. He explained to the governor that he knew who this fellow was and that he would " get him yet." In such situations party discipline is a definite and serious thing.

Municipal bosses, whose sources of power and methods of control are of the type here described, have been common, but there have been relatively few state bosses. Several years ago Professor Lancaster made a study of one such boss who continued in power for approximately two decades. J. Henry Roraback, whose regime began in 1912 and ended in the early thirties, was a big businessman and a capable executive; throughout this period he was a dominating influence in the affairs of Connecticut. The conditions favoring the establishment of such a system and its continued operation have been summarized as follows:

(1) A constitutional system under which the political center of gravity is very definitely in the legislature; this opens the door to various kinds of special legislation often conceived in the interests of the dominant group;

(2) an archaic representative system in which the small towns are vastly over-represented; (3) the persistence of certain aristocratic and deferential traditions which tend to oligarchic government; (4) the absence of machinery by which the voter may make his views felt directly upon the government and the parties; (5) the practical disappearance of an effective legislative minority; (6) the lack of an active opposition press; (7) the fact that the present boss and his lieutenants represent a desirable type of business success and therefore " fit " into their environment successfully; (8) the relatively good government provided by the present system.[3]

Party Discipline. When the party worker makes the rounds in his district before the primary or the general election, he reminds his people that he is a candidate for committeeman and that several of his friends are also on the ticket. Will the recipients of these favors support him and his friends? Of course they will — they would be ingrates if they did not. In the case of a voter who fails to support him, it is likely that further favors will be denied, at least for a time. When, following the Democratic landslide in certain wards in South Philadelphia in the Presidential election in 1928, voters came to the Republican Committeemen after election asking for favors, they were in many cases told to go and see Al Smith, that they voted for him, and he ought to take care of them. Periodically before election, the police in the same city round up minor offenders in order that the party workers may demonstrate their power and the indispensable character of the services of the organization by getting them released on a copy of the charge.

Much caustic criticism has been heaped upon party workers in the large metropolitan areas. It is true that the motives for their good deeds are offensive to many people, but no one who has had an opportunity to observe at close range the functioning of such an organization can believe that any useful purpose will be served by hurling epithets at it or its workers. Until new machinery and administrative techniques were devised to accomplish these purposes, denunciation was idle. Prior to the depression the machine rendered a necessary service in the matter of relief, and acted as a buffer between the citizen and the government of which he knew and understood so little. At that time there was no other agency capable of rendering this service so satisfactorily to those whom it benefited. Then the relief problem assumed such proportions that the party organizations were no longer able to handle it. The establishment of the social security program and of assistance as a public function,

[3] Lancaster, Lane W., " The Background of a State ' Boss ' System," *American Journal of Sociology*, March, 1930, pp. 783–798.

together with concerted efforts in many cities to eliminate corruption, have all done much to weaken the hold of the machine. Furthermore, civic education and improved standards of administration have tended to make voters more discriminating, more independent, and less inclined to accept at face value the claims of party workers.

Party organization is nevertheless a necessary and inevitable aspect of popular government. It is interesting and perhaps significant that the type of organization here described has been more or less confined to the cities of the East, and that even here it appears to be losing its grip upon the voters. Although there is in each state a branch of the national organization of each of the two major political parties, there is in fact little to bind the local and national organizations together save the desire for victory and a share in the spoils of office. The outstanding issues of a national campaign are not the important issues of a state campaign; the latter are often submerged by the national campaign, although they are important enough to be decided on their own merits. If it be true that the national party labels no longer mean anything, it is doubly true of them as applied to the issues in the various states.

THE SUFFRAGE

Much popular misunderstanding exists regarding the nature of the suffrage. It is frequently referred to as a right, using the word " right " in the sense of the natural rights upon which the Founding Fathers laid such heavy emphasis. A " right " is something which belongs to a person by virtue of his status as a human being and a citizen — something the enjoyment of which the government is not at liberty to deny him. Everyone knows that the suffrage is not such a right — that the suffrage may be, and in fact is, withheld from many persons for a wide variety of reasons. It would seem preferable, therefore, to think of the suffrage as a privilege, the exercise of which the state may either grant or withhold, rather than as a right to which one is entitled.

The states enjoy a practically unlimited control in determining qualifications for the exercise of the suffrage. This is clearly shown by reference to certain provisions of the Federal Constitution. In Article I, Section 2, it is stated that the electors for members of the House of Representatives " shall have the qualifications requisite for electors for the more numerous branch of the state legislature," while Section 4 of the same Article continues, " The times, places and manner of holding elections for Senators and Representatives shall be prescribed in each State by the legislature thereof." It thus appears that those persons who are eligible under the provisions of the state law to vote for members of the lower house in the state legislature are by virtue of that fact qualified to vote for members of the lower house of Congress. When, in 1917, Amendment XVII was adopted, providing for the direct election of Senators, this idea was extended to electors participating in Senatorial elections. Since the middle of the last century, persons possessing such qualifications have been permitted to vote for the members of the Electoral College. Consequently, the qualifications which the states impose upon voters apply to all voters, usually at all elections, within the respective states.

Three amendments to the Federal Constitution have imposed certain restrictions upon the states in the determination of qualifications. Section 2 of Amendment XIV would, if enforced, reduce the representation in Congress of states withholding the privilege of the suffrage from any considerable number of persons who might normally be considered qualified. This provision is further discussed in connection with the subject of Negro suffrage. Amendment XV provides that " no person shall be denied the right to vote on account of race, color, or previous condition of servitude "; to this, Amendment XIX would add the word " sex." It is important to note that these provisions do not guarantee to anyone, anywhere, at any time, the privilege of voting. Their effect is merely to state that no person shall be denied the suffrage for any one of the four reasons definitely indicated. It is a matter of common knowledge that the states can and do disqualify many persons for a variety of other reasons, and sometimes for these reasons under some other pretext.

In his excellent *History of Suffrage in the United States,* Professor Kirk H. Porter observes that " all of the restrictions and qualifications [on the exercise of the suffrage] can be seen to support one or the other of two fundamental principles: one may be called the ' theory of right ' and the other the ' theory of the good of the state.' Every qualification imposed had one of these two principles in view. Either it was established in order to fulfill the right which certain people were supposed to have, or else it was established in order to serve the best interests of the state. It might have been said that a man had a right to vote because he owned property, or because he was a resident or because he paid taxes, or simply because the right

Voters per State per Population in 1940
United States Bureau of the Census Figures

State	Population	Number of Potential Voters	Per Cent of Total Population	Per Cent of Total Population Voting in 1940 Election
Alabama	2,832,961	1,555,369	54.9	10.4
Arizona	499,261	363,346	52.7	30.1
Arkansas	1,949,387	1,098,986	56.4	10.3
California	6,907,387	4,455,677	64.5	47.3
Colorado	1,123,296	688,410	61.3	48.9
Connecticut	1,709,242	1,011,658	59.2	45.7
Delaware	266,505	171,856	64.5	51.2
Florida	1,897,414	1,187,827	62.6	25.6
Georgia	3,123,723	1,768,969	56.6	10.0
Idaho	524,873	305,311	58.2	44.8
Illinois	7,897,241	5,119,854	64.8	53.4
Indiana	3,427,796	2,198,935	64.2	52.0
Iowa	2,538,268	1,608,926	63.4	47.9
Kansas	1,801,028	1,144,823	63.6	47.8
Kentucky	2,845,627	1,630,772	57.3	34.1
Louisiana	2,363,880	1,364,933	57.7	15.7
Maine	847,226	493,506	58.2	37.9
Maryland	1,821,244	1,153,510	63.3	36.2
Massachusetts	4,316,721	2,575,477	59.7	47.0
Michigan	5,256,106	3,131,722	59.6	39.7
Minnesota	2,792,300	1,730,547	62.0	44.8
Mississippi	2,183,796	1,195,079	54.7	8.1
Missouri	3,784,664	2,463,726	65.1	48.5
Montana	559,456	343,180	61.3	44.3
Nebraska	1,305,834	817,280	62.1	46.8
Nevada	110,247	70,327	63.8	48.2
New Hampshire	491,524	295,859	60.2	47.9
New Jersey	4,160,165	2,592,978	62.3	47.4
New Mexico	531,818	275,227	51.8	34.4
New York	13,479,142	8,327,563	61.9	46.8
North Carolina	3,571,623	1,925,483	53.9	23.0
North Dakota	641,935	358,090	55.8	43.7
Ohio	6,907,612	4,404,423	63.8	48.1
Oklahoma	2,336,434	1,362,438	58.3	35.4
Oregon	1,089,684	717,121	65.8	44.2
Pennsylvania	9,900,180	6,031,192	60.9	41.2
Rhode Island	713,346	424,876	59.6	44.8
South Carolina	1,899,804	989,841	52.1	5.3
South Dakota	642,961	378,405	58.9	48.0
Tennessee	2,915,841	1,703,391	58.4	17.9
Texas	6,414,824	3,710,374	57.8	16.2
Utah	550,310	298,160	54.2	45.0
Vermont	359,231	214,248	59.6	39.8
Virginia	2,677,773	1,567,517	58.5	12.9
Washington	1,736,191	1,123,725	64.7	45.7
West Virginia	1,901,974	1,046,107	55.0	45.6
Wisconsin	3,137,587	1,941,603	61.9	44.8
Wyoming	250,742	150,031	59.8	44.8

to vote was a natural right. . . . Under the theory of the good of the state, men were excluded because they were not church members, because they were criminals, because they had not been residents a long enough time. It is not always possible to classify every restriction definitely, but it may be said that one of these two theories controls every modification of the suffrage." [4]

History of the Suffrage. It has been said, with much justification, that the history of civilization can be traced in the history of the suffrage — in the history of the extension of the privileges of popular participation in government. The evolution of modern government began with an absolute monarchy. In the course of time, the monarch was obliged to consult a group of nobles regarding the imposition of taxes and the requirements of military service. The story of the rise of popular government is the story of the slow but steady increase in the size of the group permitted to participate in the making of decisions on public questions. Some considerable portion of this development had already taken place before our own institutions were established. We secured by long and laborious effort a universal manhood suffrage; as recently as 1919 we achieved a universal suffrage.

Those who established the state governments had little confidence in democratic forms. They sought, as has been said, to protect the people from what they feared might be the results of their own folly. They believed in government by the best people; the best people were to be determined by the establishment of tests of religious affiliation and ownership of property. While there was no established church in the several states, as that practice is understood in European countries, it was nevertheless required that voters must be members in good standing, and contributing to the support, of the prevailing religious denomination of the state in which they lived. This same type of qualification was applied, of course, to persons desiring to hold public office. Property-owning and tax-paying qualifications were imposed both upon voters and upon candidates for public office. Some of the states established by law a scale of property qualification for each office, as in Delaware.

In fact, when the Federal Constitutional Convention met in 1787, the ownership of property in specified amounts was a prerequisite to voting in ten of the thirteen original states. In two others, New Hampshire and South Carolina, property ownership was simply one

---

[4] Porter, Kirk H., *A History of Suffrage in the United States,* pp. 5–6 (University of Chicago Press, 1918).

way of qualifying, the other being payment of taxes. These provisions were a survival from colonial times, when it was the theory of the suffrage that property was the foundation of society and that it needed protection by excluding from the vote those floaters, paupers, and apprentices who had no stake in the community. It was feared that a suffrage unrestricted by property and tax tests would threaten vested interests and stable government and would enable the poor to oppose the well-to-do.

In our time religious qualifications have been everywhere abandoned, and property qualifications have disappeared from all but three or four states. During the depression there was some talk of reviving old laws to keep the ballot from recipients of relief, but no such step was actually taken. We have come to realize that there is little or no connection between the extent of a person's wealth and his or her ability to discharge conscientiously the duties of a citizen. While such qualifications are no longer regarded as in keeping with the spirit of democracy, the Founding Fathers had a logical reason for taking the position which they did. A citizen who owns real estate is apt to have a deeper and more vital concern in the conduct of his local government than is a man who owns no such property. He may be regarded as having roots in the community and as being consequently a more stable citizen. It is possible that this is still true in many cases today, but to enforce such a qualification generally would have the effect of disqualifying those persons who own personal property only or who, like the recipients of public assistance, own neither.

General Qualifications. The qualifications prescribed for voting reflect, at any given time, the judgment of the community as to the things which are important. While we have been gradually doing away with some prerequisites as no longer pertinent or fair, we have been establishing new ones and modifying others which we still retained. Most of the qualifications have been in force for many years and are consequently well known. United States citizenship is a universal requirement, although in times past, during heavy waves of European immigration, there were instances in which states for a time conferred the privilege of the suffrage upon persons who had taken out only their first papers. The age limit of twenty-one years is in effect in every state except Georgia. Residence requirements are everywhere in force. The length of residence required within the state, the county, and the voting district varies greatly from state to state, the length of the period required diminishing from the larger

United States citizenship, and, except in Georgia, age of 21.

State	Residence in State	Residence in County	Residence in Voting Precinct	Regis-tration
Alabama	2 years	1 year	3 months	Yes
Arizona	1 year	30 days	30 days	Yes
Arkansas	1 year	6 months	30 days	Yes
California	1 year	90 days	40 days	Yes
Colorado	1 year	90 days	10 days	Yes
Connecticut	1 year	*	....	Yes
Delaware	1 year	3 months	30 days	Yes
Florida	1 year	6 months	....	Yes
Georgia	1 year	6 months	....	Yes
Idaho	6 months	30 days	....	Yes
Illinois	1 year	90 days	30 days	Yes
Indiana	6 months	†	30 days	Yes
Iowa	6 months	60 days	10 days	(a)
Kansas	6 months	30 days	30 days	(b)
Kentucky	1 year	6 months	60 days	(c)
Louisiana	2 years	1 year	3 months	Yes
Maine	6 months	3 months	3 months	Yes
Maryland	1 year	6 months	6 months	Yes
Massachusetts	6 months	....	6 months	Yes
Michigan	6 months	....	20 days	Yes
Minnesota	6 months	....	30 days	Yes
Mississippi	2 years	1 year	1 year	Yes
Missouri	1 year	60 days	60 days	(d)
Montana	1 year	30 days	30 days	Yes
Nebraska	6 months	40 days	10 days	(e)
Nevada	6 months	30 days	10 days	Yes
New Hampshire	6 months	....	6 months	Yes
New Jersey	1 year	5 months	....	Yes
New Mexico	1 year	90 days	30 days	Yes
New York	1 year	4 months	30 days	Yes
North Carolina	1 year	4 months	4 months	Yes
North Dakota	1 year	90 days	30 days	(f)
Ohio	1 year	30 days	20 days	(g)
Oklahoma	1 year	6 months	30 days	Yes
Oregon	6 months	....	....	Yes
Pennsylvania	1 year	....	60 days	Yes
Rhode Island	2 years	....	6 months	Yes
South Carolina	2 years	1 year	4 months	Yes
South Dakota	1 year	90 days	30 days	Yes
Tennessee	1 year	6 months	....	Yes
Texas	1 year	6 months	6 months	No
Utah	1 year	4 months	60 days	Yes
Vermont	1 year	....	3 months	No
Virginia	1 year	6 months	30 days	Yes
Washington	1 year	90 days	30 days	Yes
West Virginia	1 year	6 months	60 days	Yes
Wisconsin	1 year	....	10 days	(e)
Wyoming	1 year	60 days	10 days	Yes

* 6 months' residence in the town.   † 60 days in township.   (a) In certain cities. (b) In cities of first and second class.   (c) In cities of first, second, third, and fourth classes.   (d) In cities of 10,000 and over.   (e) In cities of 5,000 and over.   (f) In cities of over 1,500 population.   (g) In cities of 16,000 and over.

unit to the smaller, as is shown in the table of state voting laws on page 122.

Voting Age. Strong arguments have been presented for reducing the voting age from twenty-one to eighteen, as Georgia did by constitutional amendment in 1943. The prevailing requirement has the support of long-established usage and of conformity with legal age requirements for many other purposes. Under present conditions, however, there is much to be said for the proposal. Young people are far better informed and more mature than they were before the introduction of modern educational methods. In school and college they study social, political, and economic problems and become deeply interested in them, only to be reminded on registration day that they are not old enough to vote. Many resent this, especially when they look at some of the people who are legally entitled to vote. Some lose interest or become absorbed in other matters in the interval between the completion of school and the time at which they become of age. They are left without any effective means of expressing their interest in civic affairs. Most important of all, perhaps, is the fact that young men between the ages of eighteen and twenty-one are especially desirable for military service. If they are old enough to fight and die for their country, they should be considered old enough to vote. That a concession on voting age be made would seem to be clearly in the interests of the community and of the thousands of young men and women who would be affected.

At the present time all indications point to opposition to this change, but the passage of time has changed opinion on other questions and it may on this one. In 1939 only one in six in a Gallup poll favored the plan, although more recent polls have shown a greater degree of support. In 1943 and 1944 it is reported that measures providing for this change were introduced into the legislatures of thirty states. All of them were defeated, although in Arkansas, New York, and Wisconsin the bills passed one house and were rejected in the other. In many states the bills were never reported out of committee. A proposal for a constitutional amendment was introduced into the Seventy-eighth Congress, and a hearing was held on it by the House Committee on the Judiciary.[5]

[5] A good deal of literature has appeared on this subject: Arnall, Ellis G., " Admitting Youth to Citizenship," *State Government,* October, 1943, pp. 203–204; Dam, Loring, " Civic Plan to Bridge 18–21 Gap," *National Municipal Review,* January, 1945, pp. 10–13, 26; *Editorial Research Reports,* " The Voting Age," issue of September 9, 1944; Johnsen, Julia E., *Lowering the Voting Age* (Wilson, New York, 1944) ; *Congressional Digest,* " Should the Legal Voting Age Be Reduced to Eighteen Years? " August-September, 1944, entire issue.

Literacy Test. Connecticut in 1855, Massachusetts in 1857, both by constitutional amendment, adopted literacy tests for voting. The ability to read, or to read and write, is now a qualification for voting in approximately half of the states. Many of these states are in the South, where the qualification appears in some cases either as an alternative or as an additional test. New York adopted such an act in 1923. Dean Crawford, who made a careful study of the working of this act, testifies to its general effectiveness.[6] Basing his judgment largely upon an analysis of its operation over a period of six years, he concludes that the test has been actually enforced, 14.9 per cent having failed to pass in the six years; that there has been a steady increase in the interest of new voters in elections; that the interest in Presidential years is greater than in other elections; that women show a relatively lower percentage of interest than do men; that women are more successful than men in passing the test; and finally, that the test has developed interest in evening schools on the part of the foreign-born. To a great many people it seems that the adoption and enforcement of legislation of this character are not only justifiable but highly desirable. We have spent hundreds of millions of dollars for public education. The facilities for education have long been available. There is little excuse, therefore, for permitting persons who have failed to take advantage of them to participate in the choice of public officers and in decisions with regard to public policy.

Poll Tax. Until recently the poll tax was generally thought of as a device for keeping Negroes in certain Southern states from voting. Actually, it grew not out of the Reconstruction movement but out of the Granger movement and the Populist party activity in the last decade of the nineteenth century. The first act containing such a restriction was passed in Florida in 1889. Others followed in rapid succession, until by 1901 eight had been passed in as many states in the southeastern region. Georgia came along last in 1908. The provisions of these laws kept the poor whites as well as the Negroes from voting. They imposed high taxes and required payment many months prior to the holding of the election; and even when the tax had been paid, the colored voter was not permitted to register unless he could present his tax receipt. By setting the amount of the tax high, the assumption was that the colored voter would not have available the amount of money required, or that if he did, he would not

[6] Crawford, Finla G., *State Government*, pp. 75–79 (Holt, New York, 1931). See also his "The New York State Literacy Test," *American Political Science Review,* May, 1923, pp. 260–263, and November, 1925, pp. 788–790; and "Operation of the Literacy Test for Voters in New York," *Ibid.,* May, 1931, pp. 342–345.

be willing to spend it, many months before, for the rather doubtful chance of participating in an election. The tax was cumulative, the law requiring that the tax for all preceding years must be paid before the citizen was eligible to vote. This may constitute a financial burden sufficiently serious, especially in lower income families, white as well as Negro, to prevent participation in elections.

The subject has been one of intense controversy in both state and nation for the past several years. Throughout the South, liberals have been trying to abolish the tax. As the table on voting participation on page 119 clearly shows, in those states in which the poll tax still exists only 10 per cent or less of the total population participated in the 1940 Presidential election, whereas some fifty years or more ago, prior to the enactment of these laws, voting participation in the South compared favorably with that in other sections of the country. The poll tax requirement is undemocratic in its effects and sets apart the states that still retain it. Tennessee tried to abolish its tax in 1943, only to have the act thrown out by the courts. Under the able leadership of Governor Ellis Arnall, Georgia succeeded in abolishing its poll tax in 1945. In that year eight states remained in which some form of poll, head, or capitation tax was a prerequisite for voting.[7]

Since progress in abolishing the poll tax by state action has been so slow and uncertain, the effort has been made to secure Congressional enactment of a measure that would accomplish this purpose in all the states uniformly and simultaneously. A bill, known as the Pepper-Geyer bill, has been introduced in each session since 1940

[7] These were: Alabama, Arkansas, Mississippi, Rhode Island, South Carolina, Tennessee, Texas, and Virginia. No such tax was levied in the following thirteen states: Arizona, California, Colorado, Idaho, Iowa, Louisiana, Maryland, New Mexico, New York, Ohio, Oregon, Utah, and Wisconsin. In the remaining twenty-seven states such taxes are or may be levied, but payment is not a suffrage requirement.

The Tennessee story is told in full, by the Chairman of the Southern Electoral Reform League, in Perry, Jennings, *Democracy Begins at Home* (Lippincott, Philadelphia, 1944). Recent discussions of the subject will be found in American Council on Public Affairs, *The Poll Tax* (Washington, 1940); Arkansas State Policy Committee, *The Poll Tax and the Suffrage* (Little Rock, 1938); Bontecou, Eleanor, *The Poll Tax* (American Association of University Women, Washington, 1942); Combs, William H., and Cole, William E., *Tennessee, a Political Study*, Chapter 3 (University of Tennessee Press, 1940); Dabney, Virginius, *Below the Potomac: A Book about the New South*, Chapter 4 (Appleton-Century, New York, 1942); Eagan, D. W., *Poll Taxes in the Various States* (Tennessee State Planning Commission, Nashville, 1938); Forbush, Emory, "The Poll Tax," *Editorial Research Reports*, July 3, 1941, entire issue; "Disfranchisement by Means of the Poll Tax," a note in *Harvard Law Review*, February, 1940, pp. 645–652; Strong, Donald S., "The Poll Tax: The Case of Texas," *American Political Science Review*, August, 1944, pp. 693–709.

and has been the occasion for extended committee hearings, prolonged filibusters on the part of the Southern Senators, propaganda and counterpropaganda, crimination and recrimination. While the argument is advanced that under the Constitutional clause guaranteeing a republican form of government to the states, the Federal government has the power and the duty to pass such an act, there is, in some quarters, grave doubt as to its constitutionality. On the basis of experience up to the summer of 1945, it seems unlikely that the measure will be enacted.[8]

Negro Suffrage. The question of Negro suffrage, long one of great concern in the Southern states, is one of rapidly increasing importance in the Northern cities, where the Negroes now often hold the balance of power. In order to understand the present situation, it is necessary to review briefly the circumstances under which it developed. At the close of the Civil War, the Radical Reconstruction leaders in Congress forced through the adoption of Amendment XV, the purpose of which was to guarantee in so far as possible the privilege of the suffrage to the newly established group of Negro citizens. The period of reconstruction following the Civil War presents a story of graft and political corruption almost unparalleled in the annals of a civilized community.[9] The carpetbaggers from the North, together with the Southern scalawags, plundered the treasuries of the Southern states in a shameless fashion. Personal clothing, food, house furnishings, et cetera, were purchased in great quantities at public expense for the members of the legislature, their families and friends. These legislatures were composed largely of Negro members. Bars

[8] There has been much literature on this phase of the poll tax problem: Boudin, L. S., "State Poll Taxes and the Federal Constitution," *Virginia Law Review,* November, 1941, pp. 1–25; Briscoe, Vera, "The Poll Tax as a Voting Prerequisite," *Bulletin* of the National Tax Association, December, 1943, pp, 66–75; Dabney, Virginius, "Poll Tax Stirs Revolt," *National Municipal Review,* October, 1942, pp. 485–451; Lazere, Monroe R., "Payment of Poll Tax as a Prerequisite of Voting in a Federal Election," *Cornell Law Quarterly,* November, 1942, pp. 104–110; National Federation for Constitutional Liberties, *Poll Tax Repeal – a Priority for Victory* (New York, 1943) ; and Strong, *op. cit.* Senator Pepper based his argument in favor of the constitutionality of the bill on United States v. Classic, 313 U. S. 299, 1940.

[9] The essential facts of this era are nowhere more vividly presented than in Fleming, W. L., *Documentary History of Reconstruction,* 2 vols. (A. H. Clark Company, Cleveland, 1906–1907) . There has recently been some attempt to gloss over the abuses of this period; see Du Bois, W. E. B., *Black Reconstruction* (Harcourt, Brace, New York, 1935) , and Allen, James S., *Reconstruction; the Battle for Democracy, 1865–1876* (International Publishers, New York, 1937) . On the question of Negro suffrage, see Morton, Richard C., *The Negro in Virginia Politics, 1865–1902* (University of Virginia, 1919) ; Rose, John C., "Negro Suffrage, the Constitutional Point of View," *American Political Science Review,* November, 1906, pp. 17–43; and White, Walter, "The Negro and the Supreme Court," *Harper's Magazine,* January, 1931, pp. 238–246.

were established in close proximity to legislative chambers, the sessions in which were a riot of confusion and disorder.

In 1877 President Hayes withdrew the last of the troops from the Southern states. From this time on, the white people of the South began a very natural and proper effort to regain control of their governments. It was possible to discourage many colored persons from voting through the activities of the Ku Klux Klan, but the more enlightened Southern leaders well knew that this was neither a suitable nor a permanent solution of their problem. They cast about for techniques and methods by which the colored people could be constitutionally and legally barred from exercising the privilege of the suffrage. The first important attempt at the use of legal and constitutional means was made by Mississippi, which, in a new constitution in 1890, imposed numerous restrictions. The voter must have paid all of the taxes assessed against him, including a poll tax of two dollars; he must be able either to read any section of the state constitution or to understand it when read to him; the residence requirement was raised from one year to two years. Although there could have been little intention that these provisions would be fairly interpreted as between whites and blacks, the Supreme Court held that they did not contravene the provisions of Amendment XV.[10]

Although these methods spread rapidly through the other Southern states, they did not prove to be as effective as had been anticipated. One writer has observed that this system, although judiciously administered, failed to protect sufficiently the illiterate whites. It remained for South Carolina, in 1895, to introduce one of the most effective devices for this purpose, the grandfather clause. This device also spread rapidly through the South. Louisiana in 1898 adopted these and other restrictions, and by 1900 had reduced its registered colored electorate from the 127,000 of 1896 to 5300. North Carolina adopted such restrictions in 1900, Alabama and Maryland in 1901, and Virginia in 1902. Alabama added to other qualifications the requirement of good moral character. While the so-called grandfather provisions were temporary in character, they were extremely effective in eliminating from the list of voters the names of colored citizens, and in including whites who might otherwise have been eliminated by poll tax, educational provisions, or other tests designed to exclude Negroes. They usually covered two points, providing (1) that persons who had themselves participated in any war in which the United States was a party, or any descendants of

[10] Williams v. Mississippi, 170 U. S. 213, 1898.

such persons, might register to vote; (2) that those persons who were themselves, or whose ancestors had been before them, citizens of any recognized member of the family of nations as of January 1, 1866, might register. The effectiveness of these provisions is not difficult to understand when one recalls that prior to that date Negroes had no standing as citizens of any important country in the world. The attempt of Oklahoma to incorporate provisions of this character permanently in its constitution has been noted in a preceding chapter.[11]

The various technical and more or less devious methods which were employed prior to and along with the grandfather clauses remained in effect long after the latter had passed out of existence. In addition to the imposition of high poll taxes — taxes of three, four, or five dollars — constitution interpretation tests were widely employed. When one considers that lawyers, jurists, and students of political science spend a lifetime studying constitutional law without achieving anything more than a moderate knowledge of it, one wonders how the average layman, who has little time for or interest in such questions, could be expected to give suitable interpretations of intricate constitutional questions. The fact is, of course, that this was not the purpose of the law. If the applicant for registration did give the right answer, the chances are that the registration officer in most cases would not have recognized it as such. Nobody expected the answers to be correct; the purpose was to enable the registration clerk to say that the white man could register and that the black man could not. Some states required the prospective registrant to have been steadily employed throughout the preceding year, or to list the names and addresses of his employers during a preceding three- or five-year period.

Another device of more recent origin is the white primary. In Texas and other Southern states Negro voters are barred from participation in direct primary elections of the Democratic party by a rule of either the state or local party organization. It takes the form, says one authority, of a "declaration by the Democratic party authorities in each state that only white men [are] eligible to membership and permitted to help, in the primary elections, in the nomination of the party candidates." Since the Democratic nomination is equivalent to election in state and local contests in most of these states, debarment from participation in the nominating process is in

11 Chapter I, pp. 29–30. For an excellent discussion, see Sait, Edward M., *Political Parties and Elections,* Revised Edition, pp. 51–54 (Appleton-Century, New York, 1939) .

effect disfranchisement. This result was not achieved without a considerable struggle in the courts. The attempt of the Texas legislature in 1923 to exclude Negroes by specific legislative provision was invalidated by the Supreme Court in Nixon v. Herndon.[12] The Democratic State Executive Committee thereupon adopted a rule permitting " all white Democrats who are qualified . . and none other " to participate in party primaries. In Nixon v. Condon, in which the plaintiff was the same person who had figured in the earlier case, the Supreme Court ruled this action also invalid, on the ground that it was based upon a discriminatory legislative provision.[13]

In most states a political party is regarded as a public body; a legal solution of this problem has been possible because in certain Southern states the party is regarded by law as a private organization, which is, therefore, at liberty to make such rules as it sees fit for the management of its own affairs. In 1935 the Supreme Court held, in Grovey v. Townsend,[14] that the State Democratic Convention in Texas was not a mere instrumentality or agency of the state, so as to render its resolution limiting membership in the party to white citizens " state action," within the limitations of Amendments XIV and XV. Nine years later, in Lonnie E. Smith v. Allwright, Election Judge, et al., the Court completely reversed this decision, the only dissenter being Justice Roberts, who wrote the opinion in the earlier case. The Court caused a nationwide sensation by saying, at long last, that Amendment XV means what it says.[15]

It is easy for any impartial observer to understand why these things were done, and perhaps even to justify many of them. The situation today is somewhat changed. Negro education has made considerable progress. The urgency of the situation that necessitated the widespread exclusion of colored voters has passed. It is time for the Southern states to recognize, as some of their urban communities have already done, that those colored citizens who are able to meet the reasonable qualifications commonly imposed should be permitted to vote. There is a provision in the second section of Amendment XIV which provides that the representation of states in the House of Representatives shall be reduced in proportion to the num-

---

[12] 273 U. S. 536, 1927.
[13] 286 U. S. 73, 1932.
[14] 295 U. S. 45, 1935. See Weeks, O. Douglas, " The Texas Direct Primary System," *Southwestern Social Science Quarterly*, September, 1932, pp. 95–120, and " The White Primary," *Mississippi Law Journal*, December, 1935, pp. 135–153; also Lewison, Paul, *Race, Class and Party* (Oxford University Press, New York, 1932).
[15] 321 U. S. 649, 1944.

ber of qualified voters who are denied the privilege of the suffrage. This provision has never been enforced, and it seems reasonably safe to predict that it never will be. When, occasionally, a Northern member seeks to invoke the enforcement of this clause, the answer of the Southern members always is that they will correct their election abuses when the Northern cities prove that they can conduct elections without disorder and bloodshed, and show that their elections are reasonably decent and honest. While two wrongs do not make a right, the attitude of these Southern members is easy to understand. Under these circumstances it would be highly desirable if this clause of Amendment XIV might be repealed, for it is unfortunate to retain in the Constitution provisions which are unenforced and unenforceable.

In his *Representative Government,* John Stuart Mill advanced the theory of the ballot as an instrument for protection, and this theory was mentioned frequently during the debates in Congress. It is a mistake, however, to assume either that you can force democracy on a people or that the attempt to do so will afford them protection. It may in fact do just the opposite. Most of the problems in Negro suffrage in this country arose out of the attempt to extend the suffrage to a people wholly unprepared for it, and therefore unable to use it. This experience has been repeated many times in many lands — in Russia, in Germany under the Weimar Constitution, and in certain of the South American countries.

The problem of the Negro vote in the Northern cities has become a serious one. In recent years great numbers of Negroes have migrated to these cities because of better opportunities for employment, better living conditions, and better educational facilities for their children. Those who were unable to find work, or who were unwilling to work, found it easier to get on the relief rolls in the North than in the South. In some cities the group is large enough to hold the balance of power, and in most of them it is of sufficient size to be important on election day. The party organizations have, therefore, contended vigorously for its control. One effect of this has been a larger representation of the racial group on party tickets, in public office, and on the public payroll.

Woman Suffrage. The movement for the adoption of woman suffrage owes its origin to the famous Women's Rights Convention held in Seneca Falls, New York, in 1848. Prior to this time women had enjoyed no rights and few privileges; their mission in life was to remain at home and raise a large family. They were not permitted to maintain control over property, secure the benefits of higher education, engage in the practice of professions, appear on the public platform as speakers or musical artists, or participate in any of the other varied activities which now engage their time and attention.[16] A little group of radicals, including Elizabeth Cady Stanton, Lucretia Mott, Martha C. Wright, Mary Ann McClintock, and others, assembled for the purpose of protesting against this situation and of demanding for women opportunities of the types indicated. Although at first they were not greatly concerned with the question of suffrage, this soon became an important item in their program. The question was much debated in Congress, and when the provisions of Amendment XV were under discussion, the attempt was made to add the word " sex " to the other three items finally included. When this effort failed, a fifty-year campaign was begun, which culminated in the adoption of Amendment XIX in 1919. As astute an observer as James Bryce predicted in 1888 that nothing would ever come of the movement for at least three decades.[17] Nevertheless, one state after another, as well as a number of territories, adopted woman suffrage provisions operative within its own borders, beginning with the first territorial legislature in Wyoming in 1869 — seventy-five years ago. By the time the amendment was adopted, these were effective in approximately half the states. It was not until 1920 that women were eligible to participate in a Presidential election in all the states.

In the course of the campaign for the amendment, extravagant claims were made by the partisans on both sides. Those who opposed its adoption, including large numbers of women, predicted that the effect of woman suffrage would be calamitous. They foresaw a situation in which women would desert their families and their homes in order to take part in politics. Others thought women were incapable of intelligent participation in public affairs. The supporters of the amendment, on the other hand, painted rosy pictures of the political millennium which might be expected to follow the adoption of woman suffrage. Women, they said, with their greater sensitiveness to moral and ethical considerations, would exercise this power to eliminate graft, corruption, and political connivance. The

16 See their Declaration of Sentiments, in Anthony, Susan B., *History of Woman Suffrage*, Vol. I, pp. 67–74 (National American Women's Suffrage Association, New York, 1912). These pages also contain the text of the resolutions adopted by the Convention, together with some account of its proceedings.

17 Bryce, James, *The American Commonwealth*, First Edition, Vol. III, Chapter 93 (Macmillan, New York, 1888) ; see also Brooks, Robert C., Ed., *The American Commonwealth: Fiftieth Anniversary*, pp. 61–63 (Macmillan, New York, 1939).

claims of neither of the partisan groups which participated in the campaign have been substantiated. In general, it may be said that the amendment doubled the number of voters, giving us twice as many intelligent voters as we had before, and twice as many ignorant ones.

At this date, when women have had an opportunity to vote in all of the states for more than a quarter of a century and to participate in several Presidential elections, it is only reasonable to inquire into the effects of this participation.[18] Women accept their responsibility now as a matter of course, having largely overcome their reluctance to participate in public affairs. In general, the interest of women in politics and the effectiveness of their participation have steadily increased. In 1944 — in the midst of war — women outnumbered men on the voting lists for the first time, and played their most important role in national politics since they were enfranchised. In a few cases, particularly in local affairs and in matters relating to education and public welfare, broadly defined, it has been demonstrated that the participation of women as voters has had a distinct influence for the improvement of conditions.

While significant changes in the position of women in our society, which some people resent, are taking place, no one will argue that these changes have been due entirely or even chiefly to the participation of women in politics. Politics is but one among a series of factors, along with the depression and employment in war industry, which is causing change. And, on the other hand, there does not seem to be any appreciably greater prevalence of high moral and ethical standards in politics than there was prior to 1919. When one stops to analyze this situation, it seems strange that anyone could have seriously expected that there would be. This view was based upon an assumption that male voters went to the polling place with the deliberate intent of using their influence to perpetuate governmental inefficiency and political corruption; it assumed that their wives would deliberately go forth from the same homes and from the same social and economic environment to vote for honesty in public affairs, thereby canceling their husbands' votes. Such an assumption was little short of ridiculous. The political allegiance of individuals does not rest upon the basis of sex. People vote for one candidate or against another as they believe doing so will help them to maintain

---

[18] See Thompson, C. Mildred, "A Decade of Woman Suffrage," *Current History*, October, 1930, pp. 13–17; and "Women Voters Celebrate 25th Birthday," *National Municipal Review*, April, 1945, p. 190.

their social and economic position and privileges, if they are well off, or enable them to improve their general status in society, if they are not well off. In this important decision the interests of the husband and wife are substantially the same.

The Absentee and Soldier Vote. Absent voting legislation is not merely a convenience; it is a necessity if, in an age of great social mobility, a large number of persons whose business or professional activity requires them to be much away from home or to travel extensively are not to be virtually disfranchised. Initiated for the benefit of soldiers in service, absent voting was first used for a civilian population in Vermont in 1896. After that date the absent-voting privilege was extended until, at the beginning of World War II, there were only six states in which it was not operative, at least to a limited extent. Thirteen states enacted their laws in 1917. Maryland and New Jersey restricted the privilege to voters in the armed forces. Mississippi repealed its law in 1932 and did not replace it; Kentucky, New Mexico, and Pennsylvania lost their laws by action of the courts in 1921, 1926, and 1924 respectively. Various limitations were found in these measures — some geographical, others relating to cause of absence, type of election, et cetera. In twenty-seven states absentees were permitted to vote in all elections.[19]

A number of states liberalized their laws during World War II to facilitate voting by servicemen and servicewomen. By 1942 all states except Delaware, Kentucky, and New Mexico permitted absentee voting, although in five states servicemen alone were given the privilege — Louisiana, Maryland, Mississippi, New Jersey, and Pennsylvania. In thirty-four states absentee voting is permitted for Federal, state, and local officers in both primary and general elections, fourteen of these states extending the privilege to ordinary civilians. Registration is required in forty-five states — all except Arkansas, Texas, and Vermont. In twenty-four states servicemen need not register in person.

Thirty-five states provide that ballots of servicemen must be in the hands of the election authorities not later than election day. Thirteen allow thirty days between the time when applications for ballots may be received and the time when they must be returned;

---

[19] See Steinbicker, Paul C., " Absentee Voting in the United States," *American Political Science Review,* October, 1938, pp. 898–907; Kansas Legislative Council, *Absentee Voting* (Topeka, 1941) ; Pollock, James K., *Absentee Voting and Registration* (American Council on Public Affairs, Washington, 1940) ; also Harris, *Election Administration,* Chapter 8; Clark v. Nash, 192 Ky. 594, 234 S.W. 1, 1921; and Lancaster City's Fifth Ward Election, 281 Pa. 131, 1925.

in other states this period ranges from ten to sixty days. Military officers are given the right to attest to ballots in twenty-four states. A military balloting procedure under which voting is conducted at military and naval installations is provided for by Arkansas, Iowa, Kansas, and New York, while specific authority is given election officials to obtain names of servicemen from the War and Navy Departments by Massachusetts, New Jersey, and New York.[20]

A most bitter controversy regarding the enactment of a Federal ballot law developed before the 1944 Presidential election. The states loudly raised the issue of states' rights. In September, 1944, a tabulation showed that twenty states had adopted the Federal war ballot, the use of which was left optional. The war ballot was one in which the soldier wrote in the name of the Presidential candidate of his choice. Registration of soldiers was required, at least under some conditions, in thirty-eight states, although most of these permitted absentee registration in such cases and made registration, when effected, permanent. Additional time for the return of ballots beyond the date of the November election was authorized in eight states.[21]

REGISTRATION

It has become trite to say that " an honest electoral system lies at the very basis of popular government " — but it is none the less true. The first step in the conduct of such elections is to set the qualifications of voters; these have just been discussed. The next step is for those who are able to meet the qualifications, and are therefore eligible to vote, to establish that fact by the process of registration. The purpose of registration is to compile a list of such persons a sufficient length of time prior to the election, so that the public can have an opportunity to assure itself that none but properly qualified persons are to participate in the approaching election. Of course, if the election is properly conducted, those who have not registered can-

[20] Office of War Information, *State Absentee Voting and Registration Laws,* pp. 1–14 (Washington, 1942).

[21] *State Government,* September, 1944, inside back cover. See also " Federal vs. States' Rights in the Coming Fight for Votes," *Congressional Digest,* June-July, 1944, entire issue; Council of State Governments, " Voting by Men in Service," *State Government,* May, 1942, pp. 109, 116, " Absentee Voting for Servicemen," *ibid.,* November, 1943, p. 229, and *Voting in the United States* (Chicago, 1940) ; Lippert, David J., " The GI's Cast Their Ballots," *National Municipal Review,* December, 1944, pp, 588–590, 654; " Voting by Service Men and Women Stirs States' Rights Controversy," *ibid.,* February, 1944, pp. 87–88; National Association of Secretaries of State, *Conference Proceedings, 1944,* pp. 17–64 (Chicago, 1945) ; National Public Opinion Research Center, *Should Soldiers Vote?* (Denver, 1944) ; and Ohm, Howard F., "The Ballot Again Goes to War," *Wisconsin Counties,* February, 1944, pp. 9–11.

not vote, except in those jurisdictions where previously registered voters are permitted to vote on affidavit.

Registration as a means of establishing eligibility to vote is a relatively recent development. In the early days, when the country was predominantly rural and almost every citizen in a community was known to every other, such a process was unnecessary. At present, however, all states except Texas and Vermont have some form of registration; in Iowa, Kansas, Kentucky, Missouri, Nebraska, North Dakota, Ohio, and Wisconsin the application of the system is limited to certain cities.[22] As urbanization has continued, the idea of registration has spread and the methods of registration have been subject to development and change, the primary purpose of preventing election frauds still remaining uppermost. The various types of fraud which it is sought to prevent are: voting the graveyard, voting by persons who have moved away, voting by persons not qualified, voting under fictitious names, repeating, chain voting, and the like.

The first registration law in this country was enacted by Massachusetts in 1800; states outside New England followed slowly, South Carolina adopting such legislation for Columbia in 1819, and Pennsylvania for Philadelphia in 1836. The subject was discussed by the Constitutional Convention in New York in 1821, but it was not until 1840 that an act was passed applicable even to New York City, and this was repealed after a period of two years, apparently without protest by Governor William H. Seward, who had urged its adoption. " The spread of registration laws began about 1860 and continued until about 1910. The first laws were adopted by states with large cities, and registration was required only in those cities. As time went on it was discovered that voting frauds were not confined to the large cities, and the registration provisions were extended to smaller cities and towns, and in some states to rural sections as well." [23] The early measures provided for personal registration, and there are many jurisdictions in which this type is still used; the present tendency is in the direction of a permanent registration in accordance with such rules as will presently be described. There is too much variation in the history and development of the system in the individual states to attempt a description of any particular one.

Periodic Registration. In the operation of a registration system there are numerous questions and problems, such as the treatment of rural areas and of cities of different size. There is much difference

[22] Harris, Joseph P., *Registration of Voters in the United States*, p. 593 (Brookings Institution, Washington, 1929). This entire comment on registration is based largely on Professor Harris's work, as corrected to date.

[23] Harris, *op. cit.*, p. 72.

of opinion regarding the first; in New York, for instance, three different systems of registration are in use, according to the size of the cities concerned. Again, there is the question of the relative merits of periodic and permanent registration. There are thirty-six states which use some form of permanent registration, either on a statewide basis or in designated cities and counties. The variations show a total lack of agreement on matters of policy; some states except their large cities, as Louisiana and Maryland, while others provide for the use of the system in the cities and except the less populous areas, as Wisconsin. Periodic registration, with a frequency varying from one to six years, exists in twelve states. Of the largest cities, New York, Buffalo, and Rochester have an annual system; Los Angeles, San Francisco, Seattle, and Memphis, a biennial system; and St. Louis, Baltimore, Kansas City,[24] and New Orleans a quadrennial one. Permanent registration is used in Birmingham, Boston, Chicago, Cincinnati, Cleveland, Denver, Detroit, Louisville, Milwaukee, Minneapolis, Omaha, Portland (Oregon), and St. Paul, as well as on a statewide basis in several states.

Annual registration imposes an unnecessary burden upon the voter, and the lists so compiled are inaccurate within a few months. The biennial and quadrennial forms are less expensive in operation, if administered with a like degree of efficiency, but they are even less accurate than the annual system, and impose some inconvenience upon voters who change their address and are obliged to re-register. All these forms of registration are personal; there exists in some communities an annual nonpersonal registration, which in practice amounts to a permanent registration, since the registry boards meet as prescribed by law and copy the list of the preceding year with but few changes.[25]

Permanent Registration. A survey made by Professor Weeks in 1939 showed that three fourths of the states were using permanent registration, either on a statewide basis or in restricted areas. These systems may be fitted into two general groups: " (1) those having 'model' or approximately 'model' registration laws of recent date; and (2) those having incomplete or old laws in which most, or at least some of the necessary features of the first group are lacking. Twenty states — Eastern, Middle-western, and Western — fall into the

[24] See Civic Research Institute, *Registration and Voting in Kansas City* (Kansas City, 1934).
[25] For a good description of the quadrennial system in Louisiana, see Powell, Alden L., *Registration of Voters in Louisiana* (Bureau of Government Research, Louisiana State University, 1940).

first group; the remaining sixteen — Eastern, Southern, and Western
— into the second. The first group may be subdivided into two classifications: (a) thirteen with statewide or reasonably extensive systems,[26] and (b) seven which limit the ' model ' type to one or a few populous cities or counties.[27] The second general group of states with laws which are not ' model ' may in turn be given two subclassifications: (a) five sparsely populated Western states with recent but somewhat rudimentary systems,[28] and (b) five Eastern and seven Southern states with systems clearly of the old-fashioned type." [29]

Under such a system the voter remains registered as long as he continues to reside in the same voting district. The advantages of this are obvious. " It saves the voter the trouble of having to register frequently, and also substantially reduces the cost of registration to the taxpayer . . . and under some permanent systems provision is made for transfers, whereby the voter need register only once as long as he continues to reside in the same city or county." It is possible to operate such a system in such manner as to have a constantly accurate voting list, if public service companies are required to report new installations and discontinuances of service. Where a discontinuance is reported, the name may be automatically removed from the registry list, whereas an installation normally indicates the arrival of a new tenant and a new voter. An annual check may be made through the use of a return postcard system. Mention has already been made of voting on affidavit. This calls to mind the distinction between compulsory and noncompulsory registration systems. In the former, no one may vote who is not registered, while in the latter, unregistered persons may be permitted to " swear in " their votes at the polls. This is a system which is obviously open to abuses.[30]

One of the most serious problems affecting registration, and also

[26] California, Indiana, Kentucky, Michigan, Minnesota, Montana, Nevada, New Jersey, New Mexico, Ohio, Pennsylvania, Washington, and Wisconsin.
[27] Illinois, Iowa, Kansas, Maryland, Missouri, Nebraska, and Oklahoma.
[28] Arizona, Colorado, Idaho, Oregon, and Utah.
[29] Connecticut, Delaware, Maryland, Maine, and Massachusetts; Alabama, Florida, Georgia, Louisiana, Mississippi, North Carolina, and Virginia. Quoted from Weeks, O. Douglas, " Permanent Registration of Voters in the United States," *Temple Law Quarterly*, November, 1939, pp. 74–88. See also Horlacker, John P., " The Administration of Permanent Registration in Philadelphia," *American Political Science Review*, October, 1943, pp. 829–837; Pollock, James K., *Permanent Registration of Voters in Michigan: An Appraisal* (University of Michigan, Bureau of Government, 1937).
[30] Harris, *op. cit.*, pp. 110–112. Even permanent registration can be manipulated; see Lex, William B., " Election Frauds Go Unchecked," *National Municipal Review*, May, 1944, pp. 226–228.

the conduct of elections, is the almost total lack of state administrative control over the procedure. The power to appoint local authorities is in some cases placed in the governor; in others, in a state board of elections — in Ohio, in a state supervisor of elections.[31] New York had such an office for many years, but in 1921 abolished it because of inefficiency and expense of operation. In some states the secretary of state exercises some control, but most state officers lack power sufficient to enable them to render any real service. There is a host of problems in the solution of which they might be helpful. In addition to the organization of registration machinery and the selection of personnel, there are such questions as the maintenance of records, the procedure to be followed when registration takes place, the problem of purging registration lists and identifying voters at the polls, and control over the cost of operating the system. Local officials in communities large and small all over the country have abundantly demonstrated their inability to deal with these questions in such manner as to bring about honest elections. The reader might well study the registration and election laws of his own state to find out what forms of registration are in force there, and what solution of these problems is provided.

The Committee on Election Administration of the National Municipal League has published and kept up to date a proposed model registration system, which recommends *personal* registration on a *permanent* basis.[32] The system would be statewide, and without provision for the swearing in of voters either at the polls or after the close of registration. The administration would be centralized in a single office, with a special office for the more populous cities and counties, under an appointee of the governor or mayor. Individual registration records would be maintained on loose-leaf sheets or cards which can be bound in locked binders for use at the polls; registration would be possible at all times except in the three weeks immediately preceding an election. The correction of the lists would be made from official death notices, and provision would be made for transfers on the basis of a signed request, and for cancellation of the registrations of nonvoters after failure to respond to a written notice. This effort to keep the roll correct would be supplemented by such devices as a police census or a house to house canvass. Identification

[31] For a discussion of this point, see Fairlie, John A., and Kneier, Charles M., *County Government and Administration,* pp. 185–186 (Appleton-Century, New York, 1930).

[32] National Municipal League, *A Model Registration System,* Third Edition (New York, 1939).

of the voter at the polls would be made possible through the comparison of a signature made at that time with the signature on the registration card.

Three types of nominating machinery have been extensively used in the United States; these are, in the order in which they have served as the prevailing method of nomination: the caucus, the convention, and the direct primary. The caucus may be defined as a meeting of party members for nominating candidates and making decisions regarding party policy on public questions. The legislative caucus, as it exists for both the majority and minority parties in each legislative chamber, to some extent serves this purpose, but is not of major importance at this point. The so-called primary caucus, most important here, has endured for many years in towns and villages throughout the country. The members of the party residing in the local political subdivision concerned assemble at an appointed time and place to perform these duties. Such a caucus as an instrument of party government closely resembles the town meeting in the field of government proper. Both were based on the principle of pure democracy. Just as the male inhabitants of the town came together to decide public questions, so the members of the political party assembled to select their standard-bearers for the ensuing campaign and to determine the attitude of the party on the issues before the people.

The Convention System. Transition from these methods of direct participation to a representative system took place simultaneously in government and in the political party for precisely the same reasons. As society became more complicated and communities increased in size, it was no longer possible for all citizens to assemble at one time and place; this led to the adoption of the representative principle. In government, this meant substituting the council and the representative assembly for the town meeting; in the field of party control, it meant substituting the convention for the caucus. If the representative principle is sound when applied to governmental institutions, it should be equally sound when applied to party organization in similar geographical areas. The convention as an instrument of party control lost public confidence for two reasons.

Very often, and in many different conventions in different parts of the country, the conventions showed themselves to be responsive to the control of the party boss rather than to the wishes of the people. The late Arnold Bennett Hall used to tell of a caucus that was carried on until far into the night. The irate citizens had come to outvote the organization. As the debate continued, the irate citizens one by one got tired and went home. By 2:00 A.M., when the vote was taken, the organization slate won. Nothing had been done that was wrong. The democratic processes of discussion and debate had been used, but the "good" citizens, as usual, had grown weary of well-doing. Because they would not take the trouble, they came to believe that it was impossible for them to control the convention (or the caucus) as against the party organization.

The second charge — and one that was often justified — against the convention system was that of corruption. The depths to which a convention could descend is well illustrated by an analysis of the personnel of two Cook County conventions held in Chicago in 1885 and 1896; a description of the latter is quoted from Professor Ray:

Of the other Cook County Convention, held in 1896, a contemporary account runs as follows: "Of the delegates, those who had been on trial for murder numbered 17; sentenced to the penitentiary for murder or manslaughter and served sentence, 7; served terms in the penitentiary for burglary, 36; served terms in the penitentiary for picking pockets, 2; served terms in the penitentiary for arson, 1; ex-Bridewell and jailbirds, identified by detectives, 84; keepers of gambling-houses, 7; keepers of houses of ill-fame, 2; convicted of mayhem, 3; ex-prize fighters, 11; poolroom proprietors, 2; saloon-keepers, 265; lawyers, 14; physicians, 3; grain dealers, 2; political employees, 148; hatter, 1; stationer, 1; contractors, 4; grocer, 1; sign-painter, 1; plumbers, 4; butcher, 1; druggist, 1; furniture supplies, 1; commission merchants, 2; ex-policemen, 15; dentist, 1; speculators, 2; justices of the peace, 3; ex-constable, 1; farmers, 6; undertakers, 3; no occupation, 71; total delegates, 723." In other words, in this total of 723 delegates, 265 were saloon-keepers, 148 were officeholders, and 128 had served a term either in the house of correction or in the penitentiary.[33]

How many of the conventions were this bad it is impossible to say, but there is no reason to suppose that Chicago and Cook County were any worse than a great many other cities and counties throughout the country. These data show that there was not more than a handful of decent, respectable, law-abiding citizens and that every kind of lawbreaker and criminal, every type of antisocial element to be found in any community was abundantly represented.

When the people could no longer endure these conditions, a movement for the adoption of the direct primary system began. This break-

[33] Ray, P. Orman, *Introduction to Political Parties and Practical Politics*, Third Edition, pp. 71–72 (Scribner's, New York, 1924). This material was printed originally in the *Chicago Tribune*, March 30, 1885, and in Easley, Ralph M., "The Sine Qua Non of Caucus Reform," *Review of Reviews*, September, 1897, pp. 322–324.

down of the representative principle in party government was accompanied by a similar breakdown in official legislative bodies. The
sentiment of the people against representative institutions developed in both fields at the same time and for the same reasons. Consequently, the sentiment for the direct primary was accompanied by
a demand for the adoption of the initiative, referendum, and recall
as a partial substitute for, or supplement to, the established representative legislative body. A further discussion of this movement will
be found in the following chapters.[34]

The Direct Primary. The direct primary is used statewide in all
states except Connecticut, New Mexico, and Rhode Island. In some,
it has been in effect for many years. It seems proper, therefore, to note
what it is and to attempt an evaluation of it. A direct primary is an
election held within the limits of the membership of a particular
political party within a given jurisdiction. Just as the general electorate proceeds to the polls on election day to indicate preferences
from among the nominees of the several parties for the several offices
to be filled, so in a primary election the members of the party go to

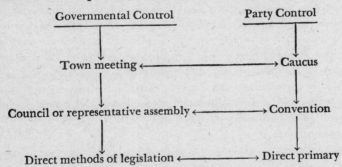

the polls on the date of the primary to select the standard bearers
for the party for the ensuing electoral campaign. These selections
are made from the slates supported by various factions or groups
within the party. Just as the voters in the general election select their
officeholders, so the members of the party in the primary select their
candidates.

Two types of direct primary are in general use — the open and
the closed. Where the closed primary is used, the voter must indicate
to the clerk at the time of registration the name of the political party
of his preference. When he appears at the polls, his name is read and,

[34] On. " The Origin of the Direct Primary," see Booser, James H., in *National
Municipal Review*, April, 1935, pp. 222-223.

subject to challenge, the clerk in charge of ballots is instructed to give him the primary ballot of this party. If voting machines are used, the machine is set for the party indicated. The chief objection to the closed primary is that it violates the principle of the secret ballot. This contention would seem to have little weight in a government operated, as ours is, through political parties. This being the case, none but a supersensitive person should object to indicating that, under normal circumstances, he has a preference for a particular political party.

The open primary used in five states enables the voter to choose, at the time he votes in the primary, the party in the selection of whose candidates he wishes to participate. In the open primary states either all the candidates of all parties may appear on the same ballot, the voter utilizing only that portion of the ballot allotted to the party of his choice, or the ballots of each party may be printed separately. At first thought, this would seem preferable to the closed primary. Experience shows, however, that under the open primary it is possible for a powerful political machine to dominate the selections in the minority as well as the majority party. Those familiar with party organization in urban communities well know the accuracy with which division committeemen and ward leaders calculate the results of the election the night before it happens. Under such circumstances, it is not at all difficult for the organization to apportion a certain number of controlled votes in each ward in excess of the number required to control the result in their own party, to be used to control the result in the minority party as well.

The nonpartisan primary is used in many states for the selection of city and county officers, as well as school and other local officers. In the state field it is frequently used for judicial officers, and in Minnesota since 1913 the members of the legislature have been elected on a nonpartisan ballot. The names of the candidates, which are placed on the ballot by petition, appear with no party designation of any kind. The two persons having the highest number of votes for each office are nominated for that office, and their names appear on the ballot in the general election without party designation. Thus a nonpartisan primary is followed by a nonpartisan election. The final election may be eliminated in some cases by a provision, such as that existing in California, to the effect that a candidate who receives a majority of the votes cast for the office he is seeking shall be declared elected.

" Run-off " elections are held in Texas and other states when no candidate at the primary receives a majority. When there is a number of candidates in the field, in a wide-open race, each with a considerable amount of support, the best that any one of them is likely to do is to win a plurality. Since a majority is required to nominate, the run-off becomes necessary; in this second primary the race is usually limited to the three highest on the list. By this process of elimination the effort is made to discover that candidate most acceptable to a majority of the party members, from among the total number presenting their names for consideration.

Advantages and Disadvantages of the Direct Primary. The supporters of the direct primary promised that it would eliminate, or help to eliminate, political manipulation. This patent political nostrum, it was said, would make it possible for the people to control party affairs in fact as well as in theory. Such has not proved to be the case. As early as 1909 Professor Charles E. Merriam observed that those who supported the primary were wondering why they had done so, while those who had opposed it were engaged in a like speculation.[35] Certain significant defects in the operation of the primary system have been abundantly demonstrated. In the first place, it is exorbitantly expensive. In the last decade, in one case after another, in one state after another, primary campaign expenditures have run into vast sums of money. Some good folk have professed to be surprised and horrified, but there is no reason why they should be. The primary system has been and will be expensive, because it makes necessary the application of practices which are commonplace in merchandising, in which advertising is a very profitable form of economic waste. The poor defenseless citizen is literally bombarded with appeals from the press, magazines, radio, billboards, and other media, exhorting him to purchase a particular brand of cigarettes, tooth paste, or breakfast food. Although this system is costly, the public has resigned itself to paying the bill.

When, in the field of politics, a system of nomination requires the

[35] The movement started in California in March, 1866, with New York following in April. Wisconsin provided for " primary meetings " in 1891; for the story of Governor La Follette's efforts to improve the system, see his *Autobiography* (Madison, 1913). For some early accounts of its operation, see *Proceedings,* American Political Science Association, 1910: Beard, Charles A., " The Direct Primary Movement in New York," pp. 187–198; Hartwell, E. M., " Primary Elections in Massachuetts," pp. 210–224; Horack, F. E., " Primary Elections in Iowa," pp. 175–186; Jones, W. Clyde, " Primary Elections in Illinois," pp. 138–162; and Loeb, Isidor, " Direct Primaries in Missouri," pp. 163–174. For later surveys, see Salter, John T., Ed., " Direct Primaries," *Annals,* March, 1923, entire issue, and Harris, Arthur, and Uhr, Carl, *Direct Primary Elections* (University of California, Bureau of Public Administration, 1941).

use of precisely the same methods and techniques, we profess to be surprised when we discover that it costs money. The candidate who wins, like the cigarette that tops the market, is the one whose name is brought most often to the attention of the voters through the largest number of channels. Many voters who go to the polls know nothing about the candidates or their qualifications; they will vote, in many cases, for the one whose name is most familiar. It is possible for a candidate to spend a million dollars for campaign purposes in any one large state without misappropriating a cent. So long as the primary system continues, candidates will continue to spend as large sums as they are able to collect, and candidates who do not have an independent income or who are not able to enlist large financial support will not run for office. This situation, in which so severe a penalty is inflicted upon the man of moderate means, cannot fail to have a serious effect upon democratic government.[36]

If it could be shown that the caliber of the candidates nominated under the primary system was conspicuously better than the caliber of those nominated by conventions, one might reconcile himself to the cost of the system. This, however, cannot be done. Indeed, it is doubtful whether the selections made under the primary are of as high a standard, on the average, as one might reasonably expect of conventions. There are a number of instances in Indiana, Pennsylvania, Wisconsin, and elsewhere where conspicuously able men have been nominated under the primary, but there are also instances, some of them in the same states, in which persons have been nominated for whom almost any party convention would have hesitated to be responsible. In great numbers of cases between these two extremes there is no evidence whatever that the voting public has shown any greater ability to select honest, able, and intelligent men than one might expect of a convention. As a matter of fact, the primary system tends to discourage men of this type, more or less dignified and reserved in character, from participating in politics; they do not like the vituperation and the hurly-burly of an electoral campaign. Many of them would, if drafted as candidates by a convention,

[36] The following figures from the 1938 gubernatorial primary in Pennsylvania are illustrative. *Republican:* James, winner, spent $470,012, of which $152,500 was put up by Pew, $22,750 by Grundy, and $5,000 each by two Kents, three Annenbergs, duPont, Widener, and Louchheim, Pinchot spent $147,862, of which $111,000 was put up by himself and his wife: *Democratic:* Jones, winner, spent $160,996 outside Philadelphia, of which $15,000 was put up by McClosky, $5,000 each by Law, Kelly, and Whalen, and $2,500 by Lee. The campaign in Philadelphia cost $61,244. Kennedy spent approximately $500,000; Margiotti, $8,992. In most cases these expenditures were tied in with those of other candidates on a slate.

go through the ordeal once, but they will not enter the primary and then go through the same trying experience a second time in an electoral campaign.

Serious objection to the direct primary may also be registered on the basis that it violates the principle of the short ballot. In general, the purpose of the short ballot is to centralize responsibility and to simplify the task which the voters are asked to perform. The direct primary does not simplify this task; it complicates it by taking the voter to the polls more times and requiring him to make a much larger number of decisions. A further discussion of the short ballot principle is included in the following chapter, but it is mentioned here because it is believed that this item, together with the excessive cost of the primary system and its failure to produce a higher quality of candidates, constitutes a sufficient indictment to make imperative a thorough and careful reconsideration of our whole system of nominating candidates for public office.

The list of arguments against the direct primary might be extended almost indefinitely. In addition to those mentioned, the authors of a recent text on political parties mention the following:

(1) It undermines party discipline and destroys party unity. (2) Only a small percentage of the voters actually participate, and under the plurality system successful nominees often represent a small minority. The result is that candidates are often hand-picked by party machines and bosses. (3) It opens the road to power to "crackpot" and "lunatic" candidates who would never "get to first base" under the convention system, and has resulted in a progressive decline in the quality of political leadership . . . . (4) It affords no opportunity for deliberation, and provides no machinery for the formulation of party platforms.[37]

Filing Fees. It happens many times that persons file, either for a primary or as an independent in a general election, who have no chance whatever of winning the election. Some do so for publicity or for bargaining power later, or for other reasons are not bona fide candidates. To discourage this practice, the filing fee system, patterned somewhat after that used in British Parliamentary elections, has been introduced. The candidate posts a specified amount, depending on the importance of the office which he seeks; if he polls a minimum specified percentage of the vote — whether he wins or not — his money is returned to him. This practice prevents cluttering up the ballot with the names of candidates who do not have, or do not think they have, some substantial support. These are sometimes re-

[37] Odegard, Peter H., and Helms, E. Allen, *American Politics*, pp. 513–521 (Harper, New York, 1938).

ferred to as "name candidates." [38] It tends, therefore, to support the principle of the short ballot, and is regarded by students as being distinctly preferable to the old-fashioned type of nominating petition.

In eleven Southern states, candidates merely file written declarations of candidacy, in three cases accompanied by a purely nominal number of signatures.[39] However, in seven of these eleven states they must pay a filing fee which, in some instances, is a fixed amount running from $1.00 for a minor local office to $100 for a statewide office, and in other cases to a percentage of the annual salary of the office. Outside of the South, approximately half of the states have no requirement for the payment of any filing fee for either the primary or general election ballots, while the remainder fall roughly into three groups. The first group consists of seven states which require a fee from primary candidates, but not from independents; seven states in the second group, chiefly Western, require the same fee of candidates independently nominated as is required of primary candidates; while in three states in a third group the candidate for the primary is given an option.[40]

Local-Primary State-Convention System Recommended. At this point one may well ask what course is open to us. We cannot go back to the caucus, and a return to the old-fashioned kind of boss-ridden party convention is out of the question. There are many who object to continuing with the direct primary in its present form. New York seems to have developed a suitable and workable alternative by retaining the primary for the nomination of candidates for local offices and returning to the state convention for the selection of candidates for state offices and for determining party policy on state questions. The results of this plan, as indicated by the choices of gubernatorial candidates from 1921, when the primary law was repealed, to date are as follows:

[38] Ramsey, Maurice M., *"Name Candidates" in Detroit Elections* (Detroit Bureau of Governmental Research, 1941).

[39] Alabama, Arkansas, Florida, Kentucky, Louisiana, Mississippi, North Carolina, Oklahoma, Tennessee, Texas, and Virginia. Tennessee and Texas require 25 signatures, and in Texas certain Congressional candidates must pay a filing fee running up to $500, which is levied by and turned over to the party. In Virginia the number of signatures is 50 for some offices, 250 for others.

[40] The states in these groups are (1) Maryland, Minnesota, Nebraska, North Dakota, Utah, West Virginia, and Wyoming; (2) California, Idaho, Missouri, Montana, Nevada, Ohio, and Washington; (3) Kansas, New Hampshire, and Oregon. See Weis, Walter M., *A Deposit System for Independent Nominations* (City Club of New York, 1939); also Dorr, Harold M., "Tightening the Direct Primary," *American Political Science Review*, June, 1936, pp. 512–522, and "Tightening the Direct Primary in Michigan; First Application of the Filing Fee." *ibid.*, February, 1937, pp. 56–65.

NEW YORK STATE GUBERNATORIAL CANDIDATES

Year	Democratic	Republican
1922	Alfred E. Smith	Nathan L. Miller
1924	Alfred E. Smith	Theodore Roosevelt, Jr.
1926	Alfred E. Smith	Ogden L. Mills
1928	Franklin D. Roosevelt	Albert Ottinger
1930	Franklin D. Roosevelt	Charles H. Tuttle
1932	Herbert H. Lehman	William J. Donovan
1934	Herbert H. Lehman	Robert Moses
1936	Herbert H. Lehman	William F. Bleakley
1938 [41]	Herbert H. Lehman	Thomas E. Dewey
1942	John J. Bennett, Jr.	Thomas E. Dewey

From this list it is evident that both parties have made use of able and distinguished men. The caliber of those selected in both parties runs high. The principle of the short ballot has been, at least in part, preserved. The whole task has been well done at a small fractional part of the cost that would have been incurred by a statewide primary for candidates for the state and Federal offices. It is to be hoped that the example of New York may influence the legislation of other states as dissatisfaction with the existing machinery for nominating candidates increases.

THE CONDUCT OF ELECTIONS

The conduct of elections presents a large number of difficult problems. It involves the expenditure of " millions of hours of time on the part of voters, electioneers, officials, and watchers." In every state the election law is sufficient to fill a large volume; the enforcement of its provisions requires the expenditure, in the aggregate, of " millions of dollars in materials, advertising, rents, and services." In fact, the cost of elections has become a matter of serious concern to students of government. It is proposed to discuss in the following paragraphs some of the more important electoral problems.

The Campaign. When the candidates have been nominated, by whatever method, when the voters have been registered and the party platforms adopted, the time is ripe for the campaign. Campaign headquarters must be established. Of the New York Republican State Committee it was reported in 1936 that they had leased the fifth floor of an office building on 42nd Street. " Approximately 7,032 square feet of floor space was divided off into some twenty

[41] For a term of four years, under a new constitutional amendment adopted in 1938.

offices and waiting rooms. . . . A large office was set up to house
the Publicity Division and newspapermen covering state headquarters." This office was equipped with telephones and typewriters for
the newspapermen and every convenience accorded them to permit
of prompt communication with their papers. A staff was set up to
assist them in contacting "news sources," to arrange press conferences, and dig up additional information desired by them. Additional offices were assigned to the Women's Division, the Speaker's
Bureau, the United Republican Finance Committee of the State of
New York, the Senate and Assembly Legislative Committee, and the
Republican State Treasurer. A suite of three rooms was assigned to
the Chairman of the State Committee, a suite of two rooms to the
Secretary. Quarters were provided for the use of the Chairman of
the Executive Committee of the State Committee, of the Veterans' Division, et cetera. " An extensive telephone service has been installed
in the new headquarters which permits direct inter-communication
with the Republican National Committee, located on the twelfth
floor, and with the National Republican Finance Committee in the
—— Building. Care has been exercised that ample space for store-
rooms be reserved, and attractive receptionists have been engaged. . . ."

Many aspects of the ordinary state campaign differ from those of
the national campaign chiefly in extent; the methods employed are
essentially the same. There is the usual round of meetings, local and
major, with their speeches, debates, and discussions. Headquarters
are set up in all centers of population, with posters, banners, and
radio or phonograph blaring forth party propaganda to all who care
to listen or to those who cannot escape because of the proximity of
their homes or their places of business. Printing presses work over-
time to turn out copies of the platform and quantities of pamphlets,
leaflets, and other printed materials. Campaign buttons and automobile stickers are distributed. Slogans and catch phrases are popular-
ized. Newspapers are filled with accounts of candidates' speeches and
of public meetings, and with copy that is sent out from the campaign
headquarters. Advertising space is reserved to point with pride or
view with alarm, as the case may be. Billboards and other forms
of commercial advertising may also be used. While all this is going
on, the party workers are busy seeing their people. The coverage is so
complete that no citizen can live through the two months before election without being aware of the candidates, the parties, and the issues
— whether or not he understands them.

There is surprisingly little that is original or different in political campaigns, although "stunts" of various sorts are often featured. Parades are largely a thing of the past; instead, motion pictures are shown on street corners, from automobiles or trucks whose sides are covered with billboards and whose interiors are equipped with amplifying devices which emit raucous sounds. In one city the wife of a candidate rode through the streets in summertime in an old sleigh — with horses, bells, and all. In the rural districts, barbecues, picnics, and outings are common; these are usually organized on the basis of allegiance to some particular leader (who pays all the expenses), or upon a county basis. In either case, it is quite an occasion for the party — the members of the party ticket are present, and the program is designed to inform the party workers and inspire them to exert a proper effort in the work of the campaign. Clambakes and outings are always popular with both city and rural workers. There is in the campaign as a whole a vast amount of hokum and showmanship.

Something more specific ought, perhaps, to be said about campaign speaking, both in rallies and by radio. There is usually, as in national campaigns, a speaker's bureau to help arrange the itinerary of the candidates and to handle the assignment of prominent speakers to the more important meetings. The tone of the discussion — indeed, the tone of the whole campaign — rests largely with the candidate at the head of the ticket. If he is a cheap and blatant showman, the campaign as a whole is likely to be of that type; if he is an able and dignified person, the tone of the campaign is bound to reflect his influence. The people have shown themselves all too willing to support candidates of the former type. In one state a candidate was elected governor who not only posed as a real dirt farmer, but who pledged himself, on the ground of economy, to plow up the lawn of the executive mansion and plant potatoes there. Although the receipts from motor vehicle taxes were needed to build and maintain the state highways, he pledged himself to reduce these fees to $3.00. One candidate used a hillbilly band, while another featured a miner's quartet. In another state a candidate for governor promised to pay all teachers' salaries out of state funds, although the amount involved was greater than the total receipts of the general fund from all sources and for all purposes.

In spite of these unfortunate occurrences, which receive more than their proper share of publicity, it is true that the general tone of political campaigns has been improving during recent years. As will

be indicated in another chapter, the governorship has been attracting a higher type of man because the position itself has been dignified
by greater power and responsibility. In many states the candidates
are outstanding men who discuss seriously, even though with partisan bias, important questions facing the state government. It is in
this field that many a state leader develops the skill which later serves
him in good stead in national politics. Governor Alfred E. Smith of
New York may not have been successful in his race for the Presidency,
but even his political opponents did not deny that he exhibited
extraordinary skill as a political technician and campaigner in his
home state. The same may be said of former Governor Gifford
Pinchot of Pennsylvania, President Roosevelt when he was Governor
of New York, and numerous others.

Radio has made an important contribution in elevating the tone
of political campaigns. It has made fewer speeches necessary, and
has indirectly aided in improving the quality of those which are
made. There are some candidates who still visit every county in the
state with an automobile entourage, meeting the people and being
seen by them, and speaking at every crossroads, but this campaign
technique is increasingly a thing of the past. With the radio, and the
use of one powerful station or a network of stations covering a whole
state, it is possible for all the important addresses of the candidates to
be heard by all who care to listen. With fewer addresses to make,
and each of those of greater significance, it is natural that greater care
should be exercised in their preparation by the candidate himself
and by the ghost writer who assists him. The radio has also short-
ened the period of active campaigning and speeded up the process.
Any important charge can be answered within a few hours or, at
the latest, the next day. Radio is expensive to use, but there is no
doubt of the benefit it has brought to political campaigning in this
country.

Ballots and Voting Machines. When the campaign is over, when
the last speech has been made and the last argument presented, the
day of reckoning arrives. The first item of interest in the conduct of
the election is the ballot. Before considering the ballot forms now
in use, the development of the balloting process may be briefly noted.
It has often been said that elections are a sort of denatured and
humanized warfare — that they are a means of determining the outcome of differences arising between opposing groups by counting
heads rather than by breaking them. In early times, when the citizen
appeared at the polls to vote, he was supposed to state in a loud

and clear voice the names of the persons for whom he wished to vote. As the process developed, paper ballots were substituted; to begin with, these were furnished by the party organizations, and were of different sizes, shapes, and colors. As more emphasis came to be placed upon the secrecy of the ballot, state laws were enacted requiring that the ballots furnished be of uniform size, shape, and color. The intent of these laws was evaded by the use of different weights of paper and slightly different shades of the same color. At this point government intervened to supervise the preparation and printing of ballots or to furnish them itself.

The Australian ballot was introduced in this country between 1887 and 1900; the term " is generally used to designate an official ballot, printed at public expense, by public officers, containing the names of all candidates duly nominated, and distributed at the polls by the election officers." [42] The original form of the Australian ballot in this country was the Indiana party column type, upon which, by placing a single cross below the party emblem, a voter could vote a straight party ticket. Later the Massachusetts office column type came into general use; this discourages straight ticket voting and makes it necessary for the voter to make a definite choice, or at least a separate cross, for each candidate for whom he wishes to vote. There are numerous variations from these two main types, and various problems with regard to the form and arrangement of ballots. The use of emblems has long been regarded as ridiculous, but organization workers, particularly in cities, have fought for their retention because they made it easier to control an illiterate vote. Sometimes the emblems are confusing even to people who can read.

The procedure used for getting names on the ballot must be simple and direct; it must effectively restrict the election to really serious contenders, and it must effectively guard against such abuses as unnecessary expense and inconvenience in operation.[43] The necessity of providing a suitable answer to these questions has been largely responsible for legislation designed to regulate and control the process of nomination, and for the spread of the direct primary. Even the order in which the names of the various candidates for a given office appear on the ballot is a matter of importance, since it has been conclusively shown that the name which appears first in the list has a distinct advantage in voting strength over other names.

[42] Harris, Joseph P., *Election Administration in the United States*, p. 154 (Brookings Institution, Washington, 1934). Chapter 5 of this important study is devoted to the ballot.

[43] *Ibid.*, p. 166.

Unless the names are rotated on the ballots in the different voting districts, the same candidate enjoys the full benefit of this advantage.

Another problem that has assumed importance in recent years is the use of voting machines. Mechanical voting devices not only eliminate some election frauds and reduce others, but in the long run they save substantial sums of money. They will last for a lifetime, and can be paid for in from five to fifteen years out of savings from the printing of paper ballots. In addition, a smaller number of precincts, a smaller number of election officers in each precinct, and, because of the shortening of working hours, a smaller compensation to the precinct officers are all possible. A considerable saving may result from avoiding expensive recounts. Students of election administration are practically unanimous in urging their adoption and use.

ARGUMENTS FOR AND AGAINST VOTING MACHINES [44]

Principal Merits	*Defects and Objections*
1. Accurate returns.	1. They slow up the voting and cause voters to have to wait in line to vote.
2. Reduction or elimination of many types of voting frauds.	2. Many voters object to their use.
3. Quick returns.	3. They are expensive to install.
4. Secrecy.	4. They are more costly to operate than paper ballots.
5. Elimination of mistakes and spoiled ballots.	5. Many voters lose their vote on the machine or vote for the wrong candidate.
6. Avoidance of recounts.	6. Many voters find them difficult to operate.
7. Reduced cost of elections.	7. They may break down at the polls.
8. Better election officers may be secured.	8. They make split voting more difficult.

The adoption of voting machine legislation has made steady progress since 1892, when the first law authorizing their use was adopted in New York. In 1940 there were only fourteen states in which no such legislation had ever been enacted.[45] States in which

44 Harris, Joseph P., *Election Administration in the United States*, pp. 259–260. See Heavenrich, Max P., Jr., *The Use of Voting Machines in Thirty-five Cities or Counties* (Flint Institute of Research and Planning, 1939) ; also *The Effect of Division Size upon Voting Conditions in Philadelphia* (Institute of Local and State Government, University of Pennsylvania, 1939) .

45 These were Delaware, Idaho, Louisiana, Mississippi, Missouri, Nevada, New Mexico, North Carolina, North Dakota, South Carolina, South Dakota, Vermont, West Virginia, and Wyoming. Data here presented from Albright, Spencer D., *Ballot Analysis and Ballot Changes Since 1930* (Council of State Governments, Chicago, 1940) . Three such laws have been declared unconstitutional by the state

laws were in force in 1940 are grouped by decades in the following table, according to the date of passage:

ENACTMENT, BY DECADES, OF VOTING MACHINE LAWS
IN FORCE IN 1945

1890–1899	*1900–1909*	*1910–1919*	*1920–1929*	*1930–1939*
1892 New York	1900 Iowa	1913 Washington	1922 Virginia	1930 Texas
1893 Michigan	1901 Kansas Maine Wisconsin	1914 Maryland	1923 California (re-enacted)	1935 Alabama New Jersey (re-enacted)
1895 Connecticut	1903 Illinois		1927 Arizona Arkansas Oklahoma	Rhode Island (re-enacted)
1897 Minnesota	1907 Montana			1937 Tennessee
1899 Indiana			1929 Florida Georgia Pennsylvania	

After the elections of 1932 and 1934 Spencer D. Albright made studies of the ballots used in representative communities in each of the forty-eight states.[46] In the latter year the party column ballot was used in twenty-eight states, while the office column type was used in nineteen. In the remaining state, South Carolina, the Australian ballot is not in use, the voter selecting a party ballot to his taste. In three of the party column ballot states, Montana, New Jersey, and Wyoming, " there was no provision for voting a straight ticket by marking a single cross, and in fourteen others voters were forced

supreme courts: Massachusetts, in 1907; Ohio, in 1909; Kentucky, in 1939; Massachusetts amended its constitution in 1911 and re-enacted a voting machine law in 1912. In Ohio, as a result of a new interpretation by the supreme court, the voting machine law was rewritten in 1929.

In eight states such legislation has been repealed: Nebraska, 1899 to 1921; Rhode Island, 1900 to 1921; New Jersey, 1902 to 1911; California, 1903 to 1921; Colorado, 1905 to 1921; Utah, 1905 to 1917; New Hampshire, 1913 to 1925; and Oregon, 1913 to 1939.

[46] Albright, Spencer D., *How Does Your Ballot Grow?* (American Legislators' Association, Chicago, 1933) ; " General Election Ballots in 1934," *Southwestern Social Science Quarterly*, March, 1936, pp. 885–895; and " Legislation on Marking Ballots," *ibid.*, December, 1940, pp. 221–226. See also Benson, Lawrence E., " Studies in Secret Ballot Technique," *Public Opinion Quarterly*, March, 1941, pp. 79–82; Jones, O. Garfield, " Exit the Party Column Ballot? " *National Municipal Review*, April, 1941, pp. 242–244; Illinois Legislative Council, *The Direct Primary Ballot* (Springfield, 1940) ; Smith, Carl O., *A Book of Ballots* (Detroit Bureau of Governmental Research, 1938) ; and Harris, *Election Administration*, Chapter 5.

to find the party of their choice without the aid of an emblem at the top of the column." Of the office column ballot states, New York alone used party emblems. Nebraska and Pennsylvania had straight ticket privileges. " The remaining thirteen of the sixteen had neither the emblem nor the privilege of voting the straight ticket by a single mark."

The study also disclosed the average size of ballots, the average number of names on ballots, the average number of propositions, the average number of parties, et cetera. Some of these data are summarized in the following table:

COMPARISON OF PARTY COLUMN AND OFFICE GROUP BALLOTS

	Party Column	Office Group
Number of states using	31	16
Average size of ballot (in square inches)	564.6	349.4
Average number of names on ballot	101.7	76.5
Average number of propositions	3.1	4.1
Average number of parties	5.3	4.9

Friends of the short ballot will note with approval that the office group type, in addition to having other notable advantages, is a third smaller than the party column type. In the figures reported, Indiana had the largest ballot of any state — a total of 2,016 square inches, or 14 square feet. Michigan, Missouri, New York, and North Dakota each had ballots with more than 1,000 square inches. The smallest ballots were in South Carolina and Virginia, measuring 28 and 72 square inches, respectively. The figures for California, Illinois, Massachusetts, New Jersey, Pennsylvania, and Wisconsin were as follows: 816, 714, 399, 560, and 384, respectively.

The total number of names on the ballot varied from 24 in Louisiana to 319 in Indiana, the average numbers being indicated in the table above. For the representative group of states already referred to, the numbers are 120, 143, 47, 134, 44, and 81, respectively. There were seventeen states in which no statewide propositions were submitted, but on the other hand, California submitted 20, Louisiana 17, and Oregon 13. " Full instructions were printed on the ballots in nineteen states, brief instructions in twenty, and in nine states every voter was presumed to know the law." One fourth of the electors in America could learn the addresses of candidates from the ballots; one third received ballots which carried numbered stubs as a safeguard against fraud. In New Mexico the ballot was printed in English and Spanish. On the ballots of four Southern states no party designations were shown. In several states voters are asked to use more than one ballot, separate ones being used for Presidential electors, judges, local officers, or propositions.

In nineteen states, where important officers numbering nine or more were elected, including governors and supreme court judges, one gets an idea of the extent to which the long ballot still survives, for this number indicates only those states holding general state elections in a single year. In five states — Kentucky, Minnesota, Missouri, North Dakota, and Virginia — all members of the Federal House of Representatives are elected at large, thus placing a heavy additional burden upon the voter. In this particular election, voters in thirty-one states were asked to pass upon 163 amendments, acts, and questions of public policy. The average number in the Pacific coast states was fourteen; in the Atlantic coast states, exclusive of Georgia, the average was very low. The author of this report concludes: " The simplest of all elections occurred in Maine where only Presidential Electors were chosen. Here, as in Maryland and Wyoming, which added Congressmen and propositions, the voting for electors was by group or separately. New Hampshire had a short state ballot. New Jersey's state-wide choices were few, as was the case in Nevada and Oklahoma. . . . Wisconsin . . . imposed only a moderate burden in the selection of state officers. . . . Among the large states in the Union, Massachusetts and Wisconsin had ballots that stood out as efficient for the voter and fair to parties and candidates."

The Conduct of Elections. Those who are now perturbed from time to time by evidences of disorder in the conduct of elections would do well to refresh their memories with regard to conditions in earlier days. In the Pennsylvania Constitutional Convention of 1837, before the registry law was enacted in that state, it was reported that " disturbances, outrages, turbulence, violence, and bloodshed existed in the city [Philadelphia] on election day, even murders being committed." [47] Because of occurrences of this character and of the existence of many types of fraud, the movement for the supervision of elections and returns was initiated. As party spirit increased, " every method was resorted to in order to secure the advantage and election boards did not escape." Important legislation was enacted

[47] Mr. Stevens, in *Debates* of the Constitutional Convention of Pennsylvania, 1837, Vol. III, p. 37. Cited by Logan, Edward B., *Supervision of the Conduct of Elections and Returns*, p. 4 (Lancaster Press, Lancaster, 1927) .

in Pennsylvania in 1836 and 1839, in New York in 1842, in New Jersey in 1855 and 1877. The general tendency was to create bipartisan boards, chosen on an elective basis; reliance was placed upon this feature and upon publicity in the determination of the applicant's right to vote and in the count of the votes. Professor Logan continues: " The first method presupposes the existence of active parties which will insure that the full quota of their members are in the election boards. The second method requires for its successful operation an electorate divided politically which can be depended upon to make challenges or insure a fair count, or an electorate actively interested in maintaining fair elections. Also the latter method requires a large element of personal acquaintanceship among the voters for its successful operation." [48]

While the framers of these acts may have been justified in expecting their successful operation, it soon became evident that they were inadequate to provide effective control over election machinery. This was notably true in Pennsylvania, where, in 1868, the legislature provided for overseers of elections, to be appointed by the Court of Common Pleas. This was the beginning of a system of multiplying the number of election officers by choosing watchers to watch those who watched the watchers. In recent years rapid progress in the improvement of election law has been made. The states have found ways of doing a better job with a smaller number of election officers, chosen by appointment on merit rather than by election, and acting under a more central supervision. Some of the problems in a modern system of election administration will now be considered.

First, there is the election call. Regular elections are provided for by law, but special elections to fill vacancies or to vote upon emergency questions occur through the issuance of a call. A serious question is presented in many jurisdictions by the frequency of such elections. Under the primary system, it is not uncommon for citizens to be asked to go to the polls four or six times in a single year. Small wonder that so many elections bring to the polls only a fraction of the eligible voters! Another question relates to the size and number of precincts or voting districts; it is well known that the maintenance of an undue number tends to increase the cost of operating the election machinery. It is necessary that polling places be accessible to the voter, but this is ordinarily possible in districts of four or five hundred voters. In some of the almost depopulated com-

[48] Logan, *op. cit.*, p. 7.

mercial wards in Philadelphia, on the other hand, there are a number of divisions with only a few dozen voters. There is, again, the question of the kind of polling place that will be used — a private home or office, a store, a garage, a school, fire house, or other public building, or a portable house. " The ideal qualifications for a polling place include the following: sufficient size to take care of the voters without crowding; well lighted; well ventilated and heated; permanent, so that the voters would not be inconvenienced by chances of location; accessible; suitable surroundings for the conduct of the election; and procurable at a reasonable cost. The polling place greatly influences the conduct of the elections, both from the standpoint of service to the voters and from that of election frauds.[49] Public buildings, such as schools, which are usually conveniently located, best meet these several requirements.

Another question involves the delivery of election equipment and supplies, and their removal at the conclusion of the balloting. A decision must be made, either by the legislature or by election officers, regarding the hours of voting; there is often little or no uniformity even within the same state. The judge of elections, or the chairman of the precinct election board together with his associates, is responsible for the conduct of the election. They are responsible for the enforcement of such rules as are provided for identification of voters, thereby preventing repeating and voting on names of voters who do not appear. There are questions as to the handling of ballots, the assistance of voters, the challenging of voters, the activities of watchers and party workers in the vicinity of the polling place, and finally the important work of counting the ballots. The rendering of assistance has been grossly abused by party workers generally; it should be permitted only in cases of actual physical disability, sworn to by the voter at the time of registration. There are numerous reasons which may justify a challenge: that the voter is not of age, is not registered, has voted before on the same day, is not a naturalized citizen, et cetera. With regard to the count, the law is usually quite explicit as to the methods to be followed; the usual procedure is to count all the votes on one ballot before proceeding

[49] Harris, *Election Administration*, pp. 214–215; see also Institute of Local and State Government, *The Effect of Division Size upon Voting Conditions in Philadelphia* (University of Pennsylvania, 1939), and Philadelphia Bureau of Municipal Research, " Election Districts," *Citizens' Business*, April 16, 1940. The topics with regard to the conduct of elections here discussed follow the outline of Chapter 6 in the Harris volume.

to the next. Professor Harris believes that it is preferable to proceed with the counting by offices or propositions.[50]

In 1930 the National Municipal League's Committee on Election Administration published its model system for election administration based largely upon the extensive field work of Professor Harris.[51] Among the provisions recommended were a state board of elections, with local control in the hands of the county clerk except in counties with a population of more than 200,000. Precinct workers would be appointed by the officer in charge of elections. An office column ballot of the Massachusetts type, from which the names of Presidential electors are omitted, is recommended, as is rotation of the names of candidates for the same office, for reasons already noted. Each voter would be required to sign his name before receiving his ballot, this signature being compared with the one on his registration card. Absent voting would be authorized. Both in primary and in general elections a candidate would be required to file a petition and deposit a sum of money equal to 5 per cent of the salary of the office which he seeks; this sum would be forfeited only in case the candidate failed to poll 10 per cent of the total vote cast for that office or nomination. A similar provision would be applied to parties which in the last gubernatorial election polled less than 5 per cent of the total vote cast. This deposit is returnable if the vote exceeds 5 per cent. An alternative to the deposit plan is provided in the form of a nomination petition.

The pessimism which is sometimes felt concerning the alertness with which a public votes is occasionally offset by demonstrations of an unusual and intelligent public interest. In the mayoralty election in New York in 1932, there were 232,501 voters who took the trouble to write in the name of Joseph V. McKee, or a total of 335,000 if unrecognized spellings of the name had been added to the official totals.[52] That there are considerable numbers of people who are really concerned about their exercise of the suffrage is still further attested by the general interest in absent voting and by the observance by employers of state laws which provide for a period of two hours off from work on election day for purposes of voting.

Election Frauds. The subject of election frauds is unfortunately

[50] Harris, *op. cit.*, p. 241; see also Eads, James K., " Indiana Experiments with Central Ballot Count," *National Municipal Review*, August, 1940, pp. 545–548, 552.

[51] " A Model Election Administration System," supplement to *National Municipal Review*, September, 1930; also Shusterman, Murray H., " Choosing Election Officers," *National Municipal Review*, March, 1940, pp. 185–193, 199.

[52] *New York Herald Tribune*, November 30, 1932.

one to which attention must be periodically directed. Because of a failure to exert a more constant interest in this important aspect of elections, all large cities are obliged to have, from time to time, grand jury or Senatorial investigations of conditions relating to election frauds. There are some indictments, and perhaps some convictions. Things then improve for a time, but before long the whole cycle has to be repeated. Conditions in many rural areas are not much better. It is with no intention of minimizing the importance of such frauds that one points out that elections today are substantially better, in this respect, than those of even a generation ago. The public today will not, in most places, tolerate the brazen and wholesale falsification of election returns that was practiced in earlier decades. This is not to say that the problem has been solved, but that progress has been made, as one might say, from burglary and larceny to petty thievery and peculation. The immediate task is to remove the latter by the development of higher standards of civic responsibility, and by the improvement of techniques of supervision and control over election machinery. This has been done, to some extent, by corrupt practices legislation.

It is impossible here to enter into any detailed discussion of election frauds — the subject is still too vast. The Senatorial investigating committee which probed into the Vare-Wilson Senatorial election of 1926 listed and classified the following types of fraud and irregularity; fraudulent returns; failure to tally votes; discrepancies in the records of the persons voting; voting by persons who were not registered or who were registered incorrectly; voting by repeaters; more ballots cast than persons voting — (in 395 out of about 1,400 divisions) ; padded lists of voters; unfolded ballots in the ballot boxes; a few persons marked many ballots, according to the testimony of a handwriting expert; ballots marked by two persons (by the addition of crosses to 738 ballots at a later time) ; ballots marked in piles; and ballots unaccounted for (18,954 in 144 election districts) .[53] There is scarcely a large city in which, from time to time, some evidence of this general character is not made public. It sometimes happens that methods and devices intended to bring about an improvement of conditions lead only to the invention of new methods of evasion.

[53] *Senatorial Campaign Expenditures,* 70 Cong., 2 Sess., Senate Report, 1858, pp. 30–40, cited by Harris, *op. cit.,* pp. 328–332. Chapter 9 of Harris's book contains an excellent discussion of election frauds. See also Minault, S. Sydney, *Corrupt Practices Legislation in the Forty-eight States* (Council of State Governments, Chicago, 1942) .

The movement for the adoption of corrupt practices legislation began in 1883, when Massachusetts and New York placed restrictions on soliciting funds from officeholders; today eighteen states have such statutes, and seventeen states make it illegal to treat voters. " Sixteen make it unlawful to solicit funds from candidates; but in Florida, Indiana, Mississippi, and North Carolina, this practice is given legal sanction as ' evidence,' to quote the Mississippi law, ' of the good faith of the candidates and an expense fund of the several political parties.' In thirteen states it is illegal to pay for conveying voters to the polls. Corporations of all kinds are forbidden to make political contributions in twenty-seven states. Nine others confine the prohibition to certain types of corporations, such as public utilities, banks, and insurance companies." [54] One of the most recent and most interesting pieces of legislation of this character is the New York law enacted in 1940, called " the little Hatch Act," patterned after the Federal law.

The Cost of Elections. Not the least important aspect of elections is their cost; and students of the subject are generally agreed that this is excessive. A recent writer has computed the average cost per vote in the larger American cities over a four-year period. The highest cost, $2.13 per vote, was found in Columbus. The following cities had an average cost of more than $1.00 but less than $2.00: Baltimore, Chicago, Cincinnati, Cleveland, Dayton, Kansas City (Missouri) , New York, and San Francisco. In the following cities, the average cost was less than $1.00: Boston, Denver, Detroit, Milwaukee, Minneapolis, Omaha, Salt Lake City, and St. Louis. In Minneapolis and Salt Lake City the cost was 37 cents, the lowest cost recorded.[55] A like situation exists in the counties of Ohio, where, in 1930, the average cost per vote in twenty-four out of eighty-eight counties was in excess of $1.00.[56] These figures are typical of election cost studies made in various parts of the country.

It may be asked why these costs have become so excessive, and why they are permitted to remain so. In the main, the answer is to be found in the fact that the administration has been political rather than professional. Personnel has been added to personnel, until in Michigan this item consumes 50 per cent of the total cost.[57] The fol-

[54] Odegard and Helms, *op. cit.*, p. 671. See also Illinois Legislative Council, *Regulation of Campaign Expenditures* (Springfield, 1940) .
[55] Harris, *op. cit.*, pp. 386–387.
[56] Harris, *op. cit.*, pp. 387–389.
[57] Pollock, James K., " Election Administration in Michigan," supplement to *National Municipal Review*, June, 1934, p. 352; also his *County Election Costs in Michigan* (Bureau of Government, University of Michigan, 1935) .

lowing table indicates the rates of pay in Michigan, the number of cities in the state represented in each salary group being shown: [58]

RATES OF PAY OF ELECTION PRECINCT OFFICIALS IN MICHIGAN

Rate of Pay	Gate-keepers	In-spectors	Rate of Pay	Gate-keepers	In-spectors
$ .30 per hour		1	$ 4.75 per day		1
.40 per hour		1	5.00 per day	2	10
.50 per hour		12	6.00 per day		8
.60 per hour		1	7.00 per day		4
.62½ per hour		1	7.50 per day		1
2.00 per day	3		8.00 per day		8
3.00 per day	4	8	9.00 per day		1
3.50 per day		2	10.00 per day	1	5
4.00 per day	1	7	12.00 per day	1	5
4.50 per day		1	15.00 per day		3

" There is little relationship between the size of the registered vote and the number of election officials. The greatest variation exists both in the rates of pay and in the number of election officials employed. Although the election law provides in a permissive way for gatekeepers, the figures show that these officials are not much used throughout the State. Only in the rural areas is much use made of gatekeepers and in those areas there is less need for gatekeepers than in the densely populated centers." Professor Harris found that the personnel cost per total vote in the cities noted above varied from 49 cents in New York City to 84 cents in Minneapolis, while the personnel cost per vote cast varied from 24 cents in Salt Lake City to $1.46 in Columbus. He found also that the salaries paid were out of all proportion to the work involved. Since most of these positions go to regular party workers, the full power of the organized local government officials is in each state thrown against any movement for improvement of the system.

The employees used in connection with election administration are of three types: the regular employees, making up the permanent clerical force which handles the registration of voters and performs various election duties; the temporary employees, who assist with the peak loads of work that develop just before and just after elections; and finally, the precinct officers whose duties are performed on election day, and whose compensation constitutes the largest

[58] Pollock, " Election Administration," p. 354.

item in both the personnel budget and the election budget as a whole. Their cost " depends upon a number of factors, including the number and kind of elections held, the size of the voting precinct, the number of officers used to the precinct, the salary paid, the use of voting machines, and the use of extra counting boards." [59] The whole system is badly organized in most jurisdictions, and is most unsatisfactory in practice.

Operating expenses in the conduct of elections include all items other than personnel — the cost of ballots, supplies, printing, rental of polling places, repairs to precinct equipment and portable houses, cartage of such equipment, storage, and advertising.[60] Professor Harris found in his selected list of cities that the ballot cost per vote varied from 1.6 cents in Minneapolis to 14.3 cents in Kansas City. Gross carelessness and waste are frequent occurrences in connection with ballot printing. In the 1932 election, 192,000 vote sheets were ordered printed a third time, at heavy expense to the taxpayers, in a densely populated county in a large Eastern state.[61] In his study of election costs in Michigan, Professor Pollock found the greatest variation in the cost of printing the same number of ballots in different counties; [62] also that the number of excess ballots prepared represents an enormous waste — a total of more than 1,600,000 ballots in excess of the number required plus the excess prescribed by law. These figures are illustrative of the manner in which election expenses are, in general, permitted to exceed any necessary or proper limits. He found also that the total election expenditures of counties bore little relation to the population of those counties or to the vote cast.

On the basis of the Michigan survey, Professor Pollock recommends that steps be taken as follows, with a view to reducing the cost and increasing the efficiency of election administration: (1) that

[59] Harris, *op. cit.*, p. 428.

[60] For a discussion of all these items, see *ibid.*, pp. 434–439.

[61] Montgomery County, Pennsylvania. Reported in *Philadelphia Record,* November 3, 1932.

[62] Pollock, " Election Administration," p. 351. He found that " in the general election in Livingston County and in Van Buren County 20,000 ballots were printed. In Livingston County these ballots cost $568.00, in Van Buren County $721.50. In the primary election in Clare County 8,450 ballots were printed which cost $131.78. Clinton County printed 8,560 ballots which cost $245.43. Ballots cost Genesee County $1,238.74, while Oakland County with fewer ballots paid $2,674.50. Luce and Keweenaw Counties with almost exactly the same populations printed 5,800 and 5,000 ballots respectively, which ballots cost $110.00 in Luce County and $351.85 in Keweenaw County. Such instances could be multiplied but they are unnecessary to prove the point that considerable attention needs to be paid to the cost of printing ballots.

contracts for the printing of ballots be awarded only after competitive bidding, to the lowest responsible bidder; (2) that the printing costs of ballots be reduced by eliminating certain unnecessary portions of the ballot; (3) that, because of the high cost of elections, fewer elections be held; (4) that the law be amended to provide more definite restrictions as to the number and pay of precinct election officers; (5) that a greater centralization of power over election matters be concentrated in the hands of the county clerks; (6) that the law be amended to provide a minimum size for precincts and greater discretion be lodged with the local election authorities in prescribing their maximum size; (7) that the system of permanent registration now mandatory for all cities and villages over 5,000 population be made to apply to the entire state; (8) that the secretary of state prepare and send out to every election authority in the state a biennial form of questionnaire which would elicit all information necessary for his guidance in the supervision of state elections; (9) that this officer be required to make an annual report of all relevant data relating to registrations and elections.[63] It may well be that not all of these items will be applicable in other jurisdictions, but their general nature is such that, considering the difficulties known to exist in states in all parts of the country, many of them — perhaps most of them — would in most jurisdictions be useful and beneficial. If anything significant is to be done in reducing the cost of government, it will be by attention to such matters as these — not through any huge and spectacular slashing of governmental expenditures generally.

SELECTED REFERENCES

Albright, Spencer D., *Ballot Analysis and Ballot Changes Since 1930* (Council of State Governments, Chicago, 1940) .

———, *The American Ballot* (American Council on Public Affairs, Washington, 1942) .

Allen, James S., *Reconstruction: The Battle for Democracy, 1865–1876* (International Publishers, New York, 1937) .

Allen, William H., *Al Smith's Tammany Hall* (Institute for Public Service, New York, 1928) .

Beals, Carleton, *The Story of Huey P. Long* (Lippincott, Philadelphia, 1935) .

Bean, Louis H., *Ballot Behavior: A Study of Presidential Elections* (American Council on Public Affairs, Washington, 1942) .

Binkley, Robert W., Jr., *Double Filing in Primary Elections* (University of California, Bureau of Public Administration, 1945) .

[63] Pollock, " Election Administration," pp. 357–359.

Binkley, Wilfred E., *American Political Parties; Their Natural History* (Knopf, New York, 1943).

Chambers, Walter, *Samuel Seabury; A Challenge* (Appleton-Century, New York, 1932).

Civic Research Institute, *Registration and Voting in Kansas City* (Kansas City, 1934).

Council of State Governments, *Voting in the United States* (Chicago, 1940).

DuBois, W. E. B., *Black Reconstruction* (Harcourt, Brace, New York, 1935).

Farley, James A., *Behind the Ballots* (Harcourt, Brace, New York, 1938).

Fleming, Walter L., *Documentary History of Reconstruction*, 2 vols. (A. H. Clark Company, Cleveland, 1906–1907).

Gassman, Benjamin, *A.B.C. of the Direct Primary Law*, Third Edition (Rosenberry, New York, 1938).

Geary, Sister Theophane, *History of Third Parties in Pennsylvania, 1840–1860* (Catholic University of America, Washington, 1938).

Gooch, George P., *Politics and Morals* (Longmans, Green, Toronto, 1935).

Gosnell, Harold F., *Boss Platt and His New York Machine* (University of Chicago Press, 1923).

——, *Machine Politics; Chicago Model* (University of Chicago Press, 1937).

——, *Negro Politicians; the Rise of Negro Politics in Chicago* (University of Chicago Press, 1935).

Harris, Arthur F., and Uhr, Carl, *Direct Primary Elections* (University of California, Bureau of Public Administration, 1941).

Harris, Joseph P., *Election Administration in the United States* (Brookings Institution, Washington, 1934).

——, *Registration of Voters in the United States* (Brookings Institution, Washington, 1929.

Harris, Thomas O., *The Kingfish: Huey P. Long, Dictator* (New Orleans, 1938).

Heavenrich, Max P., Jr., *The Use of Voting Machines in Thirty-five Cities or Counties* (Flint Institute of Research and Planning, 1939).

Hecock, Donald S., *Election Without Representation* (National Training School for Public Service, Detroit, 1945).

Herring, E. Pendleton, *The Politics of Democracy: American Parties in Action* (Norton, New York, 1940).

Howard, Paul D., Ed., *Reports of Contested Elections Cases in Massachusetts, 1923–1942*, House Document No. 1826 (Boston, 1942).

Illinois Legislative Council, *Regulation of Campaign Expenditures* (Springfield, 1940).

——, *The Direct Primary Ballot* (Springfield, 1940).

Institute of Local and State Government, *The Effect of Division Size upon Voting Conditions in Philadelphia* (University of Pennsylvania, 1939).

Johnson, John B., and Lewis, Irving J., *Registration for Voting in the United States* (Council of State Governments, Chicago, 1941).

Kent, Frank R., *The Great Game of Politics* (Doubleday, Page, New York, 1924).

——, *Political Behavior* (Morrow, New York, 1938).

Key, V. O., Jr., *Political Parties and Pressure Groups* (Crowell, New York, 1942).

Kies, Harry B., and McCandless, Carl A., *Manual on the Bill of Rights and Suffrage and Elections* (Missouri Constitutional Convention of 1943, Columbia, 1943).

Kurtzman, David H., *Methods of Controlling Votes in Philadelphia* (University of Pennsylvania, 1935).

Lasswell, Harold D., *Politics: Who Gets What, When, How* (McGraw-Hill, New York, 1936).

Lavine, Emanuel H., *" Gimme," or How Politicians Get Rich* (Vanguard Press, New York, 1931).

Lewis, Lloyd, and Smith, Henry J., *Chicago: The History of Its Reputation* (Harcourt, Brace, New York, 1929).

Lewison, Paul, *Race, Class, and Party: a History of Negro Suffrage and White Politics in the South* (Oxford University Press, New York, 1932).

Litchfield, Edward H., *Voting Behavior in a Metropolitan Area* (University of Michigan, Bureau of Government, 1941).

Logan, Edward B., Ed., *American Political Scene*, Revised Edition (Harper, New York, 1938).

Lynch, Denis T., *Boss Tweed* (Boni and Liveright, New York, 1927).

Mathews, John M., *Legislative and Judicial History of the Fifteenth Amendment,* (Johns Hopkins University Studies, Series XVII, No. 6–7, 1909).

McCulloch, Albert J., *Suffrage and Its Problems* (University Research Monographs, Baltimore, 1929).

McKean, Dayton D., *The Boss* (Houghton Mifflin, Boston, 1940).

Merriam, Charles E., *Chicago: a More Intimate View of Urban Politics* (Macmillan, New York, 1929).

——, and Overacker, Louise, *Primary Elections* (University of Chicago Press, 1928).

Minault, S. Sydney, *Corrupt Practices Legislation in the Forty-eight States* (Council of State Governments, Chicago, 1942).

Morton, Richard C., *The Negro in Virginia Politics, 1865–1902* (University of Virginia, 1919).

Munro, William B., *Personality in Politics,* Revised Edition (Macmillan, New York, 1934).

Myers, Gustavus, *The History of Tammany Hall,* Second Edition (Boni and Liveright, New York, 1917).

National Municipal League, *A Model Registration System,* Third Edition (New York, 1939).

Odegard, Peter H., and Helms, E. Allen, *American Parties* (Harper, New York, 1938).

Orth, Samuel P., *The Boss and the Machine* (Yale University Press, 1921).

Overacker, Louise, *Money in Elections* (Macmillan, New York, 1932).

Peel, Roy V., *Political Clubs in New York City* (Putnam, New York, 1935).

Perry, Jennings, *Democracy Begins at Home: The Tennessee Fight on the Poll Tax* (Lippincott, Philadelphia, 1944).

Pollock, James K., *County Election Costs in Michigan* (Bureau of Government, University of Michigan, 1935).

——, *Absentee Voting and Registration* (American Council on Public Affairs, Washington, 1940).

Pollock, James K., *Party Campaign Funds* (Knopf, New York, 1926).

——, *Permanent Registration of Voters in Michigan: an Appraisal* (Bureau of Government, University of Michigan, 1937).

——, *The Direct Primary in Michigan, 1909–1935* (Bureau of Government, University of Michigan, 1943).

——, *Voting Behavior: a Case Study* (Bureau of Government, University of Michigan, 1939).

——, and Eldersveld, Samuel J., *Michigan Politics in Transition* (Bureau of Government, University of Michigan, 1942).

Porter, Kirk H., *A History of the Suffrage in the United States* (University of Chicago Press, 1918).

Powell, Alden L., *Registration of Voters in Louisiana* (Bureau of Government Research, Louisiana State University, 1940).

Ramsey, Maurice M., *Name Candidates in Detroit Elections* (Detroit Bureau of Governmental Research, 1941).

Reynolds, George M., *Machine Politics in New Orleans, 1897–1926* (Columbia University Press, 1936).

Riordan, William L., *Plunkitt of Tammany Hall* (McClure, Phillips, New York, 1905).

Salter, John T., *Boss Rule* (Whittlesey House, New York, 1935).

——, *The Pattern of Politics* (Macmillan, New York, 1940).

——, Ed., *The American Politician* (University of North Carolina Press, 1938).

Smith, Carl O., *A Book of Ballots* (Detroit Bureau of Governmental Research, 1938).

Smith, Charles W., Jr., *The Electorate in an Alabama Community* (Bureau of Public Administration, University of Alabama, 1942).

Smith, T. V., *The Promise of American Politics* (University of Chicago Press, 1936).

Snowden, George, *Election Costs in Indiana* (Institute of Politics, Indiana University, 1941).

Steffens, Lincoln, *The Autobiography of Lincoln Steffens* (Harcourt, Brace, New York, 1931).

Titus, Charles H., *Voting Behavior in the United States* (University of California Press, 1935).

Wallis, J. H., *The Politician, His Habits, Outcries and Protective Coloring* (Stokes, New York, 1935).

Whitlock, Brand, *Forty Years of It,* Second Edition (Appleton, New York, 1925).

Wooddy, Carroll H., *The Direct Primary in Chicago* (University of Chicago Press, 1926).

——, *The Case of Frank L. Smith* (University of Chicago Press, 1931).

Zeller, Belle, *Pressure Politics in New York* (Prentice-Hall, New York, 1937).

Zink, Harold F., *City Bosses in the United States* (Duke University Press, 1930).

———

Albright, Spencer D., "Legislation on Marking Ballots," *Southwestern Social Science Quarterly,* December, 1940, pp. 221–226.

Arnall, Ellis, " Admitting Youth to Citizenship," *State Government,* October, 1943, pp. 203–204.

Benson, Lawrence E., " Studies in Secret Ballot Technique," *Public Opinion Quarterly,* March, 1941, pp. 79–82.

Briscoe, Vera, " The Poll Tax as a Voting Prerequisite," *Bulletin* of the National Tax Association, December, 1943, pp. 66–75.

Boudin, Louis S., " State Poll Taxes and the Federal Constitution," *Virginia Law Review,* November, 1941.

Dabney, Virginius," Poll Tax Stirs Revolt," *National Municipal Review,* October, 1942, pp. 485–491.

Dam, Loring, " Civic Plan to Bridge 18–21 Gap," *National Municipal Review,* January, 1945, pp. 10–13, 26.

Eads, James K., " Indiana Experiments with Central Ballot Count," *National Municipal Review,* August, 1940, pp. 545–548, 552.

" Federal vs. States' Rights in the Coming Fight for Votes," *Congressional Digest,* June-July, 1944, entire issue.

Forbush, Emory, " The Poll Tax," *Editorial Research Reports,* July 3, 1941, entire issue.

Gosnell, Harold F., and Cohen, Morris H., " Progressive Politics: Wisconsin an Example," *American Political Science Review,* October, 1940, pp. 920–935.

Horlacker, John P., " The Administration of Permanent Registration in Philadelphia," *American Political Science Review,* October, 1943, pp. 829–837.

Jones, O. Garfield, " Exit the Party Column Ballot? " *National Municipal Review,* April, 1941, pp. 242–244.

Lazere, Monroe R., " Payment of Poll Tax as a Prerequisite of Voting in a Federal Election," *Cornell Law Quarterly,* November, 1942, pp. 104–110.

Lex, William B., " Citizens, Schools Cooperate on Election Project," *National Municipal Review,* January, 1944, pp. 37–39.

———, " Election Frauds Go Unchecked," *National Municipal Review,* May, 1944, pp. 226–228.

Lippert, David J., " The GI's Cast Their Ballots," *National Municipal Review,* December, 1944, pp. 588–590, 645.

Martin, Boyd A., " The Service Vote in the Elections of 1944," *American Political Science Review,* August, 1945, pp. 720–732.

Ohm, Howard F., " The Ballot Again Goes to War," *Wisconsin Counties,* February, 1944, pp. 9–11.

" Should the Legal Voting Age Be Reduced to Eighteen Years? " *Congressional Digest,* August-September, 1944, entire issue.

Porter, Kirk H., " The Deserted Primary in Iowa," *American Political Science Review,* August, 1945, pp. 732–740

Shusterman, Murray H., " Choosing Election Officers," *National Municipal Review,* March, 1940, pp. 185–193, 199.

Starr, Joseph R., " The Legal Status of American Political Parties," *American Political Science Review,* June, 1940, pp. 439–455, and August, 1940, pp. 695–699.

Strong, Donald S., " The Poll Tax: The Case of Texas," *American Political Science Review,* August, 1944, pp. 693–709.

CHAPTER V

Popular Control of Government

POPULAR control of government necessarily, involves a number of considerations. There are those who, for many years, relied upon the extension of the suffrage; they believed that if everyone could vote, we should have democratic government, a government popularly controlled. In our day nearly everyone does vote, or perhaps, more accurately, nearly everyone can if he wants to; yet in many instances government seems to be far from popularly controlled. Still others placed their faith in changes in the mechanism of government. They urged the adoption of their favorite prescription, with the assurance that if their advice were taken, our governmental difficulties would be at an end. The initiative and referendum, the short ballot, and proportional representation have been advocated; each has been adopted in numerous jurisdictions, but the political millennium has not come. It is not meant to imply that these devices are useless or undesirable — some of them are both useful and desirable — but changes in the machinery will not, *alone,* bring popular control of government. Finally, there is a group which believes that the machinery of government should be improved where possible, but that the achievement of popular control is largely dependent upon improved methods of civic organization and civic training. This prompts a consideration, therefore, of the development and influence of civic organizations, and of certain other questions which may be grouped under the heading of popular participation in government.

DIRECT LEGISLATION

In the preceding chapter, in a discussion of nominating methods, reference was made to the various stages in the development of public sentiment regarding the application of the representative principle in the control of both governmental and party affairs. Mention was made of the spread of direct legislation as a supplement to and a partial substitute for the usual process of legislation through a representative assembly. It is now proposed to inquire more fully into the various procedures to which the term direct legislation is applied. These include the initiative, the referendum, the recall, and the recall of judicial decisions.

Prior to the Revolution, there had been some conflict between the colonial legislatures and the Royal Governors. The legislatures had defended the interests of the people, and had come to be regarded as representative of the popular will. Immediately after the Revolution, extensive powers were granted to the legislatures, but over a period of many years these powers were steadily decreased as public confidence in the legislatures declined. This decline was due to legislative inefficiency and to the undue influence of paid lobbyists and of invisible government. The movement for direct legislation as a remedy for these conditions originated in South Dakota in 1898; twenty states now have a statewide initiative and referendum, while Maryland and New Mexico have the referendum only. All but five of these are west of the Mississippi River, and most of the measures were adopted prior to 1914, many of them under the influence of the Progressive movement. There have been no additions to the list for some time, and in some cases a considerable agitation has developed for the repeal of all or part of the existing provisions.

The extent to which each of these devices has been used in California is shown in the accompanying table (page 170). In Colorado, the experience over a like period of time may be summarized. Proposals for holding a constitutional convention were voted on three times, in 1916, 1922, and 1930. The total number of constitutional amendments and laws voted on between 1912 and 1938, inclusive, was 121. In this period, 73 constitutional amendments were proposed, of which 19 were adopted and 54 rejected. Forty-eight laws were submitted, of which 19 were adopted and 29 defeated. Since 1916, not more than 10 proposals have been submitted in any one year, and the number has usually been considerably less than that.[1]

The Initiative. The idea of the popular plebiscite had long been familiar in this country; as early as 1818, Connecticut had used the referendum in adopting a new constitution. The use of the initiative

[1] Colorado Legislative Reference Office, *The Initiative and Referendum in Colorado* (Denver, 1940).

ACTION OF VOTERS ON DIRECT LEGISLATION IN CALIFORNIA, 1912–1939 [2]

Election	Initiatives		Referenda		Legislative Constitutional Amendments		Legislative Propositions	
	Approved	Rejected	Approved	Rejected	Approved	Rejected	Approved	Rejected
Nov. 5, 1912	0	3	0	3	2	0		
Nov. 3, 1914	6	11	3	1	15	7		2
*Oct. 26, 1915			0	2	0	9	3	
Nov. 7, 1916	1	3	0	1				0
Nov. 5, 1918	1	5	0	1	9	9		
*July 1, 1919					1	0		
Nov. 2, 1920	3	7	2	3	3	2		
Nov. 7, 1922	4	2	1	2	8	6	1	1
Nov. 4, 1924	2	7			10	4		
Nov. 2, 1926	1	2	0		14	4	1	
Nov. 6, 1928	0	4	2	1	14	3		0
Nov. 4, 1930	1				10	10	1	
*May 3, 1932		4	1	1				
Nov. 8, 1932	2				9	5		2
*June 27, 1933					6	2	0	
*Dec. 19, 1933			1	0			2	0
Nov. 6, 1934	6	4			6	5		
*Aug. 13, 1935					0	3		
Nov. 3, 1936	0	7	0	2	4	10		
Nov. 8, 1938	1	5	0	3	6	10		
*Nov. 7, 1939	0	2	2	1				
Totals	28	73	12	21	117	89	10	5

* Special election

[2] Table from California State Chamber of Commerce, *Initiative Legislation in California*, p. 14 (San Francisco, 1940); see also Gosnell, Harold F., and Schmidt, Margaret J., "Popular Law Making in the United States, 1924–1936," in New York State Constitutional Convention Committee, *Problems Relating to Legislative Organization and Powers*, pp. 314–335 (Albany, 1938).

owes its origin chiefly to the effort to adapt to American conditions a governmental procedure that had long been used successfully in Switzerland.[3] It permits a group of citizens especially desirous of securing enactment of a particular law to bring the subject before the voters of the state at the next general election. There are two forms of the initiative: first, the constitutional initiative under which amendments to the constitution may be proposed and voted upon; second, the statutory initiative, which may be used for ordinary legislation. Some states require a larger petition for constitutional amendments than for ordinary laws, while others make no distinction between them. The types of initiative have recently been classified as follows:

. . . Of the twenty states in which the initiative has been adopted, only thirteen permit its use for the amendment of the constitution. In eleven states the constitutional initiative is direct; in Massachusetts and Nevada the amendment is first referred to the legislature for discussion and consideration. Six states have only the indirect initiative for ordinary legislation; eleven states have only the direct initiative; California, Utah, and Washington have both the direct and indirect initiative.[4]

In each case, the law provides for a petition to be signed, usually by 8 or 10 per cent of the electors, on the basis of the vote at the last general election. The data are summarized in the table on page 172. In some cases the signatures must come from two thirds or three fourths of the counties — in order to prevent the presentation of issues which are purely local. The most common requirement with regard to filing with the secretary of state specifies four months before the election. In some states definite provision is made for publicity, although publicity for proposals is a regular feature of the plan. The pamphlets vary in size from postcards to pamphlets of considerable size and bulk, in which case the expense involved is a not inconsiderable item.[5] Certain safeguards are commonly provided, such as (in California) the requirement that the full text of the measure must appear on the petition; that the petition may be signed only by duly qualified electors; that measures must be passed or rejected by the legislature without change; and that they

[3] See Lowell, A. Lawrence, *Public Opinion and Popular Government* (Longmans, Green, New York, 1921) ; Brooks, Robert C., *The Government and Politics of Switzerland* (World Book Company, Yonkers, 1920) ; and Rappard, William E., *Government of Switzerland* (Van Nostrand, New York, 1936) .

[4] Lien, Arnold J., and Fainsod, Merle, *The American People and Their Government*, p. 410 (Appleton-Century, New York, 1934) .

[5] In Oregon, it is contended, these officially published pamphlets, reaching all voters prior to primary and general elections, have performed real public service in providing information on candidates and issues. See Josslin, William L., " Oregon Educates Its Voters," *National Municipal Review*, July, 1943, pp. 373–379.

SIGNATURE REQUIREMENTS FOR INITIATIVE PETITIONS [6]

	Statutes	Constitutional Amendments
Arizona	10%	15%
Arkansas	8%	10%
California	8%	8%
Colorado	8%	8%
Maine	12,000 signatures	Prohibited
Massachusetts	25,000 signatures	25,000 signatures
Michigan	8%	10%
Missouri	8%	8%
Montana	8%	Prohibited
Nebraska	7%	10%
Nevada	10%	10%
North Dakota	10,000 signatures	20,000 signatures
Ohio	6%	10%
Oklahoma	8%	15%
Oregon	8%	8%
South Dakota	5%	Prohibited
Utah	10%	Prohibited
Washington	10%	Prohibited

must be accompanied by the affidavit of the persons soliciting the signatures. Supplemental petitions may be permitted. As a rule, no limitation as to subject matter is placed upon initiative proposals, but time limits may be imposed, limiting the frequency with which propositions once defeated may be resubmitted. Measures, when approved, take effect immediately upon approval, upon declaration of the vote, or upon proclamation of the governor, but it is frequently specified that the governor has no veto power.

Criticism of the Initiative in Practice. The proponents of the initiative and referendum argue that these devices are more democratic in character than the ordinary process of legislation, and that they provide a method by which citizens may secure the adoption

[6] California State Chamber of Commerce, *op. cit.*, p. 4. See also Key, V. O., and Crouch, Winston W., *The Initiative and Referendum in California* (University of California Press, 1939) ; Cottrell, Edwin A., " Twenty-five Years of Direct Legislation in California," *Public Opinion Quarterly*, January, 1939, pp. 30–45; Crouch, Winston W., " John Randolph Haynes and His Work," *National Municipal Review*, September, 1938, pp. 434–440, 453, and " The Initiative and Referendum in Cities," *American Political Science Review*, June, 1943, pp. 491–504; Ketcham, Ronald M., *Voting on Charter Amendments in Los Angeles* (University of California, Bureau of Governmental Research, Los Angeles, 1940) ; Selig, John M., " San Francisco Voters Prove Sound Lawmakers," *National Municipal Review*, October, 1943, pp. 486–492. For Oklahoma and Michigan, see Ewing, Cortez A. M., " Sufficiency Certification of Initiative Signatures in Oklahoma," *American Political Science Review, February*, 1937, pp. 65–70; and University of Michigan, *Direct Government in Michigan* (Bureau of Government, 1940) .

or rejection of measures concerning which the legislature has failed to follow the popular will. The spread of the movement in the first decade of the twentieth century was due in no small part to the industry and ability of Judson King, since 1913 Director of the National Popular Government League. Viewing the experience of one third of the American voters in eighteen different states over the first third of the century in the use of the initiative and referendum, Mr. King feels that it " constitutes the most vital test of the capacity of a modern people to set up an economic, social and political system for their own well-being, of any experience in human history, as well as of their capacity to repel any kind of exploitation or tyranny by a governing class." [7]

While the theory may be good, it seems not to have operated without the development of serious objections. In the first place, a persistent effort has been made to secure better drafting of the measures enacted into law. An initiative measure may be well drafted, but if this does occur, it is likely to be rather by accident than by design. Second, the argument that this is a means of determining the popular will may be refuted by the fact that so small a percentage of voters express any preference regarding measures submitted in this way. If they are finally adopted, this result is achieved, not through the approval of the majority of citizens nor even by a majority of the voters participating in the election, but by a mere majority of that minority group sufficiently interested in the proposition to vote at all. Another important objection to the processes of direct legislation lies in their violation of the short ballot principle, the purpose of which is to simplify the voter's task by reducing the number of choices he must make. If the number of elective offices is reduced, and at the same time the ballot is lengthened by adding numerous legislative proposals, the principle of the short ballot is more harmed than aided. If the ballot must be long, it had better remain so through the necessity of electing officials, rather than through the exercise of choices on legislative proposals. However badly the voters may on occasion perform the first of these tasks, their record in the performance of the second is even more discouraging.

Other criticisms of the initiative process relate to the huge waste of money and energy required to combat unsound proposals, many of which appear on the ballot because some small group can raise sufficient funds to qualify them, and to the necessity of contending

[7] Letter to the author from Judson King, March 7, 1939.

against the same unsound proposals year after year, despite their
constant rejection by the voters each time they appear. Objection
is also raised to the growing practice of " professionalism" in conducting initiative campaigns, which some groups describe as bordering on racketeering, as well as to the tendency toward circumventing
and restricting the powers of the legislature by advocacy of those
types of measures proposing mandatory expenditures and limitations on taxation, while at the same time the legislature, with its
hands tied, has full responsibility for finding needed revenues and
imposing necessary taxes.[8]

It is true that the states using these devices attempt to inform the
voters regarding the merits of the measures proposed, in specially
prepared pamphlets. These pamphlets commonly contain a clear
and impartial statement of the provisions of each measure, with a
summary of the arguments for and against its adoption. Organizations interested in any given measure may purchase, at cost of publication, a limited amount of space in which to set forth their position regarding it. When the voters are asked to pass upon many
proposals, the pamphlet becomes a document of formidable size.
While every registered voter receives a copy of the pamphlet, one
may well ponder the extent to which these pamphlets are read and
studied by the voters prior to the election.[9] If the states had shown
the same moderation in the use of these devices which has characterized their use in Switzerland; if they had limited their use to the
effort to correct definite abuses; if they had, as Woodrow Wilson
once suggested, kept them in reserve as the settlers of old kept the
gun behind the door — rather than regarding them as a method for
the general enactment of legislation — there could be little objection
to them. Such, however, has not been the case.

Proposals for Modifying Initiative Procedure. Many attempts have
been made, more often by the enemies than by the friends of the
initiative, to modify the procedure by increasing the percentage of
signatures required on the petition, by requiring signatures to petitions to be written in the presence of a public official at some central
place such as the county court house, by prohibiting persons cir-
culating petitions from receiving pay for their services, and by
excluding such matters as taxation and bond issues from the initia-

8 California State Chamber of Commerce, *op. cit.,* p. 1.
9 See Lippmann, Walter, *The Phantom Public,* Chapter 2, " The Unattainable
Ideal " (Harcourt, Brace, New York, 1925) . In this chapter Mr. Lippmann bril-
liantly portrays one of the chief fallacies of modern democracy in general, and
of direct legislation in particular.

tive procedure.[10] While these devices would undoubtedly remedy some abuses, some of them might destroy whatever effectiveness the initiative possesses. There would seem to be no valid objection, however, to a requirement that initiative proposals be required to lie on the table at the next regular session of the legislature. If the legislature should reject them, or fail to give them consideration, it would be time enough to go over the heads of the elected representatives, directly to the people. Another desirable change would be to impose a time limit of perhaps five years on the frequency with which a proposal once rejected by the voters might again be submitted. There is no good reason why the battle of " ham and eggs," for instance, should have to be refought annually.

The Referendum. Constitutional provisions authorizing the use of the initiative usually authorize the referendum also. Like the initiative, it is of two kinds, constitutional and statutory; it may be invoked by either of two procedures. Constitutional amendments have as a matter of course in most states been submitted to a popular vote. In the case of the statutory referendum, the first method may be employed if the legislature passes an act which is objectionable to a considerable number of citizens. If 5 or 10 per cent of the voters participating in the last general election sign a petition, the proposal may be brought before the voters at the next election. This use of the referendum does not present any radical departure from established practice in American government — it is merely an extension of the method long employed and generally accepted in the case of constitutional amendments. The second method by which a referendum may be secured is dependent upon action by the legislature. If this body enacts a statute concerning which the members are in considerable doubt or for which they are unwilling to take responsibility, they may provide that this act may become law only on condition that it be approved by a majority of the voters at the polls. While no serious objection can be raised to referenda of the first type, it is certainly true that the second type tends further to undermine the prestige of the legislature. This type of referendum is a " buck passing " device, the use of which ought to be discouraged.

The constitutional and legal rules governing the referendum do not differ greatly from those governing the initiative. The percentage of signatures required for petitions is frequently less, and where a legislative referendum is initiated by the people, the petition must be filed with the secretary of state within ninety days after

[10] Key and Crouch, *op. cit.*, Chapter 8.

the close of the legislative session. The same publicity arrangements and the same safeguards apply in one case as in the other. Laws which are necessary for the public health and safety or for the support of the state government are frequently exempted from the operation of the referendum; in some states these are designated as emergency measures. In order to permit the free use of the referendum privilege, many states provide that acts of the legislature shall not take effect until ninety days after the close of the session, except in the case of exempted measures.[11] As in the case of the initiative, the governor has no veto power.

The Recall. The recall has been known in government since the time of the Greeks; its modern development began in Switzerland, where it was applied to local legislatures.[12] Its use in the American states dates from June 1, 1908, when a provision for it was incorporated in the Constitution of Oregon, although the city charter of Los Angeles had provided for it previously. It may be described as a device by which the voters may remove from office, through use of the ballot, persons who have previously been selected by the same means. The principle of the recall is applicable to officers in all three departments of the government, although its use in this country has been limited to those in the executive and judicial branches. It has not been used very extensively, having been for the most part restricted to cases of malfeasance in office. There is only one case on record in which the governor of a state has been recalled — that of Lynn J. Frazier, Non-Partisan League Governor of North Dakota in 1921. The recall has been invoked, with varying success, in the case of a number of mayors, a fairly recent case being the removal of Mayor Bowles of Detroit in 1930. An unsuccessful attempt was made to remove the mayor of Seattle in 1929.

While there is some variation in the details of procedure, that prescribed in Oregon may be taken as illustrative. In order to recall an officer, it is necessary to present a petition to which are appended the signatures of 25 per cent of the voters of the district which the officer serves. In the case of the governor, it would be 25 per cent of the voters of the state. This petition must also contain a state-

[11] But the use of the emergency clause may develop into a habit. In Oklahoma, prior to 1920, the measures including the emergency clause were never more than 62 per cent of the acts passed, while since 1920 this percentage has never fallen below 74. See Ewing, Cortez A. M., " The Emergency Epidemic," *State Government*, July, 1931, pp. 3–4; also Schumacher, Waldo, " The Emergency Clause," *Oregon Law Review*, December, 1939, pp. 73–77.

[12] Bacon, Edwin M., and Wyman, Morrill, *Direct Elections and Law-Making by Popular Vote*, pp. 50–51, 118 (Houghton Mifflin, Boston, 1912) .

ment of the reasons which, it is claimed, justify the recall. If the officer does not resign within five days, a special election is held within twenty days. On the sample ballot, the reasons for the recall must be presented in 200 words; the accused officer is allowed a like number for his defense. In this state, the officer subject to recall automatically becomes a candidate for the office at the election which follows. His opponents nominate other candidates; if re-elected, he holds his position; if not, the candidate receiving the most votes takes his place. Any officer must have been in office at least six months before he is subject to recall, an exception being made in the case of senators and representatives in the legislative assembly, where the limit is five days. After one recall election, no additional recall petitions may be circulated against the same officer until the petitioners pay into the public treasury the expenses of the preceding election.[13]

The states that adopted the recall did so — with one exception — between 1908 and 1914. The table below shows the states which use this device, together with some information as to its extent and operation. The table does not include the twelve additional states which allow the recall only in cities.[14]

WHERE THE RECALL MAY BE USED

State	Year	Extent	Per Cent of Signatures Required
Oregon	1908	Every public officer.	25
California	1911	Every elective officer.	12 — state 20 — local
Arizona	1911–12	Every elective officer.	25
Colorado	1912	Every elective officer.	25
Idaho	1912	All but judges.	—
Nevada	1912	Every public officer.	25
Washington	1912	All but judges.	25–35
Michigan	1913	All but judges.	25
Kansas	1914	Every elective and appointive officer.	10–15–25
Louisiana	1914	All but judges.	25
North Dakota	1920	Every elective officer.	25
Wisconsin	1926	Every elective officer.	25

13 Beard, Charles A., and Shulz, Bird E., *Documents on the State-wide Initiative, Referendum, and Recall,* p. 243 (Macmillan, New York, 1912) ; Barnett, James D., *The Operation of the Initiative, Referendum, and Recall in Oregon,* pp. 192–193 (Macmillan, New York, 1915) .

14 Illinois Constitutional Convention, *Bulletin* No. 2, " Initiative, Referendum, and Recall," p. 120 (Springfield, 1919) ; Hannan, William E., *Digest of Constitutions and Laws of the Various States with Respect to Recall of Public Officers*

The record shows that recall elections for mayors, councilmen, commissioners, judges, and one governor have been held among these states. Among the charges noted are the following: unfitness, favoritism, carelessness, extravagance, incompetence, inability, no benefit to public, selfishness, neglect of duties, corruption, et cetera. A tabulation of twenty-nine cases, scattered over a period of years in the states mentioned, shows seven in which the officials remained in office, seventeen in which they were removed, four upon which there was no vote, and one in which the men resigned and were returned to office in an ensuing election. All except the North Dakota case involved municipal or county officers. While the number of cases is relatively small, there are numerous instances in which the possibility of recall has been discussed, and in which the very fact of the discussion had some influence upon the conduct of the officials in question.

The principle of the recall has rarely been applied to judicial officers. Two members of the minor judiciary were removed with proper cause in San Francisco a number of years ago, but fortunately this device has not been invoked against the members of the higher judicial tribunals. Were this not true, the effect of the recall on the independence of the judiciary might have been serious. If the danger of recall proceedings were in fact great, there are many judges whose concern for the popular will in individual cases and for the security of their positions would be greater than their concern for the administration of justice. This danger was given classic statement by President Taft when in 1911 he vetoed a resolution providing for the admission of Arizona with a constitution containing provisions for the recall. In the course of this message, he said:

> This provision of the Arizona constitution, in its application to county and state judges, seems to me so pernicious in its effect, so destructive of independence in the judiciary, so likely to subject the rights of the individual to the possible tyranny of a popular majority, and, therefore, to be so injurious to the cause of free government that I must disapprove a constitution containing it. . . .[15]

(New York State Library, Albany, 1934). The twelve states are: Illinois, Iowa, Minnesota, Mississippi, Missouri, Montana, Nebraska, New Jersey, North Carolina, Ohio, South Dakota, and Wyoming. For a good summary of constitutional and statutory provisions affecting local officers, see Fairlie, John A., and Kneier, Charles M., *County Government and Administration*, pp. 195–197 (Appleton-Century, New York, 1930).

[15] President Taft, August 15, 1911; a special message published as House Document No. 106, 62 Cong., 1 Sess. For other discussions, see list of selected references, especially Brooks, *op. cit.*, Chapter 18.

Recall of Judicial Decisions. The most extreme form of direct popular participation in government — the recall of judicial decisions — was advocated by Theodore Roosevelt during the Bull Moose campaign, on the theory that the people at the polls should have it within their power to make effective, by popular vote, a statute which the highest state court had declared unconstitutional. In this way, they might in effect amend the constitution without resorting to the prescribed methods. By such a vote, they would say, not that the statute in question was constitutional, but that, even though it was unconstitutional, they desired to have it in effect. This proposal seems never to have been taken seriously, except in Colorado, where a constitutional amendment was adopted in 1912 prohibiting the lower courts from declaring statutes unconstitutional, and providing for the recall of adverse decisions by the Supreme Court, where the question of constitutionality was involved.[16]

THE SHORT BALLOT

The principle of the short ballot has for years been advocated as an antidote for that governmental monstrosity known as the long ballot. The long ballot, like Topsy, just grew. With the extension of the powers of government in many fields, the establishment of many new offices was necessary. When these offices were created by statute, it became customary, in keeping with the Jacksonian tradition, to have their incumbents selected by popular vote. Every time a new officer or group of officers was placed on the ballot, three or four times as many names were added, in order that each party might present its candidates for that office. So the ballot grew until in many elections in many states it was large enough to cover a fair portion of the side of the wall in an ordinary room. One ballot in New York, some years ago, was fourteen feet long, while ballots in many of our states have been three by five, and five by seven feet in size. A Chicago primary had over 500 names on a single ballot. Needless to say, it is practically impossible for any human being to know enough about the personalities behind so many names to vote intelligently.

Few important figures in American politics have ever done a greater disservice to the cause of popular government than Andrew

16 Article VI, Section 1, adopted November 5, 1912, after proposal by initiative petition. The State Supreme Court held it unconstitutional as a violation of due process, in People v. Western Union Telegraph Company, 70 Colo. 90, 1921; People v. Mad, 70 Colo. 100, 1921.

Jackson. His assumption was that democracy consisted in voting. If the people voted for a large number of officials, from the governor down to and including the keeper of the dog pound, and did this often enough, their government would be democratic. No ranker nonsense was ever preached, as the evidence through succeeding generations in which this principle has been applied demonstrates abundantly. Democracy does not consist in voting or in the performance of any other single act. The essence of democracy requires that the people shall maintain *control* over their government. Voting is merely one of the ways by which this is done. We have seen that an excessive amount of voting has many times, in many places, nullified the power of the people to control their government.

The principle of the short ballot in operation would restrict the officers chosen by popular election to policy-determining officers. If this principle were applied, our elections could be arranged in four-year cycles in accordance with the following general plan:

PROPOSED FOUR-YEAR ELECTION CYCLE

First Year   Electors for President and Vice-President, representatives in Congress, and a United States Senator.
Second Year   Governor, representatives in the state legislature, and city councilmen.
Third Year   Representatives in Congress, and, when required, a United States Senator.
Fourth Year   Representatives in the state legislature, and mayor, city councilmen, and county officers.

The English elect members of the county Council and of Parliament, at different times, on a ballot even smaller than a penny postcard. Under the federal plan it is impossible to achieve this extreme degree of simplicity, but the adoption of the plan suggested above would come as near this as possible.

The short ballot has a number of notable advantages. It would, in the first place, centralize responsibility and do much to insure a more efficient administration of state government. In states where a number of important department heads must still be selected by popular vote, it is impossible for the governor to exercise proper supervision and insure support of the policies of the administration. If there were no other reasons than this, one would be abundantly justified in urging the adoption of the short ballot principle. In the second place, the principle of the short ballot is in harmony with a sound concept of democracy. It recognizes the fact that popular government does not consist in the mere selection of officials, but rather in the selection of those whose key positions in government enable them to control policy and make them directly responsible to the voting public. Finally, the principle of the short ballot greatly simplifies the voter's task; this problem will be discussed more fully in a later section of this chapter.

In the foregoing chapter, where ballots were discussed as a phase of the conduct of elections, data on the form and arrangement of ballots in the various states were presented. In the conclusions of a study of ballots used in the 1932 and 1934 elections, there cited, it is shown that the most complicated local ballots were found, among cities, in Chicago, Cleveland, Denver, Detroit, Omaha, St. Louis, and Salt Lake City; among states, in Colorado, Florida, Georgia, Idaho, Iowa, Kansas, New Mexico, North Dakota, Oregon, Texas, West Virginia, and Wyoming. In each of these states there were approximately twenty local choices on the ballots examined.[17]

Even in some of the cities whose ballots were not bad enough to be included in the list above, conditions exist which are highly unsatisfactory and which indicate the need for a further extension of the short ballot principle. In Philadelphia, for instance, the Bureau of Municipal Research pointed out an interesting contrast between the appointed heads of city departments and the elective county officers:

There is a startling contrast between the city departments, under directors chosen by the mayor and the elective county officers. Although Philadelphians can elect a mayor who will appoint a director of public safety with a budget of $17,000,000 and 7,500 employees, a director of public works with a budget of $10,000,000 and 6,000 employees, and a director of public health with a budget of $4,100,000 and 2,800 employees, they are required by the constitution to go to the polls to choose a coroner, whose 1934 budget is $97,600, providing for 40 employees; a clerk of quarter sessions (budget of $257,100 and 96 employees) ; a register of wills (budget of $159,200 and 68 employees) ; a district attorney (budget of $283,750 and 83 employees) ; a recorder of deeds (budget of $290,700 and 135 employees) ; a sheriff (budget of $364,190 and 168 employees) ; a comptroller (budget of $161,960 and 59 employees) ; and a city treasurer with 47 employees and a budget of $111,900 (after eliminating large appropriations for debt service, pensions, etc., which are not indicative of the size of the job) . Then there are the county commissioners. They have 173 regular employees, 101 of them in the weights and measures bureau. They are a conduit for large appropriations which in no way measure their responsibilities. When these are eliminated, an outside figure of under $900,000 remains — several times

17 Albright, Spencer D., *How Does Your Ballot Grow?* (American Legislators' Association, Chicago, 1933) , and " General Election Ballots in 1934," *Southwestern Social Science Quarterly,* March, 1936, pp. 85–95.

larger than that of any other elected county officer, but then there are three commissioners to carry the load.

Judged by expenditures and number of employees, the elective county offices are rather small jobs. Roll them all into one and the appropriations listed above are not over 15% of the budget of the director of public safety; the number of employees is not over 12%. Why should such offices be permitted to distract attention from the really important ones that the voters must fill? But the county officers of Philadelphia County do not determine policies to any great extent. Even the county commissioners, once a legislative body, lost all of their legislative powers to city council back in 1854.[18]

Illustrations of this type could be drawn from many different states and cities. The need for extending the use of the short ballot is clear. "Students of political science generally agree," concludes Spencer D. Albright, "that precise instructions, absence of Presidential Electors, moderate burden as to positions, names, and propositions, and convenient arrangement of offices and questions are desirable features in a good ballot." On the other hand, huge ballots, excessive reading matter, lengthy voting instructions, long lists of names, great variety of offices as to both character and importance, and numerous propositions are generally condemned. " Short ballot arguments appear even more convincing after an examination of ballots throughout the nation. The handicaps set upon the workings of democracy undoubtedly undermine democratic opportunity." [19]

In olden times, when citizens gathered around the cracker barrel in the corner grocery to discuss public questions, they did so at least in part because of the absence of scores of interests, such as motion pictures, the radio, the automobile, and dozens of social and fraternal organizations, which compete for the time and attention of the average citizen today. He is actually unable, even if he were theoretically willing, to give the same attention to public questions that his father or grandfather was accustomed to give. There seems to be much justification for believing that many voters are discouraged in the performance of their civic responsibilities by the

[18] *Citizens' Business*, June 5, 1934, published by the Philadelphia Bureau of Municipal Research.

[19] Albright, *op. cit.* For another recent comment, see Pollock, James K., " New Thoughts on the Short Ballot," *National Municipal Review*, January, 1940, pp. 18–20, 47; and Jones, O. Garfield, " Is the Short Ballot Principle Obsolete? " *National Municipal Review*, April, 1943, pp. 185–187, 189.

Professor Pollock stresses the point that the arguments are the same now as they were thirty years ago, and the situation quite as serious. See *Proceedings*, American Political Science Association, 1909: Beard, Charles A., " Tendencies Affecting the Size of the Ballot," pp. 93–99; Childs, Richard S., " The Need for Simplification," pp. 65–71; and Ludington, Arthur C., " Proposed Methods of Ballot Simplification," pp. 72–91.

very complexity of the task imposed upon them. They are asked to register annually in many jurisdictions, and to vote in one or more primaries as well as in general and special elections. Not only must they make repeated trips to the polling place for registration and voting, but they must decide regarding the merits of enormous numbers of candidates with whose names they are unfamiliar, and regarding large numbers of issues concerning which they are uninformed, often through no particular fault of their own. It seems reasonable to believe that many voters who now vote unintelligently, and many others who do not vote at all, would participate more willingly and far more effectively if the time and effort required for the performance of their civic duties were made more commensurate with the amount of time and effort they are now able to spend.

TYPES OF WEIGHTED VOTING

Faults of District System of Representation. **Gross** inequalities frequently result from the application of the single member district plan of representation, due in part to the gerrymandering of districts by the legislature and in part to defects inherent in the plan. Although notable increases in the population of a given state may occur, and important shifts in population take place, the legislature frequently fails to enact a reapportionment. Even where the districts are fairly and evenly divided, a large portion of the voting population is without suitable representation. A majority of one is sufficient to determine the result of an election. While contests are seldom so close, it frequently happens that 30 or 40 per cent of the voters in a district cast their ballots for a candidate other than the one elected. To argue that under the doctrine of majority rule these persons are effectively represented by one for whom they did not vote, and with whose views they do not agree, is to substitute fiction for fact. This considerable percentage of voters in the district concerned are without anyone who can or will express, in any satisfactory manner, their views on controversial issues.

Not only are the results of the single member district plan unsatisfactory within individual districts, but the effect of the plan throughout a state may also be unsatisfactory. Pennsylvania, for instance, has a Congressional delegation of thirty-four members; for many years it was a rare election in which more than three or four or five members belonged to the minority party. It is true that the majority party in the state long maintained a substantial majority, but it is absurd to suppose that there was any such degree of unanimity of opinion on political questions as would seem to be indicated by the complexion of this delegation in Congress.[20]

These conditions affect a whole state, but the situation is just as bad — perhaps worse — when one turns to a large municipality like New York City. In eight of the elections studied there — nearly half of the time — a party with a minority of the votes elected a majority of the members. In more than a fifth of all aldermanic district contests, a minority won at the expense of a divided majority. Forty-two per cent of all the votes cast were wasted on losing candidates. In the last seven elections Democratic votes have been worth from three to twenty-five times as much as Republican votes in securing representation. In the same seven elections the Socialists have polled every time from four to ten times as many votes as the number of Democratic votes for each Democratic member elected, and have elected no aldermen at all. It has never taken as much as one third of the votes cast to elect a majority of the board for the controlling party. " In short," the author of this study concludes, " our method of trying to secure a representative body has violated every major tenet of American democracy. We have not had majority rule. We have not had fair representation for minorities. We have not even had an approach to equality of voting power." [21] In the 1935 elections the Democrats elected all but three of the sixty-eight members of the Board of Aldermen; in Philadelphia the Democrats, who polled only a few thousand less votes than the Republicans in the mayoralty contest, failed to elect a single one of the twenty-two members of the city council.

The facts with regard to the situation in New York are well presented on page 185.

Proportional Representation. To correct these abuses, various devices such as proportional representation, commonly called P.R., preferential voting, and cumulative voting have been advocated. P.R. was first proposed by the son of an obscure English clergyman, named Hare, in 1857. When the plan was published in pamphlet form, it attracted little attention until, some years later, John Stuart Mill incorporated a discussion of it in his volume on *Representative*

[20] See Hallett, George H., Jr., " Is Congress Representative? " *National Municipal Review,* June, 1933, pp. 284–285, 288–289, for an analysis of the 1932 Congressional elections.

[21] Facts and quotation from Hallett, George H., Jr., " New York City Looks toward Representative Government," *National Municipal Review,* April, 1934, pp. 221–222.

Government. From that time on, the subject has been regarded as significant; in recent years it has come to have an important practical bearing. The principle of proportional representation has been applied in two different ways: the List system, adopted in Europe; the Hare system, adopted in many communities throughout the United States.

ELECTION OF NEW YORK ALDERMEN [22]

November 7, 1933

Party [23]	Votes Cast	Seats in Proportion to Votes	Seats Won	Percentage of Votes	Percentage of Seats
Democratic and Recovery	997,601	34	49	52.7	75.4
Republican and City Fusion	782,270	27	16	41.3	24.6
Socialist	75,827	3	0	4	0
Others	38,992	1	0	2	0
Totals	1,894,690	65	65	100	100

The List system recognizes the existence of political parties and provides specifically for them; under it, each party nominates a slate of candidates, the number of which corresponds exactly to the number of positions to be filled. If we assume this number to be ten, party A, if it polls 40 per cent of the votes, will elect its first four candidates; party B, if it likewise polls 40 per cent of the votes, will elect four candidates; and party C, polling 20 per cent will elect two. This plan would appear to have considerable merit. While it has been used in Europe, it has not been tried in the United States, and its adoption here has not been widely advocated.[24]

The Hare system uses the principle of the single transferable vote for the purpose of insuring to each important element of the voting population a representation exactly in proportion to its numerical voting strength. In this plan, parties are not directly recognized although they may mobilize their voting strength behind any selection

[22] From *The Searchlight,* published by the Citizens Union of the City of New York, March, 1934; also in *National Municipal Review,* April, 1934, p. 222.

Similar tabular matter for Boston city council elections, 1925–1933, will be found in Loeffler, Herman C., " P. R. Officially Proposed in Boston," *National Municipal Review,* March, 1934, pp. 171–174.

[23] There was a great deal of overlapping between the endorsements of the Democratic and Recovery parties on the one hand, and the Republican and City Fusion parties on the other. These parties have therefore been combined in the table although in a number of cases their candidates opposed each other.

[24] See Gosnell, Harold F., " A List System with Single Candidate Preference," *American Political Science Review,* August, 1939, pp. 645–650.

```
Cincinnati
Regular City Election
NOVEMBER 7, 1939
DIRECTIONS TO VOTERS
```

Put the figure 1 in the square opposite the name of your first choice. Express your second, third and other choices by putting the figure 2 opposite the name of your second choice, and the figure 3 opposite the name of your third choice, and so on. You may express as many choices as you please, without any regard to the number being elected.

Your ballot will be counted for your first choice if it can be used to help elect him. If it can not help elect him, it will be transferred to the highest of your other choices whom it can help.

You can not hurt any of those you prefer by marking lower choices for others. The more choices you express, the surer you are to make your ballot count for one of them. But do not feel obliged to express choices which you do not really have.

Do not put the same figure opposite more than one name.

If you spoil this ballot, tear it across once, return it to the election officer in charge of the ballots and get another from him.

CANDIDATES FOR THE COUNCIL

	WILLIAM ROBERT FRY
	WILLIS D. GRADISON
	ROBERT GUNKEL
	NICHOLAS KLEIN
	JOHN M. MOLLOY
	JAMES E. O'CONNELL
	LEE PAYNE
	CARL S. RANKIN
	JAMES GARFIELD STEWART
	CHARLES P. TAFT
	CHARLES DABNEY THOMSON
	CHARLES H. TOBIAS
	DAVID D. TURPEAU
	ROBERT H. WACHENDORF
	EDWARD N. WALDVOGEL
	HOBART A. WEHKING
	ALBERT WILLMOTH
	RUSSELL WILSON
	JACK ABRAMS

SAMPLE BALLOT

of candidates they may desire. Nominations may be made by petition by any group of sufficient size and interest to secure the required number of signatures. The names of all nominees are printed on the ballot without any descriptive designation. The voter may indicate as many choices as he wishes, voting for one candidate, for a number equivalent to the number of positions to be filled, or for all the candidates whose names appear on the ballot, indicating his choices in the order of his preference. At the conclusion of the voting, the ballot boxes are taken under seal and guard to the central counting place, where a group of bank clerks and other persons accustomed to accurate checking are employed to tabulate the results. Until recently no voting machine suitable for use in P.R. elections had been perfected, but one based on the punch-card principle is now available.[25]

Preferential Voting. Preferential voting has been defined as " a device whereby a voter in a primary or general election may indicate on his ballot a first and second choice . . . with a view to combining or transferring choices when the votes are counted in such a way as to produce at least a nominal majority in favor of a particular candidate." [26] In other words, it selects the most representative

[25] See note in *National Municipal Review,* July, 1936, p. 432.

[26] Weeks, O. Douglas, " Summary of the History and Present Status of Preferential Voting in State Direct Primary Systems," *Southwestern Social Science Quarterly,* June, 1937, pp. 64–67; Dorr, Harold M., " The Nanson System: A Michigan Experiment in Voting," *Papers* of the Michigan Academy of Science, Arts, and

candidate out of any number, eliminating dark horses by a single election. The ballots are not difficult to fill out, and ordinarily they are not hard to count. Between 1907 and 1925 this system was adopted in eleven states, but it has now been abandoned by all except Maryland. The Oklahoma law was declared unconstitutional; the others were repealed. In Idaho, Indiana, Minnesota, North Dakota, Washington, and Wisconsin the plurality system was substituted for it, while in Alabama, Florida, Louisiana, and Oklahoma the run-off primary took its place. The reasons given for repeal were the failure of voters to indicate more than one choice, and the failure of party leaders to educate the voters in the use of a preferential feature. The chief weakness of this system is that a voter's second and other choices are given equal weight with his first choice, if they do not actually work against the election of his first choice.

Cumulative Voting. A system of cumulative voting is one in which a voter, with several votes at his disposal, may use all of them for one candidate if he so desires. Such a system has been in effect in Illinois for years for the choice of members of the lower house in the legislature. Professor Mathews thus describes the system:

One Senator is elected from each of the fifty-one senatorial districts, and each voter has one vote in voting for a senator; but three representatives are elected from each senatorial district and each voter has three votes which he may " plump " for one candidate or distribute in such manner as he sees fit. This is known as the system of minority representation or cumulative voting provided for in the Constitution of 1870, and is unique among the methods of electing legislative representatives found in the various states.[27]

The Hare System. It has been suggested that one might imagine all the voters in a city gathered together on a certain day and hour in the city park to select officeholders. It is assumed that, under such circumstances, each candidate for each office would have a standard erected, about which his followers might gather. When the signal was given for the citizens to indicate their choices for a particular office, such as member of council, each voter would make his way to the standard of the candidate of his choice, in order that his vote might be counted. If, as he did so, he saw that so many voters were already gathered under this standard that his favorite candidate was already assured of election, he would be foolish to increase further the number of excess votes. As a rational person he would reason that

Letters, 1942, pp. 613–621; and Kneier, Charles M., *City Government in the United States*, pp. 209–215 (Harper, New York, 1934).

[27] Mathews, John M., *American State Government*, Revised Edition, p. 235 (Appleton-Century, New York, 1934).

since the candidate of his choice was already assured of election, he might as well lend his support to his second choice. If he should find that his second choice was likewise assured of election, he might then support his third choice, and so on. This is precisely what happens when, in a proportional representation election, the excess votes of an elected candidate are distributed to the later choices indicated on these ballots.

Critics have objected to the complexity of the rules governing a P.R. count and to the time required for the work. In American cities where the plan has been used this has not proved to be a serious objection. Newspapers have welcomed the opportunity to report the progress of the count from day to day. The rules require, as a first step, the determination of the quota which represents the minimum number of votes with which a candidate may be declared elected. This number is secured by dividing the total number of valid ballots cast at the election by the number of positions to be filled, plus one. Thus, if 10,000 votes were cast and five candidates were to be elected, it would be necessary to divide 10,000 by six, in which case the quotient would be 1,666⅔. Whether or not the quotient proves to be a whole number, the rules require the use of the next highest whole number as the quota — which, in this case, would be 1,667. The second step is the tabulation of the first choices on the ballots; in this tabulation there are two methods which may be followed. Either all the first choices may be tabulated, regardless of the number which any candidate may receive, or the counters may cease tabulating first choices for any candidate as soon as the full quota has been recorded for him. In the latter case, the second choices from the elected candidate's excess ballots are added to the first choices from the rest of the ballots.

The first method of counting is more commonly employed. When this is used, it is almost certain that some candidate will have a number of votes in excess of the quota when the first check is completed, and that the number of candidates having a quota will be less than the number to be elected. When this occurs, the next step is to take from each candidate having excess votes the exact number of ballots by which he has exceeded the quota. These ballots are then rechecked, and recorded in favor of the second choice; or, if the second choice has already received the quota, in favor of the third. This process is continued until all excess ballots for all candidates have been redistributed. If it is still found that the full number of candidates to be elected have not received a quota, the next step is to cross off the name of the candidate with the lowest number of votes, redistributing his first choices to the second choices on these ballots, unless these choices have already been chosen, in which case they may be recorded for third or fourth choice. This process is continued until each of the required number of candidates has received the quota.

It has often been said that reformers fail to utilize the psychological advantage of attractive terminology as applied to their proposed improvements. This is certainly true of proportional representation, the name of which is cumbersome and forbidding. If this device had been publicized under some such name as " effective voting," it would doubtless have made more rapid progress. The purpose of P.R. is definitely to make voting more effective, to assure every voter that his ballot will influence the outcome of the election. In another way P.R. contributes to the accuracy of elections as indicators of the popular will, and to their honesty. The ballots from a P.R. election must be counted at a central counting place; the counting is done in the open, by competent persons, under able supervision. A considerable portion of the dishonesty in municipal elections has been due to " dirty work " done in the evening after the polls were closed; ballots have been spoiled, and the returns falsified. This is impossible in an election with central counting of ballots, or in jurisdictions where voting machines are used.

A serious handicap of P.R. in American politics arises from the fact that the number of officers to be chosen at one time for a city council, a state legislature, or a state delegation to Congress often exceeds practical limits regarding the number of candidates upon whom a voter can render an informed and intelligent opinion. When this system was used in Cleveland, the city was divided into four districts, each of which elected its quota of councilmen. The results were not as satisfactory as the citywide election plan used in Cincinnati. While it may be possible to choose in this way a larger number of persons at one time than had been supposed, it is certainly true that there are limits to the size of the units and to the number of officials who may be selected at one time. Districts would be necessary if P.R. were used in choosing state legislators, and, in the larger states, for the choice of Congressional delegations. The New York State Constitutional Convention Committee worked out an interesting plan in 1938 by which an assembly of sixty-four might be elected from thirteen districts, with a fixed quota of 60,000.[28] This is in line with the recommendation of the Model State Constitution.

[28] See *Problems Relating to Legislative Organization and Powers*, Chapter 4 (Albany, 1938) .

THE INFLUENCE OF CIVIC ORGANIZATIONS

During recent years citizens' organizations of various types have assumed an increasingly important role in the supervision and guidance of public affairs. Formerly these organizations were composed chiefly of reform elements who were interested in bringing about specific changes in the governmental structure. Little attention was given to the detailed supervision of regular government services, or to the study of routine problems of financial organization and administration. The depression focused attention on social, political, and economic problems, and this interest was maintained to a considerable extent during the war. The people have come to realize the necessity for an alert and well-informed citizenry if democracy is to be successful. Many organizations have been developed with this end in view, and colleges and universities, as well as programs of adult education, have laid great emphasis upon public affairs.

National Municipal League. Probably the oldest organization engaged in this work is the National Municipal League, a nonprofitmaking, nonpartisan corporation founded in 1894 by Theodore Roosevelt, James C. Carter, Horace White, R. Fulton Cutting, Washington Gladden, and others. Its former presidents include Charles Evans Hughes, Frank L. Polk, Lawson Purdy, Henry M. Waite, Richard S. Childs, Murray Seasongood, Harold W. Dodds, and Clarence A. Dykstra. While the League has confined itself largely to the field of local government, it has maintained a committee on state government, which has kept up to date the Model State Constitution (see Appendix). Since the relationship between state and local government is very close, whatever affects the one is of importance to the other.

The purposes of the League, as stated in its literature, have been: (1) to create or adapt methods by which local government could be operated more efficiently, less expensively, more responsively; (2) to maintain a clearing house service which covers all phases of local government problems and procedures; (3) to conduct educational activities which seek to crystallize public opinion in support of higher standards and better methods of administration for local government. It is the sole national organization which carries on this type of work. The methods employed and the services rendered include: *Publications: National Municipal Review,* a monthly journal; also the preparation, publication, and distribution of books, pamphlets, and other educational material on government problems. More than 300,000 pieces of literature were distributed in a recent year. *Information Service:* answers inquiries on all phases of city, county, and state government; comprehensive library available to persons seriously interested in government problems. *Speakers' Bureau:* speakers and consultants on municipal government and campaign problems supplied at cost. During the first four months of 1940, members of the League staff visited fifty-six cities to confer with citizen leaders on the manager plan and citizen organization. *Campaign Aid:* campaign plans used in other communities are supplied to local groups working for improved government, while literature suitable for educational and campaign use is supplied at cost. *Consultant Service:* makes administrative and financial surveys of local and county governments, and assists in drafting city charters, reorganizing state governments, revising state constitutions or modernizing county government, at cost. *Research Projects:* national committees of the League carry on research and develop solutions to new problems in local government. *Conferences:* national and regional conferences on government are conducted in cooperation with local groups.

The home office of the League performs the usual duties of a headquarters office, including preparation of radio programs, press releases, and other types of publicity. The influence of the League in legislative matters is frequently important. It watches over conditions in the states, and loses no opportunity to exert its influence on behalf of progressive constitutional revision, administrative reorganization, budget law reform, and many other matters. Hundreds of copies of the Model State Constitution are distributed each year, and copies are regularly supplied to members of constitutional conventions and commissions. Model registration and election codes have been prepared and publicized. In 1933, when the repeal of Amendment XVIII seemed certain, the League created a committee to draft a Model State Liquor Control Law; by the end of 1934 this law had been adopted in whole or in part by twelve states. The League has also sponsored a Model Tax Collection Law.[29]

The 1313 Group. Many other types of organizations have demonstrated a keen interest in government problems. Since 1931 a signifi-

[29] Murray Seasongood, in his address as retiring president of the League on the occasion of its fortieth anniversary, summarized admirably its contributions to the cause of good local government in the United States during that period (Pittsburgh, November 26, 1934). See *National Municipal Review*, December, 1934, pp. 644–645, 693. On its fiftieth anniversary in 1944 a special Anniversary Issue of the *Review* was published in November.

cant group of national organizations interested in various types of governmental activity has been developing in Chicago with head-quarters in a single building.[30] They are semiofficial in character; most of them would never have come into existence if there had not been developing, throughout the country, both a public and a professional interest in the organization of government and the administration of public affairs. Organizations in this list that are working in the field of state government will be discussed in a later chapter on interstate relations. The list follows:

THE 1313 GROUP

Organization	Founded	Office in Chicago since
American Public Works Association	1894	1934
International Association of Chiefs of Police	1893	1937
Municipal Finance Officers Association	1906	1932
Civil Service Assembly of the United States and Canada	1906	1935
Governors' Conference	1908	1938
International City Managers' Association	1914	1929
National Association of State Auditors, Comptrollers, and Treasurers	1915	1937
American Municipal Association	1924	1932
American Public Welfare Association	1930	1932
Public Administration Clearing House	1931	1931
Council of State Governments	1933	1933
National Association of Housing Officials	1933	1933
Public Administration Service	1933	1933
National Association of Assessing Officers	1934	1934
American Society of Planning Officials	1934	1935
Federation of Tax Administrators	1937	1937

Women's Organizations. Among women's organizations may be mentioned the National Association of Business and Professional Women, the American Association of University Women, and women's city clubs, as well as leagues or federations of women belonging to particular political parties. All of these groups have local organizations in towns and cities of any considerable size, and are showing increasing interest in public affairs. Most important, perhaps, are the branches of the National League of Women Voters, which grew out of the suffrage groups whose efforts brought about the ratification of Amendment XIX. The League is a national organization, with state and county branches, whose object is to increase the

---

[30] At 1313 East 60th Street; see Hazelrigg, Hal, " The 1313 Group in Chicago," *Annals,* September, 1938, pp. 183–189.

number of responsible voting citizens and to encourage economy and efficiency in all government affairs. It offers unbiased, factual information on political issues, carries on a continuing program of political education, and enables women of all parties and groups to work together toward common objectives. Through its various departments it carries on activities in many different fields, including government and its operation, child welfare, education, the legal status of women, and economic welfare.[31]

Commonwealth Club of California. The Commonwealth Club of California was organized in 1903 with five members as a " Public Service Club," "to investigate and discuss problems affecting the welfare of the Commonwealth and to aid in their solution " and " to maintain itself in an impartial position as an open forum for the discussion of disputed questions." It was incorporated and took its present name in 1926. Now, after a life of nearly half a century, it has a membership of over 4,000, carefully selected from the business and professional life of all parts of the West. That it has succeeded to a large extent in achieving its objectives is shown by the very high regard in which it is held, not only in the state, but throughout the nation. Its influence stems from the research of its various sections, its published *Transactions,* its meetings, and the personal contact of its members with the body politic.

The Club has organized, and maintains, as many as thirty organized bands of volunteer investigators, known as " Sections," some of them more than one hundred strong, engaged in the study of problems concerning the welfare of the Commonwealth of California; and in aid and abatement of the work of those Sections, a Research Service (established in 1926) under the general supervision of an advisory council headed by the presidents and past-presidents of Stanford University and the University of California.

An excellent idea of the nature and scope of the activities of the Club may be obtained by an examination of the annual reports of its executive secretary published in its official journal, *The Commonwealth.* Although the Club holds lecture luncheons, section luncheons, monthly dinners, and social meetings, it is not a luncheon or dinner or social organization. It is today what its founders hoped it would be, a purely investigating and reporting body. General luncheons are held weekly, on Friday, with an average attendance

---

[31] For some recent comments on the civic activities of women's organizations, see High, Stanley, " Kansas City Has Its Chin Up," *National Municipal Review,* October, 1941, pp. 561–564; Nelson, Josephine, " Business Women in a Democracy," *ibid.,* November, 1940, pp. 714–719; " New York Women's City Club Celebrates Silver Anniversary," *ibid.,* June, 1941, pp. 376–377.

for many years of around 400. The list of speakers constitutes a distinguished group of men recognized as leaders in many phases of national life. Special luncheons, ranging in number up to seven, and in combined attendance as high as eighty-eight a day, are served on Monday, Tuesday, Wednesday, and Thursday noons in adjacent rooms. Thus did twenty-four sections in 1939 hold 373 meetings, in connection with each of which there were either addresses or discussions, or both, on important problems coming within the range of interest of the several sections.

The Club has permanent headquarters in a leading hotel in the central city district, in which it maintains an extensive collection of books and magazines dealing with public questions. There is also a men's chorus and orchestra. The Club carries on various miscellaneous activities including the award of an Annual Literature Medal. Since 1922, postcard votes on topics of current interest have been conducted; in 1939 the subjects of such votes included game management and the Wagner act. The results of these votes receive wide publicity, as do many other Club activities.

The publications of the Club are important. In the course of the years, more than thirty-five volumes of *Transactions* have been published, with ten or twelve numbers per volume, each number presenting the results of a careful study of some question of current interest. Often the numbers are devoted to the same topics upon which postcard votes are taken. A review of all the public questions investigated would show that the Club has more than justified its existence. It has had an influence upon the legislation of the state and has left its imprint on the constitution. It has made studies of such important questions as taxation, judicial procedure, direct legislation, municipal water supplies, public health, public education, public morals, civil service, and various questions of conservation. *The Commonwealth* is published in two parts; Part I supplies members with extracts from Club and section talks, while Part II presents the results of the inquiries noted above.

This extensive program of activity, carried on over a period of years, has resulted in a list of tangible accomplishments of which the Club is justly proud. It is claimed that the Club influence has been directly responsible for important developments in state and local government in California, including, in addition to general questions, improvements in the administration of justice and in the election law. The general items included establishment of an effective budget system and of irrigation districts, extension of civil service, and passage of a driver's license law. A small claims court was established, the office of public defender created, the code of criminal procedure was revised, et cetera, while provision was made for absentee voting, nonpartisan elections for certain offices, and other matters relating to elections. If this Club in California is able to carry on so effective a piece of work in civic education, and to point to such a fine record of accomplishment, there is no reason why similar methods in other states might not lead to similar results.[32]

Other State Organizations. While the Commonwealth Club is outstanding among state citizen organizations, especially of broad scope, there are in most states a number of statewide citizen organizations that function within the limited fields of their own interests. Examples of these are:

> New York State Charities Aid Association
> Public Charities Association of Pennsylvania
> Pennsylvania Parks Association
> Pennsylvania Prison Society
> The Delaware Citizens Association
> The Missouri Association for Social Welfare
> The Ohio Institute

Of these, the first two are the strongest statewide organizations in the country in the field of health and welfare. While the Public Charities Association, through its Penal Affairs Division, covers legislative matters, the Prison Society concerns itself with the administration of correctional institutions and with the pardon and parole, and parole supervision, of individual prisoners. The Delaware Citizens Association, now a quarter of a century old, has concerned itself chiefly with problems in the field of education, gathering and publishing facts, conducting experiments and demonstrations, and helping in emergency situations. In Pennsylvania an Emergency Council of State Associations, with 150 member associations, was organized in 1938 " to assist in removing the principal cause of unemployment in the state — namely, excessive state taxation of business." Through its Tax Study Committee it submitted to the General Assembly a new state tax program in 1945.

All of the groups mentioned have had an important influence on legislation in their respective fields in their own states. In this work their publications, giving members up-to-date information on current

[32] This entire comment is based upon material in issues of *The Commonwealth*, supplied by the executive secretary of the Club, Mr. Stuart R. Ward. The quotations are from the same source. The *National Municipal Review*, November, 1936, pp. 682–683, contains a note on its activities in 1936.

developments, play an important part. The Public Charities Association puts out a quarterly bulletin called *The Herald* and, in legislative years, a weekly summary of the progress of welfare legislation under the title *Social Legislation*. The Delaware Citizens Association publishes a substantial monthly bulletin called *Signposts*. The Ohio Institute puts out a mimeographed bulletin, *The Ohio Citizen*, " at intervals to convey information to citizens of Ohio on topics of government."

Taxpayers' Organizations. With the advent of the depression in 1929, organizations of taxpayers sprang up in great numbers in all sections of the United States. These were for the most part born out of the spirit of discontent naturally arising in a period of economic distress. Most of these organizations were devoid of intelligent leadership. Their only concern was to batter down the tax rate. Their leaders had no conception of the duties and responsibilities of government, and no regard for the preservation and maintenance of necessary and worthwhile public services. Not content with the demand for all reasonable economies, for the elimination of duplicating and overlapping services, and of waste generally, they organized marches on city halls and pilgrimages to state capitols, to awe the members of these bodies into acquiescing to their often unreasonable demands. As the depression became less serious, many of these organizations, which had never had any constructive program, disappeared as suddenly as they had come into existence. Others developed along sound lines, and came to function with very beneficial results.

Some, capitalizing on the awakened public interest in govern. mental problems, organized on a permanent basis and secured the services of a competent staff of research workers; they are conducting scientific and impartial investigations of problems of governmental organization, of revenue, and expenditure.[33] The Pennsylvania

[33] Some of the more active state associations and their monthly publications, where the titles are known, are listed below:
State Taxpayers' Association of Arizona — *Arizona Taxpayers' Magazine.*
California Taxpayers' Association — *The Tax Digest.*
Indiana Taxpayers' Association.
Kentucky Tax Reduction Association — *News Bulletin.*
Louisiana Taxpayers' Association.
Massachusetts Federation of Taxpayers' Associations, Inc. — *Tax Talk.*
Minnesota Taxpayers' Association.
Montana Taxpayers' Association — *Montana Taxpayer.*
Nebraska Federation of County Taxpayers' Leagues.
New Jersey Taxpayers' Association — *Taxegram.*
Taxpayers' Association of New Mexico —
   See Asplund, Rupert F., " An Account of the Organization and Activities of

Economy League, for instance, set up a field organization for the collection annually of detailed financial data on every subdivision of local government in the state, so that eventually trends may be worked out. By applying a uniform system of classification of items of expenditure, accurate information on the cost and, to a certain extent, the efficiency of individual units may be determined, and fair comparisons made between different units. The League has established numerous county committees with permanent offices and secretaries. Its legislative committee has formulated a program in each legislative year, prepared carefully drafted bills, and exerted pressure through its legislative representatives to secure their adoption. It has established the Taxpayer's Forum, to publicize the results of the League's investigations, and to carry on a campaign to develop public support for the program. All of this has been done with the purpose in mind to secure " Better Government at Less Cost."

The Indiana Taxpayers' Association undertook similar studies in the field of local government, as well as a valuable study of taxpayers' associations throughout the country. The associations in New Jersey and Tennessee have prepared at regular intervals exhaustive analyses of state government finances. These may be taken as illustrative of the types of useful service which may be rendered by privately supported organizations, if they are willing to deal with governmental problems in an honest and impartial manner. Such groups may exert a powerful and beneficial influence on legislation in which they are interested; such an instance occurred in the New Jersey session of 1933, when the state taxpayers' association brought pressure to bear to secure enactment of a number of measures designed to strengthen the financial control of the executive. The story is well told by a student of financial administration in that state:

The 1933 session of the legislature dragged on for four months without the slightest prospect that any of the proposed fiscal changes would be made. Suddenly in the second week in June the public was amazed when the Senate suddenly passed the modified Kuser and Reeves bills. Until this time the Senate apparently had no intention of making any of the proposed changes in fiscal legislation. The Taxpayers' Association had previously

the Taxpayers' Association," *Bulletin* of the National Tax Association, January, 1944, pp. 1–7.

New York State Economic Council, Inc. — *Economic Council Bulletin.*
North Dakota Taxpayers' Association — *The North Dakota Taxpayer.*
Pennsylvania Economy League — *Your Dollar's Worth.*
Tennessee Taxpayers' Association.
Utah Taxpayers' Association — *Utah Taxpayer.*
Wisconsin Taxpayers' Alliance — *Wisconsin Taxpayer.*

warned the legislature that unless definite action was forthcoming it would take more vigorous measures. This was considered an idle threat until the Association called a mass meeting at Trenton to consider the advisability of conducting a state-wide tax strike until the legislature adopted its fiscal control bills. The day before this mass meeting was held the Senate passed the revised Kuser and Reeves bills without a dissenting vote. This dramatic yielding by the Senate surprised even the leaders of the Taxpayers' Association. The mass meeting was held but it was decided not to call a tax strike and to give the house of assembly an opportunity to act. At first the Taxpayers' Association insisted that its own fiscal bills should be adopted and opposed the bills which had been passed by the Senate. The leaders of the Association became persuaded, however, that to adhere to this policy would be inadvisable. They finally agreed to support the Kuser and Reeves bills with the hope that they could be improved and strengthened before final enactment.

The taxpayers already were well organized with an association in each county and numerous local organizations. Shortly after the mass meeting in Trenton the leaders of the state organization instructed each county taxpayers' association to call a special meeting to which the legislators from its district should be invited. At these conferences the advisability of supporting the fiscal reform measures was demonstrated to the members of the assembly. Largely as a result of this process of "education" assurance of sufficient votes was obtained to secure favorable action. Incidentally, before the election of last November the State Taxpayers' Association canvassed all candidates seeking election to the legislature as to their record and attitude toward the Princeton program, among other things, and published the results.[34]

This comment is illuminating. It provides both a sidelight on the processes of modern legislation and a description of the methods by which a pressure group organization carries on its work at the state capitol. The methods are in general familiar to anyone who has ever tried to secure legislative action on some subject in which he was interested.

Organizations of Municipalities and Local Officials. The movement for state leagues of municipalities began in Indiana in 1891; in 1938 there were forty such leagues actually functioning in the several states. It is estimated that 5,000 cities belong to these various leagues, and while membership is purely voluntary, all but one of the eligible cities in New York are members, while in Michigan 94 per cent of the urban population holds membership in the league.

[34] Cline, Denzel C., *Executive Control over State Expenditures in New Jersey*, pp. 14–15 (Princeton University Press, 1934). For recent data, see summary of the activities of the California association in *National Municipal Review*, November, 1937, pp. 548–550; Langmuir, John D., "Taxpayer Groups Stress Concrete Accomplishments," *ibid.*, March, 1940, pp. 210–212; and Kneier, Charles M., "Citizen Economy Movements — Why and How," *ibid.*, August, 1940, pp. 535–539.

It is unnecessary to discuss here the numerous functions which these leagues perform, since they are chiefly of interest to the student of municipal government. They do, however, undertake important legislative work. One authority observes that " the urban communities of the United States, representing more than half of the population of the country, have certain social and political problems and interests which are not readily recognized by state legislatures. The cities, through their state leagues, therefore definitely attempt to express their legitimate interests and points of view both in favor of constructive municipal legislation and against legislation which is adverse to cities." He then proceeds to list a number of outstanding legislative accomplishments in this field in widely separated states: municipal and home rule laws in Michigan and Wisconsin; zoning enabling acts in Minnesota and New Jersey; city sharing of gas tax revenue in Illinois.[35]

While the influence of state leagues of municipalities is likely to be a constructive one, quite the opposite is often true of other organizations of local government officials. In state after state, these groups range in number from one to a dozen or more, including poor directors, coroners, district attorneys, probation officers, registers of wills, sheriffs, county controllers, township commissioners, township supervisors, magistrates, justices of the peace, school directors, and many others. While they are established for the avowed purpose of discussing questions and subjects relating to their duties and of devising uniform, economical, and efficient methods of administering their affairs, they frequently assume the position of pressure groups interested in maintaining the *status quo*. When any constructive proposal is made for the improvement of local government, one may be sure both of their united opposition and of a great deal of talk about " home rule." [36]

[35] Smith, Harold D., " American Municipal Leagues," radio address in the You and Your Government Series, October 30, 1934. For the best study of these groups, by Mr. Smith and George C. S. Benson, see National Resources Committee, *Urban Government*, Vol. I, " Associations of Cities and of Municipal Officials," pp. 179–245 (Washington, 1939) ; also Ham, Clifford W., " State Leagues of Municipalities and the American Municipal Association; An Experiment in Cooperation among Municipal Officials," *American Political Science Review*, December, 1937, pp. 1132–1137. For studies of two state leagues, see Boardman, Norma, *A Study of the League of South Dakota Municipalities* (University of South Dakota, Governmental Research Bureau, 1942) , and Drury, James W., " History and Services of the Illinois Municipal League," *Illinois Municipal Review*, September, 1940, pp. 174–182.

[36] See Kurtzman, David H., " Influence of Organizations of Local Government Officials," *Annals*, January, 1938, pp. 103–109; also summary of accomplishments of the Pennsylvania State Association of Boroughs, *Borough Bulletin*, June, 1940, pp. 54–65; and *An Explanation of the Association's Work* (Hanover, April, 1942).

Local Citizen Organization. There are many types of local citizen organizations that exert a considerable influence in community affairs. In addition to city clubs, citizen committees, and service clubs, there are groups that devote their efforts to policing elections, to influencing the selection of both appointed and elected officials, et cetera. Others conduct discussion groups, and arrange for the broadcast of town meeting discussions of local issues. The city clubs of New York, Boston, Cleveland, Chicago, and other cities are well known. After the City Club of Philadelphia was given up during the depression, its old committee on public affairs continued to function as the Philadelphia Committee on Public Affairs. This group, whose membership is limited to fifty outstanding business and professional men, issues carefully prepared statements on public questions, makes recommendations to the governor and the mayor with regard to appointments, and in other ways seeks to influence the course of public affairs in the community.[37] The Rotary, Lions, Kiwanis, and other service clubs frequently have committees that engage in like activities.

One of the best known civic groups in the country is the Citizens Union of the City of New York — " a union of citizens, without regard to party, for the purpose of securing the honest and efficient government of the City of New York." In addition to the executive committee, standing committees are appointed annually on such subjects as legislation, constitutional revision, local candidates, civil service, and general reference. The annual report of the Union for 1938–1939 claimed credit for helping to remake the state constitution, for covering the legislature systematically, for following city legislation, for fighting for county reorganization, and for giving information to the voters through the famous *Voters' Directory* and otherwise. In this case, the records of officeholders were examined and 140 candidates for office personally interviewed. In many other cities, civic groups, following the lead of the Citizens Union, have made available to the public accurate information about candidates for public office.

Of a somewhat different type is the Committee of Seventy, founded in 1904 in Philadelphia, out of the remains of the old City Party, as " an organization of a permanent character whose purpose shall be to aid in securing good government in Philadelphia." It maintains standing committees on city finances, city government, civil

[37] Graves, W. Brooke, " P. C. P. A. Carries on Thirty-five Year Tradition," *National Municipal Review*, May, 1941, pp. 299–301.

service, elections, legislation, municipal work, and taxation. It is active and aggressive, particularly in all matters relating to registration and the conduct of elections. Specific items covered in the annual report (1940) were civil service and city employees, registration and elections, polling places, traffic court, purchase of supplies, city finances, public safety, mayor, gas works, budget economics, et cetera. "Through printed matter including pamphlets, digests, calendars and letters; radio broadcasts, newspaper articles and editorials; demonstrations of election and registration procedure; speeches by members of the staff and the Committee, and the giving of information by telephone or in person through the office, the Committee is constantly advocating and working for better local government and attempting to educate the voters."

Effective local organizations have been developed in many cities in support of the city manager plan. Of these, the one in Cincinnati has been notably successful and is perhaps best known.[38] Success in this type of movement is quite as possible in smaller cities and in rural communities as it is in the larger cities. In Yonkers, for instance, the Committee of 100 has given substantial proof of its effectiveness in many different aspects of municipal government. Its purpose is " to acquire information concerning the functioning of the government of the City of Yonkers, to make such information available to the public, to mobilize public opinion and to create an alert body of citizens in the affairs of said City and, in general, to secure a more efficient and economic government for the City."

An interesting attempt to promote citizen organization was carried on, until interrupted by the war, by Holland's Southern Institute for Town Service, sponsored by *Holland's,* a magazine with a considerable circulation in the South. Its aim was to encourage and aid the many groups and individuals interested in town improvement, to promote personal responsibility and cooperation for the purpose of preserving and developing " our Southern heritage of natural beauty, great human and natural resources, and rich culture." Toward this end the Institute established an Advisory Council of distinguished citizens of the Southern region, and gave awards to four communities each month for the effective carrying out of some meritorious civic project, such as an outstanding social welfare program, exceptional care for crippled children, outstanding school building improvement, a beautification program, et cetera. The pub-

[38] See *The Cincinnati Plan: Citizen Organization for Political Activity* (National Municipal League, New York, 1941).

lications of the Institute urge citizen organization in town-building institutes, supported by suitable newspaper publicity, for town rating, more effective organization, and town building.[39]

Research and Citizen Action. The municipal research movement parallels what Professor Munro has called the municipal renaissance in America. In the early years of the present century many such bureaus were established, and some are still functioning. Taxpayers associations have actively entered the field, and in some cases, because of the difficulty of obtaining adequate financial support, others have been consolidated with, or made some working arrangement with, local universities. Cases in point are the association of the New York Bureau with Columbia University as the Institute of Public Administration, and of the Detroit Bureau with Wayne University's School of Public Affairs and Social Work. Although other bureaus have had to restrict their program or to pass out of existence, there is more research work being done in the municipal field than ever before. It is, furthermore, regarded as a necessary basis for any intelligent civic action. The late Dean Mosher expressed the conviction of many when he said that each community in the country should have a well-qualified agency interested in resolving the conflict between those who would spend and those who have to pay.[40] A related type of activity includes the numerous conferences and institutes sponsored by educational institutions, such as the University of Virginia's annual Institute of Public Affairs, the University of Denver's Citizens' Conference on Government Management, the New Hampshire Institute of Public Affairs, and others.

Neither good administration nor high grade research will keep a community well governed unless there is cooperation on the part of the press and other channels of public information. William Allen White once said that " research libraries and governmental organizations have shelves filled with tried and proven methods of rendering efficient public service to the people. The great need today is to

[39] Holland's Southern Institute, R. C. Morrison, Director. See his *Organizing Our Town; Town Score Card; Town Organization Chart for Progress and Democracy* (all Dallas, 1940) , and Smith, Bernard, *Town Building* (Dallas, 1939) .

[40] See Mosher, William E., Reflections on Governmental Research," *National Municipal Review*, October, 1939, pp. 725–727; Shipman, George A., " Research and Public Action," *Journal of Politics*, February, 1939, pp. 76–86; Upson, Lent D., " Contributions of Citizen Research to Effective Government," *Annals*, September, 1938, pp. 171–175; Governmental Research Association, *Governmental Research and Citizen Control of Government*, and *Citizen Research Agencies and Taxpayers Associations* (Detroit, 1940) , Bureau of Governmental Research, *A Quarter-Century of Citizen Concern with Government, 1916–1941*, and *Citizens in the Dark — Cities in the Red* (Detroit, 1941) .

clear these shelves, to get their treasures of practical guidance into the hands and minds of our citizens." Good public reporting and good public relations on the part of research agencies can do much to bring this about.[41] Most important of all is an active and alert citizenry, effectively organized to make its wants known and to see that they are respected. This has been the key to success in every movement for good government in any American community.[42] In city after city where the city manager plan has been adopted or where improved administration has been secured under existing forms, the change has come because citizens were organized, aroused, and vigilant. The government will stay good so long — and only so long — as they remain organized, aroused, and vigilant.[43] What numerous cities have done, the states can do.

POPULAR PARTICIPATION IN GOVERNMENT

Under this heading, it is proposed to consider briefly the subject of nonvoting, the reasons for it and the methods which might be used to encourage a more general and active popular participation in voting and other governmental activities. Much has been said and written on this subject, and about the apathy of a large portion of the population toward government. In fact, this is one of the favorite themes of popular writers discoursing on government. Many of these articles and speeches are filled with denunciation. We are told that the fault lies not in our form of government but with ourselves; that corrupt political machines are able to maintain their control only by reason of the assistance given them by vote shirkers.

The extent of this nonparticipation is a matter of common knowledge. Even in Presidential years, with the tremendous ballyhoo that accompanies a national campaign, not much more than half of the

[41] For the story of fine cooperation by the press in Yonkers, see Rohrer, Miriam, "Editor Puts Civics on Page One," *National Municipal Review,* March, 1940, pp. 156–163.

[42] The two most recent studies in this field are Ewing, Russell H., *The Implementation of Municipal Research through Civic Organization* (National Bureau of Civic Research, Los Angeles, 1944) , and Gill, Norman N., *Municipal Research Bureaus, A Study of the Nation's Leading Citizen-Supported Agencies* (American Council on Public Affairs, Washington, 1944) .

[43] For recent illustrations of effective community action, see in the files of the *National Municipal Review:* Alger, Philip L., " The Charter League of the City Electric," May, 1937, pp. 234–240; Kline, Priscilla C., and Howard M., " Saginaw — a Lesson in Cooperation," November, 1939, pp. 773–780, and January, 1940, pp. 30–39; Wichman, William C., " Kenosha Citizens in Action," March, 1940, pp. 164–173; Willoughby, Alfred, " Alert Citizen Group Wins Again in Toledo," October, 1938, pp. 505–506, 517; and others.

eligible voters go to the polls. In other elections the degree of participation is much less, until in referenda on constitutional amendments and on measures submitted by initiative and referendum petitions, where usually a majority of those voting on the proposition is sufficient to adopt, important provisions are approved by the affirmative vote of small minority groups. So true is this that one distinguished scholar has undertaken to defend the thesis that government by majority rule is a fiction.[44]

Reasons for Nonvoting. There are numerous reasons, many of them more or less obvious, for failure to participate in elections. Some, however, are difficult to determine, because the citizen who failed to vote may not be able to state the real reason, or may not be willing to do so even if he is aware of it. A few years ago a careful study of the causes and methods of control of nonvoting was made for some 5,000 individuals in Chicago.[45] It was found that, in this number of cases, the percentages by age groups were substantially parallel to the percentages for the same groups for registered voters as a whole. There were approximately twice as many occasional as habitual nonvoters, and approximately twice as many women as men. The percentage of nonvoting for the native whites was slightly higher than for the Negroes, but it was more than three times as high for both of these groups as for the foreign-born.

When interviewed by well-trained and carefully selected field workers, nonvoters were asked to explain why they had failed to vote; the reasons which they gave may be grouped under five main headings. First, there were those who failed to vote because of physical difficulties, such as illness, absence from the city on election day, or being detained by a helpless member of the family. Legal and administrative obstacles deterred many others. Under this category came such excuses as insufficient legal residence, fear of the loss of business or wages, congestion at the polling places, and poor voting facilities generally. Still another group was deterred by a disbelief in woman's voting; included in this group were the antisuffragists, and those whose husbands objected to their wives' voting. The fourth

[44] Beard, Charles A., "The Fiction of Majority Rule," *Atlantic Monthly*, December, 1927, pp. 831–836.

[45] Merriam, Charles E., and Gosnell, Harold F., *Non-Voting: Causes and Methods of Control* (University of Chicago Press, 1924). The discussion which follows is based upon this study. See also Minneapolis Research Bureau, "Why Do 100,000 Minneapolis Citizens Fail to Vote?" (Mimeographed, 1941); "Getting the Answer to 'Why Voters Don't Vote,'" *National Municipal Review*, April, 1941, pp. 230–231; and Connelly, Gordon K., "The Non-Voter — Who He Is, What He Thinks," *Public Opinion Quarterly*, Summer, 1944, pp. 175–187.

group included those who were "disgusted with politics," or those who, for other reasons, disbelieved in voting. Some were disgusted with their own party, some had the idea that one vote counts for nothing, while still others would not vote because they believed that the ballot box was corrupted. A small number avowed a disbelief in all political action. Finally, there were those who failed to vote because of general indifference and inertia; this was by far the largest group — 25 per cent of the whole. The more specific reasons cited by the members of this group were: indifference to a particular election; the fact that they had intended to vote, but had neglected to do so; ignorance or timidity regarding elections; and the failure of

RÉASONS FOR NOT VOTING GIVEN BY NONVOTERS INTERVIEWED [46]

Reasons for Not Voting	Number	Per Cent Distribution
ALL REASONS	5,310	100.0
PHYSICAL DIFFICULTIES		
Illness	647	12.1
Absence	589	11.1
Detained by helpless member of family	115	2.2
LEGAL AND ADMINISTRATIVE OBSTACLES		
Insufficient legal residence	274	5.2
Fear of loss of business or wages	289	5.5
Congestion at polls	44	0.8
Poor location of polling booth	45	0.8
Fear of disclosure of age	14	0.3
DISBELIEF IN VOTING		
Disbelief in woman's voting	414	7.8
Objections of husband	54	1.0
Disgust with politics	230	4.3
Disgust with own party	105	2.0
Belief that one vote counts for nothing	79	1.5
Belief that ballot box is corrupted	40	0.7
Disbelief in all political action	22	0.4
INERTIA		
General indifference	1,347	25.4
Indifference to particular election	129	2.5
Neglect: intended to vote but failed	448	8.4
Ignorance or timidity regarding elections	378	7.1
Failure of party workers	47	7.9

[46] Merriam and Gosnell, *op. cit.,* p. 34.

the party workers, for as one committeeman observed, " People don't vote for candidates; they vote for precinct leaders." These data are clearly summarized in the table on page 205.

Quite as important as the nonvoter is the voter, and the quality and the extent of his participation. A number of recent studies show a generally upward trend in voting. While the reasons for greater interest vary from one community to another, the following may be noted: The undermining of political machines in some cities has given voters greater confidence in the electoral process. The development of parties of approximately equal strength in others has made the outcome of an election no longer a foregone conclusion. The percentage of potential voters appears to be slightly increasing, while the decline in immigration has undoubtedly reduced the proportion of unnaturalized persons ineligible to vote.[47]

Compulsory Voting. If these are the facts with regard to voting and nonvoting, what can be done about them? It does little good to draw up a bill of particulars, unless at the same time thought is given to the development of suitable remedies. There are in fact several suggested solutions: compulsory voting, the development of a new program of civic education, and the adoption of measures that will to some extent lighten the task now imposed upon the voter.

Many people have urged that compulsory voting legislation should be adopted — that people ought to vote, and if they will not do so voluntarily, we should compel them to do so by imposing some sort of penalty. If such a law were enforced, hundreds of thousands of citizens in all of our large cities would be caught — 100,000 in Minneapolis, 400,000 in Philadelphia, where in a recent poll 74 per cent opposed the idea of fining nonvoters. There are, however, precedents for the successful operation of the plan in Australia and in several European countries. Against its adoption in the United States must be mentioned the fact that conditions here are different from those existing in the countries referred to, and that the idea of compelling people to discharge their obligation to participate in government seems contrary, not only to the temper of our people, but to the whole tradition of their history and government. It is, furthermore, exceedingly doubtful whether much would be gained by such a procedure, even if the people would support the enforce-

[47] See Heavenrich, Max P., Jr., *The Participation of Flint Citizens in Elections* (Flint Institute of Research and Planning, 1938) ; Hecock, Donald S., *Detroit Voters and Recent Elections* (Detroit Bureau of Governmental Research, 1938) ; Pollock, James K., *Voting Behavior: A Case Study* (Bureau of Governmental Research, University of Michigan, 1939) .

ment of the legislation. If the functioning of democracy is to be improved, what is needed is not so much a larger number of votes as a larger number of *intelligent* votes. If the present nonvoters are not well enough informed or sufficiently interested to vote under the existing laws, it is doubtful whether their votes cast under a system of compulsion would be worth very much.[48]

Simplified Ballot and Electoral Procedure. A second suggestion relates to the extension of the short ballot principle, the simplification of the electoral process, and the lightening of the burden now placed upon the voter. This has been discussed in the section devoted to the short ballot.

Citizen Training for Youth. Until recently we had no program of citizen training worthy of the name; our efforts were confined to inflicting upon children in the public schools that abomination known as " civics," which consisted largely in memorizing and repeating, with a kind of sacred inattention, the words of the Constitution. More recently students of political parties and public opinion have given the problem serious attention. Professor Merriam edited the valuable Civic Training Series, contributing to it the significant summary volume on *The Making of Citizens.* The American Political Science Association had a Committee on Civic Training which functioned for a number of years. It made some progress, and its efforts were supplemented by weekly radio broadcasts on a nationwide hook-up over a period of three years.

Recent developments have emphasized the induction of citizens, the training of young citizens, and the community plan of action for older citizens. In years past, immigrants about to be naturalized were herded into a court room and pronounced citizens by the judge, usually a few days before election. The ceremony had no dignity and little significance; later, civic groups did give some attention to the situation, decorating a suitable room, and making a dignified public ceremony out of the act of conferring citizenship. No one ever thought that the induction of young voters should be given public notice. Then came the Manitowoc Plan. Under the leadership of the Extension Division of the University of Wisconsin, citizens in Manitowoc County organized all of the young men and women who would come of voting age during the year in clubs. These clubs were required to hold a minimum number of meetings

[48] Short of actual compulsion there are practical methods of vote stimulation which have brought beneficial results; see Gosnell, Harold F., *Getting Out the Vote* and *Why Europe Votes* (University of Chicago Press, 1927 and 1930, respectively) .

for training and discussion, but many of them held several times the minimum specified. On citizenship day, public ceremonies were held at the county seat, in which all of the new voters participated. Every band and fife and drum corps in the county took part. Each club prepared a float for the parade, depicting some principle or some event significant in American history. At the mass meeting which followed, addresses were made by the chief justice of the state, the president of the state university, and various local dignitaries. Each new citizen was given a scroll signifying entrance into the status of citizenship.

The plan immediately attracted attention in other counties and in other states, as a result of which Congress passed and the President signed in 1940 a measure providing for Citizenship Week, which should serve in each cooperating jurisdiction as the culmination of the year's work in the education and training of new citizens. In other countries, and in other institutions like the church and fraternal groups, extensive use is made of ceremonialism and symbolism; it is anticipated that the cohesive power of these forms of social control will in the years to come be extensively utilized in the United States. Other forms of political organization have managed to tell their story effectively to young people; democracy must do so too if it wishes to survive.[49]

The techniques of " I Am an American Day " and Citizenship Week have been applied in other directions toward the accomplishment of the same end. Many states regularly observe, in addition to the traditional legal holidays, September 17th as Constitution Day, and the week in which that day falls as Constitution Week, celebrating both with appropriate observances. Illinois observes, by

[49] See " Citizenship Training and Induction of New Voters," *Bulletin* of the University of Wisconsin, May, 1939; Wilson, Richard C., " Citizenship Training in Wisconsin," *Wisconsin Blue Book*, 1942, pp. 169–175; also, for use in connection with such a program, Dorr, Harold M., and Litchfield, Edward H., *Facts about Your Job as a Voting Citizen* (Edwards Brothers, Ann Arbor, 1940) ; Bonar, Hugh S., *New Voter Preparation and Recognition* (National Education Association, Washington, 1940) ; Farber, William O., *" I Am an American Day " in South Dakota* (Governmental Research Bureau, University of South Dakota, 1942) ; and in the *National Municipal Review*, June, 1944, editorial, pp. 275–276, and " Rochester, N. Y., Welcomes New Citizens with Banquet " (59th affair in twenty-five years pays tribute to 459 naturalized citizens) , pp. 307–308.

A good many states have published citizenship training manuals, as for example, Ade, Lester K., *Pennsylvania Program of Literacy and Citizenship Education* (Department of Public Instruction, Harrisburg, 1938) ; Bratton, C. A., *Elections in New York State* (New York State College of Agriculture, Ithaca, 1943) ; Garvey, Neil F., and others, *Your Business as a Voter* (University of Illinois *Bulletin*, 1941) ; and Habermann, Philip S., *A Manual of Election Procedure in Maine* (Maine Municipal Association, Hallowell, 1942) .

proclamation of the governor, Americanism Week between the birth-days of Lincoln and Washington. In December, 1941, on the occasion of the 150th anniversary of the Bill of Rights, a week was observed throughout the country in commemoration of the framing of that instrument. These " days " and " weeks," if appropriately observed, can contribute greatly to the public understanding of and respect for American political institutions.

In many cases training projects for young people have been operated in the form of boys' states, boys' cities, model legislatures, model conferences, model political conventions, et cetera. While there is danger of a model being a " small imitation of the real thing," many of these projects have been well organized and effectively carried out. In some cases, high school and college instructors have taken their classes regularly to the city hall or the state legislature and have used the material there discussed as the basis for class work.[50] One of the best organized and most successful model student groups is the Pennsylvania Intercollegiate Conference on Government, which met annually at Harrisburg from 1934 to 1942, being interrupted by the war. Attended by some 250 or 300 students from some three or four score of colleges and universities in the state, it has met as a constitutional convention, a conference on interstate co-operation, a national party convention, and several times as a unicameral legislature. Only students participate, and they take an intense interest in the work. They begin their preparation several months prior to the meeting, and most of them are well prepared by the time of the Conference, whose motto is " not to teach, not to preach, but to learn by doing." From these sessions, extending over three days and including both committee work and plenary sessions, they gain an understanding of the realities of politics such as no amount of classroom instruction or work in the library can give them.[51]

Citizen Training for Adults. A number of interesting and impor-

[50] For descriptions of other projects of this type, see Hughes, James P., " Youth Takes a Fling at Politics," *National Municipal Review,* August, 1929, pp. 592–594; Matthews, Mark, " Young Men in Action," *ibid.,* January, 1941, pp. 8–11, 62; Morris Herbert C., " Youth Builds Today for a Better Tomorrow," *ibid.,* July, 1943, pp. 357–359; Weidner, Edward W., " Boy Legislature Plan Spreading," *ibid.,* June, 1944, pp. 283–286, 294.

[51] See Webb, Malcolm L., " Collegians Steal Legislators' Fire," *National Municipal Review,* July, 1936, pp. 412–416; Gerson, Leonard B., and Zipin, Irving J., " Learning by Doing," *ibid.,* July, 1940, pp. 451–458; and " Student Solons Demonstrate Cooperation," *State Government,* June, 1938. See also Ewing, Russell H., *Can the Colleges Train Civic Leaders?* (National Bureau of Civic Research, Los Angeles, 1944) , and Burdette, Franklin L., " Education for Citizenship," *Public Opinion Quarterly,* Summer, 1942, pp. 269–279.

tant projects in community action for adult citizens have been developed. Of these, the Citizens Fact Finding Movement of Georgia, with headquarters at Atlanta, may be taken as illustrative. Tired of hearing their state referred to as " backward," a group of citizens determined to do something about it. In the summer of 1937 a central council was established, in which were represented about 130 organizations of citizens, many of them statewide and including all types of interests — chambers of commerce, service clubs, manufacturers' groups, labor organizations, agricultural groups, fraternal orders, et cetera. This council worked out a plan, according to which one important aspect of the life of the state, such as agriculture, education, and health, should be given intensive study each month for a period of one year. The member groups cooperated by furnishing information and in disseminating the results of the study to their own members, after the central office staff had had an opportunity to digest it and write it up.

A survey made at the end of five years of operation disclosed " that 317,000 of the Movement's publications had been distributed, not sent out broadcast, but furnished upon request only. Records showed that they had gone into every incorporated community in the state, to forty-two other states, to the District of Columbia, Canada, England, Alaska, Hawaii, Puerto Rico, Cuba, Argentina, and Brazil." [52] Records further revealed that these publications were being widely used in the schools and colleges of the state and were to be found in practically all the libraries. The work thus done to inform the people of the state played no small part in the civic awakening which made possible the defeat at the polls of the unspeakable Talmadge regime and the election of the able, alert, and progressive Governor Ellis Arnall.

Ever since the United States Office of Education inaugurated its community forum program on an experimental basis in the early 1930's, the public forum and discussion group idea has spread rapidly in many communities throughout the country. Interesting instances of this development are to be found in the National Policy Committee with its local branches, and in Democratic Discussions, a statewide program carried on under the auspices of the New Jersey Education Association's Committee on Long-Time Planning. In 1943–1944, 37,593 persons, located in 152 different communities in

52 Wilkins, Josephine, " Georgians Take Stock," *National Municipal Review,* June, 1943, pp. 337–339; Cohn, David L., " Georgia: These Are the Facts," *Atlantic Monthly,* August, 1941, pp. 212–219; Daniels, Jonathan, " Georgians Discover Georgia," *Survey Graphic,* March, 1939, pp. 199–203.

the twenty-one counties of the state, participated in this program —
14,000 more than in the preceding year. Any individual who is interested can organize a group of his friends and neighbors. The office of the Director gives full instructions with regard to the organization and conduct of meetings. Discussion outlines are furnished free on a variety of topics in national, international, state, and local affairs.[53]

Among smaller communities, the Dowagiac Community Plan has produced significant results,[54] affecting the social, cultural, spiritual, and economic life of a small Michigan city with a population of 5,500 persons, plus some 2,000 more of rural population who use the town as a trading center. Every organization within the area is eligible to membership, with one representative each sitting in the Community Council. The Council elects an executive board of eighteen members, from the various social and economic strata of the community. The executive committee consists of the three officers — president, vice-president, and treasurer — elected by the board. The Council meets every other month, the board every month, and the executive committee on call. The Council has hired a director, whose function is that of guidance and coordination. The work is done largely by the people themselves. In the first year of the operation of the plan, more than 1,000 persons, young and old, aided in carrying on the various projects, which are many and varied.

Ideas are brought to the Community Council from the populace, to be discussed and considered. Selections are made with care, and are considered in the light of their past usefulness in that community and elsewhere, and in the light of the opportunity they afford for cooperative community action. Not more than a dozen different undertakings are in progress at any given time. The following list will indicate something of the nature of the work: recreation, youth programs, adult education, juvenile clinics, social gatherings, church cooperation, economic betterment, vocational improvement, community music, rural education, charity drives, health services, rural-urban unity, and a number of other things. During the year 1938–1939 some two dozen projects under as many committees were carried out.

A Program for the Future. Any program of civic training and

---

[53] In addition to the discussion outlines, see *Democratic Discussions,* and *37,000 Think and Act* (New Jersey Education Association, Trenton, 1943 and 1944). The first of these is a record of activity in 1943–1944, the second a handbook for associates.

[54] Dowagiac Community Plan, *Biennial Report, a Summary of Activities,* September, 1938, to May, 1940 (Dowagiac, 1940).

citizen action, if it is to be reasonably successful, must begin with children at an early age and continue through adult life. Too long have we taken democracy for granted — too long have we assumed that democracy obviously justifies itself without explanation or effort on our part. President Dykstra some years ago outlined an excellent ten-point program:

1. First of all, a faith that our fathers were right, a faith in ourselves and in our destiny.
2. A national goal for which to strive and a willingness to sacrifice for it. To save ourselves, we must lose ourselves in a cause.
3. Some fair distribution of opportunity and the chance to succeed.
4. The elimination of special privilege by which fortunate or greedy persons or groups use power of any kind to take advantage of others. Greed is always cancerous and corrupting.
5. The development of national unity out of selfish localisms and sectionalisms.
6. The promotion of really representative governments, local and national, which will consider without fear or favor the vital interests of the American people.
7. The recruiting of some of the best ability in the nation to manage the things we require of our government.
8. Recognition of the need for a plan of nation-wide proportions which will use our man power, our resources, and our idle funds constructively in the national interest.
9. Putting our historical bill of rights to work everywhere. Democracy cannot live unless civil liberties live.
10. An intelligent and educated electorate conscious of its privileges and responsibilities.[55]

In the effort to take stock of the existing situation and to formulate ways and means of achieving these objectives of democracy, the National Municipal League summoned in May, 1940, a National Conference on Self Government at Indiana University. The conference adopted a statement of findings, following a two-day discussion, and a series of suggestions, recommending that suitable means be adopted for carrying their suggestions into effect on a continuing basis.[56] Partly as an outgrowth of this conference, although it had been under consideration for several years, there was established late in 1940 the National Foundation for Education in American Citizenship, organized by a group of citizens and educators acting

[55] Dykstra, Clarence A., " We Thought the Battle Won! " *National Municipal Review*, December, 1939, pp. 821–823, 892; also Governmental Research Association, *Citizens in the Dark — Cities in the Red* (Detroit, 1940) ; and Pollock, James K., " Plea for an Informed Citizenry," *National Municipal Review*, September, 1940, pp. 590–592.

[56] For text, see *National Municipal Review*, June, 1940, pp. 356–358.

with college and university trustees and boards of education. The chief purpose among a number of others is " to encourage and promote more effective education in citizenship and the administration of government." Other similar organizations are springing up in various parts of the country. In 1944, under the leadership of Russell H. Ewing, the National Bureau of Civic Research was established in Los Angeles, while in 1945, the work carried on for many years by Charles O. Frye led to the establishment of the American Citizenship Foundation, in Newark, New Jersey. In this same year, the American Political Science Association, through its Executive Council, authorized the establishment of a committee to study the problems involved in citizen organization and participation in government. Truly it may be said that there is a new interest in citizenship and government abroad in the land.

SELECTED REFERENCES

Ascoli, Max, *Intelligence in Politics* (George J. McLeod, New York, 1936).

Barnett, James D., *The Operation of the Initiative, Referendum, and Recall in Oregon* (Macmillan, New York, 1915).

Beard, Charles A., and Shultz, Bird E., *Documents of the State-wide Initiative, Referendum, and Recall* (Macmillan, New York, 1912).

Bird, Frederick L., and Ryan, Frances M., *The Recall of Public Officers* (Macmillan, New York, 1930).

Boardman, Norma, *A Study of the League of South Dakota Municipalities* (University of South Dakota, Governmental Research Bureau, 1944).

California Chamber of Commerce, *Initiative Legislation in California* (San Francisco, 1940).

Colorado Legislative Reference Office, *The Initiative and Referendum in Colorado* (Denver, 1940).

Council of State Governments, *Constitutional Amendments and Direct Legislation, 1940* (Chicago, 1940).

Crouch, Winston W., *The Initiative and Referendum in California* (Haynes Foundation, Los Angeles, 1943).

Dorr, Harold M., and Litchfield, Edward H., *Facts about Your Job as a Voting Citizen* (Edwards Brothers, Ann Arbor, 1940).

Ewing, Russell H., *Civic Organization and Leadership: The Science of Community Action* (To be published in 1946).

——, Ed., *A Symposium on Civic Organization: The Answer to Politi-Bosses and Machines* (To be published in 1946).

Farber, William O., *" I Am an American Day " in South Dakota* (University of South Dakota, Governmental Research Bureau, 1942).

Gill, Norman N., *Municipal Research Bureaus, A Study of the Nation's Leading Citizen-Supported Agencies* (American Council on Public Affairs, Washington, 1944).

Gosnell, Harold F., *Getting Out the Vote* (University of Chicago Press, 1927).

——, *Why Europe Votes* (University of Chicago Press, 1930).

Governmental Research Association, *Governmental Research and Citizen Control of Government* (Detroit, January, 1940).

Griffith, Ernest S., *The Impasse of Democracy* (Smith and Durrell, New York, 1939).

Gulick, Luther, *Votes in New York City on Referenda, 1920–1934, Inclusive* (Institute of Public Administration, New York, 1936).

Hallett, George H., Jr., *Proportional Representation* (National Home Library Foundation, Washington, 1937).

Harris, Joseph P., *Practical Workings of Proportional Representation in the United States and Canada,* supplement to *National Municipal Review,* May, 1930.

Heavenrich, Max P., Jr., *The Participation of Flint Citizens in Elections* (Flint Institute of Research and Planning, Flint, 1938).

Hecock, Donald S., *Detroit Voters and Recent Elections* (Detroit Bureau of Governmental Research, Detroit, 1938).

Hermens, F. A., *Democracy or Anarchy: A Study of Proportional Representation* (University of Notre Dame, 1941).

Hoag, Clarence G., and Hallett, George H., Jr., *Proportional Representation* (Macmillan, New York, 1929).

Kayanan, A. G., *Neighborhood Conservation: A Handbook for Citizen Groups* (Regional Association of Cleveland, 1943).

Key, V. O., Jr., and Crouch, Winston W., *The Initiative and Referendum in California* (University of California Press, 1939).

Lowell, A. Lawrence, *Public Opinion and Popular Government* (Longmans, Green, New York, 1921).

Luce, Robert, *Legislative Principles* (Houghton Mifflin, Boston, 1930).

McCarthy, Charles, *The Wisconsin Idea* (Macmillan, New York, 1912).

Merriam, Charles E., and Gosnell, Harold F., *Non-Voting, Causes and Methods of Control* (University of Chicago Press, 1924).

National Association of Secretaries of State, *Conference Proceedings, 1944* (Chicago, 1945).

National Municipal League, *The Cincinnati Plan: Citizen Organization for Political Activity* (New York, 1941).

Pollock, James K., *The Initiative and Referendum in Michigan* (University of Michigan, Bureau of Government, 1940).

——, *Voting Behavior: A Case Study* (University of Michigan, Bureau of Government, 1939).

Steinbicker, Paul G., and Faust, Martin L., *Manual on Amending Procedure and the Initiative and Referendum* (Missouri Constitutional Convention of 1943, Columbia, 1943).

Taft, Charles P., *The City Manager* (Farrar and Rinehart, New York, 1933).

Tharp, Claude R., *Control of Local Finances through Taxpayers' Associations and Centralized Administration* (M. Ford Publishing Company, Indianapolis, 1933).

University of Michigan, *Direct Government in Michigan* (Bureau of Government, 1940).

University of Wisconsin Bulletin, *Citizenship Training and Induction of New Voters* (Madison, 1939).

Zeitlin, Josephine V., *Initiative and Referendum: A Bibliography* (Haynes Foundation, Los Angeles, 1940).

——, *Recall: a Bibliography* (Haynes Foundation, Los Angeles, 1941).

———

Atkins, Richard A., and Ziegler, Lyman H., " Citizen Budgeting in Massachusetts," *National Municipal Review*, October, 1941, pp. 568–573.

Burdette, Franklin L., " Education for Citizenship," *Public Opinion Quarterly,* Summer, 1942, pp. 269–279.

Bush, Merrill E., " A People's Institute for Post-War Planning," *National Municipal Review,* April, 1942, pp. 175–179.

Community Service, Inc., *Community Service News* (Yellow Springs, Ohio, bi-monthly).

Connelly, Gordon M., " The Non-Voter — Who He Is, What He Thinks," *Public Opinion Quarterly*, Summer, 1944, pp. 175–187.

Crouch, Winston W., " The Initiative and Referendum in Cities," *American Political Science Review*, June, 1943, pp. 491–504.

Dorr, Harold M., " The Nanson System: A Michigan Experiment in Voting," *Papers* of the Michigan Academy of Science, Arts and Letters, 1942, pp. 613–621.

Draper, Mary, and others, " Fighting Front on Main Street," *National Municipal Review,* January, 1943, pp. 6–11.

Drury, James W., " History and Services of the Illinois Municipal League," *Illinois Municipal Review,* September, 1940, pp. 174–182.

Eliot, Charles W., " Citizen Support for Planning and Development," *Civic Planning and Comment,* April, 1945.

Evans, S. Howard, " Citizen Action through Community Councils," *National Municipal Review*, February, 1941, pp. 43–45.

Gains, Frank S., " A City Goes to Town Meeting," *National Municipal Review,* October, 1940, pp. 643–647.

Gerson, Leonard B., and Zipin, Irving J., " Learning through Doing," *National Municipal Review,* July, 1940, pp. 451–458.

Grace, Alonzo G., " Developing Responsible Citizens," *National Municipal Review,* February, 1942, pp. 88–91.

——, " From the Bottom Up," *National Municipal Review,* January, 1941, pp. 16–21.

High, Stanley, " Kansas City Has Its Chin Up," *National Municipal Review,* October, 1941, pp. 561–564.

Jones, O. Garfield, " Is the Short Ballot Principle Obsolete? " *National Municipal Review,* April, 1943, pp. 185–187, 189.

Josslin, William L., " Oregon Educates Its Voters," *National Municipal Review,* July, 1943, pp. 373–379.

Kalijarvi, Thorsten V., " New Hampshire Institute of Public Affairs," *State Government,* August, 1941, pp. 194–196.

Kline, Howard M., " Citizen Groups in Review," *National Municipal Review,* October, 1941, pp. 574–578, 612.

Kneier, Charles M., " Citizen Economy Movements: Why and How," *National Municipal Review,* August, 1940, pp. 535–539.

Langmuir, John D., " Taxpayer Groups Stress Concrete Accomplishments," *National Municipal Review,* March, 1940, pp. 210–212.

Larson, Cedric, " The Council for Democracy," *Public Opinion Quarterly,* Summer, 1942, pp. 284–290.

Lewis, John D., " Elements of Democracy," *American Political Science Review,* June, 1940, pp. 467–480.

Lex, William B., " Citizens, Schools Cooperate on Election Project," *National Municipal Review,* January, 1944, pp. 37–39.

Martin, Edward M., " Chicago's Union League Club Sponsors Many Sided Program," *National Municipal Review,* May, 1943, pp. 265–267.

Nelson, Joesphine, " Business Women in a Democracy," *National Municipal Review,* November, 1940, pp. 714–719.

Pollock, James K., " New Thoughts on the Short Ballot," *National Municipal Review,* January, 1940, pp. 18–20, 47.

——, " Plea for an Informed Citizenry," *National Municipal Review,* September, 1940, pp. 590–592.

Price, Don K., " The Promotion of the City Manager Plan," *Public Opinion Quarterly,* Winter, 1941, pp. 563–578.

Riesman David, " Government Education for Democracy," *Public Opinion Quarterly,* June, 1940, pp. 195–209.

Roher, Miriam, " Editor Puts Civics on Page One," *National Municipal Review,* March, 1940, pp. 156–163.

——, " Education of a Citizen," *National Municipal Review,* April, 1941, pp. 192–198.

Seed, Allen H., Jr., " Minneapolis Town Halls Draw 22,000," *National Municipal Review,* July, 1940, pp. 494–498.

Selig, John M., " San Francisco Voters Prove Sound Lawmakers," *National Municipal Review,* October, 1943, pp. 486–492.

Spencer, Richard C., " State Proposals Voted Upon in 1944," *Elections: 1944,* April, 1945 (U. S. Bureau of the Census).

——, " Army and Navy Voting in 1944," *Elections: 1944,* April, 1945 (U. S. Bureau of the Census).

Tugwell, Rexford G., " Implementing the Public Interest," *Public Administration Review,* Autumn, 1940, pp. 32–49.

Wells, Herman B., " New Frontiers," *National Municipal Review,* January, 1941, pp. 12–15.

Wichman, William C., " Kenosha Citizens in Action," *National Municipal Review,* March, 1940, pp. 164–173.

Wilson, M. L., " Rural America Discusses Democracy," *Public Opinion Quarterly,* June, 1941, pp. 288–294.

Part Three

THE PROCESS OF LAWMAKING

CHAPTER VI

The State Legislature: Organization

HISTORICAL DEVELOPMENT

THE antecedents of the present state legislatures include the colonial assemblies, the territorial legislatures, and those established under the constitutions adopted during the present governmental regime. Colonial assemblies existed in the thirteen original colonies, which were in time to become charter members of the Federal Union. Territorial legislatures developed in each of the other jurisdictions ultimately admitted into the Union as states. The early state legislatures immediately succeeded the colonial assemblies of the original states and the territorial assemblies of states admitted during the early constitutional period. Since that time the most outstanding group of legislatures which might warrant separate consideration here were those of the southern states during the period of reconstruction.

The Colonial Legislatures. The colonial legislatures were, for the most part, miniature reproductions of the British Parliament. In their history two facts stand out clearly: first, the lower house was almost constantly engaged in serious controversy with the executive; second, in the assembly there developed a form of unofficial party control more important than the organization provided for in the rules.[1] As noted earlier in a quotation from Professor Becker, it was the desire of the colonists to model their lives, their thinking, their culture, and their governmental institutions after the best approved English models. If there was in England a struggle between the Crown and Parliament with regard to taxation and finance, then they in their representative assemblies must wage a struggle with the

---

[1] Harlow, Ralph V., *The History of Legislative Methods in the Period before 1825* (Yale University Press, 1927).

Royal Governors regarding the same questions. Not only did these assemblies reproduce certain characteristics of the English system, but they came more and more to reflect accurately the temper of the colonists themselves. We have seen how their repeated protests against oppressive acts of the British authorities won them the complete confidence of the colonial citizens whose interests they sought to protect.

The Territorial Legislatures. By the time we had achieved independence and had come to face the problem of establishing legislative bodies in the territories, the influence of the English tradition had to some extent declined. The controlling influence in modeling the territorial assemblies was that of the older states along the Atlantic seaboard, from which the majority of the settlers in the western country had migrated. Those who are familiar with the thesis of Frederick J. Turner regarding the significance of the frontier in American history will not require any further discussion of this point.[2] Thus Congress apparently found no reason for changing the Wisconsin plan when setting up the legislature for the Territory of Iowa in 1838. This assembly consisted of thirty-nine members, thirteen of whom formed the Council and twenty-six the House of Representatives. With regard to such matters as the qualifications of members, the filling of vacancies, contested elections, term of office, oath, compensation, privileges, and immunities, the territorial legislatures were not substantially different from the state legislatures which followed them.[3] Many of these territorial legislatures were in existence for only a few years.

The Early State Legislatures. The organization and powers of the early state legislatures continued much as they had been during the preceding regime — colonial or territorial. Those which came into existence at the time the present institutions of government were established, or soon after, enjoyed to an extraordinary degree the respect and confidence of the people, and were consequently intrusted with wide powers. In North Carolina, all officers of importance were elected by the legislature, including judges and justices of the peace. The governor had not even the right to call the legisla-

[2] Turner, Frederick J., *The Frontier in American History* (Holt, New York, 1920). The original statement on this thesis was contained in his presidential address delivered before the American Historical Association in 1896.

[3] State histories available in most of the states give some information regarding the territorial and early state legislatures. A good account of the history and organization of the legislature in Iowa, by John E. Briggs, will be found in Shambaugh, Benjamin F., Ed., *Statute Law-Making in Iowa*, pp. 1–135 (State Historical Society of Iowa, Iowa City, 1916).

ture in special session in time of emergency. In Virginia, one of the gravest defects of the constitution was its grant of disproportionate powers to the legislature, especially to the lower chamber. " The latter alone could originate enactments, and though the Senate could defeat any bill, it could not amend appropriation measures. The two houses elected the principal state officers, including judges, and determined all salaries. The governor was pitifully weak, and could not even call the legislature without his council's consent." [4] These conditions were general, but for reasons that will presently be indicated the legislatures began to forfeit the right to this confidence, and in the course of time drastic limitations were imposed upon their powers.

Reconstruction Legislatures in the South. During the period of reconstruction the legislatures of the southern states, through the influence of carpetbaggers from the North and scalawags from the South, sank to almost unbelievable depths of degradation. The membership — black and white — was for the most part of the lowest type. Gambling, drunkenness, and vice characterized the private lives of a majority of members; graft, fraud, and corruption, their public life. It is difficult to exaggerate the extent to which these conditions prevailed, and they were common to all the southern states. Claude G. Bowers vividly describes some of them in the following paragraphs:

And even worse was Louisiana. . . . The Legislature we find sitting in Mechanics Hall is typical of the others we have seen in the land of jubilee. . . . The lobbies teem with laughing negroes from the plantations, with whites of the pinch-faced, parasitic type. . . . The abysmally ignorant eschew debate. . . . It is a monkey-house — with guffaws, disgusting interpolations, amendments offered that are too obscene to print, followed by shouts of glee. Bad in the beginning, the travesty grows worse. The vulgarity of the speeches increases; members stagger from the basement bar to their seats. The Speaker in righteous mood sternly forbids the introduction of liquor on the floor. A curious old planter stands in the galleries a moment looking down upon the scene, and with an exclamation, " My God! " he turns and runs, as from a pestilence, into the street. Visitors from the North organize " slumming expeditions " to the Legislature or go as to a zoo. A British member of Parliament, asking if there are any curiosities in the city, is taken forthwith to Mechanics Hall. Corruption is inevitable, and members openly charged with bribery are not offended. . . .

Worst of all, perhaps, was South Carolina:

[4] Nevins, Allan, *The American States During and After the Revolution, 1775-1789,* pp. 142, 148 (Macmillan, New York, 1924) .

Meanwhile, amid the cracking of peanuts, the shouting, laughing, stamping, members are seen leaving and returning in a strange state of exaltation — they come and go in streams . . . to the room adjoining the office of the clerk of the Senate [which] is open from eight in the morning till two or four the next morning, and now, as we push in, it is crowded. A bar-room! Solons are discussing politics over sparkling glasses of champagne, supplied by taxpayers. Here gallons of wine and whiskey are consumed daily. Members enter blear-eyed in the early morning for an eye-opener or a nightcap — some are too drunk to leave at 4 A.M. Champagne? Wine? Whiskey? Gin? Porter? Ale? — and the member orders to his taste. Does a special brand of liquor or fine cigars appeal especially? Boxes are ordered to the member's hotel or boarding house. " One box of champagne, one box port wine, one box whiskey, one box brandy, one box sherry wine, three boxes cigars " — this the order from one negro member. When the Chairman of the Claims Committee found one box of wine delivered to his lodgings, he indignantly wrote: " This is a mistake; the order calls for two boxes of wine. Please send the other." None but the finest brand of cigars were tolerated, and members, leaving, usually filled their pockets. Because of the visitors, lobbyists, State officials, enough liquor was consumed to have given each member a gallon daily, with no less than a dozen cigars. . . .

Thus stealing was a virtue, with decent citizens submerged and silenced. The only public opinion necessary to conciliate was that of thieves. Robbers included men in politics and out. Public officials made common cause against the Treasury. . . . To sustain the system a party press was required; the corruptionists created one, and then stole public funds to subsidize it. . . . The corruption in State bonds, criminally issued and divided among official gangsters, mounted into the millions, but bribery and bond-looting was not enough for this avaricious horde, which had recourse to the pay certificate steals. With thirty-five attachés in the Senate, pay certificates were issued for 350. . . . When bribery, illegal bonds, pay certificates did not suffice, the thieves bethought themselves of furnishing the State House. Within four years a people on the verge of bankruptcy was forced to put out more than $200,000 for the purpose. There was a $750 mirror to reflect the dissipated face of Moses, clocks for members in their private rooms at $480, and 200 cuspidors at $8.00 each, for the use of 124 members. The quarters of Moses at Mrs. Randall's rooming-house were elegantly furnished at the State's expense. And yet, on the expulsion of the Radicals from power, there was less than $18,000 in furniture to account for the $200,000 spent; the rest in the homes of the members and their mistresses.[5]

The Legislatures from 1875 to 1925. The decline of public confidence in the legislatures continued through the years preceding the

[5] Bowers, Claude G., *The Tragic Era* (Houghton Mifflin, Boston, 1929). Quotation on Louisiana, pp. 362–364; on South Carolina, pp. 354–357. For a contrary view, see the works by DuBois, and Allen, cited in Chapter IV; also Beale, Howard K., " On Rewriting Reconstruction History," *American Historical Review*, July, 1940, pp. 807–827.

Civil War, during the War, and in the years which immediately followed it. Conditions in the South were abnormal, but there was little about the conduct of the legislatures in other states to inspire confidence. At the outset of the period under consideration there spread through the states a move to impose vigorous constitutional restrictions upon the powers of the legislatures. State constitutions were revised at this time, as in Illinois in 1870 and Pennsylvania in 1873. These states are still suffering from the effects of the unwise limitations then imposed. The situation during this fifty-year period did not greatly change; the year 1925 marks approximately the beginning of the modern period. By that time the American Legislators' Association (now the Council of State Governments) had been organized, and due largely to its constructive work, a movement to improve the quality of the legislative output and to restore public confidence in legislative bodies began. This movement has already brought important results.

THE BICAMERAL AND UNICAMERAL SYSTEMS

For approximately a century the bicameral system of legislative organization enjoyed a universal acceptance throughout the United States; this had not always been so, nor is it entirely true today. While the bicameral plan has always been in the ascendancy, there were in the early days a number of cases in which the unicameral form was used. The colonial legislative bodies in Delaware and Pennsylvania were unicameral. When, following the Declaration of Independence, governments were organized in the several states, bicameral systems were established in all but Georgia, Pennsylvania, and Vermont. Georgia changed to a bicameral system in 1789, Pennsylvania in 1790, while in Vermont the change was delayed until 1836.

In 1784 the Committee on the Defects and Alterations of the Constitution in Pennsylvania recommended the change to the bicameral form because (1) there was an insufficient check on the proceedings of a single house, and (2) an uncontrolled power of legislation would enable the legislature to usurp judicial and executive authority. In the conclusions of a study of the unicameral legislature of Vermont for the nearly sixty years of its existence, Professor Carroll has this to say on the relative merits of the two systems of legislative organization:

Judged in the light of present-day use of the unicameral system and in the light of experience with that system in Vermont and elsewhere, the contention that the superiority of the bicameral system had been proved by the experience of all ages is interesting, but it has very little, if any, validity. Certainly, there is nothing in the experience of Vermont which justifies any such assumption of superiority.

While the arguments of those who advocated the adoption of the bicameral system in Vermont do not stand up well under searching investigation, the contentions of the Vermont leaders who opposed the change — (a) that the people were happy and prosperous, satisfied with the existing scheme, and indignant because of the proposed change, (b) that the proposed change would eliminate the unicameral system, which was the best feature of the existing constitution, (c) that it would increase the cost of government and the tax burden of the people, (d) that it would lengthen the legislative sessions without giving any compensating benefit, (e) that it would remove the government farther from the people, and (f) that it was not necessary to have a governmental organization like that of other states — appear to be amply justified.[6]

Attempts at Unicameralism in the Twentieth Century. The wide acceptance of the bicameral plan was originally based upon the belief that in a two-chamber system one body would act as a check upon and would correct the mistakes of the other. While this idea might seem reasonable and logical, the practice of the bicameral system has contributed little or no evidence in support of this theory. On the contrary, large numbers of instances indicate that politicians have played one house against the other to defeat proposals for which there was a wide public demand, and that they have in this way succeeded in avoiding personal responsibility for their action. Furthermore, the extensive number of poorly drawn statutes, filled with mistakes, with provisions that are sometimes meaningless and sometimes ridiculous, furnish abundant evidence of the failure of one house to act as an effective check upon the other. The use of the bicameral system might conceivably be justified by a difference in the representative character of the two houses. No such difference exists today; the members of both are selected by popular vote, the only difference being that the districts are somewhat larger and the terms somewhat longer in one case than in the other.

No important attempt to secure the adoption of a unicameral system was made from 1925 to 1934. Prior to the entry of the United States into the World War, and occasionally thereafter, the question

6 Carroll, Daniel R., *The Unicameral Legislature in Vermont*, p. 75 (Vermont Historical Society, Montpelier, 1933). See also Watt, Irma A., " Why Pennsylvania Abandoned Unicameralism," *State Government,* March, 1936, pp. 54–55, and *Massachusetts Law Quarterly,* April, 1936, pp. 57–59.

was submitted to the voters. It was submitted in Ohio and Oregon in 1912, and in other states from then on for several years, as indicated in the following table: [7]

STATE-WIDE REFERENDA ON UNICAMERALISM

1912   Ohio; Oregon (also in 1914)
1913   California (also in 1915, 1917, 1921, 1923, and 1925) ; Kansas; Nebraska (also in 1915 and 1919–1920)
1914   Oklahoma
1915   Alabama; Arizona (also in 1916) ; Washington (also in 1917)
1916   ——
1917   South Dakota (also in 1923 and 1925)

The Governors of Arizona, Kansas, and Washington in 1913 recommended constitutional amendments providing for a single-chamber system, and in the years immediately following, legislative committees in California, Michigan, Nebraska, and Washington recommended similar action. In most cases where the proposition was submitted to the voters, it was defeated by a majority of two to one, or more. Then in 1934 the voters of Nebraska, under the leadership of Senator Norris, voted to adopt such a change, to be effective as of January, 1937. The results have been watched with interest throughout the country; in fact, for several years thereafter numerous proposals of this character were introduced in the state legislatures.

The Nebraska Experiment. The transition from a bicameral to a unicameral system requires considerable time and a great deal of work; in Nebraska, several hundred amendments to existing statutes had to be made to bring the laws of the state in harmony with the new legislative set-up. The constitutional amendment authorized a body of not more than fifty members; the legislature of 1935 divided the state into forty-three districts, and in 1936 the first unicameral body was elected on a nonpartisan ballot for a term of two years. Thirteen of the new legislators were senators, fifteen of them representatives in the last bicameral body. They wisely devoted considerable time to organization, as a result of which a number of important changes were made, as compared with the bicameral form: [8]

1. Establishment of a legislative council, consisting of fifteen members of the Legislature, to frame a program of legislation between sessions.

[7] See Senning, John P., *The One-House Legislature* (McGraw-Hill, New York, 1937) , and Shull, Charles W., *American Experience with Unicameral Legislatures* (Detroit Bureau of Governmental Research, 1937) .
[8] See New York State Constitutional Convention Committee, *Problems Relating to Legislative Organization and Powers,* Chapter 2 (Albany, 1938) .

2. Requirement of public hearings, with five days advance notice, on all bills before passage.
3. Reduction of the number of committees from thirty-two in the Senate and thirty-six in the House to a total of sixteen, with a regular committee schedule so arranged that no member was on two committees meeting at the same time.
4. Publicity for all committee hearings as well as regular sessions.
5. Consideration of each bill after its report from the committee and before final passage at three sessions separated by at least three and two days respectively, with careful consideration of its drafting by a Committee on Enrollment and review after each of the first two considerations.
6. Requirement that every bill without exception be on the members' desks in final printed form for at least one full day before final passage.
7. Abolition of the Committee of the Whole with its *viva voce* votes and establishment of the right of any member to require a record roll call on any motion at any stage of the proceedings.
8. Employment for the session of three non-member counselors to consider the constitutionality of doubtful measures and creation for future sessions of the office of constitutional reviewer, to be appointed by the legislative council, who will give opinions on constitutionality and validity on the request of any member at any stage of the proceedings.
9. Establishment of the office of permanent secretary to the Legislature.

For purposes of comparison, a statistical summary covering certain essential points in the last bicameral and the first unicameral sessions is presented here:

The Nebraska Legislature

	1935, Bicameral	1937, Unicameral
Cost	$202,500	$150,000
Bills introduced	1,056	581
Bills passed	192	226
Vetoes	6	18
Length of session (days)	110	98

It is difficult to evaluate the Nebraska experiment in the short time it has been in operation; in general, those who favored its adoption are gratified at the result, while some of those who opposed it have changed their attitude. Professor Senning reported that the first session demonstrated an " absence of hasty legislation; a simplified and smoothly working procedure; . . . a better personnel; . . . the liberation of the legislature from the domination of the governor as the titular head of his party, and of the leaders of the political parties; and the general publicity by means of which the unicameral legislature has revived an interest among the people of the state in their lawmaking body." [9]

Future Prospects of Unicameralism. Mention has already been made of the revived interest in unicameralism since the action of the Nebraska electorate. The possibilities of the plan should be seriously considered in other states, in view of their " insulated laboratory " character. It is not certain that the plan will do all that its supporters have claimed for it; it does not necessarily touch the problems of legislative planning or of scientific bill drafting — which are perhaps the two most important problems now confronting the legislatures. The existing legislatures are, however, much too large. Serious weaknesses have developed in the operation of the bicameral system. In the large cities, the substitution of a small unicameral council for the old-fashioned large, bicameral body has been productive of much good. The experience of the Canadian provinces is also reassuring. While the conditions there differ in many respects from those in the United States, those provinces which formerly operated bicameral systems similar to our own and have substituted single chambers for them have found that the single chambers do better work and maintain public confidence and support better than the old bicameral bodies did. The experts who drafted the first Model State Constitution in 1921 recommended this change, and the recommendation has been carried on in each succeeding draft. On the other hand, it is interesting and may be important that in a nationwide poll conducted by the American Legislators' Association in 1934, only 41 per cent were in favor of one house, while 59 per cent were opposed. When, in such a poll,

9 Senning, John P., " Nebraska's First Unicameral Legislative Session," *Annals,* January, 1938, pp. 159–167. The mass of literature on this subject has of late been enormous. Some of the more important titles are cited in the footnotes and selected references; for a list of 194 titles, see Fuller, Grace S., *List of References on One Chamber and Two Chamber Legislatures* (Library of Congress, Division of Bibliography, 1937) ; Detroit Public Library, *Unicameral Legislatures, A Selected List of References* (Detroit, 1937) ; and Seager, Marguerite, *Legislative Processes: Selected Bibliography* (University of Southern California Institute of Government, 1938). Some of the most recent comments on this subject are The Citizens League, " Ten Years Test of a One House Legislature," *Greater Cleveland,* March 2, 1944, pp. 1–3; Dobbins, Harry T., " Nebraska's One House Legislature — After Six Years," *National Municipal Review,* September, 1941, pp. 511–514; Morganthau, Hans J., Ed., " Constitutional Reform in Missouri," *University of Kansas City Law Review,* December, 1942, entire issue; Senning, John P., " Unicameralism Passes Test," *National Municipal Review,* February, 1944, pp. 58–65; Trimble, Bruce R., and Stamps, Norman L., *The Structure of the Legislature: Bicameralism v. Unicameralism* (Missouri Constitutional Convention of 1943, Jefferson City, 1943).

85 per cent of the members of the American Political Science Association voted for the change, and the legislators voted against it by percentages almost as large, one wonders whether there may not be in the situation certain practical difficulties and objections to which students of government have not ascribed sufficient weight.[10]

REPRESENTATIVE CHARACTER

In general, the state legislatures are a good cross section of the American public; if they are not of as high caliber as one might wish, it may be because they are actually representative in character. It is proposed to consider here a number of phases of this question, such as the extent to which these bodies are representative of the professional and vocational interests of the general public, the extent to which urban and rural elements of the population are accurately represented, and the general question of the relations of legislators and their constituents.

Professional Classification. In recent years some attention has been paid to the representative character of the legislatures from the point of view of the business and professional affiliations of their members. Certain significant facts are evident when the effort is made to analyze the results of a professional classification of the personnel of some typical legislatures. It is clear that over a period of years one will find in such legislatures representatives of all the types of business, trades, and professions by which the members of an American community secure their livelihood, as well as persons with every conceivable educational, social, and economic background. Commenting on this fact, the authors of a standard text on American government observe:

Every degree of education is found, and in some legislatures the proportion of members who have had a high school, college, or university education is at times considerably greater than that prevailing among the people generally. Almost every profession is represented, and almost every conceivable business activity, although lawyers and farmers usually outnumber the members of other vocations. "With the farmer sits the artisan, with the banker sits the union labor agitator, with the manufacturer sits the small shopkeeper, with the preacher sits the saloon-keeper, with the professional specialist sits the Jack-of-all-trades."

10 Reported in *State Government*, October, 1934. Ballots were sent to over 6,400 persons, including all the members of Congress and of the Nebraska legislature, all the state senators, 1,900 state representatives, and sample groups of the bar, business, labor, bankers, newspaper editors, political scientists, the League of Women Voters, and the American Association of University Women.

The majority are men in the prime of life, between forty and sixty years of age; although now and then a young men barely a voter, or an octogenarian, appears. Every phase and degree of political experience is also represented: "Those who have been only voters, those who make politics a business; those who are politically torpid; the conservative and the demagogue — all are intermingled in these representative bodies. Even foreign-born citizens are well represented." And since the adoption of national woman suffrage, women legislators have appeared in increasing numbers. In the elections of 1924, nine women were elected to state senates, and no less than 106 to memberships in lower houses.[11]

It is, however, evident that there is a disproportionately large number of lawyers and farmers. The presence of these two groups in such large numbers has a significant bearing upon the character of the work done by legislatures.

Lawyers as Legislators. The following comments on lawyer legislators are not made with any known prejudice against an old and distinguished profession, the members of which have frequently made important contributions to the development of our governmental institutions. An impartial observer must admit, however, that these lawyers are not, for the most part, the ablest men in their profession. However much we may deplore the fact, the ablest lawyers are usually too busy with a lucrative practice to be able to give the time necessary for legislative work. With the exception of a few lawyers whose liking for politics and whose spirit of public service make them willing to undergo a considerable financial sacrifice, and a few able young lawyers not yet established who undertake legislative work for the purpose of developing contacts and acquaintances as a means of professional advancement, one is usually justified in the assumption that most of those members who classify

11 Ogg, Frederic A., and Ray, P. Orman, *Introduction to American Government.* Eighth Edition, p. 745 (Appleton-Century, New York, 1945). For an analysis of the composition of the state legislatures, see *Book of the States,* 1945–1946, pp. 105–113, and White, Howard, "Do Representatives Represent?" *National Municipal Review,* March, 1938, pp. 165–166. The following analyses in individual states have come to the author's attention: CALIFORNIA: McHenry, Dean E., "Legislative Personnel in California," *Annals,* January, 1938, pp. 45–52. FLORIDA: Schuck, Victoria, "Dissecting Florida's Legislature," *State Government,* March, 1940, pp. 45–46. KENTUCKY: Jones, J. Catron, "The Make-up of a State Legislature," *American Political Science Review,* February, 1931, pp. 116–119. MISSOURI: Lang, Howard B., Jr., "They Legislate for Missouri," *Annals,* January, 1938, pp. 40–44. OHIO: Orth, Samuel P., "Our State Legislatures," *Atlantic Monthly,* March, 1904, pp. 728–739. NEBRASKA: *Nebraska Legislative Manual, 1935,* "Occupations of Members of Legislature, 1901–1933," pp. 76–81. OREGON: Schumacher, Waldo, "Oregon's Legislators," *Commonwealth Review,* January, 1939, pp. 675–682. PENNSYLVANIA: Fox, William T. R., "Legislative Personnel in Pennsylvania," *Annals,* January, 1938, pp. 32–39. TEXAS: Finty, J., "Texas Makes Haste," *National Municipal Review,* November, 1923, pp. 649–654.

themselves as lawyers are not overburdened by the pressure of professional duties. Even if the lawyers who constitute so large a portion
of the total memberships were men ranking high in their profession,
the effect of their presence would still be a matter of considerable
importance. Furthermore, most of the *leaders* in legislative work are
members of this profession.

The whole training which an individual undergoes in preparation
for the practice of law is one which has a tendency to develop an
extreme degree of conservatism. The natural inclination of most
lawyers, when confronted by a given set of facts, is to look back to
see what has been done, to see what the precedents are, rather than

PROFESSIONAL CLASSIFICATION, GENERAL ASSEMBLY OF PENNSYLVANIA,
1927, 1935, 1939, AND 1943

Profession	1927		1935		1939		1943	
	House	Senate	House	Senate	House	Senate	House	Senate
Lawyers	36	17	36	17	43	22	38	21
Merchants	26	5	23	2	21	4	15	1
Clerks	20	..	11	..	8	2	5	..
Manufacturers	13	5	4	7	4	3	9	1
Farmers	10	2	16	2	9	2	12	3
Real Estate and Insur-ance Men	17	5	15	7	18	2	22	4
Editors, Publishers, and Reporters	5	2	4	2	3	2	9	1
Presidents, Managers, and Superintendents	..	..	6	1	7	..	1	..
Bankers and Brokers	7	3	5	1	8	..	6	..
Teachers	5	..	7	1	10	..	7	..
Contractors, Carpenters, and Machinists	10	1	7	2	13	1	14	4
Railroad Conductors	..	..	9	..	2	..	4	2
Coal Dealers	..	..	3	..	2	..	6	..
Clergymen	2	1	2	..	1	1	1	1
Salesmen	3	..	14	..	14	3	8	2
Retired	..	..	1	1	3	..	2	..
Lumbermen	..	..	2	..	3	..	3	..
Housewives	4	1	..	..	..	..	..	..
Physicians, Dentists, etc.	8	4	10	4	14	4	12	4
Telegraph Operators	..	..	1	..	1	..	1	..
Accountants	..	..	4	1	4	1	6	..
Automobile Men	5	..	4	1	4	2	8	3
Pharmacists	..	..	3	..	2	..	2	1
Interior Decorators and Artists	..	..	2	..	1	..	..	..
Miscellaneous	37	4	19	1	13	1	17	2
	208	50	208	50	208	50	208	50

to look to the future to see what, in accordance with the existing situation, ought to be done. Many of them see nothing incongruous in setting up against a pressing social or economic need of our own day the decision of a judge in an inferior court handed down twenty-five, fifty, or a hundred years ago. It is not meant to imply that we can or should treat each situation that arises as though it represented an experience new in the development of the race, but the attitude of the legal profession is none the less significant, because it so largely explains the difficulty of securing the passage of liberal measures of a social or economic character. The lawyer has a tendency to resist changes in the law, because of a feeling of vested right in the law as it is; he resists raising standards for admission to the bar because it would reflect on the training of many present members of the profession, and he resists progressive legislation because it is new and untried.

More important than these considerations are the frequent violations of the public confidence by lawyer legislators. After charges of bribery made on the floor of the California Senate in the 1937 session, an investigation was authorized by the Attorney General of the State and the District Attorney of Sacramento County. The investigators found that several lawyer legislators had solicited and accepted or had been proffered and accepted employment from interests directly concerned with legislation; that after accepting such employment, lawyer legislators had shown a marked tendency to vote for and otherwise act in the interests of their clients, as distinguished from impartial representation of the interests of the public. Other findings dealt with the solicitation of nonlawyer legislators, with corrupt lobbying as distinguished from open legislative representation, and with the marked tendency toward the preelection influencing of legislators by means of campaign contributions or of tangible, personal favors to prospective members of the legislature. While corruption in legislative halls is not nearly so common as it once was, it is probable that these findings could be paralleled in many other state capitols.[12]

The other side of this question is well stated by a former legislator in a large eastern state, himself a distinguished member of the bar:

> More or less prejudiced writers have, from the earliest to the present day, sustained an unintelligent critical attack upon the influence of lawyers in legislative bodies. But close study will reveal that few, if any, such writers

[12] See *Legislative Investigative Report,* submitted by H. R. Philbrick, Sacramento, December 28, 1938.

have either enjoyed the honor or borne the responsibility of membership in a legislative assembly. Only sporadically will there come, by spoken word or pen, an expression of commendation or approval of the public service rendered by the lawyer, in the legislature. Such sentiments, however, are rarely bestowed by other than one who has personally been in the service. Thus, their genuineness and sincerity are questioned if not disbelieved. The Bar, whether through lack of knowledge or want of interest in the practical phases of lawmaking, has remained inarticulate to the criticism not alone of the legislature, but as well of the services of the lawyer-legislator.[13]

It is true here as elsewhere in the public service, that any shortcoming, or even the suspicion thereof, is broadcast while little is said of the conscientious majority.

The Urban-Rural Conflict. The members from the rural districts always have constituted a majority in the state legislatures. In the early days when ours was predominantly an agricultural society, this was entirely justified; now one finds the control of the rural members no less complete, although the number who classify themselves as farmers is, for a number of reasons, much smaller than formerly. The development of an industrial civilization and of more efficient methods of agricultural production made possible a reduction in the number of farmers required to produce necessary agricultural products. High wages in the cities in war time and the greater convenience and attractiveness of urban life were contributing causes to an urban migration of considerable proportions. In addition, many members from the rural districts who might have classified themselves previously as farmers have become engaged in the management of the local bank, the local feed mill, or some other business. Owing to the lack of social prestige of farming, many of them have preferred to use this connection as a professional affiliation, although they may still have continued to own and manage one or more farm properties.

This rural control of our legislatures has given rise to what has often been appropriately called the American rotten-borough system. The problem presented is as old as the annals of recorded history; those who have resided in the great open spaces have always regarded their brethren in the cities with suspicion and distrust, and have looked upon the cities themselves as dens of iniquity. The Bible records the stories of Sodom and Gomorrah, of Tyre and Sidon.

[13] Sterling, Philip, " Some Practical Aspects of Legislation," an address before the Pennsylvania Bar Association, Bedford Springs, June 24, 1932. See also a careful study by a lawyer-political scientist, Rutherford, M. Louise, " Lawyers as Legislators," *Annals*, January, 1938, pp. 53–61.

The psychology of those days, and that evidenced in repeated instances in the intervening years, is fundamentally little different from that which prompts the rural member of a modern state legislature to impose, or to attempt to impose, all manner of restrictive regulations upon the life and activities of the cities within his state. This situation is not, however, merely an interesting analogy to conditions existing in other lands and at other times in the history of the world; it is a practical situation which confronts our people and which has a definite effect upon their social and political welfare.

The prevalence of this system means, in the first place, that rural members not only can, but must, vote upon many complicated urban problems about which they know little and care less. Members who have rarely seen a subway, and who have no knowledge of the rush of traffic in a big city at the beginning and end of a working day, must pass upon questions with regard to municipal transportation facilities and complicated problems connected with the financing of such facilities. Without ever having known anything but the ineffective and leisurely activities of their agencies of local government, they must pass upon the organization and functioning of governmental machinery for a great metropolitan community. With only such limited knowledge of electoral problems as may be gained in a small community where every inhabitant knows not only the name but the intimate details of the life and business of every other, he must consider and pass upon provisions of an election law to be used in great urban communities controlled by powerful and efficient political organizations. In addition to all this, such members frequently seek to impose upon cities all kinds of regulations with regard to Sunday sports, Sunday movies, and other matters in which they constitute themselves the moral protectors of urban dwellers.

This situation is not peculiar to any one state or group of states; it is more or less characteristic of all. It is well illustrated by the facts with regard to Pennsylvania. In this state Philadelphia County sends a delegation of 41 members, and Allegheny County a delegation of 27, representing in the lower house the cities of Philadelphia and Pittsburgh, respectively. Thus these two large urban counties control only 68 out of 208 members, although approximately half the state's total population of 10,000,000 people live in the metropolitan areas of which they are the centers. The 140 representatives from the other sixty-five counties of the Commonwealth have a regular and substantial majority on any question that brings about a division on urban-rural lines; these members commonly stand together against the two largest cities of the state, even though many of them live in and represent cities of the third class.[14]

Although the society of most of our states has definitely changed from an agricultural to an industrial one, there is little likelihood that these inequalities in representation will soon be adjusted. The rural districts have always had the majority, and they are not likely to give it up willingly even though the justification for their keeping it can no longer be supported by figures on the distribution of population. Another factor which will no doubt continue to exercise a powerful deterring influence in changing this situation is the existence of a not unjustified suspicion and distrust of the frequently corrupt political machines which urban dwellers have permitted to dominate their affairs in such centers as Philadelphia, New York, and Chicago. Up-state residents in New York and Pennsylvania and down-state residents of Illinois have naturally viewed with great apprehension the possible extension of the control of organizations of this character to the large and important machinery of the state government. This situation actually happened in Illinois, and the only reason that it did not occur in New York is the fact that Governors Smith, Roosevelt, and Lehman were never on very intimate terms with the Tammany organization. Similar situations on a somewhat smaller scale exist in many states. The present system of representation is unfair and inequitable to the urban districts, but the rural districts are unlikely to relinquish powers which they have always held, especially while dishonest and notoriously corrupt government continues to exist in many large cities.[15]

Political Complexion: the Problem of Apportionment. The problem of urban-rural representation is one phase of the general problem of apportionment; another relates to the political complexion that results from prevailing practices in apportioning representation. On the latter question, Ogg and Ray conclude:

It cannot be said, however, that all currents of political opinion find representation in legislative bodies. This defect is due mainly to the fact that, with few exceptions, both senators and members of the lower house

[14] For an analysis of the situation in Connecticut, see Lancaster, Lane W., " Rotten Boroughs and the Connecticut Legislature," *National Municipal Review,* December, 1924, pp. 678–683; MacNeil, Douglas H., " Urban Representation in State Legislatures," *State Government,* April, 1945, pp. 59–61, and " Big Cities and State Rights," *Survey Graphic,* October, 1944; Walter, David O., " Representation of Metropolitan Districts," *National Municipal Review,* March, 1938, pp. 129–137.
[15] For an illuminating comment on this situation, see Merriam, Charles E., " Breaking the Clinch," *State Government,* December, 1931, pp. 8–9. Professor Merriam lists five of the present difficulties in this field, and six possible remedies.

are chosen in small, single-member districts, and the candidate who obtains a simple plurality of the popular vote, however small, wins. This means that large minorities — even majorities, when the voters are divided among the candidates of three or more parties — are left with no spokesman in either house. A remedy for this condition would be some scheme of comparatively large electoral districts, each returning not less than three or five representatives, all elected under an arrangement which will yield each considerable political element representation in fair proportion to its voting strength, [such as might be obtained under a system of proportional representation].[16]

In an elaborate study of the personnel of a fairly recent Kentucky legislature made by the late Professor J. Catron Jones, it is shown that the relative strength of the parties in the legislature bears no relation to the normal party preferences of the voters as a whole. It may be noted that the same condition has existed for many years in Pennsylvania and other states. Professor Jones wrote:

The political complexion of this particular Assembly was 66 Democrats and 34 Republicans, while the Senate had 24 Democrats and 14 Republicans. This is, however, not a fair indication of the political complexion of the state. For example, in the last fourteen years the state has had two Republican governors and two Democratic governors. During the same time, it has had one Republican in the United States Senate all of the time, and two for a part of the time. In 1920, Cox carried the state over Harding by a bare 4,000 majority, and a Republican candidate for senator defeated his Democratic opponent by a margin of 5,000. In 1924, Coolidge carried the state by 24,000 plurality in the presidential race, while in 1928 it went Republican by 177,000 plurality. The cause of the one-sidedness in Assembly membership is a very clever gerrymander. Whereas it takes an average of 26,000 people to make a Republican legislative district, only 20,000 are required for a Democratic district. In the Senate, the ratio is 50,000 to 73,000.[17]

It is thus clear that the existing practices with regard to apportionment of members fail, first, to give adequate representation to urban communities; second, to reflect truly the partisan preferences of the voters of the states as a whole; third, to comply, either in fact or in spirit, with constitutional mandates with regard to apportionment. The constitutions frequently forbid more than one senator to a county, or by some other rule prevent urban communities from enjoying the representation to which their population entitles them. While they often provide that there shall be at least one member of the lower house from each county, other limitations coupled with rural domination prevent the cities from receiving here also their

---

16 Ogg and Ray, *op. cit.*, pp. 745–746.
17 Jones, J. Catron, *op. cit.*, pp. 116–117.

just share of representation. With regard to the second defect, that of inequitable partisan representation, gerrymandering is common. With regard to the third, the legislatures openly ignore or defy express requirements of the constitution. In all but three states in which no agency of reapportionment is specified — Delaware, Maryland, and Ohio — the legislature or the general assembly is designated as such an agency.

Every one of the forty-eight state constitutions deals with the problem of apportionment in some fashion, stating more or less clearly the basis for representation in each chamber. As Professor Farmer points out, each of them attempts to do four things: (1) to approximate the ideal of equality in representation; (2) to create a geographic unit of representation; (3) to provide flexibility in order to permit adjustment of representation to meet shifts in population; and (4) to assure stability in the legislature. In practice, the requirements of the constitution are often ignored in spirit if not in fact. The basis commonly used is the Federal census or a state census, or both, apportionments to take place every five or ten years; but frequently this requirement also is ignored. If the legislature provides no new apportionment, the old continues in effect; the longer it remains in effect, the more inequitable the representation becomes. There is, furthermore, nothing that can be done about it.[18]

Relations of Members to Their Constituents. In considering the representative character of legislative bodies, attention must be given not only to the professional affiliations of members, the urban-rural conflict, and apportionment, but also to such questions as the place of the members in their respective communities, their relations

[18] Gross inequalities frequently occur as to size of districts. In Missouri, representative districts in the 1940's ranged in population from 6,226 in Carter County to more than 91,000 in St. Louis County, while senatorial districts ranged from 44,252 in one district in the City of St. Louis to 477,828 for two districts in Jackson County. In addition to the references cited in previous editions of this book, see GENERAL: University of California, Bureau of Public Administration, *Legislative Apportionment* (Berkeley, 1941) ; Shull, Charles W., " Reapportionment: A Chronic Problem," *National Municipal Review*, February, 1941, pp. 73–79; Walter, David O., " Reapportionment of State Legislative Districts," *Illinois Law Review*, May, 1942, pp. 20–42. ALABAMA: Farmer, Hallie, *Legislative Apportionment* (University of Alabama, Bureau of Public Administration, 1944) . ILLINOIS: Illinois Legislative Council, *Reapportionment in Illinois* (Springfield, 1945) . MICHIGAN: Shull, Charles W., " Michigan Secures House Reapportionment," *National Municipal Review*, May, 1943, pp. 256–257. NEW HAMPSHIRE: Harvey, Lashley G., " America's Largest Legislature," *State Government*, March, 1942, pp. 65–66, 75. NEW YORK: see efforts to reapportion in the Constitutional Convention of 1938; and in 1942, the *Reports* of the Joint Legislative Committee on Reapportionment (Legislative Documents Nos. 57, 58, and 59, as well as the *Report and Opinion* of the Committee) .

to their constituents, and the turnover in the membership of legislative bodies. Of decided interest also is the previous preparation of the members for their job. On this matter, Professor Jones reported:

In the matter of education, 52 per cent laid claim to some high school training, while the education of 48 per cent was limited to some training in the lower grades. The writer recently had occasion to examine fifty applicants for firemen in a city of 60,000 people. The percentage of high school graduates applying was higher than the legislature's percentage in the same state. There were, however, sixteen graduates of standard colleges, and twenty others claimed to have had some college or other special training in business schools or normal schools; one had attended a theological seminary. Thus, nearly 40 per cent laid claim to some college training. I have no comparable data on legislatures in other states, and am therefore unable to determine whether this is a high, low, or average record for educational qualifications. The fact that it appears to be on about the same level as that of police applicants indicates that, absolutely if not relatively, it is low.[19]

The members are as a rule persons who are well known in their respective communities, persons who are active in local affairs and in social and fraternal organizations. Some of them are professional " joiners." In the Kentucky legislature already referred to, 80 per cent belonged to some order.

The Masonic fraternity alone could claim 50 per cent, while some reported membership in as many as five secret orders, the Ku Klux Klan not being mentioned. On the other hand, the Rotarians and Kiwanians were conspicuous by their absence. Only 10 per cent claimed membership in these mid-day oratorical societies. As might be expected, this percentage closely parallels the percentage of so-called business men found in the body.[20]

If one is surprised at the lack of educational qualifications of the members, he may be even more surprised to discover that, as politicians, a great many are, as Professor Jones said, " rank amateurs." He found that 65 per cent had never sat in a legislature before; that while 35 per cent had had some legislative experience, more than half of these had had only one term, or, in Kentucky, a total of sixty days. More than 50 per cent had never held any public office prior to their election; most of those who had such experience had occupied minor local positions. There were one ex-Congressman, two circuit court judges, and three county judges. These conclusions can be further supported by a similar analysis of the personnel of the legislature in any other state. In Pennsylvania, for instance,

19 Jones, *op. cit.*, p. 118.   20 *Ibid.*, p. 119.

prior to the Democratic overturn in 1934, it had been customary to have sixty or sixty-five new members in each regular session; as a result of this election, the number increased to ninety, or more than 43 per cent. Of approximately 7,600 state legislators, 5,500 are chosen for terms of one session, and that is all that great numbers of them ever serve. This high turnover greatly impairs the efficiency of our legislative bodies.

Professor Hyneman of Louisiana State University has made a number of significant studies of legislative tenure and turnover. If the widespread assumption of a direct correlation between legislative experience and legislative competence is sound, then it is a wonder that the legislatures function as well as they do. Of all the members of both houses in ten legislatures from 1925 to 1935, 35.4 per cent were serving their first term, 22.6 per cent their second, 12.3 per cent their third, and 8.9 per cent their fourth; 16.8 per cent had been there between five and nine terms, and 4 per cent had been there ten terms or more. The average experience in the senate is naturally higher than in the house; if the committee chairmen are men of long service, the lack of experience on the part of members is somewhat less serious. The findings of these studies are well summarized in the following paragraphs:

If one assumes that the average legislator becomes effective only after he has completed three sessions of service, he will be disappointed to find that in only four of the twenty chambers (California, New Jersey, and New York Senates and the New York House) could as many as 50 percent of the members meet this test. In seven chambers (in lower houses of California, Indiana, Iowa, Maine, New Jersey, Pennsylvania, and Washington), less than a fourth of the members could show three previous sessions of service; to reverse the English, more than 75 percent of the membership of each of these seven bodies fell short of this test. Four other chambers (Minnesota House and Indiana, Iowa, and Maine Senates) bettered this standard by a very slight margin.

If the completion of four sessions be taken as the division point between adequate and inadequate legislative equipment, then the New York House and the Senates of California, Illinois, Minnesota, New Jersey, New York, and Washington are found to be superior bodies, with more than a third of their membership in the select group; by the same measure the lower houses of Indiana, Iowa, and Maine are found to be definitely inferior.[21]

[21] Hyneman, Charles S., " Tenure and Turnover of Legislative Personnel," *Annals,* January, 1938, pp. 21–31; also, with others, " Legislative Experience of Illinois Law-Makers," *University of Chicago Law Review,* December, 1935, pp. 104–118; " Tenure and Turnover in the Indiana General Assembly," *American Political Science Review,* February, 1938, pp. 51–67, and April, 1938, pp. 311–331; and "Tenure and Turnover of the Iowa Legislature," *Iowa Law Journal,* May, 1939, pp. 673–696.

Part of the legislator's task must be performed at the state capitol; the other part involves his relations with his constituents, maintaining his contacts with them in order that he may effectively represent them at the capitol and continue to serve them in future legislative sessions. It would be interesting to have a number of case studies of the relations between members and their constituents, showing who takes the initiative in making such contacts, how citizens make their wants known to their representatives, et cetera. How many citizens adopt the " you vote for this bill or else " attitude? What other types of pressure do they attempt to use? How does a legislator feel when angry delegations wait upon him at home, or march on the capitol? The frank answers of a number of experienced legislators to these questions would be illuminating.

The evidence indicates that most of the members are " just plain folks "; their educational background is deficient, little if any better than that of a majority of their constituents. Instead of being the ruthless and successful politicians they are popularly supposed to be, a large part of them are new at the game and, judged by the high turnover, obviously ineffective. These observations are made, not in critical spirit, but as an impartial report of the facts as they exist. The reflection, if there is any, lies not upon the legislators, but upon the electorates which select the members.[22] These members have at least two functions to perform; they serve as agents for the mediation of conflicts which arise between different groups, and they develop among themselves a "we group " morale which enables them to bear up under the criticism and abuse heaped upon elective officials by a none too sympathetic or understanding public.[23]

Women Legislators. During the early years of woman suffrage the number of women legislators slowly increased, but during recent years it has shown a slight decline. The National League of Women Voters has kept a record of the number of women members, with the results indicated in the table on page 240.

In 1939 New England as usual was far in the lead, with twenty-four women legislators in New Hampshire, twenty-two in Connecticut, and fifteen in Vermont. The remaining states had from one to eight members each. In 1937 the Council of State Govern-

[22] See Hester, George C., " Whither in State Legislation," *Southwest Review*, Spring, 1931, pp. 336–350; Dodds, Harold W., " The Public's Responsibility for Legislation," *National Municipal Review*, April, 1935, pp. 200–201, 218; and the annual reports of Committee on Legislation of the Citizens Union of the City of New York.

[23] For an interesting discussion of these functions, see Smith, T. V., " Two Functions of the American State Legislator," *Annals*, January, 1938, pp. 183–188.

ments found that 44 per cent were re-elected members — a very encouraging fact. Most of those who were re-elected were serving their third, fourth, or fifth terms and four had been responding to roll calls for more than ten years. In 1938 Massachusetts had a woman

WOMEN MEMBERS OF STATE LEGISLATURES, 1921–1939

Year	Women Members	Year	Women Members
1921	29	1931	146 in 39 states
1922	33	1932	146 in 39 states
1923	84	1933	135 in 34 states
1924	86	1934	135 in 34 states
1925	125	1935	134 in 34 states
1926	130	1936	130 in 34 states
1927	124	1937	141 in 36 states
1928	126	1938	130 in 28 states
1929	149 in 38 states	1939	130 in 28 states
1930	149 in 38 states		

as presiding officer in both houses. There were, on the other hand, twenty states in 1939 in which no woman candidate was elected. The political alignment reflected the trend then current — Democrats, forty-eight as against seventy-nine in the preceding year; Republicans, seventy as against fifty-five in the preceding year. There was one Socialist, and one with Labor Party endorsement, and two were elected with the endorsement of both these parties. Three claimed " no party " endorsement and two claimed to be " independent." [24]

PLACE OF THE LEGISLATURES IN POPULAR ESTEEM

The early state legislatures were held in high regard, whereas later ones have been almost universally regarded with suspicion and distrust. Bryce used vituperative language in describing them, quite in contrast to his usual moderation.[25] It became popular to denounce legislators individually and collectively. When a session is concluded, editors, publishers, and public alike heave a sigh of relief that it is ended, at least for another year. There are a number of factors which have contributed to this unfortunate situation.

[24] " Women in State Legislatures," *State Government*, October, 1937, pp. 213–215, and Van Der Vries, Berdice T., " A Legislator Earns Her Way," *ibid.*, March, 1940, pp. 47, 54.
[25] Bryce, James, *The American Commonwealth*, First Edition, Vol. 1, Chapter 40; for a comment on this, see Reinhold, Frances L., in Brooks, Robert C., Ed., *Bryce's " American Commonwealth,"* Chapter 2 (Macmillan, New York, 1939).

Over a period of 100 years or more there were land scandals; improper granting of corporate charters; the reconstruction legislatures; the evils of special legislation and the undermining of the credit of many states, sometimes accompanied later by a repudiation of the debt; scandals in connection with the construction of state capitol buildings; and finally, limitations of legislative personnel and improper relations with persons and groups desiring legislation.

The land scandals, once frequent, no longer occur, partly because of higher standards of public morality, and partly because there are no more lands open for development. As early as 1810, a flagrant piece of dishonesty committed by the legislature of Georgia fifteen years before brought to the Supreme Court of the United States the interesting case of Fletcher v. Peck.[26] The legislature had granted a large tract of public land under circumstances which the Court agreed were wholly reprehensible; when the facts became known, an incensed electorate returned to office a new legislative personnel pledged to the revocation of the grant. The Supreme Court said in effect that corruption was unfortunate, but that the act of a preceding legislature was in the nature of a contract between the state and the persons to whom the grant was made. The rights of those who subsequently purchased portions of this land could not be affected by the fraud. The state could not, therefore, regain control over this land, since doing so would violate the obligation of contract clause in Article I, Section 10. Situations such as this were by no means uncommon.

It is well known that the corporate form of business organization owed its origin to the necessity of securing capital in large amounts for railway construction, beginning in the third decade of the nineteenth century. Gradually this form of organization was extended to other forms of business enterprise. Before the enactment of general incorporation laws, legislatures were accustomed to create corporations by special act. Under the doctrine of the Dartmouth College Case, the privileges and grants of power conferred by these charters endured through all time, without any compensation in any form coming back to the state. Rights, privileges, and property worth hundreds of thousands — and in some cases millions — of dollars were granted by corrupt legislatures as political favors.

The abuses characteristic of the reconstruction legislatures in the Southern states have already been described. The growing evil of special legislation constituted an additional cause of the declining

[26] 6 Cranch, 87, 1810.

confidence in which legislative bodies were held. The legislatures expended money and incurred enormous state debts with wanton extravagance; later, when the repayment of these loans became difficult and embarrassing, they were sometimes repudiated. More detailed discussion of this problem is reserved for a later chapter. Throughout the period during which most of the present state capitol buildings were constructed, scarcely a state escaped without evidence of gross fraud and corruption. Some of the buildings were fine, but they regularly cost the taxpayers two or three times as much as they legitimately should. Papier-mâché was substituted for oak paneling, composition materials for costly marbles, furniture was sold by the cubic yard, and inferior grades of goods were supplied at exorbitant prices — all with legislative knowledge and often with legislative connivance.[27] No one of these incidents alone, or no one type of them alone, would have brought about such a decline of public esteem for legislatures as actually occurred; the result was due to the cumulative effect of instances of nearly every type in nearly every state over a long period.

Added to all these factors was the generally inferior caliber of the legislators themselves. Mediocrity was — in many instances it still is — the rule rather than the exception. Not only have many of the members lacked native intelligence and the educational background necessary for effective legislative work, but many of them have been indifferent in the performance of their duties, and not a small number have been actually corrupt. The indifferent ones do not know and do not care what provisions the measures before them contain; they vote for or against them, regardless of their merits, as they have been instructed to do by party leaders or interest groups to whom they are under obligation.

Such was the state of affairs in which we came down into the present century. In recent years there has been a notable improve-

[27] For example, the main building of the Pennsylvania State Capitol was destroyed by fire in 1897; in 1901 the legislature appropriated $4,000,000 for a new building. For the furnishing and decoration, $8,601,922 was expended; the cost of the decorations alone was $7,720,855, while the building cost $3,932,978. The total cost without furniture was $11,653,833. When a new State Treasurer took office in 1906, he discovered a disparity between the cost and amount appropriated. Charges of graft and dishonesty were made and the 1907 legislature authorized an investigation. The net loss to the state through furniture manipulation was about $4,000,000, but the gross loss disclosed at the investigation, plus the trials of the several defendants, was $5,600,000. Apparently the actual contractors received about $1,400,000, the difference going to the conspirators. On the general problem of this section, see Hester, *op. cit.*, and Nickerson, Hoffman, " The Twilight of Legislatures," *American Mercury,* February, 1930, pp. 129–136.

ment, due to increased popular interest in public affairs, to a greater realization of the importance of the states, to higher standards of political ethics, and in no small measure to active agencies working for the improvement of legislation. As state governments have been reorganized and improved, men of greater ability and better character have been willing to devote their time and energy to legislative work. Much has been accomplished since 1925, when the American Legislators' Association began its work; since then the legislative council movement has gained momentum, and much thought has been given to the improvement of the legislative process. While the combined effect of these influences may restore the legislatures to that high position in public esteem which should be theirs, a recent poll of the members of the Oregon legislature shows a belief on the part of a substantial majority that there has been no change in the prestige of the legislature of that state.

DESCRIPTIVE FEATURES OF THE TWO HOUSES

Thus far we have been concerned with the historical development of state legislatures; with the relative merits of the unicameral and bicameral principles of legislative organization; with the representative character of these assemblies, considered from a number of different points of view; and with the long decline of the legislatures in popular esteem, with some comment on their contemporary rise. We now come to a study of the descriptive features of these bodies — their size, term, compensation, and other related matters. The discussion will be supported by tables compiled by and reproduced here through the courtesy of the Council of State Governments.[28]

Forty-seven of the forty-eight states have an upper chamber known officially as the Senate. Thirty-nine states call the lower chamber the House of Representatives. Of the remaining nine states, one, Nebraska, has since 1937 had a single chamber called the Legislature. The lower house in California, Nevada, New York, and Wisconsin is called the Assembly; in New Jersey, the General Assembly; and in Maryland, Virginia, and West Virginia, the House of Delegates. Exactly half the states call the two bodies together the Legislature; nineteen use the term General Assembly; [29] Massachusetts

---

[28] *Book of the States*, 1945–1946; also Toll, Henry W., " Today's Legislatures," *Annals*, January, 1938, pp. 1–10.

[29] These are: Arkansas, Colorado, Connecticut, Delaware, Georgia, Illinois, Indiana, Iowa, Kentucky, Maryland, Missouri, North Carolina, Ohio, Pennsylvania, Rhode Island, South Carolina, Tennessee, Vermont, and Virginia.

THE 48: NUMBERS AND DATES

Showing for Each Legislature the Numbers and Terms of Its Members and the Time of Its Sessions

State	Senate		House		Total Number of Members	Years in Which Sessions Are Held	Days on Which Sessions Convene	Regular Date of Convening, 1947
	No. of Members	Term of Years	No. of Members	Term of Years				
Alabama	35	4	106	4	141	Odd	First Tues. in May[2]	May 6
Arizona	19	2	58	2	77	Odd	Second Mon. in Jan.	Jan. 13
Arkansas	35	4	100	2	135	Odd	Second Mon. in Jan.	Jan. 13
California	40	4	80	2	120	Odd	First Mon. after first day in Jan.	Jan. 6
Colorado	35	4	65	2	100	Odd	First Wed. in Jan.	Jan. 1
Connecticut	36	2	272	2	308	Odd	Wed. after first Mon. in Jan.	Jan. 8
Delaware	17	4	35	2	52	Odd	First Tues. in Jan.	Jan. 7
Florida	38	4	95	2	133	Odd	First Tues. after first Mon. in April	April 8
Georgia	52	2	205	2	257	Odd	Second Mon. in Jan.	Jan. 13
Idaho	44	2	49	2	93	Odd	First Mon. after first day in Jan.	Jan. 6
Illinois	51	4	153	2	204	Odd	Wed. after first Mon. in Jan.	Jan. 8
Indiana	50	4	100	2	150	Odd	Thurs. after first Mon. in Jan.	Jan. 9
Iowa	50	4	108	2	158	Odd	Second Mon. in Jan.	Jan. 13
Kansas	40	4	125	2	165	Odd	Second Tues. in Jan.	Jan. 14
Kentucky	38	4	100	2	138	Even	First Tues. after first Mon. in Jan.	No Session
Louisiana	39	4	100	4	139	Even	Second Mon. in May	No Session
Maine	33	2	151	2	184	Odd	First Wed. in Jan.	Jan. 1
Maryland	29	4	123	4	152	Odd	First Wed. in Jan.	Jan. 1
Massachusetts	40	2	240	2	280	Annual	First Wed. in Jan.	Jan. 1
Michigan	32	2	100	2	132	Odd	First Wed. in Jan.	Jan. 1
Minnesota	67	4	131	2	198	Odd	Tues. after first Mon. in Jan.	Jan. 7
Mississippi	49	4	140	4	189	Even	Tues. after first Mon. in Jan.	No Session
Missouri	34	4	150	2	184	Odd	Wed. after Jan. 1.	Jan. 8
Montana	56	4	90	2	146	Odd	First Mon. in Jan.	Jan. 6

State	Senate	Term	House	Term	Total	Session	Convenes	Date
Nebraska	43[1]	2	..	..	43	Odd	First Tues. in Jan.	Jan. 7
Nevada	17	4	40	2	57	Odd	Third Mon. in Jan.	Jan. 20
New Hampshire	24	2	399	2	423	Odd	First Wed. in Jan.	Jan. 1
New Jersey	21	3	60	1	81	Annual	Second Tues. in Jan.	Jan. 14
New Mexico	24	4	49	2	73	Odd	Second Tues. in Jan.	Jan. 14
New York	56	2	150	2	206	Annual	Wed. after first Mon. in Jan.	Jan. 8
North Carolina	50	2	120	2	170	Odd	Wed. after first Mon. in Jan.	Jan. 8
North Dakota	49	4	113	2	162	Odd	Tues. after first Mon. in Jan.	Jan. 7
Ohio	33	2	136	2	169	Odd	First Mon. in Jan.	Jan. 6
Oklahoma	44	4	120	2	164	Odd	Tues. after first Mon. in Jan.	Jan. 7
Oregon	30	4	60	2	90	Odd	Second Mon. in Jan.	Jan. 13
Pennsylvania	50	4	208	2	258	Odd	First Tues. in Jan.	Jan. 7
Rhode Island	44	2	100	2	144	Annual	First Tues. in Jan.	Jan. 7
South Carolina	46	4	124	2	170	Annual	Second Tues. in Jan.	Jan. 14
South Dakota	35	2	75	2	110	Odd	Tues. after first Mon. in Jan.	Jan. 7[2]
Tennessee	33	2	99	2	132	Odd	First Mon. in Jan.	Jan. 6
Texas	31	4	150	2	181	Odd	Second Tues. in Jan.	Jan. 14
Utah	23	4	60	2	83	Odd	Second Tues. in Jan.	Jan. 13
Vermont	30	2	246	2	276	Odd	Wed. after first Mon. in Jan.	Jan. 8
Virginia	40	4	100	2	140	Even	Second Wed. in Jan.	No Session
Washington	46	4	99	2	145	Odd	Second Mon. in Jan.	Jan. 13
West Virginia	32	4	94	2	126	Odd	Second Wed. in Jan.	Jan. 8
Wisconsin	33	4	100	2	133	Odd	Second Wed. in Jan.	Jan. 8
Wyoming	27	4	56	2	83	Odd	Second Tues. in Jan.	Jan. 14
Totals	1,777		5,635		7,455			

[1] A unicameral legislature. [2] Meets second Tuesday in January after election for organization.

Reprinted from *State Government*, January, 1933, and revised from *Book of the States*, 1945-1946.

and New Hampshire call theirs the General Court; while Montana, North Dakota, and Oregon use the name Legislative Assembly.

Size. The table on pages 244–245 indicates the number of members in each house in each state, and the total number of members of each legislature. The smallest senates are in Delaware and Nevada, with 17 members each; the largest are in Minnesota, with 67, and Montana, with 56. Nine senates have less than 30 members, and only nine have 50 or more. Eighteen have between 30 and 39, twelve between 40 and 49.

The smallest lower houses are in Delaware, with 35 members, and Nevada, with 40; the largest in New Hampshire, with 399, and in Connecticut, with 272. The distribution by groups is as follows:

SIZE RANGE OF LOWER HOUSES

50 or less	3 states
51 to 100	21 states
101 to 150	16 states
151 to 200	2 states
201 to 300	5 states
301 to 400	1 state

The largest lower houses are found in the New England states, with relatively small populations and large numbers of districts, each member standing for a small constituency. Delaware and Nevada naturally have the smallest totals, with 52 and 57, respectively, while Connecticut and New Hampshire have the largest, with 308 and 423, respectively. The total number of legislators shows a slight tendency to decline. There were in the country in 1945, 1,777 senators and 5,635 representatives — 7,455 legislators in all. The average numbers per state are 37, 118, and 155, respectively, for the senate, the house, and the legislature as a whole, compared with 38, 121, and 159 a few years previously. In all states except Louisiana and Maine members are elected on the first Tuesday after the first Monday in November.

Qualifications of Members. The constitutions are specific regarding age qualifications for membership in the lower house, stating either that a person shall be twenty-one years old or that he shall be a duly qualified elector. Age qualifications for membership in the upper house differ widely. Alabama, Iowa, Oklahoma, and other states specify twenty-five years; Texas, twenty-six; while others have but one age qualification for members of both houses. In some states these qualifications must be met at the time of election (Alabama, Oklahoma, and Texas) , in others at the time of taking office (Iowa and Maine) , and in New Jersey one year next before election. The requirement of citizenship is uniform; the constitutions state either that a person must be a citizen to hold a seat in either house or that he must be a duly qualified elector. There is considerable variation with regard to length of citizenship. Maine specifies five years; Alabama and California, three; New Jersey, two; while other states have no such requirement. All the states have residence requirements for membership in either house, either express or implied, ranging from one year to five years. Prospective members must fulfill these requirements " one year next before their election " in Alabama, California, New Jersey, and Ohio; " one year next preceding their election " in Maine and Texas; and at the time of election in Iowa.

The constitutions are also specific in stating conditions which make a person ineligible to membership in the legislature. In Alabama, California, Nevada, Ohio, and Oklahoma, no person who has been convicted of embezzlement or defalcation of public funds, of bribery, perjury, or other infamous crime, or who has been adjudged guilty of a felony, may hold a seat in the legislature. No such restrictions are found, however, in Florida, Iowa, Maine, New Jersey, or Texas. All of the states here mentioned except Alabama enumerate those offices, which, when held, create ineligibility for membership in the legislature. The offices most frequently mentioned include positions under the government of the United States or of any state, and positions as collectors or holders of public moneys, judges of any court or clerk of any court of records, sheriffs, justices of the peace, secretary of state, or attorney general. Service in the armed forces is a disqualification for legislative membership in many states on the ground of dual officeholding.[30]

Length of Term. Members of the senate are elected for a four-year term in thirty-one states; in fifteen states, including all six in New England, they are elected for a two-year term.[31] New Jersey has a three-year term, while Nebraska, with its single chamber, elects for two years. Senators serve for one regular session in thirteen states;

---

[30] See Illinois Legislative Council, *Service in the Armed Forces as a Disqualification for Legislative Membership* (Springfield, 1942) . In 1940 the California legislature passed a law, which the Attorney General thought might be unconstitutional, providing for a leave of absence for military service.

[31] These are: Arizona, Connecticut, Georgia, Idaho, Maine, Massachusetts, Michigan, New Hampshire, New York, North Carolina, Ohio, Rhode Island, South Dakota, Tennessee, and Vermont.

for two regular sessions in thirty-two states; for three regular sessions in one state — New Jersey; and for four regular sessions in one state — South Carolina. In seven states, the regular session service for which a senator is elected is limited to sixty days. In the lower house, the term is two years in forty-one states. New Jersey and New York elect annually, while Alabama, Louisiana, Maryland, and Mississippi elect for four years. There are only six states in which representatives serve in two regular sessions of the legislature.

A grouping of the states by the terms accorded their senators and representatives indicates that New York is the only state with two-year senators and one-year representatives, and that there are twenty-seven states with four-year senators and two-year representatives. New Jersey has three-year senators and one-year representatives, while four southern states — Alabama, Louisiana, Maryland, and Mississippi — have four-year senators and four-year representatives.

Compensation. The question of the compensation of legislators has long been difficult and troublesome. In the early stages of the development of popular government there was no compensation; the fact that representation was permitted at all was, for many classes and groups, a great victory. It was an honor to serve. Sooner or later, as the newness wore off, those who were elected discovered that it cost money to travel back and forth to the seat of government, to maintain oneself while there, and to be absent for days at a time from one's regular calling. Before any compensation for members was secured, the situation became so serious that none but the wealthy were financially able to serve.

In our own time the per diem basis of compensation was first employed. When the public gathered the impression that sessions were unnecessarily prolonged — whether or not this was true — there developed the tendency either to limit the number of days of the session, or to adopt lump-sum payments for an unlimited session. At the present time there are twenty-seven states on a per diem basis, and all but four of these limit the length of regular sessions. Of the four exceptions, Michigan pays $3.00 per day for the elective term, which is equivalent to a salary of $2,190 for two years. Missouri, Oklahoma, and Texas do not limit the length of sessions, but they limit the number of days for which compensation, or full compensation, may be drawn. Of the lump-sum states, only five — Arkansas, Connecticut, Minnesota, Virginia, and West Virginia — limit the length of sessions.

In very few states may the amount of the compensation be considered anything like adequate. On this point Henry W. Toll has said:

When a legislator comes to the capital city, his daily hotel bill plus reasonable incidentals represents a sum between six dollars and ten dollars. In thirty-seven of the forty-eight states, the payment to the legislator amounts to ten dollars or less per day for the duration of the session. In other words, state legislators are partially or entirely reimbursed for their living expenses during the session, but almost none of them receive any compensation for their services. In short, the typical law-maker devotes to his legislative work almost his entire time during the weeks of the session, and a great deal of time during the many other months of his term. But he receives nothing for any of this time.[32]

The daily allowances in the per diem states range from $3.00 to $15; four states pay $5.00, and seven pay $10. There are only two of the twenty-seven "in which the legislator's entire payment amounts to more than a moderate allowance for living expenses — during the session only." Eighteen of the twenty-three lump-sum states hold biennial sessions, the amount of compensation ranging from $600 in Vermont to $5,000 in Illinois. The other three states hold annual sessions and pay from $500 to $2,500 to their legislators each year. Seventeen of these states pay $1,000 or less to their members, per session. *State Government* made a per diem comparison for the forty-eight states by computing the daily amount which the legislators in lump-sum states receive if their entire compensation is applied to the actual period of the session, with the results shown in the table on page 250.

The amount of compensation is set by the constitution in all but fifteen states, in which it is subject to legislative determination. Such a matter should have no place in the constitution. Mileage allowances ranging from four or five to twenty cents per mile exist in all the states except North Carolina, the usual rate being ten cents. A few states, including Delaware, Illinois, Maryland, Missouri, New Hampshire, Pennsylvania, South Carolina, and South Dakota, grant allowances for postage. The prevailing public sentiment on this question is revealed by the fact that in 1940 the voters in Louisiana, Missouri, Oregon, and Washington all rejected constitutional amendments providing pay increases for their legislators. Only Tennessee voted favorably on such a proposal.

[32] Toll, Henry W., "Should We Pay Law-Makers?" *State Government*, February, 1931. pp. 10–13.

PER DIEM COMPENSATION OF LEGISLATORS

Per Diem Payment	Number of States	States
$ 2.00	2	Connecticut, New Hampshire
3.00	3	Kansas, Michigan, Oregon
4.00	3	Maine, Tennessee, Utah
5.00	8	Idaho, Maryland, Missouri, New Mexico, North Dakota, Rhode Island, South Dakota, Washington
6.00	4	Florida, New Jersey, Oklahoma, Vermont
7.00	3	Georgia, Massachusetts, Nebraska
8.00	1	North Carolina
10.00	14	Alabama, Colorado, Delaware, Indiana, Iowa, Kentucky, Louisiana, Mississippi, Montana, Nevada, South Carolina, Texas, Wisconsin, Wyoming
11.00	1	Minnesota
12.00	1	Virginia
15.00	1	Arizona
17.00	2	Arkansas, West Virginia
20.00	1	Ohio
21.00	1	Illinois
25.00	1	California
28.00	1	Pennsylvania
30.00	1	New York

In addition to having such a ridiculously low compensation in most states, it should be remembered that each member must meet the expenses involved in his electoral campaign. It may be that the states cannot offer to able men the same compensation which they could earn in their regular business or profession, but they can and should pay enough so that members will not be obliged to undergo actual financial loss. They should offer enough to make it possible for persons of moderate means, but with ability and an interest in public affairs, to serve without financial embarrassment to themselves and their families. If, in most states, a drastic reduction in the number of members was made, a considerable increase in compensation per member could be made without additional cost to the state. If in addition the job of legislator were made a full-time job, as it should be at least in the larger states, such states would be justified in offering a compensation sufficient to enable a member to maintain his family at a decent standard, in conformity with living costs in the state or section of the country in which the state was located.

Working Conditions. A very serious obstacle to effective legislative work is the absence of suitable working conditions for members. There are elaborate, ornate, and expensive meeting chambers, but there are no offices, no secretaries, no private conference rooms, no facilities for work. Members are fortunate if they have lockers in which to leave their coats and hats during sessions. There are caucus rooms and a very small number of committee rooms, but not enough to accommodate a fourth of the standing committees at the same time. These conditions are the more serious because many of the members are accustomed to good offices and secretarial assistance at home. When they are deprived of both at the capitol, their mail must either go unanswered or be taken care of at home on their own time and at their own expense. The same situation existed in Washington until the House and Senate office buildings were constructed. It may be that few states would be able to provide comparable facilities for their legislators, but some effort should be made to provide suitable working conditions, at least for the officers and for the chairmen of committees.[33]

Privileges and Immunities of Members. A typical statement showing the nature and extent of the privileges and immunities of members of a legislature appears in Section 48 of the Virginia Constitution:

Members of the General Assembly shall, in all cases, except treason, felony, or breach of the peace, be privileged from arrest during the sessions of their respective houses; and for any speech or debate in either house shall not be questioned in any other place. They shall not be subject to arrest, under any civil process, during the sessions of the General Assembly, or the fifteen days next before the beginning or after the ending of any session.

To these privileges commonly guaranteed by the constitution there may be added numerous others under the provisions of the rules of the house. Members have the right to recognition to speak, subject to such limitations as may have been imposed upon debate, the right of the speaker to decide who is entitled to the floor, and the requirement that they confine their remarks to the subject under discussion; but they may be called to order for transgressing the rules, for the use of offensive language, and for improper conduct. Ordinarily they may not absent themselves from the sessions without a leave of absence voted by their colleagues.

[33] The *Report* of the California Assembly Committee on Legislative Organization (Sacramento, 1943) discusses the physical requirements of the legislature in the state capitol, but says nothing about these essential matters.

WHAT PRICE LAWMAKERS?

Prepared by Waldo Schumacker, Professor of Political Science, University of Oregon

State	Membership		Sessions Limit — Days		Salary		Allowances
	Senate	House	Regular	Special	Regular Session	Special Session	
Alabama	35	106	60	30	$10 per day[5]	$10 per day[5]	10¢ a mile, 1 round trip
Arizona	19	58	60[1]	20[1]	$8 per day, 60 day limit	$8 per day, 20 day limit	10¢ a mile, one way
Arkansas	35	100	60	15	$1,000 for 2 years	$6 per day, 15 day limit	5¢ a mile
California	40	80	None[2]	None	$2,400 for 2 years	[6]	Mileage, $10 per diem living expenses
Colorado	35	65	None	None	$1,000 for 2 years		Actual traveling expenses
Connecticut	35	272	5 mo.	None	$300 for 2 years		10¢ a mile
Delaware	17	35	60[1]	30[1]	$10 per day, 60 day limit	$10 per day, 30 day limit	10¢ a mile; postage $25 in reg., $10 in special, session
Florida	38	95	60	20	$6 per day	$6 per day	10¢ a mile
Georgia	52	205	70	None	$6 per day	$8 per day	10¢ a mile, 1 round trip
Idaho	44	49	60	20	$5 per day, 60 day limit	$5 per day, 20 day limit	10¢ a mile, 1 round trip
Illinois	51	153	None	None	*$5,000 for 2 years		5¢ a mile weekly round trip; postage, etc. $50 per session
Indiana	50	100	61	40	$1,200 per year[5]		$5 each 25 miles, round trip
Iowa	50	108	None	None	*$1,000 for 2 years	Not over $10 per day	10¢ a mile
Kansas	40	125	None	None	$3 per day, 50 day limit	$3 per day, 30 day limit	15¢ a mile, 1 round trip
Kentucky	38	100	60	None	*$10 per day	$10 per day	15¢ a mile
Louisiana	39	100	60	30	$10 per day	$10 per day	10¢ a mile, not over 2 trips
Maine	33	151	None	None	*$850 for 2 years	$10 per day	$2 for 10 miles, one way (once)
Maryland	29	123	90	30	$1,000 per year		20¢ a mile; stationery $25
Massachusetts	40	240	None	None	*$2,500 per year	Determined at session	4.2¢ a mile (once)
Michigan	32	100	None	None	$3 per day for elected term		10¢ a mile, 1 round trip
Minnesota	67	131	90	None	$2,000 for 2 years	Mileage only	15¢ a mile, $350 limit
Mississippi	49	140	None	None	$1,000 for 2 years	$10 per day	10¢ a mile, 1 round trip
Missouri	34	150	None	None	$125 per month	$125 per month	$1 per 10 miles round trip (once)
Montana	56	90	60	None	*$10 per day	$10 per day, 60 day limit	5¢ a mile

State					Salary	Per diem	Travel allowance
Nebraska [4]	43	.	None	None	*$1,744 for 2 years	None	Necessary mileage, 1 round trip
Nevada	17	40	60	20	*$15 per day, 60 day limit	$10 per day	10¢ a mile, shortest route
New Hampshire [2]	24	399	None	None	$200 for 2 years	$3 per day, 15 day limit	5¢ a mile, per day of attendance
New Jersey	21	60	None	None	*$500 per year	None	Transportation by railroad pass
New Mexico	24	49	60 [2]	None	$10 per day	$10 per day	10¢ a mile
New York	56	150	None	None	$2,500 per year	$10 per day, 30 day limit	Actual traveling expense, round trip once a week
North Carolina	50	120	None	20	$600 per year	$8 per day, 20 day limit	None
North Dakota	49	113	60	None	$5 per day, 60 day limit	$5 per day	10¢ a mile, 1 round trip
Ohio [2]	33	136	None	None	*$2,000 per year	None	Mileage
Oklahoma [2]	44	120	None	None	$6 per day; $2 after 60 days	$6 per day	10¢ a mile, 1 round trip
Oregon	30	60	50	20	$8 per day, 50 day limit	$8 per day, 20 day limit	10¢ a mile
Pennsylvania	50	208	None	None	*$3,000 for 2 years	$500 per session; $750 if session lasts over one month	5¢ a mile circular each week during session; postage $150 ($50 in special session)
Rhode Island	44	100	None [1]	None	$5 per day [5]	None	8¢ a mile
South Carolina	46	124	None	None	$1,000 a year	None	5¢ a mile; round trip once a week
South Dakota	35	75	60	None	$5 per day, 60 day limit	$5 per day	5¢ a mile, $300 expense a biennium
Tennessee	33	99	75 [1]	20 [1]	$4 per day, 75 day limit	$4 per day, 20 day limit	$4 for 25 miles
Texas	31	150	None	30	$10 per day; $5 after 120 days	$10 per day	$2.50 for 25 miles
Utah	23	60	60	30	$300 per year	Included in annual salary	10¢ a mile
Vermont	30	246	None	None	*$600 for 2 years	$6 per day	20¢ a mile; 10¢ a mile special session
Virginia	40	100	60 [3]	30	*$720 for 2 years	$360 per session, 30 day	10¢ a mile, nearest route
Washington	46	99	60	None	$5 per day	$5 per day, 60 day limit	10¢ a mile, 1 round trip; $10 per diem expenses
West Virginia	32	94	60 [4]	None	$500 per year [5]	None	10¢ a mile
Wisconsin	33	100	None	None	*$2,400 for 2 years [5]	None	10¢ a mile, round trip
Wyoming	27	56	40	None	*$12 per day	$12 per day	8¢ a mile, nearest route

1 No limit on sessions without pay. 2 Split or bifurcated session. 3 May be extended up to 30 days by three-fifths vote in each house. 4 Must be extended by Governor until general appropriation is passed. 5 Slightly greater compensation to officers. 6 Regular session years, $12 per session day plus balance to $1,000; non-session years, $100 monthly. * Salary fixed by statute.

Reprinted from *State Government*, January, 1935, and revised from *Book of the States*, 1945-1946.

Members are subject during the session to the discipline of the house to which they belong for conduct unbecoming a member. While legislative officers are not subject to impeachment, they may be expelled by a two-thirds vote of the house to which they belong; after expulsion they are subject to indictment and proceedings for any criminal offenses with which they may have been charged. Ordinarily, members will not be denied their seats even if they have a criminal record, if the offenses were committed prior to the date of election. The theory seems to be that if an electorate is stupid enough to elect such a person, the legislature has no right to exclude him. Nor do the houses of the legislature have the right to impose qualifications for membership in addition to those prescribed by the constitution. The question of the age of an elected member is seldom raised. Each house is the judge of contests affecting its members.

In all states technical questions arise from time to time in connection with the interpretation of these general rules. While they are fundamentally sound, at least from the long-time point of view, their application occasionally incenses the public. A case in point is that of Senator John H. McClure of Pennsylvania in 1935, who had been convicted in Federal court of conspiracy in violation of the Volstead Act. But for a decision of the United States Supreme Court which released convicts under this act when Amendment XVIII was repealed, he would have been in the penitentiary. Yet the Senate refused to expel him; in fact, it not only permitted him to remain, but kept him in an influential position as chairman of the Finance Committee. Occasionally, on the other hand, a legislative body will go to the opposite extreme, as happened in the Assembly in New York in 1920, when the five Socialist members were denied their seats, owing to the "Red" hysteria that prevailed at that time. It is generally true that any individual who has been declared elected and whose election was free from fraud is entitled to his seat.

Officers. Each house has a presiding officer, known in the lower house as the speaker and in the senate as the president, a chief clerk or a secretary, a sergeant at arms, and numerous minor officials. The major officers are chosen by vote of the members, while minor officers are appointed either by the elective officers, or, as in Wisconsin, under civil service rules. The duties of the elective officers will now be considered.

The speaker, or president, must maintain order during sessions, and conduct the business of the session, both on and off the floor.

Upon the advice of his parliamentarian, he decides all points of order, subject to appeal and the possibility of being overruled by the house. He may call upon members to preside in his temporary absence from the chair; in most states he may appoint standing and special committees, and act as chairman of the Committee of the Whole. He has control over the journals, papers, and bills of the house. When necessary, he may order the lobby and galleries cleared, assign desks to properly accredited newspaper representatives, and perform any other duties pertaining to his office as prescribed by law or by rule of the house.

The chief clerk or secretary has charge of all clerical work and of the printing of the house. He must see that the journals, other publications, and records of the house are properly kept; read or allow his assistants to read from the desk such matter as the speaker or the house shall direct; exercise general supervision over all clerks, attachés, and employees, and be responsible for their official acts and their performance of their regular duties. He must perform all duties pertaining to his office as prescribed by law or by rule of the house.

It is the duty of the sergeant at arms to attend all sessions, preserve order, guard the doors when so directed, announce all official messengers, and serve all processes issued by the house and directed by the speaker. He must see that the house chamber and the committee rooms are kept clean, heated and ventilated, and open for the use of members at all necessary times. He has assistants as required, and is responsible for their supervision. He must perform all duties pertaining to his office as prescribed by law or by rule of the house.

SESSIONS

Regular Sessions. There are four types of sessions — regular, special, split, and adjourned — the first two or all of which may be permissible in any given state. Regular sessions are most frequent and most important; they represent the normal procedure. There are forty-three states that hold regular sessions biennially, beginning usually in January of the odd-numbered years. Five states — Massachusetts, New Jersey, New York, Rhode Island, and South Carolina — still retain annual sessions. It thus happens that in odd-numbered years nearly all the state legislatures will be in session at about the same time. Most of the original state constitutions provided for annual sessions; gradually, however, biennial sessions were substituted for the annual ones — a trend which was an outgrowth of the distrust of the lawmaking machinery which developed during the nineteenth century and which resulted in the drastic limitations on the length of sessions of the legislature which are found in many states. The theory behind these restrictions seems to have been that since legislatures are necessary evils, they should be allowed as little time as possible in which to do this work. The movement to shift from annual to biennial legislative sessions came to an end in the 1880's " — only two states since then have substituted a session every two years for one every year, and one of these later rescinded its action.[34]

The agitation for biennial sessions comes chiefly from the taxpayers' associations and the economy crowd, without too much justification in fact. A study of the relative merits of annual and biennial sessions was made by the American Legislators' Association several years ago, on the basis of cost. For this purpose, the five states holding annual sessions were compared with five states of about the same population which hold biennial sessions, without constitutional limits on the length of the sessions. Since the states in the two groups had reached a similar stage of industrialization, it might be expected that they would have similar legislative problems. The results of this study are indicated in the table on page 257.

. . . The cost of legislatures represents, on the average, less than 1 per cent of the total governmental costs. During the six-year period 1927–1932 the forty-eight states spent for their legislatures and for legislative investigations a little less than $12,000,000 a year. The total cost of operating the state governments during this same period averages in excess of $1,300,-000,000. A comparison of the legislative costs in the five states having annual sessions with the legislative costs in the five comparable states shows that legislative expenses are higher in states where the lawmakers meet every year. Furthermore, a larger proportion of the state revenue is used to operate the legislative machine in the annual states. It will be observed in the table, however, that this ratio for the annual states is less than double that for the biennial states and that some of the annual states have legislative costs below those of some of the biennial states. It would seem that the cost of running the legislative establishment is due partly to the character of the problems the legislature must meet and partly to legislative customs which vary from state to state.

[34] Georgia made the change in 1924, Massachusetts in 1938, each by constitutional amendment. See Worrell, Dorothy, *Annual or Biennial Sessions for Massachusetts?* (Boston, 1938), and the report of the Special Commission on Biennial Sessions and Biennial Budgets (Massachusetts House Documents, No. 2551, 1938). Massachusetts voted a return to an annual session in 1944. Alabama changed from a quadrennial to a biennial session beginning in 1943. See Martin, Roscoe C., "Alabama Falls in Line," *State Government*, March, 1940, pp. 43–44, 63, and Pow, Alex S., " Alabama's New Legislative Process in Action," *ibid.*, December, 1943, pp. 246–247. The problem was considered in the New York Constitutional Convention of 1938, but no change was made.

COST OF LEGISLATURES, 1927–1932 [35]

State	Average Legislative Cost 1927–1932	Average Total Costs	Ratio Per Cent
Annual States			
Massachusetts [36]	$ 876,000	$ 43,317,000	2.02
New Jersey	488,000	55,998,000	0.87
New York	2,078,000	194,609,000	1.07
Rhode Island	111,000	7,279,000	1.15
South Carolina	239,000	13,274,000	1.80
Totals	3,792,000	314,477,000	
Average	758,000	62,895,000	1.21
Biennial States			
Michigan	261,000	63,456,000	0.41
Ohio	296,000	48,733,000	0.61
Pennsylvania	908,000	104,063,000	0.87
Maine	137,000	12,738,000	1.08
Mississippi	225,000	14,861,000	1.51
Totals	1,827,000	243,851,000	
Average	365,000	48,770,000	0.75

Of course, any experienced legislator knows that the efficiency of a legislative body cannot be determined by such rough tests as the number of sessions held or the amount expended for legislative work. Students of problems of legislation are quite generally agreed that one of the least desirable economies in government is the slashing of legislative expenditures. Since the amount of these expenditures is so small, in proportion to the costs of state government, the savings which could be made by biennial sessions would hardly offset the waste which might arise from the reduced opportunity for legislative scrutiny of the money appropriated for other purposes. Annual sessions offer an opportunity for legislative planning and budgeting which is difficult to achieve with biennial meetings.[37]

Special Sessions. In all states the governor is authorized by the constitution to summon the legislature in special session when, in his judgment, the circumstances require it. In seventeen states, he has complete control over the number and character of the subjects to be considered in such sessions, by virtue of his authority to include or omit them from the call. Whether the number be one or a dozen, the legislature is prohibited by the constitution from the consider-

[35] Mott, Rodney L., " Annual or Biennial Sessions," American Legislators' Association, Chicago, 1934. The figures are taken from *Financial Statistics of States*, issued annually by the United States Bureau of the Census.

[36] Five years only (1927–1931).

[37] Mott, *op. cit.*

ation of bills dealing with other subjects. Eleven states permit the governor to recommend during the special session, by special message, matters in addition to those contained in the proclamation convening the legislature. Only three states — Alabama, Arkansas, and Florida — permit the legislature itself to suggest the consideration of additional business while in special session, and such permission is considered upon a two-thirds vote of each house.[38] In some states, to be sure, the courts have given a liberal interpretation of these provisions, thereby authorizing legislation on subjects naturally and closely related to those specifically enumerated.

The number of extra sessions during the decade of the thirties was greatly increased by the repeal of Amendment XVIII, the unemployment and relief situation, and the financial problems resulting therefrom. The study of annual and biennial sessions referred to above attempted to discover the extent to which special sessions were employed in the two types of states. " During the seven and a half year period from January, 1927, to July, 1934, 158 special sessions have been called in the United States. . . . During this period, eighteen of the 158 special sessions were held in the five states having annual sessions. It should be observed, however, that five of the eighteen occurred in New Jersey in the single year 1931. The five states with biennial sessions which may be compared to those having annual sessions found it necessary to call their legislators together on the average sometimes during six years out of eight. Annual sessions would have meant for those states a meeting of the legislature in two additional years during this eight year period." [39] The number of special sessions each year rose gradually to forty-three in 1933, thirty-eight in 1934, and forty-six in 1938. From 1927 to 1940 inclusive, Illinois and Texas had nineteen each; Louisiana, fourteen; Ohio, twelve; Arizona and Kentucky, ten each. The remaining forty-

[38] New York State Constitutional Convention Committee, *Problems Relating to Legislative Organization and Powers*, p. 405 (Albany, 1938). Chapter 13 discusses the question, Shall the legislature have the power to convene itself in extraordinary session? and lists the subjects contained in the governor's calls for eighteen special sessions held in New York in the forty-year period from 1898 to 1938. This number of special sessions in an annual-session state is significant. See also Fertig, John H., *Scope of the Legislative Power of the General Assembly —* when convened in special session — (Pennsylvania Legislative Reference Bureau, Harrisburg, 1931).

[39] Mott, *op. cit.* That these sessions are costly is illustrated by a two-day session in New York in 1937, called to enact a new administrative code for New York City. The code was not enacted, but the session cost $27,400; round-trip mileage for members, $6,500; personal services of clerks and other employees, $4,400; maintenance and operation of senate and assembly, $4,500; printing, $12,000. For latest data on special sessions, see " State Legislative Overtime; 1927 to 1940," *State Government*, June, 1940, pp. 117, 119, 121.

two states each had less than ten. Nevada had one, New Jersey nine, with the rest quite evenly distributed in the range from two to eight.

Split Sessions. The split session, used for a number of years in California, was adopted in New Mexico in 1940. It was formerly used in West Virginia. Under this plan the legislature meets for a month for purposes of organization, introduction of bills, et cetera. At the expiration of this period there follows a recess of a month; it was intended that this period would enable the members to study the contents of bills which had been introduced and upon which they would be required to vote at a later date, and to determine the sentiment of their constituencies regarding important legislation. Within the last few years able students of government have made special studies of the operation of this system.[40] Their independent judgments have been that this plan has not produced legislative accomplishments of a higher order than are to be found in states operating under the usual plan. Professor Barclay points out that in California the operation of the plan since it was adopted by constitutional amendment in 1911 has resulted in the introduction of skeleton bills in considerable number; it has created a pre-recess rush not dissimilar to the familiar rush at the end of the session — which, incidentally, it has not eliminated; and it appears that constituents are in fact rarely consulted. " During the period 1915–1929, post-recess introductions averaged at each session 200 bills for the 120 members." The older and more experienced legislators are practically unanimous in desiring its abolition or modification; numerous proposals toward this end have been introduced, but the necessary majorities to secure their adoption have not been forthcoming.

Adjourned Sessions. Where the device of the split session is used, it is based upon a constitutional provision; the same result can be achieved by action of the legislature itself without any constitutional provision by the use of what is known as the adjourned session. This device has been used in a number of states. " The financial condition of Tennessee presented such a difficult problem [in 1931] that the legislature adjourned on March 20 for recess until May 25, to give the State Investigating Committee time to consider its work." [41] The legislatures of several other states recess for a month

[40] West, Victor J., " California — the Home of the Split Session," *National Municipal Review*, July, 1923, pp. 369–376; Faust, Martin L., " Results of the Split-Session System of the West Virginia Legislature," *American Political Science Review*, February, 1928, pp. 109–121; Barclay, Thomas S., " Bifurcation Out West," *State Government*, April, 1932, pp. 5–6.

[41] See note in *State Government*, May, 1931, pp. 5–6.

or more during sessions; among these are Alabama, Georgia, Ohio, Pennsylvania, and Texas. Recourse to this device in Ohio seems to have been rather frequent. Dean Crawford reports an interesting case, in which, for political reasons, the legislature took a thirty-minute recess — a recess which in fact extended from March 27, 1925, until January 15, 1926, when the members reassembled for a one-day session, after which another recess was taken.[42]

Executive Sessions. The term " executive session " is not concerned with the duration of the meeting or the time at which it is held, but rather with its essential character. Ordinarily, all legislative sessions are open — that is, members of the public are allowed in the chamber as spectators (only former members may go on the floor) as long as there is room and as long as they remain quiet and orderly. An executive session is held behind closed doors for the purpose of considering nominations sent in by the governor for confirmation. There has been a good deal of criticism of this practice on the ground that it violates the principles of democratic government, and at least one state — Michigan — amended its senate rules in 1942 to require a two-thirds vote rather than a simple majority to place that body in executive session.

Weekly Schedule of Meetings. The weekly schedule of meetings is quite different from that prevailing in Congress, where, under ordinary circumstances, daily sessions are held. Practice in the states varies, but it is customary for the state legislatures to convene sometime Monday evening for a session which may extend into the early morning hours. By this arrangement members are able to make the trip to the state capitol from their homes during the day. Many arrive at noon or shortly thereafter, devoting the afternoon to conferences and committee appointments. The same use is commonly made of Tuesday and Wednesday forenoons. On these days sessions will begin at eleven or twelve o'clock and continue until late in the afternoon. Evening sessions, similar to the one on Monday, will occur on Tuesday evening and sometimes on Wednesday. The majority of the members have returned to their homes late Wednesday night or Thursday, except in the last week or two of the session, when it may be necessary to continue meetings later in the week. This peculiar schedule is more or less necessary because the work of a legislator is only a part-time job with compensation limited accordingly; it enables members to spend the week end at home, and to exercise some supervision over their business or professional activi-

[42] Crawford, Finla G., *State Government,* p. 131 (Holt, New York, 1931).

ties — which are usually, during the session, rather seriously neglected. The following paragraphs from a representative in New Hampshire, which has the largest legislature in America, will show how this system works in that state:

In the first place, New Hampshire is a rather small state geographically, although the largest legislatively. All but a dozen of our members can reach the capitol by eleven o'clock in the forenoon if they leave their homes early in the same morning, and can reach home by evening if they leave the capitol at noon. The state pays all traveling expenses. Even a very busy man, therefore, can afford to serve his turn as a legislator without serious sacrifice in New Hampshire; there is such a short distance to travel that little time is lost, and the state assumes the expenses.

We begin our week's work on Tuesday at 11 A.M. with a short session, which rarely lasts more than an hour. At about 1 P.M. committee hearings begin; they are suspended at 3 P.M. for a second short session of each house after which the hearings are continued until 5 P.M. On Wednesday morning, hearings begin at 9.30 or 10 A.M. and continue until 11 A.M., when a general session is held. On Wednesday afternoon, the Tuesday afternoon schedule is repeated. In cases of extended debate, the 11 o'clock session may be prolonged to as late as 1 P.M. In that event, a recess is taken for lunch until 2 P.M., when the House discussion is again renewed — and the regular 3 o'clock session is delayed until 4 or 5 o'clock. The regular schedule, however, is altered but slightly; the 1 o'clock hearings for that day are simply eliminated. Thursday, the procedure of Wednesday is followed except that the work of the afternoon is advanced to the 11 o'clock session by a suspension of the rules; and that session adjourns at noon. Thus ends the week's work. Our Constitution provides that an adjournment shall not be taken for more than two days at a time. To conform to this provision, there are perfunctory sessions, by general agreement, on Friday morning and Monday evening, but these are usually attended by the clerk, the speaker pro tem, and only a few other members.

In this way our fifteen-week session dwindles to forty-five actual legislative days. As individuals, we devote Tuesdays, Wednesdays, and Thursdays to the affairs of the State, and Fridays, Saturdays, Sundays, and Mondays to our private interests at home. Thus our $2.00 per day expands to $4.00, which adequately provides for our moderate expenses. I have kept a rather accurate expense account during the last three sessions, and my expenses have never exceeded $100 per session. We are furnished stationery, stamps, and a daily paper. Of course this salary does not allow much for poker parties or for other luxuries, but that does not seem to be necessary for most of the members.[43]

Length of Sessions. Many states impose a constitutional limit of sixty days on the length of legislative sessions. This practice, as noted, grew out of the widespread distrust of legislative bodies which

[43] Duncan, George H., " 418 in One House," *State Government*, April, 1931, pp. 11–12.

reached its height in the latter part of the last century, and to the practice of compensating members on a per diem basis. In the effort to control the abuses which developed under this system, the states began to adopt a flat salary compensation for an unlimited session, or if the per diem method of compensation was retained, they limited the length of the session. In eighteen states regular sessions are limited to sixty days, while in twenty-one there is no limitation whatever. Thirty-nine states thus follow one of these two courses, the remaining nine having limitations ranging from forty days in Oregon and Wyoming to 150 days in Connecticut.[44] Thirty-three states do not limit the length of special sessions. Six states impose a limit of twenty days, six others a limit of thirty days. Arkansas sets the limit at fifteen days. Indiana at forty, and South Dakota at sixty. A " day " is variously defined by the courts, by custom, or by the constitution as a calendar day, in seventeen states, and as a meeting day, in twelve.

Much criticism has been heaped upon the limited session plan; in practice there is probably little to choose between limited and unlimited sessions. The criticism of the limited session has been based mainly upon the terrific jam which clogs the legislative machinery in the closing days of the session. While there is much justification for this criticism, precisely the same thing happens where the session is limited not by constitutional provision, but by agreement of the leaders. The same dilatory tactics are followed in both cases in the early days of the session. In states with unlimited sessions, members begin to be impatient and to demand an early closing. In the effort to keep them in line, the leaders arbitrarily set a closing date and then struggle to work their way out of a legislative jam just as severe in many cases as that which develops in states with a limited session.

THE COMMITTEE SYSTEM

As the number and scope of governmental activities have increased, the task of the legislatures has become more and more difficult, and the need for legislative committees has correspondingly increased. Economists talk much about the division of labor in industry; the committee system applies this principle to the process of legislation. The number of subjects with which a legislature must deal is large; the number of bills which it must handle is even greater. It would be a

---

[44] Data from New York State Constitutional Convention Committee, *op. cit.*, p. 396; Alabama and Kansas, fifty days; Indiana, sixty-one days; Tennessee, sixty-five days; Maryland and Minnesota, ninety days.

physical impossibility for any one member to familiarize himself with the provisions of all the measures introduced. There is, however, some subject or type of subject in which different members are interested and with regard to which they can express competent judgment. The committee system affords a member an opportunity to work on legislative subjects in which he is most interested and concerning which he is best informed; it gives the legislature the benefit of such wisdom and experience as its members may have, and it affords citizens and citizens' organizations an opportunity to present their case before legislation is enacted.

A number of important questions with regard to the operation of the committee system suggest themselves. How many committees are there, and on what subjects? How are the members commonly selected? How many members serve on the ordinary committee, and is this number more or less than it should be? How does the system operate, and is its operation reasonably satisfactory? It is difficult, in limited space, to give adequate answers to these questions, but some essential facts and some brief comment regarding them may be presented.

Number of Committees; Selection of Members. The table on page 264 shows the number of standing committees in both houses of the legislature in each of the forty-eight states as of 1931 and 1945. The number of senate committees ranges from nine in Wisconsin to fifty-one in Georgia and North Carolina, fifty-two in Oklahoma, fifty-three in Washington, and fifty-six in South Dakota. In the lower house the range is from twenty in Rhode Island to sixty-one in Georgia and South Dakota, sixty-six in Michigan, sixty-seven in Oklahoma, and seventy-five in Kentucky. Thus the variation in both chambers is wide. In some chambers the number has been purposely raised in order that most of the members of the body may serve as chairman of a committee — in which case most of the work is done by a few important committees, the others being used to placate politically ambitious members who insist on some kind of a committee chairmanship.[45] The names of standing committees in any state may be found in the legislative manual or in the *Book of the States;* for illustrative purposes the list for the Pennsylvania session of 1945 is included here, together with a proposed standard list (see page 266).

[45] Senator George Woodward wrote in *The Pennsylvania Legislator,* April, 1937: "There are thirty-four committees because there are thirty-four Democratic Senators and each Senator has to be chairman of something. If there ever are fifty Democrats, which God forbid, there will be fifty committees which seems to prove that simplicity is a work of political genius."

State	House			Senate			Number of Committee Seats in Senate	Committee Seats per Member in Senate	Average Size of Committees in Senate
	Number of Members	Number of Committees		Number of Members	Number of Committees				
		1931	1945		1931	1945			
Alabama	106	40	40	35	28	30	248	7.1	8.2
Arizona	58	27	29	19	22	22	116	6.1	5.2
Arkansas	100	41	46	35	40	53	313	8.9	5.9
California	80	58	58	40	40	20	214	5.4	10.7
Colorado	65	37	39	35	29	31	253	7.2	8.1
Connecticut [1]	272	37	34	36	37	36	106	3.0	3.0
Delaware	35	27	27	17	23	22	110	6.5	5.0
Florida	95	69	59	38	40	37	269	7.1	7.1
Georgia	205	51	61	52	48	51	952	18.3	18.9
Idaho	59	39	39	44	28	28	200	4.5	7.1
Illinois	153	32	30	51	41	35	536	10.5	15.3
Indiana [1]	100	58	42	50	48	48	379	7.5	7.9
Iowa	108	48	54	50	51	50	431	8.6	8.6
Kansas	125	37	37	40	43	44	332	8.3	7.5
Kentucky	100	66	75	38	39	44	349	9.2	7.9
Louisiana	100	37	38	39	26	29	263	6.7	8.3
Maine [1]	151	38	45	33	38	40	129	3.9	3.3
Maryland	123	35	37	29	29	31	272	9.4	8.7
Massachusetts [1]	240	30	35	40	30	33	131	3.3	4.4
Michigan	100	62	66	32	38	26	174	5.4	6.6
Minnesota	131	46	44	67	40	41	575	8.6	14.0
Mississippi [1]	140	44	46	49	42	42	356	7.2	9.6
Missouri	150	55	57	34	24	36	314	9.2	8.7
Montana	90	51	52	56	39	46	280	5.0	6.0
Nebraska [2]	..	30	..	43	31	15	119	2.8	8.0
Nevada	40	29	39	17	25	25	99	5.8	4.0
New Hampshire [1]	443	36	37	24	28	28	135	5.6	4.8
New Jersey [1]	60	38	46	21	33	32	132	6.2	4.1
New Mexico	49	31	30	24	18	15	97	4.0	6.4
New York	150	33	37	51	27	27	326	6.4	12.0
North Carolina [1]	120	59	45	50	56	51	864	15.0	15.0
North Dakota [1]	113	42	43	49	42	40	392	8.0	9.8
Ohio	136	36	27	33	21	20	158	4.5	7.9
Oklahoma	118	29	67	44	37	52	549	12.5	10.5
Oregon	60	36	37	30	35	36	194	6.5	5.4
Pennsylvania	208	44	42	50	35	26	324	6.5	12.4
Rhode Island [1]	100	20	20	44	17	18	104	2.3	6.6
South Carolina [1]	124	28	31	46	32	33	378	8.2	11.4
South Dakota	75	59	61	35	53	56	410	11.7	7.3
Tennessee	99	44	45	33	34	34	240	7.3	7.0
Texas	150	38	41	31	36	38	342	11.0	9.0
Utah	60	30	34	23	12	15	103	4.5	6.8
Vermont	246	26	27	30	31	31	163	5.4	5.2
Virginia	100	26	34	40	20	24	190	4.8	7.9
Washington	99	49	50	46	51	53	440	9.6	8.3
West Virginia [1]	94	28	28	32	26	27	267	8.3	9.9
Wisconsin [1]	100	22	22	33	9	9	47	1.4	5.2
Wyoming	55	29	19	27	25	21	99	3.7	4.5
Total	5,685	1,909	1,952	1,772	1,607	1,591			
Average	121	39.2	41.5	36.9	32.8	33.1			

[1] Joint committees are a major factor in some states: *Connecticut, 32;* Indiana, 2; *Maine, 38; Massachusetts, 29;* Mississippi, 5; New Hampshire, 4; New Jersey, 7; North Carolina, 6; North Dakota, 8; Rhode Island, 6; South Carolina, 3; West Virginia, 2; and Wisconsin, 1; the joint committees are included in the totals.

[2] Unicameral legislature since 1937.

The comparative data in the table on page 264 show a tendency for the number of committees in the lower houses to increase in spite of the fact that the number is already much too large. If the number of committees is large in one house in a given state, it is usually large in the other also. Using 1931 as a base, the number of house committees had increased by forty-eight in 1939, and by seventy-three in 1945 — and this in spite of the fact that the total was decreased by thirty when Nebraska changed from a two-chamber to a one-chamber system. The senate committees, which had increased by approximately eighty-one up to 1939, showed in 1945 a very slight net decrease, as compared with the 1931 base. It is significant that the greatest increases have occurred in the smaller chambers.

The choice of committee members in the lower house rests with the speaker except in Oklahoma, where selections are made by the Committee on Committees, and in Nebraska's unicameral legislature, where the same method of choice is used. In the selection of senate committees no such uniformity prevails.[46] In fifteen states the final choice rests with the senate itself, the nominations being made by the lieutenant governor as ex officio president in three states, by a president elected by the senate in one state, and by a nominating committee or otherwise in eleven states. In the other thirty-three states, the final authority does not rest with the senate itself; in these states, exclusive power to choose committees is vested in the lieutenant governor in twelve states, in a president elected by the senate in twelve others, in a president pro tem elected by the senate in six states, and by a committee on committees in three states.

Size of Committees. The size of committees has long been a subject of controversy. In practice most of them are fairly large, while students of legislation have almost unanimously urged that small committees would do more and better work. Senate committees vary in size from an average of two in Connecticut to an average of twenty-three in Illinois; in the lower house the range is from slightly less than five in Nevada to more than thirty-five in Georgia. A former member of the Pennsylvania legislature makes some pertinent remarks on the way this system works, as it relates to both the number and the size of committees:

Whether the existence of a particular committee is necessary to the efficient conduct of business of a legislature may well be tested by the

---

[46] "The Source of Power," accompanied by a table showing who appoints the standing committees in the forty-eight legislatures, prepared by Professor C. I. Winslow, *State Government*, March, 1931, pp. 10–12.

GENERAL ASSEMBLY OF PENNSYLVANIA

Standing Committees, 1945

House of Representatives (40)	The Senate (31)	Proposed (31)
Aeronautics	Aeronautics	Agriculture
Agriculture	Agriculture	Apportionment
Apportionment	Appropriations	Banks and Banking
Appropriations	Banking	Civil and Criminal Law
Banking	Congressional Apportionment	Claims and Audits
Boroughs	Congressional Apportionment	Commerce and Industry
Building and Loan Associations	Constitutional Change	Commerce and Industry
Building and Loan Associations	Corporations	Conservation and Planning
City and County, First Class	County Government	Conservation and Planning
City and County, First Class	Education	Constitutional Change
Cities and County, Second Class	Elections	Education
Cities and County, Second Class	Executive Nominations	Elections and Apportionment
Cities, Third Class	Federal Relations	Elections and Apportionment
Constitutional Amendments	Finance	Engrossment and Enrollment
Constitutional Amendments	Forest and Waters, Game and Fish	Engrossment and Enrollment
Corporations and Industry	Forest and Waters, Game and Fish	Finance
Corporations and Industry	Highways	Insurance
Counties	Insurance	Intergovernmental Relations
Dairy Industries	Judiciary General	Intergovernmental Relations
Education	Judiciary Special	Judiciary
Elections	Labor and Industry	Labor
Federal Relations	Law and Order	Military Affairs
Fisheries	Military Affairs	Motor Vehicles
Forestry	Mines and Mining	Municipalities
Game	Municipal Government	Passage of Bills
Highways	Public Health	Printing and Contingent Expenses
Insurance	Public Utilities	Printing and Contingent Expenses
Judiciary General	Representative Apportionment	Public Domain
Judiciary Special	Representative Apportionment	Public Health
Labor	Rules	Public Institutions
Law and Order	Senatorial Apportionment	Public Utilities
Liquor Control	Senatorial Apportionment	Public Welfare
Mines and Mining	State Government	Public Works
Motor Vehicles	Welfare, Public Assistance, and Pensions	Rules
Municipal Corporations	Welfare, Public Assistance, and Pensions	Rural Local Government
Municipal Corporations	Workmen's Compensation	Rural Local Government
Printing	Workmen's Compensation	State Government
Professional Licensure		Supervision of the Executive Department
Public Health and Sanitation		Supervision of the Executive Department
Public Utilities	State Government	Welfare
Railroads and Railways	Townships	Workmen's Compensation
Railroads and Railways	Ways and Means	Workmen's Compensation

number of bills referred to it during a session. The efficiency and success of any other business or professional undertaking is increased by the elimination of non-essentials. A like result may well be anticipated in the conduct of public business. The legislature should not be an exception. In the session of 1931 of the Pennsylvania Legislature, in the Senate (where there were thirty-five committees), six committees received no bills. Of the remaining committees, seventeen each received not more than ten bills, two each received between ten and twenty-five bills, four each received between twenty-five and thirty-five bills, two each received between thirty-five and fifty bills, and the remaining four committees each received in excess of fifty bills. To the latter group, 507 bills out of the total of 764 bills were referred as follows: to the Appropriations Committee, 174; to the Judiciary General Committee, 182 bills. The third highest number of bills were referred to Committees on Public Roads and Highways, which received ninety-four bills. To the Committee on Municipal Affairs were referred fifty-seven bills.

In the House, where there were forty standing committees, an equally uneven distribution of work prevailed. There the Appropriations Committee received 324 bills. The Committee on Counties received 126 bills. The Committee on Highways received 239 bills; the Judiciary General Committee, 232 bills. Thus of the total of 1,838 bills introduced, 911 were distributed among four committees. It will be noted that the number of appropriation bills equalled almost one-third of the total number of bills introduced into that body and that the number of bills relating to highways equalled almost one-fourth of the total number of bills introduced.[47]

This situation is by no means uncommon; in Kansas, for instance, there " are in every session two committees that regularly average 30 per cent of the total number of bills referred to committees, and seven committees that handle 61 per cent of the bills.[48] In spite of having too many and too large committees and of the uneven distribution of the work assigned to them, they none the less occupy a very important position in the legislative process. Professor Winslow, in his study of legislative committees in Maryland and Pennsylvania, found that the committee action " was really the final action in somewhat more than 92 per cent of instances in the former state, and in 83 per cent in the latter.[49]

Evaluation of the Committee System. Anyone who undertakes to study existing committee arrangements will find them haphazard and unplanned. The author made such a study of senate commit-

[47] Sterling, *op. cit.*, pp. 28–29.

[48] Kansas Legislative Council, *Expediting Legislative Procedure,* p. 4 (Topeka, 1935).

[49] Winslow, C. I., *State Legislative Committees,* Chapter 5 (Johns Hopkins Press, 1931) ; see also Horack, Frank E., " The Committee System," in Shambaugh, Benjamin F., *Statute Law-Making in Iowa,* pp. 533–609, as well as the discussions in such standard works as those of Willoughby and of Walker.

tees in the forty-eight states in 1937. In most states there were committees that were overlapping and duplicating, while at the same time, in spite of an excessive number of committees, there was none to which bills on certain subjects might be appropriately referred. This was the more surprising because there are certain problems or types of problems that are common to all the states. The lists in some were loaded with "sports." Out of a total of 1,541 senate committees, there were 553, or an average of eleven per state, which existed in no other state, and this in spite of the fact that every effort was made to group related committees together, regardless of minor differences in terminology. Kansas had only one such committee, but Kentucky, Oklahoma, and Washington had twenty or more each.

The task of developing a model list which might be usable in the several states is not easy. Established practice is slow to change, and many states have problems more or less peculiar to themselves. An attempt at such a list is made on page 266 in a third column parallel to the lists of Pennsylvania senate and house committees. It was constructed to include (1) all those committees which actually exist in any large number of states, and (2) some committee to which a bill on any ordinary legislative subject might be appropriately referred. Thus it is a compromise between the ideal and the practical. It is too long, and it may have other defects, but it is at least suggestive.

Professor Winslow, in his concluding chapter, suggests a number of objectives and theoretical tests of the results of committee work. Among the objective tests are the number of repeals and amendments of recent legislation, governors' vetoes, duplicate bills, and the referendum. The committees cannot be blamed for repeals or amendments necessitated by a changed public opinion, although they might be for such technical errors as faulty construction, incorrect references or names, ambiguities, et cetera. The vetoes by the governors appear to provide a more reliable index. " A committee system which permits the enactment of from thirty-five to forty-three, or from fifty-three to 104 defective laws (in Maryland in 1927 and 1929) needs attention. It is hardly possible that so many vetoes would be necessary if really ' careful consideration ' were given to the bills by the committees receiving them." Duplicate bills — that is, identical bills introduced in both houses and passed by each — were often referred to different committees, except in the case of appropriation bills. Local measures submitted to the referendum in Maryland were frequently rejected by the voters; "a committee system, intended to represent the local communities, should reflect local desires more accurately than is indicated in many cases."

The purposes of these committees are: " (1) to serve as a means of investigating special fields of proposed legislation and collecting information thereon [this function will be discussed in a later chapter]; (2) to deliberate upon (more time being available than in the chamber itself) and give careful consideration to matters referred to it; (3) to permit the application of specialized knowledge so that proposed legislation may be in such form as to accomplish the desired end and that the chamber may benefit by more or less expert advice; (4) finally, to recommend action." The extent to which the existing committee system succeeds in accomplishing these purposes is a matter of personal judgment. Some states do better than others. It is well known that the quality — not to mention the quantity — of work done by any committee depends largely on the ability of the chairman and the amount of time he is willing to spend on it. It often happens that the chairmen of the appropriation committees are the only members who know anything about the appropriation bills, so that the whole responsibility is largely delegated to them.

After a careful study of the system of standing committees in Alabama, Professor Hallie Farmer concludes that: [50]

1. There are too many committees.
2. Many committees are too large.
3. Work is not properly distributed among the committees.
4. The rules of both House and Senate could be revised to provide more effectively for the work of the committees.
5. The committees must have more effective means of acquiring knowledge of the bills upon which they act.

These conclusions with regard to Alabama apply with equal force to the committees in the other states. There are some changes which could be made to correct these conditions which would be highly beneficial, as has been demonstrated in those jurisdictions in which they have been tried.

The use of joint committees would help. At present separate hearings are scheduled at different times by the two committees considering the same measure. This means that citizens desiring to testify must make two trips to the capitol for the same purpose, at a con-

[50] Farmer, Hallie, *Standing Committees*, pp. 35–40 (University of Alabama, Bureau of Public Administration, 1945) ; also California Committee on Legislative Organization, *Final Report on Rational Organization of Standing Committees of the Assembly* (Sacramento, 1944) , and Illinois Legislative Council, *The Committee System of the Illinois General Assembly* (Springfield, 1940) .

siderable unnecessary expense, loss of time, and expenditure of energy. All this could be prevented if other states would follow Massachusetts and other New England states in providing for joint standing committees for all the more important subjects. Such joint committees are found in only thirteen states, and they handle the bulk of the work in only three of these — Connecticut, Maine, and Massachusetts. This plan has the additional advantage of making certain that the same data and information are presented to the representatives of both houses; under the present system this can happen only by accident, although it is obviously desirable that both groups be in possession of the same basic information. As Professor Farmer points out, if it is not desired to establish joint committees, it is possible to reduce the total number of committees by abolishing those that have outlived their usefulness, by consolidating those to which few bills are referred, or by establishing a committee setup which corresponds roughly to that of the major executive departments.

It should also be made easier for members to pry bills out of committee. Six states go so far, in one or both houses, as to require the reporting out of all bills referred.[51] While this is not necessary, since it brings to the floor many bills which stand no chance of passage, it should be possible to force out of committee any bill which has any appreciable support. In nearly every legislature there are one or more " pickling " committees, which conveniently forget to report out a great many bills. While these bills die in committee, it is often impossible to find out who killed them or why. The situation is the same, whether the bills be freaks, bills favoring some special interest, or important measures in the public interest. Where the rules require the reporting of all bills, the chairman and members of the committee must put themselves on record. Were this the general practice, or were one fifth of the members able to discharge a committee from further consideration of a bill, it is certain that many bills which are now " pickled " would be given such chance of passage as might accompany consideration on the floor. The rules in some states make such action impossible.[52]

51 In both houses in Massachusetts, North Dakota, and Vermont; in the lower houses in Texas and Utah; in the senate in Pennsylvania.

52 The methods by which a legislative body recalls a measure from committee are an interesting and important part of committee procedure. In general the states may be classified as follows into three groups according to the method used: first, that group of states in which an extraordinary vote is required; second, those in which discharge is permitted by a simple majority vote; third, a small group of states in which the bills, under certain conditions, automatically come back to the houses for action. (Winslow C. I., " Discharge Rules in State Legislatures," a memorandum in the files of the Council of State Governments.)

THE COST OF LEGISLATION

Only recently has anyone considered the cost of legislation; with rising governmental costs and decreased revenues during the depression, we have come to consider even the cost of making our laws. There has been a general impression that the cost was higher than

STATE LEGISLATIVE EXPENDITURES, UNITED STATES, FISCAL YEAR 1943*

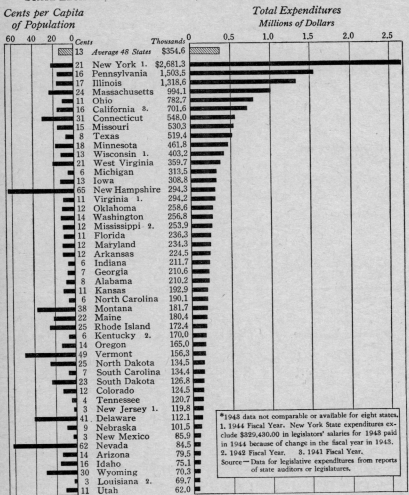

Cents		Thousands	Total Expenditures Millions of Dollars
13	*Average 48 States*	$354.6	
21	New York 1.	$2,681.3	
16	Pennsylvania	1,503.5	
17	Illinois	1,318.6	
24	Massachusetts	994.1	
11	Ohio	782.7	
16	California 3.	701.6	
31	Connecticut	548.0	
15	Missouri	530.3	
8	Texas	519.4	
18	Minnesota	461.8	
13	Wisconsin 1.	403.2	
21	West Virginia	359.7	
6	Michigan	313.5	
13	Iowa	308.8	
65	New Hampshire	294.3	
11	Virginia 1.	294.2	
12	Oklahoma	258.6	
14	Washington	256.8	
12	Mississippi 2.	253.9	
11	Florida	236.3	
12	Maryland	234.3	
12	Arkansas	224.5	
6	Indiana	211.7	
7	Georgia	210.6	
8	Alabama	210.2	
11	Kansas	192.9	
6	North Carolina	190.1	
38	Montana	181.7	
22	Maine	180.4	
25	Rhode Island	172.4	
6	Kentucky 2.	170.0	
14	Oregon	165.0	
49	Vermont	156.3	
25	North Dakota	134.5	
7	South Carolina	134.4	
23	South Dakota	126.8	
12	Colorado	124.5	
4	Tennessee	120.7	
3	New Jersey 1.	119.8	
41	Delaware	112.1	
9	Nebraska	101.5	
3	New Mexico	85.9	
62	Nevada	84.5	
14	Arizona	79.5	
16	Idaho	75.1	
30	Wyoming	70.3	
3	Louisiana 2.	69.7	
11	Utah	62.0	

*1943 data not comparable or available for eight states.
1. 1944 Fiscal Year. New York State expenditures exclude $329,430.00 in legislators' salaries for 1943 paid in 1944 because of change in the fiscal year in 1943.
2. 1942 Fiscal Year. 3. 1941 Fiscal Year.
Source—Data for legislative expenditures from reports of state auditors or legislatures.

* From New York State Joint Legislative Committee on Legislative Methods, Practices, Procedures and Expenditures, *Interim Report,* p. 23 (Legislative Document, 1945, No. 35).

it should be, but such studies as have been made do not support that view. An analysis made in 1945 by the New York State Joint Committee on Legislative Methods, Practices, Procedures and Expenditures shows that with the exception of a few of the larger states the total cost figures are not impressive, and that the per capita expendi-

COST OF LEGISLATION IN OHIO, 1937–1938 AND 1939–1940 [53]

		Bills Introduced	Bills Passed	Total Cost	Average Cost of Bills Introduced	Average Cost of Bills Passed
			Biennium 1937–1938			
Senate		368	74	$285,714.14	$573.28	$2,361.27
		6	2			
		87	28			
		37	17			
	Total	498	121			
House of Representatives		716	134	585,007.96	652.18	3,472.26
		8	4			
		110	32			
		63	10			
	Total	897	180			
Legislative Reference Bureau	S	498	121	8,806.32	6.46	29.23
	H	897	180			
	Total	1,395	301			
Total		1,395	301	$879,528.42	$631.20	$2,922.02
			Biennium 1939–1940			
Senate		325	104	$208,811.13	$642.40	$2,007.49
House of Representatives		677	121	478,489.31	706.78	3,954.45
Legislative Reference Bureau	S	325	104	8,726.84	8.71	38.78
	H	677	121			
	Total	1,002	225			
Total		1,002	225	$696,027.28	$694.63	$3,093.45

tures are negligible amounts, ranging from as little as three cents in Louisiana and New Jersey to sixty-five cents in New Hampshire. The average for all the states is thirteen cents. To take a group of representative states, the cost in California is sixteen cents; in Illinois, seventeen cents; in Massachusetts, twenty-four cents; in New York, twenty-one cents; and in Pennsylvania, sixteen cents — all for the fiscal year 1943.

A major item in the cost is the salaries of members, followed by

[53] Compiled by N. M. Yoder, and furnished to the author through the courtesy of Professor Walker of Ohio State University.

such other items as the salaries of the large group of legislative employees, the cost of legislative printing, et cetera. In Wisconsin, where legislative costs are moderate compared with those in many other states, there has been an increase of 60 per cent in twelve years. In Pennsylvania, one of the higher cost states, legislative costs during three years of the second Pinchot administration amounted to more than $3,500,000; special sessions cost $325,000, $313,000, and $300,000 in the years 1931, 1932, and 1933, respectively. The average annual cost of legislation in this state has been well over $1,000,000. It may be well to comment briefly upon the various elements that enter into this item. The chart on page 271 shows legislative expenditures for all states for the fiscal year 1943, while the table on page 272 gives a breakdown of cost figures for two fairly recent Ohio sessions.

In sharp contrast to total state expenditures, legislative costs have remained relatively stationary during the past twenty-five years. In consequence, as a percentage of total state expenditures, legislative costs have shown a sharp decline during the last century. In New York the legislature cost more than fifteen times as much to operate in 1944 as in 1850, but in this period the percentage of total expenditures represented by the cost of the legislature had declined from approximately 10 per cent to less than 1 per cent. This fact is clearly indicated in the following table:

LEGISLATIVE EXPENDITURES AS PER CENT OF
TOTAL STATE EXPENDITURES, NEW
YORK STATE, 1850–1944 [54]

| Year | Legislative Expenditures | |
	Total	Per Cent of Total State Expenditures
1850	$189,684	9.7
1860	309,096	9.1
1870	577,795	7.1
1880	507,528	6.8
1890	600,491	5.4
1900	1,343,199	6.6
1910	1,503,764	4.6
1920	1,649,254	1.8
1930	1,799,268	.7
1940	2,672,575	.7
1944	3,010,718	.8

[54] From New York State Joint Legislative Committee on Legislative Methods, Practices, Procedures and Expenditures, *Interim Report,* p. 26.

LEGISLATIVE EXPENDITURES, NEW YORK STATE [55]

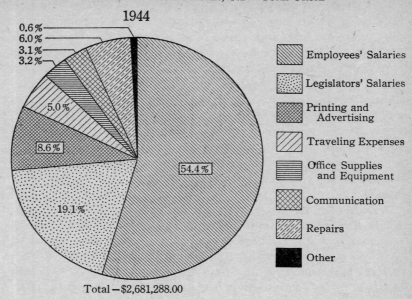

1944

0.6% —
6.0% —
3.1% —
3.2% —

5.0%

8.6%

54.4%

19.1%

Employees' Salaries

Legislators' Salaries

Printing and Advertising

Traveling Expenses

Office Supplies and Equipment

Communication

Repairs

Other

Total — $2,681,288.00

Salaries of Members. Some years ago a comprehensive report on the cost of legislation was prepared at Duke University; [56] from this one may note the percentages of total legislative costs which are accounted for by the payments of salaries to members. These data, summarized for five representative states, are as follows:

PERCENTAGE COST OF MEMBERS' SALARIES IN REPRESENTATIVE STATES

State	*Percentage of Total Cost for Senate Salaries*	*Percentage of Total Cost for Lower House Salaries*	*Percentage of Total Cost for Salaries*
California	11.63	23.83	35.46
Massachusetts	9.61	55.80	65.41
New York	7.73	21.02	28.75
Pennsylvania	10.98	41.07	52.05
Wisconsin	15.17	44.70	59.87

[55] Department of Legislative Research and Drafting. *The Cost of Legislation* (Duke University Law School, 1934).

[56] From New York State Joint Legislative Committee on Legislative Methods, Practices, Procedures and Expenditures, *Interim Report*, p. 28.

It thus appears that salary costs for members consumed approximately one third to two thirds of the total legislative costs in these states. In New York the later figures for 1944 show that less than 20 per cent of the total cost goes for salaries of members. Legislative salaries have changed little, while a greater volume of work requires more services, which must be paid for on a higher price scale. It is difficult to reduce figures such as these to a common denominator, for the sizes of the houses and the compensations authorized differ so much that comparison is difficult if not impossible.

Salaries of Legislative Employees. The accompanying pie-chart taken from the New York report shows the distribution of cost for the various major items of expenditure for the 1944 session. The salaries of employees constitute the largest single item and show a marked increase from the 1934 figures given in the Duke University report. The major employees include the secretary of the senate, clerk of the house, sergeants at arms, chaplains, engrossing and enrolling clerks, postmaster, librarian, et cetera; minor employees include a large number of clerks, stenographers, typists, pages, transcribing clerks, copy readers, pasters and folders, watchmen, custodians, and others. The data for legislative employees are presented below, for the same states and in the same form as that used for legislative salaries:

PERCENTAGE COST OF LEGISLATIVE EMPLOYEES' SALARIES IN
REPRESENTATIVE STATES

State	Percentage of Total Cost for Senate Employees' Salaries	Percentage of Total Cost for Lower House Employees' Salaries	Percentage of Total Cost for Employees' Salaries
California	3.73	3.73	7.46
Massachusetts	....	....	....
New York	15.56	15.66	31.22
Pennsylvania	13.55	14.53	28.08
Wisconsin	8.62	11.11	19.73

These figures, like the former ones, show a wide variation in expenditures. Because of temptation to employ more persons than are necessary, and to select them on the basis of political favoritism, this item of expense is one which offers considerable opportunities for savings, as is illustrated by the fact that Illinois was able to reduce its expenditures for per diem employees from $91,618 in the 55th General Assembly to $51,656 in the 56th and $59,737 in the 57th. Wisconsin has pointed the way to such savings:

> When the legislature in 1931 adjourned on June 27, only a few employees were retained beyond that date and those were laid off from day to day until the last one was dropped on July 18. The cost of legislative service in Wisconsin as compared with other jurisdictions where legislative employees are selected largely for political reasons is a practical demonstration of the value of the competitive system of selection of public employees. The state of Wisconsin spent less in 1931 for its entire personnel service in connection with the legislative session than was spent by New York State for its extra legislative employees.[57]

In addition to the personnel employed by the various legislatures when they are in session, six states have staffs of permanent employees receiving annual salaries. A majority of these remain at the capitol when the legislatures are not in session. The following table indicates the states and the number and the salary range of these employees as reported in 1936:

PERMANENT LEGISLATIVE EMPLOYEES[58]

State	Number of Senate Employees	Number of House Employees	Salary Range
Massachusetts	17	21	$2,000–$9,000
Michigan	3	3	. . . .
New York	23	31	. . . .
Ohio	5	6	1,500–4,500
Pennsylvania	22	17	1,200–7,500
Rhode Island	6	7	500–1,800

Legislative Printing. The routine legislative printing in New York includes the following items:

Bill (2,000 copies of each general bill, 1,500 copies of each local or private bill).
Index to bills.
Bound copies of Senate and Assembly bills.
Calendars (850 copies for each legislative day).
Engrossed bills (10 copies of each).
Journals (225 copies of Senate Journal; 310 copies of Assembly Journal).
Messages from the Governor for press release (850 or more).
Executive budget (1,375 copies).
Budget bills (4,000 copies).

57 " Excessive Cost of Legislative Service," *Good Government*, January, 1932.
58 American Legislators' Association, " Legislative Employees," a bulletin issued June 5, 1936.

Engrossed budget bills (20 copies).
Slip laws (250 copies of session laws).
Session laws (official edition — 2,700 copies).

In addition there are such directories and manuals as are customary in the different jurisdictions. Committees — the important ones, at least — may present printed reports; and occasionally the transcript of committee hearings will be mimeographed or printed. The costs of this printing, which are often excessive, are directly influenced by several factors:

1. The uneven volume of bills sent to the printer during the session.
2. The legislative printing contract, which may exclude a substantial part of legislative printing.
3. The lack of competition for legislative printing.
4. Waste in connection with number of copies and with the form of printing, especially of bills.[59]

As regards the last item, bill printing, such printing might well be done on cheap paper and in an inexpensive format; this is especially true of original printings, where the main purpose is immediate rather than permanent reference. In one state more copies are printed than are needed; a smooth finish paper of good grade is used for all printing, size eight and one fourth by twelve and one half inches. In 1933 the printing of 1,000 copies in pink cost $2.525; in white, $2.505. A striking illustration of the costliness of such printing may be obtained by computing the cost of the various reprints made of one of the bills in the Pennsylvania session of 1933 (see table on page 278). This bill, political in character and unsound in principle, ran through six printings, each ranging from 332 to 348 pages and each representing an expenditure of over $800. One copy of each of the six printings in one pile weighed over eight and one half pounds. The other extreme is found in Tennessee, where there is no printing of bills and where only the more important ones are mimeographed. Amendments proposed on the floor are read orally. Such a scheme obviously opens the door wide to all sorts of abuses.[60]

[59] These factors were analyzed in the report of the Moreland Commission, appointed in 1940 to investigate abuses and inefficiency in the purchase of legislative and departmental printing in New York State.

[60] Potential savings in printing costs can be made by cutting down the size of legislative journals, by the exercise of greater care in bill printing, and in other ways. See Guild, Frederic H., "Streamlining Legislative Journals," *State Government*, June, 1943, pp. 135–138. Estal E. Sparlin has done more work on state printing than probably anyone else; see his *Administration of Public Printing in the United States* (University of Missouri Studies, Columbia, 1937), and "Possible Savings in State Printing," *State Government*, June, 1945, pp. 100–101.

Legislative recording includes senate and house journals, histories of bills, and manuals. " With the exception of Pennsylvania, which prints a full verbatim record (similar to the *Congressional Record*), and of Maine, which prints a condensed verbatim record (including stenographic reports of all debates at the discussion stage of each

PRINTING COSTS OF ONE BILL IN THE PENNSYLVANIA GENERAL ASSEMBLY, 1933

Printer's Number	Notation	Number of Pages	Cost
22	In pink, as introduced	332	$ 838.30
155	As reported out of House Committee on State Government	332	831.66
193	As re-reported out of House Committee on State Government	335	839.17
409	As re-reported out of House Committee on State Government	341	854.20
839	As reported from Senate Committee on Finance	348	871.74
1102	As re-reported out of Senate Committee on Finance	348	871.74
	Total Cost		$5,106.81

bill not passed by unanimous consent), no state legislature prints a complete record of its proceedings. Records take the form, varying greatly in detail, of minutes kept by the legislative clerical staff." [61] In many states there is no permanent or adequate record of the evolution of bills enacted into law. No part of a legislative journal could lend itself so easily to standardization of form as the history of bills; yet Professor Bradley finds that no part of it is less standardized. The greatest progress has been made in Ohio and Pennsylvania, but the histories in some states are woefully inadequate. He suggests that an adequate history of bills might well contain the following data: " (1) the author or introducer of every measure; (2) committee reference; (3) committee action, with the vote of the committee — names included where recorded — on reporting out and names of those appearing before the committee; (4) action on second and third readings — on third reading, votes with the names recorded, including absences and pairs, should be listed; (5) action in other house (in the same detail for each major legislative stage) ; (6) action on conference; (7) action by gover-

[61] Bradley, Phillips, " Legislative Recording in the United States," *American Political Science Review*, February, 1935, pp. 74–83.

nor; (8) subsequent action." This would appear to be the minimum necessary to give a complete record of the activity of the legislature on each item.

State manuals or bluebooks are issued biennially in some form in most states. In addition to the manuals most states issue tiny legislative handbooks, giving the names and addresses of members, and committee assignments for each house. These usually have a very restricted circulation. The manuals themselves vary in size from small handbooks to huge volumes of 1,500 or 1,800 pages, such as are issued in Indiana, Illinois, Louisiana, New York, Pennsylvania, West Virginia, and other states. One who attempts to compare them will be amazed at the diversity of their organization and the variety of their content. The more important items include the constitutions of the United States and of the state; the names of members of the legislature, often with biographical data and individual photographs; a directory of the executive and judicial officers of the state. Many contain detailed election statistics for the state and its political subdivisions, as well as information on the history of the state, its resources, its capitol, flag, bird, flower, song, et cetera. The development of a model table of contents for these manuals, which might be a standardizing influence, is badly needed.[62]

The total cost of printing, like other items involved in the total legislative cost, consumes a widely varying proportion of the whole. In California it is as high as 41.3 per cent, but it drops to 20.4 per cent in Wisconsin, 13.64 per cent in New York, 9.25 per cent in Massachusetts, and to less than 1 per cent in New Hampshire. One may reasonably suspect that in states where the cost is less than in Massachusetts not much legislative printing is done.

Analysis of Total Legislative Costs. Brief comment has been made about each of the major items contributing to the total legislative costs. By way of summary, the table on page 280 brings together the costs for these several items, and for some minor ones, in such a way as to give a clear picture of the whole. All figures are on a per-

---

[62] See, in addition to the Bradley article: " State Manuals," a bulletin issued by the American Legislators' Association, July 7, 1934; a discussion of state yearbooks in *State Government*, June, 1936, pp. 122–125; Council of State Governments, " Legislative Digests and Indexes," a bulletin issued October 6, 1937; Swisher, I. G., " Election Statistics in the United States," *American Political Science Review*, June, 1933, pp. 422–434; and Wilcox, Jerome K., Ed., *Manual on the Use of State Publications* (American Library Association, Chicago, 1940). It is suggested that the reader secure from the secretary of state or from the legislator from his district a copy of the manual of his home state; it will be very helpful to consult it for specific information regarding his own state on many points discussed in this text.

centage basis, and are taken from data contained in the Duke University report.

DISTRIBUTION OF LEGISLATIVE COSTS

State	Salaries of Members	Salaries of Employees	Printing	Supplies and Expenses	Mileage	Miscellaneous
California	35.46	7.45	41.30	8.03	.83	...
Massachusetts	65.41	....	9.25	1.91	4.92	...
New York	28.75	31.22	13.64	12.92	.42	...
Pennsylvania	52.05	28.08	....	9.19	1.67	7.43
Wisconsin	59.87	19.73	20.40	....	...	...

IMPROVEMENTS IN ORGANIZATION

The job of the legislator is made needlessly difficult. The term is short. Re-election is uncertain and, very likely, expensive. The working conditions are poor. The compensation, in most states, is woefully inadequate. The expenses connected with the job more than consume the meager salary and allowances. While in Congress we choose men for full-time service and pay them a fair salary, we ask only part time service of our state legislators, and we scarcely pay for that. As a result, high-grade business and professional men who are willing to serve at all do so only at a personal sacrifice. Many of the legislatures are too large, and the sessions are too short and too infrequent to permit the members to do an adequate job.

The setup is conducive neither to obtaining competent legislators nor to getting relatively satisfactory performance from those whom we select. In addition to these external defects, there are others that are internal, as for instance, the failure in many states to do proper legislative planning or to set up a rational committee system. All of these conditions should be corrected, and all kinds of remedies have been proposed and tried. Consideration may be given first to the external difficulties. With the beginning of the depression, special sessions became both numerous and frequent. Under unsettled economic conditions it was and is difficult to estimate for one year — much less for two — either the probable yield of existing taxes or those expenditures which fluctuate widely, such as relief.

Some legislators in states like New York and Pennsylvania have advocated annual sessions, one in each two-year period to be devoted to general legislation, the other to be devoted exclusively to budgetary and financial problems. This proposal does not meet the need. Financial considerations are so inextricably involved in most questions of public policy that the separation of the two is impossible, and the attempt to separate them highly superficial.

More practical is the suggestion of the committee that framed the Model State Constitution. All of the factors contributing to the unsatisfactory organization of the state legislatures led this committee to propose that the legislature be more or less *continuously* in session. Regular sessions would be held quarterly, to receive a report from the governor, and would continue as long as there was business to be transacted. The members of a smaller body, paid adequately, would devote their full time to legislative work.

This proposal is not nearly so fantastic as may at first appear. Ten or fifteen years ago members attended a session, and then put legislative matters out of their minds for about a year and a half. Today the officers of the two houses, the chairmen of committees, and even ordinary members make frequent trips to the capitol — often weekly — in connection with legislative work. While their expenses may be paid, they freely give their time, often to the detriment of their personal affairs. The proposal of the Model Constitution would set up machinery suitable for the performance of the duties now imposed upon legislators.

The internal difficulties, many of which relate to procedure, could be handled by the legislators themselves without too much difficulty. Members need legislative reference service, bill drafting service, and a legislative council for planning and research. These items will be considered in another chapter. But they need also to remodel their committee setup and to modernize their committee procedures. At present there are, in most states, too many committees. They are usually too large, and they are not properly utilized if the legislature is to discharge adequately its responsibility to the citizens of the state.

SELECTED REFERENCES

Aly, Bower, Ed., *Unicameral Legislatures,* 2 vols. (Lucas Brothers, Columbia, 1937).

Bowers, Claude G., *The Tragic Era* (Houghton Mifflin, Boston, 1929).

Buck, A. E., *Modernizing Our Legislatures* (American Academy of Political and Social Science, Philadelphia, 1936).

Buehler, E. C., *Unicameral Legislatures* (Barnes and Noble, New York, 1937).

Carroll, Daniel B., *The Unicameral Legislature in Vermont* (Vermont Historical Society, Montpelier, 1933).

Chamberlain, Joseph P., *Legislative Processes: National and State* (Appleton-Century, New York, 1936).

Council of State Governments, *The Book of the States* (Chicago, biennially).

Culver, Dorothy C., *Unicameral Legislatures: A Digest of Materials* (Bureau of Public Administration, University of California, 1934).

Dunning, William A., *Reconstruction, Political and Economic* (Harper, New York, 1907).

Farmer, Hallie, *Legislative Apportionment* (University of Alabama, Bureau of Public Administration, 1944).

——, *Standing Committees* (University of Alabama, Bureau of Public Administration, 1945).

Faust, Martin L., *Manual on the Legislative Article* (Missouri Constitutional Convention of 1943, Columbia, 1943).

Fleming, Walter L., *Documentary History of Reconstruction*, 2 vols. (Clark, Cleveland, 1906–1907).

Frothingham, Richard, *The Rise of the Republic of the United States* (Little, Brown, Boston, 1899).

Graves, W. Brooke, Ed., " Our State Legislators," *Annals*, January, 1938.

Green, Harry J., *A Study of the Legislature of the State of Maryland* (Johns Hopkins Press, 1930).

Griswold, Thelma I., *Bicameralism in Ohio* (Western Reserve University, 1937).

Harlow, Ralph V., *The History of Legislative Methods in the Period before 1825* (Yale University Press, 1927).

Illinois Legislative Council, *Committee System of the Illinois General Assembly* (Springfield, 1940).

——, *Reapportionment in Illinois* (Springfield, 1945).

——, *Reapportionment in Illinois: Congressional and State Senatorial Districts* (Springfield, 1938).

Johnson, Alvin W., *The Unicameral Legislature* (University of Minnesota Press, 1938).

Luce, Robert, *Legislative Assemblies* (Houghton Mifflin, Boston, 1924).

Manning, John W., *Unicameral Legislation in the States* (University of Kentucky, 1938).

McHenry, Dean E., *A New Legislature for Modern California* (Haynes Foundation, Los Angeles, 1940).

Moore, Blaine F., *The History of Cumulative Voting and Minority Representation in Illinois, 1870–1919*, Second Edition, University of Illinois, 1920).

Nevins, Allan, *The American States during and after the Revolution, 1775–1789* (Macmillan, New York, 1924).

New York State Constitutional Convention Committee, *Problems Relating to Legislative Organization and Powers* (Albany, 1938).

New York State Joint Legislative Committee on Legislative Methods, Practices, Procedures and Expenditures, *Interim Report* (Legislative Document, 1945, No. 35).

Osgood, Herbert L., *The American Colonies in the Eighteenth Century*, 4 vols. (Columbia University Press, 1924).

Pound, Merrit B., *State Legislature: Two Houses or One* (University of Georgia, 1938).

Ray, Joseph M., *Texas Legislature: One House or Two* (University of Texas *Bulletin,* 1937).

Rousse, Thomas A., *Bicameralism vs. Unicameralism* (Nelson, New York, 1937).

Schaffter, Dorothy, *The Bicameral System in Practice* (University of Iowa, 1929).

Seager, Marguerite, *Legislative Processes: Selected Bibliography* (University of Southern California Institute of Government, 1938).

Senning, John P., *The One-House Legislature* (McGraw-Hill, New York, 1937).

Shambaugh, Benjamin F., Ed., *Statute Law-Making in Iowa* (State Historical Society of Iowa, Iowa City, 1916).

Shull, Charles W., *American Experience with Unicameral Legislatures* (Wayne University, 1937).

Smith, T. V., *The Legislative Way of Life* (University of Chicago Press, 1940).

Summers, Harrison B., *Unicameralism in Practice* (Wilson, New York, 1937).

Trimble, Bruce R., and Stamps, Norman L., *The Structure of the Legislature: Bicameral or Unicameral* (Missouri Constitutional Convention of 1943, Jefferson City, 1943).

Walch, J. Weston, *Complete Handbook on Unicameral Legislatures* (Platform News Publishing Company, Portland, Maine, 1937).

Walker, Harvey, *Law Making in the United States* (Ronald Press, New York, 1934).

Weeks, O. Douglas, *Two Legislative Houses or One* (Arnold Foundation, Dallas, 1938).

Wilcox, Jerome K., Ed., *Manual on the Use of State Publications* (American Library Association, Chicago, 1940).

Willoughby, W. F., *Principles of Legislative Organization and Administration* (Brookings Institution, Washington, 1934).

Winslow, Clinton I., *State Legislative Committees, a Study in Procedure* (Johns Hopkins Press, 1931).

Young, C. C., *The Legislature of California: Its Membership, Procedure, and Work* (Commonwealth Club of California, San Francisco, 1943).

———————

Council of State Governments, *State Government* (Chicago, monthly).

Dobbins, Harry T., " Nebraska's One House Legislature — After Six Years," *National Municipal Review,* September, 1941, pp. 511–514.

Guild, Frederic H., " Streamlining Legislative Journals," *State Government,* June, 1943, pp. 135–138.

Harvey, Lashley G., " America's Largest Legislature," *State Government,* March, 1942, pp. 65–66, 75.

Horack, Frank E., Jr., " Bicameral Legislatures Are Effective," *State Government,* April, 1941, pp. 79–80, 96.

MacNeil, Douglas H., " Urban Representation in State Legislatures," *State Government,* April, 1945, pp. 59–61.

Martin, Roscoe C., " Alabama Falls in Line," *State Government,* March, 1940, pp. 43–44, 53.

Morganthau, Hans J., Ed., " Constitutional Reform in Missouri," *University of Kansas City Law Review,* December, 1942, entire issue. Devoted chiefly to unicameralism.

Pow, Alex S., " Alabama's New Legislative Process in Action," *National Municipal Review,* December, 1943, pp. 246–247.

Senning, John P., " Unicameralism Passes Test," *National Municipal Review,* July, 1944, pp. 58–65.

Shull, Charles W., " Wrangling Reapportionment in Michigan," *National Municipal Review,* May, 1940, pp. 305–310, 314.

——, " Michigan Secures House Reapportionment," *National Municipal Review,* May, 1943, pp. 256–257.

Van der Vries, Berdice T., " A Legislator Earns Her Way," *State Government,* March, 1940, pp. 47–54.

Walter, David O., " Reapportionment of State Legislative Districts," *Illinois Law Review,* May, 1942, pp. 20–42.

CHAPTER VII

The Legislature in Action

IN the preceding chapter certain problems of legislative organization were discussed; before considering in the next chapter those relating to procedure, it seems desirable to pause long enough to present as natural and realistic a picture as possible of the legislature in action. There is a wide variation among the states in details of legislative organization and procedure, but it is believed that there are many fundamental characteristics which are more or less common. In describing some of them, an author needs to remind himself that his opportunities for observation have been relatively limited,[1] and that in reporting some of the seemingly trivial things which literally force themselves upon the observer, he is in danger of giving a false impression of the whole. On this account it is desired to emphasize here the fact that, in spite of these numerous excrescences, a large amount of serious and constructive work is normally accomplished. It is impossible to give a realistic description of what goes on in a state capitol during a session without describing absurdities, yet it is grossly unfair to judge legislative bodies solely on such a basis.

[1] So much is this true that so well recognized an authority on legislative matters as Edwin E. Witte believes that " it is almost impossible to give a description of the actual working of state legislatures which will fit the entire company." The present attempt is based primarily on Pennsylvania, but every effort has been made to indicate, by qualifying statements and in footnotes, aspects of the procedure which are known to be at variance with that of other states. In this connection the author is deeply indebted to William B. Belknap, of Kentucky, former President, American Legislators' Association; Hubert R. Gallagher, Assistant Director, Council of State Governments; Charles Kettleborough, late Director, Indiana Legislative Reference Bureau; Rodney L. Mott, Colgate University, formerly Research Consultant, American Legislators' Association; Philip Sterling of the Philadelphia Bar and former member, Pennsylvania House of Representatives; Fred B. Wood, Legislative Consultant, California; and Edwin E. Witte, former Director, Wisconsin Legislative Reference Bureau. Needless to say, the author alone is responsible for any errors in fact or in judgment that may still remain.

Legislatures are more in need of sympathetic understanding and helpful suggestions for improving their work than of denunciation and criticism. Nothing is farther from the intent of the author than to ridicule state legislatures or to overemphasize the baser features of state legislation; as one authority observes, " a legislature is not all foolishness," nor are a majority of the members either fools or knaves. No doubt if an intelligent legislator were to attempt to describe other social and political institutions, such as the universities or the press, he might be quite as critical and find much that was humorous or ridiculous. It may be noted also that legislatures conduct their business in the limelight, while other institutions and businesses are carried on with relatively little publicity.

THE OPENING OF THE SESSION

Many state capitols are located in small cities, in which case the town is likely to seem dull and the capitol half deserted when the legislature is not in session. When the date for the opening of a session arrives, there is a sudden stir of activity. The corridors of the capitol and the lobbies of the local hotels are filled with incoming members. Those who have served in previous sessions are enthusiastically greeting old friends and acquaintances, while new members are anxiously endeavoring to get located and to adjust themselves to a new and strange experience. The new member, like the freshman in college, is made the victim of a good many practical jokes. In a large eastern state a newly elected member was told to apply at the general offices of a leading railroad company to secure his pass. When he did so, it was explained to him that railways were no longer permitted to issues passes to state government officials. When he reported his inability to secure a pass, his advisers told him that he was entitled to it and that he should go back and demand it. In another instance a young woman, elected to her first term, was waiting in the hotel lobby shortly before the session was to convene, obviously ill at ease. One of the hotel employees inquired whether there was anything that he could do for her. " No," she said, " I am waiting for the state car to take me over to the capitol." The hotel man explained as tactfully as he could that there was no state car, that the entrance to the capitol was less than two blocks away, and that she could either walk or take a taxi. Old-timers around a state capitol usually have an endless supply of stories of pranks that have been played on new members, and of humorous mistakes that these members have unwittingly made.

When the session convenes, organization is the first order of business. The clerk calls the roll and the new members are sworn in. Party caucuses and conferences of the leaders have previously been held, so that candidates can be nominated and elected for the speakership, and any other elective offices. The real struggle over the choice of the speaker usually takes place in the caucus of the majority party; the action of the house is merely a formal ratification of the decision reached in the caucus. In Pennsylvania, after the speaker has been chosen, he appoints certain members of the staff of house employees, of whom there are over a hundred. The nucleus of permanent officers are paid an annual salary; the clerks at the desk are paid $1,800 or $2,000 per session; the other employees are on a per diem basis, most of them at $7.00 or $8.00. In this connection, it should be remembered that these employees must make weekly trips to and from the capitol, and that they must maintain themselves while there at a hotel or boardinghouse.[2] In Pennsylvania the speaker, the resident clerk, and the chief clerk are elected; all house employees are appointed by one of these elected officers. It is customary to employ a chaplain, but in the 1935 session, in the interest of economy, two clergyman members of the House agreed to take turns pronouncing the invocation at the beginning of each session. In Wisconsin all legislative employees are appointed by the chief clerks and the sergeants at arms of the respective houses from lists of eligibles qualified through civil service examinations.

In some states, shortly after the organization, the members draw their " prize packages." The parcels contain such items as scissors, fountain pen, pencil, comb, hairbrush, clothesbrush, diary, account book, pocketknife, memorandum book, and usually a dictionary. This practice is the cause of a good deal of merriment by outsiders. Newspapers are likely to say that the packages contain everything to make life at the state capitol comfortable, with the exception of a toothbrush (which members are supposed to furnish for themselves) , and that a reading of some of the speeches reported in the journal indicates that the inclusion of the dictionary was quite appropriate. Besides this package, the members in most states receive a mileage allowance, and in a few an allowance for stationery and

[2] For a complete list of these employees, together with the appointing authority and their compensation, see Joint Legislative Committee on Finances, *Survey of the Government of Pennsylvania*, pp. 54–55 (Harrisburg, 1934) .

postage.³ Chairmen of important committees may in addition receive an allowance for secretarial assistance. The rules of the preceding legislature are commonly adopted without important modification. While these events are taking place in the house, a similar procedure is being followed across the hall in the senate. In the early weeks of the session much work is being done, but there is little sign of accomplishment visible to the outsider. It may be well over a month before a single bill or resolution is adopted, but large numbers of bills are being introduced each week. These are being referred to the appropriate committees, and in many cases public hearings are scheduled and conferences are held with administrative officials and the representatives of private interests concerned.

THE PASSAGE OF BILLS

It is proposed here to describe the proceedings in the legislative halls while bills are in process of enactment, and to consider the origin and development of some of the rules, the reasons for their existence, and some of the ways in which the usual procedure might be improved. In general, the procedure now followed has developed through a period of many centuries. The three-reading system developed prior to the invention of the printing press as a safeguard against the railroading of legislation when those who might be opposed to the measure happened to be absent. After the invention of the printing press the same system was continued, although one and sometimes two of the readings became largely a formality. The rules in the colonial legislatures were based upon the English precedents, which continued to exercise a controlling influence until Thomas Jefferson compiled his famous *Manual*. Through all the years since, this manual has continued to be regarded as an authority on questions of parliamentary procedure; Cushing's *Manual* is now used in Massachusetts, as well as in many other states.

In attempting to give in proper order a comprehensive list of the steps through which a bill must pass in the process of enactment, it must be noted that no two states will follow the same procedure in every detail. In general, the steps are as indicated below.⁴ Motions

³ Practice with regard to this matter varies; see table, p. 240. In Wisconsin, for instance, stationery is furnished, but postage and other prerequisites (except fountain pen and pencils) are not.

⁴ The volumes by Green, Guild and Snider, Kettleborough, Patton (in Shambaugh's *Statute Law-Making in Iowa*) , and Willoughby, all listed in the Selected References to Chapter VIII, contain discussions of most of these points. The rules of each house will be found in the legislative manual of each state.

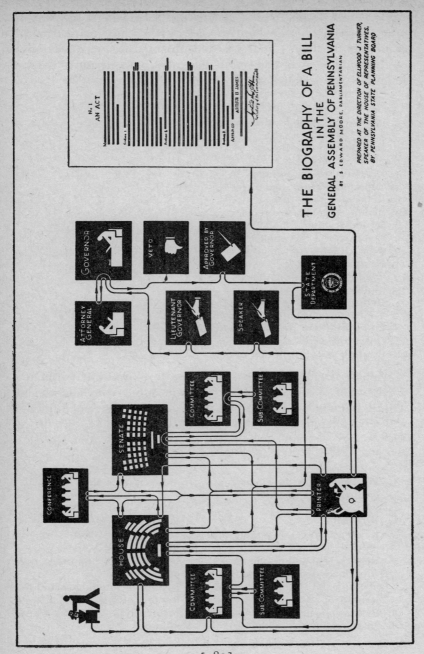

THE BIOGRAPHY OF A BILL
IN THE
GENERAL ASSEMBLY OF PENNSYLVANIA
BY S EDWARD MOORE, PARLIAMENTARIAN

PREPARED AT THE DIRECTION OF ELLWOOD J TURNER,
SPEAKER OF THE HOUSE OF REPRESENTATIVES,
BY PENNSYLVANIA STATE PLANNING BOARD

to recommit, to place on the postponed calendar, to pass over in order, et cetera, are commonly in order when a bill is under consideration on the floor. It is also possible to move for a reconsideration of the vote, in accordance with the rules, on a measure that has recently been defeated.

USUAL STEPS IN THE LEGISLATIVE PROCESS

1. Passage of general rules regulating the proceedings of a general assembly
2. Introduction of bills
3. First reading
4. Reference to committees
5. Consideration by committees
6. Reports of committees
7. Action on committee reports
8. Second reading
9. Committee of the whole
10. Third reading and final passage
11. Engrossment
12. Transmission to other house
13. Action by other house
14. Return to house of origin
15. Conference committee, when necessary
16. Enrollment and presentation to governor
17. Governor's action
18. Printing and distribution of acts

We have noted the weekly schedule with regard to sessions, but it is important to consider also the order of business at these sessions. This is commonly specified in the rules of each house; that of Indiana will serve for purposes of illustration:

ORDER OF BUSINESS IN THE LEGISLATURE OF INDIANA [5]

Senate	House
1. President takes the Chair	1. Speaker takes the Chair
2. Calling Senate to order	2. Calling House to order
3. Prayer	3. Prayer
4. Roll call	4. Roll call
5. Reading and correcting the journal	5. Reading and correcting the journal
6. Reports of standing committees	6. Disposition of unfinished business
7. Introduction of petitions, memorials, and remonstrances	7. Reports of standing committees
8. Reports of select committees	8. Reports of select committees
9. Resolutions of the Senate	9. Introduction of bills and resolutions
10. Joint resolutions of the Senate	

[5] Kettleborough, Chapter 13.

Senate	House
11. Joint resolutions of the House	10. Executive and other communications
12. Introduction of bills	
13. Messages from the House	11. Messages from the Senate and amendments proposed by the Senate to House bills
14. Senate bills on second reading	
15. Senate bills on third reading	
16. House bills on first reading	12. Senate bills and resolutions on first reading
17. House bills on second reading	
18. House bills on third reading	13. House and Senate bills and resolutions on second reading
	14. House and Senate bills and resolutions on third reading

This procedure is subject to suspension of the rules, special orders, and other parliamentary procedures which may be invoked for the handling of specially important or emergency measures. Changes in the regular order of business are made for the purpose of expediting the passage of some measure through the various steps required by the state constitution; the latter are never subject to abbreviation or modification.

Gradually, as the number of bills reported out of committee increases from week to week, the length of the calendar increases. The three-reading system is a universal practice in each house in each state except Nebraska and Utah. In most cases the first reading is by title only by the clerk at the time of introduction (although the rules may require reading in full). The speaker, hearing the title read, and judging therefrom the nature of the contents of the bill, refers it to the proper committee. The bill is ordered printed; in a few states this first printing bears some clearly distinguishing feature, such as the use of pink paper. After the committee has favorably considered the measure and reported it out, it comes out in white, at which time it is placed on the second-reading calendar.

Second Reading. The consideration on second reading is very hurried and is rarely the occasion for extended debate.[6] Measures on second reading are placed on the calendar in the order in which they are reported out by the several committees, but they need not necessarily be considered in this order. A member may call up any such bill when he is in order, or the speaker may postpone consideration of a particular measure until later in the day's session, either on his own initiative or at the request of a member. In some states

---

[6] Again there is no uniformity of procedure. In Wisconsin the second reading is the stage at which amendments are in order. This is the stage of the most extensive consideration of the bill.

it is required that such bills shall have been agreed to in committee of the whole. When bills are to be considered on second reading, the speaker announces this fact and presents each measure separately:

"The next bill on the calendar is House Bill No. 1018, Printer's No. 447."[7]

"Is this bill called up?"

"Called up by the gentleman from Cambria, Mr. Andrews. The clerk will read the first section." (The clerk reads rapidly a few words at the beginning of the section.)

"Does the House agree to this section?" (Slight pause.) "Agreed to. The clerk will read the second section." (The clerk mumbles a few words at the beginning of the second section.)

"Does the House agree to this section?" (Slight pause.) "Agreed to. The clerk will read the title."

"An Act Creating a Commission to Make a Study. . . ."

"Will the House agree to the bill on second reading?" (Slight pause.) "Agreed to. Will the House agree to having the bill transcribed and placed on the calendar for third reading? Agreed to."

If someone makes a motion to recommit, the speaker says, "The question is on the motion. Those in favor will say, 'Aye,' those opposed, 'No.' The ayes have it. The motion is agreed to." When amendments are offered, they are carried to the desk by one of the page boys and read in full. The speaker then proceeds:

"Does the House agree to the amendments?" (Slight pause.) "Agreed to. Does the House agree to the section as amended? Agreed to. Does the House agree to the bill as amended? Agreed to."

From this point on, the speaker proceeds as indicated above. There is no roll call. Motions to recommit or to pass over in order are in order with regard to any bill. At the conclusion of this procedure the speaker announces the number of the next bill, continuing the repetition of these steps until all the bills on the second reading calendar have been disposed of. This procedure can be handled so rapidly that a very long second-reading calendar can be disposed of in less than one hour.

Third Reading. When bills have passed second reading and have been placed on the calendar for third reading and final passage, the speaker announces each bill in similar fashion as follows:

---

[7] The use of a printer's number is not universal; it is useful, however, as a further means of identifying bills, avoiding errors, and insuring that one has the latest printing of a bill.

" This bill has been read three times, at length, on three separate days, considered and agreed to, and is now on its final passage. Agreeably to the provisions of the Constitution, the yeas and nays will be taken. The question is: Shall the bill pass finally? "

Having repeated the words of this liturgy in a loud voice, and in a rapid and almost mechanical fashion, the voice of the speaker booms forth at the conclusion: " The clerk will call the roll." [8] As the session wears on, the clerks have called the roll so many times that they know it from memory; it is seldom necessary for them even to glance at the roll sheets upon which the tally clerks record the votes. Pronouncing the names distinctly but with terrific speed, the voice of the clerk booms forth into the hall of the house: " Andrews, Baker, Baldi, Barnhardt, Bechtel, Beech, Bennett, Bernhard, Blumberg, Boyd, Caputo, Carey, Carson, Chervenak, Cohen, Conner . . . Wood, Woodside, Wright, Yeakel, Yourishin, Zimmerman." If the bill is important and the vote close, the clerk will proceed slowly enough so that each member's voice can be clearly and distinctly heard at the front of the chamber, and his vote recorded by the tally clerks; if the measure is not controversial, the clerk may use the so-called short roll call, racing through the first two or three dozen names at breathless speed, swinging around with a majestic wave of his hand, and concluding with " And Mr. Speaker." The speaker thereupon announces, as soon as the tally sheet reaches him from the clerk's desk, that " On final passage, the yeas were 198, the nays none. The measure is agreed to."

Special Parliamentary Procedures. An opportunity is commonly afforded, even on unimportant or noncontroversial measures, for correction of the roll before the result is announced. In such cases a member rises in his place and addresses the chair: " Mr. Speaker " — the speaker then recognizes the gentleman from Cambria, or Lehigh, or Dauphin, whatever the name of the county from which the member comes — " I desire to be recorded as voting ' No ' on this measure." The speaker then inquires: " Was the gentleman present within the hall of the House when the roll was called? " to which the usual reply is, " I was, Sir." Thereupon the speaker announces, " The gentleman will be so recorded."

In the course of these corrections amusing incidents sometimes

---

[8] In Iowa, Louisiana, Minnesota (House) , Nebraska, Texas, Virginia, and Wisconsin flash voting is used. Under this system of machine voting, about one minute is required for the entire roll call. See Kelley, Alice, " Flash Voting," *State Government*, October, 1930, pp. 6–8; reprinted in *United States Daily*, November 3, 1930.

occur. On one occasion the author heard a member from Philadelphia request permission to change his vote from " Nay " to " Yea," because, he explained, he had voted " No " in the first place merely to play a joke on his friends on the other side of the chamber. The casual manner in which many members vote is further illustrated by the story of a member who walked over to the desk of his friend during an important roll call; he had just voted " Aye ", but as he approached the desk of his friend, the latter voted " Nay." The visitor remarked: " I thought you were in favor of this bill." " No, I'm not," came the reply. " Well, well, well," exclaimed the visiting member, who turned and addressed the chair: " Mr. Speaker, I change my vote from ' Aye ' to ' Nay.' I voted under a misapprehension." [9]

After the completion of a roll call, any member has the privilege of demanding a verification of the roll. Such a verification is commonly requested following the vote on any important measure, particularly if the division is close. Two purposes are served by it. In the first place, it enables each member to assure himself that the tally clerks have correctly recorded his vote, while in the second, it affords an opportunity to challenge the vote of any member recorded as voting, but not within the hall of the house at the time the vote was taken. The procedure of the verification involves simply the reading of the list of names of those who are recorded as having voted in the affirmative, followed by an opportunity for correction, after which the same procedure is repeated with regard to the negative roll.

Sometimes the sponsors of a measure which has been defeated on final passage discover that the defeat was caused by a misunderstanding on the part of some members, or that since the vote some members have changed their minds. In such cases it is customary to move for a reconsideration within one, two, or three days after the final vote was taken, as the rules may prescribe. It is also customary for the sponsor of the bill to prepare the motion for reconsideration, which may read as follows: " The undersigned members of the House of Representatives, having voted in the negative on final passage of House Bill No. 684, Printer's No. 783, on March 13, 1939, do hereby move for a reconsideration of the vote on said bill." This motion, signed by two members who voted against the bill, must be presented to the chief clerk, together with two exact copies of the

---

[9] Some entertaining illustrations of " Humor in the Legislature " will be found in Stackpole, E. J., *Behind the Scenes with a Newspaper Man*, Chapter II (Lippincott, Philadelphia, 1927) .

tally sheet on the original vote.[10] If the members of the house agree to the motion to reconsider, the measure may then come up for another vote.

The procedure in the house during roll call has some interesting and curious aspects. If the measure is an important one, the leaders of parties and factions scurry back and forth around the chamber — doing " foot work " as it is called — giving instructions to their followers and conversing earnestly with other members whose support they hope to enlist.[11] Nearly all members of a given body can be catalogued, if one can observe them for a time. Many never cast an independent vote during an entire session, as some of them will frankly admit. The author once watched a member from a southeastern county vote " No " on a measure before the house; presently his three political satellites voted " No " as their names were called, whereupon the leader turned and said, " You see, they vote as I tell them. I do what the big boy says, and they do as I say." This kind of discipline within the party organization is well known, but rarely admitted with such frankness. On another occasion a member who had for partisan reasons delayed passage of a bill arose, secured the recognition of the chair, and said, " Mr. Speaker, I withdraw my objections. I have spoke to the sponsor of the bill and it is all right." Thus is the King's English sometimes murdered.

The Senate. The discussion thus far has been concerned with the activities of the house. Generally speaking, the conduct of affairs in the lower branch is much more interesting than in the upper house — quite the opposite of the situation existing in Washington. Measures adopted in the lower house are, of course, sent to the senate for approval; here they go through substantially the same procedure as in the house. If the second chamber makes amendments to the bill as approved by the first, these changes must be accepted by the house in which the bill originated before it can be sent to the governor. If these changes are objectionable to those who sponsored the bill originally, it is likely that their colleagues will sustain them in refusing to concur in the amendments, in which case the measure will be sent to conference. Where the bill originated in the house and amendments have been made by the senate, the speaker may put the question in this form: " Will the House concur in the amendments made by the Senate? " and the vote shall then be

---

10 In some states one signature is sufficient. In Wisconsin, for instance, any member who voted on the losing side can move for reconsideration without formality, but he must do so on the day following the vote.

11 This, of course, is impossible where a system of flash voting is used.

taken immediately. The same number of votes is required to concur in the amendments as were necessary for the original passage of the bill. If concurrence is refused, the conference committee will be appointed by the presiding officers of the respective houses, it being customary to select those members most interested and best informed regarding its subject matter. Unless the matter is badly handled, the conferees are usually able to agree on a compromise which is acceptable not only to them, but to their respective chambers.[12]

Other Problems. It is customary for the work to proceed in the manner here described until the end of the session approaches. Gradually the calendar becomes heavier and the speed of the legislative machine materially increases. Much time has been required to iron out differences in committee and to hold public hearings. As the session wears on, the members become more and more impatient in their desire to wind up the work and be relieved of their weekly journeys between their homes and the state capitol. The operation of the legislative machinery as the session advances may be likened to a great locomotive pulling a heavy train of cars out of the railway station. The first movements of the engine come slowly, laboriously, and with a terrific expenditure of effort. As the train gradually gets in motion, the speed increases and the train moves forward at great speed with little apparent effort. In similar fashion, the legislative machinery increases its speed and gathers momentum as the end of the session approaches.

This fact is responsible for the employment of various legislative shortcuts. In the course of the session, for instance, a large number of individual appropriation bills will be introduced for schools, hospitals, welfare institutions, and the like. Many of these will be passed by the house in which they originate, as a compliment to the members who introduced them, without any likelihood of their being approved by the other body or by the governor. The chairman of the appropriations committee, most influential of the two in the control of policy, may take a bill which has passed the other house providing for the appropriation of some specific sum for the biennium to a particular hospital, amend out the name of the hospital and the amount, in fact keeping nothing of the original bill except the number, and insert amendments covering several million

[12] In Wisconsin and some other states conference committees are infrequent. Senator Norris has, however, urged the frequent use of the conference committee as one of his chief objections to the bicameral system; see Burdette, F. L., " Conference Committees in the Nebraska Legislature," *American Political Science Review,* December, 1936, pp. 1114–1116.

dollars to be distributed among several scores of hospitals, the mere printing of the names of which requires several pages. The original appropriation bill thus becomes an omnibus bill by the terms of which the legislature covers all its appropriations for hospital purposes. This device is significant in two respects. If a deadline for the introduction of new bills has been set, it can be evaded by this means. And frequently this matter of appropriations is not taken up until so late in the session that the passage of an entire new bill would be impossible, a sufficient number of legislative days not being available to permit the bill to come through both houses, even if it did so within the minimum time permitted by the constitution.

An element which contributes greatly to the confusion at the end of the session is the large number of resolutions for recalling bills from the governor. Most frequently this happens when the sponsor of the measure discovers, after it has been approved by both houses and sent to the governor, that it contains some error that needs correction; sometimes this device is used to avoid a promised veto by the governor. These resolutions sometimes come through half a dozen or a dozen at a time. Nearly all of them could be avoided if the attorney general, the secretary of state, and the director of the legislative reference bureau were authorized by law to correct obvious errors in spelling and punctuation, as is provided for in the bill reproduced on page 338.

The casual observer about the legislative halls sees much that is perplexing and, partly because he does not understand it, much that seems improper.[13] Perhaps the session does not begin at the appointed hour, or perhaps there are apparently time-wasting recesses. He may not know that the printer is unable to keep up with the legislature, or that in the closing days of the session a committee may be trying to iron out the difficulties with regard to some important piece of legislation, or that the caucus of the majority party may have been held overtime through inability to come to an agreement. In the confusion of the proceedings he wonders how the members can know anything about what is going on; he does not realize that while no member can watch all the bills, some members are watching carefully the progress of every bill. He may see persons whom he suspects are lobbyists; he thinks he ought to be able to distinguish

13 For an interesting and informing account of the experience of a freshman legislator in Oregon, see Neuberger, Richard L., " I Go to the Legislature," *Survey Graphic,* July, 1941, pp. 373–376, 410–412. There are many popular descriptions of how bills become laws.

them, and is disappointed because he cannot do so with certainty.
He may listen to a mediocre debate, wherein one of the members
resorts to the common device of interrogating the sponsor of the bill
— not realizing that there are many debates of high caliber in the
course of the session. These, and many other things, perplex him.

THE END OF THE SESSION

So much has been written and said about the turmoil that develops at the end of the session that it seems appropriate to attempt
a description of it and to make some observations about its significance.[14] In most states and in most sessions it is customary for the
work to continue in an orderly and fairly dignified manner until
the middle or end of the last week. By this time the pressure has
become terrific. Anything can happen. The members are tired, and
have become increasingly anxious to complete their work and return
home. Many have put in weeks of strenuous work — anyone who
thinks that a legislative session is a " snap " little knows the facts.
The atmosphere is tense with expectation and excitement. No man
can tell at what moment, or by what seemingly innocent and commonplace occurrence, the tension may be broken and pandemonium
let loose. Perhaps some member with more zeal than wisdom may too
greatly prolong his remarks on the bill then up for consideration.
Members are visiting and talking; some of the more impatient may
already be bidding farewell to friends and preparing to leave. The
speaker raps for order without much avail. Someone shouts to the
offending member to sit down, but he continues with his speech.
Someone else picks up a huge history of bills, a bunch of old calendars, or a handful of bills and hurls them in the general direction
of the talkative member, who may succeed in dodging the first missile,
but who will be utterly unable to escape from the bombardment
which may presently descend upon him from all directions. From
that moment the show is on and it will be possible to get quiet and
orderly consideration of matters before the house only at rare intervals and for a brief time, until the hour of adjournment is reached.

The antics which occur are remarkable indeed. The majority of
the members seem suddenly to have acquired the exuberance of so
many small boys just dismissed from school. Bills and newspapers
are torn into small bits and hurled about the room until the floor is

[14] The first part of this account is based upon actual observations of several
closing sessions in Pennsylvania. Evidence from numerous other states indicates
that it is fairly typical of what happens elsewhere, although Edwin E. Witte
feels that, so far as Wisconsin is concerned, it is overdone.

carpeted with several inches of this material. Some members may bring in packages of confetti, toy squawkers, rattles, and other noise-making devices. Occasionally someone brings in a box of snuff, which he generously distributes into the atmosphere of the room, until members and spectators alike are obliged to sit with handkerchiefs tied over their noses to keep from continuous sneezing. Among certain members there has already been, and there continues to be, a liberal consumption of intoxicants. Into such an atmosphere may be injected the antics of some roughneck. The author recalls having observed a misguided enthusiast hurling water bags from the house gallery to the floor, while the helpless speaker pounded for order and called out, " Will the gentleman in the gallery please desist from hurling water bags down on the heads of members! " In Illinois, firecrackers are set off in the house in the closing hours.

As the disorder dies down, temporarily at least, the house may proceed to dispose of the remaining items on the calendar. Few questions are asked, and there is little or no discussion. Differences have been all but forgotten, compromises have been agreed to, and deals worked out so that little opportunity for discord remains. The strangest thing of all, perhaps, to a casual observer is the fact that most of the appropriation bills are passed during this general hubbub, sometimes without even a record vote. The explanation is that these bills are, and must be, drafted in committees and in conference with the spending agencies of the government, so that the members are quite unfamiliar with their details and are in no position to raise questions with regard to individual items, even if they were in the mood to do so. Few members venture to raise any questions at all, and these as a rule relate to insignificant items which, nevertheless, make good newspaper publicity. Thus, in a New England legislature a few years ago, the house debated for three quarters of an hour an item for $200 for an ornate dog trough in a public square, while no question was raised regarding other appropriation bills totaling hundreds of thousands of dollars. Such occurrences are not uncommon, but they certainly do not present a fair criterion for judging the work of a session which extends over many weeks.

A distinguished senator, in whimsical mood, has succeeded admirably in recording his reactions as he sat through a long night session immediately preceding adjournment:

It is now 2.00 A.M., June 21, the longest day of the year. The Senate badly needs the longest day of the year. We have been in session since noon of some other day behind it. It must have been yesterday. We are at this particular time voting on S1193 H2194 introduced by Mr. Ruth. It is a perfectly useless law to add to the laws that already encumber the statute books. It provides that it shall be unlawful for any board of school directors to demand, request, or accept any gift from any teacher within its employ. There is no penalty for so doing. School teachers, therefore, may present flowers to the board without fear of punishment.

S1338 H2482 provides that women shall be sentenced to the State Industrial Home instead of the State Penitentiaries. The next act provides for the establishment of the State Industrial Home for Women and providing for the commitment to said home of females between sixteen and thirty.

The next bill is to limit the operation of the rule in Shelly's case. I am voting aye, as it is now 2.30 A.M. on this longest day of the year, but I have no idea what the bill means. The only Shelly I know is the poet who wrote the " Ode To The West Wind," and what the rule is in his case will always remain a mystery.

H2499 sounds better. This act requires the licensing of portable grinding mills. They certainly ought to be licensed. It is strange that this simple act of justice has so long been neglected. Imagine a grinding mill on the loose without a license!

H1991 is the general appropriation bill. This bill has been prepared by the chairmen of the House and Senate Committees on appropriations. It covers all the expenses of government which are paid out of the general fund. All of us who are not chairmen of the two Committees take the bill for granted and vote for it on faith. There is no question about the large amount of faith displayed by law-makers at this hour of the night. . . .

The next bill in order, S1472, which we have all discovered (including the sponsor) is a racket of undertakers. It is given decent burial by being placed on the postponed calendar.

Another act is to regulate the sale of analgesic drugs. These drugs are catalogued by their awful chemical names. One glance at the names is enough. The bill passes 48 to 0. The sponsors of this drug bill are Messrs. Robelak and Sarrof. They must be Pennsylvania Germans or just chemists.

S1551 is an appropriation for the maintenance of children of soldiers, sailors, marines, female field clerks, yeomen (female) , and nurses who died in the world war. It looks like footprints on the sands of time.

We now come to the beer bill. It is a controversial bill but we must adjourn tomorrow or today whichever it is. All we know is that it is 3.15 A.M. We therefore vote down all amendments which might perhaps improve the bill because with 75 bills on our hands and our minds we must vote first and argue afterwards. The vote is ayes 30, nays 18, another statute on our statute mileage home.

That was only beer. We now approach the hard liquor bill. There is again an abortive effort to amend or perhaps make worse the proposed act of Assembly. It is now 3.23 A.M. and our thoughts are homeward. The Liquor Control Board wins, ayes 32, nays 16. Another statute step towards home.

H2109 is a model, forward looking bill of the Voters' Forum to perfect budgets of municipalities. It passes, 48–0. Fine, and there were others like that in the same collection. The Taxpayers' Forum probably did not deliberately plan the passage of the bills at 3.29 A.M. on this summer solstice. There may be a perfectly beautiful sunrise going on outside at this moment but we must wait.

At this writing we have passed three appropriation bills in three minutes, which is really encouraging.

It may be the result of writing these early morning notes, but I have precipitated a row or rather an embarrassing situation. Senator Mallery had a bill, an economy bill, but it destroys patronage. Senator from Dauphin moved to recommit which would avoid a record vote. I felt so sorry for Mallery I tried to help him defeat the motion to recommit. We won. The bill then required a roll call. That was awkward, because the senators wished to say goodbye to the bill without being recorded. There was great reluctance to answer the roll. Finally with some senators changing their votes the bill passed, yeas 28, nays 15.

We have now voted aye on another appropriation bill. Having voted aye we can read the title on the calendar which declares among other things that this appropriation is for payment of a verdict of a Federal court for personal injuries caused by a department employee while driving a Commonwealth car on which the insurance had become non-collectible. If we had more leisure we might learn something about this bill. It sounds interesting but even with this longest day we must finish the calendar.

At this writing, 4.40, the calendar has been finished. There is a fine morning light in the disheveled senate chamber. In the middle aisle are two groups arguing furiously. Instead of bowing to the rising sun and chanting God save our Keystone State, they are quarreling politely, very politely indeed, for the sunrise hour of the longest day of the year.[15]

Many legislatures have developed customs which are regularly observed in the end of the session celebration. A dinner for members and representatives of the press may be served in the rotunda of the capitol at midnight, during a brief recess which separates the sessions of two legislative days. Or it may be that the page boys who have served the members of the two houses will hold a mock session in the hall of the house, during which they occupy the seats of the members, while some of the more prominent members serve as pages. In some cases these sessions are carefully planned in advance, and represent a fine display of wit and satire. The boys introduce bills, make motions to commit and recommit, call up measures for reconsideration, and go through many complicated parliamentary maneuvers with amazing skill. In such a session in Pennsylvania one of the boys introduced a measure designed to regulate the length of women's dresses, which the presiding officer promptly referred to the Committee on Virtue and Integrity. Many of the bills and most of the speeches are take-offs on amusing incidents that have occurred

[15] Woodward, George, "The Majesty of the Law," *The Pennsylvania Legislator*, June, 1935.

during the session, and many others are intended as good-natured thrusts at the peculiarities of some of the members, many of whom may be called upon to make a few remarks.

It often happens in the closing hours that the proceedings are delayed by the inability of the printer to keep up with the demands of the two houses. These intervals are likely to be occupied by speeches and entertainment. On one occasion the author heard a young colored soprano, a gifted musical artist, render a number of selections. The political significance of this event was not to be lost. The speaker, who had aspirations for political advancement, called upon one of the colored members of the house to introduce the artist, and this member later paid eloquent tribute to the speaker for his broad-minded attitude, noting that the news of this recognition of the colored race would spread to every colored voter in the most remote portion of the state. Members may be called upon to render solos or to take part in duets and quartets. The speeches are light and entertaining, some of them displaying a considerable amount of ingenuity and wit.

Another common procedure is the presentation of gifts. Members contribute to the purchase of a handsome gift for the speaker, while checks are given to the clerks and to the page boys in appreciation of their services during the session. Before this, however, the master of ceremonies is likely to present a large number of inexpensive trifles to members of the house, each of these having some definite significance in connection with his service during the session or with his personal peculiarities. Thus a member who sponsors a Sunday baseball bill may be given a baseball and bat; the chairman of the Committee on Education, a school bag containing a pen and pencil kit; the chairman of the Fish and Game Committee, a popgun; the sponsor of a bill for Sunday fishing, a fishing rod and reel. The baldest member of the house may be given a bottle of hair tonic. A member who has made himself conspicuous by opposition to all measures providing appropriations for educational purposes may receive a scroll entitling him to free tuition in the state university. Again, a member who has continuously shown the characteristics often associated in the popular mind with farmers residing in the most backward districts may be presented with a bag of potatoes.[16]

[16] For other accounts, see Howe, Frederic C., *Confessions of a Reformer*, Chapter 16, "Making Laws at Columbus," pp. 165–166 (Scribner's, New York, 1925); on Maryland, Alexander, Holmes M., "I Hold Office," *Harper's Magazine*, September, 1933, pp. 423–424, and Suzuki, Hitoshi, "Viewing the Maryland State Legislature through Oriental Eyes," *Baltimore Sun*, April 7, 1932; and an ac-

So this great party proceeds until the final fall of the speaker's gavel marks the adjournment of another legislative session, the periods of legislative work necessary to clear up the calendar being sandwiched in between the various features of the closing hours. No matter how skillful the speaker is in guiding and directing the work of the house at the speaker's desk and in conference with party leaders, it is rarely possible for the session to adjourn promptly at the day and hour agreed upon. Frequently adjournment has to be postponed for a day or two, and rarely does it happen that a session comes to an end without one of the clerks stealthily turning back the hands of the great clock in the rear of the chamber. The final event preceding the adjournment is the adoption of a series of resolutions conferring thanks upon those who have assisted with the work of the session, and a series of laudatory speeches in which members of all parties join in paying tribute to the work done by the speaker, both as a fair and impartial presiding officer, and as a strategist in guiding and directing the legislative program during the session.

SOME EVALUATIONS

The preceding sections have been devoted to a description of a legislative session; it seems reasonable now to attempt an evaluation of these proceedings. The business of the session is normally conducted in an orderly and dignified manner. Many of the debates and discussions are of a high order, showing an understanding of the subject and some knowledge of the problems of statecraft. This the public little seems to realize. Citizens visit the legislature so seldom, and stay so short a time when they do go, that they have little opportunity to acquire an understanding of the serious work that is done there.

The public is far more familiar with the confusion at the end of the session than with any other part of the activities of the legislature. The comments of observers on this have ranged from gentle satire to vigorous and caustic denunciation. As a matter of fact, disorder and confusion in legislative halls is not peculiar either to our country or to our time. Such practices were once far more common than they are now; at present they are confined to the end of the session, and consist for the most part of harmless fun indulged in

---

count of the closing of a Louisiana session in Huey Long's day, in *Time,* July 23, 1934, p. 14. For an account of the early Virginia Legislatures, see Luce, Robert, *Legislative Procedure* (Houghton Mifflin, Boston, 1922) .

after the serious work of the session has been about completed. As Charles Kettleborough, eminent authority on legislative matters, once said: " My experience with eleven sessions in Indiana has convinced me that an average legislature is not only a very able but a very serious body of public servants and that they are entitled to indulge in the nonsense they do to maintain their poise and good humor and equilibrium." [17] Similarly, a distinguished legislator from Kentucky, the president of the American Legislators' Association, states that " my observations are that we have a very fine lot of men in most of the legislatures . . ."; while a very able and widely respected member of the Pennsylvania House of Representatives summarizes his conclusions on this point as follows:

The Pennsylvania Legislature is composed of men far above the average in every respect. On the whole, the quality of its membership is improving session after session. Perhaps there are not so many brilliant leaders as formerly, but neither are there as many stupid or corrupt men. This results from two direct causes — first, the primary election system, and second, a more sensitive and sensible consciousness on the part of the political organizations in the selection and support of candidates for the office of Senator and Representative in the State Legislature.[18]

Mr. Kettleborough also observed that the members of the Shrine, the American Legion, and other organizations indulge in pranks in their national gatherings which would scandalize their acquaintances if done elsewhere. Few people think of condemning these organizations on account of these pranks; it scarcely seems fair to condemn legislators who, at the close of a long session of arduous work, exhibit temporarily certain similar characteristics — characteristics which seem to be more typical of gatherings of men in general than peculiar to legislative bodies.

The press must accept a considerable part of the responsibility for cultivating and stimulating an unfavorable popular impression of legislatures. In any legislative year, stories and headlines can be collected by the score in which the lawmaking body is referred to in the most uncomplimentary terms — as quitters; as floundering on, hours after closing time; as incompetent and to be applauded for adjourning; as conducting the poorest session in forty years; et cetera. This attitude on the part of the press cannot have any other effect than to make people believe that their legislators are either crooks or fools, and that their legislatures are hopelessly inefficient

[17] Letter to the author from Charles Kettleborough, November 1, 1934.
[18] Sterling, Philip, " Some Practical Aspects of Legislation," an address before the Pennsylvania Bar Association, June 24, 1932, p. 11.

and incompetent. Similarly, teachers of social studies in the public schools who want their pupils to have an opportunity to see the legislature in action should select for their visit a date some time prior to adjournment, so that the students can see the legislature in normal operation.

The citizen whose impressions of the legislature are none too favorable would do well to remember that the ordinary legislature has only sixty or ninety legislative days in which to consider from two to five thousand bills and resolutions; that their task of determining the provisions of laws, and enacting them, is made more difficult by the demands which are made upon them by ourselves — their constituents — and by the fact that in many states the governmental machinery is badly out of date; that under these circumstances the average legislator acquires a feeling of utter helplessness and hopelessness. In many cases he is so paralyzed mentally that he sees no alternatives other than to follow the leaders or to oppose everything that comes up. The observer should remember also that the antics and frivolities are largely the work of the newer members, and not of the men who are doing the real work of the session. William B. Belknap observes that " the continual shifting of personnel in the legislature along with the outworn machinery is really what brings about the chaos, and that it is neither the ignorance nor the stupidity of the legislators that is really responsible." The members are, he continues, " ham-strung and hog-tied by constitutional limitations, precedents, and parliamentary procedures " of such a nature as to make the efficient operation of the legislature impossible. The chaos and confusion — when they do exist — are largely surface phenomena. The improvement of legislative procedure depends upon an understanding of certain fundamental, underlying problems, to which consideration is given in the following chapter.[19]

Professor Shumate, in an excellent reappraisal of state legislatures, notes that their prestige may be regained:

The low esteem in which the state legislature is now held is not encouraging for the future, but neither is it necessarily fatal. Other political institutions have overcome comparable obstacles and risen to positions of eminence and prestige. Democracy itself was once the most despised form of government. Membership in the United States Supreme Court was so little prized in the early years of the Republic that ambitious men rejected

[19] Letter to the author from William B. Belknap, November 3, 1934; see also Atwood, Albert W., and McGoldrick, Joseph D., " What Is the Matter with the State Legislatures? " in *Legislatures and Legislative Problems,* edited by Thomas H. Reed (University of Chicago Press, 1933) .

appointments to it in favor of election or appointment to state offices; and service in the British House of Commons was long regarded as an onerous burden, to be avoided whenever possible. Thus, it is not inconceivable that our state assemblies may rise again to positions of honor and trust in our governmental system.

No student of modern American government and politics can be blind to the faults of our state legislatures, but to admit that they have failed comes perilously close to admitting that popular government in the United States has failed. That, in turn, would be to admit that what was once regarded in foreign lands as " the American experiment " has failed, and this we are not prepared to do. If we will but free our legislatures from their constitutional hobbles, pay them decently, organize them so that they can serve adequately, and create a vigilant public opinion which insists upon responsible service of a high caliber (these are not simple reforms, to be sure) , there is no inherent reason why they cannot assume the rightful place of representative assemblies in a representative government.[20]

[20] Shumate, Roger V., " A Reappraisal of State Legislature," *Annals*, January, 1938, pp. 189–197.

CHAPTER VIII

The State Legislature: Procedure

IN the first chapter on the legislative process, the organization and structure of the lawmaking bodies were described, as well as their representative character. In the last chapter, the legislative process was presented as it might be seen by a casual observer who devoted some time to listening to and watching the obvious things which may be heard and seen around the capitol when the legislature is in session. Such material is interesting, and it is important in the sense that no one can really know state government without knowing how the legislatures operate. Such purely descriptive material, however, contributes little or nothing to one's understanding of the *how* and *why* of things. It is these questions, the less visible and more fundamental aspects of the lawmaking process, that are now to be considered.

LAWMAKING POWERS

The lawmaking powers of the legislatures are restricted by certain provisions of the Federal Constitution as well as by numerous provisions of the constitutions of the states themselves. In Chapter I, in a discussion of the nature of our Federal system, it was stated that under the provisions of Amendment X the state governments were governments of residuary powers. The legislatures are therefore, in general, free to act within that scope of governmental authority not definitely assigned to the Federal government in Article I, Section 8, or elsewhere, and not definitely prohibited to the states in Article I, Section 10. Among the acts prohibited are the making of treaties, the granting of letters of marque and reprisal and the passing of bills of attainder, the coining of money, the passing of ex post facto laws, the making of anything but gold or silver legal tender for the payment of debts, the passing of laws impairing the obligation of contract, the granting of titles of nobility, the levying of tonnage or export duties, and finally, engaging in war or keeping troops or ships of war in time of peace. Even when dealing with a subject which comes within the scope of their constitutional authority, the legislatures are restricted in the exercise of their power by important provisions of Amendment XIV; namely, those clauses which guarantee due process of law, equal protection of the laws, and the privileges and immunities of citizens.

The legislature at all times exercises its powers subject not only to the terms of the Federal Constitution and the constitution of the state, but also to such interpretations of the provisions of these instruments as the courts may choose to give them. In New York between 1914 and 1937 the Court of Appeals rendered twenty-six decisions holding legislative enactments unconstitutional. A striking illustration of the havoc that can be created by the abuse of judicial discretion in this connection occurred in Connecticut in 1929, when the State Supreme Court wiped out 1,493 laws at a single stroke. The Connecticut Constitution requires, by Article IV, Section 12, a law to be signed by the governor within three days of its passage by the legislature in order to become effective. During four preceding administrations governors, bombarded with bills at the end of the session, had studied them and signed them at their leisure. The Court, having to pass on an individual case, ruled by the letter of the law and declared that the act providing for state condemnation of a certain property was unconstitutional because the act was not signed by the governor within three calendar days of its passage. Automatically, as a consequence of this ruling, almost 1,500 other laws actually in operation were made legally ineffective. An outstanding example of the resulting confusion was found in a gasoline tax law enacted in 1925, under which at the time more than $11,000,000 had been collected. In such an emergency, of course, a special session of the legislature was required.[1]

Other Types of Legislative Power. A legislative body has execu-

[1] *Philadelphia Record,* July 30, 1929. See also: Fertig, John H., *Scope of the Legislative Power of the General Assembly* (Pennsylvania Legislative Reference Bureau, 1931); Horack, Frank E., Jr., "The Common Law of Legislation," *Iowa Law Review,* November, 1937, pp. 41–56; New York State Constitutional Convention Committee, *Problems Relating to Legislative Organization and Powers,* Chapter 5 (Albany, 1938); Ray, Joseph M., "Procedural Limitations on the Texas Legislature," *Southwestern Social Science Quarterly,* September, 1938, pp. 152–160; and "Do Legislators Think Like Judges?" *State Government,* September, 1938, pp. 163–164, 177.

tive and judicial powers as well as legislative. Both houses are responsible for exercising a general surveillance over the executive branch of the government, both with regard to its general administrative efficiency and its fiscal operations. The upper house is usually entrusted with power to act on nominations submitted by the governor. If the latter belongs to the same party as a majority of the members of the upper house, there will probably be little difficulty; but if they are of opposite parties or of different factions of the same party, all sorts of obstructive tactics are possible.

On the judicial side, the legislature must constantly make judgments with regard to the constitutionality of measures before it. More strictly judicial in character are the powers of the legislatures in connection with the impeachment process. Only executive or judicial officers are subject to impeachment. As in Congress, the charges are brought in the lower house, while the upper serves as a trial court. The process is cumbersome and time-consuming; it is frequently threatened if not actually used for political purposes, and is in general ineffective for the purpose for which it was intended, namely, relieving the public of the services of public officers who are dishonest or otherwise unfit. Other powers of a judicial or quasi-judicial character are illustrated by the dramatic attempt of Tom Mooney to secure a pardon from the California legislature in 1938, and by investigations of various sorts undertaken in other states. In the same year the General Assembly of Pennsylvania carried on an extensive investigation of charges of graft in the state administration.

Special Legislation. State constitutions establish not only restrictions on legislative power similar to those established by the Federal Constitution, but also many severe additional limitations upon the scope of that power — the result of a loss of public confidence in representative assemblies. Because legislatures in the past frequently sought to deal individually with matters relating to persons and property which should have been adequately covered by general legislation, and because they interfered in an often unintelligent and offensive manner in the regulation of purely local conditions, the restrictions apply particularly to these two types of special legislation. Abundant illustrations of these abuses can be found in the legislative history of any state; Professor Mathews cites a list of ridiculous statutes enacted in North Carolina, such as: " To prevent the throwing of sawdust in Big Ivey Creek in Buncombe County "; " To prevent the sale of malt, near-beer, and beerine in Macon

County "; " Providing that four and one-half feet shall be the lawful height of fences in Perquimans County "; " To prevent depredations by turkeys, geese, ducks, and chickens in Catawba County "; " To prevent the shooting of firecrackers within one mile of the post office at Haw River "; and " To make illegal the keeping of honey bees within 100 yards of the public roads in Pender County." [2]

In order to prevent the continuance of these unfortunate practices, many states have gone to great extremes in their constitutional provisions limiting legislative power. The legislative provisions of all the constitutions framed in the reconstruction period (for examples, see table, page 83) were based primarily on distrust of the legislature. The Pennsylvania Constitution of 1873 includes a list of twenty-eight such limitations; the California Constitution of 1879, a list of thirty-three. Of these, the following are fair examples; the reader might well compare them with the list of restrictions in the constitution of his home state.

Fifth	Granting divorces
Sixth	Changing the names of persons or places
Tenth	For the assessment or collection of taxes
Thirteenth	Extending the time for the collection of taxes
Fourteenth	Giving effect to invalid deeds, wills, or other instruments
Fifteenth	Refunding money paid under the state treasury
Twentieth	Exempting property from taxation
Twenty-first	Changing county seats
Twenty-sixth	Remitting fines, penalties, or forfeitures
Twenty-ninth	Affecting the fees or salary of any officer
Thirtieth	Changing the law of descent or succession
Thirty-first	Authorizing the adoption or legitimation of children

An examination of these items indicates that such subjects would never be dealt with by special legislation by any legislature with standards of decency and integrity, yet all were at one time or another the subject of special enactments in practically all states. In many states, as soon as constitutional restrictions such as these were adopted, the legislature proceeded promptly to set up classes of local

[2] Mathews, John M., *American State Government*, Revised Edition, pp. 247–248 (Appleton-Century, New York, 1934). For a similar list of special laws affecting the cities of New York State, see Wallace, Schuyler C., *Our Governmental Machine*, p. 112 (Knopf, New York, 1924); also Hyman, Dick, *It's the Law* (Knopf, New York, 1936), and Seagle, William, *There Ought to Be a Law* (Macaulay, New York, 1933). The compilation of lists of freak legislation has been a favorite " indoor sport " of magazine writers and feature writers for Sunday supplements. An excellent discussion of special legislation will be found in Freund, Ernst, *Legislative Regulation*, Chapter 3 (Commonwealth Fund, New York, 1932); also Mothersead, James G., " The Limitation of Legislation," *Nebraska Law Bulletin*, July, 1937, pp. 80–90.

units, by the skillful planning of which the constitutional restrictions might, to some extent, be evaded.

Other devices for protecting localities from unwanted special legislation have been tried in Michigan and New York. In the former state the constitution prohibits the passing of a local or special act in any case where a general act can be made applicable. In 1937 the United States Supreme Court threw out a statute establishing a county board of review of tax assessments applicable only to counties having a population of 500,000 or more, on the ground that it constituted a violation of this provision.[3] In New York there has long been in effect a provision requiring that a special act be accepted by a majority of the voters in the community affected before it can become effective; this provision is discussed further in a later chapter in connection with municipal home rule.

In spite of all these attempts to curb the abuses of special legislation, the number of such enactments continues to constitute a significant portion of the total legislative output. In 1945 the Tennessee legislature passed approximately 800 bills, most of them local. The Constitution of Alabama contains a series of restrictions very similar to that cited in California, yet a study of the problem in that state covering the period from 1903 to 1943 inclusive reveals that the number of local acts frequently equaled or exceeded the number of general laws. The average for this forty-year period was 35 per cent. Although exceptions at times interrupt the downward trend, the figures do show a decline from 55.9 per cent in 1903 to 30.1 per cent in 1943. The number of private acts was not large or particularly significant — about 5 per cent for the forty-year period.[4]

There are, on the other hand, some situations which can be handled only by special laws; local and special laws may be good — or at least necessary — as well as bad. The Pennsylvania legislature in 1933 repealed a section of an 1842 law entitled " An act to appoint

[3] Wayne County Board of Review, et al. v. Great Lakes Steel Corporation, 300 U. S. 29, 1937; the clause is in Michigan Constitution, Article V, Section 20.
[4] See Farmer, Hallie, *Local and Private Legislation,* p. 17 (University of Alabama, Bureau of Public Administration, 1944). This is an excellent study of experience in one state; for others, see Key, V. O., Jr., *The Problem of Local Legislation in Maryland* (State Planning Commission, 1940), and " The Problem of Local Legislation: Examples from Maryland," *State Government,* June, 1940, pp. 109–110, 118–119; Kline, Howard M., *Municipal Legislation in Maryland* (Maryland Legislative Council, 1940) ; Klitsner, Marvin E., " Constitutional Prohibition against Granting or Amending City Charters," *Wisconsin Law Review,* May, 1941, pp. 396–419; Satterfield, M. H., note on 1945 session in Tennessee, *National Municipal Review,* May, 1945, pp. 241–242; and the reports on local and special legislation put out after each session by the state leagues of municipalities.

commissioners to re-survey and mark that portion of the county line which divides the township of Bristol in the County of Philadelphia from the township of Cheltenham in the county of Montgomery, and for other purposes." Most of the items in the bill dealt with " other purposes," only a partial listing of which is possible here: a road to Dillsburg to be narrowed; four German Reformed congregations authorized to sell land; name of McKean Female Seminary changed to Troy Academy; election in Wysox to be held at the home of George Scott; new ward created in Lewistown; election of constables in Shirleysburg regulated; John Tritle and Jacob Byer authorized to sell real estate in Greencastle; survey of Saltsburg confirmed; three Tioga County townships authorized to elect additional supervisors; killing of birds regulated in Allegheny and Franklin Counties; and so on. This sort of thing, then common, is fortunately no longer possible. It ought not to be necessary for the legislature to repeal an act of 1859 " relating to billiard saloons et cetera in the counties of Chester and Delaware and extending the same to Lycoming and Clinton Counties " in order to free Lycoming County from undesired restrictions.

In 1938 it was reported that 7,466 members of forty-eight state legislatures had enacted 17,194 new laws or an average of about two and one half per legislator. For a general comment, see Gallagher, Hubert R., " Legislative Highlights of 1939," *National Municipal Review,* July, 1939, pp. 509–517, 566, and Graves, W. Brooke, article on " Legislation, Quantity of, Federal and State," in *Dictionary of American History* (Scribner's, New York, 1940) . The Library of Congress publishes three pamphlets in series: *Current Ideas in 19. . State Legislatures, Sources of Information on Legislation of 19. .–19. .,* and *State Legislation of 19. .; Summaries of Laws Currently Received in the Library of Congress.*

In addition to numerous surveys by states noted in previous editions of this book, the following have been published since 1940: CALIFORNIA: Hale, William G., " The Work of the 1943 California Legislature," *Southern California Law Review,* November, 1943, pp. 1–53 (published biennially) ; Warren, Earl, " The Work of the California Legislature during 1944," *California Law Review,* December, 1944, pp. 394–397. MINNESOTA: Minnesota Taxpayers Association, *Legislative Report for the Legislative Session of 1941* (Minneapolis, 1941, published biennially) . NEW JERSEY: Dullard, John P., Comp., *Descriptive List of Laws and Joint Resolutions Enacted by the State of New Jersey Legislative Session of 1944* (New Jersey State Library, Trenton, 1944) . NORTH CAROLINA: " A Survey of Statutory Changes in North Carolina in 1941," *North Carolina Law Review,* June, 1941, pp. 435–550 (published biennially) . VIRGINIA: Shands, William R., *Virginia Legislation of 1940* (Virginia State Bar Association, Richmond, 1940) . WISCONSIN: Ohm, Howard F., *Summary of the Action of the . . . Regular Session of the Wisconsin Legislature on Some of the More Important Questions Coming before It* (Wisconsin Legislature Reference Bureau, Madison, biennially) . All of the states publish session laws, and occasionally, as Vermont, summaries. In the state universities the law review often carries a biennial summary of important legislative action.

BILLS AND RESOLUTIONS INTRODUCED AND PASSED IN THE NORTH CAROLINA
LEGISLATURE, 1907–1945

Year	Number of Bills and Resolutions Introduced			Number of Bills Enacted	Types of Bills Enacted			Resolutions Passed
	Total	Senate	House		Public	Public Local	Private	
1907	2691			1535				37
1917	2412			1215				58
1927	1906	671	1235	1205	270	703	232	44
1929	1878	592	1286	1070	346	506	218	33
1931	2108	663	1445	1145	457	497	191	59
1933	2469	758	1711	1406	570	590	246	64
1935	2160	649	1511	1346	495	581	270	66
1936 (Extra)	13	10	3	2	2	0	0	4
1937	1803	490	1313	1163	457	65	55	60
1938 (Extra)	25	15	10	15	6	9	0	4
1939	1696	509	1187	1051	402	617	28	52
1941	1319	353	966	814	382	476	18	38
1943	1253	365	858	787	Session Laws			38
1945	1454	454	1000	1103	Session Laws			53

It may, however, be necessary to adopt special acts to meet emergency situations, to free communities from special acts passed years
ago, and to make possible the payment of legitimate claims of citizens against the state when such claims become tangled in legal technicalities. Legislatures ought to have power to meet such situations
when they arise, and the public ought to have sufficient confidence in
them to permit them to do so. Instances of this type come, at least
occasionally, to the attention of every legislator.

Quantity of Legislation. Much comment has been made on the
number of laws enacted by state legislatures. Americans seem to have
retained from Puritan times a naive idea that anything wrong can
be corrected by enactment of another statute; this has been particularly evident in the field of legislation affecting public morals. They
often forget too that an unenforced and unenforceable statute may
do more harm than good. While there has been much ground for
criticism of the quantity of legislation, there are extenuating circumstances which prevent the situation from being as bad as it is often
pictured. A large number of measures enacted are merely amendments to or modifications of earlier laws, or are validations of the
acts of public officers who have acted in good faith without proper
legal authority. Many others relate to appropriations for various purposes or are classifiable as private bills. In most cases, if the output of

ANALYSIS OF LEGISLATIVE PRODUCT, BY STATE
1939, 1941, 1943
(From *State Government*, December, 1943)

State	Bills Introduced			Bills Becoming Law			Resolutions Introduced			Resolutions Adopted		
	1939	1941	1943	1939	1941	1943	1939	1941	1943	1939	1941	1943
Alabama	1,587	(a)	1,275	599	(a)	539	134	(a)	(b)	12	(a)	39
Arizona	535	493	373	90	125	96	71	83	45	28	39	45
Arkansas	1,253	1,120	930	412	471	429	155	117	65	109	81	(b)
California	4,175	4,012	3,131	1,124	1,284	1,137	277	201	555	120	133	488
Colorado	2,085	2,256	982	176	244	200	147	102	104	84	59	72
Connecticut	2,762	5,517	2,285	903	912	982	811	1,103	542	358	382	378
Delaware	829	(b)	540	205	(b)	212	14	(b)	33	7	(b)	27
Florida	(b)	2,814	(b)	(b)	1,426	(b)	(b)	(b)	(b)	(b)	(b)	(b)
Georgia	1,059	908	890	427	468	472	294	261	250	50	54	70
Idaho	595	550	354	257	219	177	(b)	18	15	(b)	4	5
Illinois	1,759	1,707	1,501	421	563	615	(b)	204	212	(b)	159	177
Indiana	918	992	714	165	238	314	41	47	38	11	10	19
Iowa	1,185	1,121	888	310	344	306	18	15	17	5	3	9
Kansas	1,098	928	705	344	390	330	149	126	25	103	99	9
Kentucky[e]	....	....	....	....	....	....	....	....	....	....	....	....
Louisiana[e]	....	....	....	....	....	....	....	....	....	....	....	....
Maine	2,956	2,509	1,507	415	544	449	(d)	(d)	71	99	(b)	71
Maryland	1,354	1,441	1,431	603	937	948	55	48	26	18	15	12
Massachusetts	3,229	3,039	2,405e	591	731	572	16	(b)	(b)	10	96	73
Michigan	1,107	1,059	726	368	392	256	20	10	152	2	2	108
Minnesota	3,150	3,057	2,780	455	555	666	45	80	(b)	35	73	12
Mississippi[e]	....	....	(b)	....	....	....	....	....	....	....	....	....
Missouri	1,068	851	(b)	383	309	(b)	34	44	(b)	2	4	(b)
Montana	643	590	486	243	204	265	77	9	42	33	5	33

Nebraska	523	515	446	138	196	240	45	35	43	37	31	35
Nevada	488	431	304	200	192	195	64	48	38	35	22	28
New Hampshire	518	546	457	256	276	268	86	75	37	36	33	28
New Jersey	1,131	1,038	515	338	362	218	51	37	20	17	12	18
New Mexico	518	561	454	237	213	134	55	38	43	31	21	35
New York	4,638	4,381	3,594	927	955	712	194	172	137	92	70	65
North Carolina	1,695	1,319	(b)	1,052	876	(b)	(b)	(b)	(b)	52	38	(b)
North Dakota	727	552	403	258	307	281	85	(b)	92	61	46	65
Ohio	1,002	1,046	723	225	232	216	265	77	247	152	13	178
Oklahoma	984	924	700	244	348	275	283	164	141	92	79	78
Oregon	1,662	970	730	555	488	459	116	46	97	79	43	75
Pennsylvania	2,073	2,460	1,747	474	428	454	88	46	30	50	1	6
Rhode Island	837	862	702[d]	343	348	379	375	315	352	170	177	230
South Carolina	1,120	(b)	563	749	(b)	344	214	(b)	211	126	(b)	132
South Dakota	640	(b)	483	302	(b)	319	(b)	(b)	9	(b)	(b)	2
Tennessee	2,713	2,026	2,066	840	755	620	131	63	52	98	58	46
Texas	1,641	1,616	1,133	638	645	401	339	432	263	177	235	175
Utah	600	516	402	153	111	113	(b)	32	33	(b)	13	18
Vermont	520	408	297	305	245	190	222	113	56	107	94	47
Virginia[c]	.....	.....	.....	.....	.....	.....	.....	.....	.....	.....	.....	.....
Washington	1,067	1,057	733	224	266	284	79	61	46	18	22	18
West Virginia	749	623	619	184	158	116	126	142	128	74	100	69
Wisconsin	1,559	1,368	1,134	535	333	566	401	269	183	222	175	133
Wyoming	358	306	232	135	134	118	27	25	9	12	10	3
Total	60,510	58,579	42,400	17,953	18,224	15,867	5,604	4,658	4,459	2,824	2,511	3,131

[315]

a No session.　b No information available.　c Legislature meets in even-numbered years.　d Included in bills introduced.　e Includes resolves.

a whole session is analyzed and the measures of the types indicated eliminated, the number of new general laws remaining will not be found unreasonable or excessive.[5]

In many states, data on the number of bills and resolutions introduced, the number of bills and resolutions passed, and the number signed and vetoed by the governor have been tabulated over a period of years. A table containing this information for North Carolina, from 1907 to 1945, appears on page 313, while on pages 314–315 there is presented an analysis of the legislative product, by states, for the years 1939, 1941, and 1943 — a period which includes the last peacetime year, the defense period, and the first wartime session.

The following description, giving a more detailed analysis of the output in a single representative state, relates to the measures enacted by the General Assembly of Pennsylvania at the regular session of 1933:

> Historically, the session will be noted for the number of important codes enacted. The number of bills and resolutions exceeded those of any session since the Legislative Reference Bureau was created in 1909, and probably those of any prior session since the Commonwealth was established. The actual number of bills was 2,850. Of these, 781 passed both houses. The governor signed 633. Of the 633 bills signed by the governor, 300 are classified as appropriation laws, and 333 as general laws. These latter may be roughly classified as follows: amendments, 171; supplements, 8; repeals, 9; restatements, 6; appropriations, 10; salary laws, 5; temporary laws, 8; local laws, 2; validations, 20; codes, 9; new substantive laws, 85. The bulk of the legislation consists of amendments and codes which are simply corrections, consolidations, revisions, and restatements of existing law. In addition, mention should be made that 731 existing laws were wholly or partially repealed. There has been, as a result of this session, no appreciable growth of legislation.[6]

SELECTION OF LEGISLATIVE SUBJECTS

The classification of the steps in legislative procedure used here follows the outline of Professor Arthur N. Holcombe. These steps are: first, the selection of the subjects upon which legislation will be considered; second, the collection of information upon which intelli-

---

[5] Herbert Spencer's piece on "overlegislation," in his *The Man versus the State,* has produced a never ending curse of the terrible plague of laws, which the statisticians diligently perpetuate. In addition to much special and local legislation, many of the public acts deal with bridges, highways, military affairs, et cetera — measures which impose no personal restraints upon individuals. We suffer much more from the poor quality than from the excessive quantity of legislation.

[6] Statement by John H. Fertig, then Director, Pennsylvania Legislative Reference Bureau.

gent legislative action may be based; third, problems of draftsmanship; fourth, the actual consideration and enactment of bills. These subjects will be discussed in detail in the paragraphs which follow.

It is impossible to obtain a clear idea of the perplexing problems involved in the selection of subjects for legislative action, without first getting a picture of the number of bills introduced over a period of years and the disposition made thereof in one or more typical states. Figures of this type, such as were presented in the preceding section, are impressive for at least two reasons. They indicate, in the first place, a slight tendency toward the reduction of the number of bills introduced. Although the number of such bills in North Carolina in 1931 and 1933 was higher than in several of the preceding sessions, the total was still nearly 700 below the total for the first year reported, 1907. In the second place, such figures are significant because they indicate the almost staggering complexity of modern government. An analysis of these measures would show that they involve questions relating to almost every conceivable aspect of human life. This is natural when government is called upon to perform countless regulatory duties undreamed of in earlier generations, and when the scope of service in existing fields of operation is being extended and new standards of governmental efficiency are everywhere being applied.

Political Considerations. Out of this maze of subject matter someone must select those subjects on which legislation will be given serious consideration. The roots of legislation in the modern state reach deep into all parts of society. The final selection of subject matter is likely, therefore, to represent a compromise between several different and often conflicting influences, the first of which is the matter of political considerations. Some bills, sponsored by influential members, of course receive attention. The general tendency among politicians — there are exceptions in the cases of particular individuals — is to postpone action on any troublesome question as long as they can do so with impunity. Their philosophy seems to be not to trouble trouble until trouble troubles them, to " sit on the lid," so to speak, hoping that an aroused public sentiment will not blow it off. The tendency is, furthermore, to deal with a problem with palliatives, if they must deal with it at all, until some more thoroughgoing treatment of the subject can no longer be postponed.

Public Opinion and Pressure Groups. A second determining factor in the selection of legislative subjects has already been referred to — that of a well-organized and insistent public opinion or of powerful and insistent pressure groups. Unfortunately, well-organized public opinion rarely exists unless the situation has become serious. The public is large, unorganized, and largely incoherent unless it is aroused, in which case it makes its wants clearly and unmistakably known. Pressure groups are vocal because they are organized and have adequate financial support; they know what they want and they know how to get it. They have the additional drive that comes from strong self-interest. It is possible for the methods and techniques of the pressure group to be utilized in the public interest, but they rarely are.

Woodrow Wilson made some interesting observations on this point some thirty years or more ago:

> I used to wonder when I was Governor of one of the states of this great country where all the bills came from. Some of them had a very private complexion. I found upon inquiry — it was easy to find — that practically nine-tenths of the bills that were introduced had been handed to the members who introduced them by some constituent of theirs, had been drawn up by some lawyer whom they might or might not know, and were intended to do something that would be beneficial to a particular set of persons. I do not mean, necessarily, beneficial in a way that would be hurtful to the rest; they may have been perfectly honest, but they came out of cubby-holes all over the state. They did not come out of public places where men had got together and compared views. They were not the products of common counsel, but the products of private counsel, a very necessary process if there is no other, but a process which it would be a very happy thing to dispense with if we could get another. And the only other process is the process of common counsel.[7]

Professor Walker has made some studies of the sources of legislation introduced into the Ohio legislature in 1939, the results of which are summarized in the following table: [8]

OHIO LEGISLATURE, 1939 —

BILLS CLASSIFIED BY SOURCE

	Introduced		Became Law	
Individual Members	162	24%	30	25%
State Offices	89	13%	28	24%
Local Offices	55	8%	8	7%
Lobby	236	35%	47	37%
No Information on Source	135	20%	8	7%
Total	677		121	

[7] From an address on cooperation in the business of government, delivered before the United States Chamber of Commerce, February 3, 1915; Wilson, Woodrow, *Papers*, Book II, Vol. III, p. 277 (Harper, New York, 1925).

[8] Walker, Harvey, "Who Writes the Laws?" *State Government*, November, 1939, pp. 199–200, 208–209, "Where Does Legislation Originate?" *National*

As might be expected, the bills presented by lobbyists came from a wide variety of sources, the strong, well-entrenched business and professional groups with permanent organization being most successful in securing the passage of measures presented. Professor Walker concludes: " The wide range of interests represented is, one may believe, typical of the catholicity of the constituency of the typical modern legislature. It may also constitute an index to the extent of organization among our people. It is a commonplace that legislators no longer have time to consult individual constituents unless they represent an organized vote, that is, conscious groups. Pressures by these groups upon the legislature produce the resultant forces of legislation."

Influence of the Administration. An energetic, forceful, and aggressive governor, assisted by the kind of department heads that such a governor is likely to select, can exercise a profound influence, not only in the selection of subjects of legislation, but on the nature of the provisions enacted regarding them. Such a condition may be regarded as highly desirable. These men are charged with the responsiblity for the enforcement of existing laws; they should be more fully informed regarding the weaknesses and defects of these laws than anyone else, and they should be in a better position to determine the nature of the changes required for the correction of any unsatisfactory conditions that may exist. This influence is, of course, reduced almost to the vanishing point when the governor is of a weak and vacillating disposition — in which case the first two of the factors discussed exercise a controlling influence.

Two interesting studies of the extent of executive influence on legislation were published in 1942. In the first, by Edwin E. Witte, which dealt primarily with the Federal government, it was shown that " the natural result of all of the activities of the administration agencies devoted to legislation is that they have greatly influenced the action of Congress." He felt that the executive influence in the states was much less than in the Federal government, but " in some states, for instance New York, administrative departments seem to play quite as important a role in statute making as in the national government." This conclusion was borne out by a study made of the New York situation, in which it was found that " more than half of all the statutes enacted in 1941 were proposed or sponsored by state and local administrative agencies and officers, and the eighteen state

Municipal Review, September, 1929, pp. 565–567, and " Well Springs of Our Laws," *ibid.*, October, 1939, pp. 689–693.

administrative departments proposed more than a quarter of them."
In the following year the legislature accepted over three fourths of
the program advanced by the administration.[9]

THE COLLECTION OF DATA

It seems scarcely necessary to say that before enacting laws on any
important subject, the members of the legislature must have at their
disposal a considerable body of factual material. Without such information intelligent action would be impossible. As state legislatures are now organized, they have at their disposal many different
methods or techniques for securing information. Some of the fact-
finding machinery is set in motion by the members themselves to
meet a particular need existing at the time, while legislative reference bureaus, legislative councils, and other technical aids for
legislators contribute much information of both a general and
special nature. Nor can the lobby as a source of information be
ignored. The nature and extent of the service required is determined
to a large extent by the kind of people we choose to serve as members.

Ad interim Committees. The special investigating committee, ad
interim committee, or commission is usually provided for by resolution in the course of the session. Such committees may be joint, or
may function for a single house. Appointments are made by the presiding officer or officers of the two houses at the end of the session.
The usefulness of this device varies greatly from state to state, and
even from time to time in the same state. A professional jokesmith
has said that an investigating committee is a group of distinguished
persons who individually can do nothing, but who collectively decide that nothing can be done. In some states this comes very near
being true, for ad interim committees are all but worthless as fact-
finding bodies. Even though a number of such committees may be
authorized during the session, they rarely do anything unless there
is an insistent public demand for an investigation, or unless the
chairman is a person of industry and ability who takes the appointment seriously. In a good many cases the creation of such a committee
is merely a device for postponing action.

[9] Witte, Edwin E., " Administrative Agencies and Statute Lawmaking," *Public Administration Review,* Spring, 1942, pp. 116–125; Scott, Elizabeth McK., and Zeller, Belle, " State Agencies and Lawmaking," *ibid.,* Summer, 1942, pp. 205–220; Scott, Elizabeth McK., " State Executive Departments Play Growing Part in Law-making," *National Municipal Review,* November, 1943, pp. 529–534. See also Weeks, O. Douglas, " Initiation of Legislation by Administrative Agencies," *Brooklyn Law Review,* January, 1940, pp. 117–140.

In other states this device has been a most valuable source of information which has served as the basis of legislation of far-reaching importance. The New York State Commission for the Revision of the Tax Laws, for instance, was continued from year to year for twenty-two years, from 1916 to 1938, inclusive. This Commission was extremely fortunate in having continuously competent leadership and an interested and intelligent personnel. Each year it turned its attention to some pressing problem in widely separated fields relating to the establishment of a more equitable revenue system and a more even distribution of the tax burden. Altogether, twenty-nine reports were published, and at the conclusion of the work in 1938 the Commission published a large index volume covering the whole twenty-nine reports. Embodied in these reports, wrote the Commission at this time, " is the history of the New York tax system, the analysis of the fiscal and administrative problems of state and local government from early statehood to the present time, together with the well considered conclusions and recommendation of the various commissions and their personnel — composed of persons trained both in the theory and practice of taxation, economics, and government administration."

This Commission long held such a preeminent position that one may be justified in devoting some space to its history and accomplishments. The following is supplied by the clerk who served it for several years:

During the legislative session of 1915, the Joint Legislative Committee on Taxation was authorized. In 1919, the Special Joint Legislative Committee on Taxation and Retrenchment was created by the adoption of a joint resolution, which provided for an appropriation to make possible the carrying on of the necessary work. The first report of this Committee was made to the Legislature during the session of 1920. The Committee continued to function until it made its report to the Legislature, under date of February 1, 1929, — a report on the various phases of its work, which had been submitted annually to the Legislature from 1920 to 1929, inclusive.

During the legislative session of 1929, a Commission was created to make a study of old age security, and this Commission submitted a report to the Governor and Legislature under date of February 15, 1930. During the session of 1930, a New York State Commission for the Revision of the Tax Laws was created under Chapter 726 of the Laws of 1930.

In order that the reader may have a clearer idea of the valuable work done by this Commission, there is presented in the accompanying table a chronological list of the published reports from 1932 to 1938. Not only is competent leadership necessary, but adequate financial support is required. Consistently the New York Legislature appropriated from $75,000 to $100,000 a year for the work of this one investigating agency alone.[10]

LATER REPORTS OF THE NEW YORK STATE COMMISSION FOR THE REVISION OF THE TAX LAWS

1932 — Seabury C. Mastick, Chairman. Depression Taxes and Economy through Reform of Local Government, submitted February 15, 1933. Legislative Document (1933) No. 56.

1933 — Seabury C. Mastick, Chairman. Local Government Solvency through Tax Relief and Economy, submitted February 15, 1934. Legislative Document (1934) No. 56.

1934 — Seabury C. Mastick, Chairman. Reorganization of Local Government in New York State, submitted February 6, 1935. Legislative Document (1935) No. 63.

1935 — Seabury C. Mastick, Chairman. The Effect of a Two Per Cent Tax Limitation Upon Local Government in New York State, submitted January 6, 1936. Legislative Document (1936) No. 54.

1936 — Seabury C. Mastick, Chairman. Experience with Overall Tax Limitation Laws, submitted January 27, 1937. Legislative Document (1937) No. 61.

———, The Revenue Outlook for the State of New York, submitted January 27, 1937. Legislative Document (1937) No. 62.

———, Financial Control in the Suburban Areas of New York State, submitted January 27, 1937. Legislative Document (1937) No. 63.

1937 — Seabury C. Mastick, Chairman. The Revenue Outlook for the State of New York for the Fiscal Years 1937–1938 and 1938–1939, submitted January 10, 1938. Legislative Document (1938) No. 55.

———, Recent Experience with Overall Tax Limitation Laws, submitted March 8, 1938. Legislative Document (1938) No. 71.

In some states this device has been used even longer and more extensively than in New York. A study made at the University of California some years ago showed that the legislature in that state " had created 352 special committees and commissions during the period 1850–1936, or an average of seven such agencies per session. During

[10] Wisconsin appropriated $165,012 in 1933 and $128,834 in 1934 for the expenses of approximately twenty committees, some of which functioned in both years. In 1939, in Pennsylvania, $700,000 was appropriated for such committees; this was significant because of a previous unwillingness to appropriate anything for such purposes. See Whitridge, Frederick W., " Legislative Inquests," *Political Science Quarterly*, March, 1886, pp. 84–102; Herwitz, Oren C., and Mulligan, William G., Jr., " The Legislative Investigating Committee: a Survey and Critique," *Columbia Law Review*, January, 1933, pp. 1–27; Fairlie, John A., " Legislative Committees and Commissions in the United States," *Michigan Law Review*, November, 1932, pp. 25–39, and " Reports on State and Local Government," *American Political Science Review*, April, 1933, pp. 317–329.

the first session there were none, and in the 1883 session only one. Eight sessions of the legislature prior to 1909 established only two each, while three was the number created by each of six legislatures prior to 1917. The 1935 session with its forty-three special committees and commissions established the greatest number of any session to date. A definite trend upward began with the 1923 session." [11]

NUMBER AND TYPES OF SPECIAL COMMITTEES AND COMMISSIONS
CREATED BY THE CALIFORNIA LEGISLATURES, 1850–1936

Types	Total	Sessional	Interim
Senate Special Committees	80	55	25
Assembly Special Committees	125	81	44
Special Joint Committees	94	57	37
Special Mixed Commissions	11	4	7
Special Lay Commissions	42	2	40
Total	352	199	153

In this study Dr. Larsen was able to show that a surprisingly large number of major recommendations of these agencies were enacted into law within two or three sessions after they were presented to the legislature. In a similar study of such bodies established in Illinois, from 1900 to 1934, Dr. Ziegler attempted to measure the influence which such agencies have had on the enactment of law; she reports:

Forty senate and house committees and 129 joint committees and commissions which seemed definitely created to study special subjects for the purpose of aiding the legislative body in the performance of its legislative function, were studied. . . . Of the 129 joint committees and commissions, thirty-five, so far as could be ascertained, issued no written reports, but a few of these are known to have had some influence upon legislation. At least thirteen, however, were almost totally inactive. Approximately twenty-five out of a group of seventy-six committees and commissions which had issued reports and recommendations at the time this study was finished, appeared almost completely successful with their legislative programs, while about eleven were unsuccessful. Adequate criteria for determining " success " however were not available. For example, some committees and commissions may have been able to achieve complete success in the eyes of the legislature by simply being as quiet and inactive as possible. The remain-

11 Larsen, Christian L., *The Use of Special Committees and Commissions by the California Legislature* (Bureau of Public Administration, University of California, 1937) . See also Chichester, Cassius M., " Interim Activities in Virginia in Aid of Legislation," *State Government*, April, 1943, pp. 87, 97–100, and Sikes, Pressly S., " Special Interim Commissions in the Indiana Legislative Process," *American Political Science Review*, October, 1942, pp. 906–915.

ing forty which made reports seem to have had part of their recommendations adopted, eventually, although in some instances, the lapse of time was
so long that other factors or forces probably should be given chief credit.[12]

In a number of instances the interim committee has been used
either as a substitute for or as a step toward a legislative council.
The Joint State Government Commission of Pennsylvania is a case
in point. This organization is not actually a council, but both its
objectives and its methods of operation are similar to those of a
council. In Minnesota the house established the Interim Committee
on State Administration and Employment in 1943. In 1941, and again
in 1943, the House passed a bill for a legislative council, which the
Senate failed to approve, so the House went ahead with this substitute, referred to by an eminent political scientist in the state as
" a legislative council in embryo." In Missouri provision has been
made for a Legislative Research Committee which " is somewhat
similar to the legislative councils of other states, although it does not
go as far as some in preparing a program prior to the convening of
the legislature. The Legislative Committee confines itself largely to
maintaining the library and making studies at the request of members of the legislature." [13]

In 1938 the question of the powers of interim commissions was
brought before the Supreme Court of California. Can one house
of the legislature establish an ad interim committee by single house
resolution with power to function after the adjournment of the legislature and of each house thereof sine die? Witnesses summoned
before such a committee refused to answer the questions of the chairman. When the committee attempted to secure a court order directing them to testify, they questioned the validity of the committee
itself, and were supported in their objection by the decision of the
court in a five to two decision which relied upon decisions in other
states to the same effect, but implied that such a committee could
be established by statute. Immediately after this decision the State
Controller refused to honor the warrants of any ad interim committee, either of the Assembly or of the Senate. Inasmuch as some
cases had drawn a distinction between committees of the Senate and
those of the Assembly, an independent action was brought in the

[12] Ziegler, Martha J., " Legislators Work between Sessions," *State Government*,
November, 1937, pp. 236–241, including list referred to above.
[13] Short, Lloyd M., " Minnesota Interim Committee a Legislative Council in
Embryo," *National Municipal Review*, May, 1944, pp. 251–252, and editorial,
pp. 219, 228; letter to the author from Estal E. Sparlin, Legislative Analyst for the
Legislative Research Committee in Missouri, May 28, 1945.

Supreme Court directly against the Controller, to require him to honor warrants for expenses incurred by the Senate committees. This was an action for a writ of mandate directed to the Controller, ordering him to pay the expenses of the committee, and thereby putting in issue the validity of the establishment of the committee itself. The Court held in a five to two decision that the Senate could not, by a single-house resolution, or the two houses acting together could not by concurrent resolution, create an ad interim committee with power to function after the adjournment of the legislature sine die.[14] A constitutional amendment authorizing the establishment of such committees was approved by the voters in 1940.

The legislative sessions of 1943 created in the neighborhood of 200 interim committees, the states with the largest number being: California, forty; Massachusetts, twenty-one; Illinois, nineteen; New York, sixteen; Connecticut, Oregon, and Texas, thirteen each; and Minnesota, eleven — making a total of 146 in these eight states alone. While they were directed to explore many subjects, problems of the war and the postwar period predominated. Among the former were assistance to the executive in solving emergency situations, black-marketing operations, price fixing, Japanese resettlement, un-American activities, and inter-racial relations. In the latter field we find general commissions on postwar planning in ten states, with others established to study such special problems as highway and aviation plans and projects, veteran rehabilitation, veteran bonus measures, relief of businesses hard hit by the war, and many other things. As of July 15, 1944, Virginia had in operation fifteen such legislative agencies and commissions dealing with a variety of subjects.[15]

Commissions Appointed by the Governor. In the second place, the legislature may authorize the governor to appoint a special commission to investigate a particular subject, giving it the necessary power and making provision for its expenses. Agencies of this type are included in the California study already mentioned. As an illustration,

14 Special Assembly Interim Committee on Public Morals v. Southard, 13 Cal. (2d) 497, 90 Pac. (2d) 304, 1939; Swing v. Riley, 13 Cal. (2d) 513, 90 Pac. 313, 1939; McHenry, Dean E., " The Legislative Power to Investigate on the Anvil: California's Legislature Loses and Regains Investigative Authority," *State Government,* May, 1942, pp. 105–106.

15 Based on a survey made by the Council of State Governments. See *State Government,* October, 1943, p. 207, and issues of February, 1932, January and November, 1937, for earlier lists; Commonwealth of Virginia, General Assembly, *Legislative Interim Manual, 1944–1946* (Richmond, 1944). See also Legislature of the State of Alabama, *Reports of Interim Committees,* Legislative Document, 1943, No. 4 (Montgomery, 1943), and Legislative Research Committee, *Final Report for 1941–1942* (Augusta, Maine, 1942).

the General Assembly of Pennsylvania in 1925 authorized the governor to appoint a commission to investigate the condition of the blind in the state; the commission was duly appointed with a competent personnel, composed of individuals not members of the legislature, who carried on the investigation and made their report. The report outlined a program which it was recommended should be adopted. Among the items in this program was a recommendation for the establishment of a state council for the blind. The report was presented at the next regular session of the legislature, and the council provided for by legislative action, together with the necessary appropriation. This Council has now been in satisfactory operation for a period of approximately twenty-five years.

Information from Executive Departments. The legislature may by resolution direct an administrative official or a department to present a report on a designated subject falling within the range of their regular administrative activity. This method of procedure is particularly useful in the handling of questions which are largely administrative. As has been noted, the representatives of the department should be thoroughly familiar with the existing law and with the administrative problems arising under it. The information is usually supplied promptly, if not willingly, because the agency is dependent on the legislature for its appropriation, and hence is anxious to cultivate the good will of the members of that body.

Hearings by Standing Committees. Another method by which the legislature may secure information is by the conduct of hearings by its regular committees. It is customary to announce the dates of these hearings far enough in advance to enable interested parties throughout the state to gather and arrange the data which they wish to present, and to enable them to plan to be present when the hearing occurs. The weakness of the procedure in the majority of the states lies in the fact that each house maintains a separate committee, each of which schedules its hearings without regard to the corresponding committee from the other house. Thus the citizens who appear are subjected to a double loss of time and a double expense in journeying to the state capitol. This difficulty has been solved in Massachusetts and a few other states by the establishment of joint legislative committees. This device not only saves the extra time and expense which are necessary under the usual system, but it guarantees that the representatives of both houses will be furnished with precisely the same information and opinions at the same time.

There are many cases in which the members of the committee have definitely made up their minds before the hearings are held; in such cases the hearing, when it does occur, is perfunctory and may even be resorted to as a method of procrastination. In some states, however, this sort of public hearing is more or less impossible. In Wisconsin, for instance, the law requires that a list of appearances before the various legislative committees be kept. Such a list is reproduced herewith; note that in each case the corporation or interest group for which the witness speaks is recorded. This particular bill, introduced into the Senate in the regular session of 1933, dealt with the competition of municipally owned utilities with those privately owned. A similarly complete record is kept of the deliberations of the conference committee when it is necessary that such a committee be created for the consideration of any measure before the legislature.[16]

LEGISLATURE OF THE STATE OF WISCONSIN

BILL NO. 110,S., 1933 REGULAR SESSION

(By Senator Loomis)

" A bill to repeal and recreate subsection (4) of section 196.50, and to amend subsection (1) of said section 196.50 and subsection (4) of section 197.01 of the statutes, relating to municipal competition with privately owned utilities."

February 8 — Referred to Senate Committee on Corporations and Taxation.

March 8 — Hearing held.

Appearances for the bill:

Senator O. S. Loomis, Mauston, Wisconsin.

E. J. Donnelly, City Manager of Two Rivers, Wisconsin, in behalf of the Power Committee of the League of Wisconsin Municipalities.

Mayor D. W. Hoan, Milwaukee, Wisconsin, in behalf of the League of Wisconsin Municipalities.

Appearances against the bill:

Arthur J. Whitcomb, representing the Milwaukee Electric Railway and Light Company of Milwaukee, Wisconsin, one of the North American Operating companies.

Christ Kartman, representing the Farmers' Telephone Company of Lancaster, Wisconsin.

[Here follow the names of six other utility representatives who appeared.]

---

[16] Information furnished by Howard F. Ohm, Chief of the Legislative Reference Library, December 14, 1934. A similar practice prevails in Minnesota; see " Permanent Rules of the House, 1939," No. 6 in *Legislative Manual*, 1939, p. 122. See also Baker, Roscoe, " The Reference Committee of the Ohio House of Representatives," *American Political Science Review*, April, 1940, pp. 306–310.

March 23 — *Executive Session*

  Senator Reis moved that Sub. Amdt No. 1,S. be adopted; seconded by
  Senator Polakowski.
  Ayes: Senators Bolens, Reis, Polakowski, and Morris.
  Noes: None.
  Absent: Senator Edwards.

  Senator Bolens moved indefinite postponement be recommended; sec-
  onded by Senator Morris.
  Ayes: Senators Bolens, Morris, and Edwards.
  Noes: Senators Reis and Polakowski, both dissenting.
    (Note: Senator Edwards was not present but had recorded his vote
    as above with the committee.)
  Report: Adoption of Sub. Amdt. No. 1,S. and indefinite postponement,
  Senators Reis and Polakowski dissenting.

Fred H. Meyer, Clerk.

Legislative Reference Bureaus. The second major source of information mentioned was the legislative reference bureau. The movement for the establishment of such agencies, inaugurated by the
New York State Library in 1890 and the Massachusetts State Library in 1892, and expanded and developed in Wisconsin by Charles
McCarthy in 1901, has slowly spread from state to state until, in 1945,
there was in forty-four states a department or agency devoted — many
of them exclusively — to legislative reference work. In four states —
New Mexico, North Dakota, Tennessee, and Utah — there was no
legislative reference work of any kind. In approximately one fourth
of the states such work is done in the state library or the state law
library. The placement of the agency in the state government varies
widely from state to state. Thus one finds that in twenty-four states
some work is being done in the state library; in four, in the state law
library; in five, in the state historical department. Reference work
comes under the supervision of the legislature in five states, under the
governor in three, under the attorney general in four, and is separate
in three. It is under the legislative council in Illinois and Kansas, and
under the Board of University Regents in Nebraska. These figures
do not tally because some states do work of this character in two or
more different places.

The original purpose was twofold; to supply information, and to
render assistance in the drafting of bills. Such agencies may also
properly assist in the work of statute revision. Since the purpose of
these bureaus has been to provide a necessary service to legislators,
it would seem appropriate that the agency should be under legislative control, yet such is the case in only seven states, counting the

two where it is under the legislative council. With the passage of time the number and scope of the services rendered has increased. The Council of State Governments recommends that ten specific types of service be provided for, as follows: [17]

1. Carry on comprehensive research and reference service on legislative problems.
2. Summarize and digest information relating to the legislation of various governmental units.
3. Prepare reports on the effects of legislation.
4. Make such investigations into legislative and governmental institutions as will aid the legislature in its studies and deliberations.
5. Maintain a reference room and reference materials.
6. Keep and file copies of all bills, resolutions, et cetera, and maintain a card index on their status, preparing an index and digest if appropriation is made therefor.
7. Assist and cooperate with the legislative council and interim committees or commissions.
8. Cooperate and maintain an exchange reference service with other legislative reference bureaus and corresponding services of other states and with the Interstate Reference Bureau of the Council of State Governments, and with other governmental research agencies.
9. Advise legislative officers or members on any question of parliamentary law or procedure.
10. Carry on bill drafting and statutory revision work.

On the information-gathering side, it is the business of such a bureau to have on hand, properly classified and filed, up-to-date information on all the important subjects with which the legislature must deal. This information will include newspaper clippings of significant events, articles, speeches and addresses, pamphlets, court decisions, and many other more or less fugitive materials. This material must be immediately accessible, for the bureau staff never knows when some member of the legislature will come rushing in to secure, at the last minute, information regarding a subject which he feels he must talk about on the floor a few minutes hence. The work of the bureau, however, is not confined to collection of general information. In a number of states, of which Wisconsin is a good ex-

[17] *State Government*, June, 1937, pp. 120–121. The Council of State Governments, *Book of the States*, always has recent information on this subject. The most recent studies are: Laurent, Eleanore V., *Legislative Reference Work in the United States*, containing an extensive bibliography (Council of State Governments, Chicago, 1939), and Witte, Edwin E., " Technical Services for State Legislators," *Annals*, January, 1938, pp. 137–143. *Special Libraries*, October, 1941, carried a series of five articles, by recognized authorities, covering their history and growth and operation.

ample, the bureau carries on, through its regular staff members, thorough and detailed investigations of various legislative subjects, always, however, at the request of members. The bureau is furthermore a sort of clearinghouse for information regarding the state government, to which many representatives and private citizens apply. While the bureau attempts to serve all, its duties to the members of the legislature are paramount. If the members are to make the use of this service which they should, the bureau staff must do two things: it must maintain a position of absolute independence and fairness, and it must avoid any claim to credit for the work which it does. A seeker after publicity has no place on the staff of such a bureau.

The permanent staff of the Wisconsin Legislative Reference Library consists of a dozen persons, including the chief, librarians, and research assistants, stenographers and clerks, and a messenger. During the session it is necessary to make temporary additions to the staff, which is one of the largest in the country. In nine states the permanent staff are civil service employees. The cost of the service in Wisconsin is about $45,000 for the biennium; in other states the cost ranges from approximately $85,600 in New York to $3,700 in North Carolina. It is extremely difficult to compare accurately the costs of the service in different states, because in many states no separate appropriation is made for the work. There is the widest diversity in the facilities available for the use of the bureaus in the several states; Wisconsin has a catalogued collection of 75,000 or more items, and spends about $1,000 a year on books and subscriptions. In other states the facilities for the work are severely limited.

Mention should be made of other agencies of this character cooperating with the individual state bureaus. The Legislative Reference Division of the Library of Congress has been functioning since 1914; it compiles bibliographies and renders other valuable services to state legislators. Shortly after its establishment the American Legislators' Association set up, as an affiliated organization, the Interstate Reference Bureau for the purpose of assisting any legislator or legislative committee or any legislative reference bureau to secure any desired information. This service is now operated by the Joint Reference Library for all the cooperating organizations in the 1313 group. Hundreds of requests for information are answered annually from state legislators, members of Congress, and many other sources. This work has become important not only because of its extent, but because of its effort to bring about cooperation and coordination of the state services, and to eliminate so far as possible duplication of effort. State bureaus are urged to send copies of all compilations of information on any legislative subject to the Joint Reference Library; these are kept on file and, when copies are available for distribution, are listed in the weekly check list of *Recent Publications on Governmental Problems* distributed by the Public Administration Service.

The Lobby. The lobby is an outgrowth of a form of social and economic organization in which special interest groups seek to influence the course of public policy through the agency of paid representatives. The lobby has existed at state capitols for many years. In the early days its methods were crude and often objectionable — so much so, in fact, that the presence of these paid representatives aroused great popular resentment. This was reflected by the enactment of legislation in many states, such as that sponsored by Governor Robert M. La Follette in Wisconsin in 1905, requiring the registration of all such persons. In our own time the number of lobbyists in legislative halls has greatly increased. Professor Edward B. Logan said as far back as 1929 that the lobby " oftentimes outnumbers the membership in the legislature. In one state recently, more than 800 lobbyists or legislative counsel registered during a single legislative session — about half of them being paid; in another state, 140; another state, 124; another 84; and so on."

With this increase in numbers there has been a decided change in type. Many present-day lobbyists are persons of ability and education, gifted with such social graces as may enable them to move in any circle which their work may require. Many are professionals; they stay in the work year after year, first for one organization and then for another. Their faces become as familiar around the state capitol as the fittings in the legislative halls. When their presence as lobbyists is no longer a secret, much of the supposed evil of the lobbying system vanishes. No legislator can plead ignorance when buttonholed by a member of this energetic and persistent fraternity. The members of this group furnish a great deal of information, biased though it often is. It should be remembered not only that the secrecy of the lobby as an institution has largely passed, but that the efforts of one group operate very often with the effect of offsetting those of another. No important issue is decided in the legislative halls without the presence of the representatives of groups reflecting almost every conceivable position which might be taken on the issue.[18]

Legislative representation by private groups has a threefold aspect — the lobbyist himself, who is the actor in the drama; the legislator, who is the subject upon which he expends his efforts; and the public, which is affected by the outcome. A high-grade lobbyist with a social point of view is interested not merely in getting through a particular bill, but in actually being of assistance to the legislators and reflecting accurately the views of enlightened people. The public-spirited legislator is anxious to see the dependence of the members upon the lobbyist reduced by the development of accurate and impartial sources of information at the capitol readily accessible to the legislator. To the political scientist, whose point of view is to a large extent that of the public, pressure groups hold the key to the future of democratic governmental processes in America. To him it appears that the legislator carries out the public will that is determined and manipulated through channels of mass propaganda, reinforced by the old and tried methods of lobbying.[19]

The most objectionable features of the lobby as it now exists are its corrupting influence — as distinguished from legitimate legislative representation — and its cost. In an earlier chapter mention was made of the findings of a recent investigation in California. An interesting case of this sort in Michigan was reported by Paul H. Todd, former Chairman of the Michigan Public Utilities Commission, at the Anniversary Dinner of the National Popular Government League in Washington in April, 1939:

[18] In Ohio in 1924, 170 lobbyists were registered. There were 40 in New York and 77 in Massachusetts in 1928, while 127 were registered in a later California session. Professor McKean found 164 in New Jersey in 1934 and 1935; these he classifies as business, labor, agriculture, professional, religious, public employee, veteran, women, motorist, education, and reform groups; see McKean, Dayton, D., *Pressures on the Legislature of New Jersey,* Chapter 3 (Columbia University Press, 1938).

[19] *Annals,* January, 1938, included excellent articles covering the lobby from three different points of view: that of the lobbyist, Schermerhorn, Gertrude L., pp. 88–94; of the legislator, Parkman, Henry, Jr., pp. 95–102; of the political scientist, Zeller, Belle, pp. 79–87. Other recent materials include: McKean, *op. cit.,* and "A State Legislature and Group Pressure," *Annals,* May, 1935, pp. 124–130; Zeller, Belle, *Pressure Politics in New York* (Prentice-Hall, New York, 1937), "Pressure Groups and Our State Legislators," *State Government,* July, 1938, pp. 121–122, 124, and August, 1938, pp. 144–147, 155, and "Lawmaker — Legislator or Lobbyist?" *National Municipal Review,* August, 1940, pp. 523–532, 544; Ewing, Cortez A. M., "Lobbying in Nebraska's Legislature," *Public Opinion Quarterly,* July, 1937, pp. 102–104; Kalijarvi, Thorsten V., Ed., *Political Action Groups in New Hampshire* (University of New Hampshire Bulletin, July, 1940).

Official records of the Michigan Public Utilities Commission for this last year contain sworn testimony by subordinate officials of the Consumers Power Company, admitting that the Consumers Power Company paid substantial fees to a member of the Michigan State Senate while that state senator was a member of the Senate Public Utilities Committee and was ardently and successfully opposing the reporting out of four important bills which had been passed by a large majority by the State House of Representatives and had been referred to his committee in the Senate for consideration. These bills were kept buried in committee to the last. One of them would have provided for the creating of power districts by joining municipalities or other governmental districts together; another would have provided for the legal issuance of revenue bonds to pay for hydro-electric or steam power plants; a third would have facilitated rural electrification in Michigan. As a result of the death of these bills in committee through the efforts of this subsidized senator, a Michigan city was unable to sell revenue bonds for a hydro-electric plant which they wished to build. The power site is accordingly undeveloped to date.

This same senator received a check for $2,000 from this power company in 1938, and one of $395 for "legal opinions, etc.," in 1939. The case of Senator Thayer in New York in 1934 was similar. Much of this corrupt lobbying is done on a social basis at poker games, drinking parties, and other entertaining carried on in hotel rooms. This revelry often lasts until far into the night; the lobbyist pays the bills. The member knows this, and while there may be no actual bribery, he knows also what is expected of him when he accepts such hospitality. Sometimes the legislator has his room and board at the hotel taken care of by some group which desires his support. Such a system is obviously expensive to operate. In a recent North Carolina session, $82,006 were spent for lobbying services. Of this amount, "sixty-seven registered lobbyists received about $54,000 in fees and expense money or more than half the $102,000 salaries drawn by the 170 members of the Legislature. Forty-nine lobbyists reported that they drew no fees in addition to their regular salaries. Forty-six lobbyists reported that they had spent nothing." [20] Much more is spent than ever finds its way into the published reports.

The activities of the lobby are not confined to work for or against the passage of bills. Lobbyists are responsible for the introduction of a great many bills, and they are frequently in contact with administrative officers, it often being as important for them to influence the interpretation of an act as to get it passed. In fact, this is their last resort, short of court action attacking the measure on grounds

[20] *New York Times,* July 16, 1933.

of constitutionality or upon the basis of some technicality. Having been unable — for whatever reason — to prevent the passage of an unwanted bill, they must now seek to obtain an administrative determination of its meaning and effect that will produce a minimum of inconvenience or expense to the interests which they represent.

It is possible to control legitimate legislative representation to some extent by laws to regulate lobbying activities, but there is apparently no legal method of preventing the exerting of pressure on legislators through the social lobby and other corrupt methods referred to; certainly the old legislation requiring registration has not succeeded in breaking it up.[21] Nevertheless, thirty-two states have enacted such laws. In many states, however, under the present interpretation of the law, many organizations escape the necessity of registration. Under such circumstances the legislation is inadequate and insufficient to accomplish any effective control.[22] It has become customary to refer to the lobby as the third house of the legislature. It is the element of secrecy that is most objectionable. It has been suggested that this might be eliminated — that the interests represented in this way might be brought out into the open — by giving the lobbyists official standing by some system of functional representation. There are obvious difficulties of considerable magnitude in such a plan, but the idea may be worthy of consideration.

PROBLEMS OF DRAFTSMANSHIP

The statute books of every state in the Union present indisputable evidence of the failure of legislative bodies to perform the work of draftsmanship in a manner even reasonably satisfactory. Many of the statutes passed cannot be expected to mean what they say; some mean nothing, and others attempt to provide for utterly impossible things. As Professor Holcombe has observed:

Crude, almost illiterate, legislation is constantly coming to light through the proceedings of the state courts; laws which cannot be intended to mean what they say, and laws which mean nothing, are not uncommon. A regulation found in the road law of one state that no one shall operate a political steamroller or band wagon on the highway doubtless was put there in jest, but there is nothing funny about a provision, found in the same state, that proprietors of hotels shall keep the walls and floors of their rooms

[21] See the analysis of the application of the New York law in Zeller, *Pressure Politics*, pp. 252–262.

[22] See, for instance, "Indiana Lobby-Control Found Insufficient," *National Municipal Review*, November, 1938, pp. 543–544, 560; also Lowenstein, Karl, "Occupational Representation and the Idea of an Economic Parliament," *Social Science*, October, 1937, pp. 420–431.

covered with plaster. In Massachusetts, where things are supposed to be done better, one legislature, in trying to prevent the display of the red flag of anarchy upon the highway, succeeded in forbidding Harvard students from carrying their college banner to the football field.[23]

Some years ago, the Massachusetts legislature prohibited by law the wearing of hatpins protruding more than an inch beyond the crown of a woman's hat; sometime later the repeal of this statute was considered, one house voting for repeal, and the other, after serious deliberation, refusing to do so on the ground that the fashion might again occur. A legislature in South Dakota prohibited the performance within the state of a dance known at the time as the "Hoocha-coochy." Best of all, perhaps, was a statute enacted in Kansas some years ago regarding the meeting of railroad trains on a single track; the law provided that in such cases each train should take to a siding, and remain there until the other should have passed. In Ohio in 1913 the legislature provided that the coat of arms should be engraved on the officials of the state. One Pennsylvania member succeeded in getting up to a vote on final passage a bill prohibiting the shearing of hydraulic rams between November 1 and March 31. This state had managed to get along reasonably well without a state flower, and to make some progress in the development of a civilization, until 1933, when the General Assembly passed two acts providing for different flowers. The final determination of this momentous question was finally left to the wife of the governor.[24]

Governor George H. Hodges of Kansas set forth in an address before the Governors' Conference in 1913 some observations based upon his then recent experiences:

Notwithstanding the fact my executive clerk and the attorney-general did their best to scrutinize all the bills, Chapters 177 and 178, and Chapters 174 and 175, respectively, are duplicates. Chapter 75 of the laws of 1911

23 Holcombe, Arthur N., *State Government in the United States,* Third Edition, pp. 313–314 (Macmillan, New York, 1931).
24 This kind of material is constantly coming to light; see Seagle, William, "Lunatic Legislation," *Plain Talk,* April, 1929, pp. 457–466. Improper punctuation made it illegal for nine years to sleep in a hotel room in North Dakota. A New York senator in 1936 got a pension bill for Private Evael O. W. Tnesba (absent without leave) up to final passage. A jokester in California in 1937 moved along an appropriation bill for over $6,000,000 to dredge "the Pee-Wee River in the County of San Diego, which river flows two and one-fourth inches of water during three days of each year, if and when it rains." In New Jersey in 1938 a bill was presented to have all holidays fall on Monday. Sometimes old laws are resurrected either to annoy people or for ridiculous purposes; thus in 1938 a forty-one-year-old New York law was used to fine motorboat owners who failed to display lights at night, when moored.

was repealed three times. . . . Chapter 318 of the laws of 1913 was immediately amended by Chapter 319 of the laws of 1913. Chapter 82 of the laws of 1911 was repealed by Section 7 of Chapter 89 of the laws of 1913, and after being repealed was then amended and repealed by Chapter 108 of the laws of 1913.[25]

Upon the basis of a record from which the above illustrations are by no means unusual, there can be little question regarding the incompetence of the legislatures in the drafting of statutes. This difficulty has been due chiefly to two causes. In the first place, the legislators introduce large numbers of bills that come, as Woodrow Wilson observed, " out of cubby-holes all over the state." Large numbers of the measures introduced are not drafted by the members who present them but by corporations, groups, and private citizens who have some special privilege which they want conferred by legislative action. The second reason for the poor quality of draftsmanship is found in the frequent absence of any technical bill-drafting service attached to or connected with the legislative organization.

Bill-Drafting Services. There were, however, a few who realized the need for such a service. The early legislative reference bureaus attempted to combine the information service described above with technical assistance in bill drafting. In recent years great progress has been made, as is convincingly shown by the improved quality of the legislative output. Most of the states now possess some official agency whose business it is to draft, to assist in drafting, or to examine for correction bills submitted by members which have been already drafted by others. A former director of the Legislative Reference Bureau in Wisconsin states that practically all bills introduced in that state have been either drafted, or approved as to form, by the bill-drafting service. In New York and Pennsylvania competent persons estimate that at least 95 per cent of the bills introduced have at least been examined by the bill-drafting service. In one recent Pennsylvania session the Legislative Reference Bureau drafted more bills than the total number introduced in the two houses. Of course, many of those drafted were not introduced, and a few of those which were introduced were probably drawn up by others.

It is difficult for the layman to understand why any reasonably intelligent person should not be able to draft a bill. The truth is,

[25] Delivered at Colorado Springs, August 26, 1913. The text of the address may be found in the *Proceedings* of the Governors' Conference or in Ewing, Cortez A. M., and Dangerfield, Royden J., *Documentary Source Book in American Government,* pp. 641–652 (Heath, Boston, 1931) .

however, that the work is of a highly technical nature — so much so that few lawyers or political scientists are qualified to do it without special training and a period of apprenticeship. Two or three important problems are involved. The draftsman must know, in the first place, the exact nature of the provisions of the existing law; if he does not know this from practical experience, he must be able to use the tools of the lawyer quickly and effectively to secure this information. Secondly, he must know exactly what changes he desires to make. It should be self-evident that he cannot know this if he does not know what the existing provisions are. Finally, he must be able to determine a suitable means of accomplishing these changes, and to express his intention in clear, definite, and understandable language. He should have sufficient imagination to envisage the problems of enforcement which are likely to arise under each of the available methods of treating the subject. As President Wilson once observed, there is nothing easier than to draft an unworkable law, and nothing that is more difficult than attempting to enforce it.

In the early stages of its development, the movement for scientific bill drafting was linked with the official information-gathering agencies. In many cases this condition still prevails, but it is now the opinion of outstanding legislators as well as of political scientists that the two services should be separate and distinct, even though the same number of persons are still employed for their performance. This separation is already in effect in New York and in three other states and is under serious consideration elsewhere. However the service is organized, certain fundamental principles must be observed in conducting it if it is to be successful. The bill drafter cannot tell the legislator what ought to go in his bill. He must try to secure a clear understanding of the legislator's purpose and intent and then attempt to write these ideas and principles into a bill which will make their realization possible. He must be concerned with questions of constitutionality, but he cannot pass upon questions relating to the wisdom of the policies proposed. The members must be convinced that they are being given every possible attention and courtesy and that their requests are being handled in the order in which they are received, unless in some particular case there is definite justification for doing otherwise.[26]

[26] See Jones, Chester L., *Statute Law Making in the United States* (Faxon, Boston, 1923) , and Luce, Robert, *Legislative Procedure* (Houghton Mifflin, Boston, 1922) , for discussions of the technique of bill drafting. In 1937 the General Assembly of Pennsylvania passed a statutory construction act, which answers many

Printer's No.—**1975**

THE GENERAL ASSEMBLY OF PENNSYLVANIA

FILE OF THE HOUSE OF REPRESENTATIVES

No. 2333 Session of 1933

INTRODUCED BY MR. PHILIP STERLING, APRIL 19, 1933.

REFERRED TO COMMITTEE ON STATE GOVERNMENT, APRIL 19, 1933.

AN ACT

Authorizing the Secretary of the Commonwealth with the approval of the Attorney General and Director of the Legislative Reference Bureau to correct certain errors in the original copies of laws

1 Section 1 *Be it enacted by the Senate and House of Repre-*
2 *sentatives of the Commonwealth of Pennsylvania in General Assembly*
3 *met and it is hereby enacted by the authority of the same* That
4 where any law shall have been finally enacted and it
5 shall be ascertained that such law is technically defective
6 in form or contains misspelled words or typographical
7 errors or the plural or singular appears where the
8 opposite should be used the Secretary of the Common-
9 wealth in punctuating and editing such law shall have
10 authority with the approval of the Attorney General and
11 the Director of the Legislative Reference Bureau to cor-
12 rect the original copy of such law as filed in the De-
13 partment of State if such correction will not in any
14 manner affect or change the meaning intent or substance
15 of such law

PENNSYLVANIA ACT AUTHORIZING CORRECTION OF ERRORS IN LAWS

1975—Printer's No. 2

1   Section 2 Whenever any correction on any law is

2   made as hereinbefore authorized a notation thereof shall

3   be made on the original copy by the Secretary of the

4   Commonwealth together with his signature followed by the

5   approval and signatures of the Attorney General and the

6   Director of the Legislative Reference Bureau

7   Section 3 This act shall become effective immediately

8   upon its final enactment

Codification. The codification of state statutes has become a subject of great importance as the total quantity of statutory law has increased. There are many ways in which this work may be done. It may be the result of the work of either a public or a private agency. While, if the codification is to have the effect of law, it must be approved by the legislature, the work may be and usually is done by some other agency. Often this is a duty of the legislative reference bureau, although there may be a special law revision commission appointed by the governor, as happened in New York in 1934, or the legislature may itself create a commission to carry on the work. New Jersey had a commission that worked for twelve years codifying and revising the statutes of that state, reporting in 1937. The California Code Commission was established in 1929; it prepared the School Code of 1929, and from 1931 to 1937 prepared eleven additional codes. Others are in course of preparation. The codes are printed by the state printer and are available at actual cost.[27]

In other states, either because the legislature fails to provide for a codification or, as in Pennsylvania, because of a constitutional barrier, there is no official code. In such cases, private law publishers

---

questions so far as this state is concerned; see Act of May 28, 1937 (P. L. 282) , and Winsor, Mulford, " Legislative Drafting," Arizona State Library *Newsletter,* January, 1937, pp. 1–31, and January, 1941, pp. 1–47. In Oregon, Senate Concurrent Resolution No. 2, adopted January 20, 1941, was published in pamphlet form as *Legislative Style and Uniform Rules Governing and Regulating the Drafting of Bills, Memorials, and Resolutions.* Rutherford, M. Louise, *Influence of the American Bar Association on Public Opinion and Legislation,* Chapter 8, discusses the rendering of technical aid to members and the drafting of legislation (Foundation Press, Chicago, 1937) .

27 See Wood, Fred B., " Codifying Statutes of California; Classification and Revision of State Laws," *United States Daily,* May 26, 1932; also Tribble, Lewis H., " Statutory Revision in Florida," *American Bar Association Journal,* June, 1940, pp. 498–499.

may undertake the task.[28] It is important that the work be done, not only because of the great inconvenience involved in the use of the session laws, particularly by Federal officials and by persons in other states, but because of the impetus which codification gives to the systematic and orderly development of the law.

Some states provide for a periodic codification of their statutes, but this plan is much inferior to a continuous process of compilation, revision, and codification. Of the latter type, the work of the Office of the Revisor of Statutes in Kansas, created in 1929, may be taken as an illustration. This office not only does bill drafting and legislative reference work, but carries on continuous statutory revision.[29]

The revision of law has, in general, been more popular than codification, although in both cases the services of expert draftsmen are required. Professor Harvey Walker has given a clear statement of the steps in the process normally followed:

The first step is to prepare a file of all law which is still in effect in the jurisdiction. This may be done by using two original printed copies of the session laws, pasting the laws on index cards. They must then be carefully checked for amendments, repeals, and decisions as to constitutionality. The final residuum after repealed, obsolete, and unconstitutional sections have been eliminated is the " law in force." The cards must then be sorted under a comprehensive system of headings, which divides all law into categories according to its subject. The selection of the headings to be used is one of the most difficult tasks of the reviser. They may not be overlapping; they must be clear and unambiguous, and they must be inclusive. The need for uniformity between the states is nowhere clearer than in these heading lists.

After all the law in force has been properly classified, it is frequently useful to compare this body of law with that of other jurisdictions. By this process serious errors or omissions may be detected and rectified. The separate acts must then be coordinated, reconciled, and consolidated into a unified statement of the law on each topic. Such work involves many substantive changes as well as a great deal of editorial work. At this stage, hearings may be held and the ideas of competent persons concerning the changes and additions which should be made may be secured. When the re-

---

[28] Cf. Purdon's *Pennsylvania Statutes Annotated,* in forty volumes (West Publishing Company, St. Paul) . Private companies publish such editions in states which do provide an official code; see McKinney's *Annotated Statutes of the State of New York,* and the more recent Cahill's; or the Smith-Hurd *Revised Statutes of Illinois,* 1935 Edition.

[29] See Corrick, Franklin, " The Establishment and Operation of the Office of Revisor of Statutes in Kansas," *Journal of the Missouri State Bar Association,* April, 1938, pp. 64–70, and in *Journal of the Kansas State Bar Association,* May, 1938, pp. 284–294; *Report* of Revisor of Statutes of the State of Minnesota (St. Paul, 1941) .

visers have agreed upon the principle to be used, the task of drafting the sections needed may be and usually is delegated to experts on the staff of the revising commission.[30]

THE LEGISLATIVE COUNCIL MOVEMENT

Of outstanding importance have been recent efforts at legislative planning. It has become evident to all students of legislation that a considerable part of the difficulty experienced with legislative machinery grows out of the lack of planning which is largely responsible for the rush at the end of the session and for many other legislative abuses. It takes so long to decide what kinds of legislation are needed, and to revise and perfect the necessary bills and get them through the preliminary stages, that, especially in those states which impose a definite limit upon the length of sessions, no adequate opportunity remains for the proper discussion and consideration of these measures. It is reasoned that if a plan for the session could be worked out before the legislature convenes, a large part of the time now lost in the early weeks or months of the session could be saved.

Groping for Effective Planning. One method of approach to this problem is represented by the split session. Another was tried a few years ago, also in California, but as indicated in the following memorandum prepared by Paul Mason, then Assistant Secretary of the Senate in that state, without very much success:

In California, beginning in 1919, an effort was made to secure the submission and printing of bills prior to the meeting of the legislature. There was a clerk on duty who had the authority to order printed any bills submitted to him with the certification of a member or member-elect that this person intended to introduce such a bill at the session. Governor Young, who had been a member of the legislature about eighteen years and had been both Speaker of the Assembly and President of the Senate, made a determined drive to relieve the congestion of the session by securing the printing and consideration of the bills by the public and members even before the convening of the session.

[30] Walker, Harvey, *Law Making in the United States,* pp. 271–272 (Ronald Press, New York, 1934). Little seems to have been written on this subject, but see Clark, Dan E., " Codification of Statute Law in Iowa," in Shambaugh, Benjamin F., Ed., *Statute Law-Making in Iowa,* pp. 397–430 (State Historical Society of Iowa, Iowa City, 1916) ; Adams, William J., " Recodification of the North Carolina Statutes," *North Carolina Law Review,* December, 1940, pp. 27–46; Moseley, Robert, " Continuous Statute Research and Revision in North Carolina," *North Carolina Law Review,* June, 1944, pp. 281–296; and Davis, Carlton M., " What Is the Effect of a General Statute Revision? " *Kentucky Law Journal,* March, 1943, pp. 274–279.

This project failed due to the fact that members would not submit measures for printing. At the first such session there were, as I remember, 120 bills printed, and at the following session the number was reduced to about thirty, then at the third session no attempt whatever was made to secure the printing of bills prior to the session. The clerks have the authority and sometimes print important bills in advance of introduction when immediate consideration is urgent.

In 1931 Governor Philip La Follette of Wisconsin caused to be established in that state a short-lived agency which he called an Executive Council. This body is not to be confused with the executive council or council of appointments characteristic of New England. It was composed of five senators and five assemblymen, appointed as standing committees of their respective houses, and of ten other citizens appointed by the governor without confirmation. The Council was authorized to conduct economic investigations for Wisconsin firms, but its chief function was to advise the governor " in any matter which he may refer to the council," and to investigate the functioning of departments and to make studies of governmental problems (special reference being made to the possibility of consolidation and elimination of functions and departments). This Council represented an attempt on the part of the governor to perform, in cooperation with the legislature, a function which the legislatures are now, through their own councils, attempting to perform themselves.[31] The presence on the Council of so many members of the legislature was sufficient to insure some consideration of its recommendations in that body.

As a result of the election of 1932, Michigan found itself for the first time in eighty years with both the legislative and executive branches of the government under the control of the Democrats. Only a few members of the majority party in the legislature had had any experience in legislative work; the leaders made an effort to organize the body for effective action, with somewhat disappointing results. Later in the year, under the leadership of the speaker, the Michigan Legislative Council was established; it was planned that this body would be organized and functioning in the interim between the regular and a contemplated special session. It made an auspicious beginning, but in 1935, owing to a lack of cooperation on the part of the governor, its effectiveness was greatly reduced.

[31] Gaus, John M., " The Wisconsin Executive Council," *American Political Science Review*, October, 1932, pp. 914–920. The message of Governor La Follette in which the proposal was discussed was that to the Regular Session of 1931, delivered January 15, 1931; the act will be found in Wisconsin *Statutes,* Chapter 15, Sections .001–.005.

It fell into a state of " innocuous desuetude," and in 1939 a bill was passed abolishing it.[32]

Kansas Legislative Council. The objectives of legislative planning are easier to visualize and to state than to realize. Some agency must be found in which both the legislature and the administration have confidence, which has some degree of permanence and responsibility, which can work effectively, and which will not, at the same time, usurp or be subject to the charge of usurping the prerogatives of the legislature. The Kansas Legislative Council, first and most significant representative of its type, was established in 1933. Its membership includes the president of the Senate as chairman, the speaker of the House as vice chairman, and nine members from the Senate and fifteen from the House. It began its work in the special session of 1935, during which it sponsored twenty-eight measures; in the regular session of 1935 it sponsored twenty-six more. These measures were drawn up and printed in the usual form. The first report of the Council contained various reports and recommendations on such subjects as the improvement of the capitol building and grounds, and the investigation of state institutions.[33]

The lieutenant-governor of the state, who serves as chairman of the Council, thus describes the manner in which the body functions:

In general the duty of the Council is to collect information concerning the government and general welfare of the State; to examine the effects of previously enacted laws and recommend amendments thereto; to prepare a legislative program in the form of bills or otherwise, as in its opinion are required, and to present such a program at the next legislative session.

The Council is to study possible consolidations in State government, elimination of duplicate activities in personnel and equipment; to co-operate with the administration in devising means of enforcing the law and improving the effectiveness of administrative methods.

The governor is privileged to send a message to that session of the Council convening next after the adjournment of the regular session of the Legislature and may from time to time send additional messages containing his recommendations and explaining the policy of the administration.

In the discharge of its duties the Council has authority to administer oaths, issue subpoenas, to compel the attendance of witnesses and the production of papers, books, accounts and testimony. The Council may meet whenever necessary, but must meet at least once each quarter.

[32] See Dorr, Harold M., " A Legislative Council for Michigan," *American Political Science Review*, April, 1934, pp. 270–275; see also Shull, Charles W., " The Michigan Legislative Council Reports," *National Municipal Review*, May, 1935, pp. 269–270, and " The End of Michigan's Legislative Council," *ibid.*, June, 1939, pp. 470–471.

[33] *Report and Recommendations* of the Kansas Legislative Council, submitted to the Legislature, December 8, 1934; see also *Revised Statutes,* supplement of 1933, Chapter 207.

Any member of the Legislature may present his views on matters being considered by the Council but he cannot participate in any decision. The recommendations of the Council must be completed and made public thirty days prior to any legislative session at which such recommendations are to be presented. The Council members are paid three dollars per day of attendance plus actual expenses.[34]

The results have been extremely encouraging. The main objectives of the Council are to get basic and up-to-date information before the members on timely subjects when the members are in a receptive mood, to carry on research when the desired information is not at hand, and to plan the legislative program, drafting the bills that are necessary to put it into effect. The Council is not particularly interested in how many of its studies result in legislation. From the very beginning, however, many of its reports have been acted upon. The reports grow out of requests from Council members, although the interest may have been inspired by members of the research staff. The reports themselves must be couched in simple and understandable language; if the words are unfamiliar to the member, he is likely to cast the report aside as " theory." The material when completed must belong to the members — the staff members must have a " passion for anonymity." As a result of these efforts, the idea has begun to develop among the members, and throughout the state, that preparation for another legislative session should begin promptly after one session has adjourned.

Research reports have been issued on a variety of subjects, such as the sales tax, state police, old age pensions, institutional problems, et cetera. Many of these reports had a nationwide circulation and have been used in many states, not only by legislative and administrative officers, but by students and research workers. As of the

---

[34] Thompson, Charles W., " Charting Course for State Rule; Planning by Kansas Legislative Council," *United States News*, April 29–May 6, 1933. See also an extensive literature dealing with this and later councils. Bibliographies appear in Kneedler, Grace M., *Legislative Councils and Commissions* (Bureau of Public Administration, University of California, 1939), and Maryland State Planning Commission, *Legislative Councils* (Baltimore, 1939). On the Kansas experiment, see Strain, Camden S., " Kansas Legislative Council," *American Political Science Review*, October, 1933, pp. 800–803; and the following by Guild, Frederic H.: " Accomplishments of the Kansas Legislative Council," a bulletin of its Research Department, May 23, 1935, also in *American Political Science Review*, August, 1935, pp. 636–639; " Kansas' Experiment with a Legislative Council: Estimate of Accomplishments, May 15, 1933, to March 27, 1936," *Bulletin* No. 42 of its Research Department; " The Development of the Legislative Council Idea," *Annals*, January, 1938, pp. 144–150; " The Kansas Legislative Council Considers War Legislation," *State Government*, February, 1943, pp. 35, 45–47; and *Legislative Councils: An Article and a Bibliography* (Kansas Legislative Council, Publication No. 122, February, 1944).

end of 1936, research reports had been prepared on fifty-two subjects, or at the rate of nine or ten a year. The Council has proved to be much more effective than ad interim committees had been in the past; the permanent character of its organization and its adaptability have been important points in its favor. Work of this type cannot be planned far in advance — the important things are done when the opportunity offers, as when some member of the Council drops in for a visit with something on his mind. The research requires a competent director, a trained staff, and months of time.

Spread of the Council Movement. Since 1933 the legislative council idea has spread to about a dozen states; some of the details with regard to these bodies are indicated in the following table:

LEGISLATIVE COUNCILS

| Date | State | Type of Council | Size | Composition | | |
				Ex Officio Legislature Members	Legislature Members Specially Selected	Non-legislators
1933	Kansas	Legislative Council	27	2	25	..
1936	Kentucky	Legislative Council	21	..	16	5
	Virginia	Advisory Legislative Council	7	..	7	..
1937	Connecticut	Legislative Council	6	4	..	2
	Illinois	Legislative Council	22	2	20	..
	Nebraska	Legislative Council	15	1	14	..
	Pennsylvania	Joint State Government Commission	19	..	19	..
1939	Maryland	Legislative Council	14	1	13	..
	Rhode Island	Legislative	5	..	5	..

Interim committees and research committees exist in a number of states — Colorado since 1933, New Mexico since 1936, Missouri since 1939, and Maine since 1940. In the first two of these cases, the lack of a paid expert research staff hampered their work to such an extent that they cannot properly be considered as councils.

The councils range in size from five to more than twenty-five. Ex-officio membership is kept at a minimum; nonlegislative members of any type are discouraged. The lieutenant-governor is a member in two states, but not elsewhere. So far as powers and duties are concerned, the power to appoint a research staff is regularly included, as well as the power to utilize other state agencies. In most states the council may subpoena witnesses, although this is not permitted in

Illinois. Meetings are usually quarterly, although they are set semiannually in Nebraska. Adequate financial support must be provided if any really useful service is to be rendered by the council.

There are in practice many problems of interrelationships with other governmental agencies which such a council must work out — relating to the governor, the public, and the legislature, and to other agencies such as the judicial council, the legislative reference bureau, the bill-drafting service, the state university, et cetera. Many of these questions were investigated by the Maryland State Planning Commission in a comprehensive report on legislative councils, previously cited. The Kansas Council reports no definite clash with the executive, and apparently few such conflicts have developed in other states. The hostility of the executive in Michigan, however, was one of the factors which brought about the repeal of the act in that state. Public opinion seems to have been favorable except in Michigan and Illinois; in the latter state little attention has been given to the council by the press. In some cases resentment of nonmembers of the council toward members has been reported, although this will probably tend to disappear " as the true purpose and functions of the council become more evident." Members really have little reason to fear that the councils will become superlegislatures.

The problem of relations with other established agencies is more difficult, because the council supplements or supplants their activities. This is true of both standing committees and special committees or commissions of the legislature in so far as their investigating functions are concerned. These functions they are ordinarily not equipped to perform. The council does not in any way infringe upon the prerogative of standing committees in considering and deciding upon the provisions of proposed legislation. The jurisdiction of special committees is limited, while a council has the advantage of being able to investigate any proper subject of legislation. A well-organized council will to some extent overlap with the functions of a legislative reference bureau. Both must maintain a library of information on legislative subjects, but the council will normally do more and better work in the field of research than the bureaus have done in the past.

The nature of this interrelationship needs clarification. The council principle is preferable to that of the reference bureau. Under the council plan the legislative leaders work out their own program and determine the nature and scope of the research work to be done. In the reference bureau little or no planning is done, and the members are more in the position of having to accept whatever is given them by way of information. There should be no conflict with the bureaus, however, in so far as their efforts are devoted to bill drafting, nor should there be any conflict with the legislative counsel (not council) in those states where such an officer has been established to give technical assistance to legislators in bill drafting. The job of bill drafting is clearly not within the province of the legislative council. The councils should seek to avoid, as in practice they have done, any conflict with such agencies as a code commission or a judicial council, whose activities are confined to a definitely restricted field.[35] Close cooperation should be maintained with the state univeristy and other educational institutions.

IMPROVEMENTS IN PROCEDURE

The procedure followed in the enactment of legislation has been described in the preceding chapter. In the last few years a considerable interest in the improvement of this procedure has developed. Among the various proposals are those for mechanical voting and for the elimination of the three-reading system. These proposals, as well as others recommended in the Model State Constitution, look toward the saving of time and energy, the development of greater responsibility, and the improvement of the quality of the output.

Mechanical Voting. In most states the vote is taken by roll call — the time-honored viva voce, or vote by the living voice. In eleven states, in five of them since 1936, electrical voting machines are used in one or both houses; each state uses the device in the lower house, and two in the upper house as well.[36] This system, sometimes called flash voting, is a great time-saving device, but it has spread slowly, partly because of adherence to tradition, and partly because the companies which sell and install the machines have charged exorbitant prices. In 1932 an interim committee in California, appointed to study legislative procedure and to study the reduction of legislative expense, made some calculations of the loss of time that had occurred in the session in that state in 1931. From these calculations, which

---

[35] On these points, see Kneedler, *op. cit.*, as well as Guild, Frederic H., " Legislative Councils in the Spotlight," *State Government*, February, 1939, pp. 26–27, and Walker, Harvey, " Legislative Councils — an Appraisal," *National Municipal Review*, December, 1939, pp. 839–842. The Council in Maryland has more than justified its existence; see Bone, Hugh A., " Maryland's Legislative Council in Action," *National Municipal Review*, March, 1942, pp. 146–153. For Virginia, see Chichester, *op. cit.*

[36] Wisconsin, 1917; Iowa, 1921; Texas, 1922; Louisiana, House, 1922, and Senate, 1932; Virginia, House, 1924, and Senate, 1930; Nebraska (unicameral), 1933; West Virginia, 1936; California and Michigan, 1937; Minnesota, 1938; and Florida, 1939. Data from Illinois Legislative Council, *Electrical Roll-Call, Devices in Legislative Bodies* (Springfield, 1940) ; see also Kelley, Alice, " Flash Voting in Wisconsin," *State Government*, October, 1930, pp. 6–8.

were based upon the Assembly journal, it is possible to get some idea of the magnitude of the waste which commonly occurs at every session in most of our states. There were 2,344 roll calls; the committee believed the following to be a conservative estimate, based upon actual timing and their own intimate personal knowledge of the procedure.[37]

ASSEMBLY OF CALIFORNIA — 1931

TIME CONSUMED IN ROLL CALLS

Number and Classification	Total Time
1698 Unanimous affirmative viva voce calls @ 2 min.	56 hr. 36 min.
247 Affirmative viva voce rolls, 3 or less negative votes @ 2⅓ min.	9 hr. 56 min.
113 Affirmative viva voce rolls, 10 or less negative votes @ 2⅔ min.	5 hrs. 2 min.
154 Affirmative viva voce rolls, more than 10 negative votes @ 3 min.	7 hr. 42 min.
33 Unanimous negative viva voce roll calls @ 2½ min.	1 hr. 23 min.
99 Contested negative viva voce roll calls @ 3½ min.	5 hrs. 46 min.
2344 Totals	86 hr. 5 min.
Less allowance of 1½ min. saved on 819 substituted roll calls	20 hr. 28 min.
Actual time consumed by the assembly in 1931 in calling the roll	65 hr. 37 min.
2344 Rolls could have been recorded by electric roll call system, @ 10 seconds	6 hr. 30 min.
Actual time necessarily consumed calling the roll, over and above time necessary to record same number of rolls by flash voting.	59 hr. 7 min.

During 1931 there were 74 legislative, or actual meeting days, totaling 291 hours and 55 minutes. This is an average of 3 hours and 57 minutes per meeting day. Therefore, more than 15 legislative days, or three calendar weeks were actually wasted by members answering aye or nay, owing to the absence of a system of electrical voting. It seems incredible that nearly one-fourth of the actual meeting time of the Assembly is being wasted and the session needlessly prolonged more than three weeks at an added expense to the taxpayers. This is readily shown in our legislative costs for the present two-year period which total over $800,000, the major portion of which is spent during the actual time in session. Also had we not substituted 819 roll calls by unanimous consent on uncontested matters during the last session, the calling of the roll would have consumed almost one-third of the entire time we were actually in session.

[37] California Assembly Interim Committee on Legislative Procedure and Reduction of Legislative Expense, *Preliminary Report,* pp. 88–89 (Sacramento, 1932).

VIRGINIA HOUSE OF DELEGATES

NAY	AYE	NOT-VOTING
0 4 0	0 4 8	0 1 1

ROLL-CALL

ON: _____ DATE: _____

MEMORANDA: _____

_____

NAME	N	A	N-V	NAME	N	A	N-V	NAME	N	A	N-V
ADAMS, A. C.		•		FOWLER		•		POWERS		•	
ADAMS, W. H.	•			FRANCIS		•		PRESSLEY		•	
ALLMAN		•		FREEMAN			•	REASOR		•	
BADER		•		GARY		•		REID			
BAIN			•	GOAD	•			RHODES	•		
BATTLE	•			GREEAR		•		ROBERTS		•	
BEAR			•	HALL	•			RODGERS			•
BEARD	•			HARLESS		•		SCOTT		•	
BIRRELL		•		HARMAN		•		SETTLE		•	
BRAY		•		HARRISON		•		SHRADER		•	
BRENEMAN	•			HICKS	•			SISSON			•
BREWER	•			HILLARD		•		SMITH, H. T.	•		
BROWN		•		HOBSON	•			SMITH, J. C.			•
BRUCE	•			HUMPHRIES		•		SNEAD	•		
BRYANT		•		JEFFREYS	•			SPANGLER		•	
BUSTARD			•	JONES, E. B.		•		STANLEY		•	
CADMUS		•		JONES, J. P.		•		STEPHENS	•		
CHICHESTER	•			KELLY	•			STUART	•		
CLEVINGER	•			KING	•			TALIAFERRO		•	
COLEMAN, DAN.	•			LAUDERBACK	•			TERRELL		•	
COLEMAN, I. N.		•		LINCOLN	•			TOPPING		•	
COLLINGS		•		MASSENBURG		•		TUCK		•	
COSBY	•			McCAULEY	•			VELLINES	•		
CROWDER	•			McINTYRE		•		VERSER			•
DARDEN		•		McMURRAN			•	WARREN		•	
DAVIS, C. W.		•		MOFFETT			•	WARRINER	•		
DAVIS, L. N.		•		MOORE		•		WATTS		•	
DENNY	•			MORGAN	•			WHITE		•	
DEY	•			MOSS		•		WHITEHEAD	•		
DOVELL		•		NELSON	•			WITCHER	•		
DUFF	•			PAGE		•		WITTEN	•		
EGGLESTON	•			PERRY	•			WRIGHT	•		
EMBREY	•			PORTER		•		MR. SPEAKER		•	
FOLKES			•	PORTERFIELD		•					

SAMPLE RECORD FROM AN ELECTRICAL VOTING MACHINE

The arguments for and against electrical voting are summarized in the table below and on page 350.

ARGUMENTS FOR AND AGAINST ELECTRICAL VOTING

Arguments For	*Arguments Against*
1. Much time is saved in the routine work of roll call, leaving more time available for debate and consideration of issues.	1. The possible savings do not justify the extensive initial cost of the installation.

Arguments For	*Arguments Against*
2. A more accurate count on roll calls is assured.	2. Electrical voting results in hasty decisions on issues.
3. Independent voting on the part of members is encouraged.	3. It is possible for one member to vote for another who is not present.
4. Electrical voting requires members to be in their seats, thereby aiding the presiding officer in maintaining order on the floor.	4. Members may watch the progress of the vote and vote on the winning side.
5. The system eliminates noise and confusion incident to the use of the viva voce vote.	5. There is the constant danger of mechanical difficulties.
6. Electrical voting eases the rush at the end of the session, when so many votes must be taken in a short time.	6. There are legal and constitutional questions involved in the use of mechanical voting equipment.
7. Electrical voting enables the legislature to complete its business without long night and overtime sessions.	

Elimination of the Three Readings. The three-reading system originated generations ago, prior to the invention of the printing press, and was universally used to prevent the railroading of legislation. Though still generally retained in the rules, it is in practice largely a formality, and even at that, under modern conditions, a serious waster of time. Every member has a printed copy of all bills on his desk before final passage. If it were required that such copies should be distributed three days prior to vote on final passage, the members and the public would have the full protection the three-reading system was intended to give, and the legislature would be freed from a time-consuming procedure which can no longer be justified. The unicameral legislature in Nebraska eased this time-honored requirement by providing for the first two readings by title, and the third a reading in full at the time of final passage (Rule XII, Par. 5).

If one has an opportunity to study the procedure for some time, he is likely to observe that the older members, because of their greater familiarity with the rules, their acquaintance with other members, and their positions of seniority in committees, are able to pilot their bills through the intricacies of the procedure much more successfully than the newer members. He will be impressed with the great importance of committee work, commented on in an earlier chapter. He will be able to note specific instances of the influence of the lobby, and instances of vote trading, by which members help each other to secure the passage of measures in which they have a personal interest.[38]

Presession Conferences and Training Institutes. Another device that has been used for purposes of legislative planning and the improvement of procedure is the presession conference on legislative problems and the training institute on legislative procedure. The presession conference idea was begun, on a regional basis, by the American Legislators' Association in the early thirties. Some of these conferences included members from a single state, as the Colorado Conference of 1934; others included a selected group of public officials from several adjacent states, such as the Southern Conference held in Asheville in 1932. The University of Arkansas in 1936 first conducted the Institute of Legislative Procedure, a school for state legislators which has since been conducted biennially.[39]

In Pennsylvania, in 1939, when Ellwood J. Turner was Speaker of the House he conducted a series of weekly conferences or institutes dealing with problems in the field of legislative organization and procedure. These were designed particularly to aid new members and assist them to assume more quickly their full responsibilities as members. Conferences such as these have been largely experimental up to the present time, but where they have been tried they have been productive of excellent results.

Other Proposals. There have been a large number of attempts to diagnose the difficulties confronting the legislatures and to prescribe a remedy. One author has found the trouble largely outside the legislature, in the nature of the judicial process, in the attitude of the judges, and in the lack of a legislative engineer or ministry of justice.[40] Others have found the trouble largely in the antiquated procedure of the legislature itself, and have proposed, in addition to unicameralism, such remedies as alternate sessions on fiscal problems; trifurcation of other regular sessions with periods for the introduction of bills, committee hearings, and action on bills; the requiring of committees to explain the merits of measures reported; and the use of mechanical voting equipment.[41] Those who favor unicameral-

[38] See Routt, Garland C., " Interpersonal Relationships and the Legislative Process," *Annals*, January, 1938, pp. 129–136.

[39] Alexander, Henry M., " A School for State Legislators," *State Government*, February, 1941, pp. 39–40.

[40] See Mulder, John E., " Some Obstacles to Effective Legislation," *Illinois Law Review*, May, 1936, pp. 24–34.

[41] City Club of New York, *Modernize the Legislature* (New York, 1932) , and Buck, A. E., *Modernizing Our State Legislature* (American Academy of Political and Social Science, Philadelphia, 1936) .

PROPOSED IMPROVEMENTS IN LEGISLATIVE PROCEDURE, 1944

Citizens Union

1. A legislative council of leading members of both parties in both houses, to function throughout the year and to prepare a legislative program in advance of each session.

2. A permanent all-year legislative research and bill-drafting staff, to assist the committees and the legislative council.

3. Break the rules committee bottleneck by keeping assembly committees until the end of the session, as in the senate.

4. Continuance of each house for one week after ceasing to act on its own bills, to act on bills passed by the other.

5. Require committee reports in each house on all bills passed by the other.

6. Require committee reports in each house on all bills re-requested by petition of one third of the members.

Connecticut Public Expenditure Council

1. Information and instruction for new members of the legislature.

2. Streamlining the committee system.

3. Ensuring public knowledge and full and fair discussion of bills.

4. Providing for the orderly disposition of bills left in committee at the end of the session.

5. Reducing the quantity of special legislation.

6. Providing a better record of legislative proceedings.

7. Editing the reports of state departments to make them more useful to the legislature and public.

8. Effective publicity for, and legislative supervision of, the rules and regulations of state departments and agencies.

Citizens Bureau of Governmental Research (Albany)

1. That a public register of legislative employees be kept, giving full information with regard thereto.

2. That, with certain exceptions, appointments of legislative employees be made from regular civil service lists.

3. That the comptroller be instructed to audit legislative expenditures more completely, especially where same are made away from the capitol city.

4. That "vicarious payments" be discontinued.

5. That a constitutional amendment be submitted to permit certain payments to legislative leaders, for extra duties, at times other than during the regular session.

6. That travel allowances for legislative leaders on state business be provided in lieu of assigned state cars and chauffeurs.

7. Prohibit members of the legislature from seeking or accepting appointments for their constituents at the hand of administrative departments.

8. That a legislative council be established for year-

7. Joint committee meetings of the two houses to receive evidence on and also to discuss bills introduced in both houses.

8. Roll calls in committee on all bills referred to committees.

9. Electrical voting, as in ten other states, to expedite roll calls and make them more accurate.

10. Permitting joint introduction of bills by two or more members of the same house.

<table>
<tr><td>

Citizens Union

11. Permitting joint introduction of the same bill in both houses, thereby avoiding treating identical bills introduced in the two houses as separate measures.

12. Civil service for legislative assistants.

13. Use by the legislature of the state's regular purchasing and contracting agencies, instead of maintaining separate machinery of its own.

14. Appoint a secretary of the legislature with full administrative responsibility for the employment and direction of legislative assistants and the discharge of all legislative business functions which are not turned over to other agencies of the state.

</td><td>

Citizens Bureau of Governmental Research (Albany)

around study and formulation of legislative programs.

9. That legislative purchasing be done through the state Division of Standards and Purchases.

10. That legal advisers for legislative committees be employed on a permanent basis.

</td></tr>
</table>

15. A constitutional amendment to permit increased compensation for legislative leaders commensurate with their additional duties and an end to the subterfuges by which such compensation is now given illegally.

ism have found a particularly strong argument for their plan in the abuses of conference committees; Senator Norris stressed this point in the campaign for the adoption of the Nebraska amendment in 1934.[42]

It has been said that two of the most important developments of recent years affecting the work of legislative bodies are the constant expansion of the volume of work which they are called upon to perform and the increasing complexity and technicality of the subjects with which they have to deal. Obviously, if proper consideration is to be given to a large number of difficult questions, the members should be freed from unnecessarily time-consuming methods of procedure. If this were done, members would have the maximum amount of time in which to do their real work. The Kansas Legislative Council suggests that this might be accomplished by making a few very important changes in the committee system; by adopting special calendars to handle local bills and uncontested bills; by speeding up the roll call process, as indicated earlier in this chapter; and by reducing the time consumed in the reading of bills.[43]

The saving of time alone — important as that is — will not solve the problem. Planning the legislative program will help, and the

[42] Burdette, Franklin L., " Legislative Conference Committees," *State Government*, June, 1938, pp. 103–106 — based on Nebraska experience under bicameralism.

[43] Kansas Legislative Council, *Expediting Legislative Procedure* (January 1935) , and California Assembly Interim Committee on Legislative Procedure and Reduction of Legislative Expense, *Preliminary Report* (Sacramento, 1932) .

selection of abler and better trained legislators will help still more.
W. F. Willoughby devoted a full chapter to legislative aids.[44] Among
his suggestions are the delegation of authority to other agencies, in
so far as this can be done constitutionally; the drafting of bills by
executive and administrative officers and by private agencies; the
revision and codification of existing law; and interim committees and
special committees of inquiry. He would, of course, continue the
development of the legislative reference bureaus and the bill-drafting services. Some of the best thought on this subject at the close of
the war period is summarized in the accompanying table in parallel
columns which present three series of proposals for the improvement
of legislative procedure.

When further progress has been made along all these lines, there
still remain the problems of keeping legislators informed of the sentiment prevailing in their respective districts, and of supplying them
with the necessary information in usable form, so that they can intelligently assist in the task of translating the sentiment of the people
into the law of the state. In this they must eventually be assisted
in every state by efficient legislative reference bureaus with trained
and permanent staffs and by a competent bill-drafting service. All
these problems are so interrelated that all must be kept constantly
in mind. The encouraging part of the situation lies in the fact that
there is not a thing mentioned here that we cannot do effectively, if
we will. And in this task we will have the whole-hearted cooperation
and support of a fine group of able and conscientious legislators in
every state — men who want to do their work well and render real
public service, and who will welcome any real assistance that can be
given them.

44 Willoughby, W. F., *Principles of Legislative Organization and Administration*, Chapter 35 (Brookings Institution, Washington, 1934) ; see also Anderson,
Floyd E., " Legislative Reorganization in New York," *State Government*, November, 1944, pp. 435–436, 449; Council of State Governments, " Legislatures Stream-
line 1943 Sessions," *ibid.*, November, 1943, p. 228; Culver, Dorothy C., *Legislative
Reorganization* (University of California, Bureau of Public Administration,
1941) ; Hunt, Jarvis, " How Our State Legislatures Can Be Improved," *State Government*, September, 1944, pp. 400–403; Jones, Lawrence M., " Constitutional Provisions Regulating the Mechanics of Enactment in Iowa," *Iowa Law Review*, November, 1935, pp. 79–84; Luce, Charles, " Judicial Regulation of Legislative Procedure in Wisconsin," *Wisconsin Law Review*, July, 1941, pp. 439–460; Moffat,
Abbott Low, " The Legislative Process," *Cornell Law Quarterly*, February, 1939,
pp. 223–233; Weeks, O. Douglas, " Recent Developments in the State Legislative
Process," *State Government*, July, 1943, pp. 162–167.

SELECTED REFERENCES

Bentham, Jeremy, *The Theory of Legislation* (Harcourt, Brace, New York, 1931).

Buck, A. E., *Modernizing Our State Legislature* (American Academy of Political and Social Science, Philadelphia, 1936).

Chamberlain, Joseph P., *Legislative Processes: National and State* (Appleton-Century, New York, 1936).

Childs, Harwood L., *Labor and Capital in American Politics* (Ohio State University Press, 1930).

Cooley, Thomas M., *A Treatise on the Constitutional Limitations Which Rest upon the Legislative Power of the States of the American Union,* Eighth Edition, edited by Walter Carrington (Little, Brown, Boston, 1927).

Corrick, Franklin, *Report on the Validity of Special Legislation in Kansas* (Topeka, 1945).

Council of State Government, *The Book of the States* (Chicago, biennially).

Dodds, Harold W., "Procedure in State Legislatures," *Annals,* supplement, May, 1918.

Farmer, Hallie, *Local and Private Legislation* (University of Alabama, Bureau of Public Administration, 1944).

Freund, Ernst, Legislative Regulation (Commonwealth Fund, New York, 1932).

——, *Standards of American Legislation* (University of Chicago Press, 1917).

Graves, W. Brooke, *Uniform State Action* (University of North Carolina Press, 1934).

——, Ed., *Readings in Public Opinion* (Appleton, New York, 1928).

——, Ed., "Our State Legislatures," *Annals,* January, 1940.

Green, Harry J., *A Study of the Legislature of the State of Maryland* (Johns Hopkins Press, 1930).

Guild, Frederic H., *Legislative Councils: An Article and a Bibliography* (Kansas Legislative Council, Topeka, 1944).

——, and Snider, Clyde F., *Legislative Procedure in Kansas* (University of Kansas, 1930).

Haines, Charles G., *The Revival of Natural Law Concepts; a Study of the Establishment and of the Interpretation of Limits on Legislatures with Special Reference to the Development of Certain Phases of American Constitutional Law* (Harvard University Press, 1930).

Harlow, Ralph V., *The History of Legislative Methods in the Period before 1825* (Yale University Press, 1927).

Horack, Frank E., *The Sifting Committees as a Legislative Expedient* (State Historical Society of Iowa, Iowa City, 1934).

——, *Cases and Materials on Legislation* (Callaghan, Chicago, 1941).

Jones, Chester Lloyd, *Statute Law Making in the United States* (Faxon, Boston, 1923).

Kalijarvi, Thorsten V., *Political Action Groups in New Hampshire* (University of New Hampshire Bulletin, 1940).

Kansas Legislative Council, *Expediting Legislative Procedure* (Topeka, 1935).

Kettleborough, Charles, *Legislative Procedure in Indiana* (Indiana Legislative Bureau, Indianapolis, 1928).

Key, V. O., Jr., *The Problem of Local Legislation in Maryland* (State Planning Commission, Baltimore, 1940).

Kline, Howard M., *Municipal Legislation in Maryland* (Maryland Legislative Council, 1940).

Kneedler, Grace M., *Legislative Councils and Commissions* (Bureau of Public Administration, University of California, 1939).

Larsen, Christian L., *The Use of Special Committees and Commissions by the California Legislature* (Bureau of Public Administration, University of California, 1937).

Lasswell, Harold D., Casey, Ralph D., and Smith, Bruce L., *Propaganda and Promotional Activities, an Annotated Bibliography* (University of Minnesota Press, 1935).

Laurent, Eleanore V., *Legislative Reference Work in the United States* (Council of State Governments, Chicago, 1939).

Leek, John H., *Legislative Reference Work: a Comparative Study* (University of Pennsylvania, 1925).

Logan, Edward B., " Lobbying," *Annals,* supplement, July, 1929.

Luce, Robert, *Legislative Principles: The History and Theory of Law-Making by Representative Government* (Houghton Mifflin, Boston, 1930).

——, *Legislative Procedure: Parliamentary Practices and the Course of Business in the Framing of Statutes* (Houghton Mifflin, Boston, 1922).

——, *Legislative Problems: Development, Status, and Trend of Treatment and Exercise of Lawmaking Powers* (Houghton Mifflin, Boston, 1935).

Mason, Paul, *Manual of Legislative Procedure for State Legislatures* (California State Printing Office, Sacramento, 1935).

McKean, Dayton D., *Pressures on the Legislature of New Jersey* (Columbia University Press, 1938).

New York State Constitutional Convention Committee, *Problems Relating to Legislative Organization and Powers* (Albany, 1938).

New York State Joint Legislative Committee on Legislative Methods, Practices, Procedures and Expenditures, *Interim Report* (Legislative Document No. 35, 1945, Albany).

Odegard, Peter H., *Pressure Politics, the Story of the Anti-Saloon League* (Columbia University Press, 1928).

——, and Helms, E. Allen, *American Politics* (Harper, New York, 1938).

Reed, Thomas H., Ed., *Legislatures and Legislative Problems* (University of Chicago Press, 1933).

Reinsch, Paul S., *American Legislatures and Legislative Methods* (Century, New York, 1920).

Rutherford, M. Louise, *Influence of the American Bar Association on Public Opinion and Legislation* (Foundation Press, Chicago, 1937).

Shambaugh, Benjamin F., Ed., *Statute Law-Making in Iowa* (State Historical Society of Iowa, Iowa City, 1916).

Smith, Dick, *How Bills Become Laws in Texas* (University of Texas, Bureau of Municipal Research, 1945).

Spencer, Herbert, *The Man Versus the State,* Ed. by Albert J. Nock (Caxton Printers, Caldwell, Ida., 1940).

Walker, Harvey, *Law Making in the United States* (Ronald Press, New York, 1934).

Willoughby, W. F., *Principles of Legislative Organization and Administration* (Brookings Institution, Washington, 1934).

Winslow, Clinton I., *State Legislative Committee, a Study in Procedure* (Johns Hopkins Press, 1931).

Young, C. C., *The Legislature of California: Its Membership, Procedure and Work* (Commonwealth Club of California, San Francisco, 1943).

Zeller, Belle, *Pressure Politics in New York* (Prentice-Hall, New York, 1937).

Adams, William J., "Recodification of the North Carolina Statutes," *North Carolina Law Review,* December, 1940, pp. 27–46.

Alexander, Henry M., "A School for State Legislators," *State Government,* February, 1941, pp. 39–40.

Baker, Roscoe, "The Reference Committee in the Ohio House of Representatives," *American Political Science Review,* April, 1940, pp. 306–310.

Bone, Hugh, A., "Maryland's Legislative Council in Action," *National Municipal Review,* March, 1942, pp. 146–153.

Chichester, Cassius M., "Interim Activities in Virginia in Aid of Legislation," *State Government,* April, 1943, pp. 87, 97–100.

Council of State Governments, *State Government* (Chicago, monthly).

Davis, Carleton M., "What Is the Effect of a General Statute Revision?" *Kentucky Law Journal,* March, 1943, pp. 274–279.

Guild, Frederic H., "The Kansas Legislative Council Considers War Legislation," *State Government,* February, 1943, pp. 35, 45–47.

Key, V. O., Jr., "The Problem of Local Legislation: Example from Maryland," *State Government,* June, 1940, pp. 109–110, 118–119.

Klitsner, Marvin E., "Constitutional Prohibition against Granting or Amending City Charters," *Wisconsin Law Review,* May, 1941, pp. 396–419.

McHenry, Dean E., "The Legislative Power to Investigate on the Anvil," *State Government,* May, 1942, pp. 105–106.

Moseley, Robert, "Continuous Statute Research and Revision in North Carolina," *North Carolina Law Review,* June, 1944, pp. 281–296.

National Municipal League, *National Municipal Review* (New York, monthly).

Scott, Elizabeth McK., "State Executive Departments Play Growing Part in Lawmaking," *National Municipal Review,* November, 1943, pp. 529–534.

——, and Zeller, Belle, "State Agencies and Lawmaking," *Public Administration Review,* Summer, 1942, pp. 205–220.

Short, Lloyd M., "Minnesota Interim Committee a Legislative Council in Embryo," *National Municipal Review,* May, 1944, pp. 251–252.

Sikes, Pressly S., "Special Interim Commissions in the Indiana Legislative Process," *American Political Science Review,* October, 1942, pp. 906–915.

Weeks, O. Douglas, "Initiation of Legislation by Administrative Agencies," *Brooklyn Law Review,* January, 1940, pp. 117–140.

Witte, Edwin E., "Administrative Agencies and Statute Lawmaking," *Public Administration Review,* Spring, 1942, pp. 116–125.

Part Four

EXECUTIVE AND ADMINISTRATIVE PROBLEMS

CHAPTER IX

The Governor

HISTORY AND DEVELOPMENT OF THE OFFICE

THE governorship dates back to the beginning of the colonial period. The Royal Governors, in the later portion of this period, came to be regarded with suspicion and distrust — as the hated symbols of the power of a foreign oppressor. This fact greatly affected the constitutional provisions on the governorship when new constitutions were framed during and after the period of transition. The early state governors had little power; they were to a large extent figureheads created for the purpose of presiding on ceremonial occasions and making speeches. The changes of the early nineteenth century tended to establish the independence of the governor from the legislature, but to weaken his power by diffusion — a condition which continued throughout the century.[1] While there were instances in which conspicuously able men came to the governorship, they were the exception rather than the rule. There was little about the office, save the honor attached to it, to challenge the interest and the creative ability of able men.

Significant changes in the office have occurred during the twentieth century, during the whole of which there has been an increasing tendency to strengthen the governor's powers. This tendency was due in no small measure to the declining public confidence in the legislature; when the people no longer trusted that, they began to look about for some other governmental agency to which its powers might, in part at least, be assigned. Their selection of the governor for this purpose was further encouraged by the appearance in the early years of the century of a number of outstanding leaders in

[1] Lipson, Leslie, *The American Governor: From Figurehead to Leader,* Chapter 2 (University of Chicago Press, 1939).

many states, such as Johnson of California, Folk of Missouri, Cummings of Iowa, LaFollette of Wisconsin, Haney and Beveridge of Indiana, Roosevelt and Hughes of New York, Wilson of New Jersey, and many others. These leaders capitalized on a wave of democratic sentiment, popular resentment against "bossism," the desire for social legislation, and the general distrust of legislative bodies, thereby giving to the governorship a new popular appeal and a new prestige. Leaders of this type were still, however, in the minority. A study of American governors from 1900 to 1910, made in 1927 by Professor Macdonald,[2] attempted to answer the question, What becomes of our governors? Upon the basis of this study it appeared that nothing much became of them. The governorship was with few exceptions like a road with a dead end; it still led nowhere. There had been no change in the powers of the office corresponding to its changed position in public esteem.

The change in the powers of the office did not take place until 1917 and the years following. In 1917 Governor Frank O. Lowden of Illinois secured the enactment of the first program for state administrative reorganization. This set in motion a series of changes in state government which were to remain in a dominant position in the field for years to come. The influence of the changes thus inaugurated has been felt in every state in the Union. Whereas, prior to this movement, the governorship had been a position of some honor and relatively little power, it now became a position of considerable honor and great power. The change in its character brought significant changes in the character of the personnel aspiring to it. It no longer meant that a man would serve a short term and be called "Governor" for the rest of his life; it now offered him the opportunity to develop programs and inaugurate policies of far-reaching importance to the people of his state; to win for himself a reputation for able and constructive leadership upon the basis of which he might advance to important positions in the Federal government either at home or abroad.

The governorship now offered a challenge to the energy and ability of able men. It brought forth a group of public leaders of whom Smith, Roosevelt, and Lehman of New York, Pinchot of Pennsylvania, Ritchie of Maryland, and many others might be cited as illustrations. This point is supported by a study of " American Governors since 1915," made by Samuel R. Solomon in 1931, the results of which

2 Macdonald, Austin F., " American Governors, 1900–1910," *National Municipal Review,* November, 1927, pp. 715–719.

were in marked contrast to those of the Macdonald study previously cited.[3] Of the governors during this period, 113 were Republicans, 115 Democrats. Two were women; 64 per cent had attended college or university; three out of five were native sons; 41 per cent were lawyers by profession; practically all were married and had established homes. After their service as governors, 35 per cent either advanced to or tried for Federal offices. Mr. Solomon concluded that " next to the President of the United States, it is the Governor who engaged the interest of the voters."

The War Governors. Several surveys of American governors have been made since 1940; these, without exception, find their leadership still in the ascendancy, with increased administrative power and enhanced political prestige.[4] The percentage of college trained men had greatly increased and approximately one fourth had been elected to Phi Beta Kappa. Of the war governors serving in 1943, the so-called average governor was shown to be:

. . . a family man, in his early fifties, serving his first term as chief state executive, earning a yearly salary of approximately $8,000. His qualifications for his job include previous service in administrative, legislative, or judicial fields of government, and he is drawing from his experience in the nation's armed forces in past wars, or in other capacities connected with those wars, in directing his state's participation in the present victory program.

The war governors were divided exactly evenly between the two major political parties. The oldest was eighty, the youngest thirty-five, with twenty-eight between forty-six and fifty-six. One fourth were born outside the states they were governing. Illinois claimed three, and one was born abroad (Norway) . Thirty governors were serving their first terms. Through the death of one governor and the resignation of another, two had acceded to the office through the lieutenant-governorship. Thirteen were serving their second terms, and four — Leverett Saltonstall of Massachusetts, John Moses of North Da-

---

[3] Solomon, Samuel R., " American Governors since 1915," *National Municipal Review*, March, 1931, pp. 152–158.

[4] Perkins, John A., " American Governors — 1930–1940," *National Municipal Review*, March, 1940, pp. 178–184; White, Leonard D., and Sherman, Harvey, " The Governors March On," *State Government*, October, 1940, pp. 195–197, 206; Gurwell, John K., " The Governors of the States," the background and experience of America's forty-eight " War Governors " surveyed, *ibid.*, July, 1941, pp. 157–158, 172; a similar article, *ibid.*, July, 1943, pp. 154–155; Stokes, Thomas L., " The Governors," *ibid.*, June, 1944, pp. 343–345. Leonard D. White made some very bitter criticisms of the governors between the two world wars in *Public Administration Review*, Winter, 1944, pp. 68–70; see Frank Bane's reply, *ibid.*, Spring, 1944, pp. 153–155.

kota, John W. Bricker of Ohio, and Prentice Cooper of Tennessee — were serving their third terms.

Various combinations of previous governmental experience were revealed, but more governors had held administrative posts than had held the legislative or judicial positions. Eight governors had served as lieutenant-governor, eight as members of state commissions. One each had served as auditor general and adjutant general, others as state treasurer and secretary of state. Five had been mayors, six attorneys general, ten county attorneys, and six city attorneys. Two had been United States district attorneys or assistant district attorneys. Two had won nationwide fame for their energetic prosecution of racketeers — in New York and Chicago. Seven were former judges.

Twenty had had legislative experience, ten as representatives, five as senators, and five as both. Governor Neely of West Virginia had been a United States Representative and Senator. Governor Edison of New Jersey had been Assistant Secretary and Secretary of the Navy. Governor Dempsey of New Mexico had served in Congress and as Under Secretary of the Interior. Two had been Collectors of Internal Revenue. Two thirds had had some experience in the armed forces in previous wars. Among governors of the last decade who have rendered particularly distinguished service may be mentioned Ellis Arnall of Georgia, Herbert E. Lehman of New York, and James V. Allred of Texas, Democrats; Leverett Saltonstall of Massachusetts, Harold E. Stassen of Minnesota, and John G. Winant of New Hampshire, Republicans.

The Governor as Popular Leader. With the rise of the governor as popular leader have come responsibilities of two types: those that pertain to the formulation and sponsoring of policies, both with the legislature and with the people, and those that go with the occupancy of a position high in the public eye in a democratic society. As a leader in the determination of policy, the governor must interest himself in everything that concerns the welfare of the people of his state; without neglecting the performance of his routine administrative duties, he must keep himself informed regarding the needs and desires of the public. Plenty of people who want something will come to see him, but if he is to know what the people as a whole are thinking, he must "go places and see things" for himself. He must expect criticism, but he must not let it upset his poise, distort his judgment, or deter him from the pursuit of well-determined policies. He must have a genius for keeping his name on the front page of the newspapers, often with things that seem quite trivial but which appeal to the imagination of the public. He must entertain distinguished guests, making sure that the fact is reported in the papers.

He must show an interest in Boy Scouts, local anniversaries and celebrations, conventions, business and professional organizations; he may even resort to the creation of Kentucky colonels.[5] He may present packages of candy to several thousand children at an orphan's theater party, or appear in the role of Santa Claus at Christmas time. He may don a wild west outfit, or take part in an anniversary celebration of a society for the detection of horse thieves. He must attend many christenings, weddings, and funerals of the great, the near-great, and the supposed-to-be-great. He must issue proclamations galore, calling upon the people of the state to observe a day or a week devoted to the recognition of some cause — many of them worthy — the promoters of which desire publicity. He must attend numerous commencement exercises and receive honorary degrees from institutions which would never have thought of honoring him before he was elected governor. He must expect to receive and acknowledge graciously many useless gifts, and be properly grateful when someone dedicates to him a book, poem, or musical composition.

He must expect to attend countless dinners and make innumerable public addresses on the radio and in person on holidays, at places of historic interest, and on ceremonial occasions — for the people like to see and hear their governor. Numerous governors have, in recent years, made frequent " fireside chats " to the people of their states, some of them in a regular weekly program, commenting on current public questions and reporting on their stewardship. He will receive countless letters — many of them in response to these addresses — from all kinds of people about all manner of subjects, and

[5] " At a public dinner I once said, jokingly, that the constitution of our state should be amended to provide for the election of two governors — one to attend to the business of the state and the other to attend public and social functions not directly connected with the business of the state. I was prompted to make that remark by the enormous volume of invitations, supplemented by personal requests, that come to public men to attend all kinds of functions. Even a slight acquaintance at times leads people to believe that the governor should attend a wedding in the family or a christening. Invitations to attend the laying of cornerstones for private buildings, private charitable enterprises, meetings of trade bodies, anniversary celebrations of all kinds, testimonial dinners, requests for the use of the governor's name for drives for charitable and religious purposes or for donations, all pour into the governor's office. . . . When all is said and done, it seems impossible to divorce the personal equation from politics." Smith, Alfred E., *Up to Now — an Autobiography*, pp. 297-298 (Viking, New York, 1929) .

he will continue to receive them for many long years after he has left the governorship.

These writers will ask him to do all kinds of things, often assuming, without the slightest conception of the nature of the powers and duties of the office, that he has practically unlimited authority to grant favors, right wrongs, either real or imagined, and in general to remake the universe in any form that the writers might desire.[6] To men of ability, giving attention to these insignificant things is apt to be most distasteful, but the governor must do these things if he wants to maintain his following and his contact with the people. Without that contact, popular leadership is all but impossible.[7]

GENERAL CHARACTERISTICS OF THE OFFICE

Before discussing the powers of the governor, it seems desirable to consider briefly the general characteristics of the office — the qualifications, method of nomination and election, length of term, compensation, vacancies and removals, et cetera.

Qualifications. The early state constitutions prescribed much more rigid qualifications for the governorship than do the present ones. They included religious qualifications, property qualifications, and others which are not now considered necessary or desirable. The age requirement, where specified, is usually thirty years. Arizona and Oklahoma specify that only males are eligible, and Maine that only natural born citizens are eligible. Possession of the status of United States citizenship is sufficient in most states, although a few specify a definite number of years. State citizenship requirements of five or

---

6 Some of these letters are quite amusing. Former Governor Bricker of Ohio told in a public address of a farmer who wrote to him: " I have your picture on the wall, but so far it ain't done me no good." Wrote another: " My daughter ran away with an old man of forty. What can I do? " Immediately after the 1944 Presidential election, the author had an opportunity to study approximately 600 letters received by former Governor Pinchot, then out of office for nearly ten years. The letters contained requests for gifts of money and of War Bonds, expense money, aid in securing old age pensions, relief, blind assistance, new glasses, political support, and many other things. He was asked to get jobs for the writers or their relatives and friends; to get the President to revoke certain War Manpower Commission regulations; to dismiss from the government service individuals whom the writers did not like, et cetera. A high school boy, in order to win a bet, wanted the Governor to arrange for him to meet the President when the latter came to Philadelphia on his campaign trip.

7 There have been several recent accounts of gubernatorial leadership in particular states: Gilmore, Harlan W., " Louisiana Clings to Reform," *National Municipal Review*, April, 1944, pp. 164–169; and Spicer, George W., " Gubernatorial Leadership in Virginia," *Public Administration Review*, Autumn, 1941, pp. 441–457.

ten years exist in about one fourth of the states, but residence in the state up to as much as seven years is required in most. One fourth of the states require that the governor shall be an elector of the state.

These constitutional qualifications are of little practical significance, relating as they do to conditions that would be readily met by almost any person whose candidacy would receive serious consideration. The tests imposed by practical politics are of far greater significance. No candidate has any chance of receiving the nomination of his party unless he is considered politically available; under this heading are such questions as, In what part of the state does he make his home? This is important because the honors must be passed around from one section of the state to another — in New York, between the city and the up-state districts; in Illinois, between Chicago and down-state; in Pennsylvania, between Pittsburgh, Philadelphia, and the central part of the state.

Again, the candidate must have a political record that is acceptable to the party and to the voters. He must ordinarily be on good terms with the elements of the party exercising control in the state at the time. He must be personally acceptable, and suitable as a potential candidate. His previous business or professional relations must not be of such a nature as to be objectionable to large numbers of voters, or as to make him and the party needlessly vulnerable during the campaign. A candidate might conceivably have the wisdom of Solomon and all the moral virtues we profess to admire, and yet fail to secure the nomination if he was unable to meet any one or all of these practical tests. Although a large majority of recent candidates have been college or university graduates, the educational qualification is one about which candidates keep prudently silent.

Nomination and Election. It is not necessary to discuss at length the nomination and election of governors. The method of nomination will be that prescribed by the law of the state — in most cases the direct primary, while in a few states candidates for state offices are nominated by a convention. Methods of campaigning are varied. " Some resort to handshaking, back-slapping, and baby-kissing," observed Governor Prentice Cooper of Tennessee in an address before the Governors' Conference at Hershey, Pennsylvania, on " This Job of Being a Governor," in May, 1944. He continued:

Some rely heavily on a prodigious memory for names and faces; some depend upon pure eloquence to move the heart; some upon ridicule and invective to arouse prejudice; some count solely upon organization and their records to get them by; while still others rely upon music to charm away the senses. If promises are made in whatever type of campaign you are pursuing, it is my belief that the American people of today will require that you keep them. Sometimes the type of campaign is decided by the mere size of the state. No Governor of Texas, I am told, ever campaigns in all of her 254 counties, some of which are as large as the whole State of Rhode Island. Often candidates in Texas are compelled to use the airplane.

The election is always a general election, conducted in all but two states on the first Tuesday after the first Monday in November. The most important item to be considered at this point is the time at which the choice should be made, in relation to the choice of national officers. In some states governors are chosen in the years of Presidential elections. Professor Faust reports that " of the twenty-five states which fix a four-year term for the Governor, ten provide that the gubernatorial election and that of most of the other state officials shall coincide with the Presidential election; fifteen of the four-year term group hold their state elections at the intermediate period." [8] The holding of state elections to coincide with national elections is unfortunate, because it ordinarily means that little or no serious thought will be given to state problems. Citizens will vote for their preferences in the national offices and will without much consideration support the same parties for the state offices, whereas the problems of government in any one of the states are large and significant enough to the well-being of citizens to warrant a decision based upon their own merits. The selection of major state officers should not be merely an incidental aspect of national party contests. It is, of course, to the advantage of the major parties that the existing system be retained; hence the variations from it are few and more or less accidental.

Term. By the original constitutions most of the governors served for a term of one year, and none were permitted a term of more than two years. No limits were placed on re-eligibility. At present, exactly twenty-five states have a term of four years, twenty-two have a term of two years, and one state, New Jersey, has a term of three years. It was not until 1920 that the last state — Massachusetts — discontinued the practice of electing a governor annually, although there were in fact in Massachusetts few governors who served for only one year. The current tendency — supported by the weight of informed opinion — is in the direction of the four-year term; " of the twenty-two states operating under constitutions modeled since 1888, fourteen provide

---

[8] Faust, Martin L., *Manual on the Executive Article*, p. 50 (Missouri Constitutional Convention of 1943, Columbia, 1943).

four-year terms for the governors as contrasted to eight which provide two-year terms." [9]

The arguments for the four-year term may be summarized as follows: (1) It permits a more satisfactory development of administrative policies and tends to give a state more efficient government than is possible under a two-year term. (2) It makes possible greater and more consistent economy in administration; it reduces the inevitable extravagance and waste connected with more frequent changes. (3) It is in harmony with the principle of the short ballot, providing as it does for a reduction and simplification of the task which the voter is asked to perform. It is important, therefore, where the four-year term is adopted, that provision be made for holding the election at some other time than the Presidential year, although this is done in only thirteen of the twenty-four states.

The question of re-eligibility is important. Fortunately the third-term tradition of the Presidency has not affected the governorship in most states. In thirty-one states there is no limit at all: the following restrictions in other states apply to consecutive terms:

Three years (one three-year term) — New Jersey.
Four years (two two-year terms) — New Mexico.
       (one four-year term) — Alabama, Florida, Georgia, Indiana, Kentucky, Louisiana. Mississippi, Missouri, North Carolina, Oklahoma, Pennsylvania, and Virginia — twelve states.
Six years (three two-year terms) — Tennessee.
Eight years (two four-year terms) — Delaware and Oregon.

Where the two-year term is used, there are usually no limits on re-eligibility. In New York, for instance, Alfred E. Smith was a candidate in six successive elections, of which he won all but the second; Herbert H. Lehman was a candidate four times and won four times. Wilbur L. Cross was a candidate four times and won four times in Connecticut. George W. P. Hunt of Arizona became governor of that state when it was admitted to the union in 1912; he was subsequently re-elected six times, and was a candidate in nine elections. In most of the states with a four-year term, a governor is not permitted to succeed himself immediately. In practice this means that few governors are able to secure a second election at all, although there are such exceptions as those of Bibb Graves of Ala-

[9] Much of the data in this section is from a series of reports on the powers of the governor prepared by the Council of State Governments in 1936 for the Governors' Conference and printed by the New York State Constitutional Convention Committee in *Problems Relating to Executive Administration and Powers*, Chapter 1 (Albany, 1938). For a more recent study, see Ruskowski, Casimir W., *The Constitutional Governor* (Humphries, Boston, 1943).

bama and Robert E. Pattison and Gifford Pinchot of Pennsylvania. A few states have the four-year term without such a restriction, of which group Maryland with its " perpetual governor," the late Albert C. Ritchie, who served four consecutive terms, is illustrative.[10]

If one believes in democratic government, a restriction on re-eligibility seems unjustifiable; the people should have the right to re-elect an executive of whose services they approve, and the opportunity to refuse re-election to one of whose conduct they disapprove. Governor Prentice Cooper of Tennessee well stated this point in his address before the Governors' Conference:

A governor who is ineligible by law from service more than one term is in some ways at a disadvantage since he has no certain way of knowing whether he could be re-elected. He is denied the privilege of a vote of confidence by the people, and may lack means of vindication from charges of the opposition that he has done those things that he should not have done, and that he has left undone those things he should have done. (In those states where re-election is permissible), the official mortality rate among governors is unusually high.

Compensation. All of the governors receive an annual salary, the amount of which varies from $3,000 in South Dakota to $25,000 in New York. In 1945 the average was $8,083, as compared with $7,850 five years before. New Jersey pays $20,000; Pennsylvania, $18,000; Connecticut, Illinois, Louisiana, and Texas, $12,000 each; California, Kentucky, Massachusetts, North Carolina, Ohio, Virginia, and West Virginia, $10,000 each. The rest of the states pay from $4,000 to $9,000. Four states pay less than $5,000; thirty-one, or nearly two thirds, pay between $5,000 and $7,500; while thirteen, or more than one fourth, pay over $7,500. That the tendency has been toward an increase in compensation, at least before the depression, is clearly indicated in the following table:

DISTRIBUTION OF GOVERNORS' SALARIES, 1910–1945 [11]

Salary	1910	1920	1930	1940	1945
$ 2,500–$ 4,999	21	12	6	4	4
5,000– 9,999	21	29	31	34	30
10,000– 14,999	5	6	7	7	11
15,000 and over	1	1	4	3	3

10 Many of the states have had governors who served three or more terms. John T. Gilman in New Hampshire was elected to fourteen one-year terms, and John Langdon was elected to eight one-year terms. In Illinois, Richard Oglesby was elected to three four-year terms. Michigan, Minnesota, New York, North Dakota, and Wisconsin each have had two or more governors elected to three two-year terms, and the latter had one fourth-termer.

11 The first three columns are from White. Leonard D., *Trends in Public Administration*, p. 180 (McGraw-Hill, New York, 1933).

The compensation is still seriously inadequate in many states; many mayors are paid as much or more than the governors of their states. The pay of Babe Ruth a few years ago, despite a salary cut, was still greater than the combined compensation of the governors of fifteen states. The situation is still so bad that the Massachusetts Federation of Taxpayers' Association urged a doubling of the governor's salary in that state in 1945. The exact amount is usually specified by statute, but a few states have made the mistake of incorporating provisions of this character in their constitutions.

In addition to the actual salary paid, thirty-four states provide housing (two of these rent an executive mansion, but fourteen let their governors select a house themselves), and most states provide allowances for travel, servants, chauffeurs, entertaining of official guests and other items, so that the actual compensation is considerably in excess of the specified salary. In Maryland, for instance, where the official salary is $4,000, it is estimated that the compensation of the governor is approximately $55,000, of which by legislative act no audit shall be made. He has the use of an executive mansion valued at $231,000, and of a $4,000,000 yacht which the state bought in 1929 from a New York millionaire for a comparatively small sum. This policy was adopted by the legislature some years ago when a man without private income was elected to the office; before that time the office had been, like an ambassadorship, a drain upon the governor's private resources.

The holding of any important public office entails a large volume of personal expenditure, of the nature of which the average citizen is little if at all aware. If one overlooks political assessments and other political contributions, there are still demands for subscriptions to welfare, educational, and civic organizations and projects of every conceivable character. As a matter of political expediency, the governor can afford neither to ignore these appeals nor to give less than might be expected of a person in such a position.

Vacancies and Removals. There are at least six methods by which vacancies, either permanent or temporary, may occur. These include death, resignation, illness or other disability, temporary absence from the state, impeachment, and recall. In the case of temporary absences, the lieutenant-governor acts in those states where the office exists; in other states, provision must be made by law for such emergencies. The provisions with regard to illness and disability are quite as unsatisfactory in the states as in the Federal government, as witness the Horner-Steele controversy in Illinois in 1940, in which the lieutenant-governor proclaimed himself acting governor of the state.[12] Few resignations occur; most of these are occasioned by advancement to the Senate or appointment to some other Federal office.

Very unusual situations developed in Missouri in 1941 and in Wisconsin in 1942. In the first instance, Governor Stark stayed on beyond his four-year term, when the legislature attempted to steal the governorship by refusing to seat a duly elected governor who had won by a very small majority but who belonged to the opposition party. In the Wisconsin case, the governor-elect died before the inauguration. The Wisconsin Constitution of 1848, still in force, does not provide too clearly for the succession under such circumstances. Consequently the question as to whether the incumbent governor was to hold office beyond his term was presented to the court for determination. The court ruled that he should not, since the constitution was specific on this point. Under these circumstances, the only alternative was to inaugurate the new lieutenant governor, who then became acting governor of the state.[13]

Only one removal has been made and relatively few have been attempted through the use of the recall, although Governor Frazier of North Dakota was removed from office by this device in 1922. The more common method of making removals is through the use of the impeachment process, which operates in the states in a manner similar to that in which it is used in the Federal government. The lower house has the sole power of impeachment, while the trial of the accused on the charges that have been preferred against him is conducted before the senate. If convicted, the accused may be removed from office and may be debarred from holding further office of profit or public trust. Additional punishment, such as fines or imprisonment, may not be inflicted as a result of conviction in impeachment proceedings, although if the charges are such as to involve violations of the criminal law, such punishments may follow conviction in a criminal suit. Although many governors have been impeached, only a few have been convicted.[14]

It was the intent of those who incorporated the impeachment provisions in the state constitutions to establish a method by which the people might be relieved of the services of a chief executive whom,

[12] This case is discussed in Snider, Clyde F., " Gubernatorial Disability," *University of Chicago Law Review,* April, 1941, pp. 521–529.

[13] See Dilliard, Irving, " Missouri Has No Governor," *Nation,* February 15, 1941, pp. 183–184; and note on " Wisconsin Governorship," *State Government,* February, 1943, p. 48.

[14] Among the more recent convictions are the following: Sulzer of New York, 1913; Ferguson of Texas, 1917; Walton of Oklahoma, 1923; Johnston of Oklahoma, 1927. Long of Louisiana was impeached in 1929, but was not convicted.

on account of dishonesty or inefficiency, they no longer trusted. In practice, the device has failed to accomplish this purpose. Impeachment proceedings have been instituted, not as a means of protecting the public, but as a phase of the political warfare of factions or parties. The results have been determined, not by the merits of the case but by the ability of the accused to muster sufficient voting strength in the senate to retain his position. If he has been able to do this, he has remained in office; otherwise he has been removed. No more conclusive evidence of the political nature of the impeachment proceedings need be asked than the facts relating to its use in Texas and Oklahoma. In Texas, after one legislature had removed Governor Ferguson from office, another legislature removed, so far as possible, the penalties attaching to the conviction. In Oklahoma, a recent writer who had made a special study of the impeachment process in that state testifies that down to 1930 there had not been a single governor who had not been either impeached or seriously threatened with impeachment proceedings. When such use is made of this device, it ceases to be a remedy for public evils and becomes a political weapon whose use is both ridiculous and deplorable.[15]

While most governors are honest and conscientious public servants, amazing revelations are sometimes made public concerning some who are not. In 1924 Governor Len Small of Illinois was charged with having fraudulently taken more than $2,000,000 from the state during his term as state treasurer, but he was not removed from office. Governor Warren T. McCray of Indiana resigned in the same year, following conviction in a Federal court on charges of using the mails to defraud; this was only one of a series of unfortunate experiences that this state had with its governors. In 1940 Richard W. Leche, who had resigned as governor of Louisiana under fire, was convicted in Federal court of graft charges involving $111,-000, in connection with the sale of trucks to the State Highway Commission. Of this amount he was supposed to have received $31,000 as his share.

A most extraordinary exhibition occurred a few years ago in North Dakota; Governor William Langer was convicted in Federal court in 1934 of conspiracy to defraud the United States of $179.50 in relief funds. He was fined $10,000 and sentenced to eighteen months

15 Stewart, Frank M., " Impeachment in Texas," *American Political Science Review*, August, 1930, pp. 652–658; Ewing, Cortez A. M., " Impeachment of Oklahoma Governors," *ibid.*, pp. 648–652; for the most complete account, see Friedman, Jacob A., *The Impeachment of Governor William Sulzer* (Columbia University Press, 1939) .

in jail. Lieutenant-Governor Olson moved into the governor's office in the new skyscraper capitol, and attempted to take over the governor's functions.[16] The State Supreme Court ousted Governor Langer from office in the middle of the summer. In the ensuing electoral campaign, Mrs. Langer secured the Republican nomination and ran, as Mrs. Ferguson had done in Texas, to vindicate her husband. The Democratic candidate, Mr. Moodie, was elected by a comfortable majority, with the support of leading Nonpartisans. A few days after he took office, his residence in the state was questioned and impeachment proceedings against him were begun. While these proceedings were dropped, the case was taken into the courts, where early in 1935 it was decided that Mr. Moodie was lacking in proper qualifications for his office. As a result of this decision, Lieutenant-Governor Welford was elevated to the position, giving to North Dakota the distinction — if distinction it be — of having had four governors and acting governors within a period of about nine months. Occurrences of this sort are fortunately infrequent.

Powers of the Governor. Some general idea of the powers of the governor may be gained by examining the appropriate article in any state constitution; the following excerpts are from Article VI of the Constitution of Michigan:

Sec. 2. The chief executive power is vested in the governor.

Sec. 3. The governor shall take care that the laws be faithfully executed; shall transact all necessary business with the officers of the government; and may require information in writing from all executive and administrative state officers, elective and appointive, upon any subject relating to the duties of their respective offices.

Sec. 4. He shall be commander-in-chief of the military and naval forces, and may call out such forces to execute the laws, to suppress insurrection and to repel invasion.

Sec. 5. He shall communicate by message to the legislature, and at the close of his official term to the incoming legislature, the condition of the state, and recommend such measures as he may deem expedient.

Sec. 6. He shall issue writs of election to fill such vacancies as occur in the senate or house of representatives.

Sec. 7. He may convene the legislature on extraordinary occasions.

Sec. 8. He may convene the legislature at some other place when the seat of government becomes dangerous from disease or a common enemy.

Sec. 9. He may grant reprieves, commutations and pardons after convictions for all offenses, except treason and cases of impeachment. . . .

---

[16] For a graphic account of this episode, see *Time*, July 30, 1934, p. 14. For a careful analysis of the problems involved, see Miller, Roy L., " The Gubernatorial Controversy in North Dakota," *American Political Science Review*, June, 1935, pp. 418–432.

Sec. 10. Whenever a vacancy shall occur in any of the state offices, the governor shall fill the same by appointment, by and with the advice and consent of the senate, if in session.

Sec. 11. All official acts of the governor, except his approval of the laws, shall be authenticated by the great seal of the state, which shall be kept by the secretary of state.

While, in this case and in the Model State Constitution, the executive power is vested in the governor, it is true in the states generally either that the executive power is dispersed among a number of constitutional officers, or that the executive powers that the governor may exercise are enumerated. Either of these devices operates with the effect of limiting his powers quite in contrast to the situation in the Federal government, where both in theory and in fact the executive power is concentrated in the President. Even a casual examination of these provisions of the Michigan constitution reveals that the powers of the governor are of three general types: administrative and executive, legislative, and judicial or quasi-judicial. These three types will now be considered in some detail.

EXECUTIVE AND ADMINISTRATIVE POWERS

Ministerial and Discretionary Powers. In any discussion of the powers of the executive as the head of the administration, the distinction must be made between ministerial and discretionary powers. Those duties concerning the performance of which the state constitution permits of the exercise of no discretion are regarded as ministerial. Thus the state constitutions generally provide that the governor must commission all state officers when their election has been properly certified, that he must send to the senate nominations for filling certain other offices, and that he must see that the laws are faithfully executed. When, on the other hand, the decision rests with him regarding the kind of action to be taken, or indeed whether any section at all is required in a given case, the power which he exercises is said to be discretionary. An illustration is found in the provision that he may call out troops for the protection of life and property. In such a case he is the sole judge as to whether or not troops are required, and in the second place, as to the number of troops needed to deal effectively with the existing situation. Another important difference relates to the possible use of mandamus procedure. When a governor, who has taken an oath to " preserve, protect, and defend " the constitution of the state, fails to perform a ministerial act, he may be reached through mandamus proceedings instituted in the courts of the state. On the other hand, it is not possible to mandamus an executive for the purpose of compelling him to exercise his discretion by arriving at some particular decision.

Powers of Administrative Supervision. The governor is the executive head of the state government. Largely as a result of his powers of appointment and removal, of his responsibility in the matter of law enforcement, and of his powers as head of the state's military establishment, he has a general administrative supervision and control over the acts of his subordinates. In thirty-four states the constitution gives him power to require information in writing from the heads of executive departments on any subject relating to their duties, and eight of these states specify that such information shall be given under oath if the governor so requires. In units as large as many of the states, the task of supervision requires an enormous number of conferences and appointments and a careful budgeting of the governor's time.[17] This is the more true when one considers the amount of time necessarily allotted to travel, speechmaking, and ceremonial appearances.

In theory, the acts of administrative subordinates are in many cases the acts of the governor; in practice, since it is a physical impossibility for the governor to pass personally upon any considerable percentage of the total number of decisions made in his behalf by subordinates, they are accustomed to act in all but the most important cases without his knowledge. A good executive will conserve his energy by delegating all the detail work to his subordinates and reserving for his own consideration only those problems which involve decisions on important questions of policy. Where possible there should be consultation before action is taken by subordinates, but in cases in which, for any reason, this is not done the governor always has the power of review. It may happen occasionally also that divergent or conflicting policies will develop in different branches of the service. It is the duty of the governor as chief administrator to review these cases and to make decisions with regard thereto for

---

[17] The following schedule of appointments was noted in 1936, posted outside the entrance to the office of the governor of a New England state:

Monday	Members of the Legislature — 11 A.M. to 1 P.M.; 3 to 5 P.M.
Tuesday	Public, by appointment — same hours.
Wednesday	Governor's Council.
Thursday	Department officials — 11 A.M. to 3 P.M.
Friday	Legislative committee; planning committees.
Saturday	Executive business.

the purpose of unifying and coordinating the activities of the administration.

It thus happens that all important announcements, whether of appointments or of matters of policy, are given out by the governor's office. The governor performs all those acts which are suggestive of the headship and direction of the administration. He issues executive orders, orders investigations, directs his various department heads and bureau chiefs, issues proclamations, et cetera. Even though he may be responsible for the determination of major policies, and may take the credit for success as he must accept the blame for failure, he will, if he is a tactful executive, assign to his department heads and other co-workers a large part of the credit for such successes as may come to the administration. He knows that no administration succeeds without able heads of departments and bureau chiefs, and he knows that there is sufficient glory for him in having proved his ability to select such men, and to guide and coordinate their activities in such a way as to achieve some degree of administrative success.

Power of Appointment. Of all the important executive and administrative powers exercised by the governor, none is more important than the power of appointment, for the success of an administration rests in no small measure upon wise use of this power. If a governor chooses competent and able persons as advisers and for administrative positions, he can devote his energies to the general supervision of their work and the coordination of their activities. If he chooses weak and incompetent persons, he not only increases the extent of his own burdens as chief executive, but he definitely limits the effectiveness of the work done by the departments concerned and opens his administration to serious danger of fraud and corruption. No governor who has any regard for his reputation and for the success of his administration can afford to take this chance.

The governor not only has the authority to make appointments to many designated offices, but he has as well the duty to see that these positions are kept filled. A department cannot operate properly without a head, nor can a commission of three or five members function properly when vacancies exist in one or more of its positions. Some idea of the extent of the governor's power of appointment may be gained from the tabulation on page 378; not all of these offices exist in every state, and in some cases some means of selection apart from the governor may be used.

Numerous influences operate to restrict the governor's free exercise of the appointing power. He knows that he must make selections such as the senate or council will approve. In Virginia approval by both houses is necessary. The law may contain provisions with regard to the bipartisan character of administrative boards and the geographical distribution or technical qualifications of members. There may be ex officio members; it may be necessary to consider civil serv-

EXTENT OF THE POWER OF THE GOVERNOR TO APPOINT IMPORTANT STATE OFFICIALS

Officer	Appointed by Governor Alone	Appointed by Governor with Consent of Senate	Governor Has a Part in Selection	Governor Has No Part in Selection	Office or Equivalent Does Not Exist
Secretary of State......	0	7[1]	7	41	0
Comptroller...........	2	7	9	12	27
Auditor...............	3	3	6	36	6
Treasurer.............	1	0	1	47	0
Tax Commission.......	17	26	43	4	1
Education.............	2	12	14	34	0
Attorney General......	1	4	5	43	0
Budget Officer.........	16	14	30	1	17
Agriculture............	10	21	31	16	1
Labor.................	8	32	40	7	1
Health................	13	32	45	3	0
Welfare...............	26	22	48	0	0
Public Utilities........	7	21	28	18	2
Securities.............	4	18	22	21	5
Banking..............	12	31	43	5	0
Insurance.............	8	25	33	14	1
Liquor................	9	20	29	10	9
Highways.............	17	29	46	2	0
Conservation.........	15	28	43	3	2

[1] In Virginia, with the consent of both houses.

ice regulations. Then there are political considerations —the payment of campaign debts, the recognition of different factions of the party, the wishes of the state leader, et cetera. Even yet, in some states, the governor is in theory responsible for the state administration, with very little actual authority over it. In New Jersey, where, as Governor Edison expressed it in 1941, the power of the executive has been diluted to an extraordinary degree, only two state officials, the budget commissioner and the finance commissioner, are appointed by the governor and serve at his pleasure. At least eight are elected by the two houses in joint session, and nine are appointed by the governor with the consent of the Senate, usually for a five-year term, whereas the governor's term is three years. In this administrative morass, where millions of dollars are spent annually, not even the nomenclature has been standardized — there are departments, commissions, boards, bureaus, and offices.[18]

The governor is confronted by the question of whether the persons he appoints will be loyal to him and his policies. At the beginning of his second term as Governor of Pennsylvania, Gifford Pinchot required all his appointees to sign a pledge which read as follows: " I will loyally support the policies approved by the people of the Commonwealth in the last election for Governor." This policy caused wide comment and created vigorous opposition, for no appointments were forthcoming unless the pledge was signed. It seems like a drastic policy; yet a governor who is responsible for an administration ought to be entitled to the full cooperation and support of those who hold positions by virtue of his appointment. In this instance, Mr. Pinchot was doubtless influenced by his experience during his first term, which began eight years before, when he followed a much more lenient policy, and when in numerous cases it was discovered that persons holding office by virtue of his appointment, or of his continuing them in positions to which they had been appointed previously, proved disloyal to him and to the policies for which he stood. A governor can scarcely be blamed for resenting the activities of those who bore from within. From the public's point of view, such a policy is certainly dangerous if employed by a governor who is more interested in the spoils of office than in the conduct of an administration devoted to enlightened public service.

As has been suggested, the policy which a governor will pursue in his relations with the party leader and the party organization in his state is a matter of vital concern in the selection of appointees. Generally speaking, there are three possibilities open to him. He may adopt a policy of abject subservience to the state party organization; he may, at the other extreme, defy the organization; or he may adopt the more moderate and more sensible expedient of consulting the party leaders and then using his own judgment. The significance of these attitudes may be illustrated by reference to the policies of a number of well-known governors. A recent governor of a large Eastern state possessed no mind of his own in making decisions with regard to appointments. More than one applicant for a position was definitely told that the state leader would have to be consulted before a decision was made. This governor made no at-

[18] See McKean, Dayton D., *Pressures on the Legislature of New Jersey*, pp. 36–37 (Columbia University Press, 1938) .

tempt to protect his own reputation in this matter. He might easily
have said that he was not ready to make a decision or that there
were a number of applicants whose qualifications would have to
be considered, but he failed to use even these simple expedients for
avoiding a disclosure of his subservience to the organization. At the
other extreme we have the case of Governor Sulzer of New York,
who was impeached and removed from office in 1913. This man was
a professional politician of the type created by the Tammany organization; he secured his nomination and election through the influence of Charles F. Murphy. After being elected, he became impressed with the importance of the office and imbued with a desire
to administer it to the best of his ability. This led him to defy the
leader of the organization which had placed him in the position.
After some futile attempts to persuade him to change his policy, the
Democratic leader cooperated with a willing Republican majority
in the legislature to divest him of his office.[19]

The third course, not only more moderate but more sensible, is
one in which the governor consults the wishes of the party organization and its leaders, but makes the final decision himself. Of this
type of governor Theodore Roosevelt furnishes an excellent example,
as is well shown by the following account of a portion of the Barnes-
Roosevelt libel case proceedings:

Roosevelt testified that, when governor, he habitually consulted Senator
Platt, the Republican state boss, before making appointments. In recommending men for appointment to positions allotted to the minority party,
the evidence showed that Platt in his turn was accustomed to consider the
wishes of Croker, the Democratic boss. When asked why he consulted Platt,
Roosevelt answered that he had to, if he wanted to have his nominations
confirmed. Question: " That is, you had to be in alliance with the invisible
government, so-called, to get the nominations confirmed? " Answer: " To
get the nominations confirmed I had to have the support of the Senate, and
the Senate was responsive to Mr. Platt's wishes." Ordinarily Roosevelt
made no appointments of any kind, even those not dependent upon
senatorial confirmation, until he had ascertained that they would not be
objectionable to the boss. Yet Roosevelt was not a subservient governor.
In Senator Platt's autobiography, published five years before the Barnes-
Roosevelt trial, it is stated that " Roosevelt had from the first agreed
that he would consult me on all questions of appointments. . . . He re-
ligiously fulfilled this pledge, although he frequently did just what he
pleased. . . . Roosevelt told me, for instance, that he proposed to remove
Lou Payn. I protested, but he was removed, and I was consulted about the
appointment of his successor." [20]

[19] Friedman, *op. cit.*
[20] Holcombe, Arthur N., *State Government in the United States,* Third Edition, pp. 337–338 (Macmillan, New York, 1931) .

Sulzer, though a very inferior person, and of the opposite party, had the same experience. In an interview shortly after his conviction he told the press: [21]

I had several talks with Mr. Murphy, and in some of these talks I told him that I was the governor, and that I intended to be governor; that I was not going to be a proxy governor, or a rubber stamp. He laughed at me and rebuked me for this, and said that I might be governor but that he controlled the legislature; that unless I did what he wanted me to regarding legislation and appointments I could not get my nominations confirmed and that he would block everything.

While there are theoretically three courses open to the governor, there is only one course open to him if he wants to succeed — and even then he must be a strong man to succeed. It is plain that he cannot deliver himself into the hands of the organization, and that he is likely to lose his job if he defies it. His only real choice is to set certain standards of training, ability, and character and then (in the absence of civil service regulations) appoint only those persons acceptable to the organization who meet these qualifications. No one need be shocked at this suggestion. Ours is a party government and it is likely to continue to be such. We have no right to assume that a man who has the backing of the state organization must be either a fool or a rascal; there are large numbers of honest, able, and intelligent men who have associated themselves with the affairs of the major parties. The governor's task is to select men of this type, politically satisfactory to the organization, rather than men of the type all too frequently selected in the past.

Power of Removal. If administration is to be effective and responsible, the chief executive must have not only the power to appoint, but the power to investigate and remove for proper cause. An executive officer who must bear the responsibility for the record of his administration must have the power to control his subordinates; he must be in a position to insist not only that their work be well done, but that in general the policies which they pursue shall be in harmony with those of the administration as a whole. In other words, if the governor is to be held responsible for the conduct of the administration, he must have sufficient power over it to enable him to conduct an administration for which he is responsible. In recognition of this fact, many states have adopted a policy with regard to removal by the governor in harmony with the principle set forth in Myers v. United States as applying to the President.[22] This rule per-

[21] Friedman, *op. cit.*, p. 249.
[22] Frank S. Myers v. United States, 272 U. S. 52, 1926.

mits the executive to remove for proper cause, without consent of the Senate, officers for whose appointment the consent of the Senate is required, as well as to remove officers over whose appointment he has the sole power. If the principle of administrative responsibility is to be maintained, this is the only rule which could reasonably be followed.[23] There are, however, certain limitations upon the governor's power of removal, imposed by the constitution and by statute. The governor may not, except in rare instances, remove elective officers; he has no power of removal over judicial officers; and most local officers are beyond his control. He must also be mindful of the fact that, in the majority of cases, the senate must confirm the new man whom he nominates to replace the one removed; this provision furnishes a considerable practical restraint upon the exercise of the removal power.

The history of each state will provide illustrations of the type of questions which may arise in connection with attempts on the part of the governor to use his removal power. The more vigorous the governor, the more likely these contests are to arise. Frequently they have taken place in connection with the public service commissions, as attempts have been made by governors in a number of states to make these commissions either more responsive to their wishes (Talmadge of Georgia), or to the public interest (Pinchot of Pennsylvania). Governors Murray of Oklahoma and Johnson of South Carolina fought similar battles for the control of the state highway commissions. Such contests are apt to be largely political in character, and can be discouraged by the use of the device of overlapping terms — three members with a six-year term, one membership to expire every two years, or five members with a five-year term, one membership to expire annually.[24]

Power to Enforce the Law. The state constitutions have long provided that the governors should be responsible for the enforcement of the law, the protection of the lives and property of citizens, the maintenance of peace and quiet, and the quelling of domestic vio-

[23] A few months before the decision in the Myers case, the Supreme Court of Pennsylvania adopted a quite different rule in the case of Commonwealth v. Benn, 284 Pa. 421, 1925. In this case Governor Pinchot sought to remove for cause two members of the Public Service Commission. This doctrine was later modified in Commonwealth v. Stewart, 286 Pa. 511, 1927, and Commonwealth v. King, 312 Pa. 412, 1933.

[24] See New York State Constitutional Convention Committee, *Problems Relating to Executive Administration and Power*, Chapter 8, on removal of officers, and Chapter 9, on bribery and corruption of public officers, for an excellent discussion of these problems.

lence. In so-called normal times, the duties of the governors in this connection have not been very exacting; while it has always been possible for the governor to call out troops and place a troubled area under martial law, it has rarely been necessary for him to do so. Quite the opposite was true in the era of the depression, during which strikes and outbreaks of disorder from other causes were frequent. In the decade of the thirties, calling out the troops came to be a common occurrence; the practice was not confined to any one state or section of the country, nor was it attributable to the peculiarities of any particular governor. The United States District Court in Minneapolis, in a decision in 1934, upholding the use of troops by Governor Olson in a labor disturbance, used the following significant words:

Military rule is preferable under almost any circumstances to mob rule. . . . We are not prepared to find that the Governor's orders have no relation whatever to the necessities of the situation with which he is confronted and fall entirely outside the range of his discretion. While we may personally disagree with the Governor as to the manner in which he has handled the entire situation, that will not justify the relief prayed for.

There may be no great danger involved in the use of troops, but in view of events in Europe in recent years, certainly an unnecessary and unjustified use of them is to be deplored.

The governors have a responsibility in cases of lynching or threat of lynching. They cannot, however, go any further in this type of law enforcement than public sentiment will sustain them — no matter how right or courageous their stand may be. Their powers of law enforcement are not confined to the handling of emergency situations. When they do act, they must do so in accordance with the provisions of the constitution and the laws. In May, 1940, for instance, Governor Rivers of Georgia directed that the business, occupational, and professional licenses of aliens in the state be canceled as of June 1. Aliens who had applied for citizenship prior to that date were to be exempted. Such action was so clearly arbitrary and so directly in violation of the guarantees of both the Federal and state constitutions that it could not possibly stand.

In recent years numerous state administrations have assumed active leadership of law observance campaigns, of campaigns for the control and abatement of crime, for highway safety, and for other purposes. The conference of officials and interested citizens has been widely used to develop leadership and to secure publicity; this has been followed by intensive advertising campaigns by means of the press, radio, billboards, et cetera. In all such moves, the governor plays a leading part.

Military Powers. The preceding discussion gives at least a glimpse of the military power of the governor — as related to law enforcement — but there are many other aspects of it:

National Guardsmen fight forest fires, they protect Governors' families, they hunt escaped prisoners, they patrol Summer camps for wealthy children, they protect public property, they seek missing persons, they even help enforce state laws. But their chief duty, in recent weeks, has been intervention in strikes.

Thirty-five million dollars is appropriated annually for National Guard units in the forty-eight states by the Federal government, yet it has almost no control over their use.

Even when guardsmen were required to seize and stand watch over the New Orleans voting lists in Huey Long's Louisiana — a task which was considered generally as an extra-curricular activity for them — the War Department was powerless to act, even if it had wished to do so.[25]

In all forty-eight states the governor is designated as the commander in chief of the state militia; there are, however, constitutional provisions which limit or define his powers. Thirty states provide an exception when such military or naval forces shall be in the actual service of the United States. Thirty-five states specifically confer upon the governor the right to call out the militia for any one of three purposes: to repel invasion, to execute the laws, or to suppress rebellion. Thirteen states make no such provision, apparently assuming that the governor will exercise such power when required. Since two of these contingencies rarely arise, attention may be confined to the third — the use of troops in connection with the enforcement of the law. The use of troops when necessary to protect life and property is a legitimate public use; their use to aid an incumbent in office to maintain control or extend his political influence is, to say the least, questionable. In the interval between the two world wars such uses of troops were not uncommon, being made by Governors Talmadge of Georgia, Long of Louisiana, Laffoon of Kentucky, Langer of North Dakota, and Murray of Oklahoma, among others. In no case, apparently, were there any strong public protests.

Some very serious problems with regard to the Guard arose during

25 Bryant, Henry E. C., " Call Out the Guard! — Governors become virtual military dictators as the National Guard is utilized in twenty-six states," *Today*, September 1, 1934, pp. 8–9, 22. See New York State Constitutional Convention Committee, *op. cit.*, Chapter 4, and Sterling, Governor of Texas, et al., v. Constentin, et al., 287 U. S. 378, 1932.

the recent world war. Although the Guard organizations are composed of state troops rather than Federal, and have been handled under the militia clause of the Constitution rather than under the Congressional power to raise and support armies, they have tended to lose their exclusive state status and to become more and more federalized. In this war, as in the previous one, they were sworn in as a part of the armed forces of the United States, leaving the states without any organization that could be called upon to protect life and property in the case of an emergency. It became necessary, therefore, for the states to recruit a new force. This was generally done, the new organization being frequently referred to as the Home Guard. Due to the shortage of suitable personnel, these forces consisted chiefly of older men or of men who had been rejected for service in the armed forces of the United States.[26]

In addition to the use of the Guard — both legitimate and illegitimate — the governor is responsible for its organization and maintenance, its training and general well-being. The first duty comes to him as governor, the second as commander in chief of the forces. In reviews, which are often made the excuse for much ceremony and display, thousands of marching men may pass before the governor. The powers of the governor extend also to any naval forces which may be maintained by the state. In earlier times, when war as an institution was in better repute, this power was regarded as of vital importance. Even today, the military establishment in some of the larger states includes arsenals, and material and equipment for many thousands of men. In addition, the state governments are the custodians under Federal law of millions of dollars' worth of supplies and equipment. Few people realize the extensiveness of this organization.

Power to Supervise Local Units of Government. The governors of the states should have the power to remove local officers for proper cause, and to supervise the officers and agencies of local government. In most states this power is very limited, if it exists at all, because of the reverence with which the principle of local self-government has been regarded — reverence so great as to justify, in the eyes of many, the failure of the state to interfere in the case of inefficiency on the

[26] Naturally, in the war period, a number of studies have been made of these problems: Beckwith, Edmund R., and others, *Lawful Action of State Military Forces* (Random House, New York, 1944), and " Laws Relating to State Military Power," *State Government*, March, 1943, pp. 57–58, 75–77; Colby, Elbridge, and Glass, James F., " The Legal Status of the National Guard," *Virginia Law Review*, May, 1943, pp. 839–856; Council of State Governments, " War Powers of Governors," *State Government*, February, 1942, pp. 39–40, 46–47.

part of local officers. It has been assumed that democratic government requires local control of local affairs, even at the price of excessive cost and inefficiency in operation. Consequently the state police have been kept out of cities, and local communities have been permitted to exercise an almost exclusive control over school, health, and welfare problems, and have been allowed a free hand to collect taxes — sometimes even on a fee basis.

Nevertheless, some progress has been made. In New York the governor may remove district attorneys and sheriffs, provided a copy of the charges is furnished and an opportunity for a hearing is given. Similar provisions exist in Wisconsin as regards district attorneys and coroners. In Nebraska, Oklahoma, Tennessee, and Wyoming the governor may direct the attorney general or the county prosecuting officers to institute proceedings for the removal of county officers; and in Nebraska and Wyoming he may suspend such officers pending trial. In Minnesota, New York, and Wisconsin he may remove a sheriff; and in Illinois, Kansas, Michigan, and Ohio he may do so under such circumstances as the legislature may prescribe. In Maine, Maryland, and New Hampshire the governor may appoint coroners with the consent of the council or the senate, and in Massachusetts and Rhode Island, the medical examiner. Officers under the governor, in some states, appoint local enforcement officers. In Alabama the governor may appoint a special force of inspectors to assist him in enforcing the laws of the state, and in Nebraska he may call to his assistance and appoint any number of persons necessary to enforce the provisions of such laws. Many other illustrations might be cited.[27]

Governor Roosevelt of New York provided an interesting illustration of the use of the power to remove local officers when, in February, 1932, he removed Sheriff Farley of New York County on graft charges, and when, in August of the same year, he removed Mayor James J. Walker of New York City. In these cases, he personally conducted the hearings with patience, fairness, and skill. Following the decision of Mr. Roosevelt, Mayor Walker filed suit in the State Supreme Court, in the form of an application to deny the Governor's power of removal. The opinion of the Court dismissing the application had this to say:

While as a general practice arbitrary power has no place in our system of government, judicial authority is clear and well established that in the

[27] Based on Fairlie, John A., and Kneier, Charles M., *County Government and Administration*, pp. 242–245 (Appleton-Century, New York, 1930).

functioning of the departments of government, executive, legislative and judicial, the Constitution has enumerated the powers and defined the limitations of each. One cannot encroach upon the other and have the balance of power preserved.

The respondent, as Governor of the State, is immune from interference by judicial process and free from judicial control in his performance of executive powers. A sphere of duty has been established for the Executive and within that orbit of power the exercise of his judgment and authority is immune from judicial encroachment.

Courts have no power over his person and they cannot commit him for a disobedience of judicial process.[28]

LEGISLATIVE POWERS OF THE GOVERNOR

The legislative powers of the governor are of two types, constitutional and extra-constitutional. The specific constitutional powers commonly include four things: messages, regular and special; call of special sessions; the veto power; and the power to adjourn the legislature when that body is unable to agree on a date of adjournment (in those states where the session is not of definitely limited duration). The messages include information on the condition of the state and recommendations with regard to legislation. In fact, as was shown in the preceding chapter, a very substantial portion of the legislation passed arises out of the proposals and recommendations of the governor and the executive departments operating under his supervision. The constitutions of thirty-nine states provide that he shall recommend to the legislature matters which he deems it expedient to present for their consideration. The extra-constitutional powers include those acts of leadership by which the governor seeks to enlist popular support for his policies and his legislative program. Each of these powers will be briefly considered.

Reports to the Legislature. Just as the President presents an annual message to the Congress on the state of the Union, so in thirty-nine states the constitution imposes on the governor the duty of reporting to the legislature information on the condition of the state. These messages usually present in outline form the program recommended by the governor, and contain definite suggestions for legislative enactments. In many states this message is followed within a short time by the budget message, which is accompanied by a printed document setting forth the recommendations of the administration for the financial program during the ensuing fiscal period.

[28] People of the State of New York *ex rel.* James J. Walker v. Franklin D. Roosevelt, 144 Misc. 525, 1932.

In twenty-two states the governor is required by the constitution to make his reports and recommendations *from time to time,* but in eight of these cases he is required to give such information at every session.

Special messages dealing with important subjects are in order at appropriate times. Those governors who attempt to exert an aggressive leadership usually make frequent use of special messages; before such a message is delivered, the desire of the governor to address the legislature is made known to the leaders. It is then customary for the two houses to adopt concurrent resolutions calling for a joint session at a designated day and hour. It is preferable that these messages be delivered in person, and in practice they usually are.[29] Five constitutions, those of Alabama, Arkansas, Michigan, Missouri, and Nebraska, require governors to report at the close of their terms of office, but many governors in other states do so without such requirement. Such a report gives an outgoing administration a fine opportunity to summarize its accomplishments for the benefit of the people of the state as well as to report to the legislature.

Special Sessions: Adjournment. The governor is the sole judge in all matters pertaining to the calling of special sessions, except in such matters as impeachments. All of the state constitutions confer on the governor the power to convene extraordinary sessions, although three — those of Massachusetts, New Hampshire, and North Carolina — provide that he shall exercise this power with the advice of the council. In Louisiana he has not only the power but the duty to convene the legislature when so petitioned by two thirds of the elected members thereof. The governor decides whether a special session is necessary, and also the subjects to be considered. These must be specifically mentioned in the call or, in some states, in subsequent messages. In twenty-one states the legislature is without authority to consider subjects not recommended by the governor. In ten states the governor has the power to convene the senate alone in extraordinary session, and fourteen states permit him to call a special session at some place other than the ordinary seat of government if that place is in danger from war, disease, or plague. When a special session looms as a possibility, it always provokes a great deal

---

[29] These messages are usually printed in pamphlet form for general distribution. Pressure groups delight to lift paragraphs from them, to show the attitude of the governors on the subject in which they are interested. The *State Documents* Series of the United States Bureau of Census analyzes and summarizes their recommendations on all subjects. See Clickner, Louise H., " Governors' General Messages to State Legislatures in January, 1945," May, 1945, entire issue.

of discussion because of the public expense involved, and of the loss of time and inconvenience to the members. The question of special sessions has been considered more at length in the discussion of the legislature.

Eighteen states permit the governor to adjourn the legislature when the two houses are unable to agree on a time of adjournment, but only until the time of the next regular session. Massachusetts and New Hampshire limit the duration of such adjournments to ninety days and permit them only with advice of the council. Delaware limits the duration of such adjournments to three months, Kentucky and Pennsylvania to four months. In practice this power is insignificant and rarely used.

Veto Power. Under the Constitution of the United States the President has four alternatives in disposing of the bills submitted to him by Congress. With regard to any given bill, he may sign it; return it to the house in which it originated with a statement of his objections; use what is known as the pocket veto; or permit the bill to become a law without his signature, if, after a ten-day period, Congress is still in session. In twenty-one states, only the first two of these alternatives are open to the governor, and in North Carolina no veto power at all is permitted. Veto restrictions during sessions differ from those applying after adjournment. In the former case, three days are allowed in nine states (Indiana, Iowa, Kansas, Minnesota, New Mexico, North Dakota, South Carolina, South Dakota, and Wyoming); six days are allowed in four states (Alabama, Maryland, Rhode Island, and Wisconsin); ten days are allowed in twelve states (California, Colorado, Delaware, Illinois, Kentucky, Louisiana, Michigan, Missouri, New York, Ohio, Pennsylvania, and Texas); while in the remaining twenty-one states, five days are allowed.

In commenting upon the veto power, the distinction between a suspensive and an absolute veto should be noted. The suspensive veto is the one commonly authorized; it is possible for the legislature, if still in session, to pass a measure over the governor's veto by a two-thirds vote where the suspensive veto is used, whereas the absolute veto is final. The measures vetoed after the legislature has adjourned are in fact, if not in theory, absolute rather than suspensive vetoes. Prior to the widespread adoption of budget legislation by the states, the governor was able to accomplish a good deal by way of budgetary control through the use of the item veto, by means of which he could veto certain items in an appropriation bill

while approving the measure as a whole.[30] In thirty-nine state constitutions the item veto is now authorized; in the following it is not
permitted: Indiana, Iowa, Maine, New Hampshire, Nevada, Rhode
Island, Tennessee, and Vermont. While in some states the courts
have refused to sanction the practice, the governor of Pennsylvania
has power to reduce individual items. He frequently uses the power
when the amounts approved by the legislature exceed the budget
recommendations.

The veto power is exercised by the governor for a number of reasons, of which unconstitutionality accounts for an increasingly large
percentage. Others include defective drafting; objection to the policy
to be established; financial reasons, as excessive cost or failure to
provide revenue to meet a new financial obligation; or undesirable
features of measures resulting from logrolling within the legislature
itself. The following table, based on the experience in Illinois under
the Constitution of 1870, gives some idea of the increasing use of
the veto power and of the reasons for that use.[31]

The Executive Veto in Illinois

| Period | Number of Full Vetoes | Grounds for Veto | |
		Unconstitutionality	All Other
1872–1884	18	62%	38%
1884–1900	39	20%	80%
1900–1916	229	28%	72%
1916–1936	431	22%	78%

The provisions for overriding a veto likewise show a wide variation. A majority of the members present is sufficient in Connecticut,
of the members elected in the seven states of Alabama, Arkansas,
Indiana, Kentucky, New Jersey, Tennessee, and West Virginia. A
three-fifths vote of the members present is sufficient in Rhode Island,
a three-fifths vote of the members elected in Delaware, Maryland,
Nebraska, and Ohio. Florida, Idaho, Massachusetts, Montana, New
Mexico, Oregon, South Dakota, Texas, Vermont, Washington, and
Wisconsin provide for a two-thirds vote of the members present,
while the remaining twenty-two states specify a two-thirds vote of the
members elected.

In twenty-seven states the veto restrictions applying after adjourn-

[30] Wells, Roger H., " The Item Veto and State Budget Reform," *American
Political Science Review,* November, 1924, pp. 782–791.

[31] See Negley, Glenn R., " The Executive Veto in Illinois," *American Political
Science Review,* December, 1939, pp. 1049–1057; Peterson, H. A., " Veto Power of
Illinois Governor," *John Marshall Law Quarterly,* December, 1940, pp. 227–283;
and Illinois Legislative Council, *The Veto Power in Illinois,* with special relation
to the adjournment of the legislature (Springfield, 1943).

ment require the governor to dispose of all bills submitted to him within from three to thirty days after the expiration of the session; otherwise bills become law. He has three days to dispose of bills in Connecticut and North Dakota; five days in Arkansas, Florida, Montana, and New Jersey; ten days in Colorado, Delaware, Illinois, and Louisiana; and thirty days in New York and Pennsylvania. This is no small task, considering the great mass of legislation passed during the rush at the close of the session. (In New York in 1934, 750 bills were left on the governor's desk; in 1938 the number was 933.) The measures must all be carefully examined by the staff in the office of the attorney general, whose recommendations are quite generally accepted by the governor.

In the case of important measures, the signature of the governor is the occasion for much ceremony; a gold pen may be used, to be given afterward to the sponsor of the bill; news photographers may be called in. It is customary for the governor's office to make public announcement of the action taken on measures awaiting his signature; on page 392 is a typical press release, from the office of the Governor of Illinois, July 26, 1945. More extended announcements may be made in the case of important measures, whether signed or vetoed.

Of the remaining states, four — Alabama, Maine, Mississippi, and North Carolina — require their governors to return the bills that they wish to veto at the beginning of the next session of the legislature. Five states — Georgia, Kansas, Mississippi, New Hampshire, and Tennessee — prohibit their governors from approving any bills while the legislature is not in session, while pocket vetoes are allowed in the remaining twelve. In five states — California, Delaware, Iowa, Missouri, and New York — the governors have thirty days during which time bills must be signed and after which, if unsigned, they fail to become law. Montana and Oklahoma limit this period to fifteen days, Virginia to ten, Wisconsin to six, Michigan and Vermont to five, and Minnesota to three.

In 1944 the Citizens Union in New York proposed some changes in the governor's legislative powers, especially as involves his use of the veto power. It recommended that he be given more time in which to consider bills passed by the legislature, both during the session and after adjournment. This constitutes a very serious problem in many states — a problem which could be solved by amending the constitution but which is often met by subterfuge. In Connecticut the constitutional requirement was ignored for many years, with the re-

sult that a difficult problem was created (see page 308). Maryland
has contrived *to* give the governor additional time by failing to present bills to him " officially " — that is, by not affixing the Great Seal
to the bills — until he is ready to act upon them.[32] The second recommendation of the Citizens Union was that the governor's power to
veto items of appropriation which he did not himself propose be

---

NEWS RELEASE
From Executive Office of
GOV. DWIGHT H. GREEN
Springfield, Ill.
7◀▶

FOR IMMEDIATE RELEASE   487-p

    Springfield, Ill., July 26--Governor Green today vetoed Senate
Bills 514 and 516, the so-called "party circle" bills, providing
a method of indirect voting on proposed constitutional amendments
by means of the "straight" party ballot in elections.

    The Governor signed Senate Bill 515, which provides that an
explanation of any constitutional amendment submitted to the
electorate shall appear in a separate column of the official ballot,
at the left of the lists of candidates for public offices.

    In his veto message accompanying Senate Bill 514, the Governor
termed the party circle plan "an unusual, new and tricky method
of securing the approval of a constitutional amendment."

---

extended so that he could reduce items which he considered excessive
instead of being forced to accept or reject them in their entirety. As
previously indicated, this practice has long been in use in Pennsylvania, and in some other states.

Extra-Constitutional Powers. No governor in modern times who
has established a record for constructive leadership has confined his
activity in legislative matters to the use of these constitutional powers. In comparison with the extra-constitutional powers, these powers

---

[32] Everstine, Carl N., " The Signing of Legislative Acts in Maryland," a memorandum report (Legislative Council of Maryland, Baltimore, 1942).

are relatively unimportant. A governor who succeeds in getting his program through the legislature must be in more or less constant contact with the leaders of the two houses. By bargain and compromise, by threatened use of the veto power, by threat of special sessions if the work of the legislature is left uncompleted, he may steadily advance his program. By use of the radio for direct appeals to the people and by public addresses to influential groups on legislative subjects, he may build up an insistent public opinion which will demand that members give favorable consideration to measures which he sponsors. By news releases and by frequent conferences with newspapermen, the progress of his measures may be still further advanced. By frequent personal appearances before the members of the legislature, he can present the case for the administration and for the people whose support he has enlisted for the administration program. The difference between those governors who achieve a national reputation for courageous leadership and those who do not can be measured largely by the extent to which they succeed in employing these extra-constitutional powers.[33]

At the same time, it is possible for a governor to carry these tactics too far. A striking illustration of this is the attempt of Governor Bilbo of Mississippi, in 1931, to exact a signed pledge from members of the legislature that they would support his program, as a condition of his issuing a call for a special session — and this in the face of an emergency relief situation.[34] The American Legislators' Association expressed vigorously its disapproval of this procedure. Even where the governor does not go to such extremes, the members resent a dictatorial attitude on the part of the executive. On one occasion Governor Pinchot of Pennsylvania attempted to put candidates for the legislature " on the spot " regarding their attitude on the utilities question, and he and other governors have tried to stir up trouble for opposition members among their constituencies. Members deeply resent this; their attitude toward such infringement of the legislative prerogative is indicated in the following comment from a Pennsylvania senator, written before a special session to deal with the problem of relief in 1932, but after a presession conference to agree on the program:

[33] Graves, W. Brooke, *Readings in Public Opinion*, Chapter 29 (Appleton, New York, 1928) ; see also Fairlie, John A., " The Legislature and the Administration," *American Political Science Review*, April, 1936, pp. 241–256, and June, 1936, pp. 394–506; Lipson, Leslie, *op. cit.*, and " The Influence of the Governor on Legislation," *Annals*, January, 1938, pp. 72–78.

[34] "Sign on the Dotted Line," *State Government*, March, 1931, pp. 18–20.

All legislative blocs have agreed with the executive bloc upon a happy family bloc party for the benefit of the unemployed. The legislators themselves will be taken out of the ranks of the unemployed and given "made work." The executive branch, which looks like the whole tree of knowledge of good and evil, is never unemployed. The Lord walked in the Garden of Eden in the cool of the day, and we, the mere creatures of creation, shall have to appropriate our scanty assets down to our last fig leaf for relief. The Governor and the blocs are together, for a while, in the Garden of Eden. The Guardian Angel, General Schnader, has written twenty laws for the Garden's opening night. That is twice as many as the Ten Commandments, but it will take more than ten commandments to preserve harmony in our political garden. As this is an allegory, we may as well continue to remark that we, the legislators, like our grandparents, Adam and Eve, are already looking around for the tree of knowledge of good and evil. We may be beguiled into the eating thereof.[35]

As the governor's term wears on, it becomes more and more difficult for him to control his legislature. The honeymoon period of his administration fades away, he uses up his patronage, and his power and prestige decline — sometimes to the vanishing point.

This subject of executive leadership in legislation raises several important questions. Recent developments have shown that a very large part of the more important measures enacted owe their origin to the leadership of the governor or to the heads of executive departments. Many persons with opportunities for extended observation will testify to the truth of this statement, especially at those sessions which mark the middle of a four-year term of the executive.[36] This in turn raises the question as to the proper function of a representative assembly. It is the popular impression that the legislature makes the laws, but if it be true that most of the important measures originate with the executive, then the legislature really acts as a ratifying body for the proposals submitted to it, rather than in the capacity of a body actually "making" the laws which it enacts. This situation illustrates again the case in which the theory of government is at variance with the facts. One may even venture to inquire whether, in the light of the characteristics of legislative bodies already discussed and of the extreme complexity of modern social, political, and economic life, we should not modify the theory so that it might be more strictly in accord with the facts. It is true that the story of the rise of popular government records the prolonged and difficult struggle by which the power to make the laws was gradually

---

[35] Woodward, George, in *The Pennsylvania Legislator*, June, 1932.

[36] See Graves, *op. cit.* Representatives of pressure groups frequently comment upon this fact.

transferred from the King to Parliament. At that time, however, there was no responsible executive such as functions under present-day democratic institutions, nor was there the extreme complexity of governmental problems which has grown out of a mechanical and industrial civilization. It may be that these two factors will ultimately be held to justify a partial retracing of some of the steps of that development, so that the legislature may again be regarded as a safeguard for the people, passing upon and either approving or rejecting the proposals submitted to it by the executive.

Another significant problem involves the relationship between the executive and legislative branches of the government. A man of moderate ability may be able to achieve some measure of success in dealing with a friendly legislature, but it takes a genius in the art of politics to secure favorable action upon a program at the hands of a hostile legislature, whether that legislature be dominated by the opposing party or by a hostile faction of the party to which the governor belongs. The techniques to be employed in such a situation will vary as the personalities of the governors using them; in general, a policy of conciliation is more likely to be successful than one of violent opposition. As illustrations of the first, we have the success with which Governors Smith, Roosevelt, and Lehman in New York have dealt with Republican majorities in the legislature, while of the second, we have the vitriolic attacks with which Governor Pinchot from time to time assailed a hostile Republican legislature in Pennsylvania.

Governor Cooper in the address already referred to made some very interesting observations on this point. " The method a governor chooses, in dealing with his legislature," he said, " may differ according to his background," and then he proceeded to illustrate:

If he has been a Major General as our distinguished host, Governor Martin of Pennsylvania — the simple drumhead court-martial is recommended for recalcitrant members of the legislature. On the other hand, if he is a distinguished surgeon like Governor Blood of New Hampshire, simple blood-letting procedures may be resorted to. This procedure is not recommended for amateurs. . . . Governor Blood has, as a matter of fact, by skillful and constitutional operation permanently eliminated fifty-five New Hampshire legislators, body and soul, by reducing the number of his legislature from 454 to 399. If he is a dentist by profession, as is Governor Hunt of Wyoming, he can always pull the teeth of the opposition, in case of emergency. If he is a former attorney general like Earl Warren or Herbert O'Conor, he can threaten them with the penitentiary.

It is therefore apparent that the kind and degree of cooperation, as well as its effectiveness, depend largely upon the personality of the executive. A condition so essential to the smooth working of state government as the relations between these two branches ought to rest upon some more substantial basis than the chance variations in the personalities of the persons elected to the governorship. Some simple and inexpensive but permanent machinery should be provided by which effective cooperation would be assured. Some progress along this line has been made by the establishment of legislative councils in Kansas and other states. These developments were discussed in Chapter VIII.

In the effort to bridge the gap between the executive and legislative branches, it has been suggested that the governor be elected by the legislature. Such a procedure would open the way for development along either of two lines, along either or both of which experimentation might prove to be valuable. An executive so chosen might perform the functions of a manager, opening up a line of development in the states similar to that which has taken place in a large number of cities throughout the country. It is not known, of course, that such a device would operate successfully in the larger unit. The other possibility would be a development in the direction of the parliamentary system, in which the chief executive is chosen by and is responsible to the legislature, and in which he continues to hold his office so long and only so long as he can command a majority in that body. A full parliamentary system would be impossible, of course, as long as the governor was chosen for a stated term; and in view of the failure of parliamentary institutions in Europe to provide competent leadership, this alternative might be less desirable than the first one.

Ordinance and Rule-Making Power. The rule-making power of the governors has developed rapidly and extensively in recent years, largely because of the modification of previously existing legislative practices. In former days the legislatures tried to foresee and provide for every possible contingency that might arise with regard to a given subject. Acts of excessive length resulted, filled with many details and requiring constant revision. In addition, administrative agencies were frequently hampered in their work, either by the absence of needed provisions or by the fact that those which existed were no longer suitable. More recently, we have succeeded in substituting outline legislation for detailed legislation; the legislature now attempts to lay down fundamental principles and policies, but leaves matters of detail in their application to the governor and the administrative officers. This practice has somewhat reduced the quantity and improved the quality of the legislative output, but it has at the same time increased the power of administrative departments and the difficulty of their task. Most of the supplementary rules, regulations, and ordinances are drafted by the department or by an advisory board; the approval of the governor may or may not be required, although he is in general responsible. Some attention has been given to this problem so far as it relates to the Federal government, but little has been done with it at the state level.[37]

JUDICIAL POWERS

Executive Clemency. A governor may occasionally perform duties of a judicial or quasi-judicial nature. Most important of these is the exercise of executive clemency — the pardoning power, the power to parole, and the power to grant reprieves — a duty which may consume at times a great deal of time and energy. It may be in order to note first the meaning of these terms, and the differences between them. When a criminal is pardoned, the penalty is remitted; he is permitted to pass without punishment, or at least without further punishment than has already been inflicted prior to the date of the pardon. Under a parole, the prisoner is released under certain definite and specific conditions, and presumably under the supervision of a parole officer. If the conditions are in any way violated, the parole is forfeited, and the prisoner returns to serve in full the remainder of his unexpired sentence. A reprieve provides merely for a stay of execution, usually in connection with a death sentence. A reprieve is usually good for thirty days, pending the outcome of a motion for appeal or of an investigation by the governor. In New York, in March 1944, Governor Dewey gave a sixty-hour reprieve to three members of the Murder, Inc. gang "until late in the week," pending a ruling by the United States Supreme Court.

The governor also has the power of commutation — that is, of alleviating the penalty, as by changing a death sentence to one of life imprisonment or by reducing the number of years of a sentence. In addition to these various forms of executive clemency, a legisla-

---

[37] See Blachly, Frederick F., and Oatman, Miriam E., *Administrative Legislation and Adjudication* (Brookings Institution, 1934), and Griswold, Erwin N., "Government in Ignorance of the Law — a Plea for Better Publication of Executive Legislation," *Harvard Law Review*, December, 1934, pp. 198–215.

tive body may extend amnesty to a group of people who are guilty or alleged to be guilty of neglect or crime against the state, while a court may suspend all punishment prescribed by law. Under this form, which is known as probation, the court gives a convict his liberty under conditions of supervised good behavior.

The power of executive clemency exists in some form in all states, but there is the greatest diversity as to its extent and the effect of its exercise. It is most limited in Connecticut, both as to extent and duration. Fifteen states limit the pardoning power of the governor by providing for a board of pardons, the membership of which is largely ex officio.[38] In New Hampshire and Massachusetts the power is exercised subject to the consent of the council. In the remaining thirty states it is vested in the governor; but in twenty-three states he must report his reasons to the legislature, and in four others to the secretary of state. In twenty-six states additional power to remit fines or forfeitures is vested in the governor or the board of pardons. In twenty-seven states, however, the power to pardon does not ex-

TYPES OF CLEMENCY GRANTED IN NORTH CAROLINA, 1869–1930 [39]

Year	Governors	Pardons	Conditional Pardons	Commu- tations	Total
1869–1870	Holden	95	1	12	108
1873–1876	Caldwell and Brogden	219	2	18	239
1877–1880	Vance and Jarvis	150	1	21	172
1881–1884	Jarvis	187	...	25	212
1885–1888	Scales	82	...	24	106
1889–1892	Fowle and Holt	122	8	42	172
1893–1896	Carr	213	3	24	240
1897–1900	Russell	327	2	75	404
1901–1904	Aycock	369	4	85	458
1905–1908	Glenn	89	76	27	192
1909–1912	Kitchin	45	368	98	511
1913–1916	Craig	366	96	83	545
1917–1920	Bickett	97	695	205	997
1921–1924	Morrison	101	693	69	863
1925–1928	McLean	27	907	78	1,012
1929–1930	Gardner	11	909	91	1,011
	Total	2,500	3,765	977	.....

[38] These are: Alabama, Delaware, Florida, Idaho, Louisiana, Minnesota, Montana, Nebraska, Nevada, New Jersey, Pennsylvania, South Carolina, South Dakota, Texas, and Utah. In Alabama and South Carolina these boards are advisory. See New York State Constitutional Convention Committee, *op. cit.*, Chapter 3.

[39] From Cheek, Roma S., *The Pardoning Power of the Governor of North Carolina*, p. 80 (Duke University, 1932).

tend to cases of impeachment, and in eight it does not extend to cases of treason. In two states it is limited to criminal cases. In nineteen states advisory pardon boards exist, whose duty it is to investigate and make recommendations. In forty-one states the governor may not pardon until after conviction. The law usually requires that all pardons and commutations of sentence be registered in the office of the secretary of state merely as a matter of record. Only in two states — Kentucky and Texas — are the records of such cases kept elsewhere than in the governor's office. All states except Tennessee and Vermont place at least one constitutional safeguard on the exercise of the pardoning power.

It seems clear from the records in numerous states that the pardoning power has in recent years been used with increasing frequency; this is well illustrated by the table on page 398 covering its use in North Carolina from 1869 to 1930.

While some have regarded parole as an administrative procedure rather than a form of clemency, the same tendency is shown by the parole figures for New York during a shorter and more recent period. The number of persons under active supervision of the Division of Parole in that state doubled during the decade of the thirties, and has shown a further substantial increase since 1940, as indicated in the table below.

NEW YORK STATE DIVISION OF PAROLE —
NUMBER OF PERSONS UNDER SUPERVISION, 1930–1944

Year	Elmira Sentences	Indeterminate Sentences	Definite Sentences	Total
1930	....	....	...	4,177
1933	....	....	...	6,555
1936	....	....	...	7,694
1939	....	....	...	8,221
1940	3,108	4,660	728	8,496
1941	3,186	5,169	668	9,023
1942	2,678	6,081	726	9,485
1943	2,580	6,540	701	9,821
1944	2,354	6,460	620	9,434

The unfortunate men and women who may become eligible for executive clemency are in prison for almost every type of act prohibited by the criminal law; a list in a recent report of the Division of Parole of the Executive Department of the State of Maryland lists more than fifty — abduction, abortion, arson, assault of a dozen different types, burglary, bastardy, keeping of a bawdy house, carnal knowledge, carrying weapons, contributing to delinquency of minors, counterfeiting, desertion and nonsupport, embezzlement, false pretense, forgery, gambling, habitually disorderly conduct, incest, offenses against the liquor law, larceny, manslaughter, murder, rape, vagrancy, et cetera. Some of the earlier governors made extensive comments upon their emotional reactions in connection with their exercise of this power.[40] Most of them regarded it as " a most difficult and trying task," recognized that their use of it subjected them to much criticism, but contended that they had done the best they knew how. When criminals have been sentenced and their execution is pending, the governor must listen to the appeals for clemency made by distressed relatives. In such cases the governor is apt to be torn by the conflict between a desire to listen to the pleas for mercy, and the duty to see that justice is faithfully administered. In his comments on this matter former Governor Smith has been more frank and revealing than most: [41]

I gave a great deal of my time to talking to the relatives of the men in our state prisons. . . . Nothing is so distressing as the attention the governor is compelled to give to applications for executive clemency when the prisoner is to be put to death. It is impossible for a man to escape the thought that no power in the world except himself can prevent a human being from going over the brink of eternity after the Court of Appeals has sustained the verdict of the lower courts. I had very many unhappy nights when executions took place.

The governor is constantly haunted by the terrible question that if anything should develop after the execution to indicate that the prisoner was not guilty, how much of the responsibility would he be compelled to carry personally for the ending of that man's life? I studied and worked very hard, sometimes into the small hours of the morning, on the record and papers, facts and arguments in capital cases. . . .

In their despair the relatives of the condemned appeal to everybody to speak a word to the governor for them. . . . For fear of accident, it has been customary for the governor to be in touch with the prison on the night of an execution. . . . In order that I might know exactly to whom I was talking on the telephone, I had arranged a code with the Superintendent of Prisons, who was always at Sing Sing prison on the Thursday night when anybody was to be put to death. . . . Intriguing, sharp individuals might easily impersonate the Superintendent of Prisons, if for no other purpose than to delay the execution.

Mr. Smith then goes on to describe incidents of this character, and to show how the governor, in this disturbed state of mind, could easily be made the prey of plausible and unscrupulous attorneys and

---

40 See, for instance, Cheek, *op. cit.*, pp. 77–79.
41 Smith, *op. cit.*, pp. 306–308.

others pleading for the life of a condemned man. He describes vividly his experiences in the two weeks preceding the execution of Mrs. Snyder, of the Gray-Snyder murder case, and continues:

> More people were executed during my time as governor than in the term of any other governor in the state's history. This is in part due to the length of time I was in office and also to the wave of crime following the war.
>
> I gave public hearings on every capital case, and in only one instance did I find a man about to go to the electric chair for whom nobody spoke a word, whom nobody seemed to know. . . . I went over this case with the same amount of care that I devoted to all the others where a hearing was requested and given. I summoned my own counsel . . . and finally commuted the sentence of the man because I became convinced that he should have been found guilty of a lesser degree of homicide.[42]

The comments of Mr. Smith and of other governors indicate that this task is one of the most trying attached to the governorship. The suggestion has sometimes been made that the governor might well be relieved of this duty by turning it over entirely to a board of pardons. Mr. Smith expressed the belief that this would be unjustified — that the duty, difficult though it is, is a natural part of the privileges and the duties that pertain to the office. " The people of the State of New York gave the pardoning power to the Governor to use in proper cases, and the Governor who does not use it in proper cases is a coward."

One further phase of this problem remains to be considered: What are the more common reasons ascribed for decisions allowing clemency? The North Carolina study, already referred to, lists the following: [43]

Recommended by trial judge.	Ends of justice have been met.
Recommended by prominent citizens.	Family in need.
Ill health of prisoner.	Prisoner of weak mind.
Youth (or advanced age) of prisoner.	Recommended by the injured party.
	Accomplices not being punished.
Doubt of prisoner's guilt.	Prisoner has performed a meritorious deed.
Recommended by the members of the trial jury.	Good prison record.
	To correct court error.

Mr. Smith further discusses some of the less obvious and more human considerations which enter into the consideration of such cases:

[42] Smith, *op. cit.*, pp. 310–311.
[43] Cheek, *op. cit.*, pp. 92–93; also Weihofen, Henry, " The Effect of a Pardon," *University of Pennsylvania Law Review*, December, 1939, pp. 177–193.

The power of pardon is so great that it carries a corresponding responsibility. The fact of the matter is that few men are actually released from prison by pardon from the governor. The public mind is more or less confused on the question of executive clemency, because all pardons are regarded as alike in all circumstances. This is not the case.

Pardons are issued for various reasons and differ in their effects. Taking the year 1927 as a typical year during my governorship, I pardoned only five prisoners in that year, when the pardon meant their actual release from prison. In three of the five cases the pardon was extended because of the physical condition of the prisoners. They were suffering from advanced tuberculosis, and, unless pardoned, would, in all human probabilty, have died in prison. A fourth man I released from the Suffolk County jail in order that he might attend the funeral of his wife. He had but eight days more of his sentence to serve. The fifth one was pardoned on the recommendation of the district attorney and the sheriff of Onondaga County, who certified to me that the prisoner aided the state in preventing a jail delivery after several prisoners of the jail had overcome the keepers by throwing red pepper in their eyes.

A good many pardons are issued to permit aliens, convicted before they became citizens, to attain citizenship. In many cases these are minor crimes. . . . Another form is issued to prevent deportation. In many instances these are young men living in this country with their parents. All these pardons, however, are predicated on the further consideration that the conduct of the applicant while in prison was good and that he gave promise of reform. . . . Some pardons are granted to remove disability after the prisoner has completed his sentence and paid his debt to society in full for his transgression of the law. A license, for instance, will not be issued to a man to practice the business of chauffeur after having committed a crime. The pardon of the governor removes such disability. . . . Another form of pardon is for the purpose of restoring citizenship and giving to the pardoned man the right to exercise his franchise.[44]

Likewise, commutations are extended by the governor for a variety of reasons. Sometimes the officers who were responsible for convicting and sentencing the convict may be moved by information which develops later to recommend a commutation. Sometimes the governor may take such action because of the physical condition of the prisoner, and on other occasions upon the advice of a district attorney as a reward to a convict who has given information of value to the officers of the law. When the popular hysteria blows over, political prisoners may often have their sentences commuted. The problems of commutation are less serious and less nerve-wracking to the governor than those relating to the pardoning power.

Other Judicial Powers. Other powers of a judicial nature include the vetoing for constitutional reasons of bills passed by the legislature; the suspending, on rare occasions, of the writ of habeas corpus;

44 Smith, *op. cit.,* pp. 313–315.

and the making of decisions with regard to requests received from the governors of other states for the extradition of persons charged with crime. The Federal Constitution, in Article IV, requires that the governor shall hand over such persons upon request. The language of the Constitution is clear, but it has been so interpreted by the Supreme Court as to leave the course of action largely at the discretion of a governor of whom the request is made. The legal and constitutional aspect of this topic is discussed more fully in the chapter on interstate relations; it may be appropriate, however, to consider the problem here from the point of view of the burden which it imposes on the governor. With regard to this, former Governor Smith again has an interesting comment:

One of the largest single drains upon the time of the governor is his necessary attention to extradition proceedings. Every fugitive from justice from any state of the Union apprehended within the state of New York can only be returned under arrest to his own state after the governor signs three sets of papers. Similarly, fugitives from justice from our own state can only be extradited after the governor signs a similar number of papers.

When residents of the state of New York are wanted for crimes in other states and they make a request for a hearing before the governor before he signs the order to extradite, it is difficult, if not impossible, to deny it to them. Much time is taken up in listening to arguments by counsel of both sides as to whether or not extradition papers should be signed. In extradition proceedings the governor is both judge and jury. He passes, in the first instance, upon the law, and then upon the facts. It must be determined whether the prisoner was in the state on or about the time the crime was committed, whether he is the man named in the papers, and then the facts must be studied. In some cases, there are indications of grave miscarriages of justice. . . . Many extradition proceedings are for non-support, where a disagreement has arisen between man and wife. . . .[45]

SELECTED REFERENCES

Alexander, Margaret C., *Development of the Power of the Executive in New York* (Smith College Studies in History, 1917).

Beckwith, Edmund R., and others, *Lawful Action of State Military Forces* (Random House, New York, 1944).

Benson, George C. S., and Litchfield, Edward H., *The State Administrative Board in Michigan* (Bureau of Government, University of Michigan, 1938).

Black, Henry C., *The Relation of the Executive Power to Legislation* (Princeton University Press, 1919).

Chadbourne, James H., *Lynching and the Law* (University of North Carolina Press, 1933).

Cheek, Roma S., *The Pardoning Power of the Governor of North Carolina* (Duke University, 1932).

[45] Smith, *op. cit.*, pp. 304–305.

Faust, Martin L., *Manual on the Executive Article* (Missouri Constitutional Convention of 1943, Columbia, 1943).

Friedman, Jacob A., *The Impeachment of Governor William Sulzer* (Columbia University Press, 1939).

Governors' Conference, *Proceedings* (Chicago, annually, 1909–   ).

Illinois Legislative Council, *The Veto Power in Illinois* (Springfield, 1940).

Jensen, Christian, *The Pardoning Power in the American States* (University of Chicago Press, 1922).

Lipson, Leslie, *The American Governor: From Figurehead to Leader* (University of Chicago Press, 1939).

Macmillan, Margaret B., *The War Governors in the American Revolution* (Columbia University Press, 1943).

Mathews, John M., *American State Administration* (Appleton, New York, 1916).

New York State Constitutional Convention Committee, *Problems Relating to Executive Administration and Powers* (Albany, 1938).

Perkins, John A., *The Role of the Governor in Michigan in the Enactment of Appropriations* (University of Michigan, Bureau of Government, 1943).

Pfiffner, John M., *Public Administration* (Ronald Press, New York, 1935).

Porter, Kirk H., *State Administration* (Crofts, New York, 1938).

Rohr, Charles J., *The Governor of Maryland, a Constitutional Study* (Johns Hopkins Press, 1932).

Ruskowski, Casimir W., *The Constitutional Governor* (Humphries, Boston, 1943).

Smith, Alfred E., *Progressive Democracy, Addresses and State Papers* (Harcourt, Brace, New York, 1928).

Walker, Harvey, *Public Administration in the United States* (Farrar and Rinehart, New York, 1937).

White, Leonard D., *Introduction to the Study of Public Administration*, Revised Edition (Macmillan, New York, 1939).

——, *Trends in Public Administration* (McGraw-Hill, New York, 1933).

Willoughby, W. F., *Principles of Public Administration* (Brookings Institution, Washington, 1927).

———

Biographical and autobiographical accounts of some notable governorships:

Barnard, Harry, *"Eagle Forgotten": Life of John Peter Altgeld* (Bobbs-Merrill, Indianapolis, 1938).

Coolidge, Calvin, *Autobiography*, Chapter 3 (Cosmopolitan Book Corporation, New York, 1929).

Cross, Wilbur L., *An Autobiography* (Yale University Press, 1943).

Gosnell, Harold F., *Boss Platt and His New York Machine* (University of Chicago Press, 1924). Contains much material on Theodore Roosevelt as governor, and on his relations with Platt.

Hill, Louise B., *Joseph E. Brown and the Confederacy* (University of North Carolina Press, 1940).

Kearney, James, *The Political Education of Woodrow Wilson*, early chapters (Century, New York, 1926).

La Follette, Robert M., *A Personal Narrative of Political Experiences* (Published by the Author, Madison, 1913).

McElroy, Robert M., *Grover Cleveland, the Man and the Statesman*, Vol. I, Chapter 2 (Harper, New York, 1923).

Mitchell, Stewart, *Horatio Seymour of New York* (Harvard University Press, 1938).

Pringle, Henry F., *Alfred E. Smith, a Critical Study*, Book IV (Macy-Masius, New York, 1927).

——, *Theodore Roosevelt, a Biography* (Harcourt, Brace, New York, 1931).

Roosevelt, Theodore, *An Autobiography*, Chapter 8 (Macmillan, New York, 1913).

Smith, Alfred E., *Up to Now, an Autobiography* (Viking, New York, 1929).

Spaulding, E. Wilder, *His Excellency George Clinton* (Macmillan, New York, 1938).

Stackpole, Edward J., *Behind the Scenes with a Newspaperman* (Lippincott, Philadelphia, 1927). Contains material on Pennsylvania governors.

Steffens, Lincoln, *Autobiography* (Harcourt, Brace, New York, 1931).

Whitlock, Brand, *Forty Years of It* (Appleton, New York, 1914). Contains an intimate sketch of Governor Altgeld of Illinois.

———

Council of State Governments, *State Government* (Chicago, monthly).

Gilmore, Harlan W., " Louisiana Clings to Reform," *National Municipal Review*, April, 1944, p. 164–169.

Gurwell, John K., " The Governors of the States," *State Government*, July, 1941, pp. 157–158, 172.

National Municipal League, *National Municipal Review* (New York, monthly).

Perkins, John A., " American Governors — 1930–1940," *National Municipal Review*, March, 1940, pp. 178–184.

Scott, Elizabeth McK., " State Executive Departments Play Growing Part in Lawmaking," *National Municipal Review*, November, 1943, pp. 529–534.

——, and Zeller, Belle, " State Agencies and Lawmaking," *Public Administration Review*, Summer, 1942, pp. 205–220.

Snider, Clyde F., " Gubernatorial Disability," *University of Chicago Law Review*, April, 1941, pp. 521–529.

Spicer, George W., " Gubernatorial Leadership in Virginia," *Public Administration Review*, Autumn, 1941, pp. 441–457.

Stokes, Thomas L., " The Governors," *State Government*, June, 1944, pp. 343–345.

Weeks, O. Douglas, " Initiation of Legislation by Administrative Agencies," *Brooklyn Law Review*, January, 1940, pp. 117–131.

Weihofen, Henry, " Pardon: An Extraordinary Remedy," *Rocky Mountain Law Review*, February, 1940, pp. 112–120.

White, Leonard D., and Sherman, Harvey, " The Governors March On," *State Government*, October, 1940, pp. 195–197, 206.

Zeller, Belle, " Lawmaker — Legislator or Lobbyist? " *National Municipal Review*, August, 1940, pp. 523–532, 544.

CHAPTER X

Administrative Organization and Reorganization

STATE ADMINISTRATIVE ORGANIZATION

THE administrative organization of the states consists of the governor, the lieutenant-governor, the heads of the administrative departments, and the independent boards and commissions. It is the present purpose to sketch in broad outline the structure of this machinery, with some emphasis upon the important changes that have occurred in it in the last quarter of a century.

The Position of the Governor. The governor has always been, in theory, the head of the state administrative establishment; in the previous chapter the attempt was made to describe the office of governor and the powers and duties pertaining to it. Prior to the administrative reorganization movement which began in 1917, this theory was largely a fiction. In the first place, the governor had little or no control over the original, constitutional departments whose heads were chosen by popular vote. These officers owed nothing to the governor, for their power was derived from the people directly, as was his. As a rule they showed little disposition to cooperate with him, sometimes for personal reasons and sometimes for fear that they might enhance his political prestige and injure their own. The position of the governor was little better in his relations with the newer services, which had multiplied rapidly and had an almost infinite number of separate boards, commissions, and other independent agencies. The governor was thus in the unfortunate and unfair position of being held responsible for the administration of a governmental machine over which he had very limited control. In New York, for instance, there were at one time 184 administrative agencies. Under such a system, characteristic of all the states, responsible administrative control was impossible; waste, inefficiency, overlapping, and duplication were inevitable.

Professor White admirably summarized this situation in the following paragraph written in 1933:

> The American state governments until 1910 exhibited almost none of the characteristics associated with the concept of general management. Neither the governor nor any other state officer was in a position to exercise managerial power with reference to state business. The various agencies of administration had no common head and recognized little responsibility to any high executive officer. There was no central planning agency, no unified command, no administrative program, no coordinating agency, no agency to investigate and report except ineffective legislation committees, no fiscal control. American state administration was, in short, atomistic and disorganized to an exceptional degree.[1]

The administrative reorganization movement appears to have begun in Oregon in 1909 or 1910 with a proposal of the People's Power League to concentrate " executive power in the hands of the governor — checked only by an independent auditor, and to establish vital connections between the governor and the legislature." Charles E. Hughes, in his inaugural address as Governor of New York in 1910 and later in an address at Yale University, likewise urged a concentration of responsibility, with few offices and short ballots. The movement was given further impetus by the report of President Taft's Economy and Efficiency Commission in 1912. Then in 1917 the first code was enacted in Illinois under the leadership of Governor Frank O. Lowden, and a movement that was to hold a position of primary importance in the state field for the next fifteen or twenty years got under way. Under the Illinois plan, adopted subsequently in Massachusetts, New York, and Virginia by constitutional amendment and in twenty-two other states by statutory provisions, all or most of the existing agencies were abolished by law. The duties which they performed were then carefully classified under a limited number of headings, care being taken to group related services and to eliminate overlapping and duplication of functions. Each of these groups of activities was then assigned to a newly created department, the head of which was appointed by the governor. It thus became possible for the governor to establish a direct line of responsibility through the department heads, bureau

1 White, Leonard D., *Trends in Public Administration*, p. 176 (McGraw-Hill, New York, 1933). The author traces, pp. 176–180, the various events and published studies which provided the groundwork upon which the Illinois and later reorganizations were based. See also Buck, A. E., *The Reorganization of State Governments in the United States*, pp. 5–10 (Columbia University Press, 1938).

chiefs, and the heads of sections or divisions down to the minor employees of each department. The governor now became responsible in fact and not merely in theory for the conduct of his administration.

A. E. Buck has listed the following standards or principles of reorganization as applied to the executive department, but it is significant that the reorganization of state governments has extended to the legislative and judicial branches as well as to the executive and administrative structure.[2]

1. Concentration of authority and responsibility.
2. Departmentalization, or functional integration.
3. Undesirability of boards for purely administrative work.
4. Coordination of the staff services of administration.
5. Provision for an independent audit.
6. Recognition of a governor's cabinet.

These fundamental principles of the reorganization movement represent at the same time benefits to be realized after reorganization takes place. Other advantages may be noted, such as the significant financial savings which are possible through the elimination of waste, inefficiency, and the duplication of services. Second, the reorganization plan provided a much more satisfactory basis for the operation of a budget system. While it is possible to operate a system of financial planning without reorganization, it is much easier to do so under an administrative code. The centralization of control provided in the reorganization plan makes possible a proper supervision of the expenditures of spending agencies during the fiscal period. The centralization of responsibility represents a notable gain from the point of view of administrative structure. Finally, adoption of the plan inevitably results in progress toward a short ballot. It is, in fact, impossible to have any satisfactory reorganization and still retain a large number of elective state officers, for centralization of administrative responsibility cannot be obtained while this condition exists. One of the primary purposes of this plan, as Professor John M. Mathews said many years ago, is to make the governor the central pivotal point around which the whole administration revolves.

The Governor's Office. A recent survey has shown that every governor has an executive office staff, headed ordinarily by his secretary. This position is an important one, the duties of which are many and varied; it has been described as a " minister with all port-

---

[2] Buck, *op. cit.*, pp. 14–28; and on the latter point, Stafford, Paul T., " Modern Reconstruction of State Government," *Annals*, January, 1938, pp. 198–204.

folios." Among the more important duties are to keep in touch with the progress of the governor's program in the legislature; to act as liaison officer between the governor and his department heads; to investigate pardon cases (in some states) ; to absorb much of the impact of personal contact which would otherwise strike the governor directly; to devise the governor's itinerary, look after the preparation of his speeches, and handle his correspondence; to supervise the work of the office staff and answer scores of inquiries which come to the governor.

" In almost half the states the secretary, necessarily an executive himself, has one or more assistants who handle many of his routine and clerical duties. Five governors have, in addition, a personal secretary who relieves the secretary and his assistants still further by taking the responsibility for many of the routine personal duties that must be handled for the governor." Although the attorney general usually provides the governor's legal counsel, six states — Alabama, Michigan, New Hampshire, New York, Oklahoma, and West Virginia — give the governor a lawyer on his own staff.[3] The remainder of the staff is made up of clerks, stenographers, messengers, and miscellaneous employees, in varying numbers. In nineteen states there are less than five such staff members, while in twenty-six the number ranges from five to fifteen. In Massachusetts, New York, and Pennsylvania the number exceeds fifteen, there being twenty-eight in New York and forty-eight in Pennsylvania. In the latter case approximately half of these employees are accounted for by the placing of the Budget Office directly under the governor.

In New York, where the governor is the head of the Executive Department, there is, in addition to the staff connected with the executive chamber, the following list of divisions: Budget, Commerce, Military and Naval Affairs, Standards and Purchase, State Police, Parole, Alcoholic Beverage Control, State Planning, and Housing. In Pennsylvania the governor has, in addition to his immediate staff, the Budget Office and the Personnel Office. Provided in this set-up at some point should be an administration secretary, whose duty it would be to study problems of administrative organization and procedure in much the same way that the budget secre-

[3] This comment is based on " The Staffs of the Governors," a bulletin of the Governors' Conference, Chicago, May 4, 1936. In Michigan the practice regarding legal counsel is rather informal. Sometimes an assistant attorney general is assigned. Professor Dorr reports that sometimes the governor leans heavily upon one of his secretaries, selected because of his legal training. In many cases the governor unofficially takes his legal advice from some prominent attorney who holds no official post.

tary studies the financial problems of the state. The budget officer does not have the time, nor is it his duty, to consider the many problems in the field of administration.

The Governor's Council. Maine, Massachusetts, and New Hampshire maintain, by constitutional requirement, an executive council which is a survival of colonial days. These councils are small bodies of five to nine members, popularly selected (except in Maine) for two-year terms from districts. The councils meet almost continuously during legislative sessions, and on a weekly basis at other times. Members receive their expenses and a small salary for the performance of their duties in advising the governor in the executive part of the government. Their duties are numerous and varied, including supervision of state finances, state institutions, concurrence in appointments made by the governor, et cetera.[4] A somewhat similar purpose is served by the Executive Board in Pennsylvania, established under the Administrative Code of 1923, as amended. This consists of twelve members of the Governor's Cabinet, designated by him, whose duty it is to advise upon administrative matters and to pass upon organizational changes in the various departments and agencies of the state government.

The Lieutenant-Governor. The office of lieutenant-governor, first found in the colonial period, is still retained in nearly three fourths of the states.[5] It has been said that the Vice-President (except in connection with possible succession) is a fifth wheel in the Federal government. If this statement is true of the Vice-President, a similar statement would be doubly true as applied to the lieutenant-governor. Under modern conditions it is difficult to discover any useful purpose which the office serves and which could not be served more efficiently and more cheaply in other ways; [6] yet it continues to exist

4 Haynes, Evan, *Selection and Tenure of Judges,* pp. 12–16 (National Conference of Judicial Councils, 1944).

5 See Isom, Warren R., "The Office of Lieutenant-Governor in the States," *American Political Science Review,* October, 1938, pp. 921–926. There are thirteen states in which the office does not exist. In Arkansas, Florida, Georgia, Maine, Maryland, New Hampshire, New Jersey, Tennessee, and West Virginia the president of the senate serves as substitute governor; in Arizona, Oregon, Utah, and Wyoming the secretary of state so serves. See also Patterson, Robert F., *The Office of Lieutenant-Governor in the United States* (University of South Dakota, Governmental Research Bureau, 1944), and "The Lieutenant-Governor in 1944," *State Government,* June, 1944, pp. 348–349, 356.

6 The compensation in seventeen states ranges from an annual salary of $900 in Kansas to $8,000 in Pennsylvania, with an average of a little less than $2,700. In six states, reports Isom, the lieutenant-governor is paid a salary for each session over which he presides, and in others, a per diem wage. For a good discussion of the office in New York, see New York State Constitutional Convention Committee, *Problems Relating to Executive Administration and Powers,* Chapter 2 (Albany, 1938).

because the people like to elect somebody, because it provides a permanent and impartial presiding officer for the senate without robbing any district of its senator, and because it is in harmony with tradition and precedent. It was created in order to provide a successor to the governor in case of his death, resignation, or disability, but this purpose has not been fulfilled, as will presently be indicated. The occupant of the office is usually required to preside over the senate; occasionally when the governor is temporarily out of the state he functions in his stead. The latter situation has frequently led to breaks in continuity of policy and to squabbles as to whether a vacancy actually existed.

The lieutenant-governor has rarely been of much use to the governor either administratively or legislatively, because the two often belong to different factions of their party. Since the ticket must be " balanced," the nomination for lieutenant-governor is likely to be given as a consolation prize to the leading rival of the nominee for the governorship. This is almost invariably true where the convention system of nomination is used or where, in connection with the primary system, the party organization designates a slate before the primary is held. Furthermore, the ticket must ordinarily be balanced geographically, and it is extremely unlikely that both candidates will be selected from the same section of the state. Often too the nominees for this office are men of very mediocre ability.

Thus the existing plan often fails to provide a suitable successor in case the governorship becomes vacant. In most states the government is so conducted that the lieutenant-governor has little opportunity to take part in the development of administrative policies or to acquaint himself with the work of the state government. He is, in fact, seldom consulted with regard to policy and he rarely if ever attends the meetings of the cabinet. On the legislative side, he has power to appoint committees in one third of the states, and he normally acts as presiding officer where the office exists. In most states he may cast a deciding vote in case of a tie. He might conceivably be valuable as a liaison officer between the governor and the legislature; this seldom occurs, however, because he is ordinarily opposed to the governor politically. While lieutenant-governors are usually supposed to preside over the senate, they are frequently absent; they are rarely at the capitol when the legislature is not in session. The president pro tempore, who has had legislative experience, would probably be more competent as presiding officer, while the question of succession could be settled by suitable constitutional or statutory provision. In the lower house the speaker, who is always a member and therefore familiar with legislative procedure, presides more ably than a presiding officer imposed upon the house by the constitution might be expected to do.

The office of lieutenant-governor should either be abolished or developed into an important and responsible position. If it were abolished, as it might well be, the salary and maintenance expenses of the office could be saved. If it were not a constitutional office or if it were amended out, the legislature could then made suitable provision for succession, either as other states have done or in a manner similar to that which Congress adopted for Presidential succession by the Act of 1886. On the other hand, it might be possible to develop the lieutenant-governor into a kind of assistant governor, who could handle many routine duties and thereby ease the strain upon the time and strength of the governor. An experiment along this line was initiated in Indiana in 1933.

The Executive Departments. Next in the administrative set-up come the heads of executive departments, of which there are two distinct classes as indicated in the following table:

Original Officers (*Elective Heads*)	Newer Offices (*Appointed Heads*)	
Secretary of State	Agriculture	Labor
Attorney General	Banking	Mines
State Treasurer	Commerce	Property and
State Auditor	Conservation	Supplies
Superintendent of	Education (in some	Public Assistance
Education (in	states)	Public Utilities
some states)	Health	Reclamation
Other elective offices	Highways	Revenue
	Institutions	State Police
	Insurance	Welfare

An examination of this table reveals a number of interesting facts with regard to the development of state administrative machinery. The heads of the original departments are all elective, as a result of the influence of the Jacksonian tradition. Their departments are provided for in the constitutions, and their duties are confined to what students of public administration call auxiliary services. They are a survival from the day in which the services performed by government were few in number and limited in extent.

The officers listed in the right-hand columns are all of relatively recent creation, all having been established since the Civil War and some of the most important during the present century. Most of them are provided for by statute rather than by constitutional provisions, and in keeping with the newer trend the heads are appointed by the governor rather than elected. The duties performed are, for the most part, line or primary services. Only a few are auxiliary. As the reorganization movement has progressed, the heads of some of the older departments have been made appointive. The line services are a reflection of the newer concept of the social and economic responsibility of government, characterized by the increased number and scope of services.

The Secretary of State. The office of secretary of state is a very old one, existing in all forty-eight states. The occupant is elected by popular vote in all states except Delaware, Maryland, New Jersey, New York, Pennsylvania, Texas, and Virginia, where he is appointed by the governor by and with the advice and consent of the senate. In Maine, New Hampshire, and Tennessee he is elected by the legislature. He is the custodian of the great seal of the state, carries on correspondence with other states and with the Federal government, and is commonly entrusted with certain duties in connection with legislation and elections. The powers of the office have come to be of such a miscellaneous nature that it may almost be described as a sort of scrap basket of governmental authority. When there has been some new service to be performed that did not logically fit into the duties of any other department it has been assigned to the secretary of state. On this very ground it is possible to argue both that the office should be retained and that it should be abolished, although the majority of students favor the latter alternative.

The Secretary of State of New Jersey in an address delivered some years ago enumerated some of the duties for the performance of which he is responsible. He is Clerk of the Court of Pardons and of the Court of Errors and Appeals, Register of the Prerogative Court, Trustee of the School Fund, and member of the Public Library Commission and of the Public Record Commission. All wills are filed in his office, and he issues commissions to all state officers. He compiles the acts of the legislature; publishes and distributes the election law, and issues election supplies to the county officers; and files certificates of incorporation and copies of the charters of foreign corporations doing business within the state. Also, petitions of candidates for gubernatorial nomination and for nominations for national offices are filed in his office. The regular reports of the secretaries of state in other jurisdictions (many of which are poorly prepared) bear eloquent testimony to the miscellaneous character of the duties of the office.

In some states, as in Iowa, Nevada, and Oregon, the secretary of state administers the licensing of motor vehicles; in others, as in Illinois and New York, this duty was formerly performed in this department. In Nevada and Pennsylvania trademarks and fictitious names must be registered with the secretary of state (or the secretary of the commonwealth, as he is called in those states officially designated as commonwealths). In Nevada he sells state publications — statutes and reports. Among the duties mentioned in the Florida report are those pertaining to elections, to the bonding of public officials, the custody and publication of laws, the custody and maintenance of public buildings, trademark registration, nonresident service of process, corporation charters, collection of capital stock tax, and membership on various boards and commissions. Seventy-two pages of this report are taken in listing all the notaries public in the state. In the Kansas report, 126 pages out of 153 are taken in reporting primary election returns; in addition the report lists numerous officers and all the post offices in the state. Certainly there is nothing impressive about a series of these reports; all the duties performed could be assigned to other appropriate departments or handled by the governor's office or the executive department.

SOME CHARACTERISTICS OF THE REORGANIZATION MOVEMENT

Reorganization, developing as it has over a period of approximately a quarter of a century in states in every section of the country with varying social, economic, and political backgrounds, has shown little tendency toward uniformity or standardization. This is as it should be, for one of the chief merits of the federal system is found in the opportunity which it offers to member states to adapt their institutions to their own conditions and to the desires and traditions of their people. Buck, the leading authority on the reorganization movement, found four distinct types: the integrated, the partially integrated, the fiscal-control, and the commission or plural-executive types. The integrated type, which is the one recommended in the Model State Constitution, is found in New York and Virginia, where constitutional changes made it possible.

The partially integrated type is found in the original Illinois plan, and also in California, Idaho, Kentucky (1936 plan), Ohio, Pennsylvania, Rhode Island, and Washington. In these states integration has been carried as far as possible without those constitutional changes which would be essential if complete integration were to be achieved.

In the fiscal-control type the governor is given the authority " to manage the affairs of the state, not through administrative integration, but through financial supervision." This type is found in Connecticut, Maine, North Carolina, South Dakota, and Wisconsin.[7] " Under the commission, or plural-executive type, the governor becomes one of several executives, although usually the dominating one. The constitutional elective officials — a half dozen — are made to share in the administration of many consolidated departments. This type resembles the commission form of government familiar to our cities." It is found in Indiana, and formerly existed in Colorado.

Two different procedures have been followed in making these reorganizations effective. The most desirable and the most difficult to use is constitutional amendment or revision. Many of the offices that need to be eliminated or put on an appointive basis are embalmed in the constitution. As we have seen, both amendment and revision are often difficult to achieve, and in some states well-nigh impossible. In these jurisdictions the only practical alternative is to leave the constitutional offices alone, and by statutory action accomplish as much as can be done within the framework provided by the constitution. It is usually possible to deprive the constitutional officers of any policy-making powers, thereby rendering them more or less innocuous.

The maps and charts accompanying this discussion will enable the reader to visualize the reorganization movement. These include, first, an outline map of the United States, indicating clearly the nationwide interest in the improvement of the administrative machinery of state government; second, a table of the administrative departments provided in the codes of representative states; and finally, two charts showing the administrative organization of two state governments, both from states that are generally conceded to be well governed, one of which has and the other of which has not adopted a code for the administrative reorganization of its government. Wisconsin illustrates the first type, Pennsylvania the second.

A glance at the map will indicate that states in every section of the country have adopted codes; many others have undertaken analyses of their administrative organization and procedures which have resulted in substantial improvement. The only observations justified by a study of the map are, first, that perhaps the greatest interest has been evidenced along the Atlantic seaboard; and second, that the

[7] This analysis follows Buck, *op. cit.*, pp. 28–33.

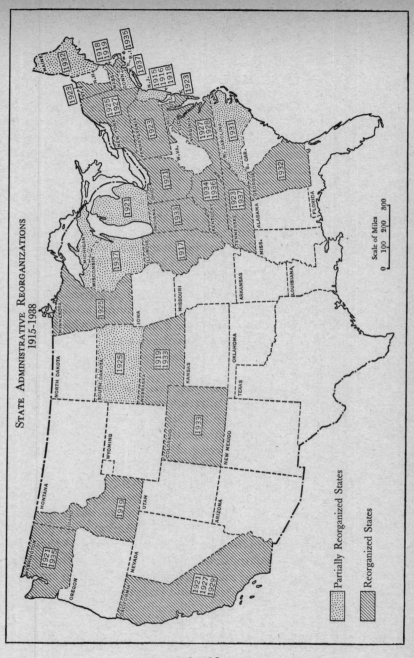

STATE ADMINISTRATIVE REORGANIZATIONS
1915-1938

Scale of Miles

0   100   200   300

Partially Reorganized States

Reorganized States

South has shown somewhat less interest in the movement than other sections of the country.

The table on page 418 shows the administrative departments and agencies established by the codes in certain reorganized states. The states are arranged in the chronological order in which their codes were adopted, and the effort has been made to carry across the table, on a single line, the names of those departments or agencies performing identical services. The table reveals, in the first place, that there are a number of fundamental problems of administration for which provision must be made in every state, regardless of variations in the details of its administrative structure. Thus every state has established a Department of Agriculture, a Department of Finance, and a Department of Labor.

In the second place, adoption of the reorganization principle does not, as noted above, require a dead level of uniformity in the administrative structure regardless of the special needs and problems of individual states. In Idaho and Pennsylvania, for instance, there is a Department of Mines. Such an administrative agency may be justified as a separate unit in states where the mining industry constitutes an important element in the economic life of the state; it would be foolish to provide for such a department in a state which had no important mining industry or mineral resources. Similarly Idaho has established a Department of Reclamation, in response to the needs of the people living in that section of the country, but such a department would be of little use in most other states. In some instances the promotion of immigration and development has been dignified by departmental status.

The table indicates, in the third place, a wide variety of terminology applied to the same or similar services. For instance, the department which supervises correctional institutions is variously designated as the Department of Institutions, the Department of Public Institutions, and the Department of Correction. In some states this service is not operated as a separate department, but as a bureau or division of the the Department of Public Welfare or of the attorney general's department. Similarly the Department of Conservation is designated as a Department of Forest and Waters in one state (where its activities are supplemented by separate commissions for fish and game), as a Department of Natural Resources in another, and as a Department of Conservation and Development in a third. The Department of Labor is variously styled as the Department of Industrial Relations, the Department of Labor and Statistics, and the

1917 Illinois	1921 Massachusetts	1921 California	1923 Pennsylvania	1925 Minnesota	1925 New York	1931 Maine
State *	Secretary of Commonwealth *	State *	Secretary of Commonwealth	State *	State *; Executive *	State
Finance	Corporations and Finance	Finance	Revenue	Administration and Finance *	Taxation and Finance	Finance
Auditor *	Auditor *		Auditor General *	Auditor *	Audit and Control	Audit
Treasurer *	Treasurer *	Treasurer *	Treasurer *	Treasurer	Treasurer	Treasurer
Agriculture	Agriculture	Agriculture	Agriculture	Agriculture, Dairy, and Food	Agriculture and Markets	
Labor	Labor and Industry [1]	Industrial Relations	Labor and Industry	Labor and Industry	Labor	Labor and Industry
Mines and Mining			Mines			
Public Works and Buildings	Public Works	Public Works	Highways	Highways	Public Works	Highways
Trade and Commerce			Commerce	Commerce		
Public Instruction *	Education	Education *	Public Instruction	Education; Rural Education	Education	Education
Registration and Education	Civil Service and Registration	Professional and Vocational Standards			Civil Service	
Purchase and Construction			Property and Supplies			
Conservation	Conservation	Natural Resources	Forests and Waters [2]	Conservation	Conservation	Forestry [3]
Public Welfare	Public Welfare	Social Welfare	Welfare, Public Assistance		Social Welfare	
Public Health	Public Health	Public Health	Health	Health	Health	Health and Welfare
Attorney General *	Law	Justice *	Justice	Attorney General *	Law *	Attorney General
	Public Safety		State Police			
	Banking and Insurance	Investments	Banking; Insurance	Board of Investments	Banking; Insurance	Banking; Insurance
	Mental Diseases				Mental Hygiene	
	Correction	Institutions Penology		Public Institutions	Correction	
	Public Utilities		Public Utilities		Public Service	Public Utilities
	Metropolitan District Commission			Drainage and Waters		
		Military Affairs	Military Affairs			Adjutant General

* Indicates elective head.   [1] There is also a Department of Industrial Accidents.
[2] In addition there are a separate Fish Commission and a separate Game Commission.
[3] In addition there are a Commissioner of Sea and Shore Fisheries and a Commissioner of Inland Fish and Game.

Department of Labor and Industry. The student of public administration must therefore look behind the name assigned to a given administrative agency in order to determine the fundamental administrative problem with which it deals.

Finally, it appears that in the years since the reorganization movement began, there has been a tendency to increase the number of departments provided for by the codes. This may be attributed to two factors. Illinois in 1917 started with nine departments and shortly found it desirable to increase this number by two. Idaho and Nebraska likewise established a minimum number, which came to be regarded as inadequate and as requiring the grouping of unrelated services under the same department. The unwisdom of this procedure was recognized in Maryland, which set up nineteen departments, including several commissions; in New York, Pennsylvania, and Virginia, with eighteen departments each; in Massachusetts with sixteen; and in Minnesota with thirteen. While the centralization of responsibility and control is highly desirable, there is no defense for carrying the principle so far as to require the grouping of unrelated services — as in Indiana, where in 1934, although no code was adopted, the Department of Health was made a division in the Department of Commerce and Industry. These later reorganizations have, furthermore, occurred in the larger and more populous states, where in the very nature of things a larger number of administrative agencies can easily be justified.

This movement for administrative reorganization was the most important single aspect of state government for nearly two decades, when the move to reorganize local government came to the fore. Both movements were practically suspended during the war period. The influence of the reorganization movement has been felt in every section of the country and in every state. While slightly more than half of the states have adopted codes, there is not a single state which has not during the last quarter of a century given thought to reorganization and to the functioning of its administrative machinery. Numerous surveys have been made and reports published; [8]

8 Among these are: CALIFORNIA: *Final Report* of the Committee on State Organization (San Francisco, 1941). KANSAS: Davis, Done E., *An Investigation of the Governmental Agencies of the State of Kansas* (Kansas State Teachers College Bulletin, Emporia, 1943). LOUISIANA: Hyneman, Charles S., " Political and Administrative Reform in the 1940 Legislature," *Louisiana Law Review*, November, 1940, pp. 1–54, and Mecklin, F. J., and Hyneman, *The Administrative System of the State of Louisiana* (Louisiana State University, Bureau of Government Research, 1940). MINNESOTA: *Report* from the Joint Senate and House Committee Covering the Acts and Activities of the Various Governmental Departments and Agencies of the State of Minnesota (St. Paul, 1940). MONTANA: Ford, Governor

although in many cases no thorough program of reorganization has been enacted, the influence of this work has been felt in numerous amendments to existing laws and in improvements and administrative procedure.

Evaluation of the Reorganization Plan. The reorganization movement seemed on the whole so sound that for years few persons raised any serious question regarding it. Professor Coker wrote, not long after the movement started, what was long considered the best critical comment. His observations were unfortunately based on one of the least satisfactory of the codes that have been adopted. Most of his objections related to matters of detail in this particular state (Ohio) and, as applied to this state, were in general well justified. His objections of a fundamental character were two:

> First, in the matter of the single headed administrative department, is it true that for all such departments unity of power and responsibility is of more importance than continuity of policy and the maintenance of a relation of mutual respect and confidence between head and staff? In the recent Ohio reorganization, have we not in too many instances sacrificed good of the latter sort in the effort to gain advantages of the former sort?
>
> Secondly, are we not in danger of carrying too far the idea that popular control is advanced chiefly by placing vast powers in one elected officer, with the expectation that this officer will feel responsibility so certainly fixed upon him that he will be more sensitive to public opinion than he would be if he possessed a narrower allotment of power? Are we not overlooking other equally potent incentives to good service — other incentives which may be weakened by this centralization of power? Are we not greatly exaggerating the ability of public opinion — even an intelligent and alert public opinion — to keep constant observance upon its representatives and to pass satisfactory judgment upon them periodically? In the last question there is reference to what may be a fundamental error of the advocates of the principles which we are examining — namely, the assumption that popular control over executive officers is applied chiefly through the election and rejection of these officers at the polls.[9]

While the author asserts that he is a strong believer in the short ballot principle, he asserts that he is " ready to part company with the short ballot advocates if they contend that, in order to be consistent, we must place the entire control of our administration in the hands of one or a few officials changeable every two or four years."

Sam C., *Reorganization Report,* submitted to the Twenty-eighth Legislative Assembly (Helena, 1943). NORTH DAKOTA: series of articles in the *North Dakota Taxpayer,* beginning March, 1943. VIRGINIA: Commission to Study the Reorganization of Certain State Departments and Agencies, *Report* (House Document No. 4, Richmond, 1941).

9 Coker, Francis W., " Dogmas of Administrative Reform," *American Political Science Review,* August, 1922, p. 409.

Subsequently the late J. Mark Jacobson questioned not so much the principles upon which the reorganization movement is based, as the possibility of measuring accurately its accomplishments, at least by the statistical method. He contended, fairly enough, that one's judgments regarding the effects of the movement center around the answers to two questions: " Has the new mechanism of administration produced increased economy or efficiency? And has this movement brought better men into public life? " He found it difficult to get any satisfactory answer to the first question by the use of statistical methods, and he concluded that the same methods were even less fruitful in deciding what, if any, economies in state expenditures are desirable. It is obviously impossible to compare exactly the capabilities of the men who held office before the adoption of the codes with those appointed to similar positions after their adoption.[10]

In recent years, after more than two decades of experience with reorganization, there has been a growing feeling that the results should be carefully studied and critically appraised. In spite of extensive and obviously beneficial results in many states, some writers have begun to complain because the scheme is not perfect and because it has not accomplished more. They apparently forget that few plans do achieve perfection and that all are subject in their operation to human limitations. They complain because so few states have achieved a complete administrative integration, forgetting that there are other purposes for which the amendment of state constitutions is difficult. Because the people of some states still choose to elect incompetent governors, these critics blame reorganization. They quibble because somebody says more agencies were abolished in a given state than somebody else, and one has even gone so far as to suggest that an acceptance of the principles or reorganization involves an adventure into theology.[11] The best answer to these argu-

[10] Jacobson, J. Mark, " Evaluating State Administrative Structure — the Fallacy of the Statistical Method," *American Political Science Review*, November, 1928, pp. 928–935; Graves, W. Brooke, " Criteria for Evaluating the Effectiveness of State Administration," *ibid.*, June, 1938, pp. 508–514.

[11] See Hyneman, Charles S., " Administrative Reorganization — an Adventure into Science and Theology " (a review of Buck's book) , *Journal of Politics*, February, 1939, pp. 62–75, and " Executive Centralization in Administration," *Proceedings*, Southern Political Science Association, 1937, pp. 13–16. For other critical comments in addition to the Coker article, see Edwards, William H., " The Position of the Governor in Recent Administrative Reorganizations in the States," in *Abstracts of Doctor's Dissertations*, pp. 61–70 (Ohio State University Press, 1937) , " A Factual Summary of State Administrative Reorganization," *Southwestern Social Science Quarterly*, June, 1938, pp. 53–67, and " Has State Reorganization Succeeded? " *State Government*, October, 1938, pp. 183–184, 192–193; Spicer, George W., " From Political Chief to Administrative Chief," in Haines, Charles G., and Dimock, Marshall E., Eds., *Essays on the Law and Practice of Governmental*

ments is that nobody, probably the critics themselves least of all, wants to go back to things as they were before reorganization changed, to some extent, the administrative picture in the states.

This is not to say that constructive criticism of the plan is undesirable. The administrative problem in the states has not been solved. It has proved difficult to get the states reorganized and equally difficult to keep them so. New York has attempted to solve this latter problem by a constitutional provision which reads as follows:

Subject to the limitations contained in this constitution, the legislature may from time to time assign by law new powers and functions to departments, officers, boards or commissions, and increase, modify or diminish their powers and functions. No new departments shall be created hereafter, but this shall not prevent the legislature from creating temporary commissions for special purposes and nothing contained in this article shall prevent the legislature from reducing the number of departments as provided for in this article, by consolidation or otherwise. — Article V, Section 3.

While a constitutional establishment of departments with such a limitation tends to prevent the establishment of miscellaneous agencies outside the limits of the reorganization plan, it is inflexible and may in time cause a grouping of unrelated services within departments. Careful attention will have to be given to this problem, as well as to the larger one of making the reorganizations more complete, and more effective in accomplishing the objectives of improved administration in the states. Continuous study and repeated surveys are necessary in each state if the administrative structure is to be adapted to the needs of the people and at the same time to be maintained on sound basis.

FORMS OF CONTROL OVER ADMINISTRATION

Many persons are apt to assume that a governor or department head endowed with proper authority is more or less a free agent in the making of decisions with regard to public questions. This is in practice far from true. Administrative officers are restricted in their freedom of decision by a variety of powerful and often dominating influences, such as public sentiment, pressure groups, political considerations, the possibility of judicial review or of legislative action,

---

Administration, pp. 94–124 (Johns Hopkins Press, 1935); Walker, Harvey, "Theory and Practice in State Administrative Reorganization," *National Municipal Review,* April, 1930, pp. 249–254, and *Public Administration in the United States,* pp. 79–81 (Farrar and Rinehart, New York, 1937).

the findings of scientific research, reports of the planning staff, and the views of superior officers in the administrative structure. These influences are deserving of brief comment.

An administrative officer must be guided in the use of the powers of his office by knowing indications of public sentiment regarding the subject at hand, or by reasonable conjectures as to the type of public reaction likely to be elicited by various methods of administrative procedure. A wise executive will refrain from arousing public criticism by the use of one procedure when such criticism might be avoided and the same ends obtained by using another. The newspapers frequently report illustrations in point. When the Pennsylvania Liquor Control Board set up the state stores system in January, 1934, it published a price list. There was an immediate and powerful sentiment that the prices were too high, whereupon the Board undertook immediate steps to meet these objections by reductions and by the listing of less expensive brands. In Iowa in 1930 the Department of Agriculture attempted to enforce a state law providing for the tuberculin testing of dairy cows. The farmers met the veterinarians with clubs and pitchforks because the Department had failed to cultivate a spirit of cooperation among them by a suitable campaign of education, such as had been used successfully in many other states, as to the value and necessity of such testing. An administrative officer must have enough of the sense of a politician to know when and how he can use the powers vested in him effectively without arousing public indignation and resentment.

Pressure groups often exert a powerful influence on administration. Representatives of citizen groups may bring pressure in the public interest; the same is not so often true of professional lobbyists, who seek not only to influence the content of legislation while it is under consideration in the legislature, but to bend the law to suit their purposes after it has been enacted. It is notoriously true that public service commissions are very frequently dominated by the very interests they are supposed to regulate and control. Instances are not lacking in which the agents of those subject to regulation have moved in and assumed control of the whole regulatory program. The effective resistance of such pressures by the administrator is not easy; it requires courage and statesmanship of a high order.

Little need be said on the subject of political influence as affecting administrative officers; illustrations of its use are too numerous and apparent, and often in direct conflict with the public interest. Political influence in the assessment of taxes, in police administration, in building inspection and the supervision of work done under government contract, in the enforcement of labor laws and election laws, and in other fields is familiar to all.

The legislative influence is manifold. With the exception of such provisions as are incorporated in the constitution, all the powers and duties of an administrative officer, as well as the organization of agencies to perform such activities, are provided for in statutes passed by the legislature. An executive must remember that an unwise or tactless use of the powers entrusted to him may lead to further legislation limiting his powers and making his work more difficult and perhaps less effective. Thus the same governmental authority that created the office and conferred certain powers upon it may, at its discretion, modify those powers or rescind its earlier action, and it may determine the means and methods of supervising the office. Furthermore, the legislature can exercise control over administration through its control over the purse. In fact, there is no more certain way of curtailing administrative activity or of impairing its efficiency than by reducing the appropriation for a service or striking out the appropriation altogether.[12]

The possibility of judicial review of the acts of an administrative officer is ever present. He must be aware that the adoption of procedures which ignore or violate the rights of citizens or groups will lead to judicial proceedings designed to attack either the constitutionality of the law or the legality of his procedure under it. In some cases such a test may be desirable from the administrative point of view, for the purpose of clarifying the powers of the officer; in others it may be unavoidable if the officer is to perform the duties required of him under the statute.

Still another control flows from the results of scientific research and the work of the planning staff. In the field of health and safety, for instance, swimming pools may be closed when an epidemic of infantile paralysis threatens, and campaigns for vaccination or immunization may be resorted to in order to combat other diseases. In such cases the findings of research take precedence over other possible controls which might conceivably influence the course of administrative action. In similar manner, the recommendations of the planning staff may indicate so clearly the proper course of action to be followed in a given situation that the administrator could not reasonably attempt to follow any other.

[12] See Fairlie, John A., " The Legislature and the Administration," *American Political Science Review*, April, 1936, pp. 241-256, and June, 1936, pp. 494-506.

Finally, administrative control over administrative officers is, or should be, an important influence. Every officer and employee should know to whom he is responsible, in what way, and to what extent, in a direct line of administrative responsibility. If he does not abide by the instructions of his superior officer or if he fails to develop his policies in harmony with those of the administration of which he is a part, he may find himself looking for another job. Executive control may extend to independent officers and may even be exercised for the purpose of harassing such officers. Some illustrations of this character came to light a few years ago in the state of Washington; they are partly administrative and partly political in character, but they will serve to indicate the possibilities of the use of the investigatory power of the governor as a coercive instrument:

The office of one elected official, who employs ten persons and handles but little money, was recently investigated for over a month, at a cost to him of almost $300. Shortly afterward the official was notified by the Department of Efficiency, acting in the capacity of budgetary control office, that he would have to reduce his rate of expenditure or overdraw his appropriation for salaries by about $300 — almost the exact amount of the cost of the investigation. The office of another elected official has been the subject of several investigations in the past seven years (during which Governor Hartley had been in office). One of the most recent took eleven months, continuously employing three or more men at a cost of about $750 a month. The enormous bill incurred was evaded by the official, who refused to pay it because he had no appropriation for doing so. In this particular instance he seems to have been more fortunate than usual. A third, semi-independent office was recently investigated at a cost of $50, which amount was deducted from the salaries of its three already underpaid employees.[13]

Space does not permit further illustration of the manner in which these various forms of control operate, but it is clear that an officer faced with a decision on an important question of policy must take into account a large number of factors of a practical nature in addition to the constitutional and legal limits of his power as defined by statutes, court decisions, rulings of the attorney general, et cetera.

RELATIVE MERITS OF BOARDS AND INDIVIDUAL COMMISSIONERS

In the forty or fifty years prior to 1917, during which state functions and administrative machinery were both greatly expanded, the commission form of organization prevailed. The idea of adminis-

[13] Roche, George S., " Executive Control of Independent Officials in Washington," *National Municipal Review*, July, 1932, p. 466.

trative responsibility made little progress, and the people were still fearful of the concentration of authority. Whenever a new activity was undertaken, a new board or commission was established to administer it. The board form was used not only because of an inherited and deepseated fear of a strong executive, but because it seemed appropriate for the performance of duties of a quasi-legislative or quasi-judicial character, involving the exercise of wide discretionary powers. Sometimes it seemed desirable to have a variety of interests represented, or to reduce by this means the influence of party politics in the administration of the service. This practice not only led to the multiplication of administrative agencies, but revealed in time a serious structural weakness in the board or commission as an administrative mechanism.

While the board was effective for purposes of deliberation and in formulation of rules and regulations, it was almost wholly unsuited to the task of administration. Responsibility was not and could not be fixed. Most of the boards were cursed with a generous sprinkling of ex-officio members who lacked either the time or the inclination to give much attention to board work or to devote much energy to it. Usually they sent a substitute, if indeed they were represented at all. With the advent of the reorganization movement, the pendulum swung in the opposite direction. Single commissioners, secretaries, or department heads were substituted for administrative boards and commissions, except in those cases where the latter were established by constitutional provision and had to be retained. This new device was often less satisfactory in the performance of rule-making activities; a single commissioner was not an adequate substitute for a board in matters requiring deliberation.

Two compromise measures have been widely adopted by the states, to meet the objections to the use of boards and of single commissioners. These are represented by the introduction of advisory boards into the departmental type of organization and the introduction of the executive secretary into the commission type. Under the first plan the department head, instead of depending upon his bureau chiefs as a council of advisers, has the aid of an advisory board or commission attached to the department. For example, the Department of Health in Pennsylvania is a highly centralized administrative agency; yet there is in addition, attached to the Department, an Advisory Health Board, the members of which are appointed by the governor. They serve without compensation for a term of four years and meet quarterly. Actual expenses incurred in attendance at meetings are returned to them. The Board is authorized to adopt rules and regulations on questions pertaining to public health; these are enforced by the Department officials on the same basis as laws enacted by the legislature.

The second type of organization is illustrated in Wisconsin, which has so far failed to adopt and retain an administrative code similar to those of other progressive states, preferring rather to continue with an antiquated form of administrative organization. This state has had the persistence and ingenuity to make it function effectively. Commission control over important functions is still maintained, but each of the boards has hired a competent person to serve during the pleasure of the board as its administrative officer and agent. Thus the Executive Secretary of the State Board of Health performs many of the duties of, and exercises much the same administrative supervision and control as, the Secretary of Health in Pennsylvania or the Commissioner of Health in New York. By the adoption of one or the other of these devices many states have made a definite effort to obtain the benefits of both types of organization without subjecting themselves to the defects most commonly associated with either of them.

In an article published in 1922, already referred to, Professor Mathews ably summarized this whole problem:

After the regrouping of the scattered administrative agencies into a few major departments has been made, it still remains to be determined what form of internal organization is desirable for these departments. Should we have at the head of the department a board, a commission, or a single commissioner? The prevalence of boards and commissions in the past has been one of the main causes of the disintegration of the administration and the diffusion of responsibility. They have amply demonstrated their incapacity for administrative work. The tendency in reorganization plans, whether proposed or in operation, has been very decidedly away from the board or commission and in the direction of the single commissioner. It is recognized, however, that for the performance of advisory, quasi-legislative, and quasi-judicial functions several heads are usually better than one, and in these cases, therefore, some concession may be made to the board or commission type of organization. Thus, in Illinois, all of the nine departments created by the Civil Administrative Code are under single commissioners, called directors; but provision is made for certain commissions, such as the tax commission and the industrial commission, which are nominally placed in the appropriate departments. Provision is also made for certain advisory and non-executive boards in some of the departments. The Illinois plan is faulty on account of the loose and ill-defined relation between the commissions and the departments in which they are nominally placed. In departments where there are quasi-legislative and quasi-judicial functions to be performed, associate directors should be provided to act with the head director for the exercise of such functions, but the head director should be solely responsible for the administrative work.[14]

The condition which Professor Mathews describes in Illinois has developed in numerous other states; this situation is met better by the plan used in New Jersey and Wisconsin than in most of the states reorganized under the code plan.

Professor John M. Pfiffner has attempted to crystallize in the following outline the general principles which may aid in determining whether a given activity should be placed under a board or a single head: [15]

Board	*Single Head*
1. Seemingly irreconciliable difference of community opinion.	1. Quick decisions and quick action essential.
2. Technology not yet developed to point of complete lay acceptance.	2. Well-developed technology commands lay confidence.
3. Deliberation necessary.	3. Discipline necessary.
a. Policy determination.	4. Almost entirely routine.
b. Quasi-legislative and quasi-judicial.	

Administrative Legislation. More and more is being said and written about the enormous growth of administrative legislation in recent years. Clearly, only a portion of law is contained in the statutes, which usually include indirectly much more than appears on the face of the bill enacted by the legislature. " The law is what the citizen meets as the end result of governmental activity — the sum total of statutes and regulations. This means that ' rules and regulations ' issued by administrative agencies may actually include more important ' legislation,' in many cases, than the law which the legislature passes." [16]

Among the advantages urged for such legislation are: economy of legislative time; availability of expert knowledge; absence of partisan conflicts concerning details; flexibility; possibility of drafting

[14] Mathews, John M., "State Administrative Reorganization," *American Political Science Review*, August, 1922, pp. 393–394. For an excellent treatment of central administrative controls by a plural executive in Michigan, see Benson, George C. S., and Litchfield, Edward H., *The State Administrative Board in Michigan* (University of Michigan Press, 1938).

[15] Pfiffner, John M., *Public Administration*, p. 72 (Ronald Press, New York, 1935). See the whole of his chapter 4, and Chapter 7 in Willoughby, W. F., *Principles of Public Administration* (Johns Hopkins Press, 1927).

[16] Kansas Legislative Council, *Legislative Functions of Administrative Agencies,* p. vii (Topeka, 1938).

under more advantageous circumstances; and completion and clarification of statutory law, with consequent avoidance of unnecessary litigation. Some of the disadvantages that have been urged are: that there may be such a scattering of sublegislative functions that inconsistencies in policy will develop; that inadequate publicity may be given either before or after the promulgation of administrative legislation; that the legislature may surrender too many of its legislative powers; and that standards may be improperly or inadequately developed. As circumstances have tended greatly to increase the volume of such legislation, the subject has become more and more a matter of controversy.[17]

CURRENT PROBLEMS AND TENDENCIES

From the foregoing discussion, certain tendencies in the field of state administration during the last few years are apparent — notably the tendencies to centralize responsibility and set up suitable agencies for financial supervision and control. A few years ago Professor White presented a careful analysis of the factors involved in these changes, including the upward trend of governors' salaries and of contingent funds under the control of the governor, the increased personnel of the governor's office, the increased powers of the governor in general financial and personnel management, the spread of the movement for state budget systems, the tendency to establish a central control over printing, and systems of centralized purchasing.[18] In his conclusions, he finds " a striking alteration in the framework of state administration " over the period from 1910 to 1930, " the key to which is the expanding power of the chief executive as general manager of state business." He concludes:

. . . In 1910 a typical state agency or institution prepared its own estimates, submitted them directly to the appropriations committee, ultimately received an independent appropriation, and spent its funds without supervision other than that provided by the auditor. Its head may or may not have been appointed by the governor in the first instance; in any case he had little effective connection with the chief executive in the ordinary course of affairs.

17 *Ibid.*, p. ix; for some recent comments, see Ray, Joseph M., " Delegation of Power to State Administrative Agencies in Texas," *Texas Law Review*, December, 1937, pp. 20–46; Stephan, Albert E., " The Extent to Which Fact-Finding Boards Should Be Bound by Rules of Evidence," *Oregon Law Review*, April, 1939, pp. 229–249; and Witte, Edwin E., " A Break for the Citizen," *State Government*, April, 1936, pp. 73–75, in which it is urged that state governments should establish more orderly procedure in the making and publication of administrative orders.

18 White, *op. cit.*, Chapter 14, on state management trends.

Now by contrast a typical administrative agency finds its estimates scrutinized and often reduced by a budget officer before presentation to the legislature; and usually the only estimates which the legislature sees are those presented by the chief executive in the approved budget. After an appropriation has been made by the legislative body, it is subject to various conditions and limitations — the purchase of materials is performed by a central purchasing office, the recruiting of personnel, its classification and rate of pay is fixed by another agency outside the department, its reports are submitted for approval before printing to still another agency; and in some jurisdictions any and all administrative operations may be called into question to ascertain whether they are " fair, just, and reasonable." [19]

These significant changes have not taken place without creating certain problems. Friction and misunderstanding between operating departments and the control agencies sometimes develop, the departments complaining that they cannot get the right kind of supplies or personnel or that they cannot get them promptly. If there is any will to do so, administrative difficulties of this type can usually be smoothed out. Again, there is the difficulty which arises from the fact that the governor, who is chief administrator, is also a politician — that he holds his office by virtue of his success at the polls and that he is the titular head of his party in the state. As Professor White says, " their managerial duties have to be construed against a traditional background which has by no means grown less significant." All the governors, at the time of their election, must be successful politicians; some of them may become competent administrators. The same authority suggests that " perhaps the most important of the tendencies of the next decade will be that which determines whether the governor is to become primarily an administrator, freed in part at least from the embarrassments of his political inheritance, or whether he is to become a political leader, leaving to another the functions of general manager."

The Minnesota Plan. The primary purpose of the reorganization movement has been to centralize administrative responsibility, eliminate overlapping and duplication of governmental services, and make possible a better integration of those services. It has often been assumed that the principle of the executive budget was an essential part of the reorganization plan although, as Professor Walker pointed out more than a decade ago, budgeting began before the reorganization movement was started and budgeting is practiced now in all states, including those which have not been reorganized as well as

[19] *Ibid.*, pp. 207–208. Stafford, Paul T., " The New Amateur in Public Administration," *American Political Science Review*, April, 1935, pp. 257–269, stresses the same point.

those which have.[20] Where reorganization has been accomplished, financial control has not always been effective. Reorganization has helped, but it has not wholly solved the problem. Consequently, further experiments are now being carried on in a number of states, notably in Minnesota.

The Minnesota reorganization act, in force from 1925 to 1939, provided for a Department of Administration and Finance, similar to that under the Massachusetts Act of 1919, headed by three gubernatorial appointees known as the State Comptroller, the State Budget Commissioner, and the State Purchasing Agent. The Comptroller was responsible for the appointment of the Public Examiner. The law gave to these three men complete authority over all state expenditures, both as to pre-audit, through the Budget Commissioner and Comptroller, and post-audit, through the Public Examiner. The State Auditor, although a constitutional officer, was left without power, in the position of an exalted bookkeeper. The act of 1939 abolished the Commission of Administration and Finance as such, and provided for an independent Public Examiner appointed by the Governor; gave to the State Auditor all of the Comptroller's rights of pre-audit; and created a Commissioner of Administration to act in the dual capacity of Commissioner of the Budget and State Purchasing Agent. Under the original reorganization act departments had from time to time exceeded their appropriations; in order to remedy this situation, the State Auditor reported that:

The Legislature authorized the Commissioner of Administration as State Purchasing Agent, first, to centralize all purchasing for all purposes and for all departments in one agency, and restricted the activities of that agency by providing, among other things, for open, advertised and competitive bids for all purchases aggregating more than $500.

Further restrictions were made by authorizing the Commissioner of Administration, as Budget Officer, to establish a quarterly allotment system. Briefly, the Commissioner and the department head discuss departmental needs for any particular quarter. . . . Having arrived at a conclusion, the Commissioner, as Budget Officer, releases for the use of the department certain sums of money for specified items; the control relative to allotments being the legislative appropriation by departments for the current fiscal year.

The Commissioner of Administration also, if he be of the opinion that current revenues are insufficient for appropriation needs, may curtail his allotments in such a degree as he deems advisable. In other words, even though appropriations are made for a department, they are not available as

[20] Walker, Harvey, address at the Institute of Public Affairs, University of Virginia, August 12, 1930.

a total to the department unless the Commissioner believes funds may be available through current revenues, nor are they available in whole or in part, only and excepting as he directs quarterly allotments.[21]

There is nothing particularly new about this procedure, as will be clearly evident in a later chapter, but it indicates an important trend toward greater financial responsibility and control. Here is a picture of a reorganized state further reorganized to accomplish the objectives of the code movement; it also illustrates the fact that the development of sound methods of fiscal control is a continuous process, and is likely to be accomplished only after prolonged effort over a period of years. The office of the commissioner of administration offers promising possibilities of development along the lines of an office of state manager. Such an officer would relieve the governor of the responsibility of personally performing many administrative duties, as the city manager relieves the mayor under a council-manager form of government. At the same time, the governor would be able to devote himself to the tasks of political leadership and policy determination, as the mayor is supposed to do under the council-manager organization.

New Emphases in Public Administration. Several important changes in emphasis in public administration seem now to be in progress. In the early days administration dealt largely with material things — the building of roads and bridges, canals, and public buildings; this was an era during which immigration was encouraged and a major portion of a continent was being opened up and developed. Then the emphasis shifted to money, to business and accounting methods, budgetary control, et cetera. Now we can observe what appears to be another shift in emphasis. " The public administrator is now concerned not chiefly with materials, not chiefly with money, but principally and predominantly with men — not merely the men he used to produce, assemble, and fabricate the materials that went into physical plant; not merely the men from whose incomes he took toll in taxes to pay for building and operating his structure — but men as human beings." Louis Brownlow, author of this statement, continues:

21 King, Stafford, " Financial Reorganization in Minnesota," in a bulletin of the National Association of State Auditors, Comptrollers and Treasurers, February, 1940. See also Short, Lloyd M., " Minnesota Brings Her Government Up-to-date," *State Government*, August, 1939, pp. 137–138, 148–149; Stassen, Harold E., " Managing Minnesota," *National Municipal Review*, July, 1939, pp. 495–498, 508, and " Minnesota Points the Way," *ibid.*, January, 1941, pp. 4–7, 21; Short, Lloyd M., and Teller, Carl W., *The Minnesota Commission of Administration and Finance, 1925–1939* (University of Minnesota Press, 1942) .

. . . The new task of the public administrator is to consider not only how much of the income of this man and that can be brought into the public treasury in taxes; but whether this man has any income at all, and whether it is sufficient to maintain him and his family in the enjoyment of that standard of living which we still like to call the American standard.

We have material — plenty of it; some say too much and say that we must restrict and reduce the production of materials. We have money — plenty of it; some say too much and that we must restrict and reduce its amount, especially when we measure its amount in terms of debts. We have men — plenty of them; but are we willing yet to say too many? Certainly we have millions of men without incomes. We have millions of men who depend today for food and clothing and shelter upon the extraordinary efforts of government, which in this respect ignores the process of budget-balancing, to save their lives. In the midst of plenty we are hungry, cold, and roofless.

We are determined, I think . . . to concentrate all our efforts on redressing this balance and striving to establish an equilibrium of production and distribution which will restore . . . that ideal which we know as the American standard of living. Differ as we may with respect to the means and methods, we have come to be all but unanimous in the conviction that the principal agency through which this equilibrium may be established is that of government. . . .

This puts the job squarely up to the public administrator. . . . At the very beginning of the crisis, the whole business of relief of the unemployed was put squarely on the door-step of the local unit of government. . . . Traditionally, it was the business of private enterprise to furnish jobs for workers, but as the depression deepened it became a task for local, and then for state, and then for Federal government. . . .

The new task of the public administrator above all else, then, is to concern himself with human relations, with human values, with those deeper economic, social, and spiritual needs of the human beings whose government, in its administrative branch, he represents.[22]

In another respect the emphasis in the organization and administration of government is changing — changing from control, from policing, from law enforcement per se, to an ideal of service. Another student of public administration has well developed this thought:

. . . On every hand, government is being forced to assume a wide variety of service functions because of the increasing helplessness of the individual in a bewilderingly complex mechanical age. If the economic and social structure of the group is to be preserved, no longer can the individual be left alone to fend for himself, appealing for public aid only in the last resort and then under public stigma. Incontrovertible evidence from all sides attests that the individual effort is alone unable to secure and main-

22 Brownlow, Louis, " The New Rôle of the Public Administrator," *National Municipal Review,* May, 1934, pp. 248–251.

tain a decent standard of living for all, and that collective measures must be undertaken on a wide scale.[23]

Thus this author arrives, by a different route, at the same point of emphasis on human values that was stated so clearly by Mr. Brownlow.

Again, there is a growing tendency to recognize the highly technical nature of government work and to regard it as professional service. Over the years the administrative reorganization movement, the spread of the short ballot principle, and the idea of the civil service have all given evidence of a growing belief that the old methods of selecting public officers were quite unsatisfactory. Civil service certainly emphasizes the idea of permanent tenure. Many now realize that more is needed than improved tenure conditions; public servants whose chief qualifications are political cannot possibly render satisfactory service in modern government. Since we had not developed a professional group of trained administrators, it was necessary during the depression to rely upon "amateur administrators" — many of them academic persons who were drafted into the public service. In the meantime the universities and colleges of the country have been emphasizing civic training and training for the public service as never before. Out of this may come the new American civil servant — a person well trained and well qualified who will, as in England, devote himself through the years to the service of his government and its people.

SELECTED REFERENCES

Benson, George C. S., and Litchfield, Edward H., *The State Administrative Board in Michigan* (University of Michigan Press, 1938).

Buck, A. E., *The Reorganization of State Governments in the United States* (Columbia University Press, 1938).

Bureau of Government, *A Manual of State Administrative Organization in Michigan* (University of Michigan, 1940).

California Supervisor of Documents, *California State Government*, Vol. I, *An Outline of Its Administrative Organization, 1850 to 1936;* Vol. II, *The Independent Agencies, 1850 to 1939* (Sacramento, 1940).

Carleton, Robert L., *Reorganization and Consolidation of State Administration in Louisiana* (University of Louisiana Press, 1937).

Coleman, James K., *State Administration in South Carolina* (Columbia University Press, 1935).

Dorr, Harold M., *Administrative Organization of State Government in Michigan* (Bureau of Government, University of Michigan, 1936).

23 Stafford, *op. cit.*, p. 263.

Dorr, Harold M., *Administrative Reorganization, 1936–1937* (Bureau of Government, University of Michigan, 1938).

Fesler, James W., *The Independence of State Regulatory Agencies* (Public Administration Service, Chicago, 1942).

Gardner, O. Max, *Public Papers and Letters of, as Governor of North Carolina, 1929–1933* (Council of State, Raleigh, 1937).

Hart, James, *An Introduction to Administrative Law, with Selected Cases* (Crofts, New York, 1940).

Hurt, Elsey, *Organizational Changes in California State Government* (Bureau of Public Administration, University of California, 1939).

Illinois Constitutional Convention, *Bulletin* No. 9, " The Executive Department " (Springfield, 1919).

Isseks, Morris S., *History of State Administrative Agencies in Oregon, 1843–1937* (Oregon State Planning Board, Portland, 1939).

Kansas Legislative Council, *Legislative Functions of Administrative Agencies* (Topeka, 1938).

——, *State Administrative Organization* (Topeka, 1937).

Martin, Roscoe C., *The Growth of State Administration in Alabama* (University of Alabama, Bureau of Public Administration, 1942).

Mathews, John M., *Principles of American State Administration* (Appleton, New York, 1917).

Michigan Commission on Reform and Modernization of Government, *Documents and Proceedings* (Lansing, 1938).

New York State Constitutional Convention Commission, *Problems Relating to Executive Administration and Powers* (Albany, 1938).

——, *State and Local Government in New York* (Albany, 1938).

Oregon State Planning Board, *History of State Administrative Agencies in Oregon, 1843–1937* (Portland, 1939).

Patterson, Robert F., *The Office of Lieutenant-Governor in the United States* (University of South Dakota, Bureau of Government Research, 1944).

Pennsylvania Joint State Government Commission, *A Survey of the Government of Pennsylvania* (Harrisburg, 1941).

Pfiffner, John M., *Public Administration* (Ronald Press, New York, 1935).

Porter, Kirk H., *State Administration* (Crofts, New York, 1938).

Putney, Bryant, *Reorganization of State Government* (Editorial Research Reports, Washington, May 23, 1938).

Short, Lloyd M., and Tiller, Carl W., *The Minnesota Commission of Administration and Finance, 1925–1939: An Administrative History* (University of Minnesota Press, 1942).

Smith, Dick, *A Layman's Guide to the Texas State Administrative Agencies* (University of Texas, Bureau of Municipal Research, 1945).

Stafford, Paul T., *State Welfare Administration in New Jersey* (Department of Institutions and Agencies, Trenton, 1934).

Taylor, Clyde W., *Public Administration in Arizona* (Scribner's, New York, 1942).

Thomas, Jack E., *Administrative Reorganization of the State Government* (Bureau of Public Administration, University of California, 1939).

University of Denver, *Reorganizing State Government in Colorado* (Denver, 1939).

Virginia State Chamber of Commerce, *Reorganization of Executive Agencies in Virginia* (Richmond, 1940).

Walker, Harvey, *Public Administration in the United States* (Farrar and Rinehart, New York, 1937).

Weiner, Grace, *Administrative Reorganization of State Governments: A Bibliography* (Joint Reference Library, Chicago, 1941).

White, Leonard D., *Introduction to the Study of Public Administration*, Revised Edition (Macmillan, New York, 1939).

——, *Trends in Public Administration* (McGraw-Hill, New York, 1933).

Willoughby, W. F., *Principles of Public Administration* (Johns Hopkins Press, Baltimore, 1927).

Wooddy, Carroll H., "The Growth of Governmental Functions," *Recent Social Trends*, pp. 1274–1330 (McGraw-Hill, New York, 1933).

———

De Lancy, Frances P., "West Virginia Explores Judicial and Administrative Reforms," *State Government*, May, 1940, pp. 87, 96–97.

Graves, W. Brooke, "Criteria for Evaluating the Effectiveness of State Administration," *American Political Science Review*, June, 1938, pp. 508–514.

Hyneman, Charles S., "Political and Administrative Reform in the 1940 Legislature," *Louisiana Law Review*, November, 1940, pp. 1–54.

Keesling, Francis W., "Keesling Committee Recommendations: Report on State Reorganization Plan Made," *Tax Digest*, May, 1941, pp. 156–159, 170–176.

Lancaster, Lane W., "Alabama's State Reorganization," *National Municipal Review*, February, 1945, pp. 69–73.

Martin, Roscoe C., "Alabama's Administrative Reorganization of 1939," *Journal of Politics*, November, 1940, pp. 436–447.

Patterson, Robert F., "The Lieutenant Governor in 1944," *State Government*, June, 1944, pp. 348–349, 356.

Smith, Dick, "Administrative Reorganization in Texas: A Reappraisal," *State Government*, May, 1945, pp. 86–87.

Stassen, Harold E., "Minnesota Points the Way," *National Municipal Review*, January, 1941, pp. 4–7, 21.

CHAPTER XI

State Administrative Services

THE three major types of administrative service — line, auxiliary, and staff — are found in the state governments as elsewhere.[1] The line functions, often spoken of as the operating services, include those which come in close contact with the people, such as activities of a regulatory character and those which furnish service or information to citizens. The control of plant and animal diseases, the enforcement of food and drug regulations, blue sky laws, public utility laws, and laws requiring the examination and licensure of practitioners of learned professions and technical trades are all examples of regulatory services. Activities of the service type, called by some writers primary services, include the farm marketing service, those phases of the plant and animal industry service which aid producers in getting a larger output at a minimum investment, public health service, free library programs, vocational and adult education programs, et cetera. The United States Bureau of the Census has grouped the services of the states under certain major headings, which are used with modifications in the following table as a basis for classifying the more common activities of the state governments.

The auxiliary services are concerned with the performance of the routine activities of government — the collection and disbursement of revenues; the custody and budgeting of the same and the supervision of their expenditure; the purchase and maintenance of property, supplies, and equipment; and the hiring and dismissing, promotion and retirement of personnel. These services, which Willoughby called the housekeeping services, are of little direct benefit to the people, and yet it would be impossible for the line services

[1] This classification follows White, Leonard D., *Introduction to the Study of Public Administration*, Revised Edition, Chapters 3–7 (Macmillan, New York, 1939) ; it differs somewhat from that used by Willoughby and other earlier writers.

to function if these auxiliary services were not regularly and efficiently maintained. These services relate, in the main, to the functions of general government provided for in the original constitutional offices.

CLASSIFICATION OF THE FUNCTIONS OF STATE GOVERNMENT

(United States Bureau of the Census classification, as modified by the author)

General Government	Governor's Office Personnel Military Affairs	State Justice State Police
Finance	Budget Office Taxation and Finance State Treasurer	State Tax Commission Property and Supplies Auditor General
Control over Business and Industry	Banking Insurance Labor Mines	Professional Licensure Public Utilities Commerce Weights and Measures
Conservation and Development of Natural Resources	Agriculture Forests and Waters Fish and Game	Geological Survey Land Planning and Use Public Lands and Parks
Transportation	Aviation Motor Vehicles Highways: Use and Safety	Highways: Construction and Maintenance
Public Health and Welfare	Health Welfare Public Assistance	Corrections Institutions Recreation
Education	Libraries Public Instruction Professional Licensure	Higher Education Adult Education

The staff services have been defined as the research and planning arm of the executive branch of the government. This function differs from that of the auxiliary services in that the latter are operating agencies, concerned with the maintenance of the existing organization and activities, but not with major policies. The staff agency is a nonoperating agency concerned with thinking, research, and advisory work, and with the revision of organization as new needs may arise. It is concerned with the formulation of major policies.[2] Some agencies are obliged to perform duties in both categories. The cen-

[2] *Ibid.*, pp. 42–43. For an excellent description of these functions in a particular state, classified by type, see New York State Constitutional Convention Committee, *State and Local Government in New York*, Chapters 3–5 (Albany, 1938).

tral personnel agency, for instance, is a staff agency for the government as a whole, and an auxiliary agency in so far as it is charged with the actual administration of the personnel function. The need for staff service in the states is great, but relatively little has been done in developing it.

Reference is made elsewhere to the tremendous increase in the number and scope of governmental services. In a later chapter we shall be concerned with this problem from the cost angle, and at that time an attempt will be made to indicate some of the reasons for the greatly increased expenditures in the field of state government.

A detailed study of the functional growth of California from 1850 to 1935 was published a few years ago. What has happened in that state is typical of the development in other states throughout the country. When California was admitted to the Union there were twenty agencies, five of which were later abolished by legislative act. By the end of 1935 over six pages in a closely printed table were required to list chronologically all of the services established in and the services rendered by the state government. The total number of entries was 452.[3] The data in this table may be summarized by ten-year periods as follows:

FUNCTIONAL GROWTH OF CALIFORNIA STATE GOVERNMENT, 1850–1935

Decade	Number of Functions Added during Decade	Total Number of Functions in State Government
1850–1859	44	44
1860–1869	18	62
1870–1879	11	73
1880–1889	32	105
1890–1899	28	133
1900–1909	47	180
1910–1919	100	280
1920–1929	117	397
1930–1935	52 (six years)	452

[3] Peirce, John M., " 420 State Activities: California Government Continues to Expand," *Tax Digest,* August, 1936, pp. 260–261, 281–286. For data on other states, see: NEW YORK: New York State Constitutional Convention Committee, *op. cit.,* Chapter 9. OREGON: Isseks, Morris S., *History of State Administrative Agencies in Oregon, 1843–1937* (Oregon State Planning Board, Portland, 1939). PENNSYLVANIA: Joint Legislative Committee on Finances, *A Survey of the Government of Pennsylvania, Introduction* (Harrisburg, 1934) ; Faught, Albert S., " The Multiplication of Administrative Agencies and Problems of Judicial Review in Pennsylvania," *Temple Law Quarterly,* November, 1938, pp. 30–54. See also Bain, Read, " Theory and Practice of State Administration," *American Political Science Review,* June, 1938, pp. 495–508.

Of the 452 functions and agencies half were created during the last twenty years covered by the survey. Among the twenty-two items added in 1935 were the following typical entries: creation of Real Estate Board, State Planning Board, and State Agricultural Adjustment Administration; regulation of Firemen's and Policemen's Benefit Associations, highway carriers, serum manufacturers, motor vehicle caravans, slaughtering of horses, motor transportation brokers, structural pest control business; registration of apiary equipment; and establishment of Southern California Prison and California Pacific Exposition Commission.

GENERAL GOVERNMENT

Under general government are grouped the following officers and agencies of the state governments:

Officers	*Departments*
Governor	Executive
Lieutenant-Governor	Executive
Secretary of State	State
Attorney General	Justice
Adjutant General	Military Affairs
Superintendent	State Police
Director	Personnel

Chapter IX has been devoted to the office of the governor, further mention of which occurs in the preceding chapter. The lieutenant-governor and secretary of state have likewise been discussed briefly in the preceding chapter. It remains, therefore, at this point to consider those services that relate to the protection of persons and property — the state police, the department of justice, and the department of military affairs. Financial administration might be regarded as an aspect of general government, but because of the size and importance of the problems involved, this topic as well as personnel will be considered separately.

The Attorney General. The attorney general is the chief law officer of the state. In those jurisdictions which maintain a department of justice he serves as its head. He may also serve ex officio as a member of various boards and commissions, such as the pardon board, the board of commissioners on uniform state laws, et cetera. The department furnishes legal advice to the governor, the administrative departments, boards, commissions, and officers of the state government. Through deputies assigned to the various departments and agencies, who become experts in the law relating to these departments, he conducts their legal business, instituting and conducting court actions when necessary to secure interpretation of the law or to prosecute offenders.

The State Police. The state police system had its origin with the Texas Rangers in the early years of the present century. The organization commonly functions under a superintendent appointed by and responsible to the governor, in the same manner as any other department. The men are carefully selected for physical vigor and mental alertness. They are well trained and disciplined, and commonly constitute an efficient force for the protection of life and property throughout the state. Their duties include such general administration of the law as is involved in the preservation of law and order.

Members of the force are commonly sent to handle large crowds wherever they are congregated for any reason. They usually render service in case of real or threatened riot or disorder or disturbance of the peace. Through their facilities for criminal identification and information they undertake the solution of crimes committed outside of municipalities with a well-organized police force of their own. They are responsible for the enforcement of motor traffic regulations throughout the state, and other duties, such as fire prevention, may be assigned to them.

Military Affairs. Mention has already been made of the governor's powers as commander-in-chief of the military or naval forces maintained for the protection of the state. Just as the Secretaries of War and Navy are responsible to the President for the maintenance of the armed forces of the nation, so the adjutant general is responsible to the governor. There is, however, one important difference. In the Federal government, there is a time-honored tradition of civilian direction of the military departments, while in the states the position is filled by a high ranking officer.

The more important duties performed by the department include the organization, training, and equipment of several thousand National Guard or Home Guard troops. This involves keeping records of drill attendance and of the physical condition of officers and men, making efficiency reports, issuing payroll requisitions, and keeping war records. The force may be called upon as an emergency state police force in case of riot, insurrection, et cetera. The department must account for and preserve Federal military property and stores valued, in the larger states, at many millions of dollars. It must maintain and repair state armories, operate homes for destitute soldiers

and sailors, and perform such other duties as rendering assistance
to veterans in presenting claims against the Federal government, administering state funds for the relief of impoverished war veterans,
and determining the amount of relief to be paid to guardsmen who
are wounded or otherwise disabled while on duty in active service.

CONTROL OVER BUSINESS AND INDUSTRY

The state services which function within the field of business and
industry include the departments of banking and insurance, of labor
and industry, and of mines, and agencies for the regulation of
public service companies, the control of weights and measures and
the sale of foods and drugs, and professional licensure. The field of
operations of each will be briefly outlined.

Department of Banking. Many of the present departments of banking were established in the later decades of the last century — that
of New York in 1880, that of Pennsylvania in 1891. The Federal
Constitution provides that the states shall not emit bills of credit;
the need for departments of banking grew out of the fact that this
clause had been evaded. If the states could not issue paper money
designed to circulate as currency, they could charter banks, which
in turn could issue paper money. During the nineteenth century we
had our era of wildcat banking, and this gave encouragement to the
move for regulation. The amount of the paper money issued by the
state banks became so great as to threaten the position of the Federal
currency; this condition prompted Congress to impose a 10 per cent
tax upon all such paper money designed to circulate as currency. The
tax was sustained in 1869 in the case of Veazie Bank v. Fenno.[4] While
this decision took care of the problem of paper money, the need of
regulation for the purpose of controlling other banking activities
steadily increased.

At the present time state departments of banking render four important services for the protection of investors: (1) the supervision
of banks and trust companies; (2) the supervision of building and
loan associations; (3) the supervision of security issues, and the protection of investors through the enforcement of blue sky laws; and
(4) the supervision of private bankers, small moneylenders, steamship ticket agents, et cetera. For the first two of these purposes
the departments maintain forces of public accountants as trained
examiners to make periodic examinations of the books and records

4 8 Wallace, 533, 1869.

of the institutions and associations under supervision. In many states it is the practice to levy such fees as will cover the actual costs of examination; in fact, some states exact fees which cover the over-head of the department as well, thereby making the department self-sustaining.

The supervision of security issues may be carried on either as a phase of the work of the department or by a commission, which in turn may be either independent or attached to the department. It is customary to license brokers and salesmen, to pass upon proposed security issues, and to carry on investigational work both before and and after issues have been approved. The private bankers are often among the largest financial organizations within the jurisdiction of the state; the small moneylenders and steamship ticket agents, on the other hand, are in a position to prey upon the less fortunate members of the community unless they are subjected to a constant and rigorous supervision.

Department of Insurance. In the early days there existed both wide-spread distrust of insurance and lack of effective regulation. The establishment of state departments of insurance became necessary when, in the case of Paul v. Virginia, the United States Supreme Court decided that insurance was not commerce, and hence not sub-ject to the regulatory power of Congress under the commerce clause. Although this decision has recently been reversed by the Court, there has been no change in the previously existing method of operation.[5] For many years the work was badly done — when, indeed, it was done at all — and the insurance business took on many of the character-istics of a modern racket. The famous Hughes investigation of in-surance companies in New York in 1911 attracted public attention to the existence of the evils, most of which have since been corrected. At the present time a well-organized insurance department will pos-sess wide inquisitorial and visitorial powers over the companies under its supervision; it will license those engaged in the business, both brokers and advisers; and it will exercise control over the financial condition of insurers, over the forms of policies, over rates and premiums, over methods of obtaining business, et cetera.

For the performance of these duties, the department may be or-ganized in accordance with either of two main principles — accord-ing to the type of company to be supervised, or according to the

[5] 8 Wallace 168, 1868; see also National Fire Insurance Company of Hartford v. Thompson, Superintendent of Insurance Department of Missouri, 281 U. S. 311, 1930. The new case is United States v. South Eastern Underwriters Association, 322 U. S. 533, 1944.

type of work to be done. New York State uses the first plan and has separate divisions for life, fire, casualty, marine, and other types of insurance. Pennsylvania uses the second plan and has in its department separate divisions for statements and audits, accounts, agents and brokers, complaints, examinations, liquidations, and actuarial work. The mere listing of these divisions serves to indicate the nature of the several types of work involved in the supervision of insurance companies, both domestic and foreign.

Department of Labor and Industry. State departments of labor, or of labor and industry, began thirty or forty years ago as bureaus of factory inspection. In the meantime the departments have grown in the larger industrial states to huge organizations employing many hundreds of persons. The movement for the establishment of such agencies was given impetus in 1895 when the United States Supreme Court decided, in the case of the United States v. E. C. Knight Sugar Refining Company, that manufacturing was not commerce — that manufacturing was a change of form, and that commerce was a change of place.[6] The type of organization varies according to the type of state. In the smaller, nonindustrial states the department is neither large nor important. In the principal industrial states the departmental form of organization is used, as in Illinois, New York, and Pennsylvania. There is, however, a third group of states that are still working under an industrial commission; important among these is Wisconsin.

The duties performed by this department are many and important. They include the protection of workers in industry — men, women, and children; the carrying on of extensive inspection services; the administration of the workmen's compensation system; and the conduct, in cooperation with the Federal government, of the public employment service. Other duties lie in the field of industrial relations and industrial standards, or may relate to matters of a miscellaneous character. Under existing court decisions men workers may be protected from excessive hours of labor in industries that are not dangerous as well as in those which are accompanied by unusual occupational hazards. They may be protected from forced labor, and aided by wage collection laws, by laws controlling the method of wage payments and the frequency thereof, by minimum wage laws in some jurisdictions, and by laws requiring payment of wages during time off to vote. All of these regulations it is the duty of the department to enforce.

[6] 156 U. S. 1, 1895. This decision, also, has since been modified.

For a great many years women and children enjoyed a preferred position before the law in the matter of protection in the field of industry. Children still do, but the effort to protect women workers in industry received a severe set-back in the decision of the United States Supreme Court in the case of Adkins v. Children's Hospital — the famous District of Columbia minimum wage case.[7] The existing legislation relates to such matters as hours of labor, minimum wage, night work, and conditions of labor. It is the business of the department to see that these regulations are enforced. The whole problem has social aspects of very great significance, yet the fact remains that very few of the states have legislation which compares favorably with the minimum standards that have been determined by competent and impartial authorities.

The inspection services represent an exceedingly important part of the work of such a department. Some of these are of a general nature, while others are more highly specialized. The general inspection work includes the inspection of manufacturing and industrial establishments for the joint purposes of enforcing the safety code and of carrying on preventive work with regard to both accidents and occupational diseases. It may be responsible for the enforcement of the fire and panic act in theaters, schools, and other places built for public assemblies. These acts regulate aisle space, seating, exits, fire escapes, emergency lighting systems, et cetera. Among the more specialized types of inspection may be mentioned that of buildings, both public and private, for observance of the requirements of the building code; the licensing of motion-picture operators; the inspection and licensing of steam boilers; elevator inspection; and the inspection of mines and quarries, of bedding and upholstery. Upon the honesty and efficiency with which this work is done depends the hourly safety of a large portion of the population of the state — old and young alike.

When an injured employee of an industrial establishment attempted to recover in a court of law, the employer was formerly able, under the common law, to set up the age-old doctrines of the assumption of risk and the fellow-servant rule, or the doctrine of contributory negligence. When these defenses were abolished by statute, we turned to a system of employer's liability, and from that to the existing system of workmen's compensation. There is the greatest diversity in the organization of existing systems of this kind — some are compulsory while others are optional; some are public and some are

[7] 261 U. S. 525, 1923.

private; some permit self-insurers while others do not. In the more progressive states there are four different agencies, each of which has a part in the administration of the compensation system. These are: (1) the bureau; (2) the referees; (3) the board; (4) the fund.

The bureau is in general responsible for the enforcement of the law. To it industrial accidents are reported; by it all but a small percentage of the cases are finally settled. It keeps the records of all cases. When it is unable to get the insurer and the insured to agree, the case may be turned over to a referee. (In New York all cases pass through the hands of the referee, although little time is spent on noncontested cases.) If the referee is unable to effect a settlement, appeal may be had to the board — a quasi-judicial body most of whose decisions are in fact final, although technically appeal may be carried to the courts on points of law. Finally, there is the fund. This is an insurance business operated by the state for the insuring of a particular type of risk; the rates are usually cheaper than those of private companies. In most states insurers are merely required to carry insurance; they may take it with private companies or with the fund, as they prefer.

The department was, until the federalization of employment offices during the war, responsible for the conduct of the state employment service. This may be true again if this function is returned to the states. In the past the employment work was commonly poorly done. The number of local offices was not adequate, and those which did exist were badly run. Only the cheapest kind of unskilled labor was benefited. During the depression the extent of the cooperation of the United States Department of Labor increased, and experimental offices were operated in Philadelphia, Rochester, and Minneapolis. The purpose was to find out how an office of this type should be run scientifically, with the hope that the discoveries made in these experimental offices might be applied to the work of public employment offices throughout the country. The development of scientific methods in this field is the more urgent because of the serious abuses that exist among private employment offices, and because of the fact that the United States Supreme Court has frowned upon state legislation designed to regulate and control the fees charged by such offices.[8]

The department is also responsible for the performance of many

8 Ribnik v. McBride, 277 U. S. 350, 1928. See also Adams v. Tanner, 244 U. S. 590, 1917, in which the Court held invalid a Washington statute designed to outlaw private employment offices.

duties of a somewhat miscellaneous character. A department of labor worthy of the name will find itself offering its good offices in the mediation and arbitration of strikes and industrial disputes; it will, in the effort to cut down the toll of accidents and deaths, carry on experimental work in its laboratories, for the purpose of discovering and perfecting safety devices and procedures. It will cooperate to the fullest possible extent with the Federal government in its industrial rehabilitation program and in the collection of labor statistics, as well as in the conduct of the public employment offices. It will have a program of cooperation with labor departments in other states and with other departments of the government in its own state. In the field of public relations it will seek to inform the people of the state concerning what is being done and why, and how it will benefit them.

Department of Mines. There is no good reason why the work of a department of mines could not be done just as well in the labor department in connection with its inspection work and its work of enforcing legislation governing hours and conditions of labor, but in some of the states, where mining is important, separate departments are maintained. This may be justified, although even in such cases the department is always a small one. It is responsible for the performance of such duties, prescribed by the mining laws, as the inspection of mines, the investigation of mine accidents, the holding of examinations for mine foremen and mine operators, the issuing of certificates to persons entitled to receive the same, and the compiling and distributing of statistical reports.

Public Service Commissions. By long and laborious effort we came finally to the establishment of public service commissions in each of the states as a means of regulating and controlling those companies affected with a public interest which supply to the general public the facilities for heat, light, power, communication, and transportation. Thus some twenty or twenty-five different types of business enterprises come under the control of the commissions. The quality of the work done by most of the commissions has not been any too encouraging, but they are none the less about the only force standing, in the interests of the public, between the public and the utilities. Under the doctrine of the decision of the United States Supreme Court in Smythe v. Ames, the utilities are entitled to a fair return upon a fair valuation.[9] The effort to interpret this rule has brought on no end of difficulty. The public does obtain, through the commis-

[9] 169 U. S. 466, 1898.

sions, some assurance of reasonable rates, adequate service, accuracy of meters through inspection, et cetera.

The procedure before the commissions is in most cases relatively simple. When the consumer has a grievance, he files with the commission a complaint which is placed on the docket for a hearing. It is not necessary for the complainant to be represented at the hearing by counsel, although of course the utilities are always so represented. In a great many cases the commissions find it possible to settle grievances informally, and this method is encouraged where possible. A typical organization includes a secretary's office; a legal bureau; a bureau of accounts, rates, and statistics; a bureau of public convenience; and a bureau of engineering, in which may be established a standardization laboratory.

The commissions provide a fairly flexible system of regulation, and insure a quicker and less costly remedy for minor grievances. Because they are permanent bodies, they are in a favorable position to collect the necessary data for the determination of rates and to maintain standards of service. The utilities are benefited in that they are protected to a considerable extent from a partisan action, and this in turn protects their securities. On the other hand, the commissions have been justly criticised for not representing the public more adequately. The laws require that their members — or part of them — shall be experienced in utility management. Obvious though the purpose of this requirement is, it has in many cases given the commissions the utility point of view. Furthermore, after their appointment the members have a large part of their contacts with the representatives of the utilities, for the public is unorganized and incoherent. The result is that many of the commissions have tended more to favor the utilities than they have to protect the public. The commissions suffer also from the fact that the public is so little informed regarding the nature of their work, and is hence not in a position to avail itself of the service and protection which the commission otherwise might give.

Professional Examination and Licensure. Few people have any idea of the extent to which the right of persons to engage in professional and business activities, or in skilled trades, is subject to state regulation, supervision, and control. The following illustrative items are selected from the California report, previously cited:

1858 — Board of Examiners.
1875 — Board of Medical Examiners.
1883 — Board of Horticultural Examiners.
1885 — Board of Dental Examiners.

1891 — Licensing of surveyors.
1901 — Board of Accountancy.
 Board of Architectural Examiners.
1905 — Registration of nurses.
1911 — Registration of commercial fishermen.
 Registration of fish dealers.
1913 — Registration of refrigeration warehouses.
 Inspection and licensing of maternity homes.
 Licensing of public weighmasters.
1915 — Licensing of private detectives.
 Board of Embalmers and Funeral Directors.
1917 — Inspection and licensing of slaughter houses.
 Inspection and licensing of swimming pools.
1921 — Inspection and licensing of bakeries.
1922 — Board of Osteopathic Examiners.
 Board of Chiropractic Examiners.
1927 — Inspection and licensing of apiaries.
 Dairy products licensing service.
 Regulation and licensing of dry cleaning establishments.
 Board of Cosmetology.
 Licensing of boarding homes.
1929 — Inspection of nurseries.
 Board of Registration of Civil Engineers.

While no comprehensive survey of the problem has ever been made, it appears that similar lists could be compiled in practically all of the states. In 1929 the Commonwealth Club of California did make a preliminary investigation, which included eighteen representative states.[10] It was estimated then that there were no less than 200 separate professions, callings, and vocations subject in one or more states to examination and licensure. The number per state is never less than a dozen and may run as high as thirty. The tendency is for the number to increase with each session of the legislature, sometimes because of the demand of the public for protection from quacks and charlatans, at other times because of the demand of those engaged in legitimate business or professional activities for protection from those who resort to unfair competitive practices.

Control over Various Aspects of Commerce. In a well-organized state government agencies are established whose business it is to maintain close supervision over weights and measures, and over the sale of food and drugs, milk, and many other types of products where adulteration, misrepresentation, and fraud are possible. Sometimes

[10] "Occupational Restrictions," *The Commonwealth*, April 19, 1927, entire issue; DeLancy, Frances P., *The Licensure of Professions in West Virginia* (Foundation Press, Chicago, 1932); Graves, W. Brooke, "Professional and Occupational Restrictions," *Temple Law Quarterly*, April, 1939, pp. 234–263; and White, Leonard D., *Introduction to the Study of Public Administration*, Revised Edition, Chapter 32 (Macmillan, New York, 1939).

the agency which supervises weights and measures is independent, while in other states it is a bureau in one of the departments. It is customary for the cities and counties to maintain inspection services, but they are seldom well organized or efficiently administered. The state agency can exercise some supervision over the work of the local agencies, and can do a great deal of testing work of its own. The authority extends to every conceivable kind of weighing and measuring device. The Bureau of Standard Weights and Measures in the Pennsylvania Department of Internal Affairs, in a recent two-year period, made over 3,250,000 inspections, approved almost 3,000,000 weighing and measuring devices, condemned nearly a quarter of a million, and adjusted over 42,000.

Since so many food products are of agricultural origin, it has become common practice to place the regulatory control over the distribution and sale of such products under the department of agriculture. The following table, taken from a Pennsylvania report, will give some idea of the nature and extent of this type of control: [11]

1876 — State Board of Agriculture established.
1895 — Department of Agriculture created.
1897 — Adulteration and Coloring of Milk or Cream Law.
Vinegar Law.
Cheese Law.
1901 — Oleomargarine Law.
Renovated Butter Law.
1905 — Fresh Meat Law.
1909 — Eggs Unfit for Food Law.
Non-Alcoholic Drink Act.
Lard Law.
Fertilizer Act.
Feeding Stuffs Act.
General Food Law.
1911 — Sausage Law.
Milk and Cream Act.
1913 — Tuberculosis Eradication Act.
1915 — Coffee and Chicory Law.
Meat and Inspection Law.
1917 — Insecticide Law.
Apple Marketing Law.

1919 — Cold Storage Law.
Agricultural Marketing Law.
Poultry and Egg Marketing Law.
Fresh Egg Law.
1921 — Apiary Inspection Act.
Butter Law.
Seed Law.
Supplement to Oleomargarine Law.
Sanitary Bottling Act.
1923 — Ice Cream Law.
Filled Milk Law.
Supplement to Filled Milk Law.
1925 — Fruit Syrup Law.
Oyster Law.
Milk Container Law.
Milk Testing Law.
Carbonated Beverage Law.
1927 — Plant Pest Act.
Nursery Inspection Act.
1929 — Grape Marketing Law.
Seed Certification Act.
1933 — Bakery Licensing and Inspection Act.

[11] Joint Legislative Committee on Finances, *A Survey of the Government of Pennsylvania*, pp. 17–18 (Harrisburg, 1934).

Milk Control work is sometimes carried on in the department of agriculture, and sometimes in the department of health. It involves testing, giving examinations for testers, issuing licenses and permits, carrying on investigations, supervising the work of local inspectors, et cetera. During the depression there was a tendency to create milk control boards in order to control the business practices of those who were engaged in retail distribution and sale of milk.

CONSERVATION AND DEVELOPMENT OF NATURAL RESOURCES

Under the heading of conservation and the development of natural resources come those state government activities carried on by the departments of agriculture, forests and waters, fish and game, mines, geological survey, and public lands and parks.

Department of Agriculture. Some administrative agency for the purpose of encouraging and assisting agriculture exists in every state but one; the function is one of the oldest among the state administrative services. The department serves the threefold purpose of protecting the farmer, protecting the consumer, and rendering technical assistance to the farmer in both the production and marketing of his crops. Besides numerous miscellaneous activities, the department carries on a large amount of regulatory work and maintains marketing and crop reporting services.

Important among the various regulatory duties are the several types of quarantine enforced to prevent the spread of both plant and animal diseases and of pests and injurious insects. While some of this work contributes to the public health, the department carries on many activities of which health is the sole aim. Among these are campaigns for the eradication of bovine tuberculosis, Bang's disease, hog cholera, and other diseases that destroy livestock; the inspection of all meats not sold under Federal inspection; and finally, the enforcement of the food law, the milk law, the carbonated beverage law, and many other types of regulatory acts affecting the distribution and sale of food products. A third type of regulatory work is designed chiefly to prevent misrepresentation and fraud: inspection of weights and measures (in some states), and enforcement of standardization and grading laws, seed inspection laws, fertilizer inspection laws, and acts providing for nursery, apiary, and poultry inspection. Finally, there is the very considerable task of enforcing the dog law, the purpose of which is to protect sheep and cattle from stray and marauding dogs.

Just as the bureaus of plant industry and of animal industry, through the regulatory activities just referred to, try to help the farmer to produce more and to get what he pays for when he buys seed, fertilizer, and other products, so the marketing and crop reporting service attempts to assist him in disposing of his products on fair and favorable terms. Toward this end the state department of agriculture, working in cooperation with the Federal department, maintains a market reporting and market analysis service, and supervises and assists in the marketing of hay and grain, fruit and vegetables, poultry and eggs, et cetera. Some inspection and supervision is given to roadside markets, and it is only a question of time before all such markets will be licensed annually. In the case of perishable products, the department will usually provide shipping-point inspection and, where needed, maintain a bonded warehouse service for the accommodation and protection of the growers of grain, tobacco, and other crops.

Other services maintained by the department include soil survey work, reclamation work if necessary; and research and educational work at the state college or university, at the argricultural experiment stations throughout the state, and in its own laboratories. It is responsible for the organization and conduct of the state fair, and for the rendering of guidance and assistance to numerous county and other fairs and exhibitions throughout the state. Of extreme importance is the whole problem of the public relations, for no other department is more dependent for its success upon the skillful handling of its work. The results of research must be put in printed form convenient for distribution, and they must be sufficiently nontechnical for popular understanding without at the same time being inaccurate. Material of current interest to farmers must be brought to them over the radio and through the newspapers, pamphlets, and other media. Constitutional problems raised by the work and intergovernmental and interdepartmental relations must receive serious consideration.

Department of Forests and Waters. The department of conservation in some states has complete charge of all conservation work; in other states there are separate departments and agencies for the different types of conservation work to be done. One of the most important types is the protection of the forest and water resources of the state. So far as the forests are concerned, the department has the twofold task of protecting existing forests and of encouraging reforestation. This involves prevention of forest fires as far as possible, and fighting forest fires where preventive methods have failed; distribution, planting, and supervision of the growth of seedlings; acquisition and management of state lands and parks; and the conduct of forest extension work.

So far as the waters of the state are concerned, the department may be responsible for surveys of the water resources of the state; for the consideration of applications for charters by water companies; for regulation of the sale, franchises, and disposition of the assets of water companies; for the granting of permits for dams and tunnel construction; and for the alteration of the current or the flow of streams. Permits may be granted to municipalities to impound water in, or to convey water over, state forests, and the department may be responsible for the regulation and inspection of freshets, floods, dams, dam sites, and flood control projects.

Protection of Fish and Game. The anglers and hunters of a state often constitute a powerful pressure group. Where they are not well organized, all of the conservation work is under the direction of a single department — as it probably should be. Where they are, they have insisted upon the maintenance of separate agencies for each type of work on the plea that no one person can be adequately informed or equally interested in all of the different phases of conservation. In either case problems of protection and of propagation are involved. For the protection work it is necessary to have game wardens and fish wardens in sufficient numbers to enforce the law, and to provide adequate protection for game refuges and game lands.

The propagation service requires the maintenance of game farms and the construction and operation of fish hatcheries. As a matter of fact, there may be as many as five types of work connected with fish propagation: construction of hatcheries and growing ponds; field service; operation of the hatcheries and other equipment; surveys of lakes, streams, and ponds in order to discover what kind of fish will thrive in each location; and the actual distribution of fish fry from the hatcheries to the waters in which they are to be planted. Bounty systems may be set up to aid in the elimination of animals which constitute a special danger to species which it is desired to protect. In many states the license fees paid by fishermen and hunters are sufficient to make the fish and game work largely if not wholly self-sustaining.

The Geological Survey. It is not necessary to discuss further at this point the work of the department of mines in the development of natural resources, nor the responsibility which rests upon the department in the matter of the supervision of public lands and parks. In the latter field much intelligent work in problems of land use has been done within the last few years. A word should be added concerning the geological survey. This work is to a large extent conducted on a cooperative basis with the Federal government. It involves the location of natural resources such as ores, coals, oils, clays, soils, fertilizers, and underground waters for purposes of surveying and mapping. It is beneficial to the agricultural, mining, and metallurgical interests of the state, as well as to the general public.

From time to time deposits of valuable substances may be found in various parts of a state; these are commonly the subject of investigation and report by the geological survey. The survey is also called upon to answer in the course of the year scores of inquiries regarding the identification of mineral substances. Of course, very few of the specimens submitted are of any value, but the fact that the survey exists to give this information saves many people from serious losses at the hands of unscrupulous promoters. The cost of the maintenance of this service is moderate indeed, and its value to the state is much greater than people generally realize.

Planning Activies. Planning represents the attempt of democracy to apply intelligence to the use of natural and human resources for the welfare and happiness of all the people. There was a considerable background of planning in many American cities, but the movement made little headway in the states until, during the depression, financial assistance was given them for the purpose by the National Resources Board. By 1940, planning legislation was or had been in effect in all but seven states. As of that date, when thirty-four laws were in effect, some of the boards were more or less inactive. Nearly all were hampered by inadequate support, which in turn meant an inadequate staff.

Before anything resembling a master plan for the state can be developed, a vast amount of material must be collected through surveys of land and water resources, public works, economic and industrial development, social institutions, and regulation. Analyses must be made of existing data. Out of all these may grow suggestions of new methods, tools, ways of doing things, which may promote a more orderly development and a fuller use of our resources. These are the objectives of planning which, in spite of objections on the part of some, represent a great forward step in the development of democratic processes.

TRANSPORTATION FACILITIES

The department of highways owes its origin, in the early years of the present century, to the desire for better roads, due first to the bicycle and later to the development of the automobile. The present administrative set-up places the responsibility for construction and maintenance under the department of highways, and the responsibility for the regulation of the use of the highways under the bureau of motor vehicles and of the state police. State aviation commissioners are responsible for the planning and development of airports and airport facilities.

The Department of Highways. The organization of the department of highways varies greatly from state to state. In some cases the work is under a department, while in others it is under the control of a commission. In some cases it is a part of the department of public works, and in others it is, as it should be, an entirely separate agency. This branch of the state government has grown until in many states it has spent during recent years as much money as all of the other departments of the state government combined, or even more. It is responsible for the construction and maintenance of the state highway system, the extent of which has increased steadily since 1910. At first the states undertook to aid the local units in roadbuilding through the subsidy system; when this method proved unsatisfactory, the actual process of taking over the roads began.

The experience in Pennsylvania has been more or less typical. The first act creating a highway department in that state was passed in 1903; construction work was under a highway commissioner from then until 1911, when the present department was created. At that time the state also took over nearly 9,000 miles of township roads, to which mileage additions have been made through the intervening years, until the state highway system comprises nearly 34,000 miles of road. In 1933 the maintenance of 48,000 more miles was undertaken without actually adding this mileage to the state highway system.

In former times the additions to the state system were made through political influence and " pull "; now additions are made by the legislature upon the basis of careful checks of the volume of traffic made by the highway department. Highways are classified as primary and secondary routes, and the type of construction and the cost are determined accordingly. The tendency in highway construction is toward an almost universal use of concrete. In any state of considerable size the highway department will be organized with a headquarters organization and a field force, the state being divided into engineering districts or divisions. Contiguous counties are grouped together for this purpose, and the counties themselves may serve as subdistricts in such a set-up. Both construction and maintenance work are handled through the same organization, although the effort is made to keep the two somewhat separate.

The headquarters office is responsible for financial supervision, for office and engineering supplies, for testing and research, for the planning of signs and safety work, and for the public relations of the department. Here also are handled the legal work, personnel work, contracts, and such forestry work as may be required for roadside planting. In the construction service, plans and specifications for roads and bridges are prepared at the central office, which advertises for bids for contracts. Separate operating units may be set up for designing and drafting highways, designing and drafting bridges, estimates and costs, and the actual work of construction. On the maintenance side, operating units may be set up for equipment; for arrangements with townships and for giving permits for road openings, et cetera; for snow removal; and for the actual work of maintenance.

Bureau of Motor Vehicles. As soon as it became apparent that the construction and maintenance of highways would be expensive, the states began to impose license fees for the operation of motor cars. The fees vary greatly in amount for passenger cars, busses, trucks, trailers, and motorcycles, there being no generally accepted principle upon the basis of which they are computed. Some states have a flat rate, some use horsepower as a basis for computing the amount of the fee, while others use net weight or gross weight. With the present exception of Georgia, the fees are generally high in the South. It is also true that the fees imposed upon trucks and busses in most states are in no wise commensurate with the damage which these vehicles do to the highways. Besides the registration fees for motor vehicles, the states commonly collect operator's licenses and gasoline taxes.

Most of the states do have, and all should have, a system of examining motor vehicle operators and chauffeurs, and a reasonable charge should be made for this service. An annual fee of one or two dollars imposes little hardship upon operators, and it may bring into the state treasury a million dollars or more a year. The gasoline tax is used in all forty-eight states, the rate ranging from two cents a gallon in a few states to a maximum rate of seven cents in others. This tax is in addition to the Federal tax collected uniformly in all states. In the past the funds from these three sources, collected by the bureau of motor vehicles, were segregated for highway purposes. During the depression there was a tendency to increase the amount of the gasoline tax and to divert portions of the receipts to relief and other purposes. This has recently led to the adoption of a number of anti-diversion amendments to state constitutions.

These registration and licensing provisions serve other purposes than the raising of revenue; they give the bureau a means of keeping unfit and incompetent drivers off the road, and a means of punishing those who are negligent by the revocation of license. In the enforcement of such regulations there is a good deal of reciprocity and cooperation among the states. In some states the bureau licenses inspection stations. The law requires either an annual or semiannual inspection of all motor vehicles within the state. This eliminates some vehicles altogether and causes much needed repairs to be made on hundreds of others. It may be true that this inspection is not always as efficient as it should be, but even so, it is of inestimable value in the saving of life and the preventing of damage to property. Some of the more progressive states have title laws for motor vehicles. Without the certificate of title, no vehicle may be sold. This device has been found to be very effective in preventing the disposition of stolen cars.

Enforcement of the Motor Vehicle Law. The work of enforcing the motor vehicle code may rest with the bureau of motor vehicles or with a separate bureau established for that purpose. In either case constant and vigorous effort is necessary if the highways are to be safe for use. Just as the department of highways is responsible for the construction of roads, so this agency is responsible for seeing that they are, in so far as possible, free from drunken and otherwise reckless drivers and safe for the use of the motoring public. This duty is assigned to the state highway patrol or to the state police. The members of this force patrol the highways for the purpose of enforcing the law and, when necessary, rendering assistance to those who are in distress.

Other Forms of Transportation. The state may be responsible for the supervision of types of transportation facilities other than motor highways. A century ago, in the internal improvement era, many of the states embarked on extensive canal-building programs. During this period New York State built the Erie Canal — about the only one that was at all successful. This remains today in the form of the new barge canal, which is operated under the supervision of the Department of Public Works. States along the seacoast, or states bordering on large inland bodies of water, may maintain port or harbor patrols, and may find it necessary to operate patrol boats to aid in the enforcement of various statutes, as for instance, to prevent the bootlegging of gasoline. Several of the states at one time owned and operated railway systems, and with the development of aviation as an important mode of transportation, the states have set up aviation commissions for the purpose of developing air routes and airport facilities in all of the larger cities and towns of the state.

PUBLIC HEALTH AND SOCIAL WELFARE

This discussion of public health and welfare services will cover, in addition to direct health and welfare service, work done in the fields of mental health, corrections, institutional management, and the establishment and operation of recreational facilities. Also included are the two relatively new major functions of relief or public assistance administration — an outgrowth of the depression years — and the social security program operated in cooperation with the Federal government for the benefit of the unemployed, the aged, dependent children, and the blind.

Department of Public Health. The states began to do a certain amount of public health work soon after the close of the Civil War. As the germ theory became established, as science demonstrated that many diseases are definitely controllable and that " within reasonable limits public health is a purchaseable commodity," expenditures have shown a steady and consistent increase.

The duties of the department are many and varied. They include work in infant and maternity hygiene, control of communicable and social diseases, sanitary engineering, food and drug control, and milk control. They embrace also such other activities as assisting in the solution of local health problems, supervising the work of local health officers, conducting clinics, licensing nurses and midwives, conducting public health laboratories for research and diagnostic purposes, keeping vital statistics records, and carrying on public health education. It is hopelessly inadequate merely to enumerate the duties performed by so large and so important a department of the state government.

Mental Health. Mental health problems have always existed, but only in recent years have they been correctly diagnosed, adequately reported, and properly treated. Persons afflicted with mental illness were regarded as " crazy " and were often thrown into prison with common criminals. Mental illness was regarded as a disgrace to the family. Now all that is changed. While the figures show a great increase in the number of mental cases, due to the nervous strain imposed by the tempo of modern life, the states have developed institutions and facilities for the treatment of such cases.

Even more important than curing those who are afflicted is the prevention of as many cases as possible for the future. In most well-organized departments of health there is a division of mental health, and in Massachusetts and New York there are separate departments. On a financial basis as well as a professional one, this is well justified. In Pennsylvania the Bureau (in the Department of Welfare) has jurisdiction over the ten state mental hospitals, and its budget is larger than that of the entire Department of Health. The agency carries on educational work in the field of mental health, operates clinics and psychiatric hospitals, supervises privately operated mental homes and hospitals, et cetera. It is just as important to prevent mental illness as to prevent physical illness. Much illness of both types is unnecessary; both cause great financial loss and much suffering.

Department of Social Welfare. The idea underlying the giving of assistance to those in need has changed very greatly in the last few years. Whereas we used to give alms to paupers, and maintain almshouses, poorhouses, and foundling asylums, now we give relief, maintain old age pension and mother's assistance systems, and try to avoid commitment to institutions. The old idea looked toward the perpetuation of a permanent class of unprosperous persons; the present system looks toward the prompt restoration of those assisted to their position as self-respecting and self-supporting members of society. The difference may be one of terminology and psychology, but it is not without significance from the point of view of social philosophy.

The location of the department in the state government varies greatly from state to state; sometimes it is an independent agency and sometimes it is part of the health department. Similar diversity exists with regard to terminology; sometimes the agency is called the department of charities, or of charities and corrections, while in other jurisdictions it is called the department of welfare or social welfare. In one state it is called the department of institutions and agencies. Furthermore, there are the same differences between the departmental form of organization and the board or commission form that have been noted in connection with the department of highways.

The services rendered by the department include numerous duties which may be classified under the general heading of community work. In connection with child welfare and mother's assistance, the department supervises adoptions; commits dependent children to institutions when necessary, and delinquent children to training schools; administers a system of juvenile probation; has charge of institutions for convalescent and crippled children; and supervises the program of aid to dependent children. It has general supervision also over private welfare institutions, and provides inspection and licensure for maternity hospitals, private nursing homes and hospitals, boarding homes for infants, and private mental hospitals. It licenses persons desiring to solicit funds for charitable purposes, and administers the system of pensions for the blind, in addition to supervising other services for the members of this group. It also administers the old age pension program.

Institutional Management. The management of the state's institutions is, in the larger states, an undertaking of no small proportions. The organization for the handling of the work varies widely. In Pennsylvania there is a Bureau of Institutional Management in the Department of Welfare; New Jersey combines the two types of service in its Department of Institutions and Agencies; California maintains a separate Department of Institutions. Even where, as in these states, there is a separate agency for institutional management, not all of the state institutions may be placed under its control; this is especially apt to be true of correctional institutions. Included are mental hospitals, mental health clinics and psychopathic hospitals, institutions for the feeble-minded, and the colony for epileptics. Louisiana and Pennsylvania make large contributions for the care of the sick-poor, the former operating charity hospitals, and the latter owning and operating ten medical and surgical hospitals in addition to making substantial appropriations for the assistance of more than 160 private hospitals throughout the Commonwealth.

Department of Corrections. The functions of charities and corrections were formerly closely associated and were often combined in same department. The recent tendency has been to regard them as separate functions, setting up a separate bureau, or preferably a separate department, for correctional work. If the bureau is attached to the department of welfare, the human aspects of the problem of corrections are likely to be emphasized; if it is attached to the department of justice, the legal and punitive aspects of the work are likely to receive greater attention. At any rate, some agency in the state government, working on one theory or the other, has to administer the penitentiaries and the homes or reformatories for women and for delinquent boys and girls.

Such an agency should, and in some states does, exercise some supervision over the county jails. These institutions have of late been much improved; they were formerly accustomed to doing everything, in the treatment of prisoners, which science has shown should not be done. There are numerous special problems for the handling of which this agency is responsible — the problem of prison industries and prison labor, the management of a fund for the operation of prison industries, and the problems of recreation and of discipline. In view of the numerous prison riots and disturbances that have occurred in many states, it is clear that these problems are large and of no slight difficulty.

Public Assistance. The function of welfare and assistance was originally regarded as being purely local in character; this belief continued during the early days of the depression. It soon became apparent that the emergency was too great for the resources of private charity, then in turn for local public charity, and finally for the states themselves. When the Federal government began to provide financial assistance through the Federal Emergency Relief Administration, it became necessary for the states to set up a relief organization that was satisfactory to the Federal authorities. In most of the states an entirely new agency was created by the legislature, often with a board to determine policy and an administrator appointed by the governor. In order to reduce, in so far as possible, the influence of politics in the distribution of relief, the Federal authorities demanded a highly centralized organization. This meant that the state relief administrations required the setting up of county boards with county administrators responsible to them. Where smaller poor relief districts existed, they were unable to function because they had no money. The influence of the emergency relief administration caused a certain degree of centralization in the handling of relief problems, which has continued down to the present time.

Social Security. The Federal social security program operates on the basis of Federal-state cooperative arrangements, under which the Federal Government reimburses the states for the administrative costs incurred, and assists with the financial burden of carrying on the program. Four specific programs are involved — unemployment compensation, old age pensions, aid for dependent children, and aid for the blind. These services may or may not be located in a single department of the state government, but in either case, participation on the part of any state is dependent upon meeting certain conditions imposed in connection with the grants-in-aid. It is required that the staff administering the work be selected on a merit basis. In some states this is the only dent the merit system has made in the system of partisan spoils politics.

The funds for the unemployment compensation program are built up from wage deductions, plus equal contributions made by the employer. Old age pensions are designed to prevent suffering on the part of older citizens and to prevent the embarrassment that goes with dependency on relatives. Aid to dependent children, or mother's assistance, is provided for the mothers of small children where the father has died or, because of illness, is unable to support his family. The system of pensions for the blind represents an attempt to provide financial assistance for a relatively small group of citizens who suffer from a very serious affliction.

Recreation. The largest expenditures for public recreation have heretofore been made by the cities rather than by the states; they have been made for public playgrounds, swimming pools and bathhouses, recreation centers, and public parks. The efforts of the states have been largely confined to the establishment of memorial parks at places of historic interest, and of camp sites in state forest lands. It seems fairly evident that the states are going to have to do much more along this line than they have previously done if the problem of the sane and profitable use of increased leisure time is to be solved. Years ago Governor Smith of New York put through his park program against tremendous opposition, but it is now recognized as having been a progressive and forward looking program. In other states similar programs will have to be undertaken in order to make suitable open spaces accessible to large urban populations.

EDUCATION

Education, like the other older functions of government, was local to begin with, and the local communities have still retained considerable control over it. Through the years state expenditures for this purpose have steadily increased, and the power of the state has been clearly recognized by the courts, although in many cases it has not been used as effectively as it might be. It is still common practice to permit groups of local citizens — well-meaning, to be sure, but totally unqualified — to determine important questions of educational policy.

The state department has an executive head, usually appointed by the governor, and a board of regents, board of control, or council of education. The major activities of the department include general supervision of school administration and school finance throughout the state; the carrying on of research work and the compilation of statistical data on the schools of the state; the conduct of the teacher certification work, and supervision of the examining boards for the learned professions; curriculum making and curriculum supervision; the school health program; vocational education; education of the deaf and blind and of other defective groups; and direction of the adult program, the rural school program, and the program for visual education. In addition, the department usually has supervision and control of the state library and the state museum; with this one exception, all of the activities here mentioned relate to the supervision of the elementary and secondary schools.

In recent years the financial problems of the public education system have become more and more difficult. The control of the states over the schools has been strengthened in the effort to solve the financial problems of the poorer school districts. For political reasons it was impossible to assist the poor districts without giving assistance to all districts. Through their grants the states have been able to set standards in many fields — teacher training, salaries, length of term, contents of curriculum, et cetera.

In the field of higher education, similar financial problems have been met without a corresponding extension of state control. In the states of the West, Middle West, and South, the governments have contributed more or less generously to state universities; in the older states of the East, it has been necessary to meet this problem of providing equal educational opportunities for all by state aid to existing private institutions. Thus the General Assembly of Pennsylvania makes sizable appropriations for the assistance of the University of Pennsylvania, Temple University, the University of Pittsburgh, and Pennsylvania State College — none of which are state institutions — as well as to a dozen other educational institutions in specialized fields, such as medical and industrial schools and the school for the blind. In addition, there is a system of free scholarships, four to each senatorial district, to be awarded on a competitive basis to young men and young women in families most in need of financial assistance to educate their children.

Selected References

Agriculture and Conservation

Baker, Gladys, *The County Agent* (University of Chicago Press, 1939).

Brinser, Ayers, and Shepard, Ward, *Our Use of the Land* (Harper, New York, 1939).

Bruner, Herbert B., and Smith, C. Mabel, *Conserving our Natural Resources* (Merrill, Chicago, 1938).

Cameron, Jenks, *Development of Forest Control in the United States* (Johns Hopkins Press, 1928).

Comey, Arhur C., and others, *State and National Planning* (Harvard University Press, 1937).

Connery, Robert H., *Governmental Probems in Wild Life Conservation* (Columbia University Press, 1935).

Dahlberg, Edwin M., *Conservation of Renewable Resources* (Nelson, Appleton, Wis., 1939).

Elsworth, R. H., and Wanstall, Grace, *Farmers Marketing and Purchasing Cooperatives, 1863–1939* (Farm Credit Administration, Washington, 1941).

Flynn, Harry E., and Perkins, Floyd E., *Conservation of the Nation's Resources* (Macmillan, New York, 1941).

Folweiler, Alfred D., *Forest Fire Prevention and Control in the United States* (Louisiana State University, 1938).

——, *Theory and Practice of Forest Fire Protection in the United States* (Louisiana State University, 1937).

Gabrielson, Ira N., *Wild Life Conservation* (Macmillan, New York, 1941).

——, *Wild Life Refuges* (Macmillan, New York, 1943).

Glover, Katherine, *America Begins Again: The Conquest of Waste in Our Natural Resources* (McGraw-Hill, New York, 1939).

Hynning, Clifford J., *State Conservation of Resources* (National Resources Commission, Washington, 1939).

Leighton, Morris M., *Summary Information on the State Geological Surveys and the United States Geological Survey* (National Research Council, Bulletin No. 88, 1932).

National Resources Planning Board, *Human Conservation; The Story of Our Wasted Resources* (Washington, 1943).

——, *National Resources Development, Report for 1943,* Part I, Postwar Plan and Program; Part II, Wartime Planning for War and Postwar (Washington, 1943).

——, State Conservation of Resources (Washington, 1942).

Neely, Wayne C., *The Agricultural Fair* (Columbia University Press, 1935).

Pryor, William C., and Helen S., *Water — Wealth or Waste* (Harcourt, Brace, New York, 1939).

Renner, George T., *Conservation of National Resources: An Educational Approach to the Problem* (Wiley, New York, 1942).

Troup, Robert S., *Forestry and State Control* (Clarendon Press, New York, 1938).

United States Department of Agriculture, *State Legislation for Better Land Use* (Washington, 1941).

Weist, Edward, *Agricultural Organization in the United States* (University of Kentucky, 1923).

Banking

American Bankers Association, *Banking Boards, Statutory and Factual Study* (New York, 1938).

——, *The Guaranty of Bank Deposits* (New York, 1933).

Anderson, Thomas J., *Federal and State Control of Banking* (Bankers Publishing Company, New York, 1934).

Bremer, Cornelius D., *American Bank Failures* (Columbia University Press, 1935).

Caldwell, Stephen A., *A Banking History of Louisiana* (Louisiana State University Press, 1935).

Council of State Governments, *Securities Regulation in the Forty-Eight States* (Chicago, 1942).

Foster, LeBaron R., *Small Loan Laws of the United Sates* (Pollok Foundation, Newton, Mass., 1939).

Gallert, David J., and others, *Small Loan Legislation* (Russell Sage Foundation, New York, 1932).

Gruchy, Allen G., *Supervision and Control of Virginia State Banks* (Appleton-Century, New York, 1937).

Robinson, Louis N., and Nugent, Rolf, *Regulation of the Small Loan Business* (Russell Sage Foundation, New York, 1935).

Rodkey, Robert C., *State Bank Failures in Michigan* (University of Michigan Studies, 1935).

Starnes, George T., *Sixty Years of Branch Banking in Virginia* (Macmillan, New York, 1931).

Welfling, Weldon, *Savings Banking in New York State* (Duke University Press, 1939).

Whitsett, James M., *Ohio Bank Suspensions and Liquidations, 1920–1937* (Ohio State University Bulletin, 1938).

——, *Banking Operations in Ohio, 1920–1940* (Ohio State University, 1941).

Woolsey, John B., *State Taxation of Banks* (University of North Carolina Press, 1935).

Commerce

Fainsod, Merle, and Gordon, Lincoln, *Government and the American Economy* (Norton, New York, 1941).

Grether, Edwald T., *Price Control under Fair Trade Legislation* (Oxford University Press, New York, 1939).

Hall, Ford P., *Government and Business,* Revised Edition (McGraw-Hill, New York, 1940).

——, *The Concept of Business Affected with a Public Interest* (Principia Press, Bloomington, Ind., 1942).

Keezer, Dexter M., and May, Stacy, *The Public Control of Business* (Harper, New York, 1930).

Koontz, Harold D., *Government Control of Business* (Houghton Mifflin, Boston, 1941).

Orth, Samuel P., *Readings on the Relations of Government to Property and Industry* (Ginn, New York, 1917).

Rohlfing, Charles C., and others, *Government and Business,* Fourth Edition (Foundation Press, Chicago, 1941).

Stone, Harlan F., *Public Control of Business* (Howell, Soskin, New York, 1940).

Tobey, James A., *Federal and State Control of Milk Prices* (International Association of Milk Dealers, Chicago, 1937).

Weigel, Stanley A., *Fair Trade Acts* (Foundation Press, Chicago, 1938).

Wilson, Stephen, *Food and Drug Regulation* (American Council on Public Affairs, Washington, 1942).

Education

Aslin, Neil C., and Bradshaw, William L., *Manual on Education* (Missouri Constitutional Convention of 1943, Columbia, 1943).

Bishop, Eugene A., *The Development of a State School System* (New Hampshire) (Columbia University, Teachers College, 1930).

Boyden, Arthur C., *Development of Education in Massachusetts, 1630–1930.* (Department of Education Bulletin, Boston, 1930).

Brody, Alexander, *The American State and Higher Education: The Legal, Political, and Constitutional Relationships* (American Council on Education, Washington, 1935).

Briscoe, Alonzo O., *Size of the Local Unit for Administration and Supervision of Public Schools* (Columbia University, Teachers College, 1935).

Chambers, Merrit M., *Some Features of State Educational-Administrative Organization* (American Council on Education, Washington, 1936).

Chism, Leslie L., *Economic Ability of the States to Support Education* (Columbia University, Teachers College, 1936).

Coffman, Lotus D., *The State University, Its Work and Problems* (University of Minnesota Press, 1934).

Cook, Katherine M., *Supervision of Instruction as a Function of State Departments of Education* (Office of Education, Washington, 1941).

Cook, William A., *Federal and State School Administration* (Crowell, New York, 1927).

Cornell, Francis G., *A Measure of Tax-paying Ability of Local School Administrative Units* (Columbia University, Teachers College, 1936).

Cubberly, Elwood P., *State School Administration* (Houghton Mifflin, Boston, 1927).

Deffenbach, W. W., and others, *State Boards of Education and Chief State School Officers* (Office of Education, Washington, 1942).

Foerster, Norman, *The American State University, Its Relation to Democracy* (University of North Carolina Press, 1937).

Frazier, Benjamin W., *Development of State Programs for the Certification of Teachers* (Office of Education, Washington, 1938).

——, *Education of Teachers as a Function of State Departments of Education* (Office of Education, Washington, 1941).

Garber, Lee O., *Education as a Function of the State: Its Legal Implications* (Educational Test Bureau, Philadelphia, 1934).

Grace, Alonzo G., and Moe, G. A., *State Aid and School Costs* (McGraw-Hill, New York, 1939).

Graves, Frank P., *Administration of American Education* (Macmillan, New York, 1932).

Hamilton, Robert R., and Mort, Paul R., *The Law and Public Education* (Foundation Press, Chicago, 1941).

Hill, David S., *Control of Tax Supported Higher Education in the United States* (Carnegie Foundation for the Advancement of Teaching, New York, 1934).

Jackson, George L., *State Control of Public Instruction in Michigan* (Michigan Historical Commission, Lansing, 1926).

Keesecker, Ward W., *Textbooks for Public School Children* (Office of Education, Washington, 1932).

——, *Teacher Retirement Systems: Principal Provisions of State Systems* (Office of Education, Washington, 1935).

Maller, Julius B., *School and Community* (McGraw-Hill, New York, 1939).

Morrison, Henry C., *School and Commonwealth* (University of Chicago Press, 1937).

Mort, Paul R., and others, *Federal Support for Public Education* (Columbia University, Teachers College, 1936).

Mulhern, James, *History of Secondary Education in Pennsylvania* (Science Press, Lancaster, 1935).

National Education Association, *Efforts of the States to Support Education* (Washington, 1936).

——, "Federal Aid for Education," *Research Bulletin,* September, 1942.

——, *Financing Public Education* (Washington, 1936).

——, "State School Finance Systems," *Research Bulletin,* November, 1942.

Noble, M. C. S., *A History of the Public Schools of North Carolina* (University of North Carolina Press, 1930).

Norton, Thomas L., *Education for Work* (McGraw-Hill, New York, 1939).

Peters, H. W., *Organization and Administration of Vocational Education in Kentucky* (Kentucky Department of Education, 1939).

Reeves, Floyd W., and others, *Adult Education* (McGraw-Hill, New York, 1939).

Schrammel, Henry E., *The Organization of State Departments of Education* (Ohio State University Press, 1926).

Schultz, Arch D., *State Aid to Common Schools* (Ohio State Chamber of Commerce, Columbus, 1935).

Shepard, E. Fenton, and Wood, William B., *The Financing of Public Schools in Michigan* (University of Michigan, 1943).

Smith, Payson, and others, *Education in the Forty-eight States* (Government Printing Office, Washington, 1939).

Soper, Wayne W., *Development of State Support of Education in New York State* (University of the State of New York Press, Albany, 1933).

Strayer, George D., *Centralizing Tendencies in the Administration of Public Education* (Columbia University, Teachers College, 1934).

Swift, Fletcher H., *Federal and State Policies in Public School Finances in the United States* (Ginn, New York, 1929).

Tidwell, Clyde J., *State Control over Textbooks* (Columbia University, Teachers College, 1928).

Troxel, Oliver L., *State Control over Secondary Education* (Warwick and York, Baltimore, 1928).

Weber, Oscar F., *The Problem of School Organization and Finance in Illinois* (University of Illinois, 1938).

Weltzin, J. Frederick, *The Legal Authority of the American Public School* (University of North Dakota, 1930).

White, Robert H., *Development of the Tennessee State Educational System* (George Peabody College for Teachers, Nashville, 1929).

Winslow, Charles E. A., *The School Health Program* (McGraw-Hill, New York, 1939).

Yakel, Ralph, *The Legal Control of the Administration of Public School Expenditures* (Columbia University Press, 1929).

Public Health

American Public Health Association, *Control of Communicable Diseases,* Sixth Edition (New York, 1945).

Anderson, Gaylord W., and Arnstein, Margaret G., *Communicable Disease Control: A Volume for the Health Officer and Public Health Nurse* (Macmillan, New York, 1941).

Bolduan, Charles F. and N. W., *Public Health and Hygiene,* Third Edition (Saunders, Philadelphia, 1941).

Buehler, Ezra C., *Free Medical Care, Socialized Medicine* (Hinds and Noble, New York, 1935).

Cabot, Hugh, *The Doctor's Bill* (Columbia University Press, 1935).

Cady, Frank C., *Dental Health Organizations in State Deparments of Health in the United States* (United States Public Health Service, Washington, 1939).

Davis, Earl H., *Birth Certificates* (Wilson, New York, 1942).

Davis, Michael M., *American Organizes Medicine* (Harper, New York, 1941).

——, *Public Medical Services, a Survey of Tax Supported Medical Care in the United States* (University of Chicago Press, 1937).

Deutsch, Albert, *The Mentally Ill in America* (Doubleday, Doran, Garden City, 1938).

Dodd, Paul A., and Penrose, E. F., *Economic Aspects of Medical Services* (Graphic Arts Press, Washington, 1939).

Falk, Isadore S., *Security against Sickness* (Doubleday, Doran, Garden City, 1936).

——, and others, *The Costs of Medical Care* (University of Chicago Press, 1933).

Havens, Leon, *The Control of Typhoid Fever, a Bacteriological Approach* (Commonwealth Fund, New York, 1934).

Hiscock, Ira V., *Community Health Organization* (Commonwealth Fund, New York, 1932).

Johnsen, Julia E., *Socialization of Medicine* (Wilson, New York, 1935).

Jordan, Edwin O., *Food Poisoning and Food-Borne Infection* (University of Chicago Press, 1931).

Kallet, Arthur, and Schlink, Frederick J., *100,000,000 Guinea Pigs* (Vanguard Press, New York, 1932).

Kendrick, John F., *Public Heath in the State and Counties of Virginia* (Virginia Department of Health, Richmond, 1939).

Kroeger, Gertrand, *The Concept of Socialized Medicine* (Julius Rosenwald Fund, Chicago, 1937).

Leonard, William A., *Organization and Administration of the Public Health Department* (Putnam's, New York, 1926).

McIntosh, William A., and Kendrick, John F., *Public Health Administration in North Carolina* (North Carolina State Board of Health, Raleigh, 1940).

Millis, Harry A., *Sickness and Insurance* (University of Chicago Press, 1937).

Mountin, Joseph W., and Flook, Evelyn, *Distribution of Health Services in the Structure of State Government*, Bulletin No. 184, Third Edition (United States Public Health Service, Washington, 1943).

Mustard, Harry S., *An Introduction to Public Health*, Second Edition (Macmillan, New York, 1944).

Paterson, Robert G., *Historical Directory of State Health Departments in the United States* (Ohio Public Health Association, Columbus, 1939).

Prescott, Samuel C., and Horwood, M. P., *Sedgwick's Principles of Sanitary Science and Public Health* (Macmillan, New York, 1935).

Reed, Louis S., *Health Insurance: The Next Step in Social Security* (Harper, New York, 1937).

Simpson, Herbert D., *Compulsory Health Insurance in the United States* (Northwestern University, 1943).

Smillie, Wilson G., *Public Health Administration in the United States*, Revised Edition (Macmillan, New York, 1940).

Tobey, James A., *Public Health Law*, Second Edition (Williams and Wilkins, Baltimore, 1939).

Turner, Clair E., *Principles of Health Education* (Heath, Boston, 1932).

Vaughan, Victor C., *Epidemiology and the Public Health*, 2 vols. (Mosby, St. Louis, 1932).

Wallace, James, *The State Health Departments of Massachusetts, Michigan, and Ohio* (Commonwealth Fund, New York, 1930).

Highways and Motor Vehicles

Agg, Thomas R., and Brindley, John E., *Highway Administration and Finance* (McGraw-Hill, New York, 1927).

Bateman, John H., *Introduction to Highway Engineering*, Third Edition (Wiley, New York, 1939).

Brown, Cecil K., *The State Highway System of North Carolina* (University of North Carolina Press, 1931).

Crawford, Finla G., *The Gasoline Tax in the United States* (Public Administration Service, Chicago, 1937).

——, and Peck, H. W., *Motor Vehicles and the Highway in New York; A Study of Social Benefits and Financial Burdens* (Syracuse University, 1927).

Curtiss, William M., *The Development of Highway Administration and Finance in New York* (Cornell University, 1927).

Dearing, Charles L., *American Highway Policy* (Brookings Institution, Washington, 1941).

DeSilva, Harry R., *Mechanical Tests for Drivers* (Cambridge, 1938) .

Ford, Robert S., and Bacon, Marvin A., *Michigan Highway Finance* (University of Michigan Press, 1943) .

Hewes, Lawrence I., *American Highway Practice* (Wiley, New York, 1942) .

Hoffman, Paul G., and Clark, N. M., *Several Roads to Safety: A Program to Reduce Automobile Accidents* (Harper, New York, 1939) .

Kansas Legislative Council, *Safety Regulation of Motor Vehicles* (Topeka, 1938) .

Kennedy, George D., *Modern Urban Highways* (Conference Committee on Urban Problems, Washington, 1944) .

Key, V. O., Jr., *The Administration of Federal Grants to the States* (Public Administration Service, Chicago, 1937) .

Levin, David R., *Public Control of Highway Access and Roadside Development* (Government Printing Office, Washington, 1943) .

McGalliard, H. W., *Guides to Highway Safety* (University of North Carolina Press, 1935) .

National Automobile Chamber of Commerce, *Facts and Figures of the Automobile Industry* (New York, annually) .

Pate, James E., *Highway Administration in the South* (Arnold Foundation, Dallas, 1935) .

Paustian, Raymond G., *Speed Regulation and Control on Rural Highways* (Highway Research Board, Washington, 1940) .

Petty, Ben H., *Some Fundamentals of Highway Improvement* (Purdue University, 1934) .

Plummer, Wilbur C., *The Road Policy of Pennsylvania* (University of Pennsylvania, 1925) .

Stewart, Frank M., *Highway Administration in Texas* (University of Texas, 1934) .

Stocker, Harry E., *Motor Traffic Management* (Prentice-Hall, New York, 1938) .

Tripp, Herbert A., *Road Traffic and Its Control* (Arnold, London, 1938) .

Trull, Edna, *Borrowing for Highways* (Dun and Bradstreet, New York, 1937) .

Tucker, Harry, and Leager, Marc C., *Highway Economics* (International Correspondence Schools, Scranton, 1942) .

Walker, John E., *Highway Tax Costs* (National Highway Users Conference, Washington, 1938) .

Insurance

Gilbert, Mort, and E. A., *Life Insurance: A Legalized Racket* (Farrar and Rinehart, New York, 1936) .

Hobbs, Clarence W., *State Regulation and State Insurance* (Milwaukee, 1927) .

Huebner, Solomon S., Ed., " Modern Insurance Developments," *Annals,* May, 1932.

McCahan, David, *State Insurance in the United States* (University of Pennsylvania Press, 1929) .

Patterson, Edwin W., *The Insurance Commissioner in the United States* (Harvard University Press, 1927) .

Tarbell, Thomas F., *Legal Requirements and State Supervision of Fire Insurance* (Insurance Society of New York, New York, 1927).

Labor

Altmeyer, Arthur J., *The Industrial Commission of Wisconsin* (University of Wisconsin, 1932).

Andrews, John B., *Administrative Labor Legislation: A Study of American Experience in the Delegation of Legislative Power* (Harper, New York, 1936).

——, *Labor Laws in Action* (Harper, New York, 1938).

Atkinson, Raymond C., and others, *Public Employment Services in the United States* (Public Administration Service, Chicago, 1938).

Baker, Helen, *Employee Counseling* (Princeton University Press, 1944).

Beckner, Earl R., *History of Labor Legislation in Illinois* (University of Chicago Press, 1931).

Beyer, Clara M., *History of Labor Legislation for Women in Three States* (Women's Bureau, Washington, 1929).

Bowers, John H., *The Kansas Court of Industrial Relations* (McClurg, Chicago, 1922).

Bowman, Dean O., *Public Control of Labor Relations* (Macmillan, New York, 1942).

Brannon, Victor DeW., *Employers Liability and Workmen's Compensation in Arizona* (University of Arizona, 1934).

Braun, Kurt, *The Settlement of Industrial Disputes* (Blakiston, Philadelphia, 1944).

Callcott, Mary S., *Labor Legislation in New York* (Macmillan, New York, 1931).

——, *Principles of Social Legislation* (Macmillan, New York, 1932).

Commons, John R., and Andrews, John B., *Principles of Labor Legislat*, Fourth Edition (Harper, New York, 1936).

Daugherty, Carroll R., *Labor Problems in American Industry* (Houghton Mifflin, Boston, 1936).

Dawson, Marshall, *Problems of Workmens Compensation Administration in the United States and Canada* (Bureau of Labor Statistics, Washington, 1940).

Donaldson, McPherrin H., *Labor Problems in the United States* (Longmans, Green, New York, 1939).

Duke University Law School, *Labor in War Time* (Durham, 1942).

Epstein, Abraham, *Insecurity: A Challenge to America,* Third Edition (Smith and Haas, New York, 1936).

Feinsinger, Nathan P., and Rice, William G., *The Wisconsin Labor Relations Act* (University of Wisconsin Bulletin, 1937).

Fuller, Raymond G., and Strong, Mabel A., *Child Labor in Massachusetts* (Houghton Mifflin, Boston, 1926).

Gagliardo, Domenico, *The Kansas Industrial Court* (University of Kansas Publication, 1941).

Hamilton, Alice, *Industrial Poisons in the United States* (Macmillan, New York, 1929).

Hopkins, Jess T., *The Emergency of a New Public Employment Service* (Public Employment Center of Rochester, 1935).

Horlacker, J. Perry, *The Results of Workmens Compensation in Pennsylvania* (Harrisburg, 1934).

Kaltenborn, Howard S., *Governmental Adjustment of Labor Disputes* (Foundation Press, Chicago, 1943).

King, Alfred S., *Unemployment Insurance* (University of California, Bureau of Public Administration, 1934).

Leiserson, William M., *Right and Wrong in Labor Relations* (University of California Press, 1942).

Macdonald, Mary E., *Federal Grants for Vocational Rehabilitation* (University of Chicago Press, 1944).

Magnusson, Leifur, *Workmens Compensation for Public Employees* (Public Administration Service, Chicago, 1943).

Mariano, John H., *Wartime Labor Relations* (National Public and Labor Relations Service Bureau, New York, 1944).

Matscheck, Walter, and Atkinson, Raymond C., *Problems and Procedures of Unemployment Compensation in the States* (Public Administration Service, Chicago, 1937).

Mayer, Marian, *Workmens Compensation Law in Louisiana* (Louisiana State University Press, 1937).

Millis, Harry A., and Montgomery, Royal E., *Labor's Risks and Social Insurance,* 2 vols. (McGraw-Hill, New York, 1938).

National Child Labor Committee, *Child Labor Law and Child Labor Facts* (New York, annually since 1929).

New York State Joint Legislative Committee on Industrial Relations, *The American Story of Industrial and Labor Relations* (Albany, 1943).

Pierson, Frank C., *Collective Bargaining Systems* (American Council on Public Affairs, Washington, 1942).

Reed, George L., *Law of Labor Relations* (Soney and Sage, Newark, 1942).

Ryan, Frederick L., *A History of Labor Legislation in Oklahoma* (University of Oklahoma Press, 1932).

Smith, Florence P., *Chronological Development of Labor Legislation for Women in the United States* (Women's Bureau, Washington, 1929).

——, *State Minimum Wage Laws and Orders* (Women's Bureau, Washington, 1929).

Stewart, Bryce M., *Planning and Administration of Unemployment Compensation in the United States* (Industrial Relations Counselors, New York, 1938).

Stilt, Louise, and Smith, Florence P., *Progress of State Minimum Wage Legislation* (Bureau of Labor Statistics, Washington, 1939).

Taylor, Albion G., *Labor Problems and Labor Law* (Prentice-Hall, New York, 1938).

Teaf, Howard M., Jr., *Self Insurance of Workmen's Compensation in Pennsylvania* (Harrisburg, 1934).

Toner, Jerome L., *The Closed Shop* (American Council on Public Affairs, Washington, 1942).

United States Department of Labor, *Monthly Labor Review* (Washington, monthly).

United States Social Security Board, *Unemployment Insurance: What and Why?* (Washington, 1937).

White, Raymond G., *Administering Unemployment Compensation* (Public Administration Service, Chicago, 1939).

Witte, Edwin E., *The Government in Labor Disputes* (McGraw-Hill, New York, 1932).

Law Enforcement and Corrections

Barnes, Harry E., and Teeters, Negley K., *New Horizons in Criminology: The American Crime Problem* (Prentice-Hall, New York, 1943).

Cantor, Nathaniel F., *Crime and Society: An Introduction to Criminology* (Holt, New York, 1939).

Carr, Lowell J., *Delinquency Control* (Harper, New York, 1941).

Fishman, Joseph F., *Crucibles of Crime* (Cosmopolitan Press, New York, 1923).

Gillin, John L., *Criminology and Penology,* Revised Edition (Appleton-Century, New York, 1935).

Glueck, Sheldon, *Crime and Justice* (Little, Brown, Boston, 1936).

——, and E. T., *Criminal Careers in Retrospect* (Commonwealth Fund, 1943).

——, *Juvenile Delinquents Grown Up* (Commonwealth Fund, 1940).

Haynes, Fred E., *The American Prison System* (McGraw-Hill, New York, 1939).

——, *Criminology,* Second Edition (McGraw-Hill, New York, 1935).

Heinberg, John G., and Breckinridge, A. C., *Law Enforcement in Missouri, 1931–1941* (University of Missouri Studies, 1942).

Hooton, Ernest A., *The American Criminal: An Anthropological Study* (Harvard University Press, 1939).

——, *Crime and the Man* (Harvard University Press, 1939).

LaRoe, Wilbur, Jr., *Parole with Honor* (Princeton University Press, 1939).

Lawes, Lewis E., *Twenty Thousand Years in Sing Sing* (Long and Smith, New York, 1932).

MacCormick, Austin H., Ed., *Handbook of American Prisons and Reformatories,* Fifth Edition (Osborne Association, New York, 1942).

Millspaugh, Arthur C., *Local Democracy and Crime Control* (Brookings Institution, Washington, 1936).

Monroe, David G., *State and Provincial Police: A Study in Police Functioning in the United States and Canada* (Northwestern University Traffic Institute, 1941).

Moos, Malcolm C., *State Penal Administration in Alabama* (University of Alabama, Bureau of Public Administration, 1942).

Olander, Oscar G., *Michigan State Police* (Michigan Police Journal Press, Lansing, 1942).

Pugmire, D. Ross, *The Administration of Personnel in Correctional Institutions in New York State* (Columbia University, Teachers College, 1937).

Reckless, Walter C., *Criminal Behavior* (McGraw-Hill, New York, 1940).

——, *The Etiology of Delinquent and Criminal Behavior* (Social Science Research Council, New York, 1943).

Robinson, Louis N., *Jails: Care and Treatment of Misdemeanant Prisoners in the United States* (Winston, Philadelphia, 1944).

Sellin, Thorsten, *The Criminality of Youth* (American Law Institute, Philadelphia, 1940).

Shaw, Clifford R., and McKay, Henry D., *Juvenile Delinquency and Urban Areas* (Iowa State University, 1942).

Smith, Bruce, *Rural Crime Control* (Institute of Public Administration, Columbia University, 1933).

——, *State Police* (Macmillan, New York, 1925).

Smith, Reginald H., *Justice and the Poor* (Carnegie Foundation, New York, 1919).

Taft, Donald R., *Criminology: An Attempt at a Synthetic Interpretation with a Cultural Emphasis* (Macmillan, New York, 1942).

Tannenbaum, Frank, *Crime and the Community* (Ginn, New York, 1938).

Tulchin, Simon H., *Intelligence and Crime* (University of Chicago Press, 1939).

Vollmer, August, and Parker, Alfred E., *Crime and the State Police* (University of California Press, 1935).

Waite, John B., *The Criminal Law in Action* (Sears, New York, 1934).

Wallack, Walter M., and others, *Education within Prison Walls* (Columbia University, Teachers College, 1939).

Weir, Eligius, *Criminology, a Scientific Study of the Modern Crime Problem* (Institute for the Scientific Study of Crime, Joliet, 1941).

Willoughby, W. F., *Principles of Judicial Administration* (Brookings Institution, Washington, 1929).

Wood, Sterling, *Riot Control by the National Guard* (Military Service Publishing Company, Harrisburg, 1940).

Young, Pauline V., *Social Treatment in Probation and Delinquency* (McGraw-Hill, New York, 1937).

Planning

Bunbury, Henry N., *Governmental Planning Machinery* (Public Administration Service, Chicago, 1938).

California State Planning Board, *An Introduction to State Planning* (Sacramento, 1937).

Cole, William E., and Crowe, Hugh P., *Recent Trends in Rural Planning* (Prentice-Hall, New York, 1937).

Goodrich, Carter, and others, *Migration and Economic Opportunity* (University of Pennsylvania Press, 1937).

Holcombe, Arthur N., *Government in a Planned Democracy* (Norton, New York, 1935).

Iowa State College, *An Introductory Series of Lectures on National, Regional, State, and Town Planning* (Ames, 1936).

Lohman, Karl B., *Regional Planning* (Edwards Brothers, Ann Arbor, 1937).

McKinley, Charles, *Five Years of Planning in the Pacific Northwest* (Northwest Regional Council, Portland, 1939).

McKinley, Findley, *Planned Society: Yesterday, Today, and Tomorrow* (Prentice-Hall, New York, 1937).

National Resources Committee, *State Planning: Progress and Accomplishments* (Washington, 1936).

——, *The Future of State Planning* (Washington, 1938).

——, *The State and Planning* (Washington, 1938).

——, *Regional Factors in National Planning* (Washington, 1935).

——, *Water Planning* (Washington, 1938).

——, *Technology and Planning* (Washington, 1937).

Odum, Howard W., *Southern Regions of the United States* (University of North Carolina Press, 1936).

——, and Moore, Harry E., *Regionalism in the United States* (Holt, New York, 1938).

Public Utilities

Barnes, Irston R., *Cases on Public Utility Regulation* (Crofts, New York, 1938).

——, *Public Utility Control in Massachusetts* (Yale University Press, 1930).

——, *The Economics of Public Utility Regulation* (Crofts, New York, 1942).

Bauer, John, *The Effective Regulation of Utilities* (Macmillan, New York, 1925).

Baum, Robert D., *The Federal Power Commission and State Utility Regulation* (American Council on Public Affairs, Washington, 1942).

Bonbright, James C., *Public Utilities and the National Power Policies* (Columbia University Press, 1940).

——, and Means, Gardner C., *The Holding Company: Its Public Significance and Its Regulation* (McGraw-Hill, New York, 1932).

Bryant, John M., and Hermann, R. R., *Elements of Utility Rate Determination* (McGraw-Hill, New York, 1940).

Burke, Henry J., *Public Utility Regulation in Maryland* (Johns Hopkins Press, 1931).

Bussing, Irvin, *Public Utility Regulation and the So-Called Sliding Scale* (Columbia University Press, 1936).

Elsbree, Hugh L., *Interstate Transmission of Electric Power — a Study in the Conflict of State and Federal Jurisdictions* (Harvard University Press, 1931).

Fesler, James W., *Independence of Regulatory Agencies* (Public Administration Service, Chicago, 1942).

Hunt, Edward M., Ed., *The Power Industry and the Public Interest* (Commonwealth Fund, New York, 1944).

Kidd, Howard C., *Railroad Consolidation and the State of Pennsylvania* (Public Service Commission, Harrisburg, 1930).

Lentz, Gilbert G., *Enforcement of the Orders of State Public Service Commissions* (University of Illinois, 1940).

Kneier, Charles M., *State Regulation of Public Utilities in Illinois* (University of Illinois, 1927).

Maltbie, William H., *Theory and Practice of Public Utility Valuation* (McGraw-Hill, New York, 1924).

Mosher, William E., Ed., *Electrical Utilities, the Crisis in Public Control* (Harper, New York, 1929).

——, and Crawford, Finla G., *Public Utility Regulation* (Harper, New York, 1933).

New York Public Service Commission, *Regulation of Public Utilities during the War* (Albany, 1943).

Pegrum, Dudley F., *Rate Theories and the California Railroad Commission* (University of California, 1932).

Reynolds, George C., *The Distribution of Power to Regulate Interstate*

Carriers between the Nation and the State (Columbia University Press, 1931).

Waltersdorf, Maurice C., *Regulation of Public Utilities in New Jersey* (Waverly Press, Trenton, 1936).

Waterman, Merwin H., *Public Utility Financing, 1930–1935* (University of Michigan Business Studies, 1936).

Public Welfare

Abbott, Edith, *Public Assistance* (University of Chicago Press, 1940).

Abbott, Grace, *From Relief to Social Security* (University of Chicago Press, 1941).

Atwater, Pierce, *Problems of Administration in Social Work* (University of Minnesota Press, 1940).

Beard, Charles A., *Public Policy and the General Welfare* (Farrar and Rinehart, New York, 1941).

Bossard, James H. S., *Social Change and Social Problems,* Revised Edition (Harper, New York, 1938).

Breckinridge, Sophanisba P., *Public Welfare Administration: Select Documents* (University of Chicago Press, 1927).

——, *Public Welfare Administration with Special Reference to the Organization of State Departments* (University of Chicago Press, 1934).

Brown, Josephine C., *Public Relief, 1929–1939* (Holt, New York, 1940).

Brown, Roy M., *Public Poor Relief in North Carolina* (University of North Carolina Press, 1928).

Butler, Amos W., *A Century of Progress, a Study of the Development of Public Charities and Corrections, 1790–1915* (State Board of Charities, Indianapolis, 1916).

Cahn, Frances, and Bary, Valeska, *Welfare Activities of Federal, State and Local Governments in California, 1850–1934* (University of California Press, 1936).

Clarke, Helen I., *Social Legislation* (Appleton-Century, New York, 1940).

Colcord, Joanna C., *Cash Relief* (Russell Sage Foundation, New York, 1936).

Deutsch, Albert, *The Mentally Ill in America* (Doubleday, Doran, Garden City, 1938).

Douglas, Paul H., *Social Security in the United States* (McGraw-Hill, New York, 1936).

Fenton, Norman, *State Child Guidance Service in California* (Department of Social Welfare, Sacramento, 1938).

Grant, Margaret, *Old-Age Security: Social and Financial Trends* (Social Science Research Council, Committee on Social Security, Washington, 1939).

Harper, Ernest B., and Gibson, Duane L., *Reorganization of Public Welfare in Michigan* (Michigan State College, 1942).

James, Arthur W., *The State Becomes a Social Worker* (Garrett and Massie, Richmond, 1942).

Indiana Department of Public Welfare, *Four Years of Public Welfare in Indiana, 1936–1940* (Indianapolis, 1941).

Kallert, John, *Child Dependency in Illinois* (State Department of Welfare, Springfield, 1941).

Kelso, Robert W., *History of Public Poor Relief in Massachusetts, 1820–1920* (Houghton Mifflin, Boston, 1922).

Klein, Alice C., *Civil Service in Public Welfare* (Russell Sage Foundation, New York, 1940).

Kurz, Russell H., Ed., *Social Work Year Book* (Russell Sage Foundation, New York, annually).

Lane, Marie D., and Steegmuller, Francis, *America on Relief* (Harcourt, Brace, New York, 1938).

Lansdale, Robert T., and others, *The Administration of Old-Age Assistance* (Public Administration Service, Chicago, 1939).

Milchrist, Elizabeth H., *State Administration of Child Welfare in Illinois* (University of Chicago Press, 1937).

Millspaugh, Arthur C., *Public Welfare Organization* (Brookings Institution, Washington, 1935).

National Resources Planning Board, *Security, Work, and Relief Policies* (Washington, 1942).

National Conference of Social Work, *Proceedings* (Columbus, annually since 1917).

Nelson, Beatrice W., *State Recreation* (National Conference of State Parks, Washington, 1928).

O'Brien, Edward J., *Child Welfare Legislation in Maryland, 1634–1936* (Catholic University of America, 1937).

Odegard, Bernett, and Keith, George M., *A History of the State Board of Control of Wisconsin and the State Institutions, 1849–1939* (State Board of Control, Madison, 1940).

Odum, Howard W., and Willard, D. W., *Systems of Public Welfare* (University of North Carolina Press, 1925).

Pennsylvania Department of Welfare, *Poor Relief Administration in Pennsylvania* (Harrisburg, 1934).

Stafford, Paul T., *State Welfare Administration in New Jersey* (Department of Institutions and Agencies, Trenton, 1934).

Stevenson, Marietta, and MacDonald, Alice, *State and Local Public Welfare Agencies* (American Public Welfare Association, Chicago, 1939).

Stewart, Bruce M., and others, *Planning and Administration of Unemployment Compensation in the United States* (Industrial Relations Counselors, New York, 1938).

Street, Elwood, *The Public Welfare Administrator* (McGraw-Hill, New York, 1940).

Troxel, Andrew G., *Outdoor Recreation Legislation and Its Effectiveness* (Columbia University Press, 1929).

White, R. Clyde, *Administration of Public Welfare* (American Book Company, New York, 1940).

—— and Mary K., *Social Aspects of Relief Policies in the Depression* (Social Science Research Council, New York, 1937).

Wisconsin Department of Public Welfare, *A Half Billion Dollars for Public Welfare in Wisconsin, 1931–1936* (Madison, 1938).

Woytinsky, Waldimir S., *Earnings and Social Security in the United States* (Social Science Research Council, Washington, 1943).

Wyatt, Birchard E., and others, *Social Security Act in Operation* (Graphic Arts Press, Washington, 1937).

CHAPTER XII

Personnel Management

THE governments of the states are so dependent on the intelligent and devoted service of thousands of employees that any general discussion of state government which failed to mention them would be incomplete indeed. A survey made in 1939 showed that one person in every nine works for the government; that the salaries and wages of public employees, excluding relief workers, exceeded $5,000,000,000 — approximately one eighth of all the wages paid in the United States.[1] By mid-1943 with the influx of war workers in industry, the ratio had dropped to one eighth, but the cost had risen to more than one billion dollars a month for nearly six and a half million employees. In succeeding months down to 1945 a downward tendency in the total number of state employees begun in 1941 continued, along with a corresponding upward trend in payrolls. The trend and the figures on both items are indicated in the accompanying graph.

Various writers have pointed out the important distinction that must be made between officers and employees. Officers are those who, in positions filled either by election or by appointment, are responsible for the administration of the several departments, boards, and commissions of the government. Certain aspects of their selection and of the organization and functions of their agencies were considered in an earlier chapter. For the present we are concerned with the state employees, including clerks, stenographers, draftsmen, technical workers, janitors, inspectors, members of the field force, and many others, all of whom are selected by appointment, under a patronage or a civil service or merit system. A distinction should also

[1] Gray, Edward R., and Divine, William R., " One in Every Nine Works for the Government," *National Municipal Review,* March, 1939, pp. 204–212, 239, and regular bulletins on government employment from the United States Bureau of the Census.

STATE AND LOCAL NONSCHOOL PUBLIC EMPLOYMENT: 1940-1945*

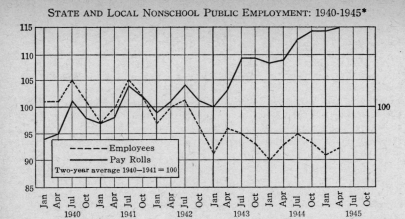

*From " Public Employment in April, 1945," in *Government Employment*, U. S. Bureau of the Census, June, 1945.

be made between a position and an employee. The position is an amount of work to be done, presumably sufficient to require the full time of an employee during business hours; once created, the position continues to exist, whether or not it is filled. The employee, on the other hand, is the person who fills the position.

The history of the state service and the operation of the spoils system, some of the fundamental problems in the field of personnel administration, the development of the civil service and merit system, and some of the current problems in the personnel field will now be briefly considered.

HISTORY OF THE STATE SERVICE

Problems of recruiting and organizing the personnel enlisted in performing the functions of government have long been important. In the early days, when the number of services performed by government was small and their extent limited, the number of public employees was small, and their duties were such that they could be performed by any ordinarily intelligent person. Studies in the history of personnel administration indicate that at a very early date such positions as were available were commonly regarded as spoils to be distributed among the party workers who supported the candidates victorious at the polls. In his *Civil Service and the Patronage* the late Professor Carl Russell Fish described in some detail early developments in such states as New York, Pennsylvania, and Massachusetts. In order that the reader may have clearly in mind the nature of the conditions existing at that time, the following excerpts from his book are included:

New York. New York was the first state in which the officers were openly and continuously used for partisan purposes. There the royal appointments had been conspicuously bad, and colonial politics especially active. This experience was probably responsible for the elaborate attempt, made in the first constitution, to limit the appointing power of the executive, and to secure proper recognition for the various geographical sections. The state was divided into four districts, each represented by an equal number of senators. . . .

The conditions which governed the working of this machinery of appointment were complicated, and do not readily admit of brief explanation. New York politics had been controlled in the colonial period by family groups or combinations, based largely on land and old manorial privileges. The power of some of these groups was broken by the Revolution, but a large part of the population lacked American political experience and ideals, and were still ready to follow leaders; hence the influence of certain families remained. The Livingstons were the most conspicuous; the Van Rensselaers were prominent for years; and the Schuylers, united with Alexander Hamilton by marriage, dominated the Federalist party. Besides these older families, the long governorship of George Clinton seems to have created a strong permanent interest, which passed to his nephew, De Witt Clinton, while in New York City the democracy was marshalled by such organizations and leaders as Tammany Hall and Aaron Burr. Although Republican formulas were used, politics continued to be a game played by a number of factions, some aristocratic, some democratic, by bosses and patrons. The political situation reproduced in miniature that of England during the eighteenth century. . . . The spoils system was particularly dangerous in New York because of the enormous extent of the patronage.[2]

Pennsylvania. Under the first constitution most appointments in Pennsylvania were controlled by the legislature, either alone or in conjunction with the president of the commonwealth who also was practically elected by it. Though no instances of removal have been found, complaint was made that offices were used to win adherents, and it is mentioned as remarkable that Rittenhouse should have held his office of treasurer for thirteen successive years, under legislatures now of one party, now of the other. In 1783, the Council of Censors called the attention of the legislature to the low standard of the holders of public offices. Mifflin, the first governor under the new constitution, began his term by refusing to reappoint certain officers who had served under the old. Although elected as a Constitutionalist, that is, as of the more democratic party, he soon turned Federalist, and apparently confined his appointments to members of that party.

Such was the situation that Thomas McKean found when, in 1799, he was elected governor, first of the *fin de siécle* Republican victors. He ac-

[2] Fish, Carl Russell, *The Civil Service and the Patronage*, pp. 86–87 (Harvard University Press, 1920).

cused of combination against him the "officers and expectants of office under the President of the United States, not only in Pennsylvania, but in neighboring states," and he wrote to John Dickinson, "I have been obliged (though no Hercules) to cleanse the Augean stable." To Jefferson, in July 1810, he outlined his theory of the civil service. "It appears," he said, "that the anti-Republicans, even those in office, are as hostile as ever, though not so insolent. To overcome them they must be shaven, for in their offices (like Samson's hair-locks) their great strength lieth; their disposition for mischief may remain, but their power of doing it will be gone. It is out of the common order of nature, to prefer enemies to friends; the despisers of the people should not be their rulers." The whole tone of this letter indicates that already in Pennsylvania the civil offices were considered as ammunition for political warfare — a fact which Jefferson must have seen clearly when he wrote to McKean, "Some states require a different regimen from others.". . .

The results of the spoils system in New York and Pennsylvania seem to have been as different as were the circumstances of its growth. The average standard of men called into the New York State service was certainly higher. Nearly always some men of eminent ability were to be found in the civil list. This was partly due to the system of family cliques which made politics fashionable, and also partly to the fact that at first the confusion of factions, and later the even balance of parties, always afforded an opportunity for talent. Many other causes might, of course, be enumerated. Besides this difference there seems to have been more actual corruption in Pennsylvania than in the neighboring state, if we except New York City. Cases of actual sale of office are reported. Niles gives an instance in which a note was actually sued out, the drawer of which had promised to pay the holder a certain sum if he were appointed to a post which the latter was about to resign, the consideration presumably being the influence of the old occupant with the governor. Naturally the offices of the national government did not escape the contagion.[3]

Massachusetts. Of the northern states, Massachusetts was perhaps the most exemplary in the conduct of the civil service; yet there, as in Rhode Island, an element existed eager for the spoils. Under the early state government there was practically no complaint as to appointments; but when the Federalists began to condemn Jefferson's removals, their opponents replied by accusing them of excluding all Republicans from office. The best vindication of their administration is found in the conduct of James Sullivan, the first Republican governor. He was a strong, conscientious man, and refused to make any removals. The radicals of the party under the lead of Levi Lincoln controlled the executive council and urged proscription, finally putting on file a protest in which they argued that to make no removals "would be arraigning the wisdom and justice of the national administration, a censure and reproach of its most deliberate acts." Had they been able to add that the conduct of the Federalist governors had been notoriously unfair, Sullivan could hardly have resisted. . . .

In 1810, another Republican, Elbridge Gerry, was elected governor. In

[3] *Ibid.*, pp. 92–93, 94–95.

his first term he made no removals and reappointed those whose commissions expired, although he doubtless found the great majority of office-holders Federalists. [Later] Governor Gerry fulfilled the wishes of his party, and was bombarded with protests from the public in general, and from dispossessed office-holders. He tried to explain and justify his conduct, arguing that the reappointment of former discredited office-holders would alarm the Republicans; that Democratic principles demanded that, when the offices fell vacant, equal consideration should be shown to all citizens, no preference being extended to incumbents. His extenuations could not, however, do away with the appearance of sharp practice. . . .[4]

The West. The frontier democracy of the West shared the characteristics of both North and South. During this period the people were divided according to personal sympathy and special issues, and consequently party lines were fluctuating. Hence there was no persistent and studied use of patronage to maintain party organization; but offices were none the less used by the leaders to promote the ends of the moment, while the people demanded that all public servants, appointive as well as elective, should be in sympathy with the majority. The conditions of this section are best illustrated by a study of Illinois, for which the career of Ninian Edwards serves as a convenient nucleus. . . .[5]

It has been customary for uninformed persons to blame the advent of the spoils system in the Federal government upon Andrew Jackson. Professor Fish makes it clear that the spoils system originated in the states, that terrific pressure was exerted upon the Presidents preceding Jackson, and that its introduction into the Federal government under Jackson represented simply the fulfillment of an insistent public demand which could not have been resisted much longer by anyone, and which Jackson had no disposition to resist at all. While occasional demands for investigations of conditions in the public service were made in Congress, it does not appear that anything important along this line occurred in the states. Even in the Federal government, the spoils system existed undisturbed for almost exactly fifty years, until in 1883 the Pendleton Act was passed.

The Civil Service Era. While some agitation for a more suitable system for the selection of public employees had begun before the Civil War, no action had been taken in any of the states. In 1880 the New York Civil Service Reform Association was organized, its name being changed later to the National Civil Service Reform League. It secured its first victory by the passage of the Pendleton Act. A few months later New York established a civil service commission, vested with the authority to prepare and administer tests for the selection of persons for the state service. Massachusetts followed in 1884. For

[4] *Ibid.,* pp. 95-97.   [5] *Ibid.,* p. 99.

more than twenty years these two states served as the sole exponents of something better than the spoils system in state government.

Early in the present century a new era of civil service reform began. In 1905 Illinois and Wisconsin set up civil service commissions and provided for the selection of state employees on a merit basis. Two years later similar action was taken in Colorado and New Jersey; in succeeding years the number of states with civil service systems has increased to approximately half of the forty-eight states. Considering the importance of the subject and the great need of reform, this is not a very impressive record. In 1929, forty-three state legislatures were in session, into five of which state civil service bills were introduced. Not one of these was adopted, but since 1935 the movement has been making more substantial progress. The Federal government has given considerable impetus to the development of civil service systems in the states, especially in the social security field.[6]

FUNDAMENTAL PROBLEMS IN PERSONNEL ADMINISTRATION

It is now generally recognized that there must be some agency in the state government charged with responsibility for handling personnel problems. The idea that the personnel agency must be independent of the operating departments and outside the general administrative plan has been largely abandoned. In modern government one finds this agency accepted and recognized as an integral part of the administrative machinery. Charles P. Messick, Secretary and Chief Examiner for the New Jersey Civil Service Commission, well states this point when he says that the personnel agency must operate as an auxiliary agency " in close cooperation with the budgeting and finance authorities and with each department and agency of the government. Its interests are not opposed to the interests of the operating department, of the executive and legislative officers, or of the people. Its interests and theirs are identical. Its attitude should be one of helpfulness, understanding, and cooperation and it should seek to cultivate and encourage a like attitude on the part of operating officers."

After a state has determined the kind of personnel system it wants and the kind of central organization that is to administer it, attention may be given to some of the major problems with which such an

---

[6] Benson, George C. S., " Federal-State Personal Relations," *Annals*, January, 1940, pp. 38–43.

organization must deal. These must be cared for in some way or other, regardless of the type of organization adopted:

1. Recruiting and Examining.
2. Appointment and Placement.
3. Classification.
4. Compensation.
5. Training.
6. Conditions of Work.
7. Employee Relations.
8. Health and Safety.
9. Changes in Status.
10. Separations.
11. Assistance to Departments.

Provision must be made for the administration of payroll and leave records, but this function will not necessarily be a responsibility of the personnel agency.

Recruiting and Examining. The finding of persons who would be willing to enter the state employ and who have the qualifications for rendering satisfactory service to the state is, in many cases, no easy task. In the past this work was often done in a perfunctory manner by announcing examinations, examining those who applied, and certifying the best of these for appointment. Little real recruiting was undertaken. During World War II the states as well as the Federal government learned that, if well-qualified persons are to be secured for consideration, it is necessary to go out and find them, and very often sell them on the desirability of the positions to be filled.[7]

Under a patronage system the applicant must come to the appointing officer with the proper political sponsorship; under a merit system, he must, by an examination, either assembled or unassembled, establish the fact that he has the qualifications requisite for the type of work to be performed. Even where a system of examinations exists, it applies only to the classified service; there remains a large number of positions in the unclassified service which must be filled by the appointment of persons whose qualifications are otherwise established.

In the larger states the volume of such work is considerable and it is constantly increasing. The Illinois Commission reported in 1942 more than 35,000 tests — written, oral, and performance — given to applicants for positions in the state service. On one single day in that year, more than 12,000 persons took examinations for positions in twenty-six different classes in the service, chiefly clerical and steno-

---

[7] On recruiting, see: Civil Service Assembly of the United States and Canada, *Recruiting Applicants for the Public Service* (Chicago, 1942) ; Graves, W. Brooke, and Herring, James M., " Recruiting Administrative Personnel in the Field," *Public Administration Review*, Autumn, 1942, pp. 302–311; Kingsley, J. Donald, " Recruitment, the Quest for Competence," *Public Personnel Review*, January, 1941, pp. 28–35.

graphic. The following table for New York, our oldest state system, shows the growth in the number of candidates examined, the number in the service, and the number and percentage of competitive, non-competitive or qualifying, and exempt positions, at five-year intervals from 1900 to 1940: [8]

NEW YORK STATE CIVIL SERVICE COMMISSION
THE DEVELOPMENT OF THE EXAMINING FUNCTION

Year	Number of Candidates	Number in Service	Competitive	Per Cent	Non-competitive	Per Cent	Exempt	Per Cent
1900	3,193	9,375	3,612	38	4,106	43	755	.08
1905	4,155	11,413	4,080	35	4,879	42	1,284	.11
1910	13,658	15,993	7,722	48	5,925	37	1,195	.07
1915	29,893	20,556	11,064	53	6,633	32	1,616	.07
1920	18,069	21,588	11,333	52	7,213	33	1,520	.07
1925	14,850	30,014	13,766	45	9,398	31	1,329	.04
1930	40,876	42,956	19,597	45	13,110	30	1,351	.03
1935	35,674	50,455	21,406	42	15,190	30	1,596	.03
1940	63,005	63,971	29,919	46	22,061	34	1,560	.02

The number of examinations of all types grows with the service. Note, however, that not only the number but the percentage of positions covered by competitive examinations shows a steady increase, with a corresponding decline in the percentage — but not the number — of non-competitive examinations. Neither the number nor the percentage of exempt positions has been very great at any time since 1900.

Appointment and Placement. After the examinations have been given, the papers are rated, and registers set up. When requisitions are received by the central personnel agency, i.e., the Commission, names are certified to the appointing officer from the top of the register, as required. In most states they operate — as does the Federal government — under the rule of three, which means that the appointing officer has the privilege of selecting one out of three for each vacancy to be filled. Having made his selection, the problem of proper placement rests with the appointing officer.

When the appointments have been made, the individuals assume their duties subject to such conditions of tenure as the laws in their jurisdiction provide — under a civil service system, always for a probationary period. Officials are commissioned by the governor, and

[8] *Fifty-Ninth Annual Report,* 1941; this report gives an excellent historical sketch of the growth of civil service in New York.

hold office as a rule for a definitely stated term, subject to the governor's power of removal; state employees, on the other hand, are not commissioned, and hold their positions at the pleasure of the appointing power or during good behavior.

Classification. The classification of positions can be made only on the basis of a job-analysis survey. It is necessary to ascertain and record the duties of all positions in both the classified and the unclassified service, grouping these positions into suitable classes, assigning descriptive titles, and preparing complete written specifications for each class.[9] When such an analysis is begun, there are likely to be opposition and a lack of cooperation on the part of some departments; there is always a tendency for employees to try to show that they are indispensable. This difficulty does not occur when the individual enters a service where the classification has already been made. It is of vital importance that this work be done, whether or not the state has a civil service system, because there is no other way in which the principle of equal pay for equal work can be made effective. In a state where no such classification has been made, it is not uncommon to find two workers in different departments doing exactly the same kind of work, one receiving twice as much pay as the other. Obviously there is no defense for such a procedure.

Compensation. Compensation — salary and wage schedules — is closely related to the classification of positions. Very often the provisions on both matters are incorporated in the same legislation. Provision should be made for the local determination of wage schedules. Generally speaking, the levels of compensation in the state service are poor. The top officials — at least in some states — receive good salaries, but the regular employees are poorly paid indeed. This condition became acute during World War II when substantial increases in the cost of living occurred, in spite of impressive efforts to prevent inflation. Cost of living increases were necessary, but since most of these were temporary in character, they cannot be regarded as having improved the general condition with regard to inadequate compensation in the state services. Provision must be made for within-grade salary advances and should include also provision for meritorious promotions. Such variations exist in the pay plans of the

9 Such classifications are put out from time to time in most jurisdictions. On the principles of classification, see Civil Service Assembly of the United States and Canada, *Position Classification in the Public Service* (Chicago, 1941) , and Baruch, Ismar, " Basic Aspects of Position Classification," *Public Personnel Review,* October, 1940, pp. 1–17, and *Facts and Fallacies about Position Classification* (Civil Service Assembly, Chicago, 1937) .

several jurisdictions that it is difficult to generalize about them further than to say that most of them provide for inadequate compensation.[10]

The most progressive and intelligent approach to the pay problem made in recent years is the sliding scale device developed in Minnesota. As applied in the State Highway Department, it provides for a guaranteed annual income as well as for employment stabilization. The same principle has been applied to the municipal employees of St. Paul. An annual adjustment of wages is made in accordance with changes in the cost of living, as revealed by standard indices; under this plan both the civil employees and the taxpayers are assured a fair deal. Under the old system pay increases follow very belatedly increases in living costs and respond rather promptly to decreases in living costs. Under the Minnesota plan, the time-lag is largely eliminated.[11]

Training. Training is being gradually recognized as an important aspect of the personnel function. Training takes place in every office or shop every day, whether formally recognized as such or not. The new employee must be inducted into service. The official tells his secretary how he wants a particular job done, or instructs her in handling a new procedure. The foreman tells his men how a new process will affect their work. Instruction may be given either in groups or on an individual basis, ordinarily on agency time.

There are various types of training — pre-induction, orientation, in-service, on-the-job, et cetera. Pre-induction training is given before the employee enters on duty. The individual may or may not be actually in the employ of the agency. Orientation training is given at the time of employment for the purpose of explaining to the new worker the organization and functioning of the agency. He must be shown where he works and given instructions necessary for the proper performance of his duties. In-service training is used during the

10 For a good study of this problem, see Nebraska Legislative Council, *The Compensation of Officers and Employees of the State and Local Governments in Nebraska* (Lincoln, 1943) ; and Riegel, John W., *Salary Determination* (University of Michigan, Bureau of Industrial Research, 1940) . See also: State of Maryland, *Standard Salary Plan*, Revised, July 1, 1944 (Annapolis, 1944) ; Nebraska Division of Personnel, *Classification and Compensation Plans of the Department of State Assistance and Child Welfare* (Lincoln, 1940) ; State of Rhode Island, *Official Pay Plan for the Classified Service* (Providence, 1942) .

11 See Pennebaker, Kenneth C., and Hart, Robert M., " Guaranteed Annual Income and Employment Stabilization Plan for State Highway Employees," *Public Personnel Review*, July, 1942, pp. 177–189; Turner, Samuel E., Jr., " St. Paul's Adjustable Salary Scale for City Employees," *National Municipal Review*, December, 1938, pp. 583–587; and Leonard, J. M., and Mohaupt Rosina, *Costs-of-Living Salary Adjustment Plans* (Detroit Bureau of Governmental Research, 1944) .

period of employment for the purpose of increasing production, increasing operating efficiency, or in preparation for promotion. On-the-job training is given on a person-to-person basis, in most cases, by the supervisor to the employee, usually at his post of duty, or under conditions simulating those existing at his post of duty.[12]

Training may be carried on either by the central personnel agency or by the departments themselves with the assistance and under the supervision of the personnel agency. The constant need for special training to improve operations in many fields is now widely recognized, although the amount, kind, and method of giving the training will vary with the agency and its problems. Health departments are training their field workers and technicians; in many states members of the state police and state highway patrol forces are put through a rigid course of training; departments of education are requiring teachers in the public schools to continue their studies if they are to advance in rank and pay; officials in charge of penal and correctional institutions are trying to help the employees under their supervision to understand better the nature of their work, and to improve themselves for the better performance of their duties. Such a list might be extended almost indefinitely.

Conditions of Work. This term covers a large group of matters affecting the employees in the service — such as determining hours of work; checking attendance; handling annual, sick, and special leaves of absence; measuring performance on the job; and effecting transfers from one department or agency to another. On all these matters there should be uniform standards, regulations, and practices throughout the service; they should not be left to the determination of heads of departments, with consequent diversity. These questions must be considered not only with the interests of the taxpayer and the efficiency of the service in mind, but from the point of view of the members of the service as well. These matters may be miscellaneous, but they are of vital importance to the worker and have much to do with the morale of the service.

Employee Relations. Employee relations work, long carried on in business and industry, has recently made its appearance in the public service. It represents an attempt on the part of management to provide the machinery for the settlement of disputes arising within the agency, and for the assistance of employees in the solution of their

[12] These various types are defined and explained in Civil Service Assembly of the United States and Canada, *Employee Training in the Public Service* (Chicago, 1941.)

personal problems. Employee counselors, skilled in interviewing and specially trained for their work, are available at all times during working hours for personal conferences. The results of exit interviews are analyzed, and corrective measures suggested to management for the elimination of major obstacles to good morale within the organization. Recreational programs, employee papers, and other types of employee activity are encouraged.[13]

Health and Safety. As an employer government has been singularly remiss in making proper provision for the health and safety of its employees. Since a large portion of government work is office work it is assumed that there are no serious hazards to safety. Numerous accidents with resulting loss of man-hours occur, however, through file drawers left open, materials piled high in insecure positions, telephones lifted across an aisle, et cetera. On the health side, free first aid and dispensary service should be available in every office of any considerable size — not merely out of consideration for the employee, but because prompt attention given to minor illnesses such as colds and sore throats may prevent the spread of infection and save untold numbers of man-hours. By doing all it can to keep its employees safe and well, an agency cuts its operating costs and goes far to insuring the efficient discharge of its responsibilities.

Changes in Status. A phrase commonly used in the Federal service is borrowed here to signify the position of the employee under the Civil Service Act, and the Rules and Regulations. As of any given time he enjoys " status " in a particular position, in a given service, at a specified grade and salary. If any of these aspects of his position are changed or modified, he is often said to have had " a change of status." Such changes commonly occur through promotion or demotion, although other types of personnel actions involving status are reemployment, reinstatement, or reassignment. Of these various types of actions, there is, perhaps, greatest interest in promotions.

Every well-organized personnel system must make provision for handling the problem of promotions. In a patronage system, promotions, like the original appointments, are likely to be based largely on political influence, but under a merit system the incentive of possible promotion must be held out to those in the service. No such system of promotions is possible without an elaborate system of record keeping — personnel records and statistics, merit ratings, et cetera,

[13] See Civil Service Assembly of the United States and Canada, *Employee Relations in the Public Service* (Chicago, 1942) .

such as are maintained in modern business organizations, both public and private. Not only the responsible administration, but any citizen in the state, as well as the governor and the members of the legislature and the heads of the various departments, ought to be able to learn quickly and accurately the size of the service, the amount of the payroll, the number and causes of additions to and separations from the service, the number and kinds of employees of various types in each department and smaller unit, and a multitude of other significant personnel facts. Such data have rarely been anything like adequate, but without them and without detailed personnel records for each individual in the service, it is impossible to work out promotion policies that are in the best interests of the service as a whole or of the individual members of it.

Separations. Separations may arise from a variety of reasons — death, resignation, transfer to another agency, removal, or retirement on age or disability. Policies must be worked out for handling the various problems which these separations create. The appointing power always has the right to remove for cause — dishonesty, lack of ability or lack of application, lack of ability to cooperate with one's fellow workers, et cetera. It is important that everything possible be done to protect the efficient, competent employees, and that the protection now inherent in many state procedures for the inefficient and incompetent be withdrawn. The problem of removals would be much easier to handle if appointing officers were more severe in their judgments during the probational period in those jurisdictions operating under a civil service system.

From the point of view of the worker, the last but by no means the least important problem in this series is that relating to retirement. In the operation of such a system it is preferable that there be some security of tenure for members of the service, but states without civil service can and do maintain public employees' retirement systems. Such systems are in operation in about half of the states. The establishment of a retirement system based upon sound actuarial standards and competently administered is a great benefit not only to the employees but to the state as well, through the opportunity which it affords to retire aged and disabled employees, and through the improved efficiency and morale in the state service as a whole. The retirement allowances should be on a graduated scale, depending upon the length of service and the age at time of retirement; they should cover all state employees, and permit temporary absences without forfeiture of service rights. Benefits may be provided not only for retirement, but also for death, disability, prior service, minimum service, et cetera. This activity is usually separately administered.[14]

Assistance to Departments. The commission is — or ought to be — the central personnel agency of the governmental unit in which it functions. In this capacity the personnel agency has two primary responsibilities. As a staff agency its first duty is the somewhat unpleasant one of policing the operating agencies, to see that there is full compliance with the rules and regulations governing state employment. Second, it is the duty of the personnel agency to assist the operating agencies in the solution of their personnel problems, and to help them handle their work with better and smaller personnel. While this is primarily a problem for the operating units themselves, many of them have done the best they could without exhausting the possibilities for improvement. Some central agency familiar with the principles and practices of modern administrative procedure is needed to furnish stimulation, make suggestions, point out ways and means, and help make adjustments when personalities are involved. The personnel agency is the state's formal agency for making personnel and procedure studies, and is in a better position than any other to be helpful along these lines.

STATE CIVIL SERVICE SYSTEMS

The first method of handling state personnel problems was the discredited but still widely used patronage system. Second came the civil service commissions. The adoption of the early laws in New York, Massachusetts, and other states has already been mentioned. Illinois and Wisconsin in 1905 were followed by Colorado and New Jersey in 1907. Other additions occurred, as shown in the table on page 492, until in August, 1945, there were twenty-three actual state-wide systems of civil service provided for.

Because of the political opposition incurred in the establishment of a civil service system, it is not an uncommon practice to have such legislation enacted in one session of the legislature and repealed shortly thereafter. This experience occurred in Arkansas (1937 to 1939), and in New Mexico (1939 to 1941). Connecticut adopted a law in 1913, repealed it in 1921, and then after eighteen years of spoils, set

---

[14] See McCamman, Dorothy F., *The Scope of Protection under State and Local Government Retirement Systems* (Social Security Board, Bureau of Research and Statistics, Washington, 1943).

up its present merit system in 1937.[15] Kansas adopted a statute in
1915 that was continuously inoperative until 1941, when the present constitutional amendment was approved. The Michigan act of
1937, exceptionally well drafted, was seriously weakened by amendments in 1939. This too is not an uncommon practice.

GROWTH OF CIVIL SERVICE SYSTEMS IN THE STATES

1883–1945

Decade	Number of States	Year	States (* indicates constitutional basis)
1880–1889	2	1883	New York *
		1884	Massachusetts
1890–1899	0	....	None
1900–1909	4	1905	Illinois, and Wisconsin.
		1907	Colorado *
		1908	New Jersey
1910–1919	2	1913	California,* and Ohio *
1920–1929	1	1920	Maryland
1930–1939	7	1937	Connecticut, Maine, Michigan,* and Tennessee
		1939	Alabama, Minnesota, and Rhode Island
1940–1945	7	1940	Louisiana *
		1941	Indiana, and Kansas *
		1942	Virginia
		1943	Georgia *
		1945	Nebraska, and Oregon

Civil service legislation affecting certain agencies was, furthermore, in operation in many other states, especially in agencies cooperating with the Federal government under the social security
program. In Pennsylvania, for instance, the Unemployment Compensation Division of the Department of Labor and Industry and
the Department of Public Assistance operate under a civil service
system. So also does the State Liquor Control Board, while the Pennsylvania State Police operates under a voluntary civil service system.
These agencies account for almost half of the total number of state
employees. In Idaho the Fish and Game Commission has civil service through the initiative, while the Department of Public Welfare,

15 Several of these systems have been the subject of recent articles: Browder,
I. J., " The Alabama State Merit System — a Report of Progress," *Public Personnel
Review*, April, 1941, pp. 101–105; French, Patterson H., " Merit System Stages Suc-
cessful Comeback in Connecticut," *National Municipal Review*, March, 1939, pp.
192–199; Pennebaker, Kenneth C., " Civil Service in Minnesota — the First Eighteen
Months," *Public Personnel Review*, April, 1941, pp. 106–113; Mitchell, James M.,
" The Trend toward the Merit System," *State Government*, June, 1941, pp. 131–
132, 150–151.

the State Comptroller's Office, and the State Police have it by legislative action. Several states, in addition, have established personnel systems which, while not providing for competitive examinations, perform many of the functions of civil service agencies.

The state civil service commissions consist of three members in nine states, of five members in five states; Maryland has a single commissioner, Ohio two commissioners, and Michigan four. Members are appointed by the governor in all states but Connecticut, the nominations in most cases being subject to senate confirmation. The term of office is six years in eight states, and varies from three years in New Mexico to ten years in California. The terms are overlapping in thirteen states, thus insuring continuity of policy. Only in Maryland, New York, and Ohio can the compensation paid members be considered anything like adequate. Per diem compensation ranges from five to twenty-five dollars, but maximum annual limits prevent members from devoting much time to the job or from regarding it as anything more than an incidental matter.

All commissions are authorized to employ an executive officer and staff. A survey made by the Maine Bureau of Personnel in 1940, covering a group of half a dozen comparable states, presented some interesting figures on a number of important points.

STATE CIVIL SERVICE COMMISSIONS

ANNUAL APPROPRIATIONS AND NUMBER OF STAFF MEMBERS — 1940

State	Number of Classified Employees	Annual Appropriation	Number of Staff Members
Colorado	3,500	$20,000	8
Maryland	4,496	33,000	13
New Mexico	4,000 *	18,000	6
Rhode Island	3,588	47,000	25
Connecticut	4,640	79,580 **	40
Maine	3,200	5,000	3

* Of this number, only 400 were classified.
** $15,000 additional was allocated from the Contingent Fund.

The size of the task entrusted to the commissions has already been indicated to some extent. In New Jersey the Commission reported an increase in the number of officers and employees from 3,930 in 1918–1919 to 10,152 in 1933–1934. The annual payroll total for the same years increased from $4,203,278 to $15,400,000, not including the appraised value of maintenance when provided. By 1940 a total of $26,141,384 was expended to employ 15,520 persons. In Michigan

GOVERNOR

CIVIL SERVICE COMMISSION

Three electors appointed by the Governor with the consent of the Senate.

Duties: To act as the Board of Trustees in assuring the orderly and proper administration of the State Civil Service Act and Rules; to represent the public interest in the improvement of personnel administration in the state service; to advise the Governor and the Director on problems concerning personnel administration; to advise and assist the Director in fostering the interest of institutions of learning, civic, professional, and employee organizations in the improvement of personnel standards in the state service; to make any investigation which it may consider desirable concerning the administration of personnel in the state service.

DIRECTOR, DEPARTMENT OF CIVIL SERVICE

Appointed by the Governor from a list of three names submitted by the Civil Service Commission as a result of open competitive examination.

Duties: To be the administrative head of the Rhode Island Department of Civil Service; to direct and supervise all its administrative and technical activities; to recommend civil service rules and amendments thereto; to attend all meetings of the Commission and act as its secretary; to establish and maintain a roster of all employees; to appoint and discharge all employees of the Department and experts and special assistants and fix their compensation; to investigate the operation of the State Civil Service Act and report findings and recommendations.

SECRETARY

Secretarial duties in answering routine inquiries, making appointments, and handling correspondence for Director; keeps minutes of Commission meetings; maintains files and other records incident to work of Director.

CLASSIFICATION DIVISION

Prepares and maintains the classification and pay plans; administers such in-service activities as service ratings, employee training projects, safety, and employee welfare programs; studies all types of positions as to duties, responsibilities and qualifications from information obtained by personal observation of jobs and written statements of duties; investigates requests received from appointing authorities and employees concerning review of allocations of positions to classes; prepares studies of wages made in private industries, other governmental organizations, and the state service incident to the maintenance of a standardized salary plan; plans and supervises the development of a service rating system and of training programs.

Class Titles:
Principal Personnel Technician—
  Classification
Personnel Technician

EXAMINATION DIVISION

Prepares, administers, and rates civil service examinations which may consist of written tests, practical tests, oral interviews, physical tests, or other measures of fitness; makes arrangements for obtaining expert consultants to serve as special examiners and to assist with the examination program; arranges for suitable examination rooms and other facilities at examination centers; makes statistical studies of test results; studies positions as to duties, qualifications, and responsibilities as a basis for obtaining information required in the examination process.

STAFF

Class Titles:
Principal Personnel Technician—
  Examination
Senior Personnel Technician—
  Social Welfare
Senior Personnel Technician—
  Skilled Trades
Personnel Technicians 2
Personnel Aides 4

ADMINISTRATION DIVISION

Maintains personnel records including planning and laying out of roster cards, procedures for handling employee status changes, time records and employment lists, the checking of pay rolls for adherence to requirements of the law and of civil service rules; supervises a clerical staff engaged in providing stenographic, typing, and clerical service to other divisions of the Department; works out problems in connection with certification of eligibles to the several departments of the state government; issues and receives applications for examination; handles general information contacts with state officials and employees and the public; assists the Director by performing administrative duties such as may be involved in the making of special studies or administrative contacts with the heads of state departments.

STAFF

Class Titles:
Principal Personnel Technician—
  Administration
Personnel Aide
Clerical Staff 12

the total number of employees increased in the ten-year period from 1925 to 1935 from 8,123 to 12,282, and the total payroll cost from $12,-424,171 to $15,031,552. Due to increases in state activities in other fields, the percentage of total operating costs spent for personal service decreased from 66 to 54 per cent. The ten-year average figures were 11,300 employees, $15,676,068 payroll cost, and 64.5 per cent. Tendencies toward a decrease in the total number of employees and further increases in costs of personal service were not apparent until the war period.

The duties performed by the commissions may be governed by as many as three different types of legal authority. Eight states, as already noted, make constitutional provision for a civil service system. The following, from the Constitution of the State of New York, is illustrative of the language of these constitutional provisions:

Appointment and promotions in the civil service of the State, and of all the civil divisions thereof, including cities and villages, shall be made according to merit and fitness, to be ascertained, so far as practicable, by examinations which, so far as practicable, shall be competitive.[16]

Then there are the statutory provisions already mentioned; where there are no constitutional provisions these are the sole basis for the civil service system. Four states restrict the activities of their commissions to the personnel of the state service; others permit a certain amount of supervision or control over their civil subdivisions, though the extent of this supervision is not the same in any two states. In Massachusetts the commission handles the recruiting of both municipal and state employees. The New Jersey commission conducts examinations for county and municipal employees, but only in those units that have voted to accept its assistance. In New York in 1941, a proposal was considered and adopted to extend the civil service law to all the small units of government in the state. Nothing of this sort had ever been attempted before. Finally, all of the commissions have, in addition to constitutional or statutory authority or both, an extensive published series of rules and regulations governing their procedure. Under this legal set-up they proceed with the performance of their duties — duties which in general

16 Article V, Section 6; see also Cornell, Herbert W., *Civil Service Provisions of State Constitutions* (Wisconsin Council on Civil Service, Madison, 1940) ; Faust, Martin L., " The State Constitution and Civil Service," in *Manual on the Executive Article*, pp. 93–103 (Missouri Constitutional Convention of 1943, Columbia, 1943) ; and Litchfield, Edward W., and McCloskey, Robert G., " Civil Service by Constitution," *National Municipal Review*, January, 1945, pp. 14–20, 56.

relate to the various personnel problems mentioned in the preceding section of this chapter. An organization chart of the Rhode Island commission is presented on pages 494–495.

Positions under a civil service system are of two types: classified and unclassified. The classified positions are filled by competitive examinations except in those cases where the technical qualifications are not high. The latter positions may be exempt, or filled by noncompetitive or qualifying tests. The unclassified positions include both those which are highest in rank and those which are lowest. Both are exempt, the highest because they are policy-determining and therefore political, the lowest, such as common laborer, because no examination is necessary. The tests which are given may be either assembled or unassembled; the former may include short-answer and free-answer questions, practical performance tests, mental and psychological tests, and character tests, as well as an evaluation of the training and experience of the applicant.[17]

Certain duties, however, are peculiar to the civil service commission form of personnel control. When an examination is to be given, competitive or noncompetitive, it is necessary to give suitable publicity throughout the state to the time and place of the examinations, and to indicate the minimum qualifications for the types of positions in question. The examinations must be made out, given, and graded; and the eligible lists must be certified to the appointing officers. The commission must deal with such other questions as temporary appointments, exemptions, et cetera. In some states employees who are dismissed have the right to appeal their cases to the commission and to have a hearing before that body.

THE MERIT SYSTEM

Of the three major methods of dealing with public personnel problems one, the spoils system, was described in the opening section of this chapter, another, the civil service system, in the third. No student of government would seriously undertake to defend the spoils system with its long record of incompetence, extravagance, and inefficiency. For years it has been customary for all "right-thinking people" to argue vigorously for the extension of civil service. Of late many thoughtful persons have had honest doubts as to whether civil service has done or can do what is required, not

[17] On these and other points, see National Municipal League, *Draft of a State Civil Service Law* (New York, 1939).

only to eliminate the glaring evils of the spoils system, but to establish sound personnel policies.

These doubts have been based upon a number of important considerations. In the first place, there have been large numbers of cases of political interference with the operation and administration of civil service systems. In some state and city systems this fact has become so widely known that the public has lost confidence in the honesty and integrity of the system. This interference has taken a wide variety of forms, ranging from crude tampering with examination scores to such refined devices as the inclusion of questions so highly specialized as to baffle those who have not been informed in advance what to expect. In several cases the intent of the civil service law has been frustrated by legislative provisions giving preferred standing to ex-servicemen. It has been necessary to work with legislatures whose members are unwilling to relinquish their control over the patronage in order to get these acts adopted, and for the same reason it has been necessary for the supporters of the act to be constantly on guard to prevent their repeal or the passage of amendments which would impair their usefulness.

There are those who feel that even if these obstacles in the enactment and administration of civil service legislation are successfully surmounted, the effect of the system upon the employee is, from the point of view of the public, undesirable. It is argued that the guarantee of a permanent tenure during good behavior encourages on the part of many workers a listless and indifferent attitude — that the system is destructive of the initiative of the individual employee. It is argued further that when private enterprise has never seen fit to guarantee permanency of tenure, there is no reason why the government should for all practical purposes divest itself of the right to remove employees who are lazy and indifferent or whose work is unsatisfactory. Of course, such employees *can* be removed, but they seldom are, for fear of charges of political interference.

Numerous other objections have been raised, some of which have less validity than those mentioned. There is a certain type of executive who believes that he can pick his employees better than anyone else can pick them for him. As Dr. Leonard D. White observed, if executives in public positions had a free hand to use the real capacity which they often possess in selecting their employees, something might be said for the point of view, but as a matter of fact they seldom do. There is no basis in fact for the popular belief that if a civil service system is inaugurated, all the existing state employees will be

Three Personnel Systems in Government

	Under the Patronage System: Spoils	Under the Old-style Civil Service System: Reform	Under the Modern Civil Service System: Merit
Finding the Man	Local bosses limit applicants to PARTY REGULARS. The test: HOW MANY VOTES?	Examinations open to ANY INDIVIDUAL. The test: ACADEMIC EXAMINATION.	Advertisements, newspapers, radio, schools, attracting QUALIFIED APPLICANTS. The test: evaluation of EDUCATION, EXPERIENCE, PHYSICAL FITNESS, INTELLIGENCE, PERSONALITY, ETC.
The Man on the Job	Politicians interfere. SALARIES USED AS BRIBES. No job records. DUTIES UNKNOWN.	Department heads lobby. PAY VARIES WIDELY. Inadequate job records. DUTIES POORLY DEFINED.	Wage and cost of living surveys. EQUAL PAY FOR EQUAL WORK. Scientific job analysis. CLASSIFICATION PLAN BASED ON DUTIES.
Keeping Up Morale	Favoritism and insecurity. GOOD MORALE IMPOSSIBLE. Political careers only. JOB CAREERS FOR NONE.	"Not our function." LITTLE CONSTRUCTIVE EFFORT. Careers for a few. BLIND ALLEYS FOR MOST.	Not paternalistic but democratic. EMPLOYEE ORGANIZATIONS, SAFETY PROGRAMS, MEDICAL CARE, CREDIT UNIONS, ETC. In-service training and promotional system. CAREER SERVICE FOR ALL.
Removing the Incompetent	Department heads powerless. POLITICAL PROTECTION FOR UNFIT.	Cumbersome. TRIAL PROCEDURE.	Eliminating the dead wood. SERVICE RATINGS.
Retiring the Superannuated	No pension plans: EMPLOYEES THROWN OUT ON STREET.	Unsound retirement plans or RETENTION THROUGH SYMPATHY.	Actuarially sound PENSION PLANS.

From Civil Service Assembly of the United States and Canada, *Newsletter*, July, 1936.

promptly thrown out of their jobs, as they are with a change of administration under the spoils system. It is customary to provide by law that these employees shall be " covered in " and thus become an integral part of the new system.

It may be of some practical significance that the psychological approach of civil service no longer fits the needs of our time. Civil service was born in an era of reform, an era in which the goal was to " chase the rascals out," and if possible, to keep them out. This represents largely a negative attitude toward the problems of the public service. The present-day American is still desirous of keeping out unqualified people, but he prefers to place the emphasis on getting competent and well qualified people in the service, and keeping them there. He knows too that selection and placement are only one aspect of the personnel function as a whole. For these reasons,

the term " merit system " is steadily coming into greater popularity as a more proper description. It is more accurate because the method of selecting employees initially is done by a system of merit through competitive examinations, and the principle of promotion is that of advancing from the ranks those who have proved they are entitled to a higher position.[18]

A real merit system should be possible which would avoid the well-known evils of the spoils system, and at the same time those evils of the civil service system which are less widely recognized but none the less real. This proposal involves an important change in attitude toward the public service.

So long as we talk of " pay-rollers " and " tax-eaters," so long as we say that every eleven Americans carry a public employee on their backs — as though that worker were not giving the community as necessary and useful a service as his neighbor who happens to work for a steel mill or a drygoods store; so long as we say of Congress that the most useful thing it can do is to adjourn, just so long will we discourage fine young men from devoting their lives to the public service. Heaven knows, the opportunities for financial reward are slight, compared with those of private enterprise. The good public servant is too often asked to let virtue be its own reward. Most of them are human enough to want in addition the esteem of their fellows. Leadership in government will come when government has prestige and respect.[19]

Commission of Inquiry on Public Service Personnel. The Social Science Research Council created the Commission of Inquiry on

[18] Phillips, James H., " Civil Service in California," *Tax Digest*, November, 1944, pp. 377–378, 385–386; and on the arguments for formal merit systems, see Belsley, C. Lyle, " Personnel Administration in the Modern State," *Social Education*, December, 1939, pp. 623–627.

[19] Brownlow, Louis, and Ascher, Charles S., *Less Government or More* (American Library Associaion, Chicago, 1933) .

Public Service Personnel to examine the problems of public personnel within the United States, to outline a program for future action, and to present its findings and recommendations to the American people. After a year's investigation, during which hearings were held in the principal centers of population in the United States and in several foreign capitals, the Commission reported in 1935: "*The time has come in the history of America to adopt an entirely new public policy in the selection and appointment of men and women to carry on the day-to-day work of government.*" The report of this Commission, the most important contribution in this field that has been published for many years, presents a practical, constructive program for the improvement of Federal, state, and local government personnel. It analyzes the failure of our 175,000 units of government, which employed, before World War II, some 3,250,000 public servants and spend $5,000,000,000 a year for salaries, to attract the best available man power to government employment.

It would be desirable, if space permitted, to quote at length from the Commission's report. It outlined a career service system, presenting certain general recommendations in support thereof; these were followed by a series of twelve recommendations of a more specific nature. Of these twelve, five have a direct bearing upon the personnel problems of the states, although the principles involved in some of the others are equally valid for the state service:

The extension of the merit system under the supervision of the United States Civil Service Commission, wherever practicable, to the personnel of state and local government agencies receiving or expending Federal funds, as a condition of the grant, with the power to utilize existing local civil service agencies which are able and willing to meet standards set by the United States Civil Serivce Commission.

The amendment of veteran preference laws so that they will adequately recognize the war service experience of veterans without conflicting with merit principles or the efficiency of the public service.

The repeal or amendment of all general provisions prescribing residence requirements or geographical apportionment of appointments.

The immediate establishment or designation in every governmental department or agency of adequate size, whether Federal, state, or local, of a personnel officer, who should in the larger departments be freed of all other responsibilities.

The increase of the appropriations for personnel administration and the Civil Service Commission in the Federal government and in state and local governments where this is necessary for the adequate maintenance of the merit system, as a step toward the ultimate development of a career service.[20]

[20] Commission of Inquiry on Public Service Personnel, *Better Government Personnel*, Specific Recommendations Nos. 6, 8, 10, 11, and 12, pp. 8–9 (McGraw-Hill, New York, 1935).

It is urgently necessary that the states take steps to carry out these recommendations. They should develop effective personnel agencies of their own, and these agencies should cooperate both with those of their local units and with the United States Civil Service Commission. Professor White, a former member of the Commission, has suggested that the state and municipal commissions might work with the Federal commission in establishing joint eligible lists for each of the more common types of positions — lists from which Federal, state, or municipal officers might make selections as the necessity arose. It seems clear that there must be an improvement in the methods of recruitment for the public service. Our techniques and processes in other phases of administration are far in advance of those in the field of personnel.

Elsewhere in this volume emphasis is laid upon the fact that the states must improve the effectiveness of their administration if they do not wish to lose still further in the struggle for power with the Federal government. " Unless the states now take steps to strengthen their governmental organization, they are almost certainly doomed to be left behind in the race for power which is now going on in this country." The depression was responsible for tremendous increases in Federal power, in the course of which direct relations between the Federal government and the cities were established, thereby short-circuiting the states with regard to such matters as relief, public works, and municipal debts. Dr. White concludes:

What I am suggesting is that the states are now face to face with a situation where they have to put their houses in order if they are to compete in the contemporary world with the more active, more aggressive, more intelligent, and more highly recognized governments of the nation on the one hand, and in many instances, of the cities on the other. Some voices have already been raised suggesting the destruction of the states and the substitution of regions more nearly adapted to the great economic problems of the present day. How far this new trend in opinion may go, it is, of course, impossible to say, but wise leadership in the state governments can no longer delay to put the state in its strongest administrative position. The adoption of the merit system is one of the essential elements of the improvement of state government.[21]

CURRENT STATE PERSONNEL PROBLEMS

There are any number of current problems in the field of personnel administration, but two or three have been selected for

[21] White, Leonard D., " The Merit System in State Government," an address before the Indiana League of Women Voters, December 7, 1934, p. 8 (Mimeographed) .

brief comment here. The question of attracting able young people into the public service and keeping them there has been a matter of concern in this country for the last fifty years, but it is still not only a current problem but one of pressing importance. From the period of the Civil War down into the present century young men of imagination and ability did not go into the public service, because the ideal of the age was to make money. Boys were brought up on the stories of Horatio Alger, the general philosophy of which was, Be good and work hard, and some day you will be rich. Adults paid millions of dollars to hear a famous lecture delivered over 6,000 times — a fine lecture, to be sure, but one which overemphasized the idea of acquiring wealth. For a period of at least two generations the public mind was saturated with this idea. Into such a scheme of things the public service did not fit. Those who went into this service with the idea of making money made it dishonestly.

In our own time people — especially young people — fortunately seem to be more concerned with making a life than with amassing a fortune. Emphasis has been shifting from material things to human values. The depression made vividly clear the weaknesses of the system of distribution in the existing economic order; with grain elevators and warehouses bursting with raw and manufactured material, thousands of people might have starved had it not been for the intervention of government. The public has been attempting to do, through the channels of government, things which it was evident could not be done through private initiative. Government has acquired a social point of view and has adopted a progressive social policy, because the people demanded it. The attitude of many people toward government has undergone a radical change; government has ceased to be typified altogether by the policeman with his club. It has come to be not only a means of law enforcement and regulation, but an agency of social service and social control. With its expanded activities and its changed point of view, it provides as never before an opportunity for young men and women imbued not so much with a reform complex as with a desire to render useful service.

Universities and colleges all over the country have sensed this and have set up courses of training for the public service. It is highly commendable to train young people in the science of administration, equipping them for careers in the service of the state, when the state is dedicated to the ideals of social security and social justice, but that is not enough. These young people, with all their fine enthusiasm and training, will not go into public work unless they can be reasonably sure that merit will be recognized and that they can make a decent living. They do not expect to get rich, but they do expect, and they have a right to demand, that they will not be in danger of being thrown out on the street after every election in which the public changes its whim with regard to party preference. More and more trained men will be available each year; the public work of a technical nature which requires their expert knowledge is here in abundance. Whether or not they will do it depends upon the vital decisions to be made by the American people within the next few years.[22]

The problem of the temporary, nonprofessional administrator, the so-called "amateur administrator" as distinguished from the permanent, professional type of administrative officer, has become conspicuous during both the depression and the war years. "Placed at the head of a staff of permanent employees, this official must serve in a dual capacity; first, he must represent the public or nonprofessional interests in administration; second, he must direct and coordinate the activities of his permanent staff.[23] The depression increased this type of administrative service. Not that the political pressure for rotation in office has been greater, but new activities in many fields have increased the demand for personnel when there were none with training or experience to be had. Many of those who have been pressed into service in the emergency have been persons from academic life. Their use would have been unnecessary if we had developed a corps of trained administrators from which selections for such positions could have been made.

Professor Stafford has suggested three essential qualifications for professional administrators: they should possess the innate qualities of leadership and intellectual competence, and they should have had technical training derived from practical experience in the administration of one or more of the functions with which their departments are concerned. There is probably no other group that meets all these qualifications as well as the members of the academic profession, although no sensible person wants a government staffed entirely by college professors. Since most of those who have been selected have served in a commendable manner, it is unfortunate that certain ones should have had an obsession for personal public-

[22] In this connection see Laski, Harold J., "Why Don't Your Young Men Care?" *Harper's Magazine*, July, 1931, pp. 129–131.
[23] Stafford, Paul T., "The New Amateur in Public Administration," *American Political Science Review*, April, 1935, pp. 257–269.

ity. One may expect a constantly increasing need for expert service in government, but the names of the experts do not belong in the headlines. The greater use of " amateur administrators " during the emergency emphasizes the need of and the opportunity for a professional administrative personnel in nation, state, and city.

In a discussion of recent developments in public personnel administration Professor Stout emphasizes five points which are characteristic not only of the states but of the Federal government and the cities as well.[24] In addition to the rapid spread of the merit system, he notes a change in the structure of agencies administering civil service: "While the three-member commission remains the typical civil service agency in this country, it is becoming increasingly common to restrict its function to those of a quasi-legislative and quasi-judicial nature and to vest the administration of technical functions in an executive officer or personnel director." Another current trend of importance is the development of interjurisdictional cooperation between cities, and between states and their local units. Again, civil service agencies are giving more and more attention to the positive aspects of public personnel administration: " Whereas they formerly concerned themselves almost exclusively with recruitment and ' fighting the spoilsmen,' today they are placing increased emphasis upon personnel management and employee welfare." Finally, there is an increased use of mechanical equipment in performing the great amount of monotonous clerical work that is necessary in connection with the administration of a modern personnel system.

SELECTED REFERENCES

Benson, George C. S., *Administration of Civil Service in Massachusetts* (Harvard University Press, 1935).

Benton, Mildred, and Buckardt, H. L., *Personnel Administration and Personnel Training: a Selected List of References* (Department of Agriculture, Soil Conservation Service, Washington, 1940).

Brown, Ann D., *A List of References on the Civil Service and Personnel Administration* (Library of Congress, 1936; supplementary lists, 1939 and 1942).

California State Personnel Board, *Salaries in the California State Civil Service* (Sacramento, 1944).

Cantor, Nathaniel, *Employee Counseling* (McGraw-Hill, New York, 1945).

Civil Service Assembly of the United States and Canada, *A Digest of State Civil Service Laws* (Chicago, 1939).

24 Stout, Hiram M., " Recent Developments in Public Personnel Administration," *American Political Science Review,* October, 1939, pp. 826–835.

Civil Service Assembly of the United States and Canada, *A Selected Bibliography in Public Personnel Administration* (Chicago, 1940).

——, *Civil Service Agencies in the United States, a 1940 Census* (Chicago, 1940).

——, *Employee Relations in the Public Service* (Chicago, 1942).

——, *Employee Training in the Public Service* (Chicago, 1941).

——, *Oral Tests in Public Personnel Selection* (Chicago, 1943).

——, *Policies and Practices in Public Personnel Administration* (Chicago, 1943).

——, *Position Classification in the Public Service* (Chicago, 1941).

——, *Public Relations in Public Personnel Agencies* (Chicago, 1941).

——, *Readings in Public Personnel Administration* (Chicago, 1942).

——, *Recruiting Applicants for the Public Service* (Chicago, 1942).

Commission of Inquiry on Public Service Personnel, *Better Government Personnel* (McGraw-Hill, New York, 1935).

——, *Problems of the American Public Service* (McGraw-Hill, New York, 1935).

Cooper, Alfred M., *Supervision of Governmental Employees* (McGraw-Hill, New York, 1943).

Cushman, Frank, *Training Procedure* (Wiley, New York, 1940).

Eggers, Rowland A., and others, *The Retirement of Public Employees in Virginia* (Appleton-Century, New York, 1934).

Faust, Martin L., *Manual on the Executive Article* (Missouri Constitutional Convention of 1943, Columbia, 1943).

Field, Oliver P., *Civil Service Law* (University of Minnesota Press, 1939).

Fish, Carl Russell, *The Civil Service and the Patronage* (Harvard University Press, 1920).

Foulke, William D., *Fighting the Spoilsmen* (Putnam, New York, 1919).

Garey, A. E., *Civil Service Procedure in the Wisconsin State Service* (American Federation of State, County and Municipal Employees, Madison, 1938).

Graham, George A., *Education for Public Administration* (Public Administration Service, Chicago, 1941).

Greer, Sarah, *A Bibliography of Civil Service and Personnel Administration* (McGraw, Hill, New York, 1935).

Gulick, Luther, Ed., " Improved Personnel in Government Service," *Annals,* January, 1937, entire volume.

Home Owners Loan Corporation, *Bibliography: Personnel and Related Subjects* (Washington, 1938).

Hormell, Orren C., *Personnel Problems in Maine: The Merit System* (Bowdoin College, 1936).

Illinois Legislative Council, *Factors Involved in Pension Legislation for Governmental Employees in Illinois* (Springfield, 1940).

——, *Right of Appeal from Removals under the Merit System* (Springfield, 1937).

Ireland, Norma O., *Supervision: Methods and Techniques, A Selected Bibliography* (University of Southern California, 1938).

Kansas Legislative Council, *Personnel Administration* (Topeka, 1938).

——, *Retirement Systems for State Employees in Kansas* (Topeka, 1937).

Klein, Alice C., *Civil Service in Public Welfare* (Russell Sage Foundation, New York, 1940).

Lefler, Grace, *Public Personnel Administration: Selected Bibliography* (University of Southern California, 1938).

McCamman, Dorothy F., *The Scope of Protection under State and Local Government Retirement Systems* (Social Security Board, Bureau of Research and Statistics, Washington, 1943).

Marx, Fritz M., Ed., *Public Management in the New Democracy* (Harper, New York, 1940).

Massachusetts State College, *Government Personnel,* a conference report (Amherst, 1942).

Meriam, Lewis, *Public Personnel Problems from the Standpoint of the Operating Officer* (Brookings Institution, Washington, 1938).

——, *Public Service and Special Training* (University of Chicago Press, 1936).

Michigan Civil Service Study Commission, *Report* (Lansing, 1936).

Minnesota Division of Administrative Management, *Improving State Employee Efficiency with an Orientation and Reference Manual* (St. Paul, 1943).

Mosher, William E., and Kingsley, J. Donald, *Public Personnel Administration,* Revised Edition (Harper, New York, 1941).

National Municipal League, *Draft of a State Civil Service Law* (New York, 1939).

Nebraska Legislative Council, *The Compensation of Officers and Employees of the State and Local Governments in Nebraska* (Lincoln, 1943).

New York State Commission on the Extension of the Civil Service, *First Report* (Legislative Document, 1940, No. 92); *Second Report,* submitted February 20, 1941.

Pfiffner, John M., *Public Administration* (Ronald Press, New York, 1935).

Porter, Kirk H., *State Administration* (Crofts, New York, 1938).

Public Administration Service, *Personnel Administration and Procedure* (Chicago, 1938).

——, *Merit System Installation* (Chicago, 1941).

Riegel, John W., *Salary Determination* (Bureau of Industrial Relations, Report No. 2, University of Michigan, 1940).

Shumate, Roger V., *State Civil Service in Nebraska* (Nebraska Legislative Council, Lincoln, 1938).

Silke, Harry, Jr., *The Administration of Public Retirement Systems in the United States* (summary of dissertation, University of Southern California, 1938).

University of Denver, *Civil Service in Colorado* (Bureau of Business and Social Research, Denver, 1945).

Walters, J. E., *Personnel Relations* (Ronald Press, New York, 1945).

White, Leonard D., *Government Career Service* (University of Chicago Press, 1935).

——, *Introduction to the Study of Public Administration,* Revised Edition (Macmillan, New York, 1939).

——, *The Prestige Value of Public Employment* (University of Chicago Press, 1929 and 1932).

White, Leonard D., *Trends in Public Administration* (McGraw-Hill, New York, 1933).

——, and Smith, T. V., *Politics and Public Service* (Harper, New York, 1939).

Willoughby, W. F., *Principles of Public Administration* (Johns Hopkins Press, 1927).

Wilmerding, Lucius, Jr., *Government by Merit* (McGraw-Hill, New York, 1935).

———————————

Baruch, Ismar, " Basic Aspects of Position Classification," *Public Personnel Review,* October, 1940, pp. 1–17.

Benson, George C. S., " Federal-State Personnel Relations," *Annals,* January, 1940, pp. 38–43.

Biren, Robert I., " Developing Adequate Class Specifications," *Public Personnel Review,* January, 1944, pp. 27–31.

Browder, I. J., " The Alabama State Merit System — a Report of Progress," *Public Personnel Review,* April, 1941, pp. 101–105.

Chamberlain, L. H., " Merit System Makes Its Debut in Idaho," *National Municipal Review,* March, 1940, pp. 204–205.

Civil Service Assembly of the United States and Canada, *Public Personnel Review* (Chicago, quarterly).

Combs, William H., " Michigan's Civil Service Amendment," *State Government,* February, 1941, pp. 34–35, 45–46.

Devoe, Maxwell A., " Administrative Relationships in Public Personnel Agencies," *Public Personnel Review,* January, 1941, pp. 18–27.

——, " Rhode Island Tries the Merit System," *National Municipal Review,* January, 1941, pp. 23–27.

Dominick, William B., " Orientation Programs for New Employees," *Public Personnel Review,* October, 1942, pp. 280–287.

Fenner, Charles P., Jr., and Moak, Lennox L., " Citizen Support of Civil Service in Louisiana," *Public Personnel Review,* October, 1943, pp. 260–265.

Graves, W. Brooke, and Herring, James M., " Recruiting Administrative Personnel in the Field," *Public Administration Review,* Autumn, 1942, pp. 302–311.

Hubbard, Henry F., " The Elements of a Comprehensive Personnel Program," *Public Personnel Review,* July, 1940, pp. 1–17.

Kingsley, J. Donald, " Recruitment, the Quest for Competence," *Public Personnel Review,* January, 1941, pp. 28–35.

Litchfield, Edward H., " Another Chapter in Michigan Civil Service Reform," *American Political Science Review,* February, 1941, pp. 76–82.

——, " The ' Open Back Door ' — a Case Study," *National Municipal Review,* February, 1941, pp. 85–89, 132.

——, and McCloskey, Robert G., " Civil Service by Constitution," *National Municipal Review,* January, 1945, pp. 14–20, 56.

Marsh, Harry W., and Powell, Norman J., " A Classification and Pay Plan for the State of New Hampshire," *Public Personnel Review,* April, 1945, pp. 109–113.

Messick, Charles P., " New Jersey's Merit System Pattern," *National Municipal Review*, March, 1941, pp. 416–418.

Mitchell, James M., " The Trend Toward the Merit System," *State Government*, June, 1941, pp. 131–132, 150–151.

National Civil Service Reform League, *Good Government* (New York, quarterly).

National Municipal League, *National Municipal Review* (New York, monthly).

Nelson, Carl J., and Drury, Robert F., " State Government Employment in 1940," *State Government*, November, 1940, pp. 221–223, 234–235.

Pennebaker, Kenneth C., " Civil Service in Minnesota — the First Eighteen Months," *Public Personnel Review*, April, 1941, pp. 106–113.

——, and Hart, Robert M., " Guaranteed Annual Income and Employment Stabilization Plan for State Highway Employees," *Public Personnel Review*, July, 1942, pp. 177–189.

Phillips, James H., " Civil Service in California," *Tax Digest*, November, 1944, pp. 377–378, 385–386.

Stalley, Marshall, " Employee Recreation as a Personnel Function," *Public Personnel Review*, July, 1945, pp. 174–178.

Stats, Herbert E., " Calling for New Ideas," *National Municipal Review*, December, 1943, pp. 577–579, 632.

Sublette, Donald J., " The Returning Veteran," *Public Personnel Review*, July, 1945, pp. 147–153.

Turner, Samuel E., Jr., " St. Paul's Adjustable Salary Scale for City Employees," *National Municipal Review*, December, 1938, pp. 583–587.

Part Five

FINANCIAL PROBLEMS

CHAPTER XIII

The Revenue System

THE financial problems of the state governments must be considered under three headings: the income derived from taxation and from sources other than taxation, including the use of the borrowing powers; the problems involved in the custody and expenditure of state revenues after they have been collected; and budgetary problems, which are concerned with the planning of the state's fiscal program and with the correlation of income and expenditure. In the present chapter we shall be concerned with the first of these problems. In the discussion of the several tax forms emphasis will be laid upon their prevalence and application, rather than upon their economic aspects.

SOURCES OF STATE INCOME

Taxation. If one were to make a careful and detailed study of the tax system in each of the forty-eight states, he would find almost every conceivable combination of the forms of taxation known to students of public finance. He would discover that some of these forms are not used frequently enough to justify including them in a general discussion of state tax systems, but that there are certain major forms of taxation each of which is used in all or nearly all the states for general fund purposes. Among these are the general property tax, corporation and business taxes, income taxes, consumption and sales taxes, excise taxes such as those on alcoholic beverages, tobacco, and gasoline, and inheritance and estate taxes. Some discussion of each of these six types is included in this chapter. The total receipts for a recent year are indicated in the table on page 514. The states raise only 25 per cent of their revenues by direct taxes, whereas the Federal and local governments raise about half of theirs in this way.

STATE TAX COLLECTIONS BY MAJOR SOURCE: 1938–1944 [1]
(In millions)

Tax Source	1944 (Prelim.)	1943	1942	1941	1940	1939	1938
Total tax collections:							
Including unemployment compensation	$5,387	$5,094	$4,975	$4,507	$4,157	$3,884	$3,834
Excluding unemployment compensation	4,068	3,923	3,899	3,606	3,313	3,085	3,132
General sales, use, or gross receipts	721	671	633	575	499	440	447
Motor vehicle fuel sales	691	777	942	913	839	801	777
Alcoholic beverage sales	267	280	256	216	193	174	175
Tobacco product sales	158	141	131	106	97	60	55
Motor vehicle and operator licenses	398	395	431	434	387	364	359
Alcoholic beverage licenses	54	55	56	56	62	54	52
Individual income	337	293	249	225	206	197	218
Corporation income	429	340	274	197	155	134	165
Property	243	258	271	268	260	259	244
Death and gift	112	109	112	118	113	133	142
Severance	71	75	62	53	53	47	58
Other, except unemployment compensation	585	530	482	445	449	422	440
Unemployment compensation tax	1,319	1,172	1,076	901	844	799	702

These revenue sources can be grouped for convenience under the six major headings which are used for section headings in this chapter:

General property — now mainly a local source.
Corporation and business taxes, including licenses and fees.
General sales, use, or gross receipts taxes.
Excise taxes, as on alcoholic beverages, gasoline, and tobacco.
Income taxes, individual and corporate.
Inheritance and estate taxes.

Social security taxes should perhaps be included, but they are so definitely earmarked for a specific purpose that they do not contribute in any way to general fund revenues. In addition to these major sources of revenue, the states collect considerable sums from

[1] From United States Bureau of the Census, "State Tax Collections in 1944," *State Finances: 1944*, p. 5 (Washington, August, 1944).

miscellaneous sources. During the depression years when the receipts from the major sources declined sharply, the states engaged in a widespread search for new revenue sources.

In 1937 the Kansas Legislative Council reported twenty-one separate and distinct new sources or possible increases in existing sources.[2] This list included special business taxes of various types, luxury taxes, amusement taxes, check taxes, increases in administrative fees, et cetera. All of these devices have been used in various jurisdictions. While the search was made for new sources, some older taxes have been reduced or abandoned.

Pennsylvania abandoned its tax on coal at the mouth of the mine, in an effort to aid the struggling coal mining industry. Several states have abandoned poll taxes and occupation taxes, either because of an adverse public opinion or because of laxity and/or expense in collection. Many states have given up the general property tax as a state source because of inequality. During the war years there have been few cases of tax reductions or of the repeal of tax laws, although with treasuries overflowing with revenues derived from the boom of war industry, there have been no new taxes. The growth in revenue receipts is clearly indicated in the table on page 514. These extra funds were used to balance budgets, retire debt, and create surpluses for postwar needs.

Sources Other than Taxation. Contrary to a widely held but mistaken popular belief, the states obtain receipts in very considerable amounts from sources other than taxation. The importance of these varies greatly from state to state. In a list of such sources one thinks first of the receipts derived from the state's borrowing power; such receipts are definitely outside the revenue classification, even though they become funds in the state treasury, subject to appropriation by the legislature and to requisition and payment at the time, and for the purpose for which, the loan was made. The loan, of course, becomes a fixed charge upon the revenues of the state, until the obligation has been met. During the depression many states made extensive use of the borrowing power, some of them to the extent of impairing their credit. As previously indicated, the retirement of much of this debt was possible during the boom of the war years.

The states derive some income from the public domain, although in most cases the amount is not large. Portions of this domain may be sold as authorized; mineral rights may be sold or leased; and

2 *Potential Sources of Additional Revenue from Taxation* (Topeka, 1937).

revenues may be derived from the rental or leasing of camp sites. The conservation and forestry movement is now old enough so that some states are able to derive some annual income from the sale of timber. This is, in fact, necessary in the interests of real conservation and good forest management, but it is a difficult policy to execute because of a general misunderstanding of the meaning of conservation. Many people seem to think that these timber reserves are to be locked up and never used, whereas failure to utilize mature timber results in waste, not conservation.

If a state maintains and operates any kind of business, any income derived therefrom is classifiable as commercial revenue. In most such cases the goods or services produced are offered to the public at cost. Illustrations include the production and sale of seedlings in order to encourage the reforestation of wastelands, and the management of public service enterprises or of a state insurance fund in connection with the enforcement of the workmen's compensation law. With the adoption of Amendment XXI, sixteen states entered the wholesale and retail liquor business; here the effort has been made to establish prices low enough to discourge bootlegging and high enough to enable the state to make a reasonable profit — often earmarked for relief or other purposes. The profits from this source were often less than was anticipated, but still reached substantial amounts.

The United States Bureau of the Census reported that, in 1941, thirty-one of the forty-eight states owned fifty-seven public service enterprises. These consisted of alcoholic beverage monopoly systems in sixteen states, and of forty-one utility or other commercial enterprises in twenty-four states. The types of enterprises and the number of states in which they operate is as follows:

Alcoholic beverage monopoly systems	16
Toll bridges	11
Port facilities	10
Ferries	5
Water conservation and irrigation works	3
Electric power systems	2
Other	8

Administrative revenues constitute a fourth such source of income; these revenues are collected through the sale of licenses and the imposition of fees. It is a universal practice to require licenses of hunters and fishermen, operators of motor vehicles, and persons desiring to practice one of the learned professions or skilled trades. The more progressive states impose fees designed to cover the cost of inspection and regulation of those types of business in which the businessmen themselves have demanded this service, or in which the public interest requires it. Thus it is customary to assess banks, not only with the actual cost incurred by the banking department in making examinations, but for their prorated portion of the overhead cost of the operation of the department. The same procedure is often applied to building and loan associations, to the inspection of buildings and the approval of plans for their construction, to the inspection of elevators, steam boilers, bedding and upholstery, and many other things. As the states have gradually expanded in the number of services rendered to the public, receipts from departmental earnings, as from other sources, have substantially increased. The Bureau of the Census reported $182,000,000 from this source in 1937 in the forty-eight states.

Yet another source of non-tax revenue is found in bookkeeping revenues, or interfund transfers. These do not represent new income, but they do provide additional funds which may be appropriated against, or spent by, the agency to which they have been transferred. Thus in Pennsylvania in 1933 the Joint Legislative Committee on Finances recommended that $500,000 be transferred from the Prison Labor Fund to the General Fund. This amount represented the total appropriation made by the General Assembly for the purchase of equipment and materials for the establishment of prison industries in the state penitentiaries. The industries had been established, were in a fairly prosperous condition, and had earned profits of more than a quarter of a million dollars. The Committee felt that this amount was sufficient to meet their needs. Thus half a million dollars might become a revenue for the General Fund, which the legislature would be free to appropriate in a period of emergency.

Last in this list are the funds received from the Federal government under the subsidy or grant-in-aid system. Such grants have normally been made under two conditions: first, that the states match the Federal grant dollar for dollar or in some other specified proportion; and second, that the total amount be expended in accordance with the conditions under which the grant is made. This system has been applied to problems in the field of education, the construction of highways, forest fire protection and reforestation projects; to a number of health problems; and to problems of agriculture, labor, and social security. The receipts of these funds is dependent upon action by the state legislatures, but the states have seldom failed to avail themselves of these offers of financial assistance. The amounts of money expended by the Federal government, and therefore received by the states from this source, increased rapidly through the twenties, but showed a decline for the original purposes after the beginning of the depression. On the other hand, the total was greatly increased through grants for relief, public works, housing, social security, and other purposes growing out of the enlarged spending program of the Roosevelt administration. The amounts spent during 1930, 1935, and 1940 are given on pages 31–32.

In addition to these major non-tax sources, there are such miscellaneous ones as special assessments, court fines, forfeits and escheats, donations, pension assessments, highway privileges, rents on investment properties, interest, et cetera. In 1937 receipts from these sources amounted to $223,000,000, which represented an increase of $81,000,000 in the five-year period since 1932. This is accounted for chiefly by receipts from public service enterprises, which the Bureau of the Census classifies as a miscellaneous source. Special assessments are really taxes levied against property owners affected by improvements or against individuals or corporations by reason of services performed. Court fines or forfeits are amounts charged for violation of criminal statutes and moneys received from forfeited bail. Escheats include debt obligations canceled after being long overdue, as well as receipts from private trust funds or accounts of which no owner could be located. Donations and gifts are self-explanatory. Pension assessments include dues or contributions from salaries of state employees for the establishment and maintenance of pension funds. Highway privilege taxes, receipts from which have greatly increased in recent years, include payments from various types of public service companies for the use of the public highways. They differ from rents, which give the payer the exclusive control and use of the property rented. The states may receive rents from properties held by them, for investment purposes or otherwise, and interest on invested capital in sinking funds, public trust funds, and investment funds.[3]

SOME FUNDAMENTAL ASPECTS OF THE TAX PROBLEM

It is difficult to overemphasize the importance of the tax power; it is impossible to exercise the other powers of government without a prior exercise of the tax power, since funds are required to main-

[3] Bureau of the Census, " State Revenues from Miscellaneous Non-taxes, 1937 and 1932," August, 1939.

tain any governmental service. It was reported in 1939 that forty-four state legislatures put 4,338 tax bills into the mill, of which 1,102 were passed. In the exercise of this power, however, the state is subject to restrictions imposed both by the Federal Constitution and by the constitutions of the states. The due process clause of Amendment **XIV,** applying as it does to the states, restricts them from any confiscatory levies. The state constitutions contain similar clauses and, in addition, usually include a statement in the clause on eminent domain which prevents the taking of private property for public use without just compensation.

Some Requirements of a Sound Tax System. It is unlikely that any two states in the Union have tax systems exactly similar. Each of the forty-eight states has combined the various possible forms of taxation into a pattern peculiar to itself. There are, nevertheless, certain tests and fundamental requirements by which students of public finance attempt to measure the soundness of tax systems. The first such test is fiscal adequacy: does the tax system yield sufficient revenue to meet the expenditure program necessary for the governmental unit concerned? This test is the simplest of all those imposed and much the easiest to meet. In the second place, any given tax should be reasonably economical in administration; the cost of collection should not run so high as to consume a considerable portion of the amount collected. A tax or a tax system which violates this requirement is bad because it removes money from the pockets of citizens without giving any return. Thus a state gasoline tax collected from retailers violates this principle, because of the number of accounts which must be carried and the overhead expense thus entailed. A similar tax can be collected from refiners and wholesalers much more thoroughly and at much less expense.

A third test requires that the burdens of taxation shall fall equitably upon the various classes in the community. A tax or a tax system which levies heavy burdens upon one group and permits another with equal ability to pay to escape its proper share of the tax burden is unfair, inequitable, and unjust. Graded taxes on income and inheritance were developed to meet this test. A fourth test relates to the ease with which the tax system may be adjusted to either an increased or decreased need for revenue; in other words, to the elasticity or flexibility of the system. It is obviously necessary that a tax system be capable of adjustment to changed conditions, supplying additional revenue by the application of higher rates when needed, or reducing the burden by imposing lower rates when such rates will yield the amount of revenue required. Fifth, the tax system as a whole and the individual acts of which it is composed should be as simple and comprehensible to the ordinary citizen as they can be made. Some income tax laws, particularly the Federal law, are flagrant offenders against this principle. The burden should not be regressive, and it is preferable that it bear much more heavily upon income than upon capital.

Finally, it is desirable that the tax system should have such diversity as will tend to stabilize the yield, regardless of general economic and business conditions. It is easy to devise systems for raising adequate revenue in prosperous times, but government must function in bad times as well as in good. In periods of depression many additional burdens are imposed on government. If it is to be prepared to meet these responsibilities, the tax program must be so designed as to bring in receipts from such a wide variety of sources that the collapse of one will not upset the entire tax program.

Distribution of the Tax Burden. In the effort to develop a system of taxation which would come near to meeting all these requirements simultaneously, we have passed through a number of stages in the development of the theory of taxation. Perhaps the earliest principle to be widely adopted was the equality principle, which is illustrated by such tax forms as the poll tax, head tax, or capitation tax. When it became evident that the distribution of the burden under this principle was inequitable, we began to rely more upon the benefit principle, in accordance with which it was assumed that each individual should contribute in proportion to the benefit which he received. This principle was particularly applicable to public improvements and is still retained, in modified form, where special assessments are used to raise a portion of the cost of such improvements. Applied to the maintenance of public schools or to police and fire protection, this principle becomes ridiculous; it is not altogether fair as applied to such improvements as streets and highways, which are used by the general public perhaps more than by abutting and adjacent property owners.

It was next concluded that the weight of the tax burden should be distributed in accordance with the ability of the taxpayer to pay. This theory has been applied in two forms, the first known as the proportionate application of the ability to pay principle. Under this plan all properties were assessed and a uniform rate applied to all, regardless of their size. The same principle was followed in the early income taxes. Although the rate in a given case might not be high, it was soon apparent that the application of this rate to a small assessment or a small income imposed upon the individual paying such a tax a far greater burden than that imposed upon the owner of extensive properties or the recipient of a large income. In the effort to eliminate this inequality we next turned to the progressive application of the ability to pay principle. This principle is now incorporated in all Federal and state laws which impose a graded tax upon income, inheritances, or estates. It is doubtless true that there is no such thing as an ideal or a perfect tax system, but serious efforts have been made to improve our tax systems and to make them more equitable.

A number of problems have arisen in connection with the effort to secure an equitable distribution of the tax burden. Advocates of the single tax have argued that an equitable distribution was possible only through the use of the single tax method. Very practical problems in the distribution of the tax burden have grown out of double, treble, and other forms of multiple taxation. The courts have told us repeatedly that multiple taxation violates due process.[4] It is obvious, moreover, that such taxes are unwise from the point of view of public policy, and that they result in an unfair distribution of the tax burden.

Tax Provisions in State Constitutions. In the foregoing paragraphs some of the economic principles governing the use of the tax power have been discussed; it is now proposed to consider briefly some of the constitutional provisions governing the use of the tax power. While these vary greatly, some are more or less common; the most common is that requiring equality or uniformity in the imposition of taxes. The clause in the Pennsylvania Constitution is typical: " All taxes shall be uniform, upon the same class of subjects, within the territorial limits of the authority levying the tax, and shall be levied and collected under general laws " (Article IX, Section 1). The courts have in some instances interpreted these clauses as prohibiting the use of graded taxes, thereby necessitating either the abandonment of the sound grading principle or the amending of the constitution. It is to be hoped that in future constitutional revisions these clauses will be omitted.[5]

[4] See First National Bank of Boston v. Maine, 284 U. S. 312, 1932; also Farmers Loan and Trust Company v. Minnesota, 280 U. S. 204, 1929; Baldwin v. Missouri, 281 U. S. 586, 1919; and Beidler v. South Carolina, 282 U. S. 1, 1930.

[5] This question is discussed fully in an excellent monograph by Girard, Richard A., *The Scope for Uniformity in State Tax Systems* (New York State Tax Commission, Albany, 1935).

Another of the usual provisions is that similar to the New York Constitution (Article III, Section 24) to the effect that no tax shall be levied except in pursuance of law and every law imposing a tax shall state distinctly the object of the tax. Some provide in effect that "no moneys arising from a tax levied for one purpose shall be used for any other purpose." Another quite common feature is the provision that "the power of taxation shall never be surrendered, suspended or contracted away;". . . in others the applicability of such provision is limited to corporations. Many of the constitutions contain rate limitations at which property may be taxed and make provision for the exemption of certain property from taxation or authorize the legislative bodies to make such exemptions.[6]

These latter provisions will be considered later in connection with the general property tax.

Many of the constitutions provide that taxes may be levied only for a public purpose. What is a public purpose? To say that it is a purpose to be contrasted with a private purpose is not enough; at the same time it is difficult to present an adequate definition, since the courts have followed in this instance their usual practice of deciding each case on its own merits. The point that taxation for a "private purpose" constitutes an invasion of the constitutional rights of the taxpayer was clarified and illustrated by the case of Loan Association v. Topeka.[7]

The practice prevailing in many municipalities of offering free factory sites to firms willing to locate within the city is familiar. The City Council of Topeka went much farther; it made a direct appropriation to a manufacturing company as an inducement to locate its plant within the city limits, the assumption being that the value of the plant to the city was sufficient to justify such a use of public funds. The Court decided that the city, which was the agent of the State of Kansas, was not justified in making such an appropriation — that the benefit to the manufacturing company was greater than that accruing to the community from the location of the plant within its boundaries.

In some form or other this is the question which the courts usually have to answer. There is, of course, no question about public buildings, highways, expenditures for salaries of public employees, the purchase of property and supplies, et cetera. Most of the questions that are brought to the courts involve borderline cases, and judgments with regard to these vary somewhat with different courts and

---

[6] Saxe, Martin, "Tax Provisions in State Constitutions," *Bulletin of the National Tax Association*, February, 1938.

[7] 21 Wallace 655, 1874.

different sections of the country, with the passage of time, and with the presence or absence of emergency situations. Purposes which would never be classified as public under ordinary circumstances may, in an emergency, become such. In general, it is also true that the courts will not sanction the use of public funds for purposes which are normally served adequately through the employment of private capital and by private initiative.

Means of Escape from Taxation. Last among these questions regarding the character of the tax power is that of the means of escape from taxation. There are at least four methods of escape, part of them legal and part illegal. The first is the shifting of the tax burden, a phenomenon which is referred to technically as the incidence of taxation. By this is meant the tendency for those who pay the tax to pass on to others as much of the actual burden as they can. Thus in normal times the landlord includes the taxes on a property in his computation of the rental; he is responsible to the tax-collecting authorities for the payment of the tax, but he passes on to his tenant the actual financial burden involved. Secondly, it is often possible to escape taxation by availing oneself of such technicalities in the law as may be employed for the purpose of avoiding, or at least diminishing, the amount of the tax burden. In the third place, many tax laws include definite exemptions; in income tax laws, for instance, it is customary to exempt persons in the lower income brackets. Finally, many persons succeed in evading all or part of their proper tax burden by illegal and unethical methods. Such tax dodgers are subject to prosecution, since they are seeking to evade a duty and responsibility which all governments place upon their citizens.

GENERAL PROPERTY TAX — REAL AND PERSONAL

The general property tax is applied to realty and to personalty or to both. It is the oldest form of taxation used in this country, and it still serves as an important source of revenue in a few states. In a number of states — California, Delaware, Illinois, Michigan, New York, North Carolina, Oklahoma, Oregon, Pennsylvania, Rhode Island, South Carolina, South Dakota, and Virginia — it has not been used for state purposes for many years. New Hampshire and Vermont levy on property only in unorganized areas. In New Jersey 90 per cent of the property tax levy is returned to the localities for school use, while in Wisconsin the .2 mill levy is for the purpose of conservation and forestry development.

The list of states abandoning this source is gradually increasing because of serious criticism of the disproportionate tax burden borne by real estate. As originally employed in Colonial America and in the early national period, the general property tax as applied to real estate was reasonable and just, as well as simple and inexpensive in administration. It was easy to designate at the town meeting some citizen to visit the various landowners in the community for the purpose of noting the number of acres of cleared land held by each and assessing this at so much an acre. In modern times, however, the assessment of property has become a difficult and highly complicated task.

Tax on Real Estate. A number of specific steps occur in the administration of the tax on real estate. There is, first, the problem of assessment. When the assessors have completed their task, opportunity must be given for the filing of complaints by dissatisfied property owners, and for hearings on the complaints before local boards of review. These agencies have not been effective in the correction of inequalities or abuses. In those states, however, where a state tax commission or a state board of equalization exists, there has been some influence toward the development of uniform and equitable assessments. Finally, after the taxing power has adopted its budget for the ensuing fiscal period and determined the rate, there is the task of collecting. The collecting agencies vary in organization and efficiency of operation all the way from the medieval system of farming out the taxes under a fee system, as in Pennsylvania, to a centralized and efficient county collection system such as is used in thirty-seven states.

In this brief outline of the steps involved in the administration of this tax, certain weaknesses of it have been indicated. Perhaps the most serious of these is the lack of uniformity, which has been recognized for the last fifty years. All but three state constitutions — those of Alabama, Arkansas, and Washington — require, but few states practice, assessment at full value. Studies of the administration of this tax in Pennsylvania, made by Richard T. Ely and Henry R. Seagers in the latter part of the last century, showed variations between adjoining counties in average rates of assessments running as high as 100 per cent. If property is assessed in one county at 45 per cent of market value and in an adjoining county at 90 per cent, and the same rate of taxation is then applied to the total assessed valuation of both counties, it is evident that the county with the 90 per cent assessment is paying actually twice as high a tax as the neighboring county with the assessment half as high. That in all these years no serious effort has been made to correct these inequalities is evident from the data presented in the following table: [8]

RATIO OF ASSESSED VALUES TO SALES VALUES OF PROPERTIES OF ALL CLASSES IN CERTAIN PENNSYLVANIA COUNTIES

County	Median	Mean	County	Median	Mean
Adams	66.7	95.6	Indiana	79.7	92.6
Chester	68.0	83.1	Mercer	59.2	72.5
Clarion	52.4	68.5	Monroe	46.0	61.9
Columbia	68.8	77.9	Montgomery	49.2	56.6
Cumberland	69.9	77.1	Philadelphia	110.2	128.7
Franklin	66.4	80.0	Snyder	76.4	93.2
Greene	49.7	63.2	Tioga	62.0	80.4
Huntingdon	92.8	98.0	Union	67.0	94.7

This situation is not quite so important where collections are made for local purposes only, but the same lack of uniformity still exists between the smaller local units, and between individual taxpayers within those units.[9] It will be impossible to secure a uniform application of the general property tax until a policy of assessment at full valuation, or at some agreed fraction, is uniformly adopted and enforced. The requirement of full value assessment is almost universally ignored for a variety of reasons disclosed in a canvass of assessors in New York in 1942. The more important of these were: belief that high assessment means high taxes, desire to minimize the share of state and county taxes paid by the area assessed, political considerations, and the assessor's desire for re-election, and difficulty in determining full value with fair accuracy.

The English system of taxing real estate on its earning power or income, instead of its market or capital value, has much to commend it. Unused vacant land and unoccupied improved property (with some exceptions) are not taxed, as they theoretically have no income or use value. Agricultural property, other than the dwellings thereon, is exempt from the real estate tax, and industrial property, includ-

[8] Based on Table 1 in Logan, Edward B., *Taxation of Real Property in Pennsylvania* (Harrisburg, 1934).

[9] The New Jersey Taxpayers' Association, in its study of the *Tax Exemption Policy in New Jersey*, shows the ratio of assessed valuation to true value in various cities throughout the state; in each city, from 300 to 700 property sales were compared with the assessed valuations to secure the data. The figures represent the percentage of true value assessed: Clifton, 44.0; Elizabeth, 54.0; Atlantic City, 66.0; Jersey City, 67.4; Camden, 65.5; Trenton, 60.0; Newark, 58.7; Bayonne, 45.5; Kearny, 50.8. In many rural taxing districts the assessed valuation is less than 40 per cent of true value (p. 11).

ing freight-transportation property, is taxed at only 25 per cent of the rate applicable to fully taxed property. These two exemptions are not essential parts of the English system, but are in the nature of subsidies to encourage agriculture and manufacturing. Three centuries of experience with taxes paid by the tenant (except in case of " compulsory compounding " of the tax on low rental properties) finds the British generally content with the steadiness of the tax, with the assessment of the tax, and with a low delinquency rate.[10]

A second major defect in administration lies in the untrained or incompetent personnel employed in the work. In the vast majority of communities, urban and rural alike, the assessor is a political hanger-on, whose political connection constitutes his only qualification. Experiments have been conducted in New York City and Cleveland, more recently in Pittsburgh and Detroit, and also in some counties, which prove that it is possible to develop and enforce definite rules for making assessments and to secure a trained and competent personnel. Many years ago, when Lawson Purdy was appointed head of the Board of Tax Appraisers in New York City, he determined to secure a competent personnel. The number of assessors employed at the time was 300. He served notice on these persons that on a certain day and hour, at a designated place, they would be required to take an examination. The questions used were such as might compose an ordinary eighth grade examination in arithmetic. Exactly half the 300 assessors appeared to take the examination, and approximately half of those who took it were entitled to a passing grade.

With this nucleus of seventy-five people Mr. Purdy began the development of a trained force of assessors. They were provided with a definite set of rules which were to be applied to all properties, the purpose being to develop a system by means of which two persons engaged independently in the appraisal of the same property might arrive at the same result. Mr. Purdy tried to meet personally those who complained about their assessments. With tax maps of the city, upon which every parcel of taxable real estate was indicated, he sat down with them to talk over the assessment. He made it a point, wherever possible, to have the complaining citizen withhold from him the amount of the assessment until their conversation was well under way. When the citizen found that there were rules, that these rules had been followed, and that he as an individual had been

[10] Collins, Arthur, " Occupancy Taxes in Britain," *National Municipal Review*, April, 1944, pp. 170–178.

treated with absolute fairness, he commonly withdrew his complaint. Without the adoption of improved methods such as these, it will probably be impossible to continue indefinitely the use of the general property tax for state purposes.

Many other criticisms have been directed against this tax. Two definite alternatives seem to be available. One is to abolish the tax, at least for state purposes; the other is to reform its administration. Some of the elements necessary for such reform have already been indicated. They include the development of a competent and adequately trained personnel; the development of workable rules that can be applied to any given property with uniform results; state supervision of local assessments through the agency of a state tax commission or board of equalization, and separation of state and local revenue sources. Because of lack of adequate appropriations and competent staff, this work is rarely well done, if indeed, it is done at all.[12]

The National Association of Assessing Officers worked out a series of forty-eight principles of a sound assessment procedure. A survey made in selected counties in New Jersey in 1941 showed that thirty-five of these were commonly violated. Almost 90 per cent of the tax districts were too small in population or in ratables to support adequately paid and qualified assessors. Consequently, the work was done on a part-time basis by political jobholders, in a great majority of districts. Supervision by the county boards of taxation and the State Tax Department was practically nil. Most of the assessing consisted in roll copying or in wholesale horizontal adjustments of the previous year's roll. In two thirds of the districts tax maps were inadequate or non-existent. In many districts the records were incomplete or inadequate, or both. In most districts no effort was made by assessors to secure adequate data pertinent to valuations, such as building costs, sale prices, rents on comparable properties, et cetera. The assessors' manual of appraising, distributed by the state, was not used or followed in the great majority of districts. And so on, ad infinitum. It is only fair, however, to say that these conditions are not in any way peculiar to New Jersey.

Early in 1945 a Joint Legislative Committee to Investigate Tax Problems reported to the Governor of Illinois; the *Report* is significant as presenting an up-to-date analysis of the defects and possible remedies, applicable to the general property tax.

[12] National Association of Assessing Officers, *Equalization Agencies* (Chicago, 1940).

ASSESSMENT AND COLLECTION OF GENERAL PROPERTY TAXES IN THE FORTY-EIGHT STATES AS OF JANUARY 1, 1940 [11]

State	Frequency of Assessment Every — Years		Assessor of County, City, or Other Unit	Separate Assessments of Land and Improvements	Percentage at Which Real Estate Is Assessed	Who Collects Taxes	Discounts Allowed
	Real Estate	Personal Property					
Alabama	1	1	County	Yes	60	County Tax Collector	No
Arizona	1	1	County	Yes	100	County Treasurer	No
Arkansas	2	1	County	Yes	50	Sheriff or Collector	No
California	1	1	County	Yes	100	Tax Collector	No
Colorado	1	1	County	Yes	100	County Treasurer	No
Connecticut	10	1	Town or City	Yes	100	Tax Collector	No
Delaware	1–4	4	County	No	100	County Treasurer	Yes
Florida	1	1	County	No	100	County Collector	Yes
Georgia	1	1	County	Yes	100	County Collector	No
Idaho	1	1	County	Yes	100	County Treasurer	No
Illinois	4	1	County	Yes	100	Treasurer or Sheriff	No
Indiana	4	1	County	Yes	100	County Treasurer	No
Iowa	4	1	Town or City	No	100	County Treasurer	No
Kansas	4	1	County	Yes	100	County Treasurer	Yes
Kentucky	1	1	County	No	100	Sheriff	Yes
Louisiana	1	1	Parish	Yes	100	Tax Collector or Sheriff	No
Maine	1	1	Town	Yes	100	Collector or Constable	Yes
Maryland	5	1	County	Yes	100	County Collector	Yes
Massachusetts	1	1	Town or City	No	100	Tax Collector	No
Michigan	1	1	Town or City	No	100	Township or City Treasurer	No
Minnesota	2	1	Town or City	No	100	County Treasurer	No
Mississippi	2	1	County	Yes	100	County Tax Collector	No
Missouri	1	1	County or Town	No	100	Collector	Yes
Montana	2	1	County	Yes	100	County Treasurer	No

11 Adapted for this volume from data in *Tax Systems of the World*, Eighth Edition (Commerce Clearing House, Chicago, 1940).

State			Unit			Collecting Officer	
Nebraska	2	1	County and Precinct	Yes	100	County Treasurer	No
Nevada	1	1	County	Yes	100	County Treasurer	No
New Hampshire	1	1	Town or City	No	100	Tax Collector or Sheriff	Yes
New Jersey	1	1	Town or City	Yes	100	Tax Collector	Yes
New Mexico	1	1	County	Yes	100	County Treasurer	No
New York	1	1	Town or City	Yes	100	Tax Collector	No
North Carolina	4	4	County	No	100	Sheriff or Tax Collector	Yes
North Dakota	2	1	Township, City, or Village	Yes	100	County Treasurer	Yes
Ohio	6	1	County	Yes	100	County Treasurer and County Auditor	No
Oklahoma	2	1	County	Yes	100	County Treasurer	No
Oregon	1	1	County	Yes	100	Sheriff	Yes
Pennsylvania	3	1	Town, Borough, and Ward	No	100	County and City Treasurer; Tax Collector in Small Units	Yes
Rhode Island	1	1	Town or City	Yes	100	Town Collector or Treasurer	Yes
South Carolina	4	1	Tax District	Yes	100	County Treasurer	Yes
South Dakota	1	1	Town or City	Yes	100	County Treasurer	No
Tennessee	2	1	County	No	100	County Trustee	Yes
Texas	1	1	County and City	No	100	Tax Collector or Sheriff	No
Utah	1	1	County	Yes	100	County Treasurer	No
Vermont	4	1	Town	No	100	Town Treasurer or Collector	Yes
Virginia	4	1	County and City	Yes	100	County and City Treasurer	No
Washington	2	1	County	Yes	50	County Treasurer	Yes
West Virginia	1	1	County	No	100	Sheriff or Munic. Collector	Yes
Wisconsin	1	1	Township or City	Yes	100	Town, City, or Village Treasurer	No
Wyoming	1	1	County	Yes	100	Treasurer	No

DEFECTS AND POSSIBLE REMEDIES APPLICABLE TO THE
GENERAL PROPERTY TAX

Defects	*Possible Remedies*
1. Instability and lack of uniformity in the application of statutory limitations on tax rates.	1. Intra-county assessment uniformity.
2. Rate discrimination within an assessment or taxing district.	2. Inter-county assessment uniformity.
3. Inequality in the apportionment of state grants-in-aid.	3. Modification of tax-rate limits.
4. Inequitability of legislative restrictions on the bonded debt of local units.	4. More equitable method of apportioning state grants-in-aid.
5. Need for property classification for purposes of taxation.	5. Actual full value assessment of real estate for tax purposes.

The application of this tax creates serious problems in many fields, usually for different reasons. In agriculture poor assessment methods result in an inequitable burden on taxpayers.[13] Some land has never been taxed at all — a Texas survey estimates that this runs to several million acres. In the taxation of forest lands, one must face the question of how much tax the owners of such lands can stand without being forced to premature cutting or wholesale slashing of forest areas. Other special problems arise with respect to mine properties, public utility properties, and many other types.

[13] Numerous studies have been made of the farm tax problem: ALABAMA: Clark, Carl M., *Rural Property Tax Problems in Alabama* (Alabama Polytechnic Institute, Auburn, 1940). INDIANA: Kessler, Sherman O., *Tax Laws Affecting the Payment of Taxes by Indiana Farmers* (Purdue University, Lafayette, 1942). KANSAS: Howe, Harold, and Miller, L. F., *Assessment and Collection of Farm Real Estate Taxes in Kansas* (Kansas Agricultural Experiment Station, Manhattan, 1940); Miller, L. F., *Kansas Oil Property Taxation in Relation to Farm Taxes* (Kansas Agricultural Experiment Station, Manhattan, 1938). MARYLAND: Miller, Earl E., and Walker, William F., *Measuring Inequalities in Farm Property Assessment in Maryland, Characteristics of Farm Property Assessments in Maryland after the Last Reassessment,* and *Extent of Changes and Equalization Produced in Farm Property Assessments by Reassessing in Maryland* (all, Agricultural Experiment Station, College Park, 1940, 1941, and 1942, respectively). MONTANA: Renne, R. R., and Lord, H. H., *Assessment of Montana Farm Lands* (Montana Agricultural Experiment Station, Bozeman, 1937). NEBRASKA: Snyder, L. B., *The Tax System of Nebraska with Special Reference to Its Relation to Agriculture* (Agricultural Experiment Station, Lincoln, 1938). NORTH CAROLINA: Forster, G. W., *Recent Changes in Tax Rates on Farm Real Estate in North Carolina* (Agricultural Experiment Station, Raleigh, 1942). OHIO: Thewlis, J. D., and Falconer, J. I., *Public Revenue in Ohio with Especial Reference to Rural Taxation* (Agricultural Experiment Station, Wooster, 1942). RHODE ISLAND: Tennant, J. L., *Farm Taxes and Farm Real Estate Transfers in Rhode Island* (Agricultural Experiment Station, Kingston, 1938). SOUTH CAROLINA: Aull, G. H., and Riley, Ernest, *Some Inequalities in the Assessment of Farm Real Estate in South Carolina* (Agricultural Experiment Station, Clemson, 1938). TENNESSEE: Allred, Charles E., and Luebke, Benjamin H., *Property Tax Burden of Tennessee Farmers* (Agricultural Experiment Station, Knoxville, 1942). TEXAS: Holden, A. W., *Report of the Texas State-Wide Tax Survey* (Works Progress Administration, Austin, 1938).

Recent Progress in Assessments. During recent years much progress has been made in the scientific assessment of real property in Pittsburgh, Detroit, Richmond, and other cities. The so-called Pittsburgh plan, which has attracted much attention, is based upon the well-known fact that city land is continually increasing in value, while the value of buildings is continually decreasing. It was provided that the tax on buildings as compared with the tax on land should be 10 per cent less for the years 1914 and 1915, and that a reduction of an additional 10 per cent in the tax on buildings should be made every third year until it was one half that on the land. That point was reached in 1930, at which time the land tax was twenty-five mills and the building tax was twelve and one half mills. A full value system of assessment has been adopted, under which there is a fixed rate for each front foot in each block, varying for the depth of the lot and its distance from the corner. This plan has increased the revenues of the city, reduced the tax rate, and lightened the burden on the small home owner.

In Detroit, tax maps are published annually and distributed. Front foot, square foot, and cube foot standards have been worked out and incorporated in an assessor's manual; these are applied successfully to 550,000 parcels of property, from which $76,000,000 were collected in 1934. There were very few appeals; the tax is computed automatically, and in the preparation of the tax bills, master metal plate records are used for printing. Mechanical methods are used in the office of the city treasurer. Unit records show the entire tax history of each parcel of property.[14] With funds provided by the Federal government and administered by state agencies, numerous other cities were able to make complete reassessments and inventories of real estate at slight cost to themselves.

In a modern assessment system the property must first be listed and described. The descriptions are often complicated, and follow the legal description of the property. Each property is located on block and lot maps and land value maps, which tends to prevent inequalities and errors. On the former, each unit is numbered, and this number is used in all official real estate records. The land value maps show the front foot value of all land in the city. Each unit is written up on a separate card or sheet suitable for loose-leaf filing, showing the entire tax history of the property. Entries are made for sales, leases, rents, foreclosures, alterations, repairs, demolitions, et

[14] See Leonard, J. M., *Suggestions for the Reorganization of Assessing Practices in the City of Detroit* (Detroit Bureau of Governmental Research, 1940) ; and Pierce, Dixwell L., " Tax Assessors Can Do Good Jobs," *State Government*, November, 1943, pp. 224–227.

cetera, so that each assessor or deputy has full information with regard to all properties assigned to him. These data are a matter of public record and are widely used by real estate men and others. A complete assessment manual gives the deputy the statutory and administrative rules which are to be followed in his work. The value of the land as though unimproved and the improvements on the land are separately determined, and added to indicate the total assessment on the property. In a progressive system, instead of treating all property alike, it is classified, depending upon the class of property, which will determine the percentage of full and true value to be used in determining valuation. Finally, the assessment roll is prepared; this is a copy of the annual record made up after valuations have been corrected.[15]

Tax Exemption. The policy of exempting certain kinds of property from taxation has been the subject of much discussion. It has been claimed, on the one hand, that such exemptions make the taxes higher for other people, and on the other, that such a policy is essential to the encouragement of many worthy purposes — religious, charitable, educational, and the like — and that the strengthening of these agencies reacts to enhance the value of other classes of property in the community. At any rate, the policy of such exemptions is well established. Most state constitutions require the uniform taxation of all property whether owned by individuals or corporations; there are, says Professor Schmidt, generally four exceptions to this universal rule:

(1) Legislatures are usually required to exempt the property of the state and its political subdivisions; (2) legislatures must usually exempt household goods, workmen's tools, et cetera, up to a given value; (3) legislatures commonly are permitted to exempt the property of educational, religious, and eleemosynary institutions (this is sometimes extended to agricultural associations, property of war veterans, et cetera); and (4) legisla-

15 For a description of the methods used, see a series of studies by the National Association of Assessing Officers: *Primary Local Assessment Districts* (Chicago, 1938). *Overlapping Local Assessment Districts* (1938), *The State as an Assessment District* (1938), *Administrative Review Agencies* (1939), *Judicial Review Agencies* (1939), and *Equalization Agencies* (1940). On classification, see *Minnesota Property Taxation, 1924–1941,* for discussion of the act of 1941 (Department of Taxation, St. Paul, 1942); Zangerle, John A., and Bethel, Walter L., *Ohio's Classification of Tax Law,* discussing the difficulties of joint state and local administration (privately printed, 1937). See also Groves, *op. cit.,* pp. 82–91; New York City Department of Taxes and Assessments, *Knowing the Department of Taxes and Assessments* (New York, 1937); and New York State Constitutional Convention Committee, *Problems Relating to Taxation and Finance,* Chapters 8 and 9 (Albany, 1938).

tures sometimes are permitted to provide for special low-rate taxation of intangible property.[16]

These constitute a group that has been called " the tax untouchables." Many additional exemptions may be provided by statute; a careful listing of the exemptions provided in the General Tax Act in New Jersey shows a total of twenty-five, some with as many as ten subdivisions. Others may be provided in specific tax acts, such as income, sales, et cetera. In a period extending from 1919 to 1933, the average percentage of exemptions allowed to public and other schools was 29.2; to public property, 33.4; to churches and charitable institutions, 20.4; to cemeteries, 1.7; all other exemptions totaled 15.3 per cent. The average per cent of exemption value in each county in New Jersey for the years 1933 and 1942 are indicated in the table below. It will be noted that in many counties there has been a marked increase in exemptions.[17]

TAX EXEMPTIONS IN NEW JERSEY, 1933 and 1942

County	Per Cent Exempt		County	Per Cent Exempt	
	1933	1942		1933	1942
Atlantic	9.2	13.3	Middlesex	30.4	34.0
Bergen	11.1	13.0	Monmouth	13.9	18.7
Burlington	14.7	26.7	Morris	18.0	20.3
Camden	17.9	18.5	Ocean	10.4	13.4
Cape May	10.3	15.6	Passaic	18.1	17.5
Cumberland	16.9	18.0	Salem	6.1	.5
Essex	14.7	17.1	Somerset	14.7	1.4
Gloucester	10.9	12.4	Sussex	6.2	8.0
Hudson	11.0	19.9	Union	9.5	11.6
Hunterdon	17.6	7.6	Warren	8.9	11.4
Mercer	25.3	29.6	State Average	17.1	17.9

In New York State in 1936, approximately $340,451,474 of Federal property, $350,000,000 of state property, and $2,199,642,513 of local property was covered by exemptions.[18]

16 Schmidt, E. B., " Problems of Homestead Tax Exemption," *Tax Magazine,* April, 1938, pp. 211–215, 248.
17 Figures for 1933 from *Tax Exemption Policy in New Jersey,* pp. 7–8, for 1942, from *Local Taxes in New Jersey,* Part 2, pp. 14–15, both from New Jersey Taxpayers Association. It is suggested that the reader make inquiry regarding tax exemptions in his own community or state.
18 New York State Constitutional Convention Committee, *op. cit.,* p. 194. On special types of property, see Bloomenthal, Lawrence R., " Taxable Status of Public Property," *Tax Magazine,* November, 1937, pp. 658–668, 692, and January, 1938, pp. 527–532, 566; Stimson, Claude W., " The Exemption of Churches from Taxation," *ibid.,* June, 1940, pp. 361–364, 397; Louisiana State Board of Com-

In spite of the opposition of students of public finance to tax exemptions, the policy has continued to spread. Once established, there is always the plea for its extension. During the depression, pressure groups worked for homestead exemption, exemption of manufacturing establishments, and other forms. A study made in 1938 showed four types of exemption and preferential treatment of homesteads existing in thirteen states, all under laws adopted since 1932. Iowa, Minnesota, and West Virginia give preferential treatment to homesteads; six states — Alabama, Arkansas, Minnesota, Mississippi, South Dakota, and Texas — grant exemptions to homesteads from state levies and from the levies of some but not all local units. Finally, Florida, Oklahoma, and Wyoming exempt homesteads from property taxes of all governmental units (with certain exemptions in the first two states). The results seem not to have been too encouraging. It is reported from Georgia that the loss to the counties amounts to $1,800,000 annually and that, unless the state comes to their aid, counties may be forced to consolidate in order to reduce costs. Iowa reports that those benefited approve of the law, but that others find the addition of sales and income taxes burdensome.[19]

Tax Delinquency. Governments, like businesses, have bad debts.

merce and Industry, *Tax Exemption to Industry in Louisiana* (Baton Rouge, 1937) ; and National Association of Assessing Officers, *Exemption of Manufacturing Plants and Machinery from Property Taxation* (Chicago, 1938) .

[19] National Association of Assessing Officers, " Exemption and Preferential Taxation of Homesteads," Bulletin No. 20 (Chicago, 1938) . Other general references include: American Legislators' Association, " Homestead Exemption Legislation," Bulletin, May 6, 1935 (Chicago) ; Bloomenthal, Lawrence R., " Tax Exemptions, Part II," *Tax Magazine*, September, 1937, pp. 527–532, 566; Carlson, R. E., " Economic Implications of Homestead Tax Exemptions," *Journal of Land and Public Utility Economics*, November, 1937, pp. 343–349; " Homestead Tax Exemption," *Federal Home Loan Bank Review*, October, 1937, pp. 6–10, 14; Groves, *op. cit.*, Chapter 21; Leonard, J. M., and Mohaupt, Rosina, *Exemption of Homesteads from Taxation* (Detroit Bureau of Governmental Research, 1937) ; Olcott, Margaret T., *Homestead Tax Exemption in the United States, a Selected List of References*, containing general references and references by states (Bureau of Agricultural Economics, Washington, 1940) ; Rose, Walter W., and Murray, E. B., " Is Homestead Tax Exemption a Good Idea? " *Freehold*, June 15, 1938, pp. 416–421; Schmidt, *op. cit.*

Numerous studies have been made in individual states; in addition to those listed in previous editions, see: CONNECTICUT: Cross, Wilbur L., " Property Tax Exemptions," *Tax Magazine*, September, 1933, pp. 338–339, 358–359. MASSACHUSETTS: Massachusetts Federation of Taxpayers Associations, *Federal Tax Exempt Property in Massachusetts* (Boston, 1944) ; MISSISSIPPI: State Tax Commission, *The Administration of the Homestead Exemption Act of 1940*, to 1943 (Jackson, 1944) ; and Satterfield, M. H., " Mississippi Provides Tax-Free Homes," *National Municipal Review*, May, 1939, pp. 365–370. OREGON: Kehrli, Herman, *The Nature and Value of Tax-Exempt Real Property* (University of Oregon, Bureau of Municipal Research and Service, 1940) ; summaries in *Commonwealth Review* and *Western City*, both, November, 1940) .

Uncle Sam collects his. Businessmen collect theirs — or write them off as uncollectible. Local governments, generally speaking, allow them to pile up. And thereby hangs a harrowing tale. The Western Division of the Pennsylvania Economy League reported in March, 1945:

> Right now, neglectful, forgetful, or indifferent taxpayers owe more than $45,000,000 to fifty-two governments in Allegheny County — the County, the City, the Pittsburgh School District, and forty-nine boroughs and townships, comprising altogether 87 per cent of the population and 90 per cent of total real estate assessments.
>
> Year after year, these delinquents are carried by people who pay their taxes. And if the debt were collected, the faithful taxpayers would enjoy a Roman holiday. $45,000,000 is equal to 27½ mills on the total assessments and would finance both the City and County governments for a year.

Tax delinquency reached acute proportions in many communities during the depression. The inability of many taxpayers to pay, and the inability of collecting officials to collect the taxes on their rolls brought many governmental units to the verge of financial ruin. Often hundreds of properties would be listed for a single sheriff's sale. The United States Bureau of the Census comprehensive study of realty tax delinquency in 1934 showed an average delinquency in all states of 20.5 per cent. These conditions led to the inauguration of pay-your-taxes campaigns on the one hand, and to all sorts of proposals for the assistance of the taxpayer on the other. Many had no money with which to pay, and others found it cheaper to rent than to continue payments of interest and principal on properties bought at the high price levels of pre-depression days.

There were widespread demands for homestead exemption and much such legislation was enacted, as were laws authorizing installment payments, discounts, staying sheriff's sales, and lengthening the period and easing the conditions under which property might be bought back. As one abatement act was piled upon another, the seriousness of the revenue problem of the local units increased. Many home owners were unaware of the changes made in the law and very often the only taxpayers who took advantage of the ameliorative legislation were the hotels and mid-city office buildings, most of which were perfectly able to pay their taxes without such assistance. Due to this legislation, then to steadily improving economic conditions through the defense boom and the war period, the trend of tax delinquency has continuously declined since 1933. A study made in 1945, covering 150 cities with a population of over 50,000, showed that the percentage of delinquency had declined from 26.35 in 1933, to 11.3 in 1937, to 3.9 per cent in 1944.[20]

Tax Limitation. Tax limitation, which will be referred to again in Chapter XXI on state-local relations, owed its recent widespread popularity to the popular psychology, fostered by taxpayers' associations, that led to taxpayers' marches on city halls and state capitols in the days of the depression. It was based upon the unthinking emotional reaction of people in a difficult financial situation, inspired by leaders who knew little and cared less about the functions and services of government. The limitations have been of a number of different types:

1. Tax limits which state a fixed maximum rate of tax.
   a. Blanket-rate limitations on the aggregate levy on each $100 value.
   b. Maximum-rate limitations for each governmental unit.
   c. Maximum-rate limitations for various purposes or funds.
2. Limitations which restrict the amount of levy to a stated percentage of the amount of some previous year, or average of certain years.
3. Limitations which restrict the amount of revenue to be raised to a fixed amount per capita.
4. Limitations which give the maximum levy permitted in terms of dollars.
5. Limitations which fix the ratio between revenues from general property taxes and revenues from other sources.

Of these types some states consistently use one, whereas others use two or more of the types jointly. In some cases one type of limitation is applied to some units of government and another to other units. The maximum-rate limitations for various purposes or funds are the oldest and most widely used type; they are usually provided for in

[20] Bird, Frederick L., *Trend of Tax Delinquency, 1930–1944* (Dun and Bradstreet, New York, 1945) ; Abbott, Peyton B., " The Collectibility of Special Assessments More than Ten Years Delinquent,"*North Carolina Law Review*, February, 1944, pp. 123–145; and in addition to the studies in particular states listed in previous editions of this volume, the following: CALIFORNIA: State Board of Equalization, *Delinquent Property Tax, 1928–29 to 1940–41* (Sacramento, 1942) . ILLINOIS: Illinois Legislative Council, *Tax Delinquency in Illinois with Particular Reference to Cook County* (Springfield, 1939) ; and City Club of Chicago, *Real Estate Tax Delinquency and Tax Foreclosure Suits* (Chicago, 1941) . MONTANA: Renne, R. R., and Brownlee, O. H., *Uncollected Property Taxes in Montana* (Agricultural Experiment Station, Boseman, 1940) . NEW YORK: Bratton, G. A., *Tax Collection and Tax Delinquency in Fifteen New York Counties* (State College of Agriculture, Ithaca, 1944) . NORTH DAKOTA: Wilner, Stanley, and Goodman, Archie B., *Taxation and Tax Delinquency of Farm Land in North Dakota* (Agricultural Experiment Station, Fargo, 1940) . OHIO: Delinquent Tax Commission of Ohio, *Final Report* (Columbus, 1940) . PENNSYLVANIA: Pennsylvania Economy League, *Tax Delinquency in Allegheny County Municipalities* (Pittsburgh, 1945) . SOUTH CAROLINA: Auhl, G. H., *The Nature and Extent of Farm Tax Delinquency in South Carolina* (Agricultural Experiment Station, Clemson, 1941) . VIRGINIA: Department of Taxation, *Virginia Local Tax Delinquency, A Ten-Year Review* (Richmond, 1944) .

the state constitution and, generally speaking, are unobjectionable. The limitations restricting the levy to a stated percentage of a previous year or years are of more recent origin, are often provided for by statute, and illustrate the type of limitation to which there is serious objection. From 1932 to 1937 nine states adopted overall rate limits, seven of them by constitutional amendment. These are shown in the table below.[21] Twenty-six states are limited either by statute or ·the constitution as to the amount of the state rate imposed on property, and forty states limit the amount minor civil divisions may raise by such levies.

It is urged that these laws do reduce property taxes and prevent increases, that they do force economy, efficiency, and a broadening of the tax base; but in practice they have proved to be a dangerous device, that has not only been disastrous to local government but that has failed to achieve its avowed purpose. In West Virginia, for instance, cities were reduced to a pitiful financial condition in 1933. Some of them were actually obliged to suspend the operation of their governments, and it took them years to recover from the effects

DIGEST OF OVERALL TAX LIMITATION LAWS IN NINE STATES

State	Constitutional or Statutory	Basic Rates		Additional Rates	
		Urban Per Cent	Rural Per Cent	Requiring No Special Authorization	Requiring Special Authorization
Indiana	S	1.5	1.0	Prior debt service	Unlimited
Michigan	C	1.5[1]	1.5	Prior debt service	3.5%
Nevada	C	5.0	5.0	None	None
New Mexico	C	2.0	2.0	All debt service	None[2]
Ohio	C	1.0[1]	1.0	None	Unlimited
Oklahoma	C	1.7[3]	1.7[3]	Prior debt service	School dists., 1%
Rhode Island	S	2.5	2.5	All debt service	Unlimited
Washington	S	2.0[4]	1.25[4]	Prior debt service	Unlimited
West Virginia	C	1.5 to 2.0	0.5 to 1.5	Prior debt service	50% of basic rates

[1] Not all incorporated cities or villages are subject to this limit.

[2] The constitution permits unlimited additional rates upon approval of a majority of voters, provided legislation to this effect is enacted.

[3] Out of this total, 0.2 per cent is reserved for counties for separate schools for whites and Negroes.

[4] Actual statutory rates are 4% and 2.5%, but property is assessable by law at only 50% of full value.

[21] Hillhouse, A. Miller, and Welch, Ronald B., *Tax Limits Appraised*, p. 2 (Public Administration Service, Chicago, 1937).

of this vicious legislation. The limitations were often evaded; taxes were not actually lowered, because ways were found by which it was legally possible to tax outside the levy.[22] Tax limitation laws, like the taxpayers associations most active in their sponsorship, thrive in periods of economic adversity. When times are good not even these associations think much about such legislation.

Collection of the Real Property Tax. In 1935 the National Municipal League published the report of one of its committees, which had been appointed to draft a Model Real Property Tax Collection Law. The nature of the tax has been discussed, some of the difficulties involved in its administration, and such questions as exemptions, delinquencies, and limitations. How, then, ought the money to be collected? Under what arrangements should the property owner be asked to make the payment of the tax moneys due? These questions are answered competently in the recommendations of the committee:

1. It should provide for the payment of taxes in semiannual, at least, preferably in quarterly, installments of which the first should be due as nearly as possible at the beginning of the fiscal year, in order to reduce the expense of borrowing in anticipation of taxes. Each installment should be separately treated with respect to liens and penalties.
2. No discount for prepayment of taxes should be allowed, because installment payments make this expense unnecessary.
3. Penalties for non-payment of taxes should be sufficient to make it unprofitable to withhold payment.
4. Tax liens should be sold at a general sale soon after the date of delinquency of the last installment. The law should make it mandatory that sales be held annually at an invariable date. . . .
5. As to legal procedure for foreclosure of the equity of redemption, it should be as simple, expeditious, and inexpensive as possible, consistent with good land titles. . . .
6. There should be personal liability for taxes so far as constitutionally possible.
7. Some elasticity should be given to enforcement machinery by the addition of such special remedies as the collection of the rents and income of delinquent real estate through statutory receiverships of income-producing property, such as have been provided by law in several states.
8. The collector should hold an appointive rather than an elective office and he should be required to give a surety bond conditioned upon the

22 The literature is voluminous; the arguments on both sides are summarized in Groves, *op. cit.*, Chapter 20; in Kansas Legislative Council, *Survey of Kansas Tax Problems* (Topeka, 1939), and *Overall Tax Limitation* (Topeka, 1941); and in New York State Constitutional Convention Committee, *op. cit.*, Chapter 1. See also Bowen, Howard R., " Overall Limitation of Property Tax Rates," *Bulletin* of National Tax Association, January, 1939, pp. 108–113, and Morris, G. M., *Tax Limitation Laws* (American Municipal Association, Chicago, 1943). Extensive lists of references by states were given in the previous editions of this book.

faithful performance of his duties, including the observance of all controlling provisions of law.[23]

This question of methods of collection is important, in view of the continued use of the fee system and other unsound practices in many states. Collection on an installment basis gained wide acceptance during the depression, and seems appropriate when so many people live on a salary. Lent D. Upson reported that in 1930 twenty-seven states provided for installment payments; during the depression official opposition to the plan practically ceased, and fourteen states were added to the list, making a total of forty-one. Some states regarded installment legislation as an emergency measure, so that in 1940 the number of states had declined to thirty-six.[24]

Declining Importance of Tax on Realty. The United States Forest Service in 1945 put out an analysis of property tax developments from 1932 to 1941 which strongly emphasized the decline of the property tax in relative importance.[25] The decline in the percentage of revenue derived from this source by the various levels of government for this period was striking. The states dropped from 13.4 per cent in 1932 to 4.3 per cent in 1941. The corresponding figures for the counties were 72.0 and 52.1 per cent; for municipalities, 75.7 and 64.3 per cent; for school districts, 74.0 and 60.4 per cent.

There are a number of factors responsible for this development. The first of these is the complete withdrawal of many states from the general property tax field and the partial withdrawal of the remainder. The second is state aids; the states have been able to abandon this tax as a major revenue source, at the same time giving financial assistance to the local communities to an extent sufficient to ease the burden on real estate at that level also.

The third factor has been the centralizing tendency — the transfer

[23] " A Model Real Property Tax Collection Law," supplement to *National Municipal Review*, May, 1935, and Cavers, David F., Ed., " The Collection of Real Property Taxes," *Law and Contemporary Problems*, June, 1936, entire issue.

[24] Upson, Lent D., " Local Government Finance in the Depression," *National Municipal Review*, October, 1935, pp. 503–511; Illinois Legislative Council, *Installment Payment of Current Property Taxes* (Springfield, 1940). Of the thirty-six states that permit installment payments of real property taxes, nineteen authorize two installments, Arkansas and Mississippi authorize three, nine states authorize four, and six provide optional numbers of installments up to twelve. Of the thirty states that permit installment payments on personal property taxes, eighteen authorize two installments, two authorize three, seven authorize four, and three a varying number. Delaware and New York have no personal property tax.

[25] Malone, Paul E., *Property Tax Developments, 1932–1941* (United States Forest Service, Washington, 1945). The Treasury Committee also analyzed the general property tax, concluding that some fundamental changes in it are essential to the reorganization of local government revenues.

of functions from the local units to the states and the consequent reduction of the local revenue needs and the burden on real estate. Tax limitation laws have contributed to this result, as has the decided trend away from special assessment financing for important improvements. A sixth factor has been the downward trend of state and local debts during the boom period of defense and war industry. Finally, improvements in property tax administration have tended to raise the percentage of collection.

Tax on Personal Property. The tax on personal property is almost as old as the tax on real estate. In its early forms it was applied to such possessions as cattle and livestock; in our own time the field of its application is much broader, including both tangible and intangible property. A recent study shows that thirty-one states have the constitutional authority to classify property for taxation; a majority of these distinguish between tangible and intangible property, and a few have classified their real property.

In general, three types of tangible property are now subjected to taxation in a number of states. In the southern states particularly, personal items such as jewelry and household possessions ranging from the lawnmower to the family silverware are assessed. The blanks used for the reporting of this tax are long, complicated, and inclusive. Motor vehicles constitute the second type; in fifteen states their original status under the general property tax has not been materially altered. In eight others the tax has been retained, and has been used practically to insure the collection of local taxes. In these states the law requires that a person licensing a motor vehicle give satisfactory evidence (usually a tax receipt) of payment of a property tax thereon. Seven states have abandoned the ad valorem base, but special taxes, licenses, and fees may be assessed. In the eighteen remaining states motor vehicles are not ordinarily subject to either general or special property taxes.[26] The third type includes manufacturing plants and machinery. In half the states these are subject to property taxes on the same terms and conditions as other tangible property. Temporary exemption for newly located or newly constructed plants is provided in sixteen states, while in the remainder such property is classified in a number of different ways.[27]

In practice, the tax on intangibles presents quite a different problem. As early as 1871 an investigating committee in New York de-

---

[26] National Association of Assessing Officers, *Property Taxation of Motor Vehicles* (Chicago, 1938).

[27] National Association of Assessing Officers, *Exemption of Manufacturing Plants and Machinery from Property Taxation* (Chicago, 1938).

clared that it was " a tax on ignorance, honesty, and helplessness."
It was then and it is now almost wholly unsatisfactory, but it is
still used in more than three fourths of the states. The number of
states in the several categories in 1944 was as follows: [28]

METHOD OF TAXING INTANGIBLES — 1944

General property taxes	6
Flat-rate annual taxes on capital value	14
Variable-rate annual taxes on capital value	4
Flat-rate annual taxes on income	9
Flat-rate nonrecurring taxes on capital value	2
Substantial exemption	13
Total	48

Some states use two or more methods of taxing intangible property,
but each has a dominant method.

The arguments against the tax on intangibles have been summarized under five points: it is extremely difficult to find such property; interest and dividend yields have been adjusted to the expectation that intangibles would not be taxed; great encouragement is
given to the concentration of owners of intangibles in low-rate " tax-
colonies "; owners of intangibles probably receive fewer direct benefits from local government than owners of real and tangible personal
property; and double taxation is likely to result whenever representative intangibles and tangibles are taxed.

Further comment on some of these points may be in order. It is
one of the time-honored canons of taxation that no tax should be
imposed upon items which can be hidden or otherwise withheld
from the knowledge of the taxing authority. It is a matter of common knowledge that there has been, since the development of the
corporate form of business organization, a steady and rapid increase
in the volume of intangibles held by our citizens. In spite of this
fact, however, and in spite of steady increases in the tax rate applied
to such holdings, the gross receipts from taxes of this character show
a steady and persistent decline. This is a striking commentary on the
honesty of the ordinary citizen in his tax-paying capacity. It indicates that the tax imposes a financial penalty upon those citizens who
are honest enough to make a correct statement of the nature and extent of their holdings. Such a tax is obviously an undesirable source
of revenue from the point of view of public policy.

[28] National Association of Assessing Officers, *Property Taxation of Intangibles*
(Chicago, 1938) ; and Governmental Research Institute, *The Taxation of Intangibles in Missouri and Other States* (St. Louis, 1944) .

The effect of the general property tax on intangibles is strikingly shown by the experiences of Kentucky, North Carolina, and Virginia. North Carolina has a personal income tax, but has continued to tax intangibles as property. The following table shows the increase in the amount of bank deposits in North Carolina, and the decrease in the amount of intangibles listed for taxation. The experience of this state is typical — not unique in any way.[29]

LISTED INTANGIBLES COMPARED TO BANK DEPOSITS IN NORTH CAROLINA
1921–1927

Year	Listed Solvent Credits (in thousands)	Percentage of Decrease under 1921	Bank Deposits (in thousands)	Percentage of Increase over 1921
1921	$192,000	....	$252,100	....
1922	185,900	3.6	275,600	9.3
1923	167,000	13.4	299,600	18.8
1924	167,600	13.0	313,100	24.2
1925	162,400	15.8	318,400	26.3
1926	164,000	15.0	352,800	39.9
1927	150,400	22.0	356,800	41.5

From another point of view this tax has shown itself to be equally objectionable. It is difficult to collect, and tax officers have frequently made no serious effort to collect it. Where such a law exists, the collections under it represent only a fractional part of the revenues due the state. The collections are " spotty," because of the varied intensity of the efforts of various collection officers. There is little or no

29 Indiana University, Bureau of Business Research, *Taxation of Intangibles,* p. 5 (Bloomington, April 15, 1930). The best recent study is that by the Governmental Research Institute, *op. cit.,* There are a number of state reports on this subject since 1940: COLORADO: *Taxation of Intangibles* (University of Denver, Bureau of Business and Social Research, 1940). CONNECTICUT: Baldwin, Roger S., *Assessment of Tangible Personal Property* (University of Connecticut, 1944). GEORGIA: Raisty, L. B., *The Intangible Tax of Georgia* (University of Georgia Bulletin, 1940). INDIANA: *The Indiana Intangibles Tax Act,* with Questions, Answers, Form, Rules and Regulations (State Board of Tax Commissioners, Indianapolis, 1939). KANSAS: Kansas State Planning Board, *Collection of Personal Property Taxes in Kansas, 1927–1936* (Topeka, 1936), and Kansas Legislative Council, *Personal Property Taxation in Kansas,* Part I, Policy and Administration; Part II, The Collection Problem (Topeka, 1940). MICHIGAN: Ford, Robert S., and Wood, William B., *Taxation of Intangibles in Michigan* (University of Michigan, Bureau of Government, 1939). MISSOURI: Governmental Research Institute study, *op. cit.,* and Howard, Robert L., *Recent Developments and Tendencies in the Taxation of Intangibles* (University of Missouri Bulletin, 1931). NEW JERSEY: Commission on the Taxation of Intangible Personal Property, *Report* (Trenton, 1945). OKLAHOMA: Oklahoma Tax Commission, *Administration of the Intangibles Tax in Oklahoma* (Oklahoma City, 1940). VIRGINIA: Virginia Advisory Legislative Council, *Classification for Taxation of Certain Tangible Personal Property* (Richmond, 1944).

disagreement among students of public finance on this point — the general property as applied to personalty, especially intangibles, should be eliminated in favor of tax forms that are more equitable, which provide less incentive for dishonesty, and which are less difficult in administration. Two steps were taken in this direction in 1945 when commissions appointed to study the subject in Missouri and New Jersey turned in reports calling for modification of the existing system in the first case, and for the repeal of the intangibles tax in the second, with the substitution of a corporation business tax measured by net worth.

CORPORATION AND BUSINESS TAXES

The rapid growth of corporations in number and size has made it necessary, for purposes of regulation and equitable taxation, that specific taxes under the administration of some central authority be levied on this type of business organization. Professor Groves has classified the taxes affecting business in two groups, general and special, as follows:

TAXES AFFECTING BUSINESS [30]

General	Special
Sales Taxes	Occupational Taxes
Property Taxes	Incorporation Fees
Excess-profits Taxes	Capital Stock Taxes
Corporate Net Income Tax	Corporate Excess Taxes
Gross Income Taxes	

The general taxes are considered elsewhere in this chapter, under appropriate headings. The present discussion will be confined to those special taxes affecting corporations, although business taxes can be, and in some jurisdictions are levied upon unincorporated businesses as well as upon corporations. A study of corporation taxes made a few years ago has this to say on the prevailing forms:

Fees and licenses which are required from corporations in many states are theoretically payments for certain services rendered by the state to corporations, or for the privilege on the part of the corporation to exercise certain rights, which without a license would be illegal; practically in many states the fees and licenses are either excise or franchise taxes on the corporation for the purpose of producing revenue for the state. Taxes on corporations are now collected as franchise taxes, license taxes, income taxes, excise taxes, corporate excess taxes, registration fees, license fees, none of

[30] Groves, Harold M., *Financing Government,* p. 272 (Holt, New York, 1939).

which has any well defined meaning. The term franchise tax is applied to a tax on net income in New York, the actual value of the capital stock in Ohio, the authorized capital stock in Texas, the nominal value of capital stock in Illinois, and the value of assets in the State of Maryland.

In a majority of the states public utilities are taxed differently from private corporations. Public utilities were the first large corporations in the United States, and consequently have been regulated for a longer period than private corporations. Likewise, the operations of public utilities are so entwined with public interest and in many cases are given a monopoly in their field or territory that regulation is more necessary than in the case of private corporations. . . .

While regulation may be accomplished through taxation, the two need in no way be considered inseparable, and it is evident that the whole system of corporate taxation in many states needs to be overhauled in order that there be a more equitable distribution of the tax burden, between the public and private corporations and between corporations as a group and individuals.[31]

The New York State corporation tax law may be taken as illustrative of legislation of this character in a large industrial state. The various elements in this law are presented in outline form in the table on page 545.[32] All companies pay the filing fee and organization tax, when they start in business, and annually thereafter, that one of the franchise taxes applicable to the type of business in which they are engaged. Corporate income taxes are considered later. There is little uniformity among the states as to the exact form of their corporation tax laws or as to the rates imposed. The total effect of these laws, however, imposes a sizeable and reasonably uniform burden on corporations of each type in all the states.

In New York, as in the majority of states, substantially the same rates are applied to foreign as to domestic corporations. The base may be different, however, in order to reach only that portion of the corporation's assets employed, or business transacted, within the state. The United States Supreme Court has established the principle that foreign corporations may not be discriminated against; they may be kept out of the state if they desire to transact only local business, but having once been admitted, they are on the same basis before the law as domestic corporations within the state engaged in the same or similar business.[33]

[31] Indiana University, Bureau of Business Research, *Taxation of Corporations,* pp. 1–2 (Bloomington, 1934).

[32] Based on data in Thull, Beulah B., *Development of the New York State Department of Taxation and Finance and the New York State Tax System,* pp. 13–25 (Department of Taxation and Finance, Albany, 1941).

[33] Western Union Telegraph Company v. Kansas, 216 U. S. 1, 1909.

Type of Tax	Domestic Corporations	Foreign Corporations
Filing fee	$50 for railroads; $40 for all others	$100
Organization tax	$\frac{1}{20}$ of 1% on authorized capital stock	$\frac{1}{8}$ of 1% on par value of stock employed in state during first year of business, and on any subsequent increase
Franchise taxes (on gross assets)		
Real estate corporations, including joint stock companies and associations	$\frac{1}{4}$ of 1 mill on each dollar of gross assets employed in state. Minimum tax, $10. Millage tax on dividends, if paid	Same
Transportation and transmission corporations and associations	1 mill per dollar of net value of stock allocated to state, with millage tax on dividends	Same
Same — additional	$\frac{1}{2}$ of 1% of gross earnings from intrastate business, for privilege of doing business as a corporation. Minimum tax, $25	Same
Cooperatives	1 mill per dollar of net value of issued stock allocated to state, with millage tax on dividends	Same
Water, gas, electric or steam heating, lighting and power companies	$\frac{1}{2}$ of 1% of gross earnings from all sources within state, and 3% on dividends paid in excess of 4% of actual paid-up capital employed in state. Minimum tax, $25	Same
Insurance corporations	2% on gross annual premiums for all except life companies, on which rate is $1\frac{3}{4}$%	Casualty, health, and surety companies, 1%; fire (outside U.S.) $1\frac{1}{2}$%; 1 to 2% on premiums received within state.
Holding corporations	1 mill per dollar of net value of issued capital stock allocated to state, with millage tax on dividends	Same

Franchise Taxes. A franchise tax is a payment to the state for the privilege of doing business as a corporation instead of as an individual or a partnership. The corporation thus continues to pay for the right to exercise the powers granted to it by the state, paid for originally by the filing fee and the organization tax. Because of the differences existing in the size of companies and in the extent of their resources, a flat rate would be inequitable and unfair. The franchise tax is, therefore, a graduated license fee, the size of which is measured by a rule prescribed by law, depending upon the size and resources of the company. As will be seen from the New York table, there are many different types of franchises and many different bases for the measurement of the tax — capital stock, gross earnings, net earnings, stock transfer, corporate excess, et cetera. This is shown even more clearly in the classification of franchises used in California.[34]

FRANCHISE TAXES COLLECTED IN CALIFORNIA

1. Agriculture and allied industries
2. Construction
3. Manufacturing
4. Motion picture production
5. Real estate and investment
6. Amusement service
7. Business and professional service
8. Personal service
9. Retail trade
10. Wholesale trade
11. Water transportation
12. Miscellaneous
13. Mining
14. Oil
15. Water
16. Utilities, car and express
17. Utilities, gas and electric
18. Utilities, transportation, highway and air
19. Utilities, railroads
20. Utilities, telephone and telegraph
21. Utilities, water, public service
22. National banks
23. State banks
24. Financial
25. Building and loan
26. Federal savings and loan

[34] Franchise Tax Commissioner, *Annual Report,* 1493 (Sacramento, 1945). A number of studies have been made of the effect of these taxes on particular types of business: Ford, Robert S., *The Allocation of Corporate Income for the Purpose of State Taxation* (New York State Tax Commission, Albany, 1933); McKinley, David, *The Corporation License Tax in Kentucky* (University of Kentucky, Bureau of Business Research, 1934); Richardson, Haynes R., " License Taxation in the Maryland Revenue System," *Tax Magazine,* April, 1939, pp. 210–212, 247–249; Gamble, Philip L., *Taxation of Insurance Companies* (New York State Tax Commission, Albany, 1937); Hogg, Robert L., *Taxation of Life Insurance under State Laws* (American Bar Association, Insurance Section, Chicago, 1938); Lutz, Harley L., *The Fiscal and Economic Aspects of the Taxation of Public Securities* (Comptroller of the State of New York, Albany, 1939), and *The Taxation of the Railroads in New Jersey* (Princeton University Press, 1940); National Tax Association, *Report* of the Committee on Taxation of Airlines (Sacramento, 1945).

Bank Taxes. Because of the peculiar nature of their business, special taxes have been devised applicable to banks. In 1864 Congress placed a narrow limitation on state taxation of national banks, but under present Federal legislation, four methods of taxing national banks are possible. The underlying principle is that they shall not be taxed at a rate higher than other capital in competition with them. In New York, banks were subject to a franchise tax until 1921, when the State Supreme Court declared the act unconstitutional. After experimenting with a tax on moneyed capital, also declared unconstitutional, the present levy on net income was adopted.

Chain Store Taxes. All of the states derive a substantial revenue from corporation taxes. While most of this comes from domestic corporations, the states sometimes seek to evade the principle of equality of treatment set up for the protection of foreign corporations by imposing cleverly devised levies particularly applicable to the latter. Among these is the chain stores tax, which had an amazing development during the decade of the thirties. Many of the laws were fostered by independent merchants and therefore intended to be discriminatory; this consideration was often more important than the revenue produced.[35] As of December 31, 1939, such laws were in existence in twenty-one states. All but three of these laws were for graduated license taxes, in which the levy was based upon the number of units in the chain. Miscellaneous types existed in Delaware, Tennessee, and Virginia. A graduated tax based on the volume of sales had previously existed in a number of states; but in 1939 state supreme courts declared the Kentucky and Pennsylvania acts unconstitutional,[36] and the Wisconsin law expired. Several others had previously been changed in form or repealed altogether.

Severance Taxes. Severance taxes are not corporation taxes, but they are business taxes. Some states impose such taxes, in lieu of or in addition to property taxes, on coal, crude oil or petroleum, mine products, natural gas, salt, sulphur, stone, sand and gravel, timber or lumber cut, turpentine, fish, oysters, clams, shells, and shrimp. Severance taxes may be general, applying to all natural products extracted from the soil, or selective, applying to a limited number of such products. Taxes of the general type exist in Arkansas and

[35] See, for instance, Liggett v. Baldridge, Attorney General of Pennsylvania, 278 U. S., 105, 1928, and Liggett, et al., v. Amos, 287 U. S. 600, 669, 1932.

[36] See Kentucky Tax Commission, *et al.*, v. Great A. & P. Tea Company, Kentucky Court of Appeals, November 24, 1939, and American Stores Company v. Boardman, Secretary of Revenue, 336 Pa. 36, 1939.

Louisiana; taxes of the selective type are in force in seventeen other states.[37] Texas reported the largest amount of revenue from this source, followed by Oklahoma, both of which states tax the production of oil, natural gas, and ores. Louisiana was the third state to adopt this tax method, with a general law covering many products at varying rates. In 1937, nineteen states collected $44,000,000 from this source.

Differences in Tax Burdens in Different States. In the large industrial states there has been much discussion about business driven out of the states by the burden of taxes. For many years there had been a migration of industry from the Northern to the Southern states, where both taxes and wages are lower. The passage of the Federal Wages and Hours Law tended to equalize wage rates as between the two sections. The tax differential still existed, but tended to be less important when the scarcity of skilled labor in the South and the nearness to markets in the North were considered. The problem is by no means a new one — the records show that it was seriously discussed in the Pennsylvania General Assembly in 1885. It is customary for some states like Nebraska and New Jersey to advertise for new industries on the basis of low taxes, but such claims are difficult to prove. Levies affecting corporations directly may be nonexistent, but it is likely that other taxes affecting them indirectly will make the burden approximately equal. It takes money to run a government and the money has to be raised by some kind of taxes, either state or local.[38]

GENERAL SALES, USE, AND GROSS RECEIPTS TAXES

In the decade of the thirties, while the sales tax was spreading so rapidly from state to state, it was calmly assumed that it represented

[37] See Davisson, Malcolm M., *Severance Taxation* (Bureau of Public Administration, University of California, December, 1934) ; Baden, Anne L., *Taxation of Natural Resources, a Bibliographical List* (Library of Congress, Division of Bibliography, 1940) ; Moses, Leslie, " Severance Taxation in Louisiana," *Taxes*, April, 1940, pp. 233–239; Farris, T. N., *Severance Taxation in Louisiana*, Part I, Historical, Constitutional and Legislative Aspects, and Part II, Administration, Receipts and Allocations (Louisiana State University Press, 1938) ; Bureau of the Census, " State Revenues from Severance Taxes," August, 1937; and Tax Policy League, *Severance Taxes* (New York, 1940) . Several states have published bulletins on this subject.

[38] For example, New Jersey claims that a typical manufacturer who would pay $66,272 in Pennsylvania and $44,094 in New York, would pay no state taxes at all in New Jersey; they do not tell that real estate levies are many times higher in New Jersey than in either of the other states, and that relief in New Jersey is supported almost wholly by the local units. See Turner, Clarence L., *Report on Comparative Study of Corporate Taxes in Fifteen Industrial States* (Pennsylvania State Chamber of Commerce, Harrisburg, 1938) ; Groves, *op. cit.*, Chapter 21; and *A Survey of Taxes Paid by Business in 1938* (Dun and Bradstreet, New York, 1939) .

a new form of taxation. As a matter of fact, it was more than a century old in the United States, and has been used in every state in the Union in some form for many years. Pennsylvania levied a general tax upon wholesale and retail transactions which has been collected since 1821. The wholesale license tax provides for an annual license fee of $5.00 plus a tax of 5 per cent on the gross annual turnover, while the retail license tax provides for an annual fee of $2.00 plus 1 per cent on the entire volume of the year's business. Virginia likewise had an early law. The Delaware gross receipts tax dates back to 1906. In 1909 Missouri authorized its municipalities to collect turnover taxes. Since 1921 Connecticut has collected a gross income tax from unincorporated manufacturing and mercantile establishments, and in the same year West Virginia adopted its gross sales tax. Georgia and Mississippi — the Mississippi law was much discussed — followed in 1929.

The term " sales tax " is used rather loosely to apply to a number of different types of tax; on this basis general sales, use, and gross receipts taxes existed in twenty-five states as of 1944. These were of two main types — taxes on general sales and taxes on the privilege of engaging in business. Seventeen states had a use tax, intended to tap the rich field of sales made in interstate commerce. Five states had a compensating tax, and one had a service tax. The laws took several different forms, such as taxes on retail sales, general sales, gross receipts, and gross income. With the exception of the early laws mentioned above, all were adopted between 1933 and 1937.[39]

The selective sales tax differs from the general type and is somewhat older; it has been defined as " a tax upon and measured by the receipts from the sale of a particular article." Every state in the

[39] The best source of current information on such matters is the latest edition of *Tax Systems of the World;* this is based on the 1940 edition. By frequent supplements the Library of Congress has kept its sales tax bibliography up to date. See also California Taxpayers Association, *The Tax Digest,* issue of July, 1937; Chernin, Milton, *Gross Income (Gross Receipts) Taxation, 1937* (University of California, Bureau of Public Administration, 1937) ; Haig, Robert M., and others, *The Sales Tax in the American States* (Columbia University Press, 1934) ; Illinois Legislative Council, *Exemption of Food under Sales Tax Statutes* (Springfield, 1940) ; Jacoby, Neil H., *Retail Sales Taxation* (Commerce Clearing House, Chicago, 1939) ; Jensen, Jens P., *The Sales Tax* (Kansas Legislative Council, 1934) ; Nelson, Carl L., and others, *Sales Taxes* (Minnesota League of Municipalities, Minneapolis, 1935) ; Nichols, Egbert R., Ed., *The State Sales Tax* (Wilson, New York, 1938) ; Schultz, Arch D., *The Sales Tax in Five States* (Ohio Chamber of Commerce, Columbus, 1934) ; Walker, William P., and Weitzell, Everett C., *The Retail Sales Tax* (University of Maryland, February, 1936) ; Waters, Lawrence L., *Use Taxes and Their Legal and Economic Background* (University of Kansas Bureau of Business Research, June, 1940) . In addition to a number of studies in particular states, cited in previous editions of this book, see Ford, Robert S., and Shepard, E. Fenton, *The Michigan Retail Sales and Use Taxes* (University of Michigan, Bureau of Government, 1941) .

Union uses at least two taxes of this type — the tax on gasoline and the tax on liquor. In addition, taxes on nonintoxicating beer exist in twenty-eight states, and taxes on nonalcoholic beverages and commodities entering into the manufacture thereof, in fifteen states. Selective sales taxes on other commodities had been adopted in 1939, as follows: public amusements, not including business licenses or inspection fees, in twenty-nine states; cigarettes and tobacco, in twenty-five states; oleomargarine, in thirty states; severance taxes, in twenty-one states; pari-mutuel betting, in twenty-three states; and taxes on electricity, per kilowatt hours generated, in four states. Since the depression there has been a marked increase in the number of states in each of these groups, and in the rates imposed, and there are a great many other miscellaneous types of excises, royalties, and licenses.[40]

The problem of exemptions is important here, as in the case of the general property tax. Most states exempt commodities already taxed under other laws, such as gasoline, cigarettes, insurance companies, and banks. Some exempt certain transactions, such as sales to the state or its subdivisions. Some formerly exempted foodstuffs or made lump-sum exemptions from the tax base, but these forms of exemption have about disappeared.[41] This problem, however, leads directly to the fundamental question of the merits of the sales tax principle. This tax form stands in the peculiar position of having scarcely a friend or defender among students of public finance, and yet of having spread rapidly from state to state.

Against all the arguments of the tax experts have been weighed two facts, in the light of the urgent need of the states for additional revenues during the depression years when nearly all of the laws were adopted: the sales tax does produce revenue in sizeable amounts, and it produces it quickly. In some states it is, in fact, the largest single source of state revenue. Receipts shot upward during the defense period, and declined somewhat with restrictions in the supply of civilian goods during the war. No one denies that the tax is burdensome to the low income group, or that it is regressive, probably to a greater extent than any other tax now in common use. While it is to be hoped that, for these reasons, the sales tax may gradually be abandoned, this is scarcely to be expected. Louisiana did repeal its

[40] See tables in *Tax Systems of the World;* also Tower, Ralph B., *Luxury Taxation and Its Place in a System of Public Revenues* (New York State Tax Commission, Albany, 1931).

[41] Illinois Legislative Council, *Exemption of Food under Sales Tax Statutes* (Springfield, 1940).

law in 1940, but it is always easier to enact new tax laws than to get rid of them, and there is no sign that the need of the states for revenue will be in any sense diminished in the postwar years.

EXCISE TAXES — LIQUOR, GASOLINE, TOBACCO

It is difficult to classify taxes because so many writers use the only terms we have to describe them in so many different ways. Very often the terms themselves are not mutually exclusive. In the discussion of sales taxes mention has been made of special levies on alcoholic beverages, gasoline, and tobacco. These taxes are usually levied in the form of sales taxes, but they are also excises. Both the general sales tax and these special sales taxes or excises may be classified as consumption taxes. There are other excises in addition to these three, but these constitute such an important part of the state revenue picture that it is deemed proper to deal with them specifically.

STATE AND LOCAL REVENUES FROM ALCOHOLIC BEVERAGES, 1944 [42]

	License States	Monopoly States	Total
Total state sales	$..........	$646,925,319	$646,925,319
State license fees	38,296,031	20,286,614	58,582,645
State ABC taxes	209,459,452	82,629,473	292,088,925
Miscellaneous state ABC taxes	1,160,485	3,742,573	4,903,058
Gross state receipts	248,915,969	753,583,979	1,002,499,948
Cost of ABC administration, collection, etc.	7,492,428	10,247,457	17,739,885
Cost of goods sold	....	501,724,502	501,724,502
Cost of sales operations	....	23,411,228	23,411,228
Total state ABC costs	7,492,428	535,383,187	542,875,615
Net state ABC revenue	241,423,541	218,200,792	459,624,333
General sales tax	27,564,366	8,517,167	36,081,533
Local ABC revenues	34,401,630	5,457,613	39,859,243
Total state and local revenue	303,389,537	232,175,572	535,565,109

Alcoholic Beverages. The states may derive revenue from the alcoholic beverage industry in either or both of two ways. They may, as sixteen states do, engage in the wholesale distribution of wines and hard liquor, realizing a substantial profit from the operation of the business. Or they may, through a central licensing agency, issue

---

[42] Distilled Spirits Institute, Inc., *Public Revenues from Alcoholic Beverages, 1944*, pp. 8–9 (Washington, 1945).

licenses or permits to taprooms, eating places, and night clubs, for the retail sale, for consumption on the premises, of wine, beers, and liquors. In all states the licensing of liquor dispensers is required as a police measure, but in some the licenses are issued locally by the county, municipality, or other civil subdivision within which they carry on their business. In either case the practice is pretty well established of turning over to the local units all or part of the revenue derived from the issuance of such licenses.

The table on page 551 shows the state and local revenues from alcoholic beverages for 1944, for both license and monopoly states, as well as the costs incurred in the administration of the alcoholic beverage commissions. The total revenue derived from this source is considerable. The monopoly system is not only a better means of controlling the traffic, but is productive of substantially greater revenues than the license system. The license states are twice as numerous as the monopoly states, but they collect only one and one half times as much revenue. During the war period the receipts from this source increased sharply, in spite of decreased supply due partly to increased demand and partly to increased tax rates.

Gasoline Taxes. The first gasoline tax law was enacted in Oregon in 1919; the rate was one cent a gallon. Colorado, New Mexico, and North Dakota followed in the same year; by the close of the legislative sessions of 1925 such legislation was in effect in all but four states, and they soon succumbed. The tax was first collected in Illinois and New Jersey in 1927, in Massachusetts in 1928, and in New York in 1929. The rates began gently enough, at one or two cents, and increased steadily through the depression period to a range of from three to five cents, with a few states collecting as much as seven cents a gallon.[43] To this must be added the one cent a gallon collected for the Federal government.

The liquid fuels tax (for the base has been broadened to include liquid fuels in general), along with motor license and operators license fees, raises in acute form the question of special or designated funds. Every special group that pays a tax or an administrative license fee wants the receipts earmarked, and their expenditure restricted to purposes beneficial to the group paying the tax. The motor car, truck, and bus owners constitute a numerous and powerful group, and have generally been successful in preventing the diversion of

---

[43] The standard title on this subject is Crawford, Finla G., *The Gasoline Tax in the United States* (Public Administration Service, Chicago, 1937); also Kansas Legislative Council, *Gasoline Tax Exemption in Kansas* (Topeka, 1937).

liquid fuels and motor license revenues to purposes other than highways. The psychology of these interest groups is readily understandable, but administratively there is little or no justification for the establishment and operation of special funds. All tax receipts belong to the state as a whole, not to any individual group of taxpayers. They should go into the general fund to be used as the financial needs of the state require.

Cigarette and Tobacco Taxes. State laws taxing the sale and consumption of tobacco are of two types, from the standpoint of the objects taxed: those applying to tobacco products as a group, and those applicable only in certain specified forms of manufactured tobacco, such as cigars and cigarettes. Only one state, South Carolina, taxes all forms of tobacco products, but more than half of the states impose special tobacco taxes of various kinds. Every state levying such taxes requires that all or some dealers be licensed to do business. In addition, many states levy a commodity tax upon the tobacco itself as a base.[44]

Cigarette smoking has become so common a practice among all ages and both sexes throughout the country that some mention may be made of the number of state levies and rates imposed upon tobacco in this particular form. Originally confined to a small number of imported tobacco-producing states, cigarette taxes are now found in twenty-nine states:

Two cent levy (one mill per cigarette) — eighteen states.
  Arizona, Connecticut, Illinois, Iowa, Kansas, Kentucky, Maine, Massachusetts, New Hampshire, New York, Ohio, Oregon, Pennsylvania, Rhode Island, Utah, Vermont, and Washington.
Three cent levy — seven states.
  Alabama, Georgia, North Dakota, South Carolina, South Dakota, Tennessee, and Texas.
Four cent levy — one state, Mississippi.
Five cent levy — three states.
  Arkansas, Louisiana, and Oklahoma.

INCOME TAXES — INDIVIDUAL AND CORPORATE

Mention has been made of the development of the theory of taxation, from one basic principle to another, in the effort to find means of distributing the tax burden more equitably. In the opinion of tax experts, the income tax meets the ability-to-pay test better than any other. State income tax legislation began in 1911, when the Wiscon-

[44] See Tower, *op. cit.*, and White, Charles P., *The Operation of Tennessee Tobacco Taxes* (University of Tennessee *Record*, January, 1937).

sin act was passed.[45] Massachusetts, Missouri, Montana, and New York had adopted such taxes by 1917, when Delaware joined the income tax states. In the meantime Amendment XVI to the Federal Constitution had made possible the Federal Act of 1913. From this time on the income tax became more and more firmly established in the tax thinking of the country. By 1918 such laws existed in twelve states; in 1923, in fourteen; in 1933, in twenty-seven, with the present total not greatly in excess of that number.

With the decline of revenue from the general property taxes and other sources during the depression, it is not surprising that there was a general extension of income tax legislation, which may be applied to either persons or corporations or both. A study of the personal income tax thus summarizes the reasons for the steady growth of this tax form:

Modern industrial development has produced conditions which indicate to some the advisability of giving a larger scope to state income taxation.

In the first place, sharp differences have developed between the distribution of property, on the one hand, and of income on the other. Some groups have property, but no income; some have income, but no taxable property; some have both. A tax on property largely exempts one group, a tax on income exempts the other. It would therefore seem logical that a tax system distributed in some rational relationship would rest on both groups and be fairer to all concerned.

Secondly, an income tax falls upon those who at least have some income, rather than those who have none, as is the case of many property holders. Such a tax would then be based on the taxpayer's ability to pay rather than upon the benefits received from the governmental unit.

In the third place, with taxes as high as they now are and likely to continue for some time, it is highly important to know who are paying the taxes levied. We know that property taxes can be, and are, shifted with such results that no one has ever been able to say just where they finally rested. One reason for a larger development of income taxation is that we can know, approximately at least, where the tax is going to rest and can form some judgment as to what its import and effects are likely to be.

Lastly, the financial stress and strain to which our state governments have been subjected during the past few years has necessitated the securing of as much revenue from as many sources as possible. These factors, coupled with the knowledge that such taxes have proved successful in both the Federal and state systems, have led thirteen states to adopt some form of income taxation during the depression.[46]

---

[45] See Slater, Harry, " Wisconsin's Income Tax Act on Its Thirtieth Birthday," *Tax Magazine*, January, 1942, pp. 27–33, and February, 1942, pp. 95–101; also Brownlee, R. Jean, *The Income Tax in Delaware* (University of Pennsylvania, 1944). The Delaware law has recently been repealed.

[46] Ferguson, Vaughn B., and Davisson, Malcolm M., *Personal Income Tax* (University of California, Bureau of Public Administration, 1934) ; see also Blakey,

In view of these considerations, the use now made of the income tax becomes an important matter. The comment which follows, and the accompanying table, have been corrected through 1944. Thirty states now have net income taxes in some form (Column 1), including in every case but one a general personal income tax (Column 2). From another approach, twenty-four states tax the income of both corporations and individuals (Column 3). Of the thirty states which now tax income in some form, seventeen have adopted their laws since 1930 (Column 4). The twenty states with a general sales or a gross income tax, with one exception, adopted their acts since 1930; thirteen of these, in 1933 (Column 5). Sixteen states which have a sales or gross income tax also have a net income tax (Column 6). Some of the items in this classification, incidentally, overlap with certain types of the sales tax group discussed earlier. Only ten states have neither a sales or gross income tax nor a net income tax (Column 7). Some of the populous and wealthy states, such as New York and Massachusetts, are among those having a net income tax; on the other hand, Illinois, Michigan, New Jersey, and Pennsylvania have no income tax legislation. Two important states, California and Ohio, have no general personal income tax. South Dakota and West Virginia repealed their income tax laws during the war, and a number of states made substantial reductions in the rates.

The rates on personal net incomes begin at 1 per cent in a majority of states, and reach a maximum of 7 per cent in North Dakota; the rates on corporate incomes range from $\frac{1}{2}$ of 1 per cent in Maryland to a maximum of 6 per cent in Minnesota. The amount of income of single persons which is exempt from the tax varies from $500 in one state to $1,500 in three states, seventeen permitting $1,000. Five states allow amounts between $500 and $1000, while five others allow a deduction of from six to ten dollars after the tax has been computed. Exemptions for married persons range from $1,200 in one state to $3,000 in another, with ten states permitting $2,500; seven states $2,000; one, $1,800; one $1,700; and the remaining five, $1,500. In the five states that allow deductions after the tax has been computed, the amounts range from twelve to thirty dollars. Five states allow small deductions for dependents, ranging from two to five dollars.[47]

These exemptions operate in such manner that a man, his wife, and three dependents pay no tax on an income of $2,000; a single

Roy G., and Johnson, Violet, *State Income Taxes* (Commerce Clearing House, Chicago, 1942).

[47] Bureau of the Census, *Digest of State Laws Relating to Net Income Taxes, 1938* (Washington, 1938).

State	Tax Net Income in Some Form	Tax General Personal Income	Tax Income of Both Corporations and Individuals	Income Tax Law Adopted since 1930	Tax General Sales or Gross Income	Tax Both Sales or Gross Income and Net Income	Do Not Tax Either Sales or Gross Income or Net Income
Alabama	X	X	X	X	X	X	
Arizona	X	X	X	X	X	X	
Arkansas	X	X	X		X	X	
California	X [1]	X	X	X	X	X	
Colorado	X	X	X	X			
Connecticut							X
Delaware	X	X			X	X	
Florida							X
Georgia	X	X	X				
Idaho	X	X	X	X			
Illinois					X		
Indiana					X		
Iowa	X	X	X	X	X	X	
Kansas	X	X	X	X			
Kentucky	X	X	X		X	X	
Louisiana	X	X	X	X			
Maine							X
Maryland	X	X	X	X			
Massachusetts	X	X	X				
Michigan					X		
Minnesota	X	X	X	X			
Mississippi	X	X	X		X	X	
Missouri	X	X	X				
Montana	X	X					
Nebraska							X
Nevada							X
New Hampshire							X
New Jersey							X
New Mexico	X	X	X	X	X	X	
New York	X	X	X		X	X	
North Carolina	X	X	X		X	X	
North Dakota	X	X	X		X	X	
Ohio				X			
Oklahoma	X	X	X		X	X	
Oregon	X	X	X	X			
Pennsylvania	X				X		
Rhode Island							X
South Carolina	X	X	X				
South Dakota	X	X	X	X	X	X	
Tennessee				X			
Texas							X
Utah	X	X		X	X	X	
Vermont	X	X		X	X	X	
Virginia	X	X	X				
Washington					X	X	
West Virginia	X	X		X	X	X	
Wisconsin	X	X	X				
Wyoming							X
	30	29	24	17	20	16	10

[1] Taxes corporations only.

[556]

man pays from $10 to $100. On an income of $5,000 a man with the family indicated may pay from $50 to $250, while the limits for a single man are the same, although in most instances the tax is somewhat higher. For an income of $25,000 the limits extend from $500 to $2,500. The state tax commission or commissioner is commonly designated as the administrative officer for this tax. After expenses of collection, which average 2 or 3 per cent, have been deducted, the money is used for refunding or for the general fund, although remainders may be assigned to schools, local governments, charities and relief, or casual deficiencies. The revenues derived from the tax represent very considerable sums, particularly in the larger industrial and commercial states. In twenty-three of the thirty-one states the revenues are turned to general fund purposes.[48]

The National Tax Association has proposed a Model Personal Income Tax Act which is based upon certain principles which the Association believes are essential to the successful imposition of such a tax. They contend that such a tax should be levied upon persons in respect to their entire net incomes from all sources, and should be collected only from persons and at the places where they are domiciled; that it should be levied on net income, operating expenses and interest on indebtedness to be deducted; that small incomes should be exempted, and that the rate should be the same for all kinds of income, the rate not being affected by the source. The rates should be progressive; the administration of the tax should be placed in the hands of state officials under a state tax commissioner; and the tax should be collected from the taxpayers upon the basis of strictly enforced and controlled returns, and without any attempt to collect at the source. The taxpayer, it is claimed, should be made to realize that *he* is paying the tax.

Certain trends have become evident in the recent application of this tax; the first is lower exemptions than were formerly customary — a trend which students of tax problems almost unanimously consider desirable. "A second significant development, based on the pioneer experiment in Wisconsin, is the practice of providing for personal exemptions by a tax offset rather than by excepting certain taxable incomes. This newer plan has the merit of giving no larger

[48] This paragraph is based on tables accompanying an article by Martin, James W., "State Income Taxes," *State Government*, April, 1934. See also publications of the Wisconsin Income Tax Study, especially *A Critical Analysis of Wisconsin Individual Income Tax Statistics* (Madison, 1939). Excellent analyses are published regularly in Minnesota, New York, and Oklahoma, and may be available in other states.

exemptions for persons receiving large incomes than are available for those receiving small ones. A still more constructive development is the recent enactment in certain states of statutes which make the maximum rate effective at a relatively low income level. This practice means steep graduation so that the maximum rate, though moderate, is attained on upper middle class incomes." The experience of the depression has shown that the productivity of the tax has been better sustained and more satisfactory than many had anticipated. Finally, the practice of requiring a filing fee, which materially reduces the administrative expense, has shown a slight gain.

INHERITANCE AND ESTATE TAXES

The inheritance tax is one of the oldest forms of tax, not only in the United States, but in the world at large. " Congress first levied a death duty in 1797; Pennsylvania in 1820 enacted the first state inheritance tax law; Louisiana and Virginia followed with laws in 1826 and 1844, respectively; and California utilized this source in 1893." The right of states to levy taxes upon the transfer of property is therefore well established by custom and usage; the main problem now is to secure a substantial yield from this source without undue hardship to the persons concerned or disruptive effect upon the organization and operation of productive enterprise.

Neither the inheritance nor the estate-tax is a tax upon property; both are taxes upon a privilege, the first levied upon the value of the estate received by the inheritor, the second upon the assessed value of the entire estate. The first is a tax on the right to receive the inheritance; the second upon the right to bequeath an estate. As of January 1, 1934 — and since — forty-seven states have had some form of death duty in force, leaving only Nevada without such a tax. Two and a half years previously (on July 1, 1932) fourteen states had had an inheritance tax only, twenty-seven had had inheritance and estate taxes, and six states had estate taxes only. The great change in so short a period was due to the pressure of the Federal government through the amendment in 1932 of the credit provision in the act of 1926. A survey in 1938 showed that eight states levy on inheritances, eight on estates, and that the remaining thirty-one levy an inheritance tax and an additional estate tax. Only six states do not take advantage of the full 80 per cent credit. In the other thirty-five states the tax is levied in the exact amount of the Federal 80 per cent credit, in most cases by direct reference to the Federal law. The following table shows the average rates and exemptions, taken for thirty-seven states having an inheritance tax on direct and collateral heirs.[49]

AVERAGE RATE AND EXEMPTION OF THIRTY-SEVEN STATES

Class	Rates	Exemption
Widow	$1\frac{1}{4}$ per cent graduated to $6\frac{1}{2}$ per cent	$16,310
Widower	$1\frac{1}{4}$ per cent graduated to 7 per cent	10,600
Child	$1\frac{1}{4}$ per cent graduated to $6\frac{3}{4}$ per cent	8,120
Brother or sister	$3\frac{1}{4}$ per cent graduated to $10\frac{3}{4}$ per cent	2,850
Uncle or aunt	$4\frac{3}{4}$ per cent graduated to $13\frac{1}{2}$ per cent	510
Stranger	6 per cent graduated to $16\frac{1}{4}$ per cent	290

It can be observed from these data that kinship is recognized in two ways, namely, by graduation of rates and by exemptions. The widow is plainly preferred over the husband and children by a larger exemption, although the rates average about the same. The widow's average exemption of $16,310 is approximately 50 per cent greater than that allowed to the husband and 100 per cent greater than that allowed to the child. It should also be observed that the rates on brothers and sisters, uncles and aunts, and more remote relatives, are substantially in excess of the rates on the surviving spouse and direct descendants. The exemptions to the collateral relatives are much less, which further increases the tax on their shares.

It must not be assumed that there is any uniformity in the rates or other features of the various state inheritance tax laws. The reverse is true, as the following data will show. Considering only thirty-seven states which have inheritance taxes on both direct and collateral heirs, and applying to residents as well as non-residents, the variations in rates on widows and direct descendants are considerable:

Eighteen states have maximum rates of 5 per cent or less.
Eight states have maximum rates of more than 5 per cent, but not more than 8 per cent.
Seven states have maximum rates of more than 8 per cent, but not more than 10 per cent.

The variation in maximum rates with regard to shares passing to strangers and remote relatives is even greater, ranging from less than 5 to 40 per cent. Graduated rates are used in thirty-four of the thirty-seven states; the upper limit, beyond which gradation of rates ceases, varies from $50,000 to $10,000,000.

[49] From King, Alfred S., and Davisson, Malcolm M., " Inheritance Taxation." (University of California, Bureau of Public Administration, 1931) . See also *Legislative Briefs,* " Estate Tax." November 1, 1938 (Arizona State Legislative Bureau, Phoenix) ; Bureau of the Census, *Digest of State Laws Relating to Inheritance and Estate Taxes* (Washington, 1938) ; Treanor, Glen R., and Blakey, Roy G., *Inheritance Taxes* (League of Minnesota Municipalities, Minneapolis, 1935) ; *Iowa Law Review,* Symposium on State Inheritance and Estate Taxation, March, 1941, entire issue; and Library of Congress reference lists on *Inheritance Taxation* (Washington, 1935 and 1940) .

SOME CURRENT TAX PROBLEMS

Tax Pattern of the States. At the conclusion of this discussion of the various types of taxes relied upon as chief sources of revenue by the states, it may be of interest to examine the tax patterns of the states — the patterns in which the several states combine these different tax forms for the purpose of securing necessary revenues. That these patterns are complicated is well illustrated by the record in California, where it was reported in 1936 that there were 101 levies in effect, adopted from 1850 to date. In 1850 the state property tax (discontinued in 1910), the poll tax, military commutation tax, foreign miner's license tax, and the auctioneer's license tax were adopted; in 1935 the legislature approved legislation for a personal income tax, a use tax, and a distilled liquor tax. In nearly every intervening legislative session one or more such acts were added to the list.[50]

The table " Tax System of the Forty-Eight States," was compiled for this volume by Dr. David H. Kurtzman of the Pennsylvania Economy League, from data in widely scattered sources, for the purpose of further illustrating the tax pattern of the states. It attempts to indicate the major sources of revenue in each of the states, and characteristics common to all or most of them. In many cases the receipts from these taxes are used for both state and local purposes. In some instances the receipts are used entirely by the state, in others, by the local units, while in still other instances they are used by both. In view of this complication, and of the fact that some are state-collected, with reimbursement to the local units, no attempt is made here to indicate the breakdown on the unit or units benefiting from the tax.

Broadening the Tax Base. In recent years there has been great dissatisfaction with the real estate tax. During the depression many property owners were unable to pay their taxes at all, while others did so with great difficulty. This situation gave rise not only to widespread delinquency, but to all sorts of measures — tax limitation, homestead exemption, and others — designed to lessen the burden. As has been shown, these devices have not solved the problem; they have provided a modicum of temporary relief and have en-

---

[50] " How California Taxes Grow," *Tax Digest,* February, 1936, pp. 41–43, and " Taxes Paid in California: Collections from 1900 to 1935 Listed," *ibid.,* pp. 50–51. See also " Varying Emphasis on Different State Taxes; the 48 States Arranged in the Order of Their Dependence upon Each of 21 Tax Types," *Tax Policy,* entire issue of August, 1940.

gendered new difficulties as great as those they were intended to relieve. In the face of this situation, many have argued a reconstruction of the whole tax program with a view to broadening the tax base. In such a program the state assumes additional responsibility for financing essential services formerly supported locally by real estate levies; to raise this money the state imposes new taxes of various sorts (often sales and income) and enlarges its grant-in-aid program so that the local units can offset this by reduced rates on real estate. The purpose is not to raise more money but to distribute the burden more equitably.

Such a program has been adopted in a number of states, including California, Colorado, Illinois, Iowa, Kansas, Michigan, New York, Ohio, and Pennsylvania; it has been discussed in many more. The results have been beneficial, but the anticipated reductions in real estate taxes have not always been realized, at least to the extent that was expected. In an era of expanding government services and increasing costs, all or part of the increased revenue intended for schools, roads, health work, et cetera, has gone into relief, public works, social security, and other new state activities. As a result, chambers of commerce and taxpayers' associations have developed a vigorous opposition to proposals to broaden the tax base.[51]

Double and Overlapping Taxation. For more than a century after the establishment of the present system of government in this country, there was a segregation of sources of revenue among the various units of government — national, state, and local — in order to avoid double and multiple taxation. Thus customs and excise duties were regarded as sources of Federal revenue, while the general property tax, inheritance taxes, and corporation taxes were regarded as sources of state revenue. The local units depended almost wholly upon the general property tax; this was the only instance of major dependence of two units upon the same source, in the whole system. When the Federal government levied the estate tax, it establishd a reciprocal arrangement under which the unfortunate effects of a double tax on inheritance have been largely avoided.

Then began the unfortunate series of events by which these distinctions were broken down, particularly during the mad scramble for new revenues during the depression. By the provisions of Amendment XVI, the states turned over to the Federal government the

51 See, for instance, New Jersey State Chamber of Commerce, *Do New Taxes Relieve the Tax Burden on Real Estate? — the Experience of Nine States* (Trenton, 1939).

Tax System of the Forty-Eight States as of 1945

State	General Property		Income		Motor Vehicles				Corporations					Sales			Miscellaneous				Total Taxing Units
	Personal	Realty	Personal	Corporate	Common Carrier	Operators	Motor Vehicles	Gasoline	Franchise	License	Chain Stores	Bank Shares	Fire and Life Insurance	Gen. Retail and Use Tax	Cigar and Tobacco	Alcoholic Beverages	Inheritance or Estate	Severance	Public Amusement	Poll	
Alabama	×	×	×	×	×	×	×	×	×	×	×	×	×	×	×	×	×	×		×	18
Arizona	×	×	×	×	×	×	×	×	×			×	×	×	×	×	×	×	×	×	15
Arkansas	×	×	×	×	×	×	×	×				×	×	×	×	×	×	×	×	×	18
California	×	×	×	×	×	×	×	×	×	×			×	×		×	×	×		×	14
Colorado	×	×	×	×	×	×	×	×			×	×	×	×		×	×	×	×	×	16
Connecticut		×			×	×	×	×	×			×	×	×		×	×			×	13
Delaware		×	×		×	×	×	×			×		×			×	×		×	×	12
Florida	×	×			×	×	×	×	×	×	×		×		×	×	×			×	14
Georgia	×	×	×	×	×	×	×	×			×	×	×			×	×			×	16
Idaho	×	×	×	×	×	×	×	×			×	×	×		×	×	×	×		×	15
Illinois	×	×			×	×	×	×		×		×		×	×	×	×				11
Indiana	×	×			×	×	×	×		×		×	×	×	×	×	×				12
Iowa	×	×	×	×	×	×	×	×			×	×	×		×	×	×	×		×	16
Kansas	×	×	×	×	×	×	×	×		×	×	×	×	×	×	×	×	×		×	16
Kentucky	×	×	×	×	×	×	×	×		×	×	×	×	×	×	×	×	×		×	18
Louisiana	×	×	×		×	×	×	×			×	×	×			×	×	×		×	18
Maine	×	×		×	×	×	×	×		×		×	×		×	×	×	×	×	×	13
Maryland	×	×	×	×	×	×	×	×			×	×	×		×	×	×				15
Massachusetts	×	×	×	×	×	×	×	×	×	×	×	×	×	×	×	×	×			×	15
Michigan	×	×	×		×	×	×	×	×		×	×				×	×	×		×	14
Minnesota	×	×	×	×	×	×	×	×	×		×	×	×	×		×	×	×		×	15

State																					Total
Mississippi	X	X	X		X	X		X	X			X	X		X	X	X			X	19
Missouri	X	X	X		X	X		X	X			X	X	X		X	X		X	X	16
Montana	X	X			X	X		X					X		X	X	X		X	X	15
Nebraska	X	X			X	X³		X		X			X			X	X			X	11
Nevada	X	X			X	X		X	X			X		X	X	X	X			X	12
New Hampshire	X	X			X	X	X	X	X		X	X	X	X		X	X		X		13
New Jersey	X	X	X	X	X	X		X					X			X	X		X	X	12
New Mexico	X	X	X	X	X	X	X	X				X			X¹	X	X		X	X	15
New York	X	X	X	X	X	X	X	X	X			X	X	X	X²	X	X	X	X		13
North Carolina	X	X	X	X	X	X		X		X	X				X	X	X	X		X	17
North Dakota	X	X	X		X	X	X	X	X				X		X	X	X		X	X	15
Ohio	X	X	X	X	X	X		X	X				X	X	X	X	X			X	13
Oklahoma	X	X	X		X	X	X	X	X	X		X	X		X	X	X				15
Oregon	X	X	X		X	X		X		X	X		X			X	X	X			12
Pennsylvania	X	X	X		X	X	X	X	X				X	X	X	X	X	X			14
Rhode Island	X	X			X	X	X	X	X		X	X		X	X	X	X		X	X	13
South Carolina	X	X			X	X³	X	X			X		X	X		X	X	X		X	16
South Dakota	X	X	X	X	X	X		X				X	X		X	X	X			X	14
Tennessee	X	X	X		X	X	X	X	X	X	X				X	X	X		X	X	16
Texas	X	X	X	X	X	X	X	X	X						X	X	X			X	14
Utah	X	X	X		X	X	X	X	X			X	X	X		X	X				13
Vermont	X	X		X	X	X	X	X	X	X		X	X			X	X	X	X	X	15
Virginia	X	X		X	X	X		X		X	X	X			X	X	X		X	X	14
Washington	X	X	X		X	X	X	X	X	X	X	X	X	X	X	X	X		X		15
West Virginia	X	X	X	X	X	X	X	X	X			X	X			X	X	X	X	X	14
Wisconsin	X	X	X		X	X	X	X	X	X	X			X	X	X	X	X	X	X	14
Wyoming	X	X			X	X		X		X		X	X			X	X	X	X	X	14
TOTALS	47	48	29	27	48	46	48	48	22	19	21	33	39	22	26	48	47	21	17	42	

[563]

¹ Gross income tax on basis of sales. ² New York City only.

³ Included as a part of ownership license or tax.

right to use the income tax; later, being short of funds, they began to use this form themselves, and have continued to do so until more than half of them now depend upon this form for a substantial portion of their revenues. Then came the tobacco taxes — at first only a few, then more, until now they exist in more than half of the states. These were state invasions of Federal fields; it was only a question of time before the Federal government would begin its invasion of the state fields. This occurred in 1932, when Secretary of the Treasury Mills proposed and Congress adopted a tax of one cent a gallon on gasoline. He said he did not approve of the states' taxing tobacco, but if they were going to do that, then the Federal government might as well tax gasoline. In other words, if the tax situation was already becoming chaotic, the Federal government might as well step in and do what it could to make it worse.

It is improbable that we shall ever again be able to segregate individual taxes to the several units in our governmental system, and unlikely that we should be able to secure an equitable distribution of the tax burden in that way. This does not seem possible, either economically or governmentally; recent decisions of the Supreme Court have shown a marked tendency to modify — if not to abandon altogether — previously accepted doctrines of intergovernmental immunity.[52] At the same time, it seems obvious that we cannot continue with the existing chaotic system, in which each unit taxes everything in sight without regard to the policies of other units.

[52] See Helvering v. Gerhardt, 304 U. S. 405, 1938, and Graves v. New York ex rel. O'Keefe, 306 U. S. 466, 1939, which makes a double repudiation of ". . . an implied constitutional immunity from income taxation of the salaries of officers or employees of a national or a state government." In Adkinson, et al., v. State Tax Commission of Oregon, et al., 303 U. S. 20, 1938, a state personal income tax imposed on an individual engaged in work on the Bonneville Dam did not involve any interference with the carrying out of the Federal project. In the Gerhardt case the Court upheld a Federal levy on the salaries of the employees of the New York Port Authority. In Allen v. Regents of the University of Georgia, 304 U. S. 439, 1938, it was held that the Federal amusements tax could be collected on the receipts from football games; this did not differ greatly from the doctrine of the earlier South Carolina v. United States, 199 U. S. 437, 1905.

The literature is voluminous. In addition to the references cited in previous editions of this volume, see Federation of Tax Administrators, *Provisions Limiting Double Taxation of Income by States* (Chicago, 1941); Fellman, David, "Intergovernmental Taxation Today," *Annals*, January, 1940, pp. 27–37; Fuller, Ambrose, Court Throws Light on a Dark Practice," on right of states to collect sales and use taxes from cost-plus-fixed-fee defense contractors, *State Government*, December, 1941, pp. 289–290, 296–298; Lepawsky, Albert, "America's Tax Dollar: A Major Problem of Government," *Annals*, January, 1940, pp. 185–193; and Martin, James W., a series of three articles on "The Problems of Duplicating Federal and State Taxes," "General Pattern of State and Federal Cooperation in Tax Administration," and "Functions of Intergovernmental Administrative Cooperation in Taxation," all in *State Government*, March, April, and May, 1944.

The available alternatives that seem workable are a system of Federally collected, state-shared taxes on the one hand, and some system by which the Federal government and the states each continue to collect their own taxes, but make some reciprocal arrangement with regard to the distribution of the revenues therefrom. At the present time, it is impossible to say which of these two plans should or will be adopted. Each has certain advantages, and each has important supporters among the authorities in the tax field.

On the basis of logic alone one would be at first disposed to favor the system of Federally collected, state-shared taxes. By this is meant that the collection of all or of certain designated taxes would be centralized in the Federal government, with the understanding that there would be turned over to the states certain agreed portions of the receipts. This would simplify the process of collection, and would probably insure the maximum degree of efficiency therein. In the case of gasoline, it would be much simpler to collect all the tax due at the refineries — or, in the case of imported gasoline, at the ports of entry — than to leave the task to forty-eight different state governments, with all the confusion and complexities that result. So with the income tax, it would be much simpler and apparently more logical to have the Federal government make the entire collection in those states which desire to use this tax form, and turn over to the state governments the portion due them; but in both cases there are serious drawbacks.

In the first place, many states feel that if they surrender the power to collect their own taxes, even though they cannot do the work as efficiently or as cheaply as the Federal government, they will be surrendering a power so vital as to undermine the states in the Federal system and reduce them to mere administrative units of the Federal government. There are those who say that this is what ought to be done. In the second place — and this is probably much more important — if the states accept this proposal, there is no assurance whatever that the Federal government will continue to hand over to the states, without restriction, their just share of the taxes collected. As early as 1934, in the now famous Hayden-Cartwright Act, Congress attempted to prevent the further diversion of state highway funds, by providing for the withholding of one third of the Federal aid that might otherwise be allowed in those states where the policy of diversion was practiced. If the independence of the states is worth saving, this is too big a chance to take.

The second alternative — by which each state continues to collect its own revenues, but with an agreement regarding the distribution of the revenues collected — is, generally speaking, strong where the first method is weak and weak where the first method is strong. It will cost a little more to duplicate, to a certain extent, the collection facilities; it will be a little less efficient; but it will insure the continued independence of the states under the Federal system, and it will make sure that they have their revenues without further restrictions imposed upon them by the Federal authorities. Those who, including the author, believe that the states are worth preserving are inclined to favor this method, viewing its weaknesses as a price which must be paid for the successful operation of a federal system.

In conclusion, it should be emphasized that the problem of conflicting taxation has many other aspects than that of Federal-state relations, such as conflicts which come from a conflicting definition of tax bases; conflicts arising from indifference of one governmental unit to the levy of another; conflicts arising because of state lines; conflicts which give rise to inadvertent maldistribution of the tax load; and conflicts arising out of dual administration.[53] The number of such cases runs into the hundreds. Of these other types the conflicts between the states are particularly important. Up to 1939 the number of interstate tax and trade barriers increased at an alarming rate; since that time, as a result of the National Conference on Trade and Tax Barriers held in Chicago in April of that year, the tendency has been to reduce the number of such barriers, although, in the early years of the war, they continued to cause considerable difficulty. These problems will be discussed further in a later chapter.[54]

SELECTED REFERENCES

Baden, Anne L., *Taxation of Natural Resources, a Bibliographical List* (Library of Congress, Division of Bibliography, 1940).

Beckman, Theodore N., and Nolen, Herman C., *The Chain Store Problem: A Critical Analysis* (McGraw-Hill, New York, 1938).

[53] See Crawford, Finla G., " Taxes Talk," *Tax Digest*, August, 1936, pp. 257, 275–278.

[54] See *Proceedings* of this Conference (Council of State Governments, Chicago, 1939); also Chrystie, T. Ludlow, " The Legal Monstrosity of Double Domicile," *Tax Magazine*, January, 1938, pp. 33, 56; Jackson, Robert H., " The Supreme Court and Interstate Barriers," *Annals*, January, 1940, pp. 70–78; Graves, Mark, " Tax Compacts," *State Government*, January, 1936, pp. 15–16; Lockhart, William B., " The Sales Tax in Interstate Commerce," *Harvard Law Review*, February, 1939, pp. 617–644; Mount, Herbert L., " Taxation: Cooperation v. Chaos," *State Government*, July, 1938, pp. 125–126, 133–134; Sachs, Leon, " The Saga of Blackstone v. Miller: a Study in Multiple State Taxation," in Mathews, John M., and Hart, James, Eds., *Essays in Political Science*, pp. 231–271 (Johns Hopkins Press, 1937).

Biscoe, Alvin B., *Sources of New Revenue in Virginia* (Virginia Education Association, Richmond, 1940).

Bitterman, Henry J., *State and Federal Grants-in-Aid* (Mentzer, Bush, Chicago, 1938).

Blakey, Roy G. and Gladys C., *Sales Taxes and Other Excises* (Public Administration Service, Chicago, 1945).

Buehler, Alfred G., *General Sales Taxation, Its History and Development* (Business Bourse, New York, 1932).

———, *Public Finance,* Second Edition (McGraw-Hill, New York, 1940).

Buehler, Ezra C., *State and Local Tax Revision* (Wilson, New York, 1932).

Bureau of Municipal Research, *An Analysis of Ad Valorem Property Tax Bases in Fort Worth* (University of Texas Press, 1941).

———, *The Assessment of Property for Ad Valorem Tax Purposes in Texas Cities* (University of Texas Press, 1939).

Clark, Kenneth R., *Inheritance and Estate Tax on Life Insurance* (Callaghan, Chicago, 1935).

Commerce Clearing House, *Sales Tax Laws* (Chicago, 1937).

———, *Tax Systems of the World,* Eighth Edition (Chicago, 1940).

———, *Tax Magazine* (Chicago, monthly).

Crawford, Finla G., *The Gasoline Tax in the United States* (Public Administration Service, Chicago, 1937).

Critz, Maurice, *The Use Tax; Its History, Administration, and Economic Effects* (Public Administration Service, Chicago, 1941).

Federation of Tax Administrators, *Recent Trends in State Revenues* (Chicago, annually since 1943).

———, *Revenue Administration, 1942* (Chicago, 1943).

Ford, Robert S., *The Allocation of Corporate Income for the Purpose of State Taxation* (New York State Tax Commission, Albany, 1933).

———, and Shepard, E. Fenton, *The Michigan Retail Sales and Use Taxes* (University of Michigan Press, 1941).

———, and Wood, William B., *Taxation of Intangibles in Michigan* (University of Michigan Press, 1939).

Girard, Richard A., *The Scope of Uniformity in State Tax Systems* (New York State Tax Commission, Albany, 1935).

Governmental Research Institute, *The Taxation of Intangibles in Missouri and Other States* (St. Louis, 1944).

Green, William R., *Theory and Practice of Modern Taxation* (Commerce Clearing House, Chicago, 1938).

Groves, Harold M., *Financing Government* (Holt, New York, 1939).

Haig, Robert M., and others, *The Sales Tax in the American States* (Columbia University Press, 1934).

Hansen, Alvin H., and Perloff, Harvey S., *State and Local Finance in the National Economy* (Norton, New York, 1944).

Harriss, C. Lowell, *Gift Taxation in the United States* (American Council on Public Affairs, Washington, 1940).

Hillhouse, A. Miller, and Welch, Ronald B., *Tax Limits Appraised* (Public Administration Service, Chicago, 1937).

Hinckley, Russell J., *State Grants-in-Aid* (New York State Tax Commission, Albany, 1935).

Hunter, Merlin H., and Allen, Harry K., *The Principles of Public Finance* (Harper, New York, 1940).

Interstate Commission on Conflicting Taxation, *Conflicting Taxation* (Chicago, 1935).

Jacoby, Neil H., *Retail Sales Taxation* (Commerce Clearing House, Chicago, 1938).

Jensen, Jens P., *Property Taxation in the United States* (University of Chicago Press, 1931).

——, *Government Finance* (Crowell, New York, 1936).

——, *The Sales Tax* (Kansas Legislative Council, Topeka, 1934).

Kendrick, M. Slade, *The New York System of Taxation* (Cornell University Extension Bulletin, 454, 1940).

Key, V. O., Jr., *Administration of Federal Grants to States* (Public Administration Service, Chicago, 1937).

Labovitz, I. M., *The Illinois Revenue System, 1818–1936* (Illinois Tax Commission, Springfield, 1936).

Lee, Maurice W., *Anti-Chain Store Tax Legislation* (University of Chicago Press, 1939).

Leet, Glen, and Paige, Robert M., *Property Tax Limitation Laws,* Revised Edition (Public Administration Service, Chicago, 1936).

Leland, Simeon E., *The Classified Property Tax in the United States* (Houghton Mifflin, Boston, 1938).

Leonard, J. M., *Suggestions for the Reorganization of Assessing Practices in the City of Detroit* (Detroit Bureau of Governmental Research, 1940).

——, and Mohaupt, Rosina, *Exemption of Homesteads from Taxation* (Detroit Bureau of Governmental Research, 1937).

Martin, James W., and Morrow, Glenn D., *Organization for Kentucky Local Tax Assessments* (University of Kentucky, 1941).

National Association of Assessing Officers, *Exemption of Institutional Real Property from Taxation* (Chicago, 1939).

——, *Equalization Agencies* (Chicago, 1940).

National Tax Association, annual *Proceedings.*

New York State Commission for the Revision of the Tax Laws, annual reports, 1919–1938 (Albany).

New York State Constitutional Convention Committee, *Problems Relating to Taxation and Finance* (Albany, 1938).

Nichols, Egbert R., and others, *The State Sales Tax* (Wilson, New York, 1938).

Olcott, Margaret T., *Homestead Tax Exemption in the United States, a Selected List of References* (Bureau of Agricultural Economics, Washington, 1940).

Pennsylvania Joint State Government Commission, *First Report on the Tax and Financial Problems of the Commonwealth of Pennsylvania* (Harrisburg, 1941).

Powell, Alden L., *National Taxation of State Instrumentalities* (University of Illinois, 1936).

Raisty, Lloyd B., *The Intangibles Tax of Georgia* (University of Georgia Bulletin, 1940).

Ratner, Sidney, *American Taxation: Its History as a Social Force in Democracy* (Norton, New York, 1942).

Rohr, Charles J., Ed., *The Problem of Taxation in Massachusetts* (Massachusetts State College, 1939).

Schmidt, E. B., *An Appraisal of the Nebraska Tax System* (University of Nebraska Press, 1941).

South Carolina State Planning Board, *Is New Industry Tax Exemption Effective?* (Columbia, 1943).

Steiner, George A., *The Tax System and Industrial Development* (University of Illinois, 1938).

Stockwell, Marvel M., *Studies in California State Taxation, 1910–1935* (University of California Press, 1939).

Stone, Harlan F., *Public Control of Business,* pp. 245–270 (Howell, Soskin, New York, 1940).

Studenski, Paul, Ed., "Government Finance in the Modern Economy," *Annals,* January, 1936).

——, Ed., *Taxation and Public Policy* (Richard R. Smith, New York, 1936).

Sundelson, J. Wilner, and Mushkin, S. J., *The Measurement of State and Local Tax Effort* (Social Security Board, Bureau of Research and Statistics, Washington, 1944).

Tax Institute, *Wartime Problems of State and Local Finance* (New York, 1943).

Tax Policy League, *Tax Exemptions* (Philadelphia, 1939).

——, *Tax Relations among Governmental Units* (Philadelphia, 1938).

Tower, Ralph B., *Luxury Taxation and Its Place in a System of Public Revenues* (New York State Tax Commission, Albany, 1931).

Tuller, Walter K., *Treatise on the Taxing Power with Particular Application to State Income Tax* (Callaghan, Chicago, 1937).

Twentieth Century Fund, *Facing the Tax Problem: a Survey of Taxation in the United States and a Program for the Future* (New York, 1937).

——, *Studies in Current Tax Problems* (New York, 1937).

United States Bureau of the Census, *Financial Statistics of the States* (Washington, annually).

——, *Digest of State Laws Relating to Inheritance and Estate Taxes, 1938* (Washington, 1938).

——, *Digest of State Laws Relating to Net Income Taxes, 1938* (Washington 1938).

——, *State Tax Collections* (Washington, annually).

Waters, Lawrence L., *Use Taxes and Their Legal and Economic Background* (University of Kansas, Bureau of Business Research, 1940).

Wycoff, V. J., and Walker, William P., *The State Fiscal Capacity of Maryland and Other Selected States* (University of Maryland, Agricultural Experiment Station, 1940).

Most of the questions discussed in this chapter are considered at length in the standard textbooks in public finance. There is also a very large body of periodical literature, much of it of high quality, the listing of which is prevented by the limits of space.

CHAPTER XIV

Public Expenditures and the Borrowing Power

IN the preceding chapter the income or revenue side of the states' financial problem was discussed; we now consider problems relating to expenditure, correlation of income and expenditure under a budget system, and methods of fiscal supervision and control. Expenditures, in a sense, are the lifeblood of the public service. The struggle for popular control of the tax power, and consequently for the power to appropriate and spend, was one of the striking features of the struggle for popular government. There is no more certain and effective way of eliminating a public service, of impairing its efficiency, or of harassing the officials in charge of it than to withhold necessary funds.

Public expenditures may be classified differently according to the point of view of the individual making the classification. Thus a student of public finance may list ordinary governmental activities, commercial enterprises, carrying and sinking fund charges necessary to discharge the public debt, trust funds and other special public funds, and finally, bookkeeping transactions, or interfund transfers.[1] A student of public administration, on the other hand, may set up classifications by funds, by appropriation heads, by organization units, by functions and activities, by character, or by object.[2] Either classification may be used, according to the purpose one has in mind.

The purposes of state expenditures include all the activities and functions of government — executive, legislative, and judicial. The legislature must appropriate for all the departments and agencies

---

[1] Lutz, Harley L., *Public Finance,* Third Edition, Chapter 3 (Appleton-Century, New York, 1936) .

[2] Willoughby, W. F., *Principles of Public Administration,* Chapter 41 (Johns Hopkins Press, 1927) .

whose activities were mentioned in Chapter X. It must provide also for its own expenses, which, as indicated in Chapter VI, are considerable, and for the salaries and operating expenses for the judicial branch of the government. The increase in the number and scope of governmental services has occurred chiefly in the executive department; the legislatures and the courts spend more than they formerly did, but the increase has not been either proportionately or actually nearly as great as in the executive branch. In Chapter X some comment was made on this increase from the point of view of the number and scope of the services rendered; the same problem from the point of view of cost will now be considered.

INCREASE IN STATE EXPENDITURES

Studies of government costs uniformly indicate a tremendous increase, 100 per cent and often more, in the cost of state government since 1900. It has been frequently assumed that this increase was largely unjustified, and that it is an indication of waste and extravagance. This explanation, although indicating a contributing cause, fails to account for important factors that have justifiably increased the expenditures of state government. In the first place, the population is much larger now than it was in 1900 or 1910; if the same services had been continued without change and other factors had remained constant, a considerable increase in expenditures would have been justified on this basis alone. When, however, it is argued that the cost of government has increased much more rapidly than population, it should be remembered that this period was also one of rising prices; in other words, of a steady decline in the purchasing power of the dollar. Indeed it is surprising that the increase in government expenditure has not been greater.

Amount of Increase. For the purpose of illustrating the exact nature of this growth in particular states, data are presented here for California, Illinois, Indiana, and Pennsylvania. The graph on page 572 shows the increase in total state and local tax collections in California from 1900 to 1939. While the cost of government had increased before 1900, it was in the early years of this century that conspicuous increases became common. In this state an increase of 1,400 per cent occurred in the seventy years from 1860 to 1930. During the first fifty years of this period the rate of increase exceeded only slightly that of the growth of population; from 1910 on, disbursements shot up at an astounding rate. No serious hardship was

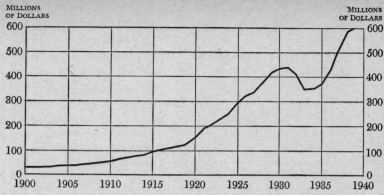

MILLIONS
OF DOLLARS

MILLIONS
OF DOLLARS

Total State and Local Tax Collections in California

caused to taxpayers as long as these increases were accompanied by increased income and increases in the assessed valuation of property. With the advent of the depression, however, the cost of government continued to mount steadily, while such indices of national economic trends as commodity prices, business activity, and factory payrolls declined at a correspondingly alarming rate. Following a slight decline during the depths of the depression, total revenues and expenditures have both continued to rise. In 1939 the California Taxpayers' Association reported a rise of 311 per cent in the last fifteen years, of 838 per cent in the last twenty years, against a population increase of 92 per cent. The present state budget for the biennium runs around $600,000,000. Viewed from another angle, this represents an increase in per capita costs for

Years of Significant Increases in Cost of Government in California

Biennium	Total State Expenditures	State Expenditures Per Capita
1888–1889	$ 7,224,493	$ 6.09
1919–1920	36,125,456	10.54
1924–1925	76,631,298	16.09
1928–1929	110,088,137	20.20
1933–1934	163,796,954	26.63
1935–1936	200,328,061	31.71
1937–1938	259,717,469	38.14

state government in a period of fifty years from 1888 to 1938 of approximately $32.00. The amounts in years of significant increase are as follows: [3]

Turning from a representative state on the Pacific coast to another on the Atlantic, one finds interesting figures on the growth of total expenditures in Pennsylvania by biennial periods from 1902 to 1945. These figures are for the General Fund only, and do not, with the exception of highways, include expenditures for purposes financed through special funds.

COMMONWEALTH OF PENNSYLVANIA EXPENDITURES, 1902–1945

Biennium	General Fund	Highway Funds [4]	Total Expenditures
1902–1904	$ 37,362,268	$	$ 37,362,268
1912–1914	67,981,590	1,175,000	69,156,590
1923–1925	135,236,493	64,866,964	200,103,457
1933–1935	208,984,164	132,306,138	341,290,302
1935–1937	340,375,072	102,932,637	443,307,709
1937–1939	421,740,717	152,077,822	573,818,539
1939–1941	476,653,696	139,037,452	615,691,148
1941–1943	444,224,718	154,467,942	598,692,660
1943–1945	417,243,914	118,466,724	535,710,639

· *Change in Major Purposes.* The two tables on page 575 present another aspect of the same general situation, showing expenditures classified according to the major purposes. The charts for Illinois on page 574 show the distribution of the general fund appropriations for 1939 and 1944. Approximately ten cents of each dollar spent by the state went for the general functions of government, described on the chart as " all other purposes."

[3] From Pierce, John M., " Trend of State Spending," *Tax Digest,* January, 1939, pp. 6–7, 20–22. See also " Forty Years of Taxes," *ibid.,* November, 1939, pp. 377–382.

[4] The Motor License Fund first operated as a separate fund in the biennium 1918–1920. Expenditures entered in this column prior to that date represent expenditures for highways from the General Fund; subsequent to that date, expenditures are included for the Motor License Fund, the State Bond Road Fund, and the Federal Trust Account, National Industrial Recovery Highway Fund. These figures are from the Joint Legislative Committee on Finances, *Survey of the Government of Pennsylvania,* p. 5 (Harrisburg, 1934), and from the Office of the Auditor General, in a letter dated October 15, 1935. See also, for similar data for Kansas, Kansas Legislative Council, *Summary History of Kansas Finance, 1861–1937* (Topeka, 1937). Similar data are now available in most states.

WHERE THE 1940 STATE DOLLAR WENT

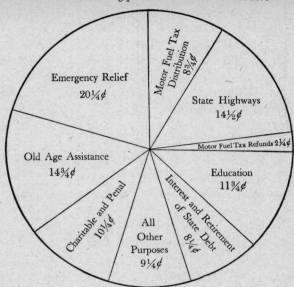

WHERE THE 1944 STATE DOLLAR WENT

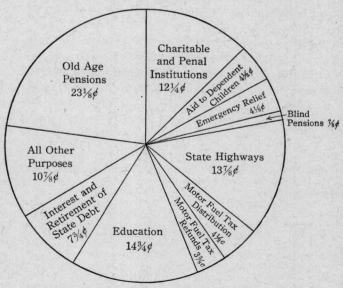

AN ANALYSIS OF STATE EXPENDITURES

(Trust funds and transfers are eliminated)

[574]

The following table shows the comparative percentages for major purposes of state expenditure for Indiana in the years 1928 and 1938:

STATE OF INDIANA

STATE GOVERNMENTAL PAYMENTS BY MAJOR FUNCTIONS, 1928–1938 [5]

Major Function	Per Cent, 1928		Per Cent, 1938	
Highways		43.8		35.1
Education		29.3		29.2
Charities, Hospitals, and Corrections		14.2		20.9
All Other				
General Government	2.5		2.9	
Protection of Persons and Property	2.9		4.0	
Health and Sanitation	1.0		.8	
Conservation	1.6		1.3	
Recreation	3.0		.5	
Miscellaneous	1.7		5.3	
		12.7		14.8
		100.0		100.0

Similar data, with both amounts and percentages, are shown below for Pennsylvania for three different bienniums separated from each other by periods of approximately fifteen years. The standard Bureau of the Census classification of objects of expenditure is used here, as in the preceding table.

COMMONWEALTH OF PENNSYLVANIA, 1898–1933 [6]

INCREASE IN EXPENDITURES FOR GOVERNMENTAL PURPOSES,

Function	1898–1900		1912–1914		1931–1933	
	Amount	Per Cent	Amount	Per Cent	Amount	Per Cent
Highway	....	....	$11,000,000	15.3	$143,562,700	41.1
Education	$12,638,800	60.8	20,200,000	28.0	93,266,700	26.6
Health and Welfare	4,099,300	19.7	25,971,400	36.0	55,000,800	15.7
Conservation	180,800	.9	1,514,990	2.1	8,067,900	2.3
Protection to Persons and Property	1,838,100	8.9	7,069,990	9.8	25,937,200	7.4
General Government	2,006,000	9.7	6,348,560	8.8	24,345,900	6.9
Total	$20,763,000	100.0	$72,104,940	100.0	$350,181,200	100.0

[5] Indiana Inter-Organization Council, *Eleven-Year Trend in Indiana State Government Payments and Receipts, 1928–1938*, p. 14 (Indianapolis, 1938).

[6] Joint Legislative Committee on Finances, *Survey of the Government of Pennsylvania*, pp. 5–6 (Harrisburg, 1934).

From the data thus far presented, certain facts stand out. Not only has the total amount of state expenditures increased but important changes in the major purposes have taken place. Practically nothing was spent for highways around 1900; expenditures for this purpose exceeded all others by 1930 and, still more important, have shown only a slight tendency to decline since. Although more is spent on education, the percentage devoted to this purpose has not materially

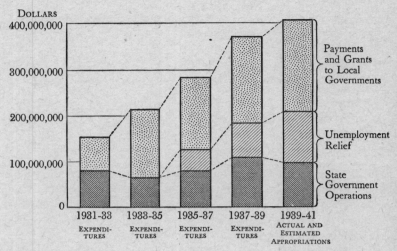

STATE OF CALIFORNIA — GENERAL FUND EXPENDITURES 1931–1941

From California Department of Finance, *The Financial Problem of California State Government, 1939–1941 Biennium*, p. 6 (Sacramento, 1939).

changed. During the depression, huge expenditures were necessary for relief and for state aid to local units. In 1938 Governor Lehman said that 56 per cent of the budget in New York reverted to the localities. In 1939, relief, schools, and roads were getting 70 per cent of the tax dollar in Pennsylvania, most of it reverting to the local units in the form of state aid. These items, together with the introduction of the social security program, account for a large part of the recent huge increases in state government costs. The regular activities of the three branches of government have not been in the past, and are not now, particularly expensive, as is clearly shown in the accompanying chart for California covering the decade 1931–1941.

Adjusted Figures on Government Costs. The report of the Joint Legislative Committee on Finances, previously cited, discusses the problem of adjusted figures, as related to the cost of government in Pennsylvania, in the following paragraph:

In order that the significance of these figures may be more clearly comprehended, there is included herewith a graphic representation of the expenditures from all operating funds of the Commonwealth for each two year fiscal period from 1912–1914 to 1931–1933 [on this page]. The increase

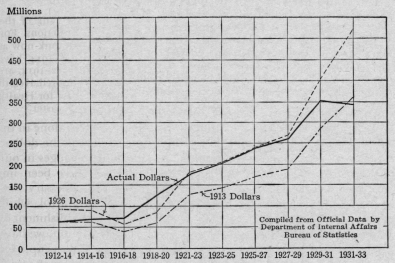

COMMONWEALTH OF PENNSYLVANIA — EXPENDITURES FROM ALL OPERATING FUNDS

in expenditures is shown by three lines, which represent, respectively, the expenditure in actual dollars, and the compensated value of expenditures based on the fluctuating value of the dollar as compared with its value in 1913 and in 1926. In arriving at the compensated value of expenditures, the monthly wholesale price index of the United States Bureau of Labor Statistics has been used as a yardstick to measure the fluctuating value of the dollar. Except for the abnormal period of the depression, governmental expenditures when adjusted for purchasing power have increased less rapidly than the figures in actual dollars would indicate. Thus from 1912–1914 to 1927–1929 actual expenditures increased about four times, whereas expenditures measured in 1913 dollars increased less than threefold.

The $350,000,000 spent in this state in 1931–1933 had a purchasing power of over $500,000,000 in terms of 1926 dollars, and much more than that in terms of the 1913 dollar. Comparisons of this type give a better picture of governmental costs than the use of per capita figures, which are frequently employed. In the above table, it is interesting to note not merely the amount expended for major functions of government, but the shifting percentages of total expenditures assigned to each. While only slight variations in percentages occur from one biennium to another, the change over a period of twenty or thirty years is striking. Commenting upon the percentages shown in the table on page 575, the Budget Secretary said:

> Such a comparison as this shows only the relative financial rank of the general functions. It does not show growth of individual functions. For example, out of the six functions four have the same financial rank now as they had twenty years ago. Highways, with third rank in 1913–1914, have taken first place, while Health and Welfare, of first rank in 1912–1914, are now in third place. This does not mean that the State has ignored Health and Welfare in favor of Highways. The fact is that expenditures for Health and Welfare have grown but Highway expenditures have grown faster.[7]

The causes of these increased costs are to be found not alone in increased populations and declining purchasing power of the dollar; developments in science and the arts and concurrent changes in our concepts of social and governmental responsibility have been important factors. Scientific developments have made necessary new and previously unheard of forms of regulation and control, while new concepts have been responsible not only for the establishment of new services but for the extension of old ones. In addition, we have developed higher standards of administrative efficiency — people expect more and better service from their government than they did a few years ago. Nor can one ignore the fact that the unplanned and unsystematic development of government services prior to the inauguration of the reorganization movement led to much overlapping, duplication, and wasteful and inefficient management. These factors are gradually being reduced to a minimum.

FINANCIAL ADMINISTRATION

In the preceding chapter attention was given to tax sources; the balance of this one is devoted to expenditure control and borrowing. It may be desirable to pause here long enough to obtain an overall view of the fiscal problem in the states, which includes five separate and more or less distinct operations as indicated in the table on page 579. The operations are listed in the order in which the problems occur, together with the state officer or agency responsible for the administration of each function.

[7] Logan, Edward B., " Costs, Trends, and Predictions Relating to Governmental Expenditures Other than Education," Schoolmen's Week *Proceedings,* p. 37 (University of Pennsylvania, 1932) .

ROUTE OF THE TAX DOLLAR THROUGH THE STATE FISCAL OFFICES

Fiscal Operation	*Department or Agency*
Assessment and collection of taxes.	Department of Revenue, Taxation and Finance, State Tax Commission, or other agency
Custody of funds (cash and securities)	State Treasurer
Financial planning and supervision	Budget Office Finance offices of departments
Procurement and Disbursement	State Treasurer Department of Purchase and Supply
Audit and control	State Treasurer Auditor General

Collection of Revenue. The collection of taxes should be carried on by a single department of revenue, or by a department of taxation and finance to which this duty is assigned by law. It is difficult to give any general description of this tax collecting agency because the number, size, and importance of the bureaus varies not only according to the size of the state but with its tax pattern. In the organization of this agency provision must be made for each of the major sources of state revenue. The Pennsylvania Department of Revenue, for instance, contains the following bureaus: Administration and Accounts, Investigations and Collections, Corporation Taxes, County Collections, Institutional Collections, and Liquid Fuels Tax. The collection of revenues for motor vehicle registrations, and operators' and chauffeurs' licenses may or may not be under the supervision and control of this department, but it should be.

In some states, where the tax collecting function has not been coordinated, one finds a situation like the following one in Michigan:

Over half a hundred state departments, boards, and commissions now act as cashiers for the state, accepting money for taxes, licenses, fees, rentals, and other miscellaneous purposes. The collection of the more important state revenues is divided among eleven of these agencies. Miscellaneous licenses and fees are collected by forty-five others.[8]

In some states a portion of the revenues are still derived from the general property tax. It is the practice to maintain a state board of equalization or a state tax commission whose duty it is to supervise the assessment of property. The purpose is to distribute the burden as fairly as possible, to prevent inequalities and, where necessary, to correct them.

[8] Michigan Public Expenditure Survey, *Save in the State to Save the Nation*, pp. 3-4 (Lansing, 1944).

Custody of Funds. The funds brought into the state treasury through the efforts of the tax collecting agency are turned over to the state treasurer, in whose custody they are kept. Usually the state treasurer is a constitutional officer and quite frequently he is elected by popular vote, although, since he is always under bond, there is no special reason why he should be elected rather than appointed. It is his duty to maintain custody of all funds after they are turned over to him by the collecting agency and to pay them out upon proper warrant. His duties " are ministerial in nature. He is controlled in all his actions by the auditor. The treasurer can no more refuse to cash a properly drawn warrant of the auditor than a bank can refuse to cash a properly drawn check." [9]

In connection with the custody of funds the state treasurer has a number of important functions to perform. The receipts bureau or division must keep record of all moneys received, giving an official receipt for the same. The bank and surety division is responsible for the selection of the banks which are used as state depositories, and for the custody of bonds and collateral to secure or indemnify state bank deposits. In the larger states securities representing very substantial amounts are kept in the vaults of the department; the coupons are clipped and the amounts credited to the proper funds. It is the duty of the department to see that the capital and surplus of banks used as depositories are in compliance with the requirement set up by the legislature and that no individual banks are over deposited.

Financial Planning and Supervision. The problem of spending public funds may be considered either from the point of view of management's function of fiscal supervision, or from that of the operating official. The former begins under the governor in the budget office, which is responsible for the formulation of the spending program of the government as a whole and for seeing that the plan is adhered to, within the limits established by the appropriation acts passed by the legislature. The preparation of the budget and the method of making and enforcing allocations to each spending agency for each fiscal period will be considered later. Each state operates on the basis of a fiscal year, a term used to designate the twelve-month period for which a government ordinarily reports on its financial

[9] Sappenfield, Max M., *Financial Administration in the States of Illinois, Ohio, and Indiana*, p. 7 (University of Illinois, 1934). See also White, *Introduction*, Chapters 16 and 17, and Faust, Martin L., *The Custody of State Funds* (National Institute of Public Administration, New York, 1925), and *The Security of Public Deposits* (Public Administration Service, Chicago, 1936).

operations. A tabulation made by the United States Bureau of the Census in 1945 showed that forty-one states end their fiscal year on June 30, as does the Federal government.[10]

No proper control is possible without a system of accounting. A study made by the National Association of State Auditors, Comptrollers, and Treasurers in 1938 showed that forty-three states had a central accounting office. In seventeen of these states accounting was set up in the office of the comptroller, while seventeen others gave accounting to the auditor. In the remaining states the function may be carried on by the budget office, or by some other agency as provided by law.[11] Whatever the form of organization, the functions to be performed are definite and specific.

The operating agencies themselves have a part in the work of financial planning. They must furnish the preliminary estimates on the basis of which the budget is prepared and, after the allocations are made, they must plan in cooperation with the budget office the further allocation of the funds to the various objects or purposes of expenditure. For purposes of internal control, they must also keep accurate records of their own operations in order that they may know at any given time what portions of their allocations are encumbered and what amounts are free for expenditure. Still another check is required in some states before any disbursements are actually made to ascertain that the expenditure has been authorized by law, that it is being charged to the proper account, and that it is in all respects regular and in accordance with law.

Disbursements. Disbursements are made by the state treasurer, to whose custody the funds of the state are entrusted. The first step in the making of disbursements is for the operating department or agency to issue a requisition. Payroll requisitions are made out for personal service, while other types are used for payments for construction work, and for necessary supplies and equipment, including rent, heat, light, power, printing, postage, and telephone and telegraph service. Payroll requisitions must be prepared well in advance of the due date in order to permit prompt issuance of checks.

The procedure involved in the making of payments for work done

10 "Financial Years of State and Local Governments," June, 1945. The seven states whose fiscal years end at some time other than June 30 are: Washington, March; New York, April; Pennsylvania, May; Texas, August; Alabama and Wyoming, September; and Ohio, December. In 1945 Missouri changed its fiscal year to end on June 30 instead of December 31.

11 *Analysis of State Fiscal Offices,* p. 49 (Chicago, 1938); for a table showing the dates of the establishment of such agencies, together with the variety of names applied to them as of 1933, see White, *Trends,* p. 183.

under contract and for materials and supplies depends upon the established financial procedure followed in any particular state. Some states have established a system of centralized control over all such matters and all states should follow this example. Others still use a decentralized system in which each spending agency makes its own contracts and goes into the market for the purchase of all needed supplies and equipment. Great waste results through favoritism, lack of knowledge of market practices, et cetera. This is especially noticeable in the renting of office space, warehouse space, and garage space, usually necessary for the housing of state activities in the field.

Under a centralized system all spending agencies requisition their needs through the central purchasing agency which makes all contracts for the state and makes all purchases (except small emergency ones) required by the several departments of the government, while in the decentralized system there are as many purchasing agencies as there are departments, boards and commissions in the state government. There are, however, difficulties in centralized purchasing which sometimes arouse criticism in the departments and which have prompted the movement in some states to substitute a system of centralized contracting for centralized purchasing. Although all requisitions would still come through one department, each operating department would be able to draw upon the manufacturer for needed supplies within budgetary limitations.

The amount of work involved in this apparently simple operation of disbursing funds has increased tremendously in recent years, owing to such things as the expanded road building program and payments for relief during the depression and the development of the social security program since. In Pennsylvania the number of checks written annually by the State Treasurer increased from 383,000 in 1923, to 2,206,323 in 1932. The mere writing of this number of checks required, in addition to the installation of modern office machinery, a very substantial increase in the number of personnel engaged in the work.

Audit and Control. The auditing function in public business as in private is intended to insure the accuracy of the records kept and to make sure that all expenditures have been made in accordance with law and for authorized purposes. The auditing officer is regularly provided for in the constitution and he is commonly elected. There are really three possible methods of choice available: election by the people, election by the legislature, and appointment by the governor. The latter method is not usually regarded with favor since it creates the somewhat anomalous situation of the executive department of the government checking upon the legality of its own expenditures and the correctness of its own records. This is not a wholly valid objection, as is clearly shown by the generally successful operation of the office of the Comptroller General in the Federal government. There is little to be said in favor of election by the legislature even though it is the legislature that provides the state revenues through the operation of its tax measures.

In many states the auditor general is responsible for the performance of a number of different functions. He must examine all invoices and accompanying requisitions before disbursements may be legally made and he must issue warrants authorizing the payment thereof. He must audit the tax collection agency's account of corporations and others, subject to the payment of taxes to the state; and finally, he must audit the accounts kept by the departments, boards, and commissions of the state government.

There are, in fact, two main types of audit: the internal or pre-audit and the external or post-audit. The former refers to the checking of revenues and receipts at the time of collection and the examination and approval of claims before payment. This is a function of management and should be done by a financial agency of the administration itself. The post-audit, on the other hand, is made after the transactions have been completed and is a review of what has taken place. To be fully effective the post-audit should be performed by an officer completely independent of the administration.

The need for the post-audit, which is the responsibility of the auditor general, is obvious. There must be some agency legally responsible for the validating of expenditures of state funds, likewise for examining the accounts of individuals and corporations subject to the payment of taxes. There are so many opportunities for an official who is so disposed to grant unwarranted exemptions and reductions that the state might lose a great deal of money if some such system of audit were not maintained. When one comes to the auditing of the accounts of the several departments and agencies numerous problems and difficulties arise.

If such audits are not made promptly — and frequently they are not — the reports are of little real value, since they have to be presented to an entirely new administration, which has no responsibility for the details of the fiscal affairs of its predecessors in office and little interest in them. If the auditing officer is of an opposite political party, there may be a lack of cooperation between the members of his staff and the various departments and agencies; if he is of the same political party, there is the possibility of too much cooperation, or at least of cooperation of a not altogether desirable type. A state may rely wholly or partially upon the services of certified public accountants engaged in commercial auditing, but it is possible for a well-organized department to do the work just as well and at a far less expense to the state.

THE BUDGET SYSTEM

Budget procedure has been maturing for nearly 600 years — since the fourteenth century when parliamentary government and civil liberties were being bought from English monarchs at the price of taxes, and the Chancellor of the Checker Table or Exchequer was carrying his estimates of revenues and expenditures into the House of Commons in a little leather bag or " bougette." The budget system in Great Britain, in the modern sense, dates from 1787, the year in which our Federal Constitution was framed, and in France from 1850.

It was not until 1921 that the Federal Budget and Accounting Law was enacted, after years of discussion and countless committee reports and recommendations. According to present standards, no state had a budget system in 1910; in 1926, systems existed in all states. The first legislation was passed in 1911 in California and Wisconsin, the last in Rhode Island in 1926. The following list shows the states grouped by the years in which their first budget legislation was enacted: [12]

1911 — California and Wisconsin
1913 — Arkansas, Oregon, and Ohio
1914 — Louisiana
1915 — Connecticut, Iowa, Minnesota, Nebraska, North Dakota, and Vermont
1916 — Maryland, New Jersey, and Washington
1917 — Delaware, Illinois, Kansas, Missouri, New Mexico, South Dakota, Tennessee, and Utah
1918 — Georgia, Kentucky, Massachusetts, Mississippi, Virginia, and West Virginia

[12] White, Leonard D., *Trends in Public Administration*, p. 189 (McGraw-Hill, New York, 1933). In a table on p. 191 Professor White groups the states according to the type of budget legislation adopted. For a classification of types of executive budget, see Carleton, R. L., *The Reorganization and Consolidation of State Administration in Louisiana*, pp. 33–36 (Louisiana State University Press, 1937). For a table on current state budgetary procedure, see *Book of the States*.

1919 — Alabama, Arizona, Colorado, Idaho, Maine, Michigan, Montana, Nevada, New Hampshire, North Carolina, Oklahoma, South Carolina, Texas, and Wyoming
1921 — Florida, Indiana, and New York
1923 — Pennsylvania
1926 — Rhode Island

When the states are grouped according to five-year periods, it is found that thirty-seven acts were passed between 1915 and 1919. In the twenties, nine states adopted the executive budget in preference to other types previously adopted.

There is a wide variety in the statutes providing for the establishment of these systems, some being executive in character, some of the board or commission type, and one legislative. The preferred form is the executive budget, now used in more than half the states; in these, the budget is under the control of the governor and a budget secretary or budget officer such as exists in New Jersey, New York, Pennsylvania, and elsewhere. A board or commission may be constituted in either of two ways: wholly of administrative officers, as is the case in ten states, or by a combination of legislative and administrative officers, as in Wisconsin. The governor is always a member of the budget board. Such a board lacks responsibility, either to the legislature in the formulation of policy or to the executive in the administration of it. The legislative type of budget has disappeared from all states. While such a system may be preferable to no budget at all, it falls far short of an approved budgetary procedure. With any of these methods, a governor who is so authorized may use the item veto in connection with appropriation bills, and thereby accomplish a good deal in the way of budgetary control.[13]

The Budget as a Plan for Spending. In present-day financial administration, a budget serves two distinct purposes. In the first place a budget is a plan for spending. A properly constructed budget will show the financial condition of the government unit concerned at the close of the last fiscal period, its expected condition at the close of the current fiscal period, and finally the recommendations for the ensuing period. It must show the condition of the finances of the government at the end of that period if the anticipated revenues are received and the recommended expenditures are made. Thus it will be possible to see where we have come from, where we are now, and where we expect to go; a summary statement with this information

[13] Fitzpatrick, Edward A., *Budget Making in a Democracy*, Chapter 11 (Macmillan, New York, 1918) , and Wells, Roger H., " The Item Veto and State Budget Reform," *American Political Science Review*, November, 1924, pp. 782–801.

should always be included. A budget is like an automobile road map. The tourist who starts out on a long trip can, after he has been on the road for a day or two, spread out his map and follow the route over which he has traveled, observe the point he has reached, and look ahead over the route leading to his destination. In similar manner, a budget serves as a guide to the financial highways over which the state must travel.[14]

In the formulation of such a plan for spending, certain principles governing public expenditures must be observed. Most important of these is the necessity for bringing about ultimately a definite correlation between the total amount of the recommended expenditures and the total amount which careful estimates indicate as probable receipts from existing tax laws during the period in question. If there is no way by which the total amount of recommended expenditures can be brought in harmony with the anticipated revenues, then the budget message should contain definite recommendations to care for this difference. If additional taxes are to be imposed, the message should indicate their nature, explain the necessity for them, and give an estimate of the revenue which may be expected from them. If a probable deficit is to be met through the exercise of the borrowing power, this recommendation should be accompanied by a similar explanation. At all events, the message must provide for revenues which it is believed will be adequate to meet the program of expenditures submitted.

Formulation of a Budget. The process by which an executive budget is formulated may be briefly outlined. A few months before the opening of the legislative session at which the new budget will be considered, the budget officer submits to the head of each executive department, board, commission, or other spending agency forms upon which estimates for the needs of the department or agency during the coming fiscal period are to be indicated. These forms with the information requested must be returned by a fixed date. The budget

[14] On this point Governor Alfred E. Smith is reported to have said: " There are two things that helped me in the Constitutional Convention, that were responsible for any knowledge that I displayed there. First, it was my knowledge of the state government that came from my studies of the appropriation bills. Whatever intimate knowledge I had about the state came from what I know about how it spent its money, for every item in the appropriation bill tells a story of state problems and state needs, or state extravagance. Secondly, it must be borne in mind that most of the great activities of the state started in 1907, when the Public Service Commission was established, and the Conservation Commission and other important agencies. Being familiar with how they started, I naturally knew something about them when they were discussed in the Constitutional Convention." — In Hapgood, Norman, and Moskowitz, Henry, *Up from the City Streets,* p. 112 Harcourt, Brace, New York, 1927) .

officer then determines the total amount requested by all agencies, well knowing that it will be vastly in excess of the most optimistic estimates of the revenues likely to be received during the period in question. He then returns the budget requests to the spending agencies together with this information so that they may reconsider their estimates with a view to reducing them.

It is at this point that the most difficult work of the budget officer begins. The reduction in the requests of the spending agencies are never sufficient to bring the total in harmony with the anticipated revenues. It now becomes the duty of the budget officer to go over these recommendations in detail with department heads, bureau chiefs, and the responsible officers of other spending agencies, considering the merits of each individual item, and the merits of each item compared with other useful purposes for which the same funds might be expended. The budget officer is thus placed in the difficult position of having to evaluate and pass judgment upon individual governmental services. He must make many decisions, many of them more or less arbitrary, keeping ever in mind his objective that the total amount shall be so expended as to bring the maximum return to the taxpayers of the state. This kind of supervision is productive of substantial savings, as has been proved many times in many jurisdictions. Reductions in department requests are possible, however, only by careful planning, based on an intimate knowledge of all state functions, by a central agency functioning for that specific purpose.

When this task has been completed, the budget must be printed and prepared for circulation among the members of the legislature and others interested, at some specified date early in the legislative session. This date might well be postponed until March, to give more adequate opportunity for a new governor to familiarize himself with the financial problems of the state and construct the budget in accordance with his plans for the state's work. While all well-prepared budgets contain much the same kind of information, there is wide variation as to details of arrangement. The budget is primarily intended as a technical working tool for the members of the legislature and the officers of administration, but the budget office also has some obligation to provide the public with information about the finances of the state government. Most of the published budgets are so technical in character and uninteresting in appearance that few citizens will even try to study them. That this does not have to be so the *Ninth Executive Budget for the State of Ohio,*

Biennium 1931–1932, prepared by Professor Harvey Walker, well demonstrates. Here was a budget document which an intelligent citizen could examine with profit and real interest.

Consideration of the Budget by the Legislature. Various writers have commented at length upon the consideration of the budget by the legislature; only a few of the more important questions can be mentioned here. In general, it may be said that the legislature ought to approve the budget as submitted. The assumption is that it has been prepared with care; the executive is responsible for it, and should be willing and able to defend it, either before the legislature or, if necessary, before the people. It would be desirable if the governor were given the power to appear before either or both houses of the legislature upon his own initiative; and correspondingly, the legislature should have the power to summon him to appear before it, either in person or through a designated representative, to defend his proposals. The budget office has or should have all necessary information; the legislature does not have it, and it is difficult for that body to secure it.

This raises a question that is of deep concern to the more intelligent legislators. The legislative branch has a real responsibility in connection with the budget; it is difficult for the members to understand the budget, both because of its technical nature and because of their lack of information. Especially when the executive and the majority of the legislature are of opposite parties, members may experience difficulty in securing information they need for intelligent action on the general appropriation bill. This has led, in some cases, to suggestions of establishing a separate budget bureau under legislative control for the service of members. This would involve needless duplication; yet the suggestion indicates the seriousness of the problem. The permanent research staff of the legislative council may be the solution. In any event, closer cooperation between the executive and legislative branches of the government than exists in most states would be extremely helpful.

It is customary for the budget to be referred to the appropriation committees of the two houses; the budget report is usually accompanied by a draft of a bill which would, if enacted, carry out the recommendations contained in the report. A joint committee, such as is common in New England, is far preferable to the usual separate committees. Legislative hearings on proposals for expenditure should in all states be an important part of the procedure; the Model State Constitution provides specifically for them in Section 704.

Council of State Governments, *Book of the States*, 1943–1944 Edition

State	Date Estimates Submitted	Budget Prepared by	Date Submitted to Legislature
Ala.	February 1	Bud. Off. of Dept. of Rev.	Second Tuesday in June
Ariz.	October 1	Governor	By 5th day reg. session
Ark.	Before session	Budget Comm. of Leg.	30 days after appt. of comm.
Calif.	July 1 or before	Dir. of Finance	January
Colo.	October 1	Bud. & Effic. Commr.	10th day of session	
Conn.	August 1	Bd. of Fin. & Control	2nd week of session
Del.	September 15	Bd. of Budget Dir.	5th day of session
Fla.	December 1	State Budget Comm.	1st day of session
Ga.	No date set	Budget Bureau	7th day of session
Idaho	September 15	Budget Director	10th day of session
Ill.	November 1	Director of Finance	4 weeks after conv.
Ind.	August 15	State Budget Comm.	With Gov's. Bud. Mess.
Iowa	October 1	Comptroller	February 15
Kan.	October 1	Budget Director	2nd Tuesday in Jan.
Ky.	November 15	Commr. of Finance	3rd Monday of session
La.	January 15 of even years	Division of Budget of Dept. of Finance	Not later than 20th day of session
Me.	November 1	State Budget Officer	4th week after conv.
Md.	As Gov. desires	Budget Director	20th day of session; 30th for new Governor
Mass.	September 15	Budget Commr.	Within 3 weeks after conv.
Mich.	December 1	Budget Director	10th day of session
Minn.	No date set	Commr. of Admin.	December 1
Miss.	No date set	Asst. Dir. of Budget Comm.	December 1
Mo.	November 1	Budget Director	2 weeks after conv.
Mont.	November 15	State Bd. of Examnrs.	10th day of session
Neb.	September 15	Commr. of Tax. & Bud.	15th day of session
Nev.	December 1	Governor	20th day of session
N.H.	October 1 of even years	Comptroller and Governor	February 15
N.J.	October 15	Budget Commr.	2nd Tuesday of Jan.
N.M.	September 15	Governor	15th day of session
N.Y.	October 15	Director of Budget	On or before Feb. 1
N.C.	September 1	Budget Director	With Gov's. Bud. Mess.
N.D.	October 1	Budget Board	10th day of session
Ohio	November 1	Supt. of Budget	2 weeks after conv.
Okla.	November 1	Budget Officer	5th day of session
Ore.	October 1	Budget Director	December 20
Pa.	November 1	Budget Secretary	No time specified
R.I.	December 15	Budget Director	Jan. 1; Feb. 1 for new Gov.
S.C.	November 1	State Budget Comm.	5th day of session
S.D.	October 15	Secy. of Finance	5th day of session
Tenn.	December 1	Div. of Acts. & Budget	January 14
Texas	Oct. 15 precedg. yr.	State Bd. of Control	January 1
Utah	No date set	Director of Budget	20th day of session
Vt.	October 1	Governor	2nd week of session
Va.	September 15	Director of Budget	5th day of session
Wash.	1st Mon. of Sept.	Director of Budget	5th day of session
W.Va.	July 1	Director of Budget	10th day of session
Wis.	November 1	Director of Budget	February 1
Wyo.	November 1	Governor	1st day of session

Eventually the bill merges in its final form. There has been much discussion of the relative merits of lump-sum and specific-allotment appropriations. Years ago, before the advent of effective methods of financial supervision, the specific-allotment form was in universal use. At present, with such methods of supervision available and in general use, the lump-sum appropriation provides an adequate protection of public funds. The old-fashioned, detailed-appropriation measure is not only no longer necessary; it is an actual obstacle or hindrance to effective administrative control.[15]

Finally, there is the question of the power of the legislature to increase or decrease the amounts recommended in the budget. In all but four states the power of the legislature to change the budget is unlimited; in Maryland, Nevada, New York, and West Virginia, it has the power to strike out or reduce, but not to raise items in the budget. Since the executive departments are rarely hesitant about asking for funds, it is a little ridiculous for the legislature to insist that executive departments need more money than has been asked for by the governor. If the three branches of the government are to be retained independently, the legislature cannot be denied the right to increase or decrease the amount of its own appropriation as compared with the budget request, although in those states where the governor has power to reduce items, an increase may later be negatived. The same right on the part of the legislature should probably exist with regard to appropriations for the judiciary.[16] If the system of control is well administered, measures providing for either supplementary appropriations or deficiency appropriations should be rare indeed.

CONTROL OF STATE EXPENDITURES

The term "control of expenditures" may be used in either of two ways; it may refer to the enforcement of the budget after the appropriation act has been approved by the legislature or to the attempt to hold within reasonable bounds the amount of the appropriations

[15] For the practice on itemization in thirty-four states, see Jones, Victor, *The Legislature and the Budget*, pp. 20–24 (University of California, Bureau of Public Administration, 1941).

[16] White, Leonard D., in his *Introduction to the Study of Public Administration, Revised Edition* (Macmillan, New York, 1939) reports, p. 220, a provision in the Maryland Constitution (Article III, Section 52) as follows: " The governor's estimates for the executive branch cannot be increased, but may be reduced . . . ; the estimates for the courts (prepared by the judges) cannot be reduced, but may be increased; and estimates for the legislative branch may be either increased or reduced."

approved as related to total income. Both aspects of the problem will be briefly considered.

Enforcement of the Budget. The making of a plan for spending, and securing its enactment, is only part of the function of a budget system; the second major purpose is to see that the plan when made and adopted is faithfully executed — that all expenditures are made in compliance with the appropriation acts. Two devices may be used to effect proper budgetary control: allotments to govern the rate of expenditure, and encumbrances to prevent commitments not in accordance with the appropriation act and the regulations of the budget office.

As soon as the general appropriation act has been passed and approved by the governor, this agency must undertake the final allocation of funds, according to purposes of expenditure, for each spending agency in the state government. This allocation is concerned not only with purposes of expenditure, but with the item element. If the state operates on an annual budget, the appropriation will be broken down into fourths for each department or spending agency; if the state has a biennial budget, half the appropriation for each spending agency must be reserved for the second year, and the yearly allotment be broken down into quarters. This quarterly allotment must then be broken down again, according to the purposes for which the spending agency in question uses its money.[17] This whole procedure should be under the immediate control of the executive.

[17] The following typical classification of the objects of expenditure is that used by Virginia:

11. PERSONAL SERVICE
    111 Salaries
    112 Wages
    113 Special payments

12. CONTRACTUAL SERVICE
    121 General repairs
    122 Motor vehicle repairs
    123 Light, heat, power, and water
    124 Traveling
    125 Transportation
    126 Communication
    127 Printing, other than office supplies
    128 Other expenses

13. SUPPLIES
    131 Food supplies
    132 Forage and veterinary supplies
    133 Fuel supplies
    134 Office supplies
    135 Medical and laboratory supplies

    136 Laundry, cleaning, and disinfecting supplies
    137 Refrigerating supplies
    138 Educational and recreational supplies
    139 Agricultural and botanical supplies
    1300 Motor vehicle supplies
    1301 Wearing apparel
    1302 Other supplies

14. MATERIALS
    141 Highway materials
    142 Building materials
    143 Sewer and water materials
    144 Other materials

15. EQUIPMENT
    151 Office equipment
    152 Household equipment
    153 Medical and laboratory equipment
    154 Live stock
    155 Motorless vehicles

An encumbrance reserves a part of an allotment at the time a commitment is made against it, in order to assure that this amount will be available to provide for payment when the goods are delivered or the service rendered. The accountant must, therefore, maintain his books on an encumbrance basis. Bills for which the accountant has already established an encumbrance will, when presented for payment, be paid out of the encumbered funds. Requisitions, on the other hand, will be charged against the unencumbered balance of the department or agency, for that particular purpose and for that particular quarterly period.

It has been demonstrated by long experience that sound budget procedure, with the accompanying advantages of economical and efficient performance of a well-balanced program of governmental services, involves certain characteristics. Some of these are as follows:

1. The budget should be formulated by the chief executive and should represent his program of work for the fiscal period.
2. It should record all — not part — of the estimated receipts and proposed expenditures of the government.
3. These proposed expenditures should not exceed the estimated revenues.
4. The expenditures should be classified in the budget document by the various " funds " involved, by the specific services to be performed, by the nature of the things to be bought.
5. In the interest of economy, the executive should exercise a large measure of control over the execution of the budget after it is approved by the legislature.

---

156 Motor vehicles
157 Educational and recreational equipment
158 Other equipment (specified)
159 State highway equipment (applies only to Highway Department)
1500 Boats and nautical equipment

16. LAND AND STRUCTURES
161 Land
162 Structures

17. CURRENT CHARGES AND OBLIGATIONS
171 Payment of State debt
172 Interest on State debt
173 Rent
174 Insurance
175 State aid (specified)
176 Contributions
177 Refunds
178 Other current charges and obligations (specified)

179 Unemployment compensation
1700 Interest on departmental or institutional debt
1701 Payment on departmental or institutional debt

18. PENSIONS AND RETIREMENT SALARIES
181 Pensions

19. ROTARY FUND
191 Imprest cash
192 Purchases of merchandise for resale

CAPITAL OUTLAYS

25. EQUIPMENT
Items 251–2500 correspond with those under No. 1.

26. LAND AND STRUCTURES
Items 261–262 correspond with those under No. 16.

— From *Classifications and Instructions for the Preparation of Budget Estimates* (Richmond, July 1, 1939).

Since no state has yet found the perfect budget system, it is probable that some changes might be made to advantage in order fully to realize these objectives in any one state.

Control of Amounts Expended. In the interests of good overall financial management, a number of techniques and methods have been used to control the amount of public expenditures. Some states have adopted tax limitations such as were discussed in the previous chapter, and further limitations upon the power to incur debt. West Virginia was the first to impose a maximum limit on the tax rate. In 1933 Ohio adopted such an amendment, and at the same time another one providing for a system of old age pensions to be financed jointly by contributions from counties and the state. The voters thus approved at the same time a measure which would inevitably increase the need for revenue and one which would impose additional limitations upon the possibility of raising it. The trouble with attempts to control public spending by such methods is that the limits established are arbitrary and inelastic; they do not represent, even at the time of adoption, any reasoned judgment with regard to the fiscal policies and needs of the state. Similar objections may be raised against certain types of constitutional limitations upon debts, but these will be discussed in a later section of this chapter in connection with the borrowing power. Other methods of control include a budget system for the state government for the purpose of planning the spending program, and an agency for the central supervision and control of the fiscal program. There should, furthermore, be an agency for rendering a prompt and careful audit.

During the depression many interesting and difficult questions arose regarding the economic aspects of public expenditures. As the depression became more serious, the practice of economy in state government became more urgent. In many states substantial savings were made through the elimination of duplication, overlapping, and waste. In some, attention was given to the problem of fees which would make regulatory services wholly or partly self-supporting. Other questions arose which were even more difficult. From many quarters there arose a demand that unnecessary and useless services be discontinued; when an effort was made to discover what these services were, it was generally found that they related to some subject that was of no concern to the group entering the complaint. Since a service which seemed unnecessary and useless to one group was a matter of vital concern to another, little could be saved by this method unless the legislature and administration were willing to engage in a reckless and wholesale elimination of existing services, such as occurred in some states following the gubernatorial elections of 1938.[18] The depression was beneficial to the extent that it caused a careful attempt to evaluate the many services rendered by state government, and to practice economy where possible without impairing essential services.

Popular Fallacies. There are a number of popular fallacies regarding public spending that have attained wide acceptance. It was long assumed, before the depression, that money spent by government was less beneficial to trade and commerce than money spent by private agencies. It is difficult to understand the basis for this belief, since a large part of such expenditures goes into salaries and wages and for the purchase of supplies, materials, and equipment, as do the expenditures of private concerns. Furthermore, such spending may be productive of greater social values than like amounts spent in the construction of new factories. Again, it is urged that government is something apart from the people, and " that every increase of the power and the activity of the government is a burden and an oppression to the people." The fallacy of this argument should be apparent to anyone. Every one of the services and activities of government is carried on either because some group demanded it for its own protection, or because the public interest required it. Before the depression one of the main problems for years had been " to dissuade large groups of citizens from going too fast and too far in demanding services from the government."

Though modern government is more a servant than a ruler, there are still complaints from many quarters that the government has gone into business, into social service, and even into the supervision of the homes of citizens. It is true that government is doing more in all these fields than ever before — and it is likely to do still more in years to come. All of the scientific developments of modern life contributing to the raising of the general standard of living bring new problems of regulation — traffic control, regulation of air waves and air routes, et cetera. The demand for these services, as Professor Anderson has pointed out, comes from every class and stratum of the population — farmers, labor, industry, home owners, and practi-

[18] The " economy bloc " found effective spokesmen either in the executive or legislative branches or both, without much regard to party control, in Colorado, Iowa, Maryland, Minnesota, Nebraska, New Jersey, New York, Ohio, Oklahoma, Pennsylvania, Utah, and Wisconsin, and probably in other states as well. In some cases the budget-hacking was done without any regard for the public welfare. See Kneier, Charles M., " Citizen Economy Movements: Why and How," *National Municipal Review,* August, 1940, pp. 535–539.

cally every organized group. As the character of our civilization changes, the needs for government and the responsibilities of government change with it.

Finally, there is the oft-repeated charge that there is wastefulness and graft in public expenditures. The assumption seems to be that the government does not receive as much in goods or service for the dollar which it spends as do private individuals. To say that, in general, government receives much more is not to deny that there are occasional instances both of wastefulness and graft. " Let any man go out and buy an education for his children, instead of sending them to public school. Or let him try to buy roads or any other thing. The idea is so silly that it, of course, does not merit further discussion. The public has asked the government to do many things for it just because the private citizen could not get a fair and economical deal in any other way." In addition, there is the fact that government, through the exercise of the taxing power, can distribute the burden of the cost of services more equitably than would otherwise be possible. Furthermore, before public expenditures are made, they must be provided for in the budget; this gives an annual opportunity for their reconsideration.[19]

THE BORROWING POWER

History of State Borrowing. There have been four periods in the history of the states when their borrowing power has been used more extensively than is usual in ordinary times: first, the period of the Revolution; second, the period of rapid internal expansion following the War of 1812, during which there was an extensive development of public works; third, the reconstruction period following the Civil War; and finally, the period of the depression which began in 1929, during which there was large borrowing for relief. The loans obtained during the first period either were paid back by the states that secured them or were assumed by the Federal government and paid off in full. They occurred so far back in our history that no extended discussion of them here is necessary. The large loans of the second period, for internal improvements, were recklessly spent on post roads, canals, and railways. In the 1840's serious difficulty arose in the payment of these obligations and many were canceled. The fact that many of them were held by foreign bond-

[19] These three paragraphs are based on an article by William Anderson, " The Other Side of the Tax Problem," *Oklahoma Municipal Review*, April, 1932, pp. 80–83.

holders led to international complications, the echoes of which have only recently died away.[20] In some of the older states the remains of some of the canals built with this money may still be seen — grim reminders of wastefulness and bad judgment, and ultimately of bad faith. The second period of default, between 1848 and 1860, was one in which the states involved were widely separated and the causes varied. Texas defaulted on the payment of a debt incurred in connection with the Mexican War, and California on a debt incurred during the inflation days of the Forty-Niners. Minnesota defaulted as a result of an ill-advised venture into state banking.

STATE DEBTS REPUDIATED AND SCALED DOWN [21]

State, and Dates of Repudiation	Repudiated	Scaled Down	Total Amount
Alabama, 1861, 1872, 1876	$ 4,700,000	$ 8,500,000	$ 13,200,000
Arkansas, 1841, 1873, 1878	7,900,000	....	7,900,000
Florida, 1840, 1873	7,900,000	....	7,900,000
Georgia, 1871, 1877	9,350,000	....	9,350,000
Louisiana, 1866, 1874, 1879	22,000,000	8,000,000	30,000,000
Michigan, 1841	....	2,500,000	2,500,000
Minnesota, 1860	....	1,137,500	1,137,500
Mississippi, 1840, 1842	7,000,000	....	7,000,000
North Carolina, 1868, 1879	12,800,000	14,000,000	26,800,000
South Carolina, 1862, 1872, 1879	6,000,000	16,000,000	22,000,000
Tennessee, 1865, 1875, 1879, 1883	....	19,000,000	19,000,000
Virginia, 1861, 1869, 1872, 1882	....	14,000,000	14,000,000
	$77,650,000	$83,137,500	$160,787,500

The loans made after the Civil War gave rise to a third period of defaults in the late seventies and early eighties; all the Southern states that had comprised the Confederacy were involved. Like many of the earlier debts, these were incurred in other sections of the country upon the basis of optimistic tales about the future of the American states, in a " setting of apparently inevitable financial stringency, followed in turn by acrimonious debates between creditors and debtors, and finally the default by some debtors unable to

20 See Monaco v. Mississippi, 292 U. S. 313, 1934.

21 No defaults have occurred in the following states: Arizona, Colorado, Connecticut, Delaware, Idaho, Iowa, Kansas, Kentucky, Maine, Massachusetts, Montana, Nebraska, Nevada, New Hampshire, New Jersey, New Mexico, New York, North Dakota, Ohio, Oklahoma, Oregon, Rhode Island, South Dakota, Utah, Vermont, Washington, Wisconsin, and Wyoming.

Defaults occurred or debts were scaled down in the following states not covered in the table: Arkansas, 1933; California, 1854; Illinois, 1844; Indiana, 1840; Maryland, 1842; Missouri, 1861; Pennsylvania, 1842; Texas, 1848; and West Virginia, 1863. These dates are taken from Jordan, David F., *Investments,* p. 86 (Prentice-Hall, New York, 1933).

adjust income to expenditures." [22] Most of the debts which were repudiated were created during the second period of borrowing; the amounts for eight states are indicated in the preceding table. This process of repudiation — total and partial — as well as of scaling down occurred mainly between 1842 and 1892; many states used the latter method, but some, as the table shows, used both. Only the major defaults are included, but the total amount involved — long before huge figures became commonplace during the two World Wars and the depression — reached the substantial total of approximately $161,000,000.

DEBT OF STATE GOVERNMENTS
(Amounts expressed in thousands)

Year	Gross Debt		Sinking Fund Assets	Gross Debt Less Total Sinking Fund Assets	
	Total	Funded or Fixed [1]		Amount	Per Capita
1880	$ 306,017	$ 286,819	$ 31,271	$ 274,746	$ 5.48
1890	258,195	238,283	46,985	211,210	3.37
1900	265,133	253,332	29,821	235,454 [2]	3.10
1910	322,949	311,093	66,814	256,143 [3]	2.78
1919	693,623	588,606	146,677	546,946	5.20
1930	2,444,122	2,238,606	449,910	1,994,212	16.35
1931	2,666,070	2,426,302	496,293	2,169,777	17.61
1932	2,907,495	2,502,665	520,577	2,386,918	19.27
1937 [4]	3,275,677	3,023,103	659,848	2,615,829	20.39
1938 [4]	3,300,648	3,116,526	664,531	2,636,117	20.47
1940	3,643,000		718,000	2,925,000	
1941	3,497,000		578,885	2,834,330	
1942	3,268,000		561,000	2,707,000	
1943	2,946,000		533,491	2,412,509	
1944	2,796,000		681,000	2,115,000	

[1] Revised to include special debt obligations to trust funds, and to agree with figures as published in state reports.

[2] Sinking fund assets exceed debt by $142,000 in one state.

[3] Sinking fund assets exceed debt by $8,000 in one state.

[4] Exclusive of public service enterprises.

Source: United States Bureau of the Census, *Wealth, Debt, and Taxation*, 1913, Vol. I, p. 38, for data for years prior to 1915; *Financial Statistics of States* (annual studies), for data for 1915 and subsequent years.

[22] See McGrane, Reginald C., *Foreign Bondholders and American State Debts* (Macmillan, New York, 1935). Each group of debts in the second and third periods is analyzed by states, with emphasis upon the origins and action by the state governments with regard to them. See also, by the same author, "Some Aspects of American State Debts in the Forties," *American Historical Review*, July, 1933, pp. 673–686.

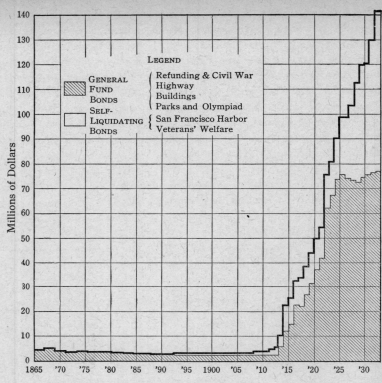

LEGEND

GENERAL FUND BONDS
{ Refunding & Civil War
Highway
Buildings
Parks and Olympiad

SELF-LIQUIDATING BONDS
{ San Francisco Harbor
Veterans' Welfare

STATE OF CALIFORNIA — GROSS DEBT, 1865–1932

The loans made during the depression which began in 1929, except those for casual deficiencies or those made on a short-term basis, have not yet come due. It seems unlikely that any considerable number will be defaulted. So far there has, with a single exception, been no move on the part of the states to escape their just payments, heavy though the burden is in some cases. The exception is Arkansas, which in 1933 practically forced the holders of its bonds paying from 4 to 5 per cent to exchange for 3 per cent bonds at par by refusing to continue interest payments on the former issues. This action actually constituted partial repudiation. In 1941 these bonds were bought by the Reconstruction Finance Corporation in a deal which may prove to be of great significance in the field of state finance.[23] Even with the heavy increases in indebtedness during the depression

[23] See Ratchford, B. U., *American State Debts*, Chapter 15, on Arkansas, a state that borrowed too much (Duke University Press, 1941), and note in *National Municipal Review*, April, 1941, pp. 238–240.

period, the states were unable in most cases to meet the extensive demands upon them without substantial assistance from the Federal government.

Growth and Present Extent of State Debts. There has been through the years, without regard to the four periods mentioned above, a steady increase in the gross debts incurred by the states, the extent of which, over the last sixty years, is indicated in the table on page 597. During this period there has been a notable increase not only in the totals, but in the per capita amounts of debt outstanding — from $5.48 in 1880 to $16.35 in 1930.[24] The chart on the gross debt of California from 1865 to 1932 (on page 598) shows what this increase has meant in the case of one representative state.[25] On June 30, 1911, the gross bonded debt of this state was $4,881,500. At no time during the preceding sixty years of statehood had the debt exceeded $5,500,000; on July 3, 1932, the gross debt was $140,574,500. That these figures are by no means unusual among the states is well shown by the table on page 601 covering state debts for all forty-eight states.

An outstanding feature of state debts is their unequal distribution among the forty-eight states. With some exceptions, those least able to meet excessive interest charges appear to have been most insistent in borrowing during the expensive period which preceded the depression.

New York showed the highest net debt of any state, in 1932, followed by Illinois, North Carolina, Arkansas, and California. The per capita figures available for 1931, however, indicate more clearly the relative burden these debts represent. On this basis, the South Atlantic States were those most heavily in debt, averaging $27.71 per capita, while those most free of debt, with a per capita figure of $10.94, comprised the East North Central group. Among individual states, Arkansas had the highest debt on a per capita basis ($86.07), followed by North Carolina ($55.07), West Virginia ($49.00), South Carolina ($44.74), Louisiana ($39.41), and Oregon ($34.59). Connecticut ($0.44) and Wisconsin $(0.43) were those most free of debt.

Wide discrepancies are also noted in the rate of increase in debt. In New England, the per capita change between 1902 and 1931 was only from $13.06 to $14.73, Massachusetts and Connecticut showing an actual decline in their indebtedness. In the Middle Atlantic States (New York, New Jersey, and Pennsylvania), on the other hand, a per capita debt of $0.53, in 1902, had mounted, by 1931, to $16.76, with New York increasing its share from $1.08, in 1902, to $24.00, in 1931. Among the East North Central States,

[24] From *Index*, May, 1934, p. 94 (New York Trust Company, New York City).
[25] *Tax Digest*, December, 1932, p. 433; for the history of the debt of other states, see New York State Constitutional Convention Committee, *Problems Relating to Taxation and Finance* (Albany, 1938); and Norman S. Taber and Company, *Reorganizing the Debt Structure of Tennessee* (Nashville, 1937).

with the lowest per capita debt of any group, a per capita average of $1.13 was reduced to $0.95, in 1912, but, by 1931, had increased to $10.84, while in the South Atlantic group, which had the highest per capita debt, the gain between 1902 and 1931 was from $4.86 to $27.71. Among these latter states, West Virginia, which prior to its debt settlement with Virginia claimed no debt, reported $40.00 per capita, in 1931, while North Carolina had a debt of $55.07, in comparison with $3.47, in 1902, and South Carolina $44.74, in comparison with $4.88, in 1902.

The percentage increase in total debt, for which figures comparing 1932 with 1912 are available, discloses even more pronounced discrepancies among the various states. Decreases are reported by Connecticut, Florida, Massachusetts, and Wisconsin, but Oregon increased its debt by 107,603 per cent, Arkansas by 13,203 per cent, Illinois by 9,641 per cent, New Jersey by 9,588 per cent and Kansas by 8,875 per cent. The average debt increase over this period, as heretofore noted, was 586 per cent.[26]

The same authority says further that these debts have, on the whole, been contracted for permanent improvements. More than half the outstanding indebtedness of 1931 had been incurred for purposes of highway construction. Among the other general purposes mentioned were park developments, charities, hospitals, corrections, schools, agriculture, and general purposes of government. Soldiers' bonuses were an important reason for borrowing in the decade of the 1920's, as was relief in the decade of the thirties. With increased tax receipts and little opportunity for spending during the defense and war period, little new borrowing took place and old debts were retired or reduced.

Constitutional Limitations on State Indebtedness. Because of large borrowings during the depression, the constitutional restrictions on the borrowing power of the states have been of particular interest. They are numerous, some of them are drastic, but the record shows that they have not been very effective in holding down the total amount of state debt. Several studies have been made of these provisions of the state constitutions.[27] Twenty-eight states have fixed sum limitations upon the amount of outstanding debt, while in nine states the limitation is based upon a percentage of the assessed valuation of taxable property. Fifteen states provide an exemption in case the proposed bond issue is ratified by popular referendum; this method of restriction has proved to be most ineffective, for there is always a tendency on the part of voters to think that someone else will have to pay most of the bills. On this point, Paul Studensky says: " The time seems ripe to abolish the requirements of referenda for

26 *Index*, May, 1934, pp. 94, 96.

27 In addition to references cited in previous editions, see Ratchford, *op. cit.*, Chapters 17–19, and Tax Foundation, a compilation of *Provisions in State Constitutions Controlling Debt* (New York, 1945).

State Debt

(Totals expressed in thousands)

State	Gross Debt Less Sinking Fund Assets				Per Cent of Increase, 1922–1932	Per Cent of Increase, 1912–1932
	1942	1932	1922	1912		
Alabama	$ 74,739	$ 82,342	$ 15,233	$13,132	440.6	527.0
Arizona	3,134	3,676	2,740	3,065	34.2	19.9
Arkansas	154,558	164,424	2,722	1,236	5,940.6	13,202.9
California	219,436	145,723	85,267	10,223	70.9	1,325.4
Colorado	24,099	6,747	12,019	3,174	43.9 [1]	112.6
Connecticut	30,213	108	6,088	7,111	98.2 [1]	98.5 [1]
Delaware	5,174	2,072	5,834	763	64.5 [1]	171.6
Florida		391	869	619	55.0 [1]	36.8 [1]
Georgia	22,967	12,488	5,419	6,934	130.4	80.1
Idaho	2,689	6,961	7,673	2,143	9.3 [1]	224.8
Illinois	149,252	221,404	13,880	2,273	1,495.1	9,640.6
Indiana	7,923	4,730	2,325	1,350	103.4	250.4
Iowa	2,038	16,495	1,457	357	1,032.1	4,520.4
Kansas	15,522	21,810	78	243	27,861.5	8,875.3
Kentucky	9,053	16,224	7,745	4,441	109.5	265.3
Louisiana	182,112	83,743	14,829	13,546	464.7	518.2
Maine	26,323	27,219	12,906	1,255	110.9	2,068.8
Maryland	57,965	31,198	22,129	7,334	41.0	325.4
Massachusetts	111,187	62,856	76,996	79,551	18.4 [1]	21.0 [1]
Michigan	41,094	60,582	50,934	7,089	18.9	754.6
Minnesota	105,221	40,156	20,308	1,345	97.7	2,885.6
Mississippi	82,998	36,320	14,864	4,461	144.3	714.2
Missouri	87,907	103,302	30,456	4,671	239.2	2,111.6
Montana	13,509	9,316	7,579	1,513	22.9	515.7
Nebraska	947	929	1,038	374	10.5 [1]	148.4
Nevada	431	1,370	1,751	608	21.8 [1]	125.3
New Hampshire	17,912	6,505	3,018	1,956	115.5	232.6
New Jersey	105,906	62,198	16,355	642	280.3	9,588.2
New Mexico	27,242	11,407	4,954	1,218	130.3	836.5
New York	703,412	463,068	186,542	86,205	148.2	437.2
North Carolina	135,445	177,210	34,713	8,059	410.5	2,098.9
North Dakota	29,971	5,005	5,913	820	15.4 [1]	510.4
Ohio	12,062	7,696	30,143	5,142	74.5 [1]	49.7
Oklahoma	40,159	11,438	4,797	6,931	138.4	65.0
Oregon	31,225	33,388	39,983	31	16.5 [1]	107,603.2
Pennsylvania	288,784	75,858	49,968		51.8	[2]
Rhode Island	29,333	16,807	9,338	5,127	80.0	227.8
South Carolina	86,537	77,984	8,729	6,190	793.4	1,159.8
South Dakota	32,056	15,510	15,431	370	.5	4,091.9
Tennessee	94,394	94,032	19,142	11,812	391.2	696.1
Texas	18,169	10,317	6,145	4,656	67.9	121.6
Utah	2,019	5,694	9,819	1,430	42.0 [1]	298.2
Vermont	6,850	9,545	2,112	570	351.9	1,574.6
Virginia	25,716	25,983	21,756	22,043	19.4	17.9
Washington	16,262	8,257	13,191	1,556	37.4 [1]	430.7
West Virginia	79,695	86,394	24,181		257.3	[2]
Wisconsin	1,184	1,184	2,164	2,251	45.3 [1]	47.4 [1]
Wyoming	3,240	5,568	4,011	122	38.8	4,463.9

[1] Decrease.   [2] Cannot be expressed.   Source: Bureau of Census.

From *Index*, May, 1934, p. 95 (New York Trust Company, New York City), and *State Government*, November, 1943.

the issuance of bonds by the states, and to vest the legislature with power to issue bonds without the approval of the people. The abuses of the state credit by legislatures ninety years ago should not be held against the legislatures of today." If these referenda are not necessary today, they are further objectionable in that they violate the prin· ciple of the short ballot.

In sixteen states borrowing for general purposes is prohibited unless authorized by the legislature and a popular referendum; borrowing is prohibited in nineteen states unless the specific purpose is authorized in the constitution, and in four states unless the loan is authorized by a vote of two thirds or three fourths of the legislature. The specific purposes for which the constitutions authorize the making of loans include the suppression of insurrection and the repelling of invasion in forty states; assistance in the defense of the United States in five states; casual deficiencies, usually to the extent of definitely specified amounts, in twenty-three states; and payment or refund of existing debts in fifteen states. Among what might be called the miscellaneous provisions affecting the borrowing power the following are the most common: prohibition upon the lending of credit to individuals or corporations in forty-one states; a maximum number of years for the maturity of state bonds in nineteen states; and the requirement that a tax to provide for the payment of interest and principal must accompany the issue in twenty-six states. In addition to the usual ease with which many of these requirements are evaded, the exigencies of the depression were responsible for many studied attempts to evade them in order to secure funds necessary for relief. Furthermore, an easy provision for amending the constitution tends to nullify any debt limitations it may contain.

Some Current Problems. One of the most important current problems in connection with the use of the borrowing power is the question of the responsibility of states for the indebtedness of their political subdivisions. There seems to be no basis upon which the states can be compelled to make good on the defaults of their municipalities and other local subdivisions, but the states should be expected so to supervise the finances of these subdivisions as to prevent defalcations. This the states in the past have not done, but the movement for state supervision of the finances of cities and other local units has been making such progress that effective supervision of this character can be expected in most states in the near future. A table compiled in 1934 showed that more than 2,000 units of local government had failed to pay the interest on their funded debts.[28]

[28] *State Government*, August, 1934.

Florida was the worst offender with 328 cases; on the other hand, Delaware, Maryland, Massachusetts, New Hampshire, Rhode Island, Vermont, and West Virginia had none. There were fifteen other states that had less than ten each.

Slightly more than a year later the *Bond Buyer,* recognized authority on municipal bonds, reported on September 1, 1935, defaults by 3,236 units. In presenting these figures, it pointed out that many of the reports were from unofficial sources and that many of the amounts were small; on the other hand, the information available in many of the states was incomplete. Florida had in this period practically doubled the number of its defaulting subdivisions; there was not a single state with an entirely clear record, although Maine had only one defaulting municipality. In addition to those in Florida, more than 100 defaulting units were reported in Arkansas, California, Illinois, Louisiana, Michigan, New Jersey, North Carolina, Ohio, and Texas. The units covered by the report included counties; cities and towns; school districts; and many special districts.

Another difficulty, affecting both states and their subdivisions, has to do with the relations of the unit of government with the bankers. There is an old maxim to the effect that he who pays the piper calls the tune; this has been all too true in the field of government. Bankers and combinations of bankers have frequently insisted upon dictating policies of government as the price of their assistance. The sounder the credit of the unit, the more independent it can afford to be. In some cases, rather than submit to the dictates of private bankers, administrations have gone directly to the banks of the state and sold their issues in that way.

In the postwar years it seems likely that the states will want to borrow fairly extensively to aid in financing the requirements of programs of social legislation and for the development of public works. It will be difficult to meet these needs entirely out of current revenues, although as a result of the boom years of defense and war the states are in a much stronger financial position than they were a few years ago. In view of the excessive and sometimes unwise use of the borrowing power in some jurisdictions in the past, by issuing bonds that equaled or exceeded the life of the improvement, the borrowing power of the states should be protected by exempting debt service from tax limitation provisions of state constitutions. In at least two states, Alabama and North Carolina, this has not been done. From the point of view of the prospective purchaser, it is preferable not only that the states pledge " full faith and credit," but that the constitutions provide unlimited taxation for debt service.

Selected References

Alyea, Paul E., *Alabama's Balancing Budget* (University of Alabama, Bureau of Public Administration, 1942).

Arkansas, State Comptroller, *Financial Analysis State Bonded Indebtedness* (Little Rock, 1939).

Benson, George C. S., and Litchfield, Edward H., *The State Administrative Board in Michigan* (University of Michigan, Bureau of Government, 1938).

Buck, A. E., *Budget Making* (Macmillan, New York, 1921).

——, *Public Budgeting* (Macmillan, New York, 1929).

——, *The Budget in Governments of Today* (Macmillan, New York, 1933).

Bureau of Governmental Research, *Louisiana's " Little Legislature,"* *A Study of the Board of Liquidation of the State Debt, 1870–1945* (New Orleans, 1945).

California Taxpayers Association, *Income and Expenditures of Government in California, 1900 to 1940* (Los Angeles, 1941).

Clark, Evans, Ed., *The Internal Debts of the United States* (Macmillan, New York, 1933).

Cline, Denzel C., *Executive Control over State Expenditures in New Jersey* (Princeton University Press, 1934).

Crouch, Winston W., *State Aid to Local Government in California* (University of California Press, 1939).

Faust, Martin L., *The Custody of State Funds* (National Institute of Public Administration, New York, 1925).

——, *The Security of Public Deposits* (Public Administration Service, Chicago, 1936).

Forbes, Russell, *Governmental Purchasing* (Harper, New York, 1929).

Groves, Harold M., *Financing Government* (Holt, New York, 1939).

Gulick, Luther H., *Evolution of the Budget in Massachusetts* (Harper, New York, 1920).

Hansen, Alvin H., and Perloff, Harvey S., *State and Local Finance in the National Economy* (Norton, New York, 1944).

Horton, Donald C., *Long Term Debts in the United States* (Washington, 1937).

Hutchinson, Ruth G., *State-Administered Locally-Shared Taxes* (Columbia University Press, New York, 1931).

Illinois Department of Finance, *The A–B–C of Illinois State Finance,* (Springfield, 1936; Revised Edition, 1940).

Indiana Inter-Organization Council, *Eleven-Year Trend in Indiana State Government Payments and Receipts, 1928–1938* (Indianapolis, 1938).

Indiana Taxpayers' Association, *Cost of Government in Indiana* (Indianapolis, annually since 1935).

Irvin, Oscar W., *State Budget Control of State Institutions of Higher Learning* (Columbia University Press, 1928).

Isseks, Morris S., *History of State Administrative Agencies in Oregon, 1843–1937* (Oregon State Planning Board, Portland, 1939).

Jones, Victor, *The Legislature and the Budget* (University of California, Bureau of Public Administration, 1941).

Kansas Legislative Council, *Cost of Government in Kansas, 1929–1936* (Topeka, annually since 1936).

——, *Summary History of Kansas Finance, 1861–1937* (Topeka, 1937).

Martin, James W., and others, *The State Auditor* (University of Kentucky, 1943).

McGrane, Reginald C., *Foreign Bondholders and American State Debts* (Macmillan, New York, 1935).

National Association of State Auditors, Comptrollers and Treasurers, *The Revenues, Cost Payments and Debts of the 48 State Governments, 1915–1937* (Chicago, 1939).

National Industrial Conference Board, *Cost of Government in the United States, 1936–1938* (New York, 1939).

New York State Constitutional Convention Committee, *Problems Relating to Taxation and Finance* (Albany, 1938).

——, *State and Local Government in New York* (Albany, 1938).

Norman S. Taber and Company, *Reorganizing the Debt Structure of Tennessee* (Nashville, 1937).

——, *Report of a Survey of the Highway Indebtedness of Texas* (New York, 1937).

Pfiffner, John M., *Public Administration* (Ronald Press, New York, 1935).

Porter, Kirk H., *State Administration* (Crofts, New York, 1938).

Providence Governmental Research Bureau, *An Analysis of State Expenditures, 1933–1938* (Providence, 1937).

Ratchford, B. U., *American State Debts* (Duke University Press, 1941).

Ray, Joseph M., *Alabama's State Dollar* (University of Alabama, Bureau of Public Administration, 1942).

——, *High Spots in Alabama Finances* (University of Alabama, Bureau of Public Administration, 1943).

Reed, Thomas H., *Federal-State-Local Fiscal Relations* (Municipal Finance Officers Association, Chicago, 1942).

Sappenfield, Max M., *Financial Administration in the States of Illinois, Ohio, and Indiana* (University of Illinois, Thesis Abstract, 1934).

Schultz, Arch D., *Tax Reduction Ahead* (Ohio Chamber of Commerce, Columbus, 1937).

Seckler-Hudson, Catheryn, *Budgeting: An Instrument of Planning,* 7 vols. (American University, Washington, 1943).

Short, Lloyd M., and Tiller, Carl W., *The Minnesota Commission of Administration and Finance, 1925–1939: An Administrative History* (University of Minnesota Press, 1942).

Social Security Board, *The Fiscal Capacity of the States: a Source Book* (Bureau of Research and Statistics, Washington, 1938).

Spangler, Frank L., *Operation of Debt and Tax Rate Limits in the State of New York* (New York State Tax Commission, Albany, 1932).

Steiner, George A., *Indiana State Disbursements* (Indiana University, Bureau of Business Research, 1939).

Studensky, Paul, *Public Borrowing* (National Municipal League, New York, 1930).

Sundelson, J. Wilner, *Budgetary Methods in National and State Governments* (New York State Tax Commission, Albany, 1938).

Tannery, Fladger F., *State Accounting Procedures* (Public Administration Service, Chicago, 1943).

Tax Foundation, *Fiscal Summary of the New England States, 1940* (New York, 1940).

Tax Institute, *Wartime Problems of State and Local Finance* (New York, 1943).

Tharp, Claude R., *State Aid in Michigan* (University of Michigan, Bureau of Government, 1942).

Trull, Edna, *Borrowing for Highways* (Dun and Bradstreet, New York, 1937).

——, *Resources and Debts of the Forty-eight States, 1937* (Dun and Bradstreet, New York, 1938).

University of Illinois, Bureau of Business Research, *State Expenditures in Illinois, 1895–1924* (Urbana, 1927).

Van de Woestyne, Royal S., *State Control of Local Finance in Massachusetts* (Harvard University Press, 1935).

Walker, Harvey, *Public Administration in the United States* (Farrar and Rinehart, New York, 1937).

White, Leonard D., *Trends in Public Administration* (McGraw-Hill, New York, 1933).

——, *An Introduction to the Study of Public Administration*, Revised Edition (Macmillan, New York, 1939).

Williams, John H., *The Flexible Budget: How to Use It* (McGraw-Hill, New York, 1934).

Williams, Juanita K., *Grants-in-Aid Under the Public Works Administration* (Columbia University Press, 1939).

Willoughby, W. F., *Principles of Public Administration* (Johns Hopkins Press, 1927).

Wisconsin Citizens Public Expenditure Survey, *A Brief Survey of Financial Administration and Organization in Wisconsin* (Madison, 1945).

Wisconsin Tax Commission, *Long-Term Indebtedness of the State and Its Political Subdivisions* (Madison, annually).

———————

Council of State Governments, *State Government* (Chicago, monthly).

——, "State Wartime Fiscal Policy," *State Government*, July, 1942, pp. 143–144.

Egger, Rowland A., "Power Is Not Enough," *State Government*, August, 1940, pp. 149–150, 160–161.

Ensley, Grover W., "A Citizen's Observations on State and Local Budgeting," *National Municipal Review*, May, 1942, pp. 265–269.

Fensel, A. C., "A Decade of State Expenditures," *Tax Digest*, February, 1941, pp. 54–58.

Ingersoll, Hugh D., "The Cost of State Government — a New Viewpoint," *State Government*, January, 1941, pp. 14–16, 26.

Martin, James W., and Briscoe, Vera, "Some Statutory Provisions for State Budgets," *State Government*, September, 1945, pp. 162–167.

Perkins, John A., "The Budget in the Legislature," *State Government*, November, 1944, pp. 446–448.

Part Six

JUDICIAL AND LEGAL PROBLEMS

CHAPTER XV

The Legal Systems of the States

THE legal systems of the states include the whole body of constitutional law, common law, and statutory law under which the governments themselves and their agencies are organized, under which they function, and which it becomes their duty to enforce throughout their respective jurisdictions. In discussing the place of the states in the Federal Union, the obligation of the states to observe and enforce those portions of the Federal Constitution which are applicable to them was noted. While the observance of these clauses constitutes a primary responsibility, the clauses are not numerous and do not require the consideration of state officers as frequently as do the provisions of the state constitutions. Just as the Federal Constitution is of paramount importance to the Federal government, its officers and agencies, so the state constitutions are paramount for the officers and agencies of the state governments except in that relatively small number of cases where provisions of the Federal Constitution apply.

In similar fashion, the states provide a fundamental law for their municipalities in the form of charters issued to or framed by them individually, the provisions of these charters being supplemented by a body of municipal law applicable to all cities or to those in a given class throughout the state. Recently a similar practice has been adopted in some states with regard to counties, townships, boroughs, and other local subdivisions.

Next in the legal system of a state comes the great body of common law, the statutory enactments, and the decisions of the courts. The significance and importance of each of these elements will be discussed in later sections of this chapter. The origin and development of the common law and of equity and the place of each in the legal system will be considered, as will also statutory law, which includes the body of public law providing for the organization and outlining the powers and duties of the various agencies of state government and the subdivisions thereof; the great mass of private law, which governs the ordinary, everyday relationships of individuals; the criminal law, which defines the different types of offenses against the state and provides punishment for the offenders; and finally, such law as the state has developed with regard to military affairs. The chapter is concluded by a discussion of the nature of the judicial process, and of the doctrine of judicial review.

THE COMMON LAW

The Supreme Court has on several occasions put the question: "What is the common law?" The answer has uniformly been in words quoted from Kent's *Commentaries:* "The common law includes those principles and security of persons and property, which do not rest for their authority upon any express and positive declaration of the will of the legislature." Others have defined the term as that body of common or customary law developed in England down to the date of the settlement at Jamestown, the date of the American independence, or some other date arbitrarily fixed, and since that time in each of the American states.[1] Developed on English soil and inherited by the American colonies, the common law forms the basis of the legal institutions of all the states except Louisiana, whose legal system was based originally upon the Napoleonic Code. Even in this instance the law of the state has been deeply influenced by the common law tradition of the surrounding states.

Before considering the development of the common law in England and America, it may be well to note briefly what is meant by saying, as we have, that the system of law in the states is based upon the common law. This system has some important characteristics that distinguish it from the Roman law, the only other legal system widely used in the western world. The principles of the common law govern the procedure of the courts, which function with a single judge in a trial court; guarantee to the individual the right to indictment by

---

[1] There is no uniformity on this matter; Virginia uses the first date, Florida and Georgia the second. New York uses April, 1775. Nevertheless, the prevailing view in both East and West favors 1607. Lawyers well know that the question has practical aspects which cannot be ignored; see Pope, Herbert, "The English Common Law in the United States," *Harvard Law Review,* November, 1910, pp. 6–30.

a grand jury in criminal cases, the right of complaint in civil cases, and the right of trial by jury; assure him that he has the presumption of innocence until proved guilty, in proceedings regularly conducted, in open court; and provide access to equity procedures when necessary in order to obtain substantial justice.

Under our system of court procedure the judge is the impartial arbiter between contending parties, while under the Roman law he represents the sovereignty of the state and actively conducts the trial. Likewise, under the Roman law, the defendant is not presumed to be either innocent or guilty. Roman law makes no provision for indictment as is understood by English speaking countries, nor for the use of equity procedures. Since juries are not used, cases are tried by the court, but the court consists, not of one judge, but of a number of judges sitting in banc.[2] This system is not without significance in the development of English law, since the Romans occupied England for a period of some 400 years. Considering the length of their occupation, the Roman system made remarkably little imprint on either the thinking or the legal practices of the British people.

In the United States, the courts originally held that the common law belonged to the states, and not to the Federal government. In 1842 Mr. Justice Story, in Swift v. Tyson,[3] enunciated the doctrine of a Federal common law in matters relating to commerce. This was extended to matters of general jurisdiction, but not to the field of crime. Consistently, the Federal courts took cognizance of, and usually abided by, the rules of the common law when they were applicable to the question before them. Then in 1938, after ninety-six years, the Court reversed the Swift case, in Erie Railroad v. Tompkins.[4]

---

[2] On the relation of these two legal systems, see Buckland, W. W., and Mc-Nair, Arnold D., *Roman Law and Common Law* (Macmillan, New York, 1936) ; Radin, Max, *Roman Law* (West Publishing Company, St. Paul, 1927) ; Dorsey, Roscoe J. C., " Roman Sources of Some English Principles of Equity and Common Law Rules," *American Law School Review*, May, 1938, pp. 1233–1243; Kirchberger, Hans, " The Significance of Roman Law for the Americas and Its Importance to Inter-American Relations," *Wisconsin Law Review*, July, 1944, pp. 249–273; and Schiller, A. Arthur, " Roman Interpretation and Anglo-American Interpretation and Construction," *Virginia Law Review,* April, 1941, pp. 733–768.

[3] 16 Peters 1, 1842; see Waterman, J. S., " The Nationalism of Swift v. Tyson," *North Carolina Law Review*, February, 1933, pp. 125–139.

[4] 304 U. S. 64, 1938; this decision brought forth numerous comments, such as: Cushman, Robert E., in *American Political Science Review*, April, 1939, pp. 246–248; Ellis, Dean, " The Implications of Erie Railroad v. Tompkins," *Oregon Law Review*, June, 1939, pp. 304–309; Grant, J. A. C., " The Search for Uniformity of the Laws," *American Political Science Review*, December, 1938, pp. 1082–1098; Stearns, Robert L., " Erie Railroad Versus Tompkins One Year After," *Rocky*

History and Development in England. The origin of the rules of the common law is found in the customs and practices of the people of England in Anglo-Saxon times, the present rules having developed through succeeding generations of English and American life. It is easy to reconstruct in imagination something of the process by which these rules developed. They were observed by the people, not because observance was required by the King or by any powerful external force, but because the rules represented the conception of the common man as to what was fair and reasonable and just. The longer they were used, the more strongly were they able to enlist the support that comes from custom and tradition. To illustrate, let us assume that in the early days, while the civilization of our ancestors was still in a crude and rudimentary state of development, a dispute arose between two neighbors over the ownership of some cattle or over the point at which the line should be drawn separating their respective properties. A few generations earlier such a dispute would have been proper justification for a trial of physical strength, but civilization had now developed to such an extent that the parties to this dispute were willing to have it settled by counting heads, rather than by breaking them. Courts, as we know them, were still in a primitive stage of development. Since the parties were unable to agree upon a solution of their problem, they resolved to take the case to one of the numerous courts for settlement. Here the facts and the arguments on both sides were heard, and decision rendered in favor of some particular solution. The parties accepted the decision, which thus became an influence in the future development of the common law.[5]

Let it now be assumed that some years later a similar dispute developed between other inhabitants of the same community. They likewise resolved to have their difficulty settled by one of the numerous local courts. Someone present remembered the earlier case, and observed that the rule there adopted seemed applicable to the

Mountain Law-Review, December, 1939, pp. 1–14; note in *Temple Law Quarterly,* July, 1938, pp. 486–496; Tunks, Lehan K., "Categorization and Federalism: 'Substance' and 'Procedure' after Erie Railroad v. Tompkins," *Illinois Law Review,* November, 1939, pp. 271–302; Eisenhart, Earl E., Jr., "Federal Decisional Law Independent of State Common Law Since Erie Railroad Company v. Tompkins," *George Washington Law Review,* February, 1941, pp. 465–473.

5 Holdsworth, W. S., in *A History of English Law,* Vol. I (Methuen, London, 1921), discusses at length the practice in the communal courts, county courts, and other types of courts. Many different types existed side by side without any system or organization; as a matter of fact, it took nearly 400 years to bring all these together into an organized judicial system. At one time all citizens were obliged to attend these numerous courts — a duty which became very burdensome.

case at hand. This point of view was accepted, and the rule became still more deeply entrenched in the life and practice of the people. It may be imagined that instances of this sort occurred at various times over a period of many years with regard to most of the important subjects coming within the range of the common law, in communities scattered all over England. By this process individual rules of law developed in separate communities over hundreds of years. As the process continued without the intervention of any unifying force, it is easy to understand the diversity which developed in the common law rules covering essential subjects, and to appreciate the need for some systematizing and unifying force.

This force was supplied over a period of years by a group of great writers including Coke, Bracton, Glanville, Blackstone, and others, who undertook the tremendous task of surveying the practices which had developed in England in the handling of various legal subjects, and of writing comments in which they pointed out prevailing tendencies. This work has been, down to the present day, an invaluable source of information to lawyers and laymen alike, interested in the history and development of the common law. " This unwritten or Common Law," wrote Blackstone, " is properly distinguishable into three kinds: (1) General customs, which are the universal rule of the whole Kingdom, and form the Common Law, in its stricter and more usual signification. (2) Particular customs, which for the most part affect only the inhabitants of particular districts. (3) Certain particular laws, which by custom are adopted and used by some particular courts of pretty general and extensive jurisdiction." [6] Blackstone, whose influence in America was the greatest, was accorded little recognition in England, where his work was regarded as elementary; it has seldom been cited by an English court.

It is exceedingly difficult to give in brief space any adequate idea of the influences and agencies that contributed to the development of the common law. Plucknett takes more than 400 pages for his *Concise History;* under the general heading of the Crown and the State, he deals successively with the various periods of English history during which significant developments in the common law took place. These begin with the Anglo-Saxon period, with its emphasis on race and religion, and end with the eighteenth century and the

---

[6] Blackstone, William, *Commentaries*, pp. 67–68; on the subject of these paragraphs, see Plucknett, Theodore F. T., *A Concise History of the Common Law* (Lawyers Coöperative Publishing Company, Rochester, 1929) .

Industrial Revolution, with such intervening topics as the period from the Conquest to Henry II, which included the beginnings of administration; the period of the Great Charters, during which law was separated from administration; the period extending from Edward I to Richard II, marked by the development of statutes and the conduct of a social revolution; the fifteenth century, with its problems of law enforcement; the Tudor period, including the Renaissance and the Reformation; and the Stuart period, with the struggle for the supremacy of law.

When the development of the common law began, such law as there was, was purely local in character and the system was dominated by the church. With the passage of centuries all this was changed. The numerous types of local courts — communal, seignioral, manorial, central, et cetera — were slowly and gradually replaced by the courts of the Crown. Meantime the jury system developed, as did the profession and literature of the law. External forces made their significant contributions to the development of the system — the civil law of Rome, the canon law of the church, the law merchant, and the system of equity. Progress was made, because of the flexibility of custom, and through the development of forms of action and of legislation and the establishment of the principle of precedent in matters of interpretation. One might also undertake the study of the history of the common law from the point of view of the development of the legal status of real property or of contractual relations. In the first instance, he would be concerned with such matters as the feudal system, the development of inheritance, fee simple and the rise of entail, common law estates, uses and trusts, conveyances, et cetera.

Development in America. The majority of the American colonies were either predominantly English at the time of their establishment, or came subsequently under the influence and control of the English. The practice with regard to social institutions — legal and otherwise — was precisely in accordance with the practice of other great colonizing powers before and since. Colonists brought with them and established in the colonies here, in modified form, the system of the common law under which they had been born and under which a majority of them had lived before their departure for America. Here the development of the rules of the common law continued under new circumstances and under conditions heretofore unknown. Pound has admirably summarized this development in the following paragraph:

Legal theory has it that the colonists brought the common law of England
with them to America. But for a long time the colonists had no need of
so advanced and technical a body of precepts as the seventeenth century
English law. It was not until the eighteenth century that there was a need
for courts manned by lawyers and for trained lawyers to advise litigants
and assist the courts. Before the American Revolution two circumstances
made for a reception of the English common law in the colonies. One was
economic. Expanding commerce, acquisition of wealth and the rise of a
more complex social structure called for tribunals of another type from
those which sufficed for the beginnings of the colonies. About 1700 colonial
legislation began definitely to run an independent course, but economic
growth became too rapid for legislation to meet its demands. The other
circumstance was political. The conditions which later led to the Revolution caused the colonists to insist on the common law as a birthright, protecting them against the Crown, the royal governors and even Parliament.
. . . The very events which were separating them from England politically
tended to make for a reception of the common law.[7]

For a considerable time after the Revolution a number of causes
operated to hold back an immediate and complete acceptance of
the English law; chief among these was the suspicion, even the hostility, with which for a time all things English were regarded. Ohio,
for instance, had on its statute books for many years an enactment
which prohibited the citation of English cases in its courts.[8] Even
more important was the religious influence; the Scriptures were regarded from an early date as a subsidiary law, especially in New
England. As time passed, many colonists were quite unfamiliar with
the common law. There were no persons trained in the law; the
judges were no exception. The proceedings of all of the colonial
courts were popular and informal. In many colonies evidence was
taken in writing — a practice utterly abhorrent to common law actions, but not to minds to which the evidence was the most important
part of the case.[9]

Pound observes that Kent's *Commentaries* (1826–1830) " and
above all, the writings of Story between 1832 and 1845 started a
current of law writing on the basis of English legal institutions which
insured that the common law should be the basis of the law in all but
one of the United States." This development has continued without

[7] Pound, Roscoe, on the Common Law, in *Encyclopaedia of the Social Sciences*,
Vol. IV, p. 52 (Macmillan, New York, 1931–1935) ; see also his *The Spirit of the
Common Law* (Marshall Jones, Boston, 1921).
[8] Long before the Revolution some of the colonies declared the common law
of England subsidiary in cases not controlled by colonial legislation; this was true
in Maryland, Virginia, and the Carolinas (American Law Schools Association,
Select Essays in Anglo-American Legal History, Vol. I, p. 410. Boston, 1907).
[9] *Ibid.*

interruption down to the present time. However, just as, before the work of Blackstone, the common law developed in England independently in a large number of communities without any coordinating or unifying force, so in the United States the same situation has existed within these forty-seven states. In recent years this fact has been a matter of concern to an increasing number of people interested in the growth of our legal institutions. The work undertaken by the American Law Institute in 1925, and in progress since, will very likely prove to have supplied, for the clarification of the rules of the common law among the states, the same kind of influence that Blackstone supplied centuries ago with regard to the rules of the common law as developed in England up to that time.

Besides the restatements of the common law, the Institute has undertaken the formulation of the *Model Code of Criminal Procedure;* this was published in 1930 and has already exerted a considerable influence among the states. Because of widespread interest this Code has already had a significant influence on the laws of the states. This effort has been extended to include a restatement of the whole substantive criminal law. A *Model Code of Evidence,* as well as other work in the field of criminal justice, has been completed. There has been no more important or helpful influence in American law than that of this Institute.[10]

Relation of the Common Law and the Statutes. When there is no statute applicable to determine the merits of a controversy between adverse parties, the common law still affords in the American states a rule and a guide. It covers the whole range of law not included in the constitutions and statutes. The term "common law" in this country is understood to mean the unwritten law of England so far as it is not inconsistent with the constitutions and statutes; it consists of broad and comprehensive principles inspired by reason and a sense of justice and receives its binding force from common consent and immemorial usage "whence the mind of man runneth not to the contrary." Therefore it may be said to have its beginning in so remote an antiquity that its source cannot be exactly traced. It is the product of evolution and not legislation, but those who presided as judges in the remote past and who rendered judicial decisions assumed there was a law not made by legislatures and that it was part of the life and custom of the people.[11]

[10] For a fuller discussion of the work of the Institute, see *The Restatement in the Courts,* Fourth Edition (American Law Institute Publishers, St. Paul, 1945), and the reports of the annual meeting in the *American Bar Association Journal.*

[11] This statement follows that of Professor Robert E. Lee, Temple University School of Law.

A statute, on the other hand, is a formal utterance of a legislative body — an enactment of a legislative body in accordance with the terms of the constitution. In this discussion it remains to note the relationship between the common law and the growing body of statutory law. In the early days, when relations between individuals were less complicated than they are today and when life itself was simple, practically all these relationships were governed by rules of the common law. With the passage of generations and of centuries, during which have occurred tremendous developments in the field of natural science, resulting in equally significant changes in the field of human relations, it has been necessary with increasing frequency to supplement or to change and modify the rules of the common law. This has been done by statute, as in the law governing the rights of injured employees, in which we have abolished the three time-honored defenses of the employer under the common law and have substituted therefor an intricate set of workmen's compensation statutes. Similarly, in most states married women have been permitted to contract and to hold property to the same extent as though unmarried — a thing which they were formerly unable to do.

In other cases the statutes have declared and put in more definite terms parts of the common law in order to establish more firmly the intent of the latter; this is known as codification. The Negotiable Instruments Act, for example, is largely a codification of the law on a subject that had for centuries been developing in the decisions of common law. Legislative bodies have the power to pass statutes modifying or suspending the common law, but until they do so, the principles of the common law as defined by the courts are as binding upon the citizens of a state as though passed by a legislative body. So, in one field after another, either a statute has been enacted to cover a modern situation to which the rules of the common law do not apply, or the common law rule has been modified when that rule seemed no longer applicable to the changed conditions of modern life. The common law must therefore be regarded more and more as a foundation upon which our legal system has been built, and less and less as a body of rules suitable and adequate for the regulation and control of present-day problems. At the same time we are coming to a situation in which we find ourselves governed more and more by the enactments of our legislatures.

The Important Writs. One writer has observed that in its widest aspect a writ is a written command in the name of the sovereign, addressed to an official or more rarely a private person, often but not always relating to the administration of justice. It is also said that the regular use of writs implies a centralized government which by this means keeps close control over a large number of distant agents. As soon as it became apparent that most forms of writ could be constantly repeated in similar circumstances in accordance with a regular routine, the regular administration of justice was simplified. The writs which have survived under the influence of the common law include: (1) the original prerogative writs, which are in very general use; (2) certain judicial writs, especially writs of execution; and (3) some of the old administrative writs.[12] No attempt will be made here to define or describe in detail the enormous number of different types of writs used in the ordinary course of legal proceedings. There are, however, a number of these writs some knowledge of the nature of which is important to the student of government, since they relate not only to technical matters in the law but to problems which frequently arise in the conduct of government. Among those to be discussed here are the following: habeas corpus, mandamus, injunction, quo warranto, error, certiorari, procedendo, prohibition, and summons.

Most important is the writ of habeas corpus — a writ named from the Latin phrase which, translated, means " you may have the body." This writ has for its object the bringing of a party before a court or a judge, especially to inquire into the cause of the person's imprisonment or detention by another, with a view to the protection of the right of personal liberty. W. F. Willoughby says concerning this important writ:

A power of the court which is of special importance is that of compelling the production in court of anyone under arrest, or deprived of his liberty through imprisonment, confinement in an institution for the insane, or in any other way, for the purpose of determining whether he is legally held. This power is exercised through what is known as a "writ of habeas corpus," which is an order addressed by the court to the officer or other person having custody of the person confined, directing him to produce such person in court and to show cause why he should not be given his liberty. It need hardly be said that the power to issue and enforce such writs constitutes one of the greatest guarantees of individual liberty to be found in our political system.[13]

The writ of mandamus is an order issued by a court commanding an officer, a corporation, or a court to perform some legal, minis-

12 See Plucknett, Theodore F. T., on Writs, *Encyclopaedia of the Social Sciences*, Vol. XV, pp. 503–504.

13 Willoughby, W. F., *Principles of Judicial Administration*, p. 225 (Brookings Institution, Washington, 1929) . At other points in the discussion the author has drawn upon this work.

terial duty, or a duty not involving discretion. Most familiar, perhaps, is the attempt made in the famous case of Marbury v. Madison to get the Supreme Court of the United States to issue such a writ commanding Madison, the new Secretary of State, to deliver a commission to Marbury, as a judge in a court in the District of Columbia. A decision of the same court in 1931 stresses the fact that the writ will issue only where the duty to be performed is ministerial and the obligation to act peremptory and plainly defined.[14] In the case of United States v. Wilbur, Secretary of the Interior, the Secretary had refused to lease certain lands to the plaintiff, although an act of Congress gave him power to grant prospecting permits under such proper and necessary rules as he might prescribe, and to lease lands upon the establishing of satisfactory proof of the discovery of valuable oil and gas deposits. Under the terms of the act it was compulsory for him to issue such leases; the plaintiff therefore had a proper case for the issuance of a writ of mandamus. The Supreme Court rendered judgment in favor of the Secretary of the Interior, holding that the duty to grant permits and issue leases was entirely discretionary. In the course of the opinion the following significant statement occurs:

Under established rules, the writ of mandamus cannot be made to serve the purpose of an ordinary suit. It will issue only where the duty to be performed is ministerial and the obligation to act peremptory and plainly defined. The law must not only authorize the demanded action, but must require it; the duty must be clear and indisputable.

A writ of injunction is a writ or process granted by a court of equity, and in some cases, under statute, by a court of law, whereby a party is required to do or to refrain from doing certain acts, according to the exigency of the writ. While a writ of mandamus is a positive writ, a writ of injunction is more often negative in character, being used as a preventive rather than as a restorative process, although it is by no means confined to this use. In those cases where the writ of injunction is positive, it is known as a mandatory injunction; where it is negative, it is called a prohibitory injunction. The writ of injunction has been used most frequently in connection with labor disputes, for the purpose of protecting property of the employer subject to possible damage at the hands of the strikers. There has, in fact, been much criticism of " government by injunction " — of the readiness with which many judges have issued such injunc-

---

[14] United States ex rel. McLennan v. Wilbur, Secretary of the Interior, 283 U. S. 414, 1931. The citation of Marbury v. Madison is 1 Cranch 137, 1803.

tions before any damage occurred, and sometimes when none was contemplated.

A writ of quo warranto was originally, in the English common law, a writ brought before the proper tribunal to inquire by what warrant a person or a corporation acted, or exercised certain powers. It is still used in that sense in the states today to test the validity of incorporations, but it is more commonly used in connection with contested elections. In such cases the contestant brings suit against the one who has been declared to have received the majority of the votes, before a final settlement of the contest, demanding that he show by what warrant he occupies the office, exercising the powers and performing the duties thereof.

The writ of error was originally the only means of reviewing decisions of law made by the central courts, but it was useful only for the purpose of reversing errors on the record of the court below; this tended to make many material matters not reversible because they did not, in fact, appear in the record. In present-day practice the writ of error has been defined as an original writ, which lies after judgment in an action at law, in a court of record, to correct some alleged error in the procedings or in the judgment of the court. The mistake may relate to matters of law or of fact. It has come to be a common method of appeal from a court of original jurisdiction to a higher court.

There are many other types of writs in common use. A writ of certiorari is a court order addressed to a public officer or inferior judicial tribunal, directing that he or it send up the papers or record in a specified case so that the court may take action in respect to it, or review the action already taken. A writ of procedendo may be used to secure an effect contrary to that of a writ of certiorari; it is defined as a writ by which a cause which has been removed on insufficient grounds from an inferior to a superior court by certiorari, or otherwise, may be sent down again to the same court to be proceeded in there. A writ of prohibition may be issued by a superior court to an inferior one, prohibiting the latter from proceeding; it is generally issued to protect the jurisdiction of the higher court. Certain other writs are employed in the effort of the creditor to get possession of property to which he has some claim.

A writ of execution is an order to the sheriff to seize and sell the property of the defendant for the satisfaction of a judgment, while a writ of ejectment orders the same officer, forcibly if necessary, to eject the defendant from the real estate which he holds, but which the court finds should belong to the complainant. It thus becomes actually a means of trying the title to real estate. The writ of summons has been defined as a warning or citation to appear in court at a specified time for the purpose of answering the plaintiff appearing as a witness, or other similar reason. It is a written notification signed by the proper officer, and is commonly served in person. Many other writs might be added to this list; it has not been intended here to attempt anything like a complete description of the various kinds of writs or orders that may be issued by courts. The aim has been merely to make clear the power of courts, by this means, to enforce the law and their decisions.

EQUITY

In order to understand the growth and development of our legal institutions, it is necessary to know something of the nature of equity, although this type of procedure is used less and less in the settlement of disputes. The term " equity " has two meanings, one professional, the other popular. When lawyers speak of equity they are thinking of that part of the law of England which is derived not from the custom of the realm nor the enactments of Parliament but from the decisions of the old courts of chancery. In this sense, equity may be defined as a system of rules originated by the King's Chancellor and the Court of Chancery to supplement the English common law, which had very early become too rigid. On the other hand, when the man in the street talks of equity, he is thinking of local justice which is not regulated by the law and may even be contrary to it. The popular meaning of equity is that which it originally bore in the Court of Chancery.[15]

History and Development. In early times the administration of the law was not altogether free from abuses of the grossest kind. The king's officers were sometimes corrupt or partial, and for a considerable period the king's courts stood in awe of unscrupulous and powerful nobles. In extreme cases the poor subject had to seek redress of his wrongs by petition to the king, who, in theory, was the ultimate fountain of justice. Originally, these petitions were heard by the sovereign himself; later, however, they were referred to the king's council. The foremost figure in this body was the chancellor. This official was the secretary to the king, head of the king's chaplains, and keeper of the royal seal. In the early days the office was always in the

---

15 Lee, Robert E., *Introduction to the Study of Law* (Mimeographed, 1935). On these points, see Plucknett, *Concise History,* Part III, Chapter 4; Cook, Walter W., *Encyclopaedia of the Social Sciences,* Vol. V, pp. 582–588. The following quotation is from Lee's *Introduction to the Study of Law.*

hands of an ecclesiastic, because of the literary qualifications demanded, In time he became the chief law member of the council as well as the most powerful executive officer of state next to the king. He was learned in the canon and moral law. He has commonly been spoken of as the " keeper of the king's conscience." It was, therefore, an easy development that after the middle of the fourteenth century all " matters of grace " were addressed directly to the chancellor; and in no long time this practice led to the establishment of a new tribunal in England which received the name of Court of Chancery.

By gradual stages there grew up a jurisdiction in chancery to grant relief in situations where the application to particular cases of rigid and general legal rules resulted in hardship or injustice. The rules applied by chancery in the exercise of this jurisdiction became known as " equity," whereas those administered by the previously established courts were designated as " common law." Three circumstances concurred to increase the jurisdiction of the chancery courts; first, the tendency of the common law rules to hardness and rigidity by reason of the deference paid to precedents; secondly, the refusal of the common law to adopt that part of the Roman law which may be called equitable, as distinguished from that which is merely *stricti juris;* and, finally, the desire to increase the dignity and importance of the office of chancellor.

For generations equity consisted of whatever the chancellor thought best in any particular case. No attention was paid to precedent or to principle; even in the time of the Stuarts, nobody thought a knowledge of law necessary for a chancellor. Sir Thomas More was the first professional lawyer chancellor. His successors were sometimes lawyers, sometimes priests, and sometimes laymen. A change, however, was impending. Young practitioners in the chancery had begun to report the court's decisions. As soon as this took place the old practitioners began to cite to the chancellor all the decisions of previous chancellors which favored the decision they desired. When the facts were identical, the chancellor felt bound, as a rule, to follow the decisions of his predecessors. As lawyers became the only chancellors, the practice grew. Soon equity hardened into a set of principles as unalterable by subsequent decision as those of the common law.

Many rights not recognized in the common law were created and enforced in equity. For example, no right existed in the common law by which a defective instrument could be reformed, a fraudulent conveyance set aside, a mistake or accident effectually relieved against, or a contract could be specifically enforced. Thus, equity became an important liberalizing agency in our legal system. Some of the things equity has jurisdiction over are: accident, mistake, fraud, mortgages, trusts, assignments, receiverships, specific performance, and injunctions. These doctrines can be better understood by considering them in connection with the various topics which form the subject matter of a law course.

For centuries law and equity were administered in England by two separate and distinct sets of courts, each applying exclusively its own system of jurisprudence, and following its own system of procedure. This dual system was abolished by the Judicature Act of 1873. By this statute the courts which had sat so many centuries at Westminster Hall were consolidated into one supreme court of which chancery became simply a division, and it was provided in substance that equitable relief should in a proper case be administered concurrently with law in each division and that in case of conflict the principles of equity should prevail over those of the common law.

Another writer, Plucknett, comments as follows on the variety of theories that have been proposed to account for the origins of Chancery jurisdiction; the result of the most recent research, he says, has been to establish an old theory first put forward by Palgrave: [16]

According to this view the Chancellor's jurisdiction was not by virtue of his office; still less had it anything to do with his supposed position of keeper of the King's conscience. At a later date, it is true, Chancery became a court of conscience, with a jurisprudence deliberately based upon this idea, but this was a later development, and will not account for the earliest period of Chancery history. It now seems clear that the Chancellor's position was originally that of a delegate of the Council. Overburdened with work of every description, the Council delegated particular matters to the Chancellor, who of all the officials was the one who was most constantly in attendance. Another advantage of this arrangement was that the Chancellor already had a well organized staff, and for a long time had exercised the power of issuing writs, both judicial and administrative, to all the King's officials, central and local. The Chancellor, therefore, commanded the machinery which sooner or later would have to be set in motion in order to give redress to the petitioners, and so nothing could be simpler than for the Council to transmit the petitions addressed to it to the Chancellor, sometimes (but not always) endorsing them with a brief instruction what to do.

It is obvious that two competing legal systems could not long endure in a well-ordered country. After years of struggle it was finally possible to work out a solution; in one sense, equity lost a great deal, while in another it gained, as it has continued to do down to the present day. It lost in the sense that its identity as a separate judicial system declined from that date on. Where there had been, originally, separate judges for the courts at law and the courts in equity, it became customary to choose judges who would at different times consider cases under both sets of rules. The extent of this development is well stated, so far as this country is concerned, by Professor Lee:

In the United States, courts of equity fall into three distinct classes: (1) In Alabama, Arkansas, Delaware, Mississippi, New Jersey, Tennessee, and Vermont there are still separate courts of common law and of equity with separate rules of procedure. (2) In the Federal courts and in Florida,

---

[16] Palgrave, Sir Francis, *Original Authority of the King's Council* (London, 1834); Baldwin, James F., *The King's Council*, pp. 236–261 (London, 1913). Quotation from Plucknett, *op. cit.*, pp. 138–139.

Illinois, Maine, Maryland, Massachusetts, Michigan, New Hampshire, Oregon, Pennsylvania, Rhode Island, Virginia, and West Virginia the same court administers both common law and equity, but the procedure is kept distinct. (3) In all the states which have not been mentioned, common law and equity are administered by the same court under the same system of procedure. Changes made from time to time in certain jurisdictions from one system of administration to another, and minor departures from the typical systems, render any such classification as this often misleading. Each jurisdiction presents its own peculiar history.[17]

It is evident therefore that separate courts of equity have disappeared from many jurisdictions; on the other hand, the influence of the principles of equity has, in the opinion of competent lawyers, steadily increased, until today they are being applied more and more in the settlement of cases coming before the courts of law.

It thus becomes important for the student of American government to know something of the nature of equity jurisdiction, and some of the more important characteristics which distinguish it from law. Since it was, and is, the primary objective of equity to right a wrong, to achieve substantial justice, it was always said that it was necessary for the parties to an equity proceeding to come into the court " with clean hands." In another form: " He who seeks equity must do equity." It is essential in all legal proceedings that the parties thereto shall tell the truth, but the very nature of equity proceedings makes it essential that they do more than that. In the conduct of equity proceedings there is no jury, since there is no oral argument; all evidence and arguments are submitted to the court in the form of briefs. Since there is no jury, the judge decides the case.

Still another difference between the two systems is to be found in the outcome of the proceedings. Suits at law terminate in judgments, while suits in equity result in decrees which may be positive demands to do or to refrain from doing certain things. Thus in a business relationship in which one of the parties to a contract has failed to do as he agreed, the injured party may in some instances either bring suit for damages, which is an action at law, or he may institute an equity proceeding. In the first instance, the amount of damages requested will represent his estimate of the loss he has suffered through the failure of the defendant to perform under the contract as he agreed. If the suit is successful, he may get the judg-

[17] Lee, *op. cit.* See also 21 *Corpus Juris* 24; Bispham, George T., *Principles of Equity*, p. 27 (Bankers Law Publishing Company, New York, 1926) ; and Emmerglick, Leonard J., " The Legal Adoption of Equitable Principles," *New Jersey Law Review,* January, 1936, pp. 53–63.

ment which states that he is entitled to collect a specified amount. The remedy is uncertain because the defendant may not have the amount specified, or may by some means succeed in evading payment. In the equity proceedings, on the other hand, the injured party may, if successful, secure a court decree calling for specific performance under the terms of the original contract. The violation of such a decree constitutes the offense of contempt of court and is punishable by fine or imprisonment. The selection of the method by which redress will be sought in any given case will depend upon the nature of the case, and upon the advice of the plaintiff's attorney.

CIVIL LAW

Civil law is a term used technically to designate the Roman jurisprudence; in another and more common sense, it is applied to that portion of the great body of municipal law which is enforced by the ordinary civil courts and which governs the great bulk of the relationships of one individual with another. In this sense it is to be distinguished from criminal law on the one hand and military law on the other. It applies to persons and to property. The body of civil law in force in the states today is based upon the heritage of the common law, supplemented by the enactments of the British Parliament prior to 1607, 1776, or some other specified date, and by the enactments of the legislatures of the states in the years subsequent to that time. The percentage of the total volume of law represented by the statutes was, until recently, very small. As the nature of our civilization has continued to change, it has been necessary to modify more and more rules of the common law through the enactment of statutes, which thereafter served as a substitute for the original rules handed down through generations and often through centuries.

The term "civil law" has been used in various ways; generally, it designates all the rules of law governing the members of a given political state. In this sense, it governs the relations of men in civil society and becomes practically synonymous with the concept of law itself. In the Middle Ages the term came to mean to Europeans private law — that is, the law governing the ordinary relations of private individuals. Its origin and basis were fundamentally Roman, but it came to include many other elements, derived from the canon law, Teutonic laws, and feudal laws. The term also has common law as well as statutory phases, but to the common law lawyer it means simply the Romanized system of Continental law in contra-distinction to the system of common law which developed in England. He rarely uses the term " civil law " in the sense of private law.[18]

Public Law and Private Law. A clear distinction must be drawn between public law and private law; this dualistic division is a historical product of a definite state of sociological development. The degree and scope of this technical differentiation, as with other branches of the law, is determined according to the unlimited discretion and the usage of the society concerned. In general, a law which applies to a class of persons, and not to individuals as such, or which, though for the benefit of individuals, includes provisions of general legislation, is a public law. On the other hand, a law for the relief of one or several specified persons, corporations, institutions, et cetera, is known as a private law. It is limited in its application and its benefits, whereas a public law relates to public matters and deals with individuals by classes only. In the past, our legislatures have often passed excessive amounts of private legislation; in more recent times, there has been a tendency to discourage this method of handling such problems, and to substitute therefor statutes of general application.

This important distinction is but one of many that have developed in our legal system. The modern legal orders, as they are called, have become divided, in the course of their historical development, into various legal branches which are determined by the character of their social functions. Constitutional law, administrative law, and criminal and canon law have long been regarded as branches of public law, while civil law and commercial law are regarded as private. Certain other branches, such as labor law and social law, have not been so definitely classified. The law of procedure has come to be regarded as public, as has also international law. Many of these classifications hold only within a given legal system, and even there they may be subject to modification with the change of time and circumstances.[19]

Substantive and Adjective Law. Another important distinction in the field of civil law involves the differences between substantive and adjective law. The former has been defined as including those rules which give recognition to rights and duties, which rules are the very foundation and substance of the law. These are static, im-

[18] Based on Declareuil, J., *Encyclopaedia of the Social Sciences*, Vol. III, pp. 502–508.

[19] Based on Walz, Gustav A., *Encyclopaedia of the Social Sciences*, Vol. XII, pp. 657–659.

mobile, and lifeless until set in motion by generic remedial rules embodied in adjective law. Substantive law includes all statutes of a generic nature, i.e., all except those regulating administrative and court procedure, as well as the greater part of case law — all except those decisions interpreting administrative regulations, codes of procedure, and court rules. Adjective law includes those rules which provide remedies for infringement of rights and failure to perform duties. While there is no clear line of division between the two, the one creates rights and obligations, while the other provides a method of enforcing and protecting them. In other words, adjective law is the law of procedure. Contracts, negotiable instruments, sales, bailments, partnerships, corporations, for example, are subjects dealt with in substantive law. Adjective law defines the nature and powers of judicial tribunals, and prescribes their methods and procedure.

Written and Unwritten Law. Statutes are frequently referred to as the " written law," in contradistinction to the common law, which is called the " unwritten law." In the beginning the decisions of the courts were not reduced to writing; hence they were called unwritten law to distinguish them from the acts of Parliament, which were always set down in writing. In course of time, these decisions were collected and published in book form, but this publication did not make the common law " written law." Being originally unwritten, it continued to be so regarded.[20]

Codification of Law. From time to time there develops in the states a demand for organizing and systematizing the great body of statutory law in effect. As the years pass, one legislative session after another enacts new measures, repeals old ones, and amends many others. The longer the state goes without a codification, the more urgent the need for it becomes; the session laws become more bulky, and it becomes increasingly difficult to follow through, with accuracy, the statutory provisions on any given subject. The work of commercial law publishers is helpful, for whether or not the state undertakes the task, these companies will usually edit and publish a series of volumes containing the annotated statutes of the state. Such series as the Hurd-Smith *Illinois Statutes,* McKinney's and later, Cahill's *Annotated Statutes of New York,* and Purdon's *Annotated Statutes of Pennsylvania* were mentioned in an earlier chapter.

It is preferable, however, that the work be done continuously, or at brief regular intervals, under public authority. The codes privately prepared and privately published may be useful for all prac-

[20] Lee, *op cit.*

tical purposes, but may lack, and may be unable to secure (because of constitutional limitations) , the official sanction which gives them the force of law. For numerous Federal officers and agencies, as well as persons in other states, it is exceedingly inconvenient to be obliged to rely upon the session laws. None the less, the work of official codification in most states proceeds slowly and irregularly. In 1908 New York created a Board of Statutory Consolidation for the revision of its laws, and this work has been continued by the Law Revision Commission at more recent dates. In 1929 California created a Code Commission, which reported in 1930; when the Commission undertook its work, the laws of the state had not been codified since 1872. The act providing for the Commission authorized it to prepare a statutory record showing the status and disposition of all acts or parts of acts adopted up to that time; to codify, consolidate, compile, or revise all statutes in force; to prepare for the express repeal of all statutes earlier which had been repealed by implication, which had been held unconstitutional by the Supreme Court of the state or of the United States, or which would be rendered obsolete by the adoption of the revision proposed by the Commission; to correct errors in form or substance, including such restatement as might best serve clearly and correctly to express the existing provisions of the law; and finally, to prepare a report, embodying therein, among other things, such legislative measures proposed by it as might be calculated to effect the adoption or enactment of the proposed revision.

In order that the reader may have some concrete idea of the scope of the subject matter of the statutory enactments of a typical state, there is included herewith, under twenty-four headings, the classification and scope notes of the code prepared by the California Commission.[21] This material was evidently prepared with care; for illustrative purposes it is superior to a list of the volumes in a set of annotated statutes, because the scope notes state briefly the nature of the subject matter covered by each heading.

CALIFORNIA CODE COMMISSION

CLASSIFICATION AND SCOPE NOTES — 1941

1. AGRICULTURAL CODE

Law relating to the agricultural industry, including the cultivation of the soil, the raising of live stock, and regulating the production, care and sale of agricultural products.

21 California Code Commission, *Report,* 1941, Appendix B (Sacramento, 1941) .

2. BANKING, BUILDING AND LOAN AND INVESTMENTS CODE

Law relating to and regulating the business of receiving money in trust or on deposit, and the business of lending of money generally.

3. BUSINESS AND PROFESSIONS CODE

Law relating to licensing and regulating certain types of business enterprise, including law relating to the adulteration, labeling, branding, care and sale of food and drugs, and regulating the practice of professions and vocations, and providing for the licensing of practitioners thereof.

4. CIVIL CODE

Provisions of substantive law that are commonly contained only in the decisions of the courts in non-code states, and that are not embraced in any of the other titles in this classification. Some examples are Property, Contracts, Trusts, Debtor and Creditor, Commercial Paper, and Sales, Mortgages and Liens, Marriage and Divorce and Domestic Relations.

5. CODE OF CIVIL PROCEDURE

Law relating to the organization and jurisdiction of the courts and the provisions of adjective or procedural law regarding the conduct of civil proceedings therein, other than such subjects as the Probate Code, which are taken care of under other titles.

6. CORPORATIONS, PARTNERSHIPS, AND ASSOCIATIONS CODE

Law relating to the formation, organization, dissolution, powers and duties of private corporations, partnerships and unincorporated associations; the regulation of the sale of corporate securities.

7. ELECTIONS CODE

Law relating to the elective franchise, registration of electors, primary, general and special elections.

8. FISH AND GAME CODE

Law relating to the preservation of fish and game, the division of the state into districts, the regulation of the taking or destruction of fish and game. This would include the provisions of the Penal Code relating to fish and game.

9. GOVERNMENT CODE

Law relating to the organization of the various state departments and the general provisions relating to state officers, and to the organization and government of the local subdivisions of the state, including counties, cities, and towns.

10. HARBORS AND NAVIGATION CODE

Law relating to the maintenance, improvement and regulation of harbors and navigation, including the control and improvement of rivers for navigation purposes.

11. HEALTH AND SAFETY CODE

Law relating to the protection of public health and safety. This title deals primarily with the protection of the public from disease or danger, such as the control of mosquitoes and the regulation as to transporting explosives.

12. INSURANCE CODE

Law relating to all types of insurance and insurance companies, including life, health, accident, fire, marine, property and title insurance.

13. LABOR CODE

Law relating to the relationship existing between employer and employee, regulation of child and female employees, and regulation of industry generally in the interests of the safety and welfare of labor.

14. MILITARY AND VETERANS CODE

Law relating to the organization and administration of the military forces of the state.

15. PUBLIC RESOURCES CODE

Law relating to the preservation and conservation of natural resources publicly or privately owned, such as minerals, oil and gas, and timber, and to the acquisition, establishment or construction and maintenance of state parks, museums, and public monuments.

16. PENAL CODE

Law defining and prescribing punishment for common law crimes and those statutory crimes of a similar nature; criminal proceedings and prisons. Penal offenses that relate specifically to a given subject or title are placed under that title.

17. PROBATE CODE

Law relating to wills, succession, estates of decedents, and guardian and ward.

18. PUBLIC UTILITIES CODE

Law relating to public utilities, including air navigation, aircraft, airmen, and airports, and providing for the regulation thereof.

19. REVENUE AND TAXATION CODE

Law relating to the assessment, levy and collection of state, county and city taxes.

20. SCHOOL CODE

Law relating to the public school system of the state, including the school code, and laws relating to public and private institutions of higher education.

21. WELFARE AND INSTITUTIONS CODE

Law relating to aid by the state in the interest of social welfare, including charities, juvenile delinquency law, and state institutions, including hospitals, homes, sanitariums, and reformatories.

22. STREETS AND HIGHWAYS CODE

Law relating to all streets, roads, highways and bridges, including municipal, county and state projects. This is confined to the establishment, construction and maintenance of said projects, the regulations of the operation of vehicles being allocated to the title " Vehicles."

23. VEHICLES CODE

Law relating to vehicles, including regulation of the use, operation, licensing and transfer thereof.

24. WATER CODE

Law relating to the waters of the state, including flood control, drainage, regulation of the appropriation and use of water by individuals and state agencies, irrigation, and conservation of water generally.

According to modern standards, a code should have three characteristics differentiating it from ordinary legislation: first, completeness in containing the law in force governing the subject of which it treats; second, a logical, scientific, and convenient arrangement; third, a clear and concise phraseology which avoids prolixity on the one hand and ambiguity on the other.[22] Some branches of the law lend themselves to codification more readily than others. Codes of law are extremely valuable for bringing organization and system into the legal structure; at the same time, they are only relatively permanent, nor can they be made more than relatively simple. They do not render resort to the courts unnecessary; yet the fact that too much should not be claimed for them should not be permitted to minimize their importance or their usefulness.

CRIMINAL LAW

Since some state constitutions outlaw prosecution for crimes under the common law, those states have been obliged to enact and others have voluntarily enacted statutory definitions of the principal crimes. With the multiplicity of laws resulting therefrom, they have later been compelled to codify their criminal law. The statutory definitions in general follow those that have come down from the common law. These codes, in addition to defining criminal acts, make provision for the trial of those who are accused of committing the acts prohibited and, so far as possible, insure that the machinery for the conviction and punishment of violators moves swiftly and certainly. A criminal code under which criminals, after having

[22] Lobinger, Charles S., *Encyclopaedia of the Social Sciences*, Vol. III, pp. 611–612.

served their sentences, are more detrimental to society than they were before they were sentenced is in serious need of overhauling. The codes in force in this country are perilously near the point where such a charge may be properly made. The prime consideration in such a code is the protection of society from the wrongful acts of individuals, rather than the reformation of the criminals; yet this latter consideration must ever be an important one.

Definition of Offenses. The various types of offenses that are prohibited in a penal code may be classified in a number of ways. There are those acts which are regarded by common consent as being wrong in and of themselves; these are technically described as *malum in se.* Other acts, not necessarily coming within this grouping, are regarded as being contrary to public policy or otherwise undesirable; these are commonly known as *malum prohibitum.* All the more serious offenses against persons and property come within the first group.

The various types of criminal offenses are classified according to their seriousness as treason, felonies, and misdemeanors. Treason, which is the only crime defined in the Federal Constitution, is declared to consist only in levying war against the United States, or adhering to their enemies, giving them aid and comfort. The same definition appears in the constitutions of many states; the crime is everywhere regarded as a fundamental attack upon the existence of the state itself, and it is for this reason that it is put in a separate category. The death penalty is provided for treason in Michigan; the same is true in other states. The famous case of John Brown at Harper's Ferry, Virginia, is perhaps the only case on record in which the extreme penalty has been inflicted for treason against a state.

A felony at common law has been defined as " any crime which occasioned a forfeiture of lands and goods, and to which might be superadded capital or other punishment." Forfeiture of lands and goods as a punishment for crime has been abolished in both England and the United States, so that the term no longer has its original meaning. " Today the term has no very definite or precise meaning, except in those states where it is defined by statute. Under these statutes, a felony is any crime punishable by death or imprisonment in a state prison. Some thirty odd states have this statutory definition of felony." [23] The crimes of murder, manslaughter, arson, burglary, larceny, and robbery are commonly classified as felonies, while the following were misdemeanors under the English common law:

[23] 16 *Corpus Juris* 55, and Lee, Robert E., *Advanced Business Law*, p. 3 (Birnbaum-Jackson Company, Philadelphia, 1934) .

conspiracy, assault and battery, false imprisonment, common nuisance, forgery and uttering, breach of the peace, unlawful assembly and riot, and libel. All these crimes are subject to severe punishment. In some states some of them have been classified as felonies, and in all states additional offenses have been added to the lists of both felonies and misdemeanors. The legal classification of these offenses is not particularly important, however, since some misdemeanors carry a heavier penalty than some felonies.

From another point of view, the various offenses prohibited by law may be classified as offenses against persons, offenses against property, and offenses against public order. The following classification is a combination of several lists: [24]

CLASSIFICATION OF CRIMINAL OFFENSES

A. OFFENSES AGAINST THE PERSON

1. Assault
2. Duels
3. Felonious assault
4. Homicide
5. Kidnapping
6. Libel
7. Maiming
8. Manslaughter
9. Murder
10. Rape
11. Robbery
12. Suicide
13. Other offenses against the person

B. OFFENSES AGAINST PROPERTY

14. Arson
15. Breaking and entering
16. Burglary
17. Destruction of ships and vessels
18. Destruction of insured property
19. Extortion
20. False personation
21. Forgery
22. Frauds in selling tickets
23. Frauds in documents of title
24. Insolvency of individuals
25. Insolvency of corporations and other frauds of management
26. Larceny, embezzlement
27. Larceny of automobile
28. Malicious mischief
29. Receiving stolen goods
30. Trespass
31. Weights and measures
32. Other offenses against property

C. OFFENSES AGAINST PUBLIC ORDER

33. Perjury
34. Forgery
35. Carrying weapons
36. Sex offenses, except rape
37. Nonsupport
38. Violating drug laws
39. Violating liquor laws
40. Driving while intoxicated
41. Drunkenness
42. Disorderly conduct

[24] Judicial Council of Massachusetts, *Sixth Report*, last page (Public Document No. 144, Boston, 1930), and Commission on the Administration of Justice in New York State, *A Proposal for the Reclassification of Crimes*, p. 17 — Legislative Document (1934) No. 50 (R).

43. Gambling
44. Violating Lord's Day
45. Violating food or health laws
46. Violating fish and game laws
47. Vagrancy

48. Violating traffic or motor vehicle laws
49. Violating municipal ordinances
50. Other offenses against public order

D. OFFENSES AGAINST THE STATE AND ITS ADMINISTRATION

51. Treason
52. Anarchy and seditious utterances
53. Riots, unlawful assemblies and societies
54. Offenses against the flag

55. Offenses against the military establishment
56. Offenses against the electoral franchise
57. Offenses affecting the public officers and official duty

The general nature of most of these offenses is sufficiently well known so that extended discussion of any of them would seem, for the present purpose, to be unnecessary. Murder may be defined as the unlawful killing of a human being with malice aforethought. Since this is unlawful, it must be distinguished from executions ordered by the state. Because murders differ with regard to the degree of premeditation with which they are committed, most jurisdictions have established by law a distinction between first and second degree murder. In those states which still use capital punishment, this is usually the penalty for first degree murder; [25] the penalty for second degree murder is a long term of imprisonment, usually life. Murder must also be distinguished from homicide, which is a more general term applying to any killing of one human being by another. Homicide may be of three kinds: justifiable, when the killing is performed in the exercise of a right or the performance of a duty; excusable, as when done, not as a duty or a right, yet without culpable or criminal intent; and felonious, involving what the law terms malice. The latter may be either manslaughter or murder.

Manslaughter is sometimes defined as unlawful homicide; a distinction is made between voluntary and involuntary types. The former is intentional, committed in a sudden passion caused by adequate provocation, but without malice aforethought; the latter is applied to an unlawful killing, either in negligence or incidentally to the commission of an unlawful act, but without specific malice. The

[25] The Library of Congress checked the session laws of the states early in 1934, and found that capital punishment had been abolished in the following states: Kansas, Maine, Michigan, Minnesota, North Dakota, Rhode Island, South Dakota, and Wisconsin. In certain instances four of these states allow capital punishment: Maine, for murder committed in prison; Michigan, for treason; North Dakota and Rhode Island, for murderous attacks on prison guards.

legal definition of rape is " sexual connection with a woman without her consent." An assault is an apparently violent attempt, or willful offer with force or violence, to do hurt to another; an attempt or offer to beat another, accompanied by a degree of violence, but without touching his person, as by lifting the fist or a cane in a threatening manner, or by striking at him and missing him. If the blow takes effect, it is battery. The distinction and the connection between assault and battery is well stated by one writer in the following words:

Assault is the threat of force or violence to do corporeal hurt to another. Battery is the unlawful touching of the person of another by the aggressor or by some substance put in motion by him. An assault may not result in battery, but every battery necessarily includes an assault. Thus, for example, to shoot or strike at another and to miss him is assault but not battery. To shoot or strike a person is assault and battery.[26]

Of the offenses against property, arson is mentioned first. The definition of this crime, which at common law meant the willful and malicious burning of the dwelling house or outhouse of another, is varied by the statutes of different countries and states. The English law has been considerably modified in the United States; in some states it has been materially enlarged, while in others various degrees of arson have been established with corresponding punishment. Robbery is the felonious and forcible taking of goods or money from the person or presence of another by violence or putting in fear, while, at common law, burglary is the breaking and entering of the dwelling house of another at night with intent to commit a felony therein. Breaking and entering is itself an offense, defined as the removal or setting aside with violence and a felonious intent of any part of a house or of the fastenings provided to secure it. Larceny is the taking and carrying away of the *personal* property of another, with intent to steal; robbery is an aggravated form of larceny, but is treated as a distinctive crime. With the widespread use of the automobile, the offense of larceny of automobile has come to be classified separately. The receiving of stolen goods is an offense if the recipient knows the goods are stolen; the seriousness of this offense varies in the several states.

It is impossible to mention all the crimes against property or to consider any of them at length; a few more may, however, be noted.

[26] Kimball, Everett, *State and Municipal Government in the United States*, pp. 254–255 (Ginn, Boston, 1922).

Malicious mischief is the term applied to wicked or malicious injury done to the property of another, while trespass is a tort or wrong committed against property by force. A tort is a civil wrong or an injury — a wrongful act — not involving a breach of contract, for which an action will lie. In some parts of the country it is a term applied to a form of action for a wrong or an injury. All in all, the offenses against public order are numerous; while many of these would be found in a list compiled for any one of the forty-eight states, there are numerous others which might be found in a few states but not in the rest.

Enforcement of Criminal Law. While the problem of enforcement is an administrative problem, the quality of the enforcement work done affects not only the crime rate but, in time, the provisions of the law itself. The administering of punishment to those convicted of crime has through the years become more humane. In England at one time there were well over one hundred offenses for which the death penalty was inflicted; in the United States in our own time there are not over four types of crime for which this extreme penalty is commonly used — first degree murder, arson, burglary, and rape. For the last named, the death penalty is used chiefly in the Southern states. In Georgia, train robbery is so punished — probably as a result of public indignation at some particular offense. Horse stealing was generally a capital offense in the Western states at one time, and still is in some of them. As a result of the Lindbergh case, kidnaping was made a capital offense in a number of states. Some of the most important crimes in connection with which this punishment is used are not defined at all by statute in many states, the definitions of the common law still being relied upon.

On the other hand, there are now eight states in which capital punishment has been wholly or partially abolished. While not a punishment for a crime, imprisonment for debt was a common occurrence; this penalty, in many of the older states, was abolished nearly a century ago. The development of civilization has brought a gradual shift of emphasis in the administering of punishment from the old *lex talionis,* or law of retaliation, to the desire and effort to assist the offender to readjust himself and return to society as a law-abiding, self-supporting, and self-respecting member of the community. " Dean Pound has told how Sir Edward Coke, in the dawn of the seventeenth century, bewailing the savagery of the criminal law and procedure of his time, made an impassioned plea for a preventive instead of a punitive justice and invoked the blessing of God upon him 'that layeth the first stone of this building.' The first stone is being laid." [27]

It is not meant to imply that this change has become completely effective. There is a more or less constant conflict between those who are anxious to exact of every offender the full measure of punishment permitted under the law, and those who tend to support the more lenient views advocated by modern criminologists and sociologists. After World War I, when there developed the so-called "crime wave," New York answered with its famous Baumes Law, the principle of which was shortly adopted in a number of other states. This was popularly known as the fourth offenders law, and provided that those convicted a fourth time should be thereafter kept in prison. While there were certain elements of reasonableness about such a measure, its rigidity proved to be a serious obstacle to the fair treatment of some prisoners and their dependents. Its effects came to be generally regarded as unfortunate.

The function of the courts should be to determine the innocence or guilt of the accused; recent developments in criminology have made it clear that members of the bench are seldom qualified by training or temperament to impose sentence. This should be done by trained technicians — psychologists, psychiatrists, and criminologists — after careful examination of the convict and study of his case record. The indeterminate sentence is preferred to the fixed sentence previously used. First offenders should be segregated and accorded a different treatment from that used in the case of hardened criminals. All persons under sentence should be under the supervision of persons with adequate technical training; parole should be more widely used in deserving cases, but with a larger staff of parole supervisors, adequate to give careful supervision to all parolees. These are only a few of the more important recommendations of this group; there are many who believe that we have just begun to uncover some of the essential facts in the treatment of prisoners — and there is much justification for such a belief.

Students of criminology now believe that speedy apprehension, arrest, trial, and conviction of guilty persons have a much more important effect as a deterrent upon crime than the severity of the sentence. In the effort to improve the functioning of the machinery for the administration of justice, and thus make speedy convictions

---

[27] Kirchwey, George W., *Encyclopaedia of the Social Sciences*, Vol. IV, p. 578; see also Radin, Max, "Pretense and Reality in Our Criminal Law," *Oregon State Bar Bulletin*, June, 1939, pp. 134–152.

possible, many reforms are now under way in the various states. Among these are the movement to establish state bureaus of criminal identification; the influence of the United States Department of Justice in bringing about cooperation and coordination of the police forces of the nation; the move to establish state departments of justice and improve and expedite judicial procedure.

Criminal Codes. Many states that have not yet reached the point of properly codifying their civil law have adopted penal or criminal codes; the general nature of the contents of such a code may be illustrated by the outline below. Since the whole problem of codification has been discussed at length in connection with civil law, and the fundamental principles governing the subject are the same wherever applied, no further comment or explanation need be given here. The following outline was prepared by the Special Advisory Committee to the Commission on the Administration of Justice in New York State in 1939:

STATE OF NEW YORK —

PROPOSED REVISION OF THE CODE OF CRIMINAL PROCEDURE [28]

I. COMPLAINT, ARREST AND EXAMINATION
   The Complaint; Arrest; Preliminary Examination
II. PROCEEDINGS BEFORE INDICTMENT OR INFORMATION
   Methods of Prosecution; Formation, Powers and Duties of the Grand Jury
III. INDICTMENT, INFORMATION AND BILL OF PARTICULARS
   Finding and Presentation of the Indictment; Indictment, Information and Bill of Particulars; Amendment of Indictment, Information and Bill of Particulars; Method of Arraignment; Setting aside Indictment and Information; Pleas; Removal of the Action before Trial
IV. PROCEEDINGS BEFORE TRIAL
   The Mode of Trial; Challenging the Jury
V. THE TRIAL
   The Trial; Conduct of Jury after Submission; the Verdict
VI. PROCEEDINGS AFTER JUDGMENT
   New Trials; Arrest of Judgment
VII. JUDGMENT, SENTENCE AND EXECUTION
   Judgment and Sentence; Suspension of Pronouncement or Execution of Sentence; Execution
VIII. APPEALS
   Appeals Generally; Certificate of Reasonable Doubt and Stay Pending Appeal; Record of Appeal; Dismissal of Appeal; Argument of Appeal; Order on Appeal
X. GENERAL PROVISIONS
   Process; Evidence; Double Jeopardy

[28] Legislative Document (1939) No. 76.

OTHER TYPES OF LAW

A survey of the various types of law under which the people in our states live must cover not only the older forms of the common law and equity and the present-day distinctions between civil law and criminal law, but also certain miscellaneous forms of more limited application, so far as the states are concerned: international law and treatise; constitutional law, involving the Federal Constitution and the acts of Congress; and finally, martial law. In Chapter I, in a section devoted to the relations of the states with foreign nations, it was pointed out that the former are forbidden by the Federal Constitution to make treaties, and that such relations as they have with foreign powers are incidental and accidental — although they may be troublesome. Since this chapter is confined to the legal system of the states, there seems to be no good reason for going into the subject of international law, even though the activities of the Federal government in that field are a matter of vital concern to every citizen of every state.

Constitutional law is more relevant to the present discussion; yet even here the law of the Federal Constitution belongs primarily to the Federal government — not to the states. Certain aspects of the subject are discussed, however, in subsequent chapters, notably those dealing with constitutional protections and the police power. The constitutions of the states are dealt with at length in an earlier part of the book. With regard to American constitutional law in general, it may be said, as Ernst Freund has done, that it " represents political action through judicial methods, dependent for success upon the ignoring, by common consent, of the political nature of the process." He continues:

. . . To judge the performance of the courts by purely legal standards is to misjudge it. The uncertainty of standards, which is a legal defect, is the salvation of the doctrine of judicial power. How much the exercise of the power has added to the stability of American institutions must be a matter of speculation. It is not even possible to speak of its effect upon the sanctity of vested rights with any assurance. . . . A comparison between American and foreign legislation in this respect would yield no definite results. The American doctrine of freedom of contract does not impress foreigners as a gain to genuine liberty. . . .

It is, on the other hand, a strong tribute to American constitutional law that it has been found possible to conduct government for a century and a half in war as well as in peace without recourse to " acts of state " or to emergency powers to suspend the constitution. While occasionally the judicial nullification of statutes has caused popular resentment, there has been substantial acquiescence in the exercise of the power and there is no disposition to doubt the soundness of the structure of which it is the corner stone.[29]

Martial Law. Martial law may, in emergency situations, become of importance in any state. Although variously defined, martial law is a legal concept by which the Anglo-American civil courts have sought in times of disorder to define the limits of the executive in military control over citizens in domestic territory. It has been said that it is regarded as the substitution of the will of the executive or the military commander for the process of the courts. " Its justification is necessity and its existence is a question of fact, the most usual test of which is to determine whether or not the courts are open." [30] Thus, when disorder or violence occurs in a given state, the proclamation of martial law by the governor does not establish, but only proclaims, the fact of its existence. Such a proclamation means in theory that the disorder is such that no court can remain open. Practically everything that can be done under martial law can also be done by troops, in aid of the civil authorities.

Since the term " martial law " is not used except to describe the suspension of the ordinary protective maxims and the procedure of domestic courts, it is not difficult to make formal distinctions between it and such concepts as " the laws and customs of war " and " military law and military government." The laws and customs of war are the rules of international law, derived from usage and international agreements, while the latter is the law applied to troops in peace as well as in war. Military government is a descriptive term which applies to any form of government by an army, with or without the aid of civil authorities. Theoretically, says Thurman Arnold, it cannot be established over citizens in domestic territory unless a revolt has become sufficiently serious to justify the recognition of the rebels as belligerents, as that term is commonly understood in connection with the laws of war. A system of martial law may be set up in enemy or alien territory, in war, or in pursuance of treaty rights, or for the protection of the lives or property of nationals. Fortunately, the need for such use of the system of martial law seldom arises among the states.

THE NATURE OF THE JUDICIAL PROCESS

Before discussing the organization and procedure of the state courts, it may be well to consider briefly the nature of judicial power

[29] Freund, Ernst, *Encyclopaedia of the Social Sciences*, Vol. IV, p. 254.
[30] Arnold, Thurman W., *Encyclopaedia of the Social Sciences*, Vol. X, pp. 162–166; much of this comment is based on Professor Arnold's article.

and of the judicial process. Judicial power has been defined as that power pertaining to the judicial department in any given case or circumstance, requisite for the attainment of the constitutional objective — justice. This great object is stated in the preambles of the Federal and state constitutions in the phrase " to establish justice " or in some similar form; its realization has been one of man's chief purposes in organized society. The existence of judicial process gives assurance to the individual that he cannot be deprived of life, liberty, or property unless a specific violation of the law is proved against him under regular procedure in open court.

Strange as it may seem, the courts which are responsible for the administration of the judicial process and largely responsible for the achievement of the ends of justice, are without any power except the confidence of the public in their integrity and the strength of public opinion to enforce their judgments:

The court does not possess the purse, neither does it brandish the sword; it is in material strength the weakest of the departments of government. It is utterly dependent for subsistence and brawn upon others. Its only power is the wisdom, if any, of its thought and the logical justice of its words. It may command, but it cannot compel obedience, when resisted by those in charge of armed force. It may seek and commission aids, but it cannot itself pay for the services rendered it. In finality, its judgments are suggestive and its planning is advisory only.[31]

In a brilliant work on the nature of the judicial process the late Justice Cardozo raised some questions which he thought an intelligent layman might like to have answered for him by a member of the bench:

What is it that I do when I decide a case? To what sources of information do I appeal for guidance? In what proportions do I permit them to contribute to the result? In what proportions ought they to contribute? If a precedent is applicable, when do I refuse to follow it? If no precedent is applicable, how do I reach the rule that will make a precedent for the future? If I am seeking logical consistency, the symmetry of the legal structure, how far shall I seek it? At what point shall the quest be halted by some discrepant custom, by some consideration of the social welfare, by my own or the common standards of justice and morals? [32]

Justice Cardozo concludes that the directive force which guides a jurist in providing logical and reasonable answers to these questions and in the determination of his opinions may be derived from a number of sources. This force may, in the first place, be exerted

[31] Riley, Fletcher, " Powers of Courts and Vitalization of Judicial Powers in Oklahoma," *Journal* of the American Judicature Society, June, 1934, pp. 8–13.

[32] Cardozo, Benjamin N., *The Nature of the Judicial Process,* p. 10 (Yale University Press, 1925).

along the line of logical progression, which he refers to as the rule of analogy or the method of philosophy; it may be exerted along the line of historical development, which he calls the method of evolution; along the line of the customs of the community, which he calls the method of tradition; or along the lines of justice, morals, and social welfare, the *mores* of the day, which he refers to as the method of sociology.

By the method of philosophy is meant the method of logical development. It has sometimes been said that a case is only an authority for what it actually decides, and that the law is not always logical. But, says Justice Cardozo, " logical consistency does not cease to be a good because it is not the supreme good," nor is logic to be ignored when experience is silent. " I am not to mar the symmetry of the legal structure by the introduction of inconsistencies and irrelevances and artificial exceptions unless for some sufficient reason, which will commonly be some consideration of history or custom or policy or justice. Lacking such a reason, I must be logical, just as I must be impartial, and upon like grounds. It will not do to decide the same question one way between one set of litigants and the opposite way between another. ' If a group of cases involves the same point, the parties expect the same decision. It would be a gross injustice to decide alternate cases on opposite principles. If a case was decided against me yesterday when I was defendant, I shall look for the same judgment today if I am plaintiff. To decide differently would raise a feeling of resentment and wrong in my breast; it would be an infringement, material and moral, of my rights.' " [33]

With regard to historical development as a directive force, it may be observed that the whole history of the law represents a continuous attempt to adapt existing legal principles to changed situations. At one point Justice Cardozo observes that " for every tendency, one seems to see a counter-tendency; for every rule its antinomy. Nothing is stable. Nothing absolute. All is fluid and changeable. There is an endless ' becoming.' " Elsewhere, he observes, quite in the manner of Justice Holmes, that " the great generalities of the Constitution have a content and a significance that vary from age to age."

If philosophy and history do not serve to fix the direction of a principle, custom may step in, although, " undoubtedly the creative energy of custom in the development of common law is less today than it was in bygone times. Even in bygone times its energy was

[33] *Ibid.*, pp. 32–34; quotation from Holmes, Oliver Wendell, *The Common Law*, p. 1 (Little, Brown, Boston, 1881).

very likely exaggerated by Blackstone and his followers. ' Today we recognize,' in the words of Pound,[34] 'that the custom is a custom of judicial decision, not of popular action.' It is ' doubtful,' says Gray, ' whether at all stages of legal history, rules laid down by judges have not generated custom, rather than custom generated the rules.' In these days, at all events, we look to custom, not so much for the creation of new rules, but for the tests and standards that are to determine how established rules shall be applied. When custom seeks to do more than this, there is a growing tendency in the law to leave development to legislation." [35]

" From history and philosophy and custom, we pass, therefore, to the force which in our day and generation is becoming the greatest of them all, the power of social justice which finds its outlet and expression in the method of sociology. The final cause of law is the welfare of society. The rule that misses its aim cannot permanently justify its existence. ' Ethical considerations can no more be excluded from the administration of justice which is the end and purpose of all civil laws than one can exclude the vital air from his room and live.' [36] Logic and custom and history have their place. We will shape the law to conform to them when we may; but only within bounds. The end which the law serves will dominate them all. . . . I mean that when they [the judges] are called upon to say how far existing rules are to be extended or restricted, they must let the welfare of society fix the path, its direction and its distance." [37]

Justice Cardozo considers at length such questions as judge-made law and the proper influence and weight of precedent in the determination of judicial opinions. With regard to the first of these questions much has been said and written. It has apparently been assumed by some that there was something inherently improper or wrong in what these critics delight in denouncing as judge-made law. Mr. Cardozo shows clearly that it is an inevitable part of the whole system of the adjudication of cases and the interpretation of laws by judicial officers. If the facts of the case are clear, and the provisions of the constitution or of the statutes specific, the task of the judge is easy. Often this is not the case. The judge is then obliged to consider

---

[34] Pound, Roscoe, " Common Law and Legislation," *Harvard Law Review*, April, 1908, pp. 383–406.
[35] Cardozo, *op. cit.*, pp. 59–60.
[36] Dillon, John F., *Laws and Jurisprudence of England and America*, p. 18 (Little, Brown, Boston, 1894) , quoted by Pound, Roscoe, in a note in *Harvard Law Review*, May, 1914, pp. 731–735.
[37] Cardozo, *op. cit.*, pp. 65–67.

the purpose and intent of the legislature, so far as it is ascertainable from the statute, and to guide himself accordingly. In such case, he is faced with the possibility of selecting one among two or more possible alternatives. No matter which he selects, he must of necessity " make law." His opinion can have no other effect than to guide or direct the current of legal development. Many of the cases with which a jurist is confronted revolve around points with regard to which the lawmaking body has made no provision, and which very often the lawmaking body did not even consider when the act was passed. In these cases his power as a lawmaker is much greater.

Likewise a great deal has been written on the doctrine of *stare decisis*, which means the decision of present cases on the basis of past precedents. Whether one likes it or not, this doctrine is " the every-day working rule " of the law in the English-speaking countries. Against the use of this principle, it is argued that it exerts an unduly conservative influence upon the development of the law, that it looks backward to see what has been rather than ahead to see what ought to be, and that consequently our current difficulties are often resolved upon the basis of decisions which are irrelevant to the facts of the current situation. In defense of the principle, it may be noted that it is first of all a time-saving and a labor-saving factor in a busy world. We cannot afford to ignore or disregard the experience of the race, and even if we could, the dockets of our courts would be far more crowded than they have ever been if we were to require our judges to enter into exhaustive research with regard to the minute details of every case that comes before them. This doctrine is not only a time-saving device but it is an important factor in the development of a reasonable continuity in the rules and principles of the law. The influence of this doctrine is not as strong in the United States as in England, and it is much weaker in the United States today than it was a few decades ago. Justice Cardozo takes the very reasonable attitude, characteristic of the more liberal jurists, that the doctrine of *stare decisis* is a guide which may properly be followed in the absence of new factors or conditions which so change the situation as to make the following of precedent clearly indefensible. The adherence of American courts to this doctrine does not mean, therefore, that decisions once made may not be reversed; they may be, and they are.[88]

---

[88] See also Shartel, Burke, " *Stare Decisis* — A practical View," *Journal* of the American Judicature Society, June, 1933, pp. 6–7; Kocourek, Albert, and Koven, Harold, " Renovation of the Common Law through *Stare Decisis*," *Illinois Law Review*, April, 1935, pp. 971–999; Pound, Roscoe, " What of *Stare Decisis?* " *Fordham Law Review*, January, 1941, pp. 1–13.

THE DOCTRINE OF JUDICIAL REVIEW

The doctrine of judicial review has been one of the most controversial in the whole field of American government. The courts have been attacked on the one hand for having " usurped " the power to nullify the action of an equal and coordinate branch of the government, and have been praised on the other as having some peculiar qualifications for determining what is right and what is wrong. Neither claim is justified, and the attempt to make a moral issue out of a clear question of governmental policy and procedure is unfortunate.

In every organization, public or private, there has to be someone in authority — some one person or some group of persons whose decision is final and from whom there is no immediate appeal. In government there are three possible agencies to which this power of final determination may be entrusted. In the monarchies of old and in the recent dictatorships this power rested with the executive — a solution of the problem which has little appeal in a democratic society. In a parliamentary government, such as that of Great Britain, it is vested in the legislature. There may be practical limits to the power of the British Parliament, but there are no legal limits. This solution has worked in a satisfactory manner in England, but governmental institutions in America did not happen to develop along this line. The third possibility is, obviously, to entrust the power to the courts, and this solution, as will presently be indicated, has its roots deep in the history and practice of American government.

Early Origins of Judicial Review. The idea of judicial review did not suddenly spring into existence in the early nineteenth century, when John Marshall handed down his famous opinion in Marbury v. Madison. This was, in fact, a crystallization of long years of practice, a strikingly clear statement of ideas long familiar and apparently generally accepted by the people in the colonies. If one refrains from citing some of the very early cases as precedents (on the ground, as Professor Corwin points out, that they were unknown to those who were responsible for the adoption of judicial review), it still appears " that the courts of the colonies, reasoning by analogy from the powers of the Privy Council, believed that in the usual and necessary procedure when cases were brought before them involving acts alleged to be beyond the provisions of their charters and laws they might refuse to give effect to such acts. Precedents which substantiate this belief are indeed rare, but the few recorded show unmistakably the notion that colonial courts did not hesitate to refuse to give effect to an order of the King or to resist an act of Parliament deemed contrary to their rights as English subjects." [39]

Although some of the cases date back more than a century earlier, as for instance, Frost v. Leighton in the Superior Court of Judicature of Massachusetts in 1639, their number increased rapidly in the latter part of the eighteenth century. The first *recorded* case appears to be Holmes v. Walton, decided in 1780 by the Supreme Court of New Jersey. Here the Court assumed the role of interpreting and enforcing upon members of the legislature the terms prescribed in their oath of office, and asserted the right to determine what constituted trial by jury according to the terms of the constitution. Some writers have ascribed to this decision great influence upon the Federal Convention; at any rate, three members of the New Jersey delegation were prominently connected with the case and were favorable to judicial control. A decade and a half later, in 1795, as many years after the Federal Convention as Holmes v. Walton preceded it, Justice Paterson in the Federal Circuit Court for the Pennsylvania district wrote these significant words:

I take it to be a clear position that if a legislative act impugns a constitutional principle, the former must give way, and be rejected on the score of repugnance. I hold it to be a position equally clear and sound, that, in such case, it will be the duty of the court to adhere to the Constitution, and to declare the act null and void. The Constitution is the basis of legislative authority; it lies at the foundation of all law, and is a rule and commission by which both legislator and judges are to proceed. It is an important principle, which, in the discussion of questions of the present kind, ought never to be lost sight of, that the judiciary in this country is not a subordinate, but a coordinate branch of the government.[40]

By 1803, the date of the Marbury case, the following states had either been definitely committed to the doctrine of judicial review by judicial decision or practically so by judicial dicta: North Carolina, 1787; New Hampshire, 1791; South Carolina, 1792; Virginia, 1788,

[39] Haines, Charles G., *The American Doctrine of Judicial Supremacy*, Revised Edition, p. 67 (University of California Press, 1932), and Corwin, Edward S., *The Establishment of Judicial Review* (Princeton University Press, 1930).

[40] Vanhorne's Lessee v. Dorrance, 2 Dallas 310. Other significant statements of similar import: Caton v. Commonwealth of Virginia, 1782; Wilson, James, in *Works*, Vol. I, pp. 415–417 (Ed., Andrews, James D.); Hamilton, Alexander, in *Federalist* No. LXXVII. Among the more useful titles are: Bizzell, William B., *Judicial Interpretation of Political Theory* (Putnam's, New York, 1914); Corwin, Edward S., *The Doctrine of Judicial Review* (Princeton University Press, 1914); McLaughlin, Andrew C., *The Courts, The Constitution, and Parties* (University of Chicago Press, 1912); McLaughlin, Andrew C., and others, Eds., *Source Problems in United States History* (Harper, New York, 1918).

1793; Pennsylvania, 1793, 1799; New Jersey, 1796; Kentucky, 1801; Maryland, 1802. The Kentucky Constitution of 1792, for instance, provided: " All laws contrary . . . to this Constitution shall be void." [41]

Present Significance. So, through decade after decade, the idea of judicial review grew and developed. The power was seldom specifically conferred upon the courts; it grew out of peculiar American concepts of a written constitution, and while not without its critics, was exercised by the courts by common consent. It was not " usurped " by the courts; it was not necessary for them to " usurp " power the right to the exercise of which was generally conceded. This historical record is clear.

The question of the wisdom of the policy is quite another matter. All power conferred on governmental officers and agencies is subject to possible abuse; the power of judicial review is no exception. On

CLASSIFICATION OF UNCONSTITUTIONAL STATUTES IN ILLINOIS
AND NEW YORK

Nature of Subject Matter	*Illinois* *1870–1941*	*New York* *1914–1937*
Constitutional Protections	45	26
Under Federal Constitution	..	7
State and Federal Due Process	..	13
Bill of Rights	45	..
Suffrage; Indictment and Trial by Jury	..	6
Distribution of Powers	4	..
Civil Service	..	7
Legislative Department	48	19
Legislative Power Vested in Legislature	5	8
Senatorial Apportionment	1	..
General Rules for Legislature	1	..
Style and Passage of Laws	12	..
Public Moneys and Appropriations	5	..
Special Legislation	24	11
Judicial Department	9	5
Education	2	..
Revenue Article	31	14
Uniformity, Exemptions, Further Taxation	12	..
Release from Taxation Forbidden	1	..
Local Improvements and Taxation	17	14
Limitation of Municipal Indebtedness	1	..
Miscellaneous	5	5
Totals	144	76

[41] Article XII; list from Corwin, *The Doctrine of Judicial Review,* p. 75.

occasion it has been abused, but it is normally exercised with sufficient moderation and restraint to avoid serious popular criticism. Two interesting studies of the use of the power in Illinois and New York have recently been made.[42] In Illinois, 144 statutes were declared unconstitutional in seventy-one years, while in New York, the number was seventy-six in a period of twenty-three years. In this state, in addition, the court decided thirteen cases in which the constitutionality of certain statutes was discussed but in which there were no direct rulings on validity. The lower courts decided twenty-one cases, which were not appealed to the Court of Appeals, in which laws were held to violate constitutional restraints, and the attorney general wrote seven opinions in which he ruled that legislative enactments were invalid. In this period the Court of Appeals ruled on the validity of approximately 232 statutes, holding that no provisions of the constitution were violated. Thus three statutes were upheld by the highest court for every one that was declared unconstitutional. The seventy-six decisions in New York and the 144 in Illinois were grouped in eight categories, as indicated in the accompanying table.

SELECTED REFERENCES

American Law Schools Association, *Select Essays in Anglo-American Legal History,* 3 vols. (Boston, 1907–1909).

Aumann, Frederick R., *The Changing American Legal System* (Ohio State University Press, 1940).

Austin, John, *Lectures on Jurisprudence* (Murray, London, 1913).

Bacon, Charles, and Morse, F. S., *The Reasonableness of the Law* (Putnam, New York, 1924).

Blackstone, William, *Commentaries on the Laws of England,* 3 vols., edited by William Draper Lewis (Rees, Welsh, Philadelphia, 1898).

Bodenheimer, Edgar, *Jurisprudence* (McGraw-Hill, New York, 1940).

Bouvier's Law Dictionary, Baldwin Century Edition (Banks Law Publishing Company, New York, 1926).

Bradway, John S., Ed., "Progress in the Law," *Annals,* March, 1928.

Bryce, James, *Studies in History and Jurisprudence* (Oxford University Press, New York, 1901).

Buckland, W. W., and McNair, Arnold D., *Roman Law and Common Law* (Macmillan, New York, 1936).

Cairns, Huntington, *Law and the Social Sciences* (Harcourt, Brace, New York, 1935).

——, *The Theory of Legal Science* (Univeristy of North Carolina Press, 1941).

[42] New York State Constitutional Convention Committee, *Problems Relating to Legislative Organization and Powers,* Chapter 5, " Judicial Restraint on Legislation, the Statistics, 1914–1937 " (Albany, 1930) ; and Illinois Legislative Council, *Problems of Constitutional Revision in Illinois,* p. 31 (Springfield, 1941).

Cardozo, Benjamin N., *The Nature of the Judicial Process* (Yale University Press, 1925).

——, *The Growth of the Law* (Yale University Press, 1924).

Cheatham, Elliott E., and others, *Cases and Materials on Conflict of Laws,* Second Edition (Foundation Press, Chicago, 1941).

Cohen, Morris R., *Law and the Social Order* (Harcourt, Brace, New York, 1933).

Coke, Sir Edward, *Institutes of the Laws of England,* 3 vols. (Brooke, Bell Yard, London, 1797).

Cook, Walter W., *The Logical and Legal Basis of the Conflict of Laws* (Harvard University Press, 1942).

Corwin, Edward S., *The Doctrine of Judicial Review* (Princeton University Press, 1914).

Dicey, Albert V., *Law and Opinion in England* (Macmillan, London, 1905).

Dillon, John F., *Laws and Jurisprudence of England and America* (Little, Brown, Boston, 1894).

Duguit, Leon, *Law in the Modern State* (Huebsch, New York, 1919).

Field, Oliver P., *Judicial Review of Legislation in Ten Selected States* (Indiana University, Bureau of Government Research, 1943).

Frank, Jerome, *If Men Were Angels* (Harper, New York, 1942).

——, *Law and the Modern Mind* (Brentano, New York, 1931).

Goodhart, Arthur L., *Essays in Jurisprudence and the Common Law* (Macmillan, New York, 1931).

Goodnow, Frank J., *Comparative Administrative Law* (Putnam, New York, 1903).

——, *Principles of Administrative Law in the United States* (Putnam, New York, 1905).

Goodrich, Herbert F., *Handbook of the Conflict of Laws,* Second Edition (West Publishing Company, St. Paul, 1938).

Gray, John C., *The Nature and Sources of the Law,* Second Edition (Macmillan, New York, 1927).

Guthrie, William D., *Magna Charta and Other Addresses* (Columbia University Press, 1916).

Hadley, Morris, *The Citizen and the 'Law* (Farrar and Rinehart, New York, 1942).

Haines, Charles G., *The American Doctrine of Judicial Supremacy,* Revised Edition (University of California Press, 1932).

——, *The Revival of Natural Law Concepts* (Harvard University Press, 1930).

Hall, Jerome, Ed., *Readings in Jurisprudence* (Bobbs-Merrill, Indianapolis, 1938).

Hart, James, *An Introduction to Administrative Law* (Crofts, New York, 1940).

Hexner, Erwin, *Studies in Legal Terminology* (University of North Carolina Press, 1941).

Holdsworth, William S., *A History of English Law,* Third Edition, 9 vols. (Methuen, London, 1921).

——, *Some Lessons from Our Legal History* (Macmillan, New York, 1928).

——, *Sources and Literature of English Law* (Clarendon Press, Oxford, 1925).

Holdsworth, William S., *The Historians of Anglo-American Law* (Columbia University Press, 1928).

Holland, Thomas E., *The Elements of Jurisprudence,* Thirteenth Edition (Clarendon Press, Oxford, 1928).

Holmes, Oliver Wendell, *The Common Law* (Little, Brown, Boston, 1881).

——, *Collected Legal Papers* (Harcourt, Brace, New York, 1921).

Jenks, Edward, *A Short History of English Law from the Earliest Times to the End of 1911,* Second Edition (Little, Brown, Boston, 1920).

Kenny, Courtney S., *Outlines of Criminal Law* (Macmillan, New York, 1936).

Kohler, Joseph, *Philosophy of Law* (Boston Book Company, Boston, 1914).

Lee, Guy C., *Historical Jurisprudence* (Macmillan, New York, 1900).

Lunt, Dudley C., *The Road to the Law* (McGraw-Hill, New York, 1937).

Lyon, Hastings, and Block, Herman, *Edward Coke; Oracle of the Law* (Houghton Mifflin, Boston, 1929).

Maine, Sir Henry S., *Ancient Law,* Third American Edition (Holt, New York, 1883).

——, *Dissertations on Early Law and Custom* (Murray, London, 1883).

Maitland, Frederic W., *Equity and the Forms of Action at Common Law,* edited by A. H. Chaytor (Cambridge University Press, London, 1909).

——, *Equity, A Course of Lectures,* edited by A. H. Chaytor and W. J. Whittaker (Macmillan, New York, 1936).

——, *Selected Essays,* edited by H. D. Hazeltine, and others (Macmillan, New York, 1936).

——, *The Forms of Action at Common Law, A Course of Lectures,* edited by A. H. Chaytor and W. J. Whittaker (Macmillan, New York, 1936).

——, and Montague, F. C., *A Sketch of English Legal History* (Putnam, New York, 1915).

McLaughlin, Andrew C., *The Courts, the Constitution and Parties* (University of Chicago Press, 1912).

——, and others, Eds., *Source Problems in United States History* (Harper, New York, 1918).

New York University School of Law, *Law; A Century of Progress, 1835–1935,* 3 vols. (New York University Press, 1937).

Plucknett, Theodore F. T., *A Concise History of the Common Law* (Lawyers Coöperative Publishing Company, Rochester, 1929).

Pollock, Frederick, *A First Book of Jurisprudence* (Macmillan, London, 1918).

——, *Essays in Jurisprudence and Ethics* (Macmillan, London, 1882).

——, *The Expansion of the Common Law* (Little, Brown, Boston, 1904).

——, and Maitland, Frederic W., *The History of English Law up to Edward I,* Second Edition, 2 vols. (Cambridge University Press, London, 1908).

Pound, Roscoe, *An Introduction to the Philosophy of Law* (Yale University Press, 1925).

——, *Interpretations of Legal History* (Cambridge University Press, London, 1923).

——, *Social Control Through Law* (Yale University Press, 1942).

Pound, Roscoe, *The Formative Era of American Law* (Little, Brown, Boston, 1938).

———, *The Spirit of the Common Law* (Marshall Jones, Boston, 1921).

———, and Plucknett, Theodore F. T., *Readings on the History and System of the Common Law* (Lawyers Coöperative Publishing Company, Rochester, 1927).

Radin, Max, *Law as Logic and Experience* (Yale University Press, 1940).

———, *Roman Law* (West Publishing Company, St. Paul, 1927).

Robson, William A., *Civilization and the Growth of Law* (Macmillan, New York, 1935).

Schramm, Gustav L., *Our Legal Heritage* (Legal Aid Society, Pittsburgh, 1929).

Schiller, A. Arthur, *Military Law and Defense Legislation, A Source of Military Law* (West Publishing Company, St. Paul, 1942).

Seagle, William, *The Quest for Law* (Knopf, New York, 1941).

Simpson, Sidney P., *Fifty Years of American Equity* (Harvard Law Review Association, 1940).

Stone, Harlan F., *The Common Law in the United States* (Harvard Law Review Association, 1936).

Timasheff, N. S., *Introduction to the Sociology of Law* (Harvard Committee on Research in the Social Sciences, 1939).

Vale, Ruby R., *Some Legal Foundations of Society,* 3 vols. (Taylor, San Francisco, 1941).

Vinogradoff, Paul, *Common Sense in Law* (Holt, New York, 1914).

———, *Historical Jurisprudence,* 2 vols. (London, 1922).

———, Ed., *Oxford Studies in Social and Legal History* (Clarendon Press, Oxford, 1909–1924).

von Moschzisker, Robert, *Stare Decisis, Res Judicata and Other Selected Papers* (C. M. Dixon, Philadelphia, 1929).

Wigmore, John H., *A Panorama of the World's Legal Systems,* 3 vols. (West Publishing Company, St. Paul, 1928).

———, *Evidence in Trials at Common Law,* Second Edition, 5 vols. (Little, Brown, Boston, 1923).

Winfield, Percy H., *The Chief Sources of English Legal History* (Harvard University Press, 1925).

Zane, John M., *Story of Law* (Ives, Washburn, London, 1927).

———

American Judicature Society, *Journal* (Ann Arbor, bimonthly).

Aronson, Moses J., "Roscoe Pound and the Resurgence of Juristic Idealism," *Journal of Social Philosophy,* October, 1940, pp. 47–83.

Eisenhart, Earl E., Jr., "Federal Decisional Law Independent of State Common Law Since Erie Railroad Company v. Tompkins," *George Washington Law Review,* February, 1941, pp. 465–473.

Field, Oliver P., "Unconstitutional Legislation in Minnesota," *American Political Science Review,* October, 1941, pp. 898–915.

Hammond, Robert S., "Specific Performance — Service by Publication," *Kentucky Law Journal,* January, 1943, pp. 174–179.

Hexner, Erwin, "The Timeless Concept of Law," *Journal of Politics,* February, 1943, pp. 48–64.

Kirchberger, Hans, " The Significance of Roman Law for the Americas and Its Importance in Inter-American Relations," *Wisconsin Law Review,* July, 1944, pp. 249–273.

Llewellyn, Karl N., " The American Common Law Tradition and Democracy," *Journal of Legal and Political Sociology,* October, 1942.

McIlwain, Charles H., " The English Common Law, Barrier Against Absolutism," *American Historical Review,* October, 1943, pp. 23–31.

Neilson, Nellie, " The Early Pattern of the Common Law," *American Historical Review,* January, 1944, pp. 199–212.

Page, William H., " Statutes as Common Law Principles," *Wisconsin Law Review,* July, 1944, pp. 175–212.

Philosophical Library, *Journal of Legal and Political Sociology* (New York, monthly).

Pound, Roscoe, " What of *Stare Decisis?* " *Fordham Law Review,* January, 1941, pp. 1–13.

Reaugh, Daniel M., " Presumptions and the Burden of Proof," *Illinois Law Review of Northwestern University,* March, 1942, pp. 703–726.

Schiller, A. Arthur, " Roman Interpretatio and Anglo-American Interpretation and Construction," *Virginia Law Review,* April, 1941, pp. 733–768.

Tönnies, Ferdinand, " The Concept and Law of Human Progress," trans. by Arndt, Karl J., and Folse, C. L., *Social Forces,* October, 1940, pp. 23–29.

Wormuth, Francis D., " The Dilemma of Jurisprudence," *American Political Science Review,* February, 1941, pp. 44–52.

CHAPTER XVI

State Courts: Organization and Jurisdiction

IT has long been regarded as one of the most important functions of government to adjudicate controversies between individuals, between individuals and officers or agencies of the government, and cases involving criminal prosecution. This function is performed by the judiciary, which is composed of various types of courts. A court may be defined as a tribunal established by the state for the administration of justice according to law. For the student of American government, the situation is complicated by the fact that there are two separate and distinct judicial systems, one for the Federal government and one for the state, exercising simultaneously jurisdiction over the same persons and within the same territory. Because the system by which the powers of government are allocated between the Federal government and the states has proved to be fairly successful, these two judicial systems are able to operate without any very serious conflicts of jurisdiction.

The state courts were organized and in operation before the Federal Constitution was framed and the Federal government established. When the Constitutional Convention met in Philadelphia in 1787, there was much discussion as to what should be done about the judiciary. The possibility of abandoning the state courts in favor of a Federal system was not even considered. There was, in fact, doubt as to whether a Federal system was needed, but this was finally resolved, for a number of reasons, in favor of the establishment of Federal courts. It was thought that they would be necessary in order to secure a uniform interpretation of the Federal Constitution and Federal laws. Again, it was feared that without such a system the various state courts would do what in practice the Federal courts have done; namely, interpret the Constitution and the laws in their own favor. If the state courts had been permitted to do this, the powers of the Federal government would have been greatly curtailed; as it is, it has been the powers of the states that have been limited in favor of the Federal government. Finally, there was the question of diverse citizenship. Where controversies arose between citizens of different states, it was feared that neither of them would want to leave the determination of the case to the courts of the state in which his opponent lived. In order to meet this situation, it was decided that a separate system of courts, organized on a national basis and impartial so far as the states were concerned, would be needed.

HISTORICAL DEVELOPMENT OF THE STATE COURTS

It is well known that the law and legal system of the states had their origin in the legal system of England. Because of the supervision of the colonies by the English authorities, colonial law was kept in line with English law, at least so far as fundamental principles were concerned. Professor Clarence N. Callender points out that the evolution of the colonial judiciary proceeded along similar lines:

. . . The charters prescribed the general character of court organization and, subsequently, acts of Parliament, royal decrees, or acts of the provincial legislatures, dominated by English governors or councils of state, established the courts themselves. In England the highest court of appeals was the House of Lords; in America for a long time the English precedent was followed, and the colonial legislatures exercised the appellate jurisdiction. In many instances similar names were used to designate the courts. The justice of the peace in America was in many respects the counterpart of the justice of the peace in England. The grand and petit juries, ancient institutions in English judicial procedure, became integral parts of the legal system in America. The system of equity jurisprudence was likewise derived from the same source. . . .

The intervention of the Revolution brought into existence the American states, and with them came many changes in the governmental organization, including some important modifications in the court system. In the first place, the appellate jurisdiction of the Privy Council disappeared, with the result that the provincial legislatures became the courts of last resort. This, however, was changed when the state constitutions were adopted. In them the theory of the separation of governmental powers between the executive, legislative, and judicial branches was introduced. Supreme courts and courts of errors and appeals supplanted the legislatures as the highest appellate bodies in all types of litigation except in certain matters of a semipolitical character, such as legislative election contests, impeachment trials, and the like. In some instances the lower courts were established by constitutional provision; in others, the authority to establish inferior courts was delegated to the legislatures. The colonial judiciary provided the framework for the new state system. Many old courts were reëstablished, with their jurisdictions substantially the same as before. The change from the old to the new order produced few changes in the main body of the substantive law. The common law of England became in general the common law in each of the states and so, in a measure, it continues to be today.

A century and a half of development has produced many changes in American institutions, but it is still remarkable how much there is in the field of law and in the organization and procedure of the courts that is similar in most essential respects to that of the English system. . . .[1]

Another student of the American judiciary notes that while the French influence was strong during the formative period, it had relatively little effect upon the courts. In a discussion of English origins and early development, he finds that judges were to proceed according to established rules so far as such rules might exist; that they were to proceed in analogy to established rules as to points which no established rule might cover; that they were to look to the common law and political institutions of England to determine what rules were established as to points not covered by local usage or legislation; that local usage or legislation might within certain limits depart from the common law and even from the political institutions of England, but that there were limits to such a departure, as it might be subject to review by a higher political or judicial authority.[2]

In 1932 an interesting study was made of the development of the judicial system of Ohio from 1787 to 1932. The history of this system is divided into twelve periods. Although it may have been subjected to a larger number of important changes than the systems in some of the other states, it may be taken as typical of what, in substance, happened in many other jurisdictions.[3] The Northwest Ordinance of 1787 provided for a simple government, consisting of a governor, a secretary, and three judges, all appointed by Congress. These three judges were to constitute the General Court, with general common law jurisdiction, both civil and criminal; later statutes provided for courts of common pleas, general quarter sessions of the peace (criminal only), probate courts, and justices of the peace. In 1795 the judges of the General Court were to act as judges in a newly established Circuit Court, and an Orphans Court was added to the

[1] Callender, Clarence N., *American Courts: Their Organization and Procedure*, pp. 18–19 (McGraw-Hill, New York, 1927). See also Williams, Nathan B., "Independent Judiciary Born in Colonial Virginia," *Journal* of the American Judicature Society, December, 1940, pp. 124–127.

[2] Baldwin, Simeon E., *The American Judiciary*, pp. 16–17 (Century, New York, 1920).

[3] Amer, Francis J., *The Development of the Judicial System of Ohio from 1787 to 1932* (Johns Hopkins Press, 1932).

established Circuit Court, and an Orphans Court was added to the system. Under the first state constitution, adopted in 1803 when the state was admitted, the system was reorganized and simplified, with a Supreme Court, a Court of Common Pleas, and the Justices of the Peace. The County Commissioners might decide highway questions, but appeals from their decisions lay to the Court of Common Pleas and the Supreme Court.

This organization continued until 1810; from 1810 to 1838 a Superior Court was added to the system for Cincinnati, concurrent with the Common Pleas in Hamilton County in all civil cases; the size of the Supreme Court was increased, and provision was made for it to sit in banc and on circuit. By 1848 a Commercial Court of Cincinnati had been established, concurrent with the Common Pleas in Hamilton County in all contract and equity cases. Thus one sees how gradually the system of specialized courts developed. In 1850 a constitutional convention was held, as a result of which, in 1852, the entire court system was reorganized, with a Supreme Court, District Courts, and Common Pleas. A separate Criminal Court was set up for Hamilton County, and provison was made for Police Courts in first-class cities, Mayors' Courts in villages and second-class cities, and Probate Courts and Justices of the Peace as before. By 1860 the Superior Court had been restored, with jurisdiction the same as Common Pleas except in certain special types of cases. The system of appellate courts that had been set up by the Constitution of 1851 had not been in operation for many years before it became apparent that it was inadequate for the needs of the state. The District Courts, composed of one Supreme Court judge and the several Common Pleas judges of the district, were the key to the whole system, and it was in the failure of the District Court that difficulty arose. In the period from 1860 to 1885 the effort was made to correct these defects.

In 1906 the judicial system was substantially the same as in 1885, with the exception of a few changes in the Supreme Court and the addition of Insolvency and Juvenile Courts. In 1913 the judicial article of the constitution was revised by amendment, defining for the first time in this state, in self-executing provisions in the constitution, the entire original jurisdiction and almost the entire appellate jurisdiction of the Supreme Court and the Court of Appeals. The framework of the judicial structure itself was changed but little; this continued to be true in 1932, in which year the judicial system of the state was essentially the same as in 1913.

STATE COURT ORGANIZATION

Courts may be classified in many ways: from the point of view of their fundamental character (administrative or judicial) ; of the type of law which they enforce (law or equity, civil or criminal) ; or of the geographical area within which they have jurisdiction (as for instance, county courts) . These attempts at classification are not mutually exclusive. There is a judiciary article in each of the state constitutions describing in more of less detail the structure of the court system for the state.[4] In spite of wide variation in the number of courts and in the nomenclature applied to them, there is none the less a skeleton organization to which all the state court systems in a general way conform. This organization is suggested by the diagram on the following page, which will be used as the basis for discussion of certain important features of the judicial system of the states. The diagram attempts to show the successive types of courts through which appeals may be taken. The discussion begins with the lower courts, because it is in them that the proceedings in the great majority of cases are instituted and finally disposed of. Thus the quality of justice which the majority of the people in a given state receive is determined by the quality of justice dispensed by the lower courts. If these courts do their work badly, the people may become dissatisfied and lose faith in the judiciary, no matter how high the quality of the work performed by the higher courts. It is more important, so far as a majority of the people are concerned, that the lower courts be run honestly and efficiently than that the higher courts be so run. It is unlikely, however, that the lower courts will be better run than the higher ones in any state, for experience shows that it is a far more difficult job to provide an effective administration of justice in the smaller local units than it is to provide an honest and efficient service in the appellate courts.

In Rural Areas — the Justice of the Peace. The office of justice of the peace as it still exists in the United States can be traced to origins developing in medieval England when transportation was slow, difficult, and expensive. It was also a part of the system of government by landed families. When the office was introduced in America, the positions were usually filled by appointment, but in the Middle

---

[4] The power of the states to establish their courts and to determine their jurisdiction within the limits of state power in such manner as they see fit was considered in Broderick, Superintendent of Banks, v. Rosner, et al., 294 U. S. 629, 1935.

Period, as a result of the spread of the Jacksonian ideas of democracy, the elective system was extended, and has since been used. As the centralization of power developed in England, the justices were taken over as a part of the national system for the administration of

STATE COURT ORGANIZATION

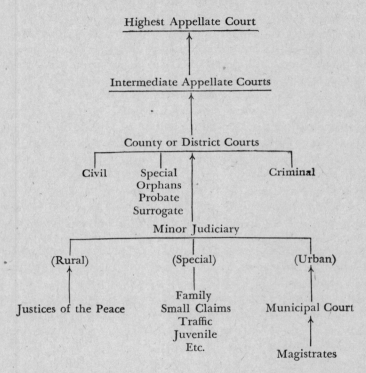

justice.[5] These courts had then, and to a certain extent still have, several useful purposes. They made justice more easily accessible and cheap for the common man. They made it unnecessary for him to travel to a distant city, with the expense and the loss of time involved — which would, in fact, have denied him an opportunity for

---

[5] Webb, Sidney and Beatrice, in their *English Local Government from the Revolution to the Municipal Corporation Act,* Vol. I (Longmans, Green, London, 1908), comment at length upon the development of the early English judicial institutions. For instance (p. 18), they say: " When it was held that the Court Baron was of private, not public nature, those words were used in a sense very different from that nowadays given to them. All that the lawyers meant was that the Court Baron was not a Court of the King, to be held only by his authority or subject to his will. . . ." In course of time, as noted, these private courts were taken over as a part of the judicial system of the realm.

the judicial settlement of his difficulties. Furthermore, there are many minor disputes between neighbors for the settlement of which intelligence, human sympathy, and common sense are more essential than a detailed knowledge of the intricacies of the law. Upon this basis, it was possible to make use of leading citizens in each community; these persons, who came to be known as justices of the peace, were vested with the necessary authority for the adjudication of minor disputes. For many years the system worked well. The men who held the offices were usually highly respected in their communities, and the office itself was regarded as a distinction. Proudly did these men sign their names " John Jones, J.P." — Justice of the Peace.

Like so many elements in American government, this system was lifted bodily from its English setting and transplanted in American soil. Here it has remained through a period of approximately three centuries without any substantial modification, few serious attempts having been made at any time in any of the forty-eight states to make such adjustments as changed conditions might have made desirable.[6] The major defects in the system are the lack of qualifications of the justices, the fee system of compensation, the practice of preying upon strangers, and the tendency to find judgment for the plaintiff. In the average American community the prestige of the office has all but vanished. The individuals who occupy it have, for the most part, no qualifications for the performance of judicial duties. They are usually men of the smallest caliber; in a day of specialization, most of them are learned neither in the law nor in anything else. They are usually small local politicians who either have no business or have never been able to succeed in the ordinary pursuits of life.

The majority are far more interested in the fees obtainable than in the attainment of justice. The fact that most justices are compensated on a fee basis rather than by salary constitutes one of the most serious defects in the system. So much is this so that the initials " J.P." have often been jocularly translated as " judgment for the plaintiff " — since only through finding judgment for the plaintiff can the justice be sure of his fees. Large numbers of them have entered

[6] Fairlie, John A., and Kneier, Charles M., report in *County Government and Administration*, pp. 156–158 (Appleton-Century, New York, 1930) : ". . . the office is at least recognized in all the state constitutions except that of California, and is definitely required in most of them. Six state constitutions authorize or permit the abolition of the office; and thirteen others provide that a competent number of justices shall be appointed or elected. Half of the state constitutions (mostly in the South and West) define or limit the jurisdiction of justices of the peace; elsewhere this may be defined by the legislature."

into dishonest arrangements with constables and other local functionaries, establishing "speed traps" for the purpose of harassing motorists. Those who are strangers in the community are their particular targets, for these people are without political influence, and are usually willing to pay their fines in order to avoid further delay. There are, of course, a few who honestly and conscientiously seek to perform the duties of their office, but the percentage of the total number who do this is pitifully small.[7]

While these comments constitute a serious indictment of the whole system, they represent the deliberate judgment of practically every person who has taken the trouble to investigate the functioning of this type of local officer. A number of studies of the justice of the peace have been recently published. As regards the occupational background of justices, there is no necessary conflict with the judicial function, although as Bruce Smith has observed, " in the majority of cases, the occupations of incumbents provide no guaranty, nor even expectation, that their experience prior to ascending the local bench would offer any degree of special qualification." In a study made by the Pennsylvania Bar Association in 1942, the following report was made:

Occupations of 3,225 justices in sixty-four counties were taken from county registration records. These occupations vary with the county, depending on the dominant occupational pattern of the county: in rural counties most of the justices were farmers, and in the urban counties most of the justices were skilled and unskilled laborers. Many justices listed their occupations as " justice of the peace," indicating that their judicial duties were their only gainful occupations. A very few were lawyers, and only a small number had any experience that would be of value in judicial work.

Nearly every occupation was represented: there were doctors, blacksmiths, reporters, bartenders, students, morticians, W.P.A. workers, and many others. The most numerous occupation listed was justice of the peace — 669 or 21 per cent of the total. Seventeen per cent or 552 were laborers and unskilled laborers; 12 per cent were farmers; 11 per cent were skilled laborers; 61 per cent of the justices and aldermen surveyed were in these four occupations.[8]

    [7] These four major defects are discussed at some length in Morris, Gail M., *Justice of the Peace Courts in Indiana* (Indiana University, Bureau of Government Research, 1942) ; see also Judicial Council of Indiana, *Fourth Annual Report* (1939), pp. 11–137 (Indianapolis, 1940).

    [8] Litke, William W., *Survey of the Minor Judiciary in Pennsylvania*, p. 27 (Pennsylvania Municipal Publications Service, State College, 1942). See also: Smith, Bruce, *Rural Crime Control*, pp. 247–248 (Institute of Public Administration, Columbia University, 1933). Similar results were obtained from occupational studies of justices in New Jersey and New York (p. 248). Chapter 7 of this volume contains a very able discussion of the office of the justice; see also Callender, *op. cit.*, Chapter 4.

A survey made in Hamilton County, Ohio, reveals some interesting facts with regard to both the income of justices and their dockets. In this county " the average annual income of justices (from all fees of whatever nature) was $415.75 . . . with yearly income ranging from $4.30 to $2,557.06. Twenty-six per cent of them earned less than $200, and sixty-eight per cent less than $300. Only eight per cent of the justices earned more than $1,000. . . . The correct concept to form of the squire is that of a judge, poorly paid and subsidized, to whom the state farms out its work in the administration of justice in the counties and townships upon the consideration that he shall collect occasionally some civil fees. If the desire for economy in local government led to the development of the present system, arithmetic proves that the desire apparently has been realized." [9] In a few cases found in Erie County, New York, salaries ranging from $2,500 to $5,000 are paid, but this is unusual; in Pennsylvania, out of 1,194 justices interrogated in an earlier survey, only five were on an exclusively salaried basis.

Under such circumstances, it is small wonder that the work is usually done badly. To refer again to the report on Hamilton County, Ohio: " The docket entries are made whenever the squire or his family have a few spare minutes. Wives and children do a considerable amount of clerical work. The report continues:

. . . A few magistrates permit their cases to accumulate until something happens to force them to bring their records up to date. On one occasion a justice sat up all night to make his entries and have them ready for the perusal of an interested party the next morning. The call of the state examiner for the records stimulates a few judges to feverish clerical activity. As a consequence of the dilatory manner of keeping official records, the dockets frequently have cases following in such sequence as March 21, 1929, December 3, 1928, January 3, 1929, October 7, 1928. One squire delighted in finding blank pages in old dockets and entering his cases. He achieved such serial order as June 10, 1925; December 6, 1930; June 12, 1925. [Although some of the justices employed systematic filing methods] one squire filed the papers of each case in the docket book. Three kept the papers in desk drawers, being sometimes able to locate the proper documents and sometimes not. In three cases the papers could not be located. In two cases papers transferred from squires to their successors were completely lost. . . . A few dockets were either lost or could not be located for examination.[10]

In 1932 the Michigan Commission of Inquiry undertook an exhaustive study of local government in that state; in connection with

[9] Douglass, Paul F., *The Justice of the Peace Courts of Hamilton County, Ohio*, p. 70, and quoted by Smith, *op. cit.*, p. 241.

[10] *Ibid.*, pp. 61, 66.

this study a careful analysis was made of the justices' courts in six typical counties. The state constitution provides that there shall be elected in each organized township not more than four justices of the peace.[11] These six counties had an aggregate of 290 justices of the peace, but all the judicial business in the counties, outside of the cities, was handled by twenty-one justices, the other 269 having no judicial business whatever. A study of the work of these twenty-one justices was then made. The situation in the individual counties was very interesting. In Kent County, for instance, where there were ninety-six justices of the peace, nine handled all the cases, five of these did 88 per cent of the business, and eighty-seven had no cases whatever. In Cass County, where there were sixty justices, five handled all the cases, one did 70 per cent of the business, and fifty-five had no cases whatever. In Luce County, the smallest of the six studied, there were sixteen justices, of whom two handled all the cases; one did 81 per cent of the business, and fourteen had no cases whatever. The situation in the other three counties was similar. The report points out that the maintenance of a magistrate's court in each township is unnecessary, that the people do not want them and do not use them. " By bringing all the judicial business in the county before one or two or a half dozen justices, the people have for practical purposes eliminated all the rest and have made them superfluous institutions."

In its general conclusions, the report condemns both the township and the smaller municipalities as units for the administration of justice, the contention being that this is a state function. With regard to the township, the report says:

> The township is not a suitable unit to be charged with the performance of any judicial duties whatever, and the Justice of the Peace, as a township officer, is wholly out of place in a modern judicial system. A county court, properly organized and housed, having a trained judge, a competent clerk, office equipment sufficient for the keeping of proper records, and sitting at such times and places as the needs of the community should indicate, ought to replace the obsolete Justice of the Peace courts.[12]

The Virginia trial justice system represents the most constructive attempt yet made to do something about the justice of the peace sys-

11 Article 7, Section 15.
12 This comment is based entirely upon Sunderland, Edson R., " The Efficiency of Justices' Courts in Michigan," published as Appendix D, *Report* on Organization and Cost of County and Township Government, by the Michigan Commission of Inquiry, 1933; reprinted in *Fourth Report* of the Judicial Council of Michigan, May, 1934, Appendix, pp. 169–172.

tem; it provides for a new type of commissioner or magistrate who is given the title of " trial justice." Herbert Harley of the American Judicature Society thus describes this notable attempt to administer justice in small cases expertly and economically throughout both urban and rural communities:

> The Virginia system is this: in counties in which the supervisors have voted to dispense with justices of the peace the circuit judge (equivalent to district judge), if he agrees, shall appoint an assistant to serve for a term of four years. This assistant of course will be a lawyer. He will take such classes of cases as may be assigned to him from time to time by his superior officer. His will be a mobile court, prepared at all times to convene court at the place most convenient to those concerned. The Virginia law provides that such an assistant judge may be appointed for any of the larger cities that realize the need. In thinly populated areas one assistant judge may serve two counties, or there may be half-time service.

After outlining various advantages of this system in operation, he continues:

> Perhaps most important of all is the obvious fact that this system creates a body of experienced, well tested, competent lawyers from which future judges are likely to be chosen. The Virginia system creates a school for judges, but the novitiates must already have met all educational requirements for the practice of law and must have spent some time at least in the service of clients. By assisting a judge of full trial jurisdiction, they round out their training and have much to offer the public in either capacity, as lawyer or as judge.[13]

In Urban Areas — the Magistrate. The justice of the peace functions in the rural districts; his urban counterpart is the magistrate, police magistrate, or alderman. If it be true that a satisfactory administration of justice in the rural districts is impossible until the justice of the peace system is either abolished or extensively modified, it is doubly true that anything approximating substantial justice in urban communities is impossible unless or until the magistrate system is abolished. If it be true that the justices of the peace are usually inefficient and often dishonest, it may be said that the record of the magistrates is very much worse — they are rarely efficient and rarely honest. In the magistrates' courts, commonly held in a police station or in a small, stuffy office, there is no dignity to the proceedings, and usually little justice results from them. Indeed, it may be said that the innocence or guilt of those who are arraigned before the magistrate has little or nothing to do with the disposition

---

[13] *Journal,* August, 1942, p. 26, and Kingdon, Arthur F., " The Trial Justice System of Virginia," *ibid.,* April, 1940, pp. 216–221.

which he makes of the cases. The decisions are determined either in a back room before the hearing takes place, or by whispered conversations carried on between the magistrate and some local politician while the hearing is in progress. Thus it is that an individual, no matter how innocent, may be held on bail or sent to jail if he is unfortunate enough to be unable to bring some political pressure to bear in his behalf, while another individual, no matter how guilty, may get off absolutely free if he is able to summon the assistance of the proper political influence.[14]

These conclusions with regard to the office of the magistrate are likewise supported by a large number of studies made by competent persons. Such a study of the magistrates' courts of Philadelphia was made by Spencer Ervin in 1931; he found that these courts were notable for the lack of any adequate reporting system — even the annual report of the chief magistrate is utterly inadequate and confused. The dockets and records of many of the individual magistrates have been kept in a " disgraceful condition," since these officers are without guidance as to the character of entries that should be made in different classes of cases. This situation has been pointed out repeatedly — in 1926 by the Law Association's Crimes Survey Committee; in 1927 by District Attorney Charles Edwin Fox; in 1928 by the famous grand jury investigation; in 1935 by the Criminal Justice Association, and by the investigation conducted by the State Department of Justice. It has also been shown repeatedly that many of the magistrates fail to make prompt return of cases to the clerk of the court of quarter sessions and to the district attorney, and that they are delinquent in making certain returns to the city controller and the city treasurer.

It is a familiar subject of comment by observers at the hearings conducted by many of the magistrates that there is a total lack of order in the room, and a lack of dignity and tact on the part of the bench. " Lateness at the hearing, conduct unbecoming a judicial officer during the hearing, and improper disposition of cases are common complaints," but unfortunately the basis of complaint does not stop here. Short shrift is often made of civil cases, and in criminal cases there are frequent and well-supported charges of intimi-

14 This comment, which one friend of the author thought " a little too strong," is certainly true as applied to New York City, Philadelphia, Pittsburgh, and many other large cities. " Rotten as they are," this commentator continued, " they are the appropriate thing in a considerable proportion of cases." It may be admitted with regard to the magistrates, as with the justices of the peace, that they can and do settle many minor disputes, and that they do, where the political influence is not too strong, render useful service in " holding for court."

dation and oppression, bail irregularities of every conceivable type, political influence in the determining of decisions, et cetera. Clearly justice is not administered " according to law." [15] In many cases the whole magistrate system is a veritable stench in the nostrils of decent people. In 1935 the situation in Philadelphia became so bad that at one time twenty-seven of the twenty-eight magistrates in the city were under indictment for various types of irregularities. While more than half these courts were formerly under the direction of ward leaders and committeemen, a legislative act of 1937 prohibits political activity on the part of magistrates. Philadelphia is by no means unique, for similar conditions are found whenever an investigation is made in any large city which still uses the magistrate system. Few persons have forgotten the sensational disclosures of corruption in New York City made by the Seabury Investigation.[16]

The following paragraphs, taken from the Philadelphia Criminal Justice Association open letter issued April 1, 1935,[17] afford specific illustrations of conditions:

The report of the Pennsylvania Crime Commission of 1929 showed that 74 per cent of all cases of major crime went no further in the process of investigation or disposition than the Magistrates' courts. This is in itself a challenging fact in the light of the fact that these offices are practically unsupervised.

Bring these figures down to 1934: These twenty-eight men dealt with 150,052 arrests by the police (although their own annual report only accounts for 140,870 cases). In addition, they disposed of 7233 arrests by constables. Eliminating every possible type of offense in the police arrests over which the Magistrates had summary power, there remain 46,785 arrests in the more important types of criminal cases. Of the latter number the Magistrates returned to the court 11,163 cases. What became of the other 36,622 criminal charges and what the Magistrates' records show with reference to them seems to us to be a proper matter of public inquiry.

Of the 103,267 cases over which the Magistrates had summary jurisdiction, 13,235 persons were committed to the county prison or the House of Correction. What about the remaining 90,032? It seems incredible that all of these arrests — nearly 250 every day of the year — were improper arrests.

Referring to the 7233 officer cases (*i.e.*, where warrants were issued by the Magistrates' offices), only one-sixth, or 1243, were returned to the court. What do the Magistrates' records show in these cases — perhaps more significant than the police arrests because the disposition of them is not even a

[15] Ervin, Spencer, *The Magistrates' Courts of Philadelphia* (Thomas Skelton Harrison Foundation, Philadelphia, 1931).

[16] Moley, Raymond, *Tribunes of the People: the Past and Future of the New York Magistrates' Courts* (Yale University Press, 1932).

[17] Addressed to the Attorney General of the Commonwealth and the District Attorney of Philadelphia, in the *Philadelphia Record*, April 2, 1935, p. 4.

matter of police record and may conceivably be the subject of private arrangements and settlements not proper in the matter of criminal charges.

An inspection of the Magistrates' statistics shows that approximately
100,000 copies of charge were issued by Magistrates — nearly 75 per
cent of all arrests. Very recently, evidence has been produced of the possibility of fraud and corruption in the matter of indiscriminate issuance
of these copies of charge. Other statistics show that 21,238 " further hearings " were accorded in the police cases, or about one in every eight arrests;
1670 " further hearings " were accorded in the cases where warrants were
issued by the Magistrates, or about one in every five cases. Since the records
do not show the cause for many of these " further hearings " an inquiry
on this subject would seem to be in order. One sinister reason generally
rumored is that opportunity is afforded between the original hearing and
the unnecessary " further hearing " for the case to be " fixed," in various
ways.

All of the foregoing shows the tremendous power of these twenty-eight
men. Some of the many complaints which have recently been voiced regarding the maladministration of their offices have to do with fraudulent
bail, summary sentences, in cases where they have no such power, permitting dishonest constables to operate in their courts, the using of criminal
warrants for the purpose of permitting creditors to collect civil debts, the
improper use of the magisterial seal upon private stationery of constables
and lawyers, the change upon their dockets of their disposition of the case
after police have left the hearing, the issuance of improper and illegal warrants, the granting of " further hearings " for corrupt purposes — and in
general terms, the connivance with gangsters, political domination or political subservience. First and last, the political aspect of the Magistrates' offices
is their worst feature.

Municipal Courts. In the larger cities, where the volume of judicial business is sufficient to justify such a course, the legislatures have
provided for the establishment of municipal courts, which serve in
the dual capacity of courts of first instance for large numbers of cases
involving small amounts of money and minor infractions of the law,
and as appellate courts for cases previously heard by magistrates. In
Chicago, Detroit, New York, and Philadelphia these courts have been
organized into divisions, set up either geographically or on a functional basis. In this development Chicago led the way in 1906. In
New York, the geographical system of organization is used:

The Municipal Court at the present time, generally speaking, has jurisdiction over civil actions in which the amount involved is not more than
$1,000 except in summary proceedings over which it has unlimited jurisdic-
tion. Appeals from its judgments and orders are made to the Appellate
Term of the Supreme Court, First and Second Departments.

Under the law the Municipal Court is intended to be a self governing
body with control vested in its Board of Justices and with an administrative
head in the person of the President-Justice. The court, structurally, is an

aggregation of twenty-eight district courts scattered among the five boroughs of the Greater City of New York — ten in Manhattan, two in the Bronx, eight in Brooklyn, six in Queens, and two in Richmond — and a Central Jury Part in Manhattan.[18]

In Chicago and Philadelphia, the functional basis of organization is used. In the latter city, where the Municipal Court functions under an act passed in 1913, there are five divisions, each of which handles cases involving a particular branch of the law, as follows:

Civil Division: For trial of cases up to $2,500.

Juvenile Division: For the hearings of boys and girls under sixteen years. There is a probation department, petition bureau, labor bureau, and house of detention for children.

Criminal Division: All criminal actions, except crimes of the most grave nature. There is a probation department for men and for women.

Domestic Relations Division: Exercises exclusive jurisdiction in all cases on nonsupport and desertion, and in all proceedings for the custody of children. There is a probation department, as well as a petition bureau and a labor bureau.

Misdemeanant's Division: For trial of incorrigibles over sixteen years. There are separate departments for women, and for men and boys, and a house of detention for women offenders.

This court, which handles more than 50,000 cases a year, has a President Judge (who has served since its establishment), eleven associate judges (one for each 200,000 population), and a large staff. The employees, except those assigned to the various divisions of the court proper, are organized in six main groups, as follows: executive office, court hearing and court proceedings, probation department, medical department, statistical department, and equipment and maintenance. Among the more important activities reported on are adoptions; the conciliation, small claims, and legal division; the medical department, with its visiting nurse staff, nursery, and laboratory; the statistical department; and the department of support accounts.[19]

---

[18] Commission on the Administration of Justice in New York State, *The Municipal Court of the City of New York,* pp. 11–12 (Albany, 1934). More recent studies of this court include: Citizens Budget Commission, *A Report on the Administration of the Judicial System in the City of New York* (New York, 1935); "Reorganization of the Judicial Structure in New York City," in *Fifth Annual Report* of the Judicial Council of the State of New York (1938), pp. 195–269. For other cities in New York, see "Uniform City Court Act for Cities Other than New York," in *Seventh Annual Report* (1941), pp. 201–266, and *Eighth Annual Report* (1942), pp. 265–322.

[19] See the exhaustive series of studies made of the Court by the Thomas Skelton Harrison Foundation, and the comprehensive annual reports of the Court, issued regularly since 1914.

In these cities and in others in many parts of the country, much progress has been made in judicial administration; the municipal court system has fully demonstrated its merit. It is possible to secure for judges in these courts lawyers of greater ability and higher ethical standards, and men with higher standards of civic responsibility, than can normally be secured for the magistrates' courts. It is clear that the line of progress in the development of city courts lies in the direction of the extension of this system. There is no reason why it cannot be introduced in cities where it has not yet been tried, nor why it cannot be extended in others by enlarging the existing set-up, thereby making possible the elimination of the magistrates. Many experiments have been tried with separate divorce courts, family courts, children's courts, small claims courts, people's courts, " poor man's courts," traffic courts, " cafeteria courts " for traffic violators, and other types.[20]

[20] Where a well-organized municipal court exists, these special types of courts are unnecessary because the function is already being performed. A few titles relating to each type are cited here:

JUVENILE COURTS: Alper, Benedict S., " Forty Years of the Juvenile Court," *American Sociological Review,* April, 1941, pp. 230–240; Children's Bureau, United States Department of Labor, *Children in the Courts,* an annual report; Consulich, Gilbert, *Juvenile Court Laws of the United States* (National Probation Association, New York, 1939) ; Reinemann, John O., " Forty Years of the Juvenile Court Movement in the United States," *Mental Hygiene,* April, 1941, pp. 256–268; Riley, Ralph J., *A Working Manual for Juvenile Court Officers* (University of Chicago Press, 1933) ; Sanders, Wiley B., and Ezell, William C., *Juvenile Court Cases in North Carolina, 1929–1934* (State Board of Charities and Public Welfare, Raleigh, 1937) ; Stern, Leon T., " Pennsylvania Juvenile Courts in War Time," reprinted from *Welfare* (Pennsylvania Welfare Conference, Winter Quarter, 1943). The most extensive work has been done in New York State, for which see: Department of Correction, *Probation, Children's Court and Related Laws* (Albany, 1941) ; Joint Legislative Committee to Investigate Jurisdiction of the Children's Court, *Report* (Legislative Document, 1939, No. 75) ; Joint Legislative Committee on Children's Court Jurisdiction, *Report* (Legislative Document, 1941, No. 56) ; Department of Correction, annual proceedings of the conference of New York State Association of Judges of Children's Courts; Joint Legislative Committee to Examine into, Investigate and Study the Existing Facilities for the Care and Treatment of Children, *Young People in the Courts of New York State* (Legislative Document, 1942, No. 55) .

FAMILY COURTS: Aumann, Frederick R., " Domestic Relations Courts in Ohio," *Journal* of the American Judicature Society, October, 1931, pp. 89–93; Entman, Sidney, " The Origins and Development of a Family Court," *Social Forces,* October, 1942, pp. 58–65.

SMALL CLAIMS COURTS: Cayton, Nathan, " Small Claims and Conciliation Courts," *Annals,* September, 1931, pp. 57–64; Commission on the People's Court of Baltimore City, *Report* (Baltimore, 1938) ; Schramm, Gustav L., *Piedpoudre Courts* (Legal Aid Society of Pittsburgh, 1928) ; Stewart, George S., Jr., and Abrahams, Robert D., " A Small Claims Court for Pennsylvania," *University of Pennsylvania Law Review,* November, 1936.

TRAFFIC COURTS: Economos, James P., " The National Program for State Traffic Court Conferences," *Journal* of the American Judicature Society, August, 1944, pp. 56–60; National Committtee on Traffic Law Enforcement, *Horse and Buggy*

County or District Courts. The county or district courts are definitely state courts rather than local, and are, with the exception of the municipal courts, the lowest courts of record in the state judicial system. Their jurisdiction extends to both civil and criminal cases, and is both original and appellate. In some New England states the county is, in fact, merely a judicial district, the officers of which are state officers, chosen and paid by the state. In densely populated states, courts of this type have been set up in each county, although occasionally, even in these states, it been found necessary to group a number of sparsely settled counties into a single district. In these states the name " county court " is most commonly used, while in the states with smaller population and a large number of counties, where a system of districting has to be used, they are commonly referred to as district courts, or in some cases, as circuit courts. New York has nine districts, Illinois seventeen, while Pennsylvania has fifty-seven — only ten less than the number of counties.[21] In any case these courts function in the state judicial system in much the same way.

In many states the same judges sitting in the same court handle cases in both civil and criminal law, as well as equity proceedings. In other states, as in Pennsylvania, separate courts have been established for civil and criminal cases, although the same judges sit in both courts. In this state the civil courts are known as courts of common pleas, which name is also used in several other states. The criminal courts are known as courts of oyer and terminer when considering the more serious offenses, and as courts of quarter sessions when hearing lesser charges. As late as 1938 Massachusetts still had part-time judges in its district courts, although this practice is now both unjustified and unusual. The jurisdiction of these county and dis-

---

Justice (Trenton, 1942) , and *Traffic Courts on Trial* (Trenton, 1944) ; National Safety Council, *Trying Traffic Cases* (Chicago, 1942) , and *Traffic Courts and Violations Bureaus* (Chicago, 1929) ; Warren, George, *Traffic Courts* (Little, Brown, Boston, 1942) and review of same by Sloan, Eldon B., in Kansas Judicial Council *Bulletin*, April, 1943, pp. 12–22; and " A Proposed Traffic Court System," *Journal* of the American Judicature Society, June, 1944, pp. 25–29.

PROBATE COURTS: Atkinson, Thomas E., series of articles on organization, principles and model code for probate courts in *Journal* of the American Judicature Society, October, 1939, pp. 93–98; December, 1939, pp. 137–142; February, 1940, pp. 183–190; and annual reports of the Kansas Judicial Council, *Bulletin*, December, 1938; April, 1939; and July, 1941.

21 See Illinois Legislative Council, *Circuit Court Redistricting in Illinois* (Springfield, 1938) ; although the state constitution requires that the districts be as compact as possible, with due regard to territory and population, they vary, like legislative districts, from 155,000 to 396,000 in population, outside of Chicago. On Massachusetts, see *Report* by the House Committee on the Judiciary of its investigation and study of the district court system (House, No. 1719, 1938) .

trict courts also varies from state to state with regard to their power to handle certain special types of cases, such as, for instance, those involving the settlement of decedents' estates. In some states these cases are a part of the general jurisdiction of these courts, while in many states separate courts, variously designated as probate courts, orphans courts, or surrogates courts, have been established to handle them.

Two other problems in connection with the operation of county courts deserve mention. One involves taking care of the state's judicial business, most of which originates at the capital. If these cases are thrown into the county court of the county in which the capital is located, they are handled by judges, elected by the voters of that county, without any special qualifications for this state work. It has been proposed, therefore, that a special tribunal with statewide jurisdiction be established, the members of which are elected for this special court by all the voters of the state. This would provide more competent service, probably at no greater cost than is involved in contributing to the support of a particular county court. Appeals from such a court would be taken directly to the state supreme court. It has also been proposed that separate labor courts be established, similar to labor courts abroad and to the court established by the ill-fated Kansas Industrial Disputes Act.

The other problem relates to the criminal work of the county court, especially in populous centers. The Behavior Clinic of the Allegheny County, Pennsylvania, courts provides an excellent illustration of effective work in this field. This Clinic was established in 1936 for the purpose of making available to the judges, and indirectly to the defendants, all the resources of modern science in the handling of criminals. During 1939 a committee of 100 citizens working through eight subcommittees, representing all walks of life and some forty-six organizations, undertook a study of the entire crime problem in the county. The staff of the Clinic includes social workers, sociologists, criminologists, psychologists, psychiatrists, and others in a position to make a contribution to the case study of the defendants brought before the court. The record of each defendant and the findings of the staff, together with their recommendations, are given to the judge before he imposes sentence. The Clinic procedure represents an extension into the county criminal courts of practices long followed in progressive municipal courts.[22]

22 Data from a letter to the author from the late Judge Ralph H. Smith, **Alle-gheny County Court of Common Pleas**, July 10, 1939. For a record of **nearly a**

Appellate Courts. Next in the organization of the state judicial system, in about one third of the states, are those courts which may be classified as intermediate appellate courts; these are the courts which stand as a buffer between the county or district courts on the one hand and the highest court of appeal on the other. The number, size, and jurisdiction of these courts will depend, in any given state, largely upon the volume of judicial business, which is in turn largely dependent upon the size of the population. In many cases there is only one of these intermediate courts, which may be designated either as a superior court or as a court of appeals. In a state like New York, with its large population and its great industrial and commercial interests, there is a Supreme Court, with trial and appellate divisions. While the bulk of the work performed by these courts is in original jurisdiction, there are many cases heard on appeal by the court sitting in banc. The Supreme Court is the only court exercising general jurisdiction in law and equity. As an additional protection to the highest court of appeal, this court is given final jurisdiction in handling several types of cases.

Finally, one comes to the capstone of the state judicial system, the highest appellate court. The most common designation applied to this court is " supreme court " although, to refer again to New York, one finds the anomalous situation of a supreme court that is not supreme, the final appellate jurisdiction resting in the Court of Appeals. In New Jersey this court is designated as the Court of Errors and Appeals. Texas has two supreme courts, one for civil matters, and another for criminal. They range in size from three to nine members. Fourteen states have five members, eighteen states have seven. The jurisdiction of the highest court is chiefly appellate in character, sometimes accompanied by a rule-making power, and sometimes enlarged by grants of original jurisdiction made in the constitution of the state. This is usually confined to the issuance of original writs — a power which in fact is seldom used. It would be extremely interesting, if space permitted, to inquire into a number of important questions relating to the organization and functioning of the highest appellate courts — questions such as the growth of these courts in number of judges, the character of the personnel, the use of commissioners and of divisional organization, et cetera. A study of judicial influence made in 1936, showing the combined

quarter of a century of this work in Detroit, see Selling, Lowell S., " The Psycopathic Clinic in a Criminal Court, Its Uses and Possibilities," *Journal* of the American Judicature Society, April, 1945, pp. 169–173.

prestige rating of these courts in the order of rank, put New York first, with the next eight as follows: Massachusetts, Illinois, New Jersey, California, Pennsylvania, Michigan, Minnesota, and Wisconsin. Some of these questions will be referred to later.[23]

Overall Organization. Considerable attention is now being given to the problems of overall organization of the state courts. While constitutional conventions, as in Georgia, Missouri, New Jersey, and New York, provide an excellent opportunity to survey the existing court organization, efforts at improvement need not be limited to such occasions, Minnesota, for instance, has had under consideration a new court plan that would provide " not only a judicial system as good as Missouri's, but a minor court system as good as Virginia's, business administration equal to that of the United States courts, along with a court organization matched by no other state, full and adequately implemented rule making power, and other advantages." [24]

One of the most urgent needs of the state courts is the establishment of some plan for an administrative officer. As one state supreme court justice has said, " It must be admitted that the legal machinery we have was designed for heavy duty and long wear, rather than for speedy and economical action." The Model State Constitution recommends, in Article VI, Section 603, that this power be vested in the chief justice. Some states have made some progress toward the solution of this problem — a problem which should not be too difficult now, with the very satisfactory Federal experience to serve as a guide. Connecticut has established by law an executive secretary to the judicial department, with the following duties, while other states are thinking and moving in the same direction: [25]

[23] See Mott, Rodney L., " Judicial Influence," *American Political Science Review*, April, 1936, pp. 295–315; and other references, cited in earlier editions of this volume. The reader should not pass over this discussion without consulting the legislative manual of his own state, or some other convenient source, in order to get clearly in mind the details of the specific organization provided for by the constitution and the laws of that state.

[24] See *Journal* of the American Judicature Society, February, 1943, pp. 133–137; *National Municipal Review*, April, 1943, p. 198; and Righter, Richard S., " The Judiciary Article of the Proposed Missouri Constitution," *Journal, supra,* August, 1944, pp. 52–55. The provisions here discussed are now in effect.

[25] See Commission to Study the Integration of the State Judicial System, *Report*, pp. 5–6, and Chandler, Henry P., " An Administrative Officer for State Courts," *Journal* of the American Judicature Society, June, 1942, pp. 7–10. On recent developments in other states, see Walsh, William C., " Court Reorganization in Maryland," *Journal, supra,* February, 1945, pp. 151–154; McCormick, Charles T., " Modernizing the Texas Judicial System," *ibid.,* June, 1944, pp. 11–19, and Alexander, James P., " An Administrative Agency for the Texas Courts," *ibid.,* October, 1943, pp. 90–92; Wickham, John E., " The Power of Superintending Control of the Wisconsin Supreme Court," *Wisconsin Law Review,* March, 1941, pp. 153–171.

1. To act as auditor for the expenditures of all state-maintained courts.
2. To keep on file information as to the expenses of conducting the judicial department.
3. To perform such duties with reference to the above matters as the judges of any state-maintained court may direct, and
4. Such duties of a non-judicial character with reference to the administration of the judicial department including municipal courts and trial judges as the judges of the superior court may direct.
5. To file an annual report as of July 1st with the chief justice.

THE SELECTION OF JUDGES

No aspect of the organization and functioning of courts is more vital than the methods used in the selection of judges. In colonial times the members of the judiciary were appointed by the Crown for life, during good behavior. When the new constitutions were framed after the independence of the colonies had been achieved, the system of selection by appointment, and usually the same conditions of tenure, were retained. The great change came in the Middle Period, when the wave of democratic sentiment swept over the country, causing a widespread substitution of popular election for appointment, and also a drastic reduction in tenure. Although few states now appoint their judges, much attention has been given to the relative merits of the two systems and to the consideration of other devices which might be used for the purpose of improving the caliber of our judges.

Appointment. It was natural that the original form of selection should have been by appointment, for the judicial function was an offshoot from the executive branch of the government. It is of the utmost importance to every individual that the independence of the judiciary be maintained, and that every effort be made to secure as jurists men of the highest character and ability. It was generally believed then, and is still believed by students, that these objectives can be much better achieved by appointment by the governor than by popular election. In an earlier chapter, it was noted that the increased powers and responsibilities of our state executives have generally served to attract men of a higher type than those who formerly served. This fact provides an additional assurance that the power of appointment will not be used for partisan and political purposes.

Popular Election. When popular election was adopted, it was believed that this was more democratic, and that it would bring to the bench men who were more concerned with the public good and more responsive to the popular will. It is a matter of record that the first of these hopes has not been realized and that the effect of the second, so far as it has been realized, has been to undermine, to a considerable extent, the independence of the judiciary. The majority of those who have studied the problem are convinced that the electoral method attracts less able men than might be secured by appointment. Men of ability and high attainments are often reluctant to enter a political campaign, particularly in states where the campaign for election must be preceded by one or more bitter primary fights. It is, furthermore, somewhat unusual to find in the same individual the qualities that are essential for a good judge and for a good candidate. Since the primary interest of the party is in winning the election, the party organization is likely to support the good candidate, regardless of his ability, qualifications, and training. Thus, under the electoral system, judges are more likely to be chosen on the basis of a friendly and engaging personality, a flair for politics, and ability as a campaign speaker, than on the basis of intellectual qualifications and general fitness for the bench.

Stuart H. Perry describes a fantastic situation in the judicial elections in Detroit and Wayne County in April, 1935, in which there was a rush of candidates for judicial nominations. This may not be typical but it is certainly illustrative. He relates:

> In the party primaries for the eighteen circuit judgeships there were 220 candidates; in the non-partisan primaries there were forty for the recorder's bench and forty-eight for the court of common pleas — a total of 308 candidates for judicial offices. More than one lawyer out of every ten in Detroit wanted to be judge. Nominations were also to be made for three non-judicial offices, which brought up the total of all primary candidates in Wayne County to about 400. . . .
>
> The number of candidates and the size of the electorate made impossible anything like an intelligent popular selection. The majority of Wayne County's 543,000 voters could not name half of the eighteen judges actually on the bench. Hardly anyone outside of the bar could name them all. Tens of thousands could barely recognize the names of a few judges, without being sure which court they belonged to, and without understanding the difference between the circuit, recorder's, and common pleas courts. An intelligent selection therefore would have been impossible even if there had been but two candidates for each position. With 220 candidates for the circuit bench and eighty-eight for other benches, the situation was fantastic.[26]

Mr. Perry then goes on to describe the huge display advertising campaign that was carried on by candidates, the humiliating and sometimes degrading methods of campaigning that were used by them, their slogans, and their campaign pledges — some impossible to keep

26 Perry, Stuart H., " Shall We Appoint Our Judges," *Annals,* September, 1935, pp. 97–108, at 99.

and some obviously ridiculous. The Polish bloc was able to exercise a disproportionate influence in the selections, getting eight out of the eighteen positions on the Democratic ticket. Among other things, he concludes that when the electorate is large, and especially when there are numerous candidates, it is impossible for most voters to appraise the judicial fitness of candidates.

CLASSIFICATION OF STATES ACCORDING TO METHOD OF CHOOSING
JUDGES OF HIGHER COURTS [27]

Partisan Ballot	Nonpartisan Ballot	Partisan Ballot with Independent Ticket Allowed	Appointment or Otherwise
Alabama	Arizona	Colorado	California
Arkansas	Idaho	Illinois	Connecticut
Florida	Michigan	Iowa	Delaware
Georgia	Minnesota	Kansas	Maine
Indiana	Montana	Kentucky	Massachusetts
Louisiana	Nebraska	Maryland	Missouri
Mississippi	Nevada	New York	New Hampshire
New Mexico	North Dakota	North Carolina	New Jersey
Pennsylvania	Ohio	Oklahoma	Rhode Island
West Virginia	Oregon	Tennessee	South Carolina
	South Dakota	Texas	Vermont
	Washington	Utah	Virginia
	Wisconsin		
	Wyoming		

Two practices have developed in some jurisdictions that tend to minimize the unfortunate effects of popular elections on the regular party ballot. Used in 1940 in about half of the states, either of them could be developed in any state. The first is the practice of re-electing sitting judges: under this plan any judge who comes to the end of his term and who desires to continue in office automatically becomes a candidate for re-election with the support of both political parties. Without partisan opposition, no campaigning is necessary. The second factor is due to the fact that most judges do seek re-election. There are consequently few of what might be called original vacancies; those vacancies which do occur arise by reason of the death or resignation of a judge in the middle of the term for which he was

[27] From Hannan, William E., and Csontos, Mildred B., *State Court Systems,* p. 17, revised and corrected to 1945 (Council of State Governments, Chicago, 1940), and Haynes, Evan, *Selection and Tenure of Judges* (National Conference of Judicial Councils, n.p., 1944).

elected. Under these circumstances, the governor usually has the power to appoint until the next election. The temporary appointee thus becomes a sitting judge, and automatically a candidate for election. Thus, in fact, most of the judges may actually be selected by appointment, even though they are elected. A study of the Common Pleas Court of Philadelphia in 1937 showed this to be true over a period of more than sixty years. Of sixty-three who served in that Court from 1873 to 1937 only eleven were originally elected; fifty-two were originally appointed. Of the twenty-one serving in the latter year only four were originally elected. The Orphans Court had had twenty judges during its existence, only the original three of whom were elected; of the six then serving all were originally appointed.[28]

Other Methods of Selection. It is unfortunate that in the minds of the general public the idea of popular election should be so deeply intrenched. In some states the mere mention of appointive judges is enough to defeat a proposal for constitutional revision. If, however, the method of election must be retained, then the election ought to be conducted on a nonpartisan ballot and at a time when the voters are not concerned with selections for important political offices. This method was used in 1940 in sixteen states. Election by the legislature is another possible method of selection used in four states. In a summary prepared by the Council of State Governments, judges were found to be nominated by party convention in six states, by party primary in twenty-one states, and by nonpartisan primary in thirteen. To summarize the practice with regard to method of selection: the governor has a part in the procedure in twelve states; the legislature makes the choice in four; twenty-two states use the party ballot; and fourteen states use the nonpartisan ballot.[29]

Some states are making progress in working out and securing the

28 *Philadelphia Record*, October 26, 1937.
29 California — Appointed by Governor from panel furnished by commission
Connecticut — By General Assembly on nomination by Governor
Delaware — Appointed by Governor with advice and consent of Senate
Maine — Appointed by Governor with advice and consent of Council
Massachusetts — Appointed by Governor with advice and consent of Council
Missouri — Appointed by Governor from panel furnished by Commission
New Hampshire — Appointed by Governor and Council
New Jersey — Appointed by Governor
Rhode Island — Elected by both houses of the legislature in grand committee
South Carolina — Elected by General Assembly, and by partisan ballot
Vermont — Elected by legislature, and by partisan ballot
Virginia — Elected by joint vote of both houses of General Assembly; all
    inferior court judges except in municipal courts (appointed by Governor)
    are elected by the people

adoption of new plans for the selection of judges. California did a pioneering job when in 1934, it adopted a constitutional amendment providing

that vacancies in judicial office shall be filled by appointment of the governor, subject to approval by a majority of a commission consisting of the chief justice of the state, the presiding justice of the appellate court of the district involved and the attorney general. The appointments are for moderate terms, superior court six years, appellate and supreme courts twelve years. On approaching the end of his term any judge may declare his candidacy and his name will be put on the ballot at the ensuing election with no opposing candidate's name.

In 1940 Missouri adopted a constitutional amendment of substantially similar character. It was attacked by its opponents, who succeeded in getting it before the electorate again in 1942. This time also, they approved it. In 1943, the Constitutional Convention carried it over, so that it is now probably in more or less permanent operation under the new constitution in that state. In brief, the plan provides for the filling of vacancies in judgeships by appointment by the governor from a panel of three for a vacancy presented by a nonpartisan commission, and for the continuation of such judges in office by vote of the people on a noncompetitive ballot.[30] It differs from the California plan only in the fact that in this case the governor is required to make his selection from the panel of names furnished to him by the commission.

The Model State Constitution (Article VI, Section 602) provides for the election of the chief justice, and vests in him the power to " appoint justices of the supreme court department and of the other departments of the general court of justice from an eligible list, containing three names for each vacancy, which shall be presented to him by the judicial council." It continues with provisions for the electorate to vote at the next regular election, on a separate ballot, on the question whether the newly appointed judge shall remain in office or be removed. If the vote is affirmative, the judge remains to

[30] For some reason, this Missouri plan obtained much more publicity than the original California plan; see: Crowdus, William W., " The Operation of the Missouri Nonpartisan Court Plan," *Journal* of the American Judicature Society, April, 1944, pp. 166–170; Hyde, Laurence M., " Selection and Tenure of Judges," American Bar Association *Journal*, December, 1941, pp. 763–765; McDonald, Thomas F., " Missouri's Ideal Judicial Selection Law," *Journal, supra*, April, 1941, pp. 194–198; Peltason, Jack W., *Missouri's Plan for the Selection of Judges* (University of Missouri, 1945) ; Philadelphia Bureau of Municipal Research, *Citizens' Business*, November 24, 1942; " Missouri Voters Approve Judicial Selection Plan," *Journal, supra*, December, 1940, pp. 118–119.

serve out his term; if not, the chief justice makes a new appointment, subject to the same type of recall.

The term of office is twelve years, at the end of the first four of which, the judge's name again appears on the ballot for a similar popular referendum on his record. Mr. Herbert Harley of the American Judicature Society describes this plan as " The best system of choosing judges and of determining how long they shall serve that has been worked out during the thirty-five years since the recall of judges movement gave the country a great scare. . . . Instead of all the judges being bedevilled every four or six years with political campaigns to save their lives, there will be only the referendum every four years, which can harm no worthy incumbent, and then eight more years of the twelve year term." [31]

Influence of Organized Bar in Selecting Judges. Whatever the final method of selection, it seems clear that in the earlier stages of the process the bar associations should be permitted to exercise some influence. It is fairly obvious that under ordinary circumstances the qualifications of a business or professional man and the quality of his work can best be judged by those who are engaged in the same profession or in the same line of work. It follows, therefore, that the members of the bar in a given state or in a given judicial district are in a better position to judge the qualifications of those who aspire to the bench than are ordinary laymen. If the final method of selection is to be by appointment, then the governor's choice should be made from a list certified to him by the bar association, containing the names of those who are regarded by their professional colleagues as possessing the qualities of mind and character desired in a judge. If the final method of selection is by popular vote, then a poll should be taken of the members of the bar in the governmental unit concerned, the result of this poll being made available to all through the

[31] Harley, Herbert, " Model Judiciary Article and Comment Thereon," *Journal* of the American Judicature Society, August, 1942, pp. 51–60. In addition to the Haynes volume, and the references cited in previous editions of this volume, see: Bomberger, Louden L., " Non-Partisan Selection of Judges," *Indiana Law Journal*, October, 1940, pp. 57–65; Feightner, Milo N., " Judicial Selection and Tenure," *ibid.*, February, 1940, pp. 215–226; Moos, Malcolm C., " Judicial Election and Partisan Endorsement of Judicial Candidates in Minnesota," *American Political Science Review*, February, 1941, pp. 69–75; Wardwell, Allen, " Selection of Judges in New York," *Journal, supra,* June, 1944, pp. 8–10, and " Judicial Selection Improvement in New York," *ibid.*, February, 1944, pp. 153–156; Winters, Glenn R., " Consensus of Judicial Selection Proposals," *ibid.*, December, 1944, pp. 107–117, with table covering proposed judicial selection plans and structure of judicial nominating commissions in all states. The current edition of the *Book of the States* also has information on this subject.

press and the other usual avenues of communication. Experiments of this type have been conducted in a number of states. The question of the organized bar is discussed in the next chapter.

Even in those states with appointive judges, politics sometimes enters into the selections made, but it is generally felt that the situation is less acute in these states than in others. The method most commonly used by bar associations for advising voters is a formal vote, many variations of which occur in different sections of the country. In many cities the bar association presents a list of acceptable candidates. In St. Louis bar referenda are held on the candidates proposed, and this list is narrowed down to the highest approved candidate. In San Francisco all members of the bar association receive biographical sketches with their ballots, summarizing the public record and achievements of each candidate; the winning candidate must receive at least one fourth of the votes, but if 40 per cent of the total vote is against him, then the candidate fails and his name is eliminated. In New Orleans the executive committee of the bar association has the power, which it occasionally exercises, of recommending candidates to the voters and having their names placed on the ballot.[32]

The Chicago Bar Association mails out long questionnaires to members to obtain detailed information about candidates before ballots are sent out in the referendum; when this information has been compiled, it is sent out with the final ballots. The candidate must get at least one third of the total vote cast; otherwise another vote must be taken with the name of the lowest candidate eliminated. In Cincinnati the majority preferential method is used for weeding out the less acceptable candidates. Other municipalities have bar associations which exact pledges from candidates to abide by the result of the referendum, pledging that if they are defeated in the bar association poll, they will not subsequently conduct a public campaign. Sometimes members of the bar suggest candidates, in which case it is necessary for the candidate to get members of the association to sign a petition sponsoring him. There are numerous other variations in the procedure followed.[33]

[32] "The Bar's Opinion on Judicial Selection," *American Bar Association Journal,* September, 1934, pp. 529–532.
[33] "Various Ways of Selecting Judges," *Journal* of the American Judicature Society, Part I, August, 1931, pp. 38–41; Part II, October, 1931, pp. 76–78. An excellent description of the bar primary conducted in Philadelphia in 1932 will be found in Reinhold, Frances L., "Philadelphia's Bar Primary," *National Municipal Review,* April, 1934, pp. 205–208.

CHARACTERISTICS OF THE JUDICIAL OFFICE

Qualifications: Politics. In the numerous studies that have been made of the courts, court procedure, and judicial personnel, little attention has been given to the formal qualifications required of judges — constitutional, professional, or otherwise. There are no constitutional or statutory requirements for Federal judges, and the same condition exists in most states. " Formal educational and professional requirements are not of too great importance," says the American Municipal Association, whose report continued: " This is especially true where there is a growing tendency to appoint or elect men as judges who are endorsed by local practicing attorneys as being reasonably capable of performing their duties." [34]

As in the case of other public positions, the unwritten and informal qualifications are likely to be more important than those specified. Many efforts have been made to divorce the judges from politics, yet in many jurisdictions, it is impossible for a lawyer to get the support necessary to be elected unless he is active politically. After he becomes a judge, his political activity becomes an even more serious problem. The American Bar Association has taken a strong stand to require judges seeking political office to resign from the bench. Most of these candidates do resign; in 1938 Judge Charles Poletti promptly resigned his judicial position when he was nominated for Lieutenant-Governor of New York. On the other hand, Arthur H. James, a member of the Superior Court of Pennsylvania nominated for Governor in the same year, refused to resign, continued to draw his salary ($18,000 a year) , and carried on his campaign for election while his colleagues faced a docket of 199 cases. When he was inaugurated, Judge James handed his resignation to Governor James. Fortunately, such violations of judicial ethics are not common.

Tenure. Members of the bench in colonial times and under the original state constitutions had a life tenure during good behavior. The democratic movement which brought about a change in the method of selection also brought about a great decrease in the length of term. In some jurisdictions this movement went so far as to reduce the term of some judges to two years. In one state where this occurred nearly every lawyer is called " judge," for there were few lawyers who had not at some time or other had an opportunity to serve on the

[34] American Municipal Association, *Formal Professional Qualifications Required of Judges* (Chicago, 1938) . See also Hannan and Csontos, *op. cit.*

bench. In recent years the tendency has been to increase somewhat the length of term. This is a wholesome sign, for if the office is to be nonpolitical in fact as well as in theory, if it does not exercise any important influence in the determination of public policy, there is certainly no justification for such very limited tenure. It is customary to provide longer terms for justices in the higher courts. A tabulation made in 1945 of the terms of supreme court justices showed a range from two years in one state to indefinite tenure in three states. Nineteen states provided a term of six years, nine states a term of eight years, six states a term of ten years, four states a term of twelve years, and the remainder, terms of various lengths.[35]

A curious situation developed in Pennsylvania, where the term for the members of the Supreme Court is twenty-one years. This would seem to be reasonable enough, since it would ordinarily provide life tenure — that is to say, a man who was old enough to aspire to this office and of sufficient standing in his profession to enable him to secure it would ordinarily, in a term of twenty-one years, serve during the remainder of his active life. A chief justice who had been elected at an early age claimed that this provision was unfair, because he was not ready to retire, and he had no group of clients to whom he might look for employment. He argued, furthermore, that long years of service on the bench had developed in his mind impartial habits of thought which actually disqualified him from pleading the cause of a particular client. It is unlikely that such a situation would arise often.

While moderately long tenure is not only desirable but necessary for the proper conduct of judicial business, there is a widespread popular prejudice against it. Albert Kales, eminent Chicago attorney, made a wise comment on this attitude some years ago when he wrote:

It is a grave mistake to suppose that judges exercise their judicial power in a distasteful and arbitrary manner merely because they hold for life or during good behavior. An arbitrary or disagreeable course of action by a judge arises principally from the fact that he is subject to no authority which can receive complaints against him and act upon those complaints by way of private or public criticism and correction of the judge. The best protection against arbitrary and disagreeable actions by judges is a duly constituted body of fellow judges who hold a position of superior power and authority and to whom complaints as to the conduct of judges may be brought and who may investigate those complaints and exercise a correc-

[35] See table, p. 683, and Swancara, Frank, " Short Terms as Deliberators of the American Judiciary," *Rocky Mountain Law Review*, June, 1939, pp. 217–232.

tive influence. When a considerable number of judges in a metropolitan district are provided with a chief justice and organized for the efficient handling of a great volume of business, the means of securing the exercise of a corrective influence over their conduct at once appears.[36]

Compensation. The compensation paid to judges has in most cases been fairly adequate. It is true that it is not generally as high as able members of the profession can earn in private practice, but there is some question as to the extent to which government should try to compete with private practice in the matter of compensation. There are connected with public positions a prestige value, an opportunity for public service, and in many jurisdictions a relative permanence of tenure through possibility of re-election, which go far to make up for the difference in income. In addition, the work is pleasant and agreeable, and often not so burdensome as private practice.

The salaries of judges in the courts of the various states are shown in the accompanying table. In addition to the salary indicated, there is in a good many states provision for allowances, expenses, and supplementary compensation. To supreme court justices, four states (Illinois, New Jersey, New York, and Pennsylvania) pay $15,000 a year or more; eleven states (Delaware, Indiana, Rhode Island, West Virginia, and Wisconsin at $10,000; California at $11,000; Connecticut, Louisiana, Michigan, and Ohio at $12,000; and Massachusetts at $14,000) pay between $10,000 and $14,999; while at the lower end of the scale, South Dakota pays $3,000, and four states (Idaho, Kentucky, North Dakota, and Utah) pay $5,000. This accounts for twenty of the forty-eight states, the salary range for the remaining twenty-eight falling between $6,000 (five states) and $8,500 (three states). Of these, four pay $7,000 and thirteen pay $7,500. The amount of compensation should be determined by statutory provision, rather than by the constitution as is done in a few states.

Retirement and Removal. There are no less than seven different methods by which judges may be removed from active service; these are: death, resignation, retirement, impeachment, recall, by concurrent resolution of the legislature, or removal by action of the supreme court. Not all of these methods of removal are operative in any one state, and some of them are of such a nature as to require

[36] Kales, Albert, " Methods of Selecting and Retiring Judges in a Metropolitan District," *Annals*, March, 1914, pp. 1–12. This subject has been one of the most widely discussed in American government; see, for instance, " Rufus Choate on Judicial Tenure," an address delivered in the Constitutional Convention of 1853, in *Journal* of the American Judicature Society, July, 1933, pp. 10–20.

	Tenure			Compensation		
	Su-preme	Inter-mediate	In-ferior	Supreme	Intermediate	Inferior
Alabama	6	6	3 & 4	7,000	6,500	5,000 to 8,000
Arizona	6	4	2	8,500	.....	4,000 to 6,000
Arkansas	8	4	2	7,500	.....	3,600 to 6,000
California	12	12	6	14,000 & 13,000	12,000	4,750 to 10,000
Colorado	10	6	4	6,500	.....	2,000 to 6,000
Connecticut	8	4	2	12,500 & 12,000	.....	9,000 to 12,000
Delaware	12	4	4	10,500, 10,000 & 7,500	.....	.....
Florida	6	6	4	7,500	.....	6,000
Georgia	6	4	2	9,000	.....	6,000
Idaho	6	4	2	5,000	.....	4,000
Illinois	9	6	4 & 6	15,000	8,000 plus per diem	8,000 to 15,000
Indiana	6	6	4	10,000	10,000	4,200 to 10,000
Iowa	6	4	2 & 4	7,500	.....	5,000
Kansas	6	4	2 & 4	6,000	.....	4,000
Kentucky	8	6	4	5,000	.....	3,000 to 5,000
Louisiana	14	8 & 12	4 & 6	14,000	8,000	7,500 to 10,000
Maine	7	7	4	9,000 & 8,000	.....	7,500
Maryland	15	15	2	11,500	.....	8,500 to 10,250
Massachusetts	**	**	3	15,000 & 14,000	13,000 & 12,000	1,200 to 10,000
Michigan	8	6	4	12,000	.....	5,000
Minnesota	6	4	2	9,000 & 8,500	.....	6,000 to 7,500
Mississippi	8	4	4	7,500	.....	5,000
Missouri	10	12	2, 4 & 6	10,000	8,500	6,000 to 8,000
Montana	6	4	2	7,500	.....	4,800
Nebraska	6	4	4	7,500	.....	5,000
Nevada	6	4	1, 2 & 4	7,500	.....	4,500 to 7,200
New Hampshire	**	**	6	7,000	.....	7,000
New Jersey	6 & 7	5	5	19,000 & 18,000	16,000	15,000
New Mexico	8	6	2	8,000	.....	6,000
New York	14	10	4 & 6	25,500 & 25,000	28,500 to 17,000	15,000 to 25,000
North Carolina	8	8	2 & 4	8,550	.....	7,550
North Dakota	10	6	2 & 4	5,500	.....	4,000
Ohio	6	6	4	12,500 & 12,000	8,000 to 12,000	3,000 to 9,000
Oklahoma	6	4	2	7,500	.....	4,000 to 7,200
Oregon	6	4	2	7,500	.....	5,000 to 6,500
Pennsylvania	21	10	5	19,000	18,500 & 18,000	9,000 to 15,000
Rhode Island	**	**	3 & 5	11,000 & 10,000	.....	10,000 & 9,500
South Carolina	10	4	2	6,750	.....	6,750
South Dakota	6	4	2	5,400	.....	4,900
Tennessee	8	8	6	7,500	6,500	5,000
Texas	6	4	2	8,000	6,500	5,000 to 7,400
Utah	10	4	4	5,000	.....	4,000
Vermont	2	2	2	6,500 & 6,000	.....	5,000
Virginia	12	8	4 & 6	8,900 & 8,500	.....	5,400 to 8,400
Washington	6	4	2	8,500	.....	6,500
West Virginia	12	8	4	10,000	.....	5,000 to 9,000
Wisconsin	10	6	4 & 2	10,000	.....	8,000
Wyoming	8	6	2	7,000	.....	6,500

* Data on tenure is from Haynes, *op. cit.*; that on salaries is from "Salaries of American Judges," *Journal* of the American Judicature Society, April, 1945, pp. 173–181.
** Good Behavior.

no comment here. There are relatively few resignations, but because the majority of the men elected or appointed are middle-aged or older, there are numerous retirements, due either to advanced age or to ill health. As has been noted in an earlier chapter, the impeachment process is effective only in theory in removing from public office those who have demonstrated their unfitness. During the entire history of the State of New York, there have been but seven proceedings for the impeachment or removal of judicial officers in the higher courts, and only two of these resulted in a judgment of removal from office. These cases all occurred between 1865 and 1939.[37]

No matter how strong the case against the accused, removal by impeachment is in practice a political proceeding. The recall is used in only about one third of the states, and in a much smaller number as applied to the judiciary. Furthermore, there are serious objections to its use in connection with judges; nowhere have these objections been better stated than in the veto message of President Taft to the resolution providing for the admission of Arizona into the Union in 1911.[38] A few states permit removal by legislative address or by the action of the supreme court.[39]

The truth of the matter is that, with the exception of those who retire from service under the provisions of a retirement law, few state judgeships are vacated. Walter F. Dodd comments thus on the subject of retirement:

Several states have express constitutional provisions for the retirement of judges on account of age. In Connecticut and New Hampshire a judge is ineligible to serve after he reaches the age of seventy. In New York a judge must retire on the last day of December after reaching the age of seventy; and in Maryland a judge must retire at seventy unless the legislature sees fit to continue him for the rest of his term. The Louisiana constitution provides for the retirement of judges on two-thirds pay after a certain number of years of service, upon reaching the age of seventy. Illinois in 1919 passed a law permitting judges who have reached the age of sixty-five and who have served twenty-four years in any one or more of the state courts to receive upon retirement an annual pension equal to one-half of the annual compensation received during their last term of service. The movement for the pensioning of judges upon retirement is making progress in the states.[40]

[37] Edelman, Albert J., *Removal of Judges,* p. 3 (City Club of New York, 1941).
[38] See discussion, *supra,* Chapter IV, Section 1.
[39] See Frothingham, Louis A., " The Removal of Judges by Legislative Address in Massachusetts," *American Political Science Review,* May, 1914, pp. 216–221.
[40] Dodd, Walter F., *State Government,* Second Edition, p. 318 (Century, New York, 1928) ; see also Willoughby, W. F., *Principles of Judicial Administration,* Chapter 29 (Brookings Institution, Washington, 1929).

Approximately half of the states make some provision for the retirement of judges. Twenty-eight provide for the retirement of supreme court judges with compensation, New Hampshire without. Age at retirement ranges from sixty-eight to eighty years, and retirement is sometimes compulsory, but usually optional. In North Carolina retired judges are subject to recall for emergency service. The period of service before a judge is eligible to retirement varies from ten to thirty years — several states specifying twenty years. Some states pay a small annuity on a monthly basis, but most pay half or two thirds of the salary received at the time of retirement. Tennessee pays the full salary, but only to the end of the term.[41]

Powers of Judges. The official powers and duties of judges vary considerably according to the type of court to which they belong. Trial judges conduct judicial proceedings in open court, and render decisions in the cases tried. In criminal proceedings their duties may also include the imposing of sentence, if the accused is convicted. Judges of appellate courts, sitting either in banc or in divisions, listen to the arguments of opposing counsel, possibly interrupting from time to time to ask questions. Oral argument is followed by a further study of the record, and discussion of the points raised. After the attitude of the court has been agreed upon in a given case, one of the justices is assigned the task of preparing the opinion of the court.

There is always a great temptation to impose upon judges responsibility for the performance of non-judicial duties. In some cases, they become responsible for the management and administration of sizeable properties and business enterprises, although they are not necessarily qualified to perform such duties. More often, they are called upon to exercise the appointing power. Because jurists are intelligent, educated, and supposedly non-political, they are frequently required to select members of school boards, tax boards, park commissioners, boards of city trusts, et cetera. Judges in Philadelphia, for instance, appoint the members of eight governmental agencies handling millions upon millions of dollars of public moneys and employing thousands of workers. Generally speaking, this is bad practice, although there are cases in which this method of selection has worked well. As a matter of principle, judges should not be required by the constitution or by statute to engage in the performance of non-judicial duties.

[41] See " Salaries of American Judges," *op. cit.,* and Haynes, *op. cit.;* also Winters, Glenn R., " Retirement Pensions for Judges," *Journal* of the American Judicature Society, December, 1943, pp. 105–112, with map showing geographical distribution of states, and tables.

ADMINISTRATIVE AND JURISDICTIONAL PROBLEMS

Many administrative problems connected with state court organization await some remedial or corrective action. While it is impossible to discuss any of them at length here, the nature of some can be suggested. There is, in the first place, the problem of the selection of clerks, bailiffs, tipstaves, and other court officers. There is the problem of reorganizing the units of judicial administration, and the desirability of eliminating justices of the peace, thereby making it possible to entrust the administration of justice in rural areas to one or more competent, full-time county judges. The urban magistrates constitute an obstacle to the administration of justice which could be remedied either by establishing well-organized municipal courts in the larger cities, or by transferring the function to a county unit in the case of the smaller ones. The administration of justice is hampered by intricate and too technical rules of procedure, by unsound practices with regard to the conduct of trials and the filing of appeals, and in many other ways.

The first and most obvious need in many states is to simplify the constitutional provisions which provide for the establishment of the judicial system. Many of these are not only needlessly long and complicated, but they freeze into the constitution a particular judicial organization which, although suitable at the time the constitution was adopted, is not adapted to modern conditions. It avails little to say that such provisions can be changed to bring them in line with present-day needs, if the amending process is as unworkable as that provided in many state constitutions. The states might well take a leaf from the experience of the Federal government, and follow the recommendation contained in the Model State Constitution.

The Federal Constitution provides in the opening sentence of Article III that " The Judicial power of the United States shall be vested in one Supreme Court, and in such inferior courts as Congress may from time to time ordain and establish." The Model State Constitution puts the idea in these words: " The judicial power of the state shall be vested in a general court of justice. . . ." The problem of correcting defects in the organization of the state courts would be a relatively simple matter if the state constitutions, in similar manner, were to provide that the judicial power of the state should be vested in a supreme court and such inferior courts as the legislature might from time to time ordain and establish.

The Unified Court System. In recent years there has been much discussion of the need for a uniform system of state courts. The prevailing practice sets up a number of different types and kinds of courts, each exercising particular types of jurisdiction, usually within definitely specified areas. The proposal is to make all courts THE COURT, in the belief that there is no reason why any judge should not hear any cause of action. This recommendation finds precedent in the provisions of the English Judicature Acts which affected important changes in the organization of the English courts. The Court of Appeals supplanted the several intermediate appellate courts which had existed before its creation; the High Court replaced the Courts of King's Bench, Common Pleas, Exchequer, Chancery, Admiralty, et cetera, and from it are drawn the Justices of Assize, who go on circuit to try criminal cases. The conditions in the states may not be quite as serious as those which had developed in England, but in many jurisdictions they are bad enough. In addition, it is urged that this highly centralized court organization gives an elasticity to the machinery for the administration of justice that is impossible where an elaborate court structure is provided for in the constitution.

The plans for unification have been numerous, but there seems to be a general agreement upon certain fundamentals in the structure of the state court system; these may be summarized as follows: [42]

First, a general court of judicature for the state.
Second, three main divisions of the court:
  I. A supreme court, with two divisions, criminal and civil, and other divisions, if necessary.
  II. District courts — intermediate courts of appeal — with original jurisdiction in a limited number of cases.
  III. County courts — with original jurisdiction over civil and criminal cases and appellate jurisdiction over cases from local magistrates; with special supervision and control over local magistrates or justices of the peace, if these officers are still retained; with authority to establish divisions for probate, juvenile cases, et cetera.
Third, the establishment of a judicial council.

There has been little agreement with regard to the degree of centralization that is either possible or desirable. The proposal for complete unification is contained in the Model State Constitution (Section 600) and has long been vigorously advocated by the American Judicature Society.

[42] Haines, Charles G., " The General Structure of Court Organization," *Annals,* May, 1933, pp. 1–11, and *Journal* of the American Judicature Society, issue of April, 1940, especially the article by Roscoe Pound, " Principles and Outline of a Modern Unified Court Organization."

It is the contention of Roscoe Pound that "unification of the courts would go far to enable the judiciary to do adequately much which we have been committing to administrative boards and commissions." The controlling principle, he points out, must be not specialized courts, but specialized judges. He would achieve this objective through unification, flexibility, conservation of judicial power, and responsibility. "Unification is called for in order to concentrate the machinery of justice upon its tasks, flexibility in order to enable it to meet speedily and efficiently the continually varying demands made upon it, responsibility in ordering that someone may always be held, and clearly stand out as the official to be held, if the judicial organization is not functioning the most efficiently that the law and the nature of its tasks permit."

Plan for an Administrative Officer. In the discussion of the overall organization of the state court system, mention has been made of the need for an administrative officer. In one way or another, a few states have recognized this need. The Constitution of Iowa provides that "the Supreme Court shall . . . exercise a supervisory control over all inferior judicial tribunals throughout the state," and sixteen other states have a more or less similar requirement. The plan for an administrative judge has its basis in the development of the English system. It has been used in the municipal courts of Cleveland and Detroit, and in the state courts of Massachusetts. In the former state the jurisdiction of the Chief Justice of the Superior Court is statewide; in the latter, the Chief Justice of the Circuit Court possesses similar jurisdiction, while an administrative judge, known as the Presiding Judge, serves in the Circuit Court of Wayne County. In Ohio there is no Chief Justice of the Court of Common Pleas with statewide jurisdiction, but there is a Chief Justice of the Court of Common Pleas of Cuyahoga County.[43]

In all these instances the adoption of the plan has brought a decided improvement both in the quality of judicial performance and in the calendar situation. In Detroit the improved calendar situation is explained by an increase in the number of juries waived and by improved executive management of the court's business, as well as by the addition of a number of judges. As applied in a state court situation, it is argued that the adoption of the plan would make possi-

[43] Commission on the Administration of Justice in New York State, *The Plan for an Administrative Judge,* pp. 5–6, Legislative Document (1934) No. 50 (H). See also *The Legal and Constitutional Status of the Plan for an Administrative Judge,* with an historical sketch of the administrative control of the Supreme Court — Legislative Document (1934) No. 50 (I).

ble (without a unified court) the assignment of judges to the more congested courts, the reduction of the number of jury trials, the development of a conciliation or settlement calendar, and improved administration of the business of the courts. The bar associations have generally approved the plan, but there has been a natural reluctance on the part of the judiciary to accept it.

Improvements Suggested for Appellate Courts. The proposal to simplify the constitutional basis of the state courts (and for a unified court system) affects the whole judicial system of a state. The proposal for an administrative judge would affect mainly the lower courts. It is now proposed to present briefly some suggestions for the improvement of the operation of the courts of review. Perhaps the best study of this subject is the one made for the Judicial Council of Michigan in 1933.[44] This report discusses ten specific proposals, the first of which is the enlargement of the membership of the court to increase its operating capacity. A tabulation of the number of regular judges of the courts of last resort for the forty-eight states shows that most of these courts began with three or five judges, and that they have since been increased to seven or, in a few cases, to nine judges. These increases have been helpful, but without accompanying improvements in the procedure of these courts, they are not of sufficient importance to solve the problem. The second proposal is the use of commissioners; this device has been resorted to for brief periods in many states since 1875, but it is nowhere regarded as anything more than a measure of temporary relief for congested calendars.

A third proposal is the temporary use of lower court judges. Virginia was the pioneer in this movement as early as 1789. Many arguments have been advanced for and against this solution, the most important of which is, perhaps, the fact that it tends to lower the prestige of the higher courts. This defect might be avoided by the creation of appellate departments of trial courts. The fourth suggestion, a more practical one for increasing the capacity of reviewing courts, calls for the setting up of a divisional organization. This method is now used in Alabama, Arkansas, Colorado, Florida, Georgia, Iowa, Kentucky, Mississippi, Missouri, Nebraska, Oregon, Texas, and Washington; it has been used at some time, for a limited period, in California, Illinois, Kansas, Louisiana, New York, Ohio,

[44] Curran, Edward O., and Sunderland, Edson R., "The Organization and Operation of Courts of Review," in *Third Report* of the Judicial Council of Michigan, 1933, pp. 50–246.

and Oklahoma. Two or three divisions are commonly used, with either a fixed or a rotating personnel. For the more important cases the court sits as a whole.[45]

The fifth suggestion is to provide judges with trained assistants, usually referred to as law clerks; this device has been used in California, Illinois, Oklahoma, and Pennsylvania, and for certain judges in Massachusetts, New Jersey, and New York. The sixth proposal is for the use of intermediate appellate courts; such courts have long been in use in the larger and more populous states, and are functioning now in about one third of the states, including Alabama, California, Georgia, Illinois, Indiana, Louisiana, Missouri, New Jersey, New York, Ohio, Pennsylvania, Tennessee, and Texas. This is one of the most important of the many proposals submitted. The seventh would impose restrictions upon the right of review. This has been done in some form in all the states, but it is obviously easier in those states which have an intermediate court of review. The eighth proposal is concerned with the methods of dealing with the problem of written opinions; it has been popularly expected and usually required by law that there would be a written opinion in every case heard by a court of review, but there is in fact little reason why such opinions should be prepared, with the consequent expenditure of time and effort, unless there is involved in the case some fundamental legal or constitutional question. This occurs in only a relatively small percentage of the cases brought before a court of review. These courts have therefore, in many jurisdictions, resorted to the use of mere orders, in some instances with — and in others without — an accompanying brief statement of reasons. This device is an enormous time-saver for the members of the court, and has not aroused the popular resentment that might have been expected. Other proposals relate to the more effective use of briefs and oral arguments, and to the problem of rehearing.

THE JUDICIAL COUNCIL MOVEMENT

The judicial council movement is one of the most important developments in recent years for the improvement of judicial organization and administration. First proposed in the Model State Constitution in 1921, the plan was first adopted in Ohio in 1923.

---

45 In addition to Chapter 5 of the Curran and Sunderland study, see Sharp, Susie M., " Supreme Courts Sitting in Divisions," *North Carolina Law Review*, June, 1932, pp. 351–365.

By 1945, it had spread to thirty-two states, as indicated in the table below. The four which are inactive are marked by an asterisk.[46]

SPREAD OF THE JUDICIAL COUNCIL MOVEMENT

1923 — Ohio
1924 — Massachusetts
1925 — Washington
1926 — California, Virginia *
1927 — Connecticut, Kansas, North Dakota
1929 — Idaho,* Illinois, Kentucky, Maryland,* Michigan, Texas, Wisconsin
1930 — New Jersey
1931 — North Carolina, Utah
1933 — New Mexico, Oklahoma, South Dakota
1934 — Missouri, New Mexico, New York, West Virginia
1935 — Indiana, Maine *
1936 — Iowa
1937 — Minnesota, Pennsylvania
1939 — Nebraska, Rhode Island

The growth of this movement has been due to a constantly increasing realization of the need for improvement in the methods of administering justice; more specifically, the causes have been stated in classic form by Roscoe Pound:

In the substantive law there has been steady growth. But growth by judicial decision, through experience of the operation of legal precepts in their application to litigated cases, is too halting to meet the needs of business in an era of rapid development of business methods. . . . Here the main difficulty is that it is no one's business to study the law functionally, to perceive how and where it falls short, and why; to discover leaks in our apparatus of precepts and doctrines and find out how to stop them. Fifty years ago the judiciary committees of the houses of the legislature were equal to the small amounts of investigation of this sort that was required for the efficient functioning of the law. Later committees of law reform in bar associations have been able to do part of this task. But today the task has become too great for these agencies. They are not continuously at work. They have no means of surveying the whole field. They can give but a fraction of their time. *We must find some agency which is always in operation, which works under conditions of permanence, independence,*

---

[46] National Conference of Judicial Councils, *Annual Handbook, 1940,* p. 109 (Newark, 1940). The *Journal* of the American Judicature Society reports on current developments, and bibliographies appear in the Conference' *Handbook*. The following articles are good: Morris, George M., " The Judicial Councils of the States," American Bar Association *Journal,* July, 1943, pp. 366–368; Pirsig, Maynard E., *Judicial Councils* (American Bar Association, monograph of Committee on Improving the Administration of Justice, Chicago, 1942) ; Saxe, Leonard S., " The Judicial Council of the State of New York: Its Objectives, Methods, and Accomplishments," *American Political Science Review,* October, 1941, pp. 933–940; and Sunderland, Edson R., " The Judicial Council as an Aid to the Administration of Justice," *ibid.,* pp. 925–933.

and assured impartiality, in which, therefore, the public may repose confidence. . . .[47]

The judicial councils have to a large extent met this need in those states in which they have been established.

Professor Sunderland, who has been intimately connected with the movement since its inception, develops more in detail the existing defects, indicating thereby the opportunities for service by the councils:

If the administration of justice is to meet the needs of the public, a thorough testing and overhauling of the organization and operation of courts, commissions, and other cognate agencies must take place. New methods must be devised and old methods reformed or applied to new uses. Venue must be made more convenient, service of process simplified, ex parte pleadings must surrender their dominant position in ligitation, greater use must be made of discovery before trial, of judicial framing of issues, and of proof by affidavit and by admissions of parties, procedural rules must be directory, not mandatory, actual prejudice must be the indispensable basis for all procedural objections, rules of evidence must be radically revised, calendars must be arranged in a way to avoid the shocking waste of time on the part of judges, lawyers, and witnesses which has become familiar practice, better coöperation between judge and jury must be reëstablished, a much more comprehensive system of references and auxiliary administrative machinery must be developed, the economic waste and legal risks of new trials must be reduced, the mechanism for the review of judgments must be enormously simplified and cheapened, courts must be unified and judicial personnel be subject to mobilization wherever needed, and better methods must be devised for the selection and retirement of judges.[48]

Organization. The organization of the councils has been simple. The Kansas statute provides that the Council shall be composed of one justice of the Supreme Court; two judges of different judicial districts, each of whom shall have served in such capacity four years previous to his appointment; four resident lawyers, each of whom shall have been admitted to practice for not less than ten years previous to his appointment; the chairman of the Judiciary Committee of the House of Representatives; and the chairman of the Judiciary Committee of the Senate. The Council in Texas is larger, but the personnel is designated in accordance with the same underlying principles: [49]

[47] Pound, Roscoe, "The Crisis in American Law," *Journal* of the American Judicature Society, June, 1926, pp. 5–11.

[48] Sunderland, Edson R., "The Function and Organization of a Judicial Council," *Indiana Law Journal*, May, 1934, pp. 479–497, at 484–486.

[49] Kansas *Laws of 1927*, Chapter 187, Sec. 1. Texas *Laws of 1929*, Chapter 309, Sec. 2.

The Chief Justice of the Supreme Court, who shall be president and chief executive officer of the Council.

An Associate Justice of the Supreme Court to be selected by that Court.

The Chief Justice of each of the Courts of Civil Appeals.

The presiding judge in each of the administrative Judicial Districts.

The Attorney General.

Two members of the Legislature who shall be chairmen, respectively, of the Senate and House committees on civil jurisprudence.

Four practicing attorneys of the state to be selected, two by the State Bar Association and two by the Supreme Court.

One member of the faculty of the State University Law School to be selected by the President of the State University.

Three laymen, citizens of this State, one of whom shall be by profession a journalist, and all of whom shall be appointed by the Governor.

After analyzing the parallel provisions of all the acts creating judicial councils, Professor Sunderland finds the most striking feature of these acts in the character of the personnel making up the membership of the councils. "Although they were drawn by lawyers, the practitioner does not occupy a dominant place upon any council. In some of them there are no representatives whatever of the practicing bar, the whole membership consisting of judges. In others the membership is divided among judges, other public officials, laymen, and practicing lawyers, but there is no state judicial council in which practicing lawyers as such predominate." [50]

Powers and Duties. The powers and duties of the councils have been variously enumerated and classified; it seems appropriate, for the present purpose, to group these powers under three general headings: (1) general administrative supervision; (2) rule-making power; (3) research and investigation. Before considering the exact nature of the work performed under these powers, it is important to emphasize the fact that, legally, the judicial council stands in a unique position. It is not a legislative body; it enacts no laws, although it may recommend legislative policies, and may draft acts for the consideration of the legislature. It is not a judicial body; it decides nothing, although it is deeply concerned with the procedure under which cases are moved through the courts, ultimately to the determination of the questions which they raise. Nor is it actually an executive or administrative body, although its powers of this type are more extensive than in the legislative and judicial fields. It is primarily an advisory and investigating body, so constituted that in most cases its recommendations are more effective

[50] Sunderland, *op. cit.*, p. 487; this article presents a detailed analysis of judicial council personnel; see also *The Judicial Council*, Appendix I, pp. 153–157.

and more likely to be translated into action than are those of most
other bodies.

Under its power of general administrative supervision of the
judicial business of the state, the council is responsible for the collection of statistics and other information showing the condition
of the dockets at all times in every civil and criminal court in the
state, and for the annual publication of these records.[51] Prior to the
establishment of the councils, data of this type were rarely if
ever available, even to the judges themselves. Upon the basis of this
information, it becomes the duty of the council, when authorized
by law, to transfer judges from districts in which the dockets are
clear, to others in which there are long calendars of cases awaiting
trial. This practice is based upon the important principle that the
state should at all times have the right to the service of its entire
judicial force. This objective has been in part achieved in some
states without judicial councils, but the assignment of judges may
itself lead to abuses unless proper safeguards are established. In
most states the councils can and should exercise the right to make
suggestions to judges, for the more efficient handling of the work
of their courts.

Rule Making. The second power usually exercised by the councils
is that of rule making. On this subject the American Judicature
Society urged, as far back as October, 1928:

. . . We should place rule making power first, as the power which dove-
tails with administrative direction, and which in every way is better vested
in a representative board of judges, than in a supreme court. The only
yielding on this point is to say that if the supreme court has complete rule
making power, as in Washington, then the judicial council should take the
initiative, do all the work of gathering data, drafting rules, discussing
proposals with the bar, and finally pass them up to the court for adoption.
All these steps are ordinarily required in drafting rules and it is not to be
presumed that any supreme court will have the time and patience to devote
to them. . . .

In 1943 the legislatures of twenty-two states had authorized the
several supreme courts to make rules of general practice not inconsistent with statutes. In numerous others the power existed but was
dormant. Congress has given similar authorization to the Supreme
Court, for the Federal Courts. These provisions are mostly of long
standing, having been enacted at various times during the last century. These enactments authorize the state courts to make rules of

51 See Pound, Roscoe, " Judicial Councils and Judicial Statistics," American
Bar Association *Journal,* February, 1942, pp. 98–105.

general practice which, when made, will supersede inconsistent legislative acts.

Seven states adopting judicial council acts prior to 1931 restored the rule-making power to the courts, as did three other states not having councils; this tendency is in conformity with the recommendations of students of judicial administration, and with the precedent established by the English Judicature Act of 1873, which established a Rules Committee with full power over court procedures. This English system of judicial administration is commonly regarded as a model. The legislature is not the proper forum in which to determine rules of court procedure, although the method has its defenders. The constitutionality of judicial rule making is now generally accepted. The arguments for judicial determination of rules and against legislative control of practice and procedure are summarized below: [52]

Arguments for Judicial Rule Making

1. Method violates no American constitutional principle.
2. Is used where justice is administered in a direct and economical manner.
3. Does not mean a return to early common law method, but alteration of a rule by judicial authority when needed, with general revisions when called for.
4. Procedure regulated by judges and attorneys in case of judicial council.
5. Bar would assist.
6. Responsible portion of bar would get a more sympathetic hearing from the bench than it gets from the legislature.
7. Changes could be made more promptly, and when needed.
8. Wider discretion left to judges — voiding defeat of substantial justice by technical rules.
9. Avoids present situation where legislated rules establish substantive rights.
10. Danger of power in hands of the judges is slight compared to power to decide cases and construe rules in specific cases.

Arguments against Legislative Rule Making

1. Members know nothing about the subject and are readily imposed upon.
2. Action is slow; meantime new difficulties arise.

[52] *Journal* of the American Judicature Society, December, 1925, pp. 122–126. In addition to the references cited in previous editions of this volume, see: Grinnell, Frank W., " To What Extent May Courts under the Rule Making Power Prescribe Rules of Evidence? " *Journal, supra,* August, 1940, pp. 41–50; Harris, Silas A., *The Rule Making Power* (American Bar Association, monograph of Committee on Improving the Administration of Justice, Chicago, 1942) ; " Judicial Rule Making Power in the United States," *Journal, supra,* August, 1943, pp. 59–60, including map of the United States; and Fifth, Ninth, and Tenth *Annual Reports* of the Judicial Council of the State of New York.

3. Consideration of rules consumes much time which could be devoted to things of which the legislature knows more.
4. Ties down judge's power to act in unforeseen situations.
5. Party may win suit by reason of opponent failing to conform to a rule which should be only the etiquette of justice.
6. Results in decisions on procedural points instead of on merits and in a complication of procedural law.
7. Prolongs trials because of procedural points and increases cost to public.
8. Deprives courts of their natural power.
9. Violates fundamental American principle of separation of powers.

Investigation and Research. The research may consist of making reports on special subjects from time to time, with recommendations to the legislature or to the governor, and of drafting acts to carry out such recommendations as an aid to the legislature. Even if the council has the rule-making power, there will be some matters that can be properly handled only by statute. The subjects under consideration are likely to be numerous and of a widely varied nature; the *First Report* of the Judicial Council of the State of New York listed sixteen, of which the following are typical: unification of the courts and the revision of the judiciary article and cognate sections of the state constitution; various changes in criminal procedure; extending procedure for examination before trial; providing more effective means for collecting money judgments; increasing costs as penalties against unreasonable claims and defenses; making more effective the official referee system; reducing expense of records and briefs on appeal, et cetera. Some of the research projects undertaken by the councils, as a basis for their recommendations, result in very extensive and valuable studies.[53]

The judicial council movement has gone so far as to bring about the organization of a National Conference of Judicial Councils, to meet annually in connection with the American Bar Association. Its purpose is to co-

[53] California makes the largest appropriation for this work, but that done by the Michigan Council has been most noteworthy. The following studies are illustrative: Ragland, George, " Procedure for Discovery before Trial," *Second Report* of the Michigan Judicial Council, 1932, pp. 83–177; Curran, Edward O., and Sunderland, Edson R., " The Organization and Operation of Courts of Review," *Third Report* of the Michigan Judicial Council, 1933, pp. 48–246; Sunderland, Edson R., " Types of Controversies in Which Declaratory Judgments Have Been Rendered," *Fourth Report* of the Michigan Judicial Council, 1934, pp. 51–168; " Statutory and Constitutional Provisions in Each State Relating to References," *Third Report* of the New Jersey Judicial Council, 1932, pp. 102–174.

For a general discussion of " The Work of Judicial Councils," see Sikes, Pressly S., *American Political Science Review*, June, 1935, pp. 456–472, and *Indiana Law Journal*, January, 1935, pp. 189–202. All the councils issue annual reports, upon which numerous comments are published, including a running series in the *Journal* of the American Judicature Society.

ordinate the work of all judicial councils and to enable all to enjoy the benefit of the study and investigations of each. If expectations are realized, we will finally have forty-eight state organizations forming a great clearing house of information and experience. All of the councils feel that the first duty is the collection of information in the form of adequate judicial statistics. A council should have power to require reports from the clerks of the courts of the state. Many of them are expressly invested with that power.

A judicial council organized with not too large a personnel, with authority to require reports from the clerks of courts, with adequate research facilities available, and with the support derived from the confidence of the public, will find unlimited possibilities for improving and developing the administration of justice.[54]

RELATIONS OF STATE AND FEDERAL COURTS

There are in the United States two parallel judicial systems, each exercising jurisdiction simultaneously within its own field over the same persons without any serious conflict. There are in practice a number of cases in which jurisdiction of the Federal and state courts is concurrent. In the field of criminal jurisdiction, situations arose, during the life of the prohibition amendment, in which the same individual could be prosecuted, tried, convicted, and sentenced for the same acts, separately and independently, in both the state and the Federal courts. In such cases it became a matter of practice for the Federal government to take precedence over the state, although if the Federal government failed to secure a conviction, it was still possible for the state concerned to attempt to do so. The control over citizenship provides an illustration of concurrent jurisdiction in the civil field. The Federal law provides that citizenship may be granted, either by the Federal courts or by a state court of record. Although the Federal government possesses full power to control this subject, the greatest diversity is permitted with regard to the conditions under which citizenship is conferred.

Another important aspect of the relation of the state and Federal courts involves the attitude of the latter toward state legislation. Since the Federal courts must interpret state law when the parties are of diverse citizenship, it has been necessary for them to develop some consistent policy with regard to such interpretation. This policy has been for the Federal courts to accept, save in exceptional cases, the interpretation of the state statute which has been adopted

54 Sunderland, Edson R., " The Judicial Council Movement," *Bulletin of the University of Minnesota*, March 5, 1931, pp. 28–35, at 35.

by the highest state court. Thus the Federal courts have properly assumed that the highest court of the state was in a better position to judge the purpose and intent of the legislature in its own jurisdiction than the Federal courts could possibly be. The question upon which the Federal court passes in cases of this sort is not, therefore, whether the state act, as they read it, is constitutional, but whether the state act as understood and interpreted by the state court is within the limits of state power, so far as the provisions of the Federal Constitution are concerned. In recent years there have been a number of cases before the Supreme Court of the United States involving various aspects of this main question.[55]

In 1936 a study was made by the Legislative Reference Service of the Library of Congress of the number of state laws declared unconstitutional by the Supreme Court. The results are indicated in the following table:

STATE ACTS HELD UNCONSTITUTIONAL BY THE
UNITED STATES SUPREME COURT [56]

Under the Commerce Clause	101
Under the Fourteenth Amendment	92
As Impairment of Contract	59
Miscellaneous	57
Total	309

Eight state supreme courts had always avoided reversals on points of constitutionality — those of Connecticut, Delaware, Idaho, New Mexico, Oregon, Rhode Island, Vermont, and Wyoming.

Finally, there are the questions of rules and of the conditions upon which appeals may lie from the state courts to the Federal. Although there are obvious advantages in a uniform system of rules in the two sets of courts, considerable diversity actually exists. It has been proposed that the states should adopt the Federal rules, and it is claimed that such adoption would not result in serious

---

[55] The United States Supreme Court will interfere with a decision of a state court only when, in the judgment, the state ruling amounts to mere arbitrary or capricious exercise of power, or is in clear conflict with those fundamental principles which have been established for the protection and enforcement of private rights; see Jacobson, J. Mark, " Federal Interpretation of State Law," *University of Pennsylvania Law Review*, February, 1938, pp. 335–369; and the following cases: American Railway Express Company v. Kentucky, 273 U. S. 269, 1927; Chicago, Milwaukee & St. Paul Railway Company v. Risty, et al., 276 U. S. 567, 1928; Coombes v. Getz, 285 U. S. 434, 1932; Adam v. Saenger, et al., 303 U. S. 59, 1938; Indiana ex rel. Anderson v. Brand, Trustee, 303 U. S. 95, 1938.

[56] *State Government*, April, 1936, p. 78.

disruption of existing procedure in the substantial majority of states which now have a so-called code procedure. A recent author states that a comparison with the varying state rules shows that, quite apart from considerations of uniformity, the merits of a given situation are largely in favor of the Federal rules.[57] Whenever a Federal court — even a District Court — acquires jurisdiction in a case by virtue of Federal questions, such court has power to determine all questions in the case, local as well as Federal.[58]

Appeals from state courts may be taken only from the highest state court to the highest Federal court. The reasons for this are obvious. There would be no purpose in the Federal courts' considering an appeal on a case properly within the jurisdiction of the state courts until the highest court in the state had had an opportunity to pass upon it. To have a case taken from the state court to any Federal court other than the Supreme Court would be an affront to that more or less mythical thing known as the sovereignty of the states.

There are several conditions upon which such appeals may be made. In the first place, the United States Supreme Court will receive on appeal a case in which the state court has declared a Federal law invalid. For obvious reasons there are few such cases, but the desirability of having a final review of them when they do arise, by the highest Federal court, is equally obvious. Any other procedure would open the way for numerous state court decisions invalidating Federal laws, thereby destroying the uniformity which is one of the virtues of Federal control, and thereby making possible a diminution of the Federal power by a series of decisions which might gradually whittle it away. In the second place, the Federal Supreme Court will review cases in which the constitutionality of a state statute has been questioned under the provisions of the Federal Constitution, and in which the highest state court has upheld the validity of the state law. If any other policy were followed, the provisions of the Federal Constitution applying to the states would soon cease to have an effective restraining power.[59] Again, under a Federal law adopted in 1914, it is possible to transfer cases from state to Federal courts by certiorari.

With regard to all these problems, evidence has accumulated

---

[57] See Gavit, Bernard C., "The New Federal Rules and State Procedure," American Bar Association *Journal*, May, 1939, pp. 367–374, 435; and "Federal Conformity to State Rules on Presumptions and the Burden of Persuasion," *Illinois Law Review*, May, 1938, pp. 101–104.

[58] Railroad Commission of California, et al., v. Pacific Gas and Electric Company, 302 U. S. 388, 1937.

[59] Callender, *op. cit.*, p. 44; Baldwin, *op. cit.*

through the years that where a dispute arises between the state and Federal courts, the latter almost invariably win their point. Professor Field has pointed out that the Federal courts may release a party who is in the custody of a state officer, if proper showings justifying issuance of the writ of habeas corpus are made.[60] The state courts may not interfere by habeas corpus with the work of Federal officers or courts.[61] The Federal Courts are careful to say that they will interfere only upon great provocation, but the fact remains that they do interfere in a manner not permitted to the states to interfere with Federal officers. Federal officers may surrender a person in their custody to the state courts if they wish to do so, but such a surrender is a matter of comity, and not one of legal obligation.[62]

" The Federal courts may enjoin state courts from proceedings with a case, and have done so occasionally,[63] but the state courts are not permitted to enjoin the Federal courts in their work." [64] Federal courts constantly interfere with state administrative officers by injunction, particularly in the field of public utility regulation and in taxation, but how often do the state courts step in to call a halt to any Federal administrative action? Congressional attempts to curtail Federal injunctive interference with state administration have been so restricted in application by the courts that they have been relatively ineffective.[65]

Diversity of citizenship cases may be removed from state to Federal courts under the provisions of a Congressional statute, and removals of this kind are legion because of the broad construction given this statute.[66] State attempts to curb removals by corporations in diversity cases have met with Supreme Court rebuffs and have proved futile.[67] Federal statutes also provide for the removal of criminal prosecutions against Federal officers in the state courts to the Federal courts; such removals have been held to be constitutional.[68]

[60] Moore v. Dempsey, 261 U. S. 86, 1923. The constitutionality of the Federal statute permitting this was sustained in Frank v. Mangum, 237 U. S. 209, 1914.

[61] Tarble's Case, 13 Wallace 397, 1872; state courts may not issue the writ to a Federal military officer to test legality of enlistment.

[62] Pomi v. Fessenden, 258 U. S. 254, 1922.

[63] United States Code (1926), Title 28, Section 379, forbids such injunctions to issue except in bankruptcy cases.

[64] Rigg v. Johnson County, 6 Wallace 166, 1867.

[65] See the fate of the " Three Judge Rule " of United States Code (1926), Title 28, Sections 380–389, as described in *Yale Law Journal*, May, 1929, pp. 955–983.

[66] An important case on removal is Gaines v. Fuentes, 92 U. S. 10, 1875. The technical law on removal, mostly district court law in fact, is in hopeless confusion.

[67] Terral v. Burke Construction Company, 257 U. S. 529, 1922.

[68] Tennessee v. Davis, 100 U. S. 257, 1879. See a later case stating rules of pleading on such a removal, Colorado v. Symes, 286 U. S. 510, 1932.

. . . The only consolation left to the states in the relations between the two judicial systems is that arising from the permission granted them by Congressional statute to try cases involving Federal questions, and that they not only decide questions arising under the Constitution of the United States in some instances, but may decide them as matters of first impression if no Federal precedent exists, and may even ignore such precedent when it exists, and evade compliance with the known rule of law for several years at a time.[69] But of course Supreme Court review substantially restricts the states in the long view, because of Congressional statutes permitting that Court to override state decisions upon Federal constitutional questions.[70] But here also, such questions are commonly brought to the Supreme Court at the initiative of the aggrieved individual rather than at the instance of the governments involved.[71]

SELECTED REFERENCES

Amer, Francis J., *The Development of the Judicial System of Ohio from 1787 to 1932* (Johns Hopkins Press, 1932).

American Municipal Association, *Formal Professional Qualifications Required of Judges* (Chicago, 1938).

Baldwin, Simeon E., *The American Judiciary* (Century, New York, 1905).

Beattie, Ronald H., *A System of Criminal Judicial Statistics for California* (University of California Press, 1936).

Beck, James M., *May It Please the Court* (Harrison Company, Atlanta, 1930).

Beman, Lamar T., Ed., *Election Versus Appointment of Judges,* Handbook Series (Wilson, New York, 1926).

Bond, Carroll T., *The Court of Appeals of Maryland* (Johns Hopkins Press, 1928).

——, Ed., *Proceedings of the Maryland Court of Appeals, 1695–1729* (American Historical Association, Washington, 1933).

Bradway, John S., Ed., " Progress in the Law," *Annals,* March, 1928.

Brown, Esther L., *Lawyers and the Promotion of Justice* (Russell Sage Foundation, New York, 1938).

Bruce, Andrew A., *The American Judge* (Macmillan, New York, 1924).

Callender, Clarence N., *American Courts: Their Organization and Procedure* (McGraw-Hill, New York, 1927).

[69] It often takes several years before state practice is really changed to conform to Supreme Court decisions on state powers, partly because a decision that a statute of one state is invalid does not automatically or immediately strike down similar statutes in other states.

[70] It seems commonly to be overlooked that statute now provides for the appellate jurisdiction of the Supreme Court, and that a repeal of the statute would leave to the state courts final jurisdiction over questions of Federal constitutional law arising in the state courts and not removed under the removal statutes. Appellate jurisdiction on this head is subject to " regulation " by Congress. Important early cases: Cohens v. Virginia, 6 Wheaton 264, 1821; Martin v. Hunter's Lessee, 1 Wheaton 304, 1816.

[71] Quotations from Field, Oliver P., " State versus Nation, and the Supreme Court," *American Political Science Review,* April, 1934, pp. 233–245.

Carpenter, William S., *Judicial Tenure in the United States* (Yale University Press, 1918).

Clark, Charles E., and Shulman, Harry, *A Study of Law Administration in Connecticut* (Yale University Press, 1937).

Cobb, W. Bruce, Ed., *Inferior Criminal Courts Act of the City of New York* (Macmillan, New York, 1925).

Cook, Wayne G., *Iowa Justice Practice* (Iowa State University, 1930).

Council of State Governments, *Book of the States,* current edition, 1945–1946 (Chicago, biennially).

Curran, Henry H., *Magistrate's Courts* (Scribner's, New York, 1942).

Douglass, Paul F., *The Justice of the Peace Courts of Hamilton County, Ohio* (Johns Hopkins Press, 1932).

Ervin, Spencer, *The Magistrates' Courts in Philadelphia* (Harrison Foundation, Philadelphia, 1931).

Furman, Abraham L., *Chief Counsel, the Ordeal of a Public Defender* (Macaulay, New York, 1933).

Gilbert, Hiram T., *The Municipal Court of Chicago* (Published by the Author, Chicago, 1928).

Goldstein, Jonah J., *The Family in Court* (Charles Boardman Company, New York, 1934).

Hannan, William E., and Csontos, Mildred B., *State Court Systems* (Council of State Governments, Chicago, 1940).

Harris, Silas A., *Appellate Courts and Appellate Procedure in Ohio* (Johns Hopkins Press, 1933).

Haynes, Evan, *The Selection and Tenure of Judges* (National Conference of Judicial Councils, n.p., 1944).

Illinois Legislative Council, *Circuit Court Redistricting in Illinois* (Springfield, 1938).

Lepawsky, Albert, *Judicial System of Metropolitan Chicago* (University of Chicago Press, 1932).

Litke, William W., *Survey of the Minor Judiciary in Pennsylvania* (Pennsylvania Municipal Publications Service, State College, 1942).

Lou, Herbert H., *Juvenile Courts in the United States* (University of North Carolina Press, 1927).

Lynch, Dennis T., *Criminals and Politicians* (Macmillan, New York, 1932).

Martin, Edward M., *The Role of the Bar in Electing the Bench in Chicago* (University of Chicago Press, 1936).

Merchant's Association of New York, *The Judicial Council* (New York, 1931).

Miller, B. R., *The Louisiana Judiciary* (Louisiana State University Press, 1932).

Moley, Raymond, *Tribunes of the People* (Yale University Press, 1932).

——, and Wallace, Schuyler C., Eds. " The Administration of Justice," *Annals,* May, 1933.

Morris, Gail M., *Justice of the Peace Courts in Indiana* (Indiana University, Bureau of Government, 1942).

National Conference of Judicial Councils, *Handbook* (Newark, annually since 1939).

New York State Constitutional Convention Committee, *Problems Relating to Judicial Administration and Organization* (Albany, 1938).

Peltason, Jack W., *Missouri Plan for the Selection of Judges* (University of Missouri, 1945).

Pound, Roscoe, *Organization of Courts* (Little, Brown, Boston, 1940).

Reticker, Ruth, *Expenditures of Public Money for the Administration of Justice in Ohio* (Johns Hopkins Press, 1933).

Schlosser, Alexander L., *Lawyers Must Eat* (Vanguard Press, New York, 1934).

Schramm, Gustav L., *Piedpoudre Courts: a Study of the Small Claims Litigant in the Pittsburgh District* (Legal Aid Society, Pittsburgh, 1928).

Smith, Bruce, *Rural Crime Control* (Institute of Public Administration, Columbia University, 1933).

Virginia Advisory Legislative Council, *Compensation and Retirement of Judges* (Richmond, 1938).

Warren, Charles, *The Supreme Court and the Sovereign States* (Princeton University Press, 1924).

Warren, George, *Traffic Courts* (Little, Brown, Boston, 1942).

Willoughby, W. F., *Principles of Judicial Administration* (Brookings Institution, Washington, 1929).

———

Alexander, James P., " An Administrative Agency for the Texas State Courts," *Journal* of the American Judicature Society, October, 1943, pp. 90–92.

Alper, Benedict S., " Forty Years of the Juvenile Court," *American Sociological Review*, April, 1941, pp. 230–240.

American Judicature Society, *Journal* (Ann Arbor, bi-monthly).

Bomberger, Louden L., " Non-Partisan Selection of Judges," *Indiana Law Journal*, October, 1940, pp. 57–65.

Chandler, Henry P., " An Administrative Office for State Courts," *Journal* of the American Judicature Society, June, 1942, pp. 7–10.

Cole, Kenneth C., " Erie v. Tompkins and the Relationship between Federal and State Courts," *American Political Science Review*, October, 1942, pp. 885–895.

Council of State Governments, *State Government* (Chicago, monthly).

Crowdus, William W., " Operation of the Missouri Non-Partisan Court Plan," *Journal* of the American Judicature Society, April, 1944, pp. 166–170.

Fairman, Charles, " Judicial Attitudes toward Federal-State Relations," *American Political Science Review*, October, 1942, pp. 880–885.

Feightner, Milo M., " Judicial Selection and Tenure," *Indiana Law Journal*, February, 1940, pp. 215–226.

Hyde, Laurence M., " Selection and Tenure of Judges," American Bar Association *Journal*, December, 1941, pp. 763–765.

Kingdon, Arthur F., " The Trial Justice System in Virginia," *Journal* of the American Judicature Society, April, 1940, pp. 216–221.

McCormick, Charles T., " Modernizing the Texas Judicial System," *Journal* of the American Judicature Society, June, 1944, pp. 11–19.

McDonald, Thomas F., " Missouri's Ideal Judicial Selection Law," *Journal* of the American Judicature Society, April, 1941, pp. 194–198.

Moos, Malcolm C., " Judicial Election and Partisan Endorsement of Judicial Candidates in Minnesota," *American Political Science Review,* February, 1941, pp. 69–75.

Morris, George M., " The Judicial Councils of the States," American Bar Association *Journal,* July, 1943, pp. 366–368.

National Municipal League, *National Municipal Review,* New York, (monthly).

Perkins, John A., " Judiciary Up to Date," *National Municipal Review,* November, 1940, pp. 736–742.

Pound, Roscoe, " Judicial Councils and Judicial Statistics," American Bar Association *Journal,* February, 1942, pp. 98–105.

Reinemann, John O., " Forty Years of the Juvenile Court Movement in the United States," *Mental Hygiene,* April, 1941, pp. 256–268.

Righter, Richard S., " The Judiciary Article of the Proposed Missouri Constitution," *Journal* of the American Judicature Society, August, 1944, pp. 52–55.

Saxe, Leonard S., " The Judicial Council of the State of New York: Its Objectives, Methods, and Accomplishments," *American Political Science Review,* October, 1941, pp. 933–940.

Selling, Lowell S., "The Psychopathic Clinic in a Criminal Court, Its Uses and Possibilities," *Journal* of the American Judicature Society, April, 1945, pp. 169–173.

Sunderland, Edson R., " The Judicial Council as an Aid to the Administration of Justice," *American Political Science Review,* October, 1941, pp. 925–933.

Walsh, William C., " Court Reorganization in Maryland," *Journal* of the American Judicature Society, February, 1945, pp. 151–154.

Wickhem, John E., " The Power of Superintending Control of the Wisconsin Supreme Court," *Wisconsin Law Review,* March, 1941, pp. 153–171.

Williams, Nathan B., " Independent Judiciary Born in Colonial Virginia," *Journal* of the American Judicature Society, December, 1940, pp. 124–127.

Winters, Glenn R., " Consensus of Judicial Selection Proposals," *Journal* of the American Judicature Society, December, 1944, pp. 107–117.

CHAPTER XVII

State Courts: Procedure

THE American courts, in spite of much criticism and of widely recognized defects, have occupied a unique position in public esteem. They have been generally admired and respected by the people, who have regarded them as the guardians of the Constitution, the custodians of the great heritage of the common law, and the protectors of their rights. While particular jurists or courts have sometimes been severely criticized, while particular decisions have been regarded with deep disapproval, the people have nevertheless cherished their judicial institutions and granted their judges more extensive powers than have the people in any other major country.

THE POWERS AND DUTIES OF COURTS

The powers of courts may be determined by constitutional or statutory provisions, or by both. Regardless of the type of court or of the nature of its jurisdiction, certain constitutional limitations are imposed upon it. From the Federal Constitution comes the limitation found in the supreme law clause of Article VI, which imposes upon the state judicial officers the duty of enforcing the Federal Constitution as well as that of the state. Due process and equal protection clauses binding upon the state courts are found in the War Amendments to the Federal Constitution and in the constitutions of all the states. In addition, the latter include, chiefly within their bills of rights, a large number of guarantees which may on occasion limit the jurisdiction of the state courts.

Some states have placed in their constitutions detailed provisions regarding the organization, powers, and duties of the courts.[1]

[1] On the unwisdom of this practice, see Callender, Clarence N., " The Shackled Judiciary," *Annals,* September, 1935, pp. 109–114, reprinted in *Journal* of the American Judicature Society, December, 1935, pp. 101–104.

Whatever the method of their determination, the powers state courts regularly exercise are of two types: inherent and jurisdictional. The inherent powers belong to the courts by virtue of the fact that they are courts, by reason of their function to determine judicially the settlement of cases brought before them. Among these are the right to preserve order within the courtroom, to punish for contempt, to employ officers, and by appropriate methods to require the enforcement of their decisions. The exercise of these powers is indispensable if the courts are to perform their duties.

There are a number of types of jurisdictional powers — original, appellate, concurrent, final, and exclusive. Original jurisdiction is exercised by courts of first instance; while these are usually lower courts, the constitution or the legislature may confer original jurisdiction upon one of the higher courts in particular types of cases. The phrase "appellate jurisdiction" is almost self-explanatory. Final jurisdiction is that from which no appeal is permitted; one commonly thinks of supreme courts as exercising this type of jurisdiction, but the legislature can and sometimes does confer final jurisdiction in particular types of cases upon the immediate appellate courts. Many instances of concurrent jurisdiction between different courts may be found. Some cases, for instance, might be taken before a magistrate, a municipal court, or a county or district court. The selection of the court in which suit is to be entered is a problem in procedure to be decided largely by the attorney handling the case. There are a few instances in which exclusive jurisdiction has been conferred upon some particular court in a particular type of case.

The work of the state courts has been classified by Dr. W. F. Willoughby under the following headings: [2]

1. The investigation and determination of facts, which function must be clearly distinguished from the work done in interpreting and applying the law to these facts.
2. The application of the law to the facts as thus determined.
3. The determination and construction of the law, resulting in the preparation of written opinions.[3]

[2] Willoughby, W. F., *Principles of Judicial Administration,* Chapter 16 (Brookings Institution, Washington, 1929).

[3] These opinions, in addition to being published in separate series for each of the states, can be found in the different units of the National Reporter System, a uniform series of reports covering the courts of last resort of all the states as well as the Federal Government. Arranged geographically, the several series are as follows: (1) *Atlantic Reporter,* 1885 to date, covering Connecticut, Delaware, Maine, Maryland, New Hampshire, New Jersey, Pennsylvania, Rhode Island, and Vermont. (2) *Northeastern Reporter,* 1885 to date, covering Illinois, Indiana, Massachusetts, New York, and Ohio. (3) *New York Supplement,* 1888 to date, covering

4. The prevention of infractions of law and the violations of rights, through the issuance of restraining orders and injunctions.
5. Advising the legislature and the executive branches of the government in respect to the law.[4]
6. Acting as public administrative agencies.
7. The administration of property, in connection with the settlement of decedents' estates, bankruptcies, receiverships, et cetera.
8. Acting as agencies for the enforcement of judicial decisions, through the compelling of the attendance of witnesses, the execution of process, et cetera.
9. The determination of the rules of judicial procedure, except in those jurisdictions in which the laws provide for legislative determination.

Volume of Judicial Business. It is not only the duty of courts to perform these functions; it is equally important that they should be able to handle promptly and efficiently such cases as may be brought before them. In recent years this has become increasingly difficult, for in all the states there have been enormous increases in the amount of judicial business. In its report for 1932 the Judicial Council for New Jersey included an interesting table [5] which showed by ten-year periods, from 1900 to 1930, the comparative increases in number of judges, population, ratables, and number of cases commenced in the

---

all intermediate and lower courts of record of New York. (4) *Southeastern Reporter*, 1887 to date, covering Georgia, North Carolina, South Carolina, Virginia, and West Virginia. (5) *Southern Reporter*, 1887 to date, covering Alabama, Florida, Louisiana, and Mississippi. (6) *Northwestern Reporter*, 1879 to date, covering Iowa, Michigan, Minnesota, Nebraska, North Dakota, South Dakota, and Wisconsin. (7) *Southwestern Reporter*, 1886 to date, covering Arkansas, Kentucky, Missouri, Tennessee, and Texas. (8) *Pacific Reporter*, 1883 to date, covering Arizona, California, Colorado, Idaho, Kansas, Montana, Nevada, New Mexico, Oklahoma, Oregon, Utah, Washington, and Wyoming. On the distinction between " opinions " and " decisions," see Rogers v. Hill, 289 U. S. 582, 1933; the terms are not equivalent, the court's *decision* of a case being its judgment thereon, and its *opinion* being the statement of reasons on which the judgment rests.

4 Advisory opinions are common, especially in the New England states. Massachusetts adopted a constitutional provision in 1780; New Hampshire, Maine, Rhode Island, Florida, Colorado, and South Dakota followed. Delaware and Alabama provided for advisory opinions by statute, and Vermont permits the governor to make inquiries concerning the rectitude of his official acts. Comprehensive statutes have been repealed in Minnesota, Missouri, and Vermont. The system has fallen into disuse in Nebraska, New York, North Carolina, Oklahoma, and Pennsylvania, the courts of these states now expressly denying their power to render advisory opinions: see New York State Constitutional Convention Committee, *Problems Relating to Legislative Organization and Powers*, Chapter 6 (Albany, 1938). While the opinions of the Massachusetts court are frequently cited, they have no binding authority; in Colorado, unfortunately, advisory opinions have the same legal effect as opinions handed down in settlement of actual cases considered by the court. It has been urged that this device be more widely adopted as a means of preventing the passing and enforcement of statutes later declared unconstitutional. The soundness of this argument is open to question.

5 From *Third Report* of the Judicial Council of New Jersey, December 15, 1932, p. 91.

supreme and circuit courts. In 1930 the last-named had increased by 935 per cent compared with 1900, while the number of judges had increased only 27 per cent. Similarly striking illustrative material could be found in practically any other state.[6] The inevitable effect of serious congestion in the courts is to deny justice to citizens.

Not only was there a tremendous increase in the volume of litigation, but there were significant changes in the major types of suits filed. Albert Smith Faught of the Philadelphia Bar studied the types of cases in the courts in 1736, 1836, and 1936. In the latter years, he used the supreme court reports; since the jurisdiction of these courts is largely appellate, the cases which they considered may be taken as a fair sample of the types handled by the lower Federal and state courts. In the comparison of 1836 and 1936 he found notable decreases in cases in business law, real estate law, and probate law and the elimination of slave cases. Torts, security law, and tax law showed the largest increases, but increases were also found in government law, criminal law, bankruptcy, family law, admiralty, and natural resources law.[7]

Current reports from judicial councils show pretty clearly that the volume of judicial business is now declining. The measures taken to deal with the congested court calendars of a few years ago — establishment of more courts, enlarging their size, changes in procedure designed to expedite business, and adoption of substitute procedures — have been successful. The data in the accompanying tables shows the effect of such measures in the State of Kansas. The volume of Supreme Court cases has declined sharply. The same is true of civil actions other than divorce, and of criminal actions in the District Courts. The increase in the number of divorce cases has been so great as to offset decreases in other types of civil actions, leaving the total number only slightly reduced. The number of jury trials has dropped to about one fourth of what it was fifteen or twenty years ago.

PROCEDURE IN CIVIL CASES

In the discussion of the legal system of the states, mention was made of the various aspects of civil law, including that governing property — real and personal; torts — against persons, against property, and against persons and property; contracts and matters re-

[6] See *Ninth Report* of the Judicial Council of Massachusetts, *Massachusetts Law Quarterly*, November, 1933, pp. 11–36; Finch, Edward F., " Excessive Litigation," *Journal* of the American Judicature Society, June, 1935, pp. 24–27.

[7] Faught, Albert S., " Three Centuries of American Litigation," *Temple Law Quarterly*, July, 1939, pp. 488–504.

Year Ending June 30	Cases Disposed of	Cases Dismissed	Cases Submitted
1928	676	200	276
1929	583	175	408
1930	633	196	437
1931	591	173	418
1932	628	210	418
1933	548	175	373
1934	521	190	331
1935	589	204	385
1936	580	206	374
1937	486	139	347
1938	461	162	299
1939	444	135	309
1940	496	147	349
1941	409	156	253
1942	343	92	251
1943	353	103	250
1944	249	71	178
Totals	8,590	2,734	5,856

DISTRICT COURTS — STATE AS A WHOLE
Cases disposed of

Year ending June 30	Civil other than Divorce	Divorce Cases	Total Civil Cases	Criminal Cases	Jury Trials
1927	10,035	3,886	13,921	3,494	1,265
1928	10,331	4,222	14,553	3,619	1,314
1929	11,229	4,827	16,056	3,726	1,340
1930	12,149	5,424	17,573	4,098	1,271
1931	12,011	5,264	17,275	4,647	1,590
1932 — no report					
1933	14,622	4,288	18,910	3,834	1,195
1934 — no report					
1935	14,621	7,312	21,933	3,456	1,001
1936 — no report					
1937	12,953	5,864	18,817	2,848	712
1938	11,915	5,576	17,491	2,930	843
1939	12,235	6,850	19,185	2,659	811
1940	10,092	5,535	15,627	2,678	806
1941	9,478	5,615	15,093	2,506	683
1942	8,918	5,930	14,848	2,081	690
1943	6,738	6,108	12,940	1,638	397

[8] Supreme Court table from Kansas Judicial Council *Bulletin*, October, 1944, pp. 88–89; District Court table, *ibid.*, July, 1944, pp. 36–46.

lating to the conduct of business, including partnerships and corporations; domestic relations, including marriage and divorce, and the status of women and children, et cetera. It now remains to consider the steps through which a civil action must normally pass. Civil actions are of two types, those at law and those in equity.

At Law. The great majority of civil actions at law — and the great bulk of litigation is confined to the civil trial courts — are heard before a magistrate or a justice of the peace; in these courts of the minor judiciary, the parties appear in person and tell their story. The " judge " decides the case. It is not necessary for attorneys to appear for the litigants, although they may do so. In more important cases, which originate in municipal, county, or district courts, the plaintiff goes to his attorney, discusses with him all the facts of the complaint, and arranges for the steps preliminary to the filing of the papers. These are well described in nontechnical language by Professor Johnson:

The attorney directs the clerk of the court which has jurisdiction to issue a writ of summons. This writ summons the defendant to appear in court at a specified time to answer the plaintiff. It is given to the sheriff, whose duty it is to find the defendant or his attorney and serve the writ. Ordinarily, the action cannot proceed until actual service has been made; but in certain cases, for example, divorce actions, where the defendant is outside the jurisdiction or residing in parts unknown, publication in newspapers is deemed sufficient. If the defendant has not already engaged a lawyer, he should do so at once; for failure to enter appearance in connection with the suit will mean that judgment will be entered against him by default. It is quite likely that he will find a lawyer, who will take the necessary steps to defend the case. This attorney " files an appearance " for his client with the clerk of the court. He then notifies the attorney for the plaintiff that the appearance has been filed, and the two attorneys thereafter notify each other of all the subsequent steps taken in the case.[9]

After these preliminary developments comes the filing of the declaration by the plaintiff (sometimes called the complaint or petition) , and the answer of the defendant; Professor Johnson continues:

The declaration must be very carefully drawn, for it must show a cause of action sufficient in law to warrant a judgment for the plaintiff. It is filed with the clerk of the court, and a copy of it is served on the defendant, together with a notice that he shall file an answer to the declaration within a certain date. The defendant, acting through his attorney, of course, may file a demurrer; that is, he may admit the facts as set forth by the plaintiff, but deny their legal sufficiency. In common parlance a demurrer is, " Yes, but what of it? " This passes the question of the sufficiency of the declaration to the judge. If he adjudges it legally sufficient, he " overrules " the

9 Johnson, Claudius O., *Government in the United States*, Third Edition, pp. 445–446 (Crowell, New York, 1945) . See also Callender, Clarence N., *American Courts*, Chapter 6 (McGraw-Hill, New York, 1927) .

demurrer and the plaintiff wins his case, unless the court, as it generally does, allows the defendant to file an answer to the declaration. If the demurrer is sustained, the defendant wins this point and would have judgment in his favor but for the fact that the court then generally permits the plaintiff to remedy his declaration by amendment. Assume, now, that the defendant answers the declaration of the opposing party. This answer or plea may admit certain allegations of the plaintiff and deny others. The points on which the declaration and answer differ are the points which will be in issue at the trial. The nature of the defendant's answer may be such as to warrant a response by the plaintiff, and in a number of states this replication (or reply) is permitted in order that all the points may be brought out clearly. It often happens that the defendant's answer does not constitute a sufficient defense. It is now the plaintiff's privilege to demur, which he does by asking the court to enter judgment for him " for want of sufficient answer," from the defendant.

As these proceedings continue, it may be possible for the attorneys to arrive at a settlement out of court of the differences between their respective clients; this is always preferable if possible, for it is well known that court actions are expensive, time-consuming, nerve-racking, and often unsatisfactory in their results. Judges are often instrumental in promoting such settlements. Judge Baldwin states dogmatically that most lawsuits never get to trial, either because the defendant has no defense and is well aware of the fact, or because the plaintiff does not care to press for a judgment, knowing that if he had it, he could not collect. This may make him the more willing to enter into any reasonable compromise, even though he may be certain that he has a good case.[10]

Much attention has been given of late to the development of formal pre-trial procedures and some progress has been made in securing their adoption. In 1945 such procedures were in regular, statewide use in Massachusetts, North Dakota, South Dakota, and Wisconsin. They were in regular use in one or more large cities and in some smaller communities in eight states; authorized by new rules with good prospects for extensive use in two states; authorized by statute or rule of court but little used in eight states; rare or occasional use by individual judges reported, without statutory action or rule of court, in fifteen states, and not used at all in eleven states.[11]

[10] Baldwin, Simeon E., *The American Judiciary*, p. 201 (Century, New York, 1905) ; Chapter 14 of this volume is devoted to trial courts for civil causes. See also Callender, *American Courts*, Chapter 7.

[11] " Use of Pre-Trial Procedure in State Courts," *Journal* of the American Judicature Society, February, 1945, pp. 156–157, with map of the United States; see also " Pre-Trial Is Readily Adapted to Rural Counties," *ibid.*, December, 1942, pp. 106–111; Laws, Bolitha J., and Stockman, Abram H., *Pre-Trial Conferences* (American Bar Association, monograph of Committee on Improving the Administration of Justice, Chicago, 1942) , and Platt, I. M., " Pre-Trial Procedure," Kansas Judicial Council *Bulletin*, December, 1938, pp. 281–284.

If the case goes to trial, the trial may be either by jury or by judge. As will be noted more fully later, the tendency is to diminish the number of civil trials by jury. If jury trial is used, the panel must be called, the members of the jury selected and sworn. The judge may then order the attorneys to proceed with the case. The counsel for the plaintiff opens the argument by informing the court and the jury of the facts in the plaintiff's case, the nature of the evidence he will offer in proof of these contentions, and the damages or redress he demands. Naturally, he " does his best to create a favorable impression with the jury for his client. His case may be won or lost by this initial effort. In some courts, this statement is immediately followed by the opening statement of the defendant's attorney; but in others, this may be delayed until the evidence for the plaintiff has been offered. In any case, the opening statement for the defendant has the same general purpose as that delivered by the plaintiff." [12]

After these opening statements, witnesses may be called, first for the plaintiff, later for the defendant. The witnesses of each party are subject to cross-examination by the attorneys for the other. Much of a lawyer's success in court depends upon the skill with which he is able, by adroit questioning, to bring out the points he desires to emphasize, and to secure admissions damaging to the case of his opponent. The examination of witnesses often makes a good " show " in court, but if the attorney is not considerate in his treatment of witnesses, he may turn the jury against his client's case. " During the examination of witnesses, one attorney may ' object ' to questions asked by the other, and the judge overrules or sustains the objection. In either case, one of the lawyers is ruled against and he may ' take an exception ' to the judge's ruling. These exceptions often constitute grounds for appealing the case." [13]

At the conclusion of these proceedings the attorneys are given an opportunity to summarize the case before it goes to the jury. The presiding judge, in his charge to the jury, is supposed to give an impartial statement of the law governing the case; he will point out clearly the nature of the verdict they should return in accordance with each of the possible findings as to the facts. Many judges acquire great skill in indicating to the jury the nature of the decision which is expected of them, by inflection, emphasis, et cetera, but without anything appearing in the record that would seem unduly to influence the jurors. Professor Johnson reports that in a number of

[12] Johnson, *op. cit.,* pp. 447–448.   [13] *Ibid.,* p. 448.

western states the judges' charge precedes the arguments of the attorneys; this procedure has been properly criticized for leaving as a last impression in the minds of the jurors the eloquence of the attorneys rather than the statement of the law made by the judge. Sooner or later the jury arrives at a verdict, which will probably be unsatisfactory to one of the litigants, and may be to both of them. Either may file a motion for a new trial, which must then be argued before the judge who presided at the trial. If the new trial is allowed, the appellate court may or may not sustain the findings of the lower court.[14]

Move to Modernize Civil Procedure. The law is notoriously conservative, but progress is being made in the effort to modernize court procedures. The new Federal rules went into effect in 1937, but five states — Arkansas, Connecticut, Illinois, Michigan, and Utah — must be credited with modernized procedures adopted prior to that date. Arizona, Colorado, South Dakota, West Virginia, and Wisconsin all have new codes adopted since 1937, and conforming substantially with the Federal rules. Quite a number of states have codes completed and awaiting adoption, or have a program for amending existing rules without adopting a code. In all of this work the state bar associations have a prominent part. In the remaining states efforts are being made to stimulate interest in a revision of the rules.[15]

Quantity of the Law. Judicial opinions are much too long and much too numerous, with the result that " the lawyer ceases to reason and becomes a mere digger in the dustheap of decisions." Back in 1915, a justice of the Wisconsin Supreme Court wrote an article on " The Courts and the Papermills," in which he quoted a remark of one practicing lawyer that he would " rather be a dog and chew rags for a papermill than have your job " (that of a Supreme Court Justice) .[16] Various arguments have been advanced to explain, if not to justify, the number and the extensiveness of the arguments in the published decisions. The result of this tremendous output has been little short of a calamity.

In 1942 a Chicago lawyer made a study of the reported decisions,

---

[14] On new trials and appeals, see Callender, *American Courts*, Chapter 6, and Willoughby, *op. cit.*, Chapter 37; Stone, Ferdinand F., *The Scope of Review and Record on Appeal* (American Bar Association, monograph of Committee on Improving the Administration of Justice, Chicago, 1942) .

[15] " States Move to Modernize Civil Procedure," *Journal* of the American Judicature Society, April, 1941, pp. 189–193, with map showing progress of the movement in the various states.

[16] Winslow, John B., *Illinois Law Review*, October, 1915, pp. 157–160, reprinted in *Journal* of the American Judicature Society, December, 1942, pp, 124–127.

Federal and state, to date, put the figures on a graph, and projected the curve into the future to 1990.[17] The results were as follows:

GROWTH IN THE VOLUME OF REPORTED CASE LAW

Period	Number of Decisions	Total Number of Decisions
1790–1840	50,000	. . . .
1840–1890	450,000	500,000
1890–1940	1,250,000	1,750,000
1940–1990	2,000,000 (est.)	3,750,000 (est.)

If the present rate of growth in the " output " of the law continues, it will become increasingly difficult as the years go by to " find " the law on any given subject, unless drastic changes are made in present methods of deciding and reporting cases.

In Equity. The origin and development of equity has already been discussed, as well as the distinction between law and equity. In an equity case the plaintiff or complainant files a bill in which he states the nature of his grievance and prays for the aid of the chancellor in securing relief. The bill is filed with the clerk of court, and a copy is served on the defendant in the mode prescribed by statute or by the rules of court; proof of service must appear in the records of the case. The defendant may plead in his defense in the form of a demurrer, as in common law, or in the form of an answer. The plaintiff may take advantage of defects in the answer of the defendant, by an exception. The case finally goes to court on the points at issue, as shown by the bill and answer. If the defendant fails to file an answer, or files one admitting the allegations of the plaintiff, the latter may have judgment by default, as at common law.

Hearings and proof constitute the next step in the proceedings; the more common methods of proof include depositions, reference to special examiners, hearings before the court, and jury trial. The judge may refer any particularly complicated question involved in the case to an examiner or master in chancery, who will investigate and report to the court. This procedure is especially common in divorce and bankruptcy cases. Jury trial is possible but uncommon in equity proceedings. In general, these proceedings move more rapidly than those at law. Equity has declined as a separate type of procedure, but as has already been suggested, the principles of equity have come to be more and more important in the consideration of all legal matters.[18]

[17] Lavery, Urban A., " The ' Findability ' of the Law," *Journal* of the American Judicature Society, June, 1943, pp. 25–28.

[18] This comment is based primarily on Callender, *American Courts*, Chapter 10, pp. 147–148.

PROCEDURE IN CRIMINAL CASES

The various steps that occur in a criminal proceeding and the significance of each will now be considered, in the order in which they normally occur. When a criminal offense has been committed and the identity of the offender is known, a warrant will be issued for his arrest, and the arrest will be made as soon as his whereabouts can be determined. If the identity of the offender in unknown, in some jurisdictions a John Doe warrant may be issued, authorizing officers of the law to take into custody persons whom, for one reason or another, they suspect. In the Federal procedure, and in that of many states, the citizen desiring to swear out a warrant must be able to describe the individual to be arrested with sufficient accuracy so that he may be identified, even though his name may not be known. Multiple arrests, in which persons are held on suspicion, occur in practice, but have no basis in law. They are not permitted in Great Britain. Persons may be held without formal charge only so long as it takes an attorney to secure a writ of habeas corpus — usually twenty-four to forty-eight hours. This requirement is sometimes evaded by holding the individual on another charge. False arrests are not uncommon here, but they are in Great Britain, where a heavy penalty attaches to them. There investigation is made first and arrest afterward.

Preliminary Hearing: Bail. As the second step, the defendant will be brought up for a preliminary hearing. The Missouri Crime Survey reported the experience of that state, which seems to be typical of what happens elsewhere:

The courts of preliminary hearing play an unimportant rôle in the administration of justice. They hear the evidence, usually only that of the state, and determine whether or not there is reasonable cause to believe that a crime has been committed, and that the accused committed it. If such cause is shown the accused is confined or released on bond if the offense is a bailable one, to answer any charge which may be lodged against him by the prosecutor or grand jury. If no charge is filed before the first day of the next regular term of the circuit or other court having jurisdiction, he is entitled to be released if in confinement, or to be discharged on his bond if at liberty on bail.[19]

In other words, if, as a result of this preliminary hearing, the charges against the accused appear to be unfounded, he may be discharged by the magistrate or the justice of the peace; if there appears to be some foundation for the charges, he may be held over for the grand jury. If the defendant is known to be a responsible person, he may be

[19] *Missouri Crime Survey,* p. 164 (Macmillan, New York, 1926).

let out on his own recognizance; if not, he will probably be retained in custody, awaiting the action of the grand jury. If he has sufficient political influence, he may be able to get out on bail anyway, in which case the amount will be determined by the magistrate who conducted the preliminary hearing. All offenses except first degree murder are or may be bailable; the abuse is found, not in the types of offenses for which bail is accepted, but rather in the kind of bail furnished and accepted.

In most states the right to bail is a constitutional right,[20] which in itself is evidence of the importance commonly attached to the right. Unfortunately, in the administration of the system, serious defects have developed in many jurisdictions. Too frequently, bail bonds are accepted in felony cases. Often there is no one responsible for compelling bondsmen to keep their qualification sheets up to date, or for a prompt and vigorous follow-up on forfeited bonds. There are few large cities in which, at one time or another, investigations have not clearly demonstrated the abuses committed by professional bondsmen. One case cited by the Missouri Crime Survey will serve to illustrate: a man whose real estate was valued at $24,100 with a mortgage of $31,500, was permitted to become surety in one year on bonds aggregating $670,295. In all probability his compensation was not less than $33,000, and it is estimated that it may have been as high as $100,000.[21] An investigation in Philadelphia in 1938 showed a widespread failure on the part of magistrates to comply with the provisions of the bail law, and a total of $250,000 in worthless bail bonds accepted during the preceding six years. A magistrate in New York was ousted in 1939, after over eleven years' service, for " cooperation " in a bail bond scandal. Such instances could be multiplied indefinitely.

Indictment. Let it be assumed that the defendant has been held in order that his case may be considered by the grand jury. The institution of the grand jury is a part of the heritage of the English common law; its function is not to try the case, but to decide whether there is sufficient evidence against the accused to justify holding him for trial. The grand jury has been defined as a body of persons chosen to inquire into offenses against the state and the conduct and management of public institutions and officers. In England, in early

20 According to the *Missouri Crime Survey*, p. 190, there are only nine states in which bail is not a constitutional right: Alabama, Georgia, Maryland, Massachusetts, New Hampshire, New York, North Carolina, Virginia, and West Virginia.

21 *Ibid.*, pp. 211–212; the whole Part V of this *Survey*, by Raymond Moley, deals with bail bonds. See also Willoughby, *op. cit.*, Chapter 39.

times, the commission of a crime was looked upon as a personal matter between the author of the crime and the person injured; gradually, however, the idea developed that crime is an offense against the peace and security of the state, and that it is to the interest of the state to proceed against the offender.[22] Maitland describes how, under the Assize of Clarendon, royal justices were sent throughout England " to inquire by the oaths of the neighbors of all robberies and other violent misdeeds." [23] This machinery, which the king kept in his own hands, thereby making it necessary for those who were accused of crime to be brought before his justices, was in full force at the time of the founding of the American colonies, and was introduced in them as an important feature of the common law. As in the case of the petty jury, the grand jury was regarded by the colonists as one of the bulwarks of their liberties, and it was retained in force after independence was achieved.

If the grand jury believes there is sufficient evidence against the accused, the foreman will bring in what is known as a true bill, in which the name of the accused must be stated with absolute accuracy, as well as the exact nature of the charges under which he is held. It must also contain a statement to the effect that the crime charged is prohibited by law. In the American states the grand jury varies in size from six men to twenty-four, plus a foreman; Michigan has experimented with a one-man grand jury. There has been much controversy in some states regarding the right of women to serve on grand juries, but their right to serve is gradually being recognized. The theory was that this body would conduct an investigation of the charges against the accused, and determine for itself whether or not he should be held for trial. Practice has come to be widely at variance with this theory. The grand jury, except in rare and exceptional instances, conducts no investigation, but confines itself to the consideration of evidence presented by the prosecuting attorney, whose recommendations are commonly followed.

This procedure is followed, not by logic, but by tradition; it is slow, cumbersome, expensive, and inefficient. There has been recently a movement in favor of indictment by information, a method which has shown itself to be quick, inexpensive, and efficient. It is argued that this method obtains substantially the same results, with-

---

[22] Willoughby, *op. cit.*, pp. 174–175; Chapter 14 is devoted to the grand jury; see also Arizona State Legislative Bureau, " Grand and Petit Juries in the United States," *Legislative Briefs*, February 15, 1940.

[23] Maitland, Frederic W., *Constitutional History*, pp. 109–110 (Cambridge University Press, 1920) .

out the loss of time and the expense involved in the consideration of routine cases by the grand jury. This does not mean that the grand jury as an institution should be abolished, but simply that in routine matters it would not be used. It would still be possible to have grand jury investigations of particular cases or situations in which such a procedure would be in the public interest.[24]

Much has been written on the question whether the intervention of a body of laymen to pass upon the action of a trained and technically qualified officer, acting under a permanent responsibility, serves any useful purpose. Dr. Willoughby quotes many authorities who believe that it does not, and summarizes their objections in the following paragraph:

The objections to the grand jury, from the standpoint of the prosecution, are: that it is in the nature of a fifth wheel; that real responsibility for the bringing of criminal charges is in fact exercised by the prosecuting attorney, the grand jury doing little or nothing more than follow suggestions; that it complicates by just so much the machinery of criminal administration; that it entails delay which is an evil in itself; that it renders prosecution more difficult through important witnesses getting beyond the jurisdiction of the court, or through memory of facts becoming weakened by lapse of time; that it entails unnecessary expense to the government; and that it imposes a great burden upon the citizens called upon to render jury service.[25]

As Dr. Willoughby points out, however, it is not enough to show that the grand jury is not an aid to the prosecution, or even that it is a positive drag and a source of avoidable expense and delay, to establish a case for its abolition. " It must also be shown that it does not render a desirable service from the standpoint of the protection of persons from being unjustifiably forced to defend themselves in court against charges of which they are innocent." This, however, can also be done,[26] not only by the production of specific data based upon studies of the operation of the system, but by reference to the fact that the grand jury is not considered an essential feature of

24 For further discussion of this proposal, see Moley, Raymond, " The Use of the Information in Criminal Cases," American Bar Association *Journal,* May, 1931, pp. 292–294.

25 Willoughby, *op. cit.,* pp. 180–186; quoted are Judge Olsen of the Chicago Municipal Court, who believes that in 95 per cent of the felony cases the grand jury cannot do any good whatever; W. F. Dodd, in his *State Government,* p. 312 (Century, New York, 1928). *The Panel,* January–February, 1935, contains an article on grand jury presentments, and articles arguing for and against the continuance of the grand jury system. Lieck, Albert H., " Abolition of the Grand Jury," *Journal of Criminal Law and Criminology,* December, 1934, pp. 623–635.

26 On this point, see Baldwin, *op. cit.,* pp. 238–239, quoted by Willoughby, *op. cit.,* pp. 184–185.

judicial administration in any country whose judicial system is derived from sources other than the common law of England.

Arraignment in Court. After indictment has been obtained, either by grand jury or by information, the case is placed on the docket awaiting trial. The court opens with the usual formalities — the "Oyez, Oyez, Oyez" of the court crier, the prayer by the chaplain, et cetera.[27] The trial may result in the conviction of the accused, or in his exoneration. It is important to note the difference of attitude toward the accused in the United States and in the countries of Continental Europe and elsewhere whose legal systems are based upon the principles of the Roman law. In the English-speaking countries there is what is known as the accusatorial system, under which it is assumed that the accused is innocent until proved guilty, whereas under the inquisitorial system, which developed under the Roman law, no assumption is made regarding the guilt or innocence of the accused. This difference in attitude toward the accused is responsible for more fundamental differences in the matter of procedure. Under our system, a large number of people who may be detained for questioning can be arrested and pending further investigation of the case, while under the system governed by the Roman law, the work of investigation has to be carried much further before charges are lodged against anyone.[28]

In this country it has been customary to try all criminal cases with a jury; in the following section certain problems in connection with jury trial will be discussed. If the accused is convicted as a result of this trial, he will either at the conclusion of the trial or some days later be brought before the court for sentence. Some consideration may be given to his attorney, if it is decided to prepare a motion for the appeal of the case. When sentence has been pronounced, the prisoner will ordinarily be moved from the city or county jail in which he has been confined during the trial, to a state penitentiary or other correctional institution.

THE JURY SYSTEM

There is no aspect of the administration of justice that has come in for greater censure, by lawyers and laymen alike, than the operation of the jury system. Trial by jury has been preserved inviolate in

[27] Baldwin, *op. cit.*, Chapter 13, discusses the formalities of judicial procedure.
[28] For full discussion, see Willoughby, *op. cit.*, Chapter 15; the criminal courts are discussed at length in Callender, *American Courts,* Chapters 12 and 13.

the state constitutions as it existed when the states achieved their independence. The constitutional guarantees, therefore, apply mainly to the essential factors of jury trial as developed in England. The United States Supreme Court has held that these were three: a jury of precisely twelve persons, a unanimous verdict, and trial before a qualified judge with power to direct the trial and instruct the jury as to the law and the evidence.[29]

History and Development. The jury system developed in medieval England on the theory that the citizen who had a grievance against his neighbor, or a person accused of crime, would be more likely to receive fair treatment at the hands of the law if the facts in his case were weighed and decision rendered by a group of his neighbors. At this time two qualifications were emphasized in selecting persons for jury duty. The juror was supposed to be acquainted with the parties to the case, or, in a criminal case, with the accused. It was assumed that a knowledge of the character and personal life of the individual would be of value in considering the legal situation in which he was involved. If the case was a civil one involving some type of business relationship, the jury was selected to include persons who had an intimate and first-hand knowledge of the subject matter involved.

A slight acquaintance with practice in selecting modern juries will be sufficient to emphasize the extent to which the early theory has been reversed. If a prospective juror admits that he is acquainted with the defendant, or with either of the parties in a civil case, his right to serve on the jury is immediately challenged by the opposing counsel. The same thing occurs when a juror admits his familiarity with the type of problem involved in the case before the court. He is not supposed to know anything about the subject at hand, and it sometimes seems that he does not know much about anything. The theory now is that all the members of the jury will start their consideration of the case with an equal background of complete ignorance, and that such technical information as may be necessary will be supplied in the course of the trial by the testimony of experts. This theory sounds reasonable enough, but it does not work.

Historians of the jury system point out that its evolution from a witness body to one composed of persons not themselves having knowledge, but having the duty of determining facts through the

[29] With regard to the last point Illinois constitutes an exception. See People v. Kelly, 179 N. E. 898, 1932. and Tennant, John S., " The Right of the Trial Judge to Comment on the Evidence," *Journal* of the American Judicature Society, June, 1932, pp. 16–20.

testimony of others, was a slow one, the details of which cannot be accurately traced. One of the writers observes:

> In the course of time, and by slow degrees — degrees so slow that we can hardly detect them — the jury put off its old and acquired a new character. Sometimes, when the jurors knew nothing of the facts, witnesses who did know the facts would be called in to supply the requisite information. As human affairs grew more complex, the neighbors whom the sheriff summoned became less and less able to perform their original duty, and more and more dependent upon the evidence given in their presence by those witnesses who were summoned by the parties. In the fifteenth century the change had taken place.[30]

Because of this change in the fundamental character of the jury, along with other factors, the caliber of the ordinary jury is very low.

Declining Effectiveness of the Jury System. In considering the causes of the decline of the jury system, it is natural to turn first to the inadequate compensation that is paid for jury service — usually three, four, or five dollars a day. If compensation were computed at the last-named rate for every day of a month excluding Sundays, the juror would receive the munificent salary of $130. Of course the service may not last a month, and the juror will not be called upon to sit every day. Thus, if the juror is engaged in business or professional life, he cannot get out of his jury service a compensation which anywhere nearly equals his normal income. In addition to the financial loss, the juror must be absent from his regular pursuits more or less continuously for a period of several weeks. This accounts, at least in part, for the almost universal desire on the part of citizens to be excused from jury service.

A second factor contributing to the low caliber of juries is the matter of exemptions. In most jurisdictions the law provides for the exemption of teachers and others whose professional activities are of such a character as to make their interruption inadvisable.[31] In addition, the majority of those called for service attempt to bring political pressure to bear in order to be excused. This is due partly to the financial reasons already noted, and partly to other causes. The net result is that the caliber of those who serve is low because the higher types of citizens are either exempted by law or excused from service by the judge.

[30] Maitland, F. W., and Montague, Francis C., *Sketch of English Legal History*, p. 57 (Putnam's, New York, 1915) ; quoted by Willoughby, *op. cit.*, p. 485; see the whole of Chapter 36 in this work.

[31] Lawyers, ministers, doctors, teachers, railroad engineers and firemen, and similar classes of persons may be excluded from jury duty, so as not to interrupt their regular work for the community. Rawlins v. Georgia, 201 U. S. 638, 1906.

There are undoubtedly many citizens whose sense of civic responsibility would be strong enough to induce them to serve in spite of financial losses and absence from their accustomed activities, if it were not that the delays of the law and the frequent miscarriages of justice have developed in their minds a sense of futility with regard to the whole undertaking. They have seen criminals set free because of some trifling inaccuracy in the indictment. They have seen weeks of labor and thousands of dollars of expense cast aside as of no account, when for some petty technical reason a new trial has been granted. They have seen juries render decisions which could not be explained by reference to the facts or to any rules of logic. They have seen juries made up of individuals who never possessed a hundred dollars, passing upon complicated business questions involving thousands of dollars of other people's money. They have seen juries " hung " by the stubbornness of a single individual, and they have seen others rush through important cases to an ill-considered decision, in order that one of the men might catch the five-fifteen train or that one of the women might keep an appointment with her hairdresser. Under such circumstances, it is not greatly to be wondered at that many conscientious and intelligent citizens have thrown up their hands in despair, and exclaimed, " What's the use! "

Should the Jury System Be Abolished? In view of the serious objections to the jury system as it now operates, there have been numerous proposals for its abolition. The proper adjudication of controversies requires the exercise of a very special faculty, usually described as judicial temperament. Dr. Willoughby contends that persons intrusted with determining individual rights should be required to perform their duties under a system of continuing responsibility; that the work of adjudication should be performed with dispatch, involve the minimum of technicalities, and entail a minimum of expense for both government and litigants. " No one of these requirements is met, even in measurable degree, by the jury system "; it would, on the other hand, " be difficult to devise a system that would be more productive of trouble, expense, and delay." [32]

" Technically considered, therefore, the jury system is defective, and all the arguments from this standpoint are in favor of the alternative system where complete responsibility for the determination of matters both of fact and the law and the rendering of the decision is vested in a permanent trained bench." This indictment applies not only to the use of the jury in civil cases, but to its use in criminal

[32] Willoughby, *op. cit.*, pp. 490–491.

cases as well. In each of the numerous surveys made in recent years of the administration of justice in one state after another, the recommendation has been made that the waiver of a jury be permitted either in all but capital cases or in all cases. A study of the attitude of bench and bar in Ohio some years ago showed that 80 per cent or more favored waiver, approximately half of them very strongly. The possibility of waiver has been in existence for years in Maryland, Ohio, and other states.[33]

Unless the jury system is to be abolished, or its use drastically reduced through the extension of the privilege of waiver, there must be significant improvements in the quality of the personnel and the functioning of the system. Charles A. Boston well states the argument for a better trained and more competent personnel:

We train recruits to bear arms, we license lawyers, physicians, dentists, midwives, veterinarians, horseshoers, and chauffeurs, but so long as a man speaks any sort of English, can hear, is on the jury list and has not formed an opinion, he is deemed a competent man to decide disputes in a court of justice. He would not be accepted to run a street car, nor to perform any number of ordinary duties for a private employer, but he is legally a fit juryman if he has these qualifications. . . .[34]

The system is not without its defenders, although some of them, like Professor John B. Waite of the University of Michigan, adopt the interesting expedient of stating the case for the system in negative form — for instance: "No enthusiast pretends that a jury is especially competent to determine guilt, but only that it is not likely to convict innocence." [35] "All its praise is in terms of advantage to the defendant, never of its efficacy in protection of society. Most of the jury's alleged virtues are negative." Again: "It is assumed that juries can profit from the greater experience of the judge in gauging witnesses and evaluating evidence. American legislators, however, have been afraid; afraid that judges would express strongly prejudicial and perhaps dishonest opinions, and afraid that juries would weakly or stupidly surrender their privilege of independent judgment and follow the judicial desires. The whole situation presents an illuminating inconsistency of insistence upon the desirability of jury verdicts, coupled with complete distrust of the jury's capacity

[33] Martin, Kenneth J., *The Waiver of Jury Trials in Criminal Cases with Special Reference to Ohio* (Johns Hopkins Press, 1933).

[34] Boston, Charles A., "Some Practical Remedies for Existing Defects in the Administration of Justice," *University of Pennsylvania Law Review*, November, 1912, pp. 1–32; quoted by Willoughby, *op. cit.*, p. 491.

[35] Waite, John B., *Criminal Law in Action*, Chapter 5 (Sears, New York, 1934).

for intelligent independence of opinion." And again: " The character of jurors depends upon the honesty of jury commissioners and the
industry and courage of trial judges. The jury system is not and cannot be better than the men who manage it." At best, the case for
the jury system is that something else might be worse.

Reconstruction of the Jury System. The defects of the jury system
are widely recognized. It is important not only to consider the various points in the indictment, but to lay even greater emphasis upon
the possible remedies. As a first step, the abolition of jury trials in
all or at least a majority of civil cases and trial by judge rather than
by jury in criminal cases where the parties agree to this procedure
might well be provided by law. In addition, everything that properly can be done to encourage the use of these alternatives should be
done. In England, where the jury system originated, such steps were
taken long ago; similar steps have now been taken in many states.

The second type of remedial action involves the use of substitute
procedures, such as quasi-judicial boards and commissions for particular types of cases, and the development of self-government in
industry for the settlement of civil cases.[36] The prevailing practice
in the enforcement of workmen's compensation legislation well illustrates the first. In former times, when the three common law defenses
might be invoked by the employer in injury cases, and under the
employer's liability system which followed, all cases involving recovery for industrial accidents were thrown into the courts and decided by juries. When, in 1915 and thereabouts, these earlier systems
were superseded by workmen's compensation legislation, an administrative bureau was placed in charge of enforcement work. Where
the bureau was unable to bring the parties to an agreement, the case
would be assigned to a compensation referee, from whose decision
still further appeal might be had to a workmen's compensation
board. Thus an enormous block of cases was lifted out of the courts
by a single piece of legislation. Technically, appeals might be carried from the board to a court, but in practice the number of such
appeals was small; when allowed, they are considered by a higher
court.

Another huge block of cases has been lifted out of the jurisdiction
of the courts and removed from consideration by juries, by the movement for self-government in industry, under which trade associations

[36] These are discussed in Elder, Robert H., " Trial by Jury; Is It Passing? "
Harper's Magazine, April, 1928, pp. 570–580; Arizona State Legislative Bureau,
op. cit.

established mediation and arbitration facilities for the settlement of differences among their members. Most of these trade associations adopted codes of ethics and standards of correct practice, the latter containing exact definitions of important trade terms. These statements represented the highest ideals of the business group, and serve as guides to mediators and arbitrators in the settlement of disputes. The more business can be encouraged to regulate itself, the less regulation it will need by government. Likewise, the more disputes it can settle through machinery it has established and administers itself, the smaller will be the burden placed upon the courts.

These first two remedies were designed to remove large numbers of cases from consideration by juries, in one case by statute, and in the other by substituting private means of settlement. For the number which remains, drastic changes in the jury system itself are proposed — changes designed to modernize and improve it and adapt it to present-day needs. The common law jury has twelve members; there is no reason why a statutory jury of six or eight members cannot be used. This expedient was adopted many years ago in Utah, and was upheld by the Supreme Court except in cases where its use might be considered ex post facto.[37] The proposal has been brought up from time to time in other states; in Kansas, for instance, in 1935 the Judicial Council suggested legislation establishing juries of six, unless twelve were requested.[38] In some states, in courts of record, the parties by agreement in open court may stipulate a smaller jury than the traditional twelve. If changes of this character were made, and if at the same time the compensation were substantially increased, some improvement in existing conditions might result.

The establishment of a system of service by professional jurymen has been suggested. If competent people were selected, and adequate training and compensation provided, this plan also might work. No one need be horrified at the suggestion, for there are in many communities political hangers-on around the courthouse who are often jestingly referred to as professional jurymen. When a panel has been exhausted without completing the jury, a number of them may be called in for this purpose.

Nor is there any good reason why the requirement of a unanimous verdict from the jury should be continued.[39] Unanimity does not

[37] Thompson v. Utah, 170 U. S. 343, 1898.
[38] Kansas Judicial Council, *Bulletin*, April, 1935, pp. 17–18.
[39] Those who disagree with this view argue that the law is not a sacred thing above the people, but an attempt to write the mores of the people into legal

carry with it any magical assurance that the case will be considered wisely and well. It rather tends to encourage either hasty and superficial consideration of cases in order to get through, or prolonged disagreements, "hung" juries, new trials, et cetera. The unanimous verdict in civil cases has not been required in California since 1879. In 1942 there were twenty-three states which permitted a verdict, in civil cases in courts of record, of a number less than the total number of jurors — in some instances, five-sixths, in some three-fourths. In addition, five permit majority verdicts in certain criminal cases.[40]

Curtis D. Wilbur, one-time Chief Justice of the California Supreme Court, has said that the results have been so satisfactory that he doubts if a single practicing attorney would advocate a return to the unanimous verdict.[41] It is difficult to understand why this requirement, as applied to juries, should be continued when people simply do not think alike, and when such a rule is applied in no other important phase of human life — in courts, in legislatures, or other public bodies entrusted with power to consider and decide vital matters.

The Selection of Jurors. The adoption of some of the suggestions here discussed would almost automatially bring about the selection of a higher type of juror. There should, however, be a planned attempt to bring this about through improvement in the methods by which the selections are made, and in their administration. The generally prevailing process of selection was described some years ago by Judge Baldwin of Connecticut:

The selection of jurors is a long process. The general plan is to commit to some local authorities in each city, town, or county the choice of a considerable number out of the inhabitants whom they may think suitable to serve in that capacity; then to have that list revised by some higher officials or persons specially appointed by the courts for the purpose, who must strike out a large part of the names; and finally to have those who are to be summoned to attend any particular term of court for jury duty chosen by drawing from the remaining names by lot. In many states special qualifications as to age, education, and intelligence are required. Out of the

sanctions. The theory is that, if twelve men selected at random unanimously agree that the accused has not outraged the mores of the community, he ought to be turned loose. He should not be subjected to punishment if there is such ground for reasonable doubt as will prompt one (or more) of these twelve men to believe him innocent.

[40] Winters, Glenn R., "Majority Verdicts in the United States," _Journal_ of the American Judicature Society, October, 1942, pp. 87–92. There is an excellent table covering all the states and territories using this system.

[41] Cited in Judicial Council of Connecticut, _Second Report_, 1930, pp. 16–18.

jurors thus summoned to attend the court, there is a further choice by lot of those to try each particular case, subject to objections made by either party to any thus drawn, for proper cause.[42]

In a study made several years ago, Professor Callender examined in detail the methods of selection of jurors used in Philadelphia and other large metropolitan centers.[43] He found considerable variation, at least with regard to the details of the methods used.

In some states the selection is made by elected jury commissioners, in some by the sheriff, in others by clerks or commissioners appointed by the judges, and in still others by the judges themselves. Choices are made, usually more or less at random, from tax lists or lists of voters, care being taken to get names that are representative of the various callings, but to omit persons belonging to legally exempted classes. These names, when chosen, are placed on individual slips in the jury wheel, in which they are indiscriminately mixed. Every precaution is taken to prevent tampering with the jury wheel, and to prevent favoritism in the final selections. When a judge needs a jury for his court, he issues a writ of venire, directing the sheriff or other officer in charge to draw at random the requisite number of names from the wheel, and to summon the persons whose names are drawn for service at the designated time. Out of this panel, it is hoped to secure a number sufficient to constitute a trial jury, after excuses and challenges.

The persons whose names are selected are interviewed at the office of the jury clerk, and checked with the police department to eliminate felons, but no effort is made either to eliminate persons of unsound mind or to determine whether a substitute has appeared for a juror who was summoned, before their names are placed on the final list. The period of service varies from one to three weeks, being in the majority of cases two weeks. In some jurisdictions, prospective jurors are allowed to select the months during which they prefer to serve. Compensation is normally three dollars a day, although in Chicago, five dollars is paid. Summons may be by personal service, although registered mail is usually used.

After the enfranchisement of women, women jurors, when occasionally one appeared, were regarded with a good deal of curiosity.

[42] Baldwin, *op. cit.,* pp. 192–193.

[43] Callender, Clarence N., *The Selection of Jurors* (University of Pennsylvania, 1927) ; see also Grant, J. A. C., " Methods of Jury Selection," *American Political Science Review*, February, 1930, pp. 117–130; and Governmental Research Institute, *The Selection of Jurors in the Circuit Court, City of St. Louis* (St. Louis, 1942) .

Gradually, the woman juror came to be less of a novelty. During the war, with so many men away in service, and others engaged in important war work, women jurors were in the majority in almost every case, both civil and criminal. It was not at all unusual to have an all-woman jury. The fitness of women for jury service ceased to be either a subject of merriment or one of serious question.

IMPROVING JUDICIAL PROCEDURE

For several years there has been a growing dissatisfaction with the prevailing methods of administering justice in the United States. One of the earliest discussions calling public attention to this situation is contained in an address delivered by Dean Roscoe Pound of the Harvard Law School in 1906. Mr. Taft, while President and throughout the remainder of his life, called attention time and again to the necessity for improving and modernizing the machinery and procedure for the administration of justice. The American Bar Association has for many years had committees at work on various aspects of the problem. The American Law Institute, organized in 1923, was a result of the culmination of these influences. This organization has recently completed an extensive program of work which is bound to have a profound effect upon the development of the American law. The program included the restatement of the law on various subjects within the field of the civil law, and the development of a *Model Code of Criminal Procedure,* which was published in 1930. It is likely that the work in the field of criminal law will be extended to include a restatement of all the substantive law. Whatever the reason, the interest which exists today in the development of more effective methods of judicial administration is greater than at any time in the past.

The Position of the Judge. There is a sharp contrast between the position of the judge in an American and in a European court. In Europe it is customary for the judge to conduct the trial. He guides and directs the proceedings, taking an active part in them, with the objective of revealing the essential facts and making more certain the proper and speedy disposition of the case. In the United States the judge presides, but cannot be said by any stretch of the imagination to conduct the case. The attorneys do that — all too often with neither dignity nor dispatch, nor, so far as one can determine, with any sincere desire to see that justice is administered. The judge is reduced to the position of referee between a couple of sparring partners, whose rounds are fought with arguments and torrents of legal verbiage, rather than with boxing gloves. Rules for this game have been agreed upon and established, and it is the business of the judge to see that neither party strikes a foul.

Professor Sunderland has elaborated upon this point in the following interesting paragraph:

> There is no difference in principle between a decision based upon a contest of procedural skill between two attorneys and a decision based upon a contest of strength between two armed champions. We smile when we are told that trial by battle, although actually obsolete, was a lawful method of trying cases in England until abrogated by Parliament only about a hundred years ago, and we marvel that a sensible nation should so long tolerate such an anomaly. But while in England trial by battle existed only in the musty pages of the law books, and was rediscovered there by accident, in the United States trial by battle flourishes throughout the length and breadth of the land, with the court rooms as the lists, the judges as the umpires, and the attorneys, armed with all the weapons of the legal armorer's cunning, as the resourceful champions of the parties. It is a system which is steadily destroying the confidence of the people in the public administration of justice.[44]

The Attitude of the Bar. It is not likely that substantial progress in the improvement of judicial procedure in either civil or criminal cases will be made until the judge is given authority to conduct the proceedings, and members of the bar have a deeper concern for the impartial administration of justice than for the winning of cases. Years ago, when the American Bar Association held its annual meeting in London, the members were interested in a murder case which developed just before they landed. The unidentified body of a young woman was discovered by the seashore late in June; there seemed to be no clues by which the mystery could be solved. By the second of August the victim had been identified, motives for the murder established, the guilty party apprehended, arrested, indicted, tried, convicted, sentenced, and executed, having had every opportunity for appeal and having enjoyed every protection to which the law of England entitled him. In this country, such a speedy and certain execution of the law is rarely achieved unless there develops a case so horrible that public sentiment is aroused to demand immediate action. In this, there is danger of the conviction and punishment of an innocent person, or of punishment as a form of vengeance.

[44] Quoted by Willoughby, *op. cit.*, p. 457; this writer devotes Chapter 34 to the role of the judge at the trial.

Observers of the English courts bring back similarly striking illustrations of the manner in which the attitude of the English barrister differs from that of great numbers of American lawyers. In one case, an English prisoner had been convicted and was standing before the bar of the court awaiting sentence. The judge had in his hand a record of the previous offenses and convictions of the prisoner. As he was about to pronounce sentence, he was addressed by the attorney *for the defense:* " Your Honor, I desire to call your attention to the fact that in one particular, this record is incomplete." He then proceeded to inform the judge that at a certain date his client had been convicted of another offense, not listed on the record. Not only have few American lawyers taken so seriously their obligation as officers of the court to see that justice is administered, but recent revelations have shown many cases in which members of the bar have worked with lawbreakers, not merely to defend them before the court (as they have every right to do), but to connive with them for the purpose of preventing their detection and of enabling them to break the law with impunity. Until the bar associations succeed in expelling from their ranks this kind of attorney, judicial administration will continue to be unsatisfactory.

The Integrated Bar. Until a few years ago, bar organization was either voluntary or federated. In 1921, Alabama and North Dakota set up an integrated bar, the characteristics of which form of organization are: (1) that choice of membership is eliminated. Every lawyer is obliged to become a member of the state association, paying the prescribed association dues, under penalty of suspension unless failure to pay is for good cause. (2) The organized bar becomes a legally recognized part of the machinery for the administration of justice. (3) The integrated bar is a self-governing body.

By 1945, the number of jurisdictions with an integrated bar had passed the half-way mark. In thirteen states the system is established by statute, and in nine jointly by statute and court rule. One state provides for integration by constitutional amendment and court rule, and two by court rule alone. One other state has provided for integration, but postponed putting it in operation until after the war.[45] Actually, the bar has little choice in the matter. There is much

---

[45] These states are: *by statute:* Alabama, Arizona, California, Idaho, Mississippi, Nevada, New Mexico, North Carolina, North Dakota, Oregon, South Dakota, Utah, and Washington. *By statute and court rule:* Kentucky, Louisiana, Michigan, Oklahoma, Texas, Virginia, West Virginia, Wisconsin, and Wyoming. *By constitutional amendment and court rule:* Arkansas. *By court rule only:* Missouri and Nebraska. *Authorized but not in effect:* Minnesota.

dissatisfaction among progressive lawyers and laymen alike over the failure of the bar in the past properly to discharge its responsibility. The profession must either adopt integration and give effective service to the state, on the one hand, or resign itself to the establishment of some form of " socialized law " on the other.[46]

Certain desirable results of an integrated organization have been demonstrated in many states. The state association becomes able to speak for the bar as a whole, every practitioner having a voice in the decisions made. The organization has better financial support, and is thus able to carry on its work more effectively. It is able to raise standards for admission to the bar and to improve bar discipline. Integration brings about a decided increase in interest and participation by lawyers in the business of the association, and, finally, local associations are so strengthened that they are able to render better service to their members. All told, integration can scarcely fail to bring about closer relationships between the bar and the legislature, the bar and the judiciary, and to improve the administration of justice generally.

Need for Statutory Revision. Another serious obstacle to the administration of justice is the excessive protection set up around accused persons. The origin of these protections is well known, and no student of history will deny that their enforcement at the time of their origin and for many years thereafter was necesssary and proper. They prevented the railroading of innocent persons, in a day which lacked the benefit of generations and centuries of the tradition of a government of law, and provided for the fair and impartial enforcement of that law by the courts. Necessary as these protections may once have been, there is no denying that in our time their continued use is a serious obstacle to the achievement of justice. Listed on page 732 are a number of those protections which have been most frequently used by ingenious and unprincipled law-

---

There is much material on this subject in the law reviews, the judicial council reports, and the *Journal* of the American Judicature Society. See Kansas Judicial Council *Bulletin,* April, 1942, and Minnesota Judicial Council, *Second Report, 1941;* in the *Journal,* notes on the progress of the movement, October, 1943, pp. 88–90; February, 1944, pp. 143–148; August, 1944, p. 55; April, 1945, pp. 165–169; June, 1945, p. 28; and the following articles: " Planning a Bar Integration Campaign," February, 1944, 149–153; Hemker, Forrest M., " Integrated Bar Created by Missouri Supreme Court," August, 1944, pp. 50–51; Shea, Edmund B., " Wisconsin's Successful Bar Integration Campaign," June, 1943, pp. 13–17; and Simmons, David A., " Stratification of the Bar," *ibid.,* pp. 7–13.

[46] See, in the *Journal* of the American Judicature Society, Osborn, Albert S., " A Layman Looks at the Law in Action," June, 1945, pp. 17–20, and Bradway, John S., " Will ' Socialized Law ' Be Next? " *ibid.,* pp. 13–17.

yers as technical grounds upon which to secure freedom or minimum penalties for defendants whose guilt was established beyond reasonable doubt: [47]

The indictment or accusation found by the grand jury does not clearly state the exact crime; or

It does not clearly state that the act is forbidden by law; or

The law itself is not sufficiently clear as to the exact criminal act which is to be punished; or

The indictment misnames or wrongly names the person accused; or

The crime was committed more than two years ago and the accused is therefore freed under the Statute of Limitations; or

In the trial itself the rights of the accused were violated by trying him in a heated state of public opinion; or

by allowing certain evidence against him to be produced which should not have been admitted; or

by refusing certain evidence in his favor; or

by the judge's decision on certain matters of fact which should have been left for the jury to decide; or by the partiality of the judge's charge, et cetera.

That the use of these technicalities is responsible for gross miscarriages of justice is well illustrated by such cases as the following. In 1938 a Philadelphia magistrate freed a doctor on charges of practicing without a license and of performing illegal operations because the affidavits on which the warrants were issued did not contain the words " County of Philadelphia." A man tried in a midwestern court for assault on a young girl, convicted and sentenced, was freed because the word " the " had been omitted from the conclusion of the indictment. Another man convicted of murder was discharged because the word " did " had been omitted from the 336-word indictment. A defendant in a Southern state was discharged because the indictment charged that he " did show " one Richard Armstrong — instead of " shoot," a typist's mistake. Many more instances might be cited.[48]

There are a number of ways in which the undesirable effect of these protections may be eliminated. In the first place, the law with regard to them may be modified. Such a result is likely to be hastened by the completion of the work of the American Law Institute. Even if the law should be permitted to remain as it is, the effect of these constitutional and statutory protections could be minimized if, as

[47] Young, James T., *The New American Government and Its Work,* Third Edition (Macmillan, New York, 1940) ; see also *Missouri Crime Survey,* Part VIII, and Waite, *op. cit.,* Chapter 4.

[48] University of Pennsylvania Bicentennial Committee, *Toward a More Effective Criminal Law* (Philadelphia, 1937) .

suggested, the concept of the function of the judge were modified, and if the members of the legal profession were to develop a higher ethical standard and a greater sense of social responsibility. These technicalities must be eliminated. They are in large measure the cause of the law's delay; and, as has often been said, justice delayed is justice denied.

The Law's Delay. Judge Baldwin devoted one chapter of his book to a discussion of the law's delays; these are common in both civil and criminal law. It has been said that whenever a case is filed in court, it ceases to be exclusively the business of the litigant and his lawyer. It has become " public business," yet an appeal is nearly always a matter of months, and the plaintiff is fortunate if it is not a matter of years. In Nebraska, for some time prior to 1901, the Supreme Court was so overwhelmed with business that it could not hear a cause until five years after it was docketed. A story is told of a brakeman injured on a New York railroad in 1882; his case went to seven appeals; in 1902, after twenty years, he was finally awarded a verdict of $4,500. The company appealed again, but was defeated. Judge Baldwin cited repeated illustrations of congested court calendars. For years after his book was written, this difficulty became more and more pronounced, as a result of World War I, prohibition, and new legislation regulating business, labor, and other subjects. The situation is now considerably improved.

The Cost of Litigation. In 1919 Reginald Heber Smith completed a study of the denial of justice to the poor, and of the agencies making more equal their position before the law.[49] He discussed three important defects in the existing system — delay, court costs and fees, and the expense of counsel. Two of these are important factors in the cost of litigation. " The actual expenses in a trial court," wrote Mr. Smith, " exclusive of witness fees, may be reduced to the writ or summons, the service of process, entry fee, calendar fee, trial fee, entry of judgment, and issuance of execution. It is proper to eliminate the jury fee, for so long as a trial by a judge is possible, no denial of justice can fairly be alleged. For similar reason, fees for attachment of garnishment are excluded. Each court uses a different combination of these items. In some, one or two payments cover everything; in others, the charges are made separately. Since our inquiry is only to determine the actual expense, all the various items may be rolled into one total. The figures given are not

[49] Smith, Reginald H., *Justice and the Poor*, Third Edition (Carnegie Foundation for the Advancement of Teaching, New York, 1924) .

absolute; they may be varied by the distance traveled for service, by the number of motions or interlocutory proceedings, and by other factors; but they fairly represent the minimum cost in an ordinary case.[50] These figures, which range from fifty-two cents in the Small Claims Courts of Cleveland to $15.51 in the Superior Court of Hartford, show an average cost of two to three dollars. They would be much higher if it were not for the advent of the municipal courts, which have done much to reduce costs; in a few instances it is provided that costs, exclusive of witness fees, shall not exceed two dollars.

In 1932 the Institute of Law of Johns Hopkins University published a survey of the cost of civil litigation in New York, made for the year 1930. The total cost for courts of all types was put at $11,000,000 a year; it was found that each inhabitant of New York City paid eight cents a year to help litigants get justice in the Municipal Court, the "poor man's court," whereas he paid fifty cents annually so that the man of larger affairs might have his disputes settled in the Supreme Court. Litigants in the Municipal Court paid 71.7 per cent of what it cost the city to dispense justice in that court, while those who made use of the City and Supreme Courts, handling claims involving much larger amounts, defrayed respectively only 7.4 per cent and 12.8 per cent of what it cost the taxpayers to operate these courts. It is unnecessary to present further figures, for from those already cited it is clear that the cost of securing justice at the hands of the courts is as much as or more than the poor man can afford to pay, and that those who are least able to pay contribute a larger percentage of the total cost.

Legal Aid. The second major item in the cost of litigation is counsel fees. To many who have a real grievance, and who are therefore entitled to legal redress, this item is so great as to prevent their turning to the courts at all for the enforcement of their rights. In a variety of ways, through agencies both public and private, the effort has been made to provide free, to such persons, the service of counsel. In the field of civil law, one finds public agencies such as the Office of the Friend of the Court in Wayne County, Michigan, and private agencies such as the Legal Aid Society of New York, which was incorporated in 1876. The Legal Aid Bureau of Philadelphia, for a few years operated as a public agency, is now private. The number of such agencies increased from fifty-five in 1923 to eighty-

●

50 *Ibid.*, pp. 24–25.

five in 1939. Professor Bradway divides the history of the movement into three periods: 1911–1923, 1923–1934, and 1934 to date. The first was the formative period, which preceded the formation of the National Association of Legal Aid Organizations in 1923. The ultimate goal is that every man, woman, and child shall receive, and none shall be denied, protection in every legal right, and redress for every legal wrong. In the field of criminal law, one finds the proposal for a public defender and, in many communities, voluntary defenders committees. In either case, the purpose is to provide counsel for those defendants who are financially unable to pay counsel fees. This may, of course, be done by the long-established practice of the assignment of counsel.

The uninformed person is apt to underestimate the value of free legal aid. He reads in his paper a summary of the annual report of the agency, observes that several hundred or several thousand persons were assisted, and then observes that only a few thousand dollars were collected. He thereupon concludes either that the service is unimportant or that the staff is inefficient, whereas the truth is that the service is tremendously important, and that in all probability it is being efficiently conducted. The amounts collected for individual clients are small, but this very fact enhances the economic and social significance of their collection. A large percentage of the cases involves wage claims — a few dollars to a washerwoman or a laboring man, to whom the loss of even a small amount is a vital concern. In many cases it means the difference between being fed and being hungry, or between paying the rent and being dispossessed. It may be that few types of social service are productive of greater benefits than this.

A voluminous literature has grown up on the subject of legal aid.[51] The National Association of Legal Aid Organizations has formulated a statement of the essential characteristics of the private legal aid agency; it is, they say, " a law office, which deals with all kinds of legal problems where the client cannot afford to pay a fee

[51] See Bradway, John S., *A Bibliography of Legal Aid Work* (National Association of Legal Aid Organizations, 1934), *Legal Aid Bureaus: a Manual of Practice* (Public Administration Service, Chicago, 1935); " Frontiers of Legal Aid Work," *Annals,* September, 1939: Smith, *op. cit.;* Smith and Bradway, *Growth of Legal Aid Work in the United States,* Revised Edition (United States Bureau of Labor Statistics, Bulletin No. 607, 1936); and three titles by Bradway, *Legal Aid Work and the Organization of the Bar* (Duke University, 1939); " Legal Service for the Indigent," *Journal* of the American Judicature Society, December, 1942, pp. 117–122, and " Wartime Opportunities in Legal Aid Work," *ibid.,* December, 1943, pp. 120–122.

and where the case is one for which a fee cannot be secured. There is a close relationship between the work of the ordinary law office and the work of this special type of law office. . . . The quality of service in a legal aid organization should be equal to that in a private law office, or the principle of equal protection of the laws means nothing in a practical sense. The legal aid organization should and does act as an observation post from which information may be made available showing how the law and the machinery for its administration are succeeding in their ultimate task of providing equal and exact justice." [52]

A legal aid organization is supposed to provide aid in criminal as well as civil cases, where there is no statute providing for the assignment of counsel or for a public defender; to provide for the investigation and handling of workmen's compensation and other special types of cases; to establish contacts with the organizations which act as contacts and serve as the sources of legal aid cases; to work for the establishment of small claims courts, domestic relations courts, and other specialized types of courts. The obstacles to the development of legal aid work include, first, the fact that most of the eligible supporters of such a movement are already involved in board membership and other phases of welfare work; second, the general impression that individual lawyers are rendering free assistance to indigent persons, just as physicians give their services freely to charity patients; finally, the hostility of some lawyers who regard legal aid as organized competition. Actually, those who are entitled to free legal service would be unable to pay counsel fees anyway. One of the chief difficulties is the cost of operation, which varies with local conditions. The form of organization varies, but there seem to be four fundamental elements: a definite place at which to meet clients; a definite time, exact office hours, et cetera; a definite personnel to carry on the work, the same person to be assigned to a case until it has been concluded; and an active advisory group.[53]

The Office of the Friend of the Court, established in 1918 in Wayne County, Michigan, is a public agency rendering a service similar to that more frequently supplied by a legal aid society. Organized by an overburdened metropolitan court to expedite the collection of alimony, the Office has developed into an important administration agency, performing a variety of functions and available for new uses as new needs arise. A year later the legislature

[52] Bradway, John S., *Legal Aid Bureaus*, pp. 2–3.
[53] *Ibid.*, pp. 10–12.

authorized by law the appointment of a friend of the court in every county, for the purpose of enforcing alimony decrees for the benefit of minor children. Over the years, the functions of the Office have been extended to include service to clients in matters relating to land contracts and mortgage foreclosures, to services as fiduciary, to bastardy proceedings, to cooperation with the Juvenile Court, and with other social agencies. In addition, the Office has succeeded in developing and maintaining a high degree of respect and confidence among the members of the bar.[54]

Assistance in the field of criminal law may be rendered by the usual legal aid bureau. Where this is not done, it may be given by a private organization of voluntary defenders, or by a public defender. Although the theory of the public defender has been widely accepted, little progress has been made in securing necessary legislation. Voluntary defenders committees exist in many cities; while in some ways they resemble other legal aid agencies, their activities are confined to the field of criminal law. The Voluntary Defenders Committee in New York, which was organized in 1917, is a good illustration; in all these years the Committee has handled thousands of cases, many of which are dismissed before trial, owing to its efforts. Because of the careful and impartial nature of their service, the lawyers of the Committee are held in high esteem by the courts. " The social service adjunct of the Committee is an asset which could not be eliminated, and through its efforts it affords defendants a far more comprehensive study than their cases would ordinarily receive, their problems being referred and directed to the proper channels. . . . No work among charitable endeavors is more worthy of support than that which helps him who is in difficulties and without the proper legal advice." [55]

Progress toward a Better Administration of Justice. It is impossible, within reasonable limits of space, to discuss all the suggestions that have been made for the improvement of the administration of justice in the states. Six of the more important have been mentioned and discussed briefly: the need for strengthening the powers of the presiding judge; the improvement of the attitude of the bar, and bar integration; the need for statutory revision, including the simplifica-

[54] Cooper, Frank E., and Dawson, John P., *The Office of the Friend of the Court in Wayne County, Michigan, a Study in Judicial Administration,* in *Fifth Annual Report* of the Judicial Council of Michigan, August, 1935, pp. 53–160.

[55] Tighe, Edward T., " Voluntary Defenders Committee Does Excellent Work," *The Panel,* January–February, 1935, pp. 4–5; Goldman, Mayer C., " Public Defenders in Criminal Cases," *Annals,* September, 1939, pp. 16–23, and " The Public Defender," *Virginia Law Review,* January, 1940, pp. 275–283.

tion of procedure and the elimination of technicalities and delay; a reduction in the cost of litigation; and the development of facilities for rendering free legal service to those who are unable to retain counsel for themselves. Pre-trial procedure might be used more extensively to save time, money, and effort, at the same time fully safeguarding the rights and interests of all parties concerned. The simplification of the appellate procedure, long so urgently needed, makes progress but slowly.[56]

Woodrow Wilson said one time that " the speediness of justice, the inexpensiveness of justice, the ready action of justice, is the greater part of justice itself." It was these considerations that Professor Sunderland had in mind when he summarized all the needed changes under three headings. Many of the rules of law which control the action of courts are uncertain and difficult to ascertain, and are often poorly adapted to contemporary conditions. The machinery by which the rules are applied has been criticized because it is too slow, too uncertain, and too expensive. All these objections are justified — and all could be corrected. Finally, the personnel engaged in the administration of justice consists primarily of the members of the bench and the bar; " to establish and maintain this personnel upon a high level of ability and ethical conduct requires adequate methods for admission to and exclusions from the bar, and for election to and retirement from the bench. These are problems of the most critical importance, and of the most baffling difficulty." These problems, too, can be solved, with the further development of the movement for an organized bar, and with the growth of a wider and more intelligent public interest in the administration of justice.[57]

SELECTED REFERENCES

Alexander, Julian P., " Presumptions: Their Use and Abuse," *Mississippi Law Journal,* March, 1945, pp. 1–18.

[56] Parker, John J., " Improvement of Jury System Must Come," *Journal* of the American Judicature Society, October, 1942, pp. 71–72.

[57] Sunderland, Edson R., " Progress toward a Better Administration of Justice," *Journal* of the American Judicature Society, August, 1933, pp. 49–55; see also Callison, I. P., " A Layman Looks at Justice," *ibid.,* April, 1933, pp. 176–181. Caplan, Oscar S., " Streamlining Our Court Procedures," *John Marshall Law Quarterly,* December, 1940, pp. 178–189; Judicial Council of Michigan, " Michigan Statute Recognizes Need for a Three-Judge Trial Court," *Journal* of the American Judicature Society, October, 1940, pp. 76–80; Loughborough, J. F., " An Arkansas Experiment in the Improvement in the Administration of Justice," American Bar Association *Journal,* May, 1942, pp. 332–333; Otis, Merrill E., " Improving the Administration of Justice," *ibid.,* 367–370; and Perry, Stuart H., " Politics and Judicial Administration," *ibid.,* February, 1934, pp. 133–139, reprinted from *Annals,* September, 1933, pp. 75–85.

Arnold, Thurman W., *Symbols of Government* (Yale University Press, 1935).

Baldwin, Simeon E., *The American Judiciary* (Century, New York, 1905).

Beattie, Ronald H., *A System of Criminal Judicial Statistics for California* (University of California Press, 1936).

Beeley, Arthur L., *The Bail System in Chicago* (University of Chicago Press, 1927).

Best, Harry, *Crime and Criminal Law in the United States* (Macmillan, New York, 1930).

Borchard, Edwin M., *Declaratory Judgments* (Banks-Baldwin, Cleveland, 1935).

——, and Lutz, E. R., *Convicting the Innocent* (Garden City Publishing Company, Garden City, N. Y., 1932).

Boudin, Louis B., *Government by Judiciary* (William Godwin, Inc., New York, 1932).

Bradway, John S., *A Bibliography of Legal Aid Work* (National Association of Legal Aid Organizations, May, 1934).

——, *Legal Aid Bureaus* (Public Administration Service, Chicago, 1935).

——, Ed., " Frontiers of Legal Aid Work," *Annals*, September, 1939.

——, *Legal Aid Work and the Organized Bar* (Duke University, 1939).

Bruce, Andrew A., *The American Judge* (Macmillan, New York, 1924).

Callender, Clarence E., *American Courts, Their Organization and Procedure* (McGraw-Hill, New York, 1927).

Cantor, Nathaniel F., *Crimes, Criminals and Criminal Justice* (Holt, New York, 1932).

Chestnut, W. Calvin, *Instructions to the Jury* (American Bar Association, Chicago, 1942).

Cincinnati Bureau of Governmental Research, *Bail Administration in the Cincinnati Region* (Cincinnati, 1932).

Clark, Charles E., and Shulman, Harry, *A Study of Law Administration in Connecticut* (Yale University Press, 1937).

Dickinson, John, *Administrative Justice and the Supremacy of the Law in the United States* (Harvard University Press, 1927).

Fuller, Hugh N., *Criminal Justice in Virginia* (Century, New York, 1932).

Goldberg, Louis P., and Levinson, Eleanore, *Lawless Judges* (Rand Book Store, New York, 1935).

Goldman, Mayer C., *The Public Defender* (Putnam, New York, 1917).

Governmental Research Institute, *The Selection of Jurors in the Circuit Court, City of St. Louis* (St. Louis, 1942).

Jensen, Christian, *The Pardoning Power in the American States* (University of Chicago Press, 1922).

Johnsen, Julia E., Ed., *Jury System,* Handbook Series (Wilson, New York, 1928).

Laws, Bolitha J., and Stockman, Abram H., *Pre-Trial Conferences* (American Bar Association, Chicago, 1942).

Lee, Howard B., *The Criminal Trial in the Virginias,* Second Edition (Michie, Charlottesville, 1940).

Lepawsky, Albert, *The Judicial System of Metropolitan Chicago* (University of Chicago Press, 1922).

Lou, Herbert H., *Juvenile Courts in the United States* (University of North Carolina Press, 1927).

Lummus, Henry T., *The Trial Judge* (Foundation Press, Chicago, 1938).

Martin, Kenneth J., *The Waiver of Jury Trial in Criminal Cases with Special Reference to Ohio* (Johns Hopkins Press, 1933).

Merriam, Charles E., and others, *The Government of the Metropolitan Region of Chicago* (University of Chicago Press, 1933).

Michael, Jerome, and Adler, Mortimer J., *Crime, Law, and Social Science* (Harcourt, Brace, New York, 1933).

——, and Wechsler, Herbert, *Criminal Law and Its Administration* (Foundation Press, Chicago, 1940).

Miller, Ben R., *The Louisiana Judiciary* (Louisiana State University Press, 1932).

Missouri Crime Survey, *Missouri Crime Survey* (Macmillan, New York, 1926).

Moley, Raymond, *Our Criminal Courts* (Minton, Balch, New York, 1930).

——, *Politics and Criminal Prosecution* (Minton, Balch, New York, 1929).

Mortenson, Ernest, *You Be the Judge* (Longmans, Green, New York, 1940).

Moschzisker, Robert von, *Trial by Jury*, Second Edition (Bisel, Philadelphia, 1930).

National Association of Legal Aid Organizations, *Papers on the Law and Social Work* (Rochester, 1941).

National Commission on Law Observance and Enforcement, *Prosecution*, Report No. 4 (Washington, 1931).

Northrop, W. B., *Insolence of Office: the Story of the Seabury Investigations* (Putnam, New York, 1932).

Orfield, Lester B., *Criminal Appeals in America* (Little, Brown, Boston, 1939).

Osborn, Albert S., *The Mind of the Juror* (The author, 233 Broadway, Albany, 1937).

Peterson, Virgil W., *Crime Commissions in the United States* (Chicago Crime Commission, 1945).

——, *The Grand Jury: Voice of Democracy* (Chicago Crime Commission, 1944).

Philadelphia Criminal Justice Association, *Annual Report.*

Pound, Roscoe, *Appellate Procedure in Civil Cases* (Little, Brown, Boston, 1941).

——, *Criminal Justice in America* (Holt, New York, 1930).

President's Research Committee on Social Trends, *Recent Social Trends in the United States*, 2 vols. (McGraw-Hill, New York, 1933).

Ragland, George, Jr., *Discovery before Trial* (Callaghan, Chicago, 1933).

Reiblich, George K., *A Study of Judicial Administration in the State of Maryland* (Johns Hopkins Press, 1929).

Rhode Island Public Expenditure Council, *Judicial Administration in Rhode Island* (Providence, 1945).

Russell, Frances T., *The Case of David Lamson* (Lamson Defense Committee, San Francisco, 1934).

Schramm, Gustav L., *Piedpoudre or Small Claims Courts* (Legal Aid Society, Pittsburgh, 1928).

Sherrill, George R., *Criminal Procedure in North Carolina as Shown by Criminal Appeals since 1890* (University of North Carolina Press, 1930).

Shientag, Bernard L., *The Trial of a Civil Jury Action in New York* (Columbia University Press, 1938).

Smith, Reginald H., *Justice and the Poor* (Carnegie Foundation for the Advancement of Teaching, New York, 1919).

——, and Bradway, John S., *Growth of Legal Aid Work in the United States,* Revised Edition (United States Bureau of Labor Statistics, Bulletin No. 607, 1936).

Stalmaster, Irvin, *What Price Jury Trials?* (Stratford Company, Boston, 1931).

Stanley, Osso W., *Instruction to Juries* (Anderson, Cincinnati, 1941).

Taft, Henry W., *Witnesses in Court* (Macmillan, New York, 1934).

Thomas Skelton Harrison Foundation, *Studies of the Municipal Court of Philadelphia* (Philadelphia, 1930–1932).

Train, Arthur, *The Prisoner at the Bar,* Second Edition (Scribner's, New York, 1908).

——, *My Day in Court* (Scribner's, New York, 1939).

Ulman, Joseph N., *A Judge Takes the Stand* (Knopf, New York, 1933).

Waite, John B., *Criminal Law in Action* (Sears, New York, 1934).

Warner, Florence M., *Juvenile Detention in the United States* (University of Chicago Press, 1933).

Warner, S. B., *Crime and Criminal Statistics in Boston* (Harvard University Press, 1934).

Weihofen, Henry, *Insanity as a Defense in Criminal Law* (Commonwealth Fund, New York, 1933).

Wellman, Francis L., *Day in Court* (Macmillan, New York, 1926).

——, *The Art of Cross-Examination,* Revised Edition (Macmillan, New York, 1931).

Willoughby, W. F., *Principles of Judicial Administration* (Brookings Institution, Washington, 1929).

Works Progress Administration of Georgia, *Survey of Criminal Court Procedure in Georgia* (Atlanta, 1937).

American Judicature Society, "Michigan Statute Recognizes Need for Three-Judge Trial Courts," *Journal,* October, 1940, pp. 76–80.

Arizona State Legislative Bureau, "Grand and Petit Juries in the United States," *Legislative Briefs,* February 15, 1940, pp. 1–27.

Bar Association of Tennessee, Junior Bar Section, "Needed Reforms in Judicial Procedure in Tennessee," *Tennessee Law Review,* December, 1940, pp. 603–609.

Barr, Allen H., "Privileges Against Self-Incrimination in California," *California Law Review,* July, 1942, pp. 547–555.

Bayes, William R., "Criminal Cases Tried to a Bench of Three Judges," *Journal* of the American Judicature Society, April, 1941, pp. 182–185.

Bradway, John S., "Legal Service for the Indigent," *Journal* of the American Judicature Society, December, 1942, pp. 117–122.

——, "Wartime Opportunities in Legal Aid Work," *Journal* of the American Judicature Society, December, 1943, pp. 120–122.

Bridewell, David A., " The Need for Foreclosure Reform in Illinois," *John Marshall Law Quarterly,* December, 1940, pp. 214–228.

Caplan, Oscar S., " Streamlining Our Court Procedure," *John Marshall Law Quarterly,* December, 1940, pp. 178–189.

Coffin, Claude C., " Jury Trial Tragic But Not Entirely Hopeless," *Journal* of the American Judicature Society, June, 1941, pp. 13–17.

Council of State Governments, *State Government* (Chicago, monthly).

Daru, Robert, " The Code of Ethics and Principles for the Prosecution and Defense of Criminal Cases," *Alabama Lawyer,* January, 1945, pp. 39–54.

DeLancey, Frances P., " West Virginia Explores Judicial and Administrative Reforms," *State Government,* May, 1940, pp. 87–88, 96–97.

Evans, Alvin E., " The Standard of Care in Emergencies," *Kentucky Law Journal,* March, 1943, pp. 207–230.

Fine, Harry G., " Unnecessary Successive Suits in Illinois Practice," *John Marshall Law Quarterly,* June, 1941, pp. 469–476.

Gilbert, Charles, " Reform of Criminal Procedure," *Tennessee Law Review,* December, 1940, pp. 489–528.

Goldman, Mayer C., " Public Defenders," *Virginia Law Review,* January, 1940, pp. 275–283.

Green, Leon, " A Practical Way to Administer Justice," *Journal* of the American Judicature Society, October, 1941, pp. 70–76.

Henry, Robert L., " Cause in the Civil Law and Consideration in the Common," *Kentucky Law Journal,* May, 1941, pp. 369–401.

Hyde, Laurence M., " Fact Finding by Special Verdict," *Journal* of the American Judicature Society, February, 1941, pp. 144–149.

Iowa Law Review, " Expert Testimony as an Invasion of the Province of the Jury," May, 1941, pp. 819–840.

Jacoby, Sidney B., " Legal Aid to the Poor," *Harvard Law Review,* April, 1940, pp. 940–976.

Loughborough, J. F., " An Arkansas Experiment in the Improvement in the Administration of Justice," *American Bar Association Journal,* May, 1942, pp. 332–333.

McClintock, H. L., " Indictment by a Grand Jury," *Minnesota Law Review,* January, 1942, pp. 153–176.

McCormick, Charles T., " Jury Verdicts upon Special Questions in Civil Cases," *Journal* of the American Judicature Society, October, 1943, pp. 84–88, with bibliography.

Morgan, Edmund M., " Further Observations on Presumptions," *Southern California Law Review,* June, 1943, pp. 245–265.

National Municipal League, *National Municipal Review* (New York, monthly).

Nims, Harry D., " Shortening Records on Appeal: a Report to the New York Judicial Council," *Journal* of the American Judicature Society, October, 1944, pp. 73–82.

Nixon, H. W., " Opinion Evidence — Experts," *Alabama Lawyer,* January, 1945, pp. 5–16.

Otis, Merrill E., " Improving the Administration of Justice," *American Bar Association Journal,* May, 1942, pp. 367–370.

——, " Methods of Preventing Delay in Disposition of Cases," *Journal* of the American Judicature Society, October, 1942, pp. 73–77.

——, "Qualifications of Jurors," *Journal* of the American Judicature Society, April, 1942, pp. 178–182.

——, "The Judge to the Jury," *Journal* of the American Judicature Society, April, 1944, pp. 171–179.

Palmer, William J., "An Essay on Appellate Courts and Procedure," *Journal* of the American Judicature Society, February, 1942, pp. 140–148.

Ramsom, Edward D., "Liberal Trend as to State Appeals," *Journal* of the American Judicature Society, April, 1941, pp. 176–181.

Reaugh, Daniel M., "Presumptions and the Burden of Proof," *Illinois Law Review of Northwestern University*, April, 1942, pp. 819–852.

Saxe, Leonard S., "New York Extends Judicial Notice to Matters of Law," *Journal* of the American Judicature Society, October, 1944, pp. 86–90.

Schwellenbach, Lewis B., "Information v. Intuition in the Imposition of Sentence," *Journal* of the American Judicature Society, April, 1943, pp. 52–55.

Simmons, Robert G., "Why New Rules of Civil Procedure Now?" *Journal* of the American Judicature Society, April, 1943, pp. 170–177.

Soper, Morris J., "The Charge to the Jury," *Journal* of the American Judicature Society, December, 1940, pp. 111–115.

Smith, T. V., "The Higher Justice in the Leaner Years," *State Government*, February, 1941, pp. 31–32, 43–44.

Stewart, William S., "Instructions to Jury in Criminal Cases," *John Marshall Law Quarterly*, March, 1941, pp. 336–343.

Sunderland, Edson R., "Arguments, Decisions and Opinions on Appeal," *Journal* of the American Judicature Society, December, 1942, pp. 102–105.

——, "Improvement of Appeals Procedure," *Journal* of the American Judicature Society, October, 1941, pp. 79–84; December, 1941, pp. 123–126; February, 1942, pp. 150–152.

Tennessee Bar Association, Proceedings, on reform of criminal procedure, *Tennessee Law Review*, December, 1940.

Tyrrell, Frank G., "Social Efficiency of the Judge," *Southern California Law Review*, June, 1943, pp. 266–274.

Warder, Smith, "Remedies Available to Convicted Defendant When New Facts Are Found," *Michigan Law Review*, April, 1941, pp. 963–976.

Watkins, David D., "Constitutional Protection of Innocence," *Journal* of the American Judicature Society, June, 1942, pp. 27–30.

Wekstein, Abraham, "Constitutional Protection Against Self-Incrimination," *Journal* of the American Judicature Society, February, 1943, pp. 154–157.

Wickhem, John D., "A Code of Evidence for Wisconsin?" *Wisconsin Law Review*, January, 1945, pp. 77–94.

Winters, Glenn R., "Majority Verdicts in the United States," *Journal* of the American Judicature Society, October, 1942, pp. 87–92.

——, "The Michigan One-Man Grand Jury," *Journal* of the American Judicature Society, February, 1945, pp. 137–151.

Wormser, Maurice, "Corroboration of Accomplices in Criminal Cases," *Fordham Law Review*, May, 1942, pp. 193–201.

CHAPTER XVIII

Constitutional Protections

THE bill of rights is one of the most important parts of any constitution; it is essential, in any state operating under a written constitution, that both persons and citizens be protected by written guarantees from infringements of their rights by the government and its officers. Thus in the Federal Constitution the citizen is guaranteed certain fundamental personal and civil rights by the first ten amendments, commonly referred to as the Bill of Rights. Similar guarantees are included in the state constitutions. Clauses intended to protect persons and citizens in the enjoyment of some of these rights as against possible infringement by the states were added to the Federal Constitution by the War Amendments. Thus the fundamental rights are guaranteed, so far as the action of the Federal government is concerned, by the Federal Constitution, and so far as the state governments are concerned, by both the state and Federal constitutions.

THE WAR AMENDMENTS

The Thirteenth Amendment. Amendments XIII, XIV, and XV were adopted in 1865, 1868, and 1870, respectively. They were framed and adopted solely for the purpose of protecting and improving the condition of the Negro, even though in later years they have been applied to the protection of almost everything and everybody except the Negro. Since these amendments include the only provisions of the Federal Constitution with regard to the duty of states to observe and protect the fundamental rights of persons, it is necessary to consider briefly the history and the wording of these guarantees.

Amendment XIII provides that " neither slavery nor involuntary servitude, except as a punishment for crime whereof the party shall have been duly convicted, shall exist within the United States, or any place subject to their jurisdiction." The history of this phraseology carries one back to the early years of the nation's history. It was a part of the Northwest Ordinance of 1787. In the years during which the controversy over slavery was being waged in Congress, it appears again and again in the resolutions introduced, and sometimes passed, through the influence of the antislavery members. One finds it in the famous Creole Resolutions introduced by Representative Joshua R. Giddings of Ohio in 1842, in the provisions of the Wilmot Proviso of 1846, in the Act of 1850 abolishing slavery in the District of Columbia. It is not strange, therefore, to find that it eventually becomes incorporated in the fundamental law. It is interesting to note, however, that in the closing days of the Buchanan Administration a resolution proposing a thirteenth amendment was introduced in Congress, designed to effect a compromise and preserve peace. The provisions of this proposal were the exact opposite of those finally adopted.

As the Constitution now stands, since the repeal of Amendment XVIII, this amendment is the only one which bears directly upon or which attempts to regulate and control in any way the conduct of individuals in their relations with each other. All other provisions relate either to the organization and the powers and duties of government, or to restraints placed upon government for the purpose of protecting the rights of persons and property. Two or three interesting questions have arisen with regard to the application of this amendment. One of these involves contracts for personal service. Strange as it may at first seem to one who recalls the original purpose and intent of the amendment, the courts have used it to prevent orders for specific performance under such contracts. Suppose, for instance, that a baseball player who has already signed a contract with one club subsequently finds that he could make more advantageous arrangements with another. While the courts are willing to enjoin him to prevent his performing under the second contract, they have regularly refused to compel specific performance under the first, on the theory that to do so would be to require an involuntary servitude as prohibited in the terms of this amendment. Similar rulings are on record with regard to sculptors, painters, musicians, and others rendering personal service of a highly specialized and technical nature.

Perhaps the most important problem arising under **Amendment XIII** is its application to the peonage laws enacted in a number of the southern states at the close of the Civil War. To understand this situation, it is necessary to refer briefly to certain historical facts. The colored people who were freed from slavery by this amendment were wholly unprepared to assume the duties and responsibilities of free members of society. In the majority of cases — in some instances through several generations — these people had assumed no responsibility for their own welfare. Under the plantation system, their cabins and food were provided for them by the owner of the plantation, and clothing suitable to the season was distributed to them in the fall and spring. When the amendment was adopted, many of the plantation owners gave the former slaves their homes, but they were obliged to provide their own food and clothing. Under the new regime, freedom to most Negroes seems to have meant absence from work. Many of them took to wandering through the country, getting food when and where they could. The landowners of the South thus found themselves suffering from considerable losses of food crops, due to this wave of vagabondage. They also found it impossible to hire dependable help to cultivate their fields.

To meet this situation, the so-called peonage laws were enacted. Without attempting to justify them, it is easy to understand the psychology which led to their enactment. The most important test case, Bailey v. Alabama,[1] was decided by the Supreme Court in 1911. Under the Alabama law it was possible for employers to hold their help by a system of indenture. The employee was forced to purchase goods, often in considerable amounts and beyond his needs, in return for which he pledged himself to work out the debt in service. Severe penalties were provided for attempts to escape. The employers so managed that the worker was constantly heavily in debt and thus unable to change his employment or to move elsewhere. The Court decided that this system was unconstitutional, inasmuch as it required the performance of an involuntary servitude within the limits set up by Amendment XIII.

The Fourteenth Amendment. Amendment XIV contains four sections, in addition to which there is the customary enforcing clause. Section 1 contains provisions which are as important as any in the whole Constitution, while Sections 2, 3, and 4 are interesting chiefly from the point of view of the student of history. In the first section

---

[1] 219 U. S. 219, 1911; see Wilson, Walter, *Forced Labor in the United States* (International Publishers, New York, 1933).

there are four important clauses, which are quoted verbatim here and numbered for convenience of discussion:

1. All persons born or naturalized in the United States, and subject to the jurisdiction thereof, are citizens of the United States and of the State wherein they reside.
2. No State shall make or enforce any law which shall abridge the privileges or immunities of citizens of the United States; [2]
3. nor shall any State deprive any person of life, liberty, or property, without due process of law;
4. nor deny to any person within its jurisdiction the equal protection of the laws.

Careful reading of these provisions indicates that those who framed the amendment, and those who voted for its adoption, were attempting to confer upon the recently freed Negroes a state of citizenship, and to guarantee to them, in so far as possible, the rights, privileges, and immunities pertaining to that status. The definition clarified the only reference to the subject of citizenship contained in the original Constitution (Article IV, Section 3); since the control over citizenship rests largely with the Federal government, no further discussion of the subject will be included here. The provisions with regard to due process and equal protection are so fundamental that they will be discussed in later sections of this chapter.

The second section of this amendment contains the much disputed provisions on the suffrage discussed in Chapter V. It provided for a reduction in the representation of any state in the Federal House of Representatives, in proportion to the number of inhabitants in such state, " being twenty-one years of age and a citizen of the United States," who should be denied the privilege of the suffrage for any reason other than participation in a rebellion or other crime. This provision has never been enforced, and so far as one can foresee, it is not likely to be enforced, for reasons earlier discussed.

The third section disqualified from membership in Congress, and from any other office of profit or public trust under the government of the United States, any person who, having previously taken an oath to support the Constitution and government of the United States, had " engaged in insurrection or rebellion . . . or given aid or comfort to the enemies " of the United States. Congress was authorized by a vote of two thirds of each house to remove such disability. While no persons are now living to whom this provision

[2] Interpreted in Colgate v. Harvey, 296 U. S. 404, 1935; see comment by Cushman, Robert E., in *American Political Science Review*, April, 1938, pp. 296–298.

might apply, it is not difficult to understand the psychology which prompted its adoption. Those who remember the intensity of the hatred of Germany which existed at the close of World War I can understand the apprehension with which the majority of the members of Congress viewed the appearance of a man like Alexander H. Stephens demanding admission to the Senate as the representative of one of the southern states. While this attitude may not now seem to have been justified, it was none the less human and understandable.

The fourth section affirmed that " the validity of the public debt of the United States, authorized by law, including debts incurred for payment of pensions and bounties for services in suppressing insurrection or rebellion, shall not be questioned." This section further provided that neither the United States nor any state should assume or pay any debt or obligation incurred in aid of insurrection or rebellion against the United States, or any claim for the loss or emancipation of any slave, all such debts, obligations, and claims being illegal and void. No one had questioned the public debt of the United States, but the Radical Reconstructionists in Congress did not want to take any chances. The second provision was intended to inform all and sundry that, from the financial point of view, insurrection and rebellion against the duly constituted authority of the United States was not a paying proposition. The clause with regard to claims for the loss or emancipation of slaves served, in the spirit of the time, as a reminder to the South that President Lincoln had offered them a plan of compensated emancipation which they had refused. Now it was too late.

The Fifteenth Amendment. This amendment provides that " the right of citizens of the United States to vote shall not be denied or abridged by the United States or by any State on account of race, color, or previous condition of servitude." These provisions were considered in Chapter V, in the discussion of the suffrage. The series of three amendments of which this is the last constitutes, for all practical purposes, a single change in the fundamental law. Amendment XIII made the Negro free; Amendment XIV defined his status as a citizen and attempted to secure for him the enjoyment of his rights as a citizen; Amendment XV attempted to insure him the privilege of the suffrage. There is in these three amendments a logical progression of ideas, the three key words for which are: free, citizen, vote.[3]

---

[3] For an account of the enactment of this amendment, see Braxton, A. Caperton, *The Fifteenth Amendment* (J. P. Bell Company, Lynchburg, 1934).

DUE PROCESS OF LAW

There are two due process clauses in the Federal Constitution, found in Amendments V and XIV, respectively. The clause in Amendment V informs us that " no person shall be deprived of life, liberty, and property without due process of law "; the provision in Amendment XIV appears in precisely the same words. While there is, therefore, an apparent repetition, none exists in fact because the Bill of Rights, of which Amendment V is a part, applies solely to the Federal government. This was made clear in the decision in Barron v. Mayor and City Council of Baltimore in 1833.[4] Baltimore had undertaken a program of harbor improvement. In executing this program, certain dredging that was done so deflected currents in the vicinity of a wharf owned by one Barron as to cause a heavy deposition of sand and silt, thereby impairing the value of the property. There was no question as to the fact of the damage or, under the theory of the common law, as to the right of Barron to recover. When, however, he based his contention on that clause of Article V which prohibits the taking of property without due process of law, the Court held that this provision (and, by implication, all of the Bill of Rights) applied only to the Federal government. Similarly, the provisions of the War Amendments apply exclusively to the governments of the states. It would thus appear that we have two kinds of due process of law — Federal and state.

It is not difficult to define Federal due process, because the elements of which it is composed are clearly and definitely enumerated in the Bill of Rights, especially in Amendments IV and V. When, on the other hand, one undertakes to define state due process, he finds himself faced with almost insuperable difficulties. Instead of dealing with a single unit of government possessing a written constitution in which the essential elements of due process are clearly stated, he must deal with forty-eight governments, each with its own constitution, set of statutes, and doctrines of judicial interpretation. It is unlikely that the student could find any two states in which precisely the same definition of due process would apply. So it is that an individual who had received due process at the hands of the government of one state might not have had due process if his case had been handled in precisely the same way in any other state. One might almost despair of finding any common elements in the various definitions of due process, had not the presence of the due process clause in Amendment XIV brought a number of cases involving its

[4] 7 Peters 243, 1833.

interpretation before the Supreme Court. From these decisions, and from the various treatises on the subject, it is possible to discover certain elements which are essential to due process in any one of the forty-eight states. These are:

1. Due notice.
2. A hearing.
3. Hearing before a competent tribunal.
4. A trial free from irregularities of procedure.
5. Freedom from arbitrary legislative action.

The first three items rest upon the decision in Twining v. New Jersey,[5] which in turn rests in part on the decision in the earlier case of Den ex dem. Murray v. Hoboken Land and Improvement Company.[6] The remaining items are based on the writings of students of constitutional law.[7]

The element of notice is required in order that the accused may be informed of the nature of the charges that have been preferred against him and have some opportunity to prepare his defense; he must be permitted to secure witnesses in his behalf and to arrange for their attendance at the trial; still more important, perhaps, he must have opportunity to employ counsel, which in turn must have some chance to prepare the defense. If this safeguard were not enforced, it would be possible for officers of the law to seize persons without warning, and to take them immediately before the bar of the court. Under such circumstances, innocent persons would be easily railroaded to a conviction. While trial by jury was commonly considered essential to due process, it has always been required that there must at least be a regular trial before some judicial body, unless, as in the case of hearings in connection with the administration of the assessment of taxes, the enforcement of such a requirement would block the operation of the whole governmental machine.[8]

The requirements regarding hearing are quite as important as those regarding notice. By the right of the accused to a hearing is meant, as noted above, the right to trial by jury — the right to one's day in court, to an opportunity to be heard and to present one's defense through one's attorney, through witnesses, and by personal testimony. Important as is the hearing itself, it is equally necessary

---

[5] 211 U. S. 78, 1908.

[6] 18 Howard 272, 1855.

[7] Mott, Rodney L., *Due Process of Law* (Bobbs-Merrill, Indianapolis, 1926). See also Burdick, Charles K., *The Law of the American Constitution* (Putnam's, New York, 1922), and Young, James T., *The New American Government and Its Work*, Third Edition, Chapter 32 (Macmillan, New York, 1933).

[8] On the subject of notice and hearing, see Mott, *op. cit.*, Chapter 13.

that it be conducted before a tribunal of competent jurisdiction. If this guarantee were not enforced, it would be possible to wear out the accused by successive trials conducted before tribunals which had no authority to adjudicate the case.

The final requirement involves, from the point of view of judicial procedure, the right to a trial free from irregularities of procedure — a trial, in other words, conducted in accordance with the requirements of the statutes and the rules of the court. Professor Mott writes on this aspect of due process under the heading of settled usage.[9] At any rate, the rules governing the submission of evidence must be observed, no rule must be enforced against the defendant that might be considered ex post facto, the accused must not be required to testify against himself, et cetera.

On the legislative side, the individual, whether a natural person or a corporation, has a right, in both civil and criminal law, to freedom from the enforcement of arbitrary and unreasonable regulations. This protection may extend to regulations which are so indefinite that the individual is unable to ascertain, even with the advice of counsel, the exact nature and extent of his rights or his duties. This principle is illustrated in the case of Connelly v. General Constructon Company,[10] in which the Supreme Court declared invalid an Oklahoma statute which required contractors engaged in state work to pay a rate of wages equaling the pay given for similar types of work in the communities in which the contractor was engaged, and for which an eight-hour day was also provided. The General Construction Company was engaged in constructing bridges for the state, but was hiring laborers on the basis of an eight-hour day and paying them $3.20, whereas the State Commissioner of Labor contended that the current rate paid in that locality for similar labor was $3.60. The Supreme Court found the requirement so vague and ambiguous as to be unenforceable, and therefore unconstitutional. The argument was similar to that in the case of the United States v. A. Cohen Grocery Company.[11] The Court found it difficult to determine the meaning of " the current rate of wages "; it was a variable depending upon a great many factors such as the efficiency of the workmen, the kind of work done, and the conditions under which the work was done. The phrase " current rate " might be construed as meaning either the lowest rate or the highest

9 *Ibid.*
10 269 U. S. 385, 1925; see also Mott, *op. cit.,* Chapter 12.
11 255 U. S. 81, 1921.

rate. Likewise, it is difficult to define concretely the word " locality." In holding the act unconstitutional, the Court held that " the constitutional guarantee of due process cannot be allowed to rest upon a support so equivocal."

Charles A. Beard observed on one occasion that Amendment XIV had become the Magna Charta of American business. This statement is true — so much so that in recent years one could prophesy with almost unerring accuracy that any regulatory measure would be tested in the courts on the grounds of a violation of due process. Walton Hamilton well expressed the current point of view when he wrote:

> In the era of constitutional law that flickers to a close, no doctrine has enjoyed greater prestige than " due process." It has come to be the symbol habitually invoked by private right, the barrier that guards the frontiers of business against the interference of the state, a sanction by which the judiciary reviews the work of the legislature. It has woven itself into the folkways of an industrial culture and called into being an august corpus of the law. . . . A novelist who made ideas his characters would not — for fear of provoking disbelief — have dared to allow his imagination to contrive such a series of events [as that by which this doctrine rose to its position of eminence in American law].[12]

This curious development of law has by no means been confined to business; it has been applied in other fields as well. The case of J. P. Waugh v. Board of Trustees of the University of Mississippi provides an excellent illustration, and one in which college students are likely to be interested.[13] It involved the attempt of the legislature of Mississippi to control college fraternities in the state university. A state law forbade fraternities and secret societies in educational institutions within the state, supported in whole or in part by state funds. Waugh was a citizen, a resident of the state, and a taxpayer, in all respects eligible to attend the state university except that he refused to sign the written pledge not to join the forbidden societies. The penalty imposed by law for refusal was no diploma, no honors — none of the customary forms of academic recognition.

---

12 Hamilton, Walton H., " The Path of Due Process of Law," in Read, Conyers, Ed., *The Constitution Reconsidered*, pp. 167–190 (Columbia University Press, 1938).

13 237 U. S. 589, 1915; for an interpretation of " liberty " under the due process clause, in relation to compulsory drill in a state university, see Hamilton v. Regents of the University of California, 293 U. S. 245, 1934, and comment of Cushman, Robert E., in *American Political Science Review*, February, 1936, pp. 79–80. For other recent interpretations, see Mooney v. Holshan, Warden of San Quentin Penitentiary, 294 U. S. 103, 1935, and Snyder v. Commonwealth of Massachusetts, 291 U. S. 97, 1934.

In his defense before the Supreme Court, Waugh's attorneys argued that the act deprived him of his liberty under Amendment XIV; that in effect it deprived him of that harmonious pursuit of happiness that goes with fraternity life; that the act was a denial of equal protection of the law, under the terms of Amendment XIV. His case was further strengthened by the fact that he was not, and that he did not contemplate becoming, a member of any chapter at the University of Mississippi. His appeal was, therefore, a matter more of principle than of personal interest. The question was whether a state might lawfully exclude members of Greek-letter fraternities from a state university and from institutions supported in part by state funds. The Court decided that it might — that the law was uniform in its application and that it presented no inequalities. The trustees had not made the law retroactive, in that they allowed students to sign a pledge which applied only during the period of residence at the state university. There was, they said, no deprivation of liberty or denial of equal protection of the law, or denial of the right to the pursuit of happiness. The situation existing between the state and the university in this case was similar to that existing between the Federal government and the states under the grant-in-aid system. This principle also operates in the law governing private inheritance.

That the amendment was adopted for the protection of individuals has already been emphasized, yet for more than half a century the Court has insisted that it applies to corporations as well as to persons. In 1938 Justice Black, in a very significant dissenting opinion, challenged this interpretation and called upon the Court to reverse its earlier decisions, so that the amendment might in fact mean what those who framed it and the states that adopted it intended that it should mean.[14] Commenting on this dissent, Professor Lerner expressed the fear that it might be nothing but a courageous gesture, after the elapse of more than fifty years. " Nor is it merely the time that has elapsed; it is the fact that the personality of the corporation has become an integral part of our constitutional law — right or wrong. The second is that his opinion would have been more complete if he had taken account of the fact that where ' person ' has been used previously in the language of the law of lawyers, it has also been construed to include the corporation. The third is that the more strategic line of attack on the abuse of power

[14] Connecticut General Life Insurance Company v. Johnson, Treasurer of California, 303 U. S. 77, 1938; see comment in Lerner, Max, " Justice Black, Dissenting," *New Republic,* March 5, 1938.

by the courts would have been to insist that 'due process' should be interpreted only to mean procedural safeguards and not substantive determinations of social policy."

The circumstances under which test cases arise are many and varied. The Constitution, however, offers no definition of due process, nor has the Supreme Court defined the term with precision. Many decades ago Cooley wrote a definition which has been accorded wide acceptance:

Due process of law in each particular case means such an exercise of the powers of the government as the settled maxims of law permit and sanction, and under such safeguards for the protection of individual rights as those maxims prescribe for the class of case to which the one in question belongs.

EQUAL PROTECTION OF THE LAW

The concept of equal protection of the law must not be confused with due process. It has been defined by the late Dean Burdick of the Cornell Law School by a transposition of the words in the original phrase as it appears in the Constitution. Equal protection of the law, he says, means for all practical purposes the right of the individual to the protection of reasonably equal law. The courts have repeatedly made it clear that the phrase requires that all persons who are similarly situated shall be treated alike; or conversely, that there shall be no discrimination in the treatment of persons in like circumstances. The Supreme Court gave an admirable expression of the doctrine of equal protection in the following paragraph from its opinion in Barbier v. Connolly:

The Fourteenth Amendment, in declaring that no state "shall deprive any person of life, liberty, or property without due process of law, nor deny to any person within its jurisdiction the equal protection of the laws," undoubtedly intended not only that there should be no arbitrary deprivation of life or liberty, or arbitrary spoliation of property, but that equal protection and security should be given to all under like circumstances in the enjoyment of their personal and civil rights; that all persons should be equally entitled to pursue their happiness and acquire and enjoy property; that they should have like access to the courts of the country for the protection of their persons and property, the prevention and redress of wrongs, and the enforcement of contracts; that no impediment should be interposed to the pursuits of anyone except as applied to the same pursuits by others under like circumstances; that no greater burdens should be laid upon one than are laid upon others in the same calling and condition, and that in the administration of criminal justice no different or higher

punishment should be imposed upon one than such as is prescribed to all
for like offenses. But neither the amendment — broad and comprehensive
as it is — nor any other amendment was designed to interfere with the
power of the state, sometimes termed its police power, to prescribe regulations to promote the health, peace, morals, education, and good order of the
people, and to legislate so as to increase the industries of the state, develop
its resources, and add to its wealth and prosperity. From the very necessities of society, legislation of a special character, having these objects in view,
must often be had in certain districts, such as for draining marshes and
irrigating arid plains. Special burdens are often necessary for general benefits — for supplying water, preventing fires, lighting districts, cleaning
streets, opening parks, and many other objects. Regulations for these purposes may press with more or less weight upon one than upon another, but
they are designed, not to impose unequal or unnecessary restrictions upon
anyone, but to promote, with as little individual inconvenience as possible,
the general good. Though in many respects necessarily special in their
character, they do not furnish just ground of complaint if they operate
alike upon all persons and property under the same circumstances and conditions. Class legislation, discriminating against some and favoring others,
is prohibited; but legislation which, in carrying out a public purpose, is
limited in its application if within the sphere of its operation it affects alike
all persons similarly situated, is not within the amendment.[15]

One of the most frequent causes of litigation under this clause are
acts involving "class legislation." In one sense, most legislation is
class legislation, for there are relatively few enactments of legislative
bodies which are of equal application and importance to all. In the
more common and popular usage, however, the phrase implies the
presence of an unfair advantage accorded to one group, or the presence of discriminatory provisions with regard to another. The fact
of discrimination is all that is necessary — it makes no difference
whether it exists by reason of legislative provisions or through improper administrative procedures. In Connolly v. Union Sewer Pipe
Company [16] the Court held invalid an Illinois antitrust law which
forbade combinations among producers to restrict competition, but
which especially exempted farmers from the provisions of the law
and thereby afforded them an advantage not given to other classes
of producers. In 1940, in Tigner v. Texas, the Court held this principle no longer controlling.[17] In both of these cases the objection

[15] 113 U. S. 27, 1885.
[16] 184 U. S. 540, 1902.
[17] 313 U. S. 635, 1940; holding that a Texas antitrust law imposing penalties
upon various forms of combination and monopoly in restraint of trade may exclude activities of agriculture and still not contravene the constitutional provision
requiring equal protection of the laws.

was to the legislation itself, but in Yick Wo v. Hopkins [18] the discrimination resulted from unfair and unjust administrative policies. San Francisco provided by ordinance that no laundries should be operated in frame dwellings without a permit or certificate from the city inspector. The apparent purpose was to reduce the fire hazard; in practice, it appeared to be to reduce the number of Chinese laundries, for permits were denied to all Chinese and were given without question to others. Thus an ordinance which was fair on its face and impartial in appearance was so applied and administered as clearly to violate the equal protection clause of Amendment XIV. The Court warned that unless these administrative practices were corrected, it might become necessary to invalidate the ordinance.

To return now to the question of the relation of due process and equal protection, it may be noted that the question has, in the words of Professor Mott, " proved one of the enigmas of constitutional law." Many authorities have held to the view that equality in application — equal protection, in other words — was an element in due process. " Even before the passage of the amendment, the state courts had worked out a fairly intensive, although far from comprehensive, body of law covering arbitrary classification. By the time of the Civil War a number of states had definitely linked this with due process of law," and this practice continued after the adoption of the amendment. The inferior Federal courts, in passing upon diverse citizenship cases, had frequently had occasion to deal with the same problem, and had adopted a somewhat similar practice. Professor Mott quotes with approval the conclusion of Dean Burdick, made after careful examination of all the evidence, that " the conception of due process does exclude legislation which inflicts inequality of burden which is clearly arbitrary and without any basis in reason." [19] Even though Chief Justice Taft, in Truax and Truax v. Corrigan, admitted that " the equality clause of the Fourteenth Amendment does not apply to congressional but only to state action," Professor

---

[18] 118 U. S. 356, 1885. For a recent case dealing with the question of classification, see Morf v. Bingaman, Commissioner of Revenue for New Mexico, 298 U. S. 407, 1936. The act taxed the privilege of dealers to bring in motor vehicles for sale, on their own wheels, imposing a flat fee without regard to mileage. Said the Court: " If a state taxing provision, of whatever form its words, results in the application of the tax to a class which may be separately taxed without denial of equal protection, those within the taxed class may not complain because the class might have been more aptly defined by the statute or because others not of that class might have been taxed."

[19] Burdick, *op. cit.*, p. 419, and quoted by Mott, *op. cit.*, p. 284. This comment is based largely on Chapter 16 of the latter volume.

Mott feels that the question still is, and is likely to remain, one of considerable uncertainty.[20]

Protection of Individuals from Private Wrongs. As noted, both the Federal and state constitutions protect citizens from infringements of their rights by the government and its officers. They do not, however, cover infringements of the rights of persons or attacks upon their property by other persons. This does not mean that persons who suffer such violations of personal or property rights are left without means of redress. The point is that the basis of their redress is to be found in the statutes as interpreted by the courts, and not in the provisions of the Constitution. In Chapter XV on the legal systems of the states, mention was made of some of the more common types of conduct which infringe upon individual and property rights. Many of these are purely personal and are protected by ordinary statutes and by recourse to judicial process; others involve violations of fundamental rights on the part of government. It is now proposed to consider the attempts that have been made by injured parties to invoke the protection of the Constitution, and to observe the results of such attempts.

The Negroes are probably the group that has suffered most from the inability to enjoy rights and privileges exercised without question by other groups in the community. For many years after the adoption of Amendment XIV, the effort was made by the Radical Reconstructionists in Congress to pass legislation assuring the Negro a large measure of social equality. In the Senate this movement was led by Charles Sumner of Massachusetts; because of constitutional difficulties, obvious to anyone familiar with constitutional law, he was unable to secure a favorable vote. After his death, however, the Senate waived its scruples with regard to constitutionality, and

---

[20] 257 U. S. 312, 1921, and Mott, *op. cit.,* pp. 298–299. For further illustrations of this uncertainty, see Finley v. California, 222 U. S. 28, 1911, affirming a California judgment which upheld a statute punishing life convicts alone with death, for an assault with a deadly weapon; Cotting v. Kansas City Stock Yards Company, 183 U. S. 79, 1901, holding invalid a Kansas statute regulating the rates of stock yards within the state doing more than a certain volume of business, an amount actually exceeded only by the yards at Kansas City; Williams v. Arkansas, 217 U. S. 79, 1910, sustaining an Arkansas statute forbidding soliciting for certain kinds of business upon trains in the state. For an excellent recent article, see Dowling, Noel T., " Equal Protection of the Laws," *Annals,* January, 1938, Supplement, pp. 65–78.

adopted, largely as a tribute to a departed friend and colleague, the Civil Rights Act of 1881.

It was not long before this act was declared unconstitutional by the Supreme Court in the famous Civil Rights Cases, decided in 1883.[21] In this decision the Court took the position that it was not the intent or purpose of those who proposed and adopted Amendment XIV to place in the Constitution a guarantee of the personal rights of individuals as against invasion by other individuals, no matter how important their enjoyment might be to the happiness of the injured parties. The facts of the case were that various colored persons had been denied by the proprietors of hotels, theaters, and railway companies the full enjoyment of accommodations, for reasons other than those excepted by the statute, the most important section of which provided as follows:

> Section 1. That all persons within the jurisdiction of the United States shall be entitled to the full and equal enjoyment of the accommodations, advantages, facilities, and privileges of inns, public conveyances on land or water, theaters, and other places of public amusement; subject only to the conditions and limitations established by law, and applicable alike to citizens of every race and color, regardless of any previous condition of servitude.

The proprietors had been indicted and sued for the penalty prescribed by the act — the forfeit of a sum of $500 for each offense to the person aggrieved, and conviction of a misdemeanor.

In its opinion the Court pointed out that " it is state action of a particular character that is prohibited " by the amendment; later, at greater length, it said that " until some state law has been passed, or some state action through its officers or agents has been taken, adverse to the rights of citizens sought to be protected by the Fourteenth Amendment, no legislation of the United States under said amendment, nor any proceeding under such legislation, can be called into activity, for the prohibitions of the amendment are against state laws and acts done under state authority." It is thus clear that if legislative action is to be taken for the purpose of protecting the civil rights of this portion of the population, it must originate in the states. A survey made in 1935 disclosed that no less than eighteen states had adopted measures forbidding segregation or discrimination against Negroes in hotels, restaurants, theaters, and shops.

---

[21] 109 U. S. 3, 1883; for an excellent discussion of constitutional rights, see Orth, Samuel P., and Cushman, Robert E., *American National Government,* Chapter 5 (Crofts, New York, 1931) .

This decision in the Civil Rights Cases and such state legislation as has been adopted may have settled certain questions of constitutional interpretation, but they have in no way contributed to the solution of a large number of vexatious questions which recur repeatedly, such as the segregation of races for purposes of residence, the operation of " Jim Crow " cars, and the right of colored persons to enjoy equally with whites the facilities of hotels, restaurants, theaters, and other places operated for and open to the general public. Perhaps two illustrative cases will suffice. In Plessy v. Ferguson [22] the Court was called upon to consider a Louisiana statute which required railway companies to provide equal, but separate, accommodations for white and colored passengers, and which made it a misdemeanor for any person to insist upon going into a coach reserved for persons of the other race. Plessy, a person of one eighth African blood, was prosecuted for violation of this statute and convicted; he appealed to the State Supreme Court, unsuccessfully, to prevent being punished under the statute, and then took a writ of error to the Supreme Court of the United States. In its opinion, this Court gave expression to a view which has been repeatedly reaffirmed in the consideration of questions of this character:

The object of the Fourteenth Amendment was undoubtedly to enforce the absolute equality of the two races before the law, but, in the nature of things, it could not have been intended to abolish distinctions based upon color, or to enforce social, as distinguished from political, equality, or a commingling of the two races upon terms unsatisfactory to either. Laws permitting, and even requiring, their separation, in places where they are liable to be brought into contact, do not necessarily imply the inferiority of either race to the other, and have been generally, if not universally, recognized as within the competency of the state legislatures in the exercise of their police power. The most common instance of this is connected with the establishment of separate schools for white and colored children, which has been held to be a valid exercise of the legislative power even by courts of states where the political rights of the colored race have been longest and most earnestly enforced.

There have been a number of cases involving the right of municipalities to establish a policy of race segregation in residential districts. Important among these is Buchanan v. Warley, decided by the Supreme Court in 1917.[23] In this case the defendant, a Negro,

[22] 163 U. S. 537, 1896. This view was supported by Chiles v. Chesapeake & Ohio Railroad Company, 218 U. S. 71, 1910, but a few years later, in McCabe v. Atcheson, Topeka & Santa Fe Railroad Company, 235 U. S. 151, 1914, it was held that Pullman accommodations on a railroad cannot be validly denied to Negroes if they are made available to white persons.

[23] 245 U. S. 60, 1917.

agreed to buy from the plaintiff, white, a lot in the city of Louisville, located in a block where there were eight residences occupied by whites and only two by blacks, on condition that the defendant should have the legal right to live in said property, although a city ordinance provided that on and after a certain date, Negroes might not move into a block in which a majority of the inhabitants were whites, and conversely, that whites might not move into a block in which the majority of inhabitants were colored. Curiously enough, the ordinance was entitled " An ordinance to prevent conflict and ill-feeling between the white and colored races in the city of Louisville, and to preserve the public peace and promote the general welfare. . . ." In the opinion of the Court, which centered around the concrete question of the right of occupancy, and to the purchase and sale of property, it was held that the ordinance could not stand, inasmuch as it involved a direct violation of the due process clause of Amendment XIV.

When the courts have considered questions involving the rights of Negroes in public places, the Negro has not always fared so well. In such cases the courts have usually held that when the lawmaking power adopted, in the interests of the public peace, a policy of segregation, as in the Louisiana statute discussed above, the fact of such segregation did not imply anything with regard to the superiority or the inferiority of either race. The assumption, of course, has always been that where a policy of segregation is adopted, the facilities provided for each race would be equal in quality and adequate in quantity to meet the needs of the group. The practice has been so far at variance with this theory, that the theory may properly be regarded in most cases as a legal fiction. In cities where separate traction facilities are provided for the two races, the equipment used for the colored people is old and dilapidated, and the service infrequent and inadequate. Even limited opportunity to observe the situation in cities where this practice is in force will be adequate to confirm this statement.

Many interesting cases have developed out of the refusal of the managers of hotels, restaurants, and theaters to permit colored people to enjoy their facilities. Hotelkeepers have frequently resorted to those common law rules which permitted them to refuse to take in persons who were drunk or disorderly or whose patronage they felt might be injurious to other established business, and to the right of innkeepers under the common law to turn away applicants for lodging when all their accommodations were engaged. A case in point arose in Philadelphia in 1910, when one Battling Nelson, of pugilistic fame, rolled up to the entrance of the Bellevue-Stratford Hotel in his limousine, entered and attempted to register.[24] The action was one for damages against the hotel for having refused lodging and accommodations. Through his agent the plaintiff had previously reserved a room at the hotel, the occupancy of which was denied him by the management when he attempted to register, on the ground that he was a prize fighter and hence an undesirable person. In the course of the trial, the hotel was able to prove that he had violated a criminal law in one of the states by engaging in a prize fight contrary to the law of that state.

The Court was called upon to decide the question whether a hotel owes an accommodation and lodging to all persons, or only to proper persons — a person having violated a criminal law being not a proper person. Judgment was rendered in favor of the defendant hotel, thereby affirming the decision of the lower court. The opinion stressed the point that while an innkeeper owes a duty to travelers applying for accommodations and tendering reasonable payment therefor – to receive and accommodate them — he may lawfully refuse to receive boisterous, intoxicated, or objectionable characters and persons who are violators of criminal laws — persons not law-abiding citizens — without being liable to such persons for damages. Since the plaintiff in the present case was a person proved to be of such character, the hotel was not liable for having failed to furnish the accommodations requested.

Nor does the colored man fare much better when he attempts to enjoy the facilities of restaurants and theaters. A favorite device employed by restaurant keepers who discourage the patronage of Negroes is to post a sign indicating a substantial cover charge; this charge is never collected — and was never intended to be collected — unless the manager discovers some patron whom he considers objectionable or likely to have an injurious effect upon his trade. In these cases, the patron would be required to pay the cover charge, and would thereby ordinarily be discouraged from returning to this establishment. The problem so far as the management of theaters is concerned is somewhat less difficult, since the usual practice in theaters sets up a range of prices, with seats on different levels, some one of which may be reserved in whole or in part for the use of colored patrons.

Another problem affecting the rights of Negroes has been arising

[24] Nelson v. Boldt, et al., 180 Fed. 779, 1910.

with increasing frequency — the question of their right to attend publicly supported institutions of higher learning. University authorities and state courts have repeatedly faced this problem, but in 1938 the Supreme Court, in Missouri ex rel. Gaines v. Canada,[25] had an opportunity to pass upon the question. Missouri maintains a separate university for Negroes which does not provide legal instruction; a statute authorizes the board of curators to arrange for scholarships to the university of any adjacent state for taking any course provided at the University of Missouri but not taught at the Negro university. The petitioner refused to avail himself of the scholarship and brought mandamus to compel his admission to the state university law school. The State Supreme Court refused the writ. Reversing the decision, the United States Supreme Court held that the out-of-state scholarship plan contravenes the equal protection clause of Amendment XIV. This decision is in accord with a growing tendency to accord to Negroes their full rights as citizens.[26]

Freedom of Speech and of the Press. There has been much popular misunderstanding with regard to the nature and extent of the liberty which may properly be enjoyed by the individual under the constitutional guarantee of freedom of speech. The right of the individual is relative, not absolute. Paradoxically enough, it is circumscribed by many restrictions which society has found it necessary to impose upon a theoretically complete freedom, in order that the individual might in fact enjoy any freedom worth mentioning. In the first place, one's freedom of speech is limited by the consequences of his action. To shout loudly " Fire! " or " Murder! " in a crowded theater or railway station might cause injury and distress too horrible to contemplate, while to do the same in open fields would be quite harmless. Furthermore, one is bound to observe the customs and conventions of society — he may not, at least in public, resort to the use of obscene, profane, or abusive language. He is bound by the law of libel — he has no right to injure or defame the reputation of another, without adequate cause and proof. He is responsible for what he says, in the sense that he may not make serious charges against another and hide behind the cloak of anonymity. If he wants to expose something, he must be willing to stand in public and de-

---

25 305 U. S. 580, 1938.

26 See Mangum, Charles S., Jr., *The Legal Status of the Negro* (University of North Carolina Press, 1940). Similarly, the Court held that exclusion of Negroes from jury lists was a violation of Amendment XIV — Hale v. Kentucky, 303 U. S. 613, 1938. A lower Federal Court held that discrimination in the rate of compensation between colored and white teachers was unconstitutional — Mills v. Board of Education of Anne Arundel County, 30 F. Supp. 245 (D. Md. 1939).

fend the charges. Again, while he may theoretically have the right to say anything he likes about any subject, at any time, and in any place, his own good judgment and a sense of the fitness of things ought to indicate to him that in fact he is not at liberty to discuss all subjects at all times and with all types of audiences. Thus freedom of speech is actually limited by many different considerations.

Many of these limitations apply with equal force to freedom of the press. In Aikens v. Wisconsin the Supreme Court decided, in 1904, an interesting case involving two defendants who were convicted in the Milwaukee municipal court of violating a statute forbidding two or more persons to combine " for the purpose of willfully or maliciously injuring another in his reputation, trade, business, or profession, by any means whatever." [27] As publishers of newspapers in Milwaukee, they had combined to refuse advertisements save at an increased rate from any person who advertised in a competing newspaper at a rate higher than their own regular rates. A conviction, affirmed by the State Supreme Court, was later affirmed by the United States Supreme Court upon the ground that when it comes to the freedom of the individual, malicious mischief and, still more, combinations for the purpose of inflicting it are familiar and proper subjects of legislative repression. In Near v. Minnesota [28] the Supreme Court was called upon to consider the attempt of the state legislature to prevent the growth of the blackmailing industry; although the Court divided sharply on the issue, the majority held " that while a malicious, defamatory publication rendered its publisher liable in damages *after* issue, any law which provided for the stopping or prevention of publication *before* issue was an interference with liberty, particularly when the publication discussed the conduct of public officers and their duty in the suppression of crime." In time of war the state may interfere to an extent that would not be permitted in time of peace, and even in time of peace it may restrict freedom of speech or of the press if there is reason for believing that the words used might be a direct incitement to violence or disorder.[29]

In recent years there have been a very large number of attempted interferences with civil liberties; some of the acts have come before the Supreme Court for review. In DeJonge v. Oregon [30] it was held

[27] 195 U. S. 194, 1904.
[28] 283 U. S. 697, 1931; for an analysis of this case, see Young, *op. cit.*, pp. 697–698.
[29] See Gitlow v. New York, 268 U. S. 652, 1925.
[30] 299 U. S. 353, 1937.

that the due process clause in Amendment XIV includes the guarantee of freedom of speech. In Nardone v. United States [31] it was held that evidence obtained through wire-tapping was inadmissible — thereby overruling, in substance, an earlier case. In two recent cases the Court upheld the right to distribute printed matter, on the ground that the right to circulate is as important as the right to print.[32] In one of these cases, Hague v. Committee for Industrial Organization, other issues were involved. Not only did Hague seek to prevent the distribution of printed material, but forbade the use of any hall in the city for a public meeting to advocate the obstruction or change of the government by any organization unless a permit had first been obtained from the Chief of Police. This the Court held to be an abridgment of the privileges and immunities clause of Amendment XIV. In Grosjean v. American Press Company,[33] the Court declared unconstitutional a Louisiana statute intended to suppress criticism of state officials by imposing a heavy tax burden on such newspapers as opposed the administration. In Minersville School District v. Gobitis, however, the Court upheld the validity of state legislation requiring pupils in the public schools to salute the flag.[34] This array of cases will be sufficient to show both the nature of the important questions affecting civil liberties in recent years, and the strong stand which the Court as now constituted has commonly taken in defending them.

PROTECTION OF PROPERTY RIGHTS

The Obligation of Contract. In Article I, Section 10, the Federal Constitution imposes upon the state a restriction that " no state shall impair the obligation of contract." This restriction was regarded by the framers of the Constitution, and has been regarded by lawyers since, as of the utmost importance in the protection of the rights of the individual. It is true that the enforcement of such a rule makes for stability in the business and economic life of the nation, but certain developments in recent times and certain aspects of the judicial

31 308 U. S. 240, 1939; see note in *Brooklyn Law Review,* January, 1940, pp. 214–221.
32 Lovell v. City of Griffin, 303 U. S. 444, 1938, and Hague v. Committee for Industrial Organization, 307 U. S. 496, 1939; see notes in *Brooklyn Law Review,* January, 1940, pp. 201–205, and *North Carolina Law Review,* December, 1939, pp. 67–71.
33 297 U. S. 233, 1936.
34 313 U. S. 690, 1940; for the brief in this case, see supplement to the *Bill of Rights Review,* Summer, 1940.

treatment of the doctrine have raised important questions. During the depression which began in 1929, wholesale execution of mortgage foreclosures took place, affecting the homes of citizens in urban communities and the farm properties which were both the homes and the means of livelihood of citizens in rural communities. Honest but helpless people were moved into the streets, so that many people wondered which our society valued more — the sacredness of human life or the sacredness of the obligation of contract. A fetish was made of a legal doctrine, the observance of which under normal conditions is admittedly for the general good. Some states went so far as to translate some of these doubts into mortgage moratorium statutes, designed to aid the debtor under the terrific strain of the depression. The Supreme Court, in its decision in the Minnesota Mortgage Moratorium Case, decided in 1934,[35] upheld the validity of such emergency legislation.

Some of the most serious difficulties with regard to this subject have grown out of the famous decision of the Supreme Court handed down by John Marshall in the Dartmouth College Case in 1819.[36] This case is interesting and important, not only because of the interpretation which the Court gave to this clause of the Constitution, but for certain incidental facts connected with the handling of the case. In 1769 King George III gave to the trustees of Dartmouth College a charter authorizing them to establish a college for the training of prospective clergymen. The charter was thus limited in its application because at that time clergymen were the only members of the community who were supposed to need any advanced education. The school was established ultimately at Hanover, New Hampshire, and apparently functioned satisfactorily. In the course of time there came to its presidency a man named Woodward, who had progressive ideas on higher education, who saw the need for the extension of its opportunities to a larger number of persons, and who had a plan by which the usefulness and scope of the work of the college might be extended. This plan he submitted to the trustees, whom he found to be opposed strongly to it in every particular.

President Woodward now applied to the New Hampshire legislature for an act modifying the original charter of the college which

[35] Home Building and Loan Association v. Blaisdell, et al., 290 U. S. 398, 1934; W. B. Worthen Company v. Kavanaugh, 295 U. S. 56, 1935; and Palitz, Max, " Legislative Relief of the Mortgage Debtor," *Temple Law Quarterly*, April, 1937, pp. 404–409.

[36] 4 Wheaton 518, 1819; in this connection, see Ellsworth, Clayton S., " Ohio's Attack upon Abolition Schools," *Mississippi Valley Historical Review*, December, 1934, pp. 379–386.

would authorize him to carry out his program. The act was passed, but as soon as the president proceeded under its terms, the trustees entered suit against him. The case was carried to the Supreme Court, before which it was argued in two successive terms. The circumstances of these arguments were indeed unusual.

Daniel Webster, Senator from Massachusetts, appeared as attorney for the trustees. It is significant, in the first place, that a leading member of the Senate should have found it possible to conduct a large and lucrative law practice in Washington, and that neither he nor anyone else should have seen any impropriety in his doing so. No Senator today undertakes to do such a thing, and there has been serious criticism of those ex-Senators who have remained in Washington for the purpose of profiting financially by representing clients before governmental agencies with whose personnel they became acquainted during service in Congress. At any rate, in Webster's time these considerations appear not to have been important. Strong political and religious rivalries and antipathies were involved in this case. Instead of discussing the legal questions in his argument before the Court, Webster dwelt at length upon these political and religious aspects of the case, delivering a highly emotional and more or less bombastic speech.

When the argument was completed and Chief Justice Marshall took a poll of the Court, he discovered that, while he was anxious to uphold the contentions of Webster and the trustees, he could not get a majority of the Court to support him. As Chief Justice he thereupon decided that the case would not be disposed of at this time, but would be held over for reargument.[37] At the term of Court the following year, Webster again appeared for the trustees, delivering a more oratorical and flamboyant speech than the original. At the conclusion of the argument, Marshall had a majority of the Court with him and handed down what we know as the decision in the Dartmouth College Case. Again it is significant to note that the

---

[37] Students of history are familiar with the extraordinary manner in which Chief Justice Marshall dominated the Supreme Court during his long tenure. In thirty-four years the Court decided 1,106 cases, of which Marshall himself wrote the opinion for 519. In all these years, he dissented from the majority of the Court in only eight cases, and wrote only one dissenting opinion — that in Ogden v. Saunders (12 Wheaton 213, 1827). This is the more remarkable when one considers the number of dissenting opinions filed by members of the Court today. Many of Marshall's contemporaries have testified to his extraordinary influence over his colleagues; brilliant young followers of the Jeffersonian philosophy were transformed into archconservatives under his influence, much to the dismay of the Anti-Federalist leaders. See Hall, James Parker, *Cases on Constitutional Law*, p. 800 (West Publishing Company, St. Paul, 1926).

trustees of the college had in the interval lavishly entertained the members of the Court, seeking thereby to place the Justices under obligation, and to influence their judgment by personal acquaintance. It is quite inconceivable that any party to a case before the Supreme Court in our own time would attempt to use such tactics, or that the members of the Court would for a moment permit themselves to be subjected to such influence. However strongly one may disagree at times with decisions of the Court, no informed person will venture to question the integrity or the sincerity of any of its members.

Webster's argument, which Marshall and a majority of the Court accepted, was to the effect that the charter granted by George III and, in theory, his successor in the exercise of the charter-granting power in New Hampshire — namely, the legislature — was a contract between the state and the trustees. It followed that a subsequent attempt on the part of the legislature to modify the charter became an attempt at the impairment of the obligation of the original contract, contrary to the provision of the Federal Constitution. This charter was not then, never had been, and is not now a contract in any generally accepted sense of that term. If the Chief Justice had been more concerned with the legal principles and the public policies involved in this case, and less concerned with matters of political and religious controversy, the decision as we now have it would never have been made.

The effect of the decision was to place the states in such a difficult and embarrassing situation that no student of state government would defend it. Not many years after this decision was made, changes were under way in our economic life, leading to a widespread substitution of the corporate form of business organization for the individual entrepreneur and the partnership. In the early days of the corporate form, every corporate charter was conferred by a separate legislative action. Under the terms of this decision, every one of these charters became an irrevocable, unmodifiable contract between the state and the persons to whom it was granted. If the legislatures had always been careful and honest in the granting of charters, the situation would have been bad enough. Unfortunately, they were often neither careful nor honest. Vast portions of the public domain were given away in connection with these charters, without any consideration whatever coming to the state, then or in the future. Rights and privileges of incalculable value were conferred for all time without restriction and without any compensation to the state therefor. The situation thus created was indeed critical.

This decision has never been officially modified or reversed, and in all probability it is now so deeply intrenched in our legal system that this is impossible. In a significant dissenting opinion, however, Justice Black, in Indiana ex rel. Anderson v. Brand, in 1937,[38] vigorously urged that this ancient wrong be corrected, that a fluid system of legislative supremacy be substituted for the plan by which property institutions have in effect frozen our economic order for more than a century. Under the circumstances, the states have been forced to invent methods of evading and circumventing the Dartmouth decision in order to bring about a control over corporations which should have been theirs without question. They have been obliged to insert in corporate charters, as a condition of their adoption, some limitation upon the life of the charter, and they have likewise inserted clauses reserving the right to modify or to abrogate the charter as the public interest may require. By such roundabout methods the states have succeeded in regaining a limited measure of control over the corporations which they themselves have created. It seems strange indeed that a decision the consequences of which have been so widely detrimental to the best interests of the states should still be regarded by many people as one of the great landmarks of our constitutional history. If the decision was great, it was so in the sense of being a great mistake, from the point of view of public policy and from the point of view of the states.[39]

Eminent Domain. The right of eminent domain has been defined as that superior dominion of the sovereign power over all the property within the state, including that previously granted by itself, which authorizes it to appropriate any part thereof to a necessary public use, reasonable compensation being made therefor. The Federal Constitution and all the state constitutions except those of Kansas, New Hampshire, and North Carolina now contain express prohibitions against the taking of private property for public use without compensation. In Kansas, corporations are also prohibited

[38] 302 U. S. 678, 1937.

[39] For the best discussions of this case, see Orton, Jesse F., " Confusion of Property with Privilege: Dartmouth College Case," *Independent*, August 19 and 26, 1909, reprinted in Orth, Samuel P., *Readings on the Relation of Government to Property and Industry*, pp. 7–24 (Ginn, Boston, 1915) ; also Lodge, Henry C., *Daniel Webster*, in American Statesmen Series (Houghton Mifflin, Boston, 1889) ; and Mott, *op. cit.*, Chapter 19. For the best recent statement of the whole problem, see Hervey, John G., " The Impairment of Obligations of Contracts," *Annals*, January, 1938, Supplement, pp. 87–120.

in the same way.[40] In these three states, substantially the same result has been reached by holding that the due process of law clause covers the matter.[41] Not only do nearly all states prohibit a taking without compensation, but a large number require compensation for property damaged or injured for public use; a case in point is that of the Tidewater Railway Company v. Shartzer, in which the Supreme Court of Virginia held the railway liable, under the damage clause of the Virginia Constitution, for annoyance from smoke, noise, dust, cinders, and danger from fire resulting to lands no part of which was taken.[42]

Like the power to tax, the power of eminent domain may be exercised only for a public purpose; generally speaking, those purposes which have been judged to be public for purposes of taxation are also public when considered in connection with the exercise of the power of eminent domain. While this power is not to be confused with the power of taxation, such a policy is reasonable and just, for both involve the taking of property, in one case to a limited extent, with a return in the form of services rendered by government, in the other, completely, with such financial return as the owner of the property may be judged to be entitled to. To state the same matter in another way, one may observe, as Professor Mott has done, that "logically, it would seem that what is a public purpose for one power of government should be also public in another, inasmuch as the publicity of the enterprise depends upon the legal privileges and obligations which have been given it." [43]

The same authority points out that the use of the power of eminent domain in aid of public service corporations did not become important before the development of railroads as a means of transportation. He continues:

. . . The power had frequently been used in aid of privately controlled turnpikes, bridges, ferries, and canals, and its constitutionality was gen-

[40] The final clause in Amendment V to the Federal Constitution reads: "nor shall private property be taken for public use, without just compensation." The state constitutions usually follow this wording exactly; these provisions are collected in Lewis, John, *Eminent Domain,* Third Edition, Secs. 15–61 (Callaghan, Chicago, 1909).

[41] In support of this statement, Hall, *op. cit.,* p. 669, cites the following: Buckwalter v. School District, 65 Kan. 603, 1902; Opinion of Justices, 66 N. H. 629, 1891; Staton v. Norfolk and Carolina Railway, 111 N. C. 278, 1892.

[42] 107 Va. 562, 1907; Hall, *op. cit.,* pp. 767–768, lists the states in which these constitutional provisions exist. For a specialized study in a particular state, for a specific purpose, see Maryland Legislative Council, *Highway Condemnation* (Baltimore, 1940).

[43] Mott, *op. cit.,* p. 471; in Chapter 22 Professor Mott deals at length with the question of public purpose.

erally taken for granted. In a few cases it was contended that the power could not be used for enterprises of this nature, but the contention was uniformly rejected by the courts. There was at first a great popular prejudice against the steam railroads and consequently the cases involving grants of public powers to them were more stubbornly fought. It was in this connection that due process of law first became an important factor in eminent domain cases.

Thus in addition to uses in connection with public buildings and other public works, the power came to be used, in behalf of the government, by private corporations such as are commonly regarded as being affected with a public interest. Even so, the power of eminent domain has been regarded as a right inherent in government, and so essential to the performance of its necessary functions that it may not be contracted away, or the right to its exercise otherwise impaired.[44]

Most authorities have found it difficult to state exactly what constitutes a public purpose; many such purposes have been established by long lines of judicial opinions, but many borderline cases still arise. Such a case was that of the Mount Vernon-Woodberry Cotton Duck Company v. Alabama Interstate Power Company, the opinion in which was written in 1916 by the late Justice Holmes.[45] The power company sought to condemn private land, water, and water rights, in order to manufacture and sell to the public power produced by water. In answer to the owner's argument that the purpose of the company was not a public one, Justice Holmes said:

In the organic relations of modern society it may sometimes be hard to draw the line that is supposed to limit the authority of the legislature to exercise or delegate the power of eminent domain. But to gather the streams from waste and to draw from them energy, labor without brains, and so to save mankind from toil that it can be spared, is to supply what, next to intellect, is the very foundation of all achievements and all our welfare. If that purpose is not public we should be at a loss to say what is.

It would be encouraging indeed to be able to feel that the courts would always take a similarly enlightened point of view.

One further point remains to be considered — the process by which the property of individuals may be taken, either by the government, or by a corporation authorized by it to exercise this power, in connection with a development of general public interest. The decision

44 See, for instance, Pennsylvania Hospital v. Philadelphia, 245 U. S. 20, 1917.
45 240 U. S. 30, 1916; for an interesting case dealing with the " market value " of land taken by a public service company, see Olson v. United States, 292 U. S. 246, 1934.

to take one's property once having been made, the individual has no recourse, for it has long been held that the right of the public to take — with just compensation — property which it needs is paramount over the right of a single individual or a corporation. The usual procedure is to appraise the value of such portion of the property as may be required by the public, and make an offer to the owner. This he may either accept or reject. It seems to be characteristic of individuals to value their property very highly when condemnation proceedings are in prospect, and to complain of overvaluation in connection with assessments. If the government or the corporation exercising the power of eminent domain is unable to arrive at a satisfactory agreement with the owner by conference, the owner may appeal to the courts, where a jury will decide what he may receive, and what he must accept, by way of compensation.[46] Most property owners are reluctant to carry a case this far, because of the expense and the uncertainties attendant upon the consideration of such a matter by a jury. It might also be added that many jurisdictions permit what is known as excess condemnation when the portion of the property that remains would be of little or no value to the owner, or when a failure to take all of it might in some way impair the value of the development for which the power was exercised.[47]

SELECTED REFERENCES

Alexander, Norman, *Rights of Aliens under the Federal Constitution* (Capitol City Press, Montpelier, 1931).

American Council on Public Affairs, *Freedom of Assembly and Anti-Democratic Groups* (Washington, 1940).

Association of American Law Schools, *Selected Essays on Constitutional Law* (Foundation Press, Chicago, 1938).

Baker, Russell, *Manual on the Law of Arrest, Search and Seizure* (Chicago Crime Commission, 1944).

Braxton, A. Caperton, *The Fifteenth Amendment* (J. P. Bell Company, Lynchburg, 1934).

Burdick, Charles K., *The Law of the American Constitution* (Putnam's, New York, 1922).

Cardozo, Benjamin N., *Paradoxes of Legal Science* (Columbia University Press, 1928).

[46] Rather comprehensive studies have been made of this procedure in at least two states: Corrick, Franklin, "A Synopsis of the Kansas Supreme Court Decisions Relating to Eminent Domain and Condemnation Procedure," Kansas Judicial Council *Bulletin*, July, 1933, entire issue; and Emory, Richard W., *Highway Condemnation* (Maryland Legislative Council, Baltimore, 1940).

[47] The standard work on this subject is by Cushman, Robert E., *Excess Condemnation* (Appleton, New York, 1917).

Chafee, Zechariah, Jr., *Freedom of Speech* (Harcourt, Brace, New York, 1920).

Cheyney, Edward P., Ed., "Freedom of Inquiry and Expression," *Annals,* November, 1938.

Collins, Charles W., *The Fourteenth Amendment and the States* (Little, Brown, Boston, 1912).

Constitution of the United States, Annotated, Revised Edition (Government Printing Office, Washington, 1938).

Cushman, Robert E., *Excess Condemnation* (Appleton, New York, 1917).

Devereaux, Harry B., *Right of Way and Land: Selected Bibliography* (University of Southern California, 1938).

Dunning, William A., *Reconstruction: Political and Economic* (Harper, New York, 1917).

Ely, Richard T., *Property and Contract in Their Relation to the Distribution of Wealth* (Macmillan, New York, 1917).

Flack, Horace E., *The Adoption of the Fourteenth Amendment* (Johns Hopkins Press, 1908).

Freund, Ernst, *Police Power* (Callaghan, Chicago, 1904).

——, *Administrative Powers over Persons and Property* (University of Chicago Press, 1928).

Goodrich, Herbert F., Ed., "Constitutional Rights," supplement to *Annals,* January, 1938.

Guild, June P., *Black Laws of Virginia, 1619–1936* (Committee for the Advancement of Negro Education, Richmond, 1936).

Guthrie, William D., *Lectures on the Fourteenth Article of Amendment to the Constitution of the United States* (Little, Brown, Boston, 1898).

Hamilton, Walton H., and Adair, Douglass, *The Power to Govern* (Norton, New York, 1937).

Hill, Helen, *George Mason, Constitutionalist* (Harvard University Press, 1938).

Hunting, Warren B., *The Obligation of Contracts Clause of the United States Constitution* (Johns Hopkins Press, 1919).

Hutcheson, Joseph C., *Law as Liberator* (Foundation Press, Chicago, 1938).

Kies, Harry B., and McCandless, Carl A., *Manual on the Bill of Rights and Suffrage and Elections* (Missouri Constitutional Convention of 1943, Columbia, 1943).

Lasson, Nelson B., *History and Development of the Fourth Amendment to the United States Constitution* (Johns Hopkins Press, 1937).

Mangum, Charles S., Jr., *The Legal Status of the Negro* (University of North Carolina Press, 1940).

Mathews, John M., *The American Constitutional System,* Second Edition (McGraw-Hill, New York, 1940).

Maxson, Charles H., *Citizenship* (Oxford University Press, New York, 1930).

McGehee, Lucius P., *Due Process of Law under the Federal Constitution* (Edward Thompson Company, Northport, New York, 1906).

McLaughlin, Andrew C., *A Constitutional History of the United States* (Appleton-Century, New York, 1935).

Moschzisker, Robert von, *Trial by Jury,* Second Edition (Bisel, Philadelphia, 1930).

Mott, Rodney L., *Due Process of Law* (Bobbs-Merrill, Indianapolis, 1926).

Nichols, Philip, *The Law of Eminent Domain*, Second Edition (Matthew Bender, Albany, 1917).

Orth, Samuel P., *Readings on the Relation of Government to Property and Industry* (Ginn, Boston, 1915).

Randall, James G., *The Civil War and Reconstruction* (Heath, Boston, 1937).

Rankin, Robert S., *When Civil Law Fails* (Duke University Press, 1939).

Read, Conyers, Ed., *The Constitution Reconsidered* (Columbia University Press, 1938).

Rohlfing, Charles C., and others, *Business and Government*, Fourth Edition (Foundation Press, Chicago, 1941).

Rottschaeffer, Henry, *Handbook of American Constitutional Law* (West Publishing Company, St. Paul, 1939).

Swisher, Carl B., *American Constitutional Development* (Houghton Mifflin, Boston, 1943).

Taylor, Hannis, *Due Process of Law and the Equal Protection of the Laws* (Callaghan, Chicago, 1917).

Tiedeman, Christopher G., *The Unwritten Constitution* (Putnam's, New York, 1890).

Van Dyne, Frederick, *Citizenship of the United States* (Lawyers Coöperative Publishing Company, Rochester, 1904).

Van Vleck, William C., *The Administrative Control of Aliens* (Commonwealth Fund, New York, 1932).

Wiley, Bell I., *Southern Negroes, 1861–1865* (Yale University Press, 1938).

Willoughby, W. W., *Principles of Constitutional Law of the United States*, Second Edition, 3 vols. (Baker, Voorhis, New York, 1929).

Wilson, Walter, *Forced Labor in the United States* (International Publishers, New York, 1933).

Wright, Benjamin F., *The Contract Clause of the Constitution* (Harvard University Press, 1938).

Young, James T., *The New American Government and Its Work*, Third Edition (Macmillan, New York, 1933).

American Bar Association, *Bill of Rights Review* (New York, quarterly, 1940–1942, then suspended during the war).

Aikin, Charles, " State Constitutional Law," in 1939–1940, *American Political Science Review*, August, 1940, pp. 700–718; in 1940–1941, *ibid.*, August, 1941, pp. 683–700; in 1941–1942, *ibid.*, August, 1942, pp. 667–688.

Cupples, H. L., " Protection of Personal Liberties under the Fourteenth Amendment: The Flag Salute," *George Washington Law Review*, May, 1940, pp. 1094–1097.

Field, Oliver P., " Property and Authority," *Journal of Politics*, August, 1941, pp. 253–275.

Haight, George I., and Lerch, Charles H., " Freedom of Religion," *Bill of Rights Review*, Winter, 1942, pp. 111–118.

Hall, Jerome, " A Proposal for Cooperative Research on the Bill of Rights," *Bulletin* of the American Association of University Professors, February, 1943, pp. 48–53.

Horack, Frank E., Jr., " Constitutional Liberties and Statutory Construction," *Iowa Law Review,* March, 1944, pp. 448–453.

Lindley, James K., " Council and Court: Handbill Ordinances, 1889–1939," *Michigan Law Review,* February, 1941, pp. 561–596.

Mulder, John E., and Comisky, Marvin, " Jehovah's Witnesses Mold Constitutional Law," *Bill of Rights Review,* Summer, 1942, pp. 262–268.

Oppenheimer, Reuben, " The Constitutional Rights of Aliens," *Bill of Rights Review,* Winter, 1941, pp. 100–111.

Ten Broek, Jacobus, " State Constitutional Law in 1942–1943," *American Political Science Review,* August, 1943, pp. 642–660.

——, and Graham, Howard J., " State Constitutional Law," in 1943–1944, *American Political Science Review,* August, 1944, pp. 670–692; in 1944–1945, *ibid.,* August, 1945, pp. 685–719.

Ward, Harry F., " Communist Party and the Ballot," *Bill of Rights Review,* Summer, 1941, pp. 286–292.

Wright, Herbert, " Religious Liberty under the Constitution of the United States," *Virginia Law Review,* November, 1940, pp. 75–87.

In the bibliography of the following chapter, the following casebooks on constitutional law are cited in full: Cushman, Dodd, Dowling, Evans, Field, Gerstenberg, Hall, Long, McGovney, Mauer, Rottschaefer, Thayer, and Wambaugh. All contain sections and cases on the topics discussed in this chapter. Mention should be made also of the numerous articles in the law journals; these are cited in the *Index of Legal Periodicals.*

CHAPTER XIX

State Police Power

THE police power has come to occupy a position of such importance that it is inconceivable that one should undertake a study of state government without considering it. The police power belongs to the states alone. While the phrase is frequently used in connection with the Federal government, one should not forget that this power has never been recognized by the Supreme Court as one of the powers or attributes of the Federal government. In using the phrase in this connection, therefore, one is taking a certain liberty with the accepted interpretation of the Court — a liberty justified only by the fact that the Court has on many occasions sanctioned the exercise of Federal powers so similar to the police power of the states that the effort to separate the two has seemed to be an effort to maintain a distinction where there was no difference.

Origin of State Police Power. While the state police power was known before the important decision of the Supreme Court in the Slaughter House Cases,[1] its extensive use in modern times dates from this decision. The case arose through the efforts of the City Council in New Orleans to remedy unsanitary conditions such as existed in many American cities at that time. The business of slaughtering animals for food was carried on by a large number of small independent dealers, each of whom maintained his own slaughter house. These establishments were scattered over the city. In the effort to rid the city of what would now be considered a public nuisance, the City Council enacted an ordinance providing for the abolition of these independent slaughter houses, and for the construction of a large municipally owned and operated abattoir in which butchers might rent time and space in accordance with their needs.

---

[1] 16 Wallace 36, 1873.

It was natural that these businessmen should seek to prevent this action, which they conceived to be an interference with the rights of private property. They instituted proceedings in the courts, which were carried by successive appeals to the Supreme Court of the United States. The attorneys for the butchers argued that the ordinance was unconstitutional, inasmuch as Amendment XIV had transferred from the states (and therefore from their creatures, the municipalities) to the Federal government the power to make and enforce regulations of this character. The Supreme Court was thus presented with the opportunity of selecting one of two diametrically opposed views with regard to the interpretation of Amendment XIV. One was the view presented by the attorneys for the butchers; the other was the view which the Court accepted in one of the most important decisions in its history; namely, the view that Amendment XIV was proposed for the purpose of protecting the rights of the newly created group of colored citizens and that it was adopted by the states with this understanding. The Court stated that there was no intention on the part of those who framed the amendment, or of the Congress which proposed it, or of the state legislatures which ratified it that it should be so construed as to disturb the long-established principles governing the allocation of powers between the Federal government and the states. It is scarcely possible to over-emphasize the significance of this decision. If the Court had chosen to adopt the alternative point of view, the whole nature of our Federal system would have been fundamentally changed. It is upon this decision that the whole doctrine of the police power rests.

Definition of the Police Power. The field in which the police power has been applied has in recent years expanded to such an extent that it is difficult to define the power in definite and concise terms. Probably the first inclination of the layman is to define it by reference to the authority of the patrolman who stands at the corner. Such a conception of the police power is correct as far as it goes; the officers of the law are an evidence of the power and duty of the state to protect life and property, to maintain peace and order, and to prevent domestic violence or disturbance of any sort. But there is another aspect of the police power, which in modern times has assumed a position of equal importance; this relates to the right of the state to impose regulations or restrictions upon our use of our property or our exercise of our personal civil rights when such use interferes with the fundamental rights or privileges of our neighbors. In practice, this doctrine means that the state has in many important respects regulated or restricted individuals and corporations in the enjoyment of the rights of both person and property. The attempts to exercise this power, whether successful or unsuccessful, can be classified under the following headings:

1. Protection of the public health
2. Protection of the public safety
3. Protection of the public convenience
4. Protection of the public morals
5. Prevention of fraud
6. Suppression of a public nuisance

Each of these will be discussed in the paragraphs which follow, with appropriate illustrations and references to Supreme Court decisions. There are few, if any, attempts at the exercise of the police power which cannot be reasonably and properly classified under one of these headings or under a combination of them.

In commenting on the legitimate objects of the exercise of the police power, the United States Supreme Court on one occasion used the following words:

Another vital principle is that, except as restrained by its own fundamental law, or by the Supreme Law of the Land, a state possesses all legislative power consistent with a republican form of government; therefore each state, when not thus restrained and so far as this court is concerned, may, by legislation, provide not only for the health, morals, and safety of its people, but for the common good, as involved in the well being, peace, happiness, and prosperity of the people.[2]

A word of caution with regard to the definition of police power is perhaps necessary. It is primarily a legislative power, although in conformity with present-day legislative practice, it tends frequently to be exercised by administrative officers under legislative authorization. Its application is very broad, but it is not unlimited. Justice Holmes, in Noble State Bank v. Haskell,[3] made the statement that the police power extends to all great public needs. This is, however, quite different from saying, as some careless commentators have done, that the police power may be exercised in the interests of the public welfare. This phrase is so broad and expansive in its application that, if it were accepted, there would be virtually no limits to the application of the police power. Such eminent constitutional authorities as Willoughby and Burdick have taken special pains to warn students of this misinterpretation.

[2] Halter v. Nebraska, 205 U. S. 40, 1907. [3] 219 U. S. 104, 1911.

The police power is not by any means an emergency power, although it is often invoked after some disaster which causes serious loss of life or property damage which might have been prevented if proper precautions had been taken. A public, shaken from its lethargy, may then take drastic action. Instances in point include the famous Triangle shirtwaist factory fire in New York in 1911,[4] the Ward's Island Fire, the insurance scandals of 1905, and the panic of 1907. A state report pointed out many years later that the first of these was responsible for a complete reorganization of the system of factory inspection; that the second had the immediate effect of securing the adoption of a $50,000,000 bond issue for state welfare institutions in 1923; while the last two called attention to the necessity for changes in the regulatory system.

To this list might be added the famous Knickerbocker Theater collapse in Washington, D. C., and the hotel fire in the capital city of Michigan in 1934 which cost the lives of seven members of the state legislature; the death of 216 persons at a fire in a swank Negro dance club in Natchez, Mississippi, in 1940; and the loss of 489 lives in the terrible Cocoanut Grove Club fire in Boston in 1942.[5] Fires cost Americans, all told, hundreds of lives a year, and approximately $1,000,000 a day. Inadequate state laws or lax local law enforcement shows up clearly in such instances. Sometimes local option in matters of police regulation leads to amusing or ridiculous situations; thus in a certain New Jersey community it is illegal on Sunday to sit on the right-hand side of a particular theater. Similarly, local option laws on the sale of liquor have sometimes given rise to situations in which the bar was removed from one side of a hotel building to the other, according to the way the vote went.

PROTECTION OF THE PUBLIC HEALTH

Regulations designed to protect the public health commonly affect property rights more than personal rights. There have, of

[4] The Triangle Fire is a milestone in I. L. G. W. U. history. Garment makers once customarily kept their workers locked in like prisoners. On the evening of March 25, 1911, fire swept through the workroom of the Triangle Waist Company in a building near Washington Square in New York City. Trapped by locked doors, 146 employees died, many by leaping to the sidewalk. Their fate shocked the nation, led to many reforms, inspired I. L. G. W. U. to fight harder than ever. Union members still make yearly pilgrimages to their graves. From *Life,* August 1, 1938, p. 23.

[5] National Fire Protection Association, *The Cocoanut Grove Night Club Fire,* Boston, November 28, 1942 (Boston, 1943) ; and Greeley, W. R., " Massachusetts Considers a New Safety Code," *State Government,* May, 1943, pp. 119–120, 126–127.

course, been some restrictions upon the conduct of persons, such as quarantine regulations or the universal rule prohibiting expectorating in public places. Illustrations of restrictions on the use of property are much more numerous. These regulations cover a wide variety of subjects; they include regulations governing the sale of food and drug products, sanitary measures to prevent the spread of contagious diseases, regulations affecting the disposition of wastes of all types, et cetera. Under food and drug control, we have such measures as those requiring the inspection and licensing of eating houses, soda fountains, soft drink establishments, and market places. These regulations are concerned not merely with the cleanliness of the premises but with " the easements of light, and air, and access."

Protection of Milk, Meat, Food and Drug Supplies. The conditions under which food products are kept and displayed and the freedom from contagious or communicable diseases of those who handle such products are most important to the public health. The rigid regulations imposed upon the production, transportation, processing, and sale of milk and milk products provide further illustrations. These include the extensive program of tuberculosis eradication which has been carried on at great expense over a period of many years; the enforcement of requirements regarding the cleanliness of barns and the care of the fluid milk before, during, and after shipment; the inspection and supervision of the pasteurizing and bottling plants; the regulation, or in some jurisdictions the prohibition, of the sale of milk in bulk. Similar laws apply to meat and meat food products. Although many regulations affecting foods and drugs had been adopted in the states before the passage of the Federal act of June 30, 1906, a great body of new legislation in support of the Federal act has grown up since. These laws cover such matters as correct labeling, net weight, claims of manufacturers with regard to curative properties, et cetera.

The manner in which such regulations get before the courts is illustrated by New York ex rel. Lieberman v. Van de Carr, decided by the Supreme Court in 1905.[6] Lieberman was arrested for violating Section 66 of the sanitary code of New York City, which provided that no milk should be received, held, kept, either for sale or delivery, in the city, " without a permit in writing from the board of health, and subject to the conditions thereof. . . ." The violation of this code was made a misdemeanor; Lieberman's writ of habeas corpus was dismissed by the State Supreme Court and this judgment was affirmed by the Appellate Division and by the Court of Appeals,

[6] 199 U. S. 552, 1905.

from which it went to the Supreme Court of the United States, where the objections to the section on Federal grounds were: first, that it conferred upon the board of health absolute and despotic powers to grant or withhold permits to milk dealers, and was not, therefore, due process of law; and second, that singling out the milk business for regulation was a denial of the equal protection of the laws to the people engaged therein. After citing an extensive list of authorities, the Court concluded:

These cases leave in no doubt the proposition that the conferring of discretionary power upon administrative boards to grant or withhold permission to carry on a trade or business which is the proper subject of regulation within the police power of the state is not violative of rights secured by the Fourteenth Amendment. There is no presumption that the power will be arbitrarily exercised, and when it is shown to be thus exercised against the individual, under sanction of state authority, this court has not hesitated to interfere for his protection, when the case has come before it in such manner as to authorize the interference of a Federal court. Yick Wo v. Hopkins, 118 U. S. 356, 1885.

There is nothing to show upon what ground the action of the board was taken. For aught that appears, he may have been conducting his business in such wise, or with such surroundings and means, as to render it dangerous to the health of the community; or his manner of selling or delivering the milk may have been objectionable. There is nothing in the record to show that the action against him was arbitrary or oppressive and without a fair and reasonable exercise of that discretion which the law reposed in the board of health. We have, then, an ordinance which, as construed in the highest court of the state, authorizes the exercise of a legal discretion in the granting or withholding of permits to transact a business which, unless controlled, may be highly dangerous to the health of the community, and no affirmative showing that the power has been exerted in so arbitrary and oppressive a manner as to deprive the appellant of his property or liberty without due process of law.

In such cases it is the settled doctrine of this Court that no Federal right is invaded, and no authority exists for declaring a law unconstitutional, duly passed by the legislative authority, and approved by the highest court of the state.

Eating and Drinking Establishments; Hotels and Lodging Houses. Public eating and drinking establishments are regulated and inspected by state and local authorities to insure the observance of minimum standards of cleanliness and sanitation in the maintenance of the premises, the sterilization of utensils and equipment (or the use of paper receptacles), the preparation and handling of food, and the cleanliness of the employees themselves. A model ordinance and code regulating such establishments, prepared by the United States Public Health Service, has been adopted in many jurisdictions.[7] This type of regulation assumes a growing importance both to individuals and to the community, in a day of great mobility of population, when so large a number of people, especially in urban communities, are accustomed to frequent public restaurants, lunchrooms, soda fountains, bars, taprooms, and cocktail lounges.

Many sanitary measures concern public utility companies and other businesses affected with a public interest. The keepers of hotels, inns, and lodging houses, for instance, are required to use cotton sheets of sufficient length to prevent blankets and bed coverings from coming in direct contact with successive guests, while other regulations require the laundering of sheets, pillow cases, and towels. Because such regulations are now universally observed, no one should assume that such has always been the case. Railways and other common carriers are prohibited from using common drinking cups and the old-fashioned roller towels in their cars and stations. Similar regulations apply to common drinking cups in rest rooms of theaters, clubs, and other public places. Barber shops and beauty shops are also subject to sanitary regulations. All these measures are designed to prevent the spread of contagious diseases by reducing to a minimum the known causes of their transmission.

Domestic Sewage and Industrial Wastes. Similarly, individuals and corporations, both public and private, are regulated in the disposition of wastes of every character which might conceivably affect the public health. Local ordinances require citizens to place garbage in covered containers, accessible to the collectors at regular intervals. Corporations are strictly regulated in most states with regard to the disposition of mine wastes, industrial wastes, et cetera, with the idea of preventing the pollution of water supplies, and in some cases for the protection of fish. Individuals are regulated and supervised in the construction of cesspools and in the use of other methods for the disposition of sewage in localities where no public sewage system exists. In cases where such systems have been constructed, the state often requires the submission of the plans, and usually inspects the system and regulates the methods of disposal.

In California Reduction Company v. Sanitary Reduction Works,

---

[7] *Ordinance and Code Regulating Eating and Drinking Establishments* (Washington, 1940) ; see also Kettleborough, Charles, " Inspection of Hotels and Public Lodging Houses," *American Political Science Review*, February, 1913, pp. 93–96. The progress that has been made in the last few years is illustrated by the fact that, as late as 1932, the Supreme Court of Utah declared that a board of health had exceeded its power in requiring sterilization of receptacles, or the use of paper receptacles.

the Court upheld a San Francisco ordinance requiring all garbage and refuse to be delivered in closed wagons at the works of the Sanitary Company, there to be cremated at the expense of the person conveying it. The Sanitary Company sought by injunction against householders and a rival reduction works to compel compliance with this ordinance, it having a fifty-year monopoly on this cremation at twenty cents a load. That the case has a relation to the use of the police power for the suppression of a public nuisance as well is clearly indicated in the following excerpt from the opinion:

. . . The garbage and refuse matter were all together, on the same premises, and, as a whole or in the mass, they constituted a nuisance which the public could abate or require to be abated, and to the continuance of which the community was not bound to submit. And when the obnoxious garbage and refuse was removed from the place of their origin, and put in covered wagons to be carried away, the municipal authorities might well have doubted whether the substances that were per se dangerous or worthless would be separated from such as could be utilized, and whether the former would be deposited by the scavenger at some place that would not endanger the public health. They might well have thought that the safety of the community could not be assured unless the entire mass of garbage and refuse constituting the nuisance, from which the danger came, was carried to a crematory, where it could be promptly destroyed by fire, and thus minimize the danger to the public health.[8]

Compulsory Vaccination. A number of states have passed compulsory vaccination laws; these have not gone without challenge on the part of the ignorant or the careless. The leading case on this subject, Jacobson v. Massachusetts, was considered by the Supreme Court in 1905.[9] The Massachusetts statute authorized local boards of health, whenever in their opinion it was necessary for protection of the public health, to require the vaccination of all inhabitants of their city or town, except such children as might present medical certificates to the effect that they were unfit subjects for vaccination. Jacobson was convicted in the Superior Court of Middlesex County of refusing to comply with such an order of the Cambridge Board of Health. The trial court declined his offer to prove that vaccination was useless to prevent small pox and that it was often dangerous. The State Supreme Court confirmed the conviction, and appeal was taken to the Supreme Court of the United States, which likewise affirmed the judgment. As usual in police power cases, the decision of the Court hinged upon the reasonableness of the regulation.

[8] 199 U. S. 306, 1905.
[9] 197 U. S. 11, 1905.

The legislature assumed that some children, by reason of their condition at the time, might not be fit subjects of vaccination; and it is suggested — and we will not say without reason — that such is the case with some adults. But the defendant did not offer to prove that, by reason of his then condition, he was in fact not a fit subject of vaccination at the time he was informed of the requirement of the regulation adopted by the board of health. . . . Until otherwise informed by the highest court of Massachusetts, we are not inclined to hold that the statute establishes the absolute rule that an adult must be vaccinated if it be apparent or can be shown with reasonable certainty that he is not at the time a fit subject of vaccination, or that vaccination, by reason of his then condition, would seriously impair his health, or probably cause his death. No such case is here presented. It is the case of an adult who, for aught that appears, was himself in perfect health and a fit subject of vaccination, and yet, while remaining in the community, refused to obey the statute and the regulation adopted in execution of its provisions for the protection of the public health and the public safety, confessedly endangered by the presence of a dangerous disease.

Premarital and Prenatal Examinations. For several years there was a growing disapproval of the hasty marriages encouraged by the " gretna greens " which were permitted to operate in a number of states. The result was the adoption of legislation in eighteen states, calling for a waiting period of from two to five days between the application for and the receipt of a marriage license. While in some states the requirements were modified somewhat for the benefit of servicemen who wished to be married during leaves of short duration, the general effect of this legislation has been a very wholesome one.[10]

Other states have gone much farther, requiring in addition to a waiting period, a premarital health examination. Since 1935, when the first legislation of this character was adopted in Connecticut, thirty-seven states have passed either premarital or prenatal examination laws, or both, thus helping to protect married couples and babies in these states from venereal disease, — and incidentally, setting an amazing record for lawmaking speed and activity. Thirty states by the end of 1944 required examination by a physician of both bride and groom, including a blood test for syphilis. Three Southern states — Alabama, Louisiana, and Texas — require examination by a physician of the groom only, for freedom from venereal

[10] See Council of State Governments, *Waiting Period for Marriage License Applicants Affecting Servicemen in Nineteen States* (Chicago, 1942). Illinois passed such a law and repealed it in 1941. The states and the waiting periods required are: Two DAYS: Maryland. THREE DAYS: California, New Jersey, Oregon, Pennsylvania, Tennessee, Washington, and West Virginia. FIVE DAYS: Connecticut, Georgia, Maine, Massachusetts, Michigan, Minnesota, Mississippi, New Hampshire, Ohio, and Wisconsin.

disease. Two — Oklahoma and Delaware — prohibit the marriage of persons with venereal diseases, but make no provisions for medical examination. Thirteen states, mostly in the South and Southwest, grant marriage licenses without regard to venereal disease infection.

Medical records show that if syphilis is discovered early enough in pregnancy cases, and adequate treatment is given, the baby has a 95 per cent chance to be born free from this infection. Accordingly, thirty states, beginning with New York in 1938, now seek to protect the health of babies by requiring that physicians and midwives see that a serological test for syphilis is included as a part of the examination of every expectant mother seeking medical care. Eighteen states, however, still do not require such a test. The use of premarital and prenatal examinations is part of a long-term plan for stamping out venereal disease, attacking the problem where the results are the most tragic — in marriage and in the family.[11]

PROTECTION OF THE PUBLIC SAFETY

Police power regulations designed for the protection of the public safety include numerous types of measures which affect the daily lives of all, such as crime control measures and the rules and regulations for the police and other law-enforcing machinery for the protection of life and property; factory inspectors and regulation of industrial safety; the regulation of common carriers, including grade crossing elimination; fireworks and firearms restrictions; building codes; and the provisions of the motor vehicle codes — to mention only a few.

Motor Vehicle Regulation. The motor vehicle codes are one of the most important evidences of the exercise of the police power in the field of public safety. They provide in most jurisdictions for the ex-

---

[11] A number of studies of these two types of legislation have been made: Bowden, Aneta E., and Gould, George, *Summary of State Legislation Requiring Premarital and Prenatal Examinations for Venereal Diseases* (American Social Hygiene Association, New York, 1941) ; Council of State Governments, " State Legislation Requiring Premarital Examinations for Venereal Disease," *State Government*, March, 1944, with table on marriage law requirements, and " State Legislation Requiring Prenatal Examinations for Venereal Disease," *ibid.*, April, 1944, with table; Edwards, Mary S., " Premarital Examination Laws in Operation," *Journal of Social Hygiene,* May, 1940; Forster, George F., and Shaughnessy, Howard J., " Premarital Examination Laws in the United States," *Journal* of the American Medical Association, March 7, 1942, pp. 790–797; Kansas Legislative Council, *Premarital Examination Laws* (Topeka, 1941) ; " State Laws to Guard Family Health," *Michigan Public Health,* February, 1945, pp. 28–29; Mahoney, J. F., " Requirements of Premarital Legislation," *Venereal Disease Information,* April, 1943, pp. 105–107.

amination and licensing of motor vehicle operators, for the periodic inspection of motor vehicles to insure their road-worthiness, and for the rules of the road — all of which are designed to protect the lives and property of both motorists and pedestrians. Many questions have arisen and many cases have been decided regarding the right of the states to enforce these measures. In 1941, for instance, in Reitz v. Mealey, the Supreme Court decided that the New York statute which authorizes the suspension of a driver's license if judgment is rendered against him for personal injuries caused by operation of an automobile, and the judgment is not satisfied or discharged otherwise than by bankruptcy, is not obnoxious to the due process clause of Amendment XIV.[12]

Factory Regulations. Another important type of regulation involves the inspection work of a state department of labor. In addition to many regulations designed to protect the health of workers, there are many others to insure safety of life and limb. These regulations require the caging of moving belts and dangerous machinery. They apply to the inspection of mines with regard to such matters as ventilation and the handling of explosive gases, inspection of electrical apparatus, inspection of hoists, shafts, and other necessary operating equipment. Such regulations need not be confined to matters affecting labor; they may apply as well to recreational activities. Examples are the regulation of amusement parks, the restrictions on the sale of fireworks for Fourth of July celebrations, and the closing of certain streets to traffic after a snowstorm, to permit coasting, or in the summertime, to permit their use as play streets.

Regulations affecting industry may be imposed for the protection of property as well as of life. Georgia v. Tennessee Copper Company, decided by the Supreme Court in 1907, raises important questions with regard to the protection of both.[13] Georgia had filed a bill in equity, in pursuance of a resolution of the legislature and by direction of the governor, to enjoin the defendant copper companies from discharging noxious gas from their works in Tennessee over the territory of Georgia. It was alleged that in consequence of such discharge there was a wholesale destruction of forests, orchards, and crops, and that other injuries were either done or threatened in five counties of the state. A preliminary injunction had been denied, but the Supreme Court ordered the injunction to issue. The case is the more interesting and the more conclusive because of the inter-

---

[12] 314 U. S. 33, 1941.   [13] 206 U. S. 230, 1907.

state feature involved, Georgia already having made application in vain to Tennessee for relief.

Regulation of Common Carriers. The cases in the field of railway regulation are an interesting group. A New York statute forbade the use of coal stoves for the heating of passenger cars; [14] an Indiana statute required the use of headlights with 1,500 candle power on all locomotives hauling trains within the state; [15] and a Pennsylvania statute required the use of safety couplers on trains operated within the limits of that Commonwealth. [16] In an Alabama case the court upheld the validity of an act requiring all engineers to pass an eye examination in order to secure a license as locomotive engineers from the state board of examiners. [17] In upholding the power of the states to regulate and control commerce, the Court even went so far as to sustain a Mississippi statute making injuries inflicted by the running of locomotives or cars prima-facie evidence of negligence on the part of railroads, and an Ohio statute permitting the Public Utilities Commission to prescribe a route for a motor common carrier even when such carrier was engaged in interstate commerce. [18]

An equal number of statutes and decisions on the other side can easily be cited. The Supreme Court rejected another Pennsylvania law which sought to regulate the size, end-rails, steps, et cetera, of the last cars on trains operated within the state. [19] In another case the Court declared unconstitutional a Texas statute forbidding any person from acting as conductor on a railroad train within the state without having previously served for two years as a brakeman or conductor on a freight train. [20] In still another, Georgia sought to impose exceedingly unreasonable restrictions upon the operation of

[14] New York, New Haven and Hartford Railroad v. New York, 165 U. S. 628, 1897.

[15] Vandalia Railroad Company v. Indiana, 242 U. S. 255, 1916; the Court held that, since the regulation was a reasonable one designed to protect the public safety, it might be enforced with regard to locomotives hauling interstate trains, as well as with regard to those hauling intrastate trains. This was contingent upon the fact that Congress had not acted. See also Atlantic Coast Line Railroad Company v. State of Georgia, 234 U. S. 280, 1914.

[16] Pennsylvania Railroad Company v. Ewing, 241 Pa. St. 581, 1913.

[17] Smith v. Alabama, 124 U. S. 465, 1888.

[18] Mobile, Jackson and Kansas City Railroad Company v. Turnispeed, 219 U. S. 35, 1910, and Bradley v. Public Utilities Commission of Ohio, 289 U. S. 92, 1933.

[19] Pennsylvania Railroad Company v. Pennsylvania, 250 U. S. 566, 1919; in this case the Federal government had acted. The Federal Safety Appliance Act and the Post Office Department both regulated the end cars on certain interstate trains.

[20] Smith v. Texas, 233 U. S. 630, 1914.

trains as to speed at grade crossings, blowing the whistle as a warning, et cetera.[21]

Grade Crossing Elimination. In the more progressive states, millions of dollars have been devoted to grade crossing elimination programs, whose sole objective has been to reduce the terrific toll of human life resulting from railway crossing accidents. There are many other regulations imposed upon the intrastate traffic of railways, trolley and bus companies, and other common carriers. These regulations cover the serviceability of equipment, adequacy of equipment for fires and for first aid, speed, distance between cars and trains, and many similar matters.

Fireworks Regulations. After the Fourth of July Celebration in 1938, the *New York Times* reported 358 dead as the holiday toll. While many of these deaths were due to traffic accidents, fireworks played their part. In 1937 there were 1,180 persons in the New York area injured through carelessness and accidents due to fireworks; as a result of a safety campaign, this number was cut in 1938 to 466. While most of the injuries were minor ones, many were not. Philadelphia in 1921 adopted a ban on the sale of fireworks within the city limits, but in spite of this, in the next seventeen years sixteen persons were killed and 1,072 were injured. In 1938, 314 persons were injured in the city, and the number who lost their lives celebrating was the highest since 1910. Although there was an interruption in the sale of fireworks during World War II, the problem is clearly of sufficient importance to justify the exercise of the state's police power.

A survey completed in 1940 showed that there were still six Southern and Western states with no legislation, while regulatory measures of some type had been adopted in thirty-three states. Nine states had practically prohibited fireworks to the ordinary user — Delaware, Indiana, Iowa, Michigan, New Jersey, Pennsylvania, Rhode Island, Utah, and West Virginia. The regulatory laws were of five general types: (1) laws making it the duty of some state administrative officials to make and enforce regulations governing the sale and use of fireworks; (2) laws granting local units permission to treat the problem as they see fit — this is the most common type; (3) laws regulating the type or content or the size of fireworks; (4) laws limiting the time or place, or both, at which firecrackers may be sold or exploded; and (5) laws providing in detail for the manufacture, storage, and sale of explosives. In some instances these laws are

---

[21] Seaboard Airline Railroad v. Elizabeth Blackwell, 244 U. S. 310, 1917.

designed to prevent industrial fires and explosions, in which case they apply only indirectly to the problem under consideration.[22]

Firearms Legislation. Problems affecting the public safety are very numerous. As an aid in the control of criminal activities, many states have adopted firearms legislation, under the terms of which sales of firearms are reported and owners must register with a state authority. These regulations, which apply especially to small firearms, do not violate the guarantee of the Federal Constitution, found in the Bill of Rights, and applying only to the Federal government.[23] As was noted in the preceding chapter, however, in the discussion of Hague v. Committee for Industrial Organization, cities may not impose severe restrictions on the right of assembly under the guise of a protection of the public safety. In some states criminal syndicalism acts have been passed for the purpose of enabling a state to protect itself against armed uprising. The courts have given conflicting judgments with regard to this type of legislation.

Crime Control. Finally, modern conditions have made it impossible for states to deal effectively with many problems affecting the public safety. The Federal government has recognized the interstate character of the white slave traffic, of the traffic in stolen motor vehicles and other forms of stolen property, and of kidnaping, racketeering, and other offenses, and has given assistance in dealing with them, in the form of the Federal Crime Laws of 1934 and the cooperation of Federal law-enforcing officers.[24]

PROTECTION OF THE PUBLIC CONVENIENCE

Questions involving the use of the police power for the protection of the public convenience are relatively few, and usually involve reasonableness of rates or adequacy of service by public utility companies. Among such questions are the number of trains or cars to be operated on a given line, the number of stops they will be required to make and the points at which they will be made, and the schedule upon which service will be maintained. Illustrative of these points are such cases as the Lake Shore and Michigan Southern Railway v.

[22] Everstine, Carl N., *Regulation of Fireworks,* and *Supplementary Report on Regulation of Fireworks* (Maryland Legislative Council, Baltimore, 1940) ; also *Model State Fireworks Law* (National Fire Prevention Association, Boston, 1938) .

[23] See International Association of Chiefs of Police, *Study of State Legislation Regulating Sale and Possession of Firearms* (Chicago, September, 1940) .

[24] For a discussion of this legislation, see Graves, W. Brooke, " Federal Leadership in State Legislation," *Temple Law Quarterly,* July, 1936, pp. 385–405, and Corwin, Edward S., *Court over Constitution* (Princeton University Press, 1938) .

Ohio; [25] Cleveland, Cincinnati, Chicago and St. Louis Railway v. Illinois; [26] and Atlantic Coast Line v. Railway Commissioners of South Carolina. [27] According to the first of these decisions, railroads may be required to furnish adequate transportation facilities at each station, and if this is not done through the service of local trains, the deficiency must be met by a sufficient number of interstate trains. It was held that an Ohio act requiring railways to stop three trains daily each way at towns on their line of 3,000 population or more was reasonable; since the act did not specify interstate trains, the companies could avoid slowing down the running time of interstate trains by providing sufficient service by local trains. Such a solution would certainly be appropriate in the service of suburban communities, such as Lakewood, outside of Cleveland, in connection with which the case arose.

In the Cleveland, Cincinnati, Chicago and St. Louis Railway case, Illinois had attempted to require the stopping of all trains at county seats; this rule applied, therefore, to both interstate and intrastate trains. If, as in the case of Hillsboro, the community already had adequate service, the state could not constitutionally require a fast interstate train, running between St. Louis and New York in competition with similar trains on other roads, to stop at this town, with consequent loss of time and slowing down of schedule. " In determining what is reasonable, the Court examines the number of trains already stopping at a given point, the population to be served, and the amount of traffic." This point is well illustrated by the Atlantic Coast Line case, in which the Railroad Commission of South Carolina had attempted to require a through train between New York and Tampa to stop at a hamlet of 453 persons which already had adequate service. These considerations are not necessarily effective if a train runs entirely within a state, even though it carries both mail and interstate passengers. [28]

A regulation of quite a different type considered by the Court as in the interests of the public convenience was dealt with in the case of Williams v. Arkansas, in 1910. [29] The constitutionality of an Arkansas statute forbidding the solicitation for certain kinds of business upon trains in the state was upheld; in the course of the opinion, this significant paragraph was included:

[25] 173 U. S. 285, 1899.
[26] 177 U. S. 514, 1900.
[27] 207 U. S. 328, 1907.
[28] See Gladsen v. Minnesota, 166 U. S. 427, 1897; for a helpful note on this subject, see Hall, James P., *Cases on Constitutional Law*, p. 1187.
[29] 217 U. S. 79, 1910.

The legislature clearly has the power to make regulations for the convenience and comfort of travelers on railroads, and this appears to be a reasonable regulation for their benefit. It prevents annoyance from the importunities of drummers. It is suggested in the argument that the statute was especially aimed at the protection of travelers to the city of Hot Springs. If this be so, we can readily see additional reason why the regulation is a wholesome one. A large percentage of those travelers are persons from distant states, who are mostly complete strangers here, and many are sick. Drummers who swarm through the trains soliciting for physicians, bath houses, hotels, et cetera, make a burden to those who are subjected to their repeated solicitations. It is true that the traveler may turn a deaf ear to these importunities, but this does not render it any the less unpleasant and annoying. The drummer may keep within the law against disorderly conduct, and still render himself a source of annoyance to travelers by his beseeching to be allowed to lead the way to a doctor or a hotel. . . .

This statute is not an unreasonable restriction upon the privilege one should enjoy to solicit for his lawful business, which, it is rightly urged, is an incident to any business. It does not prevent anyone from advertising his business, or from soliciting patronage, except upon trains, et cetera. This privilege is denied him for the public good. It is a principle which underlies every reasonable exercise of the police power, that private rights must yield to the common welfare.

PROTECTION OF THE PUBLIC MORALS

Police power regulations designed to protect the public morals affect both the rights of persons and the rights of property. In the first category, one finds prohibited by law such acts as indecent exposure, solicitation by prostitutes, procurers, bookmakers, dope peddlers,[30] distribution and sale of obscene or immoral literature, contraceptive devices, et cetera. On the property side, one finds prohibitions upon the maintenance of gambling dens, disorderly houses and dope establishments, and stringent regulation of public dance halls and the licensing and sale of wines, beer, and liquors. The theory of such regulations, of course, is that the right of the public as a whole to be protected from the influence of conditions quite generally regarded as immoral is paramount over the right of any individual in the exercise of his personal rights, or over the right of any individual to make such use of his property as he sees fit. In general, the right of government to exercise the police power for the purposes indicated is so well established as to be no longer open to serious question.

[30] See Hughes, James E., "Dope: State Narcotic Laws and the Need for the Uniform Narcotic Drug Act," *State Government*, September, 1933, pp. 11–14; Council of State Governments, *Radio Symposium on Marihuana — the Killer Drug* (Chicago, December 3, 1937).

Liquor Control. There are, however, occasional cases of a border-line nature particularly involving the use of property. In one of these, Mugler v. Kansas,[31] the principle was established that where individuals or corporations choose to invest their money in businesses the propriety of which is open to question, they have no redress if the public decides that the discontinuance of the business is desirable. Kansas had passed an act in 1881 which forbade the manufacture or sale, except for medicinal purposes, of all intoxicating liquors. Mugler was convicted, under this act, of selling beer. His attorneys argued that, since he had invested his money in a brewing business, and had done so under the sanction and with the authority of the state, he could not now be denied the right to continue the operation of his business. To require such discontinuance was, they said, to deprive him of his property contrary to the guarantee of Amendment XIV. The Court refused to accept this position. This principle of law would seem to apply similarly to such businesses as the conduct of public dance halls, the operation of a race track betting system, or the use of lotteries for charitable or other purposes.

The sale of intoxicating liquors has long been recognized as a privilege subject to regulation, rather than an inherent right. It has been subject not only to licensure, but to regulations of other types, as illustrated by the case of Crowley v. Christensen, decided by the Supreme Court in 1890.[32] In this instance the Court sustained the conviction of the defendant for violating a San Francisco ordinance forbidding the issuance of liquor licenses except to persons who obtained the written consent of a majority of the city board of police commissioners, or twelve citizens owning real estate in the block where the business was to be conducted. As the liquor business is one " attended with danger to the community, it may be entirely prohibited, or be permitted under such conditions as will limit to the utmost its evils. The manner and extent of regulation rest in the discretion of the governing authority. That authority may vest in such officers as it may deem proper the passing upon applications for permission to carry it on, and to issue licenses for that purpose. It is a matter of legislative will only." [33]

Laws Against Prostitution. The American Social Hygiene Association reports that, as early as 1909, some states saw the need to protect family and community from the moral and health hazards of com-

[31] 123 U. S. 623, 1887; see also Bartenmeyer v. Iowa, 18 Wallace 129, 1873.
[32] 137 U. S. 86, 1890.
[33] For a good discussion of the regulation of public morals, see Callcott, Mary S., *Principles of Social Legislation,* Chapter 7 (Macmillan, New York, 1932).

mercialized prostitution. Pressure of this problem during World War I and the years following spurred widespread legislative action, so that by 1929, all states had some type of law to combat this evil. The report of the Association continues:

Existence of these laws and improvement in community conditions made necessary comparatively little new legislation from 1925 to 1941, but mobilization — both military and industrial — in the national defense effort of 1939–1941, and the plunge into World War II, with a great increase in prostitution activities around strategic communities, again stimulated a drive for better laws. As of November 1, 1944, twenty-nine states and the District of Columbia had acceptable laws with only two states having laws considered inadequate.

These laws have been used during the war period to clean up conditions in many communities, but good laws will be needed more than ever in the restless postwar years. In its classification of the laws existing in the several states, the Association reports that nineteen states have adequate laws against most aspects of prostitution, and that ten more have adequate laws, with the exception of their coverage of the activities of the customers of prostitutes. Of the remaining nineteen states, all but two have laws against some activities of prostitutes and their exploiters. These two have some legislation, but it is regarded by the Association as quite inadequate.[34]

Pari-Mutuel Betting. For many years, betting on horse racing in the form of book making, pool selling, et cetera, was generally frowned upon in this country, and was in most jurisdictions prohibited by law. This did not by any means stop the practice, which was frequently carried on in barber shops, tobacco shops, and pool rooms. Gambling and lotteries, operated by the government or under close government supervision, had long been common in Europe; with the advent of the depression, there were numerous proposals to legalize these methods of raising funds for welfare and charitable purposes. Public opinion gradually changed to the point where pari-mutuel betting on horse racing is permitted in approximately half the states. A joint legislative committee in New York, investigating the first year of operation under the law in that state, thus describes the operation of the system: [35]

34 See Gould, George, " Laws Against Prostitution and Their Use," *Journal of Social Hygiene,* October, 1941, and Special Committee on Enforcement of the National Advisory Police Committee, a series of recommendations in " Techniques for Repressing Unorganized Prostitution," supplement to *Police Chiefs Newsletter,* November–December, 1942.

35 Joint Legislative Committee for the Study of the Pari-Mutuel System, *Report,* pp. 15, and 49–132, for detailed analysis of the laws of twenty-four states

Under the Pari-Mutuel System of Betting, the racing associations operate the System under regulations. The patrons purchase the tickets at windows, at varying amounts, the basic tickets costing two dollars ($2.00). Tickets may be bought for a horse to "win," "place" (place second) or may be bought for a horse to "show" (place third), and any number of tickets may be purchased on any number of horses in a race to finish in all or any of the three successful positions. All of the money bet on horses to "win," less deductions for the State and racing associations, is pro-rated among the persons holding tickets on the winning horse, and all the money for second or "place," and third or "show," are similarly divided, among those holding tickets on horses which finish second or third.

When a patron purchases a ticket, the seller presses a button which automatically releases the ticket. The same impulse records, on an electrically operated machine known as a "Totalizator," the amount of the bet, the number of the horse selected, and whether the ticket is for "win" or "place" or "show." The Totalizator adds the money bet on each horse in a race, in the three separate pools and accumulates the totals for each pool. All such statistics, and the odds for the different horses in the winning pool, are projected on a larger indicator in the infield in view of the public.

The most important feature of the Pari-Mutuel System, proven by experience, is that it makes for temperance in betting. This moderation stimulates a sense of enjoyment into the sport of horse racing, and limits its use as an instrument of gambling.

THE PREVENTION OF FRAUD

Blue Sky Laws. The state may exercise the police power for the purpose of protecting its citizens from fraud. Illustrations are to be found in Blue Sky legislation, usury laws, and laws designed to insure honest weights and measures and honest labeling of food and drug products. Blue Sky laws have been enacted in many states to prevent the sale of fraudulent securities; under their provisions, brokers and their salesmen must be registered with the state enforcing agency. Securities may not be offered for sale until the enforcing agency has been given full and complete information regarding the financial condition of the company, its credit rating, the purposes for which the funds are to be used, and other related matters. It is difficult to overestimate the importance of this type of legislation; for years the people have been "fleeced" of millions of

(Legislative Document, 1941, No. 69); Illinois Legislative Council, *Taxation of Pari-Mutuel Wagering at Horse Races* (Springfield, 1940); MacLeod, William C., "The Truth about Lotteries in American History," *South Atlantic Quarterly,* April, 1936, pp. 201–211; and Library of Congress, Division of Bibliography, *Lotteries in the United States and Foreign Countries,* a list of recent references (Washington, 1942).

dollars annually by fly-by-night salesmen offering them fabulous returns from oil wells in which there was no oil, gold mines in which there was no gold, and copper mines in which there was no copper. When sensible people had become suspicious of proposals of this character, these disreputable promoters organized fictitious companies for all sorts of other purposes. They were able to ply their trade often among supposedly intelligent people because of the almost universal human desire to get something for nothing. Many were credulous enough to believe that it could be done, but usually ended by losing the full amount of their investment.[36]

Regulation of Small Loan Companies. Another common type of fraud against which the police power has been invoked is that practiced by small loan companies. These companies advertise through the newspapers, by radio, and through the mails, presenting the benefits of their so-called service in the most glowing terms. This service was often a necessity for many small homeowners with taxes to pay or with some unusual expenses such as those incurred for illness, funerals, et cetera. When these small loan companies once had an unsuspecting borrower within their grasp, he soon found himself beset by exorbitant interest charges and every conceivable kind of sharp practice. In most states, this evil has now been brought under control.

The problem is age-old, and the need for regulation was early recognized in the United States; early attempts at control and the period of experimentation extended from 1884 to 1910. This was followed by a period of coordination and finally, in 1917, by the Uniform Small Loan Law, which has been in force in an increasing number of states since that date. These acts have been commonly based upon a system of licensure, and regulation by a public official or commission; their application has been restricted to loans of not more than, usually, $300. Interest rates have been regulated and the absolute sale of wages has in most acts been prohibited. Certain exemptions to the operation of the laws have been provided, but it is quite possible to draft them in such ways as to insure their constitutionality.[37]

---

[36] In Hall v. Geiger-Jones Company, 242 U. S. 539, 1917, the Court upheld the constitutionality of an Ohio statute forbidding any dealer to sell corporate securities in the state unless first licensed therein, even as applied to securities sent in from other states to be sold.

[37] See Gallert, David J., Hilborn, Walter S., and May, Geoffrey, *Small Loan Legislation,* Chapter 8 (Russell Sage Foundation, New York, 1932) , and Robinson, Louis N., and Nugent, Rolf, *Regulation of the Small Loan Business* (Russell Sage Foundation, New York, 1935) .

Weights and Measures. Mention has been made of the effort to prevent fraud in the sale of merchandise. The establishing and enforcing of standard weights and measures by city, state, and nation is an evidence of this type of police power regulation. A case involving constitutional questions arose in North Dakota a few years ago.[38] In 1911 the state legislature had enacted a law which provided that lard must be sold in containers holding one, three, or five pounds, respectively, or multiples of these numbers, unless the lard was sold in bulk at wholesale. In 1917 this act was amended to provide that retail sales of lard must be labeled with the quantity in the container. This change was made because practice showed that dealers were accustomed to include the weight of the container in making sales of lard. The State Food Commissioner bought a three-pound pail of lard that had been packed by Armour and Company; upon examination, he found that he acquired two pounds six ounces of lard and ten ounces of tin. Accordingly, he imposed a fine of $100 for violation of the law. In its defense in court the company contended that the act operated with the effect of depriving the company of its property without due process of law; that it represented an interference with interstate commerce; that it represented an interference with the Federal Pure Food and Drug Act; and finally, that the state had no authority to require the sale of commodities in packages of certain sizes only. The decision of the Court — that the state could fix the quantity of retail sales if the purpose was to prevent fraud — turned largely on this last point in the defense. The Court assumed that when a purchaser asked for three pounds of lard, he wanted that amount, and not a lesser amount of lard and a considerable amount of tin. It was pointed out further that the company could not be serious in its objections to the provisions of the law, since it had for many years been furnishing a grocery company in New York City with lard in containers of the sizes specified.

Misrepresentation of Merchandise. A much older case, involving a milder form of misrepresentation, Frost v. Chicago, was decided by the Supreme Court of Illinois in 1899.[39] The plaintiff in error had been found guilty in the court below of violating an ordinance of the city of Chicago, and fined fifteen dollars and costs. The ordinance provided:

[38] Armour and Company v. North Dakota, 240 U. S. 510, 1916; also Schmidlinge v. Chicago, 226 U. S. 578, 1912, upholding a weight law for loaves of bread offered for sale, and Hauge v. Chicago, 299 U. S. 387, 1937, which held that even an apparently repetitious and unreasonable weighing was constitutional.

[39] 178 Ill. 250, 1899.

Sec. 1000. Colored Netting for Covering. It shall be and is hereby made unlawful to cover any box, basket, or any other package or parcel of fruit, berries or vegetables of any kind, with any colored netting, or any other material which has a tendency to conceal the true color or quality of any such goods which may be sold, offered for sale, or had in possession for the purpose of being sold or offered for sale. Any person who shall violate the provisions of this section shall, upon conviction, be fined not less than $10 or more than $25 for such offense.

The opinion states that testimony tended to show that the defendant sold peaches in baskets covered with red tarlatan — a perforated cloth — and that these baskets had been shipped to him from Michigan put up in the same manner in which he sold them. There was some evidence that this colored netting tended to conceal the " true color or quality " of the fruit, and some to the contrary. This appeared to have been a common trade practice, preventing pilfering and loss from other causes, giving ventilation, et cetera. The Court reached the conclusion that the ordinance was " a vexatious and unreasonable interference with and restriction upon the rights of dealers in certain articles of trade and commerce," and accordingly reversed the judgment of the lower court. One cannot help wondering what will happen when the present-day practices of artificial coloring of fruit and forced ripening of fruits and vegetables are brought before a court under similar circumstances.

At the close of the nineteenth century and the beginning of the twentieth, the agricultural interests of the country were able to secure the passage of legislation to restrict the distribution and sale of oleomargarine. The product was harmless enough — more wholesome, no doubt, than much of the butter then offered for sale — but it provided competition which the farmers considered dangerous. There was, of course, the possibility that unscrupulous dealers might sell oleomargarine, artificially colored to resemble butter, as a substitute therefor, thus greatly increasing their profits. It was upon the idea of preventing this possible fraud that most of the statutes were built; the Supreme Court held that they might be enforced by the states, even as applied to the sale of goods brought in from other states.[40] These laws did not usually attempt to prevent the sale of oleomargarine, but only its sale in such manner as involved fraud; the Constitution did not secure to anyone the right to commit a fraud in the sale of merchandise, whether or not the goods were shipped in interstate commerce. A Pennsylvania statute which did

[40] Plumley v. Massachusetts, 155 U. S. 461, 1895.

forbid the " manufacture, sale, or the keeping with intent to sell " of oleomargarine was upheld by both state and Federal courts,[41] but this type of act was not enforceable as applied to a product brought into the state in interstate commerce.[42]

THE SUPPRESSION OF PUBLIC NUISANCES

The police power may be exercised, either by the state itself or by its political subdivisions, for the suppression of nuisances. Such nuisances may develop either from the inconsiderate exercise of personal rights or from a similar use of property. The Federal and state constitutions guarantee to the citizen the enjoyment of certain fundamental rights. No one is permitted, however, to make such use of these rights as will annoy his neighbors. An individual has a right to freedom of religious belief and worship, but if a person, as an act of worship, were to arise at two A.M. nightly and blow a trumpet from his window, he would clearly be exceeding his rights. Similarly, people have the right to enjoy music and to entertain guests in their homes; they have no right, however, to keep a radio blaring far into the night, nor to conduct their festivities in such a boisterous fashion as to keep all the people in the apartment house in which they live awake. Individuals have the right to maintain cats or dogs as pets, but when these animals are permitted to roam unrestrained over the property of their neighbors, the pets become a nuisance. Likewise, the dwellers in the neighborhood are under no obligation to permit frequent nocturnal cat fights, nor the continual barking of a dog through the hours of the night.

Nuisances involving the use of property may develop from a wide variety of causes, some of them deliberately conceived with the intention of annoying one's neighbors. Such a case was Rideout v. Knox, decided many years ago by the Supreme Judicial Court of Massachusetts, the opinion being written by the late Oliver Wendell Holmes when he was a member of that tribunal.[43] The Court upheld a statute making the malicious erection of a so-called "spite fence " over six feet high, for the purpose of annoying adjoining occupants, a private nuisance. Justice Holmes commented upon the limited application of the act, and observed that it would be hard to imagine a more insignificant curtailment of the rights of property; his com-

---

[41] See Powell v. Pennsylvania, 127 U. S. 678, 1887.
[42] Schollenberger v. Pennsylvania, 171 U. S. 1, 1898.
[43] 148 Mass. 368, 1889.

ment on the rules of the common law applicable to such cases is significant:

It is plain that the right to use one's property for the sole purpose of injuring others is not one of the immediate rights of ownership. It is not a right for the sake of which property is recognized by the law, but is only a more or less necessary incident of rights which are established for very different ends. It has been thought by respectable authorities that even at common law the extent of a man's rights in cases like the present might depend upon the motive with which he acted. . . . We do not so understand the common law . . . but it does not follow that the rule is the same for a boundary fence unnecessarily built more than six feet high. It may be said that the difference is only one of degree. Most differences are, when nicely analyzed.

The rules of law have so developed that the existence of a nuisance in any given instance will depend largely upon the character of the neighborhood. A machine shop or a boiler factory is a natural and legitimate part of an industrial district, but when such an establishment is set up in a residential district, where the noises emanating therefrom disturb the peace of the community and annoy the inhabitants, it becomes a public nuisance. Such nuisances may result also from the presence of disagreeable and offensive odors such as emanate from a fish glue factory or a fertilizer plant. The smoke that belches forth from the chimneys of great factories may be taken for granted (although it is no longer necessary) in an industrial district, when it would constitute a public nuisance in the commercial or residential section of the city.[44] Property may also be used in such manner as to constitute a public nuisance on moral grounds. If an individual permits the use of his premises for any one of the familiar forms of vice and crime, he may subject himself to nuisance proceedings as well as the possibility of criminal prosecution.

Classification of Nuisances. The Supreme Court of Illinois, in Laugel v. City of Bushnell, classified nuisances as follows:

. . . First, those which in their nature are nuisances per se or are so denounced by the common law or by statute; second, those which in their nature are not nuisances, but may become so by reason of their locality, surroundings, or the manner in which they may be conducted, managed,

---

[44] A smoke abatement ordinance was upheld in Northwest Laundry v. Des Moines, 239 U. S. 486, 1916; an act forbidding the conducting of a livery stable within a designated area, in Reinman v. Little Rock, 237 U. S. 171, 1914. See also: Barkley, J. E., *Some Fundamentals of Smoke Abatement* (Information Circular, United States Department of the Interior, 1939), and St. Louis Committee on Elimination of Smoke, *Report* (St. Louis, February 24, 1940).

et cetera; third, those which in their nature may be nuisances, but as to which there may be honest differences of opinion in impartial minds. The power granted by the statute to the governing bodies of municipal corporations to declare what shall be nuisances, and to abate the same, et cetera, authorizes such bodies to conclusively denounce those things falling within the first and third of these classes to be nuisances, but as to those things falling within the second class, the power possessed is only to declare such of them to be nuisances as are in fact so.[45]

It is not only difficult but probably unnecessary to cite specific court cases to illustrate the first type — nuisances per se — since the definition of many of them has come down through the rules of the common law. The common law nuisance was usually a nuisance to the sense of smell or a danger to life, such as an unsanitary building or drain.[46] Noise in extreme form was often considered a nuisance, and it is even more so in the modern city. In England, interference with the easements of light, air, and access constituted a nuisance. As far back as 1910 one writer reported a rapid increase in police power legislation of this general type. " Legislation is now eagerly desired in many states of this country," he said, " to make in certain cases that which is a nuisance to the sense of sight also a legal nuisance, as, for instance, the posting of offensive bills on the fences, or the erection of huge advertising signs in parks or on public highways. Such a law was, however, held unconstitutional in Massachusetts. There is some legislation against the blowing of steam whistles by locomotives, although I believe none against the morning whistle of factories, and some against the emission of black smoke in specified durations and quantities." [47]

It is not particularly difficult to determine whether or not a given situation is of such a character as to constitute a public nuisance. It is, however, sometimes difficult to secure the abatement of a nuisance, particularly in some of the larger cities, if the persons responsible for it have considerable political influence. In such a

---

[45] 197 Ill. 20, 1902, cited by Hall, *op. cit.*, p. 400.

[46] The following have been listed as nuisances, mostly from the standpoint of health:

Filth	Dumps	Weeds
Garbage	Wet and soggy lands	Railroad toilets
Ashes	Rodents and insect pests	Spitting in public places
Slops	Oily wastes	Keeping horses, cattle, swine
Cesspools	Defective plumbing	Dead animals
Privy vaults	Faulty cellars	Stagnant water
Sink drains	Tenement overcrowding	Smoke and dust

[47] Stimson, Frederic J., *Popular Lawmaking*, Chapter 7 (Scribner's, New York, 1910).

case, the law is clearly on the side of the plaintiff, and usually a little persistence will enable him to secure abatement. The courts have fortunately taken the position that the existence of a nuisance is sufficient to enable one to secure relief — it makes no difference whether the plaintiff moves in where the nuisance is already established or whether it is the nuisance which moves in. These nuisances are of the second type mentioned above — those which become nuisances by reason of their locality, surroundings, or the manner in which they are conducted. An interesting case in point is that of the Northwestern Fertilizer Company v. Hyde Park.[48] Hyde Park was then an exclusive suburban residential district adjacent to Chicago. A $15,000 rendering plant, with the growth of population, came to be entirely surrounded by residences; the Supreme Court sustained a decision of the highest state court compelling its abandonment as an offensive nuisance, even though plants engaged in other businesses were allowed to remain.

In 1855 the Supreme Court of New Hampshire upheld a statute which delegated the regulation of " quasi-nuisances " to municipalities, under which one of the cities of the state prohibited bowling alleys within twenty rods of any dwelling, store, shop, or church; bowling alleys conducted within that distance were to be considered nuisances.[49] A quasi-nuisance was defined as one which might become a nuisance by the manner in which it was conducted; the fact of a nuisance, it was pointed out, depended upon when, where, and how the alleys were conducted. This doctrine is one which applies to dance halls, night clubs, or tap rooms.

The third type of nuisance includes those which in their nature may be nuisances, but with regard to which there may be honest difference of opinion. This type is best illustrated, perhaps, by the numerous cases growing out of attempts to enforce billboard regulations and zoning ordinances. The early decisions on billboards

---

[48] 97 U. S. 650, 1878; in this connection see the somewhat similar brickyard case, J. C. Hadacheck v. C. E. Sebastian, Chief of Police of the City of Los Angeles, 239 U. S. 394, 1915, but an airport, landing field, or flying school is not a nuisance per se, and be regarded as such only if it is operated in such a manner as to interfere with the comfort of adjoining property owners; see Batcheller et al. v. Commonwealth ex rel University of Virginia, 10 S. E. (2nd) 529 (Virginia, 1940). The following types of business have frequently been held to be offensive trades:

Rendering works	Glue works	Tanneries
Soap works	Gas works	Varnish works
Slaughter houses	Liquor distilleries	Rubber works
Oil refineries	Breweries	Smelters
Fish handling plants	Abattoirs	

[49] State v. Noyes, 30 N. H. 279, 1855, cited by Mott, Rodney L., *Due Process of Law*, pp. 315 and 571.

were apt to be averse to such regulations,[50] but more recent decisions have been more favorable. A leading case was decided by the Supreme Court in 1917. Chicago had provided by ordinance that if a billboard were to be erected, the advertising company must first secure the consent of a majority of the property frontage on both sides of the street in the block in which the billboard was to be erected. In Thomas Cusack Company v. Chicago, the Court held that such billboards might be dangerous to the safety and decency of the district, and that the ordinance was a reasonable regulation, and therefore constitutional.[51]

Zoning. In the state courts, zoning regulations likewise met with difficulties in the early days. In 1911 the Supreme Court of California, in Ex parte Quong Wo,[52] discharged an application for a writ of habeas corpus entered by one Quong Wo. Los Angeles had by ordinance established seven industrial districts, and declared the rest of the city to be a residential area. In the residential district, it was forbidden to maintain any stone crusher, rolling mill, carpet-beating establishment, fireworks or soap factory; or any factory using mechanical power; or any hay barn, wood or lumber yard, public laundry or washhouse; or to establish anew any hospital, asylum for feeble-minded, wine or brandy manufactory, or blacksmith shop (existing ones being unaffected). Quong Wo had continued to operate a laundry, his lease upon which, at the time of his arrest, had two years to run. By 1925 the Supreme Court of Illinois, in the City of Aurora v. Burns,[53] was willing to affirm the decree of a lower court, enforcing a zoning ordinance adopted by Aurora, under the Illinois general zoning law. The defendant, Burns, was enjoined from erecting and maintaining a grocery store in a part of Aurora zoned as B residential district by the local ordinance.

Since 1909 the Supreme Court has upheld a number of acts of this character, in important decisions. In Welch v. Swasey et al.[54] it was held that regulations with respect to the height of buildings and their mode of construction in cities, made by legislative enactment for the safety, comfort, or convenience of the people, and for the benefit of property owners generally, are valid if the height and

[50] See, for instance, City of Passaic v. Patterson Bill Posting, Advertising and Sign Painting Company, 72 N. J. Law, 285, 1905.
[51] 242 U. S. 526, 1917; in 1943, the billboard decision of the Vermont Supreme Court has been described as making history in billboard control. See Kelbro, Inc., v. Myrick, Secretary of State, et al., 30 Atl. Rpts. (2), 527, 1943.
[52] 161 Cal. 220, 1911.
[53] 319 Ill. 84, 1925.
[54] 214 U. S. 91, 1909.

conditions provided for can be plainly seen not to be unreasonable or inappropriate. More recently, in 1926, in the Village of Euclid, Ohio, et al. v. Ambler Realty Company,[55] the Court said that the power to forbid the erection of particular buildings or of buildings for particular use is to be determined not by abstract considerations of buildings or use, but by considerations in connection with circumstances and locality. If the validity of the legislative classification for zoning purposes is debatable, the legislative judgment must be allowed to control; the fact that the ordinance has the effect of diverting industrial development along other lines than it might have been expected to follow does not render it invalid. To be declared unconstitutional, the ordinance must be clearly arbitrary and without substantial relation to the public health, safety, morals, et cetera. Unless such conditions exist, a zoning ordinance does not violate the due process clause, or the equal protection clause of Amendment XIV, or similar provisions to be found in the constitutions of the states.

Aesthetic Considerations. Prior to the present era, the use of the police power for aesthetic purposes was usually frowned upon by the courts, on the ground that such interests had no substantial relation to the public welfare. Where other grounds existed, such regulations were upheld even though they were in part motivated by aesthetic considerations. That beauty might have some part in public welfare was first recognized in eminent domain proceedings, and more recently in cases arising out of zoning regulations.[56] The ground for a more liberal and progressive attitude toward such attempts at the exercise of the police power was broken by the Supreme Court in Packer Corporation v. State of Utah,[57] which upheld the constitutionality of a Utah statute prohibiting the advertising of tobacco in any form on billboards, street car signs, or placards. While other questions were involved in this case, and while it cannot be denied that a moral consideration may have weighed heavily in the minds of the members of the legislature, the aesthetic aspects of the measure cannot be denied.

In 1935 the Supreme Court of Massachusetts decided the famous Massachusetts billboard cases after nearly ten years of litigation.[58]

[55] 272 U. S. 365, 1926.

[56] See note in *Harvard Law Review,* March, 1935, p. 848, for statement of these points and citation of supporting cases.

[57] 285 U. S. 105, 1932.

[58] General Outdoor Advertising Company, Inc., et al., v. Department of Public Works, 193 N. E. 799, 1935. See also the Vermont case, cited above, and for an excellent up-to-date study, the Illinois Legislative Council, *Billboard Control* (Springfield, 1944).

This decision then became "not only the leading billboard case in the country, but also the leading case on the protection of public amenity under the police power." The important aspects of this case may be summarized as follows:

Fifteen cases were decided, involving the general restrictions of the State Department of Public Works, somewhat more onerous restrictions of the town of Concord, and the refusal of the Department to renew the permit for the conspicuous Chevrolet roof-sign which overlooks and disfigures Boston Common and the State House, the latter refusal being based wholly on considerations of "taste and fitness." The regulations and the public authorities are sustained in every particular.

In barest outline the decision covers the following points, among others: (1) The billboard companies may be compelled to relocate their boards in accordance with the regulations, in spite of the expense, without compensation. (2) The billboard business is in a class by itself and may be regulated as such under the police power. (3) One basis for its regulation is the safety of travelers. There is danger both from obstruction of view and distraction of attention. Inattention causes accidents. Billboards cause inattention. (4) The regulations are also legal in that they are designed to protect travelers from the annoyance of commercial propaganda. The traveler has a right "to a peaceful and unannoyed journey." (5) Scenic beauty contributes a highly important factor to the welfare of the state; "to preserve such landscape from defacement promotes the public welfare and is a public purpose." To this end advertising on private property within public view may be controlled. Even if the regulations "did not rest upon the safety of public travel and the promotion of comfort for travelers, we think that the preservation of scenic beauty and places of historical interest would be a support for them. Considerations of taste and fitness may be a proper basis for action in granting and denying permits for advertising devices." (6) In a town of the character of Concord the restrictions may legitimately include and apply to business districts as well as to the others, without special exceptions or special concessions to the billboard business in business districts. (7) The sign overlooking Boston Common may be refused a permit upon the sole ground that it is "an inappropriate and obnoxious intrusion into that locality," without regard to considerations of safety, health, or morals. Considerations of "taste and fitness" are sufficient to exclude. (8) The effect of the 1918 amendment to the Massachusetts Constitution was to overrule a decision of the Supreme Court in 1905 limiting the police power of the State in its control over outdoor advertising. The police power over this subject is now complete. (9) The regulations in question are also wholly in accord with the Federal Constitution.[59]

[59] Bard, Albert S., "Massachusetts Supreme Court Protects Public Amenities in Billboard Decision," *National Municipal Review*, February, 1935, p. 117, and later, "Courts Expand Scope of Police Power Regulation," *ibid.*, May, 1942, pp. 280–281.

SELECTED REFERENCES

Asbury, Herbert, *Sucker's Progress* (Dodd, Mead, New York, 1938).

Association of American Law Schools, *Selected Essays on Constitutional Law* (Foundation Press, Chicago, 1938).

Bowden, Aneta, and Gould, George, *Summary of State Legislation Requiring Premarital and Prenatal Examinations for Syphilis* (American Social Hygiene Association, New York, 1941).

Burdick, Charles K., *The Law of the American Constitution* (Putnam's, New York, 1922).

Chafee, Zechariah, *State House v. Pent House: Legal Problems of the Rhode Island Race-Track Row* (Booke Shop, Providence, 1937).

Collins, Charles W., *The Fourteenth Amendment and the States* (Little, Brown, Boston, 1912).

Constitution of the United States, Annotated, Revised Edition (Government Printing Office, Washington, 1938).

Council of State Governments, *Waiting Period for Marriage License Applications Affecting Servicemen in Nineteen States* (Chicago, 1942).

Cushman, Robert E., *Leading Constitutional Decisions,* Seventh Edition (Crofts, New York, 1940).

Dodd, Walter F., *Cases and Other Authorities on Constitutional Law* (West Publishing Company, St. Paul, 1932).

Dowling, Noel T., *Cases on American Constitutional Law,* 4 vols. (New York, 1931).

Ely, Richard T., *Property and Contract in Their Relation to the Distribution of Wealth* (Macmillan, New York, 1917).

Evans, Lawrence B., *Leading Cases on American Constitutional Law,* Fourth Edition, edited by Charles G. Fenwick (Callaghan, Chicago, 1938).

Everstine, Carl N., *Regulation of Fireworks,* and *Supplement* (Maryland Legislative Council, Baltimore, 1940).

Field, Oliver P., *A Selection of Cases and Authorities on Constitutional Law* (Callaghan, Chicago, 1930).

Flack, Horace E., *The Adoption of the Fourteenth Amendment* (Johns Hopkins Press, 1908).

Freund, Ernst, *Police Power* (Callaghan, Chicago, 1904).

Gould, George, *Laws Against Prostitution and Their Use* (American Social Hygiene Association, New York, 1942).

Hall, James Parker, *Cases on Constitutional Law,* with Supplement (West Publishing Company, St. Paul, 1926).

Illinois Legislative Council, *Billboard Control* (Springfield, 1944).

International Association of Chiefs of Police, *Study of State Legislation Regulating Sale and Possession of Firearms* (Chicago, 1940).

Johnson, Bascom, Ed., *Digest of Laws and Regulations Relating to the Prevention and Control of Syphilis and Gonorrhea* (American Social Hygiene Association, New York, 1942).

——, and others, *Digest of State and Federal Laws Dealing with Prostitution and Other Sex Offenses* (American Social Hygiene Association, New York, 1942).

Kansas Legislative Council, *Premarital Examination Laws* (Topeka, 1941).

Levinson, Horace C., *Your Chance to Win* (Farrar and Rinehart, New York, 1939).

Library of Congress, *Lotteries in the United States and Foreign Countries* (Division of Bibliography, Washington, 1942).

Long, Joseph R., *Cases on Constitutional Law* (Lawyers Cooperative Publishing Company, Rochester, 1926).

Lyon, Leverett S., and others, *Government and Economic Life,* 2 vols. (Brookings Institution, Washington, 1940).

MacDougall, Michael, and Furnas, J. C., *Gamblers Don't Gamble* (Greystone Press, New York, 1939).

Mathews, John M., *The American Constitutional System,* Second Edition (McGraw-Hill, New York, 1940).

Maurer, Robert G., *Cases on Constitutional Law* (Lawyers Cooperative Publishing Company, Rochester, 1941).

McGehee, Lucius P., *Due Process of Law* (Thompson, Northport, New York, 1906).

McGovney, Dudley O., *Cases on Constitutional Law* (Bobbs-Merrill, Indianapolis, 1930).

Mott, Rodney L., *Due Process of Law* (Bobbs-Merrill, Indianapolis, 1926).

Muller, H. M., *Lotteries* (Wilson, New York, 1935).

New York State Constitutional Convention Committee, *Problems Relating to Legislative Organization and Powers* (Albany, 1938).

New York State Joint Legislative Committee for the Study of the Pari-Mutuel System *Report* (Legislative Document (1941) No. 69, Albany, 1941).

Orth, Samuel P., *Readings on the Relation of Government to Property and Industry* (Ginn, Boston, 1915).

Powell, Thomas R., *The Supreme Court and State Police Power, 1922–1930* (Michie, Charlottesville, 1932).

Rohlfing, Charles C., and others, *Business and Government,* Fourth Edition (Foundation Press, Chicago, 1941).

Rottschaefer, Henry, *Cases on Constitutional Law* (Commerce Clearing House, Chicago, 1932).

Stimson, Frederic J., *Popular Lawmaking* (Scribner's, New York, 1910).

Swisher, Carl B., *American Constitutional Development* (Houghton Mifflin, Boston, 1943).

Taylor, Hannis, *Due Process and the Equal Protection of the Laws* (Callaghan, Chicago, 1917).

Thayer, James Bradley, *Cases on Constitutional Law,* 4 vols. (C. W. Sever, Cambridge, 1894–1895).

Tiedeman, Christopher G., *The Unwritten Constitution* (Putnam's, New York, 1890).

Wambaugh, Eugene, *A Selection of Cases on Constitutional Law* (Harvard University Press, 1914–1915).

Willoughby, W. W., *Constitutional Law of the United States,* Second Edition, 3 vols. (Baker, Voorhis, New York, 1929).

Young, James T., *The New American Government and Its Work,* Third Edition (Macmillan, New York, 1933).

Anonymous, " State Regulation of Street Processions," *Bill of Rights Review,* Spring, 1941, pp. 232–235.

Council of State Governments, " State Legislation Requiring Premarital Examinations for Venereal Diseases," *State Government,* March, 1944, pp. 300–301, and table on cover.

——, " State Legislation Requiring Prenatal Examinations for Venereal Diseases," *State Government,* April, 1944, p. 319, and table on cover.

Edwards, Mary S., " Premarital Examination Laws in Operation," *Journal of Social Hygiene,* May, 1940.

Forster, George F., and Shaughnessy, Howard J., " Premarital Examination Laws in the United States," *Journal* of the American Medical Association, March 7, 1942, pp. 790–797.

Gould, George, " Laws Against Prostitution and Their Use," *Journal of Social Hygiene,* October, 1941.

Johnson, V. Webster, and Walker, Herman, Jr., " Centralization and Coordination of Police Power for Land-Control Measures," *Journal of Land and Public Utility Economics,* February, 1941, pp. 17–26.

Lade, James H., " The Legal Basis for Venereal Disease Control," *American Journal of Public Health,* October, 1945, pp. 1041–1046.

Mahoney, J. F., " Requirement of Premarital Legislation," *Venereal Disease Information,* April, 1943, pp. 105–107.

Marx, Fritz M., " Comparative Administrative Law: Exercise of Police Power," *University of Pennsylvania Law Review,* January, 1942, pp. 266–291.

National Advisory Police Committee, Special Committee on Enforcement, " Techniques for Repressing Unorganized Prostitution," Supplement to *Police Chiefs Newsletter,* November–December, 1942.

Paton, George W., " Liability for Nuisance," *Illinois Law Review,* May, 1942, pp. 1–18.

Weinstein, Charles C., " Regulation of Neon Signs," City Club of New York bulletin, 1940.

Part Seven

INTERGOVERNMENTAL RELATIONS

CHAPTER XX

The Local Units of the States

UNTIL very recently, in every period of American politics
there has been at least one unit of government which functions badly, and the study of which was largely neglected. For
some years following the Civil War — indeed until the beginning of
the present century — the states were in somewhat this position; the
reconstruction of these units did not begin until 1917. In 1887, when
Bryce published the first edition of his *American Commonwealth,*
he made the statement that the government of our cities represented
the one conspicuous failure in the American governmental system.
This judgment was supported in the early years of the present century by the literature of the muckrakers, of which Lincoln Steffens's
The Shame of the Cities is perhaps best known. The reflections which
these writers cast upon American municipal government were well
deserved; since then, however, enormous progress has been made
both in research in municipal government and in the improvement
of municipal administration. In fact, this progress has been so great
that there need be no hesitancy in asserting that, if there are still
within the United States municipalities whose governments are dishonest and inefficient, these cities have governments of this character because they do not want any other kind. Our knowledge of the
problems of municipal government and administration is sufficient
to enable us to provide honest and efficient government for any city
that wants it.

In 1917 Henry S. Gilbertson published a volume on American
county government, the subtitle of which was The Dark Continent
of American Politics.[1] This indictment was also well deserved; it

[1] Gilbertson, Henry S., *The County* (National Short Ballot Organization, New
York, 1917).

is only in the recent past that any serious study has been made of the problems of county government, or any serious effort by county officers to improve the standards of administration. There is now a steady stream of surveys and research studies issuing from the press, and political scientists are beginning to give the subject the attention which it deserves. While some improvements have resulted from these efforts, much work still remains to be done. The allusion which Mr. Gilbertson made to counties may still be applied with perfect accuracy to the smaller units of rural local government, the towns and townships, villages, boroughs, and districts.

HISTORY OF AMERICAN LOCAL GOVERNMENT

Before undertaking an analysis of the various forms of organization of local government, it is necessary that one be familiar with certain essential facts concerning the origin and development of local institutions. It is well known that the town originated in, and became characteristic of, the New England area. There were a number of definite and rather obvious reasons for this fact. The country was for the most part rocky, if not mountainous; the soil was thin and poor; the climate severe. In addition, the land was densely wooded, which constituted a serious hindrance to agriculture, as well as a source of danger to the settlers from Indians and wild animals. Taken together, these conditions present abundant justification for the small and compact forms of settlement which characterized the New England region, and for the town meeting form of government which developed in them. At a later date, the continued concentration of population in small and compact communities was further encouraged by the development of manufacturing.[2]

Just as the town, with its town meeting, came to be the prevailing form of local government in New England, so the county form came to predominate in the South. Again, there were definite reasons to account for this development. The South was from the beginning an agricultural area; the crops which early achieved a position of importance — cotton, indigo, rice, and tobacco — were all of a type requiring the cultivation of large areas of land. Under these circumstances, the plantation system developed, in sharp contrast to the

---

[2] This classification is based on Porter, Kirk H., *County and Township Government in the United States*, Chapter 4 (Macmillan, New York, 1922). Only the six New England states are included in this first group. For a good brief summary, see Tooke, Charles W., "Progress of Local Government, 1836–1936," in *Law: A Century of Progress*, Vol. II, pp. 105–143 (New York University Press, 1937).

densely populated communities in the North. In addition, the southern settlers had, except for the five tribes in the Far South, no serious danger from the Indians at any time. Under these circumstances, therefore, a broader and more extensive unit of local government was both natural and necessary. The county, in which a number of plantations were grouped together into a single unit for purposes of government, came to be the dominating type. In the West, where settlement was sparse, the same form became prevalent.[3]

Interesting questions present themselves in those areas in which these two types came in conflict, or at least in contact. In general, it may be said that the importance of each of these units varies directly in proportion to the distance from the area of its origin. That is to say, the county form steadily diminishes in importance as one travels north along the Atlantic coast; conversely, the town diminishes in importance as one travels south along this coast. The contact of these two major forms has resulted in the development of two interesting hybrid forms in New York and Pennsylvania. In these states, both the town and the county exist, and in both of them, both types of unit are important. In New York, however, the town is more important than the county, while in Pennsylvania the county is more important than the township.[4]

It is important to note the results of the contact of these various forms of local government with the settlement of the western country. In general, these forms were carried due west with little or no modification. The settlers in the western country invariably set up the same general type of local government to which they had previously become accustomed. This is, of course, in harmony with the thesis of the late Professor Turner with regard to the significance of the frontier in American history.[5] At the same time, no one should assume that these forms developed without themselves being influenced by the frontier. As early as 1787, when the Northwest Ordi-

[3] Porter, *op. cit.* The states in the South and Far West group follow (townships exist in those states whose names appear in italics, but they are merely justice of the peace districts, and do not possess the characteristic township organization): Alabama, Arizona, *California*, Colorado, Delaware, Florida, Georgia, Idaho, Kentucky, Louisiana, Maryland, Mississippi, *Montana*, *Nevada*, New Mexico, *North Carolina*, Oregon, *South Carolina*, Tennessee, Texas, Utah, Virginia, Washington, West Virginia, and Wyoming.

[4] *Ibid.* The North Central group includes Illinois, Michigan, Nebraska, New Jersey, New York, and Wisconsin, while the South Central group includes Arkansas, Indiana, Iowa, Kansas, Minnesota, Missouri, North Dakota, Ohio, Oklahoma, Pennsylvania, and South Dakota.

[5] See Goodman, A. Bristol, "Westward Movement of Local Government," *Journal of Land and Public Utility Economics*, February, 1944, pp. 20–34, and succeeding articles in this series.

nance was passed, the practice was begun of laying out the land in a very artificial way (for land in the West was more extensive and in general more level) in township units six miles square. This practice was continued under the present government, beginning with the admission of Ohio in 1803. Each township consisted of thirty-six sections, one mile square; from the beginning, one of these — and later two — was reserved for school purposes. When there developed within one of these townships a settlement of 500 or more persons, it might be incorporated as a village; a settlement of 1,000 or more might be incorporated as a city. In the course of time multitudes of special districts for roads, schools, fire, water, sanitation, lighting, drainage and sewage, and utilities were set up. School and road districts were the earliest to be established.

THE FUNCTIONS OF LOCAL GOVERNMENT

Before undertaking an analysis of the different types of organization possible for the various units of local government, it is desirable to consider briefly the functions which these local agencies have traditionally been expected to perform. The following list is fairly comprehensive, and includes some functions which were originally important but have come to be less so, functions which have always been and which still are of great importance, and still others that have recently come into a position of prominence.[6]

1. *Protection of Life and Property.* Maintenance of the peace has throughout our history been regarded as a function of local government. The colonial governments never maintained a police force, the Federal government has never maintained one, and until recently only a limited number of the states have done so. At the present time, all cities maintain police forces of their own, while in the rural districts the practice of maintaining such forces is increasing. Some experiments have been made with the county constabulary plan.[7] In the more backward districts, the enforcement of the law still rests largely in the hands of the sheriff and the constable, antiquated and unsatisfactory though this arrangement is. The character of modern crime and racketeering is making it increasingly urgent that problems of law enforcement be handled by larger units with better and more adequately trained personnel. Thus greater

---

[6] This list was originally based upon Porter, *op cit.*, Chapter 6, but has been extensively modified since. See also Satterfield, M. H., "The Growth of County Functions since 1930," *Journal of Politics,* February, 1941, pp. 76–88.

[7] Smith, Bruce, *Rural Crime Control,* Chapter 4 (Institute of Public Administration, Columbia University, 1933).

effort is being made by the states in crime control, and the Federal government has developed facilities for the handling of crime problems of an interstate character. This development is in line with long established practice in European countries, where crime control is regarded as a national rather than a local function.

2. *Judicial Functions.* The administration of justice has always been, and is still, a major function of local government. In fact, the origin of county government in Pennsylvania as well as in other states is to be attributed largely to this function; all of the original constitutional county officers had duties relating to it. The quality of justice received by the minor offenders against the criminal law and by the small claims litigant under the civil law is, in fact, the kind of justice which the majority of the people receive. These cases must be handled locally. If the parties to them receive a square deal, it is evident that a large percentage of those who become involved in court proceedings at all are receiving a square deal. It is also obvious that if the intermediate and appellate courts are of the very highest quality, they can deal with only a very small percentage of the total number of cases in which proceedings are instituted.

Not only must the quality of the work be good, but it is essential that the courts be convenient and easily accessible to all citizens. The whole theory of the common law, with its minor courts and its jury system, is based upon the belief that the citizen can and should have his disputes adjudicated in a fair and equitable manner, with the aid of his neighbors. In more than 300 years of national history Americans have not departed from this belief, and it seems unlikely that they will. This does not mean that the size of the local units may not be enlarged, nor a more adequate supervision of their work be established; in fact, it seems highly desirable that both of these things be done.

In all states the settlement of estates is administered as a local function by such officers as the register of wills, the probate judge, the surrogate, or the judges of the Orphans' Court. The purpose is twofold: to see that the property of deceased persons is disposed of in accordance with provisions of the will, where such exists; and to see that in the case of estates of persons who die intestate, the property and resources are disposed in accordance with the provisions of the law of inheritance. In connection with this work there are such additional problems as the administration of trusts and the handling of the property of minors and other persons not in the enjoyment of full legal rights.

3. *Agricultural Extension.* The promotion of agriculture was

originally a state and Federal function. It is now carried on locally by the county agricultural agent, who is employed jointly by the state college of agriculture, the United States Department of Agriculture, and the several county boards of commissioners or supervisors, and who is in charge of all extension activities carried on within the county. He works under the direction of state leaders of major phases of the program, such as home economics, extension and 4-H club activities, and is administratively responsible to the extension division of the state college of agriculture. These programs are educational in character and cover a wide variety of activities.

The duties of the county agent relate to the conservation of the soil and other natural resources, work with 4-H clubs, the securing of better livestock and crops, the marketing of farm produce, organization of groups of young farm people, control of disease and pests affecting crops and livestock, poultry raising, feed production, and assistance to the home program. The number of these agents and the exact nature of their work vary somewhat according to the needs of the state in which they serve. In Michigan, in 1941, there were seventy-three agents employed for the eighty-three counties. Of these, seven served two counties and one served four. In addition, five assistant agents were employed jointly by the Bureau of Agricultural Economics and the Division of Extension Work at the State College of Agriculture.[8]

4. *Public Welfare.* From the earliest times, poor relief was regarded as a distinctly local function. It was assumed that poverty was inevitable, and relief was provided in the form of almsgiving, as it was called, or by commitment to almshouses, poorhouses, or poor farms. In New England, every town had its town poor farm. In recent years there have been fundamental changes in the theories upon the basis of which relief is provided, the effort being made to restore persons needing relief to the position of self-supporting and self-respecting members of the community. County institutions and state institutions have replaced those formerly operated by the smaller units of local government, and there has been a steady increase in the amount of outdoor relief, based upon the theory that it is more satisfactory to the individual and more defensible from a

[8] Tharp, Claude R., *A Manual of County Administrative Organization in Michigan*, pp. 226–227 (University of Michigan, Bureau of Government, 1944). This is an excellent study of the organization, powers, and duties of all of the county government officers in a representative state. See also Baker, Gladys, *The County Agent* (University of Chicago Press, 1939).

social point of view to help the needy to maintain themselves in their own homes wherever possible. This is the theory of mothers' assistance, old age pensions, and other modern forms of relief. In the administration of these forms, both the states and the Federal government have, since 1933, assumed a very important role. While these developments will undoubtedly have a strong influence upon future practices in the field of public assistance, it is inconceivable that the functions or the responsibility of the local units in this work can ever be entirely eliminated.

5. *Maintenance of Schools*. Except in Delaware, which has a state school system, control over public schools has been from the very beginning regarded as a subject of local concern. The United States Commissioner of Education pointed out in an address a few years ago that there were 143,445 separate one-room schoolhouses in the several states. The number of separate school districts is almost as great, Illniois having the largest number, 12,138 in all; Kansas stands second with 8,632, Missouri third with 8,613, and New York fourth with 6,064. Ohio has only 1,655; Pennsylvania, 2,546, as of 1942. The numbers show a slight tendency to decline from year to year.

Originally the financing of the schools was entirely a local matter; in recent years the practice of assisting the local districts with subsidy grants has been gradually extended, and this has been accompanied by an extension of state control. Nevertheless, it is generally recognized that people in the communities take greater interest in the schools than they do in the other activities of local government. Rightly or wrongly they have insisted upon choosing by popular vote the members of the local school board or board of school directors; they have joined parent-teachers associations and have in other ways given evidence of a deep concern over the problems of the local schools. Our present major problem is to find methods of developing more efficient supervision of the schools, without antagonizing the people in the local districts and without causing them to lose their interest.

The increased amount of leisure available to workers in business and industry in this new industrial age, in which we are finding it possible to carry on our necessary business and industrial activities with a shorter work day and a shorter work week, imposes certain new responsibilities upon those in charge of local educational matters; it becomes incumbent on them to provide suitable opportunities for adult education under competent instructors. Such courses will not necessarily be confined to the conventional academic subjects, but may include current literature, drama, art, and music appreciation; courses designed to develop an understanding of current social, economic, and political questions; courses on technical and scientific subjects, et cetera. A program of this character will certainly require larger expenditures for library purposes. As the years pass, an increasing percentage of the population will have had the opportunity for high school and college training. One of the major purposes of their formal education will have been to cultivate intellectual interests and to stimulate an intellectual curiosity. If large numbers of such people are given additional leisure and the public fails to provide them with facilities for the profitable use of that time, much of the work that has already been done and much of the money that has already been spent will have been wasted.

6. *Recreation Program.* On the welfare side, the increased leisure of workers means that the local units have the duty of developing recreational facilities and a program for their use, in order to assist these people in making both a pleasant and profitable use of this time. The local units must extend their programs for the construction and maintenance of well-equipped playgrounds and parks within easy access of congested centers of population. School properties should be developed as community centers, being kept open and providing facilities for the use of adult groups. Such programs, of course, are expensive, but much less so than is the attempt to get along without them. Engaged, as it is, in an effort to reduce the amount of crime, the public can scarcely afford to fail to provide pleasant, enjoyable, and socially defensible opportunities for the use of leisure. If such a program is neglected, there need be no surprise if many persons use this time for purposes which are socially objectionable or become involved in crime.

7. *Public Health Work.* There are many public health functions for the performance of which local units are at least in part responsible. The fact that they frequently fail to perform these duties well does not lessen their responsibility. These are the units which must take action for the elimination of public nuisances affecting health conditions, for the collection and disposition of refuse, for the enforcement of quarantine regulations, for the keeping of vital statistics and records of the prevalence of contagious diseases. The local units are responsible, under state supervision and with the aid of one or more public health nurses, for the administration of child health and school health programs. In recent years the authority

of the state departments of health has been extended so that they may intervene in, or if necessary assume complete control of, health matters in communities where the local authorities fail to function effectively.[9] There should be at least one general hospital in each county of 5,000 population or more, centrally located, and adequately equipped and staffed to handle emergency cases as well as routine hospital work. The larger counties individually, and the smaller ones jointly, may maintain tuberculosis sanitaria.

8. *Highway Construction and Maintenance.* The construction and maintenance of highways were originally regarded as purely a function of local government. Streets were paved by cities, towns, and boroughs; later the counties undertook to construct roads connecting centers of population and the county seats, and when this proved to be inadequate for the development of a well-planned system of highways, the task was undertaken by the states, or by the states with the assistance of the Federal government. The construction and maintenance of the more important highway routes have therefore been transferred to the states in order to reduce the cost, secure greater efficiency, and eliminate jurisdictional disputes between local units. While there has been a definite tendency to increase the number of highways in the state highway systems, there remain in most of the states considerable numbers of miles of road still under the supervision of counties, boroughs, and townships. In some states there are units of local government for whose continued existence there would be no need if the road-building and maintenance function were taken over by the state highway department. Thus the local importance of this function, though originally great, has been steadily declining.

9. *The Collection of Taxes.* Tax collection, likewise, has always been considered a function of local government. In recent years the authorities engaged in this work have come under supervision by state departments and agencies. There have, however, been relatively few attempts at the collection by state agencies of revenues intended for purely local use. The local assessors are subject to supervision by the state tax board or board of equalization; the local collecting officers are under bond in accordance with state law, their accounts in many cases being audited by state officials, and the form in which they shall be kept being prescribed by uniform accounting acts. It is

---

[9] See Illinois Legislative Council, *County Health Departments* (Springfield, 1943) , and Stoner, John E., and Field, Oliver P., *Public Health Services in an Indiana Defense Community* (Indiana University, Bureau of Government Research, 1942) .

only within the last few years, during which the states have come to rely less on the general property tax for state purposes, and more upon business taxes, income taxes, inheritance taxes, motor vehicle and gasoline taxes, et cetera, that the function of collecting large amounts of revenue destined for local use has been transferred from the local agencies to the states.

In some of the older states, taxes are still collected on a fee basis; this procedure dates back to a time when, in the large number of units of local government and special districts which were created for a variety of purposes, it was customary to confer the taxing power upon each and to provide for a tax collecting officer. Since so many of the districts were small and the collection of taxes therefore only a part-time or temporary job, those who performed the work were paid on a fee basis rather than by salary. The conditions which have developed under this practice have been very objectionable and have constituted a strong argument for the reorganization of local government. In one instance in Pennsylvania a few years ago, a county treasurer received $34,000 for no greater exertion on his part than receiving a check and turning it over to the State Department of Revenue. This represented the fee on the tax due on a very large inheritance; it is an extreme case, but it indicates what may happen under the fee system.

10. *Administration of Elections.* The administration of elections has been regarded in all sections of the country as a function of local government. Where the town is the prevailing form of local government, the town has supervised elections; where the county is the prevailing form, control over elections has been entrusted to the board of county commissioners. In most states the state government possesses very limited powers of supervision over elections. The local authorities are responsible for the printing and distribution of the ballots, the determination of the number and the size of the voting districts, and the reporting of the returns after the close of the polls. In most cases the judges of election and other election officials, as well as the watchers and other functionaries, are under the control of the local party organization. Where this control is complete and effective, conditions such as those existing in the so-called " Zero Wards " in New York and Philadelphia develop, illustrations of which were presented in an earlier chapter.

11. *Clerical and Recording Functions.* From time immemorial the clerical and recording function has been a major responsibility of local government, performed either by the town clerk or the county

clerk. The duties of the latter include reports to state officers, on various subjects such as marriage licenses issued and certificates returned, assessment rolls, tax levies, et cetera. He is the official record keeper of the county with regard to a variety of matters, and the custodian of all kinds of papers and records. A variety of miscellaneous duties may be imposed upon him. In addition to the county clerk, there are the clerks of the various courts, the clerk of the county board, and other clerical functionaries.

The recording of land titles was originally performed by the smaller local units, but is now commonly a function of one of the county officers, either of the recorder of deeds, the abstractor of titles, or even the county clerk. The importance of having an accurate record of all transfers of land is obvious. No prudent person will purchase real estate without having a search made of the title, to make certain that the property is free from encumbrances and that the present owner is in a position to give a " clear title." These same officers may record deeds, mortgages, liens, attachments, and other instruments affecting title, and may be charged with the responsibility for maintaining a current system of indexes and abstracts thereof, so that information may be readily available to citizens, businessmen, and attorneys who have need for it.

12. *Military Organization.* Students of American history are familiar with the organization and drilling of local militia units in the colonies during colonial times; they recall also how, in the Revolutionary period, the armies were made up by a consolidation of these local units. Tradition has maintained a deep interest in and a strong attachment for local military units. Many people who are unfamiliar with the elaborate organization and the extensive properties held by a state for military purposes underestimate the present-day importance of military matters in the organization and conduct of local government. The Department of Military Affairs in Pennsylvania, for instance, had, before World War II, custody of approximately $25,000,000 worth of Federal property, for which it was responsible. This was distributed throughout the Commonwealth in some seventy-three separate armories, which served as training headquarters for nearly 150 infantry, cavalry, and other local military units. These armories themselves represent a vast investment and involve large regular expenditures for maintenance. In addition to the extensive assistance of the Federal authorities, the Commonwealth is obliged to make still further investments in order to secure the needed equipment and supplies. The attachment which the people

of the community feel to these various military units is well illustrated by the acclaim with which they were received during both World Wars.

13. *Units for Administrative Purposes.* Just as the Federal government frequently uses the states and sometimes the counties as units in the administration of many of its activities, so the states make use of the counties and other local units for administrative purposes. This is done largely as a matter of convenience; no one would seriously contend that these local units are well adapted to this purpose, but they are in existence and it is frequently easier to use them than to undertake the task of laying out new districts which might be more suitable. Since the machinery in these units is already established, the use of it may, in an emergency, make possible a considerable saving of time, as is illustrated by experiences with relief administration during the depression. This is apt to be true of some of the newer activities of government, which, as Professor Porter observes, the local areas do not and ought not to claim as being part of their functions.

LOCAL GOVERNMENT IN SMALLER UNITS

The smaller units of local government include the towns, townships, villages, boroughs, and special districts for schools, highways, and a wide variety of other purposes. The table on page 822 indicates that there are in the United States approximately 155,000 political subdivisions; it shows also the distribution of these units by states. Most of the states have, obviously, far too many — there are, as a matter of fact, so many that it is practically impossible to compute the number with accuracy. Illinois is, except for its excessive number of school districts, typical of the midwestern states; the following table contains a breakdown of the figures for that state as of 1942. The special districts are for roads, parks, sanitary purposes, forest preserves, fire protection, mosquito abatement, and public health.

It is not necessary for the present purpose to engage in a detailed discussion of the organization and functioning of these various local units. It is appropriate, however, that some mention be made of the states in which these forms exist, and the purposes for which they are employed. Most important is the township, which exists generally in Indiana, Iowa, Kansas, Michigan, Minnesota, New Jersey, New York, Ohio, Pennsylvania, and Wisconsin. In another group

STATE OF ILLINOIS —
NUMBER OF UNITS OF LOCAL GOVERNMENT

Type of Unit		Number
State		1
Counties		102
Townships		1,434
Cities, Villages, and Incorporated Towns		1,137
School Districts		12,138
Elementary School Districts	11,332	
Twelve Grade School Districts	147	
High and Non-High School Districts	659	
Special Districts		1,042

of states township organization is spotty. In Illinois there are sixteen counties, in the southern part of the state, which have no townships; in Missouri less than one fourth and in Nebraska less than one third of the counties have township organization. In North and South Dakota some townships have been organized for school purposes; in Oklahoma townships exist in less than half of the counties. In a third group of states the township exists in name, but it does not possess political organization analogous to that of the typical midwestern township. In Arkansas, townships serve primarily as judicial districts; in California they are called judicial townships; in North Carolina they are used for purposes of assessment. Similar conditions exist in Montana, Nevada, and South Carolina.

The fourth group of states includes those in which the township generally does not exist at all; here the primary districts of government are known by other names, as follows:

Beats — Mississippi
Civil districts — Tennessee
Election precincts — Alabama, Colorado, Florida, Idaho, Maryland, New Mexico, Oregon, Utah, Washington, and Wyoming
Election precincts, Justices' precincts, and School districts — Arizona
Justices' precincts, and Commissioners' precincts — Texas
Militia districts — Georgia
Police jury wards — Louisiana
Representative districts — Delaware

In a fifth and final group is found the states in which the New England town is still preserved — Connecticut, Massachusetts, Rhode Island, and, except for certain localities, the other three New England states.[10]

[10] New Hampshire, except Carroll County with two locations, and Coos County with eight grants, six purchases, six townships, and three locations; Vermont,

(From publication of the same name, United States Bureau of the Census)

STATE	All Governmental Units [1]	Counties	Townships and Towns	Municipalities Total	Municipalities Urban [2]	Municipalities Rural	School Districts	Special Districts
UNITED STATES TOTAL	155,116	3,050	18,919	16,220	3,332	12,888	108,579	8,299
Alabama	511	67	.....	275	60	215	110	58
Arizona	499	14	.....	33	16	17	397	54
Arkansas	3,705	75	.....	374	53	321	2,644	611
California	4,149	57 [3]	.....	286	167	119	2,809	996
Colorado	2,358	62 [3]	.....	239	30	209	1,937	119
Connecticut	349	8	154	37	27	10	14	135
Delaware	70	3	.....	51	8	43	14	1
Florida	503	67	.....	267	70	197	67	101
Georgia	946	159	.....	470	77	393	222	94
Idaho	1,666	44	.....	152	26	126	1,148	321
Illinois	15,854	102	1,434	1,137	208	929	12,138	1,042
Indiana	3,043	92	1,010	529	98	431	1,182	229
Iowa	7,519	99	1,608	932	89	843	4,861	18
Kansas	11,115	105	1,524	589	64	525	8,632	264
Kentucky	771	120	.....	285	56	229	261	104
Louisiana	523	63 [4]	.....	194	54	140	67	198
Maine	584	16	482	51	26	25	.....	34
Maryland	207	23	.....	142	22	120	.....	41
Massachusetts	409	13 [4]	312	39	39	.....	.....	44
Michigan	8,106	83	1,265	479	126	353	6,270	8
Minnesota	10,398	87	1,884	752	78	674	7,673	1
Mississippi	1,792	82	.....	270	48	222	1,189	250
Missouri	10,740	114	329	734	87	647	8,613	949
Montana	2,175	56	.....	115	23	92	1,932	71
Nebraska	8,307	93	476	530	36	494	7,009	198
Nevada	163	17	.....	12	5	7	115	18
New Hampshire	546	10	223	11	11	.....	231	70
New Jersey	1,143	21	235	331	164	157	490	65
New Mexico	225	31	.....	64	22	42	105	24
New York	8,339	57 [4]	932	610	202	408	6,064	675
North Carolina	603	100	.....	431	76	355	.....	71
North Dakota	4,066	53	1,399	333	12	321	2,272	8
Ohio	4,021	88	1,339	890	186	704	1,655	48
Oklahoma	5,100	77	.....	499	74	425	4,518	5
Oregon	2,332	36	.....	193	34	159	1,844	258
Pennsylvania	5,263	66 [4]	1,575	984	345	639	2,546	91
Rhode Island	54	(5)	32	7	7	.....	.....	14
South Carolina	2,057	46	.....	241	51	190	1,744	25
South Dakota	4,919	64 [6]	1,128	301	19	282	3,423	2
Tennessee	328	95	.....	206	57	149	11	15
Texas	7,360	254	.....	637	196	441	6,159	309
Utah	303	29	.....	201	25	176	40	32
Vermont	398	14	239	74	13	61	24	46
Virginia	323	100	.....	208	53	155	.....	14
Washington	1,906	39	68	221	40	181	1,148	429
West Virginia	326	55	.....	205	45	160	55	10
Wisconsin	8,508	71	1,271	515	94	421	6,569	81
Wyoming	531	23	.....	83	12	71	377	47

[1] Includes the Federal Government and the 48 State governments.
[2] Incorporated places having more than 2,500 inhabitants.
[3] The City and County of San Francisco in California and the City and County of Denver in Colorado are counted as cities and not as counties.
[4] The following counties are counted only as cities because they are wholly or very largely consolidated with the cities indicated: Orleans Parish with New Orleans City; Suffolk County with Boston City; Bronx, Kings, New York, Queens, and Richmond counties, with New York City; Philadelphia County with Philadelphia City.
[5] Counties not organized as local governments.
[6] The county areas of Armstrong, Shannon, Todd, Washabaugh, and Washington are unorganized as counties and are attached for administrative purposes to neighboring counties.

Need for Consolidation. There is a substantially unanimous agreement among students of government that these tiny units — relics of an age long past — are ill suited to the needs of the present day. Authorities in the field of judicial administration, as has been noted in a previous chapter, urge that the elected township justices of the peace be supplanted by trial justices for the county at large. In some jurisdictions the maintenance of highways is the only important function left to certain classes of townships; authorities here also urge that these roads be taken over by the counties or, as in North Carolina and Virginia, be made a part of the state highway system. Specific authorities of high standing in their respective fields might be quoted in the expression of similar ideas with regard to the work of the townships in such fields as schools, health, welfare, assessment of property — with regard to practically every important function which has ever been entrusted to township authorities. These proposals are but a part of a widespread movement now under way to reorganize the machinery of government and reallocate its functions.

These units of local government — towns and townships, boroughs and villages, and the multitude of special districts — were conceived and established to meet the needs of the colonists, and they have never been much changed since that time. The lives of the people, owing to developments in science and in the useful arts, have changed in almost every conceivable way. Small units, then necessary if government was to be accessible and convenient to citizens, have become, under modern conditions of transportation and communication, obstacles to the efficient administration of the public services. Larger units have become a practical necessity; at the same time, there must be a reallocation of the functions of government between the Federal government and the states, as well as between the states and their political subdivisions. Experience has demonstrated that functions that once had to be carried on locally if they were to be performed at all cannot now be efficiently administered in such restricted areas. It is impossible to secure the services of competent, full-time salaried personnel under such conditions. The solution of these two interrelated problems must be given serious thought and attention during the next few years.

except several unorganized townships and divisions known as grants and gores; Maine, except a number of plantations, townships, grants, gores, surpluses, and tracts. By some accident, a single town exists in Pennsylvania. See Bromage, Arthur W., " Conclusions with Respect to the Position of the Township in the Governmental Scheme," issued by the Bureau of Government, University of Michigan, February, 1932.

Local Authorities. During the depression, when many governmental units had already exhausted their borrowing capacity, the special authority was devised for the dual purposes of evading constitutional and statutory debt limitations and of making available funds necessary to carry on capital improvements. Such an authority is a special public corporation, usually organized for a single purpose, and deriving its revenues solely from receipts from the activity in which it is engaged. Its bonds are self-liquidating and tax-exempt. It has no power to tax or to levy special assessments. It is not a governmental unit in the usual sense; although it performs a governmental function, it lacks many of the powers of a municipal government. Such authorities are administered by governing boards appointed by the local units creating them.

Fairly extensive use has been made of this device in many jurisdictions. In Pennsylvania, for instance, a municipal authorities act was passed in 1935. In the ten-year period from 1935 to 1945, ninety-five such authorities were created. Of these, fifty-three have been organized by boroughs, twenty-two by townships, twelve by cities, four by counties, and four were organized jointly by two or more municipalities. Fifty of these operate a total of fifty-two projects, mostly water systems. Twenty-nine authorities purchased privately-owned water systems and eight built new ones. Nine constructed sewer projects, one built a combined theater and municipal building, one purchased a factory building and another constructed a gymnasium. It is apparent that this device can be adapted to meet almost any need for a substantial public improvement in any community.[11]

COUNTY GOVERNMENT

There are in the United States more than 3,000 counties; this type of governmental organization is found in every state. The number of counties varies from three in the tiny state of Delaware to 254 in Texas. In the majority of cases, the number seems to bear some relation to the size of the state and to population, although there are states in which it is well known that the number is too large.

Prevailing Organization. The organization of county government has remained substantially in its original form since the days of the founding. In the western states these same county institutions were

---

[11] See Pennsylvania Joint State Government Commission, *Municipal Authorities* (Harrisburg, 1945).

established by settlers from the East. While there are minor differences in the structure of county government in different states, the major characteristics have been much alike. In some states all counties maintain the same type of governmental organization, as in Mississippi; in others, the county law provides for the classification of counties according to population, as in Pennsylvania. In the larger counties the "row offices" are filled by full-time, salaried officials; in the smaller ones, by part-time officers paid on a fee basis. At the top of the governmental structure is found, irrespective of these differences, a county board, designated officially either as the board of county commissioners or as the board of county supervisors. In the South, where the county form originated, the former exists, consisting of three or five members who are elected by direct vote, either at large or from districts.

In the North, where the influence of the town form predominates, one finds the larger board of supervisors, the members of which are chosen by the electors, one from each town within the county. In Illinois, Michigan, New York, and Wisconsin the township serves as the unit of representation on the county board. Where the number of towns is considerable or where there are one or more large cities, the board of supervisors may be a large, cumbersome, and unwieldy body. A large county in western New York has such a large board, constituted as indicated in the table below.

STATE OF NEW YORK
ERIE COUNTY BOARD OF SUPERVISORS

City of Buffalo (1 from each ward)	27 members
City of Lackawanna	1 member
City of Tonawanda	1 member
Towns (1 from each town)	25 members
Total	54 members

The board in Wayne County, Michigan, has 149 members. These bodies are certainly not representative, and the duties and compensation of the members as county officers are secondary to those pertaining to their status as town officials.[12]

[12] New York State Commission for the Revision of the Tax Laws, *Report on local government*, pp. 67–70, Legislative Document (1935) No. 63. The reader may well study the more detailed facts of the set-up of county government in his home state in their relation to the data here presented; these may usually be found in the legislative manual. In 1937 New York passed an alternative county charter law (Chapter 863), the terms of which are clearly outlined in Appendix B of *State and Local Government in New York* (New York State Constitutional Convention Committee, Albany, 1938).

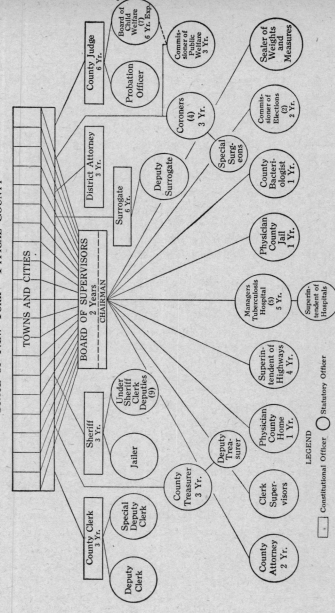

STATE OF NEW YORK — TYPICAL COUNTY

LEGEND

☐ Constitutional Officer   ◯ Statutory Officer

From Third Report of the New York State Commission for the Revision of the Tax Laws, *Depression Taxes and Economy Through Reform of Local Government*, p. 39. Legislative Document (1933) No. 56.

In addition to the county board — however constituted — there is the long list of " row offices," including county clerk, treasurer, auditor, receiver of taxes, the board of assessors; the legal officers, including the public prosecutor, district attorney, or state's attorney, and the public defender, if such exists; the sheriff, coroner, clerks of court, recorder of deeds, superintendent of schools, health officer, and the engineer or surveyor. All these officers are still chosen, in most of the states, by direct vote of the people, as indicated in the chart on page 826 illustrating the prevailing form of county organization. The duties of these several officers are somewhat familiar; no attempt will be made here to describe the duties of the individual officers as they relate to the several functions of local government previously outlined.

Reorganization of County Government. In the last few years many studies have been made of the organization and functioning of county government, the findings of which indicate clearly that some thorough overhauling of the existing machinery is imperative. While most students have come to this conclusion, there is a considerable difference of opinion with regard to the manner in which these necessary changes should be made. Without any extensive discussion of the merits and defects of the several plans, the plans themselves are outlined here.

1. *Making the Prevailing System Work Better.* The first possibility is to leave the machinery in substantially its present form, illustrated by the chart on page 826, relying upon the selection of a better type of county officeholder and upon the stimulation of a more active and intelligent interest on the part of citizens in their county government to bring about the desired results. This seems to be far from the most desirable of the alternatives available, but it is much better than nothing and there are a few cases in which it has actually been made to work. Thus in New Castle County, Delaware, the county officers have for some time been of a higher type and the work has been done in a very creditable fashion. Reports issued by some of the officers in this county are better prepared than those issued by many state departments.

2. *County President Form.* The second method of reconstructing county government, involving major changes in the organization of offices and functions, appeals strongly to those who regard the county unit as a miniature reproduction of the states. Just as in the states responsibility has been centralized by the administrative code plan, so, it is argued, administrative responsibility in the

COUNTY ORGANIZATION — PLAN A: COUNTY PRESIDENT FORM

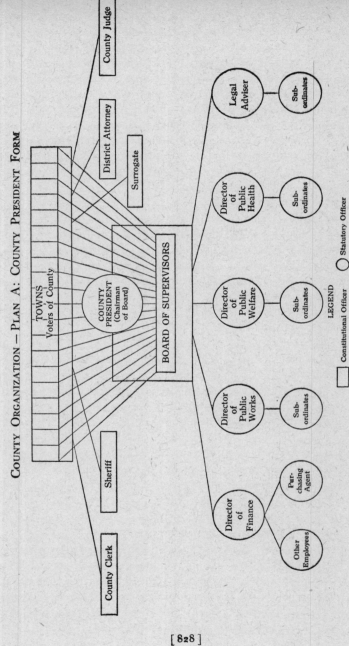

From *Depression Taxes and Economy Through Reform of Local Government,* p. 45.

counties can be centralized by the use of the same or similar methods. If this plan is adopted the resulting organization is likely to resemble that shown in the chart on page 828, which presents a graphic illustration of the county president form of county government reorganization. Here are many of the same officers and the same functions of government which were noted in the preceding chart; but the principle of the short ballot has been introduced, and the centralization of administrative responsibility secured by making all but three or four of the officers appointed by and responsible to a small, popularly elected board of county commissioners which will determine policy and supervise administration. In those cases where an advisory board seems essential to the performance of a particular service, the members of this board are selected by the county commissioners or the board of supervisors, who in turn select an executive officer. Thus the county superintendent of schools is chosen by and is responsible to a school board which has been selected by the board of county commissioners. This system makes it easier to secure efficient administration of county functions without modifying in any important respect the nature of those functions.

3. *The County Manager.* Just as the county president form of county reorganization emphasizes the points of similarity between the counties and the states, so the county manager emphasizes points of similarity between the counties and the cities. Most students of municipal government have a high regard for the city manager plan. If this is the best method of organization for the machinery of municipal government — and the problems of counties are in many respects similar to those of cities — then it follows that the county manager form may be the most desirable form of county government organization. In the operation of this plan the citizens of the county would elect a board of county commissioners, who in turn would select a properly trained and properly qualified individual, preferably from outside, to serve in the capacity of county manager. The established offices in the county government need to be somewhat revised, but when this has been done the manager will be authorized to select the heads of the several administrative agencies thus created. The proponents of this plan argue for it that it is more efficient and more businesslike and that it will more completely eliminate partisan politics from county government than the second form of organization discussed above. This form is illustrated in the chart on page 830.

County Organization — Plan B: County Manager Plan

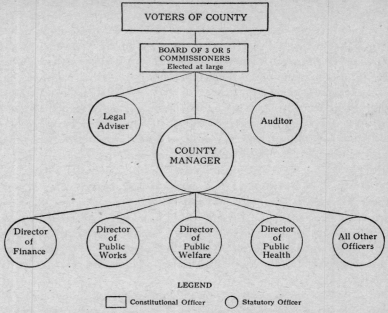

From *Depression Taxes and Economy Through Reform of Local Government*, p. 49.

This form has made relatively slow progress. In 1940, there were only seven real county manager counties; by 1945, this number had increased to eleven, distributed in six states.

County Manager Counties — 1945

State	County Manager Counties
California	Los Angeles and Sacramento
Montana	Petroleum
North Carolina	Durham and Guilford
New York	Monroe
Tennessee	Hamilton
Virginia	Albemarle, Arlington, Henrico, and Warwick

In addition, a number of counties — several in North Carolina and Virginia — had adopted various hybrid forms, lacking essential characteristics of real manager government. In a few cases like San Mateo County, California, a manager form has been adopted and later abandoned. It seems likely that the movement may make more rapid progress in the postwar years.

4. *The County Executive Plan.* The fourth form, illustrated by the chart on page 832, represents a modification of the county manager plan. It is in the main a concession to those who object to the idea of a " manager " and who fear lest the people in their local communities lose their powers of self-government. The fears may be foolish and unfounded, but they are none the less real, and may justify some concessions in the interests of getting a plan of this character accepted by the voters. The difference is more than one of terminology; this plan, which resembles somewhat the strong mayor and council form of municipal government, has found acceptance in certain counties in North Carolina and Virginia — two states which have made notable progress in the improvement of county government. Under this plan the county executive is selected by the board of supervisors and holds office during its pleasure. Like the manager under the county manager type of organization, he selects the officers who serve as heads of the various departments, and like the manager, he is responsible for their performance of their duties. This type of county organization differs from the county president type in that the county executive is selected by the board of supervisors, whereas the county president is chairman of the board.

5. *County Consolidation and County Costs.* Another group believes that the counties are much too small to serve effectively as administrative units under modern conditions. They feel that if the counties are to be retained at all, they should be kept merely as local administrative subdivisions within new and larger districts to be provided for in a thorough reorganization of the existing units of local government. If anyone had had the temerity to propose such a thing as this ten years ago, he would have been laughed out of court. Today, however, this proposal is receiving consideration. Senator George Woodward of Philadelphia has urged the adoption of such a plan of county consolidation in Pennsylvania. In the 1933 and 1934 sessions of the New Jersey legislature a bill was introduced to provide for the grouping of the twenty-one counties of the state into five administrative districts. While the bill was not passed, it received serious consideration and favorable comment. Certain newspapers have made studies of this problem in other states and have recommended plans of action to their readers.

There is much to be said in favor of county consolidation, even

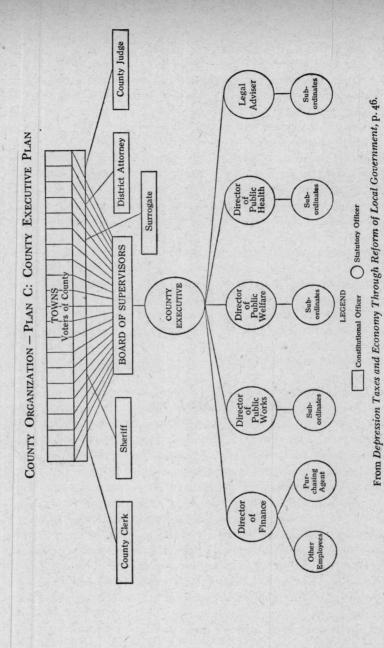

COUNTY ORGANIZATION – PLAN C: COUNTY EXECUTIVE PLAN

TOWNS
Voters of County

County Clerk

Sheriff

BOARD OF SUPERVISORS

Surrogate

District Attorney

County Judge

COUNTY EXECUTIVE

Director of Finance

Director of Public Works

Director of Public Welfare

Director of Public Health

Legal Adviser

Purchasing Agent

Other Employees

Subordinates

Subordinates

Subordinates

Subordinates

LEGEND

☐ Constitutional Officer   ◯ Statutory Officer

From Depression Taxes and Economy Through Reform of Local Government, p. 46.

[832]

though the movement has not made very extensive progress to date.[13] Proposals of this nature are being presented from time to time, from various sources, and occasionally one of them succeeds. Tennessee has had some success with consolidation, and in 1944 two counties in South Dakota were combined by legislative act. In sparsely settled areas, some counties have found it best to revert to an unorganized status and have the state or adjoining counties administer the few necessary services.

The table on page 834 presents some information on the per capita costs of county government; it appears that these costs are highest in the smallest counties, and usually lowest in those of medium size. There are a few cases in which all per capita costs are unreasonably low, indicating either that, in those states, the county is a unit of minor importance or that it does not render the services which are rendered by the counties of other states. It has been suggested that a population of at least 30,000 to 35,000 is needed for maximum service at minimum cost. Three fourths of the counties in the United States fail to meet this standard; thus consolidation may help to solve the problems of many counties.

6. *Home Rule and Optional Charter Plans.* Finally, there is the possibility of adopting, with regard to the counties, a policy of home rule somewhat resembling that used in some states in connection with cities. For this purpose there might be a general law providing for a certain amount of local autonomy, as recommended in the Model State Constitution; the counties might be specifically authorized to frame their own charters, or an optional charter plan might be used. These proposals have in their favor the usual arguments for local self-government. To offset these are the questions as to whether or not the residents of most counties have a sufficient interest in or knowledge of the problems of their counties to enable them to make these decisions wisely. For a time at least it might be preferable for the legislature to assume the initiative and take the responsibility for the reconstruction of county government.

There are many constitutional, statutory, and judicial barriers in the path of counties wishing to adopt the manager form of government — or for that matter, any of the other newer forms of county organization. In the table which follows, prepared by the National

[13] Bromage, *op cit.,* Chapter 8; also Hansen, George H., *A Regional Redistricting Plan for the State of Utah* (Brigham Young University Press, 1937); University of Denver, *County Reorganization* (Denver, 1940); Shannon, J. B., " County Consolidation," *Annals,* January, 1940, pp. 168–175; and Russell, John C., " State Regionalism in New Mexico," *Social Forces,* December, 1937, pp. 268–271.

State	Number of Counties	Average Area in Square Miles	Average Population	Average per Capita Cost of County Government			
				Population below 5,000	Population 5,000 to 25,000	Population 25,000 to 50,000	Population 50,000 to 100,000
Alabama	67	765.3	39,496.2	....	$11.24	$10.59	$17.51
Arizona	14	8,129.2	31,112.3	....	27.17	30.59	26.94
Arkansas	75	700.3	24,726.4	....	6.29	5.50	7.43
California	57	1,994.0	97,883.6	$63.56	41.59	36.65	36.55
Colorado	62	1,645.4	16,441.1	37.94	20.33	18.08	15.24
Connecticut	8	602.5	400,862.8	....	....	1.59	1.39
Delaware	3	655.0	79,460.0	....	....	11.97	....
Florida	67	818.8	21,913.6	30.31	19.50	17.76	19.56
Georgia	161	369.9	18,229.5	6.09	4.63	4.03	7.22
Idaho	44	1,894.4	10,114.3	27.62	17.20	13.90	....
Illinois	102	549.4	74,810.3	....	7.62	7.84	7.61
Indiana	92	391.7	35,201.1	16.01	11.65	10.49	8.21
Iowa	99	561.4	24,958.8	....	37.63	27.28	22.34
Kansas	105	778.6	17,914.2	....	....	....	....
Kentucky	120	334.8	21,788.2	5.96	4.28	3.54	5.14
Louisiana	64	709.5	32,837.3	....	3.60	2.88	4.12
Maine	16	1,868.4	49,838.9	....	3.60	2.99	2.25
Maryland	23	414.2	35,941.3	....	19.72	30.93	20.92
Massachusetts	13	574.2	303,543.8	5.90	....	5.76	4.80
Michigan	83	692.5	58,341.2	25.32	16.25	16.45	18.41
Minnesota	87	929.4	29,470.7	43.59	14.55	13.02	9.72
Mississippi	82	565.3	24,510.0	....	1.19	11.59	14.78
Missouri	114	602.3	24,626.3	....	....	....	....
Montana	56	2,609.4	9,600.1	27.62	20.59	16.97	13.39
Nebraska	93	825.8	14,816.8	16.63	15.02	11.12	....
Nevada	17	6,527.8	5,356.3	55.59	38.23	35.05	....
New Hampshire	10	903.1	46,529.3	....	6.97	5.36	3.28
New Jersey	21	357.8	192,444.9	....	....	27.48	13.21
New Mexico	31	3,951.7	13,655.3	8.49	5.52	5.41	....
New York	57	768.6	186,904.2	74.31	29.34	19.75	16.63
North Carolina	100	487.4	31,702.7	....	13.75	14.25	14.99
North Dakota	53	1,324.2	12,846.1	12.52	12.83	12.89	....
Ohio	88	462.9	75,536.1	....	14.95	12.86	10.96
Oklahoma	77	901.4	31,117.4	....	10.03	9.29	9.59
Oregon	36	2,655.7	26,494.0	32.21	18.31	17.72	14.88
Pennsylvania	66	669.1	143,751.4	....	4.70	6.26	6.28
Rhode Island	5	213.4	137,499.4	....	....	....	....
South Carolina	46	662.9	37,799.2	....	4.66	4.75	5.85
South Dakota	64	1,114.0	10,041.2	22.53	15.29	10.52	10.57
Tennessee	95	438.8	27,542.6	15.77	* 13.06	12.42	11.59
Texas	254	1,003.0	22,931.9	21.87	9.25	6.75	9.92
Utah	29	2,833.9	17,511.9	10.03	9.72	8.65	6.36
Vermont	14	651.7	25,686.5	.25	.16	.37	....
Virginia	100	401.2	17,188.9	17.59	13.91	16.95	12.90
Washington	39	1,713.7	40,087.1	....	....	....	....
West Virginia	55	436.7	31,440.0	....	10.35	10.47	9.36
Wisconsin	71	778.2	41,549.3	21.76	26.49	22.91	17.44
Wyoming	23	4,241.2	9,807.1	22.58	20.31	15.01	....
	3,058						

[14] Column one is taken from Anderson, *op. cit.*, p. 11; the others are taken from Manning, John W., " The County in the United States," *Southwest Review*, Spring, 1935, pp. 303–318.

Municipal League, information is given regarding the progress that has been made to date in a dozen states, in overcoming these barriers.

PROGRESS IN COUNTY STRUCTURAL REORGANIZATION [15]

State	Date	Summary of Constitutional Amendments and Statutes
California	1911	Home rule amendment authorized elected board of freeholders of fifteen members to draft charter for submission to people and ratification by legislature.
	1936	Amendment authorized county legislative body, as alternative, to propose new charter for people's approval.
Maryland	1915	Home rule amendment authorized elected charter board of five members to draft charter for submission to people; contains some restrictions as to elective officers.
Louisiana	1921	Amendment required legislature to provide optional plans of parochial (county) government.
	1924	Legislature provided for the commission form of government as an optional plan.
Georgia	1922	Legislature authorized executives for the county commissioners of roads and revenues.
Montana	1922	Amendment authorized legislature to provide " any plan, kind, manner, or form of municipal government for counties," subject to approval of electors " in the territory affected."
	1931	Legislature adopted optional county manager law.
North Carolina	1927	By statute, legislature authorized counties to adopt manager plan or variety of modified versions.
Virginia	1928	Amendment authorized legislature to provide complete optional forms of county organization.
	1930	Special act of legislature authorized Arlington County to adopt manager plan.
	1932	Legislature provided two optional plans — one, based upon the model county manager law, in which appointed manager appoints subordinates, and another in which legislative body makes all appointments upon recommendations of the manager.
Texas	1933	Home rule amendment authorized counties of 62,000 or more population to frame own charters

[15] From National Municipal League, *The County Manager Plan*, pp. 20–22 (New York, 1945).

State	Date	Summary of Constitutional Amendments and Statutes
		and smaller counties to do so with approval of two-thirds vote of state legislature. Any proposed charter change must receive a majority affirmative vote not only in whole county but also in both incorporated and unincorporated areas counted separately.
Ohio	1933	Home rule amendment authorized counties to draft own charters and adopt by popular vote; also authorized legislature to provide optional alternative forms of county government. Legislature has not yet acted.
New York	1921	Constitutional amendment authorized the legislature to provide Westchester and Nassau Counties with special forms of county government with voters' approval.
	1935	Legislature authorized a series of optional forms of county government providing restricted changes.
	1935	Amendment required legislature to provide alternative forms of county government. Amended in 1938 to provide for cases in which a transfer of functions between municipalities and the county is involved.
	1935	Legislature provided two alternative forms of government.
	1936	Legislature provided five more alternatives.
	1937	Legislature provided nine more alternatives, including permission for counties to draft charters incorporating any combination of provisions in various laws.
North Dakota	1940	Amendment required legislature to provide optional forms of county government with approval of 55 per cent of the voters required for adoption.
	1941	Legislature provided " county manager form " or " short form of county managership " may be initiated by 35 per cent of voters or majority of county board and must be approved by 55 per cent affirmative popular vote; legislature also provided " consolidated office form " reducing offices and making auditor chief administrative officer.
Oregon	1944	Amendment permitted legislature to designate county manager and county executive plans as alternative forms of county government subject to local approval.
Missouri	1945	New Constitution provides for county home rule, as well as for county consolidation or dissolution.

Importance and Growth of Cities. For centuries cities have been the centers of learning and culture. Every great advance in the arts and sciences has come from cities — in fact, it is no exaggeration to say that the greatness of a nation may be measured by the number, the size, and the development of its municipalities. The growth of cities in the United States during the last century and a half has been phenomenal. In 1790 Philadelphia was the largest city in the country, with a population of less than 60,000. By the census of 1940, New York, our largest city, had a population of about 7,000,000. So great has been the trend of urban development that since 1920, according to Census Bureau classifications, considerably more than half of our people have lived in urban communities.

In 1790 there were only six places in the United States with populations of 8,000 or over, and only two with 25,000 or more. The entire urban population, comprising all persons living in cities and incorporated villages of 2,500 or more, formed 5.1 per cent of the total population. By 1850 there were sixty-two places of 10,000 or more inhabitants, containing 11.3 per cent of the total population. By 1900 this percentage had risen to 31.7 per cent of the total population; by 1940, to 56.5 per cent, distributed according to a United States Bureau of the Census classification as indicated in the following table:

CLASSIFICATION OF CITIES ACCORDING TO SIZE — 1943

Group	Population Range	Number of Cities
I	Over 1,000,000	5
II	From 500,000 to 1,000,000	9
III	From 250,000 to 500,000	23
IV	From 100,000 to 250,000	55
V	From 50,000 to 100,000	105
VI	From 25,000 to 50,000	200
	Total	397

In 1940 there were 1,077 communities with a population of 10,000 or over. While many may not regard a community of this size as a city, the Bureau of the Census classifies as urban, communities of 2,500 or more. Such places may still serve as the center of a large and important trading and business area. The returns from the 1940 census showed a trend away from the big cities, with the exception of New York; but a continuance of the trend toward urbanism. People were moving before the war, from both the country and the large cities, to small towns and cities, to satellite cities and suburban communities; what permanent effects the dislocations of population caused by the war will have in the postwar years have yet to be disclosed.

There are a number of important reasons for this extensive development of urban communities. Not the least significant reason has been those developments in the science of agriculture which have made possible the large-scale production of necessary commodities. Without these developments, without the introduction of agricultural machinery on a large scale, a considerable percentage of those who now dwell in urban districts would be required on farms to produce necessary articles of food and clothing. In this country about 30 per cent of the people produce the nation's food supply, and there is still a large surplus to be disposed of by export or otherwise. As an emergency measure, the Agricultural Adjustment Administration found it necessary during the depression to adopt artificial methods of crop reduction. While these methods had to be abandoned, due to adverse court decisions, others of similar purpose have taken their place.

Another important factor in the growth of cities is to be found in the industrial changes growing out of the Industrial Revolution. Manufactured goods are no longer produced by hand at home for sale in the immediate community; they are produced by machinery in factories for distribution in a market often worldwide. Industry has located in those places where there was an adequate supply of labor and of power. It has settled in the cities because there it could secure better transportation, a more elastic labor supply, and large markets close at hand. The improvements and development of methods of transportation have encouraged commerce, to which nearly every great city owes its eminence. For the most part, urban workers have been able to secure a higher rate of compensation than has been possible in rural districts.

Another factor which has contributed greatly to urban growth has been the attractiveness of urban life. Man is supposed to be a gregarious animal; in addition, there are many other ways in which urban life offers opportunities which have, until very recently at least, been denied to the residents of rural districts. Among these are opportunities for recreation, education, medical and hospital care, and the many comforts enjoyed by residents of urban homes and apartments — electric lights, electric refrigeration, sanitary equipment, et cetera. It is of course true that the rural home is by no means as uncomfortable or as isolated as it was a few years ago. The extension of electric power lines and of the telephone, the construction of modern highways, the distribution of automobiles, labor-saving machinery for the home, and the radio have changed all this, and may in the future accentuate the trend away from the larger cities already under way.

Forms of Municipal Government. The discussion of municipalities has thus far been concerned with the importance of cities, their growth, and the causes of their growth. We now turn to problems connected with the organization of the various forms of municipal government. Of these there are four: the weak mayor and council plan, the strong mayor and council plan, the commission form, and the manager form. In the paragraphs which follow a brief statement will be made regarding the fundamental characteristics of each of these types.

1. *Weak Mayor and Council Form.* This form of municipal organization was the first widely used in the United States. It represented an attempt to adapt the complicated machinery of the Federal government to the governmental needs of small, compact, densely populated areas. The effort was a total failure. The form of the Federal government was devised for the purpose of controlling the public affairs of a people widely scattered over a considerable area; when the attempt was made to adapt it to the needs of even a large population in a small and compact area, the powers of government were divided into so many small segments and distributed among so many people that it became an utter impossibility for even the most conscientious and well-intentioned citizen to keep track of them. There was a mayor, but he had little real power, his duties being largely of a ceremonial nature. The legislative branch consisted of two chambers, a common council and a select council. In Philadelphia, for instance, the select council consisted of fifty members, while the common council had 150. Someone has observed that the common council was common in more than one sense of the word. At any rate, here was a legislative body for a single municipality, containing approximately 200 members. In addition, there was, of course, the judicial system, which in many communities has not been substantially changed down to the present time. It was this form of municipal government which existed throughout the country at the time Bryce penned his memorable indictment. It was under this form that there developed the famous Tweed Ring in New York, the Gas Ring

in Philadelphia, and similar rings of one sort or another in cities throughout the country.

2. *Strong Mayor and Council Form.* Out of the indictment of our municipal institutions contained in the writings of the muckrakers and the studies of an earnest group which began to analyze scientifically the problems of municipal government and administration, there gradually developed a demand for the improvement of the generally prevailing conditions in city government. The first attempts at reorganization took the form of what is now known as the strong mayor and council type. In this new plan the mayor became something more than a figurehead; he was authorized to appoint the heads of the administrative departments, who constituted an advisory board frequently called the cabinet, the members of which were directly responsible to the mayor. It thus became possible for the mayor to be in fact as well as in theory the head of the administration.

The changes made in the legislative branch of the city government were quite as striking and quite as important. The old cumbersome bicameral council was abolished and a small compact unicameral chamber substituted therefor. These new councils often had seven, nine, or eleven members; the larger ones now existing include those of Chicago with fifty aldermen, Cleveland with thirty-three, Minneapolis with twenty-six, Milwaukee with twenty-five, and Boston and Philadelphia with twenty-two each. For years New York City had the largest board of aldermen, with seventy-two members, but by the new charter in 1937 this number was reduced by more than half. The judicial branch of the government remained unchanged, at least so far as this particular form of reorganization was concerned. Where the mayor and council form of municipal organization is still in use, it is the form here discussed, for the old weak mayor and council form has practically passed out of existence.

3. *Commission Form.* Not all the efforts at improving the institutions of municipal government stopped with a modification of the existing form; some of them attempted to devise new types of organization, based upon principles which were at the time new and untried. One of these, the commission form, owed its origin to the occurrence of a great natural catastrophe — a tidal wave which swept over and largely destroyed Galveston in 1900, causing the death of 6,000 persons and a property damage of more than $17,000,000. As soon as the extent of the damage could be estimated the survivors determined to rebuild their city. They planned to construct a sea

wall of sufficient size and strength to prevent the recurrence of such a calamity. They turned to the Deepwater Committee, an organization of businessmen which had previously been formed to secure the improvement of the harbor, to undertake the planning and rebuilding of the city.

When these men had brought their work near to completion, they issued a statement in which they reminded the citizens that plans should be made to provide for the government of the reconstructed city, and suggested a group of five commissioners. This Committee had done its work honestly and efficiently. It had expended millions of dollars in the reconstruction of a city without any suggestion of graft, fraud, or corruption. Why, it was asked, could not a similar group of men govern the new city? The people liked the idea. They remembered the political stench that had emanated from the old city hall, and they resolved, if possible, to prevent a recurrence in their new city of the conditions which had existed in the old. They secured from the legislature approval of the new charter. Although a somewhat similar device had been tried years before in Sacramento and New Orleans, Galveston became the first commission-governed city to attract wide public attention.

It remained, however, for Des Moines to popularize and publicize commission government. Some time later a Board of Freeholders in Des Moines studied the Galveston plan and drew up a charter embodying its principal features, but incorporating safeguards against arbitrary action, feared under the Galveston plan. This new charter attracted wide attention; within the next few years the commission form of municipal government had spread to 200 or 300 different communities in various parts of the country. In practice this form of municipal organization developed two striking and significant weaknesses. In the first place, there was no centralization of responsibility; if something remained undone that should have been done or if something was done badly, it became a habit for each member of the commission to lay the blame on someone else. In the second place, it rarely happened that persons elected to membership in the commission were willing to serve as the heads of those executive departments concerning whose work they were best informed and for the direction of which they were best qualified.[16]

[16] For a brief summary of this development and appropriate references, see Kneier, Charles M., *City Government in the United States*, Third Edition, Chapter 22 (Harper, New York, 1945) ; *The Des Moines Plan of Commission Government* (City of Des Moines, 1939) .

4. *City Manager Form.* During the period in which municipalities were groping for better and more effective methods of organization, the little city of Staunton, Virginia, more or less by accident evolved the precedents upon which the city manager form is based. It happened that some repairs were needed in connection with the local water supply system; the city council authorized advertising for bids. The project was not a large one and should not have been either difficult or expensive, but the bids were unreasonably high. One of the members of the council discussed the project and the bids with a friend, Charles E. Ashburner, who was serving at the time as a maintenance engineer for the Chesapeake and Ohio Railroad. Mr. Ashburner studied the project and offered to perform the work for $737. He was given the contract, and actually did the work for $736, according to one version, for $712 according to another. This incident, relatively unimportant in itself, raised a question in the minds of some of the councilmen as to whether or not similar savings would not be possible in a considerable number of cases if more businesslike methods were applied to their management. Mr. Ashburner was finally persuaded to become a sort of business manager for the city of Staunton, in which position he served for about two years, giving up the position in disgust because of the extent to which his activities were hampered by political considerations. Shortly thereafter he was engaged in a similar capacity by the city of Norfolk, where he remained for several years. This man, creator of a new profession, is serving today as manager of a city in California, at a salary equal to that paid to the governor of the wealthiest and most populous state in the Union.[17]

In 1913 the city of Dayton chose a Board of Freeholders, the chairman of which was a farsighted and public-spirited citizen by the name of James M. Cox. The members of the Board took a trip to Staunton to study the organization and the functioning of the new plan; they returned to their homes to prepare a charter providing for a city manager for Dayton, the first sizable community in which the plan was tried. The spread of this new idea was extremely rapid, city manager governments being set up in cities and towns in all

[17] White, Leonard D., *The City Manager*, pp. 90–97 (University of Chicago Press, 1927) ; Kneier, *op. cit.*, Chapter 23. The Committee on Public Administration of the Social Science Research Council completed in 1940 an extensive survey of a quarter century of city manager government; see *City Manager Government in the United States; City Manager Government in Nine Cities;* and *City Manager Government in Seven Cities* (all published by Public Administration Service, Chicago, 1940) .

sections of the United States within a short time. The extension of the movement has continued until there are at present more than 500 cities, towns, and boroughs living under this form. It has been adapted to the needs of counties, and a number of states have made its adoption by these units optional.

The spread of the city manager plan indicates an increasing realization on the part of the public of the need for trained, professional service in government. Authorities in municipal government have estimated that more than 90 per cent of the work of a municipal executive consists in the performance of duties similar to those of executives in private business: the letting of contracts for goods and equipment and for construction work, the inspection and acceptance of goods received and of work done under contracts, the keeping of proper records, and the hiring, promoting, dismissing, and retirement of personnel. When an executive is chosen in private business, it is customary to select someone whose training and experience give some reasonable basis for hoping that he will be able to do the work successfully.

The city manager plan is an attempt to apply this same principle in the conduct of the public business. Under this plan it is possible to select a municipal executive on the basis of his qualifications and experience, rather than, as has been customary in this country, upon the basis of his ability to secure votes — his ability to call people by their first names, to smile pleasantly, shake hands in a friendly fashion, to notice babies, and to make more or less ambiguous speeches. Where the city manager plan works best, the occupant of this office is a man who has made a special study of public administration and who, beginning with positions of minor importance, has gradually been promoted to more responsible positions as his experience and ability warranted. He is preferably a man from outside, and therefore free from entanglement in the local political disputes of the past. City managership is a profession requiring personal qualifications of a high order. The city manager is neither a dictator nor a boss; if successful, he must have courage, poise, and tact in dealing with people. The criticism that the city manager plan is undemocratic has developed chiefly in communities where the manager was deficient in these essential qualifications.

Municipal Home Rule. To the student of state government the subject of home rule for cities is a problem of special interest. In an earlier chapter dealing with the legislature, mention was made of the extent to which cities were originally under the domination of the state legislatures. The cities owed their existence to legislative enactments, and were therefore subject to the legislative will with regard to even the most minute details of their administration. As the size and complexity of municipal problems increased, it was obviously impossible for the legislatures to perform these duties well. The size of the undertaking was appalling, even if the législators had always been, as they were not, free from the desire to gain political advantage at the expense of the cities. These conditions led to a widespread discontent, and to the organization of a movement for the establishment of municipal home rule.

The movement for home rule evolved gradually through a series of experimental stages. The first of these was the amendment to the Constitution of Ohio adopted in 1897, requiring that the legislature group the cities of the state into not more than seven classes on the basis of population. This provision proved to be quite inadequate, for the number of classes permitted was so large that the legislature was able to adjust the population limits in such manner as to include only one city in each of the first five classes, the remainder of the cities being grouped in classes six and seven. It was thus possible for the legislature to continue its domination of local affairs in all the larger communities. One act, for instance, provided for the paving of certain blocks of " Euclid Avenue in all cities of the first class." This classification plan, with a smaller number of classes, is now in effect in the majority of states having any considerable number of urban communities.

New York adopted another plan which has been quite effective in operation from the point of view of protecting the right of communities to control their own affairs, but it is a plan which has not, strangely enough, been copied in other jurisdictions. This plan provides that in those cases where the legislature adopts provisions purely local in character, the provisions shall not, even though properly passed by both houses and signed by the governor, be effective in the cities to which they apply unless, within a period of thirty days thereafter, the mayor of the city affected shall have given his consent. The author, having observed this law in operation in some New York municipalities, can testify to its effectiveness. The next step in the development of the movement for home rule also originated in New York. This was the optional charter plan, under which the legislature drew up model charters for each of the more common types of municipal government. Communities which were dissatisfied with their existing system were authorized to vote on the question of charter revision, and to choose a board of freeholders which would study the problems of the municipal government and select one of the optional charters contained in the act to be submitted to the electorate with its recommendation for adoption. Thus the communities were permitted to determine, in a general way, the form and the structure of their local government organization.

By 1915 the movement for municipal home rule had developed to the point where fifteen states had adopted constitutional amendments providing for home rule. As of that date, the late Professor Howard Lee McBain of Columbia University made a careful study. It was evidently his belief, as it certainly was that of many others, that this movement for constitutional home rule would spread rapidly through the remainder of the states, so that in the future the right of cities to determine the form of the government under which they lived would no longer be questioned. In 1933 Professor Joseph D. McGoldrick of the same institution brought the story down to 1930. During this period of fifteen years only one additional state had adopted a home rule amendment.[18]

It is thus evident that the movement had been sharply arrested. It is possible that the entry of the United States into World War I and the concentration of our attention upon international problems generally had something to do with this, but it is necessary to look elsewhere for a satisfactory explanation of the reasons why it has not since been resumed.

Metropolitan Areas. A metropolitan area or district is not — necessarily, at least — a political unit, but rather an area including all the thickly populated territory in and around a city or group of cities. The Bureau of the Census has set up for its use a metropolitan district in connection with each city of 50,000 or more inhabitants, two or more such cities sometimes being in one district. On this basis there were in 1940 approximately 63,000,000 people, or nearly half of the total population, living in 140 metropolitan areas.

Undoubtedly the most important reason for the apparent loss of interest in the home rule movement is found in the development of these areas. The urbanization movement had so increased the size of many cities that they had spread out far beyond the geographical boundaries indicated on the map. They had, regardless of county, city, borough, township, and even state lines, developed economic

[18] McBain, Howard L., *Law and Practice of Municipal Home Rule* (Columbia University Press, 1916); McGoldrick, Joseph D., *Law and Practice of Municipal Home Rule, 1916–1930* (Columbia University Press, 1933); and a series of articles on home rule in individual states in *National Municipal Review,* in 1932.

and social units centering around the originally small urban development. The need for the coordination of the essential municipal services maintained by these different units of government became more and more obvious. Where such coordination was lacking, everyone suffered loss and inconvenience. Under these circumstances many of the larger cities undertook extensive programs of metropolitan or regional planning, in which, regardless of political boundaries, the economic and social interests of the area were considered as a whole.

If progress was to be made in the solution of problems of transportation, light, power, gas, water, police, highways, sewage disposal, et cetera, it was necessary that these political barriers should be broken down or at least prevented from serious interference with service. Professor Munro in 1923 pointed out four specific ways in which this might be done: by the creation of a municipal federalism; by the outright annexation of encircling municipalities; by a compromise between these two methods, such as was developed in the city of Greater New York with its five boroughs; and by the development of cooperation between the various political units.[19] Progress has been made in many cities along one or another of these lines.

Professor Merriam suggested, as a solution of this problem, the establishment of city-states, the boundaries of which would completely ignore existing political subdivisions. Thus the city of New York would be completely separated from the up-state region, and would include as well the southwestern portion of Connecticut and the northern counties of New Jersey. The Philadelphia unit would include not only the six counties in southeastern Pennsylvania, but certain portions of southern New Jersey, including the city of Camden and its surrounding territory, and all or part of Delaware, including the city of Wilmington. The relentless logic of this proposal is inescapable; if there were no existing machinery for purposes of local government, it is not unlikely that some such plan would be adopted. Under the existing circumstances, however, it does not seem likely that much progress will be made in securing the important

[19] Munro, William Bennett, *Municipal Government and Administration,* Vol. I, p. 438 (Macmillan, New York, 1923). On other methods here mentioned, see Pinchbeck, Raymond B., " City-County Separation in Virginia," *National Municipal Review,* July, 1940, pp. 467–472; McDiarmid, John, " Los Angeles Attacks the Metropolitan Problem," *ibid.,* pp. 459–466, 508; Combs, William H., " City-County Separation and Consolidation in Tennessee," *Tennessee Law Review,* February, 1940, pp. 217–228; and Jones, Victor, " Politics of Integration in Metropolitan Areas," *Annals,* January, 1940, pp. 161–167.

constitutional changes that would be necessary in order to make this proposal effective, nor does it seem likely that the inhabitants of the several states concerned could be induced to consent to such sweeping changes in the forms and units of government to which they have become accustomed.

So little has actually been accomplished by these various methods that some attention has been given to the possibility of finding others. If consolidation or annexation cannot be accomplished, city-county separation may be a possibility. Virginia has tried this, apparently with some success. The state might take over many of the services now performed by the cities; this would relieve the cities of the financial burden involved and would be in accordance with recent tendencies to administer many functions through larger units of government. Functional consolidation among the units themselves is also a possibility. Some degree of control over the administration of certain services might be maintained by the use of state subsidies or by a system of state-collected, locally shared taxes. At present it seems more likely that progress in the field of city-state relations will be made by these means than by those earlier attempted.

Municipal Administration. Because of the limitations of space it is impossible to do more than merely suggest the nature of the more important problems of municipal administration. Books have been written on the subject — indeed, upon the individual administrative problems involved. While the Federal laws permitted unrestricted immigration, the cities had the difficult problem of assimilating the foreign-born. Now, after a number of years of either restricted immigration or no immigration at all, the problem has become more a question of providing clean, attractive, and sanitary housing facilities to replace the poorly built, congested, and unsanitary tenements which breed disease, increase fire hazards, and menace the physical and moral well-being of their inhabitants.

Under the heading of public safety are grouped both the fire and police services. The problems of fire prevention and fire fighting are quite different from those of rural districts, as are the standards of service required. With regard to crime, the statistics show that the cities contribute at least three times their proportionate quota to the crime record. Criminals have extended the field of their operations, reaching out into adjacent rural territories and making necessary the intervention of state and Federal authorities in the effort to combat kidnaping, racketeering, banditry, et cetera. Even so, crimes against property are relatively more numerous in urban communities; this is not true of crimes against persons.

In the field of public health the municipal authorities perform a great many services which in less densely populated districts are performed either directly by state authorities, or by the local authorities under a closer supervision by the state than is commonly exercised over municipalities. The density of population so increases the danger of contagion that in cities individuals cannot be left to handle their own health problems. Thus there is an infinite variety of inspections for medical and sanitary purposes, quarantines, and sanitary requirements. Such scientific knowledge and administrative techniques in public health are now available as to make many communicable diseases definitely controllable; epidemics of these diseases are inexcusable. The organization and administration of this service is one of the most important municipal functions.

It has long been known that the extremes of wealth and poverty are found in the cities. The untold suffering which developed in the cities during the depression served to emphasize this fact and to encourage constructive measures to prevent a recurrence of these conditions. In any program of national planning designed to decentralize industry and to distribute the opportunity for labor and income, the cities will have a most important part. Americans have built a great industrial civilization; the experience of the years during and since the depression has clearly shown that in many respects it must be rebuilt. Since cities have in the past been the centers of the industrial life of the nation, they will in the process of rebuilding be most affected.

The problem of transportation has been and still is of outstanding importance. In the past we have been concerned chiefly with the provision and operation of transit facilities which would carry people quickly and cheaply to and from their homes in the residential districts and the suburbs and their offices and places of business. If in the process of rebuilding our cities, we succeed in decentralizing to some extent our industrial and commercial life, the problem of transportation will be somewhat different. The peak loads which now exist in the morning and evening hours will diminish. People will be able to walk to their places of employment, and traffic will be more evenly distributed throughout the day. Those in charge of transportation facilities will be concerned with the planning of traffic routes for passenger vehicles, trucks, and busses. By-passes around congested areas and super-highways through them will become more and more common. Important in connection with the general problem of transportation are questions of street maintenance and repair.

Many of the important administrative activities of cities may be included under the general heading of public works, such as the construction and maintenance of public buildings, playgrounds, parks, et cetera; the operation of gas and electric plants and water supply systems, where these services are city-owned and city-operated; and provisions for disposition of garbage, sewage, ashes, and other refuse materials. In a large city each of these types of work is a major problem in itself, and in addition to these there are many other things which would seem to be of minor importance yet which often have significant consequences. Take, for instance, such a problem as street lighting. This would not seem difficult to solve, nor would one expect that a failure to solve it properly would do more than cause some slight annoyance and inconvenience to citizens. During World War I however, one midwestern city tried the experiment of turning off the street lights at midnight in order to conserve fuel. The experiment was of short duration, for the city was swept by an unprecedented wave of crimes against property and attacks upon persons. In many cities where, during the depression or World War II, the idea of economy in street lighting was not carried to this extreme, the number and the power of the lights provided were inadequate to give proper protection to citizens and their property.

Some mention must be made of the city's problem of educational administration. It is true that in many communities the administration of schools is separate from the rest of the city government and is under the direction of an independent board of education. The reasons for this are well known, but it is by no means certain that the separation represents sound public policy or that it prevents or minimizes politics in school administration.[20] Whatever the type of administrative control, the city is responsible for the maintenance of the public school system. It must provide suitable buildings, keep them heated, lighted, ventilated, in a sanitary condition, and in repair; it must employ and pay a qualified staff of teachers; it must purchase supplies, equipment, books, and other necessary working materials — all of this at a very great financial cost, most of which is met by the school tax upon real estate. But, as has already been said, the responsibility of the community does not stop here; a large

[20] For a significant study of this problem, see Henry, Nelson B., and Kerwin, Jerome G., *Schools and City Government* (University of Chicago Press, 1938).

portion of the public now has an unprecedented amount of leisure time, some through shorter working hours, some through enforced idleness. This raises the whole question of adult education; it means study courses, special instruction, books, vocational training, et cetera. The response of our cities to this need during the depression was often woefully inadequate; when there were more potential readers than ever before, when there were more vital issues in the field of government, economics, and sociology than in any normal time, and when more was being printed about them, drastic cuts, which have since been only partially restored, were made in budget allotments for books for our school and public libraries, on grounds of economy!

STATE SUPERVISION OF LOCAL GOVERNMENT

In the following chapter the problem of the centralization of authority in the hands of the state government will be considered. Some preliminary consideration should be given here to the problem of state supervision of the functions of local government, especially those which still remain under local control. In this respect, North Carolina, by the adoption of the Local Government Act of 1931, set an example which may well be given serious consideration by other states.[21]

The North Carolina Local Government Commission consists of nine members, including the State Treasurer, the State Auditor, the Secretary of State, the Secretary of Revenue, and five members appointed by the Governor. The four state officials are members ex officio and comprise the executive committee. It is specified that of those appointed by the Governor one shall have had experience as an executive officer of a municipality and one shall have had experience as a member of the governing board of a county at the time of their appointment. The State Treasurer is chairman of the Commission, and is also ex officio Director of Local Government. All actions required or permitted to be taken by the Commission may be taken by the Executive Committee, but the Committee shall not overrule or reverse any action of the Commission as a whole. Appeal may be taken to the whole Commission from action of the Executive

21 This comment is based upon the *Report* of the Local Government Commission (Raleigh, 1934). See also Hoffman, Samuel D., " A State Department of Local Government," *National Municipal Review*, May, 1939, pp. 348–354, and Pinchbeck, Raymond B., " The State Commission on Local Government," *ibid.*, February, 1939, pp. 80–88.

Committee. The Commission is required to meet quarterly and may hold special meetings. The members are allowed expenses for attending meetings, but receive no compensation for their services.

It is the duty of the Commission to approve the issuance of all bonds and notes of local units of government, and to keep record of all such bonds and notes that are issued in order that it may notify each unit thirty days in advance of the maturity of principal and interest of its bonds and notes, as is required by law. All contracts or agreements of local units made with any person or persons for the preparation of proceedings and forms incident to the issuance of bonds and notes, except when such agreements are made with licensed attorneys, must be approved. The Commission must furnish each local unit thirty days in advance of the annual levy of taxes an itemized statement showing the amount of principal and interest maturing in the fiscal year for which such levy is made. It shall also require of local units a report of remittances for the payment of principal and interest on bonds and notes on a form prescribed by them. It has the power to determine whether the sinking funds of local units are being adequately maintained, and to approve all proposed investments of such funds; to supervise bank deposits of local units, to approve all agreements between such units and certified public accountants with respect to audits. It may appoint an administrator to conduct the affairs of a local unit which has defaulted in the payment of principal and interest on its indebtedness.

It is the duty of the Director to visit the local units of government in the State and to advise and assist the governing bodies and other officers of these units in providing a competent, economical, and efficient administration; to suggest improved methods for levying and collecting taxes and other revenues; to suggest such changes in the organization of local units of government as will best promote the public interests, and to render assistance in carrying the same into effect. He is empowered to devise and prepare for use in the local units uniform accounting and recording systems and to require their use. It is his duty under the law to proceed, " as rapidly as possible," with the installation of such uniform records and systems of accounting in each and every local unit.

It was the claim of the Commission that in the early years of its existence it had assembled among its records more correlated information regarding the finances of the local units of government than had been done in any other state. The results of its work appear to have been significant.

From this description it is obvious that the duties of the Commission and its Director relate wholly to matters in the field of financial administration; the several types of such control will be considered more fully in the next chapter. It is desired at this point, however, to make two observations. The first is that the idea underlying the Local Government Commission is fundamentally sound and has in a measure already proved its usefulness. It is possible that this principle might be profitably extended to other fields of local administration by giving the Director power to coordinate the existing activities of those in the several departments in charge of local administration and perhaps, in some cases, to initiate new policies. The administration of specialized services would remain, as it should, under the control of the departments to which they relate, but much could be accomplished by a tactful person in the coordination of functions, and in the development of such guidance and leadership on the part of the state, for its local units, as the Federal government has long provided for the states.

In the second place, the idea conforms to well-established practice in government. National states with outlying territories have long had a colonial secretary in the cabinet. The position of the local units in one of our American states is roughly parallel to that of colonies in their relation to the parent state. If, as is suggested, the authority of the Local Government Commission were extended to other fields than finance, for the purpose of enforcing standards and securing more efficient administration, might it not be a suitable thing to set up in other states a Director of Local Government, after the plan adopted in North Carolina?

SELECTED REFERENCES

General Works, Including Items on the Smaller Units

Abercrombie, Patrick, *Town and Country Planning* (Holt, New York, 1933).

Adams, Thomas, *Outline of Town and City Planning* (Russell Sage Foundation, New York, 1935).

American Country Life Conference, American Country Life Association *Proceedings* (New York, annually).

Anderson, William, *Local Government and Finance in Minnesota* (University of Minnesota Press, 1935).

——, *The Units of Government in the United States,* Revised Edition (Public Administration Service, Chicago, 1942).

Auditor of Public Accounts of Commonwealth of Virginia, *Report* on Comparative Cost of Local Government (Richmond, annually). Similar reports are issued in New York and a few other states.

Bounds, Roger J., *A Bibliography on the Reorganization and Consolidation of Local Government* (Chamber of Commerce of the United States, Washington, April, 1934).

Bradshaw, William L., and Garrison, Milton, *Township Organization in Missouri* (University of Missouri Studies, 1936).

Bromage, Arthur W., *Recommendations on Township Government,* supplement to *National Municipal Review,* February, 1934.

——, and Reed, Thomas H., *Organization and Cost of County and Township Government* (Michigan Commission of Inquiry into County, Township, and School District Government, Detroit, 1933).

Carleton, Robert L., *Local Government and Administration in Louisiana* (Louisiana State University Press, 1935).

Carter, Edward W., *Mandatory Expenditures of Local Governments in Pennsylvania* (University of Pennsylvania, 1934).

Everstine, Carl N., *Local Government: a Comparative Study* (Maryland Legislative Council, Baltimore, 1944).

Garnett, Burt P., *Reorganization of Local Government* (Editorial Research Reports, Washington, 1933).

Haag, H. M., *Governmental Costs and Taxes in Some Rural New York Towns* (Cornell University Agricultural Experiment Station, 1933).

Hunter, Merlin H., *Costs of Township and County Government in Illinois* (University of Illinois, 1933).

Kansas State Planning Board, *Local Government Finance in Kansas* (Topeka, 1939).

——, *Miscellaneous Political Subdivisions in Kansas* (Topeka, 1939).

Lancaster, Lane W., *Government in Rural America* (Van Nostrand, New York, 1937).

MacCorkle, Stuart A., *Units of Local Government in Texas* (University of Texas Press, 1941).

Maryland State Planning Commission, *Certain Financial Aspects of Local Government in Maryland* (Baltimore, 1934).

Municipal Finance Officers Association, *The Support of Local Government Activities* (Chicago, 1939).

National Municipal League, *National Municipal Review* (New York, monthly). Contains a regular department on county and township government.

New Jersey State Department of Agriculture, *A Survey of Rural Townships* (Trenton, 1931).

New York State Constitutional Convention Commission, *Problems Relating to Home Rule and Local Government* (Albany, 1938).

——, *State and Local Government in New York* (Albany, 1938).

Ohio Tax Commission, *Financing State and Local Government in Ohio, 1900–1932* (Columbus, 1934).

Pennsylvania Joint State Government Commission, *Municipal Authorities* (Harrisburg, 1945).

Porter, Kirk H., *County and Township Government in the United States* (Macmillan, New York, 1932).

Princeton Local Government Survey, various publications.

Rush, John A., *The City-County Consolidated* (Published by the Author, Los Angeles, 1941).

Seasongood, Murray, *Local Government in the United States: a Challenge and an Opportunity* (Harvard University Press, 1933).

Shumate, Roger V., *Local Government in Nebraska* (Nebraska Legislative Council, 1939).

Sly, John F., *Town Government in Massachusetts* (Harvard University Press, 1930).

——, and Shipman, George A., *A Working Plan for Local Government in West Virginia* (Bureau of Government Research, University of West Virginia, 1933).

Smith, Bruce, *Rural Crime Control* (Institute of Public Administration, Columbia University, 1933).

Snider, Clyde F., *Township Government in Indiana* (Bureau of Business Research, Indiana University, 1932).

Sparlin, Estal E., *Special Improvement District Financing in Arkansas* (Agricultural Experiment Station, Fayetteville, 1942).

Walker, Harvey, *Village Laws and Government in Minnesota* (University of Minnesota Press, 1928).

Waller, Allen G., and Weiss, Harry B., *County and Township Taxes in New Jersey* (New Jersey State College of Agriculture, 1933).

Wasson, C. R., and Sanderson, Dwight, *Relation of Community Areas to Town Government in the State of New York* (Cornell University Agricultural Experiment Station, 1932).

Webb, Wilfred D., *An Introduction to Municipal Incorporation and Organization in Texas* (University of Texas, Bureau of Municipal Research, 1945).

——, *Cities in Society* (University of Texas, Bureau of Municipal Research, 1945).

Wells, Roger H., *American Local Government* (McGraw-Hill, New York, 1939).

County Government and Administration

Alderfer, Harold F., and others, *Pennsylvania Local Government Survey* (American Philosophical Society, Philadelphia, 1935).

Anderson, William, *Outline of County Government in Minnesota* (University of Minnesota Press, 1928).

Andrews, Columbus, *Administrative County Government in South Carolina* (University of North Carolina Press, 1933).

Atkinson, Raymond C., *Principles of a Model County Government*, supplement to *National Municipal Review*, September, 1933.

Baker, Gladys, *The County Agent* (University of Chicago Press, 1939).

Bosworth, Karl A., *Tennessee Valley County* (University of Alabama, Bureau of Public Administration, 1941).

Bradshaw, William L., *County Government Manual* (Missouri Constitutional Convention of 1943, Columbia, 1943).

Brannen, C. O., *Characteristics and Cost of County Government in Arkansas* (University of Arkansas Agricultural Experiment Station, 1937).

Bromage, Arthur W., *American County Government* (Sears, New York, 1933).

Ewing, Russell H., *County Government and Administration, a Manual and Syllabus* (University of Denver, 1940).

Fairlie, John A., and Kneier, Charles M., *County Government and Administration* (Century, New York, 1930).

Gilbertson, Henry S., *The County, the Dark Continent of American Politics* (National Short Ballot Organization, New York, 1917).

Harris, Joseph P., *County Finances in the State of Washington* (University of Washington Press, 1935).

Heckart, Scoville R., and Klemmedson, G. S., *County Consolidation in Colorado* (Colorado Agricultural College, Fort Collins, 1933).

Hellman, Florence S., *County Government in the United States, a List of Recent References* (Library of Congress, Division of Bibliography, 1940).

Hoffer, Frank W., *Counties in Transition* (Institute for Research in the Social Sciences, University of Virginia, 1929).

Hughes, Edward J., *Counties of Illinois, Their Origin and Evolution* (Secretary of State, Springfield, 1934).

Jay, C. A., *County Reorganization in Texas* (Arnold Foundation, Dallas, 1934).

Jones, Howard P., *Constitutional Barriers to Improvement in County Government* (National Municipal League, New York, 1932).

Kendrick, M. Slade, *A Comparison of the Cost of Maintenance of Large and of Small County Boards in the United States* (Cornell University Agricultural Experiment Station, 1929).

Kilpatrick, Wylie, *County Management* (University of Virginia, 1929).

——, *Problems in Contemporary County Government* (Institute for Research in the Social Sciences, University of Virginia, 1930).

Manny, Theodore B., *Rural Municipalities, a Sociological Study of Rural Government in the United States* (Century, New York, 1930).

Murphy, Wallace C., *County Government and Administration in Texas* (University of Texas, 1933).

National Municipal League, *A Model County Manager Law* (New York, 1930).

——, *The County Manager Plan* (New York, 1945).

——, *National Municipal Review*, county government numbers, August, 1932, October, 1934, and February, 1939.

New York Bureau of Municipal Research, *County Government in Virginia* (Richmond, 1928).

Prescott, Frank W., *County Finance in the South* (Arnold Foundation, Dallas, 1937).

Putney, Bryant, "Reorganization of County Government," *Editorial Research Reports*, February 24, 1938, entire issue.

Reed, Thomas H., *Twenty Years of Government in Essex County, New Jersey* (Appleton-Century, New York, 1938).

Rosenthal, Edgar P., *The County Unit of Local Government* (Mineral Point, Wisconsin, 1941).

Schmidt, Edward B., *Country Consolidation* (University of Nebraska, 1934).

Senning, John P., *Survey of the Financial Administration of Nebraska Counties* (WPA Project, Lincoln, 1938).

Snider, Clyde F., *County Government in Illinois* (Illinois Tax Commission, Springfield, 1943).

Sorrell, Vernon G., and Stuart, J. Raymond, *County Consolidation in New Mexico* (University of New Mexico Press, 1934).

Tennessee Valley Authority, *County Government and Administration in the Tennessee Valley States* (Knoxville, 1940).

Tharp, Claude R., *A Manual of County Administrative Organization in Michigan* (University of Michigan Press, 1944).

United States Bureau of the Census, *Summary of County Finances* (Washington, annually).

Wager, Paul W., *County Government in North Carolina* (University of North Carolina Press, 1928).

Walker, William P., *County Road Use and Financing in Maryland* (University of Maryland, 1942).

Weaver, Frederick P., and Alderfer, Harold F., *County Government Costs in Pennsylvania* (Pennsylvania State College, 1933).

Works, George A., and Lessor, Simon O., *Rural America Today* (University of Chicago Press, 1942).

Wright, M. A., *Administrative County Government in South Carolina* (University of North Carolina Press, 1934).

Municipal Government and Administration

Abbott, Lyndon E., and Greene, Lee S., *Municipal Government and Administration in Tennessee* (University of Tennessee Extension Series, 1939).

American City Magazine Corporation, *The American City* (New York, monthly).

Anderson, William, *American City Government* (Holt, New York, 1925).

Brown, Ann D., *A Selected List of References on Municipal Government in the United States* (Library of Congress, Division of Bibliography, 1938).

Chatters, Carl H., and Tenner, Irving, *Municipal and Governmental Accounting* (Prentice-Hall, New York, 1941).

City of Des Moines, *The Des Moines Plan of Commission Government* (Des Moines, 1939).

Cooke, Morris L., *Our Cities Awake* (Doubleday, Page, New York, 1918).

Cooper, Weldon, *Municipal Government and Administration in Alabama* (University of Alabama Bureau of Public Administration, 1940).

Forbes, Russell, *Governmental Purchasing* (Macmillan, New York, 1929).

Griffith, Ernest S., *Current Municipal Problems* (Houghton Mifflin, Boston, 1933).

——, *History of American City Government*, 2 vols. (Oxford University Press, 1938).

——, *The Modern Development of City Government in the United Kingdom and the United States*, 2 vols. (Oxford University Press, London, 1927).

Hoan, Daniel W., *City Government: The Record of the Milwaukee Experiment* (Harcourt, Brace, New York, 1936).

Hodges, Henry G., *City Management, Theory and Practice of Municipal Administration* (Crofts, New York, 1939).

International City Managers Association, *Municipal Year Book* (Chicago, annually since 1934).

——, *Public Management* (Chicago, monthly).

Jones, Victor, *Metropolitan Government* (University of Chicago Press, 1942).

Kneier, Charles M., *City Government in the United States,* Third Edition (Harper, New York, 1945).

MacCorkle, Stuart A., *Municipal Administration* (Prentice-Hall, New York, 1941).

Macdonald, Austin F., *American City Government and Administration,* Third Edition (Crowell, New York, 1941).

McBain, Howard L., *Law and Practice of Municipal Home Rule* (Columbia University Press, 1916).

McGoldrick, Joseph D., *Law and Practice of Municipal Home Rule, 1916–1930* (Columbia University Press, 1933).

Mumford, Lewis, *The Culture of Cities* (Harcourt, Brace, New York, 1938).

Munro, William B., *Municipal Administration* (Macmillan, New York, 1934).

National Institute of Municipal Law Officers, *Municipalities and the Law in Action,* Revised Edition (Washington, 1944).

National Municipal League, *National Municipal Review* (New York, monthly).

National Resources Committee, *Our Cities, Their Role in the National Economy* (Washington, 1937).

——, *Urban Government* (Washington, 1939).

Ogburn, William F., *Social Characteristics of Cities* (International City Managers Association, Chicago, 1937).

Peel, Roy V., Ed., " Better City Government," *Annals,* September, 1938.

Pfiffner, John M., *Municipal Administration* (Ronald Press, New York, 1940).

Raisty, Lloyd B., *Municipal Government and Administration in Georgia* (University of Georgia Press, 1941).

Reed, Thomas H., *Municipal Government in the United States,* Revised Edition (Appleton-Century, New York, 1934).

——, *Municipal Management* (McGraw-Hill, New York, 1941).

Ridley, Clarence E., *The City Manager Profession* (University of Chicago Press, 1934).

——, and Simon, Herbert A., *Measuring Municipal Activities* (American Municipal Association, Chicago, 1938).

——, *Specifications for the Annual Municipal Report* (International City Managers Association, Chicago, 1940).

Satterfield, M. H., and Urban, Hugh W., *Municipal Government and Administration in Mississippi* (Mississippi State Planning Commission, Jackson, 1940).

Shambaugh, Benjamin F., Ed., *Municipal Government and Administration in Iowa,* 2 vols. (Iowa State Historical Society, Iowa City, 1930).

Social Science Research Council, Committee in Public Administration, *City*

Manager Government in the United States (Public Administration Service, Chicago, 1940).

——, *City Manager Government in Nine Cities* (Public Administration Service, Chicago, 1940).

——, *City Manager Government in Seven Cities* (Public Administration Service, Chicago, 1940).

State leagues of municipalities, monthly publications.

Studenski, Paul, *The Government of Metropolitan Areas* (National Municipal League, New York, 1930).

Taft, Charles P., *City Management: The Cincinnati Experiment* (Farrar and Rinehart, New York, 1934).

United States Bureau of the Census, *Summary of City Finances* (Washington, annually).

Woolston, Howard B., *Metropolis: a Study of Urban Communities* (Appleton-Century, New York, 1938).

Zink, Harold, *Government of Cities in the United States* (Macmillan, New York, 1939).

CHAPTER XXI

State-Local Relations

THE tendency to centralize authority through the shifting of power from the smaller to the larger units of government is one of the striking trends of modern government. In discussions of American national government it is customary to devote some attention to Federal centralization, noting how, under the influence of the subsidy system, the Federal government has extended its control over such subjects as agriculture, conservation, education, health, highways, and labor — all of which had been regarded, under the doctrine of residuary powers, as belonging exclusively to the states. Similar extensions have occurred under the Federal police power, the commerce power, the tax power, and the postal power. Simultaneously with this shift of power from the states to the Federal government, there has occurred a shift of power from the local agencies to the states. In many cases where no actual diminution of the powers of the local agencies occurred, the states have extended their authority by establishing and enforcing standards. This has resulted in state supervision of local units in many of the same administrative fields in which power has been transferred from the localities to the state and from the states to the Federal government.

REASONS FOR STATE CENTRALIZATION

The reasons for this concentration of power in successively larger units of government are not difficult to discover. The development of machinery and large-scale production in industry and agriculture have made possible the growth of metropolitan areas, each with a tremendous population. Modern methods of transportation and communication have created mobility of population and channels for cheap and expeditious transmission of ideas. Under these new conditions it has become impossible to administer governmental services effectively in administrative units conceived in and suitable for the day of the oxcart, the stagecoach, and the messenger galloping on horseback.

The discovery of this fact by large numbers of people during the last few years has apparently occasioned great surprise, though there is no reason why it should. A study of the development of state control over public instruction in Michigan made a few years ago showed that from 1871 to 1919 twenty-nine new agencies had been added to the state government; while many of these represented new governmental services, many others related to services which had previously been administered locally. Since it is exceedingly difficult to get original dates, it is probable that some of these new agencies represent reorganizations rather than the original creation of the service. This list appears below: [1]

1871 — Insurance Commission
1879 — Board of Charities and Correction
1881 — State Board of Health
1883 — State Board of Dental Examiners
1885 — Board of Fish Commissioners
1885 — Board of Pharmacy
1887 — Banking Commission
1893 — Pardon Board
1893 — Dairy and Food Commission
1893 — Board of Railway and Street Crossings
1895 — Board of Law Examiners
1899 — Board of Labor Commissioners
1899 — Board of Registration in Medicine
1899 — Inspector of Oils

1903 — Board of Osteopathic Registration and Examiners
1905 — Inspector of Orchards and Nurseries
1907 — State Veterinary Board
1909 — Board of Prison Industries
1909 — Board of Optometry
1909 — Board of Registration of Nurses
1909 — Labor Commissioner
1909 — Inspector of Drugs
1912 — Industrial Accident Board
1913 — Inspector of Apiaries
1913 — Inspector of Hotels
1913 — Board of Accountancy
1915 — Board of Registration of Architects
1915 — Board of Mediation and Conciliation
1919 — Board of Control of Vocational Education

The growth of the state services by additions and by transfers from the local agencies is not to be explained wholly on the basis of developments in natural science. It has recently become evident

[1] Jackson, George L., *The Development of State Control over Public Instruction in Michigan*, pp. 331-332 (Michigan Historical Society, Lansing, 1926). See also pp. 506-514 of the present volume for discussion of the same point from a different angle.

that, to use the words of the late President Roosevelt, Americans are living under too many " layers of government." There are counties — three, four, five, six, perhaps as many as eight classes of them; cities of the first, second, third, or more classes; boroughs; towns and townships of two or more classes; villages; and administrative districts of every imaginable variety for every conceivable administrative purpose. Most of these agencies have, and use, the taxing power and the borrowing power. There are increasing numbers of government corporations, and of late, a great many " authorities " which are to a large extent exempt both from normal regulation and taxation. It has become apparent that there can be no logical justification for such a multiplicity of overlapping governmental units.

In the preceding chapter, mention was made of the number — very often the excessive number, of counties. The situation with regard to school districts — to use one type of special purpose area as an example — is even worse. In New York there are more than 9,000 school districts; in Pennsylvania there were 2,582 in 1934, of which almost half were districts with a population under 1,000. By 1941 the number had been reduced only thirty-three, the total of 2,549 being distributed among the various classes as follows: first class, two; second class, twenty; third class, 258; and fourth class, 2,269. The total number of separate governmental units in this state is 5,635 — and Pennsylvania is no worse than most of the other states. A striking illustration of the extent to which special purpose districts have been permitted to multiply is shown by the table for Los Angeles County, California, on page 862. That progress has been made in the last few years is apparent by comparing the figures in the second column with those in the first, but the number is still far too large.[2]

Local government has frequently broken down because, from one point of view there was too much of it, and from another point of view, too little of it. The units are so numerous and so small that, individually, they cannot do what needs to be done, and their efforts are so uncoordinated that they cannot function effectively as a group or on a cooperative basis. Many studies of this situation have been made. In 1945, it was shown, for instance, that there were 188 local governments in St. Louis County. The result is that the public does not receive the service that it should and that, on the basis of the taxes it pays, it has a right to expect.

[2] Morosco, A. H., " Government within Government," *Tax Digest*, February, 1932, p. 42, and Holland, J. Roy, " Taxing Units in Los Angeles," *ibid.*, November, 1940, p. 372.

LOS ANGELES COUNTY, CALIFORNIA —
COMPARISON OF NUMBER OF UNITS OF LOCAL GOVERNMENT, 1932 AND 1940

Type of Unit	1932	1940
School districts	160	144
Incorporated cities	45	45
Acquisition and improvement districts	294	42
Cemetery districts	3	3
Drainage districts	11	1
Fire protection districts	28	30
Flood control district	1	1
County library district	1	1
Lighting districts	65	64
Lighting maintenance districts	32	29
Mosquito abatement district	..	1
Park and recreation districts	..	2
Road districts (with bonds outstanding)	91	9
Sanitation districts	5	8
Sewer districts	39	29
Supervisorial road districts	5	5
County water districts	3	9
Metropolitan water district	1	1
Waterworks districts	8	12
County improvements districts — lights, water, etc.	982	368
Opening and widening districts	38	19
City and county improvement districts	5	5
Districts organized under the Act of 1915	4	2
Garbage disposal districts	..	3
Irrigation districts	..	6
Assessment bond refunding districts	..	4
Refunding bond assessment districts (1935 Act)	..	2
Library districts	..	2
Total number of districts in county	1,821	846

It has often been said that nature never permits a vacuum. Likewise, in the field of government, a governmental vacuum, a kind of governmental no-man's-land, does not long continue. If the local units break down, the states must either attempt to do the job themselves, or establish and enforce upon the local units minimum requirements for the performance of the function. The reasons why and the methods by which the power and influence of the states increase in the state-local relationship are substantially the same as those which account for the growth of Federal power in the Federal-state relationship.

Still another reason for the shift of power from the localities to the states is to be found in the fact that our people are becoming accustomed to higher standards of administrative efficiency. They expect more adequate and prompt service from their government. Service of this improved character the local units have rarely been able to give them, since they are staffed by untrained and/or part-time employees, many of whom are inadequately paid. Illustrations in support of this general thesis will be cited under appropriate headings in the paragraphs below, in which will be indicated the more important fields of government in which centralization has occurred, and the nature of and the reason for the transfer of power or the extension of supervision in each case.

STATE SUPERVISION OF LOCAL FINANCES

There is no phase of public administration of more vital concern to the average citizen than control over finances. In nearly a dozen different aspects of financial administration the states have extended their authority over local agencies. These include supervision of assessments; supervision of tax collection; limitation of tax rates; control over budgets and expenditures; limitation of debt incurrence and supervision of debt retirement; financial aid to local governments in the form of shared taxes or grants-in-aid; supervision of accounts, audits, and reporting; as well as control of receiverships and credit facilities, and control over the selection of the personnel engaged in the work.[3]

Control over local finance, as Dr. Kilpatrick points out, is not a very precise term. In any given case, it may mean all of these things, or any combination of two or more of these types of supervision. One difficulty has been that supervision has rarely been on the basis of complete coverage of the whole fiscal process in the local units concerned. Each state has regulated certain phases of the process, but few have attempted to control all phases. Those left unsupervised provided opportunities for financial leaks and for the use of unsatisfactory practices.

The scope of the supervisory function involves the setting of standards, instruction of local officials as to their meaning and observance, and finally, inspection to ascertain that they have been observed. Several methods of making supervision effective are available: constitutional, which is highly rigid; legislative, which is moderately

[3] For a tabular summary of state laws covering all of the various types of supervision of local finance, and the administrative provisions for such supervision, see Kilpatrick, Wylie, *State Supervision of Local Finance* (Public Administration Service, Chicago, 1941).

elastic; administrative, which is most elastic; and judicial. The character of the supervision which may be employed is likewise subject to wide variation. It may involve actual control of a local process or transaction. It may involve cooperation on the part of state and local officials in some part of the fiscal process. It may involve the rendering of a state service for a fee, as in auditing, where the actual costs are frequently assessed against the unit or service audited. Or it may be merely an advisory service to local officials, or even a nominal, perfunctory, and more or less sterile examination of their financial records after the transactions have been completed and it is too late to do any good.

State Supervision of Local Assessments. In an earlier chapter mention was made of the inequalities which have characterized the assessment of real estate for purposes of taxation. These have arisen through the use of untrained and politically selected assessors, the lack of accepted rules to guide assessors in their work, and the lack of a uniform basis of assessment. In adjacent or nearby units, one can find properties assessed at one third, one half, three fourths, or full valuation. In order to eliminate the worst of these inequalities, and to bring about some semblance of uniformity and justice in the treatment of taxpayers, many states long ago established state boards of equalization or state tax commissions, authorized to set up and enforce standards of assessment and to equalize assessments. More recently well-integrated state tax departments have been given extensive powers of supervision and control over the locally elected assessment officers. Such agencies now exist in more than half the states. In Virginia, for instance, under a 1927 act, the state tax commissioner may withhold the salaries of local commissioners for neglect of duty or failure to make the required reports, and he may report to the circuit court any incapacity, misconduct, or neglect of duty on the part of local commissioners, and thereby institute ouster proceedings against such officers.

In a further effort to avoid the injustices commonly associated with the general property tax, an increasing number of states have abolished the tax for state revenue purposes. Even in those states where the tax is not so used, there is still urgent need for a board of equalization, in order that the state subsidies for educational and other purposes may be distributed on a more equitable basis than is possible in the absence of such a board. Experience in Virginia shows that control over assessments is possible even where the states do not collect a real estate tax.[4] It is of course possible to improve assessments somewhat by the dissemination of information among the assessors and by control through state ordinances.

State Regulation of Local Tax Rates. The depression gave impetus to this second type of state supervision of local finances, considered in an earlier chapter under the heading of tax rate limitation. Actually, the state often controls the selection of sources, as well as the rate, by application of an almost endless number and variety of restrictions. In Pennsylvania, for instance, the Sterling Act of 1925 forbids the city of Philadelphia to levy on sources taxed by the state; the law applies regardless of which tax measure may have been first enacted. There is also the possibility that taxes imposed by local units may be thrown out by the courts on constitutional grounds. Assuming, however, that the source is available to the local unit and that the act is drawn in a manner acceptable to the courts, laws regulating rates have long been common. In the decade of the thirties, additional regulations of this character were adopted in a large number of states, often without much consideration and largely as a result of an almost hysterical desire to reduce the tax burden. The nature of these restrictions and their unfortunate effects have been discussed previously, in Chapter XIII.

Supervision of Tax Collection. In most jurisdictions, there is little state supervision over the collection of property taxes. Taxes are "received" by the treasurer, tax collector, or receiver of taxes for each local unit, such supervision as exists commonly being of the legislative variety. The law prescribes who shall collect taxes, and how, and sets up without any provision for the supervision of the process, the procedure to be followed in the collection of delinquent taxes, and the disposition of tax delinquent properties. In a few states, as in Pennsylvania, the counties collect certain types of taxes for the state; in these instances, an extensive supervision is exercised by the state revenue collecting agency.

State Control over Local Budgets. The fourth type of state financial supervision over the local units involves control over local budg-

[4] Pate, James E., "State Supervision over Local Fiscal Officers in Virginia," *American Political Science Review*, November, 1931, pp. 1004–1008. The best recent discussion of the topics of this section is Spicer, George W., "Fiscal Aspects of State-Local Relations," *Annals*, January, 1940, pp. 151–160; for comments on particular states, see Sparlin, Estal E., "State Supervision of Local Property Tax Assessments," *Tax Magazine*, August, 1939, pp. 467–468 (on Arkansas); Enslow, Harold R., "State Supervision of Assessment in New York," *ibid.*, August, 1938, pp. 458–460, 492.

ets. There are two types of such control: first, the checking of the form of local budgets to ensure their compliance with state laws; second, the exercise of discretionary powers over the purpose and amount of the various items contained in the budget. The former is used in most states where regulation exists, Indiana, Massachusetts, and North Carolina, among others, having devised budget forms for use in the localities. Massachusetts, New Jersey, New Mexico, and other states check budgets to ensure compliance with state laws. Professor Kilpatrick thus summarizes the scope of legislation requiring local budgeting:

> Thirty-nine states require the local preparation of budgets annually by all or some of their local governments. Without a formal state law governing local budgets, four other states attain similar results. The State Auditor of Maine includes estimate forms and appropriation ledgers in the accounting installations of most Maine municipalities. The same officer in Vermont gives budgetary assistance to towns requesting audits and accounts. Minnesota requires budget preparation by a few local units, and through the Public Examiner's audits checks the budget records of counties and of a few cities. The Wisconsin Division of Municipal Accounting annually distributes budget forms to counties. In total, forty-three states by statute, or administrative procedure, regulate local budget making.[5]

In Iowa and Oklahoma, it becomes the duty of the state to intervene in case any city fails to levy taxes adequate to meet the interest charges on bond issues. In Oklahoma the State Auditor must ascertain the amount of interest and sinking fund charges needed for the fiscal period and transmit the same to the county treasurer. In Iowa, in case of default of interest payments, the bondholder takes his bond to the State Auditor, who is empowered to levy a tax upon the taxable property of the municipality to the extent of the bond.[6] In several states approval of the budget is necessary. In Colorado and Kansas such approval is confined to emergency situations, while three states include all items in municipal budgets; in Iowa it is confined to certain items. The laws of the latter state provide that each municipality must prepare its budgets in accordance with forms supplied by the state and that proposed budgets, when completed, must be approved by the state. The State Board of Appeal may approve or reduce the budget, but may not make increases. In other

---

5 Kilpatrick, *op. cit.*, pp. 23–24. The eleven states without such a requirement are: Delaware, Georgia, Maine, Maryland, Michigan, Minnesota, Rhode Island, South Carolina, Tennessee, and Vermont.

6 Wallace, Schuyler C., *State Administrative Supervision over Cities in the United States*, p. 101 (Columbia University Press, 1928).

states, such as Arizona, Indiana,[7] Nevada, and North Dakota, the commission is given the power to prescribe details.

Another movement toward greater state control over local budgets was taken in California in 1929;[8] this act provides that each county official or person in charge of a county office, department, service, or institution has to file a report of estimated receipts and expenditures for the ensuing year with the county auditor. The county board of supervisors is also obliged to submit a report to the county auditor, showing construction and maintenance costs anticipated for the ensuing year. Similarly, school districts are required to submit to the Superintendent of Schools estimates of expenditures on forms prescribed by the State Department of Education. The county auditor prepares the estimate of interest and bond redemptions, and he must also prepare a statement for the county board of supervisors, showing the expenditures and the sources of revenue for the county, school districts, and special districts. This report sets forth the amount to be spent by each department and indicates the purposes of expenditure by object classifications. The county board is authorized to revise these estimates, adding to or subtracting from them as it may deem advisable. Where reductions are made, a hearing for complaints must be held. A fund known as " Unappropriated Reserves " may be set up by the county board as an emergency fund. No transfers are permitted between the general classes of expenditures or between departments. Special provision is made for the cancellation or reduction of appropriations, and for emergency expenditures by use of a warrant on moneys in the treasury. School districts are independent in carrying out their own expenditures, the only reason for their reporting being to enable the board of supervisors to compute the tax rate.

Professor Kilpatrick believes that the states should be responsible for laying down the budget procedure of their localities and for supervising its enforcement, and in this connection he sets forth four primary duties of the state: (1) by statute and administrative ruling to prescribe the procedure through which localities administer budgets; (2) to create and adequately staff supervisory agencies

---

[7] On the much publicized Indiana Plan, which seems not to have been altogether satisfactory, see: Bates, Frank G., " State Control of Local Finance in Indiana," *American Political Science Review*, May, 1926, pp. 352–360; editorial, " The Indiana Plan in Iowa," *National Municipal Review*, May, 1937; Dortch, Carl R., " The Indiana Plan in Action," *ibid.*, November, 1938, pp. 525–529.

[8] See also Johnson, Milbank, " Control of Local Expenditures," *Tax Digest*, June, 1932, pp. 184–188.

to interpret and to enforce the law and assist local units; (3) to ensure the enforcement of minimum budget and fiscal standards applicable to all local units; and (4) to assume promptly direct
budgetary and fiscal control for the duration and correction of the
breakdown in any individual units where chaotic conditions impel
state intervention and temporary control.[9]

State Control of Local Indebtedness. In this fourth method of
state control of local finances, nearly all states examine local records
in order to ensure compliance with state laws on debt limitation,
while a majority of states have constitutional limitations also. Thirty-
six state constitutions, in fact, limit local debts, and forty-four states
limit the terms of local bonds. Nearly all the limits are defined in
terms of a percentage of the assessed valuation of all property in the
municipality concerned; with the defects in the system of assessments already indicated, it is clear that this is a most inaccurate
measure of the borrowing capacity of the various units. In 1935 it
was reported that twenty-five states required serial issues, while only
ten states had done so a dozen years before. Thus is indicated a
clearly defined trend away from sinking fund bonds, with all the
abuses that have occurred in the field of sinking fund management.

In some states, supervision occurs *only* when a question of indebtedness is involved; in others, the law confers discretionary power
upon the authorities, under which they may pass upon questions of
policy and procedure, such as the necessity for the improvement for
which bonds are to be issued. Massachusetts, New Jersey, and Pennsylvania use the former method, while Indiana and Iowa employ the
latter. In about half of the states, reports and administrative ap-
provals of municipal indebtedness are sent by each city to the proper
state officials. In more than one fourth of them, such reports, in addition to being a source of information, are a necessary part of the
approval of bond issues.

In Pennsylvania, where this is the case, the Bureau of Municipalities has been able to maintain a fairly effective supervision over the
financial affairs of those cities which have applied for permission to
borrow money, checking the legality of the issues and examining
the financial records of the cities concerned, except in the case of
special assessment bonds. They have not encouraged as they might

---

[9] Kilpatrick, Wylie, *State Supervision of Local Budgeting* (National Municipal League, New York, 1939) ; see also Indiana Division of Accounting and Statistics, *Indiana Public Accounting, State Budget and Municipal Budget Laws*
(Indianapolis, 1936) . Fairlie and Kneier, *op. cit.*, pp. 399–404, have a good discussion of county budgeting.

the issuance of serial bonds. Since most of the cities have borrowed, most of them have in this way been subject to some supervision, but financial supervision of municipalities certainly ought not to be dependent in any state upon the desire to exercise the borrowing power. Such regulation should be regular and not spasmodic, and should apply to all cities, at all times, without exception, as was clearly indicated by the analysis of figures on municipal defaults during the depression beginning in 1929.

North Carolina has adopted perhaps the most drastic legislation for the purpose of controlling local bond issues. The local units in this state, like those in many others, were faced with a rapidly mounting total of indebtedness and were employing the inadequate and unsatisfactory bookkeeping and accounting methods so frequently found in local government agencies. In 1927 the legislature enacted a measure requiring every county to appoint an accountant and to operate upon a budget basis.[10] A County Government Advisory Committee consisting of trained accountants was organized to advise the county governments on financial matters. They were responsible for many improvements in financial practice and in county administration generally. In 1931 the legislature abolished the Advisory Commission and created in its place the Local Government Finance Commission, whose organization was outlined in the preceding chapter. Under the provisions of this act, no note or bond of any municipality, county, or other political subdivision is valid unless approved by the Commission. The notes or bonds are sold by the Commissioner of Revenue at Raleigh. The securities are delivered to the purchaser by the State Treasurer, who receives the proceeds and remits them to the proper local authorities. In case any local unit defaults in payment of its debt obligations, the Commissioner may appoint an Administrator of Finance to collect all taxes and disperse all funds. This subordination of the local units, this sacrifice of long-cherished rights of local self-government, has been accepted by the citizens as a price which must be paid for financial security and tax relief.[11]

A study of trends in public administration made a few years ago by Professor White has this to say regarding the development of state control in this field:

The evidence indicates that in the last fifteen years there has been considerable tendency to substitute effective state control of the incurring of local indebtedness for the mere requirements of registration or certification

---

[10] Chapter 149, Laws, 1927.   [11] Pate, *op. cit.,* pp. 996 ff.

of legality which had developed in the last quarter of the nineteenth century. The cases are still scattered and localities on the whole are still free to issue bonds, within constitutional or statutory limits, as they see fit. The present tendency is to limit this freedom by state administrative action.[12]

Elsewhere the same author observes that such controls are in effect in at least twenty-eight states.[13]

Financial Aid to Local Governments. The local units receive financial assistance from the states in the form of grants-in-aid or shared taxes. These are two separate kinds of payments, yet they are not too clearly distinguishable. Generally speaking, shared taxes go back to the governmental unit in which the revenue was collected, while grants-in-aid are distributed for a particular activity, in accordance with some prescribed formula, regardless of the origin of the funds. The movement for these forms of financial aid was stimulated originally by the desire to extend control over local units whose financial management had too often been characterized by waste, extravagance, and incompetence. It was later accentuated by the financial distress of large numbers of local units during the depression.

The growth of the system is clearly shown in the accompanying table, which indicates also the major purposes for which financial aid is given.

STATE AID BY PURPOSE: SELECTED YEARS, 1925–1941 [14]

(Amounts in millions)

Year	Total	Schools	Public Assistance	Highways	Other Specified Purposes	Unspecified
1941	$1,697.8	$735.4	$407.0	$341.7	$22.6	$191.1
1939	1,537.0	676.5	371.8	298.4	19.5	170.8
1937	1,368.5	642.6	220.5	302.0	23.4	180.0
1932	758.6	397.4	42.1	229.0	16.2	73.9
1925	535.8	254.1	3.9	150.2	19.5	108.1

A tabulation made in 1944 shows that some portion of the receipts from state liquor taxes is allocated to municipalities in nine states, while receipts from state liquor monopolies are allocated in five

12 White, Leonard D., *Trends in Public Administration*, p. 57 (McGraw-Hill, New York, 1933).

13 *Ibid.*, pp. 51–57; similar data in tabular form are presented in *State Government*, August, 1934, pp. 166–167. An older but a very good discussion of the same subject will be found in Lancaster, Lane W., *State Supervision of Municipal Indebtedness* (University of Pennsylvania, 1923).

14 From United States Bureau of the Census, *Federal and State Aid: 1941*, p. 25 (Washington, 1942); data for 1925 and 1932 are adapted from Twentieth Century Fund, *Facing the Tax Problem*, pp. 578–579 (New York, 1937).

more. Liquor dealer license receipts are allocated in seventeen states. Property tax exemptions by in lieu payments are authorized in twenty-three states. Some portion of the motor fund revenues from the liquid fuels tax, registration fees, operators' license fees, and other similiar levies are allocated in all of the states.[15]

The financial, political, and social implications of these forms of financial aid to local units are clearly outlined in the following list, compiled by Carl H. Chatters: [16]

1. A central government, national or state, uses financial aid to promote social and economic programs which it considers desirable.

2. Grants-in-aid are effective devices for assisting hard pressed areas. Great difficulties are experienced in making payments to them without giving some money also to all other governmental units of the same kind at the same level, regardless of need.

3. State and Federal aid take taxes from one area and spend them in another, thus becoming a kind of " share the wealth " program.

4. The centralization of government cannot be separated from the consideration of state and Federal aids. The two go hand in hand. " State aid implies dependency and in the end invites regulation. This is inevitable, logical and generally fair," But this dependency status of the local government may exist because something was taken away from it.

5. The larger the proportion of the expense of a particular activity paid from grants or shared taxes, the greater is likely to be the degree of control exercised.

6. Grants-in-aid may be used to raise the standard of performance of a particular activity at the local government level.

7. The temptation to use grants-in-aid for political purposes is very great. A specific project may be granted or withheld as a political club to get votes. Or, the members of a legislative body may urge large and unwarranted grants to show how well they serve their constituents.

In general it may be said that state control over finances of local agencies is spreading rapidly with regard to all types of state service. Whether local officers liked it or not, taxpayers welcomed such measure of relief as was thereby made possible, and they continue to do so.[17] The local units have demanded more and more state aid, while at the same time they have protested more and more loudly at the extension of state authority; yet, as one writer has observed, " If the

[15] See Woodworth, Leo D., *Shared Taxes* (American Municipal Association, Chicago, 1944) .

[16] *Grants-in-Aid and Shared Taxes,* special bulletin of the Municipal Finance Officers Association, Chicago, March, 1945.

[17] See Wallerstein, Morton L., " What Local Officials Think of State Financial Control," *National Municipal Review,* September, 1932, pp. 557–559; Kilpatrick, Wylie, " Reorganization Plans for State Supervision of Local Business," *Tax Digest,* June, 1933, pp. 203–208, and July, 1933, pp. 242–246; Pate, *op. cit.*

phrase 'reorganization of local government' is considered to be trite, the phrase 'local autonomy,' which is employed to combat reforms in that direction, is even more threadbare." [18]

The development of the subsidy system in the states has been generally parallel to its growth in the Federal government. The most important single purpose of state aid has been education — to secure buildings and equipment, standards of teacher training, and adequacy of curriculum. Other purposes of long standing include health and sanitation, highways, and conservation. State aid for poor relief for orphans, the aged, and the blind has in late years been supplemented by aid for unemployment relief. The system of state grants has developed under similar group pressures and with the same planlessness which has characterized the Federal grants; the same need exists in the states for some effort to see the picture as a whole, to determine in each state what portion of the total revenues are to be so expended, and how this sum shall be apportioned among the various purposes for which aid is granted.

State Supervision of Accounts. Another form of state financial supervision provides for the auditing of local accounts, and indeed for the supervision and control of the whole accounting system. Massachusetts and New Jersey did pioneer work in this field,[19] and during recent years many states have undertaken supervision of this character.[20] The most advanced legislation is that adopted by New York in 1932, under the terms of which the State Comptroller is not only permitted but required to supervise the accounts of the agencies of local government through a field force of state examiners. These men, all trained accountants, examine the records of the local agencies in a manner somewhat similar to that in which the

[18] Hinckley, Russell J., *State Grants-in-Aid*, p. 171 (New York State Tax Commission, Albany, 1935). In an extensive literature the following recent titles may be cited; Bitterman, Henry J., *State and Federal Grants-in-Aid* (Mentzer, Bush, Chicago, 1938), and Crouch, Winston W., *State Aid to Local Government in California* (University of California Press, 1939). Each of these has extensive footnotes and bibliography. See also: Stout, Randall S., *State Grants-in-Aid in Pennsylvania* (Pennsylvania State College, 1945); Tharp, Claude R., *State Aid in Michigan* (University of Michigan, Bureau of Government, 1942); Woodworth, *op. cit.*; and Wayne University, School of Public Affairs and Social Work, *Wayne County's Interest in State Grants-in-Aid* (Detroit, 1940); Wisconsin Tax Commission, *State Aids Since 1901* (Madison, 1938).

[19] Kilpatrick, Wylie, " State Supervision of Municipal Finance in New Jersey," *National Municipal Review*, August, 1925, pp. 490–501, and Lancaster, *op. cit.*

[20] A summary of the progress made in this field will be found in Haygood, T. F., " State Control of Local Expenditures through Centralization of Financial Statistics, with Special Reference to the Development of a Plan for Kentucky," *Tax Magazine*, August, 1933, pp. 301–307, 318–319; September, 1933, pp. 346–347, 353–354; *Local Government Accounting* and *Minimum Accounting Standards* (University of Tennessee Press, 1940).

bank examiners examine the records of banking institutions under their supervision and control, or in which building and loan examiners inspect the records of the building and loan associations of the state.

The New York law further provides for uniform local accounting systems, which must be used by each of the several types of local government agencies. Uniform accounting systems involving the uniform classification of the objects of expenditure are provided for cities, counties, towns, and villages. At the end of each year these several units are required to submit a detailed statement of their fiscal operations on forms which are provided by, and which must be returned to, the State Comptroller. With the introduction of such a system, it becomes possible for the first time to compare the expenditures of communities of the same size for a particular administrative purpose. Unless the items of expenditure are classified in the same way, such figures are worthless. Under such circumstances an inquirer has no way of telling whether the different totals are due to a different classification of items or whether there exist actual differences in the administrative problems confronting the communities in question sufficient to explain the variation in expenditures.

In New Mexico the law likewise provides for the installation by the state of accounting systems for the local governments. " The law also requires that local accounting records be examined either by the state or private auditors approved by the comptroller, and that the financial reports shall be published biennially. The audit costs are divided between the state and locality." [21] Virginia uses a novel method for the auditing of local accounts. The State Tax Commissioner appoints an examiner to audit the records of local commissioners of revenue with special reference to items in which the state is especially interested. If the returns on intangibles have not been properly made, the State Tax Commissioner can summon the taxpayer for an explanation. The Virginia Tax Code allows the State Tax Commissioner to withhold the salaries of local commissioners for failure to make out the required reports or for neglect of duty. He can also report to the circuit court any misconduct, incapacity, or negligence of local commissioners. This may result in ouster proceedings.[22]

[21] Tharp, Claude R., *Control of Local Finance through Taxpayers' Associations and Centralized Administration*, p. 44 (M. Ford Publishing Company, Indianapolis, 1933) .

[22] The author wishes to acknowledge at this point, and at various other places in this chapter, his indebtedness for assistance received from a former student, Dr. David H. Kurtzman, of the Pennsylvania Economy League.

A tabulation of the states supervising the accounting of local units shows that thirty-seven supervise their counties, twenty their municipalities, while thirteen supervise districts or other local units. Local accounting is state supervised for both counties and municipalities in seventeen states, and for all local units in thirteen states. The states may, for this purpose, be grouped in three general categories: first, those states with complete control; [23] second, those states with partial control; and finally, those states with no control at all.[24] About 50 per cent of the states fall in the middle group; approximately one fourth have complete control, while the remaining fourth have little or no control at all. But the movement is spreading rapidly.

One writer has pointed out the need for intelligent and adequate accounts and reporting, and listed four fundamental qualities which must be present in any adequate system of governmental accounting.[25] First, " the accounts must be classified by funds in such a way that all of the resources and obligations of each fund are clearly set out from all other accounts and the surplus or deficit of each fund clearly shown at all times. Second, a clear separation should be maintained by the accounts of current operations and those of a capital nature. The current assets and liabilities of each fund should be clearly separated from the fixed assets and bond obligations of that fund. Third, the accounts must provide for an adequate system of budgetary control. It is not sufficient merely to record the receipts and disbursements or the income and expenditures. Fourth, the system must be operated on an income and expenditure basis and not merely on a cash receipts and disbursements basis." In all such systems some recognition must be given to the different activities of local government.

State Auditing of Local Units. In Chapter XIV, mention was made of the distinction between the different types of audit — internal or operating, and postaudits. In the field of local government, the responsibility for operating audits rests clearly with the local officials, while that for postaudits is or should be a state concern, the purpose being to verify the accounts and discover any irregularities that may

[23] Complete control exists in Indiana, Iowa, Mississippi, Montana, Nebraska, New Mexico, New York, North Carolina, Ohio, Washington, and West Virginia.
[24] The states having no control are California, Delaware, Georgia, Illinois, Nebraska, North Dakota, Pennsylvania, and Utah. Five states have very limited control — Louisiana, Minnesota, Rhode Island, Tennessee, and Vermont. See Kilpatrick, *State Supervision of Local Accounting*, p. 55, and *State Supervision of Local Finance*, p. 8.
[25] Morey, Lloyd, " Uniform Accounting for Local Governments," *National Municipal Review*, July, 1934, pp. 377–379, and June, 1938, pp. 309–313.

exist, as well as any violations of statutory requirements or accepted standards. Professor Kilpatrick thus describes the coverage of the auditing process, which varies greatly among the states.[26]

Of the forty-five states with supervisory audits, Delaware and Georgia restrict their audits to school districts, leaving municipal and county records untouched. Four restrict their examinations to records of the collection of taxes and other receivables due the state. Here the question is whether the state is getting its "due," not whether local transactions are honest, legal, and efficient. In Maryland, Texas, and Utah, the state audit is confined to county finances, chiefly the county treasurers. In Pennsylvania, the examination extends to any municipal officers collecting state funds. One of the largest state auditing staffs in the country is necessary for the Pennsylvania audit.

Including these six states, the most extensive state service is for the auditing of counties in forty states. Over half, or twenty-nine of the states, make auditing services available to municipalities, or supervise private accountants who examine municipal books. Half the states audit districts, rural townships and other units. The emphasis upon counties, attributable to the county function of collecting state revenue, results in fourteen states disregarding municipalities and limiting examinations exclusively to counties. Only in the two New England states of Vermont and Rhode Island, where the county is an unimportant "shell," is state auditing exclusively for municipalities. Despite these variations in practice, twenty-one states make auditing services available to all their local governments. Even in this group, the states do not recurrently examine all local units, because local officials in some states may choose state or private examinations.

In Massachusetts the law requires the state supervisory agency to audit the accounts of local units once every two years, and they may do so annually at the request of the local units, many of which have requested an audit as often as possible. In Oklahoma the state must audit the books of county treasurers at least twice a year, but there is no requirement for the auditing of the books of cities, towns, or school districts, except upon request. The treasurers were at first hostile and uncooperative, but now most of them have their books in good shape in anticipation of the audit. During the eight years from 1926 to 1934, twenty-nine local officials were sent to the penitentiary for shortcomings in their books. This fact is no proper criterion of the value of the audit work, since most shortcomings are not criminal in character, but may be corrected by giving proper assistance and advice to the treasurer.[27]

[26] Kilpatrick, *State Supervision of Local Finance*, p. 13.
[27] See Van de Woestne, Royal S., *State Control of Local Finance in Massachusetts*, p. 109 (Harvard University Press, 1935), and Carr, Robert E., *State Control of Local Finance in Oklahoma*, p. 224 (University of Oklahoma Press, 1937).

A good illustration of what may be accomplished by such supervision is found under a Virginia law of 1927. The local treasurers,
elected by the people of the different counties and cities to collect
revenues, are used by the state to collect its revenues in the respective
localities. These collections are forwarded to the State Comptroller,
under whose supervision this work is done. The State Auditor, who is
elected by the General Assembly, audits the books of local treasurers,
since the state has an interest in the completeness and accuracy of
these records. These audits reveal an amazing lack of system in keeping local accounts. Of the 100 Virginia county treasurers, thirty-nine
were short in their accounts. Ten treasurers were removed, but the
treasurers were so strongly intrenched in local politics that no prosecution resulted — in fact, two of them were re-elected to other county
offices. In Lee County the treasurer, whose books showed a default
of $92,000, was removed by Governor Pollard, and a successor ap-
pointed. The defaulting treasurer refused to vacate and Governor
Pollard asked the Supreme Court of Appeals for a writ of mandamus;
by a vote of four to three this court refused to issue the writ, thereby
setting aside the provision of the Code under which the governor
was authorized to suspend the treasurer of any county for failure to
perform the necessary duties with reference to the collection of the
revenue of the state or of the county and city.[28]

Supervision of Local Government Reporting. It should be emphasized that budgeting, accounting, auditing, and reporting are not
separate but closely interrelated processes. Any exaggeration of the
importance of one to the neglect of the others will prevent the attain-
ing of the major goal of efficient financial administration. Uniform
reporting is really a by-product of uniform budgeting and accounting and is easily and inexpensively accomplished if these first two
steps have been properly done. Reporting is but the collecting of
information concerning local financial transactions and furnishing
of this information to the state and to the public.[29] Ten states publish comprehensive annual reports; eight publish no report.[30] The

[28] Pate, *op. cit.*, pp. 1004–1008.

[29] See Dickerson, Milton B., *State Supervision of Local Taxation and Finance
in Michigan*, Chapter 6 (Michigan State College, Lansing, 1944) ; and Miller,
Loren B., *Local Finance and Procedure* (Report to the Michigan Commission of
Inquiry into County, Township and School District Government, Detroit, 1933) .

[30] Kilpatrick, *op. cit.*, p. 19. Comprehensive report states: California, Indiana,
Iowa, Massachusetts, New Hampshire, New Jersey, New Mexico, New York, Ohio,
and Oklahoma. States with no published reports: Alabama, Delaware, Georgia,
Illinois, Nevada, Rhode Island, Pennsylvania, and Texas.

remainder publish either comprehensive reports for selected topics or units only, or reports restricted in scope.

Good reporting is essential for any comparison of the costs of governmental service in different governmental units. If — and only if — the figures are established on the basis of the same classification of items of expenditure, comparisons may be made revealing significant facts regarding the relative efficiency and economy of the spending agencies. Such data provide a sound basis for legislative action. In fact, any supervision or control, either by law or by a state agency, must be built on these local reports, which in addition, serve to inform the taxpayer what he is getting for his money, in much the same way as the financial statement of a corporation informs the investor what is being done with his money.

Control over the Selection of Personnel. No system of control can be effective unless it be administered by competent personnel; in this connection, a few states have gone so far as to provide for the appointment of local assessing officers by state agencies, and for the supervision of the choice of other local fiscal officers. For more than a decade this practice has been followed in a number of states, as reported by Professors Fairlie and Kneier:

In Maryland, the state tax commission appoints a supervisor of taxes for each county from a list proposed by the county commissioners. In West Virginia, all local boards of review are appointed by the state board of public works. In Louisiana, one member of each parish board of equalization is appointed by the state tax commission. . . . In addition to the direct state appointment of county officials, there are also significant cases of state supervision over the selection of county officers and other local functionaries. . . .

Direct state appointment to any large extent will involve a radical change from traditional methods, though it would seem to be justified in the case of some officials whose functions are most clearly those of agents of the state government. But there should be less objection to the extension, to officials whose duties call for special qualifications, of definite requirements as to such qualifications, and of state examinations for testing them or of state approval of local appointments. Such methods may well be applied further, not only in the fields of education and of health and highway administration, but also in the selection of prosecuting attorneys, sheriffs, assessors, auditors, and others.[31]

Conclusions. Although any conclusions to be drawn from such a survey must of necessity be expressed in the broadest and most general terms, the following are suggested: [32] (1) The problem is one of insuring to citizens the opportunity of intimate participation in

[31] *Op cit.*, pp. 103–104.   [32] Spicer, *op. cit.*, p. 159.

their own public affairs on the one hand, and of providing a government capable of rendering efficient service on the other. (2) The excesses of local self-government, as well as of state centralization, have seriously obstructed progress to this goal. (3) A certain measure of state supervision is not only inevitable, but essential to the general welfare. (4) Minimum standards of fiscal procedure and functional performance should be set and maintained by the state, with the opportunity on the part of local units to exceed these standards, and with responsibility on the local officials for results. (5) Every effort should be made to improve local administration from within. (6) Efficient and responsible local administration is more important than state centralization. If democracy is to work at the apex of our governmental pyramid, it must first be made to work at the base. (7) Consideration might well be given to the creation of a single central agency to serve primarily as a liaison between the state and local governments. (8) Finally, there can be no arbitrary separation of state and local responsibility for providing and supporting public services. They must cooperate, or both will suffer.

STATE SUPERVISION OF SCHOOL ADMINISTRATION

In all the states except Delaware, local control over the public schools has become an established tradition. In colonial days the early settlers built a little log schoolhouse, which in the course of time was replaced by the old-fashioned one-room country school. The people have been exceedingly reluctant to relinquish local control over their schools, even though they have often been unable, either financially or by technical training, to maintain them in a manner satisfactory from the educational viewpoint. Delaware alone has kept complete control over its schools, but there has been in the other states a steady and gradual extension of the state powers of supervision and control. Since it was impossible to proceed directly toward this end, much of the extension of state authority has taken place by such indirect means as the subsidy.

State Subsidies to Education. State subsidies to school districts have been an important means of equalizing educational opportunity and of centralizing control over the schools. Subsidies were originally offered in an attempt to equalize the tax burden for educational purposes, and to assist those districts which were financially unable to bear the cost of maintaining their own public school systems. All of the states award funds to the local districts under certain conditions and for certain purposes. Most of them regulate school age, the attendance of pupils, the training and qualifications of teachers, and the ratio of pupils to teachers; some give funds on conditions regulating the use of textbooks and the types and condition of the school buildings to be used. Four fifths of them require regular written reports to be submitted to the state authorities.

It is difficult to determine the exact basis upon which these funds are allocated, because so many laws have been passed that it becomes difficult to determine which ones are now effective.[33] There are about twenty bases used by the different states in the distribution of such funds, including population, average daily attendance, number of teaching units, and such other factors as number of pupils enrolled, salaries paid to teachers, number of school days per year, et cetera. Nor is there any clear cut pattern by which the funds appropriated are allocated to the various school levels — elementary, secondary, and junior colleges. Some appropriate for general school purposes, making little or no distinction between any school grades in the matter of school support; others make a distinction, particularly regarding the state's part of such support.

The United States Office of Education made a study of this problem in 1943.[34] They found three major plans or procedures followed among the states in the distribution of funds for education. Some make one apportionment to all grades, on a formula which has no provision for measuring the amount distributed for high schools and for the elementary schools separately. All of the states

[33] In one large eastern state, a new head of the State Department of Education found certain allocations of subsidy funds on his desk when he took office. He tried figuring these himself by every conceivable principle that he thought might have been used, but was unable by any of these methods to arrive at the results obtained by his predecessor.

[34] Covert, Timon, *State Aid for Secondary Education*, Circular No. 225, 1943. See also: Edwards, Newton, and Richey, Herman G., *The Extent of Equalization Secured through State School Funds* (Advisory Committee on Education, Washington, 1938) ; and a number of studies in individual states: CALIFORNIA: *The Administration, Organization and Financial Support of the Public School System, State of California* (State Reconstruction and Re-employment Commission, Sacramento, 1945). MASSACHUSETTS: *State Fiscal Aids to Cities and Towns for Public Elementary and Secondary Schools* (Massachusetts Federation of Taxpayers Association, Boston, 1945). NEW JERSEY: Burger, Alvin A., *Revising the System of State Aid for New Jersey Public Schools* (New Jersey State Chamber of Commerce, Newark, 1945). PENNSYLVANIA: three reports of the Joint State Government Commission: *The Distribution of State School Subsidies, School Districts on Relief,* and *Teachers' Salaries and the Commonwealth's School Subsidy Plan* (all, Harrisburg, 1945). SOUTH DAKOTA: Rishoi, Roy R., *Inequalities in the Tuition Burden of South Dakota Common School Districts: a Case Study* (University of South Dakota, Governmental Research Bureau, 1940).

provide specifically for vocational education in high school, but in seven states — Arkansas, Kansas, Kentucky, Louisiana, Oregon, South Dakota, and Virginia — no other specific reference to secondary education is made in the allocation of state school funds. Approximately half of the states provide specifically for their high schools or for special high school purposes. In some cases, such funds are for general expenses of high schools; in others, they are for special projects or purposes in connection therewith, while in still others they are provided for equalizing costs of specialized high school education throughout the state.

Publicly controlled and supported junior colleges, ordinarily offering two years beyond the four-year high school, have been established in many communities throughout the country, in some thirty-five states. In a number of states, these schools are considered a part of the local secondary school system. In seven states, the only publicly controlled junior colleges are operated by the state; in nineteen states, the only publicly controlled ones are operated by local school districts as parts of local public school systems. The report continues:

> State support for local junior colleges is not commonly provided to the extent that it is for high schools. Seven of the nineteen states — Arizona, California, Colorado, Mississippi, Missouri, Texas, and Washington — in which these junior colleges are maintained by local districts appear to provide 12 to 35 per cent of the funds used by the colleges. A few of the others provide some aid, but the amounts appear to be comparatively small, with the possible exception of the State of Utah.

General State Supervision. There are very few aspects of elementary or secondary education which do not somewhere or somehow come under state control. This control is obtained in a wide variety of ways. Under their powers of general supervision, more than half the states permit state educational authorities to require reports, and to prescribe the forms in which these reports shall be submitted and the forms in which the records of the several school districts shall be kept. In eighteen states the state is given power of ordinance making within the limits set up by the state constitution and the statutes. In about the same number of states all controversies arising under local school laws are subject to state adjudication.[35]

Control over Personnel. By the use of the system of grants-in-aid it is possible for the state to exercise an extensive control over the personnel engaged in public school work, including such matters as training, salaries, et cetera. In the matter of salary control, the

[35] Wallace, *op. cit.,* pp. 147–164.

locality is obliged to pay its teachers at the rate prescribed by law, or lose its appropriation. In five states, at least, this method was used to raise teachers' salaries, with the hope of attracting teachers of a higher type and with better qualifications. In seven states it was used for the definite purpose of raising the educational attainments of teachers, and in eleven states to secure an adequate staff to carry the teaching load. The qualifications of teachers are controlled by regulations requiring certification for permanent teaching positions in the state school system. In forty-four states examinations for teachers are administered by the state, and certificates are issued upon the passing of these examinations. In twenty-four states the supervising authorities have power to set up standards for admission to the teaching profession. Suspension or removal has been placed under the control of the supervising authorities in eleven states, removal being usually accomplished by the revocation of license.[36]

Not only do the states influence the selection of persons locally appointed, but in some instances they actually do the selecting themselves. Thus Professors Fairlie and Kneier report that the governor appoints the county boards of education in Maryland, and county school commissioners and superintendents of schools in Delaware.[37] Doubtless other similar illustrations might be cited.

Control over the Curriculum. The control over the school curriculum is a further method of centralization. Ordinances have been issued in over thirty states prescribing definite courses of study to be followed in the schools of those states. While there are instances in which these regulations have not been observed and in which enforcement has been made difficult or impossible by a lack of funds, it is still true that these regulations have provided an important means of standardization, accomplished only by invading the supposed rights of the communities to decide such questions themselves. The outstanding example of rigid enforcement of such regulations is the Regents System of New York. In this case the State Department of Education not only prescribes the subjects which shall be taught, specifying the number of weeks and the number of hours per week, but it has outlined in detail, in a series of syllabi, the exact nature of the subject matter to be presented in each course of study.

Control over Textbooks. At least twenty-nine states have established control over the choice of textbooks used in the public

---

[36] *Ibid.*, pp. 164–176. [37] *Op. cit.*, p. 102.

schools, under their ordinance-making power. In some cases this regulation has taken the form of prescribing certain books for certain courses of study, while in others a list of books acceptable to the state department is prepared and distributed to the localities. From these lists, individual selections may be made. In a few cases the state has undertaken to publish its own texts for many of the courses required.

Control over School Buildings. Many states supervise school buildings, from the point of view of exits, emergency lighting systems for auditoriums, and safety from fire hazards generally. Such buildings are usually under the control of the state administrative agency charged with building inspection and the enforcement of fire and panic regulations. Some states, however, have undertaken to pass upon building plans for schools with regard to their suitability and architectural design. In Pennsylvania, for instance, where such supervision is in effect, the Department of Public Instruction is able to assist any community in the state with the planning of a public school building of any type required. Complete blue prints of many types of buildings, which have been inspected and approved by the State Art Commission as well as construction experts, are on file.

Supervision of school buildings may become a very real and effective method of control. Some years ago, in a small town in central New York, the high school building was a dilapidated structure that had been condemned for years as unsafe and unsuitable for school purposes. The local authorities had paid no attention to the repeated pleas of the State Department of Education for the construction of a new building. In the meantime the state law was amended, giving the Department greater authority with regard to school buildings. As a result of this enactment, the Department was able to tell the local authorities that their state funds would be withheld unless they undertook immediately to plan for the new building. Needless to say, the local authorities lost no time in selecting plans, making financial arrangements, and advertising for contracts for the new building.

Thus, by the use of these several devices, most of them incidental to the distribution of state funds to the local school districts, the states have steadily extended their authority over the public school system, usually at the expense of the power of the local units. In a few instances, however, legislative acts have provided for definite transfers of authority.[38]

[38] For an excellent summary, see White, *op. cit.,* Chapter 6.

STATE SUPERVISION OVER PUBLIC HEALTH

While public health administration is one of the oldest and most important of the administrative services of modern government, it is still of rather recent origin. Students of history are familiar with the accounts of epidemics and plagues which swept over cities, taking a heavy toll of human life. Prior to the discoveries of modern science, events of this character were regarded as acts of God. They were considered inevitable, and it was generally believed that there was nothing that man could do about them. Consideration of sanitary conditions was an idea that had yet to penetrate the mind of man. Medieval cities have been described by Frederic Harrison [39] and other writers as literally reeking with filth and squalor. The sanitary conditions in early American cities were not much better. In the absence of facilities for the proper disposal of refuse, sewage, and other wastes, all of these were thrown into the back yard or into the streets. An individual walking down a street in an early American city never knew when refuse might be dumped from a window or door just ahead or behind.

With the discovery of the germ theory and the knowledge that diseases are communicable and that dirt and filth breed sickness, some attention came to be paid to conditions of this character. Most of the early supervision was entirely local. As further progress was made in science, it became evident that the local communities were badly in need of assistance. Individual communities were still more or less isolated, but the state health commissions attempted to assist them by furnishing scientific information which would enable them to cope more successfully with local conditions. This type of commission is well illustrated by that established in Massachusetts. A little later, the Indiana board was vested with powers not only to advise and assist the local authorities in the performance of their duties, but to direct their work and to remove them from office for inefficiency, negligence, or disregard of instructions received from the state board.

Reference has already been made to the changes which the development of modern science has wrought in the field of government. It may have seemed reasonable to permit local communities, under the guise of home rule, to disregard known principles of public health and sanitation, if they chose to do so, when the evil effects of that

[39] Harrison, Frederic, *The Meaning of History*, pp. 232–239 (Macmillan, London, 1894).

disregard were isolated in that single community. When, however, the development of the railroads, steamships, the automobile, and the airplane produced a mobility of population in which such a community might serve as a point of origin affecting a whole state or region, this kind of local self-government ceased to be either practical or workable. Certain aspects of these problems have become of national significance.

The Department's Local Relationships. The administration of health in the local units is well illustrated by the arrangements existing in Pennsylvania. In this state, there are ten district medical officers and 155 sanitarians, acting as a field force. The sanitarians work under the district medical health officers or under county medical directors in the local areas. The arrangements between the State Department of Health and the different types of local units are as follows:

1. In the forty-nine cities of the state, the local boards of health and health officers administer health functions generally without state aid. Only when the city health authorities request assistance, or when a health emergency exists, does the State Department of Health or its officers enter into the picture.

2. In boroughs and townships of the first-class, there are three distinct types of arrangements:

a. Where the municipality handles the local health administration through its own board of health or health officer, who are appointed by the local council or board of commissioners, and where all costs are borne by the local unit. About 800 of the 1,000 boroughs and townships operate under this arrangement. While the Department of Health stands normally in a supervisory relationship to these municipalities, actually the county medical officers and Department sanitarians located in the area are often consulted by the local authorities and render assistance upon request.

b. Where the Department of Health takes direct charge of the local health administration under the terms of the basic board of health act of the state, which gives the Secretary of Health power to take over when he finds conditions to be such as to constitute a health menace to persons living outside the boundary of the municipalities or if it be known to him that any borough or first-class township is without an existing or efficient board of health. Under this arrangement, the Department of Health is paid by the local units for its specific services.

c. Where boroughs and townships of the first-class voluntarily surrender the administration of their health functions to the State Department of Health. In such cases, all expenses incident thereto are carried by the Department of Health.

3. In all second-class townships, health administration is handled directly by district or county medical officers and their staffs employed by the

Defective

State Department of Health. There are no local health officers in second-class townships.[40]

Control over Personnel. Important among the ways in which the authority of the states over public health matters has been extended is the control over the personnel engaged in the work; this can be administered by the collecting and tabulating of data from reports furnished to the state department by each municipality or local subdivision. In twenty-three states the local health officers may be removed for failure to perform their duties, and in forty-two states failure of local officers to enforce properly rules and regulations pertaining to health matters may result in the state taking over control of these local activities. Some states go so far as to control local appointments. In twenty-five states the local registrars of vital statistics are appointed by the state. This state supervision of vital statistics is but a result of the efforts of the United States Bureau of the Census to develop complete and uniform reporting of vital statistics in the Birth Registration Area and the Death Registration Area. About eight states provide for the state appointment of regular health officers, and in two states all local health authorities must be approved by the state administrative authorities.

Maryland has developed, over a period of years extending from 1930, an excellent system of cooperation in health matters between state and county. In the beginning, a careful study was made of each county to determine its needs and conditions. After a program had been developed a local organization was set up to sell it to the county and to the board of county commissioners. As a result of this preliminary work, Maryland claims to be the only state with a trained, full-time county health officer and staff in every county in the state. The program is supported 49 per cent by the county, 51 per cent by the state, thereby insuring state control.

The personnel aspects of this program are very important. The county commissioners of each county are required by law to sit once a month as a county board of health. One of their duties is to appoint

40 See Dodson, George W., "State Health Department's Local Relationships," *Bulletin* of the Department of Internal Affairs, April, 1943, pp. 9–16, and other articles in this series of four on local health administration in Pennsylvania; also North Carolina League of Municipalities, *Municipal Health Departments of North Carolina* (Raleigh, 1941). There are many points of friction between state and local officials in the health field, not the least important of which is responsibility for the support of hospitals and sanitaria; see Philadelphia Advisory Finance Committee, *Welfare and Health Functions Burdening Philadelphia* (Philadelphia, 1937), and Committee on Legislative Research, *A Factual Report on the Question, "Should the State Take over the St. Louis Sanitarium?"* (Jefferson City, 1944).

a county health officer. The state law also requires the State Department of Health to appoint a deputy in each Senatorial District (i.e., each of the thirty-three counties of the state). In practice, the head of the State Department goes to each board of county commissioners and agrees on a man, adequately trained and carefully selected, who is then appointed to do the job. This is important, because the legislator judges the health work by what he observes in his own county.

Venereal Disease Control Work. In many states, venereal disease control work is carried on very largely as a state function; in others, this is not the case, although there are many communities that are not financially able to set up and maintain a satisfactory program in this field. To meet the needs of these communities, the State Department of Health in Illinois arranged, several years ago, to assist financially in the establishment and maintenance of clinics which serve as one phase of a well-rounded program of community social hygiene. While the Department has no intention of establishing clinics of its own, it encourages the cities to do so through subsidy grants, insisting, however, upon high standards of service in each such state-aided clinic. Otherwise the administration of the clinic is strictly a local affair.

Control over Health Ordinances. State control over health ordinances is another method of centralization. In eighteen states all local health ordinances must be submitted to the state authorities for approval. In nine of these states such approval is limited to quarantine regulations; in all others all ordinances must be so approved. Ordinances of the state boards supersede those of municipalities and other local agencies. In some cases where local health departments have been taken over by the state because of their inefficiency or the existence of an emergency, the state ordinances are paramount.[41]

Control over General Sanitary Conditions. Though the state boards of health were originally advisory groups, their control has extended into many fields. The control over general sanitary conditions has been accomplished in a number of ways. In forty-four states all sorts of health and sanitary statistics are collected. These statistics inform the state department regarding health matters throughout the state, and provide a means by which the department can measure the effectiveness of the work done by the various local officers. The mere fact that the states have the authority to collect

[41] Wallace, *op. cit.*, p. 122; centralization in public health administration is discussed in White, *op. cit.*, Chapter 7.

this information gives them a certain amount of control over the local officers, since the departments have authority to prescribe the nature and extent of the data to be furnished and the form in which they shall be presented, and since they have the power to compel local officers to comply with the request.

Inspection of local conditions by the state authorities is another method of control. In Florida the state agents may at any time visit any city for the purpose of investigating the sanitary conditions therein. Still another method of state control is maintained by the dissemination of health information through the use of the various channels of publicity, such as distribution of printed materials, radio and lecture engagements, conferences, motion pictures, correspondence, et cetera. These methods are almost universally employed. Again, the state may extend its control over general sanitary conditions through the use of its ordinance-making power, which is granted to the health authorities in forty-seven states. Illustrative of this type of control is the Pennsylvania Advisory Health Board, a nonsalaried board which holds quarterly meetings for the purpose of considering and approving sanitary and health regulations. These rulings commonly deal with matters of detail not covered in the general health laws, the provisions of which they serve to supplement and clarify.

In one other respect the states can and some of them do exercise an important control over general sanitary conditions. Many American rivers, once clear streams, have for years been little less than open sewers, loaded with mine wastes, industrial wastes, and sewage. New legislation and administrative action have sought to accomplish a purification of streams in many states. One phase of this program involves state pressure upon communities to provide proper sewage treatment works to the end that dumping sewage into streams may be eliminated and the streams purified. In Pennsylvania, for instance, the Department of Justice, working in cooperation with the Sanitary Water Board, carried on during 1944 and 1945 an aggressive campaign to prevent cities and townships from dumping sewage into the Schuylkill River and its tributaries.

Control over Sanitary Engineering Projects. Many states have established an extensive supervision over sanitary engineering projects in the various cities and other local units. These include particularly control over municipal water supplies and sewage systems; the methods used with regard to water supplies differ considerably in the various states. In twelve states reports are required, and in about forty states central inspection is maintained. State approval of all construction plans is necessary in thirty-one states, while the operation and maintenance of these plants are subject to state approval in twenty-two states. In thirty-three states, power to issue specific orders for operation has been given to the state authorities, as has the ordinance-making power in twenty-six states.

Control over sewage systems includes both construction and maintenance. In six states municipalities are required to submit reports, while in thirty-eight states the power of inspection has been given to the state. In two states, Indiana and Wyoming, the complaint must originate with the citizens of municipalities. In most states approval by the state authorities is necessary for construction and operation. Approval of plans is required in many states before any construction work is undertaken.

In many states legislation has been enacted extending the regulatory and supervisory powers of the sanitary engineers to a wide variety of subjects, such as bottling plants for mineral water and soft drinks, the inspection of public bathing places, the abatement of nuisances, housing inspection, inspection of cemeteries and mausoleums, care of environmental sanitation, and many other things.

STATE SUPERVISION OF PUBLIC WELFARE

State centralization has been extended to the field of charity and public welfare work; this tendency was much in evidence prior to the depression and has been greatly accentuated by the developments since 1929. " For centuries we have had prisons, almshouses, hospitals, and outdoor relief administered by public officials. The nineteenth century added children's institutions, parole and probation. The twentieth century has given us mother's pensions, juvenile courts, workmen's compensation, employment bureaus, housing commissions, public playgrounds and social centers, psychiatric clinics, and visiting nurses." [42]

The history of the states in the field of public welfare supervision and administration may be divided into three periods.[43] The period between 1863 and 1900 is known as the disorganized one, during which each state institution was under a separate board charged with full responsibility for its administration. In New Eng-

[42] Warner, Amos G., Queen, Stuart A., and Harper, Ernest B., *American Charities and Social Work*, p. 531, Fourth Edition (Crowell, New York, 1930) .

[43] National Conference of Social Work, *Proceedings*, 1929, pp. 523–530. See also Breckinridge, Sophonisba P., *Public Welfare Administration in the United States, Select Documents* (University of Chicago Press, 1927) .

land the town was the center of charity administration, although in Massachusetts the state took direct responsibility for this work at the beginning of the period under consideration. In New Jersey, New York, Pennsylvania, and some of the western states responsibility was divided between county and town; in the southern states the county was the center of welfare administration.[44]

Between 1900 and 1917, state boards of control were organized; these consisted of a small group of people appointed by the governor, exercising both administrative and executive control of state institutions and agencies. The first centralized board of welfare was established in Massachusetts in 1863. This was followed by the establishment of similar boards in New York and Ohio in 1867; in Illinois, North Carolina, Pennsylvania, and Rhode Island in 1869; in Michigan and Wisconsin in 1871; and in Connecticut and Kansas in 1873. All these states had unpaid boards with supervisory powers but with no centralization of authority. The authority was transferred from one board to another. In Massachusetts, the Act of 1863 provided for a Board of State Charities; in 1869 a State Board of Health was established, followed in 1879 by the Prison Commission. Finally, in 1919, when the state government was departmentalized, there were set up separate departments of health, correction, public welfare, and mental hygiene. The same process of development ocurred in Illinois and New York.

The latter part of this development falls within the third period — from 1917 to date — during which we have centralized the management and control of public charities in a single individual who serves as a member of the governor's cabinet. This type of organization represents the beginning of a new era in welfare administration, in which efforts were made to secure cooperation between departments and at the same time to centralize authority in the states so that they might control or even take over welfare institutions formerly operated by counties and cities. With the advent of the depression, emergency relief boards were established in many states; in some instances these have since been established on a permanent basis, or have been set up as departments of public assistance, leaving to the departments of welfare chiefly the functions of institutional management. In the following paragraphs illustrative types of departmental organization are described, and the techniques by which the states have extended their control over welfare problems previously regarded as purely local are emphasized.

Illustrative Types of State Organization. In 1917 North Carolina

[44] National Conference of Social Work, *Proceedings,* 1930, pp. 459–468.

enacted a law requiring the State Board of Charities and Welfare to appoint a local board of three unpaid members for each county. It was specified that the duties of these boards should be to assist the State Board in the work of the county, to act in a general advisory capacity to the county and municipal authorities in questions relating to delinquency, dependency, and social conditions generally. This law also provided for the consolidation of municipal and county welfare departments.

The New Jersey organization for welfare administration is regarded by many experts as more satisfactory than that of any other state. The governor appoints an unpaid board of eight members, which chooses a commissioner; this board is authorized to create divisions of education, medicine, labor, statistics and research, agriculture, et cetera. It also appoints boards of managers for each state institution and for noninstitutional agencies caring for the insane, feeble-minded, et cetera. The state board supervises the county, municipal, and private agencies to which state aid is given. In Massachusetts the work is divided among four departments: namely, the Department of Public Welfare, the Department of Mental Diseases, the Department of Correction, and the Commission on Probation, at the head of each of which is a commissioner appointed by the governor. The Department of Public Welfare has authority to supervise state institutions, to inspect county and municipal institutions, as well as private agencies, and to administer the public assistance program.

This centralization program has been carried on very successfully. In states like Illinois and New Jersey one finds a complete centralization, while California, Massachusetts, and New York are examples of states in which social work has been brought under state control but not under a single department. Other states, like Mississippi, Nevada, and Utah, still have no central authority to administer their charitable institutions. Eleven states still continue unpaid supervisory boards, while ten states have administrative boards that are either unpaid or ex officio. Eleven other states have salaried boards of control. Arkansas and California maintain two or more separate boards. Finally, there are ten states that have created departments, eight of these under the name of Department of Public Welfare.[45]

---

[45] Odum, Howard W., and Willard, W. D., *Systems of Public Welfare*, p. 28 (University of North Carolina Press, 1925). Recent reorganizations have added to this number.

Recent Illustrations of the Extension of State Control. We have already noted the various forms of assistance most recently undertaken by the departments of welfare. For purposes of illustration, the Mothers' Assistance movement has been selected from this list for discussion here. This movement started in 1909 at a White House Conference on Child Welfare called by President Theodore Roosevelt. The Conference stressed the importance of home life for children. The movement itself was not new, since a limited number of states had already made some provision for the assistance of orphaned children. These acts were not of statewide application. The first statewide Mothers' Aid Acts' were adopted in Illinois in 1911 and in Colorado in 1912. Missouri enacted similar legislation in 1911, but limited its application to Jackson County. By 1913 the number of such laws had increased to eighteen, while by 1931 there were forty-four — in all states except Alabama, Georgia, New Mexico, and South Carolina.[46] The provisions of these acts varied considerably from state to state. Some granted aid to deserted mothers and to mothers whose husbands were incapacitated or in penal institutions, or in institutions for the insane or feeble-minded. Some went so far as to grant aid to divorced mothers and to unmarried mothers. In six states, aid was also given to expectant mothers.[47] With the adoption of the Federal Social Security program, of which mothers' aid is a part and in which all of the states are cooperating, the problem assumed its present-day aspects.

This summary indicates the extent to which an administrative agency reached down into the communities to provide relief for persons who would formerly have been subjects of local charity. In twenty-one states such state control over mothers' aid was maintained, usually by the department of welfare. In Arizona and New Hampshire the state paid the full amount, while in twelve states the state shared the cost with the local communities, either on a fifty-fifty basis or in some other proportion. These provisions for the administration of mothers' aid are the more significant when one considers that the methods used here have been employed in somewhat similar fashion in all the newer phases of public welfare administration, notably during the depression, beginning in 1929, in the handling of emergency relief and, in some cases, programs of public works.

[46] Lenroot, Katharine F., " Mothers' Aid Legislation and Child Welfare," *American Federationist,* May, 1931, pp. 608–615.
[47] *Ibid.,* pp. 609–610.

STATE SUPERVISION OVER HIGHWAYS

In tracing the growth of centralization of control by the state governments, it is possible to draw illustrations from practically every field of administration with which they are concerned. The last function to be considered here is highways. Road building in America was, to begin with, purely a local function. It is true that in the era of internal improvements the Federal government undertook the construction or the giving of assistance in the construction of turnpikes. This, however, was later discontinued. The modern era of highway construction begins with the widespread use of the bicycle, and later of the automobile. Highways within the cities and towns were first improved; then the counties undertook to connect the various centers of population with each other and with the county seats. It soon became apparent that such a multiplicity of governmental units would be unable to develop any comprehensive system of highways. At this point the states began to enter the field of highway construction.

New Jersey appears to have originated the system of state aid for public highways by legislation enacted in 1891; this act provided for the raising of money by local authorities to build and improve roads, for which the state undertook to pay one third of the cost. In 1893 Massachusetts passed an act which provided for a State Highway Commission consisting of three men appointed by the governor with the consent of Council. The Commission was required to make investigations and to advise the counties with regard to construction, alteration, and the maintenance of roads. It was also authorized to hold a public meeting in each county at least once a year, for the purpose of discussing matters relating to roads. At approximately the same time Vermont adopted a similar method of state highway administration. By 1917 legislation of this character had been enacted by every state.[48]

The process by which control over road building passed gradually from the local units to the states is significant. As has been noted, the original state expenditures for highways were administered on the grants-in-aid basis; the roads still remained under

[48] White, *op. cit.*, p. 114. From a table presented by Dr. White, the following data are summarized:

Prior to 1900	7 states
1900–1904	8 states
1905–1909	14 states
1910–1914	13 states
1915–1917	6 states

the control of the local units, although the state authorities exercised some supervisory control over those highways for which state money was used in construction or maintenance. When it became evident that this method was inadequate, the states began to take over certain highways connecting important centers of population and county seats. These were designated as state highways. Acts of this character were adopted in many states around 1910. From that date on, the records show additions to the several state highway systems made at each successive legislative session as the financial inadequacy of the individual units and their failure to attract capable highway administrators became more and more apparent. In North Carolina all highways have been state highways since 1931, and many other states moved rapidly in the same direction. Pennsylvania, for instance, began its state highways system by an act passed in 1911, taking over 8,835 miles of road. Minor additions were made at intervals until 1931, when 20,000 miles of rural road were added to the state highway system, making a total of 33,989 miles. In the session of 1933 the General Assembly took over the maintenance of 48,500 miles of additional rural roads. While this policy was continued for a time, the pressure at the moment seems to be in the opposite direction. When the state assumes control of a piece of highway, the local residents expect a very high standard of construction and maintenance, whereas if this highway is a local responsibility, almost anything will do. With an increasing percentage of the annual receipts of the Motor License Fund absorbed in maintenance costs and with urgent needs for new construction, the department is much less anxious than formerly to assume new responsibilities.

The alternative to taking the roads over is to give financial assistance in such form and such amounts as will enable the local units properly to discharge the responsibility themselves. The allocation formula is prescribed by law. In some instances, it is extremely complicated, and may result in gross inequalities as between different local units. This has been the case in Michigan, where the Tax Study Advisory Committee reported in 1945 variations in the per capita apportionment of highway funds ranging all the way from $.80 in one county to $7.19 in another. Five other counties received less than $1.00 per capita, and thirty received less than $2.00. Thirty-four received between $2.00 and $3.00, with seventeen receiving more than $3.00.

To correct this situation, the Committee proposed a new allocation formula under which all three units of government — the state, the municipalities, and the counties — would share proportionately on a fixed percentage basis, in any increase or decrease in highway-user taxes and which would eliminate much of the existing friction between county and municipal officers. Their proposal was that all revenues from liquid fuel and motor vehicle taxes should " be commingled in one fund and then divided into three parts in the following proportions: 40 per cent to the state highway department, 35 per cent to be distributed to the counties, and 25 per cent to be distributed to incorporated cities and villages." [49]

GENERAL CONCLUSIONS

In the preceding chapter the local units were dealt with from the point of view of the organization of the machinery of government and certain suggestions were made for its improvement. The present concern is with the functions of government — with the things the government does, and the question as to what particular unit is to perform a given function. For years there has been a definite and continuous shift of power from the units of local government to the states. In some cases, as in the matter of highways, this has led — or soon may lead — to a situation in which the local communities are entirely relieved of administrative responsibility over a particular service. In other cases, as in health and welfare, a considerable transfer of power has taken place, but, owing to new conceptions of the responsibility of government, ample powers still remain in the hands of the local units.

This development is by no means limited to the important administrative fields which have here been used for purposes of illustration; others are evident on every hand. Control over the sale of liquor was formerly left in many states to " local option "; this form of control is now rare. Housing was originally regarded as a purely private concern. As a result of World War I, housing shortages developed in some cities and laws of a temporary nature were passed to curb abuses. The people thus became accustomed to some sort of supervision and control; city housing commissions

[49] Michigan Tax Study Advisory Committee, *Preliminary Report,* pp. 35–41 (Lansing, 1945) ; see also Colorado Municipal League, *The Cities' Share of Gasoline Tax Revenues in Colorado* (Boulder, 1940) ; Pennsylvania Joint State Government Commission, *Liquid Fuels Tax* (Harrisburg, 1945) ; and *State Aid from Gasoline Taxes on Texas County and Road District Bonds and Warrants* (Ranson-Davidson Company, San Antonio, 1942).

were established, to be followed, in turn, by state housing commissions. The administration of justice was once regarded as a purely local function; now, informed people in every locality are urging the abolition of the magistrate system, the establishment of centralized court systems, the establishment of a state department of justice whose head shall have supervisory powers over district attorneys, sheriffs, and other local law-enforcing officers, and the enlargement of the zones of police administration. The movement for municipal home rule, once so promising, has entirely subsided. There is, in fact, scarcely a field of government to which one might not turn to find illustrations of the tendency toward centralization.

There are a number of reasons for these significant changes in the American system of government. In the first place, the people are beginning to value efficiency and economy in public administration more than they value the long-cherished concept of home rule. In the original set-up of the units of local government, they have seen overlapping, duplication, inefficiency, and waste. These factors have been apparent to students of government for some time, but it took the hardships of the depression to bring about a wide public recognition of them. In the second place, state officials have commonly been persons of better training and qualifications, and have generally represented a higher type of personnel. Again, this centralization is a direct result of our changed economic and social structure. Matters that were formerly regarded, quite properly, as local in character have taken on a wider aspect, and have become state matters or, in many cases, matters of national concern. It is significant that the local units have not lost any power of which they have been able or willing to make a vigorous and effective use. Their losses have been due to financial inability or to ineffective administration. This, of course, is true of the tendencies toward centralization in other fields of government as well.

North Carolina has gone farther in this movement toward centralization than any other state in the Union. An able commentator from that state, in explaining the development there, has pointed out that the people were anxious to secure tax relief and that they were willing to resort to extreme measures toward that end. He suggests also that in recent years the state has been fortunate in having a number of excellent governors — a fact which has developed public confidence in the state government. This factor has certainly been operative in other states. Finally, the confidence of the people in their agencies of local government was shaken by a considerable number of scandals; the record of the state government had not been marred in this way, and consequently public confidence in it has been increased rather than diminished. In Georgia, likewise, the counties have been overshadowed by state centralization. One writer describes the counties as rapidly becoming "nonentities" as the state absorbs the administration of roads, schools, welfare, charities, and corrections, few duties being left to justify the continuance of rural local government.[50]

As this process of centralization has proceeded, each step has seemed desirable and necessary. The completion of the process now seems not only necessary but in the long run inevitable in many administrative fields. It was encouraged by the depression, when the states had more money than the local units. We have progressed far enough along this line, and have had sufficient opportunity to compare the new system with the old, so that no one need regard the culmination of this movement with apprehension. The results of centralization have proved on the whole very satisfactory — far more satisfactory than the results of the system for which centralization is a substitute. To quote again from a distinguished authority in the field of public welfare administration:

> It appears that in the field of service in which the state institution or the state agency is the appropriate authority, reasonable progress has been made in efficiency and in adequacy of service; whereas in these fields where reliance is still placed on the local unit, retardation, archaic methods and great unevenness prevail. The almshouse, outdoor relief, and the county jail remain with few exceptions the despair of the social worker and the public welfare officials.[51]

SELECTED REFERENCES

Agg, Thomas R., and Brindley, John E., *Highway Administration and Finance* (McGraw-Hill, New York, 1927).

Alexander, Ulman S., *Special Legislation Affecting the Public Schools* (Teachers College, Columbia University, 1929).

Allen, H. K., *Control of Expenditures in the Local Governmental Units of Illinois* (University of Illinois *Bulletin*, July, 1940).

American Municipal Association, *Financial Relationships between State Governments and Municipalities* (Chicago, 1933).

50 Wager, Paul W., "State Centralization in North Carolina," *American Political Science Review*, November, 1931, p. 1003, and "State Centralization in the South," *Annals*, January, 1940, pp. 144–150; Agnew, J. Thomas, "Georgia Counties Overshadowed by State Centralization," *National Municipal Review*, April, 1939, pp. 271–274, 295.

51 Breckinridge, *op. cit.*, p. 4, and Graves, W. Brooke, "Readjusting Governmental Areas and Functions," *Annals*, January, 1940, pp. 203–209.

Barclay, Thomas S., *The Movement for Municipal Home Rule in St. Louis* (Governmental Research Institute, St. Louis, 1943).

Betters, Paul V., *State Centralization in North Carolina* (Brookings Institution, Washington, 1932).

Bishop, Eugene A., *Development of a State School System in New Hampshire* (Teachers College, Columbia University, 1930).

Bitterman, Henry J., *State and Federal Grants-in-Aid* (Mentzer, Bush, Chicago, 1938).

Bradshaw, H. C., *Budgeting in Texas Counties* (Agricultural and Mechanical College of Texas, College Station, 1941).

——, *State and Local Financial Relations in Texas* (Agricultural and Mechanical College of Texas, College Station, 1942).

Brannon, Victor D., *State Auditor and Fiscal Control in Missouri Counties* (University of Missouri Studies, 1939).

Breckinridge, Sophonisba P., *Public Welfare Administration in the United States* (University of Chicago Press, 1927).

Brown, Cecil K., *The State Highway System of North Carolina* (University of North Carolina Press, 1931).

Campbell, Raymond G., *State Supervision and Regulation of Budgetary Procedure in Public School Systems* (Teachers College, Columbia University, 1935).

Carpenter, William S., *Problems in Service Levels* (Princeton University Press, 1940).

Carr, Robert K., *State Control of Local Finance in Oklahoma* (University of Oklahoma Press, 1937).

Crouch, Winston W., *State Aid to Local Government in California* (University of California Press, 1939).

Dickerson, Milton B., *State Supervision of Local Taxation and Finance in Michigan* (Michigan State College, East Lansing, 1944).

Donoghue, James R., *Intergovernmental Cooperation in Fire Protection in the Los Angeles Area* (University of California at Los Angeles, Bureau of Governmental Research, 1943).

Edwards, Newton, and Richey, Herman G., *The Extent of Equalization Secured through State School Funds* (Advisory Committee on Education, Washington, 1938).

Fairlie, John A., and Kneier, Charles M., *County Government and Administration* (Appleton-Century, New York, 1930).

Ford, Robert S., and Goodrich, Kenneth S., *State Supervision of Local Borrowing* (University of Michigan, Bureau of Government, 1942).

Graves, W. Brooke, Ed., "Intergovernmental Relations in the United States," *Annals*, January, 1940.

Grinnell, Harold C., *Studies in Local Government and Taxation in Rural New Hampshire* (University of New Hampshire, 1943).

Gruelle, Orie P., *State Insurance of Public School Property in Kentucky* (University of Kentucky, 1939).

Hansen, Alvin H., and Perloff, Harvey S., *State and Local Finance in the National Economy* (Norton, New York, 1944).

Henry, Nelson B., and Kerwin, Jerome G., *Schools and City Government* (University of Chicago Press, 1938).

Hinckley, Russell J., *State Grants-in-Aid* (New York State Tax Commission, Albany, 1935).

Hoffer, Frank W., *Counties in Transition* (University of Virginia, 1929).

Hutchinson, Ruth G., *335 State-Administered Locally-Shared Taxes* (Columbia University Press, 1931).

Illinois Legislative Council, *The Problem of Local Fiscal Control, with Special Reference to Control at the County Level* (Springfield, 1940).

Institute of Local and State Government, University of Pennsylvania, *City-State Relations* (Philadelphia, 1937).

Jackson, George L., *The Development of State Control over Public Instruction in Michigan* (Michigan Historical Society, Lansing, 1926).

Jamison, Judith N., *Intergovernmental Cooperation in Public Personnel Administration in the Los Angeles Area* (University of California at Los Angeles, Bureau of Governmental Research, 1944).

Kilpatrick, Wylie, *Problems in Contemporary County Government* (Institute for Research in the Social Sciences, University of Virginia, 1930).

——, *State Supervision of Local Budgeting* (National Municipal League, New York, 1939).

——, *State Supervision of Local Finance* (Public Administration Service, Chicago, 1941).

Kneier, Charles M., *City Government in the United States,* Third Edition (Harper, New York, 1945).

Lafferty, William A., Jr., *The Auditing of Municipal Accounts in New York State* (New York State Conference of Mayors and Other Municipal Officials, Albany, 1933).

Lancaster, Lane W., *State Supervision of Municipal Indebtedness* (University of Pennsylvania, 1923).

Leland, Simeon E., Ed., *State-Local Fiscal Relations in Illinois* (University of Chicago Press, 1941).

Lynn, Harry R., *A Decade of Change in Government and Politics* (University of Kentucky, Bureau of Government Research, 1943).

MacCorkle, Stuart A., *State Financial Control over Cities in Texas* (Arnold Foundation, Dallas, 1937).

——, *Units of Local Government in Texas* (University of Texas, Bureau of Municipal Research, 1941).

Malone, Paul E., *The Fiscal Aspects of State and Local Relationships in New York* (New York State Tax Commission, Albany, 1937).

Marr, Robert H., *Political Corporations under Louisiana Law* (Hansell, New Orleans, 1935).

Martin, Richard, *Financial Relationship of the State and the Towns* (Connecticut League of Municipalities, Manchester, 1938).

McBain, Howard L., *Law and Practice of Municipal Home Rule* (Columbia University Press, 1916).

McGoldrick, Joseph P., *Law and Practice of Municipal Home Rule, 1916–1930* (Columbia University Press, 1933).

McPheron, E. B., *A Summary of Indiana Centralization* (Bureau of Government Research, Indiana University, 1938).

McQuillan, Eugene, *Law of Municipal Corporations,* Second Edition, Supplement (Carswell, Chicago, 1932).

Merlin, Sydney, *American Taxes Shared and Allocated, 1938* (American Municipal Association, Chicago, 1939).

Mitchell, John M., *State Control and State Aid for Libraries; Statements of the Case* (Wilson, New York, 1937).

National Association of Supervisors of State Banks, Committee on Municipal Obligations, *Municipals* (Washington, 1941).

New Jersey State Chamber of Commerce, *Municipal Finances in New Jersey* (Trenton, 1939).

New York State Commission for the Revision of the Tax Laws, *Financial Control in the Suburban Areas of New York State* (Legislative Document, 1937, No. 63).

New York State Commission on State Aid to Municipal Subdivisions, *Report* (Legislative Document, 1936, No. 58).

New York State Constitutional Convention Commission, *Problems Relating to Home Rule and State Government* (Albany, 1938).

——, *State and Local Government in New York* (Albany, 1938).

Odum, Howard W., and Willard, D. W., *Systems of Public Welfare* (University of North Carolina Press, 1925).

Philadelphia Advisory Finance Committee, *Health and Welfare Functions Burdening Philadelphia* (Philadelphia, 1937).

Pontius, Dale, *State Supervision of Local Government: Its Development in Massachusetts* (American Council on Public Affairs, Washington, 1942).

Princeton Survey of New Jersey Finance, *An Improved Fiscal Structure for New Jersey* (Princeton University Press, 1941).

Reed, Thomas H., *Federal-State-Local Fiscal Relations* (Municipal Finance Officers Association, Chicago, 1942).

St. Louis Chamber of Commerce, *Tax Payments and State Aid in Missouri by Counties, 1931–1937* (St. Louis, 1939).

Scheps, Clarence, *Central Control of Municipal Accounts in Louisiana* (Louisiana State University, Bureau of Government Research, 1941).

Schulz, Ernst B., *Effect of the Contract Clause and the Fourteenth Amendment upon the Power of the States to Control Municipal Corporations* (Lehigh University, 1939).

Selko, Daniel T., *Town-Administered Special Districts and the Control of Local Finance in New York* (New York State Tax Commission, Albany, 1936).

Shepard, E. Fenton, and Wood, William B., *The Financing of Public Schools in Michigan* (University of Michigan Press, 1944).

Snavely, Tipton R., Hyde, Duncan C., and Biscoe, Alvin B., *State Grants-in-Aid in Virginia* (Century, New York, 1933).

Snider, Clyde F., *The Problem of Local Fiscal Control with Special Reference to Control at the County Level* (Springfield, 1940).

Sparlin, Estal E., *Special Improvement District Finance in Arkansas* (Agricultural Experiment Station, Fayetteville, 1942).

Stout, Randall S., *State Grants-in-Aid in Pennsylvania* (Pennsylvania State College, 1945).

Tharp, Claude R., *State Aid in Michigan* (University of Michigan, Bureau of Government, 1942).

Studensky, Paul, *The Government of Metropolitan Areas* (National Municipal League, New York, 1930) .

Troxel, Oliver L., *State Control over Secondary Education* (Warwick and York, Inc., Baltimore, 1928) .

Van de Woestyne, Royal S., *State Control of Local Finance in Massachusetts* (Harvard University Press, 1935) .

Wager, Paul W., *County Government in North Carolina* (University of North Carolina Press, 1928) .

Wallace, Schuyler C., *State Administrative Supervision over Cities in the United States* (Columbia University Press, 1928) .

Wayne University, School of Public Affairs and Social Science, *Wayne County's Interest in State Grants-in-Aid* (Detroit, 1940) .

Weaver, L. H., *School Consolidation and State-Aid in Illinois* (University of Illinois Press, 1945) .

Whetten, Nathan L., and others, *Studies of Suburbanization in Connecticut* (Connecticut State College, 1936–1939) .

White, Leonard D., *Trends in Public Administration* (McGraw-Hill, New York, 1933) .

——, *An Introduction to the Study of Public Administration*, Revised Edition (Macmillan, New York, 1939) .

Wisconsin Tax Commission, *Wisconsin's Taxes and State Aids* (Madison, annually) .

Woodworth, Leo D., *Shared Taxes* (American Municipal Association, Chicago, 1944) .

Anderson, William, " Legislative Changes in State-Local Relations in Minnesota, 1915–1939," *Minnesota Municipalities,* January, 1941, pp. 9–20.

Bradshaw, H. C., " State and Local Financial Relations in Texas," *National Municipal Review,* March, 1942, pp. 154–159, 162.

Editorial Research Reports, " State-Local Finance in the War Emergency," August 16, 1941, entire issue.

Graves, W. Brooke, and Scholz, Karl W. H., " Meeting the Needs for State and Local Revenues in the Postwar Era," *American Political Science Review,* October, 1944, pp. 904–912.

Harris, Joseph P., " The States and the Cities," *State Government,* April, 1945, pp. 55–58, 72.

Hendrickson, Robert C., and Burger, Alvin H., " New Jersey Reaps Fruits of Good Municipal Finance Laws," *National Municipal Review,* September, 1943, pp. 419–422, 436.

Hinckley, Thomas L., " Early Fiscal Plans Bear Fruit," *National Municipal Review,* May, 1944, pp. 229–233.

Hoan, Daniel W., " States, Localities, and Defense," *State Government,* January, 1941, pp. 9–12, 21–25.

Hobbs, T. G., "Annexation of Surrounding Territory by Cities in Virginia," *Virginia Law Review,* April, 1942, pp. 831–847.

Hoyt, Homer, "Forces of Urban Centralization and Decentralization," *American Journal of Sociology,* May, 1941, pp. 843–852.

Lepawsky, Albert, " America's Tax Dollar — A Key Problem in Governmental Reconstruction," *Annals,* January, 1940, pp. 185–193.

Long, Henry F., " The State and Its Political Subdivisions," *State Government,* April, 1945, pp. 62–63, 71.

MacCorkle, Stuart A., " State Control of Local Budgeting," *Southwestern Social Science Quarterly,* September, 1940.

McHenry, Dean E, " Liquor Control Ten Years After Repeal," *State Government,* October, 1943, pp. 208–210.

Marion, John H., " State Supervision in New Jersey over Municipalities in Unsound Financial Condition," *American Political Science Review,* June, 1942, pp. 502–508.

Martin, Edward M., " State Supervision of Local Finance," *Bulletin* of the Union League Club of Chicago, March, 1941, pp. 1–16.

Morrow, Glenn D., " Supervision of County Debts in Kentucky," *Public Administration Review,* Autumn, 1943, pp. 335–352.

National Municipal League, " State-Local Borrowing After Two Decades," *National Municipal Review,* January, 1945, pp. 46–47.

Peak, George, " Constitutional Limitations on County Indebtedness in Kentucky," *Kentucky Law Journal,* November, 1939, pp. 3–11.

Perkins, John A., " Government of ' Rurban ' Areas," *American Political Science Review,* April, 1943, pp. 306–313.

Peterson, Orville C., " A Survey of the Minnesota Law of Municipal Ownership of Public Utilities," *Minnesota Municipalities,* February–March, 1944.

Sheppard, Virgil, " The Middle Way — American Plan," *National Municipal Review,* March, 1940, pp. 296–300.

Spicer, George W., " Fiscal Aspects of State-Local Relations," *Annals,* January, 1940, pp. 151–160.

Wager, Paul W., " State Centralization in the South," *Annals,* January, 1940, pp. 144–150.

Weidner, Edward W., " State Supervision of Local Government in Minnesota," *Public Administration Review,* Summer, 1944, pp. 226–233.

CHAPTER XXII

Interstate Relations

FEDERAL CONSTITUTIONAL PROVISIONS

THE Federal Constitution deals with some of the problems of interstate relations. The erection of trade barriers between the states, in the form of import and export duties or both, was supposedly prohibited in Article I, Section 10. The Supreme Court is given original jurisdiction, in Article III, Section 2, over cases in which a state is a party. Most of the provisions bearing on interstate relations are in Article IV: the full faith and credit clause, one of the guarantees of the privileges and immunities of citizens, the other being in Amendment XIV; the provision for rendition of fugitives from justice; and the provision for the admission of new states. The interstate compact clause is found in Article I, Section 10.

Interstate Rendition. The Constitution says that "a person charged in any State with treason, felony, or other crime, who shall flee from justice, and be found in another State, shall, on demand of the executive authority of the State from which he fled, be delivered up, to be removed to the State having jurisdiction of the crime." This language is simple, clear, and direct, but it has none the less been responsible for a great deal of friction between the states, since the duty of determining who is a fugitive from justice rests upon the governor of the state where the accused is found. While the Court has held that the clause was intended to include every offense made punishable by the law of the state in which it was committed, governors have sometimes been unwilling to act upon this principle. If the governor of whom the request is made decides that the so-called fugitive from justice is not a fugitive — that the evidence against him is inadequate to establish a presumption of guilt, or that the offense is not sufficiently serious — there is nothing that can be done about it. Congress has provided no remedy in such cases, although there have been many of them. In a leading case, the Governor of Ohio refused, in 1860, to deliver to Kentucky a man charged with aiding the escape of a slave. The Supreme Court decided that the act of Congress passed in 1793 under this clause, declaring it to be the duty of a state to deliver upon a sufficient showing, was not mandatory. A Federal court will not, therefore, issue a mandate to compel a governor to accede to such a request.[1] While this decision greatly weakened the express intent of the Constitution and of Congress, any other decision might have raised the troublesome question of the coercion of a state.

Some of these cases attract wide public attention, and have been the cause of acrimonious struggles between the state governors concerned. Many will recall, for instance, the heated controversy between the Governors of Georgia and New Jersey in the case of one Robert E. Burns, author of *I Am a Fugitive from a Chain Gang*. Late in 1934 these questions were discussed in connection with the extradition proceedings involving the suspect in the Lindbergh kidnaping case, Bruno Richard Hauptmann, later extradited from New York, tried, convicted, and executed in New Jersey. Years ago there was the famous controversy between Pennsylvania and New York with regard to Harry K. Thaw. It has always been something of a mystery why a governor should fight to keep such persons within his jurisdiction; in 1933 the Governor of Florida well expressed this point of view when, in a controversy with the Governor of Illinois, he telegraphed a message to the latter in which he said: " If you want to keep him . . . that's your privilege." This question is discussed briefly, from another angle, in the chapter on the governor.

Privileges and Immunities. Interstate comity in the protection of the rights of citizens is provided for in Article IV, Section 2, and in the first section of Amendment XIV: " The citizens of each State shall be entitled to all privileges and immunities of citizens in the several States," and " No State shall make or enforce any law which shall abridge the privileges and immunities of citizens of the United States." An analysis of these clauses reveals that citizens have privileges and immunities both under the Federal government and under the states; it is also clear that the two are not the same. The protections of procedural rights apply to all persons, whether citizens or

[1] Kentucky v. Dennison, 24 Howard 66, 1860; see also the Massachusetts Rules of Practice in Interstate Rendition, in *Sixth Report* of the Judicial Council of Massachusetts, 1930, pp. 78–79, and Green, P. Warren, " Duties of the Asylum State under the Uniform Criminal Extradition Act," *Journal of Criminal Law and Criminology*, September–October, 1939, pp. 295–324.

not, and hence are not privileges and immunities. It was the intention of the framers of the Constitution to protect citizens against the action of the states — not against the action of other individuals. "A private individual cannot deny or abridge a right, he can at most interfere with its exercise." [2]

What are the privileges and immunities pertaining to state citizenship? They have never been completely enumerated or defined, but from a long line of judicial opinions it is possible to point out certain rights which would be included in such a definition. As Dean Burdick observed, "certain rights arise from the very nature of the relationship of a citizen to the state of which he is a member, and others arise from certain exclusive powers granted to the national government." The interpretation of this clause was dealt with by the Supreme Court in 1935 in Colgate v. Harvey.[3]

Full Faith and Credit. The Constitution provides that "full faith and credit shall be given in each State to the public acts, records, and judicial proceedings of every other State." This provision is mandatory; yet, like others, it has been weakened by judicial interpretation. The necessity for some such rule is obvious; if none existed, it would be possible for individuals who were so disposed to "beat the law" by moving into another state as soon as the law caught up with them. The Constitution further provides that "the Congress may by general laws prescribe the manner in which such acts, records, and proceedings shall be proved, and the effect thereof." In other words, the constitution and the official records of one state, properly proved and authenticated, shall have the same effect in the courts of another state as they may be presumed to have in their own. There has been a large body of judicial interpretation of this clause, but the following paragraphs give a good idea of its scope:

This clause declares the attributes and qualities which judicial proceedings and records of one state shall have when offered in evidence in the courts of another, and it implies that they shall be given the same effect in the courts of another state as they have by law and usage at home. But this provision, and the laws giving it effect, establish a rule of evidence, and not of jurisdiction; they do not operate to make records and judgments domestic for all purposes but only to give them a general validity and credit as evidence.

The full faith and credit demanded is only that faith and credit which the judicial proceedings had in the other state in and of themselves require.

[2] Burdick, Charles K., *The Law of the American Constitution*, p. 336 (Putnam's, New York, 1922); for a full discussion of this subject, see Chapter 11.
[3] 296 U. S. 404, 1935; for the interpretation of the similar clause in the Bill of Rights, see Crandall v. Nevada, 6 Wallace 35, 1867.

It does not demand that a judgment rendered by a court which has juris-diction of the person but which is in no way responsive to the issues ten-dered by the pleadings, and is rendered in the actual absence of the de-fendant, must be recognized as valid in the courts of any other state.[4]

There has been much misunderstanding with regard to the appli-cation of this clause in the field of divorce. There is obviously some-thing wrong when a person legally divorced and lawfully married again in one state may be held for bigamy in another. Such a state-ment, however, is only partly true, for ex parte divorce decrees are recognized in all but the so-called minority states — New York, North Carolina, Pennsylvania, and South Carolina. A divorce granted in the state which had always been the domicile of the plaintiff and was the only matrimonial domicile is entitled to full faith and credit in the state in which the defendant resided, although she was not personally served with process within the state where the divorce was granted.[5] Generally speaking, when a decree is rendered for alimony, and is made payable in future installments, the right to such installments becomes absolute and vested on becoming due, and is therefore protected by the full faith and credit clause, pro-vided no modification of the decree has been made to the maturity of the installments.[6] Yet, on the other hand, a judgment of divorce obtained by a husband in a state to which he had gone in disregard of his duty, upon service of process by publication by his wife who had remained in the state of the matrimonial domicile, and who did not appear in the cause, is not entitled to full faith and credit outside the state in which the decree was granted.[7]

Interstate Compacts. In Article I, Section 10, the Constitution pro-vides that "no State shall, without the consent of Congress . . . enter into any agreement or compact with another State. . . ." The application of this clause has been restricted to political agree-ments, which it was feared might be embarrassing to the central gov-ernment. Sixty-two agreements were entered into under this clause from 1789 to 1932, inclusive, to all of which the consent of Congress

[4] *Constitution*, p. 493. For excellent recent discussions, see Cataldo, Bernard F., "Full Faith and Credit," *Annals*, January, 1938, Supplement, pp. 32–45; and Cor-win, Edward S., "The Full Faith and Credit Clause," *University of Pennsylvania Law Review*, April, 1933, pp. 371–378.

[5] Atherton v. Atherton, 181 U. S. 155, 1900.

[6] Sistare v. Sistare 218 U. S, 11, 1910.

[7] Haddock v. Haddock, 201 U. S. 562, 1905. This comment is based upon data in the annotated *Constitution*, cited above. See Rodman, Karl M., "Recognition of Divorce Decrees," *Rocky Mountain Law Review*, December, 1939, pp. 16–29, and Holt, Harold W., "Any More Light on Haddock v. Haddock?" *Michigan Law Review*, March, 1941, pp. 689–718.

Number	Year	States	Subject
1	1789	Virginia and Kentucky	Interests in lands and jurisdiction over Ohio River.
2	1800	Virginia and Kentucky	Boundary agreement.
3	1820	Kentucky and Tennessee	Boundary agreement.
4	1833	New York and New Jersey	Boundary agreement and jurisdiction in New York Harbor.
5	1848	Missouri and Arkansas	Boundary agreement.
6	1853	Massachusetts and New York	Cession of territory.
56	1929	New Mexico and Arizona	Water supply of Gila and other rivers.
57	1929	Colorado, Oklahoma, and Kansas	Water supply of Arkansas and other rivers.
58	1929	Colorado, New Mexico, and Texas	Use of waters of Rio Grande above Fort Quitman, Texas.
59	1930	Oklahoma and Texas	Bridges over Red River.
60	1931	Idaho and Wyoming	Boundary agreement.
61	1932	Idaho and Wyoming	Allocation of waters of Snake and other rivers.
62	1932	Montana and Wyoming	Allocation of waters of Yellowstone River.

INTERSTATE COMPACTS WITHOUT CONGRESSIONAL CONSENT, LISTED IN CHRONOLOGICAL ORDER, 1780–1931

Number	Year	States	Subject
1	1780	Pennsylvania and Virginia	Boundary agreement.
2	1785	Virginia and Maryland	Boundary agreement.
3	1791	Virginia and North Carolina	Boundary agreement.
4	1803	Virginia and Tennessee	Boundary agreement.
5	1815	North Carolina and South Carolina	Boundary agreement.
6	1818	North Carolina and Georgia	Boundary agreement.
7	1821	North Carolina and Tennessee	Boundary agreement.
8	1825	South Carolina and Georgia	Navigation agreement.
9	1837	Georgia and Tennessee	Right of way for railroad.
10	1839	Vermont and Canada	Extradition agreement.
11	1872	Massachusetts and Connecticut	Merger of railway corporation, subjecting it to the laws of each state.
12	1886	Louisiana and Arkansas	Levee agreement.
13	1894	New Hampshire and Massachusetts	Boundary agreement.
14	1900	New York and New Jersey	Palisades Interstate Park agreement.
15	1931	Arkansas, California, Kansas, Louisiana, Oklahoma, Texas, and Wyoming	Oil, gas, and mineral committee created.
16	1931	Arizona and California	Bridge over Colorado River at Ehrenburg.

was specifically given. Only seventeen of these had been adopted before the present century. During the longer period from 1780 to 1931, inclusive, sixteen agreements were made without Congressional consent, only three of them since 1900. Illustrative entries of the first type and the complete list of agreements of the second type are listed in the tables on page 906.[8]

Few are the states that have not been a party to at least one interstate compact. Twenty-three of the agreements have dealt wholly or partly with the settlement of boundary disputes; ten have dealt with problems of jurisdiction of rivers, harbors, or boundary waters; nineteen are water supply agreements;[9] five each have dealt with the cession of territory, criminal jurisdiction, and interstate or international bridges. Two agreements dealt with conservation, while others dealt with debt agreements and the Hudson tunnels. About half the agreements not assented to by Congress related to boundaries, the remainder to such subjects as the Palisades Interstate Park, bridges, railroads, navigation, et cetera. Scholars who studied this record, with a view to determining the possible usefulness of this plan for the future, found few grounds for encouragement; they pointed to the extraordinary number of agreements dealing with such matters as boundary lines, jurisdiction over rivers and boundary waters, and water supply, and to the absence of agreements on current controversial matters.

A decade or more ago there was a greatly revived interest in interstate compacts, accompanied by a popular belief that the device might be used in the solution of some of our present difficulties. The Federal Department of Justice, through its adviser on state relations, in the early thirties, urged the use of compacts as a means of closing some of the jurisdictional gaps through which criminals have found it possible to escape.[10] Others made like recommendations with re-

[8] These figures and the data in the tables are taken from Ely, Northcutt, *Oil Conservation through Interstate Agreement*, Appendix II, Parts II and III (Federal Oil Conservation Board, 1933). A list of the acts of Congress authorizing or ratifying agreements between the states, prepared by the Legislative Reference Service of the Library of Congress, appears in the *Congressional Record*, July 17, 1935, pp. 11810–11812.

[9] See "Should the Interstate Water Compact Be Remodeled? Federal v. State Views," *State Government*, September, 1943, pp. 192–197. Gustav E. Larson, supporting the Federal view, argues that participation by the Federal government in negotiation and administration is desirable, while Clifford H. Stone, presenting the state view, contends for the preservation of the integrity of the state water laws as being of paramount importance. See also National Resources Planning Committee, *Interstate Water Compacts, 1785 to 1941* (Washington, 1942).

[10] For instance: "The murderers of Andrew Bryson shot across a state line. The state where they fired could not legally punish them; the adjacent state where

gard to milk prices in individual milkshed areas, control of the oil industry, taxation, and other subjects of common concern to a group of neighboring states. There is no constitutional reason why states far distant from each other might not enter into compacts, but for rather obvious reasons such agreements have rarely been made by states whose territory was not contiguous.

An interesting experiment with this device was carried on by the Eastern Interstate Conference on Labor Compacts, organized in 1931 for the framing of compacts on which member states might agree on minimum wages, hours, and other labor subjects. The Conference grew out of a meeting of governors assembled in Albany in 1931 on invitation of Governor Roosevelt. Another meeting was held soon after in Harrisburg on invitation of Governor Pinchot. Further meetings, involving representatives of eleven states, were held at frequent intervals during the next three or four years, about eighteen in all. After terrific effort, a minimum wage agreement was approved by the delegates, and later by one of the states. The insignificant accomplishments of this prolonged and well-directed effort to use the compact device for handling a group of highly controversial problems led many observers to conclude that further attempts in this direction would be futile.

The subsequent efforts of the Council of State Governments have produced results that are considerably more encouraging. The Interstate Parole and Probation Compact which it sponsored had, in 1945, been put in effect by thirty-eight states, and it was expected that all or most of the remaining ten would soon approve the proposal.[11] The Interstate Oil Compact Commission, which observed its tenth anniversary in 1945, stands forth as perhaps the nation's most notable example of the success and practicability of the compact method in the solution of perplexing interstate problems. One of the greatest achievements of this interstate cooperative body has been that of instilling in the minds of the public and the various branches of the state and Federal governments, confidence in its aims and objectives, and general approval of the voluntary collaboration method in correlating divergent state views and opinions.[12]

---

the bullets killed Bryson could not reach the murderers. Never having been there, they were not fugitives from the justice of that state." University of Pennsylvania Bicentennial Committee, *Toward a More Effective Criminal Law* (Philadelphia, 1937).

11 See Ellis, William J., "Interstate Parole and Probation Compact: An Appraisal After Ten Years of Operation," *State Government*, March, 1945, pp. 40–42, and inside back cover.

12 Interstate Oil Compact Commission, *The Interstate Oil Compact to Con-*

The obstacles to the success of the compact device are so formidable that they can be overcome only by the prestige, influence, and the persistent efforts of an organization like the Council. The delegates to conferences for the formulation of compact agreements have no real power; they are in a position comparable to that of delegates to an international conference. They may proceed in accordance with their instructions — if they have any — but they have no power to commit their respective governments to anything. It is always difficult to secure agreement on matters of detail, doubly so under such circumstances. Assume for the moment that they do come to an agreement on the terms of a compact; it must then be ratified by the legislature of each of the cooperating states. It is often difficult to get treaties through the United States Senate, but here the difficulties are multiplied many fold. Each legislature has two houses and there are as many legislatures as there are cooperating states.

If some of the states which took part in the negotiations fail to approve the compact, it may still be possible for the rest to proceed. Suppose, however, that one of the states, having officially approved the compact, fails to discharge its responsibility in living up to its terms. Can such a state be coerced into compliance, or must the whole plan of cooperation collapse? Probably the latter. Or suppose that all of the states observe the terms of the compact in good faith, and that the compact remains in effect until some revision is necessary. Aside from the difficulty of carrying on successfully new negotiations, and getting the resulting agreement ratified, there is the troublesome question of determining what would happen if some one or more states failed to approve the revision. How would such a cooperative venture function with some states proceeding on one basis, some on another? The complexity of these situations is such as to cause one to despair of significant accomplishment by this procedure in solving any of the controversial social and economic questions of our time.

In view, however, of numerous attempts to use the compact method, it may be well to inquire into the form which such agreements might take. Ernest L. Averill, former Attorney General of Connecticut and president of the National Association of State Attorneys General, suggested that they would probably fall into the fol-

serve *Oil and Gas, A Summary of Its Organization, Purposes and Functions* (Published by the Commission, 1942), and Webb, Wilfred D., " The Interstate Oil Compact — Theory and Practice," *Southwestern Social Science Quarterly*, March, 1941, pp. 293–301.

lowing four major groups: (1) A uniform statute preserved by compact. This is the method best suited to settling land titles and other questions requiring the preservation of a statute unaltered for a stated period. (2) A statute by each state granting reciprocal authority of jurisdiction to certain officials, but not requiring uniform regulations. The criminal law compact proposed by New Jersey in 1935 would probably come under this head. (3) Separate commissions, acting jointly, empowered to make uniform regulations by joint action, subject to each state's approval. This form has been much used and will probably be employed in many of the coming compacts on taxes, and in other regulatory laws. (4) A single administrative commission, empowered to make regulations subject to each state's approval. In many cases this form is preferable to the third method, and appropriate in the same fields, but it is sometimes difficult of adoption because of mutual jealousies or distrust between the states concerned. Its success in the Port Authority compact between New York and New Jersey is notable. The interstate compact to preserve oil and gas takes this form. Five states — California, Kansas, New Mexico, Oklahoma, and Texas — are concerned; the pact became effective within the ratifying states as soon as three had ratified and Congress had consented.[13]

UNIFORM STATE ACTION

The Need for Uniformity. Students of American government have long recognized the desirability — indeed, in many cases, the necessity — of the development of uniform rules with regard to many subjects falling within the jurisdiction of the states. Few persons there are, familiar with the problems of administration in any given field, who have not expressed the desire for the adoption and enforcement of uniform policies with regard to many of the problems within their range of interest. A few illustrations will serve to emphasize the widespread need for such uniformity. Elsewhere the author has enumerated a considerable number of subjects with appropriate references.[14] In the field of insurance, there exists a multiplicity of

[13] Quoted from a statement by Mr. Averill in *New York Times*, April 14, 1935; for an excellent recent discussion, see Routt, Garland C., " Interstate Compacts and Administrative Cooperation," *Annals*, January, 1940, pp. 93–102.

[14] Graves, W. Brooke, *Uniform State Action* (University of North Carolina Press, 1934) , and " Intergovernmental Relations in the United States," *Annals*, January, 1940, entire volume.

rules and regulations with regard to each of the aspects of insurance management commonly subjected to regulation. These rules are so different, are based upon such a variety of standards, and require the employment of such extensive personnel by each of the companies regulated, that insurance rates are far higher than would be necessary under a more rational system of regulation. The great diversity in the provisions of the state laws on marriage and divorce is a matter of common knowledge. Many citizens have lived through the futile efforts of the states to control child labor and the unsuccessful attempts to control it by Congressional legislation. They have watched the proposal of the Federal child labor amendment and the powerful opposition raised against it, which ultimately defeated it.

The states have engaged in active competition with each other in the granting of corporate charters, each one striving to attract a larger share of this profitable business. Unethical practices have been made possible on an enormous scale by the existing chaos of state laws. During the banking crisis of 1933, students of public affairs were amazed by the number of bank failures and the tremendous losses of depositors in the closed institutions. They looked across the border to Canada with its limited number of banking institutions, no one of which was closed as a result of the depression, and in no one of which a depositor lost a dollar; these banks, incidentally, were united into a single central bank in July, 1934. Confusion long existed, and in some cases still exists, regarding motor traffic regulation, naturalization procedure, provisions in workmen's compensation legislation, safety in factories, and a variety of other subjects. The need for the development of uniform policies in these fields is obvious, and in many cases it is imperative.

Interstate Tax and Trade Barriers. The most serious recent problem of interstate relations has been the development of trade and tax barriers. For a century and a half Americans prided themselves upon the complete freedom of trade in this country, and were wont to make derisive remarks about the lack of such freedom in Europe. Financial stringency, growing out of the depression, encouraged a competition for sources of revenue which resulted in the many overlapping and duplicating taxes that are now familiar to all — all with detrimental effects upon freedom of trade and commerce in the United States. Differences in wage levels, labor standards, and unemployment exaggerated by the depression induced the passage of numerous state laws favoring products produced within the state.[15]

Trade barriers are established through the exercise of the tax and license powers, police and regulatory powers, corporate and proprietary state powers, through special legislation, and also incidentally, without the support of special legislation. Illustrative of the first type may be mentioned special taxes on certain types of merchandising organization, such as chain stores; use taxes levied by sales tax states, applied to purchases from outside, as compensatory taxes; taxation of nonresident commercial motor vehicles so as to discriminate in favor of resident trucks and busses; special taxes and license fees levied on foreign corporations in return for the privilege of doing business within the states; vendor licensing by municipalities and states which apply to merchant truckers and nonresident canvassers; discretionary premium taxes on foreign insurance companies. Most of these barriers grew out of apparently legitimate attempts on the part of individual states to raise revenue, or in other ways to protect the interests of their citizens. The incidental effect was to create barriers — an effect which, while unforeseen in the vast majority of cases, was none the less serious.

In its preparation for the National Conference on Interstate Trade Barriers, the Council of State Governments concentrated its attention upon the following most common types:

1. Truck and motor vehicle regulations
2. Ports of entry
3. Oleomargarine laws
4. Horticultural products
5. Itinerant truckers
6. Use taxes (with or without compensatory tax)

15 For excellent recent statements, see Bane, Frank, *Statement before the Temporary National Economic Committee*, March 18, 1940 (Council of State Governments, Chicago, 1940) ; Corey, Herbert, " Will War Raze the State Line Trade Barriers? " *Public Utilities Fortnightly*, September 24, 1942, pp. 417–424; Downs, E. F., and Konenkamp, S. J., " Those State Trade Barriers — Fact or Fiction? " *ibid.*, April 15, 1943, and April 29, 1943; *Indiana Law Journal*, " Interstate Trade Barriers," December, 1940, entire issue; Green, Thomas S., " Combating U. S. ' Balkanization,' " *Public Opinion Quarterly*, March, 1940, pp. 162–164; Jackson, Robert H., " The Supreme Court and Interstate Barriers," Martin, James W., " Tax Competition Between States," and Melder, F. Eugene, " Trade Barriers Between States," all in *Annals*, January, 1940, pp. 54–78; Lockhart, William B., " State Trade Barriers to Interstate Trade," *Harvard Law Review*, June, 1940, pp. 1253–1288; Schlesinger, M. R., " Sales Taxes, Interstate Trade Barriers, and Congress: The Gulf Oil Case," *Michigan Law Review*, March, 1941, pp. 755–781; Tocker, Phillip, " Trade Barriers," *Texas Law Review*, April, 1940, pp. 274–294; Wolaver, Earl S., " Trade Barriers and Interstate Commerce," *American Law School Review*, May, 1941, pp. 1102–1107.

7. Milk and dairy products
8. Discriminatory laws — livestock, poultry, and general foods
9. Building material, building codes, etc.
10. Liquor laws

This comment might be extended indefinitely if the attempt were made to describe and illustrate each of these various types; the following two brief dialogues and the incident described below will suffice, perhaps, to indicate the manner in which these restrictions affect the life of the ordinary citizen. All are reported by Frank Bane of the Council of State Governments.

COP. Got a trucking license to do business in this state?

TRUCKER. Sure. Here.

COP. All right. Got a driver's license?

TRUCKER. Would I be driving a truck without one? It's right here on my cap.

COP. Okay. Got an I. C. C. license?

TRUCKER. Say, what is this? An international border or something?

COP. Well, I guess that's all. Say, wait a minute. What's the length of this truck?

TRUCKER. How do I know? I never measured it.

COP. Well, we're going to measure it right now. 5, 10, 20, 30, 35, 40, 43, 44, 45 — 45 feet and 3 inches.

TRUCKER. How long did you say?

COP. 45 feet and 3 inches. Okay, buddy, you're a lawbreaker.

TRUCKER. What do you mean, lawbreaker?

COP. Trucks over 45 feet long aren't allowed on these highways. The state law says so, and your truck is 3 inches over. Back you go over the state line.

TRUCKER. But I got green vegetables in this truck. They'll all spoil. I'll lose my job.

COP. Sorry, buddy, I don't make the law, I just enforce it.

———————

GROCER. Good mornin', Ma'm. What's your pleasure?

WOMAN. I'd like some groceries.

GROCER. You've sure 'nough come to the best store in Camden County, Georgia. Reckon you're a stranger hereabouts.

WOMAN. That's right. My husband and I have just bought the old Chinapin place.

GROCER. Happy to have your trade, Ma'm.

WOMAN. What grades of fresh eggs do you have?

GROCER. Just one. The best Georgia eggs. Thirty-seven cents a dozen.

WOMAN. That seems a little high. Only one grade, you say?

GROCER. Yes, Ma'm. We've got other eggs but they ain't " fresh."

WOMAN. You mean they're cold storage?

GROCER. No. We've got eggs from Florida but we can't call 'em " fresh."

WOMAN. Why not? The Florida line is only ten miles below here.

GROCER. I know that, Ma'm, but the law says that the only fresh eggs in Georgia is Georgia eggs.

WOMAN. What a strange ruling!

GROCER. Ain't it the truth? But we gotta protect our own hens. Now do you want fresh eggs or do you want the other kind?

WOMAN. I guess I'll have to pay the price. Even if the Florida eggs are just as fresh, I don't like the idea of buying eggs that aren't called fresh.

GROCER. Them Florida hens actually ain't the quality of ours, Ma'm. You better buy Georgia since you're in the state.

WOMAN. All right, give me a dozen. But I can't see what earthly difference it makes to a hen whether she lays an egg on one side or the other of the St. Mary's River so long as it's fresh.

GROCER. The hen ain't got nothin' to say about it, Ma'm. It's just the law, that's all.

Harry Harper, an Iowa farmer, started out for St. Louis, Missouri, to sell a load of melons he had grown. During his journey he was stopped by the Iowa Highway Patrol at night and required to put three green lights on his truck. After driving across the state line into Missouri, the Missouri police stopped him and told him it was illegal in Missouri to have three green lights on his truck, so he had to take them off.

Methods of Securing Uniformity. The methods by which uniformity may be obtained may be considered from the point of view of the units of which our Federal system is composed, or from that of the three major branches of the state governments. In the first case, one would consider the possibility of securing the adoption of uniform rules and administrative practices through the agencies of the Federal government on one hand, or the possibility of achieving the same ends by the cooperation of the states on the other. In the second case, one would concern himself with the possibilities of securing uniform rules for the control of a given subject through the adoption of identical statutes by the several state legislatures, through the adoption of uniform administrative policies enforced by cooperation among the states, or finally, by the development of uniform principles of judicial interpretation.

Since only the general question of interstate relations is being considered here, it is unnecessary to dwell on uniformity achieved — at least, in peacetime — through Federal centralization by amendment of the Federal Constitution, or through the influence of such factors as concurrent powers, the grant-in-aid system, or the leadership of Federal administrative agencies in developing uniform practices and policies among the states. Neither need we concern ourselves with such obvious influences toward uniformity as are provided by the provisions of the Federal Constitution or of Congressional legislation. During the defense period and the early part of the war, some of these obstacles to the free flow of interstate trade had a serious effect on the war effort. Corrective measures were adopted, in some cases by the states themselves, and in others by the exercise of the war powers of the Federal government, as for instance, when the Office of Defense Transportation took over full control of trucking operations.

The primary concern here is with those influences which have originated in the states, and which are organized and maintained by them for the purpose of developing uniform policies. One of these influences, interstate compacts and agreements, has already been discussed; the other, involving movements for the adoption of uniform laws and for the development of uniformity, cooperation, and reciprocity among administrative officers in different states, will be discussed briefly in the paragraphs which follow.[16] Since there has been so little actual accomplishment in the field of judicial uniformity, no further discussion of that topic will be included here.[17]

LEGISLATIVE UNIFORMITY

National Conference of Commissioners on Uniform State Laws. New York pioneered in the effort to secure uniform legislative provisions on subjects of general interest to the states, some consideration being given to this question as early as 1857. It was not, however, until 1889, when, due at least in part to the suggestion contained in a resolution adopted by the legislature of this state, the American Bar Association summoned a conference on the subject, that any really significant action was taken. Nine states were represented in this first conference; since 1912, all the states, territories, and the District of Columbia have been officially represented. The Conference is composed of three commissioners from each state, chosen usually by the governor from the legal profession to serve without compensation. They have developed an elaborate organization of regular and special committees, concerned with the drafting of uniform acts relating to a wide variety of subjects coming within the jurisdiction of the state governments.

Two short tables are presented here for the purpose of indicating,

[16] Graves, *op. cit.*, Chapter 2, and in greater detail in succeeding chapters.
[17] *Ibid.*, Chapter 18, and Hargest, William M., "Keeping the Uniform State Laws Uniform," *University of Pennsylvania Law Review*, December, 1927, pp. 178–184.

UNIFORM STATE ACTS PROPOSED AND ADOPTED, 1934 AND 1939

Section	Name	Number of Acts Proposed		Total Number of Adoptions	
		1934	1939	1934	1939
I	Commercial	10	11	188	201
II	Property	6	13	99	123
III	Public Laws	9	13	95	126
IV	Social Welfare	7	9	35	115
V	Corporations	1	5	4	6
VI	Torts and Criminal Laws	4	6	38	78
VII	Civil Procedure	11	15	154	151
	Totals	48	72	613	800

NUMBER OF ADOPTIONS OF LEADING UNIFORM STATE LAWS, 1934 AND 1939

Number	Name	Section	Adoptions	
			1934	1939
1	Bills of Lading Act	I	29	29
2	Limited Partnership	I	20	22
3	Sales Act	I	34	35
4	Warehouse Receipts Act	I	48	48
5	Negotiable Instruments Act	II	53	53
6	Stock Transfer Act	II	24	27
7	Aeronautics Act	III	22	22
8	Proof of Statutes Act	VII	23	25
9	Veterans' Guardianship Act	VII	33	35
	Total		286	296

in a general way, the scope and nature of the subject matter considered by the Conference. In the first table are listed the seven sections into which the Conference has been divided, the number of uniform acts proposed by it as of 1934 and 1939, respectively, and the number of adoptions of these acts as of the same years. In the second table are listed the nine acts which had received twenty or more adoptions in 1934, with the number of adoptions as of 1939. In the latter year, the number had nearly doubled, there being sixteen such acts, the following having been added to the list in a period of five years: Act Regulating Traffic on Highways, Act to Secure the Attendance of Witnesses from without a State in Criminal Proceedings, Criminal Extradition Act, Declaratory Judgments Act, Desertion and Non-Support Act, Narcotic Drug Act, and the Partnership Act. These sixteen acts account for 469 of the 844 adoptions reported in

1939, including adoptions of some acts which were no longer a part of the Conference program.

A number of interesting questions arise with regard to the geographical distribution of the adoptions of these uniform acts. According to data in the 1939 *Handbook,* Oklahoma and Texas had adopted three each, while Wisconsin had adopted thirty-four, and South Dakota and Utah, thirty-five each. Ten states, as well as the District of Columbia and Puerto Rico, had adopted ten each or less, while fourteen states had adopted more than twenty. Exactly half of the states and the territories of Alaska and Hawaii were in the eleven to twenty zone. These figures show a substantial increase over 1934, 1929, and other earlier years. When these data are plotted on an outline map of the United States, it is impossible to present any conclusions with regard to sectionalism, since one finds in each section states with a notably large number of adoptions and states with a very small number. The uniform laws before the states for adoption at the end of half a century of activity relate to approximately fifty subjects, nearly every law has been adopted by at least one state, while others have been approved by thirty or more.

From the data presented in the tables above, it appears that the acts proposed by the Uniform Commercial Law Acts Section and the Civil Procedure Law Acts Section have been much more successful in securing the approval of the state legislatures than acts proposed by other sections of the Conference. An outstanding example is the Uniform Negotiable Instruments Act which is in force in all states, some territories, and some Latin American countries. Others that have been widely adopted include the Warehouse Receipts Act, which makes warehouses receipts generally acceptable in business transactions, in forty-five states; and the Sales Act, which concerns the transfer of title to personal property, in thirty-two states. Seven of the acts proposed by the Commercial Section are included in the sixteen acts with twenty or more adoptions. These acts have been most frequently adopted in the industrial and commercial states of the North, in the agricultural states of the Central West, and in the mountain states of the Far West. The Civil Procedure Acts have been much less successful, but have secured large numbers of adoptions in the same sections of the country. In both cases, the Southern states have been noticeably backward.

The question has often been raised regarding the extent to which the legislatures make modifications and changes in the text of the uniform acts which they adopt. The author made a careful analysis of the data on this question as of 1930. At that time there were eighteen states, with adoptions of uniform acts totaling 170, where not a single modification of any statute had been made; there were fourteen states, with adoptions totaling 147, where in each case one act had been modified; and there were eleven states, with adoptions totaling 110, where two acts each were modified. In the remaining five states — Idaho, Louisiana, Massachusetts, North Dakota, and Pennsylvania — three or more acts were modified in each case. The author undertook to analyze these modifications in detail in a typical state, and came to the conclusion that the problem of modification was not of pressing importance. Of 139 adoptions reported in 1939 for the first ten states, only one or two per state had been modified.

In 1925, the Conference adopted an improved organization and, in 1927, the policy of dropping acts which had once been recommended but had since become obsolete was adopted. As of the same date, the Conference recognized the possible usefulness of doing a certain amount of pioneering in new fields of legislation, providing a leadership which has been of great value to the states; finally, that the movement for the adoption of the acts recommended by the Conference has been proceeding much more rapidly in the last few years. The Conference was organized in 1892; in the thirty-three years from that date to 1925, the total number of adoptions was less than 400; in 1933, only eight years later, it had increased to more than 600, and thirteen years later, to 844. While the value of the work cannot be measured solely in terms of the number of adoptions, this increase is none the less impressive. Still greater increases may be anticipated, for the Conference announced in 1940 a new cooperative arrangement with the Council of State Governments.

There has been a good deal of discussion as to the usefulness of uniform legislation. There is no denying the fact that the Conference and the Council as governmental agencies concerned with reducing interstate friction, preparing and urging the adoption of uniform acts, have made a real contribution to the cause of better government. President Dodds of Princeton commends both the progress made and the effect of this uniform legislation. " It would be difficult," he wrote in 1944, " to measure the full extent of the influence of the model laws on governmental efficiency, economy, and integration. Their impact has been very great." [18]

18. Dodds, Harold W., " Model Laws as an Aid to Progress," *National Municipal Review*, November, 1944, pp. 531–534, 544; see also Graves, *op. cit.*, Chapter

American Law Institute. The realization of the need of a closer and more effective cooperation between state governments had been developing in many quarters after World War I. In 1923 there met in Washington a conference called the Preliminary Committee for the Establishment of a Permanent Organization for the Improvement of the Law, set up by the American Bar Association the preceding year, with Elihu Root as chairman. The Institute, which grew out of this conference, was incorporated under the laws of the District of Columbia for the purpose of promoting " the clarification and simplification of the law, and its better adaptation to social needs, to secure the better administration of justice and to encourage and carry on scholarly and scientific legal work." In the first ten years of its existence the Institute embarked upon two projects of great significance in connection with the attainment of these objectives.

The first of these involved the " attempt to give orderly expression to the common law," by restating in modern form, upon the basis of exhaustive study and research by the ablest legal scholars in the country, the principles of the law. The first published result of this project was the *Restatement of the Law of Contracts,* published in 1932; others have followed, in due course, at the rate of one or two volumes a year. In 1940, fifteen volumes had appeared, covering, in addition to contracts, the following: conflict of laws, trusts, agency, torts, restitution, and property (the last in four volumes). Restatements were in course of preparation on the law relating to security (pledges of personal property, suretyship, et cetera) and judgments. The effect of this work may very likely be comparable to the effect of that done by Blackstone for the common law of England. When completed, it will not only clarify and simplify the tangled and conflicting legal rules and doctrines which had developed in this country on common law subjects over many years, but it already provides a powerful stimulus toward a more uniform application and interpretation of the principles of the common law among the several states.

The second major project of the Institute lies in the field of the criminal law. The *Model Code of Criminal Procedure,* prepared by methods similar to those followed in the restatements, was pub-

3; Mott, Rodney L., " Uniform Legislation in the United States," *Annals,* January, 1940, pp. 79–92; Schnader. William A., " Progress Toward Uniform State Laws," *State Government,* November, 1940, pp. 219–220, 231–232; and Stanley, W. E., " Progress in Uniform State Laws," *ibid.,* November, 1944, pp. 442–445.

lished in 1930. Because of the widespread interest in such matters, this code has already had a significant influence on the laws of the states. This effort has been extended to include a restatement of the whole substantive criminal law. A *Model Code of Evidence* has been prepared, as has other work in the field of criminal justice. Model statutes dealing with the arrest, trial, conviction, and treatment of youth between sixteen and twenty-one have been published, the first of these in 1940, as the Youth Correction Authority Act, which relates to the treatment of convicted youths.[19]

Other Organizations. Numerous other organizations have concerned themselves with the development of uniform statutory provisions on a wide variety of subjects. Indeed it may be said that there are few national organizations concerned with the provisions of the laws of the several states affecting subjects within their range of interest which have not at some time or other advanced the adoption of uniform measures. While in many cases they have gone so far as to prepare the drafts of model statutes, they have rarely had the financial resources or the extensive organization necessary for the successful promotion of these acts. Efforts of this type have been made by the American Judicature Society, the National Council on Uniform Aeronautic Regulatory Laws, the National Association of State Aviation Officials, the Committee on Aeronautical Law of the American Bar Association, the National Conference on Street and Highway Safety, the National Association for Labor Legislation, the Investment Bankers Association of America, the American Standards Association, the Society of Mechanical Engineers, the Mortgage Bankers Association of America, the Russell Sage Foundation, and many others.[20]

ADMINISTRATIVE COOPERATION

The cooperation of administrative officers in charge of similar services in the several states antedates the efforts to secure uniformity through legislative means, and offers on the whole a greater promise of substantial achievement. The National Convention of Insurance Commissioners was organized in 1878; the National Board of Dental Examiners was organized in 1883; two more such groups were or-

[19] Data from a letter to the author from William Draper Lewis, Director of the Institute, August 19, 1940; *The Restatement in the Courts,* Fifth Edition (American Law Institute, St. Paul, 1945), and two articles on the Youth Act, American Bar Association *Journal,* May, 1942: Lewis, for, pp. 322–324, and Hall, Jerome, against, pp. 317–321.

[20] Graves, *op. cit.,* Chapter 4.

ganized in 1884, and three in 1889, making a total of seven that were organized and functioning before the establishment of the National Conference of Commissioners on Uniform State Laws in 1892. From that time on, few years passed without the organization of one or more groups of state administrative officers. A recent effort to compile a classified list of these organizations and to study their activities revealed a much larger number than anyone had supposed, and indicated far greater achievement in the development of uniform policies and of cooperative and reciprocal relations between administrators in different states than had heretofore been known to exist.

Governors' Conferences. The first meeting of the Governors' Conference was held at the White House in Washington in 1908 at the call of President Theodore Roosevelt, for the purpose of considering the conservation of natural resources. Strangely enough, no similar meeting of governors had ever been held; this meeting was hailed by press and public, by the President,[21] and by the governors who attended as an epoch-making event in the history of American government. The second and third meetings of the Conference were held in January and November, respectively, of 1910, and were addressed by Governor Charles E. Hughes of New York and Governor Woodrow Wilson of New Jersey, both of whom outlined the advantages of conferences of this character and presented in glowing terms the possibilities they seemed to offer. Unfortunately, these possibilities have never been realized. Nothing of great importance in the history of the Conference occurred from this time until 1919, when Mr. Wilson, then President of the United States, summoned a White House Conference of Governors and Mayors to consider the problems of reemployment which faced the nation when its military forces were demobilized.

Thereafter the Conference continued to hold annual meetings (except in 1917) at various points throughout the country, with an attendance seldom exceeding 50 per cent of those eligible. The meetings have been pleasant social affairs and sightseeing expeditions. Papers were presented on a variety of more or less innocuous subjects, but the discussion of vital controversial issues has been

---

[21] With characteristic enthusiasm, Mr. Roosevelt wrote in his *Autobiography*, p. 445 (Macmillan, New York, 1913): " It is doubtful whether, except in time of war, any new idea of like importance has ever been presented to a Nation and accepted by it with such effectiveness and rapidity, as was the case with this Conservation movement when it was introduced to the American people by the Conference of Governors."

regularly banned. At the Conference in 1931 several governors tried to break down this rule but, judging by subsequent meetings, with little immediate success so far as the general policy was concerned. The meetings seemed to have little effect, either on the development of interstate cooperation or on the solution of the difficult problems arising in the field of interstate relations. A permanent secretariat was established in Chicago, in connection with the Council of State Governments, in 1935.

In the last few years, the Conferences have had much greater influence, although they have maintained many of their earlier characteristics. The maintenance of the permanent secretariat makes possible a continuity of effort previously lacking, and advance planning for the discussion of the questions of the day. At the Hershey Conference in 1944, and again at Mackinac in 1945, vital questions relating to the war effort and to postwar development were freely discussed. At these gatherings the governors showed a disposition, not merely to talk about states rights, but to do something about them. The obvious thing to do is to make the states such efficient instruments for the rendering of essential services that there will be no need for and no temptation to " run to Washington " in order to get things done.

In addition to the national Governors' Conferences, held annually, there are many sectional or regional meetings of state governors, some of them held annually, some occasionally for the consideration of a single subject, in various parts of the country. It is not unusual to find really constructive measures undertaken as a result of meetings of this character. In 1925 the New England Council was created at the suggestion of the governors of the six New England states. The governors have continued their meetings for the discussion of common problems, but the Council, with its permanent secretariat, has been able to devote a steady and persistent effort toward the advancement of the common interests of the member states. The southeastern states have established a somewhat similar council with the cooperation of the governors in that section of the country. The Western Conference of Governors has held more or less regular meetings. As illustrative of the occasional meetings, one might mention the Interstate Commission on Unemployment Insurance, which grew out of a conference of seven governors of industrial states called by Governor Roosevelt of New York in 1931; a conference of the governors of the Middle Atlantic states for the discussion of problems of state and local government called by Governor

Moore of New Jersey in 1933; and the conferences of the agricultural states in the Middle West held on a number of occasions during the period of the depression. Many such conferences of governors were held during World War II.[22]

Organizations of Department Officials. Reference has been made to the extensive organization of the heads of the various types of administrative service represented by the usual administrative departments in our state governments. A few illustrations of the work of these organizations may be in order. In agriculture, a whole series of organizations has been developed, corresponding to each of the units of government, from the largest to the smallest. Thus, in the administration of the food and drug laws, one finds the Association of Dairy, Food, and Drug Officials of the United States, seven organizations of officials in the same field organized on a sectional basis, supplemented in turn by small regional conferences of administrators. It thus becomes possible, either through the adoption of policies by the National Association, or through the influence of the United States Food and Drug Administration, to secure the uniform enforcement of rules and regulations applying to food and drug products. A similar elaborate organization of enforcement officials is to be found among those engaged in milk inspection work.[23]

The National Association of Supervisors of State Banking, the National Convention of Insurance Commissioners, and the National Conference on Weights and Measures are all organized on a similar basis for the purpose of securing the enforcement of uniform practices and the development of cooperative and reciprocal relations among the state officials engaged in supervising these phases of business activity. There are national organizations of highway officials and of motor vehicle administrators, but the latter have been more concerned with and more successful in the development of a high degree of interstate cooperation. The National Conference on Street and Highway Safety, organized and maintained under the supervision of the United States Department of Commerce, has been instrumental in developing considerable uniformity out of the previously chaotic situation with regard to the law governing the operation of motor vehicles. The American Conference of Motor Vehicle Administrators, which grew out of the Eastern Conference, has exerted a considerable influence in the direction of a uniform enforcement

[22] Graves, *op. cit.*, Chapter 5, and Nixon, H. C., "The Southern Governors' Conference as a Pressure Group," *Journal of Politics*, August, 1944, pp. 338–345.
[23] Graves, *op. cit.*, Chapter 6; also Routt, *op. cit.*

of this legislation. Further illustrations could be cited in practically every important administrative field.

Interstate Agreements. Early in the Roosevelt era, the Congress created, under the leadership of the President and Senator Norris, the Tennessee Valley Authority for flood control and for the development of the hydroelectric power and other resources of the Tennessee Valley. This agency has been well administered and has been notably successful in the accomplishment of the purposes for which it was created. Numerous proposals have been made for the establishment in similar manner of other authorities to cover the major watersheds of the country, particularly those of the Missouri and Arkansas Rivers.

In spite of the success of the TVA, and of the care which its officials have exercised in dealing with the states affected and their subdivisions, there is a feeling that this program represents a kind of compulsory regionalism. In contrast to this, the spokesmen for the states point to some outstanding illustrations of the successful operation of a voluntary regionism. Notable among these are the Interstate Commission on the Delaware River Basin, known as Incodel, the Ohio River Interstate Stream Conservation Agreement, the Interstate Commission on the Potomac River Basin,[24] which have all made significant contributions to the solution of the problems of the drainage basins affected. These agencies, along with the Atlantic States Marine Fisheries Commission, have all operated with increasing efficiency and to the satisfaction of all of the participating states. Nine states in the Missouri Valley have made progress toward a comprehensive plan for developing that great river basin.

The Ohio River Interstate Stream Conservation Agreement owes its origin to the fact that the Director of Health in Ohio discovered shortly after World War I that the water supplies of several Ohio communities were being impaired by the discharge of untreated waste from by-product coke ovens. The Director succeeded, in 1924, in entering into an agreement with the Pennsylvania and West Virginia Departments of Health, known as the Ohio River Interstate Stream Conservation Agreement. This agreement has been extended to include eleven states in the Ohio River drainage basin; the states now function as the Interstate Commission on the Ohio River Basin. The sanitary engineers in these states have already de-

[24] Kittrell, F. W., " Polution Control in the Potomac," *State Government,* April, 1942, pp. 79–80, 90, and the Commission's *An Introductory Report* (Washington, 1945) .

veloped a high degree of cooperation, whereby all downstream areas are notified promptly of any condition which might affect the taste, odor, or purity of their water supplies, regardless of the state or states in which these communities may happen to be located. This cooperative arrangement has worked well, and for the benefit of all concerned.

The Interstate Commission on the Delaware River Basin is the joint governmental agency which was created in 1936 by the states of New York, New Jersey, Pennsylvania, and Delaware for the purpose of formulating, adopting, and executing wise and constructive policies for the most appropriate development and utilization of the natural resources of the Delaware River basin and its tributaries. Each of the member states has a commission on interstate cooperation. These agencies have jointly organized Incodel, which through its technical advisory committees on Quantity of Water, Quality of Water, Research and Information, and Planning, and the staff, is developing practical programs for the use of the natural resources of the basin. The Commission, about ten years old, has a notable record of accomplishment.[25]

The Fisheries Commission, organized in 1937, has twelve member states; it functions solely in an advisory capacity. It is composed of three members from each state — the official in charge of the administration of marine fisheries, a member of the legislature appointed by the commission on interstate cooperation, and a person appointed by the governor " having a knowledge of and an interest in the marine fisheries problem." Only those states with a recognized interest in a particular species may participate in the panel dealing with such species. Panels have been set up for eight species, including lobster, oyster, striped bass, channel bass, blue crab, shrimp, shad, and clam. Four sections have been organized on a geographical basis — North, Middle, and South Atlantic, and Chesapeake Bay. Uniform acts have been generally adopted relative to a number of different species, and other types of cooperative arrangements have been made effective.[26]

[25] In addition to its numerous reports and publications, see Robinson, David W., " Voluntary Regionalism in the Control of Water Resources," *Annals,* January, 1940, pp. 116–123; *Incodel, A Report on Its Activities and Accomplishments* (Philadelphia, 1943) ; and Allen, James H., " The Delaware River Basin: A Home Rule Program for the Development of Its Resources," *Journal* of the American Waterworks Association, January, 1944.

[26] See accounts by Wayne D. Heydecker, Secretary-Treasurer, in *Book of the States,* 1943–1944, and 1945–1946; and Zimmerman, Frederick L., " Atlantic State Marine Fisheries Compact," *State Government,* April, 1941, pp. 81–83, 95; and

Before the war, as the rate of the gasoline tax was increased in many jurisdictions, there has been an added incentive to engage in the illegal distribution of gasoline in order to evade the tax. In some jurisdictions the extent to which this bootlegging is carried on is sufficient to affect appreciably the receipts from the tax. In order to check these losses, Pennsylvania and Ohio entered into an agreement whereby a border patrol is maintained twenty-four hours a day at each of the points at which a main highway crosses the boundary line. A full and detailed record is kept of every tank car of gasoline that crosses this state line. This agreement was later extended to include New York and New Jersey. The latter states already maintained patrol boats in New York Harbor and in the Delaware River.

NEW AGENCIES OF INTERSTATE COOPERATION

American Legislators' Association. The American Legislators' Association was organized in 1925, under the leadership of Henry W. Toll, then a member of the Colorado Senate. Its headquarters, first located in Denver, were later moved to Chicago. Since April, 1930, the Association and its successor, the Council of State Governments, have published a monthly magazine, *State Government,* which is sent to every member of every state legislature in the country, as well as to a considerable number of other persons interested in the problems of state government. An elaborate project of the Association was published many times during 1931; it dealt with four main proposals: first, to maintain an Interstate Legislative Reference Bureau, which it was planned would provide a variety of services to the several states; second, to maintain twelve national committees of legislators, each with an advisory board of recognized experts; third, to arrange meetings and conferences of legislators, thereby providing forums for discussion of legislative problems in national, regional, and state groups; fourth, to assist in the development of the Public Administration Clearing House, and in other efforts to coordinate work being done for the improvement of state government.

The officers of the Association proceeded in a systematic way to work out these objectives. As noted, the magazine *State Government* was published monthly. Weekly check lists of recently published materials were mimeographed and distributed in cooperation with the

"Interstate Cooperation and Fisheries," *ibid.,* August, 1942, 159–162, 166. On fisheries cooperation in the Great Lakes region, see Van Oosten, John, "The Great Lakes Fisheries," *ibid.,* November, 1942, pp. 211–212, 219–220.

Joint Legislative Library. The Association cooperated with universities, with the legislative reference bureau in each state, and with other agencies interested in legislative work. Considerable effort was expended in planning and guiding meetings of legislators, such conferences on legislative problems having been conducted in a number of Southern states, as well as regionally. Among these were the conferences on motorbus and truck regulation held in Harrisburg in 1933 and in Salt Lake City in 1934. The Association attempted the organization of a nationwide movement for the elimination of double taxation. In connection with this movement, the first interstate legislative assembly was held in Washington in 1933; out of this conference grew the Interstate Commission on Conflicting Taxation, and subsequent efforts to work out a solution of the problem of double taxation. The Association was responsible for the organization of the Interstate Commission on Crime, which has been doing an excellent work. It was instrumental in organizing the American Public Welfare Association and other national groups. During the short period of its existence, the Association took an active and intelligent part in the effort to develop cooperation between the states, and thereby made an important contribution to the smoother functioning of the machinery of American government.[27]

Council of State Governments. In 1935 the Council of State Governments, long projected, came into being. Under the direction of Henry W. Toll and former Governor John G. Winant of New Hampshire, it held its first meeting in Washington in the spring of 1935. The Council as now organized is governed by a board of managers, consisting of one member elected from the Cooperation Commission of each of the contributing states and of the governors as ex officio members. The board of managers meets annually for the determination of matters of policy. A biennial General Assembly of the Council is held for the consideration of legislative and administrative questions, including recommendations for uniform acts and procedure. These meetings are attended by three official delegates from each state, one representing the senate, one the house, and the third the governor. The Council performs research and compiles bulletins for the Governors' Conference, and for each of the following associations, which have designated the Council as their secretariat: American Legislators' Association, the National Association of Attorneys General, and the National Association of Secretaries of

[27] Graves, *op. cit.*, Chapter 4.

State. This central secretariat is maintained by the Council in a building recently erected by the Rockefeller Foundation on the University of Chicago campus.[28]

Just as the Association had sought to bring about cooperation among the legislators of the several states and to make possible a higher grade of performance by them, so the Council has directed itself to the task of bringing the executive officers and the governments themselves together. It has sought to develop a united front in resisting further extensions of Federal power, and to encourage cooperation among the states through the use of the various available methods, to the end that we may develop not merely a more perfect union, but " a more united states." Many of the activities of the American Legislators' Association were taken over and carried on by the Council. National and regional conferences of state officials have been organized; the establishment of legislative councils has been encouraged; and legislators have been given opportunities for pre-session conferences, organized and directed with the aid of the Council staff. The Council sponsors a group of regional secretariats, thus to some extent decentralizing the work of the Chicago office, and providing an opportunity for the rendering of countless services and for the development of closer contacts with the various state officials. Such offices have been functioning for several years in New York City and in Washington. This whole movement is one of the most interesting and potentially one of the most important things that have happened in American government for many years.

The Council has shown ingenuity in devising the implementation of interstate cooperation, and skill in making the new machinery work. Here were problems that were new, or that at least had never been faced; a whole new set of interlevel machinery was necessary. The informal conference procedure has been widely used. This has many advantages, not the least of which is its publicity value, if the press relations are properly handled. The National Conference on Interstate Trade Barriers is an outstanding example of this device, as is the General Interstate Assembly held biennially in Washington. More formal and more permanent organization, however, was necessary, and this need has been supplied through the state commissions on interstate cooperation and through the organization of national conferences of state administrative officials.

State Commissions on Interstate Cooperation. As has been shown,

28 At 1313 East 60th Street, Chicago; see p. 192.

attempts at interstate cooperation are not new, but they were not as effective as they might have been because they were sporadic and badly organized. There was no person or group of persons in any state government whose business it was continuously to watch for and to try to solve interstate problems. The first such agency was the New Jersey Commission on Interstate Cooperation, created in April, 1935. From that time on, the movement spread rapidly — more rapidly than civil service, legislative councils, judicial councils, or any other movement except that for the creation of budget agencies. By 1945 all forty-eight states had become members of the Council of State Governments by establishing commissions patterned after the model bill drafted by the Council.[29] Hubert R. Gallagher, who has been intimately connected with the movement from its inception, thus describes the organization of these commissions:

The commissions, with few exceptions, consist of fifteen members, including ten legislators and five administrative officials. Five of the legislative members constitute the senate standing committee on interstate cooperation, and five make up the house standing committee on interstate cooperation. These committees are appointed as are other committees of the legislatures. In most cases, the speaker appoints the house members, the president of the senate appoints the senate members, and the governor names the administrative committee, usually from the members of his cabinet.

Not only does the personnel of the commission consist of a majority of legislators, but it frequently includes the legislative leaders. This means, in practice, that when legislation is required, the commissions have someone in each house in a position to take charge of the necessary bills. Financial support is necessary, to employ an executive secretary, and in some instances, a research staff. In general, those commissions that have had the best financial support have been the most effective. The states have shown an increasing willingness to accept the idea of cooperation, and to provide the funds necessary to make it work. The commissions have tackled whatever problems were at hand, depending somewhat upon the section of the country. While these have come from a wide variety of

[29] On this movement, see Gallagher, Hubert R., " The Development of Interstate Government," *National Municipal Review,* July, 1937, pp. 345–351, and " Work of Commissions on Interstate Cooperation," *Annals,* January, 1940, pp. 103–110; also successive editions of the *Book of the States.* For the text of a California court decision upholding the state commission on interstate cooperation, and discussion thereof, see *State Government,* August, 1941, pp. 198–200, 207.

fields, those that have been most frequently recurring can be grouped
under the following headings:

Business and Industry: banking and securities, migration of industry, inter-
state trade barriers
Conservation: oil, fisheries, stream pollution, flood control, and water man-
agement
Highways: highway safety, motor truck regulation
Law Enforcement: crime, probation and parole, liquor control
Welfare: unemployment compensation, transients, marriage law

In commenting upon their work, Mr. Gallagher concludes that they
" are daily demonstrating that they can deal with these complicated
problems of interstate and Federal-state relationships in a constructive manner."

Permanent National Conferences in Particular Fields. In 1940, six
nationwide commissions were functioning in the field of interstate
cooperation. Several of these have already been mentioned. The Interstate Commission on Conflicting Taxation has accomplished
much in the field of state tax legislation and tax procedure. The
Interstate Commission on Crime has almost completed its primary
objective of obtaining uniform statutes to thwart the lawbreaker's
attempt to defeat justice at an arbitrary state line. Its 1940 annual
meeting in San Francisco was attended by representatives of more
than half of the states. The Interstate Commission on Social Security
is at work on the maze of interstate and Federal-state questions arising in the administration of public welfare laws. The Interstate
Commission on Council Development is directing its attention to
perfecting the efficiency and usefulness of the facilities of the Council of State Governments. The Interlevel Commission is at work in
an effort to bring the state governments into better adjustment with
the Federal government and with county and city governments. The
Tax Revision Council is trying to work out a more modern tax structure, particularly from the point of view of Federal-state relations.
There are in addition a number of regional commissions concerned
primarily with the solution of problems peculiar to the geographic
areas with which they are concerned.

All of these commissions are composed of representatives appointed by the cooperating states. They have a distinct advantage
over the older associations of state administrative officials, whose
rapid turnover permitted but short periods of service. Private citizens may be appointed, while many of the official members are in
positions of relatively secure tenure, which gives them an oppor-

tunity to make some real contribution. The work is not showy; it cannot be done rapidly. It requires prolonged conference and discussion, research, earnestness, and application. On this basis, these commissions have made substantial progress, and much more may reasonably be expected.

The Occasional Conference. The best illustration of the effective use of the occasional conference technique is the National Conference on Interstate Trade Barriers held in Chicago, in April, 1939. The problem which confronted this gathering has been previously outlined. Careful preparation and planning of such a conference is necessary. Months were spent in research, resulting in a series of bulletins clearly indicating the facts. Some 400 delegates registered, including a number of governors and many other officials. Although the conference listened to speeches and adopted resolutions, its influence did not stop there. Careful preparation had been made for nationwide publicity over the radio and through newspapers and magazines. Thousands of citizens who had never heard of a trade barrier before now became interested and to some extent informed. The public became " trade barrier conscious." The result was that " the drive to erect additional trade barriers in the forty-four legislatures meeting in 1939 was stopped in its tracks." Legislators who attended went home to kill bills of this character in committee, governors to use their influence against them, or to exercise their veto power if the bills were passed.[30]

UNIFORMITY AS A POSSIBLE SUBSTITUTE FOR CENTRALIZATION

There has of late been much discussion with regard, not only to the extension of the functions of the Federal government, but to the transfer to the Federal government of functions formerly regarded as belonging to the states. Many have expressed fears that the Federal government would become too large and unwieldy, that the people might become weighed down by bureaucracy, and that the states might become mere subdivisions in a great Federal administrative machine. These protests have come from responsible leaders in both of the major political parties. In these developments it has been notable that the Democrats, who were traditionally the exponents of the states' rights theory, have, under Presidents Wilson and Roosevelt, vastly extended the Federal power, while the Republi-

[30] National Conference on Interstate Trade Barriers, *Proceedings* (Council of State Governments, Chicago, 1939) .

cans, who have traditionally favored a strong central government, have of late assumed the role of spokesmen for the states' rights idea.

To the student of government it seems obvious not only that the changes which have taken place in the allocation of powers between the states and the Federal government will remain relatively permanent, but that there will be additional changes of a similar nature. These changes are but natural when one considers the extent to which scientific developments have reduced the older limitations of time and space. Government must function in larger units if it is to be reasonably efficient under modern conditions. This, together with the fact that government is expected to do more and that higher standards of performance for government service have been established, explains to some extent the reasons for these shifts in the allocation of power. It is noteworthy, however, that in all the changes which have thus far occurred, the states have not lost a single power of which they were making effective use; they have lost power only when they were either unable or unwilling to perform effectively governmental functions which the people demanded.

If these changes had taken place without justification, there might possibly have been some reason for the fears which have frequently been expressed. When, however, they present simply a part of that continuous process of adjustment of governmental institutions to the needs of a people living in a rapidly changing social and economic order, there would seem to be little reason for alarm. The state governments are larger, more powerful, and engaged in performing more necessary services than they have ever been in the past. This is due in part to the public demand for additional governmental services, to the demand for more adequate service in fields where the states are already active, and to the tendency to shift power from the local units to states, which was discussed in the preceding chapter.

Even though the reasons for these changes in Federal-state relationships are known and recognized, most students of government will agree that the states ought to retain just as large a portion of the powers which they now have as they can use effectively. The whole of the preceding discussion of uniformity and of the relation of the states to the Federal government has been predicated upon the assumption that the states can maintain all the powers which they now have, if they will further develop and use known methods and techniques for cooperation among themselves and for the development of uniform policies. The need for uniform rules and regulations in many fields of state government activity has already been emphasized. In each of these fields, uniformity will sooner or later be attained. Unless the states work out among themselves suitable methods for making uniform laws and enforcing these by uniform and cooperative administrative policies, there will be no alternative but to develop still further existing tendencies toward Federal centralization.

SELECTED REFERENCES

Bane, Frank, *Statement* before the Temporary National Economic Committee (Council of State Governments, Chicago, 1940).

Bard, Erwin W., *The Port of New York Authority* (Columbia University Press, 1941).

Bercaw, Louise O., *State Trade Barriers: Selected References* (United States Bureau of Agricultural Economics, 1939).

Buell, Raymond L., *Death by Tariff; Protectionism in State and Federal Legislation* (Public Policy Pamphlet No. 27, University of Chicago Press, 1939).

Burdick, Charles K., *The Law of the American Constitution* (Putnam's, New York, 1922).

* Carnegie Endowment for International Peace, *Interstate Compacts, Brief Reference List* (Washington, 1935).

Conference on State Defense, *The States — at the Crossroads,* address by Henry Epstein, July 25, 1938.

Council of State Governments, *Book of the States* (Chicago, biennially).

——, *Congressional Consent to Interstate Compacts, 1789–1936; State and Federal Statutes Authorizing Compacts* (Chicago, 1936).

——, *Trade Barriers among the States,* Proceedings of the National Conference on Interstate Trade Barriers (Chicago, 1939); also Research Bulletin Series, prepared for this Conference.

Ely, Northcutt, *Oil Conservation through Interstate Agreement* (Federal Oil Conservative Board, Washington, 1933).

Fite, Emerson D., *Government by Cooperation* (Macmillan, New York, 1932).

Governors Conference, *Proceedings* (Chicago, annually).

Graves, W. Brooke, *Uniform State Action: a Possible Substitute for Centralization* (University of North Carolina Press, 1934).

——, Ed., "Intergovernmental Relations in the United States," Part II, *Annals,* January, 1940.

Green, Thomas S., Jr., *Liquor Trade Barriers* (Public Administration Service, Chicago, 1940).

Hankin, Charlotte A., *Comparative Charts of State Statutes Illustrating Barriers to Trade Between States* (Works Progress Administration, Marketing Laws Survey, Washington, 1939).

Howard, J. T., *Review of References on Interstate Compacts* (New England Regional Planning Commission, Boston, 1936).

Interstate Commission on Conflicting Taxation, *Conflicting Taxation* (Chicago, 1935).

Interstate Commission on Crime, *Handbook* (Topeka, 1938; reprinted, 1940, and 1942).

Interstate Commission on the Delaware River Basin, *A Report on Its Activities and Accomplishments* (Philadelphia, 1943, and annually thereafter).

Interstate Commission on the Potomac River Basin, *An Introductory Report* (Washington, 1945).

Interstate Sanitary Commission, *The Effects of Pollution on Property in Interstate Sanitation District* (New York, 1940).

Johnsen, Julia E., Comp., *Interstate Trade Barriers* (Wilson, New York, 1940).

Kleinsorge, Paul L., *The Boulder Canyon Project: History and Economic Aspects* (Stanford University Press, 1941).

Marketing Laws Survey, *Bibliography of Barriers to Trade between States* (Department of Commerce, Washington, 1942).

Melder, F. Eugene, *State and Local Barriers to Interstate Commerce in the United States; a Study in Economic Sectionalism* (University of Maine Studies, 1937).

———, *State Trade Walls* (Public Affairs Pamphlets, New York, 1939).

National Association of Marketing Officials, *Trade Barriers, City Markets, and Advertising Farm Products,* Proceedings of 1937 Annual Meeting (Trenton, 1938).

National Associations of state officials in various administrative fields, *Proceedings* of annual meetings. See list in Graves, *op. cit.,* Appendix B.

National Conference of Commissioners on Uniform State Laws, *Handbook* (American Bar Association, Chicago, annually).

National Highway Users Conference, *State Barriers to Highway Transportation* (Washington, 1937).

National Resources Planning Board, *Interstate Water Compacts, 1785 to 1941* (Washington, 1942).

Newcomer, Mabel, *Intergovernmental Fiscal Relations in the United States: a Selected Bibliography* (Treasury Department, Washington, 1942).

Port of New York Authority, *Annual Report* (New York, annually).

Scott, James A., *Complete Exposition of the Law of Interstate Rendition* (Hight, Chicago, 1917).

Scott, James Brown, *Judicial Settlement of Controversies between States of the American Union,* 2 vols. (Clarendon Press, New York, 1918).

State commissions on interstate cooperation, annual reports.

Taylor, George R., and others, *Barriers to Internal Trade in Farm Products* (United States Bureau of Agricultural Economics, 1939).

Triborough Bridge Authority, *Fifth Anniversary* (New York, 1941).

United States Chamber of Commerce, *State Compacts, Report* (Washington, 1937).

Willoughby, W. W., *Constitutional Law of the United States,* Second Edition, 3 vols. (Baker, Voorhis, New York, 1929).

———

Allen, James H., "The Delaware River Basin: A Home Rule Program for the Development of Its Resources," *Journal* of the American Water Works Association, January, 1944.

Anonymous, " Interstate Cooperation in the Payment of Benefits," *Employment Security Review*, November, 1942, pp. 10–12.

——, " Interstate Problems in the Unemployment Compensation Program," *Illinois Law Review of Northwestern University*, April, 1942, pp. 862–872.

Bogart, George G., " Uniform Law Plans for 1943," *State Government*, December, 1942, pp. 236–237.

Carpenter, L. Hewitt, " Indiana-Kentucky Boundary: Interstate Cooperation Aids in Settling 100 Year Old Boundary Dispute," *State Government*, September, 1943, pp. 190–191 (also Treadway, William E., *ibid.*, October, 1939, p. 184).

Cohen, Sylvan M., " State Regulation of Migration of Indigent Persons," *Bill of Rights Review*, Winter, 1942, pp. 119–126.

Corey, Herbert, " Will War Raze the State Line Trade Barriers? " *Public Utility Fortnightly*, September 24, 1942, pp. 417–424.

Council of State Governments, series of five articles on interstate war problems, *State Government*, February, 1945, entire issue.

Dodds, Harold W., " Model Laws as an Aid to Progress," *National Municipal Review*, November, 1944, pp. 531–534, 544.

Downs, E. F., and Konenkamp, S. J., " Those State Trade Barriers — Fact or Fiction? " *Public Utilities Fortnightly*, April 15, 1943, and April 29, 1943.

Eccles, David, " Pacific Northwest War Industries Commission," *State Government*, April, 1943, pp. 88–89, 100–101.

Ellis, William J., " Interstate Parole and Probation Compact: An Appraisal After Ten Years of Operation," *State Government*, March, 1945, pp. 40–42, and inside back cover.

Forage, D. J., " Multiple Domiciles and Multiple Inheritance Taxes — a Possible Solution," *George Washington Law Review*, February, 1941, pp. 375–388.

Gallagher, Hubert R., " Work of the Commissions on Interstate Cooperation," *Annals*, January, 1940, pp. 103–110.

Green, Thomas S., " Combating U. S. ' Balkanization,' " *Public Opinion Quarterly*, March, 1940, pp. 162–164.

Gurwell, John K., " Governors' Conferences on War Programs," *State Government*, August, 1942, pp. 156, 167–169.

Hendrickson, Robert C., " Trade Barriers and National Unity," *State Government*, April, 1941, pp. 75–76, 88–90.

Heydecker, Wayne D., " The Northeast Cooperates," *State Government*, December, 1940, pp. 247–249, 258.

Heyman, Regina S., " Benefit Payments Across State Lines," *Employment Security Review*, April, 1941, pp. 9–14.

Hoehler, Fred H., " Relief and Resident Laws," *State Government*, May, 1942, pp. 103–104, 116.

Holt, Harold W., " Any More Light on Haddock v. Haddock? " *Michigan Law Review*, March, 1941, pp. 689–718.

Indiana Law Journal, " Interstate Trade Barriers," December, 1940, entire issue.

Jackson, Robert H., " The Supreme Court and Interstate Barriers," *Annals*, January, 1940, pp. 70–78.

Kassell, Mortimer M., " A Solution of the Double Domicile Problem," *State Government,* November, 1941, pp. 268–269, 282–283.

Kelly, William R., " Rationing the Rivers," *Rocky Mountain Law Review,* December, 1941, pp. 12–20.

Kittrell, F. W., " Pollution Control in the Potomac," *State Government,* April, 1942, pp. 79–80, 90.

Larson, Gustav E., for, and Stone, Clifford H., against, " Should the Interstate Water Compact Be Remodeled? Federal v. State Views," *State Government,* September, 1943, pp. 192–197.

Lewis, William D., for, and Hall, Jerome, against, " The Youth Correction Authority Act," American Bar Association *Journal,* May, 1942, pp. 317–324.

Lockhart, William B., " State Trade Barriers to Interstate Trade," *Harvard Law Review,* June, 1940, pp. 1253–1288.

Martin, James W., " Tax Competition Between States," *Annals,* January, 1940, pp. 62–69.

Melder, F. Eugene, " Trade Barriers Between States," *Annals,* January, 1940, pp. 54–61.

Meyer, Herbert, " State Barriers to Highway Transportation," *George Washington Law Review,* May, 1940, pp. 1070–1077.

Mott, Rodney L., " Uniform Legislation in the United States," *Annals,* January, 1940, pp. 79–92.

Nixon, H. C., " The Southern Governors' Conference as a Pressure Group," *Journal of Politics,* August, 1944, pp. 338–345.

Ostertag, Harold C., " State Rights and Interstate Cooperation," *State Government,* November, 1941, pp. 261–263, 281.

Roback, Herbert, " Legal Barriers to Interstate Migration," *Cornell Law Quarterly,* March, 1943, pp. 286–312, and June, 1943, pp. 483–526.

Routt, Garland C., " Interstate Compacts and Administrative Cooperation," *Annals,* January, 1940, pp. 93–102.

Schlesinger, M. R., " Sales Taxes, Interstate Trade Barriers, and Congress: The Gulf Oil Case," *Michigan Law Review,* March, 1941, pp. 755–781.

Schnader, William A., " Progress Toward Uniform State Laws," *State Government,* November, 1940, pp. 219–220, 231–232.

Sharp, M. Q., " Eight States and a River," *State Government,* November, 1943, pp. 221–222, 232.

Stanley, W. E., " Progress in Uniform State Laws," *State Government,* November, 1944, pp. 442–445.

Steers, Sheldon B., " Development of State Aviation Agencies," *State Government,* January, 1945, pp. 8–9, 15.

Tocker, Phillip, " Trade Barriers," *Texas Law Review,* April, 1940, pp. 274–294.

Van Oosten, John, " The Great Lakes Fisheries," *State Government,* November, 1942, pp. 211–212, 219–220.

Webb, Wilfred D., " The Interstate Oil Compact — Theory and Practice," *Southwestern Social Science Quarterly,* March, 1941, pp. 293–301.

Wolaver, Earl S., " Trade Barriers and Interstate Commerce," *American Law School Review,* May, 1941, pp. 1102–1107.

CHAPTER XXIII

Federalism in America Today[1]

SOME HISTORICAL CONSIDERATIONS

IN any consideration of the future of the American states, it is desirable at the outset to recall the circumstances of their development and of their entry into the Union. When the present Constitution was framed and adopted, the states were more than a century and a half old. Their origins were traceable, not to the date of independence, but to the granting of the letters patent to individuals and groups of individuals for the establishment of colonies in America; they had existed as colonies down to the date of independence, and had at that time, or soon after, been transformed into states. For many years after, it was the states to which the people gave their primary allegiance. Under the Articles of Confederation, the strength of the states was so great that it was impossible for the central government to function with any degree of effectiveness. It has been argued that during this period the states usurped the sovereignty of the *people of the nation,* and that in order to establish an effective government, it was necessary for the *people* to reassert their sovereign power.[2] When the Constitution was framed, the people were still greatly concerned about "states' rights," those in the smaller states contending that only by the preservation of these rights would it be possible to secure the rights of the individual.

There is much evidence to indicate that the people regarded the new central government with fear and viewed the possible extension of its powers with great apprehension. It had been possible to secure the ratification of the new Constitution only on the basis

---

[1] The author is indebted to the editor of the *American Political Science Review* for permission to reprint those portions of this chapter which appeared in that journal, February, 1936, pp. 24–50, under the title, "The Future of the American States."

[2] Burgess, John W., "The American Commonwealth," *Political Science Quarterly*, March, 1886, pp. 9–35.

of a pledge that the government to be organized under it would immediately submit to the states for adoption a series of amendments
designed to protect the rights of the individual. This was done, resulting in the Bill of Rights as we now know it. Not long thereafter,
the Supreme Court, in the case of Chisholm v. Georgia,[3] ruled that
a state might be sued in the courts of the United States without its
consent; this created such a furor that Amendment XI was promptly
proposed and ratified. It was inconceivable to the people of that
day that a sovereign state should be subjected to the indignity of
being brought into court like an ordinary citizen. Throughout the
period of controversy on the slavery question, this question of
states' rights was ever in the foreground.

The states were in the beginning, and they continued for many
years to be, the chief interest and concern and the chief object of
the governmental allegiance of the people. In the formative period
the fear was not that the central government would become too
large and too powerful, but that it would be unable to get power
and prestige enough to enable it to survive. In view of the difficulties that had been experienced by the colonists before and during the Revolution, this attitude is not surprising. When the debate on the subject of ratification was in progress, we find the
authors of the Federalist papers arguing that the powers of the
central government could not become oppressive, because, they
said, it was the tendency of the divisional governments to enlarge
and enhance their powers at the expense of any central agency that
might be created. At the time everything seemed to indicate that
they were right.[4]

The priority of the states in the Federal system continued through
the nineteenth century, down to the period of the Civil War. While
there were signs of an impending change, in the form of added
restrictions upon the legislative power, both the executive and
the judiciary were gaining in power. In the earliest constitutions
framed after 1789 " the governor was restored in large degree to
powers lost during the period of the Revolution," and during the
first three or four decades of the nineteenth century " he seemed to
hold his own." " His independence of the legislature was worked
out through the constitutional developments between 1789 and
1840, and has been preserved as a permanent principle, and a

[3] Dallas 419, 1793.
[4] *The Federalist,* Nos. XVII and XXXI, both of which were written by Hamilton. The present author has elsewhere discussed this question; see *Uniform State
Action,* Chapter 19 (University of North Carolina Press, 1934).

longer term has been accorded him." By the fifth decade of the century the tendency to limit his administrative discretion, to hedge in his pardoning power, to narrow the scope of his power to appoint and dismiss by making many officers elective by the voters, "and to place him under the surveillance of a cabinet of elective officers, not necessarily in political accord with him, whose duty it is to record his acts and report the same to the legislature," was clearly in evidence. Despite these tendencies, the governor continued in the states generally to be an important personage down to 1861.[5]

In the closing decades of the nineteenth century state government in the United States sank to its lowest depths. In the era of reconstruction in the southern states there developed an orgy of graft, corruption, and inefficiency that is quite without parallel. In the other states interest in the state governments lagged and they suffered greatly in efficiency by reason of a poor personnel and an inadequate and unsatisfactory organization. An appalling number of restrictions and limitations were placed upon the powers of the legislatures, which during this period were at their lowest point in public confidence. The restrictions upon the executive were further developed. The judiciary suffered greatly from a reduced tenure, from choice by election rather than by appointment, from an inferior quality of personnel, and from a consequent loss of dignity and influence. All these unfortunate characteristics of state government of the period were reflected in the constitutions currently framed — some of which are still in effect.

THE INDICTMENT OF THE STATES

For many years, as we have seen, the states were the hub around which the wheel of the governmental universe in America revolved; during this period the states seem to have performed fairly satisfactorily the services required of them, and it appears therefore that there was little if any serious criticism of them. When, in the latter decades of the nineteenth century, the states slumped into a long period of decline in both prestige and efficiency, there began to appear, from time to time, ringing indictments of the whole state system. Criticism of the states was fostered also by the fact that, unfortunately for the states, their decline took place at a time when

---

[5] This paragraph is based upon Burgess, *op. cit.*, from which source quotations are taken.

increasing demands were being made upon them, and at a time when people were in a position to give more thought and attention to their structure and functioning. In the days of exploration and settlement, government was and could be simple, for little was needed, or at least little was expected of it; with the advent of a new economic and industrial era, more government was needed, more was expected of it, and its shortcomings were more obvious.

Everyone knows that the boundaries of the states were often unreasonable and illogical, being determined in some cases by rather obvious geographical considerations, in others by bargain and compromise, and in still others by the arbitrary fiat of the courts. Probably no one will deny that if the task were being undertaken at the present time, we should solve the problem quite differently. The development of modern methods of communication and transportation have made the existing arrangements seem to many people more and more unsatisfactory. It is now proposed to examine a number of these indictments, with the purpose of getting clearly in mind the nature of the charges that have been brought against the states.

The first suggestions of this character that have come to the attention of the author appeared near the close of the nineteenth century, from what may now be regarded as the older school of political scientists. In 1886 Professor John W. Burgess of Columbia University, writing in the first issue of the *Political Science Quarterly*, commented at length upon the various evidences of the decline of the states and the causes of this decline, as follows:

When the colonies were planted by Great Britain upon the Atlantic shores, it was in the form of communities widely separated from each other by tracts of wilderness, in which roamed the savage and the wild beast. When they became states, these communities had encroached a little upon the surrounding wildernesses separating them from each other, and had made a few bad wagon roads in some places through the same, and a man might travel overland from one to another, or get a communication through, in about the time required for a modern steamship to go from New York to Liverpool, and with greater hardship and danger. The really settled portion of a state at the date of the Revolution was about the extent of a good large county, or, at most, of two of three counties. The state government was, therefore, at that time, real local government. But now these vast tracts of wilderness separating the original states have all been leveled. The parent communities have sent out thousands of offspring to form new communities within the waste, while thousands of other communities have been established having no such natural connection with the original settlements; and all of them are bound together by the network of tracks and wires, which enables a man to live in any one of them, and be in constant communication with anybody living in any other. No one knows now, by anything which nature has to show either in geography or ethnology, when one crosses the line which separates two commonwealths from each other.

The two natural elements in our system are now the Community and the Nation. The former is the point of real local self-government; the latter that of general self-government; and in the adjustments of the future these are the forces which will carry with them the determining power. The commonwealth government is now but a sort of middle instance, beginning to be regarded as a meddlesome intruder in both spheres — the tool of the strongest interest, the oppressor of the individual. This has been its history in other lands and other times; and the mere fact that it professes to be popular here, while it has been princely or aristocratic elsewhere, will not save it from the same fate.[6]

At about the same time another great American scholar was arriving at similar conclusions; Professor Simon N. Patton of the University of Pennsylvania, in 1890, writing in the *Annals* of the American Academy of Political and Social Science, also in the first issue, comments at length upon the lack of intelligence displayed in setting up the state boundary lines:

The old colonies grew up having common bonds of religion or of descent holding together their inhabitants. Massachusetts, New York, Pennsylvania, Virginia, and the Carolinas each stood for a special kind of civilization which gave them unity and awoke in their inhabitants common ideas which the state could realize. They were real commonwealths which protected their citizens and aided them in their development. The western states have no such origin. They were laid out before they were inhabited, and have rivers, lakes, or even worse, lines of latitude and longitude for their boundaries. Of course, such a method is an easy way to divide up a new country, but no worse way could be devised for making states. Rivers and lakes are the natural means of transit and should be in the center of states. Nothing could be more arbitrary than to make the Ohio and Mississippi rivers state boundaries. The two slopes of these rivers have a similar climate. Their inhabitants have the same centers of trade, and migrating from the same states have similar ideas as to education and government. The same facts are true of the regions about the lakes. And yet our forefathers disregarded all these considerations and threw together the most discordant elements into one state. How could the dictates of reason and experience be more rudely set aside than they were when Ohio, Indiana, and Illinois were formed? The northern and southern halves of these states have distinct climates and are fitted by nature for a very different series of crops. Add to this the fact that they were settled by two distinct currents of immigration — the one from New England and the other from the South — and what can be expected but that these states should be merely inharmonious units out of which can grow none of those common feelings which are needed to give vitality to state institutions?[7]

---

[6] Burgess, *op. cit.*, pp. 33–34.

[7] Patton, Simon N., " Decay of State and Local Governments," *Annals*, July, 1890, pp. 26–42; quotation from p. 30.

Like Burgess, Patton regarded the states as an obstacle to the growth of real local government; as being too small to serve the purposes of administrative districts, and too large and too heterogeneous in composition to serve satisfactorily as units of local government. He blamed the state system for the widespread prevalence of political corruption:

> The political problems which the American people have yet to solve do not relate to the general principles of our government. The founders of our nation were right in making vigorous state and local governments an essential part of their system. It is not the principles upon which they relied that have proved faulty, but the mechanism through which these principles act. The boundaries of a vigorous local government cannot be left to the accidental lines which a surveyor may run across our land, guided only by a compass and a measuring chain. The vitality of our states depends not on these accidents, but upon the ties of race, habits, and customs of the people, and upon the peculiarities of soil and climate. These circumstances cannot be determined until the region is settled and the social and economic conditions are fixed.
>
> It is therefore the absoluteness of our boundary lines and the unchangeableness of the territorial extent of our states, that are the sources of the present degenerate tendencies in our politics and a cause of the subordination of the individual to party power. Instead of regarding the boundaries of our states as fixed and unchangeable, we should recognize that we are only beginning to get the data upon which to decide where the boundaries of states can be properly located.[8]

Interest in the states and in government generally was greatly stimulated in the United States by the publication in 1887 of the first edition of Bryce's *American Commonwealth*.[9] While it is true that no specific attempts were made to put in practice the recommendations of these distinguished scholars, it is also true that the states did begin to make some progress in the early years of the present century. There arose in many of the states, particularly in the Middle West, a group of able and aggressive leaders who were able to rally extensive popular support, and who in the governor's office were able to arouse a new interest in state government and to bring a new vitality and efficiency to the conduct of its affairs. In 1917 the administrative reorganization movement began in Illinois, and from this date on, the progress of the states has been rapid. If there are still state governments that leave much to be desired, there are others that are on the whole well organized, well administered, and

[8] *Ibid.*, pp. 39–40.
[9] For an appraisal of the influence of this work, see Brooks, Robert C., Ed., *Bryce's " American Commonwealth ": Fiftieth Anniversary,* especially Chapter 2 by Frances L. Reinhold (Macmillan, New York, 1939) .

efficient in operation. In this period of transition, in the midst of which came our participation in World War I, the literature of dissent and criticism of the states seems for the most part to have subsided. Early in the depression many writers returned to the attack, in a new literature of criticism which developed parallel with, and in large part as a result of, the rise of cities in governmental importance.

The best known and one of the most vigorous of the new critics of the states was Professor Charles E. Merriam. In articles and addresses he repeatedly affirmed his belief that the states would neither govern the cities nor permit the cities to govern themselves. His proposal for meeting this situation will be considered later, but let us note here his attitude toward the states:

The truth is [he says] that the state itself is standing upon slippery ground as a political unit. Thirteen of our states have a historical background, but as Burgess pointed out thirty years ago, the others are the creatures of a surveyor's chain, with a few exceptions. Since the states risked all in a war with the nation over their alleged sovereignty and lost magnificently, they have gone steadily down the gentle slope. In the new German constitution the states lost even more heavily than here. Most states do not now correspond to economic or social unities and their validity as units of organization and representation may be and has been seriously challenged. The nation and the city are vigorous organs, but the state is not comparatively. Certainly as guides and guardians of cities, the states have been singularly ill-equipped and ill-qualified. Conceivably, states might be very useful to cities as administrative superiors, supervising such affairs as finances and police, but practically they have no such function as a rule and it does not seem probable they will in the near future, so far as metropolitan regions are concerned.[10]

Professor Elliott published a volume in 1935 in which he developed at some length his vision of a day in which the waste and confusion of forty-eight state governments would be wiped out. Add to these the names of Professors Peel of Indiana University, Young of the University of Pennsylvania, and Luther Gulick of the Institute of Public Administration, responsible for an intemperate denunciation of the state which began as follows: [11]

[10] Merriam, Charles E., " Metropolitan Regions," an address delivered at the University of Chicago, March 20, 1928; in the *University Record*, April, 1928, and Syllabus and Selected Readings, *Introductory General Course in the Social Sciences*, pp. 427–440 (University of Chicago Bookstore, 1933) .

[11] Gulick, Luther, " Reorganization of the State," *Civil Engineering*, August, 1933, pp. 420–422; see also Elliott, William Y., *The Need for Constitutional Reform*, Chapter 9 (McGraw-Hill, New York, 1935) ; Young, James T., " The Growing Overhead in Government," *Proceedings*, American Philosophical Society, 1933,

Is the state the appropriate instrumentality for the discharge of these sovereign functions? The answer is not a matter of conjecture or delicate appraisal. It is a matter of brutal record. The American state is finished. I do not predict that the states will go, but affirm that they have gone.

The criticisms leveled against the states through the years have, in general, centered around the fact that their boundaries were not determined in accordance with any guiding principle, the claim that they constitute an obstacle to effective local government, and the charge that they have often failed to deal adequately with many of the pressing responsibilities with which they have been confronted. The failure of the states to render efficient service and to coordinate their activities with the Federal government on the one hand and the local units on the other has brought about a number of definite tendencies in American government. In some cases the breakdown of state control has been reflected in the drift toward Federal centralization; and in the extension of the Federal subsidy system. Controversies have developed over taxation and other important subjects of general interest.

FEDERAL-STATE RELATIONS IN EMERGENCY PERIODS

The bill of particulars which has been drawn up against the states has now been presented. The high regard in which the states were held in the formative period and during succeeding years has been noted. The contrast is striking. Before one undertakes to reconcile these two widely differing points of view, it seems appropriate to consider some of the things that happened to the states in the meantime. If we can get clearly in mind why, over a long period of years, the states continued to lose prestige, perhaps we shall be in a position to discuss intelligently different solutions which now seem within the range of possibility. Prior to the twenties the scope of state functions was relatively limited. In the second place, their administrative structure was often poor, and their efforts generally ineffective when, throughout the fifty years following the Civil War, they did bestir themselves in an attempt to deal with a rising tide of important gov-

pp. 57–66; Lawrence, David, *Beyond the New Deal*, pp. 239–240 (McGraw-Hill, New York, 1934) ; Edelman, John W., " A Plan for a National Social Security System," *Annals*, March, 1935, pp. 82–87; and for a different point of view: Witte, Edwin E., " The Government and Unemployment," *American Labor Legislation Review*, March, 1935, pp. 5–12; Moley, Raymond, " Interstate Co-operation in Combating Crime," reprinted in the You and Your Government Series, April 2, 1935; Clark, Delbert, " Nine Groups instead of the 48 States," *New York Times*, Sunday, April 21, 1935, in Magazine Section.

ernmental problems. This charge became less and less true in the years following 1917. Third, the states failed in many respects to keep up with the changes that had been taking place in modern life. Finally, some mention should be made of what Professor Corwin has called the Federal spending power.

The States in the Depression. In the depression period there were numerous influences that tended to lessen still further the prestige if not the power of the states. There was a great increase in the influence of Congress and of the Federal departments and agencies in directing the course of state legislation concerning subjects of interest to them. In relief, the Federal government not only dictated the policies of the states, but further undermined their control over the relief situation by carrying on negotiations and making agreements directly with municipalities. Finally, the development of the metropolitan area raises the old problem of the urban-rural conflict in a new and acute form. Each of these will be considered briefly in the paragraphs which follow.

Even a casual observer of American government in the thirties could not fail to notice the greater Federal influence on state legislation in many different fields. Nearly all of the agencies, to be sure, denied any intention of exerting pressure on the legislatures to secure the adoption of desired legislation; the only exceptions in a survey made at the time were the Department of Labor, the Bureau of Narcotics, and the Bureau of Public Roads. Without question, these activities were undertaken with the best of motives and the legislation so sponsored was generally of a desirable character. Yet there were some pertinent questions which presented themselves regarding the effect of this practice upon the established system of American government, the ethics of the Federal government's using tax moneys for the support of propaganda, and of its carrying on pressure group activities at the state capitols.[12]

An inquiry into this general subject during legislative sessions in the depression years indicated that the number of Federal departments and agencies attempting to exert such influence was much greater than had previously been the case, and that they were better organized, knew better what they wanted, and were more insistent about getting it than in previous years. The National Recovery Administration, in 1935, through its State Relations Division, ap-

[12] Graves, W. Brooke, "Stroke Oar," *State Government*, December, 1934, pp. 259–262; "Federal Leadership in State Legislation," *Temple Law Quarterly*, July, 1936, pp. 385–405; and "Influence of Congressional Legislation on Legislation in the States," *Iowa Law Review*, May, 1938, pp. 519–528.

proached the appropriate state officials and the state party leaders in and out of the legislature in the hope of advancing its model act designed to ensure the cooperation of the states with the NRA. In the utility field, the Federal Power Commission sought supporting legislation from the states, which makes it possible for the Commission to designate the state commissions as its agents in certain aspects of utility control. A study published in 1935 revealed an extensive amount of cooperation between the Interstate Commerce Commission and the state commissions in the matter of railroad regulation.[13] The Federal Housing Administration sought and obtained legislation permitting all lending and savings institutions to make loans, where they were insured by FHA or where FHA issued the obligation.

The Bureau of Criminal Identification and the Bureau of Prisons in the Department of Justice both extended their activities in this field, sponsoring Congressional legislation, state legislation, and administrative policies, all designed to bring both greater unity in organization and greater uniformity in policy to the task of enforcing the criminal law and the administration of justice. California and several other states adopted legislation designed to ensure a maximum amount of cooperation on the part of the state with the Agricultural Adjustment Administration, and this organization sought to encourage the adoption of such legislation elsewhere. The Federal Deposit Insurance Corporation was concerned not merely with supporting legislation in the states, but with the possible modification of existing provisions of state constitutions where such provisions have interfered with the work of the Corporation; the Reconstruction Finance Corporation in some instances encountered similar problems. The Home Owners Loan Corporation drafted and advanced by such means as were at its disposal supporting legislation in the states; the most helpful thing that the states could do would be to authorize the conversion of state building and loan associations into Federal associations under the Federal law.

Most important of all, perhaps, in the significance of its influence upon the legislative policies of the states, is the social security program. In order to meet the requirements of the Federal law,

[13] Lindahl, Martin L., " Coöperation between the Interstate Commerce Commission and the State Commissions in Railroad Regulation," *Michigan Law Review*, January, 1935, pp. 338–397; Kauper, Paul G., " Utilization of State Commissioners in the Administration of the Federal Motor Carrier Act," *Michigan Law Review*, November, 1935, pp. 37–84; and Collins, John L., " Fellowship between Federal and State Commissions," *Public Utility Fortnightly*, February 28, 1935, pp. 243–248.

many states had to reorganize their whole existing legislative and adminstrative set-up for handling some of the problems included in this program. To take New York as an example, old age pensions began at age seventy, not sixty-five, and were on a fifty-fifty basis with the communities as to actual costs and costs of administration. In the same state, mothers' assistance, widows' pensions, et cetera, were entirely a local charge. When the Federal government required the states to assume part of the burden in order to qualify for Federal funds, the whole system had be reorganized. In the Federal Emergency Relief Administration the state administrators have served in a dual capacity, being at the same time for many purposes the agents of the Federal government. For this work the states were required to set up a state organization and to supervise the administration of relief by county units, thereby practically eliminating from the relief picture the old local poor boards which existed in a number of states.

The administrative agencies of the Federal government are frequently reported as doing things that would seem, under our system, to fall within the limits of state power. For instance, the Bureau of Biological Survey, in a period of three and one half months in 1934, eradicated 7,500,000 disease-carrying rodents in three states, with the aid of CWA funds, at an estimated saving to the infected areas of $8,750,000. The Department of Agriculture regulates and controls the length of hunting seasons — a practice against which, except in rare instances, there is apparently no protest. Indeed, it is no uncommon occurrence for appeals to be directed to Washington as soon the states or the people find themselves faced by some perplexing or difficult situation; this tendency has often been noted, but in view of its existence, is it any wonder that the Federal departments and agencies often seek to influence state policies, both legislatively and administratively, even when they have not been asked for assistance?

The States in the War Period. As will be indicated at greater length in the concluding chapter, the states succeeded in strengthening their position materially during the war period — financially and in other ways. They rendered many services vital to the war effort, and at the same time put their finances in so much better shape that their position in the governmental picture was substantially improved. In spite of these favorable factors, they lost temporarily, because of the exercise of the war powers of the Federal government, control over many things that have been regarded as strictly within their province

— employment service, many activities intended to benefit and protect wage earners, control of motor vehicle transportation, and many other things.

A Functional Federalism? Thus, in depression and in war, the scope of state authority has become less a question of constitutional law than one of governmental policy. Arguments over constitutional authority seem pretty sterile and purposeless in the face of urgent needs for public service. Many believe — and Professor William Anderson has well expressed the view — that the solution lies in a new " functional federalism," displacing a legal federalism based on a division of functions into non-communicating compartments, with an assumed hostility between the center and the parts. He believes that a greater degree of decentralization from Washington is required to make national administration as efficient as it should be, but that to increase the efficiency of national administration without correspondingly improving state government will contribute to a still further weakening of the states.

This question of state power has become a very practical one, the answer to which is incident — as Walter F. Dodd has said — to the form of government that will in the long run best function in this country, and the form of which will in the future be largely determined at the polls — not in the courts.[14] At this time, the nation stands at a crossroads. Contending forces struggle to control the direction of future development.

Exponents of the old constitutionalism point to the dangers of a " too big " central government, to the administrative failures of prohibition and NRA, to the waste of WPA, to the uneven quality of administration attained by OPA and other war agencies. Exponents of the new functionalism point to the urgent social and economic needs of our time, urging the extension of the Federal social security program, the need for full employment in the postwar period, and to legislation relating to the regulation and control of both business and labor. In this struggle functionalism seems definitely in the ascendency, as new patterns of federalism are shaped to meet the problems of postwar reconstruction and rehabilitation, as the nation prepares to meet the challenge of a new industrial age.

[14] See Anderson, William, " Federalism — Then and Now," *State Government,* May, 1943, pp. 107–112, and comments thereon by Oswald D. Heck, Harold W. Dodds, and William L. Chenery, *ibid.,* June, 1943, pp. 141–144; and Dodd, Walter F., " The Decreasing Importance of State Lines," American Bar Association *Journal,* February, 1941, pp. 78–84.

FEDERAL-MUNICIPAL RELATIONS

Since World War I, there has been a steady extension of Federal influence over the cities. Paul V. Betters, in a study published in 1931, went through the Federal organization department by department, noting the services rendered to cities by each bureau in each department. The table of contents of his study is an impressive bit of evidence of the extensiveness of these services. In the Department of Commerce alone, he found eight such services in the Bureau of Standards; ten in the Bureau of Mines; six in the Aeronautics Branch; four each in the Coast and Geodetic Survey and the Bureau of the Census; and additional services in the Bureau of Fisheries, the Bureau of Foreign and Domestic Commerce, the Steamboat Inspection Service, and the Bureau of Lighthouses. This type of activity has gone far enough so that press reports are frequently seen on such subjects as the manner in which the Federal crime drive prods long lethargic cities into making life less pleasant for gangdom, or the manner in which cities utilize the precise longitude and latitude bearings established by the Coast and Geodetic Survey in laying down lines of city streets and building plots.[15]

The Depression Period. During the depression period established practices were developed along new lines. The distribution of funds for relief purposes carried an urgency which was used as an excuse for short-circuiting the states, and for establishing a new pattern of direct relationships between the Federal government and the cities. Such headlines as the following became a commonplace: " Ickes Prods Cities on Works Delays. Government Stands Ready to Lend

[15] Betters, Paul V., *Federal Services to Municipal Governments* (Municipal Administration Service, New York, 1931) , *Municipal Finance Problems and Proposals for Federal Legislation* (American Municipal Association, Chicago, 1933) , and *Recent Federal-City Relations* (United States Conference of Mayors, Washington, 1936) ; Merriam, Charles E., " The Federal Government Recognizes the Cities," *National Municipal Review,* February, 1934, pp. 107–109, 116; McGoldrick, Joseph D., " Federal Financial Aid to Cities," a radio address in the You and Your Government Series, June 26, 1934.

For more recent comment, see: Betters, Paul V., " The Federal Government and the Cities: A Problem in Adjustment," *Annals,* September, 1938, pp. 190–198; Mallory, Earl D., " Federal-City Relations in 1938," *Municipal Year Book,* 1939, pp. 197–209; National Resources Committee, *Our Cities: Their Role in the National Economy* and *Urban Government* (Washington, 1937 and 1939) ; Martin, James W., " Implications of Federal and State Aid to Municipalities," *Municipal Finance,* May, 1942, pp. 27–34; Owsley, Roy H., " Current Developments in Federal-Municipal Relationships," League of Cities of the Third Class in Pennsylvania *Bulletin,* October, 1941, pp. 9–11, 15; Parran, Thomas, " The Relationship of the United States Public Health Service and American Municipalities," (bulletin of the American Municipal Association, Chicago, 1944) ; Short, Raymond S., " Municipalities and the Federal Government," *Annals,* January, 1940, pp. 44–53.

Liberally if They Will Only Act, He Says." "Federal School Aid Gives City $245,000." That both the states and the cities gave encouragement to such practices is attested by such headlines as: "Mayors Decry ' Red Tape ' — Resolution in Chicago Asks Easier Terms on Works, Warning of ' Starvation ' — $35,020,000 Federal Loans to City Backed by State Advisory Board."

Some authorities, particularly those whose interest lies chiefly in the field of municipal government, hailed these new developments with approval. The members of this school exercised, for a time at least, a controlling influence with the Federal administration. The United States Conference of Mayors urged and in time secured changes in relief organization, more Public Works Administration and Civil Works Administration money for the cities, more emphasis on planning, and the adoption of slum clearance and housing programs.[16] In addition, Congress passed the Sumners-Wilcox Act for the purpose of assisting defaulting municipalities. Although this act was declared unconstitutional by the Supreme Court in 1936, another was passed to take its place.[17] In more general terms Professor Merriam writes in approval of these policies:

In many instances the state is a fifth wheel so far as city government is concerned. The state will neither grant autonomy in the cities nor will it assume the burden of administrative supervision over them. The state will neither rule nor permit anyone else to rule over metropolitan regions.[18]

Others, whose point of view tended to emphasize the importance of the states, viewed the new development with apprehension, if not with alarm. While it is true that there were no established channels for administering such grants, these writers felt that under the existing system of government the states have a responsibility for the government of all of the people and for the supervision of all of the governmental units within their respective boundaries — even for the cities. This new development modified the procedure if not the form of the established Federal-state-local pattern, and it served to illustrate once more the fact that governmental procedures tend to follow, not established legal and conventional patterns so much as requirements dictated by necessity and human need.

16 Betters, Paul V., " What Cities Can Expect from Washington," *Public Management,* January, 1934, pp. 6–7.

17 Ashton v. Cameron County Water Improvement District, 299 U. S. 619, 1936; see also Hillhouse, A. M., " The Federal Municipal Debt Adjustment Act," *National Municipal Review,* June, 1936, pp. 328–332, 368.

18 Merriam, Charles E., " Cities Look to the Federal Government," an editorial in *Public Management,* January, 1934.

The Cities in Wartime. The cities, like all governmental units and all citizens, bore a heavy responsibility in the war effort, and in addition they were faced with many serious problems because of it. They lost heavily in personnel through the operation of Selective Service, and through the lure of high wages in war industry and in some portions of the Federal service. Losses were especially serious in police and fire services, but these same factors also made difficult local efforts at recruiting replacements, recruiting for civilian defense, and other wartime needs. Civilian defense included, in addition to protective services, other services in the field of medicine, public utilities, and transportation, not to mention an elaborate warning system to be used in case of air raid or attack.[19]

Civilian defense had a national organization and a strong state organization in every state, but much of the responsibility for its administration devolved upon the local communities. Similarly, the cities had an important role to play in providing recreational facilities for men and women in the armed forces, in bond drives, blood donor service, drives for the salvage of scrap metal and waste paper, and in a multitude of other activities familiar to all during the war period.

Financially, the cities fared well during the war, as did the states. Receipts from taxes were high, and grants in substantial amounts continued to come in for various purposes related to the war effort — defense housing, vocational training, and many other things. Professor Martin, analyzing the situation as it existed in the middle of the war, concluded that, while such grants tended to provide financial relief to the cities in the handling of emergency problems, they also encouraged laxity in fiscal policy, if not actual waste.

In the field of highways and public works, the cities were at a great disadvantage during the war, in both construction and maintenance, due to the shortage of both men and materials. In this area, they have

[19] See American Municipal Association, *Cities and the National Defense Program* (Chicago, 1941) ; Gill, Corrington, " Federal-State-City Cooperation in Congested Production Areas," *Public Administration Review,* Winter, 1945, pp. 28–33; Hoan, Daniel W., " National Defense and the Cities," *National Municipal Review,* June, 1941, pp. 359–362; Hodes, Barnet, " Civilian Defense Plans and the Civilian War Effort in Relation to Municipal Governments," *American Municipal Law Review,* October, 1942, pp. 223–226, " The War and Municipal Law," *ibid.,* April, 1942, pp. 2–6, and " Effective National Defense and Municipal Home Rule," *National Municipal Review,* October, 1941, pp. 565–567, 616; Rosinia, Michael L., " Municipal Defense Legislation," *American Municipal Law Review,* October, 1942, pp. 229–232; Taft, Charles P., " National Defense and Community Service," *National Municipal Review,* June, 1941, pp. 321–326; and United States Conference of Mayors, " Present Position of Police and Fire Departments in Relation to the Selective Training and Service Act," a bulletin issued October 29, 1943.

come to be greatly dependent upon Federal aid — and state aid as well. The Moses Survey in Portland, Oregon, in 1943, presented a $75,000,000 postwar program which could be carried out only through grants-in-aid. Nearly every city in the country, in fact, was hoping if not actually planning on Federal aid for postwar construction. The Federal Highway Act of 1944 provided funds for cities and other local units in the construction of secondary or feeder highways.

Similarly, the Public Health Service Act of 1944 authorized a broadening of the Federal-state-local relationship in cooperative health programs. It contemplated a national tuberculosis control program patterned after the venereal disease control program begun in 1938. These are only a few examples of the increasing number and scope of Federal-municipal programs and relationships.

REGIONALISM: SUB-NATIONAL AND METROPOLITAN

Thus far we have tried to do three things: to review briefly the historical background of the states, to analyze the charges that they have failed in the past and are ill suited to the needs of modern government, and to review the developments of the depression era. Whether or not one agrees with the extreme demands of those who see no solution for the shortcomings of the states except their abolition, anyone must admit that some modification of the existing practices of the states must be made, unless, as Elihu Root predicted about forty years ago, the states are to lose their power. " There has been," as one recent writer observes, " a complete lack of purpose, plan, and program on the part of the sovereign states toward integration and harmony." The possible alternatives are two. If the states are to be abolished, there must be set up in their place some system of zones or regions to serve for those administrative purposes which require a unit smaller than the central government and larger than the local units. In the second place, the state organization might be retained, with such modifications as might be deemed necessary in order to remedy the more serious defects that have become manifest in the operation of the system as it exists at present. These two alternatives will now be considered.

Proposals for Regionalism. The idea of the use of regions for administrative purposes is not new, either in Europe or in America. In Europe it has been common for at least a hundred years — in Great Britain, France, Spain, Russia, and elsewhere. Historically, it is much older, having existed in Italy under the Romans, in Manchuria under the Chinese, and in Crimea under the Russians. In the United States the problem of sectionalism was long one of great concern, and is still a favored subject for historical study and investigation. It has commonly been regarded with disapproval, because of its supposed detrimental effect upon national unity. It is therefore important to distinguish between sectionalism and regionalism; G. D. H. Cole has defined the latter " as primarily an attempt to face the difficulty of the loss of local self-government . . . by making local areas real areas, . . . to restore the influence of local spirit upon the work of social administration. It is an attempt to define areas which are at once units of social feeling and, as far as possible, also areas of economic life, and suitable to serve as units for the work of administration." [20] Professor Odum has said that " regionalism envisions the nation first, making the total national culture the final arbiter, while sectionalism sees the region first, and the nation afterward."

Professor Patton, in the paper referred to above, urged the development of regions in the following words:

. . . Instead of regarding the boundaries of our states as . . . unchangeable, we should recognize that we are only beginning to get the data upon which to decide where the boundaries of states can be properly located. If our states are to be a vital part of our political system, each section of our land which has distinct physical, social, or economic conditions should be carved out of existing states and given that independence needed to make its government reflect the sentiments of the inhabitants. A mining section should not be forced into an incongruous union with wheat-growers, nor should the latter be united with a grazing or fruit-growing region. [21]

For the most part, however, it is only recently that regionalism has been advanced by serious students as an end to be fostered and encouraged. This may be merely a characteristic of a larger movement; in Germany, for instance, Hitler abolished state lines, subdividing the Reich into approximately equal districts governed by Federal representatives, and centralizing the police power in the hands of the central government. One of the clearest statements favoring the regionalism of the United States comes from Professor Peel:

It is my proposal that they [the states] shall be divested of all the political attributes which they now have, except those which are of a historical or purely ceremonial character. These attributes, whether of status or function, I would redistribute among a series of political units, beginning with the neighborhood or community, at the base, and proceeding to the nation,

[20] Cole, G. D. H., *Social Theory*, pp. 160–161 (Stokes, New York, 1920).
[21] Patton, *op. cit.*

at the top. Midway between the units which I have named stands the *region,* by which is meant *that area within which geographic fact, economic organization, social custom, and political interest have established and fostered a sense of cohesiveness and community of interest which distinguishes it from any other area.*[22]

Proposals of this general character have in recent years been numerous. Professor Young has urged the erasure of the present state lines, and the formation of larger geographical sections in place of the present forty-eight states. The late James M. Beck suggested a new Constitution " which would revise the present artificial division of the nation by creating three or four self-governing groups of states whose economic interests are the same. . . ." Another former member of Congress, E. J. Jones, can see " no reason why groups of states could not be consolidated; . . . I would suggest that the Union consist of no more than twelve states." William K. Wallace proposed nine regional states in place of the present forty-eight. Another plea for the reconstruction of the states comes from Professor Leland:

. . . Rural government should be turned over to the state, with suitable rural administrative areas taking the place of existing counties. The states, in turn, should be divested of their legislative functions and be made administrative area of the Federal government with flexible boundaries. The anomaly of having forty-eight legislatures to solve similar problems in forty-eight different ways would be ended. Legislative chaos would be replaced by national uniformity in codes, technique, and quality of administration. The states long ago demonstrated their inability to regulate railroads, trade, commerce, or corporation finances. Conferences, conventions, and uniform law commissions have failed to solve these problems or bring order out of legal chaos. The alternative remedy of changing our form of government so as to make possible the intelligent solution of these problems has received little or no consideration. At a time when security of private banking and the revival of industrial prosperity so clearly call for unified national action, the follies of maintaining the traditional governmental set-up with its forty-eight independent states should be strikingly demonstrated. If, then, to the Federal government were transferred those problems of more than local concern, if the states met the rural needs and if the cities were given complete jurisdiction over urban problems, our major economic, social, and fiscal dilemmas would be near solution. Complete fiscal coordination would then be easily attained.[23]

[22] Peel, Roy V., " The Displacement of States by Political Regions," an address before the Conference of Metropolitan Government," New York City, October 19, 1932.

[23] Leland, Simeon E., " The Coordination of Federal, State, and Local Fiscal Systems," *Municipal Finance,* August, 1933, pp. 35–46; also Wallace, William K., *Our Obsolete Constitution,* p. 185 (John Day, New York, 1932).

The Progress of Regionalism to Date. No one can read the proposals for the establishment of regional government in the United States without being impressed by the lack of agreement among the authors, either as to the number of regions, or as to the basis upon which they should be set up. This in itself might to some extent discredit the proposals, were it not for the fact that one cannot dismiss lightly any proposal advanced by responsible persons. While the Federal government has used the states for many administrative purposes as a matter of convenience, there are many purposes for which zones have been established which disregard state boundary lines. There are literally dozens of Federal activities and services in the conduct of which a zone or regional system of administration has been in use for years. States have been employed as administrative districts in the older services and also in those created for emergency purposes. In the former class we have the United States Public Health Service, the Office of Education, the Federal Board for Vocational Education, the United States Employment Service, and many others.

In the last fifteen years, during the emergencies of depression and of defense and war, state units or directors were widely employed by Federal agencies. In the depression, in the temporary agencies set up for the administration of the agricultural, public works, and emergency relief programs, the states were used as administrative units. They were so used in the National Youth Administration, the National Resources Board, and many others. Among the war agencies, the states were used as administrative units, at first, in the Office of Price Administration and the War Production Board, later being combined into regions. The War Department, although it employs larger units also, has always made use of the states as units for certain administrative purposes.

A significant study of regionalism in the United States was made in 1935 by the National Resources Committee.[24] This covered the evi-

[24] National Resources Committee, *Regional Factors in National Planning* (Washington, 1935); Odum, Howard E., and Moore, Harry E., *American Regionalism* (Holt, New York, 1938); and White, Leonard D., *Introduction to the Study of Public Administration,* Second Edition, Chapter 12 (Macmillan, New York, 1939); for further references, see Culver, Dorothy C., "A Bibliography of Intergovernmental Relations in the United States," *Annals,* January, 1940, pp. 210–218; and the following: Durisch, Lawrence L., "Local Government and the TVA Program," *Public Administration Review,* Summer, 1941, pp. 326–334; Edelman, Alexander T., "The TVA and Intergovernmental Relations," *American Political Science Review,* June, 1943, pp. 455–469; Fesler, James W., "Criteria for Administrative Regions," *Social Forces,* October, 1943, pp. 26–32; Hagood, Margaret J., "Statistical Methods for Delineation of Regions Applied to Data on

dences of the problem, some attempts at solution, geographical factors and criteria, and finally, the integration of administrative and geographical factors in regional planning. The interstate compact and interstate cooperation were considered, along with Federal departmental procedure, as possible solutions. In the latter connection, it was found that seventy-four Federal agencies of bureau status or higher had designed sets of regions, and that there were 108 separate regional schemes in operation, with numbers of regions ranging from one to 307. Eighty-two regional schemes had 1,300 regional offices, in 195 cities. When these were plotted on a map of the country, it was found that eight metropolitan centers led by a substantial margin in the frequency of choice by Federal agencies. Thirteen cities are regional centers for twenty or more regional schemes. The Board showed various plans for establishing multi-purpose regions, ranging in number from eight to twenty, and each based upon a different principle, such as metropolitan influence, administrative convenience, et cetera.

The Merits of the Regional Plan. It is clear that the idea of regional or zone administration is not new in the United States; the current proposals would merely extend the principle, and introduce it as at least a partial substitute for other administrative devices now in use. There is nothing revolutionary about it; the important questions center rather about such considerations as its wisdom and its practicability. To the present writer, there seems to be little indeed to commend the plan for the regionalization of the United States, if by this is meant the virtual abolition of the present states and the establishment of new administrative districts in lieu thereof. So drastic a plan is not required to remedy the admitted weaknesses of the present system; even if it were, there seems to be little likeli-

Agriculture and Population," *ibid.*, March, 1943, pp. 287–297; Heberle, Rudolf, " Regionalism: Some Critical Observations," *ibid.*, pp. 280–286; Lindeman, Eduard C., " Notes on Psychological Aspects of Regionalism," *ibid.*, March, 1941, pp. 301–306; Odum, Howard W., " A Social Approach to the Study and Practice of American Regionalism," *ibid.*, May, 1942, pp. 425–436; Reimer, Svend, " Theoretical Aspects of Regionalism," *ibid.*, March, 1943, pp. 275–280; Roseman, Alvin, " The Regional Coordination of Defense, Health and Welfare Services," *Public Administration Review*, Autumn, 1941, pp. 432–440; Simpson, George, and Ivey, John E., Jr., " Regionalism and Social Planning," *Social Forces*, December, 1941, pp. 186–195; Sprague, Theodore W., " Some Notable Features in the Authority Structure of a Section," *ibid.*, March, 1943, pp. 344–350; Stanbery, V. B., " Evolution of a Regional Development Plan," *The Planners' Journal*, July–September, 1942, pp. 3–10; Vance, Rupert B., " Human Resources and Public Policy: An Essay toward Regional-National Planning," *Social Forces*, October, 1943, pp. 20–25; Watkins, James T., IV, " Regionalism and Plans for Postwar Reconstruction: the First Three Years," *ibid.*, May, 1943, pp. 379–389.

hood that its adoption could be brought about at any time in the near future.

There has developed within the states a civic cohesion, a sense of attachment, a love of locality, which cannot easily be broken down. The longer the states remain as states, the stronger this attachment becomes. To say that it is illogical and sentimental in character is to beg the issue — although it is both. There is a devotion to the soil, to the life and history and institutions of the state, to the land of one's fathers, which no one can deny who has ever come in contact with natives of California, Indiana, Maryland, Massachusetts, New York, Pennsylvania, Virginia, or any other state. In the words of Kipling:

> God gave all men all earth to love,
>   But since our hearts are small,
> Ordained for each one spot should prove
>   Beloved over all;
> That, as He watched Creation's birth,
>   So we, in godlike mood,
> May of our love create our earth
>   And see that it is good.[25]

Against such emotional attachments, the considerations of pure logic are ineffective indeed. This " persistence of the states is due to many historic facts; to the real differences in character, customs, and loyalties which obtain in colonial days; to the use of constitutional arguments by men like Taylor, Roane, and Calhoun, who were actually defending not state, but sectional interests; to geographic isolation as in California, or cultural homogeneity as in Louisiana; and to the accumulative psychological force of state pride, with its separate institutions, leaders, histories, songs, mottoes, battle-flags, and relics. And, in addition to all these forces, the state has persisted in America because it has been looked upon, even by such divergent party leaders as the late Governor Ritchie and ex-President Hoover, as the natural bulwark of local self-government." [26]

Even if one were to grant that the establishment of such a system was theoretically desirable, there is nothing in the record to indicate that it could be accomplished much before the coming of the millenium. Zones have been used by the Federal government for a wide variety of purposes, but in nearly every case the number of zones has been different. In those few instances in which the same num-

---

[25] Kipling, Rudyard, opening stanza of *Sussex*.
[26] Peel, *op. cit.*

ber of zones was set up for two or more different purposes (as in the twelve districts for the Federal Reserve Banks and for the Federal Land Banks) the boundaries of the zones have been different. This is not a criticism of what has been done; it is simply an observation upon an inevitable and inescapable fact. No one who possessed anything less than the intellect of an Aristotle, the wisdom of a Solomon, and the political acumen of a Roosevelt could possibly hope to devise and secure the adoption of a regional plan for the United States which would reconcile all the conflicting requirements of an extensive number of different administrative purposes. There is no evidence at hand to indicate that, aside from the New England group, there is any possible grouping of states that would be uniformly satisfactory. The interests of individual states would prompt them to line up in one way for one purpose and in another way for another. It seems more than likely that any grouping that might be adopted on the basis of inevitable compromises would develop deficiencies and defects just as important and just as annoying as those which now confront us; such a plan would merely be substituting one set of problems and difficulties for another.

This point is well illustrated by the failure of President Wilson at the Peace Conference at Versailles; with the magic formula of self-determination, he sought to redetermine the boundary lines of many of the countries of Europe, only to discover — or for us to discover later — that boundary lines are not merely matters of logic. The point is further illustrated by the fact that, of the many national associations of state administrative officers formed in the United States, no two use precisely the same basis for determining the number of regional groups which they will maintain, nor the same grouping of states where the number of districts is the same.[27]

Metropolitan Regions: Proposals for City-States. The growth of metropolitan areas raises in a new form the age-old problems of the urban-rural conflict. The larger centers of population have continued to grow, not only without regard to the geographical boundaries of the minor political subdivisions within the states, but without regard to the boundary lines of the states themselves. These cities and the suburban areas which surround them have problems quite distinct from the rural districts of the states, which still maintain their control of the legislative bodies. Neither group shows much understanding of or concern for the problems of the other. Out of this

[27] Many of these groupings are presented in the text and in Appendix B of the author's *Uniform State Action.*

situation develop the dissatisfaction of the urbanities with the existing state system and the pleas for its modification.

The establishment of city-states would require a complete overhauling of the existing intermediate administrative units; the states, if retained at all, would lose their present powers and serve merely in the capacity of administrative subdivisions within larger districts. There are others who would upset the existing arrangements, but in quite a different manner. Moved primarily by the desire to solve the age-long urban-rural conflict, they would create city-states out of the metropolitan areas which have grown up around our larger cities. They argue that our present arrangement is illogical and unsatisfactory, and that these areas should be considered as units, regardless of existing state boundary lines. The Tri-State Regional Planning Federation for the Philadelphia area has shown that this area in reality includes not only the city and county of Philadelphia, with the suburban counties in Pennsylvania adjacent thereto, but much of southern New Jersey from Trenton down, and northern Delaware as far south as Wilmington. Similarly, in the New York area, it is argued that socially and economically northern New Jersey and southwestern Connecticut are integral parts of the greater city of New York.

Professor Merriam has urged the adoption of this plan on many occasions. The city-states which he visualizes would answer many of the problems now confronting local government; they would resemble closely such units existing in several European countries, notably Germany. They would have an autonomous government, divorced from state control, transcending state boundaries, and having their own legislative, administrative, and judicial bodies. In every state containing large metropolitan areas — California, Michigan, New York and Pennsylvania, for example — a divergence of interests exists between those areas and the rest of the state. Constant friction arises between representatives of the rural and the urban populations in state legislatures; in many instances this has developed into a bitter hostility. Elsewhere he observes:

. . . In the Chicago region, for example, which we construe as fifty miles from State and Madison streets, there are not less than 1,500 independent governing agencies undertaking to carry on the governmental functions incidental to the life of a community of three and a half million people. Metropolitan Chicago extends into four different states, Illinois, Wisconsin, Indiana, and a corner of Michigan; it includes fifteen counties and an innumerable array of cities, villages, towns, townships, school districts, park districts, drainage districts. . . . It is conservatively estimated that the population of the Chicago area in 1950 will approach eight million. Problems of regional organization are presented not only in American cities such as Boston, Philadelphia, Pittsburgh, Cincinnati, San Francisco, but in the great cities all over the world.[28]

This situation makes it difficult to carry on efficiently in almost the whole range of public activities. Meanwhile, the emigration from the central urban areas continues: " There are more Bostonians outside of Boston than inside the corporate limits, in the ratio of 750,000 in, to 1,000,024 out. There are 205,000 Cincinnatians outside the city and 400,000 inside. There are over 600,000 Pittsburghers outside the city. There are two and a quarter million New Yorkers who are outside the town. Chicago has half a million Chicagoans who are not in the city and three million who are." On the subject of municipal home rule, the same authority contends that the cities have been given too much power without supervision, or not enough with wise and temperate supervision.

Professor Merriam believes that " the urban community is a more effective counter-weight to the centralizing tendencies of Federal government than the feebly struggling states which now make such ineffectual resistance to the continuous pressure of national consolidation." On the basis of the size of the cities, as compared with many of the states, he believes the proposal a reasonable one. " Already there are seventeen cities of a population of over 500,000; nine states with less population than that. And if economic resources and prestige are added to number, the contrast is far more striking."

Whatever solution is finally made of these difficult questions will be determined very largely on the basis of financial considerations. The facts with regard to this aspect of the subject seem to favor the Merriam proposal:

Fiscally, the cities are more important than the states; the Federal government outranks either. In 1930, the revenues of the national government were almost seven times greater than those of New York City, the second largest governmental unit in the country. The state of New York outranked Chicago and the state of Pennsylvania, but Los Angeles, Detroit, and Philadelphia came ahead of California and Michigan. Thus the ten largest governments are the Federal government, five cities, and four states. One hundred sixty-five governments must be listed to include all of the forty-eight states. Nevada which comes last on the list is separated from New Mexico by fifty-six cities. The eight cities of New York, Chicago, Los Angeles, Detroit, Boston, St. Louis, Baltimore, and Seattle are more important

28 Merriam, *op. cit.,* p. 428.

fiscally than the states which contain them. Cleveland and Cincinnati together spend more than the state of Ohio, but with state expenditures on highways excluded, the fiscal operations of Cincinnati practically equal those of the state. . . . New York City spent more on education in 1930 than the receipts of any one of the 160 fiscally largest governments, a list which included forty-six states. It spent more on the retirement of city employees, or on the retirement of teachers, or on its health department or board of child welfare than was raised by the state of Nevada for all purposes. The continued expenditures of that city for these four services exceeded the combined expenditures of Nevada, New Mexico, and Arizona. The expenditures of New York City on its police department exceeded the revenues of Indiana, or Missouri, or any one of thirty-five other states. Its fire department spent more than Florida, Arkansas, or West Virginia not to mention eighteen other states. The Chicago police department cost more than the state governments of Mississippi, or Delaware, or Utah. It spent more on street cleaning and garbage removal than was expended for all governmental purposes by the state of Nevada. The combined expenditures of New York and Chicago on police and fire departments exceeded in 1930 the aggregate expenditures of any one of the 155 fiscally most important governments. These expenditures on fire and police protection exceeded the revenues collected by any one of forty-four states. The fiscal importance of cities, it seems, should soon be recognized.[29]

These statements may all be true, but somehow they fail to convince one that the whole state system should be overhauled and reorganized. The objections raised to the former plan apply with like effect to this one. Nowhere has the situation with regard to the cities and the states been better summarized than in the address delivered by President Dodds of Princeton Univerity on the occasion of his election to the presidency of the National Municipal League:

I do not wish to be understood as predicting the immutability of the states as at present constituted. In many instances, state boundary lines are today historic survivals whose values are largely sentimental. I am thinking of the state as a unit of government intermediate between the locality and the nation and such a unit has value and constant possibilities. In the course of the years the present circumstances of area and function of the states may

[29] Leland, *op. cit.*, pp. 35–36; among recent comments on metropolitanism may be noted: Hoyt, Homer, "Forces of Urban Centralization and Decentralization," *American Journal of Sociology*, May, 1941, pp. 843–852; May, Samuel C., and Ward, Robert E., "Coordinating Defense Activities in a Metropolitan Region," *Public Administration Review*, Spring, 1942, pp. 104–112; Ketcham, Roland M., *Intergovernmental Cooperation in the Los Angeles Area* (University of California at Los Angeles, Bureau of Governmental Research, 1941) ; New York State Teachers Association, "Metropolitan Areas and Future School Problems," *Public Education Research Bulletin*, December 15, 1951; Pinney, Harvey F., and others, "Proposals for Organization and Operation of Regional Councils in Metropolitan Areas," *The American City*, June, 1943, pp. 79, 81, 83, 85; Price, Daniel O., "Factor Analysis in the Study of Metropolitan Centers," *Social Forces*, May, 1942, pp. 449–455.

be modified but I do not foresee an abandonment of the principle of national federalism, although its internal structure may be changed as time progresses.[30]

THE FUTURE OF THE STATES

At a meeting of the governing board of the American Legislators' Association in Washington in January, 1935, President William B. Belknap observed that the states are historically and in every other way very independent; they are, he said, so independent that they are going to commit suicide independently, if we do not watch out. This is literally true. The prestige of the states has declined because of their failure to function effectively in important fields; it has declined as the number of states has increased; there is, without doubt, a larger number of states than can be logically justified. Territorially, at least, some of the eastern states are too small and some of the western too large, while some of the latter are also too small, on the basis of wealth and population.

The states have suffered, either because they were not doing the the things that needed to be done or because they were not doing them well enough. In either case, they were ill prepared to offer effective resistance to Federal encroachments upon their powers. Reference has already been made to the changing character of Federal-state relations — to the shift from a legal and constitutional to a functional federalism. But the future of the states is also dependent, in part, upon the relations of states with each other, and upon the effectiveness with which they put in order their own internal organization and their relations with their own subdivisions.

Interstate Relations. The problem of the relations of the states with one another has, for our present purpose, two aspects: their relations with their immediate neighbors, and their relations with the other forty-seven states in the Union. Informal cooperation between neighboring states may accomplish much; where a more formal agreement is required, there is the possibility of the interstate compact.[31] It is conceivable that regions of adjacent states with similar problems and interests might be developed more or less informally without adopting the extreme form of regionalism previously discussed. The New England states have carried on such cooperative arrangements for several years; groups of states in the South and West and in the Middle Atlantic region have experimented along

---

[30] Dodds, Harold W., " The Future of Municipal Government," *National Municipal Review*, December, 1934, pp. 646–649.

[31] The effectiveness of this method is open to serious question: see Chapter 22.

the same line. There is no reason why such cooperation should not be encouraged, and every reason to believe that its encouragement would be highly useful.

There are problems, such as those of river valleys, that affect the interests of several states and yet do not directly concern either the nation or other groups of states. We are in the process of developing new methods of solving them, and it is too early yet to predict which type of solution will be found most generally useful. The Federal government has by act of Congress created the Tennessee Valley Authority, and proposals have been presented and considered for the extension of this type of agency into other comparable areas. In contrast to this, we have a sort of voluntary regionalism operating in the Delaware, Potomac, and Ohio River valleys, in the form of the Interstate Commission on the Delaware River Basin, the Interstate Commission on the Ohio River Basin, and so forth. In these cases the states concerned have by joint action undertaken to work out the solution of their own problems. Here is presented a clear-cut alternative between having the Federal government do things for the states without any necessary regard for local sentiment, and having the states solve their own problems in their own way.

In the field of interstate relations on the larger scale, much has already been written. Machinery already in existence for the development and enforcement of uniform policies must be perfected and made more effective. A distinguished former legislator in one of the eastern states writes:

. . . The time is come when complete cooperation between the states must be implemented. Unless a plan and an agency is set up to provide the states with a method by and through which such integration can be accomplished and maintained, an even further federalization of the American government will result. . . . Although the exact scope of the jurisdiction of the Federal government is yet unknown, there still remains a broad area in which the Federal government does not have jurisdiction. In this field, we have chaos — resulting not through the fault of the Federal government . . . but rather resulting from inertia on the part of the governments of the several states.[32]

In 1789 the framers of our Federal Constitution stated as one of their purposes and objectives the formation of a more perfect union; we who live a century and a half later must dedicate ourselves to the task of recreating the union which they established into one more perfect still. This can be done only through the successful develop-

[32] Sterling, *op. cit.*

ment of interstate cooperation, under the leadership of such organization as the Council of State Governments and its affiliated organizations; in addition, we must perfect the existing associations of state administrative officers, and perfect the techniques of Federal-state cooperation, not leaving to the Federal government the entire responsibility for the development of such cooperation.[33]

Internal Reorganization: Structure. The states must, as the slang phrase goes, " put up or shut up "; either they must produce results or they must expect to continue to lose power and prestige, and look forward eventually to some readjustments of the boundaries of the intermediate administrative areas, standing between the Federal government and the local units. The causes of the decline of the states and of their loss of prestige are well known. The methods or techniques by which the states may redeem themselves are, therefore, quite clear. By setting their houses in order the states may halt the existing tendencies and restore some of their lost prestige.

Competent authorities agree that the states must be retained. They still have many essential — indeed, indispensable — functions to perform.[34] The most desirable solution would seem to be for the states to improve their organization and administrative efficiency, and so far as is consistent with efficiency, cut their costs. Governor O'Conor argued in 1943 that executive competence and vigorous state action would restore power to the states.[35] Without doubt, some reorganization of governmental machinery is needed, as well as a reallocation of the functions of government. The smaller units are, however, the ones that should be eliminated, the powers of government in the urban areas being concentrated in the municipalities, those in the rural areas being concentrated in the counties, keeping the states as the important units of general government and as the intermediaries between the Federal government on the one hand and the cities and counties on the other. If this is done there will remain but the question of securing a more effective cooperation among the states.

Internal Reorganization: Reallocation of Functions. It has been repeatedly said that modern methods of communication and transportation have greatly reduced the significance of factors of time

[33] See the suggested program for the hastening of uniformity in Chapter 20 and the classified list of organizations of administrative officers in Appendix B, Graves, *Uniform State Action.*

[34] Cf. Mott, Rodney L., " Still the United States," *National Municipal Review,* May, 1934, pp. 264–267.

[35] See O'Conor, Herbert R., " The Challenge to the States," *State Government,* March, 1943, pp. 51–52, 66–68.

and distance. When our present units were established they were purposely made small, so that government might be convenient and accessible to the ordinary citizen. The activities of government were limited in number and restricted in extent. In our own day the opposite is true; these services must be performed in larger units if they are to be performed efficiently in the kind of society that modern methods of communication and transportation have created. The tendency of modern government is to move the functions of government to successively larger units; this leaves the smallest of the older units with no functions to perform and with no excuse for their continued existence.

Towns and townships, villages, and most of the boroughs, special districts for schools and highways and water and sewers and for innumerable other purposes could then be dispensed with. This would leave a rational governmental structure, suited to the conditions and needs of the day in which we live. The functions of local government in urban areas would then be concentrated in municipalities, and the functions of local government in rural areas concentrated in the counties. Under modern conditions, government will still be close to the citizen, and yet the unit of administration will be large enough to employ the services of full-time, trained personnel and to operate efficiently. The state will supervise and coordinate the activities of the various cities and counties, render important services of its own, and carry on all necessary relations both with neighboring states and with the Federal government.

The Council of State Governments. Outstanding organization for the improvement of state government is their own Council — the Council of State Governments, and its related and affiliated groups. These organizations are constantly working to assist and inspire the states to do a better job — organizationally, legislatively, administratively. The paragraphs which follow indicate very briefly the nature and scope of their activities.

"Legislation is — or should be — a profession." For several years the American Legislators' Association functioned as the professional organization of the 7,500 state legislators. It studied the means for securing better qualified legislators, for improving the organization and procedure of the legislatures, for developing worthy professional standards, and for providing better technical assistance to all legislators through state reference bureaus and through the Joint Reference Library. It endeavored to broaden the perspective of legislators by state conferences, regional conferences, and national conferences,

as well as by other means. This work is tremendously important if
state government is to function effectively, but unfortunately, much
of it has been permitted to lag. The work in the field of interstate
cooperation done by the Council of State Governments is important
too, but this work in the field of legislation should be resumed and
expended at an early date.

" The Council of State Governments is primarily concerned with
those governmental spheres over which the Federal government has
no jurisdiction. It seeks to develop better coordination and more
active cooperation between groups of states in the various regions
of the United States, and also between the forty-eight states as a
whole. It also seeks to bring the state governments into better adjustment with the Federal government — and with town and city governments."

The Joint Reference Bureau is a clearing house of information
concerning problems of *state* government. It was " originally established for the use of state legislators and is now rendering service
also to executive and administrative officials of the states. Since
Federal policies relating to many subjects cannot be determined intelligently without accurate information concerning the statutes on
the same subjects in each of the forty-eight states, the Bureau is being
consulted frequently by Federal officials."

The Interstate Assembly, which was organized in 1932 and 1933
with the support of two successive Presidents of the United States,
is composed of three delegates from each state: one designated by
the governor, one by the house of representatives, and one by the
senate of the state. Like the Council of State Governments, whose governing body it is, it views governmental problems as a whole; like the
Council, it brings " together alert officials who are interested in coordinating the legislative, administrative, and executive activities
of state government, and strives to perfect the machinery for attacking the problems of state government as a related whole." These
agencies are assisted by a rapidly increasing number of interstate
boards and commissions, functioning in a wide variety of fields. In
addition to all of these, there is the magazine *State Government,*
which is the only periodical in the country exclusively devoted to the
improvement of state laws and state government.

At present " the laws of the states conflict, their practices diverge,
their policies are antagonistic. In the face of a universal demand for
harmony, the states are functioning as forty-eight sovereign nations,
each going its own sovereign way. Such chaos cannot continue. One

of two courses is inevitable. Either many of the remaining functions of the states will rapidly pass into Federal control, or else the states must hasten to cooperate with each other as they have never cooperated before." Organizations of the type described here, with adequate financial support and suitable publicity, together with the national and regional organizations of state administrative officers, offer the main hope for the future of the states. If these organizations fail, the states fail. If the states fail in these critical times, the Union must inevitably cease to be " the Union as it was."

SELECTED REFERENCES

Advisory Committee on Education, *Selected Legal Problems in Providing Federal Aid for Education* (Washington, 1938).

Aiken, George D., *Speaking from Vermont* (Stokes, New York, 1938).

American Association of State Highway Officials, *The History and Accomplishment of Twenty-five Years of Federal Aid for Highways* (Washington, 1944).

American Legislators' Association, *Conflicting Taxation* (Chicago, 1935).

American Municipal Association, *Cities and the National Defense Program* (Chicago, 1941).

Association of American Law Schools, *Selected Essays in Constitutional Law,* Part III (Foundation Press, Chicago, 1938).

Baden, Anne L., *Federal Aid to Specific Activities in the United States: a Selected List of Recent Writings* (Library of Congress, 1935).

Baker, Gladys, *The County Agent* (University of Chicago Press, 1939).

Ball, Carleton R., *Federal, State, and Local Administrative Relationships in Agriculture,* 2 vols. (University of California Press, 1938).

Beman, L. T., *Selected Articles on State Rights* (Wilson, New York, 1926).

Benson, George C. S., *The New Centralization* (Farrar and Rinehart, New York, 1941).

Betters, Paul V., *Federal Services to Municipal Governments* (Municipal Administration Service, New York, 1931).

——, *Recent Federal-City Relations* (United States Conference of Mayors, Washington, 1936).

Bitterman, Henry J., *State and Federal Grants-in-Aid* (Mentzer, Bush, Chicago, 1938).

Boddy, Francis M., *Federal Expenditures in Minnesota; Their Significance for the Economic Welfare of the State* (University of Minnesota Press, 1935).

Brown, Ann D., *Centralization in the Government of the United States Including States Rights: a Selected List of References* (Library of Congress, 1940).

Burdine, J. Alton, *National-State Cooperation, with Special Reference to Texas* (Arnold Foundation, Dallas, 1935).

Clark, Jane P., *The Rise of a New Federalism: Federal-State Cooperation in the United States* (Columbia University Press, 1938).

Cohen, Julius H., *Increasing Federal Encroachments upon the Powers and*

Properties of the States (Chamber of Commerce of the State of New York, New York, 1938).

Council of State Governments, *Book of the States* (Chicago, biennially).

——, *Grants-in-Aid and Other Federal Expenditures within the States,* with supplements (Chicago, 1945).

Davidson, Donald, *The Attack on Leviathan: Regionalism and Nationalism in the United States* (University of North Carolina Press, 1938).

Educational Policies Commission, *Federal Activities in Education* (Washington, 1939).

Elliott, William Y., *The Need for Constitutional Reform* (Whittlesey House, New York, 1935).

Fite, Emerson D., *Government by Coöperation* (Macmillan, New York, 1932).

Graves, W. Brooke, *Uniform State Action* (University of North Carolina Press, 1934).

——, Ed., "Intergovernmental Relations in the United States," *Annals,* January, 1940, entire issue.

Hansen, Alvin H., and Perloff, Harvey S., *State and Local Finance in the National Economy* (Norton, New York, 1944).

Holcombe, Arthur N., *Political Parties of Today* (Harper, New York, 1934).

Howard, Donald S., *The W.P.A. and Federal Relief Policy* (Russell Sage Foundation, New York, 1943).

International City Managers' Association, *Municipal Year Book* (Chicago, annually).

Jamison, Judith N., *Intergovernmental Cooperation in Public Personnel Administration in the Los Angeles Area* (University of California at Los Angeles, Bureau of Governmental Research, 1944).

Kallenback, Joseph E., *Federal Cooperation with the States under the Commerce Clause* (University of Michigan Press, 1942).

Ketcham, Roland M., *Intergovernmental Cooperation in the Los Angeles Area* (University of California at Los Angeles, Bureau of Governmental Research, 1941).

Key, V. O., Jr., *The Administration of Federal Grants to States* (Public Administration Service, Chicago, 1937).

Lee, F. P., *New Federal-State Relationships* (University of Virginia Institute of Public Affairs, 1938).

Leigh, Robert D., *Federal Health Administration in the United States* (Harper, New York, 1927).

Millett, John D., *The Works Progress Administration in New York City* (Public Administration Service, Chicago, 1938).

Mumford, Lewis, *The Culture of Cities* (Harcourt, Brace, New York, 1938).

National Resources Planning Board, *Regional Factors in National Planning* (Washington, 1935).

——, *Our Cities, Their Role in the National Economy* (Washington, 1937).

——, *Urban Government* (Washington, 1939).

——, *Federal Relations with Local Planning* (Washington, 1940).

Nevins, Allan, *The American States During and After the Revolution, 1775–1789* (Macmillan, New York, 1924).

Northwest Regional Council, *Discovering Anew the Pacific Northwest* (Portland, 1940).

Northwest Regional Council, *A Report of Progress, 1941–1943* (Portland, 1943).

Odum, Howard W., *Southern Regions* (University of North Carolina Press, 1936).

——, and Moore, Harry E., *American Regionalism: A Cultural-Historical Approach to National Integration* (Holt, New York, 1938).

Pate, James E., *The Decline of States' Rights* (Arnold Foundation, Dallas, 1936).

Pound, Roscoe, and others, *Federalism as a Democratic Process* (Princeton University Press, 1942).

Reed, Thomas H., Ed., *Federal-State-Local Fiscal Relations* (Municipal Finance Officers Association, Chicago, 1942).

Ribble, Frederick D. G., *State and National Power over Commerce* (Columbia University Press, 1937).

Ridley, Clarence E., and Nolting, Orren, Eds., *What the Depression Has Done to Cities* (International City Managers' Association, Chicago, 1935).

Rosen, Dorothy E., *Federal Grants-in-Aid: Selected Bibliography* (University of Southern California, 1938).

Studensky, Paul, *Government of Metropolitan Areas* (National Municipal League, New York, 1930).

Summers, Harrison B. and Robert E., *Increasing Federal Powers* (Wilson, New York, 1940).

Thompson, Dorothy C., *Social and Economic Problems Arising Out of World War II: A Bibliography* (Public Administration Service, Chicago, 1941).

Treasury Department, Committee on Intergovernmental Fiscal Relations, *Intergovernmental Fiscal Relations* (Washington, 1943).

Turner, Frederick J., *The Frontier in American History* (Holt, New York, 1920).

——, *The Significance of Sections in American History* (Holt, New York, 1932).

Vance, Rupert B., *Human Geography of the South: A Study in Regional Resources and Human Geography* (University of North Carolina Press, 1932).

Walker, Harvey, *Federal Limitations on Municipal Ordnance Making* (Ohio State University Press, 1929).

Wallace, William K., *Our Obsolete Constitution* (John Day, New York, 1932).

Wilk, Kurt, *Decentralizing Governmental Work* (Columbia University, Institute of Public Administration, 1942).

Williams, J. Kerwin, *Grants-in-Aid under the Public Works Administration* (Columbia University Press, 1939).

Zuber, Leo J., *Federal Aid in Tennessee* (Tennessee State Planning Commission, 1939).

———

Anderson, William, "Federalism — Then and Now," *State Government*, May, 1943, pp. 107–112, and comments thereon, *ibid.*, June, 1943, pp. 141–144.

Bane, Frank, " Mr. Bane and States Rights," *State Government,* March, 1945, pp. 48–49.

Bennett, Walter H., " Early American Theories of Federalism," *Journal of Politics,* August, 1942, pp. 383–395.

Broughton, J. Melville, " The Future of the States," *State Government,* March, 1943, pp. 53–54, 70–71, 74.

Carr, Ralph L., and others, articles on Arkansas Valley Authority proposal, *Rocky Mountain Law Review,* April, 1941, pp. 175–219.

Culver, Dorothy C., " A Bibliography of Intergovernmental Relations in the United States," *Annals,* January, 1940, pp. 210–218.

Davidson, Donald, " Political Regionalism and Administrative Regionalism," *Annals,* January, 1940, pp. 138–143.

Davis, J. William, " The Conflict between the Federal Commerce Power and the Taxing Power of the States," *Southwestern Social Science Quarterly,* September, 1940, pp. 149–162.

Dodd, Walter F., " The Decreasing Importance of State Lines," American Bar Association *Journal,* February, 1941, pp. 78–84.

Dowling, Noel T., " Interstate Commerce and State Power," *Virginia Law Review,* November, 1940, pp. 1–28.

Durisch, Lawrence L., " Local Government and the TVA Program," *Public Administration Review,* Summer, 1941, pp. 326–334.

Edelmann, Alexander T., " The TVA and Intergovernmental Relations," *American Political Science Review,* June, 1943, pp. 455–469.

Engelbert, Ernest, and Wernimont, Kenneth, " Administrative Aspects of the Federal-State Legislative Relationship," *Public Administration Review,* Spring, 1942, pp. 126–140.

Fesler, James W., " Areas of Industrial Mobilization," *Public Administration Review,* Winter, 1941, pp. 149–166.

Gill, Corrington, " Federal-State-City Cooperation in Congested Production Areas," *Public Administration Review,* Winter, 1945, pp. 28–33.

Graves, W. Brooke, " Readjusting Governmental Areas and Functions," *Annals,* January, 1940, pp. 203–209.

Hagood, Margaret J., " Statistical Methods for Delineation of Regions Applied to Data on Agriculture and Population," *Social Forces,* March, 1943, pp. 287–297.

Heberle, Rudolf, " Regionalism: Some Critical Observations," *Social Forces,* March, 1943, pp. 280–286.

Hoan, Daniel W., " National Defense and the Cities," *National Municipal Review,* June, 1941, pp. 359–362.

Hodes, Barnet, " Civilian Defense Plans and the Civilian War Effort in Relation to Municipal Governments," *American Municipal Law Review,* October, 1942, pp. 223–226.

——, " Effective National Defense and Municipal Home Rule," *National Municipal Review,* October, 1941, pp. 565–567, 616.

——, " The War and Municipal Law," *American Municipal Law Review,* April, 1942, pp. 2–6.

Hoyt, Homer, " Forces of Urban Centralization and Decentralization," *American Journal of Sociology,* May, 1941, pp. 843–852.

Leland, Simeon E., " Wanted: More Equity in Tax Division," *National Municipal Review,* February, 1942, pp. 73–78, 109.

Lepawsky, Albert, "America's Tax Dollar — A Key Problem in Governmental Reconstruction," *Annals,* January, 1940, pp. 185–193.

Lindeman, Eduard C., " Notes on Psychological Aspects of Regionalism," *Social Forces,* March, 1941, pp. 301–306.

McCall, Charles C., " The Development of Federal-Municipal Relations Under P.W.A. and the Defense Public Works Program," *American Municipal Law Review,* April, 1942, pp. 35–44.

Martin, James W., " Federal-State Tax Cooperation," *National Municipal Review,* January, 1945, pp. 21–26.

———, " General Pattern of State and Federal Cooperation in Tax Administration," *State Government,* April, 1944, pp. 307–311, 320–321.

———, " Implications of State and Federal Aid to Municipalities," *Municipal Finance,* May, 1942, pp. 27–34.

———, " Possibilities of Federal Tax Administration as a Solution for Tax Conflicts," *Journal of Politics,* August, 1944, pp. 294–322.

———, " The Problem of Duplicating Federal and State Taxes," *State Government,* March, 1944, pp. 287–289.

May, Samuel C., and Ward, Robert E., " Coordinating Defense Activities in a Metropolitan Region," *Public Administration Review,* Spring, 1942, pp. 104–112.

Merriam, Charles E., " Urbanism," *American Journal of Sociology,* March, 1940, pp. 720–730.

Nelson, Roger S., " Federal Aid for Urban Land Acquisition," *Journal of Land and Public Utility Economics,* May, 1945, pp. 125–135.

New York State Teachers Association, " Metropolitan Areas and Future School Problems," *Public Education Research Bulletin,* December 15, 1941.

O'Conor, Herbert R., " The Challenge to the States," *State Government,* March, 1943, pp. 51–52, 68.

Odum, Howard W., " A Social Approach to the Study and Practice of American Regionalism," *Social Forces,* May, 1942, pp. 425–436.

Owsley, Roy H., " Current Developments in Federal-Municipal Relationships," *Bulletin* of League of Cities of the Third Class in Pennsylvania, October, 1941, pp. 9–11, 15.

———, " The Municipalities' Stake in Federal Action," *New England Townsman,* November, 1940, pp. 3–6, 8–9.

Pinney, Harvey F., and others, " Proposals for Organization and Operation of Regional Councils in Metropolitan Areas," *The American City,* June, 1943, pp. 79, 81, 83, 85.

Pond, Walter, " Intergovernmental Immunity," *Iowa Law Review,* January, 1941, pp. 272–301.

Powell, Thomas R., " Intergovernmental Tax Immunities," *George Washington Law Review,* June, 1940, pp. 1213–1220.

Price, Daniel O., " Factor Analysis in the Study of Metropolitan Centers," *Social Forces,* May, 1942, pp. 449–455.

Reimer, Svend, " Theoretical Aspects of Regionalism," *Social Forces,* March, 1943, pp. 275–280.

Rice, Stuart A., " Government Statistics Lack Integration," *State Government*, February, 1940, pp. 27–28.

Richberg, Donald R., " Should the Power of the Federal Government Be Increased? " *Michigan Law Review*, April, 1941, pp. 845–855.

Robinson, David W., " Voluntary Regionalism in the Control of Water Resources," *Annals*, January, 1940, pp. 116–123.

Roseman, Alvin, " The Regional Coordination of Defense, Health and Welfare Services," *Public Administration Review*, Autumn, 1941, pp. 432–440.

Rosinia, Michael L., " Municipal Defense Legislation," *American Municipal Law Review*, October, 1942, pp. 229–232.

Short, Raymond S., " Municipalities and the Federal Government," *Annals*, January, 1940, pp. 44–53.

Simpson, George, and Ivey, John E., Jr., " Regionalism and Social Planning," *Social Forces*, December, 1941, pp. 186–195.

Sprague, Theodore W., " Some Notable Features in the Authority Structure of a Section," *Social Forces*, March, 1943, pp. 344–350.

Stanbery, V. B., " Evolution of a Regional Development Plan," *The Planners' Journal*, July–September, 1942, pp. 3–10.

Stassen, Harold E., " E Pluribus Unum," *Public Administration Review*, Summer, 1942, pp. 187–194.

Taft, Charles P., " National Defense and Community Service," *National Municipal Review*, June, 1941, pp. 321–326.

Thatcher, Harold W., " Calhoun and Federal Reinforcement of State Laws," *American Political Science Review*, October, 1942, pp. 873–880.

Vance, Rupert B., " Human Resources and Public Policy: An Essay Toward Regional-National Planning," *Social Forces*, October, 1943, pp. 20–25.

Watkins, James T., IV, " Regionalism and Plans for Postwar Reconstruction: The First Three Years," *Social Forces*, May, 1943, pp. 379–389.

CHAPTER XXIV

The States in the War and the Postwar

IT is often assumed that the responsibility of the states in the prosecution of a war is slight, but, as experience in World War II has again clearly shown, nothing could be farther from the truth. It is true that the war powers are conferred upon the central government in Article I, Section 8, in the most lengthy provisions devoted to any single subject in the Federal Constitution, and that by the same instrument, the states are restricted in Article I, Section 10, in their activities in the defense field. Yet, when war comes, the states can and do make a significant contribution to the success of the Nation's war effort.

It is the purpose of this concluding chapter to consider the nature and extent of this contribution of the states to the war effort, and to present an overall view of the effect of the impact of the war upon the states. In other words, what did the states do in the war, and what did the war do to the states? What plans have the states made for their development in the postwar era — their social and economic development, their plans for building construction and highways, and for the development of their physical resources? Finally, one ought to have some idea of their plans for aiding and absorbing into productive employment, their large numbers of returning veterans.

VITAL SERVICES RENDERED TO THE WAR EFFORT

The contribution of the states to the war effort was very great. In some cases it was indirect and not clearly apparent, but in many others the states were responsible for the performance of duties highly essential to the successful prosecution of the war. Most important of the latter was the administration of the Selective Service System, and of civilian defense. In addition, the National Guard units of the states were taken over in toto by the Federal government, as units in the new citizens' army. In state after state, active steps were taken toward the development and encouragement of war industry, while both public and private agencies in the smaller local units of government contributed to the war effort in a variety of ways.[1]

Administration of Selective Service. The administration of the draft in each state is placed by law in the hands of the governor, who is the responsible head. He appoints the draft boards and must see that the law is fairly and promptly administered. He may — and usually does — delegate responsibility for administration either to the adjutant general or to a state director of selective service. In World War I, the local draft boards operated under fairly definite and explicit instructions governing what they could or could not do, under various conditions. Some objection was raised to this plan because it failed to give to the local boards any appreciable opportunity for the exercise of independent judgment.

Before the United States became involved in World War II, the Selective Service and Training Act was enacted by the Congress. It provided for local boards, similar to those that had functioned in the previous emergency, but it modified the plan so that each local board operated almost as an autonomous unit. Although the task to be performed was, in many ways, larger and more difficult, experience proved that the system used in World War I was clearly preferable. Under the more recent plan, the only instructions binding upon the local boards were their quotas. These they were supposed to meet, but they were left with " a wide latitude for the exercise of independent judgment " as to the manner in which the necessary individuals might be secured.

When the program was inaugurated, all males of serviceable age were required to register.[2] Each registrant was then classified by his local draft board, according to the facts pertaining to his individual case, in one of four classes, each of which had a number of subdivisions:

> Class 　I — Available for service
> Class 　II — Deferred because of occupational status
> Class III — Deferred because of dependents
> Class IV — Deferred specifically by law or because of
> 　　　　　obvious unfitness for military service

[1] The Council of State Governments in 1942 put out a weekly *Governors' Bulletin,* the successive issues of which not only summarize the recommendations contained in the governors' messages, but give a clear idea of the nature and scope of the activities of the states in behalf of the war effort.

[2] See Draper, William H., " The Role of the States in Registration Under the Selective Service Law," *State Government,* October, 1940, pp. 203, 206.

Those in Class IV with only minor defects were eligible for limited service, and might still be drafted. At the beginning of the program, the number of men called for service each month depended largely on the ability of the camps to absorb trainees. Later, it depended on the estimated needs of the armed forces.

Instructions were issued to the local boards from the state head-quarters of Selective Service, but these boards appeared to be able to ignore them with impunity. As a result of this situation, and the fact that some boards were " tough " while others were " easy," and that some boards had within their jurisdiction a larger proportion of eligible males who could be drafted, there developed a conspicuous lack of uniformity in dealing with cases that were more or less parallel. The public relations aspect of such situations was bad. Here were two boys similarly situated, living on opposite sides of the street, under the jurisdiction of two different boards. Both were single, both were employed in war work, yet one was drafted and the other was not. This lack of uniformity in procedure not only did not make sense, but in many cases, resulted in gross unfairness to individuals and to families.

So much difficulty was experienced as a result of the drafting of men not " occupationally adapted " to military service, that many states set up screening programs for draft registrants, to determine by means of neuropsychiatric tests their fitness or unfitness for military service. This was done in response to instructions from national headquarters of Selective Service, to the effect that " registrants whose condition is such as positively indicates physical or mental breakdown, or failure to adjust themselves to the responsibilities of military service " should be rejected. The New Jersey program, carried on in cooperation with members of the medical, social work, and nursing professions and with public and private welfare and health organizations, was well administered, and has been fully described by the Department concerned.[3]

Absorption of National Guard Units. The National Guard, the nation's second line of defense, had its origin in the state militia of the original thirteen states. These states retained their militia, and every state created thereafter provided in its constitution for a state militia. Actually, the militia of the several states includes

[3] See Franel, Emil, " Social Histories as Aids in the Selection of Members of the Armed Forces," (1943) ; " Neuropsychiatric Screening of Selective Service Registrants in New Jersey," (1944) ; and " Incidence of Previous Institutional Care Among Selective Service Registrants — the New Jersey Experience of 100,000 Men," (1944) — all duplicated by the Department of Institutions and Agencies, Trenton.

every male between the ages of eighteen and forty-five, who is physically able to bear arms and mentally competent to use them, but the term as commonly used applies only to the *organized* militia, known as the National Guard. Citizens qualified to bear arms who are not members of the National Guard are classified as " militia reserve."

The Army of the United States consists of three component parts, the Regular Army, the National Guard, and the Officers Reserve Corps. For many years, the organization, training, and equipment of the militia units were seriously defective. Some improvements were made after the Spanish-American War, and more after World War I. At that time, the defenses of the country were so poorly organized that there was no way of transferring the National Guard units from the states to the Federal service, as units of the United States Army. In the meantime, legislation correcting this situation had been enacted, so that it was possible upon our entry into World War II, for the Federal government to take over state units of the National Guard in their entirety. Thus the Pennsylvania National Guard became the famous 28th Division in the United States Army, which served in the campaigns in Germany.

As these changes occurred, the militia ceased to be primarily a state organization under state control; today, it is a national organization under the control of the Federal government. Even so, the governors of the several states still retain the right to appoint the various officers in their respective Guard units, but these appointments are not effective unless the appointees have met the military requirements of the United States Army. The organization is extensive and costly to maintain, even in a small state like South Dakota:

The State's part is to maintain armories, pay the salary of the State Adjutant General and his necessary clerical help, while the Federal government provides all uniforms and equipment, pays the guardsmen, provides rations, gasoline and oil, and other necessary expenses. In dollars and cents, the State of South Dakota appropriated only $18,000 for its National Guard last year while the Federal government provided about $320,000 or eighteen times as much.[4]

4 See Strathman, Earl, *South Dakota's Contribution to National Defense,* pp. 11–15 (University of South Dakota, Governmental Research Bureau, 1941). See also: Bacon, George W., " The Model State Guard Act," *Fordham Law Review,* January, 1941, pp. 41–63; Beckwith, Edmund R., " Laws Relating to State Military Power," *State Government,* March, 1943, pp. 57–58, 75–77; Conway, Francis X., " A State's Power of Defense under the Constitution," *Fordham Law Review,* May, 1942, pp. 169–192; Illinois State Planning Commission, *United States War Department Activities in Illinois* (Springfield, 1939).

In a large state like Illinois, at about the same time, the Federal government was providing almost $2,000,000 a year, to maintain more than sixty different units or organizations.

Reference has already been made, in Chapter X, to the fact that the absorption of the National Guard units of the state left them without any organized force at their disposal with which to protect life and property at home, should the need for doing so arise. This situation was met by the recruiting of new state guard or home guard forces, which were trained and disciplined for the purpose of providing such an emergency force.

Civilian Defense. State councils of defense functioned in all the states, but the names applied to them varied considerably from one state to another. Most of them were established in 1940 and 1941, at first by executive order.[5] By the end of 1942, all but a very few had been set up by legislative act, modeled usually after the war powers act drafted by the Council of State Governments. In practically all states, the members were appointed by the governor, who served as chairman. The number of members varied all the way from five in Kentucky to more than 150 in Massachusetts, with a range between fifteen and twenty-five in a majority of states. Members received no compensation other than their expenses. The tenure was indefinite, usually at the pleasure of the governor. Although the councils had important advisory functions, they frequently set up advisory committees to assist them. This led, in some cases, to the establishment of a " double-headed " organization, consisting of an advisory council and an administrative board.

It was originally suggested by the Office of Civilian Defense that, organizationally, six functional committees be set up to carry out the work of the council; in New York, it was decided that ten committees were necessary to make a plan of civilian defense effective throughout the state. Most of the states conformed to this general pattern. These lists are shown in parallel columns on page 978; space limitations prevent any attempt at describing the activities of these various phases of the civilian defense program.

Provision was usually made for a staff, the nucleus of which was often obtained from the state planning board. Some states seem to have relied mainly on volunteer service, while others provided substantial appropriations for expenses. Since no one knew how much

[5] Similar organizations were established during World War I; see Carey, William D., " State Councils of Defense: 1917 and 1941 Models," *State Government*, May, 1941, pp. 105–106, 117–120, 123, and June, 1941, pp. 133–135, 145–146, 151.

STATE CIVILIAN DEFENSE ORGANIZATION

OCD Recommendations	*New York State List*
Agricultural resources and production	Police
Civil protection	Fire
Health, welfare and consumer interest	Water supply
Housing, works and facilities	Health and sanitation
Human resources and skills	Evacuation
Industrial resources and production	Transportation
	Communications
	Shelter and food
	Air raids
	Administration and records

would be required, there was no rhyme or reason to some of the amounts provided. The legislature of New York appropriated $1,475,000 for 1942, while that of Pennsylvania provided $25,000. Nevada provided $10,000 and Utah $125,000. Mississippi put up half a million.[6]

All of the councils functioned of necessity through organizations in the local communities, and elaborate plans were developed for the organization and direction of regional, county, and municipal defense councils. In Oregon, a manual was put out respecting the organization of county councils, each of which was to have divisions on planning, protection, necessities, communication, and public utilities. Not only were regional councils set up in Virginia, but the 100 counties of the state were grouped into zones or districts for special defense purposes. Thus there were four civil protective mobilization zones and twenty fire protection mobilization zones. There were eight regions for general civilian defense purposes, whose functions were essentially those of a coordinating agency for all the various phases of the program.[7]

[6] *State Councils of Defense* (University of California, Bureau of Public Administration, May, 1941, and revised, December, 1942) is about the best source of information. A tremendous amount of material was published on the subject. Helen F. Conover, of the Division of Bibliography, Library of Congress, prepared *Civilian Defense: A Selective List of Recent References*, in 1941. Many of the articles in the professional journals are cited in the selected references at the end of this chapter. Two of the best state manuals were prepared in California and Indiana: State Director of Civilian Defense, *War Council Manual* (Sacramento, 1943), and Indiana State Defense Council, *Civilian Defense in Indiana*, Fifth Revision (Indianapolis, 1943). See also: Furlong, Harold A., Administrator, *Organization, History, and Fields of Activity of the Michigan Council of Defense* (Lansing, 1942), and New York State Council of Defense, *Report on New York State Defense Program* (Legislative Document, 1942, No. 26, Albany).

[7] See Oregon Civilian Defense Council, *Organizing for Civilian Defense: County Defense Councils* (Salem, 1941), and Virginia Defense Council, *A Manual for Regional Defense Councils*, in twelve separate sections (Richmond, 1941); also Virginia Council on Public Administration, "Regional Defense Areas," *Public Administration Notes*, January 6, 1941, entire issue.

In addition to these major phases of the civilian defense program, the organization in each state carried on, through its state and local units, a multitude of special programs, among which the following may be mentioned:

Aluminum Collection — in the early days of the war, when this metal was critically scarce.

Clean-up for Victory Campaign — a home inspection campaign to remove fire hazards.

Fire Prevention Week — special promotion efforts made.

V-Home Campaign — awarding window stickers to families which had made proper air raid precautions and performed other services useful in the war effort.

Victory Garden Campaign — giving aid to amateur gardeners in the effort to increase to the maximum the supply of food.

Security of War Information Campaign — designed to inform the public and especially the families of service men of the dangers of revealing military information.

Home Safety Mobilization — promoting the use of a checklist of home hazards responsible for the injury and death of thousands of persons each year.

War Film Council — distribution of moving pictures on war and civilian defense subjects.

Scrap Drives — to collect scarce metals, waste paper, fats and oils, and other critical substances essential to the war effort.

Auto License Plate Campaign — to collect old license plates from cars and trucks for reprocessing.

Educational Campaigns — conduct of defense institutes, plant protection schools, and training institutes for various purposes.

Publicity — conduct of a speakers' bureau, publicity bureau, using all available media for informing the public regarding the program.

Securing Maximum Production. In time of peace the states carry on extensive campaigns to convince manufacturers of the advantages of locating their plants within their borders, emphasizing nearness to markets, good transportation facilities, low taxes, desirable living and working conditions, et cetera. In time of war, they did all of these things and many more, with the dual purpose of helping the war effort and of advancing their own interests. Some states seized upon President Roosevelt's slogan, "Make America the Arsenal of Democracy," supplementing it, as did Pennsylvania, with some phrase of its own, such as "Make Pennsylvania the Arsenal of America."

The states turned over their employment services to the Federal government for the emergency — somewhat under protest, to be sure — but they still waged an intensive campaign to recruit workers for defense and war industries. They undertook to guard the migration of workers, and through cooperation with the various training agencies such as the vocational schools, WPA, NYA, TWI, CCC, and ESMWT, to prepare new workers for war jobs, and to increase the productiveness of those who were already employed. Efforts were made to utilize the total labor supply by bringing in inexperienced youth, and calling back over-age workers, many of whom had retired; by calling upon housewives and others not ordinarily employed in industry, Negro workers, the physically impaired, and whenever possible, returning veterans.

The prisons were another source of increased manpower, long neglected and ignored. Many prisoners were quite as anxious as others in the population to help in the war effort; in fact, many of them felt that, by doing so, they would have an opportunity to redeem themselves in the eyes of society. There were at least three ways in which they were ultimately able to be of service. Those who were confined in institutions because of relatively minor offenses, and who were otherwise acceptable for military service, were permitted to serve. It was estimated that about one fourth of the male prison population fell within this group. There was another large group that could not be released, but could be trained in prison for needed industrial skills. This represented sound policy; the skills so learned would not only contribute to the war effort, but would stand the prisoners in good stead in their efforts later to adjust themselves to normal conditions of life. Finally, it was possible to utilize inmate labor for the production of materials needed for civilian defense and lend-lease purposes.[8]

In addition to all these methods used to increase the amount of available manpower and get more people to work, other devices were adopted for the purpose of conserving manpower and increasing its production. To protect workers from possible injury, extensive campaigns placing a heavy emphasis on the safety factor in war industry were organized. Other devices used were defense training and the modification of existing labor laws, in order to permit full cooperation in the war effort. Stringent laws regulating child labor and the hours and conditions of work for women are highly desirable in normal times, but in time of emergency such regulations can properly be modified. Thus many states lowered the minimum

---

[8] For an excellent report of progress of state prison industries under the Government Division of the War Production Board, see Maverick, Maury, and Burke, William H., *Prisons in Wartime* (War Production Board, Washington, 1943); also Joint Legislative Committee to Study the Use of New York State Prisoners in War Service, *Preliminary Report* (Legislative Document, 1943, No. 8). On women in wartime industry, see Women's Bureau, *State Labor Laws for Women with Wartime Modifications,* in four parts (Washington, 1945).

age limits for employment and eased the conditions governing the issuance of working papers for minors, while the regulations governing night work in war plants for women workers were relaxed.

Tremendous training programs were inaugurated throughout the country. State departments of education, aided by Federal funds, undertook supervision of local efforts to provide several different types of defense and war training courses, vocational in character. Those included were:

Supplementary or trade extension courses designed to increase the efficiency and knowledge of persons already employed in defense industries.

Preemployment or refresher courses designed for the unemployed.

Specialized technical courses offered for employed workers in technical occupations requiring training in the new technical procedures developed in defense production.

Supervisory or foremanship courses providing training to increase the efficiency of men already serving in supervisory capacity, or to train men selected as possible supervisory material.

These efforts were supplemented by within-plant training programs carried on in many war plants, both public and private, chiefly with the aid of instructors trained in the War Manpower Commission's TWI program, or in ESMWT courses offered, with Federal aid, in the various colleges and universities.[9]

Mention should also be made of the fact that the efforts of the states in this field were not confined to recruiting and training for industry, but extended to the field of agriculture as well. They sought to encourage maximum production in this field by educational campaigns with regard to the most efficient methods of cultivation and by encouraging the extension of the areas cultivated. They did all that they could to aid in the recruiting of essential farm labor, transporting school and college students to farm areas for harvest work and, with the cooperation of the Federal government, importing farm labor from far distant points, sometimes outside of continental United States. They gave vigorous support to the effort to increase the number, the size, and the productiveness of victory gardens.

In addition to these efforts to fill essential jobs in war industry, and to train the incumbents of these positions, the state gave assistance to the recruiting efforts for various specialized types of Federal service. They recruited women as nurses and as nurse's aides. They

[9] There was a tremendous pamphlet literature in all of the states on the subject of war training. For a good discussion of the effect of the defense and war training program on the activities and financing of education in the states, see Studebaker, John W., " The States, Education and National Defense," *State Government*, May, 1941, pp. 103–104, 115–116.

helped in securing men for service in the Seabees. Under the direction of the governors, they launched long drives for the recruiting of Wacs and Waves, who were needed for vital services in the armed forces. In some jurisdictions, prizes were offered to high school students for the best essays on such recruiting campaigns. The part played by the states in the manpower situation was indeed a vital one.

Assistance in Rationing. Although the entire rationing program was conceived by the Federal government and was administered by OPA, state administrative officers rendered important assistance in carrying it out. The voluntary cooperation of state gasoline tax officials, for instance, in the administration of the gasoline regulations of the mileage rationing program was described as a unique development in Federal-state cooperation. Many of these officials assumed greatly increased burdens in both expense and effort, in order to aid in passing on to the public all the information necessary for compliance with rationing regulations. Similar efforts were made in connection with the tire rationing program.

The purposes of these efforts — as of the rationing program as a whole, which included at various times shoes, and such food products as butter and oleomargarine, sugar, coffee, meat and fats, canned goods and processed foods — was to insure an equitable distribution among civilians of scarce commodities, and to do as much as could be done to prevent inflation.[10] Since the OPA lacked sufficient funds and personnel properly to enforce its regulations, some of the states took up with energy and determination the task of eliminating the black market in certain food products, in gasoline and tires, and of stamping out racketeering in ration stamps. When the supply of liquor was drastically curtailed, many states assumed full responsibility for the inauguration and administration of a rationing program.

Conservation of War Transportation. The states and the local communities did many things to assist in the conservation of war transportation. The Office of Defense Transportation requested each governor to enlist the services of the State Highway Traffic Advisory Committee, whose chairman served as the liaison between the national committee and the state committee. In most instances, the state

10 Several articles on this subject include: Henderson, Leon, " Problems of Price and Supply in Wartime," *State Government*, January, 1942, pp. 11, 29; Parkman, Henry, " The Local Rationing Board in Massachusetts," *Public Administration Review*, Summer, 1942, pp. 195–198; Routt, Garland C., " Tire Rationing: A Federal-State-Local Job," *State Government*, February, 1942, pp. 35–36, 44; Watson, George H., " State Gasoline Tax Administrators and the Mileage Rationing Program," *ibid.*, June, 1943, pp. 131–134; and " State Participation in Gasoline Rationing," *Public Administration Review*, Summer, 1943, pp. 213–222.

committees were obliged to appoint a full-time state administrator to advise and assist the many local units, which, under this leadership, took steps to control war traffic, making plans to spread peak loads on the basis of traffic surveys under the new conditions brought about by war industry.

Staggering working hours seemed to offer the best means of relief from traffic congestion and overloading of street cars and busses due to the war production load and automobile tire and gasoline rationing. Intraplant, interplant, and interindustry staggering plans were worked out, to supplement what was known as the natural staggering due to long standing differences in the practices of different industries with regard to hours of work. State campaigns gave powerful impetus to share-the-ride and swap-ride plans for transporting war workers. Laws requiring reduced driving speeds were strictly enforced, while important savings of critical materials and money were affected by controlled use of motor vehicles owned and operated by the states themselves. All of these changes produced important modifications of previously existing driving practices and work schedules.[11]

A canvass of Federal war agencies made by OWI in 1943 revealed that the Federal government was receiving wholehearted cooperation on war problems from state and local governments. Some of these evidences of cooperation were found in the field of transportation. For instance, uniform rules were adopted, permitting most trucks carrying materials to cross state lines unhampered; during the defense period, these interstate barriers had been a serious impediment to the program. Interstate reciprocal licensing of passenger vehicles was extended, to make it easier for war workers to travel from state to state.[12]

[11] See Barber, A. B., " Staggered Hours and Local Passenger Transport," an address before the Midwest Safety Conference in Chicago, May 6, 1942; Brewster, R. Wallace, and others, " The States and Mileage Conservation," *State Government*, October, 1943, pp. 211–213; Chamber of Commerce of the United States, *Staggered Hours* (Washington, November, 1941, and supplement, February, 1942); MacDonald, Thomas H., " The American Motorist in Wartime," *State Government*, June, 1943, pp. 140, 146–147; National Highway Users Conference, *Our Highways and the Nation's Defense* (Washington, n.d.); Office of Defense Transportation, *Conservation of Vital War Transportation* (Washington, n.d.).

Among the many state manuals issued on this subject, the following may be noted: Governor's Coordinating Safety Committee, *Official Manual of the Indiana War Transportation Conservation Program* (Indianapolis, 1942); State War Council, *New York State War Transportation Manual* (Albany, 1942); Ohio War Transportation Committee, *Ohio Manual on Conservation of Vital War Transportation* (Columbus, 1942); State Defense Council, *War Highway Traffic Control in Pennsylvania* (Harrisburg, n.d.).

[12] See Office of War Information, report on Federal-state cooperation on war problems, September 6, 1943, and *National Municipal Review*, October, 1943, pp. 499–500.

Local Citizen Services. The conduct of modern warfare requires mechanized operations on a very large scale, but these operations are utterly impossible without an effective mobilization of manpower and materials on the home front. The overall planning as to policy and some of the administrative work must be done in the nation's capital, but the successful operation of the program on the home front that is desired cannot be secured without the full cooperation and active support of the civilian population. The things that the people did to help in the war effort were legion. The ways they worked in the rendering of essential services, very often without compensation, constitute an outstanding record of accomplishment, and of patriotism and loyalty to the nation.

It should be remembered that all of this was done under most unusual and most difficult circumstances. The needs for production of war and civilian goods were enormous — without precedent in our history. Time was of the essence. We had to turn out, not only the war materials and equipment for our armed forces, but a far greater output of food, clothing, and other essential needs than had been required previously in peace time, for our armed forces, for ourselves, and for our allies. With millions of our most robust and able-bodied workers in uniform, the balance of the population had to perform this overwhelming task. In order to accomplish it, the over-aged, the under-aged, the physically impaired, and the retired were all pressed into service and untold numbers of women, many of whom had never been employed in business or industry, took war jobs. Holidays and long week ends vanished. People worked forty-eight hours as a standard work-week, and many worked far in excess of that amount.

It was from individuals so situated that the states, the local units, and private organizations recruited the workers that were needed to carry on the war effort in the local communities. These busy citizens — hundreds of them — were drafted to serve long hours each week on draft boards, war, price and rationing boards, and in many other capacities. The responsibility on draft board members was onerous and in many ways obviously unpleasant. In the early days of the Office of Price Administration, citizens were called upon to serve on rationing boards when they had no place to work, and nothing to work with — when they had to use orange crates for filing cases. Other citizens who had worked all day in a war plant, continued well into the night on civilian defense work, port patrol duties, work in victory gardens, and on countless other tasks.

Local organizations, sometimes working independently, and sometimes in cooperation with state and national groups, tackled all manner of problems. Bar associations established facilities through which servicemen and women could obtain free legal advice. Women organized and maintained army leagues, navy leagues, and relief services to aid the stricken peoples of many lands. They carried on the Red Cross Blood Donor Service, Red Cross canteens, USO entertainment centers, and gave assistance in war bond drives, hospital work, preparation of bandages, and many other things.[13] All citizens aided in drives for salvage of metals and papers, and for books for service people.

Local defense councils were organized during the defense campaign — in Pennsylvania, there were 450 of them operating before Pearl Harbor. Their activities included a wide variety of programs, in all of which they had the cooperation and assistance of their respective local governments. The local governments gave them financial aid, and together they developed blackout measures and air raid precautions, regulations governing employees going into military service, restrictions upon the use of municipal automobiles during the emergency, wartime building and plumbing code restrictions, defense housing regulations, plans for public works reserves, rules governing municipal liability for injury in blackouts, plans for auxiliary police, et cetera.[14]

[13] The State Council of Defense of Pennsylvania put out an excellent bulletin by Mrs. William J. Clothier, on "What the Women of Pennsylvania Can Do in the Defense Program," listing under volunteer defense activities for women, three types of work — work in established community services, defense activities created by the emergency, and war relief. Possible defense training courses for women were also listed. Many women gave valuable assistance on fair rent committees, and in other phases of community protection, as well as in homes registration work.

[14] A good many states published manuals for their local defense councils: California State Council of Defense, *Organizing for Defense, a Manual for the Cities and Counties of California* (Sacramento, 1941); Illinois State Council of Defense, *Civilian Defense, General Outline of Organization and Duties of Local Councils* (Springfield, 1943); New Jersey Defense Council, *Official Municipal Plan of Defense* (Trenton, 1940); New York State Council of Defense, *Manual for Local Defense Councils* (Albany, 1941); State Council of Defense of Pennsylvania, *A Manual for the Organization of Local Councils of Defense in Pennsylvania*, and *Organization and Guidance of Consumer Committees of Local Councils of Defense* (Harrisburg, 1941). See also Civic Research Institute: *Gearing for War, A Study of the Department of Public Works* (Kansas City, 1943), and City of Portland and Multnomah County Civilian Defense Council, *Organization Manual* (Portland, 1944). Some of these programs were described, either in reports or in newspaper articles: *Portsmouth Herald, Portsmouth and National Defense* (Portsmouth, 1941), and San Francisco Civil Defense Council, *Report* (San Francisco, 1941).

Several articles were published on the activities of these councils: Dixon, Frank K., "Federal-State Relations in Wartime," *State Government*, August, 1942, pp. 153–154, 163–166; Ellis, William J., "War Services of Community Agencies," *ibid.*,

Law Enforcement. The Federal Constitution makes the prevention of sabotage in most cases a state rather than a Federal function, except in time of war. The successful performance of this function depends primarily on alert and intelligent police work, aided by whole-hearted public cooperation. A committee established by the Federal-State Conference on Law Enforcement Problems of National Defense in 1940 urged that changes be made in the state laws to make the work easier, proposing the enactment of model laws on sabotage prevention, explosives, interstate public property, state guard, and providing for fresh pursuits by military forces.[15]

War Legislation. Reference has just been made to proposals for war legislation to enable the states to discharge their responsibilities in a particular field. Actually, through the efforts of the Council of State Governments, the attention of the states was called to needed legislation in many fields, if they were to meet their war responsibilities adequately. The Council, through its committees, sought to develop a set of legislative principles covering such subjects as: emergency war powers, precautions against attack, mobilization for fire defense, military traffic control, emergency health and sanitation areas, acceptance of Federal grants, defense housing, and zoning for defense areas.[16]

In addition to these attempts to draft legislation covering new fields of activity, efforts were also made to eliminate barriers arising out of existing legislation. Changes of this character in the highway field have already been referred to; others, mentioned in the same OWI survey, included such specific items as the following:

April, 1942, pp. 81–82, 91; Hoan, Daniel W., "States, Localities, and Defense," *ibid.,* January, 1941, pp. 9–11, 21–25, and "States and Cities in the Defense Program," *National Municipal Review,* March, 1941, pp. 141–146, 159.

[15] See the following items in *State Government:* "Federal-State Conference to Consider Law Enforcement Problems of National Defense," August, 1940, pp. 146, 155; "Federal-State Conference Adopts Law Enforcement Plans for Defense," September, 1940, pp. 166–168, 180–184; and Smith, Bruce, "Civil Defense in the National Emergency, State Plans for Effecting a General Mobilization of Police at the Scene of Disorders," October, 1940, pp. 198–201. See also: State of New Jersey, Executive Department, *Police War Plans* (Trenton, 1942) ; and Office of the Joint Conference Committee, *A Legislative Program for Defense* (Washington, 1940) ; and Harrison, Earl G., "How State and Local Officials Can Assist in the Alien Registration Program," *State Government,* October, 1940, pp. 204–205.

[16] In addition to the reports issued each year by the Council, see the following articles which are listed in chronological order: Bogart, George G., "Progress in Adoption of State Defense Laws," *State Government,* July, 1941, pp. 162–163, 174–175; "State War Legislation," *ibid.,* February, 1942, pp. 41–42, 49–52; "Progress Report on State War Legislation," *ibid.,* May, 1942, pp. 107–108, 113; "State Legislative Highlights — 1943," *National Municipal Review,* July, 1943, pp. 360–366, 372; "State and Local Aid Given War Agencies," *ibid.,* October, 1943, pp. 499–500; "Suggested State Legislation for 1945," *State Government,* January, 1945, pp. 10–12.

Recognition of legal documents executed by servicemen before commissioned officers instead of notaries, without indicating where such documents were executed (hitherto mandatory in many state laws).

Relaxation of stringent laws governing powers of attorney, to make it possible for servicemen's dependents to act for them during long absence or when they are reported missing.

Standard laws on weights and measures to prevent deviation in size or weight of munitions and war weapons, and to help maintain price ceilings.

Lifting of restrictions on state banks, making possible local financing of large war contracts.

Changing of state housing laws and building codes to meet Federal regulations dictated by scarcity of materials and the necessity for war housing.

Alteration of state laws governing prison labor, resulting in millions of dollars' worth of war goods by thousands of prison inmates.

At the same time, while cooperating with one another and with the Federal government, states and municipalities jealously guarded their traditional American concepts of self-government. Some municipalities refused to pass civilian defense ordinances so phrased as to appear to make local rule subservient to Federal regulations. Another instance of local individualism was the decision of three states to abandon War Time.

THE IMPACT OF THE WAR UPON THE STATES

No one can expect, certainly not in a few paragraphs, to say as early as the Fall of 1945 what the ultimate effects of the war upon the states will be. Certain general observations can, however, be made, for some of the results of the impact of the war, as it has affected them up to V–J Day and beyond, are quite clearly apparent. These can, for convenience, be grouped under five headings, as follows: curtailment of services, suspension of governmental improvements, severe losses of personnel, improved financial condition, and further losses of power to the Federal government.[17]

Scope of Services Rendered. It was a general characteristic of the states in the war period, and of the local units as well, that many types of governmental services were greatly reduced. Essential services were drastically cut, and those that were regarded as less essential or as " frills " were dispensed with altogether. This was not due

[17] Anderson, C. Arnold, and Ryan, Bryce, *War Came to the Iowa Community* (Iowa Agricultural Experiment Station, Ames, 1941) ; Beers, Howard W., *Effects of War on Farm Populations in Kentucky* (Kentucky Agricultural Experiment Station, Bulletin 456, Lexington, 1944) ; Farmer, Hallie, Ed., *War Comes to Alabama* (University of Alabama, Bureau of Public Administration, 1943) ; Pennsylvania Historical Commission, *Pennsylvania's First Year at War, December 7, 1941–December 7, 1942* (Harrisburg, 1943) ; and United States Bureau of Labor Statistics, *Impact of the War on the St. Louis Area* (Washington, 1944).

to a lack of funds with which to provide them, as we shall see, but rather to a number of other factors. First and foremost, perhaps, was the universal desire to get along as best one could, and at all costs to refrain from any use of men or money or materials that might possibly impede the war effort. A second consideration was the shortage of manpower. Some things might have been attempted, but in a tight labor market it was often utterly impossible to obtain qualified people to do them. Therefore these projects were either postponed indefinitely or abandoned altogether.

At the same time, some services essential to the war effort had to be expanded, and some new ones instituted. The states were asked to do all sorts of new and unusual things. The Governor of Illinois, in 1943, issued a list that had been compiled by the State Historical Librarian, of the names of twenty-four men and one woman, all prominent in the history of the state, which had been submitted to the United States Maritime Commission, in response to a request from that agency for names for use in connection with the naming of Liberty ships. Extensive studies were made in many states of defense resources — minerals, power, population, manufacturing, et cetera.[18] Most important extensions of service occurred in the health and welfare fields, and in those portions of the state program related to the production of essential food products and war materials.[19] Some of these efforts have been mentioned in the preceding section.

The departments of highways found continuance of their operations especially difficult. Their work was of first importance, due to the vital nature of the transportation of war workers and war materials, yet new construction was, except under unusual circumstances, out of the question. Maintenance of existing construction was likewise difficult, due to scarcity of materials and parts, higher costs, higher wage levels, and loss of personnel. These factors compelled states to revise their programs, and to postpone many projects that would otherwise have been regarded as necessary.[20] All highway

[18] See Illinois Geological Survey, Circular No. 104, containing papers on war mineral research (Urbana, 1941); Washington State Planning Council, *Defense Resources* (Olympia, 1941); and War Production Board, *Federal Aids for War Mineral Production* (Washington, n.d.).

[19] See, for instance, "Conference Studies Defense Problems," *State Government*, April, 1941, pp. 85, 98–99 — a consideration of subcontracting and of the welfare problems of defense areas, and Department of Public Welfare, *Defense Developments in Alabama* (Montgomery, 1941).

[20] "Defense Needs Create New Problems," *Better Roads*, September, 1941, pp. 17–18, 32; and Clark, Frank W., "National Defense Demands Compel Some Revisions and Postponements of Projects in State Highway Budget," *California Highways and Public Works*, November, 1941, pp. 1–3, 13.

department forces operated under strict rules with regard to conservation of supplies, equipment, and materials.

Suspension of Governmental Improvements. The fact that the time and energy of officials and civic-minded citizens was so engrossed in the war effort accounts to a large extent for a general slowing up of efforts for civic reform and improvement of governmental organization and administration at the state and local levels. This is a regrettable and somewhat curious effect of the war, in view of the surge of popular interest in social and economic problems in other governmental areas. There was, in national and international politics, a widespread and more lively interest than ever before. This was demonstrated in the Presidential election of 1944, and by the generally high degree of interest shown throughout the country in the terms of the international organization to preserve peace, as well as in the terms of the peace treaty itself. In the field of state and local government, however, no such interest has existed. With certain notable exceptions, it was the policy to postpone governmental reorganization, extension of the merit system, constitutional revision, and other similar matters.

In some cases, items such as these are on the agenda for the post-war period. Constitutional revisions were attempted in Georgia, Missouri, and New Jersey, successfully in the first two states, and are in serious contemplation in other jurisdictions. The merit system made headway in a few jurisdictions but was impaired and impeded in others, sometimes by legislative, sometimes by executive action, and usually on the pretext that if enforced it would be " unfair to the boys in the service." The net result has been practically to suspend progress in governmental improvements although, as has been said, the nation could not, while its sons were fighting to preserve democracy in far away lands, strengthen it at home by declaring a moratorium on efforts designed to correct existing abuses.

Severe Losses of Personnel. During the war, the states lost scores and hundreds of employees whom it was difficult if not impossible to replace. The losses due to the operation of Selective Service were not unique — they occurred in all organizations, public and private alike. As early as November, 1942, the State of Illinois reported a total of 1,688 state officials and employees as having gone into the Nation's war service, of whom approximately 750 were under civil service. Thirty-five of them were women. The largest numbers included 450 from the Department of Welfare, 383 from the University of Illinois, with four other departments reporting numbers in excess of 100.

Losses from other causes were due to the poor salary and wage scales existing in most states, on the one hand, and the lure of better paying jobs in war industry, on the other. The turnover rates grew into proportions that were both amazing and alarming. The Federal government itself had some responsibility in this matter. While no Federal recruiting was carried on among the employees of the state and local units, many of their employees came seeking Federal employment, being attracted by the higher Federal pay scales in lower grade positions. By April, 1943, it was reported that the number of state employees was at a five-year low. The very factors responsible for the original losses operated to make it practically impossible to secure suitable replacements.

The seriousness of the problem is well illustrated by facts cited in the Annual Report of the Maine Department of Personnel for 1942:

During the past year, the turnover in employees at the Bangor State hospital has run to more than 100 per cent. A close approximation of this figure was experienced at the Augusta State Hospital, 90 per cent at the Northern Maine Sanatorium, 60 per cent at the School for the Deaf, and in the other departments, the percentages ran all the way from 5 per cent in the more fortunate ones, to 50 per cent and over in others.

This sort of thing costs money, plenty of it, but the State loses in many other ways when experienced employees leave and have to be replaced by new ones. First, and what should be of definite interest to the taxpayer, is a loss in the efficiency of service rendered to the public. This must be obvious to anyone who gives the matter even a passing thought. Second, it holds up administrative detail and processes all along the line and immediately throws an undue workload on those employees who stay on the job.

Thus it was that the turnover was high in all the states, in all branches of the service, but it was highest in the institutions. The result was that in institutions of all types, many of them filled to capacity if not overcrowded, there was such a serious condition of understaffing that it was impossible to give proper care to patients or proper supervision to inmates. In many departments and offices, necessary work fell far behind schedule.

Vigorous measures had to be taken to meet this situation. In order to obtain as many replacements as possible, recruiting activities were expanded, and examining procedures expedited. In many jurisdictions, continuous recruitment was undertaken for the filling of those types of vacancies where the shortage was greatest — clerical and stenographic positions, certain types of case workers, and others, and various expedients were adopted to speed up the examining and certification procedures. The Maine Department of Personnel reported on this point:

Where, in normal times, such examinations would be conducted once in two years, we have since early in 1941, accelerated the giving of these tests, first to yearly intervals, then six months, and since early in October, 1942, a plan has been in operation whereby examinations may be conducted as fast as a sufficient number of applications are received. . . .

As a further aid in securing eligibles, the examination processes themselves have been reduced and simplified to the minimum consistent with reasonable maintenance of standards. One of the latest steps in the program of speeding up recruiting is the plan of maintaining " open lists " for all clerical, typist, and stenographic positions. In this connection, a new type of announcement or " flyer " is being used to acquaint the public generally with the opportunities and advantages that exist in the State Service.

A survey conducted by the Civil Service Assembly of the United States and Canada revealed that the following methods were also being employed in an effort to supply the need for personnel: [21]

> Use of retired employees
> More jobs opened to women
> Waiving residence requirements
> Lower training, experience, or physical qualifications
> Increase in pay rates
> Use of physically handicapped persons
> Increase in number of examination centers
> Use of unassembled examinations
> Scheduling more examinations and speeding process
> Raising maximum and lowering minimum age limits
> Continuously open eligible registers
> Use of eligible lists prepared by other jurisdictions
> ·Greater use of transfers
> Use of training programs
> Securing increased appropriations for the agency

[21] Civil Service Assembly *News Letter,* August, 1942, and November, 1943. See also: Donovan, Jeremiah J., " Manpower Conservation — A ' Must ' for Management," *State Government,* November, 1942, pp. 215–216, 223–224; Drummond, Helen C., " The Wartime Program of the National Civil Service Reform League," *Public Personnel Review,* October, 1942, pp. 288–292; Mitchell, James M., " Overcoming Wartime Personnel Shortages," *Public Management,* August, 1942, pp. 232–233; and War Manpower Commission, *Personnel Survey of the United States Employment Service: Three Wartime Years Under Federal Civil Service, January 1, 1942–December 31, 1944* (Washington, 1945) .

The states not only adopted new methods for filling vacancies, but they struggled to keep the employees they already had, and to reduce the turnover, in order to keep their activities functioning. Toward this end, they resorted to such devices as longer working hours, over-time pay, and cost-of-living bonuses. The use of these devices resulted in larger payroll amounts, despite fewer employees on the payroll. The United States Bureau of the Census called attention to the fact that the majority of the governors' budget and general messages submitted to their legislatures in 1944 and 1945 discussed the pressure of increased living costs on state employees, and the competition of war industries, recommending remedial legislation. In many jurisdictions, these recommendations were subsequently enacted into law.

Improved Financial Condition. Financially, the states profited very greatly from the war effort. They were able, without imposing any new taxes or raising the rates on existing taxes, to balance their budgets, accelerate the reduction of their outstanding debt, and accumulate considerable surpluses — all accomplished simultaneously from swollen tax receipts. No unusual skill in financial management was required to accomplish these results, in spite of the claims made by some candidates for office. The facts were that the boom in war industry so increased the receipts from existing taxes that all the states had to do was to sit by and watch the money flow into the treasury. It was reported for the fiscal year 1944 that 6.6 billion dollars was collected, and only 5.9 billions expended, with receipts exceeding expenditures in all but three states.

It would have been possible to reduce taxes, when many services were being curtailed and revenues were increasing, but this was not done for a number of reasons. The idea of reducing the debt and building up a surplus for postwar needs made a strong appeal. There was a hesitancy to reduce or remove tax levies that might later have to be restored, but most important was the desire to avoid increasing at the time and under the circumstances the amount of spendable income in the pockets of citizens, through tax reduction. Maintaining taxes on the then existing basis was one more check upon inflation. It was one further way in which the states could — and did — render assistance to the Federal government in the prosecution of the war.

Under these circumstances, wartime legislative sessions in many states were able to enact legislation materially strengthening the financial position of the state governments. In California, for instance, during the special session in June, 1944, $129,792,667 was appropriated for a postwar expenditures and reserves fund, thus bringing the total for this purpose up to $788,336,289 for the 1943–1945 biennium alone. Similar accomplishments, depending upon the size and wealth of the state, are reported in state after state, across the country.

In 1941, the Council of State Governments appointed a tax committee, whose report was approved by the Executive Committee of the Governors' Conference and by the Board of Managers of the Council. The report recommended six policies to all state and local governments: [22]

1. That in adjusting their own services and programs, these governments give priority to activities which will best promote defense work within their territories.

2. That these governments postpone non-defense public works and adjust their other services in order to release the utmost manpower and materials for the defense effort.

3. That these governments contribute further to the conservation of manpower and materials by maintaining essential public facilities and improvements in good condition, by simplifying specifications, perfecting purchasing procedures, and developing cooperative buying arrangements, and making other improvements in administrative organization and methods.

4. That these governments begin now to prepare programs and plans for useful public works, to the end that the consummation of such works may help in the process of adjusting the economy to peacetime pursuits. This planning will avoid wasteful make-work projects later.

5. That these governments begin now to prepare for the critical fiscal demands of the post-defense readjustment by applying all available revenue to the retirement of debt or accumulation of reserves if such excess revenue can be applied to debt retirement or accumulated reserves adequately protected against invasion.

6. That these governments seek, by all measures compatible with the objectives of the defense program, to safeguard and preserve their own essential activities in order that the state and local governments may continue in their vital role as basic service institutions in a free democracy. This is imperative for public morale and effective economic functioning in this period of defense; it may be even more important in the return to peace.

This was sound advice. To the extent that it was followed, it tended to put the states as a group in a comparatively better finan-

---

[22] Council of State Governments, " Wartime Fiscal Policies for State and Local Governments," *State Government,* December, 1942, pp. 241–244, and *State Legislative Developments, 1941–1943,* pp. 7–11 (Chicago, 1943); Chatters, Carl H., " States Face Problems of Wartime Finance," *State Government,* February, 1942, pp. 37–38, 47; Langum, John K., " A Constructive Emergency Tax Program," *ibid.,* July, 1942, pp. 137–138, 146–148; McKibbin, George B., " Wartime Fiscal Problems in Illinois," *ibid.,* November, 1942, pp. 213–214, 220–222, 224.

cial position after the war than the Federal government, thereby reversing the situation existing prior to the war. At that time, the Federal government and the states had contracted sizable debts in making relief payments and in fighting the depression. The former, with its broader taxing base and greater debt capacity, was in a stronger position than most of the states. During the war, while the Federal debt skyrocketed upward, due to war costs, the states were, as has been indicated, able to reduce or pay off their debts and to accumulate considerable surpluses to care for postwar needs.

Further Loss of Power to the Federal Government. One of the outstanding characteristics of governmental development in recent years has been the gradual and constant shift of power from the state capitals to Washington. This trend, which has been accentuated in many fields during the war, is well illustrated by the activities of the War Manpower Commission. The United States Employment Service, functioning under WMC, took over in their entirety the placement services formerly operated under state authority. The states resented this move and vigorously asserted their intention to demand the return of this function to state control at the end of the war.

Parallel with this move affecting placements in private employment was the move to control public employment at state and local levels. The United States Civil Service Commission, also functioning under WMC, was made responsible for the general supervision of all matters relating to government employment, at all levels. Actually, this power of supervision was very little used. There was much complaint from state and local officials because so many clerical and stenographic employees resigned to take positions in the Federal service. Actually, these employees came of their own accord, because of the salary differential; the Commission scrupulously refrained from recruiting efforts among the employees of other governmental units.

Of similar centralizing effect were the controls exercised over labor disputes. Whereas in the past such problems had been handled largely by the state departments of labor, all control over them shifted to the Federal government during the last decade. The move started with the National Labor Relations Board in the prewar years, and continued under the National War Labor Board during the war. Most of the disputes which arose — no matter how local they might appear to be — involved, or could be reasonably claimed to involve, the war effort. Under these conditions, local controls, while theoretically continuing, practically ceased to exist.

POSTWAR PLANS FOR SOCIAL AND ECONOMIC DEVELOPMENT

The social and economic problems that will confront the state and local governments in the postwar era will be quite as challenging and far-reaching as those of the war itself. Governor Prentis Cooper of Tennessee, in an address before the Governors' Conference at Hershey in May, 1944, discussed some of these, and expressed the view that, " to plan adequately for postwar America, we shall have to cope with six dominant influences that will exist, no matter how long the war will last: "

1. At the end of the war, there will be a huge labor surplus. . . .
2. A large number of war plants valued at $20,000,000,000 and an enormous surplus of war materials, estimated at $50,000,000,000 will need disposition.
3. The end of the war will find an excessive concentration of power in Washington.
4. Potential inflationary conditions will exist in a considerable degree. Savings are now accumulating at the rate of $35,000,000,000 per year.
5. The Federal government will be burdened with an unprecedented indebtedness.
6. When peace comes, there will be a serious depletion of many basic materials necessary for the continued well-being of this Nation, requiring new conservation policies.

In anticipation of the problems of peace and reconversion, the states established separate postwar planning commissions, although most of them already had planning commissions quite capable of handling the problems involved. These were variously designated as follows: [23]

> California Reconstruction and Reemployment Commission
> Agricultural and Industrial Development Board of Georgia
> Illinois Postwar Planning Commission
> Economic Development Committee of Louisiana
> Oregon Postwar Readjustment and Development Commission
> Pennsylvania Postwar Planning Commission

The organization and structure of these commissions varies greatly according to the differences existing in the problems of the several states. The Illinois Commission, which appears to be well organized, had a list of fifteen committees which may be taken as illustrative of the types of problems with which these commissions have concerned themselves:

[23] For a good summary of information on postwar planning agencies, see Council of State Governments, *State Legislative Developments, 1941–1943*, pp. 1–7 (Chicago, 1943). For an excellent account of what one such agency has done and what it plans to do, see Agricultural and Industrial Development Board of Georgia, *Georgia Goes Forward* (Athens, 1945).

Aeronautics
Agriculture
Drainage Basins and Flood Control
Industrial Plants and Opportunities
Inventory of Labor
Local Planning and Urban Areas
Organic Law and Legislation
Markets and Consumer Demand

Public Works
Resources
Services
Special Problem Areas
State and Municipal Finances
Transportation
Veterans Care

In the paragraphs which follow, brief consideration will be given to some of the social and economic aspects of postwar planning in the states — to such problems as education; housing; fair employment practices, including race relations; social security, including liberalization of unemployment compensation; the co-operative movement; and the postwar fiscal outlook. In the following section, attention will be given to problems relating to the construction and development of the physical resources of the states.

In both of these areas, the problem of Federal-state-local relations will be of paramount importance. The thesis has been advanced that " the most important factor in determining the position of state and local governments after the war is the extent to which the Federal government dominates all activity during the war. If in wartime the national government must be supreme and overshadow all other governmental units, the question may well be raised as to the status of the other levels of government after the war." In this connection, it is pointed out that there were during the war four different patterns or types of procedure in the field of intergovernmental relations: [24]

1. Direct Federal operation
2. Modified direct Federal operation by locally appointed Federal officials
3. Indirect Federal operation, direct state operation
4. Indirect Federal operation, direct local operation

Education. After World War I, the states faced a tremendous problem of combatting illiteracy. They face equally great — though different — problems in the field of education after World War II. There will undoubtedly be huge increases in school and college enrollments. In the America of today, nearly everyone has an opportunity for elementary schooling. As minimum age limits for working papers have been steadily raised, a larger and larger per-

[24] See Rightor, C. E., and Ingersoll, Hugh D., " State and Local Government After the War," *National Municipal Review,* July, 1942, pp. 305–310.

centage of the population has had high school training, and an increasing number have gone on to college or university work. The postwar problems in education seem to fall into about five major fields.

Elementary education must be improved, especially in many rural areas. Consolidated schools must be built, and better facilities provided. Better trained teachers are needed. During the war, age limits for school attendance were lowered, in order to ease the manpower shortage. The earlier requirements must now be restored, and adequate provision made for high school and junior college training, at public expense, to provide for all who are able to profit by it.

Next, more attention must be given than heretofore to the development of trade or vocational training. There are large numbers of pupils who are not interested in and who are not able to profit to any great extent from the conventional types of secondary school training, designed largely for those who are planning to attend college. Many of those would make good artisans, and society needs the services of persons skilled in working with their hands. Again, it is essential that there be developed — as was indicated in an earlier chapter — adult education programs and programs for recreation and leisure time, for the constructive utilization of the greater amount of such time that all employed persons may expect to have in the postwar era.

All of these programs cost money — more money than some of the states are in a position to provide. There is no reason why those who happen to live in the poorer states, economically, should suffer from the lack of advantages that the nation is abundantly able to provide. After all, to paraphrase Wendell Willkie, this is "one country." Readjustments in recent years have resulted in increased state support for education, the quality of which has benefited thereby. The question is now presented as to whether even that is sufficient. Perhaps the answer will be found in the much disputed proposal of Federal aid for education, which would have a very wholesome effect in raising standards, especially in those jurisdictions lacking in resources, and lacking progressive leadership.[25]

[25] For recent discussions of this subject, see: Burger, Alvin A., *Should the Federal Government Subsidize Education?* (New Jersey State Chamber of Commerce, Newark, 1945); *Iowa Law Review*, "A Symposium in Federal Legislation Relating to Education," January, 1945, entire issue; Quattlebaum, Charles A., *Federal Aid to the States for Education* (Library of Congress, Legislative Reference Service, Washington, 1944).

Housing. No one familiar with our large cities need be reminded of the blight that has spread over the central sections of many of them, like an apple rotting at the core. Frequently, nothing has been done save to moan about the disloyalty of those who have moved their families to the suburbs in search of a decent place to live. Providing decent living quarters for urban residents in the postwar years involves not only the physical problems of building construction, but the much more difficult problems of saving the cities from further decay, and of providing living conditions for all citizens such as will permit of a decent life and of the achievement of some of the ideals of democracy.

The longer this problem is postponed, the larger its proportions and the more difficult becomes its solution. Aside from some war houses — cheap and poor and temporary — constructed during the war, few new homes were built in America between 1940 and 1945. As men return from service in the armed forces to establish their own homes, as the doubling up processes of the war period come to an end, the extreme scarcity of desirable homes and apartments in many communities becomes apparent. The meeting of this need, which should be one of the major projects of the postwar years, will require the cooperation of all three levels of government. The problem has been very clearly stated in a report of the National Lawyer's Guild: [26]

Prior to the war, some 40,000,000 Americans lived in 10,000,000 substandard dwellings. Most of them inhabited the slums of our country, which constituted a standing threat to the national health and welfare. The urgent need for clearing these blighted areas and for replacing these dwellings by new decent dwellings still exists. In addition, the increase in the population, the large number of newly-married couples, the cessation of normal construction, and the suspension of major repairs during the war, have increased the need for new homes. It is estimated that a sound postwar housing program must cope with the need for 15,000,000 new dwellings. Such a program must necessarily be formulated on the practical basis of a plan spaced over a term of years. A Ten Year Plan has been proposed and would appear to be feasible. Such a plan would mean a program of construction of 1,000,000 to 1,500,000 new dwellings each year for ten years.

[26] See National Lawyer's Guild, *A Postwar Low-Rent Public Housing Program*, pp. 3–4 (Washington, 1945) ; Curtis Publishing Company, *Urban Housing Survey* (Philadelphia, 1945) ; Housing Authority of the City of Newark, *A Study of the Social Effects of Public Housing in Newark, N. J.* (Newark, 1944) ; Weinfeld, Edward, "New York State Faces War Housing Issues," *National Municipal Review*, December, 1942, pp. 584–590; and Blandford, John B., Jr., "Our Postwar Housing Problem," in *Papers Presented at the Eleventh National Conference on Assessment Administration*, pp. 9–15 (National Association of Assessing Officers, Chicago, 1945) ; Illinois State Housing Board, *Your State Plan for Slum Clearance and Better Housing* (Chicago, 1945).

A postwar housing program is clearly an indispensable part of any program for full employment after the war. Such a program would by itself provide a substantial portion of the national income and national employment. It would, of course, provide employment not only for the construction industry directly, but would enormously stimulate all capital goods and consumer goods industries. It would underpin prosperity for the nation as a whole.

In similar vein, a current survey of urban housing points out that, because the housing industry cuts across so many different fields of business activity, it probably exerts a greater influence on the overall economy than any other single industry. For this reason, postwar market possibilities of the housing industry and its employment potentials have become matters of widespread interest and concern to states and cities throughout the land.

Fair Employment Practices. During the war, fair employment practices were enforced by the President's Committee on Fair Employment Practices, established by an Executive Order based upon his war powers, and functioning until Congress withheld from it funds for operation beyond June 30, 1945. In the meantime, the legislature of New York had passed in 1944 an act of like purpose and intent, and similar bills were considered in the legislatures of a number of states in 1945. Less sweeping in their effect, but still of vital importance in the cause of good race relations are the state commissions on interracial relations in Connecticut and Illinois, established in 1943, and the New Jersey Good-Will Commission, established as early as 1938. In New York, a Committee on Discrimination in Employment, an agency of the State War Council, functioned prior to the enactment of the Ives-Quinn Act in that state.

Legislation prohibiting discrimination in various fields of employment has been appearing with increasing frequency since 1933, as is shown by the table on page 1000. While committees on race relations have long functioned to good purpose in the Southern states, their appearance in the North is relatively recent. That the idea is taking hold is shown by the fact that the State Commission in Illinois succeeded in establishing, in a little over a year, no less than eight municipal commissions in localities throughout the state. If the states are really in earnest about checking the influence of the Federal government, here is a golden opportunity for them to demonstrate by prompt and decisive action that they can deal effectively with new problems, the solution of which is necessary to the achievement of real democracy in America.[27]

[27] American Council on Race Relations, *State FEPC — What the People Say* (Chicago, 1945); Duffy, John F., Jr., *State Organization for Fair Employment*

STATE LEGISLATION PROHIBITING DISCRIMINATION
IN VARIOUS FIELDS OF EMPLOYMENT [28]

State	Work Relief Projects Public Works	Civil Service	Labor Unions	Defense and War Contracts	Public Utilities	Teachers (Religion)	Non-Teaching Jobs in Schools
California	1939	1941					1935
Connecticut		1943					
Illinois	1933 1935			1941			
Indiana	1933						
Kansas	1937		1941				
Massachusetts	1941	1920			1920 [1]		
Michigan		Constitution [2]					
Minnesota	1941	1939					
Nebraska			1941	1943		1937	
New Jersey	1933			1942		1920	
New York	1935		1940	1942	1933 [3]		
Ohio	1935					1932	
Pennsylvania	1935		1937				
Wisconsin		1937 [4]					

[1] In any department of a street railway company operated, owned, controlled or financially aided in any way by the Commonwealth, or by any political subdivision thereof.
[2] Article VI, Section 22, adopted in 1940.
[3] Any public utility.
[4] Refers to religious discrimination only.

Full Employment. The pressures of war made drastic and far-reaching changes in the national economy. Some of these were temporary, but many will prove either to be permanent, or to have permanent effects upon the states and communities affected. Selective Service withdrew millions of men from their normal productive activities, while at the same time war industry caused tremendous migrations of workers from one locality to another. Whole towns and cities were built where there had been no development before. Other communities grew in size rapidly, while still others not adapted to the development of war industry decreased in size. Some of these war workers will return to their original locations after the war, but many will not, either because they do not want to, or because their original jobs have been abolished.

These situations pose tremendously serious problems for the states and cities. It has been the function of the postwar planning agencies to try to solve them. By surveys of population and resources, of po-

Practices (University of California, Bureau of Public Administration, 1944); Illinois Inter-Racial Commission, *First Annual Report* (Springfield, 1944); New York State Commission Against Discrimination, *Report* (Legislative Document, 1945, No. 6).
[28] From Duffy, *op. cit.,* p. 4.

tential markets and transportation facilities, they have tried to evolve plans according to which an orderly reconversion to peacetime industry may be effected. The major objective is to provide jobs for all who are able and willing to work. So far as the states and cities are concerned, the problem is complicated by the presence of many uncertain factors, such as the exact number of jobs that will be required, the times at which they should be available as war contracts are terminated and servicemen return, the effect of strikes, the uncertainty as to where war workers and returned servicemen will settle down, and many other things. The solution of these problems will depend to a large extent on national policies, but there is still a large sphere within which the states and local units can function to good advantage.[29]

Social Security. In the postwar period, increasing attention will be given to various phases of the social security program. While the program of the states will be greatly affected by what the Federal government does, there is here also a considerable sphere within which the states may take independent action. Urgent demands are being made upon the states to raise the ceiling of the weekly payments under unemployment compensation. The Illinois State Industrial Union Council demanded $35.00 a week, in 1945. In the fall of that year, Congress refused to approve the President's recommendation to establish a uniform $25.00 weekly payment. Without such Federal legislation, the problem can be solved only by appropriate action in the individual states. Careful studies preparatory to such action have been made in many states.[30]

Unemployment compensation is only one phase of a huge program, which has many phases and ramifications. Others include in-

[29] Much information on these questions will be found in the reports of the several postwar planning commissions; in addition, see: Baldwin, Raymond E., "Employment in the Postwar Period," *State Government*, August, 1945, pp. 129–131, 139; Kelly, Harry F., "Postwar Problems of Employment and Unemployment," *ibid.*, May, 1943, pp. 113–114, 125–126; Smullyan, Emile B., "War Distortions and Postwar Demobilization: The Problems of the States," *ibid.*, January, 1944, pp. 255–259. Some of the postwar planning commissions put out guides and checklists designed to aid business men in sizing up their situation, and in making plans for the future, as for instance, Illinois Postwar Planning Commission, *Your Business After the War: A Guide for Illinois Small Business* (Chicago, 1944), and *Preparing for War Contract Termination: A Checklist* (Chicago, 1944).

[30] For example, California Senate Committee on Unemployment Insurance, *Preliminary Report*, 1943, and *Report*, 1945; Pennsylvania Joint State Government Commission, *Unemployment Compensation — Proposals for Increased Benefits and Benefits for Partial Unemployment* (Harrisburg, 1945); Reticker, Ruth, "State Unemployment Compensation Laws of 1945," *Social Security Bulletin*, July, 1945, pp. 1–18, and Altmeyer, A. J., "Ten Years of Social Security," *ibid.*, August, 1945, pp. 1–56.

surance for medical care, to provide for a vital need that has up to
this time, been met inadequately and only in limited areas by private
associations. Rhode Island, by its cash sickness compensation program, begun in 1943, has undertaken a pioneer venture in this phase
of social security. This program, designed to protect at a reasonable
cost those persons who received no compensation while they were
unemployed because of illness, is financed entirely by a tax of 1 per
cent levied on the first $3,000 earned by a worker in any given year.[31]

There are many phases of labor law that will need to be strengthened in the postwar period. In some cases, these subjects have been
covered by Federal legislation in effect during the war and will, now
that the war is over, revert back to the states. More than half of the
states, with many years of successful experience in the enforcement
of minimum wage laws for women, may want to extend these laws
to men, thereby covering individuals not affected by the Fair Labor
Standards Act.

The Cooperative Movement. Cooperatives are now operating in
every state in the Union. The extent to which they have developed
may not be fully realized; actually, they play a leading role in the
economic life of the American people. In almost every county, the
services of a cooperative of one kind or another are now available.
A very large number of farmers — perhaps 3,000,000 or half of the
total number — belong to some kind of cooperative, while in urban
communities, cooperative food stores are common. The total volume
of marketing and purchasing associations alone aggregated more
than $5,000,000,000 in 1943.

In 1945, the Inter-Bureau Committee on Postwar Programs of the
United States Department of Agriculture reported that the last two
decades have been characterized by many improvements in local
cooperatives and by expansion of local cooperative services.[32] This
report continues:

Many new fields of cooperative activity have been opened, such as cotton
ginning, cotton warehousing, forest management, cooperative auctions for
various products, rural electric cooperatives, rural health associations, cooperative slaughter houses, cold-storage locker enterprises, artificial breed-
ing associations, and cooperative farm machinery groups.

Certain objectives are outlined for the development of cooperatives
in the postwar period. Although their ability to survive the trials of

[31] See Newton, Mortimer W., " The Rhode Island Cash Sickness Compensation Program," *State Government*, September, 1945, pp. 156–159, 161.
[32] United States Department of Agriculture, *Agricultural Cooperatives in the
Postwar Period* (Washington, July, 1945) .

the war years without serious setbacks would seem to prove that their management is not less efficient than other types of business, they should strive, even so, further to increase their operating efficiency. A second objective should be to explore new fields of cooperative activity and to develop new types of cooperative services. Still another should be the development of farmer cooperatives in regions and localities where the use of the cooperative method is not now established. Under the leadership of the Federal and state departments of agriculture, the achievement of these purposes should be fulfilled.

Fiscal Problems. Some observations have been made earlier regarding the effects of the war on state finance. At this point, one may inquire regarding the fiscal problems that will confront the states in the postwar era. They have accumulated considerable surpluses. Termination of war contracts will produce — temporarily, at least — a reduction in tax receipts, but if conversion proceeds rapidly, the reduction in revenue need not be too great or too serious. Programs for social and economic advancement and for construction purposes will require substantial sums, but with balanced budgets, accumulated surpluses, and debts reduced during the war, their credit should be excellent. Furthermore, the states will receive funds for some purposes from the Federal government in the form of Federal aid, while the local units will receive aid from both the states and the Federal government.

On the expenditure side, the demand for funds will be great. Expenditures for personal service will be higher than before or during the war. The rates of compensation may not be as high for some types of work, but the work-week will be shorter and there will be more employees to be paid. Long postponed plans for many purposes and programs will be approved for expenditure. These will include supplies and equipment, as well as the needs for some of the items discussed in this section for development in the social and economic fields, and for highways, public buildings, and other public works, as well as for the development of such physical resources of the states as their land and water resources.[33]

[33] For recent comments on these problems, see Blakey, Roy G., " Postwar Tax Problems," *State Government,* September, 1944, pp. 422–423, 432; Council of State Governments, *Grants-in-Aid and Other Federal Expenditures within the States* (Chicago, 1945) , and *State Legislative Developments, 1941–1943* (Chicago, 1943) ; Graves, W. Brooke, and Scholz, Karl W. H., " Meeting the Needs for State and Local Revenues in the Postwar Era," *American Political Science Review,* October, 1944, pp. 904–912; Ruml, Beardsley, " Taxes After the War," *State Government,* July, 1945, pp. 113–114.

POSTWAR PLANS FOR CONSTRUCTION AND PHYSICAL DEVELOPMENT

Extensive programs of public works are planned in the states for the postwar years. These new facilities will be needed, partly as an aid in achieving full employment, and, after the long interruption in construction activities during the war period, to meet actual needs for new highways and for new and more adequate physical plant and resources for state institutions and services. New programs will be undertaken for the promotion of agriculture and for the conservation of natural resources.

It is generally assumed that a serious slump in business activity is more or less inevitable — sooner or later — after the war. A period of readjustment and conversion, accompanied by numerous strikes and labor disturbances, with considerable unemployment, followed V–J Day. Then began a period of industrial activity during which manufacturers sought to catch up in production for an accumulated demand for many types of civilian goods. When these demands have been met and new markets for these goods exploited, the serious slump may be expected. Just when, for just how long, and just how serious, nobody knows.

There has been a good deal of discussion of the usefulness of public expenditures as an aid to economic stability.[34] The states were handicapped in this respect during the depression because so many of them had not only spent every cent they had received, but had gone heavily into debt. The successful working of such a program demands that the states, when economic conditions are good, shall not only live within their incomes, but create a reserve fund. This the states have been able to do during the war period, as has been previously indicated.

State Institutions. The states are responsible for the construction, maintenance, and operation of a growing list of institutions — educational, health, welfare, penal and correctional, military, et cetera. In many cases, these institutions have in the past been provided for most inadequately. In the health and welfare institutions especially, there have never been enough beds properly to accommodate the existing number of patients, to say nothing of those on long waiting lists. Overcrowding and inadequate staffing have made it impossible

---

[34] United States Chamber of Commerce, Construction and Civic Development Department, *The Use of Public Works to Sustain Construction Activity* (Washington, 1945) .

to render proper service to those who were, often through no fault of their own, the unfortunate wards of the state.

Slowly but surely the public is becoming more concerned about the adequacy of the facilities and the kind of care that are provided for the inmates of these institutions. Short-range plans provide for the repair and modernization of existing structures. In many jurisdictions, long-range plans for new construction have been made, based upon surveys of existing facilities, and on statistical studies of institutional populations over a period of years. These programs of construction will be made possible, partly by the use of funds already available and in some cases earmarked for the purpose, and in others by borrowing all or part of the money required.

California, as has been shown, provides an excellent example of a state that has, by careful advance planning, made provision for meeting the cost of a substantial part of its postwar construction program out of surpluses created during the war years. During legislative sessions in wartime, some surplus funds were set aside in a postwar unemployment reserve, while others were allocated for specific postwar purposes, to meet the needs of the state university, of agriculture, of the state itself for office space, et cetera. In Pennsylvania, the Postwar Planning Commission developed an extensive program of construction for state institutions — penal, mental, and medical-surgical. A number of the state commissions put out manuals for the guidance of local units in the development of postwar public works projects.[35]

Highways. Little highway construction was undertaken during wartime. Due to the shortages of manpower and materials, even maintenance work was held at an absolute minimum. During this period of suspension of construction activity, the need for new construction grew steadily more urgent. Old roads, especially those car-

[35] See American Society of Civil Engineers, *Postwar Construction* (New York, 1944), and Moses, Robert, *Function and Degree of Participation of the Federal Government in the Construction of Postwar Federal, State, and Local Public Works* (Triborough Bridge Authority, New York, 1944). Among the better reports on state projects, see: Federal Reserve Bank of Atlanta, *The Alabama State Docks* (Atlanta, 1945); Maryland Commission on Postwar Construction and Development, *Maryland Postwar Public Works Manual* (Baltimore, 1944), and *Program and Activities of the Maryland Commission on Postwar Construction and Development, 1943–1944*, and *Six Year Capital Improvement Program for Maryland* (both, Baltimore, 1945); Michigan Planning Commission, *Recommended Allocations from the Proposed State Building Fund* (Lansing, 1944); Pennsylvania Postwar Planning Commission, *Penal, Mental and Medical-Surgical Institutions in Pennsylvania* (Harrisburg, 1945); Commonwealth of Virginia, Governor's Office, *Manual on the Planning and Execution of State Capital Outlays* (Richmond, 1944).

rying heavy loads of wartime truck and bus traffic, were wearing out, while the need for modern express highways to speed traffic in congested areas grew daily more acute. Postwar highway construction plans designed to meet these needs have been developed in many jurisdictions, awaiting only the availability of men and materials before actual construction work is undertaken.

The goal of rational highway planning is to provide roads to fit the type and volume of traffic to be carried. In rural areas, this means heavy duty trunk line highways between centers of population, with feeder roads or farm-to-market roads branching out to the back country. In the cities, it means wide arterial highways for through traffic, with overpasses or underpasses where necessary, and suitable ramps at intervals to permit local traffic to enter or leave the arterial highway. Examples of this modern type of construction are found in the Beltline in Chicago, the West Side Highway, the Merritt Parkway, and the Pulaski Skyway in the New York metropolitan area, and other similar constructions in the Detroit and Los Angeles areas. The state highway departments in California and New Jersey have done more in developing this type of construction than in most other states.[36]

Aviation and Airport Problems. It now appears that air travel will be as common in the postwar era as rail and steamship travel have been in the past. In this new era of air travel, states and cities will have to give the same attention to airport development that they gave in the past to the development of rail terminals and port facilities. Some states have established boards or bureaus of aeronautics, which will concern themselves with the solution of these problems. While some states have never spent money for airport development, others like Louisiana, Michigan, and Pennsylvania have made substantial appropriations for this purpose. The ten-year airport plan in the latter state calls for construction and development at a total cost of $34,512,700. Since airport construction requires large expenditures, many states and cities will require the aid of Federal funds.[37]

[36] Pennsylvania Motor Federation, *Straight Thinking About Highways* (Harrisburg, n.d.) ; Sheets, Frank T., *The Development of Primary Roads During the Next Quarter Century* (American Association of State Highway Officials, Washington, 1940) , and *The Rational Planning of a Public Highway Program in a State* (Portland Cement Association, Chicago, 1939) ; Iowa Postwar Rehabilitation Commission, *Final Report by the Highway Committee* (Des Moines, 1944) ; Portland Cement Association, *Express Highways: How They Serve Millions of Motorists* (Philadelphia, n.d.) , *The Highway of Tomorrow* (Philadelphia, 1937) , and *Concrete Highways and Public Improvements* (Chicago, monthly) ; Public Roads Administration, *Highways in the United States: 1945* (Washington, 1945) .
[37] McKenna, Coe A., " State Aviation and Airport Problems," *State Government,* September, 1945, pp. 160–161; Council of State Governments, " The States

War Memorials. After every war, there develops in each community an urge to erect some kind of permanent memorial to the memory of those who gave their lives in the service of their country. In times past, these memorials often turned out to be hideous monuments or architectural monstrosities of some sort. In the twentieth century, these memorials have often been constructed in the form of useful public works — memorial bridges (in Harrisburg), state office buildings (Nashville), airports, or other permanent improvements. It is to be hoped that attempts to memorialize the dead of World War II will be channeled into the construction of similarly useful types of public works of permanent value.[38]

Conservation Projects. In the postwar era, much attention will be given to the improvement of agriculture and the development of conservation projects. Conservation means the wise use of our natural resources, for the greatest benefit and enjoyment of all the people. It includes soil conservation, forestation projects and the proper utilization of existing timber stands, stream purification and water conservation, power development, mineral development, improvement of facilities for hunting and fishing, development of state parks and recreation projects, and many similar things. It may include also the preservation and proper marking of places of historic interest.[39]

---

and a National System of Airports," *ibid.*, May, 1945, pp. 81–84; Department of Public Works, *Louisiana Aviation* (Baton Rouge, 1944); State-Wide Aviation Conference, *New York State Building an Aviation Future* (Albany, 1945); Missouri State Department of Resources and Development, *Missouri Skyways* (Jefferson City, 1945); United States Senate Committee on Commerce, *Federal Aid for Public Airports* (Report of hearings, March 13–23, 1945); and Waterman, Patricia L., *The Role of the States in Postwar Aviation* (University of California, Bureau of Public Administration, 1945).

[38] A group calling itself the American Commission for Living War Memorials, having a special interest in athletics and physical fitness, has put out two elaborate brochures containing suggestions for the use of recreational facilities as war memorials, including camps, reservations and trails; parks and playgrounds; fields for team play; indoor sports centers; community physical fitness centers; water fronts; swimming facilities; winter sports centers; stadiums; and auxiliary projects. See *Memorials That Live* (Columbus, 1944), and *More About Memorials That Live* (Columbus, 1945).

[39] See Illinois Postwar Planning Commission, Committee on Agriculture, *Report* (Chicago, 1945); Sparks, Chauncey, "A Constructive Postwar Program for Agriculture," *State Government*, September, 1945, pp. 152–153, 167; and United States Chamber of Commerce, Agricultural Department, *Agricultural Imports and Exports in Relation to American Agriculture* (Washington, 1945); and on conservation: Department of Conservation, *Outdoor Indiana of the Future: Postwar and Longrange Program* (Indianapolis, 1944); Leighton, Morris M., *Illinois Resources: An Atlas* (Illinois Postwar Planning Commission, Springfield, 1945); Michigan Department of Conservation, *A Five-Year Program of Improvements in Michigan's State Parks and Recreation Areas* (Lansing, 1945); State Board of Park Supervisors, *Mississippi State Parks* (Jackson, n.d.); Strouse, Don, *Conservation Means You* (Ohio Postwar Program Commission, Columbus, 1944).

Any one of these projects might be discussed at length. Under current conditions, however, the anti-stream pollution program assumes a position of great significance. The rivers and streams, once clear and clean, now carry off mine wastes, industrial wastes, and domestic sewage to such an extent that municipal water supplies require chemical treatment to prevent contamination. Fish cannot live in the water, nor wild life exist upon it; in some cases, it is so bad as to injure the paint on the seagoing vessels that come into port. In view of the seriousness of the problem, Pennsylvania and other states are waging an aggressive campaign to purify their streams.[40]

One of the most important fields of activity from the point of view of both agriculture and conservation, is the development of electric power and the extension of rural electrification. Tremendous progress in the latter field has been made in the last twenty years, but it still appears that less than half of the farms in the country receive central station electric service. The Inter-Bureau Committee on Postwar Programs of the United States Department of Agriculture proposes four objectives for a postwar program in this field: [41]

1. Electric service for all rural people
2. Full use of electricity on the farmstead
3. Full use of electricity for rural welfare
4. Use of electricity in developing local rural industries

The Committee estimates that:

A vigorous five-year program by private utilities, cooperatives, and public agencies can provide service to 3,655,000 additional rural families and will require about 2¾ million man-years of employment. This will involve the expenditure of about one billion dollars for line construction and expenditures by old and new rural customers, amounting to about 750 million dollars for plumbing installations, and about three billion dollars for electric appliance and equipment purchases, or a total expenditure of about 5½ billion dollars.

Such a program will be a tremendous stimulus to private employment. Since it is projected as a self-liquidating program, it means no burden to the taxpayers and will correspondingly reduce the need of tax supported public works programs during the reconversion and readjustment period. It will bring rural electrification in the United States on a par with that of other advanced countries; it will help to make farm life pleasanter and more attractive, farming easier and more profitable; and it will create a better social, economic, and cultural environment for our rural population generally.

[40] Pennsylvania Economy League, *Stream Pollution Abatement as It Concerns Political Sub-Divisions in Pennsylvania* (Pittsburgh, 1945), and " Abatement of Stream Pollution in Pennsylvania," *P. E. L. Newsletter*, September, 1945.

[41] United States Department of Agriculture, *Rural Electrification After the War* (Washington, February, 1945).

THE STATES AND THE VETERAN

Although the Federal government has indicated, in the terms of the Selective Service Act, the G.I. Bill of Rights, and the Starnes-Scrugham Act of 1945, that it intends to see that all necessary steps are taken to protect the interests of returning veterans, the states too have a responsibility. In recognition thereof, old veteran legislation is being revised in one state after another and new legislation is being enacted, to the end that they shall be in a position to do everything possible to supplement the Federal effort. From the point of view of the states, the veteran problem involves the community responsibility for giving information, advice, and assistance to the returning serviceman or woman; provision for rehabilitation, including both hospitalization and training or re-training; the problem of employment or reemployment, including the finding of new jobs, reinstatement in old ones, and preference in the state service; and finally, provision for grants, bonuses, and financial assistance, including temporary or emergency relief for the veteran and his family.

Veteran Legislation. By the middle of 1944, state service officers had been established by law in twenty-one states, state service commissions in fourteen states, with miscellaneous arrangements in the remainder. Among the more interesting pieces of new legislation may be mentioned the Michigan act creating an Office of Veterans' Affairs, the Minnesota act creating a Veterans' Reserve Fund, and the New Jersey act creating a Veterans' Loan Guarantee Fund, all passed in 1944. Under the leadership of Governor Baldwin, the State of Connecticut in 1943 developed what is known as the Connecticut Plan, based on collaboration between manufacturers, state welfare and educational agencies, veterans' organizations, labor unions, and many other individuals and groups. This Plan, which will be described later, is administered by the Connecticut Re-Employment Commission, created by executive order, and is based on the theory that veterans want jobs, not a dole.[42]

[42] State veterans' laws are usually treated as a separate title in the annotated codes of the several states. For the information of the public, compilations of these laws are often published in pamphlet form, as for example: Cook, Frederick W., Comp., *Laws Relating to Veterans and Their Organizations,* revised to include 1943 legislation (Boston, 1944); New Jersey Legislature's Veterans' Commission, *Synopsis of State Veteran Legislation of 1944* (Trenton, 1944); and Cote, Armand H., Comp., *Legislation of Interest to Servicemen and Veterans* (Providence, 1943). The most useful compilation is House of Representatives, Committee on Pensions, *State Veterans Laws,* revised to January 1, 1943 (77 Cong., 2 Sess., House Committee Print No. 9) which includes for all states, laws granting rights, benefits, and privileges to veterans, their dependents, and their organizations.

Community Responsibility for Advice and Assistance. At the discharge centers, service personnel are given full information regarding their rights and privileges under the law, and are given literature on the subject. Skilled interviewers are available to talk with them about employment and other problems. Most of them are not interested at that time; they want to get out of the service and return home. They do not listen to what they are told, and they do not take the literature. Consequently, after they have been at home for a time, and are ready to seek employment, the job of giving information and advice has to be done all over again. That is the responsibility of the home community.

Most communities want to do this job well, but it is difficult for them to do so because every church, lodge, club, and other organization wants to develop a veterans' assistance program of its own. Where such a condition is permitted to exist, the poor veteran is likely to receive what is commonly known as the good old American " run-around." Everywhere the veteran goes, he is sent somewhere else, or given a different answer to his questions. After being subjected to this treatment, the veteran naturally becomes disgusted, and is likely to develop a state of mind in which no one can help him.

In those communities where the job is done properly, there is one central veterans' information center, with skilled and specialized personnel ready to give him information with regard to any of his problems, whether they are disability benefits, educational benefits, employment, hospitalization, veterans' organizations, community services, or what not. In such a setup, there are representatives of the various divisions of the Veterans Administration, the United States Employment Service, the United States Civil Service Commission, the state and local civil service commissions if such exist, local welfare agencies, et cetera — all under one roof, and preferably all on one floor.

Rehabilitation. Rehabilitation for returning servicemen may involve either hospitalization and/or training and retraining. In either case, Federal funds help defray the expenses, but in the case of training, the administration is carried on locally. In addition, the state legislatures may authorize, and many of them have authorized, benefits over and above those provided for by Federal legislation. In some cases, these involve remission of tuition or fees. Oregon grants monthly allowances for expense while in training to veterans who were residents of the state for at least one year prior to their entry into the service. In New Hampshire and West Virginia, specific benefits for educational purposes are provided for the children of veterans. Massachusetts established in 1941 a special board for the purpose of providing opportunities for young people.[43]

When hospitalization is required, it may be provided in an army or navy hospital or in a Veterans Administration facility. In other cases, additional beds may be provided in designated and approved state institutions, in which case the cost of service is defrayed by Federal funds. In the field of education, no problem is created by those veterans who desire higher education or professional training; in such cases, enrollment is effected in a college or university of recognized standing. When vocational training is required, this must be provided by locally supported and administered institutions. This involves Federal-local relationships. A Massachusetts Commission thus outlines the service which the vocational schools may render to returning servicemen: [44]

1. Disabled veterans referred to vocational schools by the Veterans Administration. These servicemen will be given instruction in the vocational schools on an individual basis or in groups if the numbers warrant it, tuition to be paid by the Veterans Administration under a contract between that agency and the local schools.

2. Disabled servicemen referred to the vocational schools by the Rehabilitation Section of the State Department of Education. These veterans would receive training in vocational schools as in Group 1 above, the expense being shared by the local community and the State, under the provisions of state law, plus Federal funds for extra teachers if such are required.

3. Non-disabled servicemen. These men would receive training in local vocational schools, under the same conditions as described in Group 2 above.

It should be remembered that vocational training includes training not only for entry into various industrial occupations, but for agriculture as well. In states largely agricultural in character, this type of training is extremely important.

Vocational rehabilitation involves another factor, after physical therapy and vocational training have been completed, namely, assistance in locating a suitable opportunity for gainful employment, in which the veteran will be able to utilize his newly acquired skills. The entire process of diagnosis and treatment, training and placement of the disabled has been very clearly outlined by the Director of the Ohio Bureau of Vocational Education, as follows: [45]

[43] Council of State Governments, *State Legislative Developments, 1941–1943*, pp. 13–14 (Chicago, 1943).

[44] Massachusetts Postwar Rehabilitation Commission, *Preliminary Report*, pp. 13–14 (House Document No. 1906, 1944).

[45] Perrin, Marlow B., "Bureau of Vocational Rehabilitation," reprint from *Ohio Schools Progress Report* of 1944. Other pertinent discussions include: Cham-

1. Early location of persons in need of rehabilitation to prevent the demoralizing effects of idleness and hopelessness.

2. Medical diagnosis and prognosis, coupled with a vocational diagnosis as the basis for determining an appropriate plan for the individual.

3. Vocational counseling to select suitable fields of work, by relating occupational capacities to job requirements and community occupational opportunities.

4. Medical and surgical treatment to afford physical restoration and medical advice in the type of training to be given and in the work tolerance of the individual.

5. Physical and occupational therapy and psychiatric treatment where needed.

6. Vocational training to furnish new skills where physical impairments incapacitate for normal occupations, or where skills become obsolete due to changing industrial needs.

7. Financial assistance to provide maintenance and transportation during training.

8. Placement in employment to afford the best use of abilities and skills in accordance with the individual's physical condition and temperament, with due regard to safeguarding against further injuries.

9. Follow-up on performance in employment to afford adjustments that may be necessary, to provide further medical care if needed, to supplement training if desired.

After every war there are many cases requiring psychiatric treatment. Some of these require hospitalization, part of them permanently, part temporarily. Other veterans, whose plight is not so serious, can be adequately cared for in mental hygiene clinics, and by cooperation with local health and welfare agencies.[46]

Employment and Reemployment. The responsibility of the states in the field of employment is three-fold: they must give assistance to veterans who wish to return to their old jobs (reemployment and reinstatement) ; they must help them to find new jobs if their old

---

ber of Commerce of the United States, Committee on Education, *Education and Training for Demobilized Service Personnel*, and *Retraining War Workers for Peacetime Activities* (Washington, 1944) ; State Board of Control for Vocational Education, *Vocational Rehabilitation of Michigan's Disabled Manpower* (Lansing, n.d.) ; Bureau of Vocational Rehabilitation, *The Ohio Plan for the Administration of Vocational Rehabilitation for Disabled People* (Columbus, 1944) ; MacDonald, Mary E., *Federal Grants for Vocational Rehabilitation* (University of Chicago Press, 1944) ; Odum, Edward E., " Federal-State Cooperation in Relation to Veterans' Affairs," *State Government*, December, 1944, pp. 455–458; West, Warren R., " Educational Programs for Veterans in Tennessee," *Tennessee Planner*, June, 1945, pp. 146–151; and " Federal Funds Asked for Area Schools — Postwar Plans Should Include Vocational Education Program," *National Municipal Review*, December, 1944, pp. 639–641. For discussions of both Federal and state legislation affecting disabled veterans, see Mousman, Gerald, *Annals*, May, 1945, pp. 38–45, and Caldwell, Lynton K., *ibid.*, pp. 46–52.

[46] See Department of Institutions and Agencies, " Plans for the Psychiatric Rehabilitation of Veterans in New Jersey," (Trenton, July, 1945) .

ones have been abolished or they do not wish to return to their previous employment; and they must — or at least they will — give them preference in connection with employment in the state service.

In order to avoid the devastating experience of widespread postwar unemployment, the United States Bureau of Labor Statistics has suggested six points:

1. Rapid reconversion of industry from war to peacetime production.
2. A public works program to supply jobs during industrial reconversion.
3. Financial assistance, during the period of transition, to returning servicemen and demobilized war workers.
4. A gradual demobilization of the armed forces to level out the impact of unemployment.
5. Voluntary withdrawal from labor markets of as many women, school-age youths, and over-age employees as possible.
6. A Federal job placement service to direct workers to available jobs and help rehabilitate the war-wounded.

While the states are cooperating with the Federal government along these lines of general policy, there is still much that they can do in rendering assistance to specific individuals returning from war service.

The guidance and placement of returned servicemen and women will present some unusual and difficult situations. In general, the men can be divided into four groups: (1) The physically disabled, whose rehabilitation has just been discussed; (2) Men who want to and are physically qualified to go back to their old jobs. This group includes men who have not acquired any new skills in the military services and others who, despite the acquisition of new skills, prefer their old jobs. (3) Men who have received technical training or whose war experience has created dissatisfaction with pre-induction jobs and an expectation of placement in better or more responsible positions, such as the office boy who, as an officer, has been piloting a four-motor bomber. (4) Men who never had a job before they went into the armed forces. In spite of the fact that such men have had little experience and possess little or no understanding of business and industrial operations, they have had a varied and active service experience which, with skillful vocational guidance, can be profitably utilized, both for them and for their future employers.[47]

[47] Based on Kirkpatrick, Forrest H., " A Look at Postwar Employment Adjustment," *The Scientific Monthly*, April, 1945, pp. 254–256; see also: American Society of Civil Engineers, Committee on Postwar Construction, *Nine Million Jobs* (New York, 1945) ; Chamber of Commerce of the United States, Department of Manufacturing, *Employment of Veterans* (Washington, 1945) ; Committee for Economic Development, *Postwar Jobs and Growth in Small Communities* (New

Reference has already been made to the Connecticut Plan, a basic part of which is the testing of servicemen and displaced war workers to determine what training or education should be given them before they seek a job. This information is supplemented by intelligence and aptitude tests, together with medical and psychiatric findings, and the record of the individual in civilian life. A Job Training Program under the leadership of one of the state's leading industrialists, which it is claimed is the most extensive and efficient technical training system in the country, has been established.[48]

This whole program emphasizes the determination on the part of the states to seek the return of the employment service function to the states, when the period of the emergency is over. It is argued that, since the unemployment compensation plan is firmly established on a state basis, control of the job placement function is essential, and the states propose to do all in their power to attain this end. It should be noted, incidentally, that there can be no effective planning for jobs without planning for the industry which is to provide the jobs. As has been seen in an earlier section of this chapter, the states are doing that also.

One of the most difficult problems facing America today, in connection with the returning serviceman, is that of preference in the public service. In this respect, the Federal government has set an example which, in substance, the states and cities are following. Exactly half of the states, in the 1943–1944 legislative sessions alone, revised their laws to give preference to veterans of World War II. The pressure of the veterans' organizations was probably greater than could be withstood, but current developments give friends of a real merit system cause for concern. The provisions of the laws sound reasonable enough; only those veterans who are qualified are to be appointed. But if civil service finds a veteran who is not qualified, there is a loud protest.

York, 1945) ; Labor Relations Institute, *Practical Guide to Rehiring of Veterans* (New York, 1944) ; Myers, Charles A., *Personnel Problems of the Postwar Transition Period* (Committee for Economic Development, New York, 1944) ; North Dakota Postwar Planning Board, *Report* (Bismarck, 1944) ; Petroleum Industry War Council, *Reemployment of Veterans* (Washington, 1944) ; " Reemployment and Readjustment Rights of Veterans," *North Carolina Law Review*, February, 1945, pp. 107–128; and Sublette, Donald J., " The Returning Veteran," *Public Personnel Review*, July, 1945, pp. 147–153.

48 Baldwin, Raymond E., " Jobs, Not a Dole, for the Veteran," *New York Times*, Magazine Section, May 28, 1944, pp. 13, 39–40; Connecticut Reemployment Commission, *First Annual Report* (Hartford, 1944) ; and Council on Intergovernmental Relations, *Governmental Cooperation and the Returning Veteran in Connecticut Communities* (Washington, 1945) .

It is said immediately that the law granting preference means nothing, that the examination was not a fair one, that the standards were unreasonable, et cetera. Appeal is made to veteran organizations, to the legislator from the applicant's district, and the pressure begins. Unless the civil service commissions are staffed with persons of courage and integrity, the consequences of the continued application of these pressures are horrible to contemplate.[49]

The legislation so far has, for the most part, been reasonable enough, but it may not always be so. There are, in fact, disturbing signs that it will not be. In November, 1945, the electorate in New York approved a constitutional amendment which, in effect, limits the public service to veterans for years to come. As a result of a sentimental attitude toward the veteran, and pressure from veteran organizations, other proposals for constitutional amendments and legislation of similar character may be expected in the future.[50]

Grants, Bonuses, and Financial Assistance. Nearly all of the services previously described cost money; but, generally speaking, these are among the less expensive items, in so far as state veteran programs are concerned. Tax exemption provisions applicable to veterans already exist in twenty states. Special provisions for loans to veterans existed on January 1, 1945, in four states, and will probably exist before long in many more. Bonuses were paid to veterans of World War I in many states; so far, only two bonus laws exist from that war, but many new laws of this character may be expected.

Provisions for veteran relief are on the books in seventeen states from World War I, with seven more added to date from World War II. Expenditures for this purpose in all the states already run to many millions of dollars annually. In 1943, the total expenditures for states and local units was $12.3 million, of which $6.5 was spent by the states, $5.8 by the cities and counties. Provisions for burial exist in twenty-six states — thirteen old laws, thirteen new ones. The situation with regard to this legislation is clearly shown in the table on

[49] On these questions, see Donovan, Jeremiah J., "Planning Postwar Personnel Policies," *Public Management*, January, 1945, pp. 4–9; Ordway, Samuel H., Jr., "The Veteran and the Civil Service," *Annals*, March, 1945, pp. 133–139; Richey, Carl L., "Preparing for Postwar Personnel Administration," *Public Personnel Review*, April, 1944, pp. 101–107; Brainerd, Carol P., "Public Employment and Pay Rolls in the United States, 1929–1939, and Postwar Implications," *Monthly Labor Review*, February, 1945, pp. 1–31; White, Leonard D., *Veterans' Preference — A Challenge and An Opportunity* (Civil Service Assembly of the United States and Canada, Chicago, 1944).

[50] See Weintraub, Ruth G., and Touch, Rosalind, "Veterans Preferred, Unlimited," *National Municipal Review*, October, 1945, pp. 437–439, 444.

Types of Services and Benefits Available to Veterans of World War II, under State Laws, by State, as of January 1, 1945[1]

State	Veterans' Service Office	Employment Preference	Tax Exemptions	Educational benefits — Loans	Educational benefits — Veterans	Educational benefits — Children of Veterans	Bonus	Care in State institutions — Homes	Care in State institutions — Hospitals	Relief	Burial
Total	19(X) 17(XX)	20(X) 12(XX)	16(X) 20(XX)	4(X)	10(X)	17(X)	(3X)	10(X) 10(XX)	4(X) 3(XX)	17(X) 7(XX)	13(X) 13(XX)
Alabama	X	XX	X							X	
Arizona	XX	XX	XX					XX	XX	XX	XX
Arkansas	XX	XX									XX
California	X	X	XX	X	X	X					
Colorado	X	X	X					XX		X	X
Connecticut		X	XX			X		X	X	XX	XX
Delaware	XX		X			X				XX	
Florida	X					X					
Georgia	XX	XX	X					X		X	
Idaho		XX	X					XX		XX	XX
Illinois	X	X			X	X		X		X	X
Indiana		XX	XX			X		XX	XX	X	
Iowa			XX					XX		X	XX
Kansas		X	X							X	X
Kentucky	XX		XX								
Louisiana	XX	XX									
Maine			X	X	X					X	
Maryland	XX	X		X	X	X		X		XX	XX
Massachusetts		X	XX					XX		X	XX
Michigan	X		X			X			X	X	X

[1016]

State										
Minnesota	X	X	X		X		X		X	X
Mississippi	XX	X	XX		X		X		X	XX
Missouri	X		XX							
Montana		X		X	X			XX		XX
Nebraska	XX	X	X		X		X			XX
Nevada	XX	XX	X	X	XX	X	XX		XX	X
New Hampshire	X	X	X		XX		XX	XX	X	XX
New Jersey	XX	X	X		XX		XX		X	XX
New Mexico	XX	XX	XX		XX				X	XX
New York	X	X	X	X	XX		X	X		XX
North Carolina	X	XX	XX						X	XX
North Dakota		X		X			XX		X	XX
Ohio	XX	X	XX	X	X		X	X	XX	XX
Oklahoma	X	XX	X		XX		X	X	XX	X
Oregon	XX	X	XX	XX	XX		X		XX	X
Pennsylvania					X				XX	X
Rhode Island	X	X	X				X		X	X
South Carolina	XX	X	XX	X	X		XX			XX
South Dakota	X	X	XX	X	X		X	X	X	X
Tennessee	X	XX	XX					X		
Texas	X	X	XX	X	X		X		X	X
Utah	XX	X	XX		XX	X	XX		XX	XX
Vermont	XX	X	X		XX		X		X	X
Virginia	XX	XX	XX		X		XX			
Washington	XX	X	XX		XX		XX	X	XX	X
West Virginia	XX	X			X		X		X	X
Wisconsin	XX	XX	XX	X	XX		XX	X	X	XX
Wyoming	XX	XX	XX		XX		XX		XX	XX

¹ X indicates that recent legislation has been enacted to provide the particular type of benefit; XX indicates that the legislation on the statutes prior to World War II has been extended to cover veterans of that war or that the laws can be interpreted to include such veterans. From Aaronson and Rosenbloom, *op. cit.*

pages 1016–1017. The public can look forward to huge increases in this type of expenditure during the next few years.[51]

SELECTED REFERENCES

American Council on Public Affairs, *Design for Defense* (Washington, 1941).

American Public Works Association, *The States of Public Works Planning and Its Relation to Full Employment* (Chicago, 1945).

Association of Land-Grant Colleges and Universities, *Post War Agricultural Policy* (University of Minnesota, 1944).

Biddle, Eric H., *Mobilization of the Home Front* (Public Administration Service, Chicago, 1942).

Buck, A. E., *Politico-Economic Prospects of Rhode Island* (Rhode Island Public Expenditures Council, Providence, 1945).

Bureau of Public Administration, *State Councils of Defense* (University of California, May, 1941, and Revised, December, 1942).

California Reconstruction and Reemployment Commission, *Postwar Housing in California* (Sacramento, 1945).

Commerce, Department of, *Federal-State Conferences on War Restrictions* (Washington, 1942).

Conover, Helen F., *Civilian Defense: A Selective List of Recent References* (Library of Congress, Division of Bibliography, 1941).

Council for Democracy, *Defense on Main Street* (New York, 1941).

Council of State Governments, *Grants-in-Aid and Other Federal Expenditures Within the States* (Chicago, 1945).

——, *Public Works and the States* (Chicago, 1945).

——, *State Provisions for Veterans' Benefits Enacted During 1943 and 1944* (Chicago, 1944).

——, *State Legislative Developments on Postwar Problems, 1941–1943* (Chicago, 1943).

——, *State Veterans' Programs* (Chicago, 1945).

——, *Suggested State War Legislation for 1943* (Chicago, 1942); *for 1944–1945* (Chicago, 1944); *for 1945* (Chicago, 1944).

Dowling, Lee C., *Today's Problems and Tomorrow's Horizons for Servicemen and Their Families* (New York State Department of Social Welfare, Albany, 1943).

---

[51] The best summary of this legislation will be found in Aaronson, Franklin, and Rosenbloom, Hilda, "State Aid to Veterans," *Social Security Bulletin*, February, 1945, pp. 12–20; see also Bane, Frank, "State Plans for Aid to Veterans," *Annals*, March, 1945, pp. 71–76; Griswold, Dwight, "Better Than a Bonus: Nebraska's Plan for Assistance to Ex-Servicemen Places Administration of State Fund Relief in Hands of Veterans Themselves," *State Government*, August, 1944, pp. 375–376, 385–386; Skilton, Robert H., "Moratoria and the Soldiers' and Sailors' Civil Relief Act," *Annals*, May, 1943, pp. 28–34. Several compilations and analyses of state veteran benefit laws have appeared: Council of State Governments, *Recent State Action Providing for Returning Veterans: Summarization of Reports from Forty-five States*, and *State Provisions for Veterans' Benefits Enacted During 1943 and 1944* (both, Chicago, 1944); Tax Foundation, *State Veterans Legislation* (New York, 1944).

Duffy, John F., Jr., *State Organization for Fair Employment Practices* (University of California, Bureau of Public Administration, 1944).

Farmer, Hallie, Ed., *War Comes to Alabama* (University of Alabama, Bureau of Public Administration, 1943).

Florida State Planning Board, *Florida Wartime Fiscal Problems* (Tallahassee, 1943).

Governmental Research Institute, *You and the War,* a Series of Bibliographies; No. 2, Home Defense (University of South Dakota, 1942).

Governors' Conference, *Proceedings* (Chicago, annually).

Gurwell, John K., *Veterans' Information Centers* (Public Administration Service, Chicago, 1945.

Housing Authority of the City of Newark, *The Social Effects of Public Housing* (Newark, 1944).

Howard, L. Vaughan, and Bone, Hugh A., *Current American Government: Wartime Developments* (Appleton-Century, New York, 1943).

Illinois State Planning Commission, *United States War Department Activities in Illinois* (Chicago, 1939).

Kidder, Peabody & Company, *Post-War Housing* (New York, 1945).

Leonard, J. M., and Woodworth, L. N., *Gearing for War: A Study of the Department of Public Works* (Civic Research Institute, Kansas City, 1943).

Lorwin, Lewis L., *Time for Planning* (Harper, New York, 1945).

MacDonald, Mary E., *Federal Grants for Vocational Rehabilitation* (University of Chicago Press, 1944).

Martin, Roscoe C., Ed., *National Defense and State Finance* (University of Alabama, Bureau of Public Administration, 1941).

Maverick, Maury, and Burke, William H., *Prisons in Wartime* (War Production Board, Washington, 1943).

Michigan Office of Veterans' Affairs, *How to Organize a Local Council of Veterans' Affairs and a Veterans' Counseling Center* (Lansing, 1945).

Michigan Unemployment Compensation Commission, *Mobilizing Michigan Manpower for Defense* (Detroit, 1941).

National Housing Agency, *Housing After World War I* (Washington, 1945).

National Resources Planning Board, *After Defense — What?* (Washington, 1941).

New England Council, *New England and the National Defense: the First Year* (Boston, 1941).

New York State Division of Commerce, *Handbook of War Agencies* (Albany, 1942).

New York State War Council, *New York State War Emergency Act and Other War Emergency Laws, 1941, 1942, and 1943* (Albany, 1943).

Quattlebaum, Charles A., *Federal Aid to the States for Education* (Library of Congress, Legislative Reference Service, 1945).

Schiller, A. Arthur, *Military Law and Defense Legislation* (West Publishing Company, St. Paul, 1941).

Stevens, S. K., and others, *Pennsylvania's First Year at War, 1941–1942* (Harrisburg, 1944).

——, *Pennsylvania's Second Year at War, 1942–1943* (Harrisburg, 1945).

Strathman, Earl, Ed., *South Dakota's Contribution to National Defense* (University of South Dakota, Bureau of Governmental Research, 1941).

Straus, Nathan, *The Seven Myths of Housing* (Knopf, New York, 1944).

Summers, Harrison B., and Robert E., *Increasing Federal Power* (Wilson, New York, 1940).

——, *Planned Economy, A Supplement* (Wilson, New York, 1940).

Tax Foundation, *State Veteran Legislation* (New York, 1944).

Tax Institute, *Wartime Problems of State and Local Finance* (New York, 1943).

Tompkins, Dorothy C., *Social and Economic Problems Arising out of World War II: A Bibliography* (Public Administration Service, Chicago, 1942).

Time, Inc., *Reemployment of Veterans* (New York, 1945).

United States Department of Labor, *Impact of the War on Employment in 181 Centers of War Activity* (Bulletin No. 826, Washington, 1945).

Waller, Willard, *The Veteran Comes Back* (Dryden Press, New York, 1944).

War Manpower Commission, *Personnel Survey of the United States Employment Service: Three Wartime Years Under the Federal Civil Service* (Washington, 1945).

Waterman, Patricia L., *The Role of the States in Postwar Aviation* (University of California, Bureau of Public Administration, 1945).

Watson, George H., *State Gasoline Tax Administrators and the Mileage Rationing Program* (Federation of Tax Administrators, Chicago, 1943).

White, Leonard D., *Veterans' Preference — A Challenge and An Opportunity* (Civil Service Assembly of the United States and Canada, Chicago, 1944).

Wilcox, Jerome H., *Official Defense Publications* (University of California, Bureau of Public Administration, 1941, and Supplement, 1942).

Aaronson, Franklin, and Rosenbloom, Hilda, "State Aid to Veterans," *Social Security Bulletin*, February, 1945, pp. 12–20.

Altmeyer, A. J., "The First Decade in Social Security," *Social Security Bulletin*, August, 1945, pp. 1–26.

Anonymous, "Reemployment and Readjustment Rights of Veterans," *North Carolina Law Review*, February, 1945, pp. 107–128.

Bacon, George W., "The Model State Guard Act," *Fordham Law Review*, January, 1941, pp. 41–63.

Baldwin, Raymond E., "Employment in the Postwar Period," *State Government*, August, 1945, pp. 129–131, 139.

Bane, Frank, "Cooperative Government in Wartime," *Public Administration Review*, Spring, 1942, pp. 95–103.

——, "State Plans for Aid to Veterans," *Annals*, March, 1945, pp. 71–76.

Beckwith, Edmund J., "Laws Relating to State Military Power," *State Government*, March, 1943, pp. 57–58, 75.

Biddle, Francis, "Federal-State Cooperation in Wartime," *State Government*, April, 1943, pp. 90–91, 101.

Blakey, Roy G., "Postwar Tax Problems," *State Government*, September, 1944, pp. 422–423, 432.

Bogart, George G., " Progress in Adoption of State Defense Laws," *State Government,* July, 1941, pp. 162–163, 174–175.

Brewster, R. Wallace, and others, " The States and Mileage Cooperation," *State Government,* October, 1943, pp. 211–213.

Broughton, J. Melville, " Organizing the States for the Future," *State Government,* January, 1945, pp. 3, 14–15.

——, " The Future of the States," *State Government,* March, 1943, pp. 55–56, 70–71, 74.

Caldwell, Lynton K., " Veteran — Disabled, State Legislation," *Annals,* May, 1945, pp. 46–52.

Carey, William D., " State Councils for Defense, 1917 and 1941 Models," *State Government,* May, 1941, pp. 105–106, 117–120, 123, and June, 1941, pp. 133–135, 145–146, 151.

Chatters, Carl H., " State Face Problems of Wartime Finance," *State Government,* February, 1942, pp. 37–38, 47.

Clarke, Frank W., " National Defense Demands Compel Some Revisions and Postponements of Projects in State Highway Budget," *California Highways and Public Works,* November, 1941, pp. 1–2, 13.

Conway, Francis X., " A State's Power of Defense Under the Constitution," *Fordham Law Review,* May, 1942, pp. 169–192.

Council of State Governments, " Conference Studies Defense Problems," *State Government,* April, 1941, pp. 85, 98–99.

——, " Progress Report on State War Legislation," *State Government,* May, 1942, pp. 107–108, 113.

——, " State War Legislation," *State Government,* February, 1942, pp. 41–42, 49–52.

——, " Suggested State Legislation for 1945," *State Government,* January, 1945, pp. 10–12.

——, " War Records Project," *State Government,* May, 1944, pp. 336–337.

——, " Wartime Fiscal Policies for State and Local Governments," *State Government,* December, 1942, pp. 241–244.

——, " Western States Study Defense Situation," *State Government,* November, 1941, pp. 273, 284.

Dixon, Frank M., " Civilian Defense in the States," *State Government,* August, 1941, pp. 183–185, 202–204.

——, " Federal-State Relations in Wartime," *State Government,* August, 1942, pp. 153–154, 163–166.

Donovan, Jeremiah J., " Manpower Conservation — A ' Must ' for Management," *State Government,* November, 1942, pp. 215–216, 223–224.

——, " Planning Postwar Personnel Policies," *Public Management,* January, 1945, pp. 4–9.

Draper, William H., " The Role of the States in Registration Under the Selective Service Law," *State Government,* October, 1940, pp. 203, 206.

Drummond, Helen C., " The Wartime Program of the National Civil Service Reform League," *Public Personnel Review,* October, 1942, pp. 288–292.

Ellis, William J., " War Services of Community Agencies," *State Government,* April, 1942, pp. 81–82, 91.

Fesler, James W., " Areas of Industrial Mobilization, 1917–1918," *Public Administration Review,* Winter, 1941, pp. 149–166.

Gill, Corrington, " Federal-State-City Cooperation in Congested Production Areas," *Public Administration Review,* Winter, 1945, pp. 28–33.

Graves, W. Brooke, and Scholz, Karl W. H., " Meeting the Needs for State and Local Revenues in the Postwar Era," *American Political Science Review,* October, 1944, pp. 904–912.

Griswold, Dwight, " Better Than a Bonus," *State Government,* August, 1944, pp. 375–376, 385–386.

Gurwell, John K., and Price, Don K., " National Defense and Relief Highlight Fifth General Assembly Deliberations," *State Government,* March, 1941, pp. 59–64.

Harrison, Earl G., " How State and Local Officials Can Assist in the Alien Registration Program," *State Government,* October, 1940, pp. 204–206.

Henderson, Leon, " Problems of Price and Supply in Wartime," *State Government,* January, 1942, pp. 11, 29.

Hoan, Daniel W., " States, Localities and Defense," *State Government,* January, 1941, pp. 9–11, 21–25.

——, " States and Cities in the Defense Program," *National Municipal Review,* March, 1941, pp. 141–146, 159.

Ice, Willard, and Stickgold, Simon, " The Role of State Grants in the Postwar Era," *American Political Science Review,* December, 1942, pp. 1103–1108.

Jackson, Clarence A., " Indiana Civilian Defense Program," *State Government,* October, 1941, pp. 241, 254.

Kelly, Harry F., " Postwar Problems of Employment and Unemployment," *State Government,* May, 1943, pp. 113–114, 125.

Kirkpatrick, Forrest H., " A Look at Postwar Employment Adjustment," *Scientific Monthly,* April, 1945, pp. 254–256.

LaGuardia, Fiorello H., " Civilian Protection in Wartime," *State Government,* January, 1942, pp. 12–14, 23–24.

Langum, John K., " A Constructive Emergency Tax Program," *State Government,* July, 1942, pp. 137–138, 146–148.

Lehman, Herbert H., " The States and the Present Emergency," *State Government,* March, 1941, pp. 55–57, 71.

Loeffler, Herman C., " Price Control Is Felt by States and Cities," *National Municipal Review,* March, 1943, pp. 135–138, 141.

McGrath, J. Howard, " An Adequate Social Security Program," *State Government,* August, 1945, pp. 132–139.

——, " State Settlement Laws Delay Victory," *State Government,* February, 1943, pp. 31–33.

McKenna, Coe A., " State Aviation and Airport Problems," *State Government,* September, 1945, pp. 160–161.

McKibbin, George B., " Wartime Fiscal Policies in Illinois," *State Government,* November, 1942, pp. 213–214, 220–222, 224.

McNutt, Paul V., " Health and Welfare Sectors of Defense," *State Government,* January, 1942, pp. 8–10, 24.

MacDonald, Norman, " Organization for Civilian Defense," *State Government,* March, 1942, pp. 61–62, 72.

MacDonald, Thomas H., "The American Motorist in Wartime," *State Government*, June, 1943, pp. 140, 146–147.

Martin, Edward, "The Returning Veterans," *State Government*, August, 1945, pp. 123–125.

Martz, Arnaud C., "The Work of the State Council of Defense," League of Cities of the Third Class in Pennsylvania *Bulletin*, October, 1941, pp. 7–8, 14.

Neufeld, Maurice F., "The New York State Defense Production Plan," *Public Administration Review*, Autumn, 1941, pp. 421–431.

Newton, Mortimer W., "The Rhode Island Cash Sickness Compensation Plan," *State Government*, September, 1945, pp. 156–159, 161.

O'Conor, Herbert R., "The Challenge to the States," *State Government*, March, 1943, pp. 51–52, 66–68.

——, "The Sovereign States," *State Government*, August, 1945, pp. 126–128.

Odum, Edward E., "Federal-State Cooperation in Relation to Veterans' Affairs," *State Government*, December, 1944, pp. 455–458.

Ordway, Samuel H., Jr., "The Veteran in the Civil Service," *Annals*, March, 1945, pp. 133–139.

Owen, Jerrold, "Oregon Prepares for War Emergencies," *State Government*, April, 1942, pp. 85–86, 93.

Parkman, Henry, Jr., "The Local Rationing Board in Massachusetts," *Public Administration Review*, Summer, 1942, pp. 195–198.

Purcell, C. H., "Highways for National Defense," *California Highways and Public Works*, November, 1940, pp. 1–5.

Reticker, Ruth, "State Unemployment Compensation Laws of 1945," *Social Security Bulletin*, July, 1945, pp. 1–18.

Richey, Carl L., "Preparing Now for Postwar Personnel Administration," *Public Personnel Review*, April, 1944, pp. 101–107.

Rightor, C. E., and Ingersoll, Hugh D., "State and Local Government After the War," *National Municipal Review*, July, 1942, pp. 306–310.

Routt, Garland C., "Tire Rationing: A Federal-State-Local Job," *State Government*, February, 1942, pp. 35–36, 44.

Ruml, Beardsley, "Taxes After the War," *State Government*, July, 1945, pp. 113–114.

Skilton, Robert H., "Moratoria and the Soldiers' and Sailors' Civil Relief Act," *Annals*, May, 1943, pp. 28–34.

Smith, Bruce, "Civil Defense in the National Emergency," *State Government*, October, 1940, pp. 198–199, 201.

Smullyan, Emile B., "War Distortions and Postwar Demobilization: The Problem of the States," *State Government*, January, 1944, pp. 255–259.

Sparks, Chauncey, "A Constructive Postwar Program for Agriculture," *State Government*, September, 1945, pp. 152–153, 167.

Stassen, Harold E., "Duties of the States in National Defense," *State Government*, March, 1941, pp. 53–54, 72.

——, "Our Democracy and the War," *State Government*, August, 1942, pp. 151–152, 166.

——, "State Participation in the War Effort," *State Government*, June, 1942, pp. 3–5, 24.

Studebaker, John W., "The States, Education and National Defense," *State Government*, May, 1941, pp. 103–104, 115–116.

Sublette, Donald J., "The Returning Veterans," *Public Personnel Review*, July, 1945, pp. 147–153.

Tormey, Thomas J., "The War Services Side of Civilian Defense in California," *Western City*, September, 1943, pp. 56–58, 60.

Warren, Earl, and Edison, Charles, "Postwar Problems," *State Government*, April, 1943, pp. 83–84, 103.

Watson, George H., "State Gasoline Tax Administrators and the Mileage Rationing Program," *State Government*, June, 1943, pp. 131–134.

——, "State Participation in Gasoline Rationing," *Public Administration Review*, Summer, 1943, pp. 213–222.

Weinfeld, Edward, "New York State Faces War Housing Issues," *National Municipal Review*, December, 1942, pp. 584–590.

Weintraub, Ruth G., and Tough, Rosalind, "Veterans Preferred, Unlimited," *National Municipal Review*, October, 1945, pp. 437–438, 444.

Williams, John F., "Kentucky's Approved Facilities for the Education and Training of Veterans," *Educational Bulletin*, Frankfort, August, 1945.

Wilson, Richard H., "Federal Defense Road Program in California Presents Serious Financial and Traffic Problems," *California Highways and Public Works*, February, 1941, pp. 1–7, 26.

Wiltsee, Herbert, "State Legislative Highlights — 1943," *National Municipal Review*, July, 1943, pp. 360–366, 372.

Appendix

NOTE: The Fourth Edition of the Model State Constitution was published by the National Municipal League in 1941, with explanatory material. The document was first published in 1921, revisions appearing in 1928 and 1933. The present edition is the result of nearly two years' work by the League's Committee on State Government. The form of the Constitution has been improved, and the text itself subjected to a thoroughgoing revision, resulting in many important changes. For approximately two decades the Model State Constitution has had a wide influence on thinking with respect to problems of state constitutional law and the relations of the states with their units of local government. The Committee hopes that this edition may merit a continuance of that influence.

The membership of the Committee on State Government which is responsible for this document is as follows: Frank Bane, Council of State Governments; Charles A. Beard, Milford, Connecticut; George C. S. Benson, Northwestern University (on leave) ; A. E. Buck, Institute of Public Administration; J. Alton Burdine, University of Texas; Finla G. Crawford, Syracuse University; Walter F. Dodd, Chicago, Illinois; John A. Fairlie, University of Illinois; Hubert R. Gallagher, Council of State Governments; Frederick H. Guild, Kansas Legislative Council; Arthur N. Holcombe, Harvard University; Rodney L. Mott, Colgate University (on leave) ; Robert S. Rankin, Duke University; Frank M. Stewart, University of California at Los Angeles; Paul T. Stafford, Princeton University; with W. Brooke Graves, Bryn Mawr College, as Chairman, and Wilbert L. Hindman, University of Southern California, as Secretary. The Committee had valuable assistance from about seventy distinguished authorities who are specialists in particular problems dealt with in the Constitution; the names of these persons were included in the official text of the document as published by the League.

Appendix

MODEL STATE CONSTITUTION
Fourth Edition, 1941

ARTICLE I

BILL OF RIGHTS

Section 100. *Political Power.*[1] All political power of this state is inherent in the people, and all government herein is founded on their authority.

Section 101. *Inherent Rights.* All men are by nature equally free and independent and have certain inherent rights; namely, the enjoyment of life and liberty, with the means of acquiring and possessing property, and pursuing and obtaining happiness and safety.[2] These rights carry with them certain corresponding duties to the state.

Section 102. *Legal Rights.* No citizen shall be disfranchised, or deprived of any of the rights or privileges secured to any other citizen, unless by the law of the land or the judgment of his peers; nor shall any person be deprived of due process of law, or be denied the equal protection of the laws. There shall be no imprisonment for debt and a reasonable amount of the property of individuals may be exempted from seizure or sale for payment of any debt or liabilities.

Section 103. *Right to Organize.* Citizens shall have the right to organize, except in military or semi-military organizations not under the supervision of the state, and except for purposes of resisting the duly constituted authority of this state or of the United States. Employees shall have the right to bargain collectively through representatives of their own choosing.

Section 104. *Searches and Seizures.* The right of the people to be secure in their persons, houses, papers and effects, against unreasonable searches and seizures, shall not be violated; and no warrants shall issue but upon probable cause supported by oath or affirmation, and particularly describing the place to be searched, and the persons or things to be seized. Evidence obtained in violation of this section shall not be admissible in any court against any person.

[1] The Committee has adopted the policy of inserting short headings at the beginning of each paragraph; these are intended as aids to reference and have nothing to do with the legal operation or judicial interpretation of the sections.

[2] Virginia Constitution, Article I, Section 1.

Section 105. *Writ of Habeas Corpus.* The privilege of the writ of h̲
corpus shall not be suspended, unless, in case of rebellion or invasi̲
public safety requires it, and then only in such manner as shall be prescr̲
by law.

Section 106. *Rights of Accused Persons.* In all criminal prosecutions, the
accused shall have the right to demand a specific statement of the charges
against him, and to appear and defend himself in person and by counsel;
to meet the witnesses against him face to face; to have process to compel
the attendance of witnesses in his behalf; and to have a speedy public trial
in the county or district in which the offense is alleged to have been committed, unless he shall waive this right in order to secure a change of venue.

Section 107. *Double Jeopardy; Excessive Bail.* No person shall, after ac-
quittal, be tried for the same offense. All persons shall, before conviction,
be bailable by sufficient sureties, except for capital offenses when the proof
is evident or the presumption great.[3]

Section 108. *Right of Assembly.* The right of the people peaceably to
assemble, and to petition the government, or any department thereof, shall
never be abridged.

Section 109. *Freedom of Speech.* No law shall be passed abridging the
freedom of speech or of the press.[4]

Section 110. *Freedom of Religion.* No law shall be passed respecting the
establishment of religion, or prohibiting the free exercise thereof.

Section 111. *Appropriations for Private Purposes.* No tax shall be levied
or appropriation of public money or property be made, either directly or
indirectly, except for a public purpose, and no public money or property
shall ever be appropriated, applied, donated, or used directly or indirectly,
for any sect, church, denomination, or sectarian institution. No public
money or property shall be appropriated for a charitable, industrial, educational or benevolent purpose except to a department, office, agency or
civil division of the state.

Section 112. *Freedom from Legislative Abuses.* The power of the state to
act in the general welfare shall never be impaired by the making of any
irrevocable grant of special privileges or immunities.

Section 113. *Eminent Domain.* Private property shall not be taken or
damaged for public use without just compensation.

ARTICLE II

SUFFRAGE AND ELECTIONS

Section 200. *Qualifications for Voting.* Every duly registered citizen of the
age of twenty-one years who shall have been a citizen for ninety days, and
an inhabitant of this state for one year next preceding an election, and for
the last ninety days a resident of the county and for the last thirty days a
resident of the election district in which he or she may offer his or her vote,
shall be entitled to vote at such election in the election district of which he
or she shall at the time be a resident, and not elsewhere, except as herein-
after provided, in the election of all officers that are now or hereafter may

[3] Based on provisions in the Iowa and New Jersey bills of rights.
[4] Constitution of the United States, Amendment I.

· elective by the people, and upon all questions which may be submitted to the vote of the people, provided that no person shall become entitled to vote unless such person is also able, except for physical disability, to read and write English; and suitable laws shall be passed by the legislature to enforce this provision.

Section 201. *Absent Voting.* The legislature may, by general law, provide a manner in which qualified voters who may be absent from the state or county of their residence may register and vote, and for the return and canvass of their votes in the election district in which they reside.

Section 202. *Disqualifications from Voting.* No person who shall receive, accept, or offer to receive, or pay, offer or promise to pay, or withdraw or withhold or threaten to withdraw or withhold any money or other valuable consideration as a compensation or reward for the giving or withholding of a vote at an election shall vote at such election. No person under conviction of bribery or of any infamous crime shall exercise the privilege of the suffrage.

Section 203. *Residence.* For the purpose of voting, no person shall be deemed to have gained or lost a residence, by reason of his presence or absence, while employed in the service of the United States; nor while engaged in the navigation of the waters of this state, or of the United States, or of the high seas; nor while a student at any institution of learning; nor while kept at any almshouse, or other asylum, or institution wholly or partly supported at public expense or by charity; nor while confined in any public prison.

Section 204. *Registration of Voters.* Laws shall be made for ascertaining, by proper proofs, the citizens who shall be entitled to the privilege of the suffrage and for the registration of all qualified voters. Registration shall be upon personal application, in the case of the first registration of any voter and shall be completed at least ten days before each election. Such registration shall be effective so long as the voter shall remain qualified to vote from the same address or for such other period as the legislature may prescribe.

Section 205. *Methods of Voting.* Voting at all elections or on referenda shall be by voting machine or by such other method as may be prescribed by law, provided that secrecy of voting be preserved.

Section 206. *Election Officers.* All officers and employees charged with the direction or administration of the election system of the state and of its civil divisions shall be appointed in such manner as the legislature may by law direct, provided that appointment shall be made according to merit and fitness, to be determined, so far as practicable, by competitive examination.

Article III

THE LEGISLATURE

Section 300. *Legislative Power.* The legislative power shall be vested in a legislature, which may delegate to other public officers the power to supplement statutes by ordinances, general orders, rules, and regulations, provided a general standard or principle has been enacted to which such delegated legislation shall conform. All such delegated legislation, promulgated state officers, departments, offices, or agencies shall be reported to the legislative council, and shall be adopted and published in accordance with a fair procedure prescribed by law.

Section 301. *Composition of the Legislature.* The legislature shall be composed of a single chamber of such number of members as may be prescribed by law, but not to exceed ———— members. Except as otherwise provided in this constitution, any qualified voter shall be eligible to membership in the legislature.[5]

Section 302. *Election of Members.* The members of the legislature shall be chosen by the qualified voters of the state for a term of two years by proportional representation, under a method to be prescribed by law. For the purpose of electing members of the legislature, the state shall be divided into districts, composed of contiguous and compact territory, from each of which there shall be elected from three to seven members, in accordance with the population of the respective districts. The term of members of the legislature shall begin on the first day of December next following their election.

Section 303. *Apportionment.* After each decennial census, the secretary of the legislature shall reallot the number of members assigned to each district, in accordance with the changes in the population of the several districts. The boundaries of the districts and the total number of members may be altered only by law and not more frequently than once in each census period.

Section 304. *Time of Election.* The election of members of the legislature shall be held on the Tuesday next following the first Monday in November in the odd numbered years, beginning in 19———.

Section 305. *Vacancies.* Whenever a vacancy shall occur in the legislature, it shall be filled by a majority vote of the remaining members from the district in which said vacancy occurs. If, after thirty days following the occurrence of a vacancy, it remains unfilled, the governor shall appoint some eligible person for the unexpired term.[6]

Section 306. *Compensation of Members.* The members of the legislature shall receive an annual salary, as may be prescribed by law, but the amount thereof shall neither be increased nor diminished during the term for which they are elected.

---

[5] The Committee has followed previous drafts in recommending a unicameral legislature, recognizing, however, that the bicameral system now generally prevails, and that it is likely to continue to do so for some time. The Committee believes that most of the recommendations in this Model Constitution are applicable to the bicameral system, with slight modifications. The chief recommendations in a model draft for a bicameral legislature would involve: reduction in the size of the two houses; redefinition of the basis of apportionment; establishment of joint committees; and representation of the two houses on the legislative council. The size of the body, which should be substantially smaller than most of the existing legislative bodies, will depend somewhat on the size of the state, the size and density of its population.

[6] Some authorities prefer a recount of the ballots cast at the original election in the district which has been left unrepresented as a result of the vacancy. This prevents a district majority from appropriating to itself a vacated seat of a district minority.

Section 307. *Sessions.* The legislature shall be deemed a continuous body during the biennium for which its members were elected. It shall meet in regular sessions quarterly or at such other times as may be prescribed by law. Special sessions may be called by the governor or by a majority of the members of the legislative council.

Section 308. *Organization and Procedure.* The legislature shall be judge of the election, returns and qualifications of its members, and may by law vest in the courts the trial and determination of contested elections of members. It shall choose its presiding officer, and a secretary who shall serve for an indefinite term. It shall determine its rules of procedure; it may compel the attendance of absent members, punish its members for disorderly conduct and, with the concurrence of two-thirds of all the members, expel a member; and it shall have power to compel the attendance and testimony of witnesses and the production of books and papers either before the legislature as a whole or before any committee thereof.

Section 309. *Legislative Immunity.* For any speech or debate in the legislature, the members shall not be questioned in any other place.

Section 310. *Local and Special Legislation.* The legislature shall pass no special act in any case where a general act can be made applicable, and whether a general act can be made applicable shall be a matter for judicial determination. No local act shall take effect until approved by a majority of the qualified voters voting thereon in the district to be affected, except acts repealing local or special acts in effect before the adoption of this constitution and receiving a two-thirds vote of all members of the legislature on the question of their repeal.

Section 311. *Transaction of Business.* A majority of all the members of the legislature shall constitute a quorum to do business but a smaller number may adjourn from day to day and compel the attendance of absent members. The legislature shall keep a journal of its proceedings which shall be published from day to day. The legislature shall prescribe the methods of voting on legislative matters, but a record vote, with the yeas and nays entered in the journal, shall be taken on any question on the demand of one-fifth of the members present. Mechanical devices may be employed to record the votes of members.

Section 312. *Committees.* The legislature may establish such committees as may be necessary for the efficient conduct of its business. Each committee shall keep a journal of its proceedings, as a public record. One-third of the members of the legislature shall have power to relieve a committee of further consideration of a bill when the committee to which it was assigned has not reported on it. Notice of all committee hearings and a clear statement of all subjects to be considered at each hearing, shall be published one week in advance, in the journal.

Section 313. *Bills and Titles of Bills.* No law shall be passed except by bill. Every bill, except bills for appropriations and bills for the codification, revision or rearrangement of existing laws, shall be confined to one subject, which shall be expressed in the title. Bills for appropriations shall be confined to appropriations.

Section 314. *Passage of Bills.* No bill shall become a law unless it has been read on three different days, has been printed and upon the desks of the members in final form at least three legislative days prior to final passage, and has received the assent of a majority of all of the members of the legislature. No act shall become effective until published, as provided by law.

Section 315. *Action by the Governor*. Every bill which shall have passed the legislature shall be presented to the governor; if he approves he shall sign it, but if not he shall return it with his objections to the legislature. Any bill so returned by the governor shall be reconsidered by the legislature and if, upon reconsideration, two-thirds of the members present shall agree to pass the bill it shall become a law. In all such cases the vote of the legislature shall be by roll call, and entered on the journal.

If any bill shall not be signed or returned by the governor within fifteen days after it shall have been presented to him, it shall be a law in like manner as if he had signed it, except that, if the legislature shall be in recess at end of such fifteen day period, the governor may return it with his objections upon the reconvening of the legislature, and if the legislature shall adjourn finally before the governor has acted on a bill that has been presented to him less than fifteen days before, it shall not become law unless the governor signs it within thirty days after such adjournment.

Section 316. *Referendum on Legislation*. Any bill failing of passage by the legislature may be submitted to referendum by order of the governor, either in its original form or with such amendments which were considered by the legislature, as he may designate. Any bill which, having passed the legislature, is returned thereto by the governor with objections and, upon reconsideration is not approved by a two-thirds vote of all the members but is approved by at least a majority thereof, may be submitted to referendum by a majority of all the members of the legislature. Bills thus submitted to referendum shall be voted on at the next succeeding general election occurring at least sixty days after action is taken to submit them, unless the legislature shall provide for their submission at an earlier date.

Section 317. *Legislative Council*. There shall be a legislative council consisting of not less than seven nor more than fifteen members, chosen by and from the legislature. Members of the legislative council shall be chosen by the legislature at its first session after the adoption of this constitution and at each subsequent session following a general election. Members of the legislative council shall be elected in such manner as the legislature shall direct, and when elected shall continue in office until their successors are chosen and have qualified. The legislature, by a majority vote of all its members, may dissolve the legislative council at any time and proceed to the election of a successor thereto.

Section 318. *Organization of Legislative Council*. The legislative council shall meet as often as may be necessary to perform its duties. It shall choose one of its members as chairman, and shall appoint a director of research; it shall adopt its own rules of procedure, except as such rules may be established by law. The secretary of the legislature shall serve ex-officio as secretary of the council.

Section 319. *Duties of the Legislative Council*. It shall be the duty of the legislative council to collect information concerning the government and general welfare of the state and to report thereon to the legislature. Measures for proposed legislation may be submitted to it at any time, and shall be considered, and reported to the legislature with its recommendations thereon. The legislative council may also recommend such legislation, in the form of bills or otherwise, as in its opinion the welfare of the state may require. Other powers and duties may be assigned to the legislative council by law. The legislature may delegate to the legislative council authority to supplement existing legislation by general orders. No such general orders shall be effective until published as provided by law.

Section 320. *Compensation of Members of the Legislative Council.* Members of the legislative council shall receive such compensation, additional to their compensation as members of the legislature, as may be provided by law.

ARTICLE IV

INITIATIVE AND REFERENDUM

Section 400. *The Initiative.* The people reserve to themselves power by petition to propose laws and amendments to this constitution, and directly to enact or reject such laws and amendments at the polls. This reserved power shall be known as the initiative.

Section 401. *Initiative Procedure.* An initiative petition shall contain either the full text of the measure proposed, or an adequate summary thereof, and, to be valid, shall be signed by qualified voters equal in number to at least ———— per cent of the total vote cast for governor in the last preceding general election at which a governor was chosen. An initiative petition proposing a constitutional amendment shall be signed by ———— (a greater) per cent of the qualified voters of the state than is required for a petition proposing a law. Not more than one-fourth of the signatures counted on any completed petition shall be those of the voters of any one county. Initiative petitions shall be filed with the secretary of the legislature, and the question of adopting any measure therein set forth shall be submitted by him to the qualified voters at the first regular state election held not less than sixty days after such filing, except that a constitutional amendment so proposed shall be submitted at the second regular state election after such filing.

Section 402. *The Referendum.* The people also reserve to themselves power to require, by petition, that measures enacted by the legislature be submitted to the qualified voters for their approval or rejection. This reserved power shall be known as the referendum.

Section 403. *Referendum Procedure.* A referendum petition against any measure passed by the legislature shall be filed with the secretary of the legislature within ninety days after the adjournment of the session at which such measure was enacted, and to be valid, shall be signed by qualified voters equal in number to not less than ———— per cent of the total vote cast for governor at the last preceding general election at which a governor was chosen. Not more than one-fourth of the signatures counted on any completed petition shall be those of the voters of any one county. The question of approving any measure against which a valid referendum petition is filed shall be submitted to the voters at the first regular or special state election held not less than thirty days after such filing.

Section 404. *Effect of Referendum.* A referendum may be ordered upon any act or part of an act, except acts continuing existing taxes and acts making appropriations in amounts not in excess of those for the preceding fiscal year. When the referendum is ordered upon an act, or any part of an act, it shall suspend the operation thereof until such act, or part, is approved by the voters.

The filing of a referendum petition against one or more items, sections, or parts of an act shall not delay the remainder of the measure from becoming operative. No act shall take effect earlier than ninety days after the adjournment of the legislative session at which it was enacted, except acts declared to be emergency measures. If it be necessary for the immediate preservation of the public peace, health, or safety that a measure become effective without delay, the facts constituting such necessity shall be stated in a separate section, and if, upon a record vote entered in the journal, two-thirds of the members elected to the legislature shall declare the measure to be an emergency measure, it shall become effective at the time specified therein; but no act granting or amending a franchise or special privilege, or creating any vested right or interest, other than in the state, shall be declared an emergency measure. If a referendum petition be filed against an emergency measure, such measure shall be operative until voted upon, and if not approved by a majority of the qualified voters voting thereon, it shall be deemed repealed.

Section 405. *Special Elections.* Any referendum measure shall be submitted to the qualified voters at a special election, if so ordered by the governor, or if a separate petition requesting a special election be signed by ———— per cent of the qualified voters. Any such special election shall be held not less than one hundred and twenty nor more than one hundred and fifty days after the adjournment of the legislative session at which the act was passed.

Section 406. *Passage of Constitutional Amendments and Laws by the Initiative and Referendum.* Each measure shall be submitted by a ballot title, which shall be descriptive, but not argumentative or prejudicial. The ballot title of any initiated or referred measure shall be prepared by the legal department of the state, subject to review by the courts. The veto power of the governor shall not extend to measures initiated by, or referred to, the qualified voters. Any measure submitted to a vote of the qualified voters shall become law or a part of the constitution only when approved by a majority of the votes cast thereon, provided that, in addition, no initiative measure or constitutional amendment shall become effective unless the affirmative votes cast therefor shall equal 30 per cent of the total vote cast for governor at the last preceding general election at which a governor was chosen. Each measure so approved shall take effect thirty days after the date of the vote thereon, unless otherwise provided in the measure. If conflicting measures referred to the people at the same election shall be approved by a majority of the votes cast thereon, the one receiving the highest number of affirmative votes shall prevail to the extent of such conflict.

Section 407. *Restrictions on Direct Legislation Procedure.* The initiative shall not be used as a means of making appropriations of public funds, nor for the enactment of local or special legislation. No measure submitted by the initiative shall contain therein the name of any person to be designated as administrator of any department, office or agency to be established by the proposed law or constitutional amendment.

Section 408. *Provisions Self-Executing.* The initiative and referendum provisions of this constitution shall be self-executing, and shall be treated as mandatory. Laws may be enacted to facilitate their operation, including provision for verification of signatures on petitions, but no law shall be enacted to hamper, restrict or impair the exercise of the powers herein reserved to the people. No measure adopted by vote of the qualified voters under the initiative and referendum provisions of this constitution shall be repealed or amended by the legislature within a period of three years except by a two-thirds vote of all of the members of the legislature.

ARTICLE V

THE EXECUTIVE

Section 500. *Establishment of the Executive.* The executive power of the state shall be vested in a governor, who shall be chosen by the direct vote of the people for a term of four years beginning on the first day of December next following his election.

Section 501. *Election of the Governor.* The election for governor shall be held on the Tuesday next following the first Monday in November in each alternate odd numbered year, beginning in 19———. Any qualified voter of the state shall be eligible to the office of governor.

Section 502. *Legislative Powers.* The governor shall, at the beginning of each session, and may at other times, give to the legislature information as to the affairs of the state, and recommend such measures as he shall deem expedient. He shall have the power of veto over bills approved by the legislature, as in this constitution prescribed.

Section 503. *Executive and Administrative Powers.* The governor shall take care that the laws are faithfully executed. He shall commission all officers of the state. He may at any time require information, in writing or otherwise, from the officers of any administrative department, office or agency upon any subject relating to their respective offices. He shall be commander-in-chief of the armed forces of the state (except when they shall be called into the service of the United States), and may call out the same to execute the laws, to suppress insurrection or to repel invasion.

Section 504. *Judicial Powers.* The governor shall have power to grant reprieves, commutations and pardons, after conviction, for all offenses, subject to such regulations as may be prescribed by law relative to the manner of applying therefor.

Section 505. *Oath of Office.* The governor and all officers of the state, and all civil divisions thereof shall, before entering upon the duties of their respective offices, take, and subscribe the following oath or affirmation: " I do solemnly swear (or affirm) that I will support and defend the Constitution of the United States and the Constitution of the State of ———, and that I will faithfully discharge the duties of the office of ——— to the best of my ability."

Section 506. *Administrative Manager.* The governor shall appoint an administrative manager of state affairs, whose term shall be indefinite at the pleasure of the governor. The governor may delegate any or all of his administrative powers to the administrative manager. The administrative manager shall be assisted by such aides as may be provided by law, but all such aides shall be appointed and shall hold office under civil service regulations.

Section 507. *Administrative Departments.* There shall be such administrative departments, not to exceed twenty in number, as may be established by law, with such powers and duties as may be prescribed by law. Subject to the limitations contained in this constitution, the legislature may from time to time assign by law new powers and functions to departments, offices and agencies, and it may increase, modify, or diminish the powers and functions of such departments, offices or agencies. All new powers or functions shall be assigned to departments, offices or agencies in such manner as will tend to maintain an orderly arrangement in the administrative pattern of the state government. The legislature may create temporary commissions for special purposes or reduce the number of departments by consolidation or otherwise.[7]

The heads of all administrative departments shall be appointed by and may be removed by the governor. All other offices in the administrative service of the state shall be appointed by the governor or by the heads of administrative departments; as provided by Article IX of this constitution and by supporting legislation. No executive order governing the work of the state or the administration of one or more departments, offices or agencies shall become effective until published as provided by law.

Section 508. *Executive-Legislative Relations.* The governor, the administrative manager, and the heads of administrative departments shall be entitled to seats in the legislature, may introduce bills therein, and take part in the discussion of measures, but shall have no vote.

Section 509. *Removal of the Governor.* The legislature shall have the power of impeachment by a two-thirds vote of the members elected thereto, and it shall provide by law a procedure for the trial and removal from office of all officers of this state. No officer shall be convicted on impeachment by a vote of less than two-thirds of the members of the court hearing the charges.

Section 510. *Succession to Governorship.* In case of the failure of the governor to qualify, or of his impeachment, or of his removal from office, death, resignation, inability to discharge the powers and duties of his office, or absence from the state, the powers and duties of the office shall devolve upon the presiding officer of the legislature for the remainder of the term, or until the disability be removed.

ARTICLE VI

THE JUDICIARY

Section 600. *Establishment of the Judiciary.* The judicial power of the state shall be vested in a General Court of Justice, which shall on and after January 1, ———, exercise the judicial power heretofore vested in any court in the state. The legislature shall provide by law for a supreme court

---

[7] Follows New York State Constitution, Article V, Section 3.

department, and for such other departments, divisions, or special tribunals, and for such judges as may be required to handle the judicial business of the state properly.

Section 601. *Jurisdiction of the Courts.* The General Court of Justice shall have jurisdiction to hear claims against the state, and such other powers and jurisdiction as may be conferred upon it by law. The legislature may delegate to the judicial council the power to determine by general rules the jurisdiction of departments of the General Court of Justice other than the supreme court department.

Section 602. *Selection of Judges.* The chief justice shall be elected by the qualified voters of the state at a general election on the first Tuesday after the first Monday in November, in an odd numbered year, beginning two years after the first election of governor under this constitution. He shall hold office for a term of eight years, beginning on the first day of December next following his election.

The chief justice shall be a member of the supreme court department and shall appoint the judges of the various departments of the General Court of Justice from an eligible list containing three names for such vacancy, which shall be presented to him by the judicial council. The term of office of each judge so appointed shall be twelve years, subject to removal as hereafter provided. After any judge appointed by the chief justice shall have served for four years, the qualified voters of the state or of the judicial district which he is serving shall decide at the next regular election whether such judge shall be retained or removed from office. A separate ballot shall be used (unless voting machines are employed) in such election on which there shall appear no other question than that of the retention or removal of such judge. If a majority of the votes cast are against retaining such judge in office, the chief justice shall appoint his successor for a term of twelve years, subject to recall as provided in this section. If a majority of the votes cast are in favor of retaining such judge, he shall continue in office until the end of his term. All vacancies caused by death, resignation, or retirement shall be filled in like manner, for the full term.

Section 603. *Powers of the Chief Justice.* The chief justice shall be the presiding justice of the supreme court department and a member of any division thereof. He shall preside over meetings of the judicial council, and shall be the executive head of the General Court of Justice, exercising such powers as are herein conferred or may be hereafter conferred by law, or by rules not in conflict herewith or with the the statutes, made by the judicial council. It shall be the duty of the chief justice to organize and administer the General Court of Justice. He shall cause to be published an annual report covering the business done by each department of the General Court of Justice and stating the condition of the dockets at the close of the year. He may require periodic or special reports from the presiding justices of the several departments on the state of judicial business and operation of said departments. He shall appoint the clerk and such other ministerial agents of the supreme court department as may be authorized by law.

Section 604. *Judicial Districts.* The judicial council shall have power to alter the districts into which the state may be divided for the handling of judicial business, in so far as the legislature does not otherwise provide, but any such order of the council may be amended or revoked by the legislature.

Section 605. *Judges of Inferior Court Departments.* The chief justice shall assign the judges of the inferior court departments to the several districts. Any judge shall be eligible to sit under temporary assignment in any district.

There shall be a presiding justice in each district who shall be appointed by the chief justice from among the judges of such district, and who shall serve until his retirement or his removal as presiding justice by the judicial council. The presiding justice in each district shall have control over the calendars in the courts in his district and over the assignment of judges within his district, subject to rules made by the judicial council, and shall appoint clerks, magistrates, and such other ministerial agents as are authorized by law for his district.

Section 606. *Establishment of Judicial Council.* There shall be a judicial council, to consist of the chief justice, and one justice of the supreme court department and two judges of the inferior court departments to be designated for four years, by the chief justice; three practicing lawyers, to be appointed by the governor for overlapping terms of three years, from an eligible list containing three times as many names as there are appointments to be made and presented to him by the governing board of the state bar association; three laymen citizens of the state, to be appointed by the governor for overlapping terms of three years; and the chairman of the judiciary committee of the legislature. The judicial council shall meet at least once in each quarter, at a time and place to be designated by the chief justice.

Section 607. *Powers of the Judicial Council.* The judicial council, in addition to other powers herein conferred upon it, or hereafter conferred by law, shall have power to make or alter the rules relating to pleading, practice, or procedure in the General Court of Justice, and to prescribe generally by rules the duties and jurisdiction of masters and magistrates; and also to makes rules and regulations respecting the duties and the business of the clerk of the General Court of Justice and his subordinates and all ministerial officers of the General Court of Justice, its departments, divisions, or branches. The legislature may repeal, alter, or supplement any rule of pleading, practice, or procedure, by a law limited to that specific purpose. No such rule made by the judicial council shall be effective until published as provided by law.

Section 608. *Removal of Judges.* The legislature may, upon due notice given and opportunity for defense, remove from office any judge, upon the concurrence of two-thirds of all the members elected. Judges of the inferior departments of the General Court of Justice and all ministerial agents of the General Court of Justice may be removed, for cause, after due notice and opportunity for defense, by the judicial council.

Section 609. *Compensation of Judges.* All remuneration for the services of judges and court officials provided for under this constitution shall be paid from an appropriation by the legislature. The annual compensation paid to any judge shall be neither increased nor diminished during the term of office to which he shall be elected or appointed. The legislature may by law provide for the apportionment among the several counties of the state of the expense of the maintenance of the General Court of Justice.

Section 610. *Fees, Costs, and Fines.* All fees collected in any department of the General Court of Justice and all masters fees shall be paid to the clerk of said court and shall be accounted for by him monthly and paid to the state treasury. The judicial council shall have power to establish or alter fees to be collected in the several court departments of this state, subject to such general regulations as the legislature may by law establish.

Section 611. *Ineligibility of Judges to Other Offices.* No judge shall hold any office or public employment, other than a judicial office, during the term for which he shall have been elected or appointed,[8] and no judge shall engage in the practice of law or other private employment during his continuance in office.[9] No judge shall be eligible for election to any non-judicial office until two years after the expiration of the full term for which he was appointed or elected.

Section 612. *Disqualifications in Certain Cases.* No judge shall sit in any case wherein he may be interested, or where either of the parties may be connected with him by affinity or consanguinity within such degrees as may be prescribed by law or where he shall have been of counsel in the case,[10] or in the trial of which he presided in any inferior court.[11]

Section 613. *Writ of Habeas Corpus.* Each judge of any department of the General Court of Justice shall have power to issue writs of habeas corpus.

ARTICLE VII

FINANCE

Section 700. *Powers of Taxation.* The power of taxation shall never be surrendered, suspended, or contracted away.

Section 701. *Borrowing Power.* The credit of the state or any civil division thereof shall not in any manner, directly or indirectly, be given or lent to or used in aid of any individual, association, or private corporation.

Section 702. *Debt Limitations.* No debt shall be contracted by or in behalf of this state unless such debts shall be authorized by law for a single project or object to be distinctly specified therein; and no such law shall, except for the purpose of repelling invasion, suppressing insurrection, defending the state in war, meeting natural catastrophes, or redeeming the indebtedness of the state outstanding at the time this constitution is approved, take effect until it shall have been submitted to the qualified voters at a general election and have received a favorable majority of all votes cast upon such question at such election; except that the state may by law borrow money to meet appropriations for any fiscal year, in anticipation of the collection of the revenues of such year, but all debts so contracted in anticipation of revenues shall be paid within one year.

Section 703. *The Budget.* Three months before the opening of the fiscal year, the governor shall submit to the legislature a budget setting forth a complete plan of proposed expenditures and anticipated income of all de-

---

[8] Arizona Constitution, Article VI, Section 11.
[9] Alabama Constitution, Article VI, Section 102.
[10] Maryland Constitution, Article IV, Section 7.
[11] New Mexico Constitution, Article VII, Section 18.

partments, offices, and agencies of the state for the next ensuing fiscal year. For the preparation of the budget the various departments, offices and agencies shall furnish the governor such information, in such form as he may require. At the time of submitting the budget to the legislature, the governor shall introduce therein a general appropriation bill to authorize all the proposed expenditures set forth in the budget. At the same time he shall introduce in the legislature a bill or bills covering all recommendations in the budget for new or additional revenues or for borrowing by which the proposed expenditures are to be met.

Section 704. *Legislative Budget Procedure.* No special appropriation bill shall be passed until the general appropriation bill, as introduced by the governor and amended by the legislature, shall have been enacted, unless the governor shall recommend the passage of an emergency appropriation or appropriations, which shall continue in force only until the general appropriation bill shall become effective. The legislature shall provide for one or more public hearings on the budget, either before a committee or before the entire legislature in committee of the whole. When requested by not less than one-fifth of the members of the legislature, it shall be the duty of the governor to appear in person or by a designated representative before the legislature, or before a committee thereof, to answer any inquiries with respect to the budget.

The legislature shall make no appropriation for any fiscal period in excess of the income provided for that period. The governor may strike out, or reduce items in appropriation bills passed by the legislature, and the procedure in such cases shall be the same as in case of the disapproval of an entire bill by the governor.

Section 705. *Expenditure of Money.* No money shall be withdrawn from the treasury except in accordance with appropriations made by law, nor shall any obligation for the payment of money be incurred except as authorized by law. No appropriation shall confer authority to incur an obligation after the termination of the fiscal period to which it relates. The governor shall have authority to reduce expenditures of state departments, offices and agencies under appropriations whenever actual revenues fall below the revenue estimates upon which the appropriations were based, and, through allotments or otherwise, to control the rate at which such appropriations are expended during the fiscal year, provided that the legislature may exempt specific appropriations from the exercise of this power by the governor.

Section 706. *Purchasing Methods.* All public purchases made by the government of this state, or by any of its cities, counties, or other civil divisions, shall, so far as practicable, be made under a system of competitive bidding. Centralized purchasing shall be practiced, wherever practicable, within individual civil divisions, and the legislature may by law authorize cooperative purchasing by two or more civil divisions.

Section 707. *Post-auditing.* The legislature shall, by a majority vote of all its members, appoint an auditor who shall serve during its pleasure.[12] It

12 Or it may be provided that the legislature shall contract with qualified public accountants to conduct all post-audits for the state. The auditor or auditors should, in any case, be certified public accountants.

shall be the duty of the auditor to conduct post-audits of all transactions and of all accounts kept by or for all departments, offices and agencies of the state government, to certify to the accuracy of all financial statements issued by accounting officers of the state, and to report his findings and criticisms to the governor and to a special committee of the legislature quarterly, and to the legislature at the end of each fiscal year. He shall also make such additional reports to the legislature and the proper legislative committee, and conduct such investigation of the financial affairs of the state, or of any department, office or agency thereof, as either of such bodies may require.

Section 708. *Excess Condemnation.* The state, or any civil division thereof appropriating or otherwise acquiring property for public use, may, in furtherance of such public use, appropriate or acquire an excess over that actually to be occupied by the improvement, and may sell such excess with such restrictions as shall be appropriate to preserve the improvement made. Bonds may be issued to supply the funds in whole or in part to pay for the excess property so appropriated or acquired; and such bonds, when made a lien only against the property so appropriated or acquired, shall not be subject to the restrictions or limitations on the amount of indebtedness of any civil divisions prescribed by law.[13]

ARTICLE VIII
LOCAL GOVERNMENT

Section 800. *Organization of Local Government.* Provision shall be made by general law, for the incorporation of counties, cities, and other civil divisions; and for the alteration of boundaries, the consolidation of neighboring civil divisions, and the dissolution of any such civil divisions.

Provision shall also be made by general law (which may provide optional plans of organization and government) for the organization and government of counties, cities, and other civil divisions which do not adopt locally framed and adopted charters in accordance with the provisions of Section 801, but no such law hereafter enacted shall become operative in any county, city, or other civil division until submitted to the qualified voters thereof and approved by a majority of those voting thereon.

Section 801. *Home Rule for Local Units.* Any county or city may frame and adopt a charter for its own government in the following manner, subject to such further regulations as to the manner of framing and adopting a charter as may be provided by general law:

(a) The legislative authority of the county or city may, by a majority vote of its members, and upon petition of 10 per cent of the qualified voters thereof shall forthwith, provide by ordinance or resolution for submission to the qualified voters of the question, " Shall a commission be chosen to frame a charter for the county (or city) of ———? " The ordinance of resolution shall require that the question be submitted to the qualified voters at the next regular election, if one shall occur not less than sixty nor more than one hundred and twenty days after its passage; otherwise, at a special

[13] Follows Ohio Constitution, Article XVIII, Section 10.

election to be called and held within the time aforesaid. The ballot containing such question shall also contain the names of candidates for the proposed commission, but without party designation. Such candidates shall be nominated by petition signed by not less than 1 per cent of the qualified voters of such county or city and filed with the election authorities at least thirty days before such election, provided however that in any case the signatures of 1,000 qualified voters shall be sufficient for the nomination of any candidate. If a majority of the qualified voters voting on the question of choosing a commission shall vote in the affirmative, then the nine candidates receiving the highest number of votes (or if the legislative authority of the state provides by general law for the election of such commissioners by means of proportional representation, then the nine chosen in the manner required by such general law) shall constitute the charter commission and shall proceed to frame a charter for such county or city. The legislative authority of such county or city shall, if so requested by the charter commission, appropriate money to provide for the reasonable expenses of the commission and for the printing of any completed charter and any separate and alternative provisions thereof and their distribution to the qualified voters as required by subsection (b) of this section.

(b) Any charter framed as provided in subsection (a) of this section shall be submitted to the qualified voters of the county or city at an election to be held at a time to be determined by the charter commission, but at least thirty days subsequent to the completion of the charter and its distribution among the qualified voters and not more than one year after the election of the charter commission. Any part of such a charter, or any provision alternative to a part thereof, may be submitted to be voted upon separately. The commission shall make provision for its distribution, not less than fifteen days before any such election, of copies of the proposed charter, and of any separate parts and alternative provisions thereof, to the qualified voters of such county or city. Any charter so proposed which is approved by a majority of the qualified voters voting thereon, with the addition of such parts and as modified by such alternative provisions as may have been separately submitted and similarly approved by a majority of those voting on any such part or provisions, shall become the organic law of the county or city at the time fixed in such charter, and shall supersede any existing charter and all laws affecting the organization and government of the county or city which are in conflict therewith. Within thirty days after its approval the election authorities shall certify a copy of the charter to the state officer charged by law with the supervision of civil divisions, who shall file it as a public record in his office and publish it as an appendix to the session laws enacted by the legislature.

(c) Amendments to any such charter may be framed and submitted by a charter commission in the same manner as provided in subsections (a) and (b) for framing and adopting a charter. Amendments may also be proposed by a majority vote of the legislative authority of the county or city, or by petition of 10 per cent of the qualified voters thereof; and any such amendment, after due public hearing before such legislative authority, shall be submitted to the qualified voters of such county or city at a regular or special election as in the case of the submission of the question of choosing a charter commission. Copies of all proposed amendments shall be sent to the qualified voters. Any such amendment approved by a majority of the qualified voters voting thereon shall become a part of the charter of the county or city at the time fixed in the amendment and shall be certified to and filed and published by the state officer charged by law with the supervision of civil divisions, as in the case of a charter.

Section 802. *Powers of Local Units.* Counties shall have such powers as shall be provided by general or optional law. Any city or other civil division may, by agreement, subject to a local referendum and the approval of a majority of the qualified voters voting on any such question, transfer to the county in which it is located any of its functions or powers and may revoke the transfer of any such function or power, under regulations provided by general law; and any county may, in like manner, transfer to another county or to a city within its boundaries or adjacent thereto any of its functions or powers, and may revoke the transfer of any such function or power.

Section 803. *County Government.* Any county charter shall provide the form of government of the county and shall determine which of its officers shall be elected and the manner of their election. It shall provide for the exercise of all powers vested in, and the performance of all duties imposed upon counties and county officers by law. Such charter may provide for the concurrent or exclusive exercise by the county, in all or in part of its area, of all or of any designated powers vested by the constitution or laws of this state in cities and other civil divisions; it may provide for the succession by the county to the rights, properties, and obligations of cities and other civil divisions therein incident to the powers so vested in the county, and for the division of the county into districts for purposes of administration or of taxation or of both. No provision of any charter or amendment vesting in the county any powers of a city or other civil division shall become effective unless it shall have been approved by a majority of those voting thereon (1) in the county, (2) in any city containing more than 25 per cent of the total population of the county, and (3) in the county outside of such city or cities.

Section 804. *City Government.* Except as provided in Sections 802 and 803, each city is hereby granted full power and authority to pass laws and ordinances relating to its local affairs, property and government; and no enumeration of powers in this constitution shall be deemed to limit or restrict the general grant of authority hereby conferred; but this grant of authority shall not be deemed to limit or restrict the power of the legislature to enact laws of statewide concern uniformly applicable to every city.[14]

The following shall be deemed to be a part of the powers conferred upon cities by this section:

(a) To adopt and enforce within their limits local police, sanitary and other similar regulations, not in conflict with general laws uniformly applicable to all cities.

(b) To levy, assess and collect taxes, and to borrow money and issue bonds, within the limits prescribed by general laws uniformly applicable

[14] General grant follows New York Constitution. Last clause follows Wisconsin Constitution.

to all cities; and to levy and collect special assessments for benefits conferred.

(c) To furnish all local public services; and to acquire and maintain, either within or without its corporate limits, cemeteries, hospitals, infirmaries, parks and boulevards, water supplies, and all works which involve the public health and safety.[15]

(d) To maintain art institutes, museums, theatres, operas, or orchestras, and to make any other provision for the cultural needs of the residents.

(e) To establish and alter the location of streets, to make local public improvements, and to acquire by condemnation or otherwise property, within its corporate limits, necessary for such improvements, and also to acquire additional property in order to preserve and protect such improvements, and to lease or sell such additional property, with restrictions to preserve and protect the improvements.

(f) To acquire, construct, hire, maintain and operate or lease local public utilities; to acquire, by condemnation or otherwise, within or without the corporate limits, property necessary for any such purposes, subject to restrictions imposed by general law for the protection of other communities; and to grant local public utility franchises and regulate the exercise thereof.

(g) To issue and sell bonds, outside of any general debt limit imposed by law, on the security in whole or in part, of any public utility or property owned by the city, or of the revenues thereof, or of both, including in the case of a public utility, if deemed desirable by the city, a franchise stating the terms upon which, in case of foreclosure, the purchaser may operate such utility.

(h) To organize and administer public schools and libraries, subject to the general laws establishing a standard of education for the state.

(i) To provide for slum clearance, the rehabilitation of blighted areas, and safe and sanitary housing for families of low income, and for recreational and other facilities incidental or appurtenant thereto; and gifts of money or property, or loans of money or credit for such purposes, shall be deemed to be for a city purpose.[16]

Section 805. *Public Reporting.* Counties, cities and other civil divisions shall adopt an annual budget in such form as the legislature shall prescribe, and the legislature shall by general law provide for the examination by qualified auditors, of the accounts of all such civil divisions, and of public utilities owned or operated by such civil divisions, and providing for reports from such civil divisions as to their transactions and financial conditions.

Section 806. *Conduct of Elections.* All elections and submissions of questions provided for in this article or in any charter or law adopted in accordance herewith shall be conducted by the election authorities provided by general law.

[15] Michigan Constitution, Article VIII, Section 22.
[16] Paragraph (b) gives general bonding power, subject to general limitation by general law and paragraph (g) gives additional bonding power for public utilities, et cetera. Paragraph (i) is an addition agreed to by the Committee on Revision of the Model City Charter.

ARTICLE IX
THE CIVIL SERVICE [17]

Section 900. *General Provisions.* In the civil service of the state and all of its civil divisions, all offices and positions shall be classified according to duties and responsibilities, salary ranges shall be established for the various classes, and all appointments and promotions shall be made according to merit and fitness to be ascertained, so far as practicable, by examinations, which, so far as practicable, shall be competitive.[18]

Section 901. *Administration and Enforcement.* There shall be a department of civil service which shall, in accordance with the provisions of this article and the laws enacted pursuant thereto, administer the personnel functions of the state and of such of its civil divisions as elect to come under the jurisdiction of the department. For the administration of the personnel functions of civil divisions that do not elect to come under the jurisdiction of the department, and which do not make provisions for the administration of their personnel functions in a home rule charter adopted pursuant to Section 801 of this constitution, provision shall be made by law. No payment for any employment hereunder shall be made without the affirmative certification by the department, or of a designated local authority in the case of a civil division over which the department does not have jurisdiction, on each payroll or claim as to the legality of such employment. The legislature shall enact laws necessary to carry out the provisions of this article and the department shall make such rules as may be necessary to carry out the provisions and intent of such laws.

Section 902. *Legislative and Judicial Employees.* Employees of the legislature shall be selected in conformity with the provisions of this article and shall be appointed and supervised by the secretary of the legislature. Employees of the courts, including clerks of the courts, bailiffs, probation officers, parole officers and other technical employees likewise shall be selected in conformity with the provisions of this article, and shall be appointed and supervised as provided in this constitution or as may be prescribed by law.

ARTICLE X
PUBLIC WELFARE

Section 1000. *Public Education.* The legislature shall provide for the maintenance and support of a system of free common schools, wherein all the children of this state may be educated,[19] and of such other educational institutions, including institutions of higher learning, as may be deemed desirable.

Section 1001. *Public Health.* The protection and promotion of the health of the inhabitants of the state are matters of public concern and provision therefor shall be made by the state and by such of its civil divisions and

[17] Draft prepared through the cooperation of committees representing the National Municipal League, the Civil Service Assembly of the United States and Canada, and the National Civil Service Reform League.

[18] In part from New York State Constitution, Article V, Section 6.

[19] New York State Constitution, Article IX, Section 1.

in such manner, and by such means as the legislature shall from time to time determine.[20]

Section 1002. *Public Relief.* The maintenance and distribution, at reasonable rates or free of charge, of a sufficient supply of food, fuel, clothing, and other common necessities of life, and the providing of shelter, are public functions, and the state and its civil divisions may provide for the same for their inhabitants in such manner, and by such means as may be prescribed by law.[21]

Section 1003. *Public Inspection of Private Charitable, Correctional, or Health Institutions and Agencies.* The state shall have the power to provide for the inspection by such state departments, offices or agencies, and in such manner as the legislature may determine, of all private institutions and agencies in the state, whether incorporated or not incorporated, which are engaged in charitable, correctional, or health activities.[22]

Section 1004. *Public Housing.* The state may provide for low rent housing for persons of low income as defined by law, or for the clearance, replanning, reconstruction and rehabilitation of substandard and insanitary areas, or for both such purposes, and for recreational and other facilities incidental or appurtenant thereto, in such manner, by such means, and upon such terms and conditions as may be prescribed by law.[23]

Section 1005. *Conservation.* The conservation, development and utilization of the agricultural, mineral, forest, water and other natural resources of the state are public uses, and the legislature shall have power to provide for the same, and to enact legislation necessary or expedient therefor.[24]

Section 1006. *Sightliness, Order and Historic Associations.* The natural beauty, historic associations, sightliness and physical good order of the state and its parts contribute to the general welfare and shall be conserved and developed as a part of the patrimony of the people, and to that end private property shall be subject to reasonable regulation and control.

Section 1007. *Powers of the State.* The enumeration in this article of specified functions shall not be construed as a limitation upon the powers of the state government. The state government shall have full power to act for the government and good order of the state and for the health, safety, and welfare of its citizens, by all necessary and convenient means, subject only to the limitations prescribed in this constitution and in the Constitution of the United States.

ARTICLE XI

INTERGOVERNMENTAL RELATIONS

Section 1100. *Federal-State Relations.* Nothing in this constitution shall be construed in such manner as to impair the constitutionality of any act passed by the legislature, for the purpose of making effective the coopera-

[20] New York State Constitution, Article XVII, Section 3.
[21] Combines New York State Constitution, Article XVII, Section 1, and the Massachusetts Constitution, Amendments, Article XLVII.
[22] Adapted from New York State Constitution, Article XVII, Section 2.
[23] Adapted from New York State Constitution, Article XVIII, Section 1.
[24] Adapted from Massachusetts Constitution, Amendments, Article XLIX.

tion of the state with the Federal government, under any legislation which Congress has the power to enact.

Section 1101. *Interstate Relations.* The legislature shall provide by law for the establishment of such agencies as may be necessary and desirable to promote cooperation on the part of this state with the other states of the Union. The legislature may appropriate such sums as may be necessary to finance its fair share of the cost of any interstate activities.

Section 1102. *Cooperation of Governmental Units.* Agreements may be made by any county, city, or other civil divisions with any other such civil divisions or with the state, or with the United States for a cooperative or joint administration of any of its functions or powers, and the legislature shall have power to facilitate such arrangements.

Section 1103. *Consolidation and Cooperation of Local Units.* The legislature may, by appropriate legislation, facilitate and encourage the consolidation of existing civil divisions, or the establishment of cooperative enterprises on the part of such civil divisions.

ARTICLE XII

CONSTITUTIONAL REVISION

Section 1200. *Amending Procedure.* Amendments to this constitution may be proposed by the legislature at any two regular sessions, a period of six months having intervened between each passage of such a proposal, or by the initiative as provided in Section 401. Any such amendment presented in the legislature and twice agreed to by a majority of all the members shall be entered each time on the journal, with a record of the roll call vote, and submitted after the second legislative action to a vote of the qualified voters by the legislature, at the first regular or special state election held not less than three months after date of adjournment.

Section 1201. *Constitutional Conventions.* The legislature, by vote of a majority of all the members entered by roll call vote on the journal, may at any regular session provide for the submission of the question, " Shall there be a convention to amend or revise the constitution? " to the qualified voters of the state at any regular election. If approved by a majority of the qualified voters voting on said question, the legislature shall at its next session provide by law for convening such a convention four months after the date of the election of the delegates thereof, and it shall provide for a preparatory commission to assemble information relating to constitutional questions for the assistance of the delegates. The secretary of the legislature shall submit the question, " Shall there be a convention to amend or revise the constitution? " to the qualified voters at the general election in 19——, and in every twentieth year thereafter.

Delegates to the convention shall be chosen at a special election to be held not less than three months nor more than six months after approval of the proposition to call a convention. Delegates shall be elected in the same manner as members of the legislature, by proportional representation. Except as otherwise provided herein, any qualified voter of the state shall be eligible to membership in the convention. Three delegates shall be elected to the convention from each existing legislative district; in addition, there shall be elected from the state at large, by the Hare system of proportional representation, a number of delegates equalling one-fifth of the membership of the legislature.

No proposal shall be submitted by the convention to the qualified voters as herein provided, unless it has been read on three different days, in the convention, has been printed and upon the desks of the delegates in final form at least three days on which the convention was in session, prior to final passage therein, and has received the assent of a majority of all the delegates. The yeas and nays on any question shall, upon request of one-tenth of the delegates present, be entered in the journal. The proposals of the convention shall be submitted to the qualified voters at the next regular election held not less than three months after the adjournment of the convention, either as a whole or in such parts and with such alternatives as the convention may determine. All such proposals approved by a majority of such qualified voters voting thereon shall become effective thirty days after the date of the vote thereon, unless a different time is provided therein, provided that the affirmative vote thereon shall equal 30 per cent of the total vote cast for governor in the last preceding general election at which a governor was chosen.

Section 1202. *Self-Executing Character of Provisions.* The provisions of the constitution affecting its amendment or revision shall be self-executing, but legislation may be adopted to facilitate their operation. If conflicting measures submitted to the qualified voters at the same election shall be approved, the one receiving the highest number of affirmative votes shall become law as to all conflicting provisions.

Article XIII

SCHEDULE

Section 1300. *Former Laws to Remain in Force.* All laws in force in this state at the time of the adoption of this constitution, not inconsistent therewith, shall continue in force until specifically amended by the legislature, as if this constitution had not been adopted; and all rights, actions, prosecutions, and contracts shall continue except as modified thereby.

Section 1301. *Officers.* All officers now filling any office by election or appointment shall continue to exercise the duties thereof, according to their respective commissions or appointments, until their successors shall have been selected in accordance with this constitution or the laws enacted pursuant thereto and shall have qualified.

Section 1302. *Choice of Officers.* The first election of governor under this constitution shall be in 19——. The first election of chief justice under this constitution shall be in 19——. The first election of members of the legislature under this constitution shall be in 19——.

Section 1303. *Establishment of the Legislature.* Until otherwise provided by law, members of the legislature shall be elected from the following districts: The first district shall consist of the counties of —— and ——, and said district shall be entitled to —— members in the legislature, etc.

(The description of all the districts from which the first legislature will be elected should be inserted in similar language).

A system of proportional representation for the election of the members of the legislature shall be prescribed by law. In the event that no such system shall be provided by law, the members of the first legislature under this constitution shall be selected by the Hare system of proportional representation, each voter having a single transferable vote, under regulations promulgated by the governor.

Section 1304. *Establishment of the Judiciary.* All courts in this state existing at the time when this constitution becomes effective shall constitute departments or divisions of the General Court of Justice until the legislature or the judicial council, subject to legislative approval, shall otherwise provide. The justices of the (here name the highest court of the state) and the judges of the (here name all the courts of the state except justice of the peace courts) holding office on the first day of January, 19——, shall constitute the first judges of the General Court of Justice, and shall continue to serve as such for the remainder of their respective terms and until their successors shall have qualified.

The justices of the (here name highest court of the state) shall become justices of the supreme court department of the General Court of Justice, and the judges of the existing inferior courts shall be assigned by the chief justice to the other departments of the General Court of Justice, due regard being had to their position in the existing judicial structure. As nearly as may be, each judge shall be assigned to a district containing all or part of the district in which he served regularly as a judge prior to the adoption of this constitution.

Justices of the peace shall be attached as magistrates to that department of the General Court of Justice exercising general jurisdiction in the county in which they reside. The judicial council may reduce the number of such magistrates in any county as vacancies occur.

Section 1305. *Judicial Districts.* Subject to alteration by the judicial council or by law, the state shall be divided into the following judicial districts, namely:

First District: The first district shall comprise (and so forth).

Section 1306. *Judicial Rules.* The rules in force at the time the General Court of Justice shall be established, regulating pleading, practice, and procedure in the courts consolidated by this constitution, which are not inconsistent herewith, shall constitute the first rules of court for the appropriate departments of the General Court of Justice, but subject to the power of the judicial council to make or alter such rules.

Table of Cases

Index

court organization, 689, 690; judicial council, 691; court reports, 707; advisory opinions in, 707; crime survey of, quoted, 715, 716; race segregation of students in, 762; local government, 811, 821, 822, 834; education, 815, 880; county reorganization, 836; state supervision of local accounting, 874; interstate relations in, 906, 913; size of government, 961; veterans' benefits, 1017

Missouri Association for Social Welfare, 195–196

Missouri Crime Survey, quoted, 715, 716

Model State Constitution: 79–80; on legislative organization, 28, 1030; amendment provisions of, 70, 1047–1048; influence of, in Nebraska, 80; recommendation of, on P.R., 189; sponsored by National Municipal League, 190, 191; recommendation of, on unicameralism, 227, 1030; recommendation of, for improvement of legislative procedure, 347, 1031–1033; recommendation of, on governorship, 375, 1035–1036; recommendations of, on reorganization, 414, 1036; provides for joint committees, 588; on judicial administration, 672, 1037–1039; selection of judges in, 677–678, 1037; on judicial power, 686, 687, 1036; on county government, 833, 1043

Montana: amending procedure in, 66; adoption of existing constitution, 83; calling constitutional conventions in, 84; voters in, in 1940, 119; qualifications for voting in, 122; extensive system of registration, 137; petition requirements of, 146, 172; voting machine law, 153; ballot forms in, 153; uses recall in cities only, 178; legislature, data on members, sessions, and salary, 244, 246, 250, 252, 271; Legislative Assembly in, 246; committee system, 264; analysis of legislative production in, 314; veto powers of governor, 390, 391; pardoning board, 398; tax pattern, 528, 554, 556, 563; budget system, 585, 589; debt, 596, 601; selection, tenure and salary of judges, 675, 683; court reports, 707; local government, 811, 821, 822, 834; county reorganization, 830, 835; state supervision of local accounting, 874; interstate compacts in, 906; veterans' benefits, 1017

Montesquieu, influence of, on American institutions, 55, 57

Moodie, Thomas H., in North Dakota governorship tangle, 374

Mooney, Tom, attempt of, to secure legislative pardon, 308

Moore, A. Harry, calls regional conference of governors, 922–923

Mortgages and liens, moratoria on, 765

Moses, John, as governor, 363

Mothers' aid, legislation on, 891

Motor vehicles: control of, 456–457; tax on, 540; in civil code, 631; regulation of, 784–785; interstate barriers in operation of, 912–914; uniform legislation for regulation of, 916; control of, in wartime, 982–983

Municipal courts, 666–668

Municipal leagues, influence of, on legislation, 198–199

Murphy, Charles F., relations of, with Governor Sulzer, 380–381

Murray, William H., use of removal powers by, 382; use of troops by, 384

National Association of Assessing Officers, 192, 527; on tax on intangibles, 540

National Association of Legal Aid Organizations, 735

National Association of Secretaries of State, secretariat of, 927–928

National Association of State Attorneys General, 909–910; secretariat of, 927

National Association of State Auditors, Comptrollers, and Treasurers, 192, 581

National Association of State Aviation Officials, sponsors uniform legislation, 920

National Association of Supervisors of State Banking, organization of, 923

National Board of Dental Examiners, organization of, 920

National Civil Service Reform League, 482, 1045

National Conference of Commissioners on Uniform State Laws: work of, 915–918; organization of, 921

National Conference of Judicial Councils, 696–697

National Conference on Street and Highway Safety, 920, 923

National Conference on Trade and Tax Barriers, 566, 928, 931

National Conference on Weights and Measures, organization of, 923

National Convention of Insurance Commissioners, organization of, 920, 923

National Council on Uniform Aeronautic Regulatory Laws, sponsors uniform legislation, 920

National Foundation for Education in American Citizenship, organized, 212

National Guard: use of, in states, 384–

review in, 647–648; court organization, 661, 669, 671, 672, 689, 690; selection, tenure, salary and retirement of judges, 675, 682, 693, 684; judicial council of, 691, 696; court reports, 706; advisory opinions in, 707; bail situation in, 716; law's delay in, 733; cost of litigation in, 734; prenatal examinations in, 784; driver's license law in, 785; regulation of common carriers in, 786; pari-mutuel betting in, 792; local government, 811, 820, 822, 834, 861; education, 815; county reorganization, 830, 836; size of government, 837; home rule and optional charter plans, 844–845; metropolitan areas, 846, 959; state supervision of local accounting, 872–873, 874; state control over schools, 881, 882; public welfare organization, 889, 890; interstate relations in, 903, 906, 910, 915, 926; divorce law in, 905; cooperation of, with Social Security Board, 947; state council of defense, 977–978; passes fair employment practice legislation, 999–1000; veterans' preference and benefits, 1015, 1017

New York State Charities Aid Association, 195–196

New York Times: publishes *Constitutional Convention Almanac*, 98; report of, on holiday accidents, 787

Nineteenth Amendment, 118, 131

Nomination: systems of, 138–139; and election of governor, 367–368

Nonpartisan primary, 142

Non-voting: reasons for, 203–206; possible solutions of, 206–213

Norris, George W.: sponsors Nebraska unicameral experiment, 225–227; opposes use of conference committee, 296, 353; sponsors TVA legislation, 924

North Carolina: early trade discriminations against, 39; early legislature in, 54, 220–221; amending procedure in, 67; adoption of existing constitution, 73; constitutional conventions in, 84; voters in, in 1940, 119; qualifications for voting in, 123, 127; inadequate system of registration, 137; petition requirements in, 146; voting machines not used, 152; permits solicitation of funds from candidates, 160; uses recall in cities only, 178; General Assembly in, 243; legislature, data on members, term, sessions, cost and salary, 245, 247, 249, 250, 253, 271, 388; committee system, 263, 264; special legislation in, 309–310; analysis of legislative production in, 313, 314,

315, 317; cost of legislative reference work in, 330; expenditures for lobbying in, 333; term and salary of governor, 369, 370; veto power in, 389, 391; executive clemency in, 398, 399, 400; type of reorganization, 415; general property tax system, 523, 529; tax pattern, 542, 556, 563; budget system, 585, 589; debt, 596, 599, 600, 601; local defalcations in, 603; development of law in, 615; judicial review in, 646; selection, tenure and salary of judges, 675, 683, 685; judicial council of, 691; court reports in, 707; advisory opinions in, 707; bail in, 716; integrated bar, 730; eminent domain in, 768–769; local government, 811, 821, 822, 831, 834; extension of state control over highways in, 823, 893; county reorganization, 830, 835; Local Government Commission, 850–852; state supervision of local finances, 866, 869, 874; public welfare organization, 889–890; extensive centralization in, 895–896; divorce law in, 905; interstate compacts in, 906; veterans' benefits, 1017

North Dakota: compact of, with United States, 42; amending procedure in, 67, 68; adoption of existing constitution, 83; voters in, in 1940, 119; qualifications for voting in, 123; limited registration in, 135; petition requirements in, 146, 172; voting machines not used, 152; size of ballot in, 154, 181; elects Representatives at large, 155; recalls Governor Frazier, 176, 372; use of recall in, 177; preferential voting abandoned in, 187; legislature, data on members, sessions, cost and salary, 245, 250, 253, 271; Legislative Assembly of, 246; committee system, 264, 270; analysis of legislative production in, 315; no legislative reference work in, 328; freak legislation, 335; Moses as governor, 363; reeligibility of governor, 370; fraud charges against Governor Langer, 373; controversy over governorship, 374; use of troops in, by Governor Langer, 384; veto power in, 389; tax pattern, 529, 552, 553, 555, 556, 563; budget system, 584, 589; debt, 596, 601; capital punishment abolished in, 634; selection, tenure and salary of judges, 675, 682, 683; judicial council in, 691; court reports, 707; pre-trial procedure in, 711; integrated bar, 730; regulation of weights and measures, 795; local government, 811, 821, 822, 834; county reorganization, 836; state su-